AF696941

American Health Law

EDITORIAL ADVISORY BOARD

Little, Brown and Company
Law Book Division

Richard A. Epstein
James Parker Hall Professor of Law
University of Chicago

E. Allan Farnsworth
Alfred McCormack Professor of Law
Columbia University

Ronald J. Gilson
Professor of Law
Stanford Law School

Geoffrey C. Hazard, Jr.
Sterling Professor of Law
Yale University

James E. Krier
Earl Warren DeLano Professor of Law
University of Michigan

Elizabeth Warren
Professor of Law
University of Pennsylvania Law School

Bernard Wolfman
Fessenden Professor of Law
Harvard University

American Health Law

George J. Annas
Utley Professor of Health Law
Boston University Schools of Medicine and Public Health

Sylvia A. Law
Professor of Law
New York University School of Law

Rand E. Rosenblatt
Professor of Law
Rutgers University School of Law - Camden

Kenneth R. Wing
Professor of Law
University of North Carolina School of Law
and University of North Carolina School of Public Health

LAW SCHOOL CASEBOOK SERIES

Little, Brown and Company
Boston Toronto London

Copyright © 1990 by George J. Annas, Sylvia A. Law,
Rand E. Rosenblatt, and Kenneth R. Wing

All rights reserved. No part of this book may be reproduced in any form or by any electronic or mechanical means including information storage and retrieval systems without permission in writing from the publisher, except by a reviewer who may quote brief passages in a review.

Library of Congress Catalog Card No. 89-84760

ISBN 0-316-04309-5

HAD

Published simultaneously in Canada
by Little, Brown & Company (Canada) Limited

Printed in the United States of America

To all those who struggle for justice in health care

especially to

Justice Harry A. Blackmun

The National Health Law Program

and

Edward V. Sparer (1928-1983)

Summary of Contents

Contents

III

Health Care Financing: Provider Reimbursement and Cost Containment 211

V
Quality of Care and the Law: Defining Standards and Structuring Enforcement 377

VI
Patient Rights 561

VII
Medical Personnel 667

IX
Organ Transplantation 855

Preface

The study of health law presents a unique opportunity to apply law and legal analysis to an industry that dramatically affects all our lives, is undergoing tremendous change, and is filled with challenges that the thoughtful application of law can help us to meet constructively. Few fields of applied law match the richness of health law. Changes in medicine directly affect not just what humans can do, but how we think about what it means to be human; issues of social justice and resource allocation arise more starkly and more compellingly in the health care context than in any other; and health law introduces us to the problems confronted by another major profession, medicine.

As the title of this book asserts, uniquely American values are reflected and challenged in our health care system. Human anatomy and physiology are the same worldwide, but the organization and delivery of health care reflect individual cultures. Americans, for example, are probably more health conscious than any other culture. It is thus both ironic and disturbing that, with the exception of South Africa, we remain the only industrialized country that does not have a system of national health insurance. Cost is often given as the rationale for this inhumane policy. Nevertheless, we are already inefficiently spending more than 12 percent of our gross national product on health care and seem unable to control even government expenditures on medical care. We pride ourselves on having the "best" medical care in the world, but its quality varies greatly, and even where it is recognized as first rate, measures of quality are problematic. America is the home of other paradoxes as well. For example, although human rights are a focal point of our Constitution and legal tradition, it is often extremely difficult for individual patients to exercise such basic rights as refusing treatment in the modern American hospital.

As the 1990s open, there seems little doubt that this decade will witness major changes in our health care delivery system. A 1989 national opinion poll, for example, found that 89 percent of Americans thought that the health care system needed "fundamental change." We possess what has been accurately described as the most expensive, least well-liked, least equitable, and perhaps least efficient system of health care delivery in the world. Of course, because of continuing and dynamic change, any book on health law quickly faces at least partial obsolescence. But such change also presents unique study opportunities. Health care provides a real-world laboratory to examine how several bodies of law shape and are shaped by the organization of medical care in the United States.

Bodies of doctrinal law explored in this text include: tort standards of duty and medical malpractice, traditional insurance law as well as more contemporary insurance measures to control costs and assure access, labor law, constitutional principles, FDA law, state licensing programs for people and institutions, antitrust, as well as state and federal programs for financing medical care and education. In addition to exploring the often critical issues of doctrinal detail, the book addresses the interplay between courts, legislatures, administrative agencies, lawyers representing the wide range of interests, and more general cultural forces such as technology, ideology, and social movements.

This book highlights social justice and social choice in health care delivery. It provides a conceptual framework for understanding the processes by which the law allocates choice to professional prerogative, free market transactions, state or federal regulatory mechanisms, courts, or others. Identifying patterns of social choice and concepts of social justice does not provide easy answers or formulas, but rather illuminates the questions that help us understand contending and often controversial concepts and social forces.

New medical technologies present new legal challenges so intrinsically fascinating that they appear on the front pages of newspapers and magazines. Thus there is little trouble capturing the attention of even harassed second-year law students or hardened third-year law students. Relationships between lawyers and physicians have become increasingly adversarial, and increased knowledge of the health care field may help restore more reasonable and socially beneficial interaction. Moreover, the advice lawyers give their clients in the health care field often has a direct impact on matters of health, birth, life, and death. Professional responsibility has an immediacy in this field that is lacking in many others.

Full treatment of all of these issues in one book is, of course, impossible. This book introduces all of these issues and provides the student with a framework for analyzing them, with problems to focus discussion, and references for further study. This text is designed to be used in an introductory law school course, which could be followed by specialized courses in medical malpractice law, bioethics, law and health care economics, and so forth. It draws from a wide variety of materials, not just appellate decisions, and seeks to acquaint the student with the facts of health care delivery before confronting the legal problems that dominate the field. As will be seen, although they can be separately described and discussed, issues of cost, quality, access, and human rights cannot be compartmentalized in the real world. All of them must be understood to deal adequately with any of them.

The text is divided into an introduction (which outlines how our current health care system was developed) and ten chapters. Chapter 1 deals with access to care both because this is a central social justice issue and because it is perhaps the most "accessible" subject for law students. Chapters 2 and 3 detail health care financing, perhaps the most difficult material in the text, but essential for anyone who seeks to understand our changing health care system. Chapter 4 introduces what has become the central issue in health care delivery: the development and use of new medical technology. It can be followed by Chapter 5, which focuses on defining and enforcing standards of quality care, or by Chapter 9, a case study of the most expensive and seductive medical technology: organ transplantation. Chapter 6 deals with the rights of patients, and 7 with the legal issues involving health care personnel. Chapter 10, the case study on reproductive health, can be left to the end or can follow either of these two chapters. Finally, Chapter 8 presents various economic approaches to deal with the issues of cost, quality, and access and explores application of antitrust law to health care.

Although we all worked on the entire book, George Annas had primary responsibility for Chapters 4, 6, and 9; Sylvia Law for Chapters 1, 7, 8, and 10; Rand Rosenblatt for Chapter 5 and Section H (value conflicts) of the Introduction; and Kenneth Wing for the Introduction (Sections A-G) and Chapters 2 and 3.

We expect that after taking a course in health law, many students will agree with us that health law is perhaps the most intrinsically fascinating area of law. But even if students who take this course never advise a health care client, they will be hospitalized an average of seven times during their lives, will have almost yearly personal visits to physicians and clinics, and, as consumers and voters, will confront the problem we all share as a society: securing and financing adequate care of acceptable quality for all Americans.

Each of us has been teaching health law for approximately 15 years. Obviously, our students have had a significant influence on how we teach and the subject matter on which we focus. In addition, we wish to acknowledge specifically the generous support and constructive criticism of our colleagues in helping us to prepare this text, John D. Blum, Patricia Butler, Geraldine Dallek, Claire Dalton, Barry Ensminger, Margaret Farrell, Martha Field, Eleanor Fox, Leonard H. Glantz, Joel Handler, Joseph Healey, Lewis Kornhauser, Mark Lyons, Randall E. Robbins, Andreas Schneider, and Barbara Swartz. Research assistance was admirably provided by George Biaggi, Barry Bridges, Sherrill Hicks Canedo, Margaret Costella, Laura Gilbert, Cindy Harbin, Victoria Kristian, Patricia LaPierre, Gwenda Laws, Maureen McCarthy, Fretta Miller, Jean M. Mohrbacher, Martha Neary, Selina Nomeir, Brynn Parker, John Purcell, Patricia Rinaldi-Johnston, Sarah Rosenfield, Jennifer H. Rothschild, and Gerald Studzinski.

Some people deserve special mention. Edward V. Sparer created the first community-based legal services program for the poor and the first legal services support center. These programs, and the political and intellectual analysis that Sparer brought to health care, have had profound impact on some of the developments described in this book. Much in these materials is derived from the work of the former and present staff of the National Health

Law Program (NHeLP), the backup center for the nation's legal services programs on matters related to health care. These include NHeLP's work in various legislative, administrative, and judicial forums on behalf of the poor and health care consumers generally. Justice Harry A. Blackmun's deep understanding of the world of medical practice and his empathy for both physicians and patients are a source of inspiration to all of us. Justice Blackmun has been able to be an eloquent advocate for patient rights, while simultaneously supporting reasonable autonomy for physicians. Professors Frances Miller and Wendy K. Mariner have provided special insight and support to us and have gone above and beyond what could reasonably be expected of colleagues in reviewing and critiquing these materials.

October 1989

George J. Annas
Sylvia A. Law
Rand E. Rosenblatt
Kenneth R. Wing

Acknowledgments

We wish to thank the authors and copyright holders of the following works, who permitted their inclusion in this book.

Ad hoc Committee on Brain Death, A Definition of Irreversible Coma, 205 J.A.M.A. 337-340 (1968). Copyright 1968, American Medical Association.

American College of Obstetricians and Gynecologists: Department of Professional Liability, Alert: Professional Liability Implications of AFP Tests (May 1985).

American College of Obstetricians and Gynecologists: Prenatal Detection of Neural Tube Defects (ACOG Technical Bulletin 99). Washington D.C., ACOG, 1986.

American Hospital Association, A Patient's Bill of Rights (1972). Reprinted with permission of the American Hospital Association, copyright 1972.

Annas, Malpractice in Perspective, 1988 Medical and Health Annual 261 (A. Bernstein ed.). Reprinted with permission from the Medical and Health Annual, copyright © 1986 by Encyclopedia Britannica, Inc.

Anon., It's Over, Debbie, 259 J.A.M.A. 272 (1988). Copyright 1988, American Medical Association.

Blackhall, Must We Always Use CPR?, 317 N. Engl. J. Med. 1281 (1987).

Blake, Patricia, Incident Investigation, A Complete Guide, 15 Nursing Management 39-41 (Nov. 1984). Reprinted with permission.

C. Bosk, Forgive and Remember: Managing Medical Failure 37-50 (1979). © 1979 by the University of Chicago. All rights reserved.

D. Breo, Extraordinary Care 198-206 (1986). Excerpted from Extraordinary Care by Dennis L. Breo, Chicago Review Press, 1986.

D. Callahan, Setting Limits: Medical Goals in an Aging Society 171-173 (1987).

Clifford & Inculano, AIDS and Insurance: The Rationale for AIDS-Related Testing, 100 Harv. L. Rev. 1086 (1987). Copyright © 1987 by the Harvard Law Review Association.

Dunne, New York City: Gay Men's Health Crisis, in AIDS: Public Policy

Dimensions (1987). Reprinted with permission from AIDS: Public Policy Dimensions, United Hospital Fund of New York, 1987.

Elias & Annas, Routine Prenatal Screening, 317 N. Engl. J. Med. 650-658 (1987). Copyright 1987 Massachusetts Medical Society.

Enthoven, Consumer Choice Health Plan, 298 N. Engl. J. Med. 650-658 (1978). Copyright 1978 Massachusetts Medical Society.

Fein, Social and Economic Attitudes Shaping American Health Policy, 58 Milbank Mem. Fund Q. 349, 376-385 (1980).

Friedland, Introduction and Background: Private Initiatives to Contain Health Care Expenditures, in The Changing Health Care Market (F. McArdle ed.). From The Changing Health Care Market, Frank B. McArdle, ed., (Washington D.C.: Employee Benefit Research Institute, 1987). Reprinted with permission.

M. Friedman, Capitalism and Freedom, 139-160 (1962).

Ginzberg, For-Profit Medicine, 319 N. Engl. J. Med. 757-760 (1988). Copyright 1988 Massachusetts Medical Society.

Hallowell, Challenging the HMO system of incentives, Philadelphia Inquirer, Mar. 28, 1989, at 1-B:2. From the Philadelphia Inquirer, March 28, 1989. Used by permission.

Havighurst, Altering the Applicable Standard of Care, 49 Law & Contemp. Prob. at 265, 271, 273 (Spring 1986). Copyright 1986, Duke University School of Law.

Havighurst & Hackbarth, Private Cost Containment, 300 N. Engl. J. Med. 1298-1305 (1979). Copyright 1979 Massachusetts Medical Society.

Health Care Committee, American Bar Association, An Antitrust Overview (1988).

Hemminki, Content of Prenatal Care in the U.S., 26 Medical Care 199 (1988).

Hilfiker, Facing Our Mistakes, 310 N. Engl. J. Med. 118, 118-122 (1984). Copyright 1984 Massachusetts Medical Society.

D. Hilfiker, Healing the Wounds 45-47 (1985). From Healing the Wounds by David Hilfiker, M.D., ©, 1985 by David Hilfiker, M.D. Reprinted by permission of Pantheon Books, a division of Random House, Inc.

Hillman, Financial Incentives for Physicians in HMOs: Is There a Conflict of Interest?, 317 N. Engl. J. Med. 1743, 1744 (1987). Copyright 1987 Massachusetts Medical Society.

Iglehart, Congress Moves to Bolster Peer Review: The Health Care Quality Improvement Act of 1986, 316 N. Engl. J. Med. 960 (1987). Copyright 1987 Massachusetts Medical Society.

Jensen & Gabel, The Erosion of Purchased Health Insurance, 25 Inquiry 328 (1988).

J. Katz, The Silent World of Doctor and Patient 177-184 (1984).

Law & Emsinger, Negotiating Physicians' Fees: Individual Patients or Society?, 61 N.Y.U.L. Rev. 1, 12-20 (1986).

Lohr et al., Use of Medical Care in the Rand Health Insurance Experiment: Diagnosis- and Service-Specific Analyses in a Randomized Controlled Trial, 24 Medical Care S1, S72-S81 (Sept. 1986).

K. Ludmerer, Learning to Heal: The Development of American Medical Education, 3-7, 16 (1988).

M. Lynch, Peau d'Orange, in Sutured Words (J. Muquand ed. 1987). By permission of Aviva Press, Brookline, MA.

M. Macdonald, K. Meyer & B. Essig, Health Care Law; A Practical Guide s12.03[2] at 12-10 to 11 (1988 ed.). Copyright © 1988 by Matthew Bender & Co., Inc., and reprinted with permission from Health Care Law: A Practical Guide.

McKinley, From "Promising Report" to "Standard Procedure": The Seven Stages in the Career of a Medical Innovation, 59 Milbank Mem. Fund Q. 374-411 (1981).

Mansell, M.D. Anderson Hospital and Tumor Institute, in AIDS: Public Policy Dimensions (United Hospital Fund of New York 1987).

Morone & Dunham, Slouching Towards National Health Insurance: The New Health Care Politics, Yale J. on Reg. 263, 276-284 (1985).

Oberg & Polich, Medicaid: Entering the Third Decade, Health Affairs 90 (Fall 1988).

Perry, The NIH Consensus Development Program: A Decade Later, 317 N. Engl. J. Med. 485 (1987).

Rakich & Darr, Hospital Organization and Management: Text and Readings 26 (1983). Reprinted by permission from *Hospital Organization and Management: Text and Readings,* 3rd edition, Jonathon S. Rakich and Kurt Darr, eds. (New York: SP Medical & Scientific Books, 1983), p.26. All rights reserved.

S. Reiser, Medicine and the Reign of Technology, 229-230 (1978).

Roberts, The Economics of Organ Transplants, 25 Jurimetrics J. 256 (1985).

C. Rosenberg, Healing Hands: Nursing in the Hospital, in The Care of Strangers: The Rise of America's Hospital System 213-236, 334 (1987).

Rosenblatt, Health Care Reform and Administrative Law: A Structural Approach, 88 Yale L.J. 243, 247-253 (1988).

Rosenblatt, Health Care Markets and Democratic Values, 34 Vand. L. Rev. 1067, 1079-1082 (1981). Copyright 1981 by the Vanderbilt Law Review.

Rosenblatt, Medicaid Primary Care Case Management, the Doctor-Patient Relationship, and the Politics of Privatization, 36 Case W. Res. L. Rev. 915 (1986).

Rosoff, Not Just Teenagers, 20 Family Planning Perspectives 52 (No. 2 1988). Source: J. Rosoff, "Not Just Teenagers," *Family Planning Perspectives,* Vol. 20, No. 2 (March/April 1988), p. 52. Copyright The Alan Guttmacher Institute.

Schatz, The AIDS Insurance Crisis: Underwriting or Overreaching?, 100 Harv. L. Rev. 1782 (1988). Copyright 1988 by the President and Fellows of Harvard College.

Simpson, State Certificate of Need Programs: The Current Status, 75 Am. J. Pub. Health 1225, 1226-1227 (1985).

E. Sparer, Medical School Accountability in the Public Hospital, 14-26 (1974).

Sullivan & Field, AIDS and the Coercive Power of the State, 23 Harv. Civ. Rts.-Civ. Lib. L. Rev. 139 (1988). Copyright 1988 by the President and Fellows of Harvard College.

Thomas, The Technology of Medicine, 285 N. Engl. J. Med. 1366-1368 (1971).

Vladeck, The Market v. Regulation: The Case for Regulation, 59 Milbank Mem. Fund Q. 209 (1981).

Vladeck, Medicare Hospital Payment by Diagnosis-Related Groups, 100 Annals Internal Med. (1984).

Wennberg, Dealing with Medical Practice Variations: A Proposal for Action, 3 Health Affairs at 6, 9-10, 12, 15, 30-31 (Summer 1984).

Wing, American Health Policy in the 1980s, 36 Case W. Res. L. Rev. 608 (1986).

Wing, The Impact of Reagan-Era Politics on the Federal Medicaid Program, 33 Catholic L. Rev. 1-15 (1983).

American Health Law

Introduction to Health Care Delivery in the United States

John Smith, a retired Iowa City machinist, has advanced Alzheimer's disease. When his wife found she could no longer care for him in the home, her personal trauma was followed by a further shock: neither Medicare nor the private health insurance paid for by his former employer would cover his $3000 per month nursing home bills. Mr. Smith will eventually qualify for the state's Medicaid program, but only after the Smiths' life savings have been exhausted and after all but a small portion of their retirement income has been "spent down" on medical bills. Mrs. Smith's only "practical" way to secure public support for her husband's care — and to avoid poverty — is to legally separate from her husband.

The Smiths' circumstances are neither aberrational nor unusual. As numerous government reports have documented, catastrophic medical expenses force thousands of the nation's elderly into poverty each year. Nor is the risk of catastrophic medical expenses confined to the elderly. At least 35 million and perhaps as many as 50 million Americans *under the age of 65* had no health insurance coverage during 1988. All indications are that the ranks of the nation's "underinsured" will continue to grow.

The Smiths' circumstances may be very dramatic, but they are not the only Americans facing difficult choices. In the halls of Congress, a subcommittee chairman with jurisdiction over federal health programs is given reconciliation instructions to, once again, "tighten" Medicare and Medicaid expenditures by several billion dollars annually — and unwritten instructions from party leaders to do so without the appearance of program cutbacks. His circumstances are not unusual either. Indeed, by the late 1980s, the dance of federal health legislation would be well rehearsed: grand flourishes of reform; sympathetic postures towards the hapless consumer, the beleaguered states, the frustrated providers; and, in the end, a health budget and a federal health policy driven largely by fiscal considerations and budget deficit politics.

While both the details and the direction of federal policy will have considerable impact on the medical director of a public hospital in Oakland, California, her immediate worries are thousands of miles away: finding an empty bed in an already crowded facility, cajoling her clinic's physicians to understand the culture — and language — of their patients, and battling with neighboring hospitals who dump their difficult or nonpaying patients at the emergency room door. These are just today's problems. Tomorrow she will be told that her pleas for newer equipment and a modernized facility are unrealistic. Public or charitable sources of capital for health facilities have all but disappeared, and in the upscale world of tax exempt bonds and commercial paper, joint ventures and proprietary marketing practices, a "poor person's hospital" is unlikely to compete favorably for capital financing.

This textbook begins with these anecdotes not to claim that they present the most serious or the most fundamental problems of contemporary health policy. In fact the relative importance of these and other problems, and whether they are fundamental or merely symptomatic, are questions that a good portion of these materials will attempt to assess. These anecdotes are intended only to illustrate the range and the seriousness of the problems that arise in the delivery of health care. Other scenes in other places might serve this purpose equally well. An acutely ill diabetic is "escorted" from a Tennessee hospital emergency room and left in the parking lot to die — apparently because he had not paid his previous bill. A North Carolina family pleads on the nightly news for an organ donor for their infant child. William Bartling, suffering from five fatal diseases is kept "alive" for the last six months in intensive care despite his demands that his respirator be disconnected so he would die in peace. An economist speaking to an audience of manufacturers blames rising health care costs — and, implicitly, consumers' lack of discipline — for economic inflation, flagging productivity, and the decline of the nation's competitiveness in international markets.

Health care delivery in the United States today confronts not simply a single or fundamental problem or, as critics keep insisting, a pending crisis. Health care confronts a series of related but distinct and conflicting problems involving the accessibility and adequacy of the nation's health services; the costs of those services to various levels of government, to private third party payers, and to individual consumers; and the quality and efficacy of the services that are provided. These problems draw us, collectively and individually, into divisive political controversies wherein the definition of the problem that needs to be addressed is often as controversial as the fashioning of the remedy, and the remedy for one problem, as often as not, only exacerbates the problem of another.

The materials in the chapters to follow describe our current health care delivery system in more detail, identify contemporary health care-related problems, and analyze the political and legal controversies that they present. The remainder of this chapter provides a basic historical account of the development of American health care from its origins in 19th century medicine through the 1970s, the starting point for the descriptions to follow in subsequent chapters; sketches the major political and social forces that have shaped this development; and suggests some recurring themes in our history.

A. The Physician and American Medicine

The structure of health care delivery in the United States has been in large part defined by the evolution of the American medical profession.

While historians can trace the role of the physician and the practice of medicine as far back as the earliest records of civilization, the story of American medicine essentially begins in the mid-nineteenth century. The physician of the 1850s had neither a firm intellectual foundation nor a clear social role. Many types of "healers" competed for the public's respect and a share of its pocketbook: midwives, abortionists, eclectics, homeopathics, herbalists, faith healers, and even "patent medicine" or "snake oil" salesmen. In fact, none was particularly successful, therapeutically or otherwise. In part by preference, in part by economic necessity, most people received their medical care in the home from the women of their family, following traditional healing practices.

Only slowly did the edicts of science for the practice of medicine emerge and take hold. If germs, not moral failure or a vindictive deity, caused disease then a properly trained physician could diagnose an illness, evaluate and prescribe a remedy. If infections could be prevented by antiseptic technique — the advantages of cleanliness in the operating room were not discovered in this country until the 1870s — then surgery could be less a heroic, last ditch effort to save life and more a restorative, professional skill. Above all, if science could rationalize medical practice, then both the therapeutic value of medicine and the social and economic status of its practitioners could be greatly enhanced. It should be noted, however, that while many new techniques represented genuine scientific progress, they were also understood and implemented within the dominant political and cultural attitudes of the day. Thus, for example, new methods of anesthesia were reserved for whites, because it was believed, as a matter of science, that blacks were less sensitive to pain.

The battle of "regular" or "alleopathic" medicine for the respect of the public was as slow as that to conquer disease. Nineteenth-century Americans were reluctant to accept scientific medicine and its consequent implications for the role of its practitioners. As early as the late 1700s, a few states had attempted to impose limits on who could practice medicine; but medical licensing legislation, granting exclusive control over treatment and diagnosis of disease and illness to those who were properly credentialed or trained,

A Selected Chronology of 19th Century American Medicine

1789 Maryland adopts legislation allowing the state medical society to license physicians (repealed 1838).

1818 Valentine Mott, a New York physician, performs first successful cardiovascular operation (the patient survived for one month).

1846 First use of ether as an anesthetic, during surgery at Massachusetts General Hospital by William Thomas Morton (that same year, the American Medical Association is founded). Chloroform soon becomes more widely used.

1873 Texas adopts the first "modern" medical licensing law. (A similar statute in Virginia is upheld as constitutional by the Supreme Court in 1883.)

1881 President Garfield is shot by an assassin and dies three months later. While the original wound may have caused his death, contributing factors include the repeated examination of the wound with unwashed hands and unclean instruments and, on several occasions, the "squeezing" of the wound to encourage suppuration.

1887 The Pennsylvania Hospital first offers service to paying patients, building a private villa, "to meet a demand for a more liberal accommodation for a limited number of patients . . . [so that they might enjoy the comfort] to which they were accustomed . . . and for which they were willing and able to pay."

1890 First use of rubber gloves during surgery (by William Halsted at Johns Hopkins).

1893 Surgeons remove cancer-ridden portion of President Cleveland's upper jaw. Operation performed on board a yacht on the East River in New York. The successful operation is kept secret until revealed 24 years later.

1901 Rockefeller Institute for Medical Research is established.

1909 Abraham Flexner submits his final report to the Carnegie Foundation.

1911 "I believe firmly that more patients have died from the use of gloves than have ever been saved from infection by their use." W. P. Carr (a prominent Boston surgeon).

despite the efforts of local and state medical associations, was highly controversial in America before the Civil War, suffering several waves of popularity and repeal. Not until the end of the century did all states require all medical practitioners to hold a medical license. And it would not be until the year 1912, we are told by one Harvard researcher, "when for the first time in human history . . . a random patient with a random disease consulting a doctor chosen at random stood better than a 50-50 chance of benefiting from the encounter."[1] Whatever the technical accuracy of the claim, it accurately reflects the legacy of nineteenth-century American medicine.

More critically, although a scientific foundation for medical practice was being more adequately secured, the social and economic foundations of medical practice remained precarious. Neither the imprimatur of licensing legislation nor the physician's claims to the advances of science had an immediate impact on medicine's nontraditional competitors. The promised miracles of science as applied to medicine and those of the homeopath, or even the quack, were still hard to distinguish in the late nineteenth century. Indeed, it was at this time of rapid scientific advances that the patent medicine and cure-all nostrum reached the height of their popularity.

The twentieth-century physician commanded much more respect than his nineteenth-century counterpart, as scientific medicine became more sophisticated and as the profession became more effectively organized. In the first quarter of this century, licensing laws were made stricter and more uniform, allowing alleopathic physicians a virtual monopoly over the treatment of illness and disease. And in fashioning medical licensing laws, the states established a political pattern that would be repeated often in future health-related legislation: most of the control over licensing standards and their application was ceded to the state and local medical associations. In some states, chiropractors, Christian Scientists, and a few other alternative providers also managed to secure the recognition of licensing legislation or at least to escape the reach of medical licensure laws. But in practice as well as in legal doctrine, the alternative provider would be vastly overshadowed in the twentieth century by the medical physician.

The most immediate and concrete effect of state medical licensing requirements, however, was not to diminish the popularity of alternative healers but to increase the value of a medical school diploma. One hundred fourteen medical schools were founded between 1875 and 1900. Most were small institutions offering little more than an apprenticeship and a diploma. Many physicians, even with growing confidence in their abilities, bitterly claimed that the resulting oversupply of physicians, coupled with the continued competition from without the profession, made the maintenance of a viable medical practice both professionally and financially unrewarding.

The connection between medical education requirements and medical li-

1. Quoted in R. Harris, A Sacred Trust 5 (1966).

censure eventually allowed the profession to gain control over the supply of physicians and to secure the social and economic status that the profession would enjoy in the twentieth-century. Nineteenth-century medical education had been a reflection of nineteenth-century medicine: neither had a strong scientific foundation. Until the last decades of the century, most American physicians had learned their craft as an apprentice to another physician. A few traveled to Europe for more sophisticated training. The proliferation of medical schools in the last several decades of the century did little to improve the quality of American medical education.

In 1909, Abraham Flexner surveyed the nation's medical schools at the behest of the Carnegie Foundation. He found poorly equipped and unsanitary clinics, schools with optional attendance, two year "diploma mills" that were more a matter of good business for the faculty members who owned them than of good education for their students. As he tactfully put it, he had found "the best in the world side by side with the worst." Flexner recommended that medical education be upgraded following the pattern of European, university-based education, and that medical licensure be limited to physicians who graduated from schools that met these upgraded educational standards. His intention was not only to enhance the quality of medical practice, but also to limit the number of those admitted to the profession. What we needed, according to Flexner, was better but also fewer physicians.

Flexner's much publicized report was more the chronicle than the cause of a process driven by economic realities and pressure from the increasingly powerful medical profession. Nonetheless, his vision of reform was soon realized. From 166 medical schools in 1904 — the year that the AMA founded its Council on Medical Education (CME) to establish standards for accrediting medical schools — the number of schools dropped to 133 in 1910 and to 104 in 1915. During this period, the annual number of medical school graduates dropped by more than 50 percent (although by the 1930s, the number of medical school graduates had risen again to pre-Flexner levels.) In the schools that remained, both admission and graduation standards were upgraded and standardized. In keeping with the demands of medicine's new scientific basis, both laboratory and clinical work were expanded. By 1920, all states had made accreditation by the Council on Medical Education essentially mandatory. (Later, in the 1950s and 1960s, when internships and residency programs became a regular part of medical training for virtually all physicians, these programs also became subject to the profession's accreditation.) In fact, for the next fifty years, AMA policy and American medical education policy would be virtually synonymous.

The implications of the Flexner-era reforms were enormous. The scientific quality of medical education and practice was improved dramatically. The medical school emerged as an elite, academically based graduate institution for both training and research that would eventually dominate both education and practice. Its graduates were comparably elevated. In the words of

E. Richard Brown, from 1890 to 1925 the medical profession "ascended from ignominy and frustrated ambition to prestige, power, and considerable wealth," largely on the wings of medical education reform.[2] The public commitment to medical education also grew. Student fees could no longer support the expense of more sophisticated laboratories and research facilities, longer training, and expanded teaching clinics and hospitals. Driven by pressure from the medical profession and by the publicity of Flexner and other reformers, both public and private sources made unprecedented investments in what had been previously considered largely a proprietary enterprise. State legislatures funneled substantial tax revenues into state university medical schools. The Carnegie and Rockefeller foundations and other private philanthropies embarked on major campaigns to fund medical education and research projects, particularly in the elite private universities. The Rockefeller Foundation alone gave $82 million in grants to medical schools between 1915 and 1930.

By the mid-1920s, Flexner's vision had been partially realized. There were fewer and better medical schools producing fewer and better physicians.

There was, of course, a downside to these reforms. First, during this era, five of seven schools that had admitted blacks and all but three of the women's schools were closed. Both groups were discriminated against by the new elite schools. In addition, the twentieth-century American physician-scientist relied predominantly on a biological understanding of health and disease, encouraging an individual and curative orientation to medical treatment. The lay healer and the alternative provider had been subjugated to medicine's dominance. Even within the medical profession, the social or economic factors that contributed to disease or illness received little attention, despite the obvious role played by preventive and community techniques in improving health at the turn of the century. (See sidebar infra.) Some critics have argued that private philanthropy's enthusiastic support of scientific medicine and its practitioners deterred physicians from addressing other causes of ill health — occupational injuries, environmental hazards and social dislocations that medicine's benefactors had done so much to create.[3]

The most important impact of these reforms in medical education, however, was on the profession itself. By the 1920s, on the eve of the several technological revolutions in medical care that would follow, medicine already had become the textbook prototype for a sovereign profession: granted a virtual monopoly over a valued service; allowed to self-regulate its practice and education; held only to its own self-determined notions of appropriate conduct and ethical behavior, even in its commercial dealings. The profession converted its increasing public respect into growing political power. It had successfully limited competition from other types of healers as well as dissent

2. E. R. Brown, Rockefeller Medicine Men 192 (1979).

3. Id. at 98-134; see also T. McKeown, The Role of Medicine: Dream, Mirage, or Nemesis? (1979); L. Doyal, The Political Economy of Health (1981).

from within its own ranks. In the years to follow, the medical profession would use this same political clout to resist external influence of medical practice and to shape programs for financing health care. Medicine had achieved all this because of the growing value of medical services, but also because physicians had successfully organized a cohesive and highly disciplined professional structure. Not surprisingly, through the next several decades, the AMA and the state and local medical associations would be among the most successful actors in the complicated landscape of American health politics.

SIDEBAR: PRIVATE MEDICINE AND PUBLIC HEALTH, ADVANCES IN HEALTH CARE AT THE TURN OF THE CENTURY

Progress in the health of Americans at the turn of the century could be measured in leaps and bounds.

Within a few decades, mortality from tuberculosis, pneumonia, and other respiratory diseases, among the leading causes of death for the previous three centuries, was dramatically reduced. Similar trends were seen for the "childhood" killers: measles, whooping cough, diphtheria, and scarlet fever. Advances in prophylactic vaccination and chemotherapy had given the nation the means to respond to the recurring epidemics of cholera, smallpox, and typhoid that had killed tens of thousands in the 1800s. Even when disease or illness occurred, advances in medicine offered hope that the resulting condition might be treatable and transitory, and rarely, as had often been the case a generation earlier, a life threatening or disabling condition that could linger through a lifetime.

Prior to 1900 two-thirds of Americans died before the age of 50. Between 1900 and 1930 mortality rates for all age groups between 10 and 35 years of age were halved. It has been estimated that out of ten children born in the early 1800s, two to three died in the first year of their life, five or six died by their sixth birthday, and only three lived to maturity. Even by 1915, one out of ten children would die in the first year of life; by 1930, that number also had been halved. Childbirth in the nineteenth century had been almost as risky for the mother. By the 1930s, survival could be expected for both mother and child.

Such advances in the human condition must have been visible and startling. Simply put, most Americans could expect to live better and longer. Average life expectancy at birth was less than 35 in the 1800s; it increased to over 45 by 1900, and to over 60 by the 1930s; this trend of increasing life expectancy would moderate but continue uninterrupted until the 1970s.

Medical historians remind us that medicine *per se* was only partially responsible for these achievements. The war on infectious disease was fought by public health workers — sanitarians, health inspectors, public health nurses — in the streets as much as by physicians at the bedside. The techniques for control of most infectious diseases was less a matter of individual medical care and treatment and more a matter of preventive or public health techniques: mass vaccination programs, identification and isolation of outbreaks, improvements in sanitation and water supply.

Although medicine's new scientific approach was undeniably a vast improvement over the primitive therapeutics of an earlier century, medicine as practiced by the 20th century physician was — and is — focused largely on the individual patient and the biological causes of an illness or disease. There may be many contributing causes to health problems, not all of which are biological or responsive to individual medical care. Treatment and, in particular, prevention of disease or illness may be achieved by "treating" the environmental, social, or economic causes as well as and, in some cases, better than by treating individual patients.

George Rosen, in his assessment of the combined efforts of individual medical care and public health techniques in the early part of this century, uses the successful campaign against tuberculosis as an illustration:

> Tuberculosis . . . provides a model of a disease resulting from a complex interaction of biological socioeconomic and cultural factors. Although a specific etiologic agent has been known for almost a hundred years, a high degree of prevention and control has not been achieved by a frontal attack on the organism, but by drying up the sources of infection through isolation of patients, pasteurization of milk, by reducing overcrowding in dwellings, improving nutrition, and in general raising living standards and making it possible for people to maintain them by increasing their economic resources.[4]

In fact, as Rosen points out, mortality and morbidity from many of the "dread" diseases of the nineteenth century had already begun to decline markedly even before vaccines were available or effective treatment had been developed, simply as a result of improvements in housing, nutrition, and other social and economic conditions.

The point is not to understate the achievements of medicine or the value of medical practitioners. The practice of medicine was becoming increasingly effective in the early 1900s. Americans would soon witness the introduction of sulphanomides, penicillin, and the other "magic bullets" that would be described as the "antibiotic revolution" of the twentieth century. Advances in surgical and obstetric technique would make successful childbirth more commonplace. Deaths from such conditions as appendicitis, once common, would become rare, avoidable tragedies. But the role of medicine in achieving these visible advances in health care must be viewed in the context of the other social and economic advances of the early twentieth century. Protection

4. G. Rosen, Preventive Medicine in the United States 295 (1982).

and maintenance of health requires both good medicine and other conditions, and the lack of either can be significant.

B. The Evolution of the American Hospital

The twentieth century saw Americans turn from traditional healing to medicine and from comfort and palliation in the home to treatment in the physician's office — and in the hospital.

The early forerunners of the American hospital were public institutions — the infirmaries of public "almshouses" and, later, separate state or local institutions for the sick called "hospitals," but still primarily serving to house the poor and the homeless. In the late eighteenth and early nineteenth centuries, private, "voluntary" hospitals, generally financed by bequest or donation, supplemented the public institutions. Voluntary hospitals purported to provide care — mostly convalescent not curative — for patients with some prospect of recovery. The incurable, the destitute, the homeless elderly, and those with infectious diseases were sent to the public almshouse.

All nineteenth-century hospitals, however, were institutions for the poor. Patients with adequate means were treated in the physician's office or, most often, in their home. Abysmal hygienic conditions, overcrowded wards, the primitive state of medical knowledge made the hospital the choice of only the most desperate. Indeed, the poor did not always go willingly to the hospital, although many were forced to apply to the institution's patrons for sponsorship for admission. Even surgery, such as it was, was often practiced outside of the hospital. The average nineteenth-century physician had little contact with either public or private hospitals.

By the late 1800s, however, the increased efficacy of modern medicine and the demands of increasingly sophisticated surgical techniques had enhanced both the medical persona of the hospital and its public image. Still primarily an institution for the care of the poor, the hospital also had begun to take on its twentieth-century function as the "physician's workshop," particularly as the scientific breakthroughs of the nineteenth century — antisepsis, anesthesia, x-ray diagnosis — became more widely available and widely practiced. The late nineteenth-century hospital also took on an important role in the training of physicians. Physicians fortunate enough to secure a volunteer position in a hospital — the nineteenth-century physician considered it unethical to charge a fee to a hospital ward patient — could learn and practice the latest in medical and surgical technique, often under the tutelage of one of the recognized leaders of what was becoming an increasingly hierarchical profession. The result improved the physician's medical skills as well as his reputation with his private — and paying — patients.

The evolution of the hospital had a comparable influence over the development of the nursing profession. Mid-nineteenth-century hospitals drew no sharp lines between nursing and domestic service, or between the services of nurses and patients. Particularly in the almshouses, more able "inmates" became nurses, and then nursing supervisors. Beginning in England in the 1860s, however, the movement inspired by Florence Nightingale sought to train women to bring the order, cleanliness, and morality associated with middle class femininity to grim hospital wards. Many American hospitals established nursing schools in the 1870s and quickly learned that student nurses provided an inexpensive and stable workforce. Students worked 60 to 70 hours a week, in exchange for room, board, and a stipend for books. Discipline was severe and unremitting. The best nursing programs provided little classroom training, and the worst provided none. A small hospital could establish a "school" with as few as five students. After training on the wards, hospitals sent student nurses to care for more wealthy patients in their homes; fees for nursing service were paid directly to the hospital. Still, women sought nursing work because it was one of the few forms of wage work available to them, and because the training could be obtained by women of modest means, who could then make a living in private nursing practice.

Efforts to improve these conditions and upgrade the education and status of nurses met resistance from both physicians and hospital managers. While some in the medical profession saw the value of better trained and more highly skilled nurses, others were threatened by a fear that trained nurses would "prove restless in their subordination."[5] Further, many hospitals, particularly smaller ones, with a weak financial base, resisted educational reform for nurses. These hospitals perceived that they could not afford a nurse training program that met more rigorous standards, and, at the same time, use low cost student nurses to meet their staffing needs.

Sheer numbers reflect the rapid growth and increasing importance of the American hospital. In 1873 there were only 178 hospitals in the United States (about one-third were institutions for the mentally ill). By 1900 there were over 4000 hospitals. By 1930 there were nearly 7000. From 35,500 hospital beds in 1900, the American hospital industry grew to 922,000 beds by 1930.

As their numbers grew, their size and distribution varied considerably, but they took on a pattern that would remain largely unchanged for the next fifty years. More hospitals were in the more populated Northeast, and most were in urban areas. Most were organized as voluntary or charitable institutions, and many were affiliated with religious groups. A few small institutions were "for profit" or proprietary enterprises, generally owned by a group of physicians for their exclusive use. Some of the largest were publicly sponsored, and many — but not all — of these retained their original mission to serve the poor. The largest and most influential hospitals were those affiliated with medical schools.

5. C. Rosenberg, The Care of Strangers: The Rise of America's Hospital System 232 (1987).

The transformation from warehouse for the poor to medical institution for the general public was essentially completed by the 1930s. During the first three decades of this century, many of the techniques were pioneered that became the more visible miracles of modern medicine: vascular, neurological, and thoracic surgery; x-ray and other techniques of internal diagnosis; orthopedic repair and replacement. The modern hospital became a source of hope, perhaps even wonder, rather than despair. Both public expectations and public demand increased accordingly.

As hospital-based medicine became more sophisticated, a complex and unique institution emerged, built around a bifurcated organizational structure: an administrative staff to provide the equipment, facilities, and non-physician staff supervision for the convalescence of the patient and the support of the physician; and a medical staff, which was organizationally part of the management structure but in practice a self-regulating organization of private, independent contractors. This institutional structure, along with the physician's legally sanctioned monopoly over medical treatment, allowed the medical profession to exercise considerable control over all patient care issues within the hospital: admission and discharge, patient management, staff privileges.

At the same time, physicians and hospitals became more mutually dependent on one another. By the 1930s, seven out of ten physicians had some affiliation with a hospital, and hospital-based practice represented a growing proportion of annual physician income. Hospitals were even more dependent upon physicians, the more successful of whom could choose among several hospitals for the care of their paying patients. The physician, by standing between the hospital and the patient had effectively co-opted the hospital's resources and could expect and demand fealty from the hospital's nursing and administrative staff, even from its management and board of trustees.

Hospital-based medicine also created strong pressures towards intraprofessional loyalty and discipline. As staff privileges and the specialty referrals generated by hospital-based practice became more important to the livelihood of many physicians, they found it increasingly difficult to give even the appearance of disloyalty to the professional or to the ideological commitments of organized medicine (as the physicians who became involved in prepaid group practices and other forms of "contract medicine" would quickly learn).

Significantly, by the 1930s, hospital-based medicine was consuming a growing proportion of the nation's health care dollar. In 1929 (the first year for which national health spending data were collected) physician services represented 28 percent of all expenditures for health care. In the next thirty years that proportion would shrink to less than 20 percent. In contrast, hospitals consumed 19 percent of all health spending in 1929; by the 1960s that share had grown to 40 percent of all national health expenditures.

This increase in the importance of hospital services laid the groundwork for major structural changes in health care financing and, eventually, more direct public involvement in health care delivery. As hospitals became more sophisticated, their traditional public and private sponsors found themselves unable to continue supporting them. Even at the turn of the century, some private hospitals had turned to patient-generated revenues to cover expenditures. In 1900 most hospitals had only a small number of paying patients; by the 1920s approximately one-half of hospital patients were paying fees for their services, and over two-thirds of all hospital income in the United States came from individual patient charges. But by the early years of the Depression, reliance on out of pocket payments by patients had proven to be an insufficient basis for financing hospital care. Hospital occupancy had dropped dramatically. Some facilities were forced to close. On the other side of the financial equation, American consumers, already shocked by unprecedented unemployment and widespread financial hardship, faced a further threat of financial ruin: catastrophic medical bills. Thus, from a variety of sources, but most critically from some leaders of the hospital industry, there arose considerable pressure to develop some sort of prepayment or insurance financing for hospital care.

C. The Politics of Health Care Reform From the Progressive Era to the New Deal

Some amount of political support for public financing of health care had been generated in this country as early as the turn of the twentieth century. Many of the industrialized European countries had adopted some form of "sickness insurance." Progressive reformers and some — though not all — labor leaders sought similar programs in the United States. The successful movement to adopt state worker compensation programs to pay workers for losses from industrial accidents (and to limit the liability of their employers) encouraged those who sought broader financing for health services. Mandatory national health insurance was a plank of Theodore Roosevelt's unsuccessful presidential campaign in 1912. The AMA even briefly supported what they labeled "social insurance," although this posture was quickly reversed by more conservative elements within the organization. Political interest, however, waned during World War I (nationalized health insurance, after all, had been "invented" by the Germans) and remained dormant during the laissez-faire politics of the 1920s.

The hardships of the Depression rekindled interest in government financing of health care, as well as other health care reforms. Even earlier, in 1927, the Carnegie Foundation had organized the Committee on the Costs of Medical Care (CCMC), a private commission of leaders from business and government, public health and medical experts, to study and evaluate health and medicine in the United States. In 1932, the CCMC issued a report recommending 1) the organization of all professional services on a group practice basis; 2) the extension of basic public health services, by both private and public agencies, to all Americans; 3) the establishment of prepayment mechanisms for medical services through either private insurance or government-financed programs; and 4) the establishment of local and state agencies for the study and coordination of medical services.

SIDEBAR: THE GAUNTLET IS [CAREFULLY] THROWN DOWN . . .

When the Committee on the Costs of Medical Care issued its final report — and the first national assessment of health and medical care — its findings were stark and direct: the recently witnessed progress in medicine held out tremendous potential for the American people; but those benefits were poorly and unequally distributed. Many people were denied medical care altogether. Few people, largely due to economic reasons, were receiving what they needed. "Medical care," the CCMC proclaimed, "is essential."

The CCMC's recommendations were equally important but more cautiously stated, with evident concern for the reaction they would inspire (see sidebar infra).

> The Committee recommends that medical service, both preventive and therapeutic, should be furnished largely by organized groups of physicians, dentists, nurses, pharmacists, and other associated personnel. Such groups should be organized, preferably around a hospital, for rendering complete home, office and hospital care. The form of organization should encourage the maintenance of high standards and the development or preservation of a personal relation between patient and physician.
>
> The Committee recommends the extension of all basic public health services — whether provided by governmental or non-governmental agencies — so that they will be available to the entire population according to its needs. Primarily this extension requires increased financial support for official health departments and full-time trained health officers and members of their staffs whose tenure is dependent only upon professional and administrative competence.
>
> The Committee recommends that the costs of medical care be placed on a group payment basis, through the use of insurance, through the use of taxation, or through the use of both these methods. This is not meant to preclude the continuation of medical service provided on an individual fee basis for those who prefer the present method. Cash benefits, i.e., compensation for wage-loss due to illness, if and when provided, should be separate and distinct from medical services.
>
> The Committee recommends that the study, evaluation, and coordination of medical service be considered important functions for every state and local community, that agencies be formed to exercise these functions, and that the coordination of rural with urban services receive special attention. . . . [The

Committee on the Costs of Medical Care, Medical Care for the American People xvi (October 1932).]

The report had carefully downplayed the implications of the recommendations for government involvement in medical care; indeed, it was conspicuously silent about how these recommendations would be achieved. Nonetheless, the implications of the report were not lost on the medical profession. The response of the AMA was understandable albeit hyperbolic. The encouragement of group practice, AMA leaders claimed, was no less than "the establishment of medical soviets." Government financing of medical care, voluntary or not, would be the "first step towards socialized medicine."

The AMA's rhetoric highlighted the profession's primary concern and the concern that would be voiced with equal vehemence in the decades to follow to virtually all attempts to reform health care delivery or financing. What organized medicine feared was not just the threat to its economic self-interest, but also what it viewed as "socialized medicine," or any inroad, public *or* private, on the autonomy of the individual practitioner or on the control over medical practice exercised by the profession itself. Most physicians perceived — and later history would validate their perception — that external control and loss of their autonomy would be the necessary incidents of any reform of solo, fee-for-service medicine, or any third party prepayment scheme for financing medical services. Even though many physicians suffered financially during the Depression, most were convinced that any economic advantage that might accrue from third party financing would be offset by the loss of their autonomy and professional control. Thus while physicians later gave ground to private prepayment schemes, they did so reluctantly and under conditions where the traditions and ideology of American medicine were carefully protected.

The vehement opposition of the AMA to government-financed health insurance and to other structural changes in health care delivery of the type proposed by the CCMC also demonstrated much about the politics of health care reform from the 1930s to contemporary times. The perceived concerns of the medical profession for its sovereignty closely aligned with those of political conservatives, at least to the extent that both opposed further expansion of government authority, particularly from the federal level. Only later when the inherent differences between "private medicine" as viewed by the inherently conservative profession and "private *and competitive* medicine," as envisioned by some economic conservatives, became clearer would this alignment begin to diverge. But in the 1930s, notwithstanding Roosevelt's liberal majority, this conservative coalition was formidable. When some officials within the Roosevelt Administration initially, and then again at the beginning of his second term, urged the inclusion of mandatory health insurance as part of the domestic reforms of the New Deal, the opposition marshalled by the medical community and conservative politicians convinced the President that further support of health insurance would jeopardize support for his Social Security, welfare, and other New Deal domestic reforms. Federal health insurance was reduced to a political bargaining chip, a position it would occupy for several decades.

In response to rising political support for the CCMC reforms, the AMA sponsored a series of critical reports and public statements emphasizing the evils of what they labeled "sickness insurance." At the annual meeting of the AMA House of Delegates in 1934, the efforts culminated in what could be regarded as the profession's manifesto for private insurance.

Sidebar: The AMA Responds . . .

First: All features of medical service in any method of medical practice should be under the control of the medical profession. No other body or individual is legally or educationally equipped to exercise such control.

Second: No third party must be permitted to come between the patient and his physician in any medical relation. All responsibility for the character of medical service must be borne by the profession.

Third: Patients must have absolute freedom to choose a duly qualified doctor of medicine who will serve them from among all those qualified to practice and who are willing to give service.

Fourth: The method of giving the service must retain a permanent, confidential relation between the patient and a "family physician." This relation must be the fundamental and dominating feature of any system.

Fifth: All medical phases of all institutions involved in the medical service should be under professional control, it being understood that hospital service and medical service should be considered separately. These institutions are but expansions of the equipment of the physician. He is the only one whom the laws of all nations recognize as competent to use them in the delivery of service. The medical profession alone can determine the adequacy and character of such institutions. Their value depends on their operation according to medical standards.

Sixth: However the cost of medical service may be distributed, the immediate cost should be borne by the patient if able to pay at the time the service is rendered.

Seventh: Medical service must have no connection with any cash benefits.

Eighth: Any form of medical service should include within its scope all qualified physicians of the locality covered by its operation who wish to give service under the conditions established.

Ninth: Systems for the relief of low income classes should be limited strictly to those below the "comfort level" standard of incomes.

Tenth: There should be no restrictions on treatment or prescribing not formulated and enforced by the organized medical profession.

[American Medical Association, Sickness Insurance Problems in the United States (June 30, 1934).]

It is somewhat ironic that most of CCMC reforms were eventually adopted. In fact, the outlines of the agenda suggested by the CCMC — the reorganization and integration of medical services, the extension of private and public prepayment mechanisms, the collective planning of health care resources — essentially outlined the central issues that dominated American health policy debates for the next forty years.

Health care reform had emerged by the end of the 1930s as an important and complex public policy issue. As the CCMC had recognized, whatever the advantages and potential of health care for the American people, it also had raised fundamental questions of cost, accessibility, and equity; health care had become "essential"; what they did not say but clearly implied was that health care had also become problematic and controversial.

D. The Emergence of Private Health Insurance and the "Birth of the Blues"

The growing concerns for the costs and adequacy of health care, on the one hand, and the strong political opposition to publicly sponsored reforms, on the other, set the stage for the growth of privately initiated prepayment schemes.

Much to the chagrin — and often to the active opposition of the medical profession — a number of experiments with "contract medicine" emerged in the 1920s and 1930s. Probably the most important were attempts by employee groups and "medical cooperatives" to form "closed panel" prepayment schemes for physician and other medical services, the forerunners of what would later be called prepaid health plans or health maintenance organizations. A few hospitals attempted similar arrangements, offering coverage for specified hospital benefits in exchange for a fixed annual or monthly premium, protecting the enrolled consumer from the unpredictable threat of hospitalization costs, and offering some measure of economic stability to the contracting hospital.

As these prepayment experiments became more widespread, they encountered both political and legal constraints. Despite the eagerness of the hospital industry to find a more suitable source of financing, most hospitals viewed themselves as "charitable" and medical institutions. The notion of competition between hospitals for the exclusive enrollment of patients threatened both these traditions. Legal questions were also raised concerning the applicability of state insurance laws to these schemes, particularly the organizational and reserve requirements imposed by states on most other forms of insurance. Physicians also opposed hospital-based prepayment plans because they profoundly altered the power relationship between physicians and hospitals.

In an effort to steer these developments in a direction more acceptable to the medical profession and the hospital industry, the increasingly visible American Hospital Association (AHA), along with state and local hospital groups, sought state legislation authorizing tax-exempt hospital "service-benefit" plans and exempting these plans from general insurance laws. These plans were also exempted from federal taxation on their income and premiums. To qualify for tax exemption, "service-benefit" plans had to be structured according to what the industry regarded as proper and ethical standards, including:

1) the assurance that such plans would be open to the whole community;
2) the requirements that such plans offer "freedom of choice" to both provider and subscriber, that is, any hospital would be allowed the "freedom" to join the plan and any subscriber would have the "freedom" to choose any participating hospital;
3) and the requirement that the majority of the directors of these plans be representatives of the hospital industry.

From these efforts emerged what several observers have called the "Birth of the Blues."[6] As states were adopting "service-benefit" authorizing legislation, the AHA was sponsoring the formation of a national Blue Cross Association (BCA). BCA offered to any hospital "service-benefit" plan meeting the membership requirements of BCA — not the least of which was the requirement that any BCA member show that 75 percent of the hospitals in its geographic area were participants in the plan — was entitled to use the name and emblem of Blue Cross. As a result, while theoretically any number of hospital "service-benefit" plans might have been formed in a region, most Blue Cross plans were assured a de facto monopoly over a unique and important form of hospital financing.

Fueled by both the public demand and the hospital industry's interest, Blue Cross plans spread rapidly. By 1938, 1.4 million people had enrolled in 38 plans across the country. By contrast, at that time private indemnity insurance covered only 100,000 people for hospital care. By the end of 1946, nearly one out of five Americans had enrolled in Blue Cross hospital "service-benefit" plans.

American physicians were more reluctant to embrace third party insurance, even "service-benefit" plans tailored to the needs and traditions of med-

6. See, e.g., P. Starr, The Social Transformation of American Medicine 295 (1982).

icine. Throughout the 1930s, many individual and organization efforts were made to discourage participation by physicians in any insurance or prepayment plans. Several states gave judicial or statutory recognition of the "corporate practice of medicine" doctrine, which effectively prohibited any form of medical care financing or delivery that allowed nonphysician control over medical practice. By the 1940s, however, physicians in many states were, in the words of Rosemary Stevens, turning a necessity into a virtue.[7] In California, Oregon, and Washington, local medical associations established "medical service associations," that paid participating physicians on a prorated fee-for-service basis for services provided to subscribers. In other states, Blue Cross plans underwrote and, in some cases, administered "Blue Shield" plans, incorporating arrangements parallel to those of Blue Cross for physician control, and "freedom of choice" guarantees for both the consumer-subscriber and for the participating physician. The official Blue Shield emblem was created in 1946: the initials "A.M.A." over a caduceus emblazoned on a blue shield. Between 1939 and 1945, 26 states enacted special enabling legislation for medical "service-benefit" plans. By 1947, 4.4 million people, 4 percent of the American population, were members of Blue Shield or medical "service-benefit" plans, although nearly two-thirds were in five states.

A number of factors encouraged the growth of "service-benefit" plans and, eventually, other forms of private health insurance. First, as concern for the costs of health care continued but the political likelihood of publicly sponsored health care financing dimmed, health insurance became increasingly popular as an employment benefit. This trend was given an additional boost when wage controls were imposed during and after World War II, but fringe benefit increases up to 5 percent of wages were exempted from these controls. Perhaps more important for long term policy, the Internal Revenue Service ruled in 1943 that employer-contributions to group health insurance (expanded in 1954 to cover all employer-purchased health insurance) were exempt from the employee's taxable income.

While these factors fostered continued growth of the Blues, they also sparked the interest of many commercial insurance companies. Until the 1940s, most insurance experts had insisted that indemnity insurance against medical bills was inherently unprofitable: the losses were actuarially unpredictable and biased by what economic experts call "moral hazard," that is, the insured's ability to influence whether a claim could be made. But the convenience of selling group insurance through employers, combined with the success of the Blues, encouraged commercial insurers to enter the health insurance market. During the 1940s, commercial health insurance coverage in the United States jumped dramatically. By 1951, nearly 80 million Americans had hospital insurance coverage, over 40 million through various indemnity policies, a slightly smaller share through Blue Cross plans. By the

7. R. Stevens, American Medicine and the Public Interest 418-426 (1971).

end of the decade, over 80 percent of the work force had employer-purchased health insurance benefits. By the 1960s — and even after the enactment of Medicaid and Medicare — a stable pattern had emerged: roughly 80 percent of the nonelderly population has some hospital insurance coverage, most of which was employment-based; slightly less than half of this insurance was provided by some form of "service-benefit plan," and a slightly larger proportion by private commercial insurers. Until the 1980s, few employers were "self-insured." Only a small but stable proportion of the health insurance market was held by closed panel, prepaid health plans, or health maintenance organizations. About 60 percent of the population had some coverage for physician services — distributed in a roughly similar pattern.

The competition during the 1940s and 1950s between commercial insurance companies and Blue Cross and Blue Shield plans had a major impact on the character of health care financing in this country. As originally conceived, nonprofit "service-benefit" plans were designed as much for political and social purposes as for economic objectives. The sponsors of Blue Cross and Blue Shield envisioned themselves as providing the private alternative to government financing, securing the reimbursement of providers for their services while meeting the public's needs for collective prepayment. Thus the original Blues offered "community rating" (all subscribers in a geographic area paid the same price), minimal co-payment and deductibles, broad coverage of services, and guaranteed service: enrolled subscribers were assured that they would be accepted by all participating providers. Some plans went further and provided discounted rates to low income people and to large families. Blue Cross subscribers were also assured that participating hospitals would accept assignment of claims, that is, accept the Blue Cross payment as payment in full. (Even physicians who were willing to participate in Blue Shield programs preferred to set their own fees and charge directly to their patients; thus Blue Shield reimbursements generally have been paid on an indemnity basis to the patient.)

Commercial indemnity insurers have no contractual relations with either hospitals or physicians. The commercial insurer simply contracts to pay the patient a fixed rate or, for a substantially higher premium, to pay whatever the provider charges. Commercial insurers have never sought to provide coverage to entire communities, but rather seek to avoid insuring people who are at high risk and to vary the rates charged in accordance with the risk that the individual or group will use insured services.

But while the features of "service-benefit" plans were attractive to providers and to many consumers, other consumers, particularly those at low risk and some employers, preferred to purchase the most limited coverage and indemnity insurance and, of course, the resulting reductions in premiums.

As a consequence of the competition with commercial insurers, Blue Cross and Blue Shield plans abandoned some of the features of "service-benefit" plans and began to charge different groups and individuals different rates on an experience basis. Likewise, there was some pressure on indemnity insurance companies to offer policies that more closely resembled the deeper and more comprehensive coverage of typical "service-benefit" plans. As a result, as indemnity insurers and "service-benefit" plans have settled into a relatively stable division of the private insurance market, the original distinctions between them have been somewhat blurred.

The result also has been a uniquely American form of health service financing. Unlike virtually every other industrialized country, Americans rely predominantly on private, employment-based, insurance-type financing schemes and on schemes that largely have divorced the financing of services from their delivery. Neither "service-benefit" plans nor indemnity insurers integrate the provider into the financing scheme, nor do they often attempt to control directly the behavior of physicians, hospitals, or other providers.

The potential for doing so has always been there. HMOs and other closed panel prepayment schemes had provided successful experiments with direct control over providers as early as the 1930s. Prior to the emergence of the Blues, such programs had been attempted by a few individual hospitals. For decades the United Mine Workers union ran a program on this model for its workers, constructing facilities, hiring health personnel and providing service to meet its members' needs. The largest program of this type was organized by the Kaiser Aluminum Company to provide health services to its workers and their families, and eventually to others in the communities where it operated. Organized medicine, however, has strongly opposed such arrangements, perceiving them as a threat to physician autonomy. Further, with the growth of the Blues and indemnity insurance, few employers, unions, or communities felt the need to undertake the challenging job of creating an integrated health service delivery program, particularly in the face of deep provider opposition.

But there were two weak links in this dominant pattern of private, employment-based health insurance, weaknesses that would eventually lead to controversy and reform. First, fee-for-service reimbursement and the lack of control exercised over provider behavior by third party payers set the stage for the rapid increases in the costs of their services that would become increasingly problematic by the 1960s and "critical" by the 1970s and 1980s. Under the private, insurance-type financing that became predominant in the United States, providers had little incentive even to consider the costs of the services they delivered. In fact, as economists would later insist, the reimbursement arrangements built into most health insurance schemes created economic incentives to provide marginally beneficial and even unnecessary care. But so long as third party payers could raise their premiums to cover these reimbursement costs, there would be little pressure on the commercial insurance companies or the Blues to reform these arrangements. And so long as the consumer, insulated by government subsidy and by employer contributions, was more concerned with the extent of health insurance coverage than with rising premium costs or increase in out-of-pocket payments, political pressure to reform health care financing from the purchasers of insurance would not emerge. The seeds of the cost problem that would eventually dominate health care policy debates were sown into the character of the private third-party financing of health care that developed in the 1940s and the 1950s, but the perception of this "cost problem" would emerge only later.

More immediate pressure to reform would first come from the other weak link in this pattern of American health care financing. Private employment-based health insurance had also failed to secure financing for the care of the elderly and the poor.

E. The Evolution of the Government's Role in Health Care: Public Health and Private Medicine

As noted earlier, there were antecedents for government involvement in health care as far back as the late 1700s. Nonetheless, these efforts were quite limited, limited largely to state and local government, and strictly confined within the boundaries of legitimate "public health" — in contrast to "private medicine" — activities.

The federal role, in particular, was quite narrow until nearly the middle of the twentieth century. The first federal quarantine laws were not enacted until the 1870s and then only following an intense congressional debate over the constitutionality of such legislation. The first major federal health-related regulatory program was created in 1906, prohibiting interstate commerce in misbranded or adulterated food and drugs (amended in 1938 to regulate drug safety and in 1962 to require testing of the efficacy of new drugs).

American politics, however, traditionally demanded that most public health activities, to the extent they were appropriate at all, were the responsibility of the state or local government. In the second half of the nineteenth century, government programs to control sewage, maintain water quality, and to report and control contagious disease were exclusively state and local government activities. By the early 1900s, these traditional public health activities had been extended to include more regulatory controls; for instance, compulsory vaccination programs, mandatory testing prior to marriage or for public-contact occupations, inspection and licensing of restaurants and other businesses. Such regulations, however, did not lose their state or local character; the federal role was virtually negligible. Moreover, even at the state and local levels, government authority over health and health care was begrudgingly conceded by nineteenth and early twentieth-century Americans. Even when faced with epidemics of yellow fever, typhoid, and cholera, the public mistrust and political resistance to remedial public health measures were remarkably persistent.

Understandably, government activities that encroached directly on the practice of "private medicine" were even more proscribed. Most of the exceptions to the rule — medical licensing laws, public funding for medical education, tax exemption of health insurance and authorization of "service-benefit plans" — only demonstrated the distinct political origins of these exceptions: government might legitimately encourage and protect the practice of medicine without crossing the public-health/private-medicine boundary; but government did so almost always at the behest of medical practitioners, and any resulting control over the practice of medicine was generally delegated back to the providers themselves.

The only governmental programs that directly involved provision of medical care were more aptly described as "public" or "welfare medicine": programs providing care for public wards and for the poor. The 18th century public almshouse gave way to public hospitals in some state and urban areas (generally mandated to serve *only* the poor). State hospitals for the confinement and treatment, such that it was, of the mentally ill and, later, other people with disabilities or contagious diseases were established in the last half of the nineteenth century.

At the turn of the century, a few local governments briefly experimented with dispensaries and clinics to provide medical care for the poor. In each case, these programs were carefully limited to avoid competition with "private medicine." Within similar boundaries, the federal government historically provided medical care to military personnel, veterans, American Indians and other federal wards. These state and federal programs provided historical precedents for government involvement in both public health and medical care-related activities. They also provided the testing ground for judicial consideration of the constitutional limits on government authority over health care, limits that proved to be quite broad. At least through the first quarter of this century, however, political constraints severely limited government to "public health" activities, and "public health" generally ended where "private medicine" began.

As with so many other American social and political phenomena, the 1930s marked the watershed for a redefinition of the course of government health policy. As noted in the previous section, the growing importance of medical care, paired with the harsh economic realities of the Depression, created substantial political efforts to adopt federally sponsored health insurance as part of the New Deal reforms. While those efforts were eventually rebuffed, the Social Security programs did include increased federal funding for maternal and child health programs and other federally-funded, state administered public health services. Other New Deal programs also represented modest extensions of the federal role in health care; for instance, the Federal Emergency Relief Administration financed medical care for the unemployed; the Work Projects Administration funded some public clinic and hospital construction.

The 1930s also saw the beginning of what would become a major federal responsibility, the funding of biomedical research. In 1930, the National Institute for Health (NIH) was established, to be followed in 1937 by the National Cancer Institute, and thereafter a succession of research institutes for specific diseases. By the 1950s, federal spending for biomedical research was over $70 million; by 1960, $500 million. By the early 1970s, the federal government would be spending several billion dollars annually to conduct and finance biomedical and health services research.

The program that most clearly demonstrated the emergence of federal leadership and the new direction of twentieth-century health policy, however, was the Hill-Burton hospital survey and construction program enacted in 1946. During the 1930s and the 1940s, there was a growing recognition that hospitals were poorly and inequitably distributed. Many areas, particularly in the rural South, had no hospitals at all. Moreover, while the growth of prepayment schemes offered some basis for financing hospital services, the high costs of the initial capital investment and the periodic modernization and replacement of hospital facilities — particularly during a period of rapid technological change — left the traditional sources of hospital capital funding — that is, community fundraising and private philanthropy — inadequate. World War II had also dramatized two realities. As the CCMC had claimed a decade earlier, the health status of many Americans was unimpressive. Reports of the high percentage of American males who flunked their preinduction draft physicals, as high as 50 percent in some states, frequently claimed that this poor health status was a result of a lack of available medical and hospital care — a dubious but politically volatile observation. The war also gave visibility to many of the new developments of modern medicine: penicillin and other "wonder drugs," restorative surgery, new techniques for the treatment of trauma, burns, and the like. It also tended to legitimize a federal role in the distribution of these medical breakthroughs. For many Americans, military service during World War II meant that for the first time they had access to modern medical care on a regular basis.

Political liberals attempted to convert this public concern into support for nationalized health insurance (NHI) and other structural reforms in health care delivery. President Roosevelt was apparently warming to the idea of NHI shortly before his death. His successor, Harry Truman, bluntly embraced national health insurance in his first domestic policy message to Congress following the war. Political conservatives, desperate to find some acceptable alternative as they moved into the second decade of Democratic dominance, found nationalized federal financing an anathema, but were increasingly willing to consider an extended but limited federal role in health care, particularly one that would not directly affront the traditional interests of health care providers.

The final Hill-Burton hospital construction legislation, sponsored by a moderate Republican from Ohio and a conservative Democrat from Alabama, captured these politics. Hill-Burton authorized federal funds for each state to survey needs and to develop the plans for the development of hospital facilities. It also provided matching funds and loans for the construction of public and nonprofit facilities that met the needs outlined in the state's plan. In later years, the program was expanded to allow the funding of other types of health facilities and, in 1964, the modernization of existing facilities. Funded projects had to comply with a number of requirements outlined in the federal law concerning the safety and adequacy of the facilities, as well as provisions — largely overlooked — to provide a reasonable volume of uncompensated care and not to discriminate on the basis of race (the latter was expanded in 1964 to a general "community service" requirement).

Hill-Burton represented an unprecedented federal initiative and the first major investment of federal funds into mainstream health care. In the first 25 years of the program, over half of the hospitals in the country received Hill-Burton assistance, to finance facility construction and modernization. Hill-Burton also broke another barrier: for the first time, government agencies were authorized to plan for and allocate health care resources, a foreshadowing of the more serious planning efforts that would follow.

Nonetheless, the regulatory features of Hill-Burton were more symbolic than real. The program was structured and administered more as a conduit for federal assistance than as an attempt to collectively rationalize the distribution of hospital resources. While the federal requirement that states have licensing programs in order to participate in Hill-Burton spurred some interest in state regulation of quality standards, that movement was sidetracked by hospitals and physicians through the creation of a private, provider-dominated program to review and certify the quality of medical care: the Joint Commission on the Accreditation of Hospitals. As they had with virtually all previous state and federal government health programs, providers had once again managed to secure the benefits of government intervention, in this case public financing of their capital costs, without conceding much control over those resources or over their professional activities.

F. The Evolution of Health Policy from the Post-War Era to the 1960s

If there were "glory days" for American medicine, they must have been in the 1950s. In the name of the public's welfare, medicine had successfully claimed the protection of licensing laws, public and philanthropic support for medical education, and freedom from both external control and internal competition. Private but publicly encouraged third party payment schemes were now available, assuring reimbursement for medical services, but carefully structured to avoid "socializing" medical practice. State and federal money was being spent in increasing amounts for public health services, "welfare medicine," biomedical research, and hospital construction. Both individual and institutional providers were able to claim both the cloak of free enterprise and the mantle of service to the public's health in their successful efforts to protect their autonomy and their respected social status.

American medicine could also claim that all these advantages were more than justified by what they now could provide. In the first quarter of the century, American medicine had started on the road to professional sovereignty and economic security on the wings of an unsecured promise of hope: what science had discovered today, medicine would provide, left to its private practice, tomorrow. By the 1950s, the promise had been replaced by an assertion that would become medicine's permanent political banner: "Americans," we were proudly told, "have the best medical care in the world."[8]

As an assessment of the nation's technical capability, the claim was quite certainly true. As in other fields, American medical technology had assumed a position of leadership following World War II. As a description of medical practice, however, American medicine's claim to supremacy was an understandable exaggeration, statistical improvements in health status notwithstanding. Only some Americans had access to the "best medical care in the world." Despite Hill-Burton and other government efforts, there were still areas of the country that could claim a need for hospital services. More critically, the limited supply of physicians and the unwillingness of many practitioners to practice in "undesirable" areas left a shortage of physician services in many rural areas and, particularly, urban poor areas. Even when medical care was available, the necessary concomitant of better medical care — higher medical costs — posed financial barriers, particularly for those who fell into the gaps between private insurance coverage, despite its rapid growth, and the limited government "welfare medicine" programs.

The political irony of American medicine's adamant claim to provide the best medical care in the world was not that its accuracy was disputed; it was that the proposition was so readily accepted. But while for its authors the claim implied that private medicine's sovereignty and privileged status should be left intact, for others it had quite a different meaning. In the best medical care system in the world, those who are denied that care become all the more visible, and their calls for remedial measures become increasingly popular. American politics did not abandon altogether the political constraints that had shaped public policy previously, but for the next several decades those constraints would be continually weakened by the pervasive egalitarian notion that all Americans were *entitled* to the best medical care available.

8. See The Causes, Control, and Remedies of the Principal Diseases of Mankind: Hearings Before the House Comm. on Interstate and Foreign Commerce, 83rd Cong., 1st Sess. 2 (1953) (statement of Charles A. Wolverton, Comm. Chairman); see also American Medical Association, The Case Against the King-Anderson Bill 16 (1963) (published text of congressional testimony); see also Medical Care for the Aged: Hearings on H.R. 3920 Before the House Comm. on Ways and Means, 88th Cong., 1st Sess. 766 (1963) (statement of the American Medical Association).

The 1950s saw a continuation of the trend of growth for government spending for health care, although, at least at the federal level, there was a hiatus in the creation of new government programs. Congressional debates over public financing of health care continued, although more often those debates focused on the needs of the elderly and the poor. Significantly, President Eisenhower flatly disavowed any support for mandatory federal health insurance, although he advocated the creation of a private, voluntary national program. (Equally indicative of the politics of the 1950s, the President allowed the AMA to hand pick the first Secretary of Health, Education, and Welfare.)

The 1960s, however, saw the return of liberal politics to both Congress and the White House and, coincidentally, the beginning of an era of unprecedented growth in both the economy generally and in federal tax revenues. The result was a literal flood of federal domestic legislation, in which accelerated health spending and new health programs were most prominent.

Federal assistance was extended to virtually all health-related services and activities. Public health service funding was increased; new programs of grants to states for alcoholism and drug abuse were created. New federal programs were also established to fund research and services for the mentally retarded. Federal funds were made available directly — not through state agencies — to fund comprehensive mental health centers. The initial success with OEO-funded health clinics led to the establishment of a separately funded program to support neighborhood health centers. A similar program to provide migrant health services was also enacted. All told, from 1960 to 1965 federal spending for health-related programs nearly doubled, only to be tripled again in the next five years with the initial implementation of Medicare and Medicaid.

By 1970, there were over 250 different health-related programs funded in the federal budget, an annual expenditure of $17.7 billion, nearly 25 percent of all health care spending. In the next decade, that effort would continue to grow in both absolute and relative terms.

Medical education funding provided an interesting demonstration of prevailing politics. Traditionally, the AMA had opposed any attempt to provide federal funds for medical education, although the growth of federal funding of biomedical research had indirectly achieved the same result. Beginning in 1960, however, the concern for what was viewed as a "doctor shortage" and the maldistribution of physicians virtually reversed the federal role. Substantial federal funds were made available for medical and other health professional schools. Programs were funded for student grants and loans. By the mid-1960s, each medical school was receiving a flat grant of assistance plus additional funds tied to increases in student body size.

The results were dramatic. Medical school enrollment rose sharply. Between 1960 and 1975, 40 new medical schools were opened. By the late 1970s, the problem of a "doctor shortage" would be replaced by predictions of a "doctor surplus." But the notion of federal funding for medical schools, once a matter of principled opposition for many conservatives and for the medical profession, was no longer seriously questioned.

As Congress was investing more funds in health services and other activities, it also expanded the government's role in various health planning efforts. In 1965, it enacted the Regional Medical Program (RMP). In theory, regional agencies with representatives from medical schools, teaching hospitals, state and local health departments, practitioners, and consumers, were to fund projects coordinating research and the distribution of information from research institutions to medical practitioners, particularly for the "killer diseases," cancer, heart disease, and stroke. In practice, RMP programs made little progress towards the coordinated effort that was the original objective of the program. Much like Hill-Burton, RMP agencies became primarily conduits for federal funds, responding primarily to local concerns and politics.

In 1966, Congress enacted the Comprehensive Health Planning Program (CHP), providing for the first time a national network of state and local health planning agencies. Each state was given funds to maintain a state health planning agency and a consumer-dominated advisory council, and to develop a plan for the distribution of all health resources. The federal law also provided funds for local, nonprofit agencies to develop similar plans for each locality. Functionally, these agencies were to encourage voluntary compliance with these plans and to establish a grand "Partnership for Health" among government, providers, and consumers.

Understandably, the reality of CHP fell far short of these ambitions. The state and local agencies were unable to overcome either political or technical barriers to the establishment of the health planning network envisioned in the original legislation. Chronically understaffed, heavily dependent on private sources for a share of their resources, and with no real regulatory authority to require compliance with their planning efforts, CHP provided the testing grounds for various planning efforts but had little demonstrable impact on the actual distribution of health care resources.

More serious efforts to control health care resources directly were made by states that adopted certificate of need (CON) legislation requiring state approval for broad categories of capital expenditures by hospitals and some other institutional providers. Some states attempted to coordinate the federally funded CHP planning efforts with the state authorized CON programs, giving more authority to CHP planning. The federal government also made some not too successful efforts to coordinate federal funding decisions under various discretionary programs with the recommendations of CHP agencies.

The significance of the planning programs initiated in the 1960s did not lie in their actual impact or the level of federal investment they represented. Their symbolic value, nonetheless, was enormous. However limited they were in authority, they represented a direct government attempt to "plan" the distribution of hospitals and other resources, and indirectly, the distribution and character of health care services. Paired with state certificate of need laws and the planning and regulatory efforts that would be attempted in the 1970s, they were the foundation of the "regulatory" strategy that American politics would consider as one fundamental option for contemporary health care policy.

G. The Enactment of Medicare and Medicaid

The rapid increases in federal spending during the 1960s for public health services and programs, and the initiation of federal and state efforts to plan for the distribution of health facilities marked major shifts in government policy. Nonetheless, the enactment of Medicare and Medicaid in 1965 represented by far the most significant federal health policy initiatives of the twentieth century.

Medicare, in particular, irrevocably breached the traditional barrier between private medicine and public health; and it did so directly in the face of an expensive and heavy-handed campaign by organized medicine to prevent its enactment. Indeed, political scientists would later argue that the AMA's campaign against Medicare was also at an expense to its public image that it would never fully recover.

As noted earlier, the public financing debate had shifted during the 1950s to focus largely on proposals to finance health care for the elderly, the most visible and politically organized of the groups that could claim an inability to meet the rising costs of medical care. In fact, health care financing for the elderly emerged as one of the major domestic issues in the presidential and congressional elections of 1960.

Not surprisingly, Congress, shortly before the election, enacted the Kerr-Mills program, offering federal funds to states that extended medical benefits to elderly welfare recipients, as well as to some nonwelfare elderly who could "spend down" to meet the program eligibility standards. Kerr-Mills provided a rehearsal for many of the problems that would later plague Medicaid: the costs of the program increased much faster than expected; yet even with federal matching, some states were unable, or at least reluctant, to participate. As with all welfare-based programs, coverage varied widely among the states. By 1964, five states with 30 percent of the nation's population were receiving over 60 percent of the federal funds.

In the meantime, a battle ensued in Congress over extending federal assistance to the large portion of the elderly population beyond Kerr-Mills' reach. The White House — both President Kennedy and later President Johnson made the enactment of Medicare one of their top priorities — and liberal Democrats were backed by labor, consumer, and elderly groups. They were opposed by conservative Republicans with the support of most business interests, insurers, and health care providers, most particularly organized medicine. The struggle for undecided votes and for the support of the political center was heated, even for the tumultuous politics of the early 1960s, and revealed much about the quixotic complexities of contemporary health care politics. Many Southern Democrats, for instance, eschewed party loyalty and opposed Medicare, fearful of the loss of state sovereignty (and patronage) that a federally funded *and* administered health program for the elderly would represent. Others saw these same characteristics as advantageous, an opportunity for their state to escape some of the growing burdens of state-administered welfare medicine. Still other Southern Congressmen were wooed to oppose Medicare by the AMA's suddenly lenient stand on the health hazards of smoking. Some Republicans, on the other hand, were tempted across party lines despite their political and budgetary objections to Medicare and their traditional loyalties by the increasingly sophisticated "senior vote." Above all, no one, regardless of personal or political inclination, wanted to be publicly characterized as unwilling to "do something" about "the problem."

The details of the political machinations during the Medicare debate have been recounted elsewhere, at great length and in many different voices.[9] All observers unanimously agree on at least one thing: the landslide victory of the Democrats in 1964 was the critical event that assured the passage of some form of federal health insurance for the elderly. Nonetheless, the political circumstances were more in the nature of a temporary break in the political log jam that the public financing debate had represented for several decades; as a result, both the process and the resulting legislation can only be understood in their peculiar historical context.

Ironically, the Social Security Amendments of 1965 went several steps beyond most of the proposals that had been under congressional consideration, establishing three distinct medical benefits programs: a mandatory federal program to finance hospital and related services for retired Social Security recipients, funded through payroll deductions, Medicare Part A; a voluntary federal program covering physician and outpatient services, financed by a monthly premium supplemented by federal general revenues, Medicare Part B; and a state-administered program to finance medical care for the poor, essentially an extension of the Kerr-Mills program to all welfare categories (indigents who are elderly, blind, disabled, or families with dependent children) funded by 50-80 percent federal funds, Medicaid.

Whereas the origins of Medicare parts A and B can be traced in detail through highly publicized and lengthy political debates, Medicaid emerged

9. See Harris, supra note 2; Starr, supra note 7 at 363-379; A. Somers & H. Somers, Medicare and the Hospitals: Issues and Prospects 1-25 (1967); T. Marmor, The Politics of Medicare (1973).

rather unexpectedly from the last minute Medicare deliberations and with no formal legislative history, apparently part of the political compromise that was necessary to secure the enactment of Medicare. And while Medicare was an extension of the Social Security program, Medicaid was gerrymandered to fit the contours of existing federal welfare programs. Participating states were given a great deal of discretion in determining eligibility standards and the scope and nature of covered services. And by affixing Medicaid to existing federal welfare programs, Medicaid was limited to groups traditionally defined as the "deserving poor": the aged, blind, disabled, and families with dependent children.

Nonetheless, Medicaid was more than an extension of Kerr-Mills. The minimum federal requirements for participating states and, implicitly, the amount of federal oversight they would require were far greater than those under the earlier federal program. More importantly, as originally enacted the federal Medicaid legislation included a time table — later repealed — requiring participating states to move towards an "ultimate goal" of "comprehensive care" for all eligible individuals. Medicaid was also more generous than Kerr-Mills in its computation of the federal financial share, an attempt to encourage more states to participate. Medicaid was, in effect, an open-ended federal commitment to share in the expenditures of any state that opted to provide a Medicaid program.

Indeed, Medicaid *and* Medicare represented unprecedented and open-ended commitments to program beneficiaries. Both programs offered federal funding to finance all services within the scope of their authorization statutes for all people who could meet the programs' eligibility requirements, in contrast to government programs of discretionary authority or with fixed budgetary ceilings. In addition, Medicare and Medicaid were enacted with permanent authorization, at least suggesting that once enacted these statutory "entitlements" were a fixed political commitment.

It is equally significant, however, that in enacting Medicaid and Medicare Congress, quite deliberately, did little to change the character of American health care delivery or to exercise control over the practice of medicine. At least as initially enacted, Medicaid and Medicare did little more than add two public third party payers that in large part paralleled the private third party payment schemes that had developed in the 1940s and 1950s, particularly the "service-benefit" plans. The debates over Medicare and the manner in which the program, once enacted, was initially administered were heavily colored by the fear that unless the program was acceptable to most hospitals and physicians, providers would refuse to participate and thereby undermine the underlying objective of assuring access to medical care for the elderly. The preamble to the original Medicare statute includes a prohibition against federal "supervision or control over the practice of medicine or the manner in which medical services are provided . . . or the administration of any . . . institution, agency, or person [providing medical services.]" More significantly, in implementing the program the responsibility for the day-to-day administration of the program, the assessment of quality, and the disbursement of funds was in large part assigned to private organizations controlled by providers, as had been demanded by industry representatives. In essence, in adopting Medicare, the federal government attempted to provide access to health care for the elderly by buying into the existing institutions that dominated American health care delivery. As a strategy to overcome the political resistance that had historically blocked further federal involvement in health care delivery, purchasing access for the elderly into "mainstream medicine" was a remarkable success. But by undertaking a program that did so little to control what services would be provided, or the costs or quality of those services, the enactment of Medicare also set the stage for the health policy debates that would emerge in the 1970s and 1980s.

Medicaid can be viewed similarly. The enactment of a federal entitlement program extending health care to many — though not all — of the nation's poor was also a remarkable political success. But as originally enacted, Medicaid delegated a good portion of the policymaking responsibility and all of the day-to-day administrative responsibility to the individual states. In particular, the federal Medicaid statute was virtually silent on the amount of control that would be exercised by the federal government or the states over providers in matters relating to reimbursement, utilization, or quality. These issues would quickly emerge as critical problems in the 1970s and 1980s.

H. Conflicting Values in Health Care

At the beginning of this introduction, we suggested that American health care delivery today confronts not a single "problem" or "crisis," but rather a complex network of intersecting problems, the definitions of which are often matters of fierce controversy. Having examined these problems in their different concrete contexts, we now wish to articulate one general theme. The issues of access, quality, and costs, and of professional autonomy, government regulation, and market competition, have been profoundly affected by an underlying tension between two contrasting principles or ideals. The first, often termed a principle of equality, holds that health care should be distributed without regard to what are considered irrelevant factors, such as race, gender, income, and social status. Proponents of this principle ask: when a physician or other health care provider confronts a patient seeking care, what factors should influence the response? As between two women in the process of childbirth or between two victims of heart attack, kidney failure, or automobile accident, do we really want doctors to deny one of them care, or provide markedly inferior care, because the patient cannot pay for it or is considered socially less worthy? The second principle, often termed one of market competition, comes close to answering yes, albeit with qualifications that attempt to avoid some of the harsher consequences. This view holds that most or all health care should be treated as a commodity, that ability to pay is a legitimate criterion of allocation, and that differing "tiers" of health care are necessary for economic efficiency and individual liberty. Proponents of this principle ask whether individuals should be prevented from spending their own money in order to obtain the best possible treatment, because society cannot afford to subsidize similar services for everybody? Should those who want to spend less on health care be prohibited from buying limited insurance plans or a lower standard of care, because of a doctor-defined ideal?

Although concepts of equality and competition are sharply distinct as principles, in the world of practical policy and politics they often appear to be points on a spectrum, with "conservative" proposals to promote equal access merging into "liberal" competition views.[10] Details of particular reform proposals are considered in Chapter 2 and elsewhere. While touching on some reform debates here, the main purpose of this section is to explore the two contrasting principles and their underlying rationales, and the critical dialogue between them.

1. HEALTH CARE: THE PRINCIPLE OF EQUALITY

The principle of equality holds that health care should be allocated according to need, the anticipated benefits of treatment, and patients' own values. In other words, the persons with the greatest health care needs should have the correspondingly greatest claims on health care resources, subject to four important limiting principles. First, society should be able to limit overall health expenditures to preserve resources for other important social needs, such as education and environmental protection. Second, within the sphere of health

10. Not surprisingly, the pressures of contending philosophical and political views have generated efforts to find compromises, not only in particular reform proposals but also at the conceptual level. Thus, in its 1983 report on access to health care, the President's Commission for the Study of Ethical Problems in Medicine and Biomedical and Behavioral Research (hereinafter "the President's Commission") articulated a position somewhat straddling the concepts of equality and competition. Responding to a statutory mandate to report on the ethical and legal implications of "differences in the availability of health services as determined by . . . income or residence . . . ," see 42 U.S.C. §300v-1(D) (1982), the President's Commission collected extensive empirical data on access inequalities and concluded that "[s]ociety has a moral obligation to ensure that everyone has access to adequate care without being subject to excessive burdens." President's Commission, 1 Securing Access to Health Care: Report 22 (1983) (hereinafter Access Report). The Commission noted that by a "societal" moral obligation it meant not only, or perhaps even primarily, government, but rather individuals and institutions of all types, all of which "play a role in discharging societal obligations." Id. Moreover, the Commission denied that its version of "moral obligation" gave rise to any "corresponding right" of any individual to receive adequate care. Id. at 34. The commission's concept of societal moral obligation is thus considerably less than a concept of a right to equal access, although it may mean something more than unregulated competition. For critiques of the commission's reasoning, see Arras, Retreat from the Right to Health Care, 6 Cardozo L. Rev. 321 (1984); Bayer, Ethics, Politics, and Access to Health Care, 6 Cardozo L. Rev. 303 (1984).

care delivery, society should also be able to make cost-benefit decisions — to decide that it is more valuable to provide large numbers of people with an important low-cost service (for instance, prenatal care) than to provide a very small number of people with an extremely expensive (and perhaps dubiously beneficial) service (for instance, heart transplants). Third, it is important that health insurance be designed so that the concept of "need" is not grossly distorted by providers' desire to maximize their incomes and patients' desire to minimize their uninsured costs. Fourth, it is important that patients and (in the case of incompetent patients) their families be able to define their own needs and to decline care that purports to "prolong life" in ways that people find oppressive. Health economist Rashi Fein sums up the first two of these principles as a two-part "right to health care" — the right to have a reasonable overall level of health care expenditures in relation to other needs and the right to an equitable distribution of the health care budget, "where equitable means that the distribution of care reflects medical need and the costs and benefits of care rather than individual income, wealth, political power, or social status."[11]

The principle of equal access on the basis of need and fairly applied social judgments of costs and benefits is reflected throughout health law and health care delivery. Important expressions of medical ethics — such as the declaration of the World Health Organization, the hospital accreditation standards of the Joint Commission on the Accreditation of the Health Care Organizations, and various patients' bills of rights — enjoin physicians with varying specificity to provide care on the basis of medical need rather than economic and social factors and to treat all patients with equal consideration. The federal Hill-Burton Act and civil rights laws prohibit racial and other forms of discrimination in hospital care, and the 1986 COBRA legislation and similar state laws explicitly require hospitals to provide emergency care without regard to ability to pay. Proposals and programs that condition access to scarce resources — such as kidney and other organ transplants — on ability to pay or explicit judgments of social worthiness, encounter strong criticism. Even after years of reductions in social welfare programs under the Reagan Administration, the rhetoric of the "right to health care" remains powerful.

Philosophically, the concept of distributing health care on the basis of need, rather than as a commodity, has been defended on several grounds. At the most general level are arguments that do not focus on health care alone, but rather hold that equal respect for all human beings requires egalitarian provision for important human needs, including health care.[12] But given the

11. See R. Fein, Medical Care, Medical Costs 194-195 (1986).

12. According to this view, people should be treated with equal respect for two reasons: (1) the existence of common basic human needs — minimally the means to life and health — without which no one can function in a recognizably human manner and (2) the existence of common basic human capacities such as consciousness of purposes and alternatives, choice of actions and relationships, and development of one's own skills and capabilities to achieve one's chosen ends. Although individuals' specific needs and capacities may differ in various ways, this view stresses the commonalities among them. A society committed to equality of

powerful political hostility to broad egalitarianism in the United States, American philosophers have tended to focus on why health care is "special," and should be treated to a significant extent as a noncommodity even in the midst of a generally commodified society. The President's Commission's Securing Access to Health Care, discussed in footnote 10 supra, could be read in part as an extended answer to the skeptic's question, "Why is health care special?"[13] Among the Commission's responses were the special importance of health care to achieving virtually all life plans, preferences, and values; the need for health care to provide essential information about our own futures; the unevenness and unpredictability of health care needs; the lack of individual control over — and the environmental or occupational source of — many health care risks; the impact of health care on equal opportunity; and the unusual interpersonal significance of health care needs, which makes access to health care "a measure of [a society's] sense of solidarity in the face of suffering and death."[14]

Varying concepts of equality have also been expressed in the politics of health care reform. At the most egalitarian end of the spectrum, exemplified by Congressman Ron Dellums' 1975 National Health Service bill, equality in health care is conceived as part of a more general restructuring of American society, in which social welfare functions are divorced as far as possible from private profit. More modest but still substantial reform is contemplated by the "Canadian model," somewhat approximated by Senator Edward Kennedy's National Health Insurance bills of the mid-1970s, in which the private practice of medicine and private control of hospitals are maintained, but under much stricter government budgetary control. The version of equality that has won legislative approval has been even less reformist than this, channeling public funds for Medicare and Medicaid entitlements through largely unregulated, privately owned, and highly profitable hospitals and private medical practices.

For all their flaws and compromises, the institutions of "the welfare state" — social security, unemployment insurance, food stamps, cash public assistance, and public health insurance (primarily Medicare and Medicaid), have helped to protect millions of Americans from the continual threat of econom-

---

respect of this sort would attempt to ensure that all its members were "equally free from political control, social pressure, and economic deprivation and insecurity to engage in valued pursuits, and [had] . . . equal access to the means of self-development." S. Lukes, Socialism and Equality, in The Socialist Ideal: A Reappraisal 74, 82 (L. Kolakowski & S. Hampshire, eds. 1974), reprinted in S. Lukes, Essays in Social Theory 96, 104 (1977).

13. See Arras, supra note 10, at 324.

14. Access Report, supra note 10, at 17. For a superb restatement of the Commission's arguments, see Arras, supra note 10. See also B. Williams, The Idea of Equality in Philosophy, Politics and Society (2nd Series) 110 (P. Laslett & W. Runciman ed. 1962), reprinted in Justice and Equality (H. Bedau ed. 1971) (arguing that since the function, or raison d'être, of health care is to respond to illness and disability, illness and disability are the only justifiable criteria of distribution); N. Daniels, Just Health Care 66-67, 78-85 (1985); Gutman, For and Against Equal Access to Health Care in In Search of Equity 43 (R. Bayer, A. Caplan & N. Daniels ed. 1983); M. Walzer, Spheres of Justice 86-91 (1983); Buchanan, The Right to a Decent Minimum of Health Care, 13 Phil. & Pub. Aff. 55 (1984).

ic dislocation caused by business cycle downturns, shifting regional patterns of investment, and long-term structural changes in the economy that "leave millions stranded with obsolete skills and scanty resources."[15] Yet for complex reasons beyond the scope of this book, a broad-based political coalition committed to an egalitarian welfare state along the lines of the European social democracies has not developed in the United States, leaving most social welfare programs exceptionally vulnerable to repeated attacks by American business, often joined in complex ways in the area of health care by the formidable power of the American Medical Association and other sectors of the health care industry.[16] Rather than confront the general problem of meeting basic human needs, including health care, on an equitable basis, American politics has tended to fragment the issues, leaving each subgroup (the aged, the handicapped, victims of AIDS or kidney failure etc.) to struggle for its own special entitlements and programs, in a political environment increasingly dominated by the ideal of market competition.

2. HEALTH CARE: THE PRINCIPLE OF MARKET COMPETITION

Advocates of the market competition principle rose to prominence in the United States in the 1970s by launching three major attacks on the previously dominant equality ideal. First, they argued that most health care was not a matter of life and death, but of comfort and convenience. They conceded that there was some "core" of life and death services that might be regarded as a human and social necessity, but they viewed the rest — by implication the vast majority of health care expenditures — as discretionary consumption choices. They claimed support for this view in the small area studies by Dr. John Wennberg and others, which showed that widely varying rates in surgical procedures and hospitalization could not be explained by demographic factors. If rates of hysterectomies and hospitalization for pneumonia could not be justified by demographic data regarding age or incidence of illness, the argument went, then these procedures were less an objective necessity

15. F. Block, R. Cloward, B. Ehrenreich & F. Piven, The Mean Season ix (1987).

16. On business attacks on the welfare state, see id. at xii-xiii; T. Edsall, The New Politics of Inequality 67-140 (1984); on the role of organized medicine in opposing and then dominating publicly-financed health insurance, see P. Starr, The Social Transformation of American Medicine 363-378 (1982). The Republican Party and other business-dominated groups tend to pursue two somewhat inconsistent goals: reducing the budgetary size of public spending for health and turning over as much publicly-financed health care as possible to minimally regulated, private, for-profit entities. The hospital industry and medical profession tend to push for maximum governmental reimbursement and minimal regulation of their own services and thus endanger services less linked to doctors and hospitals. Depending on shifting political and programmatic details, these two agendas may overlap at some points (minimal regulation, maximum profit) and diverge at others (budgetary constraints, hospital and physician reimbursement).

than a "choice" shaped by medical fashion and/or patients' own culturally influenced expectations.[17]

Second, with a secure base in American capitalist ideology, the market advocates had what the liberals often lacked: the courage to launch a direct attack on the medical profession and hospital industry. Despite rhetoric about health care as something special and noncommodified, American doctors and hospitals insisted on fee-for-service and cost based reimbursement, putting a price on every action performed. If doctors and hospitals were going to treat health care as a commodity for their own benefit, the argument went, it was ludicrous to deny consumers and third-party payers whatever economic leverage they could bring to bear through bargaining and market competition.[18]

Third, having highlighted the dangers of monopolistic and self-interested practices by doctors and hospitals, the market advocates denied that government regulation could provide any solution. Regulatory programs were notoriously subject to "capture" by the powerful and well organized regulated interests (in this context, doctors and hospitals), as the history of Blue Cross/Blue Shield, Hill-Burton, Medicare, Medicaid, and health planning seemed to confirm. Moreover, governmental agencies simply lacked the technical skills and political authority to direct or even seriously influence the powerful forces of economic self-interest that operated in the health care industry as anywhere else. The only force that could discipline providers in the interest of consumers, and provide consumers with genuine freedom of choice to allocate their own resources according to their own values, was the same one that operated in other sectors of the American economy: market competition.[19]

Like the principle of equality, the principle of market competition has generated a number of different reform proposals, reflecting varying concerns with equality and varying commitments to pure market principles. Some market advocates focus on increasing out of pocket costs to individual patients at the point of illness, hoping to stimulate price shopping and cost-conscious decisionmaking. Others advocate changes in the income tax and employment-based health insurance to penalize consumers for choosing expensive, comprehensive, fee-for-service insurance, and reward consumers for choosing insurance plans characterized by patient cost sharing, limited benefits, and provider financial risk. Still others advocate government encouragement of large scale "alternative delivery systems," which would compete among themselves in a market relatively tightly regulated to insure equitable access and adequate quality. Most market advocates make some reference to

17. See Havighurst & Blumstein, Coping and Quality/Cost Trade-Offs in Medical Care: The Role of PSROs, 70 N.W.U.L. Rev. 6, 12 (1975); A. Enthoven, Health Plan, xvi, 6 (1980).

18. See, e.g., Relman & Reinhardt, Debating For-Profit Health Care and the Ethics of Physicians, 5 Health Affairs 5, 10 (Summer 1986).

19. See, e.g., A. Enthoven, supra note 17, at 93-113.

the need for subsidizing some health care for some part of the population, but most do not supply or even propose the crucial details.[20]

3. THE EGALITARIAN RESPONSE TO MARKET COMPETITION

Advocates of the equality principle have offered several responses to the positions advanced by the proponents of market competition.[21] First, egalitarians dispute the assertion that if individuals were only liberated from the tyranny of comprehensive, tax-subsidized health insurance, they would happily purchase more limited or lower quality health care in order to engage in other, more immediately gratifying consumption. Much to the consternation of the market advocates, Americans seem to want broad health insurance coverage, although they quite reasonably also want it to be less expensive. More fundamentally, egalitarians question the idea that people's current consumption patterns, made under economic and social pressures and influences of all sorts, are a uniquely valid basis of social policy. An individual's choice to buy minimal health care coverage may be an exercise of deeply felt personal values, but it is at least as likely to reflect a painful compromise in the face of economic necessity and limited social options.

Second, the market advocates' critique of the "failure" of governmental programs is fundamentally flawed by the fact that egalitarian governmental regulation and provision of health care (and of much else) has never been fairly or seriously tried in United States. Instead, when markets fail, as they do in providing health care for the aged, the poor, and increasingly for middle-income families, government intervention typically takes a "hybrid" form that combines "substantial government involvement with opportunities for private profit. [This often results in] the worst of both worlds: insulation from market discipline and strong incentives for the running up of costs."[22] As Bruce Vladeck concludes in his impressive study of nursing homes, Americans seem to want government to fail, design financing and regulatory programs in ways that insure that failure, and then find in that failure

20. See, e.g., Rosenblatt, Rationing "Normal" Health Care Through Market Mechanisms: A Response to Professor Blumstein, 60 Tex. L. Rev. 919, 921 (1982). Alain Enthoven is a notable exception among market advocates in this regard. See A. Enthoven, supra note 17, at 114-144.

21. Elaboration of these egalitarian responses can be found in the following works: Rosenblatt, Health Care, Markets, and Democratic Values, 34 Vand. L. Rev. 1067 (1981); Rosenblatt, Rationing "Normal" Health Care: The Hidden Legal Issues, 59 Tex. L. Rev. 1401 (1981); Rosenblatt, Rationing "Normal" Health Care Through Market Mechanisms: A Response to Professor Blumstein, 60 Vand. L. Rev. 919 (1982); Arras, The Neoconservative Health Strategy: Vouchers and the Rhetoric of Equity, in In Search of Equity 125 (R. Bayer, A. Caplan & N. Daniels ed., 1983); R. Fein, supra note 11, at 162-192. See also The Mean Season, supra note 6, for similar arguments regarding the entire welfare state.

22. Block, Rethinking the Political Economy of the Welfare State, in The Mean Season, supra note 15, at 149.

confirmation of their faith in market competition.[23] Needless to say, this is hardly a fair comparison of the two approaches, and even in the United States, one can find occasional examples of well managed governmental or nonprofit programs that strongly outperform their for-profit rivals.[24]

Third, and relatedly, it is not at all clear that market competition in health care, at least in its contemporary form in the current American political and professional context, actually promotes efficiency and consumer sovereignty. To be sure, there is some evidence that it does tend in these directions; for example, the increasing numbers of physicians, and increased competition among physicians for paying patients, have in some localities probably generated increased doctor responsiveness to consumer wishes regarding styles of practice, geographic location, and even price. But for a variety of well known reasons — such as consumer ignorance and dependence, the difficulty of comparing services and prices, and the strongly felt need for insurance — it seems unlikely that market competition in health care will generate major advances in efficiency. Moreover, there are far easier ways to make money in health care than by delivering efficient, consumer-responsive, good quality services — notably by "skimming" the healthiest and best insured patients and most highly reimbursed services, and leaving the more serious problems to underfunded public programs and institutions.

Fourth, as one might expect, the market competition model seems very weak on the issue of equality. As noted above, most market competition advocates acknowledge briefly the need to subsidize health care for some part of the population, but fail to develop serious proposals or link them to their broader calls for market competition. On its face, if a society is deeply committed to the market as the mechanism for allocating vital health care resources, it is unlikely to be generous in its subsidies or careful in their implementation, a point repeatedly confirmed by recent American history. Indeed, the Institute of Medicine recently proclaimed the plight of millions of patients without health insurance in the United States, and hence increasingly denied essential medical care, as a national crisis equal in seriousness to that posed by AIDS.

Finally, advocates of the equality principle accept the need for efficiency in implementing broader access to health care. Indeed, there is bitter irony in the charge by market advocates that egalitarians simply want to "throw government money" at the problem of health care and pay whatever doctors and hospitals define as the costs. The truth is that some of the earliest and most detailed critiques of waste and profiteering in governmental (and nongovernmental) health care financing came from scholars and policy analysts committed to equality and true public responsibility for health care delivery.[25]

23. B. Vladeck, Unloving Care: The Nursing Home Tragedy 6, 264-265 (1980).

24. See, e.g., B. Vladeck, supra note 23, at 122-127 (noting the superior performance of some voluntary nursing homes and also the complexity of the issue).

25. See, e.g., S. Law, Blue Cross: What Went Wrong? (1974, 2nd ed. 1976); Sparer, Gordian Knots: The Situation of Health Care Advocacy for the Poor Today, 15 Clearing-

The political power of the medical profession, hospital industry, and insurance industry prevented these insights from being translated into actual policy in the late 1960s and early 1970s, just as they also often blocked market competition proposals in the late 1970s and 1980s. It is to be hoped that a new constellation of constituencies in the 1990s may form the basis for a synthesis of the most effective and humane elements of both perspectives.

---

house Rev. 1 (1981); Health-PAC, The American Health Empire (1970); Schneider & Stern, Health Maintenance Organizations and the Poor: Problems and Prospects, 70 N.W.U.L. Rev. 90 (1975).

Bibliography

Annas, G. J., The Rights of Patients (2d ed. 1989).

Annas, G. J., Judging Medicine (1988).

Annas, G. J., Glantz, L., & Katz, B., The Rights of Doctors, Nurses & Allied Health Professionals (1981).

Brieger, G., Medical America in the Nineteenth Century: Readings from the Literature (1972).

Brieger, G., Theory and Practice in American Medicine (1976).

Brown, E. R., Rockefeller Medicine Men (1979).

Carlson, R., The End of Medicine (1975).

The Committee on the Cost of Medical Care, Medical Care for the American People (1932) (Final report; for all the studies, see Falk et al.).

Daniels, N., Just Health Care (1985).

Derbyshire, R., Medical Licensure in the United States (1969).

Doyal, L., The Political Economy of Health (1979).

Earle, A., Surgery in America (2nd ed. 1983).

Elias, S., & Annas, G. J., Reproductive Genetics & the Law (1987).

Evans, R., Strained Mercy: The Economics of Canadian Health Care (1984).

Falk, I., Roem, C., Ring, M., The Costs of Medical Care (1933, rep. 1972).

Fein, R., Medical Care, Medical Cost: The Search for a Health Insurance Policy (1986).

Flexner, A., Medical Education in the United States and Canada, (1910).

Friedson, E., Profession of Medicine (1970).

Fuchs, V., Who Shall Live? (1974).

Grossinger, R., Planet Medicine (rev. ed. 1982).

Harris, R., A Sacred Trust (1966).

Illich, I., Limits to Medicine (5th ed. 1976).

Lagemann, C., Nursing History: New Perspectives and Possibilities (1983).

Law, S., Blue Cross: What Went Wrong? (1974).

Law, S. & Polan, S., Pain and Profit: The Politics of Malpractice (1978).

Ludmerer, K., Learning to Heal: the Development of American Medical Education (1985).

Luft, H., Health Maintenance Organizations (1981).

McKeown, T., The Role of Medicine: Dream, Mirage, or Nemesis? (1979).

Melosh, B., The Physician's Hand (1982).

Navarro, The Crisis of the International Capitalist Order and Its Implications for the Welfare State, 12 Intl. J. Health Serv. 169 (1982).
Navarro, V., Medicine Under Capitalism (2d ed. 1977).
A New Approach to the Economics of Health Care (M. Olsen, ed. 1981).
President's Commission on the Health Needs of the Nation, Report to the President, Building America's Health (1952).
Reed, L., Blue Cross and Medical Service Plans (1947).
Reverby, S., & Rosner, D., Health Care in America: Essays in Social History (1979).
Roemer, M., Ambulatory Health Services in America: Past, Present, and Future (1981).
Rosen, G., Preventive Medicine in the United States (1977).
Rosen, G. The Structure of American Medical Practice 1875-1941 (C. Rosenberg ed. 1983).
Rosenberg, C., The Care of Strangers: The Rise of America's Hospital System (1987).
Starr, P., The Social Transformation of American Medicine (1982).
Stevens, R., American Medicine and the Public Interest (1971).
Stevens, R., Statutory History of the United States: Income Security (1970).
Stevens, R., & Steven, R., Welfare Medicine in America: A Case Study of the Medicaid Program (1974).
Williams, S., & Torrens, P., Introduction to Health Services (2d ed. 1984).
Wing, K., The Law & the Public's Health (2d. ed. 1985).
Vogel, M., The Invention of the Modern Hospital: Boston 1870-1930 (1980).
Young, J., The Toadstool Millionaires: A Social History of Patent Medicines in America Before Federal Regulation (1961).

CHAPTER

I

Access to Health Services

A. Introduction

The Constitution of the World Health Organization provides, "The enjoyment of the highest attainable standard of health is one of the fundamental rights of every human being without distinction of race, religion, political belief, economic or social condition."

For decades, ringing proclamations that health care is a basic human right have been found, not only in the speeches of American reformers, but in the assertions of American Presidents and presidential-level commissions. J. Arras, Retreat from the Right to Health Care: The President's Commission and Access to Health Care, 6 Cardozo L. Rev. 321 (1984). In 1952, for example, a commission established by President Truman proclaimed that "access to the means for attainment and preservation of health is a basic human right." President's Commission on the Health Needs of the Nation 3 (1953). According to sociologist Paul Starr, during the 1960s and 1970s, the assertion that health care is a matter of right, not privilege, was "so widely acknowledged as almost to be uncontroversial." The Social Transformation of American Medicine, 389 (1982). Even Ronald Reagan, who generally sought to limit the role of government in meeting human needs, states, "We cannot and will not scrimp on the health of America's citizens." 19 U.S. Weekly Compilation of Presidential Documents 916 (1983). For a good general discussion of the concept of health care as a right see J. Arras, Id.

Most Americans agree that no one should be denied necessary medical care simply for lack of money to pay for it. Even in times of fiscal austerity and taxpayer revolt, most Americans are willing to pay more taxes to provide medical care to those who need it. For example, in 1986, a Gallup poll found that, despite concern about the federal budget deficit, 88 percent of those polled opposed "cuts in 'entitlement' programs such as Social Security, Medicare and the like." See Blendon & Altman, Public Attitudes About Health-Care Costs, 311 N. Engl. J. Med. 613 (1984).

These notions — that an individual has a right to help in time of need and that essential medical care should not be contingent upon anything except medical need — clash with important strains of American political and legal philosophy. Dr. Robert M. Sade disputes the concept of a right to medical care.

> The concept of medical care as the patient's right is immoral because it denies the most fundamental of all rights, that of a man to his own life and the freedom of action to support it. Medical care is neither a right nor a privilege: it is a service that is provided by doctors and others to people who wish to purchase it. It is the provision of this service that a doctor depends upon for his livelihood, and is his means of supporting his own life. If the right to health care belongs to the patient, he starts out owning the services of a doctor without the necessity of either earning them or receiving them as a gift from the only man who has the right to give them: the doctor himself. . . . [Sade, Medical Care as a Right: A Refutation, 285 N. Engl. J. Med. 1288 (1971).]

If individuals have a "right" to essential medical care, who has a duty to provide it? The right to medical care and individual liberty conflict starkly when a doctor or hospital refuses to provide essential medical care to an individual who needs it. The first part of this chapter examines the common law principles developed when American courts have been asked to reconcile patient's and medical provider's conflicting claims of right.

Throughout American history, government has attempted to mediate this conflict. Sometimes state government seeks to assure medical care by imposing duties upon hospitals. In addition, states often require that local communities assure that citizens can obtain necessary medical care. Section C of this chapter further explores these legal mandates.

In the second half of the twentieth century, government has encouraged the provision of necessary medical care by requiring that organizations receiving government benefits provide services to people who need them. Section D examines the legal requirements attached to state and federal tax exemption. Sections E and F describe federal laws that condition benefits upon a hospital's agreement to provide necessary services. Section G discusses limited programs for direct, government sponsored provision of medical care. The final section of this Chapter describes the particular challenge that the AIDS crisis has posed for people seeking access to medical care and illustrates the diversity of approaches adopted in different areas of the country.

Most people obtain access to medical care by purchasing health insurance or by qualifying for government sponsored health insurance. Chapters 3-4 explore the laws defining the availability of health insurance and the financing of medicare care.

The United States is the only industrialized country, apart from South Africa, that does not have a national system to finance or organize medical care for all people. Indeed, many nations of the third world aspire to provide all people access to basic health services. At the federal level, interest in national health insurance has waxed and waned since the 1930s. In the 1980s, with no realistic prospect of federal action to assure all people access to basic medical services, several states, including Massachusetts and New Jersey, have adopted programs described as "universal health insurance." These financing programs are discussed, after consideration of our current financing system for medical care, in Chapter 3.

B. The Ambivalent Tradition of the Common Law

Hurley v. Eddingfield

156 Ind. 400, 59 N.E. 1058 (1901)

BAKER, J. The appellant sued appellee for $10,000 damages for wrongfully causing the death of his intestate. The court sustained appellee's demurrer to the complaint, and this ruling is assigned as error. . . .

At and for years before decedent's death appellee was a practicing physician at Mace, in Montgomery county, duly licensed under the laws of the state. He held himself out to the public as a general practitioner of medicine. He had been decedent's family physician. Decedent became dangerously ill, and sent for appellee. The messenger informed appellee of decedent's violent sickness, tendered him his fee for his services, and stated to him that no other physician was procurable in time, and that decedent relied on him for attention. No other physician was procurable in time to be of any use, and decedent did rely on appellee for medical assistance. Without any reason whatever, appellee refused to render aid to decedent. No other patients were requiring appellee's immediate service, and he could have gone to the relief of decedent if he had been willing to do so. Death ensued, without decedent's fault, and wholly from appellee's wrongful act. The alleged wrongful act was appellee's refusal to enter into a contract of employment. . . .

In obtaining the state's license (permission) to practice medicine, the state does not require, and the licensee does not engage, that he will practice at all or on other terms than he may choose to accept. Counsel's analogies, drawn from the obligations to the public on the part of innkeepers, common carriers, and the like are beside the mark. Judgment affirmed.

Manlove v. Wilmington General Hospital

54 Del. 15, 174 A.2d 135 (1961)

This case concerns the liability of a private hospital for the death of an infant who was refused treatment at the emergency ward of the hospital. . . .

On January 4, 1959, Darien E. Manlove, . . . then four months old, developed diarrhea. The next morning his parents consulted Dr. Hershon. They asked whether the medicine they had for him was all right and the doctor said that it was. In the evening of the same day Mrs. Manlove took the baby's temperature. It was higher than normal. They called Dr. Hershon, and he prescribed additional medication. . . .

Mrs. Manlove stayed up with the child that night. He did not sleep. On the morning of January 6th the parents took the infant to Dr. Hershon's office. Dr. Thomas examined the child and treated him for sore throat and diarrhea. He prescribed a liquid diet and some medicine.

On the morning of January 7th (a Wednesday) his temperature was still above normal — 102. Mr. and Mrs. Manlove . . . knew that Dr. Hershon and Dr. Thomas were not in their offices on Wednesdays, and they took their infant to the emergency ward of the Wilmington General Hospital.

A nurse was on duty. They explained to the nurse what was wrong with the child. . . . The nurse explained to the parents that the hospital could not give treatment because the child was under the care of a physician. . . . The nurse did not examine the child. . . . The child was not in convulsions, and was not coughing or crying. There was no particular area of body tenderness.

The nurse tried to get in touch with Dr. Hershon or Dr. Thomas in the hospital and at their offices, but was unable to do so. She suggested that the parents bring the baby Thursday morning to the pediatric clinic.

Mr. and Mrs. Manlove returned home. Mrs. Manlove made an appointment by telephone to see Dr. Hershon or Dr. Thomas that night at eight o'clock. At eight minutes past three o'clock in the afternoon the baby died of bronchial pneumonia. . . .

The issues made by the parties below were in effect two: 1. whether the hospital was under any duty to furnish medical treatment to any applicant for it, even in an emergency; 2. whether the existence of an apparent emergency was a material fact in dispute. . . .

It was assumed by both parties below that the hospital was a private hospital and not a public one. . . . The trial court disagreed, finding a quasi-public status in the receipt of grants of public money and tax exemptions. . . . Hence, the court concluded, liability may be imposed on the defendant in an emergency case.

We are compelled to disagree with the view that the defendant has become a public (or quasi-public) hospital. It is admitted . . . that it is privately owned and operated. [S]uch a hospital may, at least in the absence of control by the legislature, conduct its business largely as it sees fit. . . .

Moreover, the holding that the receipt of grants of public money requires the hospital to care for emergency cases, as distinguished from others, is not logical. Why emergency cases? If the holding is sound it must apply to all the hospital services, and that conclusion, as we shall see, is clearly unsound. . . . What, then, is the liability of a private hospital in this respect?

Since such an institution as the defendant is privately owned and operated, it would follow logically that its trustees or governing board alone have the right to determine who shall be admitted to it as patients. No other rule would be sensible or workable. Such authority as we have found supports this rule. "A private hospital owes the public no duty to accept any patient not desired by it, and it is not necessary to assign any reason for its refusal to accept a patient for hospital service." 41 C.J.S. Hospitals Sec. 8, p. 345. . . .

Does that rule apply to the fullest extent to patients applying for treatment at an emergency ward? . . . It may be conceded that a private hospital is under no legal obligation to the public to maintain an emergency ward, or, for that matter, a public clinic. . . . But the maintenance of such a ward to render first-aid to injured persons has become a well-established adjunct to the main business of a hospital. If a person, seriously hurt, applies for such aid at an emergency ward, relying on the established custom to render it, is it still the right of the hospital to turn him away without any reason? In such a case, it seems to us, such a refusal might well result in worsening the condition of the injured person, because of the time lost in a useless attempt to obtain medical aid. Such a set of circumstances is analogous to the case of the negligent termination of gratuitous services, which creates a tort liability. . . .

But this is not a case in which the hospital assumed to treat the patient. The claim is that it should have treated him, and that the nurse was negligent in failing to have the infant examined by the interne on duty, because an apparent emergency existed.

This leads to the inquiry: What is the duty of a nurse to one applying for admission as an emergency case? Obviously, if an emergency is claimed, some one on behalf of the hospital must make a *prima facie* decision whether it exists. The hospital cannot reasonably be expected to station an interne at all times in the receiving room. It therefore keeps a nurse on duty. If the nurse makes an honest decision that there is no unmistakable indication of an emergency, and that decision is not clearly unreasonable in the light of the nurse's training, how can there be any liability on the part of the hospital? . . .

Applying this rule here, we inquire, was there an unmistakable emergency? Certainly the record does not support the view that the infant's condition was so desperate that a layman could reasonably say that he was in immediate danger. The learned judge indicated that the fact that death followed in a few hours showed an emergency; but with this we cannot agree. It is hindsight. And it is to be noted that the attending physician, after prescribing for the child on morning before, did not think another examination that night or the next morning was required. . . .

We do not think that the record made below satisfactorily developed the pertinent facts. What is standard hospital practice when an applicant for aid seeks medical aid for sickness at the emergency ward? Is it the practice for the nurse to determine whether or not an emergency exists, or is it her duty to call the interne in every case? Assuming (as seems probable) that it is her duty to make such a determination, was her determination in this case within the reasonable limits of judgment of a graduate nurse, even though mistaken. . . ? To resolve these questions additional evidence, probably expert opinion, would seem to be required. . . .

[The case was remanded.]

Campbell v. Mincey

413 F. Supp. 16 (D. Miss. 1975), aff'd., *542 F.2d 573 (6th Cir. 1976)*

On the morning of March 21, 1974, Hattie Mae Campbell gave birth to her third child, a son whom she named Frederick, under circumstances which counsel for plaintiffs in this case maintains would "disgrace a nation of savages." . . . The plaintiffs alleged that on the occasion of the birth of her son, Ms. Campbell was refused admittance to the Marshall County Hospital and its emergency room because of her race (she is black) and financial condition (she is indigent). . . .

The course of events giving rise to this litigation began in the early morning hours of March 21, 1974, when Ms. Campbell was awakened by labor contractions. . . . Ms. Campbell, accompanied by her sister, secured the services of a neighbor to drive her from their home some eight miles north of Holly Springs, Mississippi, to Oxford, Mississippi, where Ms. Campbell received prenatal care from a local physician. Upon reaching Holly Springs, the occupants of the automobile concluded that it would not be possible for them to arrive at the Oxford-Lafayette County Hospital, located some thirty miles south of Holly Springs, prior to the birth of Ms. Campbell's child.

Upon arrival at the Marshall County Hospital, Ms. Campbell and her sister entered the emergency room where they encountered a staff nurse. Upon learning that Ms. Campbell was of the opinion that she was about to deliver, the nurse informed Ms. Campbell and her sister that they should go to the hospital in Oxford where Ms. Campbell had received prenatal care and have the baby delivered there. The nurse did call the emergency room doctor. . . , and informed him that Ms. Campbell's labor contractions were occurring at the rate of one every five minutes, that her water was intact, and that she had been seeing a doctor in Oxford. The emergency room doctor then affirmed the nurse's directive to Ms. Campbell that she should go to Oxford. . . .

Ms. Campbell and her sister returned to the parking lot where she gave birth on the front seat of the neighbor's automobile. After Frederick's birth, Ms. Campbell's sister again went into the hospital and requested the nurse to admit Ms. Campbell and her newly-born son. Once again the nurse refused to admit plaintiffs but did go out into the parking lot to look over the mother and child. The only assistance which the nurse provided was in the form of a sheet in which the baby could be wrapped. The nurse did not notify the emergency doctor of the birth of the child and no other post-natal care was afforded mother or child. . . . The staff did, however, summons a Holly

Springs ambulance which delivered the mother and child to the Oxford-Lafayette County Hospital. . . . The evidence shows that the mother and son suffered no physical injury. . . . The report of the attending physician at the Oxford hospital indicates Ms. Campbell's delivery was normal in all respects other than the location and the absence of a doctor at the immediate time of the birth. . . .

[Plaintiffs] claim that defendants' conduct . . . constitutes a breach of a common law duty owed plaintiffs; it is plaintiffs' position that both public and private hospitals in this state operating an emergency room must accept, treat, and admit every individual who comes to them seeking assistance. [T]he court has noted the existence of what may be described as a "trend" in the common law of this country toward imposing liability upon a hospital which refuses to admit and treat, on an emergency basis, a seriously injured person. [I]n most instances, liability was predicated upon the defendant's arbitrary refusal to treat the plaintiff in question, which refusal was a marked departure from previous hospital custom and procedure. The refusal of the staff of the Marshall County Hospital to admit or treat the plaintiffs here was in compliance with, rather than a departure from hospital policy not to admit patients who are not referred by local physicians.

The following excerpts from the bylaws of the Marshall County Hospital furnished the motivation underlying the defendants' refusal to treat or admit plaintiffs:

> All inpatients shall be admitted and attended only by members of the medical staff. If during an emergency the attending physician is unavailable then the on call or staff physician may be asked to serve in the emergency. . . . In the case of an emergency the physician attending the patient shall be expected to do all in his power to save the life of the patient. . . . For the purpose of this section an emergency is defined as a condition in which the life of the patient is in imminent danger and in which any delay in administering treatment would increase the danger.

Both the administrator and chief of staff of the hospital testified [that there] are no staff physicians on duty at the hospital between 6:30 P.M. and 7:00 A.M. During those hours, the only physician on duty is the emergency room doctor. The . . . University of Tennessee Medical School at Memphis . . . supplies the hospital with doctors who have completed their general medicine degrees and are pursuing a specialty residence. . . . The emergency room doctors are not considered to be members of the medical staff of the Marshall County Hospital in the contemplation of the afore-quoted bylaws. Because the emergency room doctors are not available to afford follow-up or continuing treatment for in-patients, patients may be admitted to the hospital only upon the authorization of a local physician who is a member of the medical staff.

According to hospital policy, when an individual appears at the emergency room seeking treatment between the hours of 6:30 P.M. and 7:00 A.M., and such individual has not been referred for treatment and/or admission by a local physician, the emergency room doctor will see the individual but only for the limited purpose of determining whether the patient should be treated at the Marshall County Hospital. . . . That is, the emergency room doctor exercises his medical judgment as to whether the individual in question can best be treated at the Marshall County Hospital or should be referred to a hospital with better accommodations, expertise, or equipment.

Plaintiffs in the case at bar were twice examined by a staff nurse who determined that no "emergency," as that term is defined by the regulations of the hospital, existed. The nurse's determination that no emergency existed prior to Frederick's birth was confirmed by the emergency room doctor. The nurse's conclusion that no emergency existed after Frederick's birth was confirmed by the report of treating physician in Oxford who recorded his observation that Ms. Campbell's delivery and post-partum recovery was "uneventful" except for a loss of blood during the ambulance trip. . . .

Turning finally to the constitutional issues raised in the complaint, the plaintiffs claim that they were refused . . . treatment in the emergency room because of their race and indigency. The overwhelming weight of the evidence in the record is to the effect that the plaintiffs' race and financial condition had nothing at all to do with the defendants' refusal to admit or treat plaintiffs. . . .

1. BARRIERS TO ACCESS TO MEDICAL CARE

How common are cases in which hospitals or doctors refuse to provide medical treatment to individuals in need? This section explores a) the extent to which people lack the financial ability to purchase necessary care; b) other factors that make it difficult for people to obtain care; c) the amount of charitable care provided by various types of hospitals; d) evidence whether patients denied are thereby injured.

a. Patients Unable to Pay for Medical Treatment

In early 1984, about 35 million American people under age sixty-five, or about 17 percent of this population, had *no* health insurance. The uninsured population grew during the 1980s. For a general discussion, see Bovbjerg & Kopit, Coverage and Care for the Medically Indigent: Public and Private Options, 19 Ind. L. Rev. 857 (1986). Several factors contribute to increases in the numbers of people without insurance. Most people purchase health insurance through employment. When unemployment rises, so too do the number of people without health insurance. Changes in employment patterns also increase the numbers of uninsured. Health insurance is more often

TABLE 1
Increase in the Uninsured Over Time
(Selected Survey Estimates, Under Age 65)

Year	*Millions of Uninsured*	*Percentage of Population*
1977	26.2	13.8%
1978	26.0	13.7%
1980	28.6	14.6%
1982	30.7	15.2%
1983	32.7	16.1%
1984	35.1	17.1%

Source: Bovbjerg & Kopit, Coverage and Care for the Medically Indigent: Public and Private Options, 19 Ind. L. Rev. 857, 861 (1986). (Adapted from M. Sulvetta & K. Swartz, The Uninsured and Uncompensated Care, 3, Table 1 (1986).)

provided to unionized workers, those who work for large employers, and workers in the primary wage labor market. As union membership declines and jobs shift from manufacturing to service, the number of workers in secondary, marginal labor markets increases. These employees are less likely to have health insurance. See Monheit, Hagen, Berk & Farley, The Employed Uninsured and the Role of Public Policy, 22 Inquiry 348 (1985). In addition, federal and state cutbacks in the Medicaid program contribute to increases in the number of people without health insurance. See Chapter 2, infra.

The uninsured fit no simple stereotype. While racial minorities as well as the poor, the unemployed, and the young, are disproportionately represented among the uninsured, most families without health insurance are employed, white, earning incomes above the poverty line.

Some groups are particularly likely to be uninsured. In 1984, 17 percent of all American women of childbearing age had no insurance for obstetrical care. See discussion Chap. 10, infra. A survey of widows and children receiving Social Security benefits revealed that 31 percent were uninsured at the time of the husband's death, and 34 percent of those with children under age six were uninsured at the time of the survey. S. Rosenbaum, Defining the Problem of the Medically Needy 34 (1985).

The uninsured receive less medical care than those who have insurance, even though they generally have greater medical needs than those with insurance. Uninsured people are also less likely to have a regular source of medical care.

Often people who have some form of health insurance are not entitled to payment for many essential services. For example, Medicare does not cover prescribed drugs, preventive health services, routine dental care or most long-term care. Most elderly people who purchase supplemental private coverage remain uninsured for items and services not covered by Medicare. Private,

TABLE 2
The Share of the Uninsured Contributed by Groups With Certain Characteristics (1984)

Characteristic	*Percentages* of Under-65 Uninsured Who Are*	
Family Income (All Ages)	Below Poverty	35.6%
	1 to 2x Poverty	29.3%
	2 to 3x Poverty	15.4%
	Over 3x Poverty	19.7%
Employment Status (Adults, 18-64)	Employed	56.5%
	Housekeeping	15.2%
	School	7.2%
	Unemployed	12.1%
	Unable to work, early retirement	8.9%
Age	0–17	33.0%
	18–24	23.6%
	25–44	27.4%
	45–64	16.0%
Race (Adults)	White	79.3%
	Black	17.3%
	Other	3.5%

*Percentages in each group may not add to 100.0% because of rounding.
Bovbjerg & Kopit, supra at 863.

employment-based insurance rarely covers preventive care or dental services. Even when coverage is provided, it is often subject to high deductibles and co-insurance payments that deter people from obtaining necessary care.

b. Other Barriers to Medical Care

Factors other than ability to pay affect access to medical care. Many rural and inner city areas lack adequate hospital and physician services. See Note, Maintaining Health Care in the Inner City: Title VI and Hospital Relocations, 55 N.Y.U.L. Rev. 271 (1980).

In the late 1980s, the rich as well as the poor sometimes find that even emergency care is unobtainable. In 1988 the California Medical Center, which serves a major portion of downtown Los Angeles, ordered all ambulances diverted to other hospitals. California's public support for medical care was seriously constrained in the 1980s, and the hospital asserted that it could no longer afford to maintain an emergency room because too many of the people who were brought there could not pay for the service the hospital provided. The chief of the Los Angeles County paramedic and trauma hos-

TABLE 3
How Insurance Status Affects Medical Care

Indicator of Medical Use	*Insured*	*Uninsured*
Physician visits per person under age 65 in 1977	3.7	2.4
Hospital patient days per 100 persons under age 65 in 1977	90.0	47.0
Families who needed care but did not receive it in 1982	4.8%	15.0%
Families who did not see a physician in 1982	17.1%	32.9%
People with no regular source of health care in 1982	9.7%	23.1%

Bovbjerg & Kopit, supra at 864. (Adapted from M. Sulvetta and K. Swartz, The Uninsured and Uncompensated Care, supra at 51.)

pital programs explained, "On a Friday or Saturday night, it is not unusual to have 17 or 18 hospitals all closed, beginning in the central city and fanning out. . . . Many people mistakenly think this is a problem for the poor. But if there is no emergency room, it is not there for anybody. If the wealthiest person in the state is at a conference downtown and has chest pains, he will be taken to a county hospital." R. Reinhold, Crisis in Emergency Rooms: More Symptoms Than Cures, N.Y. Times, July 28, 1988, at A-1, col. 1. In New York City, acutely ill people are often unable to obtain prompt emergency treatment, whether or not they are able to pay. H. French, Crisis in Hospitals: New York Health System's Problems Resist Quick or Inexpensive Solutions, N.Y. Times, Jan. 7, 1989, at A-31.

In 1987, many Florida neurosurgeons refused to provide emergency care to protest rising malpractice premiums and avoid the risk of suit, which they believe to be greater in providing emergency care to patients they do not know. Edwina Haynes was shot in the back and seriously injured. Glades General Hospital, to which she was taken, did not have a neurosurgeon on staff. Hospital personnel contacted 14 neurosurgeons and 6 hospitals before Tampa General, 150 miles away, agreed to allow Ms. Haynes to be flown to it for treatment. Woman in Florida Shot in Back, Waits 13 Hours for Surgery, N.Y. Times, Aug. 9, 1987, at A-21.

Racial minorities face special barriers. Even though, on the average, minorities have greater needs for medical care, they do not receive more hospital or physician care than whites. Low use of dental services and nursing home care among blacks is particularly striking. Academy of Science, Institute of Medicine, Health Care in a Context of Civil Rights 5-6 (1981). R. Blendon et al., Access to Medical Care for Black and White Americans, 261 J.A.M.A. 278 (1989). Low income whites are more likely to receive care from private physicians than are *any* nonwhites, regardless of income. Congressional Budget Office, Health Differentials Between White and Nonwhite Americans 12 (1977). Minority physicians generally provide care to minority people; such doctors are twice as likely as their white counterparts to provide primary care services. K. Gray, The Geographic and Functional Distribution of Black Physicians: Some Research and Policy Considerations, 67 Am. J. Public Health 519 (1977). However, in 1985 there were only 53.7 black physicians per 100,000 black people compared to 218.5 total physicians per 100,000 total U.S. population. R. Hanft & C. White, Constraining the Supply of Physicians: Effects on Black Physicians, 65 Milbank Mem. Fund Q. 249, 250 (1987). More generally, see Currents of Health Policy: Impacts on Black Americans, 65 Milbank Q. Supp. 1 and 2 (1987).

c. The Organizational Structure of American Hospitals and the Provision of Charitable Care

Traditionally hospitals have been classified according to two variables: ownership and clinical scope. Ownership is divided between public (that is, governmental) and private, and private is further subdivided between profit and nonprofit, or voluntary. Clinical scope is classified as general, treating all or most types of patients, or special, focusing on children, cancer patients, veterans, or other classes of patients. Hospitals can also be classified according to the sophistication of their technology and services. The first level, "primary care," refers to procedures and services typically delivered in a doctor's office or outpatient clinic. The average community hospital delivers "secondary care," and large urban teaching hospitals deliver more complex, "tertiary care."

Manlove suggests that the public/private ownership distinction is critical to the question of patients' access rights, and indeed it sometimes is. State statutes and local ordinances often require public hospitals to accept poor patients or to accept patients without regard to ability to pay. See §G of this chapter. In other cases, such as Campbell v. Mincey, the court considers public ownership relevant only to the applicability of the federal Constitution; certainly the court does not suggest that public ownership imposes on the hospital a duty to provide care without regard to income or other nonmedical factors. An underlying theme of the cases is whether a hospital is simply a passive "workshop" in which doctors pursue the private practice of medicine on their own terms or whether it has institutional obligations to the community, including the low income community, that doctors must satisfy as a condition of membership on the hospital staff.

Most hospitals in America are organized as nonprofit corporations. In 1980 69.9 percent of hospital beds were in nonprofit hospitals; 21.3 percent

TABLE 4
Hospitals in the United States with a High or Low Volume of Uninsured Admissions by Type of Ownership as of 1981

Type of Hospital	*Number of Hospitals*	*Hospitals with Less Than 3% Uninsured Admissions %*	*Hospitals with More Than 25% Uninsured Admissions %*
For-profit	732	58.6	3.1
Not-for-profit	3,324	44.5	4.1
Public	1,641	29.8	10.7
All hospitals	5,697	42.1	5.8

Source: Office for Civil Rights, DHHS Data reported in Rowland (1984).

were in public hospitals and 8.8 percent in profit making institutions. State and federal law provide that nonprofit hospitals may, in some circumstances, be exempt from payment of taxes. See Section D.

American hospitals provide a significant volume of care for which they are not paid. The amount of uncompensated care varies with history, location, ownership, and institutional ethos.

While most American hospitals are nonprofit, in California, Florida, Tennessee, Texas, and Virginia profit making hospitals have become an important source of medical care. With the exception of California, which has an extensive system of public hospitals, data show that profit making hospitals in these states provide significantly less uncompensated care than do nonprofit institutions.

Geographic location also affects the amount of uncompensated care a hospital is likely to provide. Hospitals in the south provide the greatest proportion of uncompensated care, relative to the volume of care for which they are paid. Urban hospitals bear a disproportionate share of the total charges for uncompensated care; hospitals in the 10 largest cities represent 39 percent of total hospital charges and almost half of all uncompensated care. Major teaching hospitals have only 17 percent of the nation's hospital beds but provide 36 percent of the uncompensated care. This data is collected in M. Sulvetta & K. Swartz, The Uninsured and Uncompensated Care, supra.

While the amount of charity care varies significantly by type of hospital ownership, even greater differences can be seen among the individual hospitals of each category. Some public hospitals and nonprofit hospitals avoid providing charitable care, while others are stretched beyond their limits.

d. Studies of Patient Dumping

Throughout the 1980s, hospitals turned away or transferred growing numbers of uninsured people. For example, in Dallas in 1984, indigent pa-

TABLE 5
Hospital Uncompensated Care as Percentage of Gross Patient Revenues in Various States, 1981–1983

Type of Ownership	*California 1981–1982*	*Florida 1982*	*Tennessee 1983*	*Texas 1983*	*Virginia 1982*
Public	7	12.1	18.7	12.4	21.5
Not-for-profit chain	2	6.6	9.0	6.5	5.5
Not-for-profit independent			8.7		
Investor-owned chain	2	3.8	3.4	3.5	3.5
Proprietary independent	3		4.6		

Reprinted in For Profit Enterprise in Health Care, supra, 103.

tients were transferred to the public Parkland Memorial Hospital at the rate of 200 a month, three times the 1983 average. D. Himmelstein, et al., Patient Transfers: Medical Practice as Social Triage, 74 Am. J. Public Health 494 (1984). Transfer to Chicago's Cook County Hospital rose steadily from 1295 in 1980 to 6769 in 1983. R. Schiff, et al., Transfers to a Public Hospital: A Prospective Study of 467 Patients, 314 N. Engl. J. Med. 552 (1986). Only 4 percent of the patients transferred to Cook County had private insurance and 3 percent were eligible for Medicare. Of the transferring hospitals, 87 percent cited the lack of insurance as the sole reason for the transfer. A. Relman, Economic Considerations in Emergency Care: What Are Hospitals For? 312 N. Engl. J. Med. 372 (1985); K. Wrenn, No Insurance, No Admission, 312 N. Engl. J. Med. 373 (1985). Transfers to D.C. General Hospital rose from 169 to nearly 1000 annually between 1981 and 1984. Hospitals in Cost Squeeze "Dump" More Patients Who Can't Pay Bills, Wall Street J., March 8, 1985, at 33. Two physician researchers estimate that in 1986, 250,000 patients in need of emergency care were transferred for economic reasons. D. Ansell & R. Schiff, Patient Dumping: Status, Implications, and Policy Recommendations, 257 J.A.M.A. 1500 (1987).

Transfers are often harmful to patients. Harvard Medical School researchers found that the lives of 33 of 458 patients transferred to the emergency department of Highland General Hospital in Oakland were jeopardized by the transfer. Of those endangered by the transfer, 85 percent lacked insurance. Social Triage, supra at 495. In the Cook County study, all of the four participating physician researchers agreed that 24 percent of the transferred patients were in unstable condition. See also M. Holmes and H. Reyes, A Critical Review of Urban Pediatric Trauma, 24 J. Trauma 253 (1984).

Some physicians speculate that transfers may be beneficial to patients.

> In hospitals where full-time qualified surgeons are present at all times and 24-hour staffing of the operating room is provided, the long transit times for admission to the operating room caused by bringing in the surgical consultant

> and operating team are avoided. . . . As it stands now, the poor in need of emergency surgical care probably benefit from transfer, especially when in an unstable condition, and it is the paying patient who may be at a disadvantage, since transfer is rarely considered. [O. Jonasson & J. Barrett, Transfer of Unstable Patients: Dumping or Duty, 257 J.A.M.A. 1519 (1987).]

2. COMMON LAW PRINCIPLES

a. The No Duty Principle

Tort law historically draws a sharp distinction between action and inaction. It holds people liable when careless actions cause injury to others, but does not require affirmative action to help others in distress, even when essential help could be provided without inconvenience or danger. The "no duty to rescue" principle reflects both a moral vision and a practical concern about the difficulty of defining the duty to help. See M. Shapo, The Duty to Act: Tort Law, Power, and Public Policy (1977). Its morality rests on a rugged individualism that has long been challenged as blind to moral values of interdependence and community. See Bohlen, The Moral Duty to Aid Others as a Basis of Tort Liability, 56 U. Pa. L. Rev. 217 (1908). For a defense of the autonomy protected by the no duty principle, applied to a woman's right to choose abortion, see D. Regan, Rewriting Roe v. Wade, 77 Mich. L. Rev. 1569 (1979).

The no duty principle also rests on very practical concerns. How can a hospital operate efficiently if it must serve every person who appears at its door? How can it assure every patient an ongoing relationship with a physician if it must serve everyone? Do hospitals refuse to serve people in need for these reasons or to maximize revenue and convenience? Can the law possibly distinguish these motives?

Today nearly every state imposes some duty on hospitals to provide emergency care, either through common law doctrine or through the state statutes discussed infra, §§C. and D. Alabama may be an exception. See Harper v. Baptist Medical Center-Princeton, 341 So. 2d 133 (Ala. 1976). Nonetheless, the rhetoric and morality of the no duty principle continue.

In *Campbell,* for example, the court adopts an extraordinarily narrow view of "injury" in suggesting that the plaintiff was not harmed when she gave birth in the parking lot, lost blood, and was delayed in obtaining medical care. There is a very broad consensus in the medical profession that hospital care is necessary to prevent and treat complications that may occur during labor and delivery. This is not to say that all women and infants born outside a hospital will die or suffer grave injury. But risks are greatly increased when laboring women are not provided clean surroundings and trained personnel to help. See G. Dallek, Labor and Delivery as a Medical Emergency, 8 Clearinghouse Rev. 250 (1979), and Chap. 10. See also Floyd v. Willacy County

Hospital District, 706 S.W.2d 731 (Tex. Ct. App. 1986) (public hospital owed no duty to patient who died of a heart attack after being denied care. Though county had waived immunity for injuries caused by negligent actions, waiver did not encompass negligent failure to act).

b. Detrimental Reliance

Other courts, following *Manlove,* have held hospitals liable for failure to provide emergency care when patients have reasonably relied upon the hospital's prior practice of providing service. See Santurf v. Sipes, 447 S.W.2d 558, 35 A.L.R. 834 (Mo. 1969) (holding that where the hospital had a long established custom of accepting all persons for emergency treatment upon payment of $25, and plaintiff relied on the custom, the hospital had a duty to provide care).

c. Hospitals' Undertaking to Provide Care

General tort principles require that even if an individual has no duty to help, anyone who undertakes to provide aid must continue to act with reasonable care. Courts often find that a hospital has undertaken to provide care. In O'Neill v. Montefiore Hospital, 11 A.D.2d 132, 202 N.Y.S.2d 436 (1960), the emergency room nurse called the personal physician of a patient suffering a heart attack; the court held that the jury could determine whether the hospital had thereby undertaken to care for the patient. Fjerstad v. Knutson, 271 N.W.2d 8 (S.D. 1978) held that, even though no staff physician was on duty, a hospital had undertaken to provide reasonable care when an intern examined a patient, took a throat culture and a blood test, and discharged the patient, who died shortly thereafter. Le Juene Rd. Hospital, Inc. v. Watson, 171 So. 2d 202 (Fla. Ct. App. 1965), found that the patient's continued presence in the hospital rendered hospital liable for failure to treat.

d. Other Bases of Hospitals' Common Law Duty

The lower court in *Manlove* predicated liability on a finding that the hospital was a "quasi-public" institution because it was tax exempt, received public funds, and was publicly licensed and regulated. Generally, courts considering whether a hospital has a common law obligation to provide emergency care have not drawn distinctions on the basis of hospital ownership. But Williams v. Hospital Authority of Hall County, 119 G. App. 626, 168 S.E.2d 336 (1969), held that public hospitals have an obligation to provide emergency service.

Mercy Medical Center of Oshkosh, Inc. v. Winnebago Co., 58 Wis. 2d

260, 206 N.W.2d 198 (1973), recognized a hospital's duty to provide essential care, saying:

> It would shock the public conscience if a person in need of medical emergency aid would be turned down at the door of a hospital having emergency service because that person could not at that moment assure payment for the service. The public expects such service; the public support of a hospital and the governmental grants in aid to hospitals to increase their facilities all substantiate the fact that hospitals with emergency service cannot refuse it to the needy. [Id. at 201.]

General tort law prohibits certain actors — common carriers, innkeepers, and public utilities — from denying service on an arbitrary basis unrelated to the purpose of the enterprise. Doe v. Bridgeton, 71 N.J. 478, 366 A.2d 641 (1976), *cert. denied,* 433 U.S. 914 (1977), applied this concept to invalidate a hospital policy that prohibited physicians and patients from using the facility to provide abortion services. Common carriers and innkeepers may, of course, limit their services to those who are able to pay.

e. Physician's Duties Arising from the Doctor/Patient Relationship

The "undertaking" issue is particularly important in cases in which a physician, rather than a hospital, has failed to provide care. Courts scrutinize the complexity of patient/doctor interactions to determine whether the jury should be allowed to determine that the physician has undertaken to care for the patient. Clanton v. Von Haam, 177 Ga. App. 694, 340 S.E.2d 627 (1986), held that the fact that a doctor returned a patient's calls and counseled her over the phone did not create a relationship of duty. Courts have divided on whether a physician who is contractually obligated to be on call at a hospital emergency room owes a duty of care to individuals who seek treatment there. In Childs v. Weis, 440 S.W.2d 104 (Tex. Civ. App. 1969), the physician on call refused to come to the hospital to see a woman from another town who was in labor. She gave birth on the highway an hour later, and the baby died shortly thereafter. The court held, as a matter of law, that the physician owed the patient no duty. But Hiser v. Randolph, 126 Ariz. 608, 617 P.2d 774 (Ct. App. 1980), held that a doctor who agrees to be on call owes a duty to patients seeking emergency aid. The patient died when treatment for an acute diabetic episode was delayed. Her husband alleged that the doctor refused care because the husband was a lawyer.

A physician who has undertaken to care for a patient may terminate that relationship "only by the cessation of the necessity which gave rise to the relationship, or by the discharge of the physician by the patient, or by the withdrawal from the case by the physician after giving the patient reasonable notice so as to enable the patient to secure other medical attention." Ricks v. Budge, 91 Utah 307, 64 P.2d 208 (1937).

In Lyons v. Grether, 218 Va. 630, 239 S.E.2d 103 (1977), a blind woman called a doctor's office and made an appointment to be seen for "treatment of a vaginal infection." When she arrived, accompanied by her guide dog, the physician evicted her from his office. The court, while recognizing that merely having an appointment did not establish a doctor-patient relation, found that such a relationship did exist in this instance. "The unmistakable implication is that plaintiff had sought and defendant had granted an appointment at a designated time and place for the performance of a specific medical service, one within the defendant's professional competence. . . ." Id. at 105. State law prohibited discrimination against blind people accompanied by guide dogs.

In Walker v. Pierce, 560 F.2d 609 (4th Cir. 1977), *cert. denied,* 434 U.S. 1075 (1978), a woman pregnant with her fourth child challenged the physician's policy of conditioning his obstetrical services upon her consent to be sterilized. Dr. Pierce testified:

> My policy was with people who were unable to financially support themselves, whether they be on Medicaid or just unable to pay their own bills, if they were having a third child, to request they voluntarily submit to sterilization following the delivery of the third child. If they did not wish this as a condition for my care, then I requested that they seek another physician. . . . [Id. at 611.]

The plaintiff refused to consent throughout her prenatal care and then, during labor, signed forms consenting to be sterilized. The court found "no reason why Dr. Pierce could not establish and pursue the policy he has publicly and freely announced. Nor are we cited to judicial precedent or statute inhibiting this personal economic philosophy. Particularly is this so when all persons coming to him as patients are reasonably made fully aware of his professional attitude toward the increase in offspring and his determination to see it prevail. At no time is he shown to have forced his view upon any mother." Id. at 613.

What are the similarities and differences between Lyons v. Grether and Walker v. Pierce? Would Dr. Grether's actions be accepted if he made it plain from the outset that he did not accept blind patients with guide dogs? Does a doctor's personal opposition to helping poor women bear more than three children carry more moral weight than opposition to blind people with guide dogs? Should it be unethical or illegal for a physician to discriminate against patients on the basis of the patient's choice in relation to reproduction or to medical treatment? Ms. Walker was black and Ms. Lyons white; does that explain the difference in the cases?

In Payton v. Weaver, 131 Cal. App. 3d 38, 182 Cal. Rptr. 225 (1982), Dr. Weaver provided Ms. Payton hemodialysis for three years. The patient's life depended upon having her blood cleaned through a machine three times a week. Her condition also made it extraordinarily dangerous for her to use drugs or alcohol or to eat certain foods. Nonetheless she persisted in these self-destructive behaviors. In addition, she often disrupted the dialysis center. Dr. Weaver attempted to work with and to support her. She held him in great respect. She said: "Dr. Weaver is and was and still is the man between me and death . . . other than God, I don't think of nobody higher than I do Dr. Weaver." Id. Finally, the doctor notified Ms. Payton that unless she changed her habits and entered therapy, he would no longer treat her. He advised her of other sources of dialysis treatment. Ms. Payton sought to compel the doctor to continue to provide her with care. The court rejected her claim. Think about the similarities and differences among Ms. Payton, Ms. Walker, and Ms. Lyons and their physicians.

The *Payton* court also rejected plaintiff's claim that the hospital had violated the state statute requiring provision of emergency care. Nonetheless, the court found,

> It does not necessarily follow that a hospital, or other health care facility, is without obligation to patients in need of continuing medical services for their survival. [I]t is questionable whether a hospital which receives public funding . . . can reasonably be said to be "private." . . . Rather, where such a hospital contains a unique, or scarce, medical resource needed to preserve life, it is arguably in the nature of a "public service enterprise," and should not be permitted to withhold its services arbitrarily, or without reasonable cause. . . . And, while disruptive conduct on the part of a patient may constitute good cause for an individual hospital to refuse continued treatment, since it would be unfair to impose serious inconvenience upon a hospital simply because such a patient selected it, it may be that there exists a *collective* responsibility on the part of the provider of scarce health resources in a community, enforceable through equity, to *share* the burden of difficult patients over time, through an appropriately devised contingency plan. . . . Whatever the merits of such an approach, . . . it cannot serve as a basis for imposition of responsibility upon these respondents under the circumstances present here. . . . Whatever collective responsibility may exist, it is clearly not absolute, or independent of the patient's own responsibility. [131 Cal. App. 3d 143.]

How can a court, even in "equity," enforce "collective" responsibilities on hospitals?

f. Good Samaritan Laws

Every state has sought to encourage doctors to provide treatment at roadside emergencies through Good Samaritan statutes that provide immunity from liability for negligence. D. Louisell & H. Williams, Medical Malpractice 21-23 (1985). Such laws have had little impact in encouraging doctors to provide care in emergencies. See S. Law & L. Polan, Pain and Profit: The

Politics of Malpractice 247 (1977). One state, Massachusetts, in response to a proposal by the state medical society, requires that licensed physicians "render medical services to a person experiencing a medical emergency, whether or not the person is able to pay." Quoted in Annas, Beyond the Good Samaritan: Should Doctors Be Required to Provide Essential Services? Hastings Cent. Rep., April 1977, at 16.

Some courts have held that Good Samaritan statutes immunize physicians from liability when they provide emergency care in the hospital to patients who are under the care of other physicians. See McKenna v. Cedars of Lebanon Hospital, 93 Cal. App. 3d 282. 155 Cal. Rptr. 631 (1979); Burciaga v. St. John's Hospital, 187 Cal. App. 3d 710, 232 Cal. Rptr. 75 (1986). See Note, Good Samaritans and Hospital Emergencies, 54 S. Cal. L. Rev. 417 (1981).

g. Medical Ethics

The American Medical Association, Code of Ethics provides that "A physician may choose whom he shall serve. In an emergency, however, he should render service to the best of his ability." American Medical Association, Principles of Medical Ethics, §VI (1980). Prior to 1957, the AMA Principles contained an ethical duty to render charitable care. Chapter 7, §1 (1955). Some physicians continue to regard care for those unable to pay as an ethical duty, while others reject such ethical concepts on economic or political grounds. See discussion in R. Rosenblatt, Medicaid Primary Care Case Management, the Doctor-Patient Relationship, and the Politics of Privitization, 36 Case W. Res. L. Rev. 915, 925 n.37 (1986). No court has given legal force to these ethical obligations.

h. Emergency

In *Manlove,* as under the state statutes discussed below, if hospitals have emergency room, the duty to treat turns on a determination whether a medical "emergency" exists. New Biloxi Hospital, Inc. v. Frazier, 245 Miss. 185, 146 So. 2d 882 (1962), found an emergency in which a patient with a gun shot wound was left untreated for two hours before he was transferred to another hospital, where he died. The Court defined emergency treatment as that which is "immediately and reasonably necessary for the preservation of life, limb or health." Id. at 882. In Jones V. City of New York Hospital for Joint Diseases, 134 N.Y.S.2d 779 (Sup. Ct. 1954), *rev'd,* 286 A.D. 825, 143 N.Y.S.2d 628 (1955), a patient with a stab wound was transferred to a public hospital, one hour away, where she died. The court upheld a jury determination of emergency, though the physician who ordered the transfer testified that he did not regard the patient's condition as emergent. Various professional organizations have promulgated definitions of medical emergency. See discussion, Wing, The Emergency Room Admission: How Far Does the "Open Door" Go?, 63 U. Det. L. Rev. 119 (1985).

In *Manlove,* the court held that a nurse could normally make an initial determination whether an emergency existed. Citizens Hospital Association v. Schoulin, 48 Ala. App. 101, 262 So. 2d 303 (Civ. App. 1972), held a hospital negligent when a nurse refused to call a physician for an accident victim experiencing severe back pain, and, the next day, another hospital discovered that his back was broken. Should the law require that a physician make this assessment? By the late 1980s, most states require that hospital emergency rooms be staffed by a physician, who can determine the need for emergency care and provide it. See Chap. V, infra.

i. Proximate Cause

The determination of proximate cause is colored by the tension between the general no duty principle and the ethical appeal of a patient in emergent need of care. Judicial ambivalence is reflected in a broad or a narrow approach to the issue of proximate cause. Harper v. Baptist Medical Center-Princeton, 341 So.2d 133 (Ala. 1976), held that the plaintiff's injury was caused solely by the original accident, not by the delay in obtaining medical care. Where a state statute establishes a duty to provide care, courts are more likely to find proximate cause. See Thompson v. Sun City, infra.

j. The Duty to Provide Medical Care to People in State Custody

The constitutional prohibition on cruel and unusual punishment bars prison officials from acting with deliberate indifference to serious medical needs of incarcerated people. Estelle v. Gamble, 429 U.S. 97 (1976). "Deliberate indifference" can be proved by either actual intent or reckless disregard for the prisoner's health and well being. Benson v. Cady, 761 F.2d 335, 339 (7th Cir. 1985). While a detainee has a constitutional right to adequate medical care, that right does not tell us who must pay for it. Revere v. Massachusetts General Hospital, 463 U.S. 239 (1983). Wideman v. Shallowford Community Hospitals, Inc, 826 F.2d 1030 (11th Cir. 1987), rejected a claim that a county had assumed custody of a patient when a county-operated ambulance refused to take her to the hospital where her doctor was waiting but instead took her to a county-preferred hospital where care was delayed. She gave birth to a premature infant who died in four hours.

k. Large Movements in the Values Emphasized by the Common Law

The study of contracts and torts suggests one standard way to understand the development of the common law in the past 100 years is as a progressive development from the bad old "no duty" rules of brutal individualism to the good, humane, liberal protective rules of our current civilized era. Or, in somewhat different words, the law has moved from the status based relations of the medieval period to the contract based arrangements of industrialism, to an understanding that large differences in power often preclude meaningful bargain and agreement. The converse view is also prominent today — that the older cases wisely promoted individual choice and that newer efforts to regulate market transactions undermine productivity and human liberty. *Hurley* has been criticized sharply as inconsistent with modern developments in both torts and contracts. See, for instance, Prosser and Keeton, Torts at 375 (5th ed. 1984); Contracts Cases and Materials (F. Kessler, G. Gilmore & A. Kronman, eds.) at 56-58 (3rd ed. 1986). How do these changes in common law principles relate to the conflicts in political values discussed in the Introduction?

See generally Fine, Opening the Closed Doors: The Duty of Hospitals to Treat Emergency Patients, 24 Wash. U.J. Urb. & Contemp. L. 123 (1983); M. Dowell, Indigent Access to Hospital Emergency Room Services, 18 Clearinghouse Rev. 483 (1984); L. Powers, Hospital Emergency Services and the Open Door, 66 Mich. L. Rev. 1455 (1968); Note, Duty of a Private Hospital to Render Emergency Treatment, 1974 Wis. L. Rev. 279; Note, To Treat or Not to Treat: A Hospital's Duty to Provide Emergency Care, 15 U.C. Davis L. Rev. 1047 (1982).

C. State Efforts to Encourage Hospitals and Localities to Provide Essential Medical Care

Thompson v. Sun City

141 Ariz. 597, 688 P.2d 605 (1984)

Michael Jessee, plaintiff's son, was injured on the evening of September 4, 1976. Jessee was 13 years old. . . . He was rushed by ambulance . . . to the Boswell Memorial Hospital. . . . Among Jessee's injuries was a transected or partially transected femoral artery. . . . Upon arrival at the emergency room at 8:22 P.M., Jessee was examined and initially treated by Dr. Steven Lipsky, the emergency room physician. Fluids were administered and blood was ordered. The leg injury prompted Dr. Lipsky to summon Dr. Alivina Sabanas, an orthopedic surgeon. She examined Jessee's leg and determined that he needed surgery. Dr. Jon Hillegas, a vascular surgeon, was consulted by phone.

At some time after 9:30 P.M. Jessee's condition "stabilized" and the decision was made to transfer him to County Hospital. There is no clear indication in the record of who ordered the transfer. Dr. Lipsky determined that Jessee was "medically transferable" but stated that "Michael Jessee was transferred for economic reasons after we found him to be medically transferable." Dr. Lipsky had no authority to admit patients to Boswell. Dr. Sabanas, who did have such authority and who knew that Jessee needed vascular surgery, claimed that Jessee was transferable from an orthopedic standpoint. Dr. Hillegas told Dr. Lipsky that Jessee could be transferred when "stabilized." A witness for the plaintiff testified that "The doctor at Boswell (apparently Dr. Lipsky) said (to Ada Thompson), 'I have the shitty detail of telling you that Mike will be transferred to County. . . .'" A Boswell administrator testified that emergency "charity" patients are transferred . . . whenever a physician, in his professional judgment, determines that "a transfer could occur."

Thus, at 10:13 Jessee was . . . taken to County. The doctors who attended to him at County began administering fluids and ordered blood. They testified that Jessee's condition worsened but that he was eventually "stabilized" and taken to surgery at about 1:00 A.M. He survived but has residual impairment of his left leg. . . .

The trial record reveals a confusion of the issues of duty of care and causation. In any case such as this there are two types of causation questions. The first, relating to the question of breach of duty, pertains to the cause for the transfer to another hospital. Was the patient transferred for medical or other reasons? The second question relates to the cause of injury and is concerned with whether the transfer, with its attendant movement and delay, caused a new or additional injury or aggravated any injury which already existed. The first question was answered by defense counsel . . . : "We admit and stipulate that the plaintiff in this case was transferred from Boswell to County Hospital for financial reasons. There is no question about it."

In this state, the duty which a hospital owes a patient in need of emergency care is determined by the statutes and regulations interpreted by this court in Guerrero v. Copper Queen Hospital, 112 Ariz. 104, 537 P.2d 1329 (1975). Construing the statutory and regulatory scheme governing health care and the licensing of hospitals as of 1972, we held that it was the "public policy of this state" that a general "hospital may not deny emergency care to any patient without cause." Id. at 106, 537 P.2d at 1331.

Principles governing the functioning of hospitals were not left in the abstract. Specific regulations, adopted in 1976, . . . concerning "emergency departments," provided that "general hospitals shall provide facilities for emergency care." In addition, such hospitals were required "to have on call one or more physicians licensed to practice medicine and surgery in Arizona or resident physician or intern physician." Our holding in *Guerrero* is reinforced by . . . [an Arizona statute providing]:

> A. When an indigent emergency medical patient is received by an emergency receiving facility from a (licensed) ambulance . . . , the county shall be liable . . . to the ambulance service for the cost of transporting the patient and to the facility for the reasonable costs of all medical services rendered to such indigent by the facility until such patient is transferred by the county to the county hospital. . . .

The quoted statute . . . provides the answer to a serious problem. Charging hospitals with a legal duty to render emergency care to indigent patients does not ignore the distinctions between private and public hospitals. Imposition of a duty to render emergency care to indigents simply charges private hospitals with the same duty as public hospitals under a statutory plan which permits reimbursement from public funds for the emergency care charges incurred at the private hospital.

[A]s a matter of public policy, licensed hospitals in this state are required to accept and render emergency care to all patients who present themselves in need of such care. The patient may not be transferred until all medically indicated emergency care has been completed. . . . Interpreting the standard of care in accordance with the public policy defined in *Guerrero,* we hold that reasonable "cause" for transfer before completion of emergency care refers to medical considerations relevant to the welfare of the patient and not economic considerations relevant to the welfare of the hospital. A transfer based on the forbidden criterion of economic considerations may be for the convenience of the hospital but it is hardly "medically indicated." Given the duty imposed in Arizona — that a general hospital may not deny emergency care to any person without valid cause — there are three possible defenses a hospital may raise in an appropriate fact situation: (1) that the hospital is not obligated (or capable) under its state license to provide the necessary emergency care, (2) there is a valid medical cause to refuse emergency care, (3) there is no true emergency requiring care and thus no emergency care which is medically indicated.

Neither of the first two defenses are at issue. . . . The third is more troublesome. . . . What constitutes an emergency is a matter of some disagreement. There are various definitions; the need for immediate attention seems to be the common thread. Ordinarily it is for the jury to determine the factual question of the duration of an emergency and the treatment modalities that are a necessary component of emergency care.

Given the stipulation that Boswell ordered the transfer of Jessee to County Hospital because of financial reasons, the relevant inquiries in the case at bench [were] . . . whether, before transfer, the hospital had rendered the emergency care medically indicated for this patient. . . . Dr. Hillegas testified that ". . . you want to repair the arterial injury just as soon as you can." Dr. Lipsky knew Jessee needed surgery. Dr. Sabanas believed Jessee needed emergency surgery. . . . Thus the undisputed evidence established that the patient was transferred for financial reasons while emergency care was medically indicated. As a matter of law this was a breach of the hospital's duty. Thus, the only question before the jury on the issue of the hospital's liability was whether its breach of duty was a cause of some compensable damage.

The duty of care owed by a physician to a patient is different from the hospital's duty. No statute requires the physician to provide services separate and apart from those which the hospital is required to provide. Thus, the duty of care owed by a physician is determined by common law principles which require reference to that which is usually done by members of the profession. . . . Dr. Lipsky was not a specialist in either orthopedic or vascular surgery. He was an emergency room physician. . . . Lipsky had no power to admit and could not have admitted Jessee if he had wanted to do so. . . . Nothing in the record indicates that any act or omission of Dr. Lipsky was a cause of the refusal to admit Jessee. . . .

Plaintiff argues . . . that the vascular surgeon [Dr. Hillegas] breached his duty in failing to come to the hospital to attend Jessee. [P]hysicians were on duty and present at Boswell to care for emergency patients; specialists were "on call" prepared to come to the hospital and treat patients who needed specialized attention. . . . Boswell did not request this physician to come. To the contrary, Boswell's refusal to admit Jessee would have made Dr. Hillegas' arrival at the hospital an empty gesture. . . .

Boswell's theory of the case was that the breach of duty, if any, in transferring the patient had caused no damage, since Jessee's serious injuries might have led to precisely the residual injury which he did sustain. At defendant's request, the court instructed the jury that plaintiff could not recover absent proof of a probability that the acts or omissions of the defendant had aggravated the original injury. Plaintiff sought an additional instruction that such cause was established if plaintiff had proved that defendant's acts or omissions had "increased the risk of harm" to plaintiff. . . .

Generally, two different rules have evolved. The first holds that the plaintiff must introduce evidence from which the jury may find a probability that because of the defendant's negligence the ultimate result was different from or greater than that attributable to the original injury or condition. . . . Under this rule, plaintiff fails in his burden of proof and a verdict is directed if the evidence does not warrant a finding that the chance of recovery or survival absent defendant's negligence, was over 50 percent.

Under the second rule, even if the evidence permits only a finding that the defendant's negligence increased the risk of harm or deprived plaintiff of some significant chance of survival or better recovery, it is left for the jury to decide whether there is a probability that defendant's negligence was a cause in fact of the injury. . . .

There is much to be said against the . . . [first] rule. It puts a premium on each party's search for the willing witness. [F]or every expert witness who evaluates the lost chance at 49 percent there is another who estimates it at closer to 51 percent. Also, the rule tends to defeat one of the primary functions of the tort system — deterrence of negligent conduct. . . .

We caution that this [second] rule fits only in those situations where the courts traditionally have allowed juries to deal more loosely with causation — the cases where the duty breached was one imposed to prevent the type of harm which plaintiff ultimately sustained. [W]here the law governing duty encompassed "the chance interest within (its) range of protection" (and the harm from which defendant was to have protected the plaintiff occurred), greater latitude is given to the trier of fact to find causation under any plausible theory. . . . "Hence the interest which the law is protecting is the chance itself, and the chief problem is the evaluation of the chance, which is a function peculiarly within the province of the jury." . . . This formulation, of course, merely recognizes that juries often discount damages according to the statistical evidence in order to accurately evaluate the true loss. . . .

We hold, therefore, that because the protection of the chance interest was within the range of the duty breached by defendant and the harm which followed was the type from which the defendant was to have protected the plaintiff, the jury may be allowed to consider the increase in the chance of harm on the issue of causation. If the jury finds that defendant's failure to exercise reasonable care increased the risk of the harm he undertook to prevent, it may from this fact find a "probability" that defendant's negligence was the cause of the damage. . . .

This rule, of course, is . . . for the court. That defendant is "subject to liability" means that the issue of causation may go to the jury upon proof of increase in the risk of harm. The jury is left to decide the issue of probability. . . .

1. STATE REQUIREMENTS THAT ALL HOSPITALS PROVIDE EMERGENCY CARE

Twenty-two states require hospitals to provide emergency medical care regardless of a patient's ability to pay. Most statutes do not define what constitutes an emergency. Others define an emergency narrowly as "a condition requiring prompt lifesaving treatment," while yet others define it more broadly to encompass "any injury or acute medical condition which might cause death or severe injury or illness." Dowell, Indigent Access to Hospital Emergency Room Services, 18 Clearinghouse Rev. 483 (1984). Only seven state statutes provide any penalty for their violation, and most of these remedies are weak. Georgia and Kentucky allow $100 to $500 fines. Enforcement actions are rare.

In the late 1980s, several states strengthened the legal obligations on hospitals to provide emergency care. Texas led the way in 1986. Tex. Health and Safety Code Ann., §4438(a) (Vernon Supp. 1986), defines emergency services as those

> that are usually and customarily available at the respective hospital and that must be provided immediately to sustain a person's life, to prevent serious permanent disfigurement or loss or impairment of the function of a bodily member or organ, or to provide for the care of a woman in active labor if the hospital is so equipped and, if the hospital is not so equipped, to provide necessary treatment to allow the woman to travel to a more appropriate facility without undue risk of serious harm.

Perhaps more significant, the regulations implementing the Texas statute set guidelines for hospital transfers. No transfer may be made unless the patient has been stabilized, the receiving hospital agrees to accept the patient, appropriate medical service is provided during transfer, and medical records are sent with the patient. Rules Governing Hospital Patient Transfer Policies, Tex. Admin. Code tit. 25, §133.21 (1986). Texas physicians or hospital personnel who violate the statute may be punished with up to 10 years imprisonment and $5,000 fines.

California and Maryland adopted similar laws: 1987 Cal. Stat. Ch. 1225, 1240; Md. Health-Gen. Code Ann. §19-308.2 (1987). In 1987, Pennsylvania required, as a condition of hospital licensure, that providers "should offer and provide medically necessary, lifesaving and emergency health care services to every person . . . regardless of financial status or ability to pay." Pa. Stat. Ann. tit. 35, §449.8 (Purdon Supp. 1987). Tennessee adopted a similar law in 1986. Tenn. Code Ann. §§68-11-701 – 705 (1986). In 1987, the New York Legislature added a new requirement that "[n]o general hospital shall transfer any patient to another hospital or health care facility on the grounds that the patient is unable to pay or guarantee payment for services rendered." N.Y. Pub. Health Law, §2805(b) (1)(McKinney 1988). Florida responded to physicians who protested malpractice premiums by refusing to treat emergency patients. The 1988 law provides that licensed physicians "may not instigate or engage in a concerted effort to refuse to render services to a patient in a hospital emergency room. . . ." 1988 Fla. Sess. Law Serv., Ch. 88-1, §458.3295. A 1986 Louisiana statute requires that a person "in need of emergency services" at a hospital must be diagnosed by a licensed physician, regardless of ability to pay. A person diagnosed as "requiring emergency service" may not be denied services available in the hospital. La. Rev. Stat. Ann, §40:2113.6 (West Supp. 1988). In 1986, Massachusetts prohibited any involuntary transfers made on the basis of ability to pay. It is not limited to emergency situations. Mass. Ann. Laws ch. 111, §70E(n) (Law. Co-op. Supp. 1988). Virginia amended its state hospital licensure law to "require that each licensed hospital that provides obstetrical services establish a protocol for admission or transfer of any pregnant woman who presents herself while in labor." Va. Code Ann, §32.1-127(c). See Waxman & Dorn, States Take the Lead in Preventing Patient Dumping, 21 Clearinghouse Rev. 136 (1988).

As you study the material in the balance of this chapter, and the following chapters on financing medical care, think about the factors that, in the late 1980s, led so many states to impose more stringent emergency care requirements.

The impact of state laws requiring private hospitals to provide emergency care is not clear. Most patients denied care will not institute a malpractice claim, even if they are injured by the hospital's refusal to care for them. When many emergency patients have no means of paying for care, it may be more costly for a hospital to provide care, than it is to deny it and risk liability.

2. HISTORIC STATE AND LOCAL OBLIGATIONS TO CARE FOR THE POOR

Our Nation has a deep tradition of local obligation to care for those in need, when their families are unable to do so. The English Elizabethan poor law, 43 Eliz., c.2 (1602), provided that "the church wardens of every parish, and four . . . substantial householders there . . . shall be called the overseers of the poor of the same parish. . . . By taxation of every inhabitant . . . [they shall raise] competent sums of money for and toward the necessary relief of the lame, impotent, old, blind, and such others among them, being poor and not able to work."

American colonies and states adopted this pattern, enacting laws that required localities to assume responsibility to provide essential services for the poor, including medical care. Until the late nineteenth century localities met this responsibility by creating almshouses, and the first hospitals were the dispensaries of these institutions. B. J. Stern, Medical Services by Government, Ch. 6 (1946).

This tradition of local responsibility for the provision of medical care means that the legal duties and actual practices of hospitals vary widely from place to place. Local taxes are generally raised on a more regressive basis than state or federal revenues. Local property and sales taxes impose disproportionately large burdens on low income people, as compared with the income-graduated federal and state income taxes. The mobility of capital means that if a locality attempts to tax on a progressive basis, people and businesses with money will move. Communities where need is greatest are often least able to generate the resources to meet it. Thus in the 1930s and 1960s state and federal governments assumed greater responsibility to finance essential services for needy people. See Chapter 2, infra. The tradition of local responsibility has also been altered by the increasing intensity and complexity of medical care and the rising costs of providing it. See Chapter 3, infra. Nonetheless, in many states the laws imposing responsibility on localities remain on the books, and localities continue to bear residual responsibility for care of those not included in state and federal programs.

In the late 1980s, all but three states have constitutional or statutory provisions declaring a state or local responsibility to provide necessary medical care for the indigent; in twenty states, that bottom line responsibility is assigned to local government. Localities meet these responsibilities in three ways: maintenance of public hospitals, programs that make individual poor people eligible for particular medical benefits, and arrangements under which hospitals are reimbursed for care provided to the poor. P. Butler, Legal Obligations of State and Local Governments for Indigent Health Care, Table 1, in Academy for State and Local Government, Access to Care for the Medically Indigent: A Resource Document for State and Local Officials 13 (1985). See discussion Bovbjerg & Kopit, Coverage and Care for the Medically Indigent: Public and Private Options, 19 Ind. L. Rev. 857 (1986).

3. JUDICIAL ENFORCEMENT OF STATE LAWS REQUIRING LOCALITIES TO PAY FOR CARE THAT PRIVATE HOSPITALS PROVIDE TO POOR PEOPLE

Actions to enforce historic state laws assigning localities responsibility for care of the indigent have most often been brought by hospitals seeking reimbursement for care they have provided. Judicial reaction has been sharply divided.

Many courts have required that localities pay private hospitals for necessary care provided to the indigent. In Illinois, many cases have enforced a state law requiring that indigent people "shall be given such care as may be necessary and proper, including transportation, and if he dies he shall be decently buried." See Lakeview Medical Center v. Richardson, 76 Ill. App. 3d 953, 395 N.E.2d 405 (Ct. App. 1979) and cases cited therein. Washoe County v. Wittenberg, 100 Nev. 143, 676 P.2d 808 (1984), held that while the county could generally insist that indigent people seek medical care at the county hospital, when a private hospital provided emergency service to an indigent person state law demanded county reimbursement. Similarly, University of Utah Hospital & Medical Center v. Bethke, 101 Idaho 245, 611 P.2d 1030 (1980), required an Idaho county to pay a hospital that was neither under contract nor even within the state. Welborn Memorial Baptist Hospital v. County Department of Public Welfare, 442 N.E.2d 372 (Ind. App. 1982), held, over a strong dissent, that a statute requiring that counties pay the "cost of treatment for indigents suffering from any disease, defect, or deformity" prohibits an arbitrary five day limit on inpatient treatment for drug and alcohol addiction. But see Lutheran Hospital v. Department of Public Welfare, 397 N.E.2d 638 (Ind. App. 1979) (statute does not require payment for costs of normal childbirth). Wisconsin courts require counties to pay private hospitals for emergency care provided to indigent people. See, for instance, Clintonville Community Hospital Association v. Clintonville, 87 Wis. 2d 635, 275 N.W.2d 655 (1979). Montana requires that counties reimburse doctors and hospitals for necessary services provided to indigent people. Michels v. Department of Social and Rehabilitation Services, 187 Mont. 173, 609 P.2d 271 (1980), refused to enforce a requirement that application be made for county aid within five days of medical care, on grounds that demanding compliance would subvert the beneficial purpose of the state mandate. Arizona courts have read a state statute authorizing counties to care for the sick as imposing a duty to do so. Industrial Commission v. Navajo County, 64 Ariz. 172, 167 P.2d 113 (1946). Ohio law mandates counties to appropriate the funds necessary to support essential medical care. St. Thomas Hospital v. Schmidt, 62 Ohio St.2d 439, 406 N.E.2d 819 (1980).

New Hampshire requires counties to finance necessary medical care for indigent people. Until 1976 county officials made judgments of both financial and medical need on an individualized, ad hoc basis. Baker-Chaput v. Cammett, 406 F. Supp. 1134 (D.N.H. 1976), applying constitutional due process norms, required that the county articulate eligibility standards. Hall v. Hillsborough County, 122 N.H. 448, 445 A.2d 1125 (1982), required that the county pay the nursing home costs of an individual whose income exceeded fixed eligibility standards. The court recognized that its ruling leads "to the irrational result that every time the taxpayers decide to limit the State Medicaid benefits . . . [the county] will have to provide local welfare for those who become ineligible for state welfare. . . ." Id. at 1128.

Other courts have refused to require counties to finance care that private hospitals provide to indigents. In Dade County v. American Hospital of Miami, Inc., 502 So.2d 1230 (Fla. 1987), private hospitals sought to force the county to compensate them for post-emergency care provided to indigent patients. Ordinarily indigent patients who seek care at private hospitals are transferred to the public hospital when their condition is stabilized. Sometimes, however, the public hospital is filled to capacity, and it simply cannot accept additional patients. American Hospital sought payment for these services arguing that a provision of the 1885 Florida constitution requires that "the respective counties of the State shall provide, in the manner prescribed by law, for those of the inhabitants who by reason of age, infirmity or misfortune, may have claims upon the aid and sympathy of society. . . ." Id. at 1232. The Florida Supreme Court held that this provision had been repealed in subsequent constitutional revisions. American Hospital also relied on a 1977 statute expressing a legislative intent "to place the ultimate financial obligation for the medical treatment of indigents on the county in which the indigent resides, for all those costs not fully reimbursed by other governmental programs or third-party payors." Id. at 1233. The court held, over vigorous dissent, that this provision only applies when an indigent resident of one county receives care in a public hospital in another county. The court observed that courts "are ill equipped to investigate and evaluate changing public needs in this area. Post-emergency, indigent health care is a problem for legislative solution." Id. at 1234.

Even though California statutes impose strong obligations upon counties to provide necessary medical care to the indigent, California courts have given counties broad discretion in meeting these duties. See Union of American Physicians v. Santa Clara County, 149 Cal. App. 3d 45, 196 Cal. Rptr. 602 (Ct. App. 1983) (physicians not entitled to payment from county); Bay General Community Hospital v. San Diego County, 156 Cal. App. 3d 944, 203 Cal. Rptr. 184 (Ct. App. 1984)(private hospitals not entitled to reimbursement from county). Under Iowa law counties have broad discretion to determine the form and amount of support for the indigent. Collins v. Hoke, 705 F.2d 959 (8th Cir. 1983).

D. Obligations Attached to State and Federal Tax Exemption

1. FEDERAL TAX LAW AND POLICY

Hospitals and other health organizations may qualify for federal tax exempt status under §501(c)(3) of the Internal Revenue Code if they are 1) organized for "charitable purposes," that is do not distribute net earnings to owners, and 2) operate to fulfill those charitable purposes. Qualified hospitals do not have to pay federal income tax, and contributions to them are deductible to the donor. In addition, benefits from the federal government and private foundations are often restricted to nonprofit organizations.

Until 1969, IRS regulations required that a tax exempt hospital "be operated to the extent of its financial ability for those not able to pay. . . ." The IRS monitored and enforced this requirement. Revenue Ruling 69-545 (1969) changed that policy and specified two factors to be used to determine whether a hospital is "charitable" for federal tax purposes: 1) the operation of an emergency room open to all persons, and 2) the provision of hospital care to all persons in the community able to pay the cost of services, either directly or through third party insurers such as Medicare, Medicaid, or Blue Cross/Blue Shield. Poor people sought to challenge this shift in policy, but the Supreme Court held that they had not demonstrated a sufficiently personal and concrete injury to establish standing. Simon v. Eastern Kentucky Welfare Rights Organization, 426 U.S. 26 (1976).

A 1983 Revenue Ruling further broadens the grounds upon which a hospital may qualify as a charitable institution for federal tax purposes. Hospitals may be considered charitable if they offer education and training programs, serve a disproportionate number of Medicaid or Medicare patients, or provide community health programs or specialty hospital services, such as cancer control. Rev. Ruling 83-157, 1983-42 I.R.B. 9. See Hopkins & Beckwith, The Federal Tax Law of Hospitals: Basic Principles and Current Developments, 24 Dug. L. Rev. 691 (1985).

Some people question the wisdom of the federal tax exemption for hospitals. Representative Fortney H. Stark, Chair of the Health Subcommittee of the House Committee on Ways and Means, argues that the federal tax exemption for nonprofit hospitals is unwarranted because the tax revenue lost often exceeds the value of the charity care provided. "[T]he community often gets a bum bargain. Many nonprofit hospitals appear to be cruising by on an unjustifiable public subsidy and can hardly be distinguished from proprietary hospitals." R. Pear, Tax Exemption Questioned for the Non-Profit Hospitals, N.Y. Times, July 15, 1987, at A-21. Mr. Stark argues that nonprofit hospitals should be required to demonstrate the benefits they provide to the community through charitable care and suggests that tax deductions for such care might be more appropriate than a blanket tax exemption. Id.

In a letter to the New York Times, J. David Seay, Vice President of the New York United Hospital Fund, responded to Representative Stark's comments:

> [T]o be around to give community service, whether it is charity care, medical education and training, . . . biomedical research or any of the other forms voluntary community service can take, the hospital or institution must be able to stay afloat. . . . [Non-profit hospitals'] very presence, or being there — in good "markets" and bad — is itself a service to a community that is difficult to measure in monetary terms. Removing the tax exemption of the voluntary, not-for-profit hospitals and healthcare institutions would be tantamount to turning them into for-profit companies, and that would be a big public mistake. Our nation has consistently rejected government as the sole guarantor of health care services, relying instead upon a pluralistic approach, involving government, the private charitable section and, to a lesser extent, for-profit businesses. [N.Y. Times, July 29, 1987, at A-22.]

2. STATE TAX LAW AND POLICY

This debate divided the Utah Supreme Court in Utah County v. Intermountain Health Care, Inc., 709 P.2d 265 (1985). The court denied tax exempt status to two nonprofit hospitals that made "every effort . . . to recover payment for services rendered" and devoted less than one percent of their gross revenues to providing charity care. The majority rejected the hospitals' argument that they were charitable because they provided a service that government would otherwise have to organize. The evidence showed that the local counties paid the hospitals significant amounts for services provided to the indigent and that the hospitals sometimes turned people away from their emergency rooms if the county would not authorize payment for their care.

The dissenting judges criticized the majority's concept of charity as inappropriately narrow. The "alternatives are not for-profit or nonprofit hospitals, [but] . . . nonprofit hospital care or no hospital care at all. . . ." Id. at 289. Because profit making institutions must be concerned with making money, "for-profit hospitals in Utah have invested to a limited extent in high volume, low cost services such as pediatric, psychiatric, and obstetrical-gynecological services, but not in high cost, lower volume kinds of services" that are provided by the nonprofit hospitals. Id. at 290.

Utah voters rejected a referendum to exempt all hospitals from tax payment. Tax Issues Could Plague Not-for-Profits, 62 Hosps. 24 (1988). Intermountain opened a clinic to treat homeless men and women, began providing health services at soup kitchens, and expanded health services on Indian reservations. Tolchin, Hospitals Use Charity to Fend off Tax Collectors, N.Y. Times, May 3, 1988, at C-3, col. 1.

In the late 1980s, tax commissioners and courts in other states, including Illinois and Pennsylvania, have insisted that nonprofit hospitals either pay taxes or provide charity care. See Fairview Haven v. Department of Revenue, 153 Ill. App. 3d 763, 506 N.E.2d 341 (1987); Highland Park Hospital v. Illinois Department of Revenue, 155 Ill. App. 3d 272, 506 N.E.2d 1331 (Ill. App. Ct. 1987); Lutheran Home at Topton v. Board of Assessment, 100 Pa. Commw. 244, 515 A.2d 59 (Pa. Commw. Ct. 1986). See generally Perkins & Dowell, Tax Exemptions for Health Care Facilities: Charity Care Enters the Picture, 22 Clearinghouse Rev. 247 (1988).

E. The Hill-Burton Act

American Hospital Association v. Schweiker

721 F.2d 170 (7th Cir. 1983), cert. denied, *466 U.S. 958 (1984)*

This case involves a challenge to certain regulations issued on May 18, 1979, by the Secretary of Health, Education and Welfare (now Health and Human Services) (the "Secretary") pursuant to Title VI (the "Hill-Burton Act") and Title XVI of the Public Health Service Act, 42 U.S.C. §§291, 300o et seq. (1976). The regulations, published at 42 C.F.R. §124, Subparts F and G, impose specified obligations for community service and uncompensated care upon hospitals which received funds under the Hill-Burton Act. The American Hospital Association ("AHA"), on behalf of those hospitals, sued to have the 1979 regulations declared invalid, arguing that they violated statutory, contractual and constitutional rights. The district court granted summary judgment in favor of the Secretary. We affirm. . . .

In 1946, in response to President Truman's call to enact legislation which would ensure adequate health care for all Americans . . . , Congress passed the Hospital Survey and Construction Act, . . . presently codified as Title VI of the Public Health Service Act, 42 U.S.C. §291. Title VI, commonly known as the Hill-Burton Act, was intended to address post-Depression and post-war problems with respect to the adequacy and distribution of health service facilities by means of a program of grants-in-aid to the states. . . . The stated purpose of the Hill-Burton Act, in addition to the development and improvement of physical facilities and the promotion of research, was:

> to assist the several States in the carrying out of their programs for the construction and modernization of such public or other nonprofit community hospitals and other medical facilities as may be necessary, in conjunction with existing facilities, to furnish adequate hospital, clinic, or similar services to all their people. . . . 42 U.S.C. §291.

States wishing to obtain the federal financial assistance — outright grants, loans and loan guaranties — were required to submit to the Surgeon General for his approval a state plan for carrying out the congressional purpose. 42 U.S.C. §291d.

Most importantly to the issues involved in this litigation, the Hill-Burton Act provided that:

> The Surgeon General . . . shall by general regulations prescribe —
>
> (e) that the State plan shall provide for adequate hospitals, and other facilities for which aid under this part is available, for all persons residing in the State, and adequate hospitals (and such other facilities) to furnish needed services for persons unable to pay therefor. Such regulations may also require that before approval of an application . . . assurance shall be received by the State from the applicant that
>
> (1) the facility or portion thereof to be constructed or modernized will be made available to all persons residing in the territorial area of the applicant; and
>
> (2) there will be made available . . . a reasonable volume of services to persons unable to pay therefor, but an exception shall be made if such a requirement is not feasible from a financial viewpoint. 42 U.S.C. §291c(e).

. . . These two assurances have become known, respectively, as the "community service assurance" and the "reasonable volume" or "uncompensated care assurance."

The regulations issued from 1947 to 1972 in implementation of this statutory provision essentially tracked the language of the statute . . . and, although over $4.4 billion in grants and $2 billion in loans and loan guaranties were authorized between 1947 and 1974, . . . the hospitals receiving aid displayed a marked reluctance to give even the most token charitable care. See Comment, Provision of Free Medical Services by Hill-Burton Hospitals, 8 Harv. C.R.-C.L.L. Rev. 351, 352 (1973). After — and apparently in response to — a series of lawsuits . . . against federally assisted hospitals to enforce compliance with the Hill-Burton obligations, . . . the Secretary began in 1972 to issue regulations which defined standards for compliance with the assurances. . . .

In 1975 a new federal assistance program for hospital construction and modernization was established to replace Title VI. This later program, Title XVI of the Public Health Service Act, . . . provides for assurances similar to those in Title VI but adds teeth to the Title VI requirements as well. . . . Apparently in recognition of the compliance problems which had arisen under the Hill-Burton program, Title XVI mandates, rather than permits, the Secretary to prescribe by regulation the manner in which all recipients of financial assistance under either Title VI or Title XVI "shall be required to comply with the assurances required to be made at the time such assistance was received and the means by which such entity shall be required to demonstrate compliance with such assurances." . . .

The regulations which have given rise to the instant litigation were issued by the Secretary in response to this mandate. . . . Briefly, the 1979 regulations apply to all health facilities which gave assurances under either Title VI or Title XVI. The [free and below cost care] obligations . . . are made to continue for twenty years after the completion of construction or until the amount of the grant or loan is repaid, . . . although they have no retroactive application to the period prior to the effective date of the regulations. . . . [Community service obligations are not limited to any period of time.] In carrying out the uncompensated care assurance, Subpart F of the regulations sets a quantitative annual standard of compliance by requiring uncompensated care equal to the lesser of either 3 percent of the facility's operating cost for the last fiscal year or 10 percent of all federal assistance received by the facility, adjusted to make allowance for inflation for each year after 1979 (in effect prescribing the meeting of the obligation in the equivalent of 1979 dollars). . . . If in any year a facility is financially unable to meet this standard, the deficit may be made up in the following year, or in years subsequent to that, and, if necessary, at the end of the twenty-year period of obligation. Excesses will similarly be applied as credits against subsequent years' obligations. . . . The regulations also specify that amounts received as reimbursement from insurance programs or under Medicare or Medicaid may not be counted in computing the amount of uncompensated services rendered.

With respect to the community service assurances, Subpart G of the regulations requires that the federally assisted health facilities be made available to all residents and prohibits the exclusion of anyone in the area served by the hospital on the basis of any factor unrelated to need. The facility may, however, deny services to individuals unable to pay for them if the facility is not required to accept these patients under the uncompensated care requirements. . . . The regulations also specifically address certain denials of medical services which are impermissible. These denials include refusals to participate in the Medicare and Medicaid programs or discrimination against individuals who are recipients of aid under those programs. . . . The regulations also prohibit adherence to certain admissions policies which would have the effect of excluding individuals on impermissible grounds. . . . As an example of such prohibited practices, the regulations cite a policy of accepting only patients with private physicians who have staff privileges at the hospital. The rules require that the facility make alternative arrangements to ensure that its services are available to patients of this kind, and the regulations contain illustrative examples of such arrangements — the extension of temporary privileges to the person's physician; the referral of patients to a doctor with staff privileges; the establishment of a clinic through which such patients may be treated and, if necessary, admitted; the entering into contracts with qualified physicians and other arrangements. . . . Similarly, if most physicians on the staff of a Hill-Burton hospital refuse to accept Medicare and Medicaid patients, so that beneficiaries of such aid are effectively excluded from admission, the hospital must establish alternative arrangements to make facilities available to such persons. . . . The requirement of a pre-admission deposit which acts to exclude otherwise eligible individuals is also prohibited. . . . The regulations also contain provisions regarding notice to patients of the facilities' obligations, reporting and record-keeping requirements and mechanisms for investigation and enforcement. . . .

We must first inquire whether the Secretary, in promulgating the 1979 regulations, acted within the scope of his statutory authority. . . . If we conclude that he was so acting, the regulations cannot be set aside unless we find that they are "arbitrary, capricious, an abuse of discretion, or otherwise not in accordance with law." . . . This standard of review . . . affirms the agency decision if it has any rational basis. . . .

We think it is clear that the Secretary was acting within the scope of his statutory mandate. . . . Although the AHA contends that the Hill-Burton Act was merely a construction statute with a nondiscrimination clause attached, such a contention is difficult to reconcile with the specific statutory language requiring assurances that the facilities constructed be available to all residents and in particular to those unable to pay for medical services.

Moreover, the legislative history of the Hill-Burton Act . . . , indicates that it was intended to be more than a construction statute. Although the assurances were not in the original bill introduced by Senator Hill in 1945, . . . the records of the Senate hearings demonstrate that the provision of medical services to indigents was a recurrent theme. . . . A particularly revealing colloquy took place among Senator Ellender, Senator Pepper, Senator Taft and Dr. Frederick D. Mott, an official of the Department of Agriculture, on March 12, 1945:

> *Senator Taft.* . . . You would say a hospital accepting aid of this kind should have an obligation to take care of a certain number of indigent patients. Most of them do, but I mean if they are going to have Federal money, should there not be a definite obligation to handle a certain number of indigent patients?
>
> *Dr. Mott.* Senator, I would think there would certainly be an obligation to meet the needs of all the people of that hospital service area for which the hospital was designed, which would, of course, include many indigent and medically indigent.
>
> *Senator Pepper.* This is what occurred to me, Senator, . . . that in determining the burden which the hospital would be expected to carry, they might not be able to get Federal aid unless they agreed to take a fixed number of indigent patients.
>
> *Senator Taft.* That is what I mean. I imagine every hospital of a general nature would be lucky if they did not have 20 percent of indigent patients. . . .
>
> *Senator Ellender.* If people in all localities were able to pay for hospitalization there would be no need for this bill. It seems to me that our primary purpose should be to devise means to take care of those who cannot take care of themselves. My reason for supporting a bill providing for Federal aid to build hospitals is to make it easy for the community in which a hospital may be built to give aid to the indigent. . . .
>
> *Senator Taft.* My interest in it is like in a public works bill, just to provide construction. But beyond that, these facilities must be available to the people. 1945 Hearings at 190-191.

This discussion indicates that provision of medical services for the indigent was a major concern among supporters of the bill; it also points out the contemporary assumption that hospitals would voluntarily provide charitable services at low or no cost to the poor. . . .

The provision adding the community service and uncompensated care obligations to the Hill-Burton Act first appeared in late 1945 in the report of a subcommittee of the Senate Committee on Education and Labor. . . . In any event, one may infer from the provisions' mere presence in the statute that the free care obligation was intended to have some effect. Moreover, the very fact that the Act authorized an exception to the obligation to provide uncompensated care, if a facility was financially unable to furnish it, indicates that the Act contemplated that the hospital would be required to devote some of its own resources to fulfilling the assurances. See Rosenblatt, Health Care Reform and Administrative Law: A Structural Approach, 88 Yale L. Rev. 243 (1978). . . .

The premise, assumed in 1945, that hospitals would voluntarily provide services to all residents, including the indigent, out of their history of charitable service, proved to be unjustified; their apparent failure resulted in litigation to enforce the federally assisted hospitals' community service and uncompensated care obligations in the early 1970s. See, for instance, Corum v. Beth Israel Medical Center, 359 F. Supp. 909 (S.D.N.Y.1973); Euresti v.

Stenner, 458 F.2d 1115 (10th Cir. 1972); Cook v. Ochsner Foundation Hospital, 319 F. Supp. 603 (E.D. La.1970). The regulations which were issued in 1972 and 1974 were to some extent a response to this litigation. For the first time, they set specific standards for compliance with the hospitals' obligations — standards which are in many respects similar to the ones embodied in the 1979 regulations at issue here. . . .

Congress passed Title XVI in 1975, after the passage of the more stringent regulations under Title VI. . . . The Senate report indicates that the inclusion of these stronger provisions, and the extension of their application to facilities which had received funds under Title VI as well, was the result of a conviction that the Secretary, state agencies and health care facilities had all been deplorably lax in complying with the community service and uncompensated care obligations:

> . . . the GAO report states that "the implementation of the free service requirement is in its infancy at the State agency and local facility level." It states that "while the State plans reviewed contained provisions which essentially met the Federal requirements, none of the State agencies had an active program for monitoring compliance with the requirement. Most intend to rely on complaints to monitor compliance. Also, some facilities have not informed the State agencies how they intend to meet the reasonable volume of free services requirement." This seems to the Committee to be a sorry performance by the Department and the State Hill-Burton agencies in implementing a provision which has been in law for over 20 years, and which has recently been reemphasized. Senate Comm. on Labor and Public Welfare, S. Rep. No. 1285, 93d Cong., 2d Sess., reprinted in 1974 U.S. Code Cong. & Ad. News 7842, 7900. . . .

This . . . legislative history . . . provides abundant evidence that Congress . . . strongly intended that the words of the statutory assurances be given a practical reality. . . .

The AHA challenges the compliance levels set in 42 C.F.R. §124.503(a) on several accounts. . . . In determining the precise level which reflects that "reasonable volume," this court may not substitute its own idea of reasonableness for that of the agency unless the regulation is clearly inconsistent with the purposes of the [Act]. . . . We find no such inconsistency here.

Appellants' arguments to the contrary appear to be based upon a conception of the Hill-Burton program as a relationship between the hospital as a private debtor and the government as a commercial lender entitled merely to a market rate of return upon capital. Thus they complain about the addition of an inflation factor to the 10 percent of assistance level and the inclusion of other federal assistance in the base amount, or, alternatively, about the use of operating costs of the entire facility rather than of the assisted portion alone. But the 1946 program was not simply a commercial lending transaction; rather, it was a program, having broad public implications, under which Congress extended aid for the construction of hospitals and expected those hospitals in return to offer services to all the residents in their communities, including those who were indigent. When this expectation was not met, percentage compliance amounts were established. But those amounts, it is important to remember, do not constitute a loan repayment schedule; they are instead a rough means of monitoring compliance with the obligation to provide uncompensated care. [The Secretary contends that, "The financial burden of providing uncompensated services amounting to 10 percent of federal assistance received for twenty years is the same as the burden of repaying a loan over twenty years at 7.75 percent interest, without some of the major risks a loan would ordinarily entail for the borrower."] [T]he inflation factor is a rational means of preserving a real dollar amount as a reasonable measure of the volume of services which the facilities are expected to provide. . . .

As a related matter, the AHA challenges the regulation . . . which prohibits hospitals from crediting against their uncompensated care obligation the difference between the cost of care for a patient and the amount actually reimbursed under the Medicaid program, which may be less than actual cost. [T]he fact that reimbursement under the Medicaid program may fall short of cost is a problem that Hill-Burton hospitals share with all other hospitals participating in Medicaid. It is neither reasonable nor just that Hill-Burton hospitals should fare better in relation to this problem than do hospitals which have received no federal assistance under the program. . . .

The AHA argues that the various regulations affecting hospital admissions policies violate the statutory prohibition against federal control over the administration and operation of hospitals and the conduct of physicians. . . . The particular regulations under challenge in this respect are those which prohibit certain admissions policies having the effect of excluding persons on impermissible grounds: exclusion of patients who do not have a doctor with staff privileges, exclusion of Medicaid patients because few or none of the staff physicians treat Medicaid patients and the requirement of a pre-admission deposit. . . . If these policies should apply, the regulations require that an assisted facility make other arrangements so that individuals excluded by these policies may be treated; various alternatives are suggested, such as referrals to physicians on the staff. [T]he alternatives are offered only as suggestions; the only mandate is the prohibition of certain practices if their effect is exclusionary.

We find the argument that such a prohibition constitutes supervision or control over the administration of a hospital to be most implausible. . . . If exclusion is the result, the hospitals must make other arrangements, but no particular solution is imposed. . . . Since there is, moreover, abundant evidence in the record that the three prohibited practices did in fact prevent many otherwise eligible persons from receiving care at Hill-Burton facilities, we cannot set these provisions aside as arbitrary and capricious. . . .

We turn now to the contractual and constitutional challenges to the 1979 regulations. The AHA alleges that the regulations impermissibly impair the assisted hospitals' contractual rights by adding conditions to which the hospitals did not assent at the time they entered into their agreements with the government; this impairment of contract rights and retroactive alteration of the hospitals' obligations, according to the AHA, constitute a violation of the facilities' rights under the due process clause of the Fifth Amendment. . . .

[T]he relationship between the government and the hospitals here cannot be wholly captured by the term "contract." . . . Rather than a voluntary agreement negotiated between two parties, a grant-in-aid program like that under the Hill-Burton Act is an exercise by the federal government of its authority under the spending power to bring about certain public policy goals. The government acts by inducing a state or private party to cooperate with the federal policy by conditioning receipt of federal aid upon compliance by the recipient with federal statutory and administrative directives. . . . The "conditions" of this arrangement are not the result of a negotiated agreement between the parties but rather are provided by the statute under which the program is administered. Determination of statutory intent, therefore, is of more relevance to the interpretation of these conditions than is an inquiry into the intent of the two parties at the moment of the initial agreement. The contract analogy thus has only limited application. . . .

Even assuming for the moment the contractual nature of the obligations at issue here, . . . we conclude without difficulty that the 1979 regulations do not violate those principles. The "contracts" entered into here consisted not only of the forms signed by the applicants for aid (on which general statements of the assurances were printed) but also of the statutory obligation under 42 U.S.C. Sec. 291c(e). . . .

APPENDIX [to AMERICAN HOSPITAL ASSOCIATION V. SCHWEIKER]

Subpart G — Community Service

Sec. 124.603 Provision of services.

(a) General.

(1) In order to comply with its community service assurance, a facility shall make the services provided in the facility or portion thereof constructed, modernized, or converted with Federal assistance . . . available to all persons residing . . . in the facility's service area without discrimination on the ground of race, color, national origin, creed, or any other ground unrelated to an individual's need for the service or the availability of the needed service in the facility. Subject to paragraph (b) (concerning emergency services) a facility may deny services to persons who are unable to pay for them unless those persons are required to be provided uncompensated services under the provisions of Subpart F. . . .

[(b) Emergency Services.

(1) A facility may not deny emergency services to any person who resides (or, in the case of facilities assisted under Title XVI of the Act, is

employed) in the facility's service area on the ground that the person is unable to pay for those services.

(2) A facility may discharge a person that has received emergency services, or may transfer the person to another facility able to provide necessary services, when the appropriate medical personnel determine that discharge or transfer will not subject the person to a substantial risk of deterioration in medical condition.

(c) Third party payor programs.

(1) The facility shall make arrangements, if eligible to do so, for reimbursement for services with:

(i) Those principal State and local governmental third-party payors that provide reimbursement for services that is not less than the actual costs, as determined in accordance with accepted cost accounting principles; and

(ii) Federal governmental third-party programs, such as medicare and medicaid.

(2) The facility shall take any necessary steps to insure that admission to and services of the facility are available to beneficiaries of the governmental programs specified in paragraph (c)(1) of this section without discrimination or preference because they are beneficiaries of those programs.

(d) Exclusionary admissions policies. A facility is out of compliance with its community service assurance if it uses an admission policy that has the effect of excluding persons on a ground other than those permitted under paragraph (a) of this section. Illustrative applications of this requirement are described in the following paragraphs:

(1) A facility has a policy or practice of admitting only those patients who are referred by physicians with staff privileges at the facility. . . . The facility is not required to abolish its staff physician admissions policy as a usual method for admission. However, to be in compliance with its community service assurance it must make alternative arrangements to assist area residents who would otherwise be unable to gain admission to obtain services available in the facility. Examples of alternative arrangements a facility might use include:

(i) Authorizing the individual's physician, if licensed and otherwise qualified, to treat the patient at the facility even though the physician does not have staff privileges at the facility;

(ii) For those patients who have no physician, obtaining the voluntary agreement of physicians with staff privileges at the facility to accept referrals of such patients, perhaps on a rotating basis;

(iii) If an insufficient number of physicians with staff privileges agree to participate in a referral arrangement, requiring acceptance of referrals as a condition to obtaining or renewing staff privileges;

(iv) Establishing a hospital-based primary care clinic through which patients needing hospitalization may be admitted; or

(v) Hiring or contracting with qualified physicians to treat patients who do not have private physicians.

(2) A facility, as required, is a qualified provider under Title XIX medicaid program, but few or none of the physicians with staff privileges at the facility or in a particular department or sub-department of the facility will treat medicaid patients. If the effect is that some medicaid patients are excluded from the facility or from any service provided in the facility, the facility is not in compliance with its community service assurance. To be in compliance a facility does not have to require all of its staff physicians to accept medicaid. However, it must take steps to ensure that medicaid beneficiaries have full access to all of its available services. . . .

(3) A facility requires advance deposits (pre-admission or pre-service deposits) before admitting or serving patients. If the effect of this practice is that some persons are denied admission or service or face substantial delays in gaining admission or service solely because they do not have the necessary cash on hand, this would constitute a violation of the community service assurance. While the facility is not required to forego the use of a deposit policy in all situations, it is required to make alternative arrangements to ensure that persons who probably can pay for the services are not denied them simply because they do not have the available cash at the time services are requested. For example, many employed persons and persons with other collateral do not have savings, but can pay hospital bills on an installment basis, or can pay a small deposit. Such persons may not be excluded from admission or denied services because of their inability to pay a deposit.

Clair v. Centre Community Hospital

317 Pa. Super. 25, 463 A.2d 1065 (1983)

. . . At the direct insistence of the . . . [state Commissioner of Health], appellee-hospital adopted certain by-laws. They required, in their application, that appellant accept as a patient every third indigent obstetrical or gynecological patient at the hospital. (At the time there were two other such specialists at the hospital.) The Commissioners were concerned that the hospital conform with the State's community service regulations, which were, in turn, established to ensure conformity with Federal Hill-Burton regulations. . . .

[Appellant refused to comply.]

Appellant's staff privileges were then suspended, pending an indication of his willingness, in writing, to comply with the bylaw. . . . Appellant's case is based on an alleged violation of his right to due process of law as guaranteed by the Fourteenth Amendment to the Federal Constitution.

[The court found that the state involvement in the hospital's decision making process was sufficient that the denial of staff privileges could be characterized as state action, subject to constitutional constraints. The court further found that denial of hospital staff privileges is an important liberty interest protected by the due process guarantee of the 14th Amendment.]

. . . Not all governmental actions restricting protected liberty interests are impermissible. . . . [Dr. Clair's] claim is that the actions taken against him contravene substantive due process. . . . It is not an easy task to have an action held invalid in substantive due process terms. Nor should it be. State actions are "endowed with a presumption of legislative validity," and the burden is on respondent to show that there is no rational connection between the Board's action and its conceded interest.

. . . The regulations imposed must be reasonably related to the public health and welfare and must not amount to an arbitrary or unreasonable interference with the right to practice one's profession. . . . The governmental interest served by the hospital bylaw was the provision of medical care to indigent individuals. This is a clearly permissible governmental goal and the action has a rational relationship to its accomplishment.

We do not minimize the serious nature of the interference with appellant's right to practice his profession that resulted from the termination of his staff privileges. Nor do we think it inconsequential that he was required, as a condition of remaining a staff member, to treat every third indigent obstetrical or gynecological patient who comes to the hospital. . . . Even in the face of these factors, we are unable to say that the requirement is arbitrary or unreasonable. . . . The requirement that appellant accept indigent patients is onerous yet reasonable. It is both severe and not arbitrary. In short, it does not work a violation of substantive due process.

1. THE COMPLEX INTERRELATIONSHIPS OF HOSPITALS, NEEDY PEOPLE, LAWYERS, COURTS, CONGRESS, AND ADMINISTRATIVE AGENCIES

AHA v. Schweiker, supra, notes that even though the Hill-Burton free care and community service requirements existed since 1946, it was not until the 1970s that anyone attempted to enforce them. The creation of the legal services program, in the late 1960s, provided lawyers for indigent people, who filed the law suits that in turn provided the impetus for enforcing Hill-Burton requirements.

The early suits received mixed reception in the federal courts. Cook v. Ochsner Foundation Hospital, 319 F. Supp. 603 (E.D. La. 1970), was the first case to recognize that potential beneficiaries of the Hill-Burton Act could enforce its requirements. When *Cook* was filed, poor people in New Orleans had a difficult time obtaining hospital care, whether or not they were eligible for Medicaid or Medicare. All but one of the private Hill-Burton hospitals in New Orleans served white people; one private hospital served black people. Charity, the public hospital, was integrated, but like most public hospitals was underfunded and overcrowded. Most of the private hospitals in New Orleans did not accept patients insured by Medicaid and had no emergency rooms or clinics. Patients were accepted solely on referral from physicians with admitting privileges and paid substantial cash deposits prior to admission. One of the named plaintiffs died when he was denied admission to a private hospital, because he could not pay the cash deposit, and denied admission to Charity, because they had no room for him.

The initial *Cook* decision simply denied defendants' motion to dismiss. Plaintiffs had stated a justiciable cause of action and had standing to enforce the requirements of the Act. Judge Comiskey recognized that the Act "contains no section expressly authorizing a private individual [such as the plaintiffs] to judicially enforce its provisions." Id. at 606. He opined, however, that the free care requirement must mean something. He decided that since the Act "makes it plain that persons unable to pay for medical services are one of the chief sets of beneficiaries of this legislation," the court "must conclude that a private civil action may be implied under the Act. Id. at 606.

In another early case, Judge Gessel in Perry v. The Greater Southeast Community Hospital Foundation, Civ. No. 729-71 (D.D.C. 1972), reacted differently to efforts to enforce the community service requirements of the Act. Plaintiffs were black, low income residents of the District of Columbia who complained that the hospital limited its services by requiring referrals from staff physicians, who in turn served a population that was primarily white and suburban. The court dismissed the plaintiffs' claims, characterizing the federal statutory free care requirement as "purely a statement out of the blue. The Court cannot determine what a reasonable volume of free care is, any more than the learned and qualified counsel that is considering the matter can agree even among themselves." Id.

Judge Comiskey had no more guidance as to the meaning of this vague federal mandate than Judge Gessel, but he was willing to interpret the statute in light of its broader substantive purposes. Many factors cause judges to treat similar legal claims in such different ways: the judge's personality, political beliefs, and conceptions of the functions of courts; the style and skill of all the attorneys; the factual situation of the named plaintiffs and of the hospital practices; the scope of relief sought by the plaintiffs.

As events developed, the courts were not left wholly at sea to determine the meaning of the Act. The federal agency and eventually the Congress, responded to the judicial recognition of plaintiffs' claims with increasingly specific regulations.

The hospitals' argument, rejected in AHA v. Schweiker, was that the 25 year history of nonenforcement accurately reflected the Congressional intent that these requirements are merely symbolic and precatory. James Blumstein argues that the free care and community service requirements were "a sop to access egalitarians" that were easy for Congress to enact, precisely because

Congress provided no effective mechanism by which they could be enforced. J. Blumstein, Court Action: Agency Reaction: The Hill-Burton Act as a Case Study, 69 Iowa L. Rev. 1227, 1235 (1984).

One of the authors of this volume, Rand Rosenblatt, offers a different perspective:

> Congress can, and occasionally does, explicitly delegate public regulatory power to private interest . . . more typically, however, private control is maintained by a pattern of "symbolic" public regulation. Under this pattern, social control is apparently created by general statutory and regulatory provisions, but is simultaneously undermined by a lack of enforcement. Federal health care statutes promote government passivity of this sort through two common devices: the statement of substantive goals and powers in general terms, which leaves their implementation to relatively unstructured agency discretion; and the absence of clearly articulated and accessible remedies for consumer beneficiaries. Federal and state agencies continue the process of nonenforcement by failing to translate statutory goals into operational standards, failing to enforce whatever standards exist, and denying consumer beneficiaries access to agency decision making or avenues for complaint and relief. . . .
>
> [A]lthough providers need public funds to finance the rising cost of their services, including profit, they strongly oppose public regulation of their traditional power over the price and other conditions of medical practice. The expansion of government financing and regulation of health care has thus taken place in a political context in which largely unorganized consumers seek relief from the rising costs and declining accessibility of care, while well organized providers seek public subsidies for a health care system that remains largely under private control.
>
> The government policies that emerge from this context are heavily influenced by the distribution of power between providers and consumers at different stages of the political process. Congress will generally act on behalf of consumers only when the issue of health care has achieved a high political visibility, creating at least a potential for consumer mobilization. Providers, however, retain considerable legislative influence even during periods of intense consumer pressure. The resulting legislation usually attempts to satisfy both constituencies by stating a general commitment to meet consumer needs while preserving a regulated and subsidized private health care system. The task of developing an operational program of financial inducement and regulatory control is then delegated with little legislative guidance to federal and state agencies, where the crucial policy and enforcement decisions have much less public visibility than the original legislation. At the administrative stage, organized provider interests are better able than unorganized consumers to extract tangible benefits and to shape the programs to their own ends. . . .
>
> The result is that consumer demands for substantive health care benefits become entwined with judicial decisions about the internal structure of government. [T]he implementation of substantive health care reform tends to become linked to what has been called the jurisprudence of remedies: the standards by which courts decide when "interests" embodied in statutes should be given the type of judicial protection traditionally associated with enforceable individual

"rights." [Rosenblatt, Health Care Reform and Administrative Law: A Structural Approach, 88 Yale L.J. 243, 247-251 (1978).]

2. ENFORCEMENT OF HILL-BURTON OBLIGATIONS

Since 1975 federal regulations have provided three enforcement mechanisms: 1) hospitals must adopt procedures designed to assure that eligible individuals are aware of hospitals' obligations to provide free and below cost care and that hospitals have an equitable plan for determining how that care is to be distributed; 2) the federal Office of Civil Rights monitors hospital compliance; and 3) aggrieved individuals may institute suit if complaints are not redressed in the administrative process.

a. THE ENFORCEMENT PROCESS WITHIN INDIVIDUAL HOSPITALS

Regulations require that hospitals post notices informing patients that the hospital provides free and below cost care and telling them how they may go about applying for such service. Individual written notice must also be provided to people seeking care. 42 C.F.R. Sec. 124.505(d)(1987). The hospital must develop and publicize a plan for the distribution of free and below cost care. In most cases the amount of care that the hospital is required to provide is far less than the amount needed to meet the essential medical needs of eligible people. Under the regulations, individuals are entitled to a fair process to inform them that they are, or more often are not, entitled to free or below cost care.

Rosenblatt argues that a useful function is served in requiring a fair process to allocate the relatively small amount of free and below cost care required of Hill-Burton hospitals.

> [A]rticulated standards and fair procedures [may] . . . more fairly allocate limited resources to those patients most in need. More importantly, by raising the visibility of the need for hospital care, due process techniques may contribute to political efforts to increase the amount of resources available. In this sense, structural due process functions as a mode of political participation by requiring the agency to expose itself and the community to the facts and values inherent in its decisions. This may in turn encourage the development of an adequately funded, substantive entitlement to hospital care. [Rosenblatt, supra at 284.]

Is this wishful thinking? What, in addition to a fair process hearing, is required to produce political efforts to change the nature and quality of health services available? Courts have divided on whether Hill-Burton creates individual rights entitled to constitutional protection. Contrast Newsom v. Vanderbilt, 653 F.2d 1100 (6th Cir. 1981), with Davis v. Ball Memorial Hospital Association, Inc., 640 F.2d 30 (7th Cir. 1980).

b. Federal Administrative Enforcement

The 1979 regulations require the Office of Civil Rights of the federal Department of Health and Human Services to monitor and enforce hospital compliance with the free care obligations. Hospitals must file regular reports. 42 C.F.R. §124.510 (1987). The federal agency must conduct periodic investigations to assure compliance and also investigate in response to individual complaints. 42 C.F.R. §124.511 (1987). If HHS finds that a hospital is not in compliance, the department may seek a voluntary agreement or ask the Attorney General to institute suit. From 1982 to 1986, federal administrative actions seeking compliance with Hill-Burton free care requirements declined by 300 percent. In 1986, only 38 administrative decisions were rendered on free and below cost care complaints, and all but four of them were decided in favor of the hospital. M. Dowell, Hill-Burton, New Developments, National Health Law Program (June 1987).

The 1975 statute also authorizes individual actions to enforce compliance with free care obligations. Individual complainants must first file a complaint with the Secretary. If the Secretary dismisses the complaint, or if the Attorney General has not pursued it within six months, the individual may seek relief in federal court. 42 C.F.R. §124.511 (1987). Gillis v. U.S. Department of Health and Human Services, 759 F.2d 565 (6th Cir. 1985), dismissed a complaint in which Detroit consumers alleged that the federal agency had systematically failed to enforce the regulations. The court found that the federal statute did not permit an action directly against the federal agency. See generally, Rosenblatt, Health Care Reform and Administrative Law: A Structural Approach, 88 Yale L.J. 243 (1978).

Some states have sought to enforce Hill-Burton requirements. One New York study found "a consistent pattern of non-compliance. In some cases, more than half of the amount of the claims could not be substantiated." Office of Attorney General Robert Abrams, Serving the Medically Indigent: A report on Hospitals' Compliance in New York State With the Federal Hill-Burton Act. 28 (1983). The report is sharply critical of the HHS enforcement. On other state enforcement efforts, see Extension of Health Planning Program; Hearings on H.R. 6084, H.R. 6173 and H.R. 4554, Before the Subcommittee on Health and the Environment, Committee on Energy and Commerce, 97th Cong., 2d Sess. 735-755 (1982); K. O'Neill, Site Visits at 21 Hill-Burton Facilities Reveal Extensive Noncompliance, 16 Clearinghouse Rev. 404 (1982).

For a discussion of the community service provisions see K. Wing, The Community Service Obligation of Hill-Burton Health Facilities, 23 B.C.L.

Rev. 577 (1982). Systemic federal enforcement of the community service regulations has been lax. See M. Dowell, Indigent Access to Hospital Emergency Room Services, 18 Clearinghouse Rev. 483 (1984); A. Freifeld, Putting Flesh on the Bones of the Hill-Burton Community Service Regulations, 19 Clearinghouse Rev. 14 (1985).

However, in response to individual complaints, the HHS Office of Civil Rights has taken some actions to enforce community service requirements. For instance, In re Madera Community Hospital (O.C.R. Region IX, 1981) disapproved a hospital policy that limited obstetrical services to patients who had a physician on the staff of the hospital. The hospital was required to make its services available to all women seeking them, including those who sought delivery services, but had not received prenatal care. Community groups have argued successfully that hospitals must assure that physicians in every major specialty are available to individuals eligible for Medicaid and Medicare.

c. The Hospital Collection Defense

Another enforcement mechanism may be invoked by an individual poor person who is not given an opportunity to quality for free or below cost care, is provided with service, and is then subjected to debt collection action. Prior to 1979, several courts rejected efforts by potential Hill-Burton beneficiaries to use the hospital's failure to meet its free care obligations as an affirmative defense to a bill collection action. These courts held that the individual patient could not show that "she is personally entitled to free or below cost medical services." Valley Credit Service, Inc. v. Mair, 35 Or. App. 637, 582 P.2d 47,49 (1978). See also Yale-New Haven Hospital v. Matthews, 32 Conn. Supp. 539, 343 A.2d 661 (Com. Pl. 1974), *cert. denied,* 423 U.S. 1024 (1975); Falmouth Hospital v. Lopes, 376 Mass. 580, 382 N.E.2d 1042 (Mass. 1979).

Since the 1979 regulations provided a uniform federal definition of financial eligibility for care, courts in at least one state have allowed patients in hospital bill collection actions to argue an affirmative defense that a Hill-Burton hospital has failed to comply with federal regulations. See Hospital Center at Orange v. Cook, 177 N.J. Super 289, 426 A.2d 526 (App. Div. 1981); Cooper Medical Center v. Boyd, 179 N.J. Super 53, 430 A.2d 261 (Super. Ct. Div. 1981).

3. FINANCING "FREE" SERVICES

How is a hospital supposed to finance the free and below cost care that it is required to provide to patients who are unable to pay? Blue Cross and Medicare pay, on a reasonable cost basis, for services provided to patients who are insured through these programs. Blue Cross reimbursement sometimes includes an allocation for "community service." See Chap. 3, infra. Until 1982, hospitals claimed Medicare reimbursement for the costs of providing the free care required by Hill-Burton. Federal courts divided on whether such costs could properly be charged to Medicare. See Comment, The Propriety of Reimbursement by Medicare for Hill-Burton Free Care, 130 U. Pa. L. Rev. 892 (1982). Section 106 of the Tax Equity and Fiscal Responsibility Act of 1982 (TEFRA) provides: "the intended beneficiaries of the Hill-Burton Act are indigent patients who have no Medicare or Medicaid coverage and no private health insurance coverage. Since the individuals are not covered by Medicare, the program will not recognize as reasonable the cost of a hospital in delivering services to such individuals."

PROBLEM

Assume that you are a legal services attorney in Marshall County, Mississippi. Further assume that the county hospital has not altered its policy since Campbell v. Mincey. Consider the possibility of litigation under the Hill-Burton Act by individual women who are pregnant or actually in labor. Think about whether there are ways of getting a government agency to take action, and if so, which agency, what kind of action, and with what prospects of success?

Alternatively, assume that you represent the hospital that would like to continue its current policy.

F. FEDERAL EMERGENCY CARE ACT OF 1986

Consolidated Social Security Amendments of 1986, Examination and Treatment for Emergency Medical Conditions and Women in Active Labor

42 U.S.C.A. §§1395 DD

(a) *Medical screening requirement.* In the case of a hospital that has a hospital emergency department, if any individual (whether or not eligible for benefits under [Medicare]) comes to the emergency department and a request is made on the individual's behalf for examination or treatment for a medical condition, the hospital must provide for an appropriate medical screening examination within the capability of the hospital's emergency department to determine whether or not an emergency medical condition (within the meaning of subsection (e)(1) of this section) exists or to determine if the individual is in active labor (within the meaning of subsection (e)(2) of this section).

(b)(1) *In general.* If any individual (whether or not eligible for benefits under this subchapter) comes to a hospital and the hospital determines that the individual has an emergency medical condition or is in active labor, the hospital must provide either —

(A) within the staff and facilities available at the hospital, for such further medical examination and such treatment as may be required to stabilize the medical condition or to provide for treatment of the labor, or,

(B) for transfer of the individual to another medical facility in accordance with subsection (c) of this section. . . .

(c) *Restricting transfers until patient stabilized* —

(c)(1) *Rule.* If a patient at a hospital has an emergency medical condition which has not been stabilized (within the meaning of subsection (e)(4)(B) of this section) or is in active labor, the hospital may not transfer the patient unless —

(A)(i) the patient (or a legally responsible person acting on the patient's behalf) requests that the transfer be effected, or

(A)(ii) a physician . . . , or other qualified medical personnel when a physician is not readily available in the emergency department, has signed a certification that, based upon the reasonable risks and benefits to the patient, and based upon the information available at the time, the medical benefits reasonably expected from the provision of appropriate medical treatment at another medical facility outweigh the increased risks to the individual's medical condition from effecting the transfer; and

(B) the transfer is an appropriate transfer (within the meaning of paragraph (2)) to that facility.

(c)(2) *Appropriate transfer.* An appropriate transfer to a medical facility is a transfer —

(A) in which the receiving facility —

(A)(i) has available space and qualified personnel for the treatment of the patient, and,

(A)(ii) has agreed to accept transfer of the patient and to provide appropriate medical treatment;

(B) in which the transferring hospital provides the receiving facility with appropriate medical records (or copies thereof) of the examination and treatment effected at the transferring hospital;

(C) in which the transfer is effected through qualified personnel and transportation equipment, as required including the use of necessary and medically appropriate life support measures during the transfer; and

(D) which meets such other requirements as the Secretary may find necessary in the interest of the health and safety of patients transferred.

(d) *Enforcement*

(d)(1) As requirement of Medicare provider agreement, if a hospital knowingly and willfully, or negligently, fails to meet the requirements of this section, such hospital is subject to —

(A) termination of its provider agreement under [Medicare], or

(B) at the option of the Secretary, suspension of such agreement for such period of time as the Secretary determines to be appropriate, upon reasonable notice to the hospital and to the public. . . .

(d)(2) Civil monetary penalties. In addition to the other grounds for imposition of a civil money penalty under . . . this title, a participating hospital that knowingly violates a requirement of this section and the responsible physician in the hospital with respect to such a violation are each subject, under that section, to a civil money penalty of not more than $50,000 for each such violation. As used in the previous sentence, the term "responsible physician" means, with respect to a hospital's violation of a requirement of this section, a physician who —

(A) is employed by, or under contract with, the participating hospital, and

(B) acting as such an employee or under such a contract, has professional responsibility for the provision of examinations or treatments for the individual, or transfers of the individual, with respect to which the violation occurred.

(d)(3) *Civil enforcement.*

(A) Personal harm. Any individual who suffers personal harm as a direct result of a participating hospital's violation of a requirement of this section may, in a civil action against the participating hospital, obtain those damages available for personal injury under the law of the State in which the hospital is located, and such equitable relief as is appropriate.

(B) Financial loss to other medical facility. Any medical facility that suffers a financial loss as a direct result of a participating hospital's violation of a requirement of this section may, in a civil action against the participating hospital, obtain those damages available for financial loss, under the law of the State in which the hospital is located, and such equitable relief as is appropriate. . . .

(e) Definitions. In this section:

(e)(1) The term "*emergency medical condition*" means a medical condition manifesting itself by acute symptoms of sufficient severity (including severe pain) such that the absence of immediate medical attention could reasonably be expected to result in –

(A) placing the patient's health in serious jeopardy,

(B) serious impairment to bodily functions, or

(C) serious dysfunction of any bodily organ or part.

(e)(2) The term "*active labor*" means labor at a time at which —

(A) delivery is imminent,

(B) there is inadequate time to effect safe transfer to another hospital prior to delivery, or

(C) a transfer may pose a threat of the health and safety of the patient or the unborn child.

(e)(3) The term "*participating hospital*" means hospital that has entered into a provider agreement under §1395cc of this title.

(e)(4)(A) The term "*to stabilize*" means, with respect to an emergency medical condition, to provide such medical treatment of the condition as may be necessary to assure, within reasonable medical probability, that no material deterioration of the condition is likely to result from the transfer of the individual from a facility.

(B) The term "*stabilized*" means, with respect to an emergency medical condition, that no material deterioration of the condition is likely, within reasonable medical probability, to result from the transfer of the individual from a facility.

(e)(5) The term "*transfer*" means the movement (including the discharge) of a patient outside a hospital's facilities at the direction of any person employed by (or affiliated or associated, directly or indirectly, with) the hospital, but does not include such a movement of a patient who

(A) has been declared dead, or

(B) leaves the facility without the permission of any such person.

(f) *Preemption*. The provisions of this section do not preempt any State or local law requirement, except to the extent that the requirement directly conflicts with a requirement of this section.

House Committee on Government Operations, Equal Access to Health Care: Patient Dumping

H.R. Rep. No. 531, 100th Cong., 2nd Sess. (1988)

I. INTRODUCTION

Under the rules of the House of Representatives, the Committee on Government Operations has responsibility for studying, on a continuing basis, the operation of Government activities at all levels. The committee has assigned this responsibility, as it pertains to the Department of Health and Human Services [HHS], to the Subcommittee on Human Resources and Intergovernmental Relations.

Pursuant to its authority, the subcommittee conducted a review of HHS' role and responsibilities with regard to "patient dumping" — the transfer of patients from one hospital to another primarily for economic reasons.

HHS is responsible for the enforcement of several Federal laws that pertain to patient transfers. The Office for Civil Rights [OCR] has responsibility for a portion of the Hill-Burton Act, initially adopted in 1946 and later amended, which provides funding for the construction of hospitals and other health facilities.

Title VI of the Civil Rights Act of 1964 prohibits discrimination on the basis of race, color, or national origin in any facility that receives Federal funds. Section 504 of the Rehabilitation Act of 1973 forbids discrimination in federally funded facilities against persons based on their handicap. These laws are also enforced in HHS by OCR, and apply to all hospitals that are certified to participate in the Medicare Program — which includes virtually all hospitals.

In April 1986, Congress adopted the Consolidated Omnibus Budget Reconciliation Act of 1985 [COBRA]. An amendment to COBRA, that took effect on August 1, 1987, establishes criteria for the safe transfer between hospitals of critically ill or injured patients, and women in active labor.

The Health Care Financing Administration [HFCA] has primary responsibility for enforcing the COBRA antidumping law, and the Office of the Inspector General [OIG] is responsible for applying certain sanctions under the statute.

Patient dumping can take many forms. The most common is the transfer of a patient from one hospital emergency room to another for economic reasons, that is, lack of insurance and inability to pay. Dumping may occur from any part of a hospital, but the majority of these incidents take place from emergency rooms. It can mean turning patients away who may be actually ill, seriously injured, or in active labor, and it can be accomplished by transferring patients to other hospitals, refusing to treat them, or subjecting them to long delays before providing care. These transfers may involve discrimination on the basis of poverty, race, ethnicity, or appearance. Dumping can result from hospital policies and practices that include (1) requiring advance payment under certain circumstances, (2) refusing to accept Medicaid, (3) refusing patients who don't have a personal physician on staff, or (4) refusal to treat patients with "undesirable" conditions such as intoxication or overdose symptoms. . . .

B. *The Failure of the Department of Health and Human Services to Issue Regulations Implementing the 1986 Antidumping Amendment Has Left Thousands of Patients at Increased Risk of Illegal Transfers*

The COBRA antidumping amendment imposes on Medicare-participating hospitals new requirements for the treatment and transfer of patients seeking emergency care. The legislation, enacted on April 7, 1986, became effective on August 1, 1986. However, even proposed rules for the implementation and enforcement of this critical legislation still have not been published. Dr. William Roper, Administrator of HCFA, testified that the law is "self-implementing," meaning regulations are not needed to set the law in motion. However, the following example of a mishandled case suggests otherwise.

An internal HCFA document obtained by the subcommittee described a case which was investigated for a violation of the Federal law. A St. Louis hospital was found out of compliance but was "not terminated through procedural error." The dumping victim was a "pregnant girl" who arrived at the hospital on May 30, 1987, complaining of abdominal pain and vaginal bleeding. The transfer of the girl was agreed to by another hospital, but "prior to being transferred she began active labor and delivered a stillborn 5-month-old fetus." The hospital proceeded with the transfer "even though the umbilical cord was not cut and the placenta not delivered."

This hospital was never sanctioned for what appears to be a serious violation of the COBRA amendment. Had strong regulations been in place that were energetically enforced, this type of oversight would have been much less likely to occur.

Until as late as mid-December 1986, the Health Care Financing Administration had not communicated in writing with its regional offices regarding the antidumping law. On December 12, HCFA headquarters sent a memorandum to all associate regional administrators "directing them to require States to send all Medicare participating hospitals: (1) a copy of the statute, and (2) a letter describing their new obligation . . . and directing them to sign a revised provider agreement." Before this memo was sent, HHS had not informed hospitals of the existence of the new law and how it affected them. The subcommittee's investigation found that there had been no direction of any kind given to regional office staff or any other responsible parties as to how the law was to be implemented, or how to handle the complaints that had started to trickle into HHS.

On June 4, 1987, six months later, HCFA sent a second memo to the regional offices. . . .

These interim instructions . . . fail to provide any substantive guidelines either for the hospitals to follow, or the regional offices to enforce. For example:

1. While the Regional Administrator is directed to send the complainant a letter telling him whether or not the investigation is warranted, there is no standard for what constitutes a warranted investigation.

2. The Regional Administrator is told to direct the State agency to investigate the complaint if it is warranted. However, the interim instructions do not propose standards, criteria, or guidelines for making judgments as to whether a hospital has violated the law.

There is no requirement, for example, that the patient's condition when leaving the transferring hospital or his condition on arrival at the receiving hospital be established. The instructions do not suggest that the investigator interview staff at the hospital receiving the transferred patient or seek independent medical judgment about the patient's condition if it is at issue.

Until comprehensive regulations are issued, the HCFA regional offices, the State agencies, and the OIG regional offices will have no further guidance as they decide which complaints to investigate, undertake those warranting investigation, draw conclusions as to the validity of the allegations, and determine what sanctions should be applied. . . .

C. HCFA has Failed to Use its Enforcement Powers Under the COBRA Antidumping Statute and Failed to Notify Hospitals, Doctors, Patients, and the General Public of the Law's Prohibitions

No matter how strong the statute, it is useless without enforcement. Dr. William Roper, HCFA Administrator said at the hearing that the COBRA amendment was meant to serve as a deterrent; however, it can only serve as a deterrent if it is enforced. A law sitting quietly on the books will not serve as an obstacle to violations.

During the 18 months between the amendment's effective date of August 1, 1986, and January 31, 1988, only 129 allegations of COBRA violations were filed. When compared with the 250,000 patients transferred annually for economic reasons, suggested by Dr. David Ansell of Cook County Hospital, it appears that the public has little knowledge of the law and that it is not being enforced.

The following case is an example of HHS' reluctance to use its enforcement powers. On September 17, 1986, a young man, Terry Takewell, died at his home in Somerville, TN, after having been dumped in the parking lot at Methodist Hospital in Somerville. Mr. Takewell had been a diabetic for years and on the day before he died, neighbors found him at his home, suffering with acute ketoacidosis. Mrs. Zettie Mae Hill sent Mr. Takewell by ambulance to his doctor, who was familiar with his medical history. The doctor ordered Mr. Takewell to go immediately to the hospital for emergency treatment, so Mr. Takewell proceeded by ambulance to the hospital. According to eyewitnesses, the acting hospital administrator appeared at Mr. Takewell's bedside, picked him up under the arms, lifted him out of bed, and still supporting him, walked him out of the hospital to the parking lot where he left him without shirt or shoes. Mrs. Zettie Mae Hill testified at the subcommittee hearing that Mr. Takewell told her that he was refused care because he had no insurance and still owed the hospital for previous treatment. Mrs. Hill confirmed this in a call to the hospital. Mr. Takewell died at his home the next day.

The next month, a COBRA complaint against Methodist Hospital was filed with HHS by a community organization in Tennessee. Following an investigation by the Tennessee State Board of Licensure, the hospital was found in compliance with both State and Federal law. It was not even threatened with the mildest sanction HHS could apply.

During its investigation, the subcommittee learned that HHS often fails to respond to attempts to obtain relief for clients who have been dumped from hospital emergency rooms. Judith Waxman of the National Health Law Project testified:

> When we hear of dumping problems, we advise lawyers to send complaints to HHS, citing the COBRA statute and the other statutes that have been mentioned today that are within the agency's jurisdiction. Frankly, lawyers are hesitant to use this process because they have one of two experiences; either they never hear a response at all from the agency, or the response is so delayed that their clients are totally discouraged by the wait and the meagerness of the ultimate results. . . .

HCFA refers all cases in which violations are found to OIG for review. But OIG very rarely uses the authority it has to sanction hospitals for serious violations of the COBRA amendment. OIG has the authority to impose a civil monetary penalty of up to $50,000 per violation on a hospital or physician whose actions do not conform to the COBRA amendment. Through January 31, 1988, civil monetary penalties have been levied against only two hospitals for violations of the antidumping law. For the most severe cases of patient dumping, OIG can suspend a hospital from the Medicare Program. But according to OIG staff, it has never suspended a hospital.

The small number of complaints — 129 cases as of January 31, 1988 — filed under COBRA by patients or their representatives who have experienced unlawful transfers is in large part a result of the lack of knowledge of the law among the general public, and especially among persons entering hospital emergency rooms. The clusters of dumping complaints filed in Texas and California as compared with just a few in the rest of the United States most likely result from publicity centered on antidumping measures being considered by the two State legislatures. In order for a complaint to be filed, the groups to whom this amendment applies must at least know of it so that, in the case of a hospital or physician, it can be obeyed; or, in the case of a patient, they can claim their rights under it. The Federal Government must enforce it.

The following exchange between Chairman Weiss and the doctors at the hearing suggest serious problems regarding the effectiveness of the COBRA amendment:

> *Mr. Weiss.* . . . Has the new Federal law, that is the COBRA legislation, had any impact on your hospitals?
>
> *Dr. Ansell.* None.

Dr. Kellermann. I have seen no perceptible impact whatsoever.

Mr. Weiss. Would you be able to tell us why you think it has had no impact?

Dr. Ansell. I don't think anybody knows about it. . . . We have actually called HCFA to see what the rules and regulations are, and have not been able to get them.

D. *The COBRA Antidumping Amendment is not an Effective Weapon Against Patient Dumping and Should Be Strengthened*

The committee believes that there are several modifications in the COBRA amendment which would make it easier to implement and a more effective weapon against inappropriate patient transfers.

Some of the recommendations would require statutory changes; others could be accomplished through regulation or through actions by the hospitals themselves.

1. *Stabilizing the Patient Prior to Transfer*

The statute requires that emergency room patients who are deemed to have an emergency medical condition or to be in active labor be given such treatment as may be required "to stabilize" their medical condition before being transferred. Several witnesses testified at the hearing that there are often difficulties associated with determining the stability of emergency patients. As Dr. Arnold Relman, noted New England Journal editor writes, "'Stabilization' of emergency cases is a notion used by hospital managers to justify transfers for economic reasons, but it is an elusive and dangerous concept."

Similarly, there is no legal definition of a stable condition that can be uniformly applied to all patients. Judith Waxman, National Health Law Program attorney, stated at the hearing that "one doctor's stabilized is another doctor's dump." Stabilization of an emergency patient can require surgery, or days in the intensive care unit. Additionally, apparent stability in an emergency patient can erode during the trip from one hospital to another.

The committee strongly supports the contention that treatment delays resulting from transfers can be justified only in cases in which the transfer is made in order to provide treatment that is not available at the transferring hospital or made at the patient's request. Thus, the committee believes the transfers of patients solely because they are not privately insured or cannot otherwise cover the cost of treatment should not be tolerated.

2. *Memorandum of Transfer*

The committee believes that in order to protect patients from illegal transfers, all hospitals should be required to maintain a record of each transfer including all available information on each patient transferred, evidence of communication between the transferring and receiving hospitals, the reasons for transfer, the patient's condition at the time of transfer, and the risks and benefits of such transfer. This document should be kept on file in the transferring hospital and a copy sent with the patient to the receiving hospital. . . .

3. *Informed Consent and Patient Notification*

There is no requirement for informed consent in the COBRA antidumping amendment. Both Dr. David Ansell, the coauthor of a study of emergency room transfers, and Dr. Arthur Kellermann, an emergency room doctor, testified that the transfer of a patient from one hospital to another is a potentially harmful procedure. It is established practice that patients provide informed consent before any procedure that may be risky to the patient. However, without a requirement for informed consent in the law, most transfer cases will proceed without it. Dr. Ansell found in his study at Cook County Hospital that only 6 percent of the patients in the study had signed consent for transfer. . . .

There is no requirement for providing notification to the patient of his or her rights under the COBRA amendment. Patients and their families and friends are usually unaware of the law. This is evidenced by the fact that they do not refuse inappropriate transfers, nor do they often complain to authorities when their rights have been violated. Dr. Kellermann suggested at the hearing that any consent document include reference to the Federal law so the patient will be informed of his or her right to refuse transfer for nonmedical reasons. . . .

4. *Reverse Dumping*

The subcommittee learned of numerous instances in which it is necessary to transfer a patient from one hospital emergency room to another because the patient's condition requires a level of care which that hospital is unequipped to provide or because there is no physician available there who can adequately treat the patient. But often when the second hospital refuses to accept the transfer and treat the patient, this is referred to as "reverse dumping."

The subcommittee learned of one case, for example, that occurred in Texas which resulted in the unnecessary death of a young man. McAllen Medical Center, a large tertiary care hospital in McAllen, Texas, established a blanket policy that it would not accept uninsured or Medicaid transfers from the smaller hospitals in its area. A tragic result of this policy occurred when a small hospital in the area telephoned McAllen Medical Center and was refused the right to transfer a 17-year-old boy with a bullet lodged in his brain. The smaller hospital counseled the boy's family to take him to McAllen's emergency room on their own. Once he arrived, the COBRA amendment required them to treat him, but by then 8 hours had elapsed and he could not be saved.

The committee believes this sort of violation might be less likely if the COBRA language were strengthened. Tertiary hospitals must be required to accept patients from small, unequipped hospitals.

5. *Review of Hospital Transfer Records*

There are many hospitals of last resort — often the public hospitals — that regularly receive patients who are transferred because they cannot pay for treatment or have only Medicaid coverage — the so-called economic transfers. The COBRA amendment allows the administrator of a hospital that is dumped on to bring a private right of action against the sending hospital. However, numerous factors can prevent the receiving hospitals from reporting these violations to HCFA, much less from bringing a law suit. Public hospital administrators explained that good relationships must be maintained between hospitals within a given area for many reasons and thus hospital administrators and individual physicians are often reluctant to "squeal" on their fellow providers. . . .

Dr. Kellermann recommended that the hospital receiving transferred patients require reports of all dumping cases to be filed and that these files be audited periodically to detect illegal transfers which were not reported to Federal officials. He explained that this system would be more effective for detecting and regulating dumping than relying on complaints alone. Dr. Kellermann suggested that an organization such as the Joint Commission on Accreditation of Healthcare Organizations periodically review these files.

The committee agrees that hospitals receiving dumped patients might well be reluctant to file a complaint against the sending hospital, even if there were a requirement for such in the law. This is an enforcement responsibility and, therefore, the committee suggests that HCFA be required to develop a system for the periodic, random review of hospital transfer records and further be required to investigate all possible violations of the COBRA amendment.

6. *Attorney's Fees*

The COBRA antidumping language establishes a private right of action on behalf of any individual who suffers personal harm resulting from a hospital's violation of the statute. This threat of civil enforcement of the COBRA amendment should have a preventive effect. However, the subcommittee review found that private attorneys would most likely be reluctant to bring suit to enforce the statute, unless the patient has been severely harmed by the illegal transfer, because their expenses and fees might not be paid. But the preventive effect of the statute is diluted if only those cases which command a large damage award are brought.

The award of attorney's fees in successful private law suits to enforce the COBRA amendment would correct this problem. . . .

Notes and Questions: Proposed Emergency Care Regulations of 1988

On June 16, 1988, the Department of Health and Human Services published proposed regulations implementing COBRA's emergency care requirements. 53 Fed. Reg. 22513. The proposed regulations track the language of the statute.

They provide that "termination of a provider agreement would be the initial action contemplated against a hospital that knowingly and willfully, or negligently failed to meet the requirements . . ." of the Act. Id. at 22518. Why does HHS make termination of Medicare participation, rather than financial penalties, the remedy of choice?

While the statute authorizes the Secretary to specify "other requirements" that must be met before a transfer is appropriate, the Secretary declined to do so. 53 Fed. Reg. 22517. What other requirements might be helpful?

The statute requires hospitals with emergency rooms to provide an "appropriate medical screening" to determine whether an emergency exists. The proposed regulations "would allow hospitals maximum flexibility in their utilization of emergency care personnel by not including specific requirements concerning education or credentials for individuals conducting emergency medical examinations." Ibid.

The Act provides that an individual who suffers personal harm, or a medical facility that suffers a financial loss, as a result of a hospital's violation of the antidumping provisions may bring a civil action in federal court for money damages and equitable relief. The regulations state that the "federal district court will apply the law of the State in which the hospital is located." 53 Fed. Reg. 22520. What does that mean? Is it consistent with the federal statute?

The proposed regulations add a new provision, not addressed by the statute: "If a hospital receives a patient transferred in suspected violation [of the Act], it must report the incident promptly to the State survey agency and to HCFA. . . . HCFA may terminate the hospital for failure to report the incident." 42 C.F.R. §489.24(f). The receiving hospital must report each incident within 72 hours. Is this new requirement sensible? Is it authorized by the statute?

NOTE: HEALTH LAW BAR REACTS TO COBRA

Not surprisingly, informed legal reaction varies, depending upon whom the lawyer represents. One counsel to private hospitals in Dallas explains, "Most hospitals transfer patients in a professional manner. If an indigent shows up at a private facility, most of these hospitals will ignore economic concerns and treat the patient as best they can. [T]he new network of legislation imposes additional pressures on hospitals already financially strapped and adds just another potential for malpractice litigation." G. Taylor, Cracking Down on Patient Dumping, Natl. L.J., June 6, 1988, at 1. The legal affairs director of Dallas' public hospital, Parkland Memorial, retorts, "Dumping patients has been such a standard practice for so many hospitals that they don't even know they are doing something wrong." Id.

R. Dooley, of the large health law firm, Wood, Lucksinger and Epstein, characterizes COBRA as "a litigation time bomb waiting to explode. [W]hat

RICO has been in the last few years to business fraud, this statute may soon be to medical malpractice. . . . If a sending hospital should have known that the doctors [at the receiving hospital] were below par, it can be held liable for any mishaps." R. Dooley, New Federal Law Helps Medical Malpractice Plaintiffs, 6 Health Alert 330 (1987).

For a point of view more sensitive to patients, see K. Treiger, Preventing Patient Dumping: Sharpening The Cobra's Fangs, 61 N.Y.U.L. Rev. 401 (1987). Treiger makes several recommendations: HHS should employ the civil remedy of money penalties more often than the draconian revocation or suspension of a hospital's Medicare contract; regulations should clarify that patients do not need to suffer substantial physical harm in order to state a claim for illegal dumping; HHS should be required to provide written decisions in response to every complaint, stating the facts that justify the decision; and hospitals should be required to inform individuals of their rights under the antidumping act.

JUDICIAL ENFORCEMENT

Few reported cases have adjudicated the remedies available when the COBRA provisions are violated. Bryant v. Riddle Memorial Hospital, 689 F. Supp. 490 (E.D. Pa. 1988), rejected a hospital's claim that the federal statute created no federally justiciable cause of action for a patient discharged before her condition had stabilized. In Reid v. Indianapolis Osteopathic Medical Hospital Inc., 709 F. Supp. 853 (S.D. Ind. 1989), defendant transferred an auto accident victim to another hospital, where she died. Her husband alleged that she was moved before she was stable in violation of COBRA's antidumping provisions. The hospital moved to dismiss the federal action, arguing that COBRA's language limiting damages to those "available for personal injury under the law of the state in which the hospital was located," required that plaintiff first comply with Indiana's procedures for screening medical malpractice claims. The court rejected the claim that the federal statute had incorporated state procedural limitations on a federal cause of action in a federal court. The Indiana malpractice screening panel applies a negligence standard, "whereas the federal antidumping statute was based on a strict liability standard." 709 F. Supp. 856. However, the court upheld the hospital's claim that the federal act incorporates Indiana's cap on malpractice damages to limit plaintiff's potential recovery. Is this decision consistent with the language and spirit of the federal act?

PROBLEMS

Reconsider the problem presented at the end of the Hill-Burton section, p. 91 supra. In what ways does COBRA change parties' rights and obligations?

Does Michael Jessee Thompson have a winnable case against Sun City Hospital under COBRA? Could he secure administrative enforcement, and if so, how?

Does Edwina Haynes, p. 53 supra, have a winning case under COBRA against all of the hospitals that refused her care? Could she secure administrative review, and if so, how?

Now assume that you are a lawyer in a small private practice. You support yourself with contingency fees for personal injury actions and with direct client payments for routine matters such as drawing wills and real estate closings. Each of the patients in the preceding cases seeks your help. The clients emphasize that they wish to collect as much money as possible from the hospital that denied them care. What can you do? Do your responses to these questions change if, rather than focusing on the desire for cash recompense, the clients express concern that no one else should have to go through the difficulty they experienced?

You are a lawyer representing the hospitals to which each of these three patients was transferred; what are the legal remedies available to your client? As counsel to the hospitals that transferred these patients, defend a client who believes that its policies are sound and would like to continue to operate as it has in the past. Your client fears that dramatic changes could undermine the fiscal and medical strength of the institution. What do you advise?

G. Direct Public Provision of Medical Care

1. DO PUBLIC HOSPITALS SERVE THE POOR?

The hospital that refused care to Hattie Mae Campbell is a public hospital. Still, most public hospitals serve people unable to pay — particularly the large urban general hospitals. Nationally, public hospitals bear a disproportionate share of the burden of serving the uninsured, as well as those people who are eligible for Medicaid. Public hospitals also provide a relatively large share of the care to aliens and to people who are regarded as undesirable for social reasons — addicts, disruptive psychiatric patients, prisoners, people with AIDS, and the homeless. In addition, public hospitals provide a large amount of care for patients with conditions that are expensive and difficult to treat: badly burned patients, distressed newborns, high risk pregnant women, victims of life threatening trauma or crime. E. Freidman, Public Hospitals: Is "Relevance" in the Eye of the Beholder? Hospitals, May 1, 1980, at 82.

Public hospitals increase access to medical care for uninsured people. One study compared the volume of uncompensated care provided to the uninsured poor in cities with public hospitals with that provided in cities without a public hospital, and found that uninsured people are significantly more likely to receive hospital care if they live in a city with a public hospital. K. Thorpe & C. Brecher, Improved Access to Care for the Uninsured Poor in Large Cities: Do Public Hospitals Make a Difference? 12 J. Health Polit., Policy L. 313 (1987). This analysis suggests that local tax support for public hospitals does not merely offset other sources of uncompensated care but rather increases the amount of care provided.

2. PUBLIC HOSPITALS AS FAMILY DOCTOR

In 1975, public hospitals in the 100 largest cities provided 14.4 outpatient visits per inpatient admission, as compared to only 5.3 outpatient visits per admission in private hospitals in those cities. Report of the Commission on Public-General Hospitals, The Future of the Public-General Hospital: An Agenda for Transition, (Hosp. Research and Ed. Trust, 1978). This pattern is particularly pronounced in New York City. In 1979, public hospitals had less than one-fifth of the inpatient beds, but provided over half of all hospital-based ambulatory care. Between 1969 and 1978, the number of primary care practitioners in the city declined by 45 percent. Despite the large numbers of doctors in the city, in 1979 2.3 million people, nearly one-third of the city's population, lived in areas federally designated as medically under served. See A Decade of Change in New York City Hospital Services, (United Hospital Fund, 1981).

3. FISCAL PROBLEMS OF PUBLIC HOSPITALS

The fiscal crisis of the mid-1970s had a dramatic impact on municipal finances and health services. See Craig & Koleda, The Urban Fiscal Crisis in the United States, National Health Insurance, and Municipal Hospitals. 8 Int. J. of Health Services, 329 (1978); Brown, Public Hospitals on the Brink: Their Problems and Their Options, 7 J. of Health Politics, Policy and Law 927 (1983). In the 1980s, reductions in Medicaid and Medicare adversely affected the financial status of public hospitals which serve disproportionate numbers of people insured under these programs. Dallek, The Continuing Plight of Public Hospitals, 16 Clearinghouse Rev. 97 (1982); Feder, Hadley & Mullner, Poor People and Poor Hospitals: Implications for Public Policy, 9 J. Health Politics, Policy and Law 237 (1984). These issues are discussed more fully in Chap. 3, infra.

Since the mid-1970s, many public hospitals have used private management services in an effort to restrain costs. Most management contractors attempt to achieve savings by restricting services, and most contracts show few or no benefits for the substantial costs involved. Shonick & Roemer, Private Management of California County Hospital: Experience and Performance, 23 Publ. Affairs 1 (1982); Shonick, Expanding Contracting: Private Management of Public Hospitals in California, 13 Health/PAC. Bull. 7 (1982).

4. LOCAL OBLIGATIONS TO MAINTAIN PUBLIC HOSPITALS

Even though many localities are legally obligated to provide medical care for the needy, courts have not demanded that they maintain a public hospital. In the 1970s, poor people opposed to the closing of Philadelphia General Hospital argued that a 1766 state law required the city to maintain a hospital for the poor. The court recognized that 200 years of statutes "might be construed as imposing a duty upon the city to provide health care for the indigent, but we can see no basis . . . for the proposition that Philadelphia must maintain the [public hospital] as such." Preston v. City of Philadelphia, 26 Pa. Commw. 106, 362 A.2d 452 (1976). The city has "power to contract for the provision of those same services elsewhere." Ibid. The hospital was closed in 1978.

Since 1974, California has required that if a county proposes to close or sell a public hospital it must hold formal hearings, with opportunity for public participation, and determine that such reductions would not have a "detrimental impact" on the health of the indigent. One detailed analysis of the law concludes that it has "probably resulted in a lower rate of county hospital and health service closures than would have prevailed without the statutes. However, the laws have been inadequate to maintain existing levels of health services to the poor." Brown & Cousineau, Effectiveness of State Mandates to Maintain Local Government Health Services for the Poor, 9 J. Health Politics, Policy and Law 223, 233 (1984).

H. The AIDS Crisis and Access to Medical Care

Legal rules are not necessarily the most important variable influencing access to medical care. The ability to obtain care depends upon where people live, their financial circumstances, and their medical needs. This note examines the situation of people who seek treatment for AIDS. For discussion of people with other medical needs, see Chapter 2, §C on routine screening and treatment for low income children, Chapter 9 on organ transplants, and Chapter 10 on prenatal care and reproductive health services. For an excellent collection of articles dealing with legal issues in relation to AIDS, see Symposium, AIDS, Public Policy and the Law, 7 St. Louis Univ. L. Rev. 1 (1988).

1. WHAT IS AIDS?

Acquired Immune Deficiency Syndrome, or AIDS, was first reported in the United States in 1981. By 1988, 52,000 cases had been reported, and half of those people had died. By the end of 1991, 270,000 cases of AIDS are expected. The Centers for Disease Control estimates that in 1988 between 945,000 and 1.4 million people in the United States are infected with the HIV virus.

AIDS is incurable and fatal. It involves a breakdown of the body's immune system that disables its victims from fighting infectious diseases. The virus that causes it, HIV, attaches to white blood cells. A person may be infected with HIV for months before developing antibodies to the virus and thus testing positive. It often takes seven years or more after infection with the virus before symptoms of the disease develop.

The HIV virus is not easily transmitted. It can be spread by sexual intercourse; needle sharing for intravenous injection; transfusion of infected blood; transplantation of infected organs; and transmission to a fetus from an infected mother. In 1987, three cases of HIV transmission were reported from infected blood that had splashed into unprotected skin lesions or mucous membranes of hospital workers. Casual contact — even sharing a household, towels, or even a toothbrush with an infected person — does not spread the disease. Kissing does not spread AIDS.

Although much has been learned about HIV transmission, much remains unknown. Two tests are used to identify the presence of antibodies to the HIV virus. Testing contains the spread of AIDS, particularly through blood, organ, and semen donation. However, even when both tests are used, false positives are reported. False negatives may occur when people are tested during the period between infection and development of antibodies.

Cases of AIDS and HIV infection have been disproportionately concentrated in gay men and intravenous drug users; 20 to 25 percent of the homosexual men, or 500,000 to 625,000 people have been infected; 25 percent of regular intravenous drug users, or 225,000 people. Together these groups comprise 90 percent of the persons with AIDS in the United States. AIDS has afflicted disproportionately more blacks and Hispanics than whites, and disproportionately more men than women. Seventy percent of hemophilia A patients, or 8700 people, are infected.

The federal Centers for Disease Control (CDC) have played a central role in gathering and disseminating information about AIDS. When the HIV virus was identified in 1984, the CDC advised that all donated blood and plasma be tested for HIV antibody. In consultation with experts and affected communities, the agency has developed guidelines addressing many concrete problems associated with AIDS: such as safety in schools and work places; precautions for surgery and other invasive procedures; guidelines on immunization of children infected with HIV; and recommendations on preventing perinatal transmission.

In 1987, Ronald Reagan appointed a Presidential Commission on AIDS, which issued a comprehensive report in 1988. Its central recommendation called for strong new federal laws to prevent discrimination against people who carry the AIDS virus, so that individuals at risk can be encouraged to be tested. Report of the Presidential Commission on the Human Immunodeficiency Virus Epidemic, July 24, 1988. (Hereinafter President's AIDS Commission.) President Reagan rejected the Commission's core recommendation for new federal antidiscrimination legislation and instead ordered federal agencies to adopt antidiscrimination guidelines. Johnson, Reagan, Spurning Tougher Moves, Orders Anti-bias Rules on AIDS, N.Y. Times, A-1, Aug. 3, 1988.

2. PREVENTING AIDS TRANSMISSION

AIDS is transmitted by conduct and therefore the risk of transmission can be reduced by modifying behavior. Homosexual men have transformed their behavior to reduce the transmission of AIDS in that community. The fact that AIDS is spread by conduct and the stark fatality of the disease invite aggressive public policies to encourage self-protective changes in behavior. Unfortunately, however, the actions by which AIDS is transmitted — sex and IV drug use — are behaviors not easily addressed in contemporary culture and not easily changed.

a. Preventing AIDS: Quarantine and Criminal Prosecution

The President's AIDS Commission recommends that states consider adopting a special law that would punish those who know they are HIV-infected and fail to disclose their condition to sexual partners, to obtain their partners' knowing consent, and to use precautions. Id. at 131. The commission also cautions that criminal sanction should be "employed only when all other public health and civil actions fail to produce responsible behavior." Id. at 130. The commission rejects quarantine based only on HIV status, without consideration of an individual's behavior. However, it approves application of a range of coercive measures against people who are infectious and "reasonably likely to transmit the infectious agent." Id. at 130. The commission asserts that the standards of proof applicable to the civil commitment of the mentally ill should govern coercive treatment to prevent AIDS transmission. Id. at 77-78. For an excellent discussion see Sullivan & Field, AIDS and the Coercive Power of the State, 23 Harv. Civ. Rts.-Civ. Lib. L. Rev. 139 (1988).

b. Preventing AIDS: Protecting the Blood Supply

The President's Commission found that "[t]he initial response of the nation's blood banking industry to the possibility of contamination of the nation's blood by a new infectious agent was unnecessarily slow." Id. at 78. In part, hospitals rely upon transfused blood because reimbursement pays for blood transfused from others, but not for autologous transfusion therapy, in which patients anticipating elective surgery or childbirth bank their own blood. The commission recommends notifying anyone who received transfused blood since 1977 of the risk of HIV exposure. It also recommends that reimbursement be provided to support autologous transfusion.

Kozup v. Georgetown, 663 F. Supp. 1048 (D.D.C. 1987) rejected a malpractice claim brought by parents whose child died from AIDS after a blood transfusion in 1983. The court found that the medical community did not understand that AIDS could be transmitted through blood transfusions until 1984 and that the defendants were not negligent for failing to guard against a then unknown danger. However, the findings of the President's Commission suggest that further suits of this nature are likely and could be successful if the contaminated blood was transfused after 1984.

c. Preventing AIDS: Safer Sex

The most successful efforts to stop the spread of AIDS have been undertaken by private groups in the gay community. As the understanding of AIDS has grown, organizations and periodicals have disseminated detailed, graphic information describing which sexual practices are dangerous and which are safe. Altering sexual behavior requires more than simply information. These groups have also undertaken to eroticize safer sex and to create a sexual morality of caring and concern.

A physician involved in the development of safer sex programs explains:

> The use of street language rather than clinical terms is important for two reasons. First, educated and uneducated people alike understand these terms. In contrast, "insertive anal intercourse with ejaculation" is not understood by all.

> Second, many people at risk for AIDS are more likely to adopt advice that appears to originate in their own cultural community than that coming from government or health authorities. [D]rawings and pictures that show safe sex in an erotic light have aroused the most intense controversy. Many people think of safe sex as unfulfilling, boring, and unsatisfying. In contrast, they are exposed to a wealth of highly erotic images of unsafe sex. . . . Sex is not primarily a rational activity. Thus, factual information may impart knowledge about what is safe, but it does not change attitudes about what is satisfying and erotic. [Whyte, Teaching Safe Sex, 318 N. Engl. J. Med. 387 (1988).]

By 1987, the rate of new HIV infections in San Francisco had been reduced to 1 percent among uninfected gay men. The city's Director of Public Health termed it a "stunning success story for public health." The new cases appear primarily among minority and adolescent homosexuals. Staver, San Francisco Successful in Cutting HIV Infection Rate, Am. Med. News, Nov. 27, 1987, at 25. W. Winkelstein, et al. The San Francisco Men's Health Study: Continued Decline in HIV Seroconversion Rates Among Homosexual/Bisexual Men, 78 Am. J. Public Health 1472 (1988).

Outside the gay community, there have been minimal efforts to provide education or moral leadership to encourage safer sex. The Institute of Medicine, National Academy of Science reports, "Surveys of high school students reveal an alarming degree of misinformation about AIDS. Even many students living in San Francisco, an AIDS epicenter, were seriously misinformed as late as 1986." Institute of Medicine, National Academy of Sciences, Confronting AIDS: Directions for Public Health, Health Care, and Research at 101 (1986). A few states have developed and mandated educational programs for schools. California and Virginia require that information about AIDS and safe sex be provided to people seeking a marriage license.

The federal government and many states have actively frustrated AIDS education. In 1987, Congress adopted an amendment to the CDC's appropriations bill forbidding any AIDS education and preventing materials or activities that "promote or encourage, directly or indirectly, homosexual sexual activities," and requiring emphasis on "abstinence from sexual activity outside a sexually monogamous marriage (including abstinence from homosexual sexual activity)." The amendment, offered by Senator Jesse Helms, swept through the Congress with little opposition, though it was weakened by the removal of the word "indirectly." See Outcomes of Conference Committee on J.H. Res. 395, Continuing Resolution for FY 88 Appropriations: Helms Amendment, 133 Cong. Rec. 14,220 (1987). Following the federal lead, several states have adopted similar restrictions. A 1987 Indiana statute requires the state board of education to develop sex education material "stressing the moral aspects of abstinence from sexual activity . . . [and stating] that the best way to avoid AIDS is for young people to refrain from sexual activity until . . . marriage." 16 Ind. Code Ann. §16-1-9. 6-1 (1987).

d. Preventing AIDS: IV Drug Users

The burgeoning medical/legal literature on AIDS devotes little attention to people addicted to intravenous drugs. This is alarming because AIDS is spreading rapidly through this population, their sexual partners, and their children. On the other hand, the lack of attention is quite predictable. Addicts lack the organizational and financial resources necessary to provide community based services or to pressure the larger community to do so. Intravenous drug users are disproportionately poor and black or Hispanic. Community based organizations serving these groups have received little financial support, either public or private. President's AIDS Commission at 110. See also Against All Odds: Grassroots Minority Groups Fight AIDS, 18 Health PAC Bull. 4 (1988).

In 1988, in nine states — including New York and New Jersey, where most IV drug use related AIDS cases have developed — intravenous needles can only be purchased with a prescription. Demand for sterile needles has soared in response to AIDS. In 1987, New Jersey instituted a small experimental program to distribute sterile needles to people addicted to IV drugs. Law enforcement officials, however, maintain that selling clean needles over the counter would condone and encourage drug use. See Comment on Law and Medicine, Legalization of Non-Prescription Sale of Hypodermic Needles: A Response to the AIDS Crisis, 41 Record of N.Y.C.B.A. 809 (1986). The President's Commission did not address this issue.

Fear of AIDS has induced many people addicted to IV drugs to seek treatment. Demand far outstrips supply, and people must wait for months to enter a treatment program. The President's AIDS Commission recommends large expansion of federal support for treatment for people addicted to drugs. Id. at 99.

3. PROVIDING CARE TO PEOPLE WITH AIDS

a. Tales of Two Cities: New York and San Francisco

The two U.S. cities with the largest numbers of AIDS patients have divergent approaches to care, reflecting more general differences between them. This note relies on United Hospital Fund and Institute for Health Policy Studies, AIDS: Public Policy Dimensions (1987); the New York Times; Arno & Hughes, Local Policy Responses to the AIDS Epidemic: New York and San Francisco, N.Y. State J. Med., May 1987, 264; Pinkney, New York Hospitals Spilling Over, Am. Med. News, Feb. 5, 1988, 1; NYC United

Hospital Fund, Blueprint, Fall, 1987; and the President's AIDS Commission, supra.

In 1986, 98 percent of the AIDS patients in San Francisco were gay men, and 88 percent were white. In New York in 1988, more new cases of AIDS were reported among intravenous drug users than among gay men. In New York's public hospitals, 62 percent of the AIDS patients were heterosexual drug users, 11 percent were their sexual partners, and 5 percent were children. Although New York has 28 percent of AIDS cases nationwide, it has 51 percent of the cases linked to IV drug use, 42 percent of the cases of women with AIDS, and 36 percent of the cases of children with AIDS.

Overall, San Francisco is a more affluent community, particularly among patients with AIDS. San Francisco AIDS patients are more likely to have private insurance, at least at the beginning of their illness. In San Francisco, 69 percent of AIDS patients in private hospitals are covered by private insurance, while only 40 percent of those patients are covered in New York. The gay community is a much more significant force in the political life of San Francisco than are the gay or drug addicted populations in New York. While New York's gay community is somewhat larger than that of San Francisco, the entire New York population is ten times as large.

The medical cultures are distinct. New York has 11 public hospitals, over 70 voluntary hospitals, and seven medical schools, while San Francisco has only one public hospital, one medical school and 13 other hospitals. In San Francisco, one agency — the City Health Department — coordinates public health work, outpatient clinics, and administration of the public hospital. In New York, three large, uncoordinated city bureaucracies — the Health Department, the Health and Hospitals Corporation, and the Human Resources Administration — are partially responsible for services to people with AIDS. San Francisco has a stronger tradition of community-based care, group practice, and nonphysician health care providers.

Only San Francisco provides coordinated care, with an emphasis on outpatient service. In 1981, the San Francisco Health Department developed a centralized system of reporting and referral for AIDS cases. In 1982, San Francisco General established a multidisciplinary, outpatient AIDS clinic. In 1983, the Health Department instituted the first inpatient ward for AIDS, staffed with volunteer employees, and established an AIDS Activity Office to coordinate care, identify service gaps, and develop plans to address them. This office also oversees and supports AIDS-related contract services and maintains liaisons with community groups.

New York had no coordinated AIDS policy until late in 1984, and citywide coordination and planning has remained weak. New York's first outpatient AIDS clinic opened in 1984, providing service in Brooklyn two afternoons a week. There was no ambulatory care service in Manhattan until 1985. Over 90 percent of the City's expenditures for AIDS care subsidize inpatient services. Only 25 percent of San Francisco AIDS funding supports inpatient care.

Although volunteer labor is tremendously important in AIDS care in both cities, the local governments respond very differently. In 1984, San Francisco provided over 60 percent of the funds supporting voluntary organizations serving AIDS patients, while in 1984 New York provided only 3 percent of the resources of such groups. The ratio of volunteer to paid staff hours is about twice as high in New York. Neither nursing homes nor home health care services are available to New York patients with AIDS. For an excellent analysis see D. Felix et al, AIDS in the Long-Term Care Setting, 7 St. Louis U. Pub. L. Rev. 115 (1988).

San Francisco AIDS patients spend less time in the hospital than New York AIDS patients — in 1985 an average of 12 days vs. an average of 21, down from 26 days in 1982. In 1985, about 22 percent of all AIDS patients in New York were hospitalized at any time, while the comparable figure in San Francisco was 10 percent. The longer hospitalizations make AIDS care far more costly in New York. In 1984, the average charge per admission of an AIDS patient was $20,320, while in San Francisco it was $9,024, despite comparable per diem costs.

The pattern follows a general one of longer hospitalizations in New York. The difference in AIDS demographics also contribute to the disparity in lengths of hospitalization. Children require longer hospitalizations than adults. IV drug users are more apt to contract *Pneumocystis carinii,* which requires longer hospitalization, while gay patients are more apt to contact Kaposi's sarcoma, which can often be treated on an outpatient basis. New York AIDS patients are more likely to be poor or homeless. On any day in 1987, more than 1000 people with AIDS-related illnesses are hospitalized in New York City, constituting 5 percent of all hospital patients. The city hospitals, which contain 16 percent of the total hospital beds, serve 36 percent of the AIDS patients.

Both public and private New York hospitals protest inadequate reimbursement for care for AIDS patients. The state rate regulation program is discussed in Chapter 3. Because AIDS patients often require intensive medical care, "average" per diem reimbursement is less than the cost of providing it. Further, New York's rate setting methodology penalizes hospitals when patients remain hospitalized for longer than average numbers of days, as AIDS patients often do.

In 1986, the New York State Health Department sought to encourage more integrated forms of care by offering substantially increased reimbursement to hospitals that created a center for AIDS patients. Such hospitals are paid $584 a day for AIDS patients, an increase of nearly $250 over the standard rate. To qualify, the hospital must create an AIDS inpatient care unit; provide ambulatory services for screening, diagnosis and treatment; offer emergency services on a 24 hour basis; provide home health care, education, crisis counseling and specialized diagnostic and therapeutic services; and arrange for residential health care services appropriate to AIDS patients. In New York City, seven private hospitals and eight municipal medical centers are AIDS centers. Outside of the City, only one hospital serves as a center for AIDS care.

b. Providing Care: Integration vs. Segregation?

Are AIDS patients likely to receive better care if they are integrated in the mainstream of hospital service or segregated in specialized units? A segregated care unit could become a "leper colony" where rejected people are sent to die. Personnel might resist working there. On the other hand, a successful focused care unit could offer high quality care to AIDS patients.

In 1983, when San Francisco General first established its AIDS unit, many sensitive physicians and community leaders were concerned. However, favorable reports by informed observers, and high patient demand, testify to the success of the unit. It has recruited knowledgeable, self-selected staff and provides private rooms, following the preferred model for cancer care treatment. The unit encourages patients to make choices about intensive care procedures early in the course of their illness. Most reject heroic maintenance. This exemplary model of focused care for AIDS patients does not deny the dangers of segregation. The San Francisco General AIDS ward cares for a homogeneous, middle class gay population, with extensive community support. Different problems might arise in an AIDS unit serving patients who are more economically and ethnically diverse, who lack a sympathetic community to support them.

c. Health Care Workers

The President's AIDS Commission identified problems recruiting, training and supporting people to care for AIDS patients. Professional education does not prepare graduates to treat people infected with the HIV virus. Id. at 24. Many specialties most needed in AIDS treatment are underenrolled. Some health care workers avoid practices that risk exposure to AIDS. The Commission calls for expanded federal programs. See Chapter 7.

Health care workers confront risks of exposure to HIV infected blood or other bodily fluids. The Center for Disease Control (CDC) identifies three ways a health care worker might be exposed to HIV virus: parenteral (such as a needlestick or cut), mucous membrane (such as a splash to the eye or mouth), and cutaneous (e.g., when chapped or cut hands are exposed to large amounts of blood). In 1988, the CDC identified three cases in which health care workers developed HIV infection from exposure in the course of their work. Data assembled by the President's Commission and the CDC indicate that fewer than one percent of workers exposed become infected. Id. at 31. Nonetheless, given the fatal consequences of AIDS, precautions are essential.

Past infectious disease control efforts have not been effective. Each year between 12,000 and 15,000 health care workers become infected with hepatitis B, leading to over 200 deaths a year. HIV is far more difficult to transmit than hepatitis B. The risk of infection from a single needlestick exposure to HIV infected blood is 0.5 percent, while the rate of infection following a single needlestick exposure to blood infected with hepatitis B virus is 10 to 15 percent. President's AIDS Commission at 32.

The CDC advises health workers how to minimize the risk of exposure to AIDS, hepatitis B and other conditions. See Hermann & Gorman, Hospital Liability and AIDS Treatment: The Need for a National Standard of Care, 20 U.C. Davis L. Rev. 441 (1987). But the CDC has no authority to enforce hospital compliance. The Occupational Safety and Health Administration (OSHA) enforces workplace safety. The Health Care Financing Administration, in conjunction with the private Joint Commission on Accreditation of Hospitals (JCAH), enforces hospital quality standards. See Chapter 5. Hermann and Gordon argue that the CDC guidelines should be adopted by courts to determine whether hospitals are liable when a health worker contracts AIDS. Think about the processes by which that might happen. Is the risk of tort liability likely to encourage compliance?

One controversial proposal would require hospital patients to be tested for the HIV virus so workers could take additional precautions. Most medical and public health professionals reject such testing. Precautions should now be routine to protect workers against AIDS, hepatitis B, and other infectious diseases. Screening a low-risk population would require testing 1,300,000 individuals to prevent one case of AIDS infection. Hagen, Routine Preoperative Screening for HIV, 259 J.A.M.A. 1357 (1988). Some, however, urge screening of both physicians and patients for surgical procedures likely to be particularly bloody. Fear of infection is only one factor discouraging people from providing care to AIDS patients. Health professionals are trained to cure. Care of patients with AIDS offers no opportunity for victory. This is especially tragic since most AIDS patients are young. People who care for AIDS patients often work in conditions made extraordinarily harsh by inadequate staff and resources.

d. The Financial Costs of AIDS

An early national study by the Center for Disease Control estimated the lifetime medical care costs for an AIDS patient at $147,000. Hardy, The Economic Impact of the First 10,000 Cases of Acquired Immunodeficiency Syndrome in the United States, 255 J.A.M.A. 209 (1986). More recent studies have found the actual lifetime medical costs of people with AIDS substantially lower: $46,505 in Boston and $27,571 in San Francisco. Seage et al. Medical Care Costs of AIDS in Massachusetts, 256 J.A.M.A. 3107 (1986); Scitovsky et al. Medical Care Costs of Patients With AIDS in San Francisco, 256 J.A.M.A. 3103 (1986). Both fewer hospitalizations and shorter hospital stays explained these lower costs. The well organized gay community in San Francisco provides support services to enable people to leave the hospital sooner or to stay out of the hospital completely.

These studies compare the costs of AIDS treatment with other major illnesses. The Boston study notes that the mean medical care costs for nonelderly persons with terminal cancer during their final year is $30,280. The San Francisco study observes that mean lifetime medical care costs of patients with end stage renal disease who are undergoing dialysis is about $158,000. Estimates of the proportion of direct health care costs devoted to the care of AIDS patients range from a low of 0.3 percent of 1986 expenditures to a high projection of 2.4 percent of total personal health care expenditures in 1990. Costs are concentrated in few facilities in few communities, that is public and teaching hospitals in New York and San Francisco.

Medicaid is the principal source of payment for care for AIDS care, paying about 54 percent of these costs. Private insurance pays approximately 17 percent of AIDS costs and only 2 percent of AIDS patients qualify for Medicare. Medicaid eligibility varies enormously. In the Northeast, 60 percent of patients with AIDS are covered by Medicaid, while only 15 percent are covered in the South. See Chapter 2. Hospitals — principally public and urban teaching institutions — shoulder the balance of the costs of providing care to AIDS patients. Andrulius, The Provision and Financing of Medical Care for AIDS Patients in U.S. Public and Private Teaching Hospitals, 258 J.A.M.A. 1343 (1987).

4. DENYING CARE TO PEOPLE WITH AIDS

Many health care providers refuse to serve patients who suffer from AIDS, may carry the virus, or are in a high risk group. In New York City complaints have become so numerous that the Commission on Human Rights has established a Special AIDS Discrimination Unit. The Commission's Report on Discrimination Against People With AIDS and People Perceived to have AIDS, at 16-20 (August, 1987), recounts these complaints. A private hospital informs people with sexually transmitted disease that they can only be served in the public hospitals. A group health plan refuses treatment to gay plan members, citing "health concerns." A private clinic advertises its services in the gay press, provides dangerously poor quality service, and charges patients amounts far in excess of originally quoted prices. Several drug rehabilitation programs refuse to treat people who are HIV antibody positive. Some public hospitals, which care for most AIDS patients, are alleged to treat AIDS patients, including children, in abusive and offensive ways. Most nursing homes "categorically deny access to patients with AIDS. . . . The scope of service rejections is devastating." Id. at 19.

Virtually every hospital and nursing home receives federal funds from Medicare and is hence subject to federal rules prohibiting discrimination on the basis of handicap. See United States v. Baylor University Medical Center, 736 F.2d 1039 (5th Cir.), *cert. denied,* 469 U.S. 1189 (1984), and the Civil Rights Restoration Act of 1987, 42 U.S.C. §§2000d–4a.

A person who tests positive for the HIV virus is a "handicapped individual," both because the immune system is impaired and because others perceive the person as handicapped. Doe v. Centinela Hospital, 27 F.E.P. Cases 1036, 57 U.S.L.W. 2034 (C.D. Calif. 1988), held that an HIV antibody positive man who was excluded from participation in a residential drug rehabilitation program was an "individual with handicaps" under §504 of the Rehabilitation Act because he was "regarded as handicapped." The court said that "discrimination based solely on fear of contagion is discrimination based on a handicap when the impairment has that effect on others." Id. The court ordered a trial on the question of whether the plaintiff is "otherwise qualified" to participate in the program. See also Local 1812, American Federation of Government Employees v. United States Department of State, 662 F. Supp. 50, 54 (D.D.C. 1987); Chalk v. United States District Court, 832 F.2d 1158 (9th Cir. 1987); District 27 Community School Board v. Board of Education of the City of New York, 130 Misc. 2d 398, 502 N.Y.S.2d 325, (Sup. Ct. 1986).

The more difficult determination is whether the individual is "otherwise qualified," for treatment. The antidiscrimination law allows recipients of federal funds to give "appropriate weight to such legitimate concerns of the grantees as avoiding exposing others to significant health and safety risks." School Board of Nassau County v. Arline, 480 U.S. 273, 282 (1987). What does that mean in the AIDS context? Hospitals or nursing homes that seek to exclude patients with AIDS will cite other reasons for their actions, such as lack of beds or necessary specialized services, or a policy of admitting only patients under the care of a physician with staff privileges. What evidence would illuminate whether a person with AIDS was excluded solely on the basis of handicap? Discrimination by insurance companies is discussed in Chapter 2.

In Dallas Gay Alliance v. Parkland Memorial Hospital, No. 88-6346-A (4th Dist Dallas Co., May 20, 1988), a state court ordered the Parkland Hospital to abolish all bed quotas for HIV-positive patients, allocate hospital beds to AIDS patients on the basis of need, and dispense AZT and aerosolized pentamidine inhalation treatment to patients qualified on the basis of need. The hospital, the major provider of AIDS services in the Dallas area, maintained that staff shortages precluded it from providing more service to patients needing drugs that must be administered under physician supervision. The hospital claimed that it was unable to recruit more people to care for AIDS patients. The plaintiffs asserted that the AIDS service was the only one through which medical students and residents did not rotate routinely.

Think about the implications for AIDS care of the Hill-Burton community service requirements, and COBRA's Emergency Care requirements of 1986. In response to this injunction, the hospital modified all of the practices about which the plaintiffs complained, except the policy of not requiring medical students to rotate through the AIDS clinic. At the hospital's request the suit was removed to federal court. The federal court refused to certify a class action and dismissed the claim as moot and non-justiciable. Some of the named plaintiffs had died and others were then receiving the services they needed.

Do health workers have a legal duty to treat AIDS patients? It may be useful to distinguish treating AIDS, which may involve knowledge and skill necessary to treat a particular disease, from treating a person infected with HIV virus, which involves knowing the precautions necessary to avoid infection while treating a different condition. In 1987, the Council on Ethical and Judicial Affairs of the AMA issued a statement that a physician "may not ethically refuse to treat a patient whose condition is within the physician's current realm of competence," solely because the patient has AIDS or is infected with HIV. "Ethical Issues Involved in the Growing AIDS Crisis, 259 J.A.M.A. 1360 (1988). "A person who is afflicted with AIDS needs competent, compassionate treatment. Neither those who have the disease nor those who have been infected with the virus should be subjected to discrimination based on fear or prejudice, least of all by members of the health care community. Physicians should respond to the best of their ability in cases of emergency where first aid treatment is essential, and physicians should not abandon patients whose care they have undertaken." Id. This statement was undercut by AMA Executive Vice-President James Sammons, who commented that physicians with a "psychological hang-up" that interferes with their ability to treat AIDS patients may decline to do so. G. J. Annas, Not Saints, But Healers: The Legal Duties of Health Care Professionals in the AIDS Epidemic, 7 Am. J. Pub. Health 1, 3 (1988). Most state medical associations have not addressed the issue. The Texas Medical Association affirmed doctor's "traditional freedom" to choose whom to serve. Id. at 1. The Massachusetts Board of Registration in Medicine declared that

> [l]icensed professionals should accord persons with AIDS . . . the same respect and quality of service delivered to non-infected individuals. . . . Caring for routine problems associated with AIDS . . . is a skill all professionals need to master. If care for specialized AIDS manifestations is a skill which an up-to-date professional needs to master, then continuing professional competence would require mastering and offering those skills as well. Therefore, when a person with AIDS develops problems that would normally be in the area of expertise of . . . a skilled professional, referral to another professional would be generally not in conformity with the intent of these guidelines. [Id. AIDS Guidelines.]

The New Jersey medical licensing board's AIDS policy provides that "A licensee of this Board may not categorically refuse to treat a patient who has AIDS or AIDS-related complex, or an HIV positive blood test, when he or she possesses the skill and experience to treat the condition presented." Id. When the physician is unable to render care, "the licensee retains the responsibility to make alternative arrangements for the proper care of a patient." By contrast, the Arizona Board of Medical Examiners has stated that their licensees have the right to refuse continued treatment to AIDS patients, Id. at 4.

Hospitals have greatest power to prevent discrimination against people with AIDS, by insisting upon nondiscrimination as a condition of employment or of staff privileges. In 1987, the Associated Medical Schools of New York decreed that physicians have a "most fundamental responsibility" to treat AIDS patients, and that any faculty member, house staff or medical student who refused to treat an AIDS patient would be dismissed. Sullivan, Thirteen Medical Colleges Say Staffs Must Treat AIDS, N.Y. Times, Dec. 9, 1987, B-3.

C H A P T E R

II

Health Care Financing: Who Pays for Health Care?

A. An Introduction to the Costs of American Health Care

Viewed in the aggregate, the costs of health care in this country are extraordinarily expensive. According to the most reliable government estimates, national health expenditures (NHEs) were nearly $500 billion in 1987, 11.1 percent of the Gross National Product (GNP). Personal health services, roughly the equivalent of individual medical care, accounted for approximately 90 percent of this total. For an earlier treatment of these issues, see Wing, American Health Policy in the 1980's, 36 Case W. Res. L. Rev. 608, 618-628 (1986).

Table I highlights the growing importance and problematic character of these expenditures for the American economy.

National health expenditures have been dramatically and steadily increasing for at least forty years, in both absolute and relative terms. In 1950, essentially the eve of the technological revolution in modern medicine, Americans were spending $12.7 billion annually for their health care, 4.4 percent of the nation's GNP. What followed was several decades of continually increasing growth. Through the 1960s, NHEs increased at an average annual rate of over 8 percent per year, accelerated to an average annual growth rate of 12 percent after the implementation of Medicaid and Medicare and through the mid-1970s, and grew by an average rate of over 13 percent from 1975 to 1983. More important, this accelerating growth rate for NHEs, with only a few exceptions, continually exceeded the annual growth in the rest of the economy.

The rate of NHE growth moderated somewhat in the mid-1980s, falling to a low of 7.8 percent in 1985, the lowest rate of increase in 25 years. Nonetheless, the overall trend of growth continues; with the exception of 1984, NHEs have continued in this decade to consume a larger share of the GNP each year. Although future estimates are necessarily speculative, gov-

TABLE 1
Aggregate National Health Expenditures 1929–2000

Year	*NHE (in billions)*	*Annual Growth Rate (% of NHE)*	*% Total GNP*
2000	$1500	—	15%
1990	690	—	12.3
1987	500	9.8	11.1
1986	456	8.6	10.7
1985	419	7.8	10.4
1984	389	9.3	10.3
1983	357	10.4	10.5
1982	324	12.9	10.2
1981	287	15.7	9.4
1980	248	15.6	9.1
1979	215	13.2	8.9
1978	190	11.7	8.8
1977	170	12.9	8.9
1976	151	13.6	8.8
1975	133	12.1	8.6
1974	116	12.5	8.1
1973	103	10.0	7.8
1972	94	12.5	7.9
1971	84	11.4	7.7
1970	75	13.4	7.6
1969	66	12.7	7.0
1968	58	13.1	6.7
1967	52	10.8	6.4
1966	46	10.3	6.1
1965	42	9.3	6.1
1960	27	5.3	5.3
1955	18	7.0	4.4
1950	13	12.2	4.4
1940	4	0.8	4.0
1929	4	—	3.5

Source: Division of National Cost Estimates, Office of the Actuary, Health Care Financing Administration.

ernment experts have predicted that this trend will continue into the next decade and that NHEs could be over $1.5 trillion by the end of the century, representing over 15 percent of the GNP.

Moreover, whatever the exact level of future increases, NHEs have already grown at a rapid rate for at least four decades, have continually grown faster than the rest of the economy, and have therefore represented a sizable and virtually relentless shifting of economic resources from other goods and services to the purchase of health care. International comparisons reveal similar trends in most other industrialized countries, but, at least in the last ten years, in no other economy has the level of spending for health care or the rate of its growth matched that of the United States.

Whether this represents a problem of fundamental importance, however, is a matter of debate. To some extent this rapid growth in NHEs, and the consequent shifting of economic resources during the last several decades, was predictable. To oversimplify, there was much more medical care to purchase in 1987 than there was in 1950. . . .

In addition, the American population has grown during this period of NHE growth, and, particularly in the last decade, the age composition of that population has changed. Elderly Americans now represent a much larger proportion of the population; while healthier than their earlier counterparts, the elderly still need and use more medical care than their younger contemporaries. Recent data indicate that the average spending on the elderly is as much as three and one-half times that of the rest of the population, with spending on the growing number of the "very old" even higher. It is also generally accepted in the economic literature that, as an economy "matures," consumers have more resources to spend and tend to spend more of their discretionary resources on medical care and related services. Indeed, a few critics have attempted to argue that there is nothing inherently wrong with a "mature economy" or a wealthy society spending 12 percent, 15 percent or, for that matter, 20 percent of its economic output on health care, if that is what consumers want to purchase with their available wealth.

But while these factors have been and will continue to be influential, their relative contribution to increases in NHEs, particularly during the 1980s, should not be misunderstood or overstated, nor should they be weighed too heavily in formulating contemporary health policy.

Of much greater importance has been the proportion of NHE increases that can be attributed to two factors: higher rates of utilization of health care services and the greater number of services being rendered to each patient per visit or episode and price inflation, meaning inflation in the generally accepted economic sense: increases in what economists call "inputs," or increases in the cost of "inputs," for what are regarded as essentially the same goods or services. At least since the mid-1970s, 50-80 percent of the annual increase in total health spending can be attributed to inflation in prices. In fact, inflation has been a factor of continuing and *growing* importance, an observation of crucial significance in both defining the exact nature of the "fundamental problem," and in evaluating the need for and the nature of appropriate remedial responses. Americans are essentially paying more for their medical care in the most literal sense; indeed, the latest estimates of rates of utilization of services indicate that they may be paying more and receiving slightly less.

This price inflation has been driven in large part by the inflation in the economy in general, but it also represents a higher level of inflation in health care prices that is specific to health care services. In 1984, for example, 52 percent of the increase in health spending was attributed to inflation in the economy. Another 25 percent was attributed to an additional industry-specific inflation. In 1986, economy-wide inflation represented only 32 percent of the increase. Again, nearly a quarter of the annual increase was due to an additional industry-specific inflation. As measured by the Medical Care Price Index (MCPI), price inflation in national health care spending during the last twenty years has continually and significantly exceeded the Consumer Price Index (CPI), the generally accepted measure of inflation in the general economy. The annual percentage change in the MCPI has exceeded that of the CPI in all but two of the years since 1965, and in some years the MCPI has grown at twice the rate of the CPI. This trend was sustained even during years when the inflation in the general economy was itself regarded as reaching critical levels.

No other major item in the economy — food, housing, transportation, or even energy costs — has matched these levels of specific-price inflation. Thus during the last two decades and, more importantly, during the last ten years, the period of the greatest increases in the costs of health care, Americans have been paying higher prices for their medical care, due to a rate of inflation that cannot be explained simply by reference to prevailing economic conditions or other mitigating factors.

A relevant economic, as well as political, lesson can be learned from an analysis of the cost data for the last several years, when, ironically, the "fundamental problem" was somewhat obscured by the apparent decline in the rate of increase in NHEs. In 1984, for example, growth of NHEs was slightly less than that of the general economy, and government reports and media accounts were heralding a slowing in the rate of health care "inflation." But, in fact, the longterm trend of price inflation, driven both by inflation generally and by the inflation specific to health services, was continuing to influence health care spending at a relatively high level. The rate of increase in total NHEs in 1984 was slightly lower than the percentage growth of the GNP only because the rate of productivity of health services declined and was significantly lower than that for the rest of the economy. The MCPI was still 6.2 percent, 150 percent of the rate of general price inflation, as measured by the CPI.

This emphasis on the continuing role of price inflation in health care costs is not meant to suggest that other factors that have contributed to the growth of NHEs, or the shifting of economic resources, should be disregarded in evaluating either historic trends or the need for cost containment. Changes in demographics, in the patterns of utilization or service, or in our social or economic circumstances will continue to have an influential impact on NHEs. Some experts, for example, have warned that the "graying" of the American population will become one of the dominant factors contributing to future increases in health spending, particularly towards the end of this century. Conversely, induced or incidental changes in such factors as "intensity" (for instance, a reduction in the rate of hospitalization) can contribute to the containment of rising health care costs, even if they do so only by disguising the influence of price inflation or of other factors, as they have in some years. But such short-term success notwithstanding, the principal health care cost problem of the 1980s, the one that appears to have the most significant economic consequences and the one that has not been contained in any realistic sense, is price inflation. Price inflation, driven by inflation in the economy but continually exceeding the level of inflation — not "staggering" levels of aggregate spending, a growing or aging population, or significant increases in demand — is the most problematic characteristic of contemporary American health care.

To blame price inflation for increases in health care costs is, of course, only a symptomatic analysis, not the isolation or the evaluation of underlying causes. And, as with the rise in aggregate national spending, price inflation can in some respects be explained, perhaps even justified, by our social and economic circumstances and by the inherent nature of the services involved. The slow growth of productivity in health care may not be able to keep pace with the growth of public expectations, leading, economists have argued, to inflation in prices. Some amount of inflation in the costs of a valuable service may be part of the price we pay for a maturing economy. For that matter, estimates of price inflation, technically an attempt to measure increases in the cost of the "inputs" used to produce the same product or service or changes in those "inputs," only roughly distinguish between changes in "inputs" and changes in the "intensity" of the service. Surely the same services — a day in the hospital or a visit to the physician — are not being provided today as they were yesterday, even in the most basic sense. But the relative influence of price inflation on health care costs, both historically and, in particular, through the last decade, is too significant and too consistent to be dismissed as the product of either of these somewhat mitigating circumstances or the difficulty of separating real price inflation from changes in the nature of the services delivered.

Indeed, experts from a variety of disciplines — economists, public policy analysts, health services researchers, and virtually everyone that has studied the "fundamental problem" — have uniformly agreed that inflation in health care prices and the resulting impact on health care costs and, as a result, on the economy, must be traced to other, more retributional factors, deriving from the manner in which health care is financed and organized. There is little agreement on the relative influence of various systemic characteristics. The literature abounds in debate over the causal relationship between health care cost increases and a number of factors: cost based or fee-for-service reimbursement; comprehensive third party coverage; "freedom of choice"; government payment or tax subsidy for health services; or other structural or financial characteristics of American health care delivery. But the central theme of this criticism is fairly unanimous: the methods by which health services in this country have been traditionally delivered and financed have created the circumstances in which both providers and their patients are relatively insulated from the costs of the services that are delivered. At the very least, the immediate and direct impact of those costs has been greatly reduced. Under such circumstances, providers may be inclined to provide more, for both the best and the worst of motives; and patients may be inclined to request — and accept — more. To some extent, then, the historic increases in utilization of services and the continuing increases in "intensity" of services may also be attributed in part to these systemic characteristics.

But more importantly, there is little incentive under such circumstances to offset the various pressures on physicians, hospitals, and other health service providers to increase the costs of the various goods and services they provide or, at least, to tolerate such increases. To address such a fundamental problem and to contain the rising costs of health care, these systemic characteristics must somehow be modified or reformed. As a matter of sound public policy, such systemic reform should be designed to impact on the inflating prices of medical care services as much as, if not more than, on other factors that influence health care costs.

Obviously, any significant improvement in the general economy — a slowing of general inflation, an increase in productivity, or a change in any other "health indicator" of our economic status — can reduce, or at least mask, the economic effects of inflating health care costs. In fact, the health of our economy, rather than the economics of health care itself, may be the best predictor of the day of reckoning for cost containment of health care. But just as it is difficult to predict any significant or long lasting improvements in the American economy, it is equally difficult to foresee the advent of any other mitigating factor to offset the problematic character of health care costs to that economy. In particular, it is difficult to suggest that the historic trend of price inflation, in the technically correct sense of that term, is moderating.

The rising costs of health care may not have been a crisis for the economy in the 1980s; they may not even constitute a problem of fundamental proportions. Nonetheless, strong arguments still can be made that rising health care costs deserve serious attention. Health care continues to demand more and more of our economic output. Health care is purchased at the expense of other economic activities. Every dollar spent on health care cannot be spent elsewhere. When one out of every ten dollars is spent on health care, the economic effect of that spending can be said, with only slight exaggeration, to influence virtually everything: interest rates, social and domestic spending, even international competitiveness. All of these economic effects have been muted in recent years by the moderation of the rise in total spending. But health care costs continue to rise and continue to inflate. Given the underlying causes of these trends, it is clear that these costs should be of immediate concern, and it is likely that they will become increasingly problematic, particularly if one assumes that the availability and distribution of health care should be maintained at current levels.

B. Private Third Party Payers

1. An Overview of Private Health Insurance

Fein, Social and Economic Attitudes Shaping American Health Policy

58 Milbank Mem. Fund Q. 349, 376-381 (1980)

INSURANCE AND EXPENDITURES

Existing financing and reimbursement arrangements provide incentives for the public to seek and providers to deliver more care than knowledgeable physicians deem appropriate or necessary; for hospitals to be overbuilt; for technology to run rampant; and for costs, prices, and expenditures to keep escalating. In spite of rules and regulations, the incentives create a situation in which the health care system appears out of control. The free-marketeer suggests that this is the inevitable outcome of a set of policies that have interfered with the market by introducing government funding for health care and resource development and by encouraging the expansion of health insurance coverage. He attaches special blame to health insurance that eliminates, or significantly reduces, the patient's monetary payment at the time that the particular service is sought. Given the absence of a price barrier, we find more physician visits, hospital days, and drugs than patients need or would choose in a nondistorted market. Given federal and state regulations, licensing practices, and reimbursement and payment arrangements, prices and expenditures inevitably rise.

Overbedding and other excesses thus are partly explained by the surge of demand for care. Insurance makes it possible to translate the consumer's presumed taste for medical care, for physician visits, hospital days, CAT scans into effective demand. Nor is it surprising that supply increases to meet that demand. Physicians, hospital administrators, equipment manufacturers, all find expansion rewarding in monetary and prestige terms and sometimes in both. The normal constraints, the ability to sell wares or services or fill beds, are no longer present. Absent the market, there is an explosive expansion.

True, each of us is aware that our own behavior contributes to the escalation of premiums. But each of us is also aware that our individual contribution is negligible and that premiums would not be different if we "behaved" ourselves while others did not — and why should we assume *they* would? Indeed, if we assume that others would take advantage of the system, we feel encouraged to do so ourselves. . . .

The argument sounds powerful; yet there is even more. How is it that, knowing the outcome, we purchase the insurance nonetheless, and purchase it though it covers events many of us could finance out-of-pocket? Why should we form voluntary association with those who will abuse the system? Ignoring the psychological security provided by insurance and our willingness to pay for risk aversion, the explanation for our behavior is sought in government tax policy, which, in the United States, encourages the purchase of insurance by reducing its true price. . . .

This argument, though captivating, is incomplete or, perhaps because it is incomplete, it appears simple and captivating. It ignores the externalities, the social benefits of insurance, the welfare gains associated with security, the unequal distribution of income and of purchasing power. It assumes that insurance pays the full fee without deductibles or coinsurance and overlooks the fact that the physician's fee is only one part of the cost of care. Some people lose wages when they visit a physician; for others, transport costs may represent a barrier. It ignores the fact that, even in the presence of insurance or "free care," it is often necessary to have outreach programs to achieve greater utilization, that some people are afraid to visit their physician lest he confirm their worst fears or cause them pain, and that others have no ready source of care. It ignores the fact that our attitudes and behavior toward medical care are not the same as, say, toward ice cream cones. The argument defines the free-market allocation of resources as optimal and assumes that except for insurance we would, in fact, have a free market. It says that voting with dollars is somehow more appropriate than voting with ballots and that being "free to choose" in the market will yield better outcomes than being "free to choose" in the political sphere, as if, for example, each of us should buy clean air and not collectively legislate about it.

FOSTERING THE MARKET

Many economists in the United States find the previous arguments about tax subsidies, the expansion of insurance, and the increase in demand compelling. Nor do they stop with the analysis. They use the analysis as a basis for policy prescriptions and that set of prescriptions is, of course, fairly obvious: eliminate government tax incentives that stimulate the purchase of insurance by distorting its real price, and make certain that insurance policies require significant cost-sharing by the consumer. Some proposals suggest utilizing a high deductible in which the patient might pay for his medical expenses on his own up to, say, 5 percent of family income. . . . Above that, he would face a coinsurance rate of 50 percent for the next 10 percent of income. . . . The maximum risk, therefore, would be a full 10 percent of income. . . . Above that figure, catastrophic insurance would take over, providing the financial protection that is "really" needed. The various cost-sharing devices, it is assumed, would lead to more responsible behavior on the part of patients and on the part of physicians, acting as the patients' agent. The fact that most care would be paid for by the patient would deter the use of services, bring price consciousness, induce price competition, and lead to greater efficiency. Though we have different health care needs and different incomes, the proposals rely on price rationing to supply the discipline, the control mechanisms, that the health care system lacks. . . .

NEGLECTED ISSUES.

Wherein lies the fallacy? What is at error in the proposed solution? Let me try to answer that question in two ways. First, I should like to mention some matters that, I believe, call into question the idea that the answer to the economic problems of the United States health sector, to resource misallocation, and to rising expenditures lies in increasing cost-sharing or charges and in reducing government support for, and provision of, insurance. I question the notion that these devices would maximize "efficiency." But I shall not leave it at that, for I should also like to raise a more basic question that relates to the question of equity, the needs that health services address, and the role of health activities.

The more technical questions that can be raised can be listed:

1. Does a proposal that erects a substantial economic barrier to the receipt of noncatastrophic medical care respond to the area of prevention and early treatment, on the one hand, or to the financial impact of chronic illness, on the other? Does such an approach represent good medicine? . . .

2. Does the emphasis on cost sharing meet the clear desire expressed by individuals in their voting and personal behavior and in union-management collective bargaining agreements for a budgeting device that reduces the impact of the nonforeseeable illness? Everything we observe suggests that individuals who can afford it rush to buy insurance to fill in the uncovered bits and pieces (and do so at rates that, because of the costs of administration, often are actuarially unsound). They are looking for security, predictability, budgeting devices. Is this irrational? If we do believe in individual choice, why rule out these choices, why rule out individual choices collectively expressed?

3. Can economic deterrents work with equal impact on families and individuals with unequal economic resources? Will not the poor face barriers that will impede access to early treatment? Can we really expect that the only care that will be affected is that which really was "unnecessary"?

4. If we conceive of a program that is income-related or means-tested, we will need to know income and to pay the costs of ascertaining and monitoring the requisite data. We will also have to pay the costs of keeping track of the deductibles and other elements of cost-sharing. These costs will be substantial. Each program refinement that is added in order to deal with equity adds to these costs. . . .

5. The assumption of competitive behavior on the part of providers and

price shopping on the part of consumers in seeking care is questionable at best and foolish at worst. Can we really expect the benefits of price competition? . . . Furthermore, consumers, confronted by illness, are hardly in a position to shop, are not privy to the information required, and might (as all of us do so often) assume that higher price means higher quality. If so, they are hardly likely to feel comfortable about seeking low-cost care for themselves or their dependents.

6. Given the administrative costs, the insurance purchased to fill in the gaps, the use of price as proxy for quality, will the nation's total health expenditures stabilize or will expenditures continue to escalate? Is the control mechanism of price sufficient unto the task?

It seems to me we solve little in the American health care problem by adopting a solution that assumes unreal conditions: that consumers have, or could acquire, perfect knowledge; that providers could compete; and that cost-sharing and income data would spew out of the computer at little cost. If one is searching for a frame of reference, some understanding of how the system would behave, that frame of reference is not to be found in textbook descriptions of pure competition, which are useful for didactic purposes only because they abstract from reality. Instead, look to an examination of the behavior of real markets populated by real people, people with fears, emotions, and passions. Regrettably, our understanding of these markets and of the people in them, their goals, desires, and behavior, leaves much to be desired. So, too, with our understanding of the dynamic purposes that create the situations, the imperfections, that subsequently are deplored.

a. Who Buys Health Insurance, What Do They Buy, and Why Do They Buy It?

i. Extent and Coverage of Private Insurance

According to insurance industry estimates, 180 million Americans held some form of private health insurance policy at the end of 1986, representing roughly 80 percent of the population under 65, but also nearly 14 million people over the age of 65. These figures, however, are somewhat misleading and exaggerate both the number of people covered and the extent of their coverage. Not all of these people have insurance throughout the year. Further, while most private health insurance includes some form of hospital coverage, coverage for physician services and, particularly, other services is not as extensive. Even when a policy covers these categories of services, coverage is often limited by a fixed dollar ceiling, durational limits, specific exclusions, or by other cost sharing provisions. In addition, a number of these policies are supplemental, as in the case of Medi-gap policies for Medicare beneficiaries, and many people purchase two or more such policies — in some cases providing duplicative and unnecessary coverage.

These limitations on the scope of private health insurance policies are reflected by the proportion of health care actually purchased with private health insurance. Private health insurers paid for nearly $130 billion in health benefits in 1986, roughly 30 percent of personal health expenditures. By way of comparison, public third party payers, primarily Medicaid and Medicare, paid for around 40 percent of total expenditures. The remaining 30 percent primarily represents individual consumer out of pocket payments (cost sharing, payments for services not covered by insurance, and payments by the uninsured).

Because of more extensive coverage, private health insurance pays for a much larger share of hospital and physician services than it does for other services. Over 80 percent of privately purchased hospital services and 50 percent of privately purchased physician services were paid for by private health insurers. On the other hand, private health insurance pays for less than 5 percent of nursing home care.

The portion of personal health expenditures purchased with private insurance grew steadily from the 1940s to the most recent decade, reaching a high of 32 percent in 1983. In the most recent years, however, that share has stabilized. As the extent of coverage has expanded over the last forty years, and particularly as the costs of health care services have increased, the costs of purchasing private health insurance have also increased rapidly. Total premiums for private health insurance have grown at an average annual rate of 14 percent since 1950 and increased fourfold from 1973 to 1983. In the 1980s, growth has been more moderate, but significantly, insurance *premiums* have continued to grow and to grow faster than the rate of increase of the *benefits* purchased with those expenditures. This has been attributed to the increase in the administrative costs of private health insurance during a period of market instability, the development and marketing of new plans, and, ironically, the expense of various efforts to control costs.

With the costs of health care rising rapidly and the administrative costs of health insurance also increasing, not unexpectedly, private health insurance policies have become a less profitable business. In the mid-1980s many insurers were claiming underwriting losses. Some were getting out of the health insurance business altogether. For this reason, most experts predict that there will be considerable pressure on private health insurers to raise premiums even faster in the next several years.

Obviously the impact of these rising premium costs falls most heavily on those individuals who purchase their own insurance. But for a large portion of the population, the impact of these rising costs has been at least partially disguised. A majority of Americans receive their health insurance as part of their employment benefits, benefits that are not subject to federal income or Social Security taxation. See discussion infra. Many former workers also receive health insurance from their employers as part of their retirement benefits. It has been estimated that nationwide employers pay all or almost all of the premiums for nearly one-half of their employees (and their dependents) and as much as 75 percent of all private health insurance premiums, although there is a great deal of variation between employment and income categories, and across geographic regions.

Understandably, those employers who are paying all or a large part of the health insurance premiums for their employees and their dependents, and for their retired workers, are becoming increasingly sensitive to increases in insurance premiums. Again, there is wide variation, but some employers are claiming "leaps" in health insurance premium costs as high as 100 percent per year. General Motors, for example, claims to have spent over $2.2 billion for health care in 1983, a 50 percent increase in five years, translating to over $3000 for every GM family, including retirees, and over $5000 per active employee per year. Some insurance analysts are also claiming that most employers have grossly underestimated their commitments to fund health benefits for their retired employees. See Employee Benefit Research Institute, Measuring and Funding Corporate Liability for Retiree Health Benefits (1987). This may lead to considerable political and legal controversy in future years. See, for instance, Moore v. Metropolitan Life Insurance Co. 856 F.2d 488 (2d Cir. 1988).

If their share of the contribution to the Medicare trust fund is included, an expenditure that has also been rapidly rising in recent years, employers can legitimately claim that the costs of their employees' health-related benefits have been skyrocketing in the 1980s. Even in relative terms, the employers' burden appears increasingly problematic. Employers' total contribution for health benefits has been growing faster than total employee compensation for at least a decade. The same mechanism that has tended historically to insulate many consumers from the impact of the rising costs of privately financed health expenditures — employer-purchased and tax-subsidized health insurance premiums — may be having the opposite effect on their employers. Those that have committed themselves to providing broad health insurance coverage as part of their employee compensation package now find that this is an increasingly expensive commitment. Thus among the most significant trends in private health insurance in the 1980s have been the efforts of employers to shift more of the cost of premiums to their employees, increase employee cost sharing liability, increase utilization review and other administrative controls, and experiment with self-insurance, health maintenance organizations, and other alternative arrangements. In fact, the rapid increase in the number of employers engaged in some form of self-insurance will clearly have many far reaching consequences. For a discussion of these alternative strategies, see Friedland, Introduction and Background: Private Initiatives to Contain Health Care Expenditures in The Changing Health Care Market 1 (F. McArdle ed. 1987). For sources and updates on the data cited above, see Division of National Cost Estimates, Office of the Actuary, Health Care

Financing Administration, National Health Expenditures, 1986-2000, 8 Health Care Fin. Rev. 1 (1987); Health Insurance Association of America, 1988 Update: Source Book of Health Insurance Data (1987).

ii. Structure of Private Insurance Mechanisms

While there are a wide variety of individual and group health insurance schemes available in the United States, and while the current economic and political circumstances dictate that there will be considerable change and innovation in the industry, for introductory purposes, private health insurance can be viewed as falling into three broad generic categories: "service-benefit" plans, indemnity insurance, and independent or self-insured plans.

Until the turmoil of the 1980s, the distribution of the private health insurance market was fairly stable: roughly 40 percent of private health insurance policies were "service-benefit" plans sold by Blue Cross and Blue Shield. Altogether, the various indemnity insurers sold just over 50 percent of the health insurance policies. Independent plans and self-insurers represented a relatively small portion of the health insurance market. By 1988, the Blues' share had shrunk dramatically, and HMOs' percentage share was approaching 15 percent.

As described in the introductory chapter, Blue Cross and Blue Shield premiums originally were community rated: all people in a particular region paid the same premium regardless of health status or other characteristics. They also offered fairly comprehensive coverage, few maximum liability limits, and only modest cost sharing. When commercial insurers began to compete for the Blues' market share, some of the original features of these "service benefit" plans had to be abandoned. More critically, in the most recent years, Blue Cross and Blue Shield have begun to sponsor HMOs, preferred provider plans, indemnity-type arrangements, and a range of other third party payment schemes; thus, the structural distinctions between insurers are becoming harder to characterize.

Notwithstanding, there are still essential differences between the "service-benefit" plans typically offered by the Blues and the more traditional indemnity-type insurance generally offered by commercial carriers. Under a "service-benefit" plan, the Blues contract with providers who agree to provide covered services to the plan's subscribers under specified terms of reimbursement. Subscribers are assured of the availability of the covered service and of the amount of their out of pocket liability. Subscribers are also offered the "freedom of choice," at least among those providers who have agreed to participate in the plan.

The major difference between indemnity insurance and a "service-benefit" plan has to do with the relationship between the insurer and the provider. The traditional indemnity policy merely reimburses the insured following an incurred liability; in its purest form, the patient pays the hospital or the physician, and the insurer reimburses the patient/insured according to prearranged reimbursement terms, terms that are independent of the provider's charges. The indemnity insurer has essentially no agreement or other relationship with the provider.

The indemnity insurance policy will often exclude routine services from coverage, limit reimbursement to a fixed cap, require the consumer to pay percentage (co-payments) or first dollar coverage (deductibles), and impose other limits on the range or depth of the policy's coverage. As noted above, most "service-benefit" plans also incorporate some of these conditions. Also as noted earlier, indemnity insurance policy premiums are generally based on risk experience, considering such factors as age, health status, etc., in determining premiums, particularly for individual policies.

As noted above, a small but rapidly growing share of the private health insurance market belongs to HMOs, other prepaid group practice plans, and employer or employee sponsored groups that act as self-insurers. Indeed, the proliferation of independent plans and self-insurers is at the heart of many of the important political and policy controversies that will be discussed in more detail in Chapter 8.

The larger and more established HMOs, such as the Kaiser-Permanente plans, represent a full integration of financing and service. The plan accepts premium payments from the subscriber and provides the services covered by the plan's policy through its own physicians, hospitals, and other providers. In the case of Kaiser, the parent corporation actually owns the facilities, and the subsidiary Permanente Group employs the physicians who provide the plan's medical services and staff its hospitals. Kaiser also allows its group physicians to share in the plan's profits. In other HMO arrangements, the insurer is more of a broker, contracting with physicians, hospitals, and other providers on a fee-for-service or capitated basis. In essence, consumers who enroll in HMOs are assured of the availability of services but only from the "closed panel" of providers that are part of or contracting with the plan; the subscriber's "freedom of choice," therefore, is necessarily curtailed. In addition, HMOs and similar arrangements typically rely more heavily on nonphysician providers, particularly in their clinics and other outpatient services, and generally utilize more peer review and other administrative controls over their providers. In return, most HMOs offer comprehensive coverage and minimal cost sharing liability. And while HMOs offering comprehensive coverage often are actually more expensive than traditional indemnity or "service-benefit" arrangements, some offer more inexpensive premiums than their traditional competitors.

One of the most significant differences inherent in this integration of financing with service delivery is the rearrangement of the financial incentives for the providers responsible for delivering the covered services. To the extent that the entity providing the service ultimately bears the risk for the resulting costs, that provider, unlike providers reimbursed on a fee-for-service basis by other third party payers (or paid directly by consumers) have, in theory, at least some incentive to minimize costs, use services more efficiently, and arguably, as the name implies, maintain the health of the enrolled consumer. On the other hand, critics of HMOs and similar arrangements argue that these same incentives may also discourage utilization of services by the plan's providers, even when those services are necessary.

Obviously HMOs and other independent plans have been a source of economic competition, as they offer alternatives to the more traditional forms of private health insurance that have historically dominated the private health insurance market. But HMOs also have been the source of controversy because they deviate so greatly from fee-for-service and "freedom of choice" reimbursement, and challenge other closely held values of traditional medicine. Indeed, in the 1940s and 1950s, Kaiser and other prepaid health plans were often accused of "socializing" medicine, a technically inaccurate characterization, but one reflecting the depth of the opposition to HMOs from organized medicine. And while HMOs became more accepted in the 1980s, some physicians continue to oppose HMOs on ideological grounds.

Some variations on the HMO model have been designed, in part, to be more acceptable to the traditional medical community. Thus, in a few areas of the country, medical care foundations have been developed under the sponsorship of local medical associations. Under these plans, the foundation contracts with the physicians in an area who agree to provide services to the foundation's subscribers; these physicians are typically reimbursed on a fee-for-service basis, much as they are under "service-benefit" arrangements, but they also share in the financial risk (for instance, they agree to take a discounted level of reimbursement if payouts exceed predicted levels). Physicians participating in a foundation-type arrangement also agree to periodic audits or reviews of their services, thus ceding some, but not all, of their autonomy.

Another alternative form of prepaid health plan that merges some of the characteristics of the "service-benefit" plan and the HMO is the preferred provider organization (PPO). In a PPO the insurer contracts with various physicians and other providers to provide covered services at a discounted or low rate, and subscribers are either required or encouraged to use these "preferred" providers: for instance, consumers get full reimbursement if they use preferred providers but reduced reimbursement if they use other providers.

A more recent variation on prepaid health insurance involves the "case management" concept. Under this arrangement, a "gatekeeper," usually a physician, contracts with the insurer on a fee-for-service or capitation basis to deliver medical services, to refer the insured to specialists or to hospitals. The insurer will pay only for referrals or institutional care ordered by the "gatekeeper." In some cases, the "gatekeeper" bears partial risk for the cost of referral services.

For a detailed description of alternative health insurance schemes, see Employee Benefit Research Institute, Fundamentals of Employee Benefit Programs (1987).

iii. The Economics of Insurance

Under the traditional economic view of insurance, health insurance, whether purchased from an indemnity insurer, a "service-benefit" plan, or an alternative arrangement, is basically an attempt by the consumer to spread the costs of health care evenly over time and to minimize the uncertain risk of high medical bills by pooling these with those of other consumers. As Fein points out, it is a view that relies heavily on a supply and demand model to describe and evaluate the behavior of consumers and insurers and assumes the primacy and appropriateness of market forces in determining who will buy what kind of insurance from whom.

While the economist's description of health insurance is used extensively and is a useful vehicle for understanding the whys and wherefores of health insurance — indeed it is almost impossible to discuss any aspect of health care financing without the convenient rhetoric of supply and demand, market and competition — it is important to note that the traditional economic analysis of private health insurance is as much normative as it is descriptive. That is to say, it is a statement of how consumers ought to behave, assuming they can and will respond to economic considerations. Whether such analysis describes what they actually do is a separate question. In fact, in the "real world" what people actually buy and who they buy it from are matters that are only partially determined by economic considerations. Among other things, as noted above, most people receive their health insurance as part of their employment benefits; to view this as consumers and suppliers bargaining in a competitive market place is at best only a rough approximation of the actual transaction.

The traditional economic analysis of private health insurance is also heavily skewed by its inherent ideology, and the political agenda that that ideology necessarily implies. For example, "free marketeers" assume that private health insurance is appropriately structured — "meets the standards of economic efficiency" — when each consumer is paying no more and no less than the expected cost of his or her future health needs. Under such conditions, each individual will engage in the "optimal, least cost-strategy of risk management." Feigenbaum, Risk Bearing in Health Care Finance, in Health Care and Its Costs 122-130 (C. Schramm ed. 1987). The result will be good for the individual and good for the economy. To do otherwise would require that some people spend money on health care that they would under proper economic conditions rather spend on other goods and services; others would be unjustly enriched — and have little incentive to avoid risks to health or to purchase medical care efficiently. Differentials in consumers' ability to pay are largely irrelevant to this view, except at the point where low income — or high medical bills — may justify some sort of collective subsidy. But even under these circumstances, subsidized insurance or other attempts by government to make insurance more equitable, for instance, prohibitions on discrimination, mandatory benefit laws, etc., have to be carefully, almost suspiciously, tailored, to achieve the traditional economists' primary objective of making individuals bear the costs of their own health needs.

As Fein demonstrates, even viewed through the glasses of an economist, these assumptions are not necessarily compelled. Fein's article, in fact, is clearly intended to parody much of the traditional economic view of health insurance, the assumptions that underlie that traditional view, and their implications for public policy. As Fein points out, the economist's market model of supply and demand only raises — not necessarily answers — important questions. Economists claim that making people pay more at the point of purchase of medical care may mean that they will buy less. Is that true? If so, is that what we want? People frequently buy more insurance than is actuarily sound; is that bad economics or merely a demonstration that economics alone cannot describe human behavior? Is economic efficiency so important that government subsidies and other attempts to achieve equity should be avoided?

Fein's answer to these questions (in a portion of his article omitted from our text) is both a critique of the traditional economic view of health insurance and a repudiation of the implied political agenda of his traditional counterparts:

> None of us lives in an economy. We live in a society. That society is something bigger than the economy, prices, balance of payments, and exchange rates. A society's goals and aspirations, the way it works, what it calls forth from us, the way we see ourselves and others, how we behave, all these are more than economics. Surely economic arrangements influence those matters, and that is just the point. Since economic arrangements do have an impact on the fabric of the society, we dare not evaluate those economic arrangements solely on the basis of their presumed *economic* benefits, on what they might do to investment or production. We must consider what impact they might have on the social fabric. Does it avail us to have a higher gross national product if the cost is hostility and alienation? Indeed, in the long run, can we have that higher GNP if each of us behaves as an island unto one's self?
>
> If the problem of equity is not addressed, we shall continue to ration health care services by price. The impersonal market, the interplay of prices and unequal incomes, will distribute resources as it distributes cars, phonograph records, books, and fine wine. Researchers may suggest that medical care is not as helpful as the public thinks, that it does not offer value for money, but both patients and physicians are unlikely to accept that argument. Those with low income and inadequate care, observing the behavior of those with money, will be more impressed by the behavior of the rich in seeking care than by the words of those who say the rich are wasting their money in doing so. They will conclude, and rightly so, that budget cuts and new constraints will not affect the provision of care and cure for the individual who can pay the price, but will affect *their* opportunities. They will conclude that the social benefit-cost criteria will apply to them but not to others. They will wonder why, if efficiency is really so desirable, it should not be sought everywhere, not solely in the publicly supported programs. They will wonder how a society can proclaim the right to

a decent existence and yet permit — in Arthur Okun's words — "dollars to transgress on rights." [Fein, supra, at 381-382.]

b. The Tax Treatment of Employer-Purchased Health Insurance

Whether or not it is consistent with sound economic principles, the public subsidy of private health insurance through tax exemption is virtually a political given. As described in the Introduction, the exclusion of employer-purchased health insurance from the computation of income and payroll taxes was adopted administratively during World War II and codified in the Internal Revenue Code in 1954. While it is not clear whether it was intended to be so at the time, this indirect subsidy of most (but not all) private health insurance has become an important element of federal health policy.

It has also become a major fiscal effort. As illustrated in the chart below, the federal "tax expenditure" or revenue loss attributable to the tax treatment of employer-purchased health insurance could be as much as $60 billion annually by 1993. The largest portion of this "tax expenditure" is the revenue lost from the exclusion of employer-purchased health insurance from gross income. If an employer makes a contribution towards the purchase of a health insurance policy for the employee or the employee's dependents, or establishes a self-insurance scheme to pay the employee's medical bills, these contributions, unlike wages and most other forms of employee compensation, are not subject to either federal income or payroll tax. See 26 U.S.C.§105(b), 106(a) (Supp. 1983-1987); 26 U.S.C. §§3101, 3102, 3121 (Supp. 1983-1987). Self-employed individuals, such as lawyers and other professionals, can achieve these same tax advantages through incorporation or through forming an employee-employer relationship with a client. See B. Bittker & J. Eustice, Federal Income Taxation of Corporations and Shareholders §2.06 (1987).

Additional tax expenditures result from the deductibility of some medical bills, including individual payments for health insurance premiums, in excess of 7.5 percent of gross income (5 percent before 1987), 26 U.S.C. §213 (1982 and Supp. 1983-1987).

Recent changes in the federal law also allow individual employees to shelter health insurance contributions and other out of pocket medical expenses through the use of "salary reductions" and "flexible spending arrangements." 26 U.S.C. §125 (1982 and Supp. 1983-1987).

Most states follow the federal law and therefore employer-purchased health insurance receives the same treatment for state income tax purposes, and, consequently, there is an additional public tax expenditure hidden in the loss of state revenues as well. For further discussion, see Congressional Budget Office, Tax Subsidies for Medical Care: Current Policies and Possible

TABLE 2
Federal Tax Expenditures for Health Care, Fiscal Years 1985, 1989, 1993

	1985	*1989*	*1993*
Exclusion of employer contribution for insurance premiums or medical care	$20.2 b.	$27.6 b.	$45.8 b.
Deductions for medical expenses	$ 3.2 b.	$ 2.5 b.	$ 9.8 b.
Payroll tax exclusions (Medicare contributions)	$ 4.8 b.	$ 6.5 b.	$ 9.8 b.

Source: House Committee on Ways and Means, 100th Cong., 2d Sess., Background Material and Data on Programs within the Jurisdiction of the Committee on Ways and Means (Comm. Print 1988)

Alternatives (1980); Ginsburg, Altering the Tax Treatment of Employment-Based Health Plans, 59 Milbank Mem. Fund. Q 224 (1982).

Some of the implications of the tax treatment of employer-purchased health insurance can be highlighted with an example:

Suppose the employee makes $36,000; as such, he will pay approximately 30% of gross income in federal income and payroll taxes. If his employer also contributes $1200 towards the purchase of a health insurance policy for the employee and his family, the employee pays no tax on the benefit. In essence, the employee receives the full $1200. In contrast, if the employer contributes $1200 in additional cash wages, the employee receives only $840 ($1200 – 30 percent of $1200). Conversely, if the employee purchases the health insurance policy out of net income, he must earn $1715 ($1200 = 70 percent of $1715) in order to receive the "after tax dollars" to buy the same benefits that the employer can purchase for him for $1200. Obviously both employer and employee gain by converting cash earnings into health care benefits. Note, however, that the effect of the subsidy is skewed by the employee's tax bracket. If the employee is in a lower tax bracket, for example 15 percent, there is still a financial gain to the employee if the employer purchases the health insurance, but it is greatly reduced.

Traditional economists are heavily critical of this subsidy, arguing principally that it immunizes the consumer from the real costs of health care and provides disincentive to efficient shopping for both insurance coverage and delivery of services. But even critics who accept the tax treatment of health insurance as a political given have made strong arguments against the present policy. As Alain Enthoven has argued, the current tax incentives are most favorable to those in higher income brackets, less favorable to those in lower brackets, and offer no help to those in the most need: the unemployed, those in marginal jobs, or the self-employed. Enthoven, Health Policy Mismatch, 4 Health Affairs 10-11 (Winter 1985). For a discussion of alternatives to the present policy, including proposals by Enthoven and others to radically restructure the tax subsidy of health insurance along "neo-conservative" lines, see Chapter 5.

c. Cost-Sharing and the Economics of Third Party Payment

As Fein points out, some traditional economists insist that substantial cost-sharing arrangements should be built into all third party payment schemes. According to the tenets of traditional economics, the purpose of cost-sharing is to offset the undesirable effect of third party payment. Simply put, if insulated from the "true costs" of medical care, people will utilize more services; cost-sharing mitigates that effect. Some economists even argue that without cost-sharing to make people share in the financial burden of their ill health, people will be more likely to smoke, gain weight, or engage in other unhealthy lifestyles, knowing that they will not have to pay the costs of their resulting medical problems. See Feigenbaum, Risk Bearing in Health Care Finance in Health Care and Its Costs 105 (C. Schramm ed. 1987).

While the theory that people will get sick if it doesn't cost anything seems a little far fetched, the former proposition — that people will utilize more medical care if they are insulated from the cost of that care by third party payment — has been fairly well documented in the literature. The real question, however, is not whether cost sharing works, that is, does it have a quanitative effect on utilization; obviously it does. The real question involves *how* it works; that is, what are the qualitative effects on utilization? The traditional economic view assumes that the net result of people shopping with their own dollars for health care will be the elimination of unnecessary or at least marginally necessary services, the efficient outcome produced by the competitive market to which the traditional economist aspires. Unfortunately, there is little evidence that this actually happens.

In the early 1980s, the Rand Corporation attempted to study the effect of various cost sharing arrangements on the use of outpatient medical services. Their conclusions indicated that the traditional economic view is simplistic if not wholly inaccurate.

> This monograph presents analyses . . . on the use of outpatient medical care for specific diagnoses. The HIE was a large-scale randomized controlled trial of alternative forms of health care financing that ran for 3 to 5 years . . . in six sites around the country. It enrolled more than 7,700 nonaged persons . . . in one of several experimental health insurance plans that differed either in the amount of cost-sharing borne by the families or in the organization through which they received their care. . . .
>
> Cost-sharing reduced outpatient medical use principally by deterring people from seeking any care at all. It did not decrease the intensity or "size" of an episode of care for a given diagnosis, measured by the number or amount of services provided per episode once people entered the medical care system. Physicians evidently did not adjust their practice patterns to their patients' insurance status. . . . We conclude that insurance that requires patients to share in the costs of their care will not necessarily change the *per-episode* use of outpatient

services but will importantly influence the number of episodes for which care is sought.

. . . We found no evidence that the imposition of cost-sharing led individuals to make appropriately selective decisions about the problems for which they will seek care.

Not all complaints and symptoms require medical attention, so cost-sharing does reduce ostensibly inappropriate use of ambulatory care. For some problems, such as a cold, medical care may bring little, if any, tangible benefit because self-care would be equally effective. This favorable outcome of cost-sharing comes at the price, however, of reductions in appropriate care; that is, it appears to invoke a considerable risk of foreclosing medical diagnosis and treatment for conditions in which such intervention can be expected to be effective and to benefit the patient. . . .

These risks of cost-sharing are not uniformly distributed across socioeconomic strata of the population. Almost always in these analyses, disadvantaged individuals had less use than more well-off persons. Cost-sharing appeared to exert its greatest impact on poor children. [Lohr et al.; Use of Medical Care in the Rand Health Insurance Experiment: Diagnosis- and Service-Specific Analyses in a Randomized Controlled Trial, 24 Med. Care Sl, S72-81 (Sept. 1986).]

In a similar analysis of the use of hospital care by participants in this study, the authors of the Rand study found that a considerable proportion of the inpatient care provided to the studied population was "inappropriate." In a randomized sample, 23 percent of the hospital admissions were inappropriate, while another 17 percent of the admissions could have been avoided by ambulatory surgery. There was considerable variation across geographic regions, but, curiously, areas with low rates of admission did not necessarily have low rates of inappropriate admissions. Most importantly, plans with cost sharing had about the same level of inappropriate admissions as plans that had less cost sharing. Thus, since cost sharing reduced hospital admissions, the authors concluded, as they had in the article excerpted above, that cost sharing reduces inappropriate use of services only at the price of reducing appropriate services as well. Siu et al., Inappropriate Use of Hospitals in A Randomized Trial of Health Insurance Plans, 315 N. Engl. J. Med. 1259 (1986).

It must be noted that in the first study, the Rand authors raised but did not answer a more complicated question: will a reduction in the use of care — whether appropriate or not — result in poorer health status for those who receive less care? In the outpatient study, the authors found negligible effects of cost sharing (and the consequent reduction in utilization) on general health indices (for instance, mortality rates) and only a few measurable disease-specific consequences. They did find, however, that those consequences that were found were predominately among the poor and low income children. The Rand authors were understandably surprised that they did not find more obvious health consequences from the reductions in appropriate medical care but were unwilling to conclude whether these results were valid or simply proof of the difficulty of measuring health outcomes from statistical data. For a discussion by the Rand authors, see Lohr at 80-81; for a similar study with somewhat different results, see Lurie et al., Termination of Medical Benefits: A Followup Study One Year Later, 314 N. Engl. J. Med. 1266 (1985) (study of impact of complete termination of Medicaid coverage found to have measurable impact on health status of the poor). For further discussion of the relationship between utilization and health outcome and the difficulty of measuring the quality of medical care, see Chapter 5.

2. PUBLIC REGULATION OF PRIVATE INSURANCE

Metropolitan Life Insurance v. Massachusetts

471 U.S. 724 (1985)

Justice BLACKMUN delivered the opinion of the Court.

A Massachusetts statute requires that specified minimum mental-health-care benefits be provided a Massachusetts resident who is insured under a general insurance policy, an accident or sickness insurance policy, or an employee health care plan that covers hospital and surgical expenses. The . . . question before us in these cases is whether the state statute, as applied to insurance policies purchased by employee health care plans regulated by the federal Employee Retirement Income Security Act of 1974, is preempted by that Act. . . .

General health insurance typically is sold as group insurance to an employer or other group. Group insurance presently is subject to extensive state regulation. . . . Mandated-benefit laws, that require an insurer to provide a certain kind of benefit to cover a specified illness or procedure whenever someone purchases a certain kind of insurance, are a subclass of such content regulation. . . .

The substantive terms of group-health insurance contracts . . . have been extensively regulated by the States. For example, the majority of States currently require that coverage for dependents continue beyond any contractually imposed age limitation when the dependent is incapable of self-sustaining employment because of mental or physical handicap; such statutes date back to the early 1960s. And over the last 15 years all 50 States have required that coverage of infants begin at birth, rather than at some time shortly after birth, as had been the prior practice in the unregulated market. . . .

Mandated-benefit statutes . . . are only one variety of a matrix of state laws that regulate the substantive content of health-insurance policies to further state health policy. . . . With respect to a Massachusetts resident, it requires any general health-insurance policy that provides hospital and surgical coverage, or any benefit plan that has such coverage, to provide as well a certain minimum of mental-health protection. In particular, §47B requires that a health-insurance policy provide 60 days of coverage for confinement in a mental hospital, coverage for confinement in a general hospital equal to that provided by the policy for nonmental illness, and certain minimum outpatient benefits.

Section 47B was designed to address problems encountered in treating mental illness in Massachusetts. The Commonwealth determined that its working people needed to be protected against the high cost of treatment for such illness. It also believed that, without insurance, mentally ill workers were often institutionalized in large state mental hospitals, and that mandatory insurance would lead to a higher incidence of more effective treatment in private community mental-health centers. . . .

In addition, the Commonwealth concluded that the voluntary insurance market was not adequately providing mental-health coverage. . . : good insurance risks were not purchasing coverage, and this drove up the price of coverage for those who otherwise might purchase mental-health insurance. The legislature believed that the public interest required that it correct the insurance market . . . by mandating minimum-coverage levels, effectively forcing the good-risk individuals to become part of the risk pool, and enabling insurers to price the insurance at an average market rather than a market retracted due to adverse selection. Section 47B, then, was intended to help safeguard the public against the high costs of . . . mental-health care, . . . shift the delivery of treatment from inpatient to outpatient services, and relieve the Commonwealth of some of the financial burden it otherwise would encounter. . . .

It is our task in these cases to decide whether such insurance regulation violates or is inconsistent with federal law.

The federal Employee Retirement Income Security Act of 1974, 88 Stat. 829, as amended, 29 U.S.C. §1001 et seq. (ERISA), comprehensively regulates employee pension and welfare plans. An employee welfare-benefit plan or welfare plan is defined as one which provides to employees "medical, surgical, or hospital care or benefits, or benefits in the event of sickness, accident, disability [or] death," whether these benefits are provided "through the purchase of insurance or otherwise." Plans may self-insure or they may purchase insurance for their participants. Plans that purchase insurance — so-called "insured plans" — are directly affected by state laws that regulate the insurance industry.

ERISA imposes upon pension plans a variety of substantive requirements relating to participation, funding, and vesting. It also establishes various uniform procedural standards concerning reporting, disclosure, and fiduciary responsibility for both pension and welfare plans. It does not regulate the substantive content of welfare-benefit plans.

. . . It does, however, contain a broad pre-emption provision declaring that the statute shall "supersede any and all State laws insofar as they may now or hereafter relate to any employee benefit plan.". . . Metropolitan . . . argues that ERISA preempts Massachusetts' mandated-benefit law insofar as §47B restricts the kinds of insurance policies that benefit plans may purchase.

While §514(a) of ERISA broadly preempts state laws that relate to an employee-benefit plan, that pre-emption is substantially qualified by an "insurance saving clause," §514(b)(2)(A), . . . which broadly states that, with one exception, nothing in ERISA "shall be construed to exempt or relieve any person from any law of any State which regulates insurance, banking, or securities." The specified exception to the saving clause is found in §514(b)(2)(B) . . . the so-called "deemer clause," which states that no employee-benefit plan, with certain exceptions not relevant here, "shall be deemed to be an insurance company or other insurer, bank, trust company, or investment company or to be engaged in the business of insurance or banking for purposes of any law of any State purporting to regulate insurance companies, insurance contracts, banks, trust companies, or investment companies." Massachusetts argues that its mandated-benefit law, as applied to insurance companies that sell insurance to benefit plans, is a "law which regulates insurance," and therefore is saved from the effect of the general preemption clause of ERISA. . . .

Section 47B clearly "relate[s] to" pension plans governed by ERISA so as to fall within the reach of ERISA's pre-emption provision, §514(a). . . .

Nonetheless . . . [t]he insurance saving clause preserves any state law "which regulates insurance, banking, or securities." [W]hile the general preemption clause broadly preempts state law, the saving clause appears broadly to preserve the States' lawmaking power over much of the same regulation. . . .

Fully aware of this statutory complexity, we still have no choice but to "begin with the language employed by Congress and the assumption that the ordinary meaning of that language accurately expresses the legislative purpose." We also must presume that Congress did not intend to preempt areas of traditional state regulation. . . .

To state the obvious, §47B regulates the terms of certain insurance contracts, and so seems to be saved from pre-emption by the saving clause as a law "which regulates insurance.". . .

The insurers nonetheless argue that §47B is in reality a health law that merely operates on insurance contracts to accomplish its end, and that it is not the kind of traditional insurance law intended to be saved by §514(b)(2)(A). We find this argument unpersuasive.

Initially, nothing in §514(b)(2)(A) . . . purports to distinguish between traditional and innovative insurance laws. The presumption is against preemption, and we are not inclined to read limitations into federal statutes in order to enlarge their pre-emptive scope. Further, there is no indication in the legislative history that Congress had such a distinction in mind. . . .

Moreover, it is both historically and conceptually inaccurate to assert that mandated-benefit laws are not traditional insurance laws. As we have indicated, state laws regulating the substantive terms of insurance contracts were commonplace well before the mid-70s, when Congress considered ERISA. . . .

Nothing in the legislative history of ERISA suggests a different result. There is no discussion in that history of the relationship between the general pre-emption clause and the saving clause, and indeed very little discussion of the saving clause at all. . . . There is a complete absence of evidence that Congress intended the narrow reading of the saving clause suggested by appellants here. . . .

We are aware that our decision results in a distinction between insured and uninsured plans, leaving the former open to indirect regulation while the latter are not. By so doing we merely give life to a distinction created by Congress in the "deemer clause," a distinction Congress is aware of and one it has chosen not to alter. We also are aware that appellants' construction of the statute would eliminate some of the disuniformities currently facing national plans that enter into local markets to purchase insurance. Such disuniformities, however, are the inevitable result of the congressional decision to "save" local insurance regulation. Arguments as to the wisdom of these policy choices must be directed at Congress.

NOTES: PUBLIC REGULATION OF PRIVATE HEALTH INSURANCE

State Regulation of Health Insurance

As the Court acknowledges in *Metropolitan Life,* there is a long and extensive tradition for state regulation of insurance generally, and health insurance in particular. As noted earlier, who are covered by private health insurance and what they receive are matters heavily dependent in this country on one's employment status; nonetheless, there are some significant public controls over those benefits.

Public control over the Blues has been substantial from their very inception. The Blues were created by special enabling legislation, allowing for their nonprofit structure, exempting them from many other state insurance law requirements, and essentially providing them with a publicly approved monopoly over "service-benefit" type health insurance. At the same time, the enabling legislation also imposed requirements relating to the benefits offered by these plans, the kind and nature of their relationship with providers, and the rates they can charge to subscribers. See discussion of reimbursement in Chapter III. Courts have had little trouble upholding the states' discretion to create or regulate the Blues, or to treat them preferentially or differently from other health insurers. Borland v. Bayonne Hospital, 72 N.J. 152, 369 A.2d 1 (1977); *cert. denied,* 434 U.S. 817 (1977); Godfrey v. Massachusetts Medical Service, 359 Mass. 610, 270 N.E.2d 804 (1971).

While the amount and kind of state control exercised over other health insurers has not been as extensive as the public control of the Blues, the states have also undertaken a variety of attempts to regulate the cost, adequacy, and quality of private health insurance. All states impose mandatory reserve and other financial requirements on health insurers. Most states have some sort of review or other regulatory authority over the rates charged for private health insurance. Some states also have exercised considerable authority over the reimbursement paid under these policies under hospital rate setting programs. See Chapter 3. There is also a variety of state laws relating to the sale and advertising of private health insurance, such as mandatory disclosure of benefits and exclusions.

As the Court points out in *Metropolitan Life,* in recent decades many states have also attempted to directly regulate the content of private health insurance policies. In addition to the examples cited by the Court, some states require insurers to allow people to convert from a group to an individual policy when the subscriber's employment ends. New York requires that hospital insurance benefits include benefits for normal vaginal delivery. (Prior industry practice had been to pay only for caesarian section.) States frequently mandate coverage of certain categories of providers, such as podiatrists, chiropractors or midwives, on the same terms as traditional practitioners. Similarly, other states mandate that private health insurance policies include coverage for drug rehabilitation, psychiatric services, hospice, or other categories of services traditionally omitted from private health insurance policies. Again, the courts have had little trouble upholding the authority of states to enact this type of legislation. Attorney General v. Travelers, Insurance Co., 391 Mass. 730, 463 N.E.2d 548 (1984), *aff'd,* 471 U.S. 724 (1985); Guardian Life Insurance Co. of America v. Insurance Commissioner of Maryland, 293 Md. 629, 446 A.2d 1140 (1982).

ERISA Preemption and State Regulation

As *Metropolitan Life* demonstrates, so long as a mandated benefit requirement or other state law intended to regulate or reform private health insurance is viewed as an "insurance law," such legislation will not have ERISA preemption problems. Other state regulatory or reform measures, however, may be invalidated by ERISA. One of the first and most comprehensive state health insurance programs was adopted in Hawaii in 1974, requiring all employers to provide a minimum package of health benefits to their employees. Hawaii Rev. Stat. §§393-1 to 393-53 (1985). Following the enactment of ERISA, the Hawaii legislation was held to be preempted by the federal legislation. Standard Oil v. Agsalud, 633 F.2d 760 (9th Cir. 1980), *aff'd,* 454 U.S. 801 (1981).

Subsequent to *Standard Oil,* Congress exempted Hawaii's legislation from the ERISA preemption, at least to the extent that "it governs matters" not addressed by ERISA. Pub. L. No. 97-473, §301(b), 96 Stat. 2605, 29 U.S.C. §1144 (b)(5)(c) (1982). The language of this exemption makes it clear that this is only a "grandfather" clause; the requirements of the Hawaii legislation may not be expanded beyond those that existed at the time ERISA was established. It is also apparent from a reading of the legislative history that Congress does not intend to encourage other states to follow Hawaii.

Presumably most forms of state legislation mandating benefits, requiring coverage of employees or dependents, or virtually any other regulatory measures directed towards the benefits offered employees would be similarly invalidated. See, for instance, St. Paul Electrical Workers Welfare Fund v. Markman, 490 F. Supp. 931 (D. Minn. 1980); but cf. Rebaldo v. Cuomo, 749 F.2d 133 (2d Cir. 1984), *cert. denied,* 472 U.S. 1008 (1985).

In the spring of 1988, Massachusetts enacted an ambitious state "universal health insurance for all" bill attempting, among other things, to avoid ERISA problems while still requiring most employers to purchase health insurance for their employees. "An Act to Make Health Security Available to All Citizens of the Commonwealth and to Improve Hospital Financing," 1988 Mass. Acts 23, codified as Mass. Gen. L. ch. 118 F, §9 (1988). First, the Massachusetts program expands Medicaid coverage (see discussion infra); second, it creates a new program to purchase health insurance for the uninsured, funded by a tax on employers; finally, payments by employers for employee health insurance will reduce or eliminate the employer's new tax obligation. Essentially, the state law attempts to coerce rather than directly require employers into purchasing health insurance. Whether this will survive a challenge under ERISA is not clear. For a discussion, see Sager, Making Universal Health Insurance Work in Massachusetts, 17 Law, Med., Health Care — (No. 3 1989). Note also that as of 1989, the revenue for this program had not been appropriated and the Massachusetts program requires further legislative approval before it is fully implemented.

One important result of the ERISA preemption of some forms of state regulation of health insurance has been the growth of self-insurance schemes by employers. Since the "savings" clause only rescues laws that regulate insurance from ERISA preemption, and the ERISA "deemer" clause prohibits states from treating self-insurers as "insurance plans," ERISA essentially preempts any state regulation of self-insured benefit plans. As noted earlier in this chapter, historically only a small portion of the private health insurance market was represented by self-insured or independent plans, but in recent years that market share has skyrocketed. While there are many reasons for doing so, avoiding state mandated benefit and other regulatory measures is clearly one important consideration. The resulting politics are significant:

any state measure to reform or regulate health insurance can only be applied to those employers who purchase health insurance through an insurer.

Federal Regulation of Private Insurance

Another result may be to shift the focus from state regulation to federal regulation. Historically, federal policy has built upon and reinforced the tradition of state responsibility for the regulation of health insurance. In 1944, the Supreme Court held that the sale of insurance was a "transaction in commerce" and therefore subject to federal antitrust jurisdiction. In response, Congress quickly enacted the McCarran-Ferguson Act of 1945 exempting insurance from the reach of the antitrust laws. Since that time, McCarran-Ferguson has provided broad protection for the state regulation of insurance. In 1957, the Supreme Court refused to allow federal courts to scrutinize whether state regulation was in fact sufficiently effective to justify exclusion of otherwise applicable federal law. Federal Trade Commission v. National Casualty Co., 357 U.S. 560 (1958).

In recent years, however, the principle that the states, not the federal government, are responsible for the regulation of health insurance has been challenged in two important ways. First, the Supreme Court has narrowed the interpretation of McCarran-Ferguson. See discussion infra Chapter VII. Second, the enactment of ERISA, while exempting state regulation of health insurance, obviously increases federal control (and limits state authority) over employer-purchased health insurance plans.

There are other possible extensions of federal authority in this area. From time to time, especially when unemployment is high, Congress has considered whether to require employers to provide some form of health insurance coverage as a supplement to the federally mandated unemployment benefits. In 1985, Congress required employers with 20 or more employees to offer health care continuation coverage (at the employee's expense) for up to 18 months for employees who quit or who have been laid off and for up to 36 months for widows, divorced spouses, and dependents of covered workers. 29 U.S.C. §§1161-1168 (Supp. 1983-1987). The Tax Reform Act of 1986 may also have the effect of expanding employer coverage by severely limiting an employer's discretion to discriminate between high level and lower level employees in providing health insurance coverage. Pub. L. No. 99-514, §§1111-1115, 100 Stat. 2089, 2435-2454 (1986).

More far-reaching proposals for federal involvement have been given considerable attention in recent years. In 1987, Congressman Waxman and Senator Kennedy proposed legislation to require all employers to provide minimum benefits to employees who work more than 17 hours a week. H.R. 2508, S.1265, 100th Cong., 1st Sess. (1987). In 1988, Congressman Stark offered legislation that would subject employers to a tax if they failed to provide employees with health benefits similar to those covered by Medicare. H.R. 4951, 100th Cong., 2d Sess. (1988).

A federal mandated benefits law would, of course, avoid ERISA problems; it would also make health insurance coverage more uniform from state to state. Some states have been discouraged from enacting mandatory benefit laws by the arguments that such legislation would create an "undesirable" business climate and that self-insurers can avoid any state requirements. On the other hand, any requirement imposed on employers, whether state or federal, will still be strenuously opposed by the business community, particularly small businesses, which are generally hit hardest by such legislation. Mandatory health benefits law also operate as a hidden tax — which has both advantages and disadvantages.

For a good discussion of the economic and political implications of both state and federal mandated benefits programs, see Employee Benefit Research Institute, Government Mandating of Employee Benefits (1987).

Private Insurance and Coverage of AIDS

Another problem that is certain to receive considerable attention in the next few years involves the difficulty faced by AIDS patients who may be excluded from private insurance coverage.

Representatives of the private insurance industry have argued that insurers have a right to engage in "fair discrimination" between people with AIDS and other insureds. Clifford & Inculano, AIDS and Insurance: The Rationale for AIDS-Related Testing, 100 Harv. L. Rev. 1806 (1987). Others have argued that the concerns of insurers are overstated and that attempts by insurers to identify those who have been infected will have a number of undesirable effects. See Schatz, The AIDS Insurance Crisis: Underwriting or Overreaching?, 100 Harv. L. Rev. 1782 (1987).

Currently, many insurers routinely refuse to issue individual policies to people with AIDS or AIDS-related diseases or to people who test positive for exposure. Others attempt to avoid writing policies for homosexual men or even for unmarried men between ages 25 and 40. Discrimination on the basis of sexual orientation has been prohibited in a few jurisdictions. Legislation in Washington, D.C., prohibits discrimination against those who have been infected with the virus (although not those diagnosed with the disease). See American Council of Life Insurance v. District of Columbia, 645 F. Supp. 84 (D.D.C. 1986). In many other jurisdictions, however, there may be no legal barrier.

Many AIDS patients have also argued that insurers under both group and individual plans have been unusually aggressive in applying pre-existing condition limitations to them. More concretely, many insurers claim that a positive antibody test obtained prior to the time that the insurance is issued constitutes a pre-existing condition. Some also have argued that seeking treatment for fatigue or malaise prior to the issuance of an insurance policy is a "pre-existing condition" and thus bars coverage for subsequently diagnosed AIDS. Problems also arise for AIDS patients when they are no longer able to work. Unless subject to federal or state conversion laws, many employers terminate the patient's health insurance benefits. For a review of these problems and possible responses, see Scherzer, Insurance and AIDS-Related Issues, in AIDS Practice Manual: A Legal and Educational Guide VIII-1 (National Gay Rights Advocates and the National Lawyers Guild AIDS Network, 2d ed. 1988).

3. ISSUES IN COVERAGE

Sarchett v. Blue Shield of California

43 Cal.3d 1, 729 P.2d 267, 233 Cal. Rptr. 76 (1987)

BROUSSARD, Justice.

In 1966, John Sarchett . . . elected to be insured under a group policy provided by Blue Shield. In January 1976, Sarchett was hospitalized for three days by his family physician, Dr. Bruce Van Vranken, who is a member physician of Blue Shield. Dr. Van Vranken testified that Sarchett . . . reported symptoms during January of fatigue, tremor, disorientation, painful swelling and distension of the stomach and back, changing bowel habits and peculiar stools. His blood test showed low hemoglobin and low white blood cell counts. . . . Dr. Van Vranken feared Sarchett might be suffering from a life-threatening bleeding duodenal ulcer or leukemia.

Blue Shield paid Sarchett's medical and diagnostic testing bills, but denied his claim for the hospital stay . . . based on two separate provisions of Sarchett's policy: (1) an exclusion for "[s]ervices when hospitalized primarily for diagnostic purposes or medical observation, rest or convalescent care". . . and (2) exclusion for services not "medically necessary." . . . Blue Shield contended that Dr. Van Vranken's orders for Sarchett's care in the hospital were inconsistent with a belief that Sarchett was seriously ill and hospitalized for medical treatment.

Plaintiff, Dr. Van Vranken, and the hospital utilization review committee protested the denial of coverage. . . .

. . . Only after six months of correspondence and repeated protests did Blue Shield first mention the possibility of peer review. . . . This belated offer to submit the dispute to peer review was made conditional upon the production of further "solid" information in support of Sarchett's claim. . . .

The trial court . . . found that Sarchett's policy failed to reserve for Blue Shield the right to review the "medical necessity" of a procedure ordered by his physician and not excluded from coverage by the contract. It found that Blue Shield had violated the covenant of good faith and fair dealing by "disagreeing with the judgment of the treating physician to hospitalize his patient solely on the basis of retrospective review of hospital files . . . where the subscriber [was] not clearly informed of this procedure in the health plan." . . .

The trial court found that the Blue Shield policy was ambiguous because it did not indicate who would determine when the diagnostic services or medical necessity exclusion barred coverage. Construing that ambiguity in favor of the member, it concluded that he should be able to rely on the judgment of his treating physician as to the purpose and necessity of hospitalization, and that Blue Shield could not question that judgment. Blue Shield contends that . . . its right to review claims is inherent in the insurance contract. Sarchett, on the other hand, maintains that only the addition of an explicit statement asserting the insurer's right of retrospective review would cure the ambiguity and . . . argues that regardless of policy language retrospective review should be banned as contrary to public policy.

We begin with the specific language of the policy. The diagnostic exclusion denies coverage for "[s]ervices when hospitalized primarily for diagnostic purposes or medical observation, rest or convalescent care." The "medical necessity" provision provides coverage "only for such services . . . as are reasonably intended, in the exercise of good medical practice, for the treatment of illness or injury." When the two provisions are read together, certain ambiguities appear. In some cases, for example, some diagnostic procedures may be so difficult or hazardous that hospitalization is medically necessary. In others a patient's medical condition may be so serious as to require hospitalization even though the physician is unable to treat that condition without diagnostic tests which ordinarily could be performed on an outpatient basis. . . .

At oral argument, however, counsel for Blue Shield explained that the diagnostic exclusion is intended as a subset of the implied exclusion for unnecessary medical treatment, and that the insurer would cover "medically necessary" hospitalization even if done for diagnostic purposes. Consequently, coverage for plaintiff's hospitalization does not turn on whether he was hospitalized for diagnosis, but simply on whether hospitalization was "medically necessary." . . .

Plaintiff's insurance coverage would therefore appear to depend upon three questions of fact: (1) whether Dr. Van Vranken ordered hospitalization with the intention of treating plaintiff's illness or injury, (2) whether the physician's intention was reasonable, and (3) whether that intention conforms to good medical practice. . . .

Plaintiff, however, seeks to eliminate even these factual questions, arguing that the policy is ambiguous as to who decides whether hospitalization is medically necessary. . . .

Upon review of the entire policy, however, we find no ambiguity in this respect. . . . Blue Shield has provided a separate provision . . . which applies to all disputes under the policy. That section first provides that "[a] dispute concerning the therapeutic justification for any services rendered to the member shall be resolved by the decision of the appropriate review committee of that medical society . . . for the geographical area in which such services were provided. . . ." It then states that "disputes with respect to the decisions of the medical society . . . shall be resolved . . . in accordance with the Rules of the American Arbitration Association."

[S]ince the policy itself provides unambiguously how disputes are to be resolved . . . there is no room for the argument that the policy contains an ambiguity which, construed in plaintiff's favor, would vest the final determination of medical necessity in the treating physician. . . .

Plaintiff argues, however, even if the policy is not ambiguous upon close reading, it should still be construed in light of the "reasonable expectation of the insured,". . . [who] would reasonably expect to be covered for hospitalization recommended by the treating physician. [W]e doubt that [this expectation] arises from any belief that Blue Shield will cover all treatment recommended by a physician, however unreasonable the recommendation. Instead, the subscriber expects coverage because he trusts that his physician has recommended a reasonable treatment consistent with good medical practice. Consequently we believe the subscriber's expectations can be best fulfilled not by giving his physician an unreviewable power to determine coverage, but by construing the policy language liberally, so that uncertainties about the reasonableness of treatment will be resolved in favor of coverage.

Finally, plaintiff argues that . . . the courts as a matter of public policy should bar insurers from refusing coverage for hospitalization ordered by the treating physician. He points to the dilemma faced by the subscriber when his doctor tells him that hospitalization is necessary. . . . If he follows the recommendation, he takes the risk that the insurer may later deny coverage, leaving the subscriber liable for a hospital bill he cannot afford. Yet if he does not follow the recommendation, he may be foregoing needed treatment. Faced with this dilemma, most subscribers would follow their doctor's recommendation and risk the denial of insurance coverage. Subscribers purchase insurance not only for financial advantage, but to obtain the peace of mind and sense of security that follows from assured payment and retrospective review frustrates those objectives.

There are, however, countervailing policy considerations. Sarchett had a choice between the Blue Shield plan, which offered him unlimited selection of physicians but provided for retrospective review, and alternative plans which would require him to choose from among a limited list of physicians but guaranteed payment. A holding that retrospective review is against public policy would narrow the range of choices available to the prospective subscriber, since it is unlikely that any insurer could permit the subscriber free selection of a physician if it were required to accept without question the physician's view of reasonable treatment and good medical practice. If the treating physician makes the final decision whether the treatment he prescribes is covered by the policy, inevitably a few will abuse that power by overutilization of medical procedures, imposing excessive costs on the insurer. . . .

The second ground for the trial court's finding of a violation of the good faith duty was that Blue Shield repeatedly denied Sarchett's claim for hospital benefits without advising him of his contractual right to impartial review and arbitration of the disputed claim. . . . Blue Shield's denial letter was couched in terms of finality. The short letter concluded: "*We are sorry that we cannot be of more help to the subscriber in this instance,* but point out that we must adhere closely to the terms of the subscriber agreement in order to keep dues at a reasonable level." (Italics added.) The italicized language could be read, in the absence of any mention of appeal procedures, as a statement that no further recourse may be had.

[A]fter six months of correspondence and repeated protests from Sarchett . . . , Blue Shield offered to submit the claim to peer review *only if* more "solid" information were provided, even though Sarchett claimed that all relevant information had already been furnished to Blue Shield. Blue Shield had no right to place any conditions on Sarchett's access to impartial review of his claim, since his policy provided unconditionally that "dispute[s] *shall* be resolved" by review and arbitration. Furthermore, Blue Shield never advised Sarchett himself of his review rights, but instead mentioned them to the utilization review committee of the hospital. . . . This offer did not disclose that peer review was a matter of right under Sarchett's contract. . . .

We appreciate the concern, voiced by the dissent, that it may appear inconsistent for us to hold that an arbitration clause is clear and conspicuous, and therefore binding on the subscriber, but that Blue Shield was in bad faith because it failed to call his attention to the clause. The problem, however, disappears when each holding is viewed in context. When a court is reviewing claims under an insurance policy, it must hold the insured bound by clear and conspicuous provisions in the policy even if evidence suggests that the insured did not read or understand them. Once it becomes clear to the insurer that its insured disputes its denial of coverage, however, the duty of good faith does not permit the insurer passively to assume that its insured is aware of his rights under the policy. The insurer must instead take affirmative steps to make sure that the insured is informed of his remedial rights.

. . . Blue Shield had reason to know that Sarchett was uninformed of his rights, since he repeatedly protested the denial without demanding review by an impartial panel of physicians. Blue Shield nevertheless denied Sarchett's claim several times without mentioning his right to review by anyone other than the single hired consultant who initially and repeatedly denied the claim. This course of conduct appears designed to mislead subscribers into forfeiting their contractual right to impartial review and arbitration of disputed claims, and therefore we must affirm the trial court's ruling on this issue. . . .

MOSK, J., dissenting

. . . In my view, the policy is ambiguous because . . . it does not state that Blue Shield had the right, on the basis of a retrospective review, to disagree with the judgment of the treating physician to hospitalize Sarchett.

The majority admit that the diagnostic exclusion is ambiguous when read in the light of the medical necessity exclusion. However, because of an explanation offered by Blue Shield at oral argument, the majority fail to apply the usual rule of interpreting ambiguous language in favor of the insured. But the question of ambiguity cannot be determined from the 11th-hour concession of an insurer before this court as to the meaning of the policy. It must be decided from the terms of the policy itself. . . .

Nor do I agree with the majority's second reason for finding that the "medical necessity" exclusion is unambiguous. They conclude because the policy contains a provision that disputes relating to the "therapeutic justification" for services are to be resolved by a review committee, a subscriber is unambiguously notified that Blue Shield may second-guess the subscriber's physician on the issue of medical necessity.

. . . The burden is on the insurer to "phrase exceptions and exclusions in clear and unmistakable language" and to "draft its policy to avoid any misinterpretation by the average layman.". . .

The provision relating to resolution of disputes does not meet the foregoing standard. It does not state that Blue Shield reserves the right to second-guess the judgment of the subscriber's doctor as to medical necessity. At most, it allows the subscriber, if he ponders the subject at length, to draw an inference that because there exists a right to review of disputes concerning "therapeutic justification" for services, Blue Shield may challenge the judgment of his doctor. [T]he provision relied on by the majority does not even appear on the same page in the subscriber's brochure as the "medical necessity" exclusion. Thus I do not see how it can be said that the power which Blue Shield seeks to exercise is set forth in language clear and unmistakable to the average layman.

In addition, there is a significant incompatibility between the conclusions reached by the majority in Part I and Part II of the opinion. Part I holds that the provision relating to resolution of disputes unambiguously states that Blue Shield reserved the right to second-guess the judgment of Sarchett's doctor. . . . In Part II the majority decide that Blue Shield was guilty of bad faith because it must have known that Sarchett was ignorant of that procedure and Blue Shield violated its duty to bring it to his attention. Nevertheless, they conclude the existence of the provision in the policy precludes Sarchett from successfully challenging Blue Shield's failure to reserve the right to determine after the fact whether his hospitalization was medically necessary. My colleagues fail to explain how a policy provision of which Sarchett had neither actual nor constructive notice can serve as the basis for its holding in Part I.

Finally, I am unable to concur in the determination . . . that Sarchett did not have a reasonable expectation of coverage. The opinion states a subscriber could not reasonably expect that Blue Shield would cover all treatment recommended by his physician "however unreasonable the recommendation." A subscriber, unless he is knowledgeable in medical science, is unable to assess the reasonableness of his physician's recommendation for hospitalization. Since in this sense he is controlled by the opinion of his doctor, it is not unreasonable for him to expect that his insurer would likewise be bound by his doctor's judgment . . . absent clear notification to the contrary.

The failure of Blue Shield to make clear its claimed right to decide after-the-fact that hospitalization was not a medical necessity deprives a subscriber of his opportunity to make a meaningful selection between various available types of health plans. If the policy and the brochure had made it known to Sarchett that Blue Shield claimed this right, he could have made a meaningful choice between the plan offered by Blue Shield and one with a limited choice of physicians but guaranteed payment.

BIRD, C.J., and REYNOSO, J., concur.

NOTES: *SARCHETT* AND RELATED CASES

Legal Principles Regulating "Medically Necessary" Exclusions

Insurers often deny coverage for services, claiming that they are "medically unnecessary." Indeed, the "medically necessary" requirement written into virtually all health insurance policies is a frequently overlooked but important limitation on the liability of the insurer and on the depth of the coverage extended to the subscriber.

In the *Van Vactor* decision, discussed in *Sarchett,* the Illinois appellate court essentially held that since nothing in the policy explicitly allowed the insurer or anyone other than the subscriber's physician to make judgments about the necessity of the rendered care, the insurer was prohibited from claiming that the policy implicitly allowed the insurer to disagree with the physician's judgment. In the court's view, this was a proper application of the insurance law principle that ambiguous provisions or equivocal expressions whereby an insurer seeks to limit liability are to be strongly construed in favor of the insured. Van Vactor v. Blue Cross Association, 50 Ill. App. 3d 709, 717, 365 N.E.2d 638, 645 (1977).

In Siegal v. Health Care Service Corp., 81 Ill. App. 3d 784, 401 N.E.2d 1037 (1980), that same court indicated that it still approved of the *Van Vactor* ruling in situations where it perceives an ambiguity in the language of the policy, but held that where there is no ambiguity, the question of "medically necessary" becomes one of objective fact to be decided by a jury. This latter interpretation, as the court in *Sarchett* indicated, appears to be the majority interpretation of "medically neccessary" provisions. And, in any event, insurers can always avoid the *Van Vactor*-type logic by properly wording their policies.

There is also the possibility, rejected in *Sarchett,* that retroactive denial of liability based on a "medically necessary" requirement may be voided on public policy grounds. See, for instance, Weissman v. Blue Cross of Western New

York, 116 misc. 2d 1063, 457 N.Y.S.2d 392 (Sup. Ct. 1982), *rev'd*, 126 Misc. 2d 341, 482 N.Y.S.2d 659 (Co. Ct. 1984).

It is also possible that these disputes will be governed not by contract or tort principles but by state insurance legislation. As described supra, health insurance policies are heavily regulated. The enabling legislation for the Blues, and for the HMOs and other integrated plans, and to a lesser extent other health insurance regulatory schemes, often include provisions regulating the scope and terms of coverage. HMO enabling statutes, for example, frequently include a "hold harmless" clause, requiring the HMO to indemnify their subscribers for the costs of services purchased outside of the plan under appropriate circumstances. Other states regulate the remedies available to all private health insurance subscribers in disputes with their insurers, for example by attaching statutory penalties for late or withheld payments. See Lopez v. Blue Cross of Louisiana, 397 So. 2d 1343 (La. 1981).

Practical Difficulties with Subscriber Remedies

The most obvious inequity created by "medically necessary" requirements is demonstrated in *Sarchett*. The patient-subscriber is told that, in the opinion of his physician, he needs to be hospitalized or treated. Only later is he told that, in the opinion of his insurer, the service was "unnecessary" and that, therefore, he must pay for the service out of pocket. Not only does the insurer have a great deal of discretion over its own financial liability, but that discretion is exercised only after the financial liability of the subscriber has already been incurred, and incurred under circumstances where the patient-subscriber is hardly in the position to challenge the judgment of the provider.

As the *Sarchett* court points out, there are some ways to avoid at least the element of retroactivity. Many insurance policies require either a second opinion from another physician or approval of the service from the insurer prior to the service. See discussion of peer review in Chapter V infra. While this limits the autonomy and convenience of the subscriber, it does eliminate prospectively some potential controversies. The risk of retroactive denial is also avoided if the patient subscribes to an HMO or other health insurance plan where the insurer both delivers and finances the services. Indeed, the court in *Sarchett* points out that the plaintiff had the option of enrolling in an HMO. Note, however, that under HMO arrangements, there are still risks of inequity. In the event that the insurer/HMO refuses to recognize the medical necessity for a particular service, it then leaves the subscriber with both the risk of substantial out of pocket liability and the need to find another provider outside of the plan to provide the service. Presumably, under such circumstances, courts may apply the reasoning of *Sarchett* or *Siegal*, or the dictates of a "hold harmless" clause, and hold the HMO liable to the subscriber for failing to provide services under the terms of their agreement. For a discussion of these possible theories and their problems, see Stern, Bad Faith Suits: Are they Applicable to Health Maintenance Organizations?, 85 W. Va. L. Rev. 911 (1983).

The more subtle inequity has to do with the practical constraints on pursuing remedies against insurers. As virtually all observers agree, disputes are frequent between subscribers and insurers over the medical necessity of provided services and over other conditions on liability. Yet there are few litigated disputes and surprisingly few appellate decisions. Some industry experts claim that this is because disputes over coverage are either negotiated informally or handled through formal arbitration. As illustrated by *Sarchett,* many health insurance policies explicitly require arbitration of these and most other disputes over coverage or eligibility. But it is also apparent that the size of the claim and the nature of the available remedy are also controlling factors. To the extent that the claim is based solely on a contract theory, the judgment is likely to be only for the amount of the disputed claim, an amount that may not justify the time and expense of litigation. It is only in cases such as *Sarchett* where the plaintiff can claim a tort action and, possibly, punitive damages that the pursuit of a judicial remedy may be practical.

ERISA Implications

A recent decision by the Supreme Court has apparently limited the applicability of *Sarchett* and related decisions, at least as applied to employer purchased health insurance policies. In Pilot Life Insurance Co. v. Dedeaux, 481 U.S. 41 (1987), the insurer refused to make payments on an employer-purchased disability benefits policy. The employee sued alleging bad faith breach of contract and other state tort and contract remedies. The court of appeals upheld the validity of the action based on their reading of *Metropolitan Life*. The Supreme Court reversed, holding that the state common law principles applied by the lower courts were laws that "relate to any employee benefit plan" and were, therefore, preempted by the federal ERISA legislation. Further, the Court held, the state common law actions were not saved as laws that "regulate insurance":

> Certainly a common sense understanding of the phrase "regulates insurance" does not support the argument that the Mississippi law of bad faith falls under the saving clause. A common sense view of the word "regulates" would lead to the conclusion that in order to regulate insurance, a law must not just have an impact on the insurance industry, but must be specifically directed towards that industry. Even though the Mississippi Supreme Court has identified its law of bad faith with the insurance industry, the roots of this law are firmly planted in the general principles of Mississippi tort and contract law. Any breach of contract, and not merely breach of an insurance contract, may lead to liability for punitive damages. . . . [481 U.S. at 49.]

Thus claimants under employer-purchased health insurance schemes can only pursue the remedies available under ERISA and not the more favorable remedies available under some state common law principles. Presumably, a state cause of action created by a statutory scheme might still survive the ERISA exemption. Likewise, in a dispute involving an individually purchased health insurance policy — as opposed to an employment-based policy — claimants can still pursue the remedies available under state contract or tort law. But in the vast majority of cases, it would appear that employees are limited to the remedies provided by ERISA and may not proceed under state common law.

The distinction here is more than technical. Under the terms of ERISA, the employee must exhaust all available administrative remedies before filing a judicial suit; ERISA claimants are not entitled to a jury trial; the court hearing an ERISA claim is limited in its review to deciding whether the plan acted arbitrarily or capriciously; perhaps most importantly, the ERISA claimant is not entitled to noncontractual or punitive damages. The employer may be liable for civil penalties of $100 a day for delay in payment, but delay in payment does not create a cause of action for the claimant. See 29 U.S.C. §§1109, 1133 (1982); 29 U.S.C. §1132 (1982 and Supp. 1983-1987).

4. OUT-OF-POCKET-PAYERS AND THE "UNINSURED"

a. Who Pays Out-Of-Pocket?

While private insurance pays for approximately 30 percent of national health expenditures, an equal amount represents direct or out of pocket expenditures by the individual consumer. Taken in the aggregate, the relative share of personal health care expenditures paid directly by consumers had been steadily and dramatically *decreasing* until the mid 1980s. In 1965, just prior to the enactment of Medicare and Medicaid, consumers were paying over one-half of the costs of their health care. By 1975, that share had dropped to less than a third, and by the early 1980s to just over 25 percent. In the 1980s, that share appears to have stabilized. Nonetheless, insurance experts predict that with the increased reliance on cost sharing and other mechanisms that shift costs from third party payers to consumers and with the growing size of the uninsured and the "underinsured" populations, that share can only increase in the years to come.

While out of pocket spending represented nearly $500 per person in 1987, it is important to note that these costs were unevenly distributed across the population. Many people pay a relatively modest amount through cost sharing incident to insurance covered services or for those services that are not covered by their insurance policies, such as outpatient visits, eye or dental care. And, of course, in any given year, some people incur no direct medical expenses at all. On the other hand, some people incur extraordinary or catastrophic expenses. One study (using 1980 data) estimated that over two-thirds of all families spend less than 3 percent of their income for out of pocket medical expenses in any given year, with at least one half spending less than 2 percent. That same study estimated that 10 percent of all families had out of pocket expenses in excess of 10 percent of their incomes, and over 4 percent had direct payment in excess of 20 percent. A small, but not insignificant number of families, however, had direct costs that ran into hundreds of thousands of dollars.

Who are the people who must bear this burden? The fact that so little is known about these consumers is itself a political commentary. As discussed in Chapter I, the "uninsured" include people who are insured only part of the year, as well as those who have no insurance at all; and while they include the unemployed, many are people who work part time or in low paying jobs or are dependents of such workers. Others have only partial or inadequate insurance, the "underinsured." Medicaid and Medicare are important programs, but, as will be detailed in the next section, they cover only a fraction of the poor and the "uninsured." And even people who have some form of public or private third party coverage are not insulated from the possible and growing risk of high or even catastrophic health expenses, and for those who are "uninsured," even a single illness can mean facing the choice between financial ruin or foregoing health care. As Robert Blendon of the Robert Wood Johnson Foundation has put it, our current economic and political circumstances may be creating a new class of Americans, "the medically homeless." Blendon, Health Policy Choices for the 1990s, Issues in Science and Technology, Summer 1986, at 65-73.

b. Recent State Efforts to Finance Health Care for the "Uninsured."

Many state policymakers have been searching, albeit somewhat unsuccessfully, for appropriate remedial responses to this problem. Some of the difficulties that they face in this search are best demonstrated by the experience of those states that have experimented with health insurance "risk pools."

In 1986, six states (Connecticut, Florida, Indiana, Minnesota, North Dakota, and Wisconsin) were providing some type of private health insurance for the otherwise uninsured through "risk pooling" arrangements. A number of other states were in the process of instituting similar programs. Although the details of these programs vary from state to state, the basic scheme is to guarantee the availability of a health insurance policy to anyone who is willing to purchase a policy, regardless of health status or other characteristics, by requiring private health insurance companies to form an organization that offers private insurance to people who cannot buy it from individual insurers. (Proposed federal legislation would amend ERISA to allow states to mandate that self-insurers also participate in the pool.) The policies available under this pooling arrangement must meet state guidelines relating to benefits, premiums, deductibles, etc. In some states, anyone can buy insurance from the pool. In other states, subscribers must first be rejected by other private insurers. All states have some form of prior condition exclusion or mandatory waiting period, apparently to discourage people from "gaming" the system and subscribing only after they need health care.

Risk pool coverage is generally very broad, but states allow a range of deductibles and other cost sharing obligations to be imposed on the subscriber. Out of pocket liability for subscribers to the pool can be as high as several thousand dollars in some states. Premiums vary and can also be very expensive. But most states cap the highest premium at some fixed percentage (such as 150 percent) of the actual cost of such a policy if it were purchased from an individual private insurer.

For this and other reasons, all "risk pools" operate at a net loss. With broad coverage and a maximum cap on the premium, the premiums cannot be expected to pay the full cost of the services purchased under these policies. Most states finance the loss by assessing the members of the insurance pool according to their proportionate share of the state health insurance market. (Although, as discussed supra, self-insurers are exempt under ERISA.) In some states these assessments are in turn subsidized through tax rebates on state tax liability. Other states simply fund the pool's loss directly out of state revenues.

The obvious advantage of a "risk pool" is the political appeal of a program for the "uninsured" that relies heavily on the existing private health insurance mechanisms and has only a limited governmental role. The obvious problem, however, is that such programs are either very expensive, and consequently lose some of their political appeal, or they benefit only a very small group of people. Some people can afford to pay all or nearly all of the actuarial cost of their health insurance, but because they are high risks, insurers are still reluctant to sell them individual policies; unless they can obtain health insurance through their employment, private health insurance simply is not available to them. Forcing private insurers to accept a proportionate share of these bad risks — and perhaps bear a small loss on these policies — may be a reasonable and politically acceptable solution to the problem. But the actual cost of insurance for most of the people who would benefit from a risk pool is much greater than the premiums that they can afford to pay. For the largest segment of the "uninsured," health insurance is not just unavailable, it is also unaffordable. Thus the greater the portion of the "uninsured" that is potentially affected by a risk pooling arrangement, the more revenue will be needed to finance the pool — either from an assessment on the insurers or directly from public coffers.

Not surprisingly, thus far, most states have preferred the course of least resistance, maintaining programs that help only a very few people at a modest cost. For a further discussion of "risk pool" arrangements, their problems, and their performance, see Bovbjerg & Koller, State Health Insurance Pools: Current Performance, Future Prospects, 23 Inquiry 111 (1986).

Only a few states have experimented with catastrophic health insurance programs, that is, making the state the payer of last resort for those people with very high medical bills. These programs have encountered the same dilemma as "risk pools": either the program helps only a small number of people or it becomes extremely expensive. For discussion see Perkins, Dallek, Dowell & Waxman, State-Financing of Indigent Health Care: Promise and Problems, 20 Clearinghouse Rev. 372 (1986). Similar constraints have played a significant role in the deliberations over federal catastrophic insurance: see discussion infra.

A few states have considered mandating that employers offer health insurance to their employees, a requirement that could have far reaching impact on the surprisingly large number of people who are "uninsured" but employed; however, such programs face ERISA problems. See discussion of Hawaii and Massachusetts supra. Another potentially effective way to finance the care for the "underinsured" involves the attempts in some states to fund "uncompensated care" by adjustments in hospital rate setting mechanisms; for a full discussion, see Chapter 3. Another obvious option available to states to finance care for the "underinsured" involves expanding the state's Medicaid program. Medicaid will be discussed in great length in the next section of this chapter.

Recent legislation in the State of Washington may provide the foundation for the most innovative — and also the most costly — state effort thus far. Starting in January 1989, the state will pay up to 90 percent of the cost of health insurance for families (in two selected counties) whose income is less than double the federal poverty standard ($23,000 a year). Thirty thousand people, about 4 percent of the state's "uninsured," will be covered for the first five years of the program, nearly half of whom will be under the age of 25. Without this subsidy, health insurance premiums would average $250 per month; with the program premiums for the covered families will vary between $7.50 and $38 per month, depending upon family size and income. Participating families can buy traditional insurance or buy into HMOs.

The problem of financing health care for the "uninsured," as these notes reflect, raises complicated problems for state policymakers. As the next part of this chapter will make clear, beginning with the enactment of Medicaid and Medicare, the federal government's role in financing health care is extensive, and considerable attention in the last two decades has been given to an expansion of these programs, and, on occasion, to broader programs of nationalized public insurance. Recent political trends have made a broadening of the federal role less likely; in fact, the growing number of the "uninsured" can be attributed in some part to the cutbacks in these federal programs. As a consequence, the states have been more active in attempting to find ways to increase access for the "uninsured" to private insurance and to find other options for financing their health care that essentially concede that the federal programs will not be significantly expanded. Nonetheless, federal policymakers have made some efforts to expand the availability of private health insurance; much like the state efforts, these initiatives have been rather piecemeal, and at best have affected only a small number of people. See, for instance, discussion of COBRA amendments pp. 99-104 supra.

c. Programs to Finance "Uncompensated Care"

Another aspect of the problem of the "uninsured" that is currently receiving considerable political attention involves the financial stress created for those providers who choose (or are required by law) to provide services to those who do not have private insurance or other sources of third party payment. Indeed, the frequency with which the plight of the "uninsured" is referred to as the problem of "uncompensated care" reflects the political power of provider interests to draw attention to that aspect of the problem that has the most direct impact on their financial security.

The dimensions of "uncompensated care," meaning the actual costs of services provided to people for whom the provider receives no reimbursement, are difficult to assess. Some providers insist that any difference between their expenses and their revenues should be regarded as "uncompensated care." Others insist that the difference between their charges and the reimbursement they receive from third party payers should be included. Obviously for some purposes providers have incentives to exaggerate the amount of "uncompensated care;" in other situations they want to downplay any suggestion that they are not efficient or profitable. Thus any attempt to provide assistance to these providers is immediately complicated by the difficulty of determining which costs should be subsidized and of ensuring that the assistance actually translates into care for the targeted population.

Some experts believe that the amount of services delivered by providers to people who do not pay, at least in an institutional setting, is surprisingly small; they argue that the problem of "uncompensated care" is more with the *distribution* of "uncompensated care" between providers rather than the absolute *amount*. A study in 1982 found that of $6.2 billion in "uncompensated care" reported by hospitals, $4.5 billion were costs associated with bad debts, patients who were billed but did not pay, and only $1.7 billion was for "charity" care patients, patients for whom no payments were expected. (Presumably some small portion of the bad debt could be attributed to people who did not pay for other than financial reasons.) This $6.2 billion represented less than 6 percent of the total hospital revenues, a figure not all that dissimilar from the bad debt of other businesses. But some hospitals, particularly publicly sponsored hospitals and some (but not all) teaching hospitals, were bearing a disproportionate and growing share of this burden. On the average, public hospitals were providing three times the amount of "uncompensated care" as other hospitals. Obviously some public hospitals were bearing even greater shares of this amount. Given that the number of "uninsured" people is increasing, the number of those people who will go to public hospitals is also certain to increase as well. At the same time, many private hospitals are taking steps to reduce the amount of "uncompensated care" they provide. Thus the disproportionate burden of "uncompensated care" is almost certain to become an even more serious problem, even if the aggregate level of "uncompensated care" is not regarded as problematic. For a more detailed discussion of these findings and their implications, see Wilensky, Solving Uncompensated Hospital Care: Targeting the Indigent and the Uninsured, 3 Health Affairs 50 (Winter 1984).

Another study found that hospitals that are heavily involved with providing services to the "uninsured" were predominately urban public teaching hospitals; it also found that they were twice as likely to be financially stressed and less likely to have the capacity to generate financial surplus through private patient care. Feder, Hadley, & Mullner, Poor People and Poor Hospitals: Implications for Public Policy, 9 J. Health Polit. Policy Law 237 (1984). This study is particularly interesting since it also found that the costs of "poor hospitals" were on the average 30 percent higher than those of other hospitals, a finding that the authors claim was not due to their low occupancy rates, their patterns of utilizing services, or other problems of inefficiency at the "poor hospitals" (as some critics frequently assume). According to this study, the high costs of "poor hospitals" are due to such factors as the location of these hospitals in urban (and more expensive) environments, the more complicated case-mix inherent in the provision of care to a poor population, and the greater needs for staff and physicians incident to the research and teaching activities in these institutions.

d. Human and Health Impact on the Uninsured

While the costs of the care for the "uninsured" may be responsible for creating the financial stress of some providers, those same costs may be having an equally important if somewhat less visible impact on the "uninsured." Nationwide, it has been estimated that people without insurance are only two-thirds as likely to use physicians' services and almost half as likely to use hospital services as those with private or public insurance. Attempts to explain this by differences in health status between the insured and the "uninsured" have been unsuccessful. Government estimates indicate that the sick among the poor without insurance use no more than half the medical care of full year Medicaid recipients who have comparable levels of illness and other demographic characteristics. While these estimates are somewhat rough cuts — again data on people who pay out of pocket are very sparse — no one disputes the fact that a significant number of people are either delaying or forgoing medical care because of a lack of financial resources. See also data on Cost-Sharing and Third Party Payment pp. 142-144 supra. This only highlights the irony of defining the problem of the "underinsured" in terms of "uncompensated care." The cost of the problem is reflected both by the dollars spent and those *not* spent, the latter measurable only by the death, disability, and discomfort of those who find that medical care is financially inaccessible.

This human cost is most often recounted anecdotally. "Horror stories" of treatment denied, patient dumping, medical bankruptcy, etc. are all too frequent. But there are also some statistical indicators of the growing human cost of those who cannot pay for their health care. Maternal and child health experts are now documenting a slowdown in the historic decline in overall infant mortality in this country, a nationwide *rise* in the postneonatal mortality rate (deaths in the first year of life), and increases in both the percentages of low birth weight babies and the number of women who have late or no prenatal care. While these trends have many causes, the principal reason, they assert, is that many pregnant women lack the financial resources for prenatal care. D. Hughes, K. Johnson, J. Simons & S. Rosenbaum, Maternal and Child Health Data Book: The Health of America's Children (Children's Defense Fund 1986).

C. Public Third Party Payers

The role of the government in financing health care has changed dramatically in the last two decades. In 1965, local, state, and federal government programs combined spent only $11 billion for health care, 26 percent of total NHEs. A good portion of this represented state and local public hospitals and other programs for the poor. See discussion of government programs in the introductory chapter. Only two years later, following the implementation of Medicaid and Medicare, total government spending for health had jumped to $19 billion and had grown to nearly 37 percent of all health expenditures. Between 1968 and 1980, government spending continued to grow rapidly, increasing at an average annual rate of over 14 percent and bringing with it increased government involvement in virtually every aspect of health care delivery. By 1980, the government was spending over $100 billion a year for health care, 42 percent of all health spending and over 50 percent of all hospital care.

All told, this growth exceeded the rate of the growth of NHEs by a significant margin and exceeded the growth of the GNP during this period by nearly 50 percent. Most of the accelerated growth was between 1965 and 1975 and can be attributed to the implementation of Medicaid and Medicare. In fact, virtually all of the increase in the government's role in providing health care since 1965 has been a result of an increase in federal spending. The state and local share has actually declined from 13 percent to 10 percent of all health spending from 1967 to 1983. Moreover, most of the rapid growth came in the first ten years of Medicaid and Medicare.

The government's proportionate share of all health spending essentially stabilized between 1975 and 1983, and in the most recent years the rate of growth of both state and federal spending has been slightly slower than that of NHEs. On the other hand, the ability — and willingness — of both state and federal government to continue to commit resources to these programs has been a matter of considerable controversy during the past decade, and government health spending, even as it has moderated in its rate of growth, has become an increasingly visible target for policymakers concerned with limited revenues bases and growing deficits.

Thus, by the mid-1980s, Medicaid and Medicare, financing health care for one out of five Americans and representing three-quarters of all public spending for health care, have become both the primary vehicles for government health care policy and a source of continuing controversy over their adequacy, impact, and cost.

1. THE MEDICAID PROGRAM

a. An Introduction to Medicaid

The original Medicaid program was a creature of peculiar origins. It evolved somewhat unexpectedly from the political debates over the enactment of the Medicare program and was predesigned in large part by the patchwork of state and federal social welfare programs spawned by the New Deal and its Great Society progeny. As originally conceived, it was principally a state-administered, federally funded medical care reimbursement program, financing benefits to the four categories of federal welfare recipients and, at the option of each state, to other indigent people. Nonetheless, it offered the potential for a nationwide catastrophic health insurance program — an opportunity for the nation's poor to participate in the mainstream of American medicine. For an earlier discussion of these issues, see Wing, The Impact of Reagan-Era Politics on the Federal Medicaid Program, 33 Cath. U.L. Rev. 1 (1984).

In implementation, however, Medicaid has been far less. Even under the most ambitious state programs, Medicaid has offered medical benefits to only a fraction of the people who live below the poverty line, and its benefits have been distributed in a pattern that is neither wholly rational nor fully understood.

Medicaid, like any medical care financing scheme, is inherently complicated. The morass of service coverage and exceptions, the limitations on reimbursement, and the terms and conditions of eligibility virtually defy thorough understanding. In effect, Medicaid is not one, but a series of programs, differing from state to state (and sometimes within a state) and further complicated by the several tiers of governmental responsibilities for its financing and administration.

The minimum requirements for each state's program are outlined in the

FIGURE 2.1

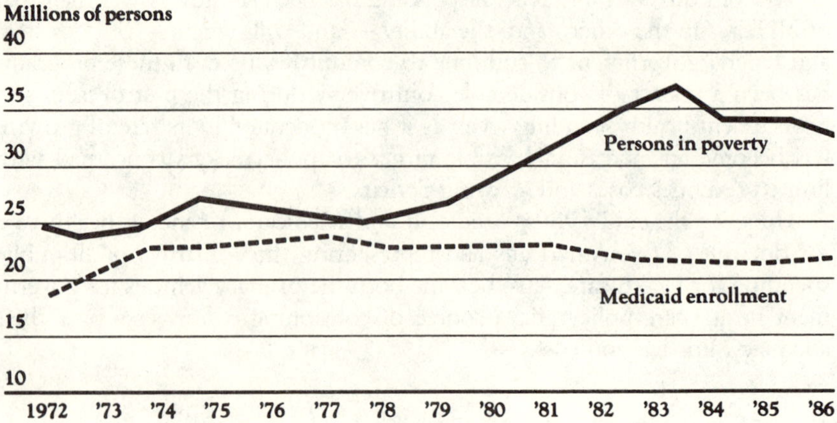

federal law; beyond that, each state is allowed a series of options in terms of the services offered, the population covered, and the terms of reimbursement. The federal government shares the cost of each state's program — such shares range from 50 percent to 78 percent — with no maximum ceiling on federal financial participation.

Because of the complexities of the federal and state eligibility requirements, the Medicaid population is difficult to describe with any specificity. Twenty-three million people received Medicaid benefits in 1986, though over 27 million people may have been eligible. Most were recipients of Supplemental Security Income (SSI) or Aid to Families with Dependent Children (AFDC), the basic welfare cash grant programs; the vast majority were children; many were disabled or in need of constant nursing care. Notwithstanding popular stereotypes of welfare recipients, extremely few were able-bodied adults with any real opportunity to support themselves or to find other means to pay for their medical care. All were by definition very poor and, in some states, virtually destitute. AFDC families, who account for over 60 percent of the nation's Medicaid recipients, rarely receive more than $400 a month in cash grant assistance and in some states receive much less.

Even so, many poor people are not eligible, eliminated by the "categorical" requirements of the program, by stringent income and resource restrictions, or by the various nonfinancial eligibility requirements characteristic of welfare programs. In 1986, about one-half of the nation's population living below the federal poverty line were ineligible. See Figure 2.1. Nor do all welfare recipients qualify.

The Medicaid benefit structure is also complicated and difficult to encapsulize. To give a grossly over-simplified account, a participant state is required by federal law to provide all "mandatory eligibles" with a basic set of services and is allowed to provide a wide range of additional services. States opting to provide Medicaid to the "medically needy" have greater latitude in the range of services offered to these beneficiaries. In many states, the services covered by Medicaid are generally limited to the federally mandated services and are only available to the "mandatory eligibles." Other states can boast that their Medicaid programs cover a broader range of services than most private insurance policies. But in all states, and particularly in recent years, the scope of services covered is a source of continuing controversy. Few states are generous, and all are becoming increasingly willing to cut back on Medicaid coverage, to impose cost sharing requirements on recipients, and to utilize a variety of restrictive administrative techniques, all with the effect of limiting the availability and use of services. Twenty-day limits on inpatient hospital use, once-a-month limits on physician visits, and the elimination of coverage for dental care, hearing aids, or other services are typical Medicaid coverage limitations. Even for that portion of the nation's poor that are eligible, Medicaid offers only limited coverage for a restricted list of services.

For eligible beneficiaries, an equally serious shortcoming of Medicaid is the limited reimbursement available in most states and the resulting reluctance of many providers to accept Medicaid patients. States traditionally have reimbursed providers on a fee-for-service basis. Federal law requires states to allow virtually any qualified provider to participate in Medicaid, but the federal law does not require even qualified providers to accept any particular patient. On the other hand, the federal law grants each state considerable discretion in determining rates of reimbursement, authority that states are increasingly willing to exploit as Medicaid costs continue to rise.

As a result of restricted reimbursement policies and several other factors, the Medicaid recipient's access to covered services is far from assured. Many providers, and particularly private physicians, are reluctant to participate in the Medicaid program. Medicaid is a voluntary program and therefore does not guarantee the availability of services, but only assures that providers will be reimbursed for services actually provided. In many areas of the country Medicaid is a realistic source of medical care for the eligible poor only through public sector clinics and hospitals, through the so-called "Medicaid mills," and through the efforts of some dedicated but frequently disgruntled providers.

Although Medicaid has proven to be an important source of medical care for millions of people, the implied promise that Medicaid would provide the nation's indigent with access to "mainstream medicine" has been, at best, only partially fulfilled.

The remainder of this section will focus on the discretion of the state and federal governments to limit Medicaid eligibility and service coverage. For a further discussion of Medicaid reimbursement mechanisms and their role in containing costs, see Chapter 3. For a discussion of health maintenance organizations, case management programs, and other limits on the freedom of choice of Medicaid recipients, see Chapter 8. For a further discussion of the role of utilization review and its role in containing program costs, see Chapter 5.

b. Medicaid Eligibility

i. Who are the "Worthy Poor"?

Ever since the Elizabethan Poor Laws, core aims of welfare policy have been to distinguish between the "worthy" and "unworthy" poor, to avoid undermining incentives for work, to encourage family support and care, and to limit public expenditures. As discussed in the introductory chapter, until the twentieth century, aid to the poor was generally regarded as a function of private charity, or of state or local government. Such views were typified by alms houses, intentionally designed to be harsh and degrading.

In the twentieth century, and particularly during the depression of the late 1930s, when more than a quarter of the U.S. population could not find work, reliance on these traditional sources became increasingly untenable and inadequate. The New Deal sought to provide federal support for subsistence for the poor and, at the same time, to avoid undermining traditional notions of social welfare. Thus the New Deal programs incorporated two key elements. First, they distinguished between people who were presumed able to work and those who were not expected to do so. Aid was targeted to the aged, blind, and disabled, and to children who had been deprived of the support of a parent. Second, the New Deal welfare programs respected state discretion. They were built on a model of "cooperative federalism," under which the federal government provided funding for state-administered programs that met minimal federal conditions. States were given wide latitude to determine who was needy, so that no one would be allowed to choose state subsidy over the least attractive wage labor that might be available in a particular locality.

Medicaid was built on this New Deal tradition, through reliance on traditional categories of the "worthy" poor and through deference to state discretion to determine who was needy. To qualify for Medicaid, individuals must meet financial requirements determined primarily by the state *and* the categorical requirements outlined by the federal statute.

The categorical qualifications of Medicaid basically limit eligibility to the poor who are aged, blind, or disabled, and to poor children deprived of parental support. Who is excluded from the "worthy poor"? One obvious group are people who live in two-parent families. In 1972, one Iowa family challenged this exclusion. Both parents lived at home and worked but did not earn enough to support the family. One son was seriously disabled and had enormous medical bills. The family argued that the rules denying them Medicaid created a destructive and unfair pressure for one of the parents, probably the father, to leave so that the children could qualify as "deprived of parental support." They further claimed that even if welfare might undermine incentives for wage work, paying children's medical bills was unlikely to have that effect. Medical expenses tend to be large, episodic, and unpredictable, whereas the need for food and shelter is more regular. Medical services are apt to be undesired necessities, whereas food and shelter are desired goods. Despite these arguments, the court held that the government was constitutionally free to limit Medicaid to poor children who were deprived of the support of a parent. Dimery v. Iowa, 334 F. Supp. 1181 (D. Iowa 1972). Cf. discussion infra.

Significantly, state welfare programs have historically been more generous to the aged, blind, or disabled than to mothers and children. In part, this reflects a moral disapprobation of women who, for whatever reason, do not have a man to support and protect them and their children. Race bias may also explain the disparity, for while the aged, blind, and disabled belong to all races, poor women and children are disproportionately black or hispanic. In fashioning Medicaid policy, Congress has attempted to ameliorate some of the harsher effects of these disparities. As discussed infra, the federal Medicaid statute requires that states provide comparable treatment to all "categorically needy" recipients. In addition, the federal statute allows states to provide Medicaid to people who fall into the recognized categories but who have income above welfare cash assistance levels, the "medically needy." See discussion infra.

Federal Medicaid policy with regard to eligibility for aliens has been more ambivalent. In 1973, the first federal regulation was issued limiting Medicaid eligibility to citizens, lawful permanent residents, and "persons permanently residing in the United States under color of law" (PRUCOLs). In Lewis v. Gross, 663 F. Supp. 1164 (E.D.N.Y. 1986) the court invalidated the federal regulation, holding that it was inconsistent with the federal statute. In 1986, however, Congress revised the federal statute to, again, limit Medicaid eligibility to citizens, lawful residents, and PRUCOLs. See 42 U.S.C. §1396(b)(v)(1) (Supp. 1983-1987). The definition of a PRUCOL remains complex and controversial. See, e.g., Lewis v. Grinker, 660 F. Supp. 169 (E.D.N.Y. 1987). Note that in 1986 Congress also authorized emergency services to be covered under Medicaid regardless of alienage. 42 U.S.C. §1396(b)(v)(2)(A)(Supp. 1983-1987). Further, women who are otherwise eligible for Medicaid are entitled to prenatal care, regardless of alienage (on the grounds that the fetus will be a citizen when born). 42 U.S.C. §1396(b)(v)(2)(B) (Supp. 1983-1987). But while many aliens are eligible for Medicaid, many seek to avoid involvement with Medicaid for fear that such action will jeopardize their future immigration status by allowing the Immigration and Naturalization Service to exclude them as persons who are likely to become a public charge. For a discussion, see Stowe, Undocumented Aliens and Emergency Care, 22 Clearinghouse Rev. 619 (1988).

In the 1980s, Medicaid has further broken with poor law traditions by extending coverage to a number of groups of people who do not qualify for cash assistance. In 1986, the federal law was amended to require states to provide Medicaid for all poor children under the age of five, whatever their family situation. 42 U.S.C. §§1396(a)(10)(A)(i)(III) (1982 and Supp. 1983-1987) & 1396d(n)(2) (Supp. 1983-1987). States also were allowed to expand eligibility for other pregnant women and children.

The Family Support Act of 1988 further expanded Medicaid eligibility. In 1990, states must make Medicaid available to two-parent families in which one parent has a work history and is now unemployed. In addition, when a recipient of Aid to Families With Dependent Children obtains work and leaves welfare, Medicaid coverage must continue for six months (and may continue for an additional six months under specified circumstances). Pub. L. No. 100-485, §401, 102 Stat. 2351, 2393-2397 (1988); codified at 42 U.S.C. §1396a(10)(A)(i) (1989).

ii. Who is "Needy"?

As noted above, a core principle of American social welfare programs is that states have broad discretion to determine who is needy and hence eligible for needs-based subsistence and medical care programs. As one consequence, the income eligibility levels for Medicaid vary widely from state to state.

Traditionally, needy families with children receive much more meager aid than the aged, blind, or disabled. In 1973, Congress federalized this pattern by adopting a national floor on the income eligibility level that qualifies the aged, blind, or disabled both for cash subsidy and a guaranteed federally funded subsidy for cash assistance to these groups. Since 1974, the aged, blind, and disabled have received cash subsidy through the federally financed Supplemental Security Income program (SSI). In 1983, SSI benefits and Medicaid income eligibility standards exceeded those for AFDC families of comparable size in every state. In 22 states, SSI benefits exceeded benefits for needy women and children by more than 100 percent. In 6 states, SSI benefits exceed AFDC benefits by 400 percent. Why do we provide greater federal protection and subsidy for the aged, blind, and disabled than for women and children? For a view that this pattern reflects a deep hostility toward women, see Law, Women, Work, Welfare and the Preservation of Patriarchy, 131 U. Pa. L. Rev. 1249 (1983).

The complexity of Medicaid eligibility was exacerbated by measures adopted in 1973 to protect states when the SSI program was created. Because federal SSI payments were higher than the amounts that many states paid to the aged, blind, and disabled, Congress did not want to burden these low benefit states by requiring that they provide Medicaid to a large new class of people. Hence Congress allowed states to elect to provide Medicaid only to those individuals who would have been eligible under the state Medicaid plan in effect on January 1, 1972. States choosing that option are known as "209(b)" states, while states providing Medicaid to all SSI beneficiaries are known as SSI states. Federal law provides a different set of rules for evaluating income of Medicaid beneficiaries in these two categories of states. See Schweiker v. Gray Panthers, 453 U.S. 34 (1981).

The complexity of Medicaid income eligibility standards has been yet further exacerbated by federal provisions adopted to protect the aged, blind, and disabled. When these categories of aid were federalized with the creation of the SSI program, Congress sought to ensure that the change would not damage any individuals who were then receiving aid. The Pickle Amendment of 1977, Pub. L. No. 94-566, §503, 90 Stat. 2667, 2685, assures that people who receive both SSI and Social Security (OASDI) do not lose Medicaid eligibility because of annual cost-of-living increases in their Social Security benefits. For an illustration, see Ciampa v. Secretary of Health and Human Services, 687 F.2d 518 (1st Cir. 1982), holding that the federal and Massachusetts regulations interpreting this complex statute were unduly restrictive. One commentator has emphasized the potential impact of the Pickle Amendment: "The income criteria applied to [individuals who qualify under the Pickle Amendment] are substantially more liberal than those that ordinarily govern entitlement to Medicaid coverage. Moreover, the Pickle criteria become more liberal with each passing year, and the number of people eligible under the amendment therefore grows accordingly. Once thought of as a narrow grandfather clause, it is now more useful to understand and apply the Pickle Amendment as a separate, important category of Medicaid eligibility. . . ." Bonnyman, Medicaid Eligibility in a Time Warp, 22 Clearinghouse Rev. 120 (1988).

c. Medicaid Eligibility: "Deeming" Income Available to Meet Needs

Vance v. Hegstrom

793 F.2d 1018 (9th Cir. 1986)

Thompson, Circuit Judge:

. . . The sole issue on appeal is whether sibling income, which a state must include in computing income available to a family to determine AFDC eligibility . . . may be included in computing that family's available income to deny Medicaid benefits. We hold that it cannot. . . .

This case involves an interpretation of Title XIX of the Social Security Act (Medicaid) and its relation to Title IV-A of the Social Security Act, . . . more commonly known as Aid to Families with Dependent Children (AFDC). Both programs are cooperative federal-state efforts that enable states to provide assistance to needy families and individuals. Although states are not required to participate in the AFDC or Medicaid programs, participating states must have their programs approved by the Secretary of Health and Human Services. Oregon has elected to participate in both programs.

1. *MEDICAID*

States electing to provide Medicaid benefits must cover "categorically needy" individuals, [that is] . . . those persons receiving AFDC or those "who would be eligible for AFDC except for an eligibility requirement used in that program that is specifically prohibited under [Medicaid]."

[A] . . . state's Medicaid plan must:

> [I]nclude reasonable standards . . . for determining eligibility for and the extent of medical assistance under the plan which. . . .
>
> (B) provide for taking into account only such income and resources as are, as determined in accordance with standards prescribed by the Secretary, available to the applicant or recipient and . . .
>
> (D) do not take into account the financial responsibility of any individual for any applicant or recipient of assistance under the plan unless such applicant or recipient is such individual's spouse or such individual's child who is under age 21 or . . . is blind or permanently and totally disabled. . . . [42 U.S.C. §1396a(a)(17).]

Subsection (17)(B) grants the Secretary broad powers to set standards to determine what income is available to a Medicaid recipient. However, subsection (17)(D) precludes a state from "deeming," as income available to a Medicaid applicant, income from persons other than the applicant's spouse, or parent if the applicant is under twenty-one, blind, or disabled.

2. *AFDC*

Aid to Families with Dependent Children was enacted to "encourag[e] the care of dependent children in their own homes or in the homes of relatives. . . ."

The Secretary's regulations require that states provide Medicaid to individuals receiving AFDC. . . .

Applicants for AFDC are called family filing units. Prior to 1984, a family applying for AFDC benefits could exclude from the filing unit those family members whose income and/or resources, if counted in the overall family income and resources, would make the family ineligible for AFDC benefits. For example, prior to 1984, if one child in a family received $300 per month in social security benefits, that child and his income could have been excluded from the family filing unit, thus enabling the remainder of the family to qualify for and receive AFDC benefits.

This procedure changed in 1984 when Congress passed the Deficit Reduction Act of 1984 [which] . . . no longer allows an applicant for AFDC to exclude children from the filing unit. . . . Thus, siblings who were previously excluded from the family filing unit are now members of the unit and their income is considered available to all members of the filing unit.

Appellees . . . are two mothers who, with their children, received AFDC and Medicaid benefits prior to 1984. Each had one child who was excluded from the AFDC and Medicaid filing units prior to 1984 because they received social security benefits. Following the enactment of DEFRA, those children were made members of the family filing unit. The social security benefits received by those children made their families ineligible for AFDC benefits and consequently those benefits were terminated by Oregon. In addition to the termination of these AFDC benefits, which is not at issue in this case, Oregon also terminated appellees' Medicaid benefits. It was Oregon's position that . . . when a family became ineligible for AFDC because of the sibling income provisions of DEFRA, the family was also ineligible for Medicaid.

In response to an inquiry from the state, the Health Care Financing Administration (HCFA) of the Department of Health and Human Services informed Oregon that this position fully complied with the Medicaid statutes and regulations. HCFA administers the Medicaid program at the federal level and is responsible for assuring that states operate their programs in accordance with their approved plans and in compliance with all applicable requirements. . . . HCFA further informed Oregon that it could lose matching federal Medicaid funds if it provided Medicaid to a family ineligible for AFDC because of the sibling income provisions of DEFRA.

. . . [Appellees] claimed . . . that the termination of their Medicaid benefits violated Medicaid statutes prohibiting deeming of sibling income. . . .

Appellants contend the Secretary's definition of a Medicaid filing unit, which includes siblings and their income, is a proper exercise of his authority under subsection (17)(B). They argue that the Secretary has not "deemed" income to a filing unit in violation of subsection (17)(D). . . . Rather, he has exercised his authority under subsection (17)(B) to determine what income is available to a filing unit by defining the filing unit. . . . The Secretary distinguishes his definition of a filing unit from deeming of income by arguing that deeming cases involve attribution of income to the Medicaid applicant in the filing unit from someone *outside* the unit, whereas here it is the income of individuals *within* the filing unit that is being included in the total income of the family unit. Thus, according to the Secretary, subsection (17)(D) would be relevant only after the filing unit was defined; it would not be relevant to the definition of the filing unit.

Although the Secretary has been granted broad authority under subsection (17)(B) to prescribe standards setting eligibility requirements for state Medicaid plans . . . the Secretary's statutory authority is not unlimited. [T]he Secretary may not read subsection (17)(B) independently of subsection (17)(D). Both subsections place a limit on the extent to which an applicant's income may be deemed to include contributions from other sources. In structuring a Medicaid filing unit by defining it in such a way as to include sibling income, the Secretary is doing through subsection (17)(B) that which he is expressly precluded from doing by subsection (17)(D). . . .

[T]he plain language of subsection (17)(D) explicitly prohibits the deeming of income from persons other than a Medicaid applicant's spouse, or a parent in the case of a child who is under twenty-one, blind or permanently and totally disabled. . . .

The Secretary attempts to avoid the plain language of subsection (17)(D) by arguing that Congress clearly expressed an intent that the subsection apply only to relatives outside the nuclear family household and that it fully intended for the nuclear family to remain responsible for a Medicaid applicant. However, the legislative history relied on by the Secretary does not support such a conclusion. The term "nuclear family" does not appear in the legislative history. The legislative history refers only to a spouse, or the parent of a minor child, or the parent of children over twenty-one who are blind or permanently and totally disabled. . . .

The Secretary also contends that his definition of a Medicaid filing unit is consistent with Congress's reason for passing DEFRA, which was to reduce spending in light of a huge federal deficit. . . . It does not follow, however, that Congress intended to deny persons such as appellees Medicaid benefits when it enacted the AFDC amendments. . . . The statute finally enacted by Congress which required states to include sibling income when determining AFDC eligibility is directed solely to the provisions of . . . the AFDC statute, and not to subsection (17)(D). We must assume that Congress was aware of subsection (17)(D) when it enacted the AFDC amendments, could have amended subsection (17)(D), and chose not to do so. . . .

Finally, we note that the Secretary's current position appears to be directly opposite to that taken in an analogous situation in early 1984. At that time, a recent amendment to AFDC allowed the deeming of stepparent income in determining AFDC eligibility. . . . However, the Secretary concluded that states were prohibited . . . from considering the stepparent's income for purposes of determining Medicaid eligibility. See Malloy v. Eichler, 628 F. Supp. 582, 596 (D. Del. 1986). . . .

NOTE: "DEEMING" INCOME: "DEFINING" FAMILY-BASED OBLIGATION

Recognition that a need-based welfare program should take "into account only such income and resources as are [actually] available to the applicant or recipient . . . ." 42 U.S.C. §1396a(a)(17), was a major victory of the welfare rights movement that existed in the United States in the late 1960s. The principle was established in the context of challenges to state rules that "assumed" that men who had sexual or social relationships with women could be expected to support those women's children. In King v. Smith, 392 U.S. 309 (1968), the Supreme Court interpreted the federal AFDC statute to prohibit states from "assuming" these men supported children unless a) there was evidence that the men in fact did so, or b) the men were legally obligated to do so under a "state law of general applicability." No state requires stepfathers, much less "boy friends," to support the children of women they date or even the children of women they marry. For obvious reasons, state legislatures are not likely to impose such obligations. However, many states do require that a variety of blood relatives — adult children, grandparents, siblings — support blood relatives who would otherwise be financially dependent upon the state for subsistence.

One of the liberalizing features of the Medicaid legislation was to limit the category of relatives who could be required to provide financial support for medical needs to parents for minor or disabled children, and to a spouse for a spouse. The Reagan Administration sought to undermine this principle in a variety of ways. *Vance* is one of several federal court decisions that rejected the Reagan Administration's effort to assume that sibling income is available to pay for medical care. The Seventh, Eighth, Ninth, and Tenth Circuits have followed the reasoning in *Vance*. The only court that supported the government was the Sixth Circuit, but that decision was reversed en banc. See Sundberg v. Mansour, 831 F.2d 610 (6th Cir. 1987).The Omnibus Reconciliation Act of 1987 added a provision affirming that the *Vance* court's interpretation of the federal statute is correct. Pub. L. No. 100-203, §4101(e)(6)(C), 101 Stat. 1330-142 (1987). However, as of late 1988, the Secretary continued to defend the effort to "deem" sibling income in the federal circuit courts.

d. "Spending Down" to Medicaid Eligibility

i. "Medically Needy" Program Requirements

A significant provision of the original Medicaid legislation was a requirement that states disregard the amounts that individuals spend on medical care in determining whether they qualify for further medical assistance. Essentially, the federal law recognized that when people, as a result of medical expenses, have available income no greater than those on public assistance, they need help to pay their medical bills. The provision was highly significant in breaking down the divisive lines between the welfare poor and other poor people. This provision, however, has been interpreted to apply only to those states that opt to provide a "medically needy" program.

To simplify somewhat, "medically needy" includes those people who fall within the categorical requirements but who have income or resources above the financial cut-off levels to qualify for Medicaid. A state *may* provide Medicaid benefits to the "medically needy" when their medical expenses reduce their net income and resources below a certain level. States have wide discretion in structuring their "medically needy" program, within the following federal guidelines:

1) Any state with a "medically needy" program *must* at least include certain categories of pregnant women and children under age 18. They also have the option of including additional children, eligible children's caretaker relatives, pregnant women up to 60 days following delivery, and *any* of the other three categories of welfare recipients (the blind, the disabled, or the elderly).

2) A state may set the "medically needy" financial eligibility level at any dollar amount up to a ceiling of 133 percent of the state AFDC level. Any "medically needy" person whose income is below this level automatically receives Medicaid. Any person who incurs liability for or "spends down" income and other resources on *medical expenses* receives Medicaid for a prescribed period (between one month and six months), and Medicaid will pay for any *additional* medical expenses incurred during that period.

3) A state *may* offer more restrictive coverage for the "medically needy" than that which the state chooses to cover for other Medicaid recipients. See discussion infra.

4) A state that covers the "medically needy" *must* use uniform financial eligibility requirements for all categories covered.

A "medically needy" program works much like a catastrophic health insurance program — at least for those people who fall within the categorical limits and meet other eligibility requirements. The 133 percent of AFDC ceiling on the "medically needy" spend down level, however, and the other financial requirements on eligibility generally mean that people must be either very poor — essentially destitute — or very sick to qualify as "medically needy." Nonetheless, whether or not a state chooses to have a "medically needy" program can represent an extremely important public policy choice. As of January 1988, 30 states had opted to offer "medically needy" programs.

By its nature, a "medically needy" program is an expensive commitment. Since many "medically needy" people obtain eligibility only at a time when they have high medical bills, "medically needy" recipients are more expensive, a fact not lost on states' policymakers. Adding a "medically needy" recipient to the state's program will cost two to three times as much as a "categorically needy" recipient; and adding a "medically needy" program to a state's Medicaid program has been estimated to raise program costs anywhere from 10 percent to as much as 50 percent, depending on the state.

Somewhat ironically, experts also estimate that most people who are eligible for the "medically needy" programs do not receive Medicaid benefits, even when they technically qualify, as a result of the complications of "spend down" requirements, state reluctance to promote eligibility, and the failure of many providers to assist their patients in seeking eligibility.

ii. Mechanics of "Spending Down"

Schweiker v. Hogan, 457 U.S. 569 (1982), provides a good illustration of how the "medically needy" "spend down" requirement works; it also illustrates some of the inequities that can exist even in a state that attempts to be generous to (some) recipients.

In *Hogan,* Massachusetts chose to supplement the federal cash grants received by the state's SSI recipients. Thus, at the time of the suit, SSI recipients were receiving a total cash grant of $513 a month. Since Massachusetts is not a "209(b)" state, these recipients were also automatically eligible for Medicaid as "categorically needy." Massachusetts also had a "medically needy" program. As noted above, under federal law, the "medically needy" financial requirements are capped at 133 percent of the AFDC cash grant level. At the time of the suit, the state set the AFDC cash grant level at $300 per month. Thus, even if an applicant for the "medically needy" program met the categorical and other requirements, the applicant would have to have a net income (income minus incurred medical expenses) under $400 to be eligible for Medicaid as "medically needy."

Hogan, a retired former wage earner, received $534 per month in Social Security benefits. For purposes of SSI eligibility, $20 in income was disregarded in determining his SSI and supplemental payment eligibility. But with an income just over the financial standard, Hogan did not qualify for a cash grant; accordingly, he did not qualify as a "categorically needy" Medicaid recipient. Hogan did have high medical bills; thus, he had to "spend down" over $114 to qualify as "medically needy." Ironically, if the federal government under Social Security had given him $1 less, he would have received Medicaid automatically and coverage for all his medical expenses.

Despite the inequity between recipients of public assistance and the hardship this caused Hogan, the Supreme Court held that neither the overall structure of the Medicaid program nor any particular provision of the federal statute invalidated the state's "medically needy" financial requirements. It also denied Hogan's argument that the Massachusetts eligibility requirements were a violation of equal protection. See discussion of constitutional principles infra.

A *Hogan*-type inequity also occurs whenever a Social Security cost of living increase raises the income of Social Security recipients. Even if the combined effect is to raise their income, ironically, some recipients lose their Medicaid benefits as a result of this attempt to adjust their benefits to reflect increases in their cost of living. Note that the "Pickle Amendment," discussed supra, eliminates the inequity for the "categorically needy" but does not apply to those who are "medically needy."

iii. State Discretion to Discriminate

The extent to which a state has the discretion to discriminate between categories of the "medically needy" and, in particular, between the "categorically needy" and the "medically needy," has a long and controversial history. As noted supra, the states are required to use the same income and resource eligibility standards for all covered categories of the "medically needy." They are also required to use the same methodology for determining "medically needy" financial requirements as they do for the appropriate "categorically needy" programs. 42 U.S.C. §1396a(10)(C) (1982). States, however, may use higher standards for determining eligibility for institutionalized recipients, presumably because they are subject to different needs. Beyond this, current federal law allows a state to use different standards (although the same methodology must be followed) for the "categorically needy" and the "medically needy" in setting income, resource, and other financial eligibility restrictions (as well as in determining service coverage for the two relevant groups, as discussed infra.) For a discussion, see Atkins v. Rivera, 477 U.S. 154 (1986).

iv. Spending Down Resources

The federal statute is silent about whether resources, as well as income, also may be spent down. In 1980 HHS issued a transmittal to the states claiming that resource "spend down" was not permitted. The courts have disagreed about whether the transmittal is binding. In Hession v. Illinois Department of Public Aid, 163 Ill. App. 3d 553, 516 N.E.2d 820 (1987), plaintiff, an SSI medically needy applicant, was denied Medicaid when he had incurred medical bills of $16,000 in a single month because his resources for that month, a savings account of $1953.05, exceeded Illinois's resource limit of $1500. Illinois had adopted the federal rule prohibiting the spend down of resources. The court upheld plaintiff's claim that he should be able to offset his bills by the amount of his excess resources, reasoning that resource spend down was not prohibited by the federal statute. The court also found that resource spend down was required under Illinois law, which emphasized the importance of allowing the medically indigent to "preserve their limited resources for ordinary maintenance needs to prevent their total or substantial dependency." See also Haley v. Commissioner of Public Welfare, 394 Mass. 466, 476 N.E.2d 572 (1985). On the other hand, Hamer v. Department of Human Services, District of Columbia, 492 A.2d 1253 (D.C. App. 1985), upheld a District of Columbia ruling eliminating resource spend down, in response to the Secretary's directive.

As a matter of policy, is there any reason to treat resources differently from income in terms of allowing people to spend down to qualify for Medicaid?

Consider the following contrast in the way that income and resources are distinguished for purposes of establishing eligibility for AFDC. Under the AFDC provision, 42 U.S.C. §602(a)(7) (1982 and Supp. 1983-1987), incorporated into Medicaid regulations by 42 C.F.R. §435.711 (1987), AFDC recipients who receive a sum classified as *income* that exceeds the state's income limit are ineligible for as many months as that income would last if the recipient spent an amount equal to the state's standard of need each month. If the sum is classified as a *resource,* however, the recipient of the sum is ineligible only for so long as the resource is actually available.

In Lukhard v. Reed, 481 U.S. 368 (1987), the Supreme Court considered a Virginia rule classifying a lump sum personal injury award as income for the purposes of that state's AFDC program. Plaintiffs, disqualified from AFDC for a statutory period after receiving personal injury and workers' compensation awards, contended that personal injury awards should be classified as resources because they are compensatory and the common definition of "income" involves gain. They also argued that since personal injury awards are not considered income under the tax code, the food stamp program, or HHS poverty guidelines, they should not be considered income for AFDC. The Court ruled that personal injury awards could be considered income because they compensate for the "lost gain" of lost wages and general and legal sources also define "income" as "any money that comes in." Four dissenting judges argued that the effect of including personal injury awards as income was to deprive AFDC families of the benefit of state tort and workers' compensation remedies and that it was inequitable to treat compensation for property damage as a resource but compensation for personal injury as income. After the suit was filed, HHS promulgated a rule requiring states to treat all lump sum payments, including property damage awards, as income for AFDC purposes. 45 C.F.R. §233.20(a)(3)(vii)(F) (1988).

e. "Spend Down" and Medicaid Eligibility for Nursing Home Residents

Medicaid nursing home recipients go through a two-step income determination process. First, their income is calculated for eligibility purposes. Second, after eligibility is established, an additional calculation is made to determine how much of the recipient's income and resources must be applied to nursing home care. This latter amount is referred to as the resident's "share of cost." The state agency then pays the difference between the resident's "share of cost" and the state-established Medicaid nursing home reimbursement rate.

Residents are allowed to retain a small amount — about $20 a month in the late 1980s — for personal needs. In addition, some states allow residents to deduct amounts that they spent on medical care not provided by the home or by Medicaid, for instance, eye glasses or dental care. Several courts have interpreted the federal statute as requiring that states allow these deductions for medical costs. Recently, however, HHS has attempted to prohibit deductions of some medical expenses. 42 C.F.R. §§432.722, 432.725, 432.733, 432.832 (1988).

Another difficult problem, involving how much a spouse must contribute, has led to enormously different results from state to state. Common law property rules, which apply in all but a handful of American jurisdictions, incorporate the "name-on-the-check" rule of ownership: that is, Medicaid eligibility is determined by the amount of money an applicant receives in his or her name, regardless of the portion that may belong to the spouse under state community property law. The usual situation is that the husband is both the first to need nursing home care and the one to whom the family's checks are written. In common-law-property states, the issue becomes the extent to which the income of the spouse in the nursing home can be treated as the income of the spouse outside the institution.

Sometimes the spouse at home can obtain a judicial order of support against the spouse in the nursing home. In re Rose Septuagenarian, 126 Misc. 2d 699, 483 N.Y.S.2d 932 (Fam. Ct. 1984), ordered support for a 72-year-old woman from the pension fund of her husband, who was in a nursing home where his care was financed by Medicaid. The court found

> [t]o deprive women, and particularly women of petitioner's generation who, in many cases, were denied an equal opportunity to fulfill their potential in the employment market and are, therefore, dependent on their husbands for support, access to their husbands' pensions and assets in their later years effectively sentences many of them to tremendous hardship and a complete disruption of their lives at a time when they are extremely vulnerable." [126 Misc. 2d at 702, 483 N.Y.S.2d at 934.]

In 1988 the Reagan Administration issued regulations providing that funds owed under judicially enforceable support orders must be considered in determining medical eligibility. 20 C.F.R. §§416.2101-2176 (1988).

The extent to which the spouse outside the home is required to contribute has also turned, in part, on the historical accident of whether the state has chosen to be an SSI state or a "209(b)" state. Federal regulations provide that in "209(b)" states, all of the income and resources of the noninstitutionalized spouse, in excess of that allowed by the standards of need in effect in 1973 standards, may be "deemed" available to pay for the nursing home care of the institutionalized spouse. In SSI states, if the spouse living in the community is not receiving SSI or Medicaid, the state may only "consider the income and resources of the ineligible spouse that are actually contributed to the eligible spouse." 42 C.F.R. §435.723(d) (1988), upheld in Herweg v. Ray, 455 U.S. 265 (1982).

The Catastrophic Coverage Act of 1988, discussed infra at 188-189, amends the way Medicaid pays for nursing home care. It provides that all resources held by either spouse, as of the date of the application for Medicaid, are presumed available to the institutionalized spouse. The spouse living outside the nursing home is entitled to retain an allowance which is the greater of: half of the marital assets, not to exceed $60,000; or a level set between $12,000 and $60,000, to be established by the state. If the spouse living outside the nursing home needs more, he or she can request a welfare department fair hearing or obtain a family court order of support. However, if the spouse living outside the nursing home fails to contribute these amounts, Medicaid will not be denied to the patient spouse so long as he or she assigns to Medicaid the right to sue for support. (The new legislation also allows the patient to transfer *any* amount to the spouse living outside the nursing home without application of the transfer of assets waiting period rules, described below.)

States may deny Medicaid to those who become financially eligible because they have transferred property for less than fair market value within 30 months of application for aid. While this applies to all Medicaid applicants, transfer of asset problems most frequently arise with nursing home residents. Any transfer of assets will be presumed to have been made for the purpose of establishing eligibility for Medicaid unless the individual furnishes convincing evidence that it was for some other purpose. Randall v. Lukhard, 729 F.2d 966 (4th Cir. 1984), *cert. denied,* 469 U.S. 872 (1984), discusses the meaning of "convincing evidence." The period of ineligibility is a minimum of two years, and states may set longer periods where the uncompensated value of the assets is greater than $12,000. For a discussion of the computation of periods of ineligibility, see Lewis v. Hegstrom, 767 F.2d 1371 (9th Cir. 1985).

Homesteads may be transferred to certain close relatives within 30 months of qualifying for Medicaid. These relatives include a spouse, a dependent child under 21, a blind or disabled child of any age, a sibling with an equity interest who was residing in the home for at least one year prior to the transfer, and a son or daughter residing in the home who was a primary caregiver for the Medicaid applicant. 42 U.S.C. §1396p(c)(B)(iii) (1982).

f. Medicaid Coverage

White v. Beal

555 F.2d 1146 (3d Cir. 1977)

Weis, Circuit Judge.

In administering its federally aided medical assistance program, Pennsylvania chose to limit its expenditures for eyeglasses by making them available on the basis of etiology rather than medical necessity. The district court determined that the classification was in conflict with the underlying federal statute, and enjoined application of the restrictive state regulations. We affirm.

The plaintiff class . . . are poor persons who, though not suffering from eye disease, need eyeglasses to correct refractive error. Under the Pennsylvania Department of Public Welfare's regulations, eyeglasses are provided only for treatment of eye disease or pathology. Accordingly, the state refused to furnish this benefit to plaintiffs. . . .

. . . Title XIX is intended to aid the needy in meeting the expense of health care. The Act requires a participating state to provide five specified health services to the "categorically needy," those in the most severe financial straits. If the state wishes to maintain a more comprehensive program, it may provide seven of sixteen listed benefits to the less poor, characterized as the "medically needy." 42 U.S.C. §1396a(a)(13)(C). A state providing specific services for the "medically needy" must also provide them for the "categorically needy." Moreover, all persons within a given category must be treated equally. The defendants do not dispute these general propositions. Basically, they contend that because of limited resources, the state has chosen to restrict payment for eyeglasses to those individuals it considers most in need of the aid, those having pathology or disease of the eye. The . . . state's interest in financial responsibility may not be treated lightly. Nevertheless, we do not believe that the state has applied a permissible method of obtaining economies in its administration of the medical assistance program. . . .

Congress recognized the financial pressures upon the states and provided that, if a medical assistance plan was adopted, the state could pay . . . "part or all of the cost of the . . . care and services." 42 U.S.C. §1396d(a). The state interprets this authorization essentially as permission to meet part of the total cost by paying the expenses of some who would benefit (those requiring eyeglasses because of pathology) but paying nothing to others (those requiring them because of eye defects). . . . In our view, the statute does not grant such discretion to the state. Rather, it requires an equitable distribution of the total funds available among all in need of the service, with a consequent sharing of benefit and hardship.

The optional service at issue, for which a state may choose to pay all or part, is set out in 42 U.S.C. §1396d(a)(12):

> . . . eyeglasses prescribed by a physician skilled in diseases of the eye or by an optometrist, whichever the individual may select. . . .

Significantly, the only statutory restriction on furnishing eyeglasses is that they be prescribed by a physician or an optometrist. The state regulations add another qualification. The glasses must be necessary because of pathology. Limitation of eligibility is based on the state's assumption that this class of visually handicapped persons is most in need of spectacles. Assuming that medical need is a valid measurement of eligibility, the state's factual premise, however, is not supported by the record.

The plaintiffs submitted the affidavits of two qualified ophthalmologists stating that some persons with refractive error, but without eye pathology, may be far more visually handicapped than those who have a disease of the eye. Moreover, the physicians maintain that, while eyeglasses will correct a refractive error, they are not helpful in many cases of eye disease.

The state has not controverted these affidavits. Thus, the restriction on furnishing eyeglasses results neither in furnishing them to those who are the most visually handicapped (and thus most in need) nor to those whose impairment would most likely be improved. On this record, therefore, the state's classification, based on diagnosis, is little more relevant to health care needs than one based on the color of eyes. We find nothing in the federal statute that permits discrimination based upon etiology rather than need for the service. By permitting the state plans to provide only part of the cost, the statute must be construed to envision an evenhanded sharing of benefits and burdens among those having the same needs. The state plan's classification is arbitrary since it is based upon a factor not reasonably related to the medical need. We conclude that when a state decides to distribute a service . . . the service must be distributed in a manner which bears a rational relationship to the underlying federal purpose of providing the service to those in greatest need of it.

Further support for our conclusion is found in the regulations promulgated by the Department of Health, Education, and Welfare. 45 C.F.R. §249.10(a)(5)(i) provides that a state plan must:

> Specify the amount and/or duration of each item of medical and remedial care and services that will be provided to the categorically needy and to the medically needy, if the plan includes this latter group. Such items must be sufficient in amount, duration, and scope to reasonably achieve their purpose. With respect to the required services for the categorically needy . . . *and the medically needy* . . . the State may not arbitrarily deny or reduce the amount, duration, or scope of, such services to an otherwise eligible individual solely because of the diagnosis, type of illness or condition. Appropriate limits may be placed on services based on such criteria as medical necessity. . . .

The regulations permit discrimination in benefits based upon the degree of medical necessity but not upon the medical disorder from which the person suffers. Thus, a state plan providing eyeglasses only to those with a specified amount of visual impairment, regardless of its cause, would be consistent with the regulations. The reason for the prohibition against the deprivation of benefits based on diagnosis is illustrated by the situation described in the ophthalmologists' affidavits. A person who cannot see clearly beyond a short distance from his face because of a refractive error may not be given eyeglasses under the Pennsylvania plan, but a person with only slightly impaired vision, caused by pathology, may receive aid. . . .

NOTES: THE SCOPE AND EXTENT OF MEDICAID COVERAGE

Federal Limits on State Discretion

As of 1988 the federal statute requires that states that participate in Medicaid *must* provide coverage for a rather broad range of services:

- inpatient hospital services
- outpatient hospital services
- rural health clinic services staffed by nurse practitioners or physician assistants (where permitted by law)
- physician services
- laboratory and x-ray services
- skilled nursing home services
- early and periodic screening diagnosis and treatment (EPSDT)
- family planning services
- home health services
- nurse midwife services (where permitted by state law)

States have the *option* of covering virtually any other medical service; the only major exception is the federal prohibition on the coverage of most abortions. See pp. 201-206. In fact, in terms of the categories of services that are covered, many states offer Medicaid programs that are more comprehensive than many private health insurance policies. For instance, many states cover prescription drugs, dental care, nursing home services, rehabilitation, eye glasses, and other items frequently not included in private insurance policies. Significantly, all states have opted to cover nursing home services in intermediate care facilities (ICFs) despite the fact that this can represent an extremely expensive commitment. In some states, services to patients in ICFs can represent 40 to 50 percent of the Medicaid program costs.

But while the list of services covered can appear to be rather comprehensive, the actual extent of coverage can be limited in a number of other ways. As summarized by the court in *Beal*, states have been given considerable discretion under the federal law to limit the amount, scope, and duration of Medicaid coverage. States frequently limit the maximum number of physician visits, hospital days, or other services available to Medicaid recipients. In some states these restrictions are particularly harsh; for instance, a limit of no more than 12 hospital days a year. States are also allowed by the federal law to impose prior authorization, pre-admission screening, and other forms of utilization controls that also effectively limit which services are covered. See discussion in Chapter 5.

In addition to mandating that certain categories of services must be covered by a state, the federal Medicaid statute requires that the services covered by Medicaid must be "comparable" for all covered groups; this has been generally interpreted to mean that the services and limits on their coverage must be identical for all Medicaid eligibles. The major exception is that the federal statute explicitly allows the state to provide more limited services to the "medically needy." See, for instance, DeJesus v. Perales, 770 F.2d 316 (2d Cir. 1985), *cert. denied,* 478 U.S. 1007 (1986); see also Hogan v. Heckler, 769 F.2d 886 (1st Cir. 1985), *cert. denied,* 478 U.S. 1007 (1986).

Cost Sharing Limitations

States can also impose cost sharing requirements on Medicaid recipients, although federal law limits the states' discretion. Prior to 1982, states were allowed to impose cost sharing only on the medically needy; all cost sharing had to be "nominal." Since the 1982 amendments, "nominal" deductibles and co-payments can be imposed on both the medically needy and the categorically needy, with the following exceptions:

- no cost sharing may be imposed on individuals under 18 years of age
- no cost sharing may be imposed on pregnancy-related services
- no cost sharing may be imposed on institutionalized individuals
- no cost sharing may be imposed on emergency services
- no cost sharing may be imposed on family planning services
- no cost sharing may be imposed by HMOs on the categorically needy

Amount, Scope, and Duration Limits

The federal Medicaid statute requires that a state in determining the amount, scope, and duration of coverage of a service "include reasonable standards . . . for determining . . . the extent of medical assistance which are consistent with the objectives of the [state Medicaid] plan." 42 U.S.C. §1396a(a)(17) (1982 and Supp. 1983-1987). It also provides that the state must "provide such safeguards as may be necessary to assure that . . . care and services will be provided in a manner consistent with simplicity of administration and the best interests of recipients. . . ." 42 U.S.C. §1396a(a)(19). As discussed in *Beal,* the federal Medicaid regulations also limit the states' discretion to impose amount, scope, or durational limits on covered services. See 42 C.F.R. §440.230, for the most recent codification.

Beal and some other courts have relied on this authority to invalidate various coverage limits, particularly where the net result of the state's restriction would be to deny a needed service to a particular recipient. See, for instance, Pinneke v. Preisser, 623 F.2d 546 (8th Cir. 1980) (invalidating a refusal to fund transsexual surgery). On the other hand, the courts have frequently upheld challenges to state-imposed limits on the amount, scope, and duration of a covered service, generally arguing that so long as the needs of most recipients are met the restrictions are "reasonable." See, for instance, Charleston Memorial Hospital v. Conrad, 693 F.2d 324 (4th Cir. 1982) (upholding an 18 day maximum on inpatient hospital days as reasonable because most recipients would need fewer than 18 days of coverage); see also Alexander v. Choate, 469 U.S. 287 (1985) (upholding a 14 day maximum for inpatient hospital services challenged as a violation of federal law prohibiting discrimination against the handicapped).

It would appear that some courts are attempting to mix a certain amount of proper judicial deference to the state with a certain amount of ad hoc judicial equity. It is clear, however, that most courts have been reluctant to read the language of the federal Medicaid regulations or the Medicaid statute to require any demanding judicial scrutiny of the connection between the Medicaid program's overall objectives and the specific details of the program's coverage.

A few courts, however, have inferred from the statutory and regulatory language a requirement that within a covered service, all medically necessary services should be provided despite the discretion apparently allowed by the language of §440.230. The most notable authority for this view can be found in the Supreme Court's opinion in Beal v. Doe, 432 U.S. 438 (1977). While the Court upheld the state's discretion to exclude nontherapeutic abortions (see pp. 201-206), it indicated in dictum that "serious statutory questions might be raised if a state Medicaid plan excluded necessary medical treatment." Id. at 444.

Questioning the state's exclusion of medically necessary treatment focuses attention on a critical issue: the extent to which the state will be allowed to second guess the medical judgment of the recipient's physician or other provider. See similar discussion in notes following *Sarchett* supra. In *Pinneke,* the court characterized the choice as allowing the decision of the patient's physician to predominate over the decision of "clerical personnel or government officials." Not surprisingly, the *Pinneke* court sided with the physician. With other factual situations, deference to the decision of the provider might not be so easily justified, particularly when the judgment as to the medical necessity of the service is based on a peer review or on other medical third party mechanisms with medical expertise. See Ringer v. Heckler, Chapter 3; see also Cowan v. Myers, 187 Cal. App. 3d 968, 232 Cal. Rptr. 299 (1987), *cert. denied*, — U.S. — (1987).

Difficulties in Obtaining Covered Services

For the most part, Medicaid is a "voluntary" program for providers. Medicaid eligibility entitles recipients to have payment made on their behalf to participating providers for covered services. The state is generally not required to make affirmative efforts to assure that these covered services are available; the major exception involves the federal requirement that a state *must provide* for early and periodic screening, diagnosis and treatment (EPSDT) for eligible children. Unfortunately, neither the federal agency nor the states have been eager to comply with the EPSDT requirement, even under court order to do so. See Philadelphia Welfare Rights Organization v. Shapp, 602 F.2d 1114 (3d Cir. 1979), *cert. denied,* 444 U.S. 1026 (1980), Mitchell v. Johnson, 701 F.2d 337 (5th Cir. 1983). Other courts rejected recipient challenges to the adequacy of state EPSDT programs. Woodruff v. Lavine, 417 F. Supp. 824 (S.D.N.Y. 1976); Wisconsin Welfare Rights Organization v. Newgent, 433 F. Supp. 204 (E.D. Wisc. 1977). And unless the court and the plaintiffs are willing and able to persist in pushing for implementation of an effective program, a recalcitrant state can easily avoid doing so. States in which courts have ordered implementation of EPSDT have not implemented programs of particular excellence. Conversely, Wisconsin, where the court refused to order the state to establish a program, has in fact established a very strong one. See K. Erdmann & S. Wolfe, Poor Health Care For Poor Americans: A Ranking of State Medicaid Programs 215 (1987).

Similarly, providers generally are not required by the state or federal Medicaid law to participate in the program. Consequently, many providers, claiming that Medicaid reimbursement is inadequate or that the program's "red tape" and administrative controls are burdensome, are reluctant to accept Medicaid patients or, in particular, take new Medicaid patients. As a result, in many areas of the country Medicaid is a realistic source of medical care for recipients only through public sector clinics or hospitals, or through the efforts of some dedicated but frequently disgruntled physicians. For a further discussion, see Perkins, Increasing Provider Participation in the Medicaid Program: Is There a Doctor in the House? 26 Hous. L. Rev. 77 (1988).

A few states have attempted to require physicians to participate in Medicaid as a condition of their medical licensure. Hospitals and other institutional providers may be required to accept Medicaid (or Medicare) patients as a condition of licensure, as part of the community service obligation of Hill-Burton recipients (see discussion Chapter 1), or as a condition of their tax exempt status. See, for instance, Armstrong v. Fairmont Community Hospital, 659 F. Supp. 1524 (D. Minn. 1987).

2. THE MEDICARE PROGRAM

a. Eligibility for Medicare

Since Medicare is a uniform federal program and there is no "means test," eligibility for people over 65 is fairly simple. People who have paid the Social Security payroll tax for a sufficient length of time receive retirement benefits when they reach age 65 (nearly 30 million people in 1988). They are also automatically eligible for Medicare Part A (including, after 1986, all former federal and state employees). People who are over 65 and do not qualify for Social Security may "buy in" to Medicare Part A by paying a monthly premium ($156 in 1989). Part A recipients are also entitled to enroll in Part B by paying a monthly premium ($31.90 in 1989).

Eligibility for disabled people who are not over 65 is more complex. Social Security cash grants are paid to people who have been subject to the payroll tax who are "totally and permanently disabled." After a one-year waiting period, they also become eligible for Medicare. Determinations of who is "disabled" have become increasingly controversial; the Reagan Administration attempted to narrow the definition of disability and require more frequent redeterminations. See Bowen v. Yuckert, 482 U.S. 137 (1987). On the other hand, Medicare eligibility rules were amended by Congress in 1988 to allow Social Security disability recipients with AIDS to qualify for Medicare without waiting one year. As of 1988, nearly 3,000,000 disabled people were Medicare recipients. Apart from requirements of age or disability, Medicare eligibility is also available to people with end stage renal disease (over 80,000 people in 1988).

b. Medicare Service Coverage and Limitations

Since there are no income or resource limits on Medicare eligibility and since eligibility is automatic for Part A, there have been relatively few eligibility related legal controversies (at least as compared to Medicaid). The scope of Medicare coverage has, however, been a source of continuing legislative and judicial controversy.

As with Medicaid, the scope of covered services can at first glance appear comprehensive. Medicare Part A essentially pays for all hospital inpatient care including diagnostic and related services, with very few exclusions. Part A does, however, impose limits on the amount, scope, and duration of covered services, as well as substantial cost sharing requirements, although Medicare cost sharing was simplified and reduced by the 1988 Catastrophic Coverage Amendments. See discussion infra.

As of 1989, Part A beneficiaries are entitled to 365 days of inpatient hospital services. (Previously, coverage was limited to 90 days per spell of illness plus a once in a lifetime 60 day reserve.) Medicare also covers up to 150 days in a skilled nursing home, some home health services, and hospice care for the terminally ill. Part A beneficiaries pay a deductible calculated to be approximately the cost of the first day in a hospital ($564 in 1989). Part A imposes a daily co-insurance of 20 percent of the cost of a day in a skilled nursing home for the first eight days ($25.50 in 1989).

Part B covers virtually all physician and other related services. But Part B excludes coverage of routine physicals, most preventive services, and eye and dental care. Neither Part A nor Part B covers custodial or intermediate care in a nursing home. There is an annual deductible for all Part B coverage ($75.00 in 1989), and co-insurance of 20 percent on all Part B services. For an illustration of how this is calculated, see Chapter 3 p. 256.

Medicare coverage was also expanded by the 1988 catastrophic coverage legislation to cover — with significant co-insurance and deductibles — the costs of outpatient prescription drugs, previously excluded from Part A and Part B. Starting in 1990, Medicare will cover home intravenously administered antibiotics and other drugs (with a 20 percent co-insurance) and extend its coverage of drugs used in immunosuppressive therapy (with a 50 percent co-insurance) in years beyond the first. The beneficiary, however, is liable for the first $550 of these costs in 1990. In 1991, Medicare will cover all other outpatient prescription drugs (with a 50 percent co-insurance). The deductible will rise to $600 in 1991. The co-insurance requirement is scheduled to be reduced to 40 percent in 1992 and 20 percent in 1993, while the deductible requirement is scheduled for comparable increases.

The Part B monthly premium is calculated to represent 25 percent of Part B program costs. Originally Part B premiums were to be adjusted to represent 50 percent of program costs, but amendments in the 1970s reduced the percentage to 25 percent and capped Part B premium increases to no more than annual Social Security cash grant increases. The catastrophic coverage amendments of 1988 scheduled a series of increases in the premiums ($4 in 1989, rising to $10.20 in 1993) to cover the costs of the additional service coverage created by the amendments. These are in addition to the Part B premium increases that must be made each year to ensure that Part B premiums reflect 25 percent of other Part B costs. Note that the total premium increase for any individual is still subject to the rule that no beneficiary can have a premium increase greater than the Social Security increase for that year.

The 1988 catastrophic coverage amendments also created another source of Medicare revenue. Starting in 1989, all Medicare beneficiaries will be subject to what has been labeled a "supplemental premium," in fact a surtax on the income tax liability of middle and higher income Medicare beneficiaries. The amount of the "supplemental premium" is determined by dividing the individual's tax liability by $150. That result is then multiplied by the "supplemental tax rate" for that year. The 1988 legislation scheduled the rates as $22.50 for 1989, $37.50 for 1990, $39.00 for 1991, and $40.50 for 1992. The ceiling on each individual's liability for this new tax is $800 for 1989, $850 for 1990, $900 for 1991, and $950 for 1992. There are special rules for married and single beneficiaries. (Note, however, that this tax has been extremely unpopular and is likely to be repealed or modified.)

c. Utilization Review and "Reasonable and Necessary" Limits on Medicare Coverage

Kuebler v. Secretary of Department of Health and Human Services

579 F. Supp. 1436 (E.D.N.Y. 1984)

Wexler, District Judge.

Plaintiff brings this action pursuant to Sections 205(g) and 1869(b) of the Social Security Act ("Act"), as amended, 42 U.S.C. Sections 405(g), 1395ff(b), to review the final determination of the Secretary of Health and Human Services ("Secretary") denying plaintiff [Medicare] reimbursement for 100 days of care in a skilled nursing facility. . . . Plaintiff and defendant cross-move for judgment on the pleadings. . . .

On February 12, 1981, Mrs. Alice Kuebler was transferred from Eastern Long Island Hospital to San Simeon by the Sound Nursing Home ("San Simeon"), a skilled nursing facility. Plaintiff was notified that her care at San Simeon would not be covered by Medicare as it was custodial in nature. On reconsideration this determination was upheld. A hearing was held at plaintiff's request on June 15, 1982. After *de novo* consideration the Administrative Law Judge found Mrs. Kuebler not entitled to reimbursement. . . . The Appeals Council upheld the ALJ's determination. . . .

At the time of her admission to San Simeon, plaintiff was 71 years old. She was admitted directly from the hospital after six days of confinement there occasioned by a fall at her home. Plaintiff's treating physician, Dr. Arnold Urist, strongly recommended that plaintiff's husband, Reverend Kuebler, place his wife in a nursing home and certified her need for continuing skilled nursing care. [P]laintiff was evaluated by the Utilization Review Committee ("URC") of the nursing home, which also certified her need. . . . In two subsequent evaluations the URC determined there was continued need for skilled nursing care.

On admission to San Simeon plaintiff's diagnosis was kyphoses, osteoporosis, a possible compression fracture of the L-4 vertebra and concommitant lowback syndrome, progressive cerebral arteriosclerosis with brain atrophy, a urinary tract infection, early Parkinson's disease, and chronic depressive reaction by history. Plaintiff suffered from periods of confusion during which she did not recognize her husband and did not know her name. She also had episodes of agitated, assaultive and abusive behavior and a history of wandering about, both at her home and at San Simeon. . . .

. . . Haldol, a psychotropic drug, was prescribed as needed to control agitation. The plaintiff was evaluated to be in unstable condition with a need for daily observation and modification of dosage in connection with administration of the Haldol. . . .

[T]hree principles applicable to the case at hand have been established by district courts reviewing a denial of Medicare benefits for skilled nursing facility care. The first is that the Court's review of the Secretary's determination is not limited to the substantial evidence standard, but extends to a review of the Secretary's interpretation of the law. The second is that the correct legal standard for determining Medicare coverage is consideration of the patient's condition as a whole. The third is that where there is no directly conflicting evidence the treating physician's opinion must be given great weight.

The Secretary contends that Mrs. Kuebler's care at San Simeon was purely "custodial.". . . Under the regulations custodial care is defined as administrating routine medication, routine care of incontinence, assistance in dressing, eating, and going to the toilet, and exercise supervision not done by a physical therapist. 42 C.F.R. §405.127(d). The courts have interpreted custodial care to be care that can be provided by a lay person without special skills and not requiring or entailing the continued attention of trained or skilled personnel. Such custodial care is excluded from Medicare payments. . . .

The Secretary urges on this Court the standard of review articulated in the statute, 42 U.S.C. §405(g), and in Richardson v. Perales, 402 U.S. 389 (1971), limiting the scope of the district court's review to a determination of whether the Secretary's findings of fact are supported by substantial evidence on the record. Findings that are so supported are deemed conclusive. The Secretary, however, ignores another well-established standard. . . . For while the district court may be compelled to accept the Secretary's supported findings of fact, it is not bound to accept . . . her application of an incorrect legal standard. [T]he Secretary contends that her examination . . . of the treatment and services rendered by San Simeon is the correct standard for determining the nature of Mrs. Kuebler's care.

The courts, however, have on numerous occasions rejected this analysis. [T]he legal standard for determining the need for skilled nursing care is not an analysis of services provided but *consideration of the patient's condition as a whole.* [A]s Chief Judge Northrop pointedly observed:

> [T]he purpose of the custodial care disqualification in §1395y(a)(9) was not to disentitle old, chronically ill and basically helpless, bewildered and confused people . . . from the broad remedy which Congress intended to provide for our senior citizens. Rather, the provision was intended to stop cold-blooded and thoughtless relatives from relegating an oldster who could care for him or herself to the care of an [Extended Care Facility] merely so that the oldster would have a place to eat, sleep, or watch television. But when a person is sick, especially a helpless old person, and when those who love that person are not skilled enough to take care of that person, Congress has provided a remedy in the

> Medicare Act, and that remedy should not be eclipsed by an application of the law and findings of fact which are blinded by bureaucratic economics to the purpose of the Congress.

Repeatedly the Secretary has urged on the courts the limiting technical definition and analysis of custodial care presented . . . [here]. Repeatedly the courts have rejected them. Observing that "custodial care" is not defined by statute the courts have consistently interpreted the term in light of the statute's benevolent cogressional purpose . . . consider[ing] . . . the needs and underlying condition of the claimant insured as a whole. . . .

. . . Although many specific services rendered to Mrs. Kuebler were routine and seemingly unskilled, in the aggregate they were treatment of her medical condition. And although taken singly Mrs. Kuebler's ailments might not seem to require skilled nursing care, taken together they made her a chronically ill, disabled old woman in need of monitoring and care by skilled personnel in order to maintain what health she had left and prevent any further injury. To contend that her care was merely custodial and therefore could have been provided by a lay person is to ignore the fact that a lay person, in the form of her husband, was unable to provide adequate care. In sum, this Court concludes that considering Mrs. Kuebler's condition as a whole she required the skilled care rendered by San Simeon.

[T]he Secretary's determination has also ignored an important principle in evaluating and weighing the evidence on the record. While the opinion of Dr. Urist, the attending physician, is not binding on the Secretary, where there is no direct conflicting evidence his decision has great weight. . . .

Under the Act physician certification for the specific level of care provided is required before Medicare will pay. Here, Dr. Urist not only recommended that Mrs. Kuebler be placed in a skilled nursing facility, but repeatedly certified the need for this level of care. The Utilization Review Committee for San Simeon also reviewed Mrs. Kuebler's condition and concluded there was need for skilled nursing services. . . . There is no directly contrary medical evidence cited or presented. It is clear that the Secretary has assessed the list of services rendered by San Simeon and found her medical judgment more sound than that of medical professionals. . . .

Notes on Medicare Utilization Review

Brief History of Medicare Utilization Review

The scope of Medicare coverage is limited by several conditions intended to assure that Medicare services are, in fact, necessary. The Health Care Financing Administration (HCFA) also has a complicated process for determining what new procedures and technologies will be covered Medicare benefits.

See discussion in Chapter 4. Covered services under both Part A and Part B must be "reasonable and necessary." Medicare services must also meet other prescribed conditions and definitions; in addition, certain services, for instance custodial care, are specifically excluded. All of these determinations essentially require that a decision be made whether services provided are covered, necessary, and provided in an appropriate setting. The various mechanisms that have attempted to do so throughout the history of the program, however, rarely have been regarded as successful.

The original Medicare legislation only required that physicians ordering services certify that the services were necessary, appropriate, and in accordance with other conditions of coverage. It also required hospitals and nursing homes to establish in-house utilization review committees to evaluate both the quality and necessity of Medicare services.

Not surprisingly, these utilization review mechanisms did not function very effectively and often did not function at all. In response, in the early years of the program, HEW instructed the fiscal intermediaries (insurance companies handling reimbursement for Medicare) to institute programs of retroactive review of claims for medical necessity. Despite the lack of explicit statutory authority to do so, many intermediaries implemented their programs enthusiastically. Most hired nurses to review claims against standardized grids; decisions to deny reimbursement were reviewed by physicians. Hundreds of claims, particularly for nursing home care, were denied. Medicare beneficiaries often found themselves in the confusing situation of receiving a bill for services ordered by their providers but for which Medicare later refused to pay.

In 1972, Congress sought to correct some of these problems and established a program of Professional Standards Review Organizations (PSROs) that would organize local physicians to review the quality, necessity, and appropriateness of Medicare (and Medicaid) institutional services. The underlying notion was that groups of physicians independent of a particular institution would have more expertise and more independence than prior mechanisms. The program would, therefore, both reduce Medicare expenditures and improve the quality of covered services. Unfortunately, the PSRO program was not particularly successful for a variety of reasons. Many physicians aggressively resisted forming PSRO organizations. Those that formed them often delegated all responsibilities back to individual hospitals. In fact, only a small percentage of Medicare services were actually reviewed for necessity and quality by PSROs.

In 1982, Congress replaced the PSRO program with the Peer Review of Utilization and Quality Program (PRO). PROs are similar to the PSROs they replaced but have some significant differences. There are fewer, larger PROs. While PSROs were nonprofit organizations controlled by physicians, PROs can be any group that contracts with the Secretary to perform the review functions. The scope and kinds of services reviewed and other PRO functions are negotiated in these contracts. Whether PROs will improve on the track record of PSROs or of other utilization review mechanisms—or even be continued—remains to be seen.

For a more detailed discussion of PSROs, PROs, and their effectiveness, see Chapter 5. For a description of the appeals procedures for beneficiaries and providers, see Chapter 3.

Utilization Review in Skilled Nursing Homes

The primary focus of the PRO program is on inpatient hospital services, as had been the focus of its predecessor programs. Nonetheless, the new PRO contracts provide for review of nursing home as well as hospital services. Whether PROs will be successful in reviewing nursing home services, however, is also difficult to predict. In many areas, Medicare review of the need for and appropriateness of skilled nursing home care continues to function much like the administrative practice adopted for both nursing homes and hospitals during the period 1965 to 1972. Not surprisingly, therefore, some of the same problems persist, as demonstrated by *Kuebler.*

Beneficiaries have frequently challenged the validity of individual decisions as in the *Kuebler* case. Dozens of federal court decisions have required Medicare payment relying on the principles set forth in *Kuebler.* Courts in dozens of other cases have given greater deference to the Secretary's determination that care was unnecessary or merely custodial. See, for instance, Johnson v. Richardson, 336 F. Supp. 390 (E.D. Pa. 1971).

In Fox v. Bowen, 656 F. Supp. 1236 (D. Conn. 1987), the federal court condemned the practice of arbitrarily denying skilled nursing home coverage to patients requiring daily physical therapy treatments, finding a violation of the due process clause of the Fifth Amendment. (But the court rejected, without statutory analysis, the claim that ex post facto review also violates the federal statute.) The court did, however, attempt to rework the government's administrative process and to eliminate some of the inequities. A special master appointed by the court developed procedures requiring the fiscal intermediaries to review beneficiary records in a manner most favorable to finding eligibility. The court ordered that ambiguities or insufficiencies in the beneficiary's record are not sufficient to support a retroactive denial of payment unless there is no plausible way to support eligibility. Working with a panel of expert physical therapists, the master developed an evaluation form to be used as the primary coverage assessment instrument for patients entering a skilled nursing facility. If eligibility is established under these standards, the fiscal intermediary may reverse only with the agreements of a physical therapist, who shall describe with great specificity why the therapy involved does not qualify the patient for skilled nursing home benefits. The court has retained jurisdiction to review the operation of these new procedures. See also New York State Department of Social Services v. Bowen, 846 F.2d 129 (2d Cir. 1988).

In a recent decision factually similar to *Kuebler,* the Second Circuit required Medicare to cover skilled nursing home services for a patient who remained in the hospital because no skilled nursing bed could be located. The lower court had upheld the agency's finding that the patient required only custodial care. The circuit court held that since the patient was under restraint and required injections of psychotropic drugs, there was no evidentiary basis for the agency's decision. Further, since no skilled nursing home bed was available, Medicare was required to pay for the in-hospital skilled nursing services. Hurley v. Bowen, 857 F.2d 907 (2d Cir. 1988).

Who Bears the Liability when Services are Denied?

As a general rule, when a Medicare claim is denied — for any reason — the liability for the provider's bill falls on the beneficiary. Under prior law, this had been true even when the denial was based on the necessity or appropriateness of the service or when it was made retroactively. As a result, in many cases a beneficiary can be liable for services that are not covered by Medicare even though she acted in good faith and had no reason to believe the services were not covered, and even when the provider is at fault or the services are inappropriate or unnecessary.

Subsequent to *Kuebler,* the federal statute was amended. As of 1989, a beneficiary who does not know and does not have reason to know that services are not covered cannot be billed by the provider in three specific situations: (1) when the services are found to be not reasonable or necessary, including level of care determinations; (2) when custodial care is involved; and (3) when home health care benefits are denied because the beneficiary is not "homebound." See 42 U.S.C. §1395pp(a) (1982 and Supp. 1989); 42 C.F.R. §405.330 (1988).

If a beneficiary has no knowledge, the provider can only bill the beneficiary for cost sharing liability. If both the provider and the beneficiary do not know the service is not covered, Medicare will accept liability. There are also various other situations in which Medicare will accept liability for "noncovered" services: for instance, there is a limited grace period following notice of noncoverage of some institutional services.

d. Medicare Financing and Revenue Reform

Since the first full year of its implementation, total Medicare expenditures have risen from $3.4 billion to over $90 billion in 1988, representing nearly 50 percent of all government spending for personal health care. The rate of this increase has been dramatic, nearly doubling the aggregate growth rate of NHEs during the last two decades and growing as much as 20 percent in some years. In the most recent years, however, the rate of Medicare expenditure growth, as with other health care spending, has moderated. Indeed, the growth rates in 1986 and 1987 were dramatically lower than in previous years and notably lower than the growth rates of NHEs for those same years. All of the moderation, however, was in Part A costs. Part B costs continued to skyrocket. For a full discussion, see Chapter 3. Moreover, most experts insist that Medicare expenditures will continue to grow in the future at rates that will *exceed* those for health care generally and, as a consequence, will continue to demand even larger portions of the federal budget. The Medicare population continues to grow faster than the general population; there is a trend of increasing "intensity" of services for the Medicare population, in contrast to the trend for the rest of the population; and, of course, it is universally accepted that medical care prices will continue to inflate at rates faster than those of prices in the rest of the economy.

While the rising costs of Medicare have many implications, they are sure to focus significant attention on the peculiar revenue structure of Medicare. A portion of the Social Security payroll tax is put in a separate Part A trust fund from which all Part A expenditures are paid. For the first two decades of the program, the Part A trust fund had annual surpluses. More recently, as Medicare Part A costs have risen rapidly, the payroll tax revenues have been rising more slowly. Annual deficits are now predicted, and the Part A trust fund will eventually be depleted. According to congressional sources in 1988, recent changes in Medicare reimbursement and other cost containing measures (see discussion below), should allow the surplus in the Part A trust fund to carry the fund through the next decade. Given present assumptions, the trust fund is not expected to be depleted until some time after the turn of the century. For a discussion, see House Committee on Ways and Means, 100th Cong. 2d Sess., Background Material on Programs Within the Jurisdiction of the Committee on Ways and Means 136-142 (1988).

The financial picture for the Part B trust fund is somewhat different. The Part B trust fund receives general revenues each year to supplement the approximately 25 percent of program costs paid by beneficiary premiums. Thus the trust fund cannot be automatically depleted. It nevertheless represents a growing portion of general revenue expenditures. The most recent predictions by congressional experts indicate that Part B expenditures will grow at an average annual rate of over 13 percent through 1993, much faster than the growth of federal general revenues. Id. at 137.

What is at stake here is substantial. The Medicare Part A shortfall could be as much as $100 billion a year by the end of the 1990s. New general revenues for Medicare Part B (or reductions in Part B expenditures) may require as much as $20 billion annually by the end of the 1990s. For a more detailed discussion, see Ginsburg and Moon, An Introduction to the Medicare Financing Problem, 62 Milbank Mem. Fund Q. 167 (1984).

The Reagan Administration, as it had for Medicaid and other domestic spending programs, envisioned substantial structural changes in Medicare, in order to contain its fiscal impact and to reorient the program in accordance with the Administration's conservative agenda. But the Administration was only partially successful in reducing federal expenditures for Medicare; it has been estimated that as much as $25 billion in budget reductions (actual Medicare program costs as compared to projected costs if the program had not been changed) were enacted from 1981 to 1985. See Background Materials on Programs Within the Jurisdiction of the Committee on Ways and Means, supra, at 144-147. Yet despite the Administration's efforts to restructure the program, Medicare emerged from the Reagan years essentially unchanged. More importantly, as noted above, recent changes only delayed the depletion of the Part A trust fund and did little to correct the imbalance built into the Medicare revenues structure.

Most of the Administration's more radical proposals to limit program coverage, means test eligibility, or shift Medicare towards a voucher-based program, were rejected altogether. On the beneficiary side, Congress enacted a few relatively minor program reductions, but made notable increases in beneficiary cost sharing. All told, congressional experts have estimated that out-of-pocket spending for health by the elderly was increased from $966 per individual annually in 1980 to $2,394 annually in 1988 — mainly from increases in Medicare cost sharing. The enactment of the 1988 catastrophic coverage amendments will only partially soften this impact. While the impact of these changes on the individual Medicare recipient has been substantial, in aggregate terms most of the Medicare budget savings in the 1980s, however, can be attributed to major changes in provider reimbursement policy enacted during this period, particularly the revisions in Medicare hospital reimbursement. See full discussion of these changes in Chapter 3. But regardless of whether these reimbursement changes are continued or expanded, the sheer size of the Medicare "cost problem(s)" dictates that further changes will be considered in the cost sharing required of Medicare beneficiaries and, in particular, in the revenue structure that will only support the program for a few more years.

Medicare has long been billed as an insurance scheme, paid for by future beneficiaries through a tax on their current earnings. The additional revenues that will be needed to continue the program as it is currently structured could be realized by further increases in the Social Security payroll tax rate. Medicare Part A payroll tax revenues could also be supplemented by a portion of general revenues, much as Part B revenues currently are, although this would require a further erosion of the notion of "Medicare-as-insurance."

It has also been suggested that new forms of taxation could be undertaken, with the revenues from these taxes to be earmarked for Medicare. Some critics have advocated a national value-added tax or a national revenue-producing lottery as sources of Medicare revenues. It has also been frequently argued that certain excise taxes, such as those on tobacco and alcohol, could be appropriately designated for Medicare funding.

Other potential sources of new revenue for Medicare focus more exclusively on the beneficiary population. Obviously, as urged by the Reagan Administration, the Medicare revenue shortfall could be avoided by increasing beneficiary cost sharing at the time of delivery of service or by increasing the co-insurance or deductibles paid by recipients with a resulting reduction in trust fund liability. See discussion Chapter 8. There also has been some discussion of further increasing the premiums paid for Part B eligibility, as was done in 1988 either across the board or by "means testing," maintaining universal eligibility for all recipients but requiring higher income recipients to pay higher premiums. The income tax surcharge imposed in 1988, albeit unpopular, has spawned further proposals to tax the income of the elderly and to earmark the resulting revenues for the Medicare trust fund(s). A similar result could be achieved by treating Medicare benefits as taxable income.

Aside from the technical problems of designing a revenue reform that will produce the desired increase in revenue, these reforms raise some basic social and political issues. As noted above, Medicare was originally structured to parallel an insurance program wherein workers' payroll tax revenues financed their future benefits. If additional revenues are required to finance the future of the program, should this "pay as you go" concept be retained? Similarly, if beneficiaries are asked to pay a larger portion of Medicare's cost, should all beneficiaries pay the same amount, or should the revenue burden be "means tested"? Should all eligibles pay more or only "users"? For a good discussion of these proposals, concerning both intragenerational and intergenerational equity questions, and other related issues, see Long & Smeeding, Alternative Medicare Financing Sources, 62 Milbank Mem. Fund Q. 325 (1984).

3. CONSTITUTIONAL CONSTRAINTS ON THE SCOPE OF GOVERNMENT SPONSORED HEALTH INSURANCE PROGRAMS

Memorial Hospital v. Maricopa County

415 U.S. 250 (1974)

Mr. Justice MARSHALL delivered the opinion of the Court.

This case presents an appeal from a decision of the Arizona Supreme Court upholding an Arizona statute requiring a year's residence in a county as a condition to receiving nonemergency hospitalization or medical care at the county's expense. The constitutional question presented is whether this durational residence requirement is repugnant to the Equal Protection Clause as applied by this Court in Shapiro v. Thompson, 394 U.S. 61 (1969).

Appellant Henry Evaro is an indigent suffering from a chronic asthmatic and bronchial illness. In early June 1971, Mr. Evaro moved from New Mexico to Phoenix in Maricopa County, Arizona. On July 8, 1971, Evaro had a severe respiratory attack and was sent by his attending physician to appellant Memorial Hospital, a nonprofit private community hospital. Pursuant to the

Arizona statute governing medical care for indigents, Memorial notified the Maricopa County Board of Supervisors that it had in its charge an indigent who might qualify for county care and requested that Evaro be transferred to the county's public hospital facility. In accordance with the approved procedures, Memorial also claimed reimbursement from the County in the amount of $1,202.60, for the care and services it had provided Evaro.

Under Arizona law, the individual county governments are charged with the mandatory duty of providing necessary hospital and medical care for their indigent sick. But the statute requires an indigent to have been a resident of the County for the preceding 12 months in order to be eligible for free nonemergency medical care. Maricopa County refused to admit Evaro to its public hospital or to reimburse Memorial solely because Evaro had not been a resident of the County for the preceding year. Appellees do not dispute that Evaro is an indigent or that he is a bona fide resident of Maricopa County. . . .

The trial court held the residence requirement unconstitutional as a violation of the Equal Protection Clause. [T]he Arizona Supreme Court upheld the challenged requirement. [W]e reverse the judgment of the Arizona Supreme Court.

In determining whether the challenged durational residence provision violates the Equal Protection Clause, we must first determine what burden of justification the classification created thereby must meet, by looking to the nature of the classification and the individual interests affected. The Court considered similar durational residence requirements for welfare assistance in Shapiro v. Thompson, 394 U.S. 618 (1969). The Court observed that those requirements created two classes of needy residents "indistinguishable from each other except that one is composed of residents who have resided a year or more, and the second of residents who have resided less than a year, in the jurisdiction. On the basis of this sole difference the first class [was] granted and second class [was] denied welfare aid upon which may depend the ability . . . to obtain the very means to subsist — food, shelter, and other necessities of life." Id. at 627. The Court found that because this classification impinged on the constitutionally guaranteed right of interstate travel, it was to be judged by the standard of whether it promoted a compelling state interest. Finding such an interest wanting, the Court held the challenged residence requirements unconstitutional.

Appellees argue that the residence requirement before us is distinguishable from those in *Shapiro,* while appellants urge that *Shapiro* is controlling. We agree with appellants that Arizona's durational residence requirement for free medical care must be justified by a compelling state interest and that, such interests being lacking, the requirement is unconstitutional.

The right of interstate travel has repeatedly been recognized as a basic constitutional freedom. Whatever its ultimate scope, however, the right to travel was involved in only a limited sense in *Shapiro*. The Court was there concerned only with the right to migrate, "with intent to settle and abide" or, as the Court put it, "to migrate, resettle, find a new job, and start a new life." Id. at 629. Even a bona fide residence requirement would burden the right to travel, if travel meant merely movement. But, in *Shapiro*, the Court explained that "[t]he residence requirement and the one-year waiting-period requirement are distinct and independent prerequisites" for assistance and only the latter was held to be unconstitutional. Id. at 636. . . .

It is true, as appellees argue, that there is no evidence in the record before us that anyone was actually deterred from traveling by the challenged restriction. But neither did the majority in *Shapiro* find any reason "to dispute the 'evidence that few welfare recipients have in fact been deterred [from moving] by residence requirements.' Indeed, none of the litigants had themselves been deterred." Dunn [v. Blumstein,], 405 U.S. at 340 (1972). An attempt to distinguish *Shapiro* by urging that a durational residence requirement for voter registration did not deter travel was found to be a "fundamental misunderstanding of the law" in *Dunn,* supra, at 339-340. "*Shapiro* did not rest upon a finding that denial of welfare actually deterred travel. Nor have other 'right to travel' cases in this Court always relied on the presence of actual deterrence. In *Shapiro* we explicitly stated that the compelling-state-interest test would be triggered by 'any classification which serves to *penalize* the exercise of that right [to travel].'". . .

Whatever the ultimate parameters of the *Shapiro* penalty analysis, it is at least clear that medical care is as much "a basic necessity of life" to an indigent as welfare assistance. And, governmental privileges or benefits necessary to basic sustenance have often been viewed as being of greater constitutional significance than less essential forms of governmental entitlements. It would be odd, indeed, to find that the State of Arizona was required to afford Evaro welfare assistance to keep him from the discomfort of inadequate housing or the pangs of hunger but could deny him the medical care necessary to relieve him from the wheezing and gasping for breath that attend his illness.

Nor does the fact that the durational residence requirement is inapplicable to the provision of emergency medical care save the challenged provision from constitutional doubt. As the Arizona Supreme Court observed, appellant "Evaro was an indigent person who *required* continued medical care for the preservation of his health and well being . . . ," even if he did not require immediate emergency care. The State could not deny Evaro care just because, although gasping for breath, he was not in immediate danger of stopping breathing altogether. To allow a serious illness to go untreated until it requires emergency hospitalization is to subject the sufferer to the danger of a substantial and irrevocable deterioration in his health. Cancer, heart disease, or respiratory illness, if untreated for a year, may become all but irreversible paths to pain, disability, and even loss of life. The denial of medical care is all the more cruel in this context, falling as it does on indigents who are often without the means to obtain alternative treatment.

We turn now to the question of whether the State has shown that its durational residence requirement is "legitimately defensible," in that it furthers a compelling state interest. A number of purposes are asserted to be served by the requirement, and we must determine whether these satisfy the appellees' heavy burden of justification, and insure that the State, in pursuing its asserted objectives, has chosen means that do not unnecessarily burden constitutionally protected interests.

The County . . . attempts to sustain the requirement as a necessary means to insure the fiscal integrity of its free medical care program by discouraging an influx of indigents, particularly those entering the County for the sole purpose of obtaining the benefits of its hospital facilities.

First, a State may not protect the public fisc by drawing an invidious distinction between classes of its citizens, so appellees must do more than show that denying free medical care to new residents saves money. . . .

Second, to the extent the purpose of the requirement is to inhibit the immigration of indigents generally, that goal is constitutionally impermissible. And, to the extent the purpose is to deter only those indigents who take up residence in the County solely to utilize its new and modern public medical facilities, the requirement at issue is clearly overinclusive. The challenged durational residence requirement treats every indigent, in his first year of residence, as if he came to the jurisdiction solely to obtain free medical care. . . .

In addition, the County's claimed fiscal savings may well be illusory. The lack of timely medical care could cause a patient's condition to deteriorate to a point where more expensive emergency hospitalization (for which no durational residence requirement applies) is needed. And, the disability that may result from letting an untreated condition deteriorate may well result in the patient and his family becoming a burden on the State's welfare rolls for the duration of his emergency care, or permanently, if his capacity to work is impaired. . . .

The appellees also argue that the challenged statute serves some administrative objectives. They claim that the one-year waiting period is a convenient rule of thumb to determine bona fide residence. Besides not being factually defensible, this test is certainly overbroad to accomplish its avowed purpose. . . . Less drastic means, which do not impinge on the right of interstate travel, are available and employed to ascertain an individual's true intentions, without exacting a protracted waiting period which may have dire economic and health consequences for certain citizens. . . .

Harris v. McRae

448 U.S. 297 (1980)

Mr. Justice STEWART delivered the opinion of the Court.

This case presents statutory and constitutional questions concerning the public funding of abortions under . . . the "Medicaid" Act, and recent annual Appropriations Acts containing the so-called "Hyde Amendment.". . .

[T]he Hyde Amendment . . . provides:

> [N]one of the funds provided by this joint resolution shall be used to perform abortions except where the life of the mother would be endangered if the fetus were carried to term; or except where such medical procedures are necessary for victims of rape or incest. . . .

We address first the appellee's argument that the Hyde Amendment, by restricting the availability of certain medically necessary abortions under Medicaid, impinges on the "liberty" protected by the Due Process Clause as recognized in Roe v. Wade, 410 U.S. 113, and its progeny.

The Hyde Amendment, like the Connecticut welfare regulation at issue in Maher [v. Roe], places no governmental obstacle in the path of a woman who chooses to terminate her pregnancy, but rather, by means of unequal subsidization of abortion and other medical services, encourages alternative activity deemed in the public interest. The present case does differ factually from *Maher* insofar as that case involved a failure to fund nontherapeutic abortions, whereas the Hyde Amendment affects a significant interest not present or asserted in *Maher* — the interest of a woman in protecting her health during pregnancy — and because that interest lies at the core of the personal constitutional freedom recognized in *Wade,* the present case is constitutionally different from *Maher*. . . .

But, regardless of whether the freedom of a woman to choose to terminate her pregnancy for health reasons lies at the core or the periphery of the due process liberty recognized in *Wade,* it simply does not follow that a woman's freedom of choice carries with it a constitutional entitlement to the financial resources to avail herself of the full range of protected choices. The reason why was explained in *Maher*: although government may not place obstacles in the path of a woman's exercise of her freedom of choice, it need not remove those not of its own creation. Indigency falls in the latter category. The financial constraints that restrict an indigent woman's ability to enjoy the full range of constitutionally protected freedom of choice are the product not of governmental restrictions on access to abortions, but rather of her indigency. Although Congress has opted to subsidize medically necessary services generally, but not certain medically necessary abortions, the fact remains that the Hyde Amendment leaves an indigent woman with at least the same range of choice in deciding whether to obtain a medically necessary abortion as she would have had if Congress had chosen to subsidize no health care costs at all. . . .

It remains to be determined whether the Hyde Amendment violates the equal protection component of the Fifth Amendment. This challenge is premised on the fact that, although federal reimbursement is available under Medicaid for medically necessary services generally, the Hyde Amendment does not permit federal reimbursement of all medically necessary abortions. The District Court held, and the appellees argue here, that this selective subsidization violates the constitutional guarantee of equal protection.

The guarantee of equal protection under the Fifth Amendment is not a source of substantive rights or liberties, but rather a right to be free from invidious discrimination in statutory classifications and other governmental activity. It is well-settled that where a statutory classification does not itself impinge on a right or liberty protected by the Constitution, the validity of classification must be sustained unless "the classification rests on grounds wholly irrelevant to the achievement of [any legitimate governmental] objective." This presumption of constitutional validity, however, disappears if a statutory classification is predicated on criteria that are, in a constitutional sense, "suspect," the principal example of which is a classification based on race. . . .

The remaining question then is whether the Hyde Amendment is rationally related to a legitimate governmental objective. It is the Government's position that the Hyde Amendment bears a rational relationship to its legitimate interest in protecting the potential life of the fetus. We agree.

In *Wade,* the Court recognized that the State has "an important and legitimate interest in protecting the potentiality of human life." That interest was found to exist throughout a pregnancy, "grow[ing] in substantiality as the woman approaches term." Moreover, in *Maher,* the Court held that Connecticut's decision to fund the costs associated with childbirth but not those associated with nontherapeutic abortions was a rational means of advancing the legitimate state interest in protecting potential life by encouraging childbirth.

It follows that the Hyde Amendment, by encouraging childbirth except in the most urgent circumstances, is rationally related to the legitimate governmental objective of protecting potential life. By subsidizing the medical expenses of indigent women who carry their pregnancies to term while not subsidizing the comparable expenses of women who undergo abortions (except those whose lives are threatened), Congress has established incentives that make childbirth a more attractive alternative than abortion for persons eligible for Medicaid. These incentives bear a direct relationship to the legitimate congressional interest in protecting potential life. Nor is it irrational that Congress has authorized federal reimbursement for medically necessary services generally, but not for certain medically necessary abortions. Abortion is inherently different from other medical procedures, because no other procedure involves the purposeful termination of a potential life. . . .

Where, as here, the Congress has neither invaded a substantive constitutional right or freedom, nor enacted legislation that purposefully operates to the detriment of a suspect class, the only requirement of equal protection is that congressional action be rationally related to a legitimate governmental interest. The Hyde Amendment satisfies that standard. It is not the mission of this Court or any other to decide whether the balance of competing interests reflected in the Hyde Amendment is wise social policy. If that were our mission, not every Justice who has subscribed to the judgment of the Court today could have done so. But we cannot, in the name of the Constitution, overturn duly enacted statutes simply "because they may be unwise, improvident, or out of harmony with a particular school of thought.". . .

Mr. Justice BRENNAN, with whom Mr. Justice MARSHALL and Mr. Justice BLACKMUN join, dissenting.

I agree entirely with my Brother Stevens that the State's interest in protecting the potential life of the fetus cannot justify the exclusion of financially and medically needy women from the benefits to which they would otherwise be entitled solely because the treatment that a doctor has concluded is medically necessary involves an abortion. I write separately to express my continuing disagreement with the Court's mischaracterization of the nature of the fundamental right recognized in Roe v. Wade, 410 U.S. 113 (1973), and its misconception of the manner in which that right is infringed by federal and state legislation withdrawing all funding for medically necessary abortions.

Roe v. Wade held that the constitutional right to personal privacy encompasses a woman's decision whether or not to terminate her pregnancy. *Roe* and its progeny established that the pregnant woman has a right to be free from state interference with her choice to have an abortion — a right which, at least prior to the end of the first trimester, absolutely prohibits any governmental regulation of that highly personal decision. The proposition for which these cases stand thus is not that the State is under an affirmative obligation to ensure access to abortions for all who may desire them; it is that the State must refrain from wielding its enormous power and influence in a manner that might burden the pregnant woman's freedom to choose whether to have an abortion. The Hyde Amendment's denial of public funds for medically necessary abortions plainly intrudes upon this constitutionally protected decision, for both by design and in effect it serves to coerce indigent pregnant woman to bear children that they would otherwise elect not to have.

When viewed in the context of the Medicaid program to which it is appended, it is obvious that the Hyde Amendment is nothing less than an attempt by Congress to circumvent the dictates of the Constitution and achieve indirectly what Roe v. Wade said it could not do directly. . . . As my Brother Stevens persuasively demonstrates, exclusion of medically necessary abortions from Medicaid coverage cannot be justified as a cost-saving device. Rather, the Hyde Amendment is a transparent attempt by the Legislative Branch to impose the political majority's judgment of the morally acceptable and socially desirable preference on a sensitive and intimate decision that the Constitution entrusts to the individual. Worse yet, the Hyde Amendment does not foist that majoritarian viewpoint with equal measure upon everyone in our Nation, rich and poor alike; rather, it imposes that viewpoint only upon that segment of our society which, because of its position of political powerlessness, is least able to defend its privacy rights from encroachments of state-mandated morality. . . .

Moreover, it is clear that the Hyde Amendment not only was designed to inhibit, but does in fact inhibit the woman's freedom to choose abortion over childbirth. . . .

A poor woman in the early stages of pregnancy confronts two alternatives: she may elect either to carry the fetus to term or to have an abortion. In the abstract, of course, this choice is hers alone. . . . But the reality of the situation is that the Hyde Amendment has effectively removed this choice from the indigent woman's hands. By funding all of the expenses associated with childbirth and none of the expenses incurred in terminating pregnancy, the Government literally makes an offer that the indigent woman cannot afford to refuse. It matters not that in this instance the Government has used the carrot rather than the stick. What is critical is the realization that as a practical matter, many poverty-stricken women will choose to carry their pregnancy to term simply because the Government provides funds for the associated medical services, even though these same women would have chosen to have an abortion if the Government had also paid for that option, or indeed if the Government had stayed out of the picture altogether and had defrayed the costs of neither procedure. . . .

It would belabor the obvious to expound at any great length on the illegitimacy of a state policy that interferes with the exercise of fundamental rights through the selective bestowal of governmental favors. It suffices to note that we have heretofore never hesitated to invalidate any scheme of granting or withholding financial benefits that incidentally or intentionally burdens one manner of exercising a constitutionally protected choice. . . .

Mr. Justice MARSHALL, dissenting. . . .

This case is perhaps the most dramatic illustration to date of the deficiencies in the Court's obsolete "two-tiered" approach to the Equal Protection Clause. . . . With all deference, I am unable to understand how the Court can afford the same level of scrutiny to the legislation involved here — whose cruel impact falls exclusively on indigent pregnant women — that it has given to legislation distinguishing opticians from ophthalmologists, or to other legislation that makes distinctions between economic interests more than able to protect themselves in the political process. . . . I do not believe that legislation that imposes a crushing burden on indigent women can be treated with the same deference given to legislation distinguishing among business interests.

The Hyde Amendment, of course, distinguishes between medically necessary abortions and other medically necessary expenses. As I explained in Maher v. Roe, supra, such classifications must be assessed by weighing "'the importance of the governmental benefits denied, the character of the class, and the asserted state interests,'" id., at 458, quoting Massachusetts Board of Retirement v. Murgia, [427 U.S.] at 322. Under that approach, the Hyde Amendment is clearly invalid.

As in *Maher*, the governmental benefits at issue here are "of absolutely vital importance in the lives of the recipients." Maher v. Roe, at 458 (Marshal, J., dissenting). . . .

The class burdened by the Hyde Amendment consists of indigent women, a substantial proportion of whom are members of minority races. . . .

. . . In *Maher*, the Court found a permissible state interest in encouraging normal childbirth. The governmental interest in the present case is substantially weaker than in *Maher*, for under the Hyde Amendment funding is refused even in cases in which normal childbirth will not result: one can scarcely speak of "normal childbirth" in cases where the fetus will die shortly after birth, or in which the mother's life will be shortened or her health otherwise gravely impaired by the birth. . . . In these circumstances, I am unable to see how even a minimally rational legislature could conclude that the interest in fetal life outweighs the brutal effect of the Hyde Amendment on indigent women. Moreover, both the legislation in *Maher* and the Hyde Amendment were designed to deprive poor and minority women of the constitutional right to choose abortion. That purpose is not constitutionally permitted under Roe v. Wade. . . .

Ultimately, the result reached today may be traced to the Court's unwillingness to apply the constraints of the Constitution to decisions involving the expenditure of governmental funds. . . . The Court perceives this result as simply a distinction between a "limitation on governmental power" and "an affirmative funding obligation." For a poor person attempting to exercise her "right" to freedom of choice, the difference is imperceptible. . . .

In this case, the Federal Government has taken upon itself the burden of financing practically all medically necessary expenditures. One category of medically necessary expenditure has been singled out for exclusion, and the sole basis for the exclusion is a premise repudiated for purposes of constitutional law in Roe v. Wade. The consequence is a devastating impact on the lives and health of poor women. I do not believe that a Constitution committed to the equal protection of the laws can tolerate this result. . . .

NOTES: CONSTITUTIONAL CONSTRAINTS ON GOVERNMENT-SPONSORED HEALTH INSURANCE PROGRAMS

The Constitutional Idea of Equality

Since the 1960s, constitutional jurisprudence has been dominated by a two-tiered equal protection analysis. The first tier, applicable to all state action, requires that the government must have some reasonable basis for distinguishing between citizens in the distribution of penalties and benefits. In applying this core rationality requirement, the Court is highly deferential to the government and will uphold any classification based "upon a state of facts that reasonably can be conceived to constitute a distinction, or difference in state policy. . . ."

The second tier of equality analysis requires more demanding scrutiny of both state purposes and the "fit" between the classification drawn and the goals served. This more rigorous scrutiny is triggered by a finding that the challenged classification is either drawn on a suspect basis or that it burdens the exercise of a fundamental constitutionally protected right.

Race is the classic suspect classification. Lines drawn on nationality, ancestry, or the basis of the marital status of children's parents are also suspect. More generally, many commentators and some justices have urged that the suspect classification concept should protect against any government action tainted by "prejudice against discrete and insular minorities," the sort of prejudice "which tends . . . to curtail the operation of those political processes ordinarily to be relied upon to protect minorities" in our society. United States v. Carolene Products Co. 304 U.S. 144, 152-53, n. 4 (1938).

More rigorous equality scrutiny is also required when government action burdens the exercise of fundamental rights. For example, in Skinner v. Oklahoma, 316 U.S. 535 (1942), the Court struck down a law requiring the sterilization of recidivist criminals but exempting those convicted of white collar crimes. See also Sherbert v. Verner, 374 U.S. 398 (1963).

Maricopa is one of many decisions striking down state policies drawing classifications that burden the exercise of important rights. The rights that trigger this more searching equal protection review include those explicitly protected by the Constitution, such as freedom of religion or speech, as well as other important interests that enjoy only implicit constitutional protection such as the right to vote, Dunn v. Blumstein, 405 U.S. 330 (1972), and the right to travel from state to state, Shapiro v. Thompson, 394 U.S. 618 (1969).

As *Maricopa* illustrates, the second tier of equal protection scrutiny, applicable if a classification is drawn on a suspect basis or burdens the exercise of a fundamental right, places a high burden of justification upon the state. The "strict scrutiny" applied in these cases is, in Professor Gunther's words, "strict" in theory and "fatal" in fact. Gunther, The Supreme Court, 1971 Term — Foreword: In Search of Evolving Doctrine on a Changing Court: A Model for a Newer Equal Protection, 86 Harv. L. Rev. 1, 8 (1972). The two-tiered approach to equal protection analysis is highly dichotomized. The basic rationality requirement of the first tier is highly deferential to state discretion. But if a classification draws lines on a suspect basis or burdens a fundamental right, the state must demonstrate a "compelling" reason for its action.

This dichotomized, two-tier, mode of equality analysis has been challenged from several directions. Women and handicapped people have argued that gender and handicap should be treated as suspect classifications, like race. There are powerful analogies among race, gender, and handicap. Each is obvious, immutable, and not attributable to any individual fault. Gender is like race in that it does not correlate with ability to perform or contribute. But most fundamentally, women, blacks, and handicapped people share a history of oppression and exclusion from mainstream political processes.

Nonetheless, the Court, perceiving that there may be circumstances in which it might be legitimate to differentiate on the basis of gender or handicap, has refused to characterize classifications based on these factors as "suspect." Rather, the Court has described classifications based on gender or handicap as "quasi-suspect" and has required that they be supported by "important" state interests that might be something less than "compelling." Craig v. Boren, 429 U.S. 190 (1976); Cleburne v. Cleburne Living Center, 473 U.S. 432 (1985).

The two-tiered analysis also has been challenged by many cases involving welfare programs. As noted supra, welfare programs have historically sought to encourage work and distinguish the "worthy" from the "unworthy" poor. People are often granted or denied aid on the basis of their family composition. On the other hand, private choices about family composition are of fundamental human importance. In Dandridge v. Williams, 397 U.S. 471 (1970), welfare recipients challenged a Maryland rule that placed a fixed maximum on the aid available to large families. Despite the argument that the result was to give a smaller grant per person to people in larger families, the Court in a 5-4 decision supported state discretion to fix welfare grant levels.

Is it possible to reconcile the Court's decisions in *Maricopa* and *Harris*? In both, the Court had previously recognized an independent constitutional right — to travel and to privacy — that was burdened by the government's funding distinctions. For several reasons, *Harris* seems an easier case. The practical consequence of *Maricopa* was to impose new financial burdens on the county. In contrast, in *Harris* the government could not argue that denying payment for medically necessary abortions saves public funds. Further, no evidence supported the assumption that Maricopa County's policy would, in fact, deter people like Mr. Evaro from exercising their constitutionally protected right to travel from state to state, while substantial evidence showed that denying Medicaid for medically necessary abortions actually deters poor women's exercise of the constitutional rights recognized in Roe v. Wade, 410 U.S. 113 (1973). Finally, the Medicaid statute incorporates a very strong principle prohibiting discrimination on the basis of diagnosis. Congress has abrogated that principle only in relation to abortion.

For a good critique, see Perry, Why the Supreme Court Was Plainly Wrong in the Hyde Amendment Case: A Brief Comment on Harris v. McRae, 32 Stan. L. Rev. 1113 (1980). For a good defense, see Appleton Beyond the Limits of Reproductive Choice: The Contributions of the Abortion Funding Cases to the Fundamental-Rights Analysis and to the Welfare-Rights Thesis, 81 Colum. L. Rev. 721 (1981).

An Affirmative Constitutional Right to Medical Care?

There is substantial rhetorical and political support for a "right" to health care. However, as a constitutional matter, there are large obstacles to the recognition of such a right. First, the Constitution constrains only the state, not "private" actors. So, for example, when a "private" doctor informs his poor pregnant patients that he will not deliver their babies unless they agree to be sterilized, there is no basis for constitutional challenge because there is no state action. A second pervasive obstacle to recognition of a constitutional right to medical care that would actually guarantee people the care they need and want is the constitutional analogue of the common law's "no duty" principle. *Maricopa* and *Harris* both affirm the principle that the government has no duty to provide essential medical services. It is only when the government has undertaken to provide medical care that constitutional guarantees of equality and fair treatment come into play. Even then, as these cases demonstrate, the government has broad discretion to limit the coverage provided.

Constitutional claims are most likely to contribute to assuring access to medical care when used to challenge affirmative state actions restricting access to services. Andrews v. Ballard, 498 F. Supp. 1038 (S.D. Tex. 1980), for example, strikes down a broad prohibition on acupuncture as unconstitutional. And Roe v. Wade struck down criminal sanctions against abortion. See Chapter 10. These are, however, the high water marks of constitutional protection against state policies restricting access to medical care.

Note: Critical Dimensions of Third Party Payment

	Coverage	*Exclusions/Limits*	*Cost Sharing*	*Terms of Reimbursement*	*Conditions on Reimbursement*	*Integration Providers*
Medicare Part A	comprehensive — most inpatient hospital care	durational limits; long term care excluded	substantial co-insurance and deductibles	prospective DRG reimbursement (no assignment)	voluntary participation but PRO and other conditions imposed on participants	generally no (some Medicaid HMOs)
Medicare Part B	comprehensive — most M.D. and outpatient services	dental care, glasses, preventive care excluded	co-insurance 20% on all services; substantial deductible	customary, prevailing, reasonable (assignment)	voluntary participation with minor conditions on participants	(same as above)
Medicaid	variable (mandatory services plus options)	variable; scope, amount, durational limits; exclusions; other "gaps" in coverage	(limited co-insurance and deductibles)	cost-related reimbursement for hospitals; prospective fee schedules or CPR for M.D. (no assignment)	voluntary with PRO and other conditions; also case management for some beneficiaries	(some HMOs)
Service-Benefit Plans	generally comprehensive	variable; service exclusions and durational limits; maximum liability limits	substantial co-insurance and deductibles	cost-related for hospitals; usual, customary, reasonable for M.D. (assignment varies)	(some) utilization, prior authorization, and other admin. controls	participating providers agree to accept plan enrollees
Indemnity Insurance	variable	(same as above)	(same as above)	fee schedules (assignment)	usually none	none
HMOs	comprehensive	excludes "out of plan" services; generally no other limits	generally no cost sharing	budget or capitation for hospitals; salary or capitation for M.D.	utilization review and other in-house controls	plan's providers obligated to treat enrollees; enrollees cannot go outside plan

CHAPTER

III

Health Care Financing: Provider Reimbursement and Cost Containment

A. The Reimbursement of Hospitals

1. EXPENDITURES FOR HOSPITAL SERVICES

Tracking virtually the same longterm course as total NHEs, aggregate spending for hospital services rapidly increased from $10.9 billion in 1950 to $195 billion in 1987, averaging nearly a 14 percent increase per year from 1965 to 1983. In the mid-1980s, along with other health spending, the rate of growth of hospital expenditures moderated; in fact, from 1984 to 1986 the rate of growth of hospital spending was *lower* than that of NHEs, dropping to a three decade low of only 6.3 percent in 1984. As Table 1 illustrates, current government estimates indicate, however, the rate of hospital spending will start to grow again in the 1990s, although it is unlikely to return to the double digit increases of the 1970s and early 1980s. For an earlier discussion of these issues, see Wing, American Health Policy in the 1980s, 56 Case W. Res. L. Rev. 608, 628-636 (1986).

Notwithstanding the apparent trend of slower growth in the mid-1980s, spending for hospital services during the last forty years has, with a few interesting exceptions, increased rapidly and measurably faster than the rest of the economy as measured by GNP growth. See Table 1. With the exceptions of the mid-1980s, the annual growth rate of hospital spending has also generally exceeded the annual growth rate of total NHEs.

The importance of hospital expenditures in defining health policy issues cannot be overstated. Historically, hospital spending has been the largest portion of the national health budget. That share has steadily grown over the last four decades; while it appears to have stabilized in the most recent years, hospital services still command over one-half of all spending for personal health services and roughly 40 percent of all NHEs. Perhaps more critical from a policy perspective, hospital expenditures have represented even higher

TABLE 1
Annual Growth Rates of Health Expenditures by Type of Service

Year	*Hospitals*	*Doctors*	*Nursing Homes*	*GNP*
2000	9.5%	8.9%	8.8%	6.4%
1995	9.5	9.5	9.2	6.6
1990	9.1	9.3	9.4	6.9
1987	9.1	12.1	8.6	6.8
1986	7.0	12.5	7.8	5.6
1985	6.7	9.4	9.8	6.4
1984	6.3	8.7	7.5	10.7
1980	16.7	16.9	14.7	8.9
1970	15.7	13.5	24.0	5.3

Division of National Cost Estimates, Office of the Actuary, Health Care Financing Administration.

proportions of total government expenditures. Moreover, these figures represent only direct hospital charges. If physician charges to hospitalized patients, spending for separately billed procedures, and rehabilitation following hospitalization were included, total spending associated with hospitalization would represent over 80 percent of all health spending. Particularly in the light of the dominant role of the hospital in modern American medicine, the analysis of the underlying causes of the growth in hospital expenditures becomes critically important for evaluating both the need for cost containment and the appropriate response to the need.

As with increases in total health care spending, price inflation has apparently played a primary and continuing role in the growth of expenditures for hospital services, even as the rate of increase in total spending has begun to moderate in recent years. Indeed, the role of price inflation in rising expenditures for hospital services in the 1980s has been particularly dominant, since utilization of hospital services during that time apparently leveled off, and even declined according to some measures.

Data collected by the hospital industry indicate that the utilization of hospital services was increasing through the 1970s. During the early 1980s, however, both the rate of inpatient admissions and the average length of an inpatient stay markedly declined. It should be noted that at the same time, the rate of admissions for outpatient services increased, as did the number of surgical procedures per admission. These changes in the utilization patterns for hospitals — particularly the decline in inpatient services — must be ranked among the most significant phenomena of the 1980s and are generally attributed to the influence of the reimbursement, peer review, and other cost containment measures that have been instituted during the past decade, as discussed infra. It should also be noted that there was no significant increase in the number of hospitals or hospital beds, or any other indication that either a change in the supply of hospital services or in the utilization of those services had been primarily responsible for the rapid growth in hospital expenditures during the 1970s. Nor did these factors play a greater role in the continuing but moderated rates of growth in the 1980s. One expert estimated that from 1966 to 1980, less than 13 percent of the increase in hospital expenditures during this period could be attributed to either increased utilization or to increases in population. The remaining 87 percent was attributable to sizable increases in expenditures per patient day of service, reflecting either inflation in the prices of hospital services or increases in the "intensity" of the services rendered to each patient.

Unfortunately, distinguishing price inflation from "intensity" in the hospital context is a particularly difficult task, confounded by some peculiar characteristics of American hospital care, not the least of which are the significant variations in utilization rates of hospital services from state to state and even within the same state — variations for which no satisfactory explanation is available. (See discussion in Chapter 5.) But even given this complication, it is fairly clear that price inflation, driven by inflation in the general economy, in addition to a rate of inflation specific to hospital services that is higher than that of the general economy, has played and continues to play a primary role in rising expenditures for hospital services. Estimates for the decade from 1973 to 1983 indicate that increases in the intensity of service per admission were responsible for less than 25 percent of the increase in total hospital expenditures. Roughly 65 percent of the increase during this period can be attributed to inflation, 50 percent of which was inflation in the general economy, and 15 percent the result of an additional hospital-specific price inflation. While more recent data are not as yet available, with the rate of inpatient admissions and the average length of stay apparently declining, the combined roles of intensity and price inflation in driving hospital expenditures must be even greater in the mid-1980s than in previous years.

The implications of these data are confirmed by other estimates of the rate of increase of hospital price inflation. As measured by average room rate increases, hospital price inflation was 11.3 percent in 1983, when the Medical Care Price Index (MCPI) was 8.7 percent, and the overall Consumer Price Index (CPI) was 3.2 percent. In 1984, hospital price inflation was only 8.3 percent, the first time that figure has dropped below double digits in nearly twenty years. Nonetheless, this rate of hospital price inflation still exceeded the MCPI by wide margins and was nearly twice the rate of the CPI for 1984. In both 1985 and 1986, the rate of hospital price inflation dropped below 6 percent and below the rates of MCPI for those years, but was still well above the CPI rates for those years.

It appears that price inflation, and to a lesser extent, increases in the intensity of the services provided, have been the driving forces behind hospital spending increases, both historically and during the most recent years, and will likely continue to be so.

2. HOSPITAL REIMBURSEMENT

The story of hospital reimbursement tracks the evolution from charge or cost based reimbursement to various attempts to limit or disallow costs, to prospective reimbursement schemes, and, most recently, to diagnosis-based prospective reimbursement and capitation schemes.

The original Blue Cross "service-benefit" plans reimbursed hospitals on a fee-for-service, per diem basis determined by the hospital's charges or a percentage of its charges. Payment levels were essentially arbitrary, depending largely on the relative negotiating strength of the hospital and Blue Cross. No comparison was made between hospitals or between costs and charges.

Even when charge based reimbursement evolved into "reasonable cost" reimbursement, the focus was to tighten accounting methodology and to disallow certain unnecessary or expensive elements of an individual hospital's expenditures. Indeed, "reasonable cost" reimbursement had little to do with reasonableness. As applied by Blue Cross through the 1960s, the average daily cost of hospital care was determined essentially by dividing the hospital's expenditures, as retrospectively accounted, by the total number of patient days. The underlying assumptions, endorsed by both the hospital industry and Blue Cross, were that each hospital should be reimbursed for its legitimate expenses and that doing so would insure access to hospital care and the highest standards of service.

When Medicare was adopted in 1965, there was never any doubt that Congress would declare that providers would be paid their "reasonable costs." In its effort to secure the support of hospitals and other providers, Congress essentially adopted the reimbursement practices urged by the American Hospital Association and its then affiliated insurers, Blue Cross plans.

In implementing Medicare, two related principles emerged from this congressional compromise. First, Medicare payment should treat all hospitals fairly; second, Medicare payment should assure beneficiaries quality or mainstream medical care. The results were significant. Feder and Spitz recount,

> Although both the AHA and Congress recognized that one hospital's costs could be "excessive" relative to other hospitals' costs, cost differences were treated as a result of differences in quality and intensity of care. . . . Congress promised that hospitals' incurred costs would be paid, "however widely they may vary. . . ."
>
> Equal treatment, however, went beyond actual costs. In some areas, policy makers were willing to pay more than actual costs to avoid the "inequity" of paying some hospitals less than others. . . . Equity meant that payment options designed to solve fiscal problems of some institutions should be available to all, whether or not the problem applied. . . .
>
> Concern with "mainstream medicine" and quality care had a similar effect. If government financing was to replace charity care, it was argued, the govern-

> ment had to cover the full cost of care for its beneficiaries. The expected result was an increase in hospital revenues. The conventional wisdom of the period when Medicare and Medicaid were established . . . was that more revenue meant more and better services, and that hospital growth and development were in the public interest. . . .
>
> Payment policy that treats each hospital's incurred costs as "reasonable," equitable, and supportive of quality care has had two major consequences. First, this policy has provided financial resources for individual hospitals to spend as they see fit, and has thereby encouraged an upward spiral in hospital expenditures. Second, it has established standards of adequate and appropriate hospital payment that have been almost impossible to challenge. [Feder & Spitz, The Politics of Hospital Payment, in J. Feder, J. Holohan & T. Marmor, National Health Insurance: Conflicting Goals and Policy Choices 301, 305-306 (1979).]

Despite the reluctance of many public and private third party payers to challenge either "reasonable cost" reimbursement or its underlying assumptions, rapid and continual increases in hospital expenditures through the 1970s eventually led to various attempts at reform. Individual Blue Cross plans and, as described infra, some state insurance commissioners pursued various strategies to reform traditional cost-related methodologies, for instance, by capping payment levels with industry-wide averages or by imputing occupancy rates. Prospective hospital reimbursement schemes were also adopted by some public and private payers. They retained fee-for-service, cost-based reimbursement methodology but factored an institution's actual costs in a base year according to various inflation indices and measures of change in service. They also set — in advance — a maximum on the per diem rate allowed for that institution. Some states experimented with prospective reimbursement schemes, both as a means to control their Medicaid expenditures and to control the costs of hospital services to other patients. Throughout the 1970s, a number of states adopted various hospital rate setting programs negotiating rates to be charged Blue Cross and Medicaid patients; providing annual budget reviews for all hospitals; and, in a few states, creating mandatory "all payer" rate setting agencies not unlike agencies that regulate public utilities. See discussion infra. Nonetheless, the hospital industry and even some third party payers clung to the notion that "reasonable cost" reimbursement should still primarily reflect the costs of each individual institution. At the same time, hospital expenditures continued to spiral upward.

One major shift in the political logjam came in 1982, with congressional enactment of a system of Medicare hospital reimbursement that borrowed heavily from some of the more successful state rate setting programs: a prospective payment scheme based on diagnostic-related groups (PPS/DRG). PPS/DRG not only pays the hospital prospectively but shifts away from the traditional notions that hospitals should be reimbursed on the basis of their costs, on a fee-for-service basis, and on a per diem basis. The new scheme reimburses hospitals on a cost-related basis and on the basis of the patient's primary diagnosis. Whether this is the first step in a total restructuring of public and private policy towards hospital reimbursement is not yet clear. Nor is it clear whether this will be the foundation for controlling hospital costs. Curiously, both conservatives and liberals have claimed PPS/DRG as a victorious first step towards their preferred future strategy. Nonetheless, both the details of PPS/DRG reimbursement and its actual impact of the new scheme are still unfolding.

3. STATE EFFORTS TO CONTROL HOSPITAL COSTS THROUGH REIMBURSEMENT REFORM

Insurance Department v. Saint Lukes Hospital of Bethlehem

342 A.2d 773, 21 Pa. Commw. 10 (1975)

MENCER, Judge

These are appeals from the Insurance Department's refusal to approve a reimbursement contract between the Hospital Service Plan of Lehigh Valley (Blue Cross) and its contracting hospitals (appellants). [Pennsylvania law] . . . provides:

> (a) General rule. — The rates charged to subscribers by hospital plan corporations, all rates of payments to hospitals made by such corporations pursuant to the contracts provided for in this chapter, all acquisition costs in connection with the solicitation of subscribers to such hospital plans, the reserves to be maintained by such corporations, the certificates issued by such corporations representing their agreements with subscribers, and any and all contracts entered into by any such corporation with any hospital, shall, at all times, be subject to the prior approval of the department.

Each of the appellants is a hospital providing medical services to subscribers of Blue Cross, and they were member hospitals of Blue Cross until July 1, 1972, when their last contract expired. Appellants have negotiated jointly with Blue Cross as to the form of the reimbursement contract, and such negotiations have been going on since July of 1972. These hospitals have been reimbursed on an interim basis since July of 1972, but no final settlements have been held for the ensuing period. . . .

On November 18, 1974, the Insurance Department refused to approve the contract in question . . . [stating]:

> I am disapproving the contract for the following specified reasons:
>
> (1) Section 5(E) of the proposed contract reads "Hospital agrees to make

every effort to minimize costs and actively promote programs which will increase efficiency and minimize expenditures, and to give consideration to suggestions in this regard from all sources."

This provision is so general and non-specific as to be virtually meaningless. No standards exist to evaluate and therefore enforce the requirements of making "every effort," and "actively promoting." A committment [sic] merely to "consider" suggestions represents no commitment at all.

[T]he current filing is so vague and nonspecific as to be . . . unacceptable. . . . At the very least, hospitals' committment [sic] to specific required cost saving and other programs should be clearly set forth in the contract.

(2) The proposed contract does not contain a provision requiring submission of hospital budgets to Blue Cross and at the very minimum provide Blue Cross with the right of review and comment.

I believe this to be one of the most basic methods of cost containment and assuring public accountability of hospitals. In view of Blue Cross's agreement to pay hospital costs, I believe that Blue Cross has an affirmative obligation to know what those costs are and to evaluate their reasonableness. Failure to make such evaluations gives hospitals a virtual blank check which Blue Cross must pay, and therefore is a primary factor in Blue Cross's repeated requests for rate increases.

. . . (3) The proposed contract does not contain a reasonable cost ceiling. While we all realize that hospitals, like us all, are living in an inflationary economy, and are thus concerned about unreasonable ceilings perhaps causing them to be unable to meet incurred expenses, I do not believe this to be an excuse for no ceilings at all. The absence of any cost ceiling for reimbursement removes an incentive for hospitals to contain their costs and cost increases. Again this is a major factor in Blue Cross's all too frequent requests for rate increases.

(4) While the proposed contract does contain a limitation on reimbursement when hospital occupancy falls below a minimum level, the proposed limitation (90 percent of the average percentages of occupancy of all member hospitals) does not effectively limit reimbursement during periods of low or declining occupancy and overbedding in your service area. Thus there is no incentive for hospitals to remove expensive and unused beds from service since Blue Cross will pay for them anyway. A lower limit on occupancy per individual hospital would be more appropriate, and in fact was contained in the hospital contract approved for use from July 1, 1971 to June 30, 1972. . . .

[W]e have reviewed the record in this case and conclude that the Insurance Department's refusal to approve the contract here in question must be affirmed.

. . . [The Insurance Commissioner's] reasons relate to the contractual rates of payment to hospitals by Blue Cross. . . .

. . . The proposed contract does not contain a provision requiring submission of hospital budgets to Blue Cross. Our analysis of this reason, when viewed from the standpoint that the rates charged to subscribers by Blue Cross are subject to approval by the Insurance Department, convinces us that it does not constitute a manifest and flagrant abuse of the Department's discretion. Since Blue Cross has contracted to pay the hospital costs for inpatient-covered services furnished to its eligible subscribers, it would seem axiomatic that Blue Cross would need to know, as nearly as possible, what the costs will be, as projected by budget estimates. Without such information, the rates of payments to the hospitals are virtually open ended, with Blue Cross obligated to make payment of final cost figures. This practice fuels a further request by Blue Cross for rate increases and encourages hospitals to operate with less cost consciousness.

The third stated reason — the proposed contract does not contain a reasonable cost ceiling — is merely a corollary to the second reason. The lack of budget information and absence of a reasonable cost ceiling unnecessarily increase the likelihood of higher rates of payment to hospitals by Blue Cross. Fixed rates established by negotiation and based on realistic budget estimates are certainly more susceptible to approval than the undetermined blanket cost commitment proposed here.

We think that the fourth reason advanced was a reasonable one . . . both self-explanatory and persuasive. . . .

Although we agree that the first reason advanced by the Insurance Department is not sufficient to warrant a refusal to approve the contract, since the Insurance Department is without authority to compel contractual adoption of the Insurance Commissioner's recommendations and guidelines, we do conclude that [the other] reasons . . . are of substance and therefore there has not been, in the instant case, a manifest and flagrant abuse of discretion or a purely arbitrary execution of the Insurance Department's duties or functions. . . .

BOWMAN, Presiding Judge (dissenting). . . .

As I understand the majority opinion of this Court, the Commissioner acted beyond the bounds of his authority in disapproving the proposed contract because it did not require the contracting parties to follow his recommendations and/or department regulations regarding hospital cost programs as found in previously published "guidelines," or otherwise. I share this view.

I dissent, however, from the majority view that the remaining contested reasons assigned by him in disapproving the contract are within his power to impress upon the contracting parties.

The remaining . . . reasons . . . demonstrate his intent and attempt to inject himself into the role of superadministrator of hospitals participating in such health delivery programs, a subject on which his expertise is not acknowledged.

As I view the role of the Commissioner and the Insurance Department under this statute, it cannot be questioned that rates to subscribers and rates of payments to hospitals are subject to his approval after appropriate hearing on the subject of such rates. However, he cannot under his authority to approve "contracts entered into by any such [hospital plan] corporation with any hospital," as a condition to such approval, require adoption of hospital cost programs or hospital management and administrative policies representative of what he conceives to be programs or policies which, if adopted, *may* reduce costs and hence, *may* reduce rates.

By conferring upon the Commissioner the limited powers expressed in section 6124, the legislature certainly did not intend to repose in him the role of autocrat of the health delivery system in Pennsylvania.

A review of the history of this controversy . . . discloses . . . a blatant attempt by the former Commissioner and followed by the present Commissioner to indirectly do what he is without authority to directly do, namely, assume superintendency over hospital administration and fiscal management. Even if one assumes that he has power and authority to insist upon inclusion in such contracts provisions covering the subjects of his second, third and fourth reasons for disapproving the proffered contract, I think the record can only support a conclusion that he abused his discretion in doing so. . . .

a. State Efforts to Control Costs Through Reimbursement Reforms

i. Early Insurance Efforts to Restrain Hospital Costs

In the early 1970s, as Medicaid costs continued to escalate and as both consumers and employers began to protest the costs of insurance premiums, various efforts were made at the state level to control rising hospital costs. (Medicare costs were also rising, but the political impact of rising hospital costs was felt initially more strongly at the state level.)

As demonstrated in *Saint Lukes,* one approach was to use the authority of the commissioner of insurance to approve Blue Cross premium increases in order to encourage Blue Cross to force reform measures on participating hospitals. Insurance commissioners in a few other states, such as Michigan, Ohio, West Virginia, and New Hampshire, made similar efforts. Both Blue Cross and the hospitals resisted these efforts, however, and it eventually became clear that both as a matter of law and as a matter of politics the authority of state insurance regulators to require cost containment measures was quite limited. In fact, as the dissenting judge in *Saint Lukes* observes, most insurance commissioners have little expertise, as well as little interest, in regulating hospital costs.

Judicial attitudes towards these efforts also varied. In West Virginia, for example, the state supreme court upheld the agency's authority to evaluate the reasonableness of the charges paid to hospitals in approving rate increases. In re Rate Filing of Blue Cross Hospital Service, Inc., 214 S.E.2d 339 (W. Va. 1975). Other courts interpreted the agency's authority under rate approval more narrowly. See, for example, New Hampshire-Vermont Hospitalization Service v. Commissioner of Banking and Insurance, 132 Vt. 592, 326 A.2d 163 (1974).

ii. "First Generation" Rate Regulation Programs

In other states, programs were established to directly regulate the rates paid for services to Medicaid patients and, in some cases, to other patients as well. In Massachusetts, for example, a hospital rate setting program was established in 1971 that divided each institution's costs for a base year by its allowed number of inpatient days. See Massachusetts General Hospital v. Weiner, 569 F.2d 1156 (1st Cir. 1978). This per diem rate was then increased by an inflation factor for subsequent years. An institution with actual per diem costs that exceeded this rate would receive a per diem "reasonable cost" rate for services to Medicaid patients that was in fact less than its average daily cost of providing care in that institution. Conversely, an institution that managed to provide care efficiently (or at least inexpensively) would receive a per diem "reasonable cost" rate for each Medicaid patient day that exceeded its average daily expenditures.

The specific incentives of this and other rate setting methodologies deserve careful consideration. The resulting impact on the cost, access, and quality of services varies significantly from scheme to scheme. Providing the same care to the same patients more efficiently is only one way that an institution might respond to Massachusetts-type limits on per diem reimbursement. An institution might also respond to these same limits by providing fewer — and arguably poorer quality — services or by making efforts to avoid patients who need the most intensive care and, consequently, demand more of the institution's resources. Perhaps more importantly, any time Medicaid, or any other third party payer, attempts to contain costs by adopting restrictive rates, an affected institution may respond simply by refusing or discouraging admission of patients covered by that particular payer. Indeed, the differential that has existed in many states between Medicaid reimbursement and reimbursement from other third party payers — a differential that has often been defended as a means to encourage hospitals to provide services to Medicaid patients more efficiently — often has made institutions reluctant to accept Medicaid patients.

A prospective rate setting scheme similar to that of Massachusetts, but one with more complicated incentives, had been adopted a few years earlier in New York. Under the New York scheme, Medicaid per diem reimbursement of "reasonable cost" for a particular hospital was based on the facility's historic costs from a base year, excluding any costs for certain items that exceeded 105 percent of the industrywide average cost for that item. For purposes of estimating the total number of patient days for the facility, the state imputed a level of occupancy, again based on industrywide averages. Finally, there was no reimbursement allowed for any additional patient days that exceeded the average length of stay for various diagnostic categories, again calculated on an industrywide average for each diagnosis. The resulting incentives for the hospital were again noteworthy. As in the Massachusetts scheme discussed in *Weiner,* there was considerable pressure on each hospital to limit its per diem costs. Indeed, the manner in which New York determined the hospital's base year costs was even more demanding, excluding some historic costs that exceeded industrywide averages and reducing the share of the hospital's expenditures apportioned to Medicaid patients by imputing occupancy of the institution's beds. In addition, limits on the length of stay inhibited the institution from keeping patients in the institution for additional days. (It should also be noted that Blue Cross had adopted a similar hospital reimbursement methodology in New York at that time, somewhat mitigating the likelihood that hospitals would respond to this reimbursement scheme by discouraging the treatment of Medicaid patients.)

Despite these various exclusions and limits, the federal court of appeals held that New York's scheme for estimating "reasonable cost" did not violate New York state law; nor did it violate the limits on the state's discretion established by the federal Medicaid statute. New York City Health and Hospital Corp. v. Blum, 708 F.2d 880 (2d Cir. 1983). In one particularly interesting part of the decision, the court held that the length of stay norms and disallowances were not inconsistent with the PSRO controls then in effect (see discussion of PSROs and other forms of peer review in Chapter 2 and Chapter 5), even though this reimbursement limitation was effectively denying reimbursement for some days of patient care to Medicaid patients that had received the specific approval of the federally-inspired PSRO program. See id. at 885.

iii. Federal Limits on State Discretion to Reform Medicaid Reimbursement

At least until 1980, the federal Medicaid statute had required that the states pay hospitals on the same "reasonable cost" basis as the federal Medicare program. Significantly, the states' discretion was made much broader under the Medicaid reforms adopted during the Reagan years. As part of the Medicaid amendments adopted in 1981, the "reasonable cost" language was amended to require that hospital rates paid by Medicaid must be "reasonable and adequate to meet the costs that must be incurred by efficiently and economically operated facilities." 42 U.S.C. §1396(a)(13) (1982 and Supp. 1983-1987). The *legal* effect of this language is illustrated by *Blum* and gives even further legitimacy to prospective reimbursement, industrywide averaging, and other cost containing schemes in the reimbursement of hospitals under Medicaid. The *practical* effect was to encourage more states to adopt these more stringent reimbursement methodologies and to further widen the gaps between actual cost and "reasonable cost," and between Medicaid reimbursement rates and the rates paid by Medicare (at least until the PPS/DRG scheme was implemented) and other third party payers.

The discretion allowed to the states in fashioning hospital reimbursement schemes for their Medicaid programs should not be overstated. The federal Medicaid statute and interpretive regulations still impose some substantive limits on the states' discretion, as well as impose fairly complicated procedural obligations on states that attempt to modify their Medicaid reimbursement schemes. See, for instance, New England Memorial Hospital v. Rate Setting Commission 394 Mass. 296, 475 N.E.2d 740 (1985); Virginia Hospital Association v. Baliles, 830 F.2d 1308 (4th Cir. 1989).

iv. Constitutional Limits on State Reimbursement Reform

While providers have had some success in challenging state and federal government reimbursement policies on statutory grounds, constitutional challenges to limits on "cost reimbursement," on methods for determining costs, or on conditions imposed on providers participating in Medicaid (or Medicare) have rarely been successful.

As one example of the wide discretion allowed to legislative prerogatives, in 1976 Minnesota adopted a prospective reimbursement scheme for nursing homes serving Medicaid patients. In addition, the legislation required participating nursing homes to agree to limit their charges to non-Medicaid patients to no more than 110 percent of the Medicaid per diem rate. As one result of the legislation, many institutions raised their non-Medicaid rates to the statutory ceiling of 110 percent. The legislature then amended the statute to require participating institutions to charge no more than they had been charging to non-Medicaid patients on the date of the enactment of the original legislation and to require the restitution of any excess charge collected subsequent to that date. The state nursing home association challenged the constitutionality of both statutes.

The Court of Appeals for the Eighth Circuit held that the limits on charges to non-Medicaid patients were not a violation of the due process clause of the Fourteenth Amendment, primarily because the court viewed participation in Medicaid as voluntary. Minnesota Association of Health Care Facilities, Inc. v. Minnesota Department of Public Welfare, 742 F.2d, 442 (8th Cir. 1984), *cert. denied*, 469 U.S. 1215 (1985). The court reasoned that a condition on participation in a voluntary program need only bear a rational relationship to a legitimate state interest. In doing so, the court rejected the argument of the nursing homes that the statute constituted an uncompensated taking of their property. The court did, however, indicate that had the rate regulation been mandatory, then the scheme would have been more akin to a "taking" and would have been subjected at least to a more demanding judicial review:

> Rates which are not sufficient to yield a reasonable return on the value of the property used at the time it is being used to render the service are unjust, unreasonable, and confiscatory, and their enforcement deprives the public utility company of its property in violation of the Fourteenth Amendment.
>
> Cases concerning public utilities are inapposite, however, because the present case simply does not involve a forced taking of property by the state. Minnesota nursing homes, unlike public utilities, have freedom to decide whether to remain in business and thus subject themselves voluntarily to the limits imposed by Minnesota on the return they obtain from investment of their assets in nursing home operation. . . . Moreover, the state does not require that nursing homes admit medical assistance residents and participate in the Medicaid program. . . . [Id. at 446.]

The court also held that the statute did not violate the requirements of equal protection in discriminating between institutions that participated in Medicaid and those that did not or in regulating nursing homes but not other Medicaid providers. The court did, however, declare that the portion of the statute that declared unlawful the charges that had already been collected from non-Medicaid patients at the time of the enactment of the second statute was an unconstitutional impairment of contract. For a further discussion of the "taking" argument and the consequent limits on government discretion in setting rates, see discussion infra at 258-259, 289-291.

b. "All-Payer" Rate Setting

Prince George's Doctors Hospital, Inc. v. Health Services Cost Rev. Commission.

302 Md. 193, 486 A.2d 744 (1985)

SMITH, Judge.

Appellant Prince George's Doctors' Hospital, Inc., (the Hospital) is of the view that the Health Services Cost Review Commission (the Commission) was too stingy in its allowance of rates to it. On the other hand, Group Hospitalization, Inc. (Group Hospitalization), Blue Cross for the District of Columbia metropolitan area, believes the Commission was entirely too generous with the Hospital. We think the Commission had it about right. Hence, we shall affirm in both appeals.

The Hospital is a proprietary (for-profit) 240-bed acute care medical/surgical hospital owned and operated by physicians. . . .

On November 7, 1983, the Commission issued its final order in a ratemaking proceeding involving the Hospital. Group Hospitalization, which insures approximately 35 percent of the patients at the Hospital, intervened as an interested party before the Commission. The Hospital had requested rates that would generate in excess of $41.5 million in gross revenue per year. The Commission's final rate order approved rates for the Hospital that, according to the Commission, would generate $35.1 million in gross revenue. The Commission found that the Hospital had overcharged its patients by some $16.8 million since September 1982 when it placed its requested rates into effect. . . .

. . . Under our act the Commission is vested with jurisdiction over the costs and rates of hospitals, health care institutions, and related institutions located in Maryland. . . .

The Commission's powers relative to the controversy here before us are found in §19-216, which provides:

> (a) *Rate reviewing power.* — The Commission may review costs and rates and make any investigation that the Commission considers necessary to assure each purchaser of health care facility services that:
>
> (1) The total costs of the facility are related reasonably to the total services that the facility offers;
>
> (2) The aggregate rates of the facility are related reasonably to the aggregate costs of the facility; and
>
> (3) The rates are set equitably among all purchasers or classes of purchasers without undue discrimination or preference.
>
> (b) *Rate approval power.* —
>
> (1) To carry out its powers under subsection (a) of this section, the Commission may review and approve or disapprove the reasonableness of any rate that a facility sets or requests.
>
> (2) A facility shall charge for services only at a rate set in accordance with this subtitle. . . .

. . . The Hospital first contends that "the Commission exceeded its statutory powers in imposing the guaranteed inpatient revenue system upon the Hospital effective July 1, 1985." A definition of such a system was set forth for the Court by Judge Davidson in *Health Services Cost Review v. Lutheran Hospital,* 298 Md. 651, 472 A.2d 55 (1984):

> According to the Commission, a guaranteed inpatient revenue system (GIR) is a "diagnostic-based rate-setting approach" "that is designed to provide incentives to reduce unnecessary or marginal ancillary testing, to reduce length of stay, and to promote pre-admission testing," and is "Maryland's most promising inflation control methodology" as well as "the linchpin of the current efforts by the Commission to control hospital costs in Maryland."
>
> Before the Commission attempted to impose a GIR, rates for services such as laboratory tests were based upon the price per unit of service. A GIR, however, establishes an approved rate for the total costs incurred for the treatment of a given patient's diagnosis regardless of the units of service rendered. If more units of service are provided to a given patient than are covered by the approved rate, the amount of the excess is offset against cases involving similar diagnosis

> in which fewer services are provided than are covered by the approved rate. At the end of the fiscal year, a hospital will be denied reimbursement for the aggregate amount of charges in excess of the GIR rate for a particular diagnosis. . . .

The Hospital contends that the Commission lacks the authority to impose this system because its statutory duty is to determine the reasonableness of costs, not to regulate the quality or quantity of services. It claims: "The system . . . places a cap on revenues by creating an irrebutable presumption that every class above the cap is medically unnecessary and therefore not reimbursable. It places a limit on the amount a Hospital will be allowed per patient stay without regard to reasonableness of the costs for the total services actually provided."

Judge Ross said in the trial court on the issue of the guaranteed inpatient revenue system:

> Utilization of the Guaranteed Inpatient Revenue System (GIR) to establish rates is within the power of the Commission. The argument that the GIR is beyond the authority of the Commission because the nature of the system is to constrain revenues is without merit. The power to approve or disapprove rates is the power to constrain revenues. Nor is the GIR an unlawful interference with hospital management. It is difficult to see how the power to regulate rates can fail to impact on management decisions. Indeed, the underlying purpose of this regulatory statute would seem to be to require hospital management to become more efficient and to reduce costs. The expert testimony is to the effect that rather than adversely affecting quality GIR not only effectively reduces costs but tends to improve quality. The net of the Hospital's testimony with respect to GIR is that as a method it has imperfections. . . . However, there is substantial evidence that this imperfect method works. . . . The Hospital's contention that GIR restricts introduction of new technology is answered by the inclusion of the 1 percent of gross revenue and the evidence to the effect that in practice the GIR has not restricted the introduction of new technology.

. . . We regard the guaranteed inpatient revenue system as falling within [the Commission's broad] authorization. . . .

The Hospital next attacks the application of the Commission's "market basket" methodology. It claims that the rate set on that basis should be reversed because [the "market basket" methodology was not *prima facie* validated, was arbitrary and capricious, was illegally used as an absolute rule, and was made upon unlawful procedure.] . . .

Despite the Hospital's attempt to cull five or six distinct issues from the Commission's use of the market basket methodology, there is really only one question here: is use of the methodology within the Commission's power . . . ? It will be recalled, once again, that "to promote the most efficient and effective use of health care facility services" the Commission is authorized to "promote and approve alternate methods of rate determination and payment that are of an experimental nature."

[The lower court held]:

> There is nothing inherently illegal, capricious or arbitrary about the Market Basket methodology per se. It is a form of peer group comparison. There is expert testimony that peer group comparison is an established and proper tool for hospital rate setting. . . .
>
> The Commission did not totally ignore the "actual costs of the Hospital." It compared them to the market basket averages and gave the Hospital opportunity to demonstrate that its higher costs were warranted. The Hospital chose to justify its costs by showing they had been actually incurred and attempting to show all were reasonable and necessary. The net effect was to pit the cost based reimbursement method championed by the Hospital against the disparate peer comparison method uniformly applied by the Commission with the predictable result that the Hospital in large measure failed to explain by credible evidence why the costs it had actually incurred and anticipated it would incur were so far out of line with those of its peers. There is substantial evidence that the cost based reimbursement method has been discredited and has been replaced by peer comparison, which is now widely accepted. The Commission did not arbitrarily apply the market basket as an absolute rule but used it as a basis for comparison. It found that the evidence did in part support the Hospital's principal contention that its greater intensity accounted for its higher costs and made adjustments accordingly in establishing the rates.

. . . We reject the contention that the Commission arbitrarily applied the market basket averages as an absolute rule. . . . The market basket methodology imposes no absolute rules concerning cost factors. It is simply a method of comparison. . . .

The Hospital and Group Hospitalization each contest the implementation. . . .

. . . On October 5, 1983, the Commission issued a proposed opinion, which was distributed to all interested parties. Its final decision was rendered on November 4, 1983. The following is contained within the implementation portion of its decision:

> While the evidence presented supports rates 2 percent above the Market Basket averages, the Hospital's requested rates are 71 percent above Market Basket I and 64 percent above Market Basket II. These rates are clearly far in excess of reasonable rates justified by the evidence and have been in effect since September 1, 1982 by operation of law.
>
> [T]he Commission recognizes that immediate imposition of *appropriate* underlying rates would cause a drastic reduction in income to the Hospital. It is recognized that the Hospital is not entitled to the excessive revenue it has been receiving, but its cost structure could not immediately absorb an abrupt reduction to a level of reasonable rates.
>
> . . . Since the Hospital's rates prior to implementation of requested rates

> were approximately 13 percent above its peers, the entire amount of increase was unwarranted and must be *returned prospectively* over 20 months. . . . [The Hospital is permitted] to retain any interest it earned on the excessive rates during the 13 months they were in effect. . . .
>
> In being lenient towards the Hospital in this order, the Commission does not require repayment of interest earned (estimated at $1,850,000) on the excess charges for the period [in which the hospital contested the Commission's orders.] . . .

The Hospital contends that the order is confiscatory, constitutes retroactive rate-setting, and sets rates far into the future on the basis of evidence having no reasonable relationship to the rates set and without giving the Hospital the procedural protections to which it is statutorily and constitutionally entitled.

Group Hospitalization claims that the trial court erred in affirming the Commission decision, which required only prospective repayment, without interest estimated at $1.85 million, for unreasonable overcharges [from 1982 to 1985]. It further claims the court erred in affirming a Commission decision which, on grounds of "leniency," failed to require repayment of unreasonable overcharges or interest, in the amount of $13.691 million, for the period [1980 to 1982]. . . .

[The lower court said:]

> The Hospital's contention that the Commission's power is circumscribed by the budget year of the data it chose to submit in support of its amended application is specious. The Hospital may only charge Commission-approved rates. The latest previous general rate approval order was in 1978. . . . [R]ates . . . were expressly made subject to refund in the event that the Commission's determination of final rates showed they were excessive. . . .
>
> While [Group Hospitalization's] contentions with respect to refunds, which were presented with force and clarity, are not unpersuasive, it cannot be said that the Commission's decision with respect to refund is beyond its power or is arbitrary and capricious. It is true the method used by the Commission in calculating the rates for the several years in question utilized an adjusted market basket average, which it designated as a reasonable rate. However, the net effect of the total decision which involved adjustments including forbearance of requiring refunds, was to establish what the Commission deemed to be reasonable rates for each of the years in question. . . . In effect, the Commission granted varying rates during an interim period to allow the Hospital to alter its cost structure to accommodate an ultimate rate structure substantially lower than that which the Hospital had requested and that for which its existing cost structure had been designed. Its decision is not without rational basis nor beyond its statutory mandate.
>
> There is substantial evidence to support the conclusion that the rates set by the Commission are not confiscatory and do not threaten the solvency of the Hospital. The statute does not require the Commission to guarantee the solvency of a hospital. It merely requires that the rates be set in such a manner

that the hospital can be operated on a solvent basis and, if proprietary, receive a fair return on fair value of its assets. There is substantial evidence that the rates approved by the Commission will permit this hospital to be so operated, if it is operated efficiently. Acceptance of the Hospital's contention that the Commission must approve rates which would assure solvency and a fair return on the basis of the Hospital's actual costs or projected actual costs would defeat the purpose of the statute. . . .

NOTES: "ALL-PAYER" RATE SETTING PROGRAMS

Existing State "All-Payer" Programs

A number of states have established what could be described as "all-payer" rate setting programs similar to that discussed in *Prince George*. In fact, the distinction between "all-payer" programs and other attempts to regulate hospital rates is more conceptual than real. Only some of the "all-payer" programs exercise direct and mandatory controls over the rates charged by hospitals and some other institutional providers for essentially all categories of patients. Other states have attempted to control hospital rates by programs of public disclosure of rates or budgets, or by establishing a public agency to periodically scrutinize — but not directly control — hospital budgets. Moreover, even in states with "all-payer" programs, Medicare payments to hospitals are still subject to federal law; see discussion infra. For a discussion of these various programs and their political history, see Schramm, State Hospital Cost Containment: An Analysis of Legislative Initiatives, 19 Ind. L. Rev. 919 (1986).

Thus far, there are remarkably few cases in which regulated hospitals have challenged these decisions. See, for instance, Brooklyn Hospital v. Axelrod, 97 A.D.2d 493, 467 N.Y.S.2d 687 (1983), *aff'd,* 61 N.Y.2d 1012, 463 N.E.2d 1233, 475 N.Y.S.2d 381, (1984); Pentucket Manor Chronic Hospital, Inc. v. Rate Setting Commission, 394 Mass. 233, 475 N.E.2d 1201 (1985).

Political Motivation for "All-Payer" Programs

The complicated politics inspired by proposals for rate setting account for some of the reasons why only some states move towards "all-payer" rate setting programs and why the scope and structure of these programs vary so much from state to state. These politics go far beyond a battle between the competing ideologies of competition and regulation, or between the needs of the consumer public and those of powerful providers. Commenting on the cumbersome and protracted legislative battles that accompany debates over state rate setting programs, Schramm has identified at least twelve distinguishable interest groups — nonprofit hospitals, proprietary hospitals, hospital trustees, Blue Cross, commercial insurers, representatives of Medicaid and Medicare, business interests, organized labor, consumer groups, and various individual providers — from which a political coalition must emerge to secure enactment of legislation. As he argues:

> As a result of the large number of interested parties, hospital rate setting proposals present a curious legislative phenomenon; namely, unpredictable coalition behavior among the interest groups depending on the positions they adopt from state to state. Indeed, several of these groups have taken diametrically opposing positions in different jurisdictions. Compounding matters is the unpredictable identity of the "initiator" party from state to state. [Schramm, supra, at 927.]

The "curious" politics of state rate setting are best reflected in the ambiguous posture of the private insurance industry towards this form of regulation. During the 1970s, for example, private insurers viewed "all-payer" rate setting as a means to improve their competitive position against Blue Cross and Blue Shield plans. On the other hand, as insurers start to experiment with HMOs, PPOs, and other alternative arrangements, they may prefer a nonregulated environment. Westwater & Prottas, The Future of All-Payer Reimbursement Systems, Bus. & Health, June 1987, at 36-38.

The Economics of Rate Setting Programs

As noted earlier, one of the disadvantages of limits on reimbursement or other cost containment schemes that apply to some but not all payers is that some institutions will attempt to discourage or to avoid patients reimbursed under the restricted reimbursement scheme. Alternatively, hospitals may also react to differentials in rates of reimbursement by attempting to shift the cost of their unreimbursed expenditures to those payers that use more generous methods of reimbursement. The "cost shifting" problem may persist even in situations where all or most payers are engaging in some sort of rate regulation, but different agencies may have different responsibilities for different types of payments: for instance, the federal government determines Medicare rates; the state health or welfare department may set rates for Medicaid; the state insurance departments may influence or regulate Blue Cross and other health insurance companies. A truly comprehensive "all-payer" rate setting program would avoid these problems and allow the agency responsible for the reimbursement of hospitals to more carefully target the resulting incentives on cost containment and on hospital behavior. Nonetheless, as noted earlier, not all states have adopted programs that allow such sweeping authority to one rate setting agency.

Even if a comprehensive "all-payer" rate setting program is adopted, the state has a wide range of choices in determining the methodology to be followed and the principles to be applied. As Spitz and Feder argue, these choices can have important consequences:

> Prospective payment methods can be divided into two broad types, the formula or target budget approach and the budget review and negotiation approach. . . . With the formula or target budget approach, hospital payment in the coming year is based on cost or revenue experience in an earlier year projected forward for inflation. The base-year experience may be either that of each individual hospital or an average of several hospitals, and the target set may be a payment ceiling or an actual rate. The primary advantages of this approach are its administrative control and the simplicity of a statistical method; its disadvantages are its tendency to perpetuate the base distribution of resources and its limited capacity to respond to particular circumstances.
>
> Alternatively, payment may be set by budget review and negotiation. With this approach, the payer or regulator reviews and evaluates each hospital's proposed expenditures, and a final budget is negotiated and approved. The budget review method allows review of resource distribution and individual treatment of hospitals; but at the same time it poses a considerable administrative burden on regulators and offers hospitals an opportunity to exert political pressure. Features of the formula and budget review methods can be combined. A budget review system can use statistical norms as guidelines or triggers for review; formulas can incorporate standards for resource allocation. Moreover, a formula can be used to set an aggregate limit on expenditures for a group of hospitals and individual budgets can be negotiated within that limit. Finally, proposed budgets can be reviewed periodically, such as every three to five years, with a formula applied between reviews. The objectives of the combination are to enhance control, to minimize administrative burdens, and to provide flexibility in resource allocation. [Spitz & Feder, *supra* at 319-320.]

Rate Setting and Employee Compensation

One example of how the specific contours of the rate setting methodology can have important and controversial consequences involves the treatment of a facility's employee wage and benefit compensation.

In Washington State Nurses Association v. Washington State Hospital Commission, 773 F.2d 1044 (9th Cir. 1985), the plaintiffs claimed that the state rate setting methodology interfered with state and federal statutory rights to bargain for wage increases. Under the Washington state "budget review" legislation then in effect (and applicable only to Medicaid patients), all wage increases that exceed 105 percent of the preceding year's total wages triggered a review by the state agency, comparing the wage increases to the average wage increase of other hospitals of comparable size and location. Any increase that exceeded this average had to be approved by the agency.

The federal court held that the state statute was not inconsistent with either the state or federal labor laws, primarily because the rate setting scheme did not directly regulate the wages paid to any employee or employee group. Total wage payments in excess of the 105 percent of the ceiling might be excluded from reimbursement, but, as the court argued, hospitals were "free to contract to pay wages at any level so long as they were able to meet their obligations either by obtaining revenue from other sources or by reducing costs in other areas." Id. at 1045. For a similar case, see Massachusetts Nurses Association v. Dukakis, 726 F.2d 41 (1st Cir. 1984).

A somewhat similar factual setting led to a different result in Riverside General Hospital v. New Jersey Hospital Rate Setting Commission, 98 N.J. 458, 487 A.2d 714 (1985). The state supreme court overturned a decision by the state agency that had refused to include the costs of new employee dental and pension plan benefits in determining the rate of reimbursement for the hospital under the New Jersey "all-payer" program. The hospital had instituted the employee benefits *after* the base year from which the hospital's reimbursement rates were prospectively calculated; consequently, the new benefits were treated as increases in the facility's costs and the commission, with little discussion of its basis for doing so, refused to recognize these "cost increases" as "reasonable." (The commission was apparently swayed by the fact that the hospital, a proprietary hospital owned by the facility's physicians, had generated a revenue surplus from which some profits were distributed to the facility's owners.) The court ruled that the hospital was not automatically entitled to the inclusion of these costs in its reimbursement rate, but that the agency would have to find some basis for their exclusion in its statutory and regulatory authority and make properly documented evidentiary findings to support the conclusion that these costs were not reasonable.

The Effectiveness of "All-Payer" Rate Setting Programs

Whether or not "all-payer" rate setting programs have been successful in containing hospital costs is not clear. Schramm has argued that an "examination of the regulatory period from 1976 to the present has consistently shown statistically significant reductions in the rate of hospital cost inflation in the regulated states." Schramm, supra, at 925-926. See also Schramm, Renn & Biles, Controlling Hospital Cost Inflation: New Perspectives on State Rate Setting, 4 Health Affairs 22 (Fall 1986). Sloan, on the other hand, has argued that the apparent success of the states with mandatory "all-payer" rate setting programs during that same period could best be described as a temporary slowing of the rise in hospital costs initially, and since that time the rate of increase in those states has mirrored that in other states. Sloan, Rate Regulation as a Strategy for Hospital Cost Control: Evidence from the Last Decade, 61 Milbank Mem. Fund Q. 195 (1983).

Rate Setting and Uncompensated Care

Another important issue in rate setting involves the extent to which the reimbursement scheme allows for the recovery of bad debt or uncompensated care. Traditionally, care provided to the uninsured was factored into reimbursement in a variety of ways. Blue Cross, for example, typically allowed an allowance for a "plus factor" or "bad debts." Similarly, Medicare paid hospitals a "plus factor" over other allowable costs — whether or not they actually provide uncompensated care. "All-payer" rate setting programs provide states with similar choices — and an opportunity to have a significant impact on the level of uncompensated care.

New Jersey not only provides for the treatment of these items as "reasonable costs," but provides a methodology for doing so that could be viewed as a de facto program for the medically indigent. As described by the staff of the New Jersey Department of Health,

> According to the state law which enacted New Jersey's all-payer hospital rate setting system, the cost of care provided to medically indigent persons (charity care) and the cost of bad debts may be included in each hospital's rates which are then paid by all purchasers of hospital coverage in New Jersey.
>
> A state wide Uncompensated Care Trust Fund was enacted and implemented in 1987 . . . in New Jersey to refine previous law. The primary objective of the legislation was to spread the cost of uncompensated care more evenly, more equitably, across hospitals in the state. Before this legislation was passed all uncompensated care reimbursement was hospital-specific. Each hospital collected through its *own* rates the funds to pay for its *own* uncompensated care. Uncompensated care add-ons ranged from a low of 1 percent to a high of 25 percent. Hospitals with disproportionately high numbers of uninsured and low income patients had to add higher-than-average uncompensated care charges to the bills of their paying patients, putting these hospitals at a competitive disadvantage with hospitals that had very low numbers of uninsured patients.
>
> Under the new law . . . all hospitals use the same statewide uncompensated care add-on to the bills of their patients — the overwhelming number of which are insured. This uniform add-on — which for the second half of 1987 is 9.7 percent — replaces the 89 hospital-specific add-ons across the State. It is calculated semi-annually to meet the projected aggregate cost of hospital uncompensated care in New Jersey. All 89 acute-care hospitals in the State continue to be paid for the amount of uncompensated care which they provide and all collect money through their rates via the statewide add-on. Approximately two-thirds of the State's hospitals provide a lower-than-average volume of uncompensated care and forward part of what they collect, their "excess" (the difference between the statewide add-on, which they collect through their rates, and their *own* approved uncompensated care expenses), to the Trust Fund. The Trust Fund then redistributes this money to the remaining one-third of the State's hospitals that provide a higher-than-average volume of uncompensated care. . . .
>
> Medicare, Medicaid, Blue Cross/Blue Shield, commercial insurers, health maintenance organizations, and self-insured employers each contribute their proportional share of uncompensated care costs based on their share of total hospital revenue in the State. These public and private insurers and self-insured businesses pay for the cost of uncompensated care through the add-on to the hospital bills of the persons for whom they provide health coverage. The insurers, in turn, collectively spread the cost of uncompensated care across the 89 percent of the population (almost 7 million persons) who is insured by including it in their premium costs. This method of financing is frequently and incorrectly conceptualized as a "sick tax." This view is inaccurate in that it assumes that *only* people who are sick and hospitalized pay for uncompensated care. This

is not the case, as the number of hospitalized persons who actually pay out-of-pocket for hospitalization is relatively small. Rather, the uncompensated care add-on is paid by all those who pay for third party coverage.

The Trust Fund does not draw any additional monies into the hospital payment system, nor does it represent any aggregate increase in hospitals' bills over the system in existence prior to the Trust Fund's enactment. It simply introduces a uniform statewide add-on to replace 89 hospital-specific add-ons. [Division of Research, Policy, and Planning, New Jersey Department of Health, New Jersey's Uncompensated Care Trust Fund: An Initiative to Promote Access to Needed Health Care 1-2 (1987).]

Federal Limits on State Discretion

The federal government has been somewhat reluctant to allow control of Medicare reimbursement to be ceded to the states, apparently for both fiscal and ideological reasons. These problems have been magnified by the enactment of the Medicare DRG/PPS legislation. (A more detailed discussion of Medicare reimbursement follows in Section 4.)

From 1972 to 1982, federal law authorized Medicare to pay hospitals on a different basis from the one provided in the federal statute only if the hospital agreed to this arrangement and the state rate setting scheme met with the approval of the Secretary of HHS. Since 1982, the federal law has provided that the "Secretary may provide, in his discretion, that payments with respect to services provided by a hospital in a State may be made in accordance with a hospital reimbursement control system in a State, rather than in accordance with the [Medicare system] if the . . . state requests such treatment and if . . . the Secretary has been provided satisfactory assurances that . . . the amount of payment made under [Medicare] . . . will not exceed the amount . . . which otherwise have been made. . . ." 42 U.S.C. §1395ww(c)(1)(C) (1982 and Supp. 1983-1987). In 1983, Congress *mandated* that HHS allow Medicare payments to be made under state rate setting programs in specified states (Maryland, New York, New Jersey, and Massachusetts) that had demonstrated the cost effectiveness of their programs or in states that could in the future make such a showing. Despite this congressional mandate, the Reagan Administration was reluctant to allow Medicare "waivers." For a detailed discussion of the legal issues and one chapter in this long-running political controversy between the states and the federal government, see Kean v. Heckler, 799 F.2d 895 (3d Cir. 1986).

4. MEDICARE REIMBURSEMENT

INTRODUCTORY NOTE TO MEDICARE REIMBURSEMENT

As discussed in the beginning of this chapter, until 1983 Medicare reimbursed hospitals on a fee-for-service, retroactively determined, "reasonable cost" basis. However, starting in 1982, Congress amended Medicare reimbursement to allow for prospective and, eventually, diagnosis-based reimbursement for most hospitals. (Medicare continues to reimburse some hospitals and some costs for all hospitals on a "reasonable cost" basis.) The result has been one of the most significant reforms in hospital reimbursement since the enactment of Medicare.

The Tax Equity and Fiscal Responsibility Act of 1982 (TEFRA), Pub. L. No. 97-248, 96 Stat. 324, modified Medicare in a number of ways. First, TEFRA modified Medicare's per diem, "reasonable cost" reimbursement of hospitals by capping the maximum reimbursement allowed to a hospital at 110 percent of the average *per case* of comparable hospitals. TEFRA also placed a limit on the rate of increase allowed for a hospital's routine operating costs. While the statutory language still described this as "reasonable cost" reimbursement, together with other adjustments in the reimbursement methodology, these amendments essentially shifted Medicare reimbursement of hospitals away from a scheme that focused almost exclusively on the actual costs of each facility and towards a system of cost-averaged, prospective reimbursement. Most importantly, HHS was instructed in the 1982 legislation to prepare for Congress a proposal for a comprehensive prospective reimbursement scheme for hospitals.

As an additional part of TEFRA, Congress enacted the Peer Review Improvement Act of 1982, codified as 42 U.S.C. §§1320c-1–12 (1982 and Supp. 1983-1987). Although administratively separate from the PPS/DRG scheme, these peer review organizations eventually were given various functional roles relating to PPS/DRG reimbursement, and the design of the peer review program was intended to act as a quality control to offset the service reduction incentives that would be inherent in PPS/DRG. (For a full description of the peer review program, see Chapters 2 and 5.)

The recommendations of HHS for a prospective reimbursement scheme for hospitals were submitted to Congress in December 1982. Although Congress substantially modified these recommendations, the final legislation moved rapidly through Congress and was enacted in March of 1983 as one part of a broad legislative package that included, among other things, massive reforms in Social Security financing. Pub. L. No. 98-21, Title VI; 97 Stat. 149-172. The basic provisions of the new PPS/DRG scheme and its impact on hospitals are described in the article and the notes that follow.

Vladeck, Medicare Hospital Payment by Diagnosis-Related Groups

100 Annals Internal Med. 576 (1984)

On 1 October 1983, the system by which hospital care is financed in the United States began its most significant transformation in almost two decades. Medicare, which accounts for roughly 40 percent of total hospital revenues, began a phased transition from a system in which each hospital was paid, subject to relatively minor adjustments, the actual, retrospectively determined cost incurred in its treatment of Medicare beneficiaries, to one in which every hospital in the United States will eventually be paid on the basis of a uniform national rate for each of 468 diagnosis-related groups (DRGs).

Concern with the continuing increase in hospital and Medicare costs was primarily responsible for the adoption of the Medicare DRG system. However, the initial development of DRG-based hospital payment resulted in part from a desire to change the ways in which hospitals are managed, the ways in which physicians practice in hospitals, and the relation between hospitals and physicians. . . .

RATIONALE FOR CASE-MIX BASED PAYMENT SYSTEMS

The Medicare DRG system is a result of two related streams of development: first, the implementation of hospital prospective payment systems and the analysis of hospital costs that underlies them; second, the development of DRGs as a measure of case-mix. . . .

Once one recognizes that case-mix is a critical measure of hospital activity, it is easy to conceive of paying hospitals on a per-case basis. Treating identifiable patients with identifiable illnesses is, for the most part, what hospitals do. If the costs of treating a particular case or a group of patients with definable characteristics is the fairest comparative measure of hospital costs, then it should also provide a plausible basis for hospital payment.

Using the appropriately defined case as the basis for hospital payment as well as cost analysis becomes attractive if one considers the incentive and managerial effects of alternative pricing schemes. Using the case, rather than the average day or the individual itemized unit of service (such as a roentgenogram of the head or dose of antibiotic), as a definition of the hospital's "product" permits the development of hospital reporting and cost accounting systems that evaluate the component costs of producing given "products." At the same time, use of the case provides a clear signal to hospital administrators, employees, and attending physicians that the process of cost containment requires a focus on the mix of services (inputs) required for the production of the hospital's outputs. . . .

DIAGNOSIS-RELATED GROUPS AS A MEASURE OF CASE-MIX

Diagnosis-related groups were first developed as part of an effort to establish length of stay norms for use by the professional standards review organizations. The original classification of DRGs arose as much from the availability of statistical techniques for grouping large volumes of data as from any specific set of clinical concerns. The original notion was that if length of stay was defined as the dependent variable, one should be able to identify, in broad clinical categories, a relatively small number of independent variables that could be used to cluster cases into a manageable number of groups that were relatively homogeneous with respect to the dependent variable. . . .

Early efforts in New Jersey to develop a DRG-based reimbursement system . . . made it apparent that . . . refinements in the methods of creating DRGs would be required. First, clinicians were made uneasy by a number of groupings that had been statistically created, because they appeared to mix types of cases that, although similar in terms of length of stay, were clinically dissimilar. Second, the failure of the original methodology to distinguish among secondary diagnoses, in conjunction with the relatively lax practices in many hospital medical records rooms relative to the ordering of secondary diagnoses on discharge summary sheets, inadequately distinguished between significant complicating conditions and minor secondary diagnoses, creating the possibility of artificial manipulation of discharge reporting once DRGs became the basis for hospital payment. . . . There were also concerns that the original classification of DRGs, while treating age as an independent variable, was insufficiently sensitive to it; analyses done in New Jersey in 1978 and 1979 showed that, within DRGs, patients over 65 used consistently more days of care than patients under 65. . . .

There appears to be general consensus that the new DRGs are a substantial qualitative improvement over their predecessors. There is also a substantially less explicit consensus that they provide the best currently available method of case-mix classification that is administratively feasible and economical to operate. The principal criticisms of DRGs as a classification method fall into four broad categories: the inherent limitations of any classification system; the inadequacy of the data on which DRG assignments are made; the failure of DRGs to adequately show differences in "intensity" or "severity" of illness within a given diagnostic category; and the degree to which DRGs represent a classification based on the existing prevailing patterns of medical practice for defined diagnostic entities, rather than normative standards of practice.

The objection to classification systems such as DRGs on generic grounds is essentially philosophical and conceptual, and difficult to address. However, it is extremely important to emphasize that, for purposes of a Medicare — or any other — reimbursement system, one must distinguish between the individual case and the consistent reliability of relatively large statistical aggregations. Even a relatively small hospital will discharge 2000 to 3000 Medicare patients a year, with more half of them falling into the 10 or 15 highest-volume DRGs. The idiosyncracies of individual cases can, as a statistical matter, at least for purposes of cost analysis and reimbursement, be expected to even out. . . . Further, since the original effort to develop DRGs, it has been clear that no classification system can ever account for all cases. There will always be statistical outliers. Just how broadly, and on what basis, outliers should be defined remains a matter of some concern, but as is the case with most statistically describable phenomena, a substantial reduction in total variance can be achieved by factoring out as few as 5 percent of all cases. . . .

The criticism that DRGs fail to adequately account for differential intensity has engendered the most comment, no doubt because of the perception on the part of many of those engaged in academic medicine that major teaching hospitals are likely to treat a disproportionate share of patients with atypically intense manifestations of particular illnesses. At the moment there is no convincing evidence to show that academic centers systematically treat more intense illnesses within DRGs than other institutions, nor that more intense illnesses, by nontautologic definitions, are more expensive to treat. Again, the question is largely an empirical one, relating to the distribution of intensity in DRGs across hospitals and hospital types. Significant research in this area is already underway and will undoubtedly grow in the near future. In the meantime the treatment of the indirect costs of medical education under the Medicare Prospective Payment System has made the intensity issue moot, at least as a matter of immediate financial concern.

THE MEDICARE DIAGNOSIS-RELATED GROUP SYSTEM

In a way characteristic of many regulatory interventions in the American political system, the Medicare DRG System is conceptually simple and straightforward in its broad outlines, but extremely complex when all its exceptions, refinements, and special adjustments are included. . . .

At the conceptual level, the amount paid to a hospital for any Medicare patient is the product of two numbers: a standardized, adjusted amount per case; and the relative weight assigned to the DRG in which the case is classified. The relative weight of DRGs is uniform across hospitals and the nation, derived from both Medicare records and special studies of data from Maryland and Michigan for 109 DRGs for which the Medicare data files contained insufficient information. . . . A primary question about the future of the Medicare DRG system is the extent to which the relative weights, along with the DRG classification itself, can and should be regularly "recalibrated." . . .

A hospital's standardized adjusted payment amount per case will be determined, once the Medicare DRG system is fully phased in after 1 October 1986, by three factors: whether the hospital is in an urban or rural area; the extent of its graduate medical education activities; and the relative wage rates in the labor market in which the hospital is located. In the intervening period, a process of phased transition towards national uniformity also considers the census region in which the hospital is located and the hospital's own historic costs.

In the fully phased-in system, the Secretary of Health and Human Services will each year promulgate two numbers: a national standardized urban amount per case and a national standardized rural amount per case. These figures can be determined deductively, by a procedure established in regulation that derives them from the average Medicare per-case costs in 1981, adjusted for inflation and standardized for case-mix, wage differences, and teaching activity. But — critically — the figures can also be determined by first setting a target budget for total Medicare inpatient expenditures, and then running the calculations backwards to produce the correct per-case amounts. . . .

Once the national per-case amount has been determined, any given hospital's per-case amount is determined by making two adjustments to the national number. First is the wage adjustment. That portion of the national standardized amount attributed to labor-related costs . . . is multiplied by an area wage index derived from Bureau of Labor Statistics data for standard metropolitan statistical areas and non-metropolitan areas. . . . Such adjustments have been used, with general acceptance but much specific quibbling, both by Medicare and other rate-setting programs for almost a decade.

The other adjustment, applied to "outlier" cases . . . as well as cases paid on a DRG basis, and paid to the hospital as an annual lump sum amount, is meant to account for the indirect costs of medical education activities. The ratio of fulltime interns and residents in approved programs to the hospital's certified bed complement is divided by 0.1, the result multiplied by 0.1159, and the amounts otherwise payable to the hospital are multiplied by that product. . . .

Once the system is fully phased in, a hospital's payment from Medicare will be based on its adjusted payment rate multiplied times the case-mix index for each Medicare inpatient. That amount will comprise the total Medicare inpatient reimbursement to the hospital with only five exceptions: payments for outliers, capital costs, direct medical education, patients transferred to other hospitals, and costs associated with kidney transplantation for approved transplant centers.

A central criterion in evaluating any categorization scheme is what it leaves out. The question of which cases should be treated as "outliers" and paid differently from inlier cases has been a central concern, with important policy considerations. The fewer the outliers, the greater the budgetary predictability for payers and the stronger the incentive effect for hospitals, but the greater the likelihood of extremely arbitrary or inequitable squeezing of unusual cases into the DRG classifications. This issue was regarded by the Congress as so important that, although it left many other fiscally significant issues about Medicare Prospective Payment to administrative discretion, it mandated that total payments for outliers comprise between 5 percent and 6 percent of total prospective payment amounts. . . .

PROFESSIONAL REVIEW

In a process concurrent with, but to a considerable degree independent from, the development of the prospective payment system, Congress also significantly revised the legislation concerning what had been professional standards review organizations. What will now be called professional review organizations have, in fact, increasingly come to be recognized as vital and integral components of the new payment system.

Concerns about the quality, appropriateness, and necessity of care rendered to Medicare and Medicaid beneficiaries existed before the development of DRG-based payment systems, but at least some characteristics of the new system seem especially to reinforce the need for improved external oversight of those issues. Prospective payment — in any form — may give hospitals an incentive to underprovide needed services, as opposed to cost-based reimbursement, which may encourage the overprovision of services. Similarly, although per diem payments, set prospectively or retrospectively, may encourage excessively long inpatient stays, DRG-based payments may encourage prematurely early discharge, because the hospital's revenue is fixed regardless of the length of stay. Payment on a per case basis may also encourage increases in admissions of marginally appropriate or even inappropriate cases.

Although the organizational relation and performance standards for professional review organizations are still in the process of formation, they will be assigned several central tasks in the implementation of Medicare prospective payment. These tasks include monitoring admissions patterns and reviewing admissions for necessity and appropriateness; seeking to identify and even prevent premature discharges or the underprovision of clinical services; and, perhaps critically, monitoring the accuracy of medical records reporting on which DRG assignment, and hospital revenue, will be based.

Notes on PPS/DRGs

The Implementation of the PPS/DRG Scheme

As Vladeck describes, the original PPS/DRG authorization legislation anticipated that by the end of fiscal year (FY) 1986 there would be a national schedule of PPS/DRG rates; after 1987, the only differentials between the basic rate of PPS/DRG payment by Medicare to various hospitals for a given diagnosis would be determined by whether the hospital was urban or rural and by the relative wage rate in its locality (in addition to the exceptions and additional payments described below). The basic PPS/DRG rates and these adjustment factors would be revised annually by HHS with the recommendations of the newly created Prospective Payment Assessment Commission (PROPAC), an advisory body made up of industry experts. Prior to the end of the FY 1986, however, the federal legislation allowed for a transitional phase during which only a portion of a hospital's reimbursement rate would be based on the PPS/DRG methodology. The remainder would be based on its actual costs. Also, the PPS/DRG rate during this period was a blend of national rates and separately determined regional PPS/DRG rates, reflecting cost differentials in different parts of the country. Both the use of actual costs as a portion of reimbursement and the use of regional PPS/DRG rates were to be gradually phased out by the end of FY 1986.

As it turned out, the transition to a single, national PPS/DRG scheme was neither smooth nor complete. In each of the years since the initiation of the PPS/DRG scheme, heated battles have raged between the Congress and the Administration, as well as with the increasingly political PROPAC. The battles ranged from technical debates over the appropriateness of various DRG categories, to the need to exclude institutions that face exceptional circumstances, to essentially political debates over the need to adopt a single national rate. The timetable for the phase-out of regional rates and hospital-specific costs has been repeatedly delayed. The various inflation factors have been frequently contested and revised. The determinations of adjustment factors and other findings by the agency also have been a continuing source of controversy. In FY 1986 for example, HHS attempted to freeze the FY 1986 PPS/DRG rate at the FY 1985 level, arguing that the rates calculated in 1985 had been overly generous (largely because of unanticipated changes in the case mix of Medicare patients experienced by the nation's hospitals during that fiscal year). Congress, however, first preempted the Secretary's proposal, by postponing the effective date of the FY 1986 rates through March 1986, and then mandated a .5 percent increase over the FY 1985 for the remainder of FY 1986. When the FY 1987 rates were proposed by the agency, Congress again enacted legislation requiring the agency to revise its timetable for a national rate and reworking many of the adjustments that the agency had proposed.

This transitional period and the accompanying politics have delayed and somewhat complicated the movement towards a national PPS/DRG rate. But while the transition to PPS/DRG and the details of its computation have been controversial, neither the Executive Branch nor the Congress have waivered in its resolve to implement a prospectively determined, per case reimbursement scheme, notwithstanding the controversies over the time table for its implementation, the need for exceptions and modifications, and other complicating issues. And while there are still some hospitals and some expenditures reimbursed on traditional cost basis (see notes infra), as of FY 1988, the movement towards the national PPS/DRG rate was virtually complete. For purposes of PPS/DRG reimbursement, national adjusted payment rates have been set for urban and for rural hospitals. (Only new hospitals continue to receive a blend of national and regional adjusted payment rates.) The FY 1988 adjusted payment rates were determined (following a protracted negotiation between the Administration, Congress, and PROPAC) by increasing the FY 1987 payment rates by a hospital-specific "market basket" inflation index, minus 2 percentage points, resulting in a modest increase of only 1.15 percent over the FY 1987 amounts.

To illustrate, in FY 1988, a payment to Grand Hospital, a nonteaching, urban institution, for treatment of a tonsil bypass would be computed in the following manner:

DRG standardized amount for FY 1988 (for urban hospitals):

— labor component: $2400
— nonlabor component: $500
— Grand Hospital's area wage index: 1.1
— Case DRG weighing factor for tonsil bypass: 1.875

The labor component of the DRG standardized amount is adjusted for the area wage index: $2400 × 1.1 = $2640. The total adjusted standardized amount is $2640 + $500 = $3140. The total adjusted standardized amount is multiplied by the DRG weighing factor for the particular diagnosis. $3140 × 1.875 = $5888. The hospital will receive $5888 as the PPS/DRG payment for the patient (plus additional reimbursement for other expenditures, such as capital costs, and other adjustments, if applicable, for the indirect costs of medical education, "outliers," and service to a disproportionate number of low income patients, as described below).

For updates and additional details on PPS/DRG rates and their computation, see 42 C.F.R. §412 (1987); see also annual reports to the Secretary of HHS from PROPAC.

Exceptions and Exclusions to PPS/DRG

Even under a fully nationalized PPS/DRG scheme, the original legislation provided for a number of exceptions to PPS/DRG reimbursement: psychiatric hospitals, rehabilitation services, and some other hospital and hospital-related services were exempted from the original legislation and continue to be reimbursed under Medicare Part A according to traditional cost reimbursement principles. Also, as noted in the previous section, in a few states, rate setting waivers have been granted, and Medicare reimbursement follows the methodology used by the state's rate setting program.

There are also some particular categories of expenditures that, unless the original legislative scheme is amended, will continue to be excluded from the PPS/DRG rate and to be reimbursed separately. At least through 1987, reimbursement for "outliers," direct medical education expenses, bad debts attributable to Medicare patients, capital expenses, and a few other itemized expenditures were specifically excluded from the PPS/DRG scheme. Hospitals treating Medicare patients will be reimbursed for these items according to the traditional Medicare cost principles.

The exclusion of capital expenditures provides the most interesting and, perhaps, controversial example. As originally implemented, capital expenditures, including such items as depreciation and other capital-related expenses, were exempted altogether from the PPS/DRG scheme. However, the initial

PPS/DRG authorization legislation required HHS to develop a methodology for inclusion of these expenditures and envisioned a phase-in of capital expenditures into the PPS/DRG scheme beginning in 1987. Under political pressure from providers, however, that time table was postponed under the Omnibus Reconciliation Act of 1987, and capital costs are now not scheduled to be combined with other expenses covered by PPS/DRG until after 1992. For a summary of one proposal for reimbursing capital costs on a PPS/DRG basis, see 52 Fed. Reg. 33168-33208 (1987).

One reason for the exemption of capital-related costs is largely technical: since capital expenditures are not uniform from year to year or from facility to facility, the use of a single base year and an industrywide average cost as the basis for reimbursement would cause hardships for some hospitals, windfalls for others. Also, construction costs vary widely from area to area, requiring some adjustments to any scheme based on a single national rate. The hospital industry has also argued that capital expenditures, like routine costs, occasionally encounter "outlier" expenditures. Since capital expenditures tend to be larger and fewer, the averaging out of overpayments and underpayments over time and across institutions is less likely to offset the inequity of the impact of a "capital outlier" on an individual institution.

Ironically, the original legislation also provided that if capital expenditures were not included in PPS/DRG reimbursement by 1987, then Medicare and Medicaid would cease payment for new capital expenditures by any facility, unless the facility was in a state that had a Section 1122 capital expenditure review program that had approved the capital costs involved (for a description, see infra at p. 278). Whether this alternative form of control over capital expenditures will be triggered has been complicated by the fact that the federally funded health planning programs have, in the meantime, expired, and it is not clear whether many states will continue to maintain 1122 programs that could perform this function. See discussion infra at pp. 282-283.

PPS/DRG "Outliers."

In addition to the above, hospitals may also qualify for additional "outlier" payments. A "cost outlier" is a case in which the costs of the patient's care are extraordinary when compared to other patients in the same DRG. A "day outlier" is a case in which the patient has an extraordinary length of stay when compared to other patients in the same DRG.

For services provided in 1987, a facility was entitled to a "day outlier" payment if the length of stay for a patient exceeded the average length of stay for that DRG by the lesser of 17 days or 1.94 standard deviations from that average. If so, the PPS/DRG payment was supplemented by an amount equal to 60 percent of the average daily cost of treatment of patients in that DRG for each additional "outlier" day. Alternatively, in 1987 a facility was entitled to a supplemental payment if the cost of providing care to a given case exceeded the lesser of $13,500 or two times the national PPS/DRG rate for that DRG. If so, the difference between the "outlier" threshold amount and the actual cost to the facility was multiplied by 60 percent to determine the additional payment. 42 C.F.R. §412. 82 (1988).

HHS used the 60 percent factor to determine appropriate "outliers" in accordance with the statutory mandate that the additional payment approximate the marginal cost of care beyond the outlier cutoff. The federal statute also mandates that this factor be determined in a manner so that the Medicare program under PPS/DRG will make no less than 5 percent and no more than 6 percent of total payments for "outliers." As a consequence, the specific details of "outlier" payments and their computations will be annually revised.

Criticism of the National Rate

The use of national rate for PPS/DRG determinations has been repeatedly questioned, even by those who have applauded the underlying approach of PPS/DRG reimbursement. As Judith Lave has argued,

> Hospital care like all services is locally produced and consumed. Even after controlling for wage differences, teaching, and location (urban/rural), there remain significant differences in the cost per case by region. Some of this difference is due to regional patterns in length of stay, some is due to differences in the prices which hospitals have to pay for factors of production such as food and electricity, and the rest [is due] to less quantifiable variables including physician and consumer tastes. Factor price information is consistently available at the local level only for wages. However, other prices also vary. . . .
>
> . . . After controlling for wages, case mix, and teaching, the Medicare cost per case of urban hospitals is approximately 20 percent higher in the East North Central Region than it is in the East South Central Region. Additionally, under a system with national rates, 62 percent of the hospitals in the East North Central Region would receive an average 13 percent reduction in their payments. These large reductions in some regions would be occurring at the same time hospitals would be experiencing considerable pressure because of the overall limit imposed on how much the rates, on average, can increase. [Lave, "Hospital Reimbursement Under Medicare," 62 Milbank Mem. Fund Q. 251, 254-55 (1984).]

Lave's argument has been repeated by others. Even if the incentives of averaged costs (not individual institutional costs) and of prices based on diagnosis (not length of stay) are assumed, what is the purpose of a national average — as opposed to an average for a region or other grouping of institutions?

The Urban Institute has taken the argument one step farther. In an interesting study comparing the experience of hospitals during the years from 1982 to 1984, when Medicare prospective reimbursement and the PPS/DRG scheme were being phased in, the Urban Institute found that hospitals did, in fact, respond to the resulting profit motive, that is, the opportunity to keep the difference between their Medicare revenues and their actual costs. They also found that hospitals did so under both prospective reimbursement based on historic costs and prospective reimbursement based on DRGs. Based on these findings, the Urban Institute questioned whether it is necessary to use average, national rates and to allow low cost hospitals to keep the difference between their costs and the nationally determined rates — with the resulting redistribution of revenues. They claim that a prospective reimbursement scheme based on actual costs could work just as effectively. Their proposal parallels that of Lave, and it would eliminate inequities between hospitals inherent in the hard to measure but real differences between hospitals. It would also, according to their estimates, allow Medicare to achieve the hoped for incentives at a lower cost; hospitals would make equivalent efforts to contain costs even without what the Urban Institute views as the opportunity for windfall profits. For a full discussion, see Feder, Hadley & Zuckerman, How Did Medicare's Prospective Payment System Affect Hospitals? 317 N. Engl. J. Med. 867 (1987). For a similar analysis, see Sheingold, Unintended Results of Medicare's National Prospective Payment Rates, 5 Health Affairs 5 (Winter 1986).

This argument must be read, however, in light of the data compiled by Wennberg and others that examines the differences in costs and utilization within a region and finds them not attributable to legitimate differences but to "styles" of practice. See discussion of Wennberg in Chapter 5.

The Economics of PPS/DRG

In essential economic terms, PPS/DRG shifts hospitals from reimbursement that is related to their actual costs per patient day to reimbursement that is based on average costs per case for all hospitals. The result, as noted above, has been defended as rewarding the efficient hospitals with a profit and providing incentives to hospitals that are inefficient to reduce their costs. As Vladeck points out — somewhat facetiously — the primary impact of all this may be to require hospital managers to manage their facilities — something that many critics have claimed hospitals have traditionally failed to do.

Certainly hospitals will need to understand and to understand quickly a great deal of information about the services they are providing and the costs associated with them. Rather than focus on occupancy, hospitals may have to focus on "throughput," the speed and efficiency with which patients are moved from admission to discharge. Some hospitals may make efforts to vertically integrate (see discussion in Chapter 8), that is, integrate their facilities with both pre-hospitalization and post-hospitalization services and facilities, again something critics have often cited as a failing of many hospitals.

Most controversially, however, hospitals will have to exercise a great deal more control over the practices of the physicians on their medical staff. Thus, even if physician services continue to be reimbursed on a fee-for-service basis, physicians practicing in hospitals will be under considerable pressure to alter their practices. Vladeck also predicts that the function of the organized medical staff will likely be expanded to take on management tasks, particularly as analyzing and controlling patterns of care become increasingly important. Similarly, the amount of peer review, by PROs as well as by institutionally created internal mechanisms, is likely to increase, particularly as more data are collected on the differences in patterns of practice between various practitioners.

Among other things, both physicians and hospitals will respond to the incentives for more efficient behavior and for more profit, with a variety of gaming techniques: discouraging "unprofitable" admissions, transferring potentially complicated cases, eliminating costly specialties, and so forth. Already the Medicare lexicon has been expanded to include "DRG creep," the tendency to diagnose patients with multiple problems in DRG categories with the highest possible level of reimbursement.

Congress has also evidenced some concern that these incentives for efficiency will result in undesirable consequences. One provision of the Sixth Omnibus Budget Reconciliation Act of 1986 requires "discharge planning" as a condition of participation in Medicare. Pub. L. No. 99-509, §9305(c), 100 Stat. 1874, 1989, codified as 42 U.S.C. §1395x(e)(6) (1982 and Supp. 1983-1987).

Exceptions for "Disproportionate Share" Hospitals and "Sole Community Providers."

While PPS/DRG reimbursement may provide positive incentives to economize for those hospitals that now provide services inefficiently, the scheme also will have an adverse impact — apparently unintended — on those hospitals that provide a high proportion of care to low income patients, many of whom are Medicare beneficiaries. A number of sources have compiled data indicating that the costs (per case) of treating the poor are inherently higher. See references cited in Kotelchuck, Poor Diagnosis, Poor Treatment: How the DRG System Affects Hospitals that Serve the Poor, 16 Health PAC Bull. 1, 7-15 (1985). The reasons for this difference likely involve a number of factors: poor people frequently have more severe and more complicated problems; they also have a greater need for supportive services both during and following treatment. For these and other reasons, the costs associated with facilities located in low income areas can be substantially higher. Refinements in the DRG categories cannot be expected to eliminate all of these differences, nor can the exceptions allowed for "outliers" be sensitive enough to allow for all "expensive" patients.

Congress attempted to provide some relief in the statutory scheme itself. The original legislation included language which required HHS to make adjustments to the PPS/DRG payment *as the Secretary deems appropriate,* to take into account the special needs of public or other hospitals that serve a significantly disproportionate number of patients who have low income and a disproportionate number of Medicare patients. 42 U.S.C. §1395ww(d)(5)(C)(i) (1982 and Supp. 1983-1987).

After HHS exhibited a reluctance to act under this authority, the statute was amended in 1984 to require the agency to issue a definition of the "disproportionate share hospitals" and to identify those hospitals that meet the definition. See Deficit Reduction Act, Pub. L. No. 98-369, §2315(h), 98 Stat. 494, 1080 (1984).

When the agency issued regulations finding only 89 (of nearly 6000) hospitals as "disproportionate share" institutions and finding that there was no evidence to support additional payments to these institutions, several lawsuits were filed asking the federal courts to require the issuance of further regulations. In Samaritan Health Center v. Heckler, 636 F. Supp. 503 (D.D.C. 1985), the federal district court ruled that the part of the statute requiring the agency to issue a definition of "disproportionate share" was a mandatory obligation, but ruled that the "exceptions and adjustments" to be made for these institutions were discretionary acts, based on both a reading of the statute and a lengthy review of the legislative history. Cf. Redbud Hospital District v. Heckler, 473 U.S. 1308 (1985) (district court ruling requiring issuance of implementing regulations was held to be improper order pending determination on the merits).

In 1985, Congress again amended the legislation, requiring the agency to pay additional amounts under PPS/DRG reimbursement (1) for both urban and rural hospitals that serve a significant portion of low income patients and (2) for urban hospitals with more than 100 beds that can show that more than 30 percent of their revenue comes from state or local government payments for indigent patients not covered by Medicaid or Medicare. Significant share is defined as 15 percent of inpatient days for urban hospitals with more than 100 beds, 40 percent for urban hospitals with fewer than 100 beds, or 45 percent for rural hospitals with fewer than 500 beds. (Those with more than 500 beds receive special treatment under a slightly different methodology.) For the most recent interpretation of this statutory mandate, see 42 C.F.R. §412.106 (1988). For a critique of the implementation of "disproportionate share" hospitals requirement, see Office of Inspector General, Office of Audit, Report on Disproportionate Share Payments to Hospitals Under PPS (1988) (reprinted at 2 CCH Medicare and Medicaid Guide §37,105).

Similarly, the PPS/DRG legislation provides for exceptional treatment of hospitals that are designated as the "sole community provider" for Medicare patients either because of location, weather, or travel conditions or because of the inaccessibility of other hospitals. 42 U.S.C. §1395ww(a)(2)(A) (1982 and Supp. 1983-1987). If the agency finds that a facility is a "sole community provider," it is entitled to a rate determined by 75 percent of the hospital's actual costs and 25 percent of the *regional* PPS/DRG rate. In addition, the institution is entitled to additional adjustments in its PPS/DRG payment if it experienced more than a 5 percent decrease in its total patient discharge in a given year. For implementing regulations, see 42 C.F.R. §412.90 (1988).

The Impact of PPS/DRGs on Hospital Expenditures

It was anticipated that PPS/DRG reimbursement would provide incentives for hospitals to increase the volume of admissions and to decrease the length of stay. Length of stay, which had been declining prior to PPS/DRGs, did, in fact, decline even faster after its implementation. The expected increase in admissions did not materialize. There was, however, a significant increase in the number of outpatient services. For a full discussion, see Guterman & Dobson, Impact of the Medicare Prospective Payment System for Hospitals, 7 Health Care Financing Rev. 97, 103-12 (Spring 1986). At the same time, it has been reported that hospitals have been showing dramatic increases in "profit", i.e., net revenue over expenditures. It is not clear whether any or all of these trends can be traced to the influence of PPS/DRGs. See id. at 103. Some experts have speculated that PPS/DRGs have in fact had substantial effect on the practice of medicine and on the manner in which hospital care is delivered. Sloan & Valvona, Why Has Hospital Length of Stay Declined? An Evaluation of Alternative Theories, 22 Soc. Sci. Med. 63 (1986).

Policy Implications of PPS/DRG Reimbursement

In terms of the overall policy direction, PPS/DRG reimbursement clearly represents a move towards reimbursement of hospitals more on the basis of "price" and less on a basis of their actual costs. Neoconservatives, in fact, have hailed the enactment of PPS/DRG as one part of a larger movement towards the establishment of a market-oriented health care financing system. (See Chapter 8 for full discussion.) But is this less or more government involvement in health care? Is this half a glass of competition or another spoonful of regulation? Surely providers seeking to maintain their autonomy — which they frequently but inaccurately equate with private competition — view PPS/DRGs, particularly when paired with the PRO utilization controls, more as a regulatory burden than as an increase in their (economic) freedom.

Morone and Dunham have argued that PPS/DRGs are not only more governmental control, but will lead inexorably to even more governmental involvement:

> While DRGs ostensibly thrust hospitals into competition, the real world of DRGs is a good deal more Calvinist — redemption and perdition turn on a number of factors entirely beyond a hospital's control. [In a partially regulated system, hospitals compete] . . . for the right mix of patients. Winning and losing will be less a consequence of efficiency than of who — if anyone — is paying the bills. . . .
>
> . . . Prices for the unregulated payors will swiftly balloon. . . . Congress is

already hearing the balloon metaphors. Once again the commercial insurers will be paying for a government attempt to control its program costs while failing to address the underlying problem of general medical inflation.

Commercial insurers will pass on the costs, largely to corporations which pay insurance premiums for their employees. Corporations and labor unions are already troubled by rising health care costs; soaring rates will substantially increase their concern. Many will demand action. . . .

In short, Medicare DRGs are likely to be devastating for hospitals that treat mainly Medicare beneficiaries and patients who cannot fully pay their bills. [It] will threaten the commercial health insurers and constitute a growing problem to the corporations that pay the insurance premiums. For all the problems it creates, the program will prove insufficient to balance the Medicare trust fund or to ease the federal deficit. The present DRG system will generate pressure for its reform. . . .

When a future Congress or blue-ribbon Presidential Commission confronts these problems, where can it turn? There will continue to be few plausible alternatives, even fewer politically expedient ones. . . . The most likely reform is what occurred in New Jersey: an extension of DRGs to cover all payors, factoring into the rates the costs of uncompensated care. . . .

Unlike previous public health insurance schemes, this one would not look like welfare or socialized medicine. In fact, it would not directly help the poor, only the hospitals that serve them — a politically crucial difference.

[E]xtending DRGs to all payors and including the cost of uncompensated care would sound less like a radical new program than like a technical adjustment to an existing one. It differs from past reform proposals by conforming to the incremental bias of the American political process. . . .

Despite the relatively quiescent politics that would accompany the change, extending DRGs and factoring in the cost of uncompensated care would establish a national health system of sorts. Government officials would set rates for all payers in all hospitals. These changes would amount to an unprecedented public intervention into the practice of medicine, and a broad subsidy for hospital care to the poor. . . .

After a half century of political thunder over the socialized medicine implicit in programs such as Medicare or national health insurance, the state is poised to assume a role at the center of the American health system. [N]ational health insurance may arrive quietly, with scarcely an interest demurring. [Morone & Dunham, Slouching Towards National Health Insurance: The New Health Care Politics, 2 Yale J. Reg. 263, 276-84 (1985).]

B. The Reimbursement of Physicians

1. EXPENDITURES FOR PHYSICIAN SERVICES

As with other health care expenditures, spending for physician services has steadily increased during the last forty years, growing from $2.7 billion in total spending in 1950, to $14 billion in 1965, to $103 billion in 1987. The rate of this growth has roughly paralleled that of other health expenditures, accelerating through the 1970s, peaking at over 17 percent per year in 1975, and continuing to grow rapidly, but at somewhat more moderate rates in the 1980s. Overall, the rate of increase of physician expenditures has been much higher than the rate of increase of NHEs or of the GNP, although it has been more variable than that of hospital or other services. For an earlier treatment of these issues, see Wing, American Health Policy in the 1980s, 36 Case W. Res. L. Rev. 608, 635-639 (1986).

Most importantly, the slowing of the rate of growth of physician spending in the 1980s has not been as marked as that of hospital and other health spending. Physician spending in 1984 rose 12.6 percent. In 1985, it slowed to a rate of 9.8 percent. But by 1987 it had risen to 12.1 percent. These figures should be compared to those for hospital services in Table 1 in this chapter, as well as those for aggregate NHEs in Table 1 in Chapter 2.

Physician expenditures historically have represented a relatively constant and, to some observers, relatively small share of total health spending, averaging just over 20 percent of all health expenditures. But in addition to their direct costs, the services of physicians also indirectly affect other expenditures for health care. Virtually all other medical care, most notably services in hospitals and other institutions, is ordered or prescribed by a physician, usually incident to the delivery of some direct service. The proprietization of hospital care and the modest growth in recent years of alternative delivery systems may somewhat dilute the traditional autonomy of physicians; their role in determining who gets what kind and what level of service may be thereby reduced. But the physician's role in determining the utilization and "intensity" of all services — and consequently the cost of those services — should be considered as important as the direct costs of physician services in evaluating the need for cost containment and the appropriate remedial responses.

As with hospital expenditures and expenditures for most other health services, the rate of growth of physician expenditures can be traced primarily to two factors: 1) inflation in the price of physician services, reflecting inflation for the general economy as well as an additional factor of inflation specific to physician fees, and 2) increases in the "intensity" of physician services.

The latter factor, increases in the "intensity" of physician services, is perhaps the most intriguing. The utilization of physician services as measured by the average number of physician visits per person and by other factors was remarkably constant from the mid-1960s, following enactment of Medicaid and Medicare, to the mid-1980s. Starting in the mid-1980s, however, experts were reporting indications that both the rate of physician visits and the number and kind of physician services were on the increase and were, in part, responsible for the relatively high rates of growth of physician expenditures in those years. Utilization rates for Medicare Part B recipients, which had been increasing gradually from 1975 to the mid-1980s, were also higher in the mid-1980s. (See discussion of Medicare Part B pp. 257-259.) How much of these increases in physician services are attributable to shifts in services from an inpatient setting to an outpatient setting — spurred by PPS/DRG reimbursement and other hospital cost containment measures — and how much actually reflects more frequent visits to a physician or additional treatment or diagnosis per visit is difficult to assess. But if these trends are confirmed and continue, increasing "intensity" of physician services will become increasingly problematic for cost containment strategies.

In any event, what has been steadily increasing during the last thirty years and throughout the 1980s has been the level of physician fees. The rate of growth of the price of physician services increased through the 1970s and remained relatively high until the early 1980s, far exceeding the overall growth of the Consumer Price Index (CPI). Through the mid-1980s, inflation in physician fees moderated but continued at rates well above those for the rest of the economy. In 1986, the price index for physician fees rose 7.2 percent, when the CPI was only 1.4 percent. In 1987, physician fees rose 7.3 percent, and the CPI was 4 percent.

As these data indicate, some portion of the increase in physician expenditures can be traced to inflation in the economy, but physician fees have been subject to an additional factor of inflation specific to physician services. Again, as with hospitals, there is some problem divorcing changes in the "intensity" of a physician service from the inflation in its price. The nature of the services delivered by physicians may be changing in various respects; moreover, the costs of providing the same "inputs" for the service would be expected to change roughly at the rate of the CPI or other indicators of general economic inflation. Nonetheless, the inflation of physician fees has clearly exceeded these expectations. Various studies that have attempted to compare actual expenses of maintaining a physician practice also have confirmed that the fees charged by physicians are rising faster than the increases in the expenses associated with those fees. Thus, as with rising expenditures for hospital services and for health expenditures in the aggregate, if expenditures for physician services are considered problematic, one principal focus of attention should be on the continuing inflation of the prices paid for these services.

2. SETTING FEES

Law & Ensminger, Negotiating Physicians' Fees: Individual Patients or Society? (A Case Study in Federalism)

61 N.Y.U.L. Rev. *1, 12-20 (1986)*

Insurance that allows patients to select physicians at the time of treatment reimburses them for doctors' fees in one of three ways: actual charges, fee schedules, or charge-based reimbursement. Insurance that pays actual charges is simple, but expensive. Under a fee schedule, the insurance program sets the fees that it will pay. Such schedules can be set high or low and adjusted to account for a number of variables including: the diagnosis; the service provided; the training, experience, and specialty status of the doctor; and the setting in which care is given.

Charge-based reimbursement pays doctors amounts based on the historical charges of individual physicians and their medical colleagues at some period in the recent past. Private insurance calls this usual, customary, and reasonable reimbursement (UCR), and Medicare calls it the customary, prevailing, and reasonable charge method (CPR). In both cases the insurance program pays the lesser of: the individual physician's actual billed charge; the amount that he or she customarily charges for that procedure, as defined by the median of actual charges; or the prevailing charge in the community, defined as some percentile of customary charges within a given medical specialty and geographic locality. Since the payment a doctor receives is determined by the stated charges at some time in the recent past, doctors have strong economic incentives to keep stated charges high. As a result, insurance programs using charge-based reimbursement most often pay the prevailing charge in the community.

With the growth of Blue Shield and the enactment of Medicare, charge-based reimbursement became the primary method of paying for physicians' services. When Congress enacted Medicare in 1965, the AMA was strongly opposed, and many feared that physicians would boycott the program. To encourage physicians' participation, Congress gave the doctor-sponsored Blue Shield programs responsibility for paying doctors and required that Medicare follow the Blue Shield practice of paying doctors based on physicians' customary, prevailing, and reasonable charges. Congress gave the states discretion to decide how Medicaid was to pay physicians for services provided to poor people. About one-half of the states pay doctors on the basis of fee schedules, while the others provide some form of charge-based reimbursement.

Theoretically, under a charge-based reimbursement system, unjustifiable increases in physicians' fees are prevented by market constraint on underlying charges. But with widespread use of charge-based reimbursement, usual fees "have little relation to actual average payments per service," particularly for surgical procedures, and "tend to lose all meaning, becoming an instrument in physicians' hands to maximize third-party payments."

From 1966 to 1972, Medicare's prevailing charges were adjusted each July to take account of individual doctor's charge increases in the prior year. Because prevailing charges rose rapidly, Congress limited increases in 1973 by applying an economic index reflecting a weighted average of the cost of physicians' office practice and general wage rates. Because physicians' charges have continued to rise faster than the economic index, the Medicare reimbursement structure has gradually changed to a fee schedule that rises annually, maintaining the ratios among fees that were in effect in 1973.

Prior to 1974, Blue Shield and Medicare kept customary charge profiles secret, in the hope that physicians would price their services without reference to other doctors' charges. When the Medicare profiles were made public in 1974, the information produced a dramatic escalation in "gaming by physicians to increase income by raising charges." As the President of Massachusetts Blue Shield stated, "[W]hen the numbers were disclosed, physicians became aware of the fact that others in the same specialty were receiving a higher rate of reimbursement for procedures. The impact was for physicians to upgrade their charges in order to receive the maximum."

CONTINUING FINANCIAL BARRIERS TO CARE AND OTHER CONUNDRUMS

Both the cost and the accessibility of physicians' services are influenced in fundamentally different ways, depending on whether an insurance program contracts with doctors and requires them to accept program fees as full payment or pays fixed amounts and allows doctors to impose additional charges on patients. Any insurance program's capacity to constrain physicians' costs or to change the relative value of various services is limited by the concern that patient access will be impaired if total physicians' payments are too low.

With insurance plans that pay fixed amounts and allow doctors to charge more if payments are too low, insurers can constrain their costs and premiums by limiting payments to doctors and shifting the burden of rising fees to the patient. Patients, however, may have difficulty paying the difference between the insurance payment and the doctor's bill. With such insurance, the incentive and power to constrain costs or to change the relative value of various services rests with the individual patient. Theoretically, patients forced to confront out-of-pocket costs will shop and negotiate for a reasonably priced service.

By contrast, under an insurance program that requires participating doctors to accept program fees as full payment, the incentive and power to constrain fees rests with the insurance program, for insurance costs rise directly with physicians' payments. If fees are too low, doctors may refuse to participate in the program or may reduce services to patients insured by it. Physicians' ability to refuse participation is affected by the number and nature of patients insured by a particular program. It is much easier for a doctor to refuse to participate in a program that insures few patients or one that insures patients whom the doctor perceives as socially or medically uninteresting or undesirable.

Blue Shield programs have direct relationships with participating physicians. In the early years, many programs required physicians to accept program payments as full compensation for most services provided. Commercial insurers, on the other hand, do not have the relationships with physicians that make it possible to impose such requirements. Commercial insurers guarantee payments to insured patients, who in turn deal with physicians. As competitive pressures from commercial insurers pressed Blue Shield to keep premium rates low, most Blue Shield plans found that it was easier to allow physicians to charge patients amounts in excess of Blue Shield rates than to constrain physicians' fees. Today, Blue Shield of Massachusetts seems to be unique in limiting payment to participating doctors who agree to accept program fees as payment in full.

The federal health insurance programs, Medicaid and Medicare, require providers — doctors and hospitals — to enter into participation agreements with the program. Under both Medicaid and Medicare Part A, hospitals are prohibited from charging patients amounts in excess of the rates paid by the program. Because Medicaid insures the very poor, federal Medicaid law both prohibits doctors from charging amounts in addition to the amount that the state program pays and limits state freedom to require deductibles and coinsurance. Medicare, on the other hand, allows doctors to decide whether to accept the fees the program provides or bill patients at higher rates. If higher rates are billed, patients must collect what they can directly from Medicare. In Medicare jargon, the doctor's decision to accept the program's payment instead of billing the patient is described as "accepting assignment." Doctors are free to decide whether to accept assignment on a patient by patient, procedure by procedure basis. Because Medicare reimbursement rates have tightened, fewer doctors accept assignment of Medicare claims. Elderly patients find it difficult to find a doctor who will care for them for the fees that Medicare provides. Under Medicaid, access problems to the poor are even more acute. In states where Medicaid payments to physicians are low, many patients eligible for Medicaid cannot find physicians to serve them.

Physicians' charges in excess of insurance program payments are not the only financial costs that insured patients must bear at time of illness. Medicare and most private insurance policies also require patients to pay fixed deductibles before insurance coverage begins and copayments assessed as a fixed amount per service or a percent of service cost. The costs of deductibles and coinsurance are substantial. The elderly now pay the same percentage out of pocket medical costs as they did prior to the enactment of Medicare. Such costs are so high that 65 percent of all Medicare beneficiaries buy private supplemental insurance. These supplemental policies are expensive and often do not provide comprehensive supplementation, even for acute care services.

Escalating program and patient costs and financial barriers to access are not the only problems in our present arrangements for paying doctors' fees. Payment on a fee for service basis, where doctors are paid for each separate service they provide, creates financial incentives for marginally useful care. Those incentives are exacerbated by the uncertainties inherent in medical practice and by excess hospital and physician capacity, particularly in the surgical subspecialties. Further, financial rewards for various types of medical practice are inappropriately disparate. Existing payment patterns favor specialists over generalists, practitioners in urban areas over those in rural areas, inpatient treatment over ambulatory care, and surgery over primary, chronic, or psychiatric care. These disparities are fueled by two forces. First, patients choose, for perfectly rational reasons, to purchase insurance against catastrophic need rather than more predictable, less costly routine care. Because acute care services are more likely to be insured, they command higher prices. Second, some types of physicians — notably surgeons and other practitioners of heroic medicine — have historically enjoyed greater status and political power within the profession and hence have greater capacity to negotiate favorable reimbursement rates with insurers.

3. THE EVOLUTION OF PHYSICIAN REIMBURSEMENT

a. Physician Reimbursement Under Various Third Party Payers

As Law and Emsinger point out, historically most third party payment programs have reimbursed physicians on a fee-for-service basis, calculated using either an actual charge, a fee schedule, or an "averaged" charge (either UCR or CPR) methodology. Some physicians, such as those working in administrative or teaching capacities in a hospital or group practice, have been reimbursed on a salary basis, for at least a portion of their work. More recently, physicians participating in HMO-type arrangements have been reimbursed on either a salary basis or a capitation basis, receiving at least some portion of their compensation on the basis of a fixed fee per enrolled patient, regardless of the amount of care provided to the patient. There also have been proposals to reimburse physicians on a *per case* or *per diagnosis* basis; see discussion infra pp. 259-260.

As of 1989, Medicare continues to use a fee-for-service CPR, "averaged" charge reimbursement scheme, although the exact methodology has been complicated by various cost ceilings, periodic freezes in rate adjustments, and various other cost-containing limits that have been adopted for Medicare Part B payments. See pp. 257-258. Private third party payers use a wide variety of arrangements for reimbursing physicians. Indemnity insurers typically use fee schedules; most Blue Shield and other service-benefit plans use some variation on UCR or CPR reimbursement.

States have varied widely in the schemes adopted to reimburse physicians under their Medicaid programs. Many states use variations of the Medicare CPR scheme. Others use fee schedules. Interesting but politically volatile variations on traditional Medicaid reimbursement involve capitation arrangements under which Medicaid recipients enroll with an HMO, IPA, or other provider for all covered services, in return for which the provider receives an annual payment per enrollee. Also, many states are attempting to integrate capitation payments with "case management" arrangements. See discussion in Chapter 8. But regardless of the methodology, the net result is that the rates of physician reimbursement under Medicaid are generally lower than the reimbursement of physicians for the same services available under Medicare or under many private insurance schemes. In some cases, Medicaid reimbursement for some physician services is dramatically lower, one of the reasons Medicaid recipients frequently have problems finding a physician who will accept Medicaid patients.

For additional discussion of physician reimbursement, alternative arrangements, and related health policy issues, see Holohan, Physician Reimbursement, in J. Feder, J. Holohan & T. Marmor, National Health Insurance, Conflicting Goals and Policy Choices 73-128 (1979); Capron, Containing Health Care Costs: Ethical and Legal Implications of Changes in the Methods of Paying Physicians, 36 Case W. Res. L. Rev. 708 (1986); Burney, Hickman, Paradise & Scheiber, Medicare Physician Payment, Participation, and Reform, 3 Health Affairs 5 (Winter 1984). U.S. Cong., Office of Technology Assessment, Payment for Physician Services: Strategies for Medicare (1986).

b. Assignment and "Balance Billing"

In addition to the reimbursement methodology, another critical characteristic of a reimbursement scheme that has special significance for physician reimbursement involves the amount of the provider's bill paid by the patient. As discussed in Chapter 2, even when a service is covered, the patient often faces substantial cost-sharing requirements. In addition, under virtually any reimbursement methodology, there will be a difference between the third party payment and the provider's actual or preferred charges. Under some reimbursement schemes, the provider is allowed to bill the patient separately and may either a) "balance bill" the patient for both the cost sharing requirement *and* the difference between the third party payment and actual charges or b) bill the patient for the whole amount of the actual charge, requiring the patient to recover the reimbursable amount directly from the third party payer. Under other schemes, the provider is required to take "assignment" of the bill and must accept the amount of reimbursement paid by the third party payer as payment in full. The patient is only liable to the provider for the cost sharing requirement. (And if the provider refuses to accept assignment, the patient must pay the provider directly and will not be reimbursed by the third party payer.)

Medicare Part B and most private insurers both impose substantial cost sharing requirements on eligible beneficiaries *and* allow physicians the option of accepting assignment. Medicaid payments to physicians, on the other hand, must be accepted as payment in full, except for the modest co-payments and deductibles that states are allowed to impose on Medicaid beneficiaries. By way of contrast, under Medicaid, Medicare Part A, and some but not all service benefit plans, hospitals must accept assignment of claims for covered inpatient services and cannot bill the patient for the remainder of the bill, other than the patient's cost sharing obligation. (Nor can the patient receive reimbursement directly from the program if the hospital bills the patient directly.)

The practical consequences of assignment can best be illustrated by an example from Medicare Part B. A patient visits his physician on two occasions for services covered by Medicare Part B. The physician would actually charge $100 for each visit if the patient were paying out of pocket. Medicare under CPR determines that the physician's reimbursement should be $80. As of 1989, Medicare required the beneficiary to pay the first $75 of Part B claims during a fiscal year; it also required the beneficiary to pay 20 percent of each Part B bill as co-insurance.

First visit

— Physician's charge: $100
— Medicare CPR: $80
— Patient's cost sharing liability: $75 plus 20 percent of the remainder — $76
— Medicare will pay: $4

If the physician takes assignment, she receives $4 from Medicare, $76 from the patient; if the physician does not accept assignment, Medicare will pay the patient $4 and the physician can bill the patient $100.

Second visit (during the same year)

— Physician's charge: $100
— Medicare CPR: $80
— Patient's cost sharing liability: 20% of CPR — $16
— Medicare will pay $64

If the physician takes assignment, she receives $64 from Medicare, $16 from the patient; if the physician does not take assignment, Medicare pays $64 to the patient, and the physician will bill the patient $100.

As the illustration demonstrates, whether or not the physician opts to accept assignment can have a substantial impact on the patient's liability out of pocket, particularly where the patient also has cost sharing obligations. And even supplemental insurance policies that many Medicare beneficiaries purchase that pay the cost sharing obligations under Part B generally do not cover the difference between Part B reimbursement and actual charges by a physician. On the other hand, while assignment can make billing and collection more convenient and predictable for the physician, it can also result in a much lower rate of reimbursement. Most important, from an economic point of view, since the difference between a third party payer's reimbursement and a physician's actual or preferred charge is generally intended to contain the costs of the service, assignment, in effect, determines whether the impact of the cost containment will be borne by the physician or the patient. (See discussion infra of assignment rates following the 1984 Medicare reimbursement reforms.)

c. Medicare Reforms of Physician Reimbursement

Until the mid-1980s, few attempts were made to reform either the terms or methodology of Medicare Part B reimbursement or, for that matter, of the physician reimbursement schemes of any third party payer. As described in the Introduction, Medicare had attempted to closely parallel the practices of Blue Shield and other private insurers; it was generally assumed that a continuation of "averaged-charge" reimbursement and voluntary assignment was necessary to secure the participation of physicians in the program. Private insurers, with few exceptions, had little interest in breaking with their traditional reimbursement practices. Even when Medicare came under increased political scrutiny in the 1980s, more attention was focused on what was regarded as the most pressing problem, containing hospital costs. After the enactment of the PPS/DRG scheme for hospitals, however, the political spotlight shifted to reform of physician payment.

In fact, it is not surprising that physician reimbursement would be subject to such attention. As described in Chapter 2, the peculiar revenue structure of Medicare may have somewhat disguised the rising costs of physician expenditures under Medicare Part B, but, nonetheless, those costs had been rising rapidly throughout the history of the program and, as noted at the beginning of this section, were continuing to do so in the 1980s, even when the rates of increase in spending for other services began to moderate. Fueled by inflation in physician fees, a growing Medicare population, *and* marked increases in the "intensity" of Medicare Part B services, Medicare Part B costs had grown at an average of 17 percent a year from 1975 to 1986 — a rate even higher than that for hospitals during that decade — and one that was particularly visible as hospital spending rates began to decline in the mid-1980s. By 1987, experts were predicting that Part B spending would soon represent over 40 percent of all Medicare program costs, and some form of physician payment reform was becoming a political certainty.

In 1984, Congress mandated a series of reimbursement reforms, billed as temporary measures pending more comprehensive and permanent reforms. The most notable measure was a 15-month freeze on physician reimbursement rate increases through September 1985. At the same time, Congress required all physicians participating in the program to declare whether they were "participating" or "nonparticipating" physicians. Congress enacted two conditions on reimbursement, intended to encourage physicians to become "participating" physicians: a) "nonparticipating" physicians were prohibited during 1985 and 1986 from charging Medicare patients more than their actual charges as of April 1984 — even if they refused to accept assignment; and b) it was announced that increases in actual charges (to all patients) during the freeze by "nonparticipating" physicians would not be included in the calculation of Medicare Part B rates after the freeze was lifted, but would be included in the rate increases of "participating physicians."

Despite the political "promise" that these reforms would be temporary, the rate freeze was extended the following year. "Participating" physicians were not allowed rate increases until May of 1986. "Nonparticipating physicians" were not allowed increases until January 1987 and these increases were subject to the disallowances discussed above. Through 1989, Medicare continued to restrict allowable increases in reimbursement rates for unassigned claims.

The economic effect of the Part B rate freeze and other reforms enacted in 1984 was also only temporary. The rate of increase in Part B spending dropped to only 8 percent in 1984 — the lowest rate in two decades — but Part B spending grew at an annual rate of nearly 18 percent from 1985 to 1989 (despite the continuation of the freeze and other limits), largely due to measurable increases in the "intensity" of Part B services.

The 1984 reforms also had some effect on physician participation in Medicare Part B. Data for 1985 and 1986 indicate that nearly 70 percent of Medicare Part B claims were accepted as payment in full by physicians in those years. This was a notable increase over the assignment rate for the years prior to the 1984 reforms, when the overall assignment rate averaged just over 50 percent. On the other hand, only about 30 percent of physicians opted to be "participating" physicians in 1985 and 1986. Apparently many physicians were willing to accept assignment for some patients, and, for some reason, the rate of assignment was increasing. Physicians, however, were still unwilling — for either economic or ideological reasons — to give in to government pressure to accept assignment for all Medicare patients. It should be noted that there was considerable variation by specialty and that physicians were more willing to accept assignment for hospital-based services than for services in private offices. There was also considerable variation across regions of the country. In 1985, for example, Maryland had 84 percent of its claims accepted in full. In the same year, Wyoming had a rate of only 41 percent. In states where the rate of acceptance of assignment was high, it is also apparent that the rate was heavily influenced by a few physicians who had a high volume of Medicare patients, not by widespread participation. See U.S. Government Accounting Office, Medicare: Physicians Income by Specialty and Place of Service 33-41 (HRD-86-90BR 1986); see also Physician Payment Review Commission, Medicare Physician Payment: An Agenda for Reform 57-64 (1987).

Physician resistance to the rate freeze and participation incentives was also reflected in a lawsuit challenging the constitutionality of the 1984 reforms and arguing, among other things, that the rates paid by the government must provide an administrative mechanism to ensure that all physicians are guaranteed a "reasonable profit." In rejecting the physicians' claim that the legislation was a violation of substantive due process, the Eleventh Circuit held:

> Under the particular facts and circumstances of this case, we conclude that the legislative purposes are legitimate — *i.e.,* to control federal spending in order to alleviate deficit problems, and to promote the public welfare by precluding physicians from shifting the burden of the reductions onto Medicare beneficiaries — and we conclude that the means chosen by Congress are not unreasonable — *i.e.,* the fees are fixed at what this physician himself charged in the recent past (the quarter immediately preceding the freeze period), and the freeze is temporary pending a study which can form the basis for more permanent legislation. Under these circumstances, we hold that due process does not require Congress to follow the ratemaking procedures suggested by appellants. We are not confronted with the issue of whether due process would require ratemaking or other such procedures in the case of permanent legislation, and we express no opinion thereon. [Whitney v. Heckler, 780 F.2d 963, 971-72, (11th Cir. 1986), *cert. denied,* 479 U.S. 813 (1987).]

For a further discussion of the constitutional issues raised in the *Whitney* decision and of the discretion of state and federal governments to mandate rate controls, see discussion pp. 222-223, 289-291.

d. Future Reforms of Physician Reimbursement: DRGs for Physicians

As noted above, one significant and potentially controversial reform in physician reimbursement would be to reimburse physicians under Medicare Part B (or any other third party payment scheme) on a *per case* or *per diagnosis* basis, rather than per visit or per service, paralleling the PPS/DRG reimbursement scheme now applied by Medicare to hospital reimbursement. See discussion supra. In fact, the original PPS/DRG legislation mandated a study by HHS of the feasibility of including physician reimbursement for services provided on an inpatient basis under the PPS/DRG scheme. See §603(a)(2)(B) of Pub. L. No. 98-21. In 1987, the Reagan Administration did propose such a scheme for the reimbursement of radiologists, anesthesiologists, and pathologists performing services incident to inpatient care. The so-called "DRG/RAP" payment would have been a lump sum given to the hospital in addition to the PPS/DRG payment. The hospital would be given the discretion to negotiate with these physicians for their actual payment by the hospital. (Also, under the proposed plan, the physician would be allowed to "balance bill" the patient.) In theory, the result would be to create incentives for physicians to provide services efficiently — or at least inexpensively — and to eliminate unnecessary or marginal services. It would also tend to make Medicare payments for hospital-based physician services more predictable for federal policymakers.

The "DRG/RAP" proposal was sharply criticized by the medical profession and generated little political momentum. Some critics have argued that whatever the merits of PPS/DRG reimbursement for hospitals, it should not be automatically assumed that a per case or per diagnosis reimbursement scheme would have the same results if applied to physicians. In addition, many critics have argued that the continued use of independent, fee-for-service reimbursement for physicians performing services in hospitals acts as a counterbalance to the economic incentives for the hospital to discharge patients prematurely created by PPS/DRG reimbursement. Also, some studies have indicated that the variation among fees charged by physicians for the same service is much more dramatic than the variation among hospital charges; if a single DRG rate were used for all physicians, there would be many more "winners" and "losers." Also, individual physicians see fewer Medicare cases per year; an "expensive" case would have a greater impact on a physician than on a hospital where PPS/DRG cases tend to average out over a period of time. Several expensive cases could theoretically have a catastrophic effect on a physician (unless some kind of "outlier" exception were allowed). Some of this risk of catastrophe could be eliminated if the physician DRG scheme incorporated a kind of risk pooling, paying the physician DRG payment to a group practice, to an entire medical staff, or to a hospital, allowing the group to continue to reimburse individual physicians on a fee schedule or other charge basis, as the "DRG/RAP" scheme contemplated. The trade off, however, is obvious: the larger the group receiving the DRG, the less incentive there is for an individual physician to respond to the financial pressures for efficient or cheaper services that per case or per diagnosis reimbursement would theoretically create. For a more extended discussion of the potential impact of per case or per diagnosis reimbursement for physicians, see Burney, Hickman, Paradise & Scheiber, supra, at 17-20.

e. Future Reforms of Physician Reimbursement: Resource-Based RVS

Another possible reform of Medicare Part B reimbursement that has received considerable attention is the possibility of replacing the existing CPR scheme with a fee schedule based on a relative value scale (RVS), eliminating some of the inequities in payments and other recognized disadvantages of the current Medicare Part B methodology and, possibly, containing the costs of Part B payments.

In 1985, Congress created the Physician Payment Review Commission (PPRC). The PPRC was mandated to report annually to Congress on possible reforms of the Medicare physician payment scheme. Somewhat surprisingly, in its first reports in 1987 and 1988, the PPRC strongly advocated that Medicare's CPR methodology be replaced by a national fee schedule based on a RVS.

Neither fee schedules nor relative value scales are novel ideas. As Law and Ensminger point out, many private insurers have traditionally relied on RVSs and fee schedules to reimburse physicians. Somewhat oversimplified, a RVS is a weighted ranking of medical procedures. Once determined, a RVS can be converted into a fee schedule simply by multiplying the relative value of a service times a fixed dollar value. The dollar value can be periodically adjusted to reflect inflation and other economic changes. The relative value scale also can be adjusted for geographic differences in cost, variations in patterns of practice, or other factors. While these adjustments can create both technical and practical problems, the essence of this methodology is the weighted rankings of each service, reflecting the perceived qualitative differences between various services. Significantly, private insurers have generally adopted RVSs that have been developed by medical associations or other physician groups.

What is new about the PPRC's proposal is not just that the methodology would be determined independently by the Medicare program (giving the government much more leverage over the levels of reimbursement), but also that the new proposal anticipated the development of a fee schedule that would rely on a relative value scale more accurately reflecting the actual resources that physicians employ in providing services. The immediate result of such a fee schedule, according to the PPRC, would be more equitable, eliminating overpayment and underpayment, and encouraging more physicians to participate. The longterm result would be more control over reimbursement increases and Part B costs.

The PPRC proposal was also somewhat of a political compromise, a fee-for-service alternative to proposals to reimburse physicians on a per case or per diagnosis basis. The proposal would dilute physician control over reimbursement, form a somewhat different pattern of "winners" and "losers," and, eventually allow for more control over the costs of the program. It would, however, retain at least one of the profession's most cherished values: fee-for-service reimbursement.

Some of the political and economic implications of this proposal can best be illustrated by the results of a study commissioned by the PPRC at the Harvard School of Public Health as the first step in the development of the critical feature of the PPRC proposal: a resource-based relative value scheme. The study was intended to rate, among other things, the technical skills, mental effort, potential risk to patients or providers, uncertainty and anxiety involved, and other "resources" required for various medical procedures; and to compare these resources to the existing CPR reimbursement. The results of this study — applauded by some and jeered at by others — confirmed many of the conclusions that had earlier been released by the PPRC: as a result of Medicare Part B payment, some physicians are overpaid; others are underpaid. Medicare skimps on reimbursement of cognitive services and splurges on surgical procedures. If a fee schedule based on the study's relative value scale were adopted, surgeons' fees under Medicare Part B would shrink as much as 30 percent, but rates for family practitioners and internists should increase by virtually the same amount.

While it did not specifically adopt the recommendations of the Harvard study, the final PPRC report urged Congress to abandon the current Medicare physician reimbursement scheme and adopt a national, resource-based fee schedule for all physician services starting in 1990. (Geographic variations would be recognized only in the calculation of overhead costs.) For obvious political reasons, the PPRC recommended that the new reimbursement scheme be "budget neutral": total outlays for the first year would be the same as would be expected under the existing physician reimbursement scheme. In subsequent years, however, the PPRC recommended that a target budget be set. In years when the target budget for physician services is exceeded, the cost-of-living increase for the succeeding year would be adjusted to offset the unexpected increase. In theory, this will discourage physicians from attempting to offset per service losses by increasing the volume of services rendered. The PPRC report also included several proposals to encourage participating physicians to accept assignment of claims. (See discussion infra.) For a full discussion of these and other recommendations of the PPRC, see Physician Payment Review Commn., Annual Report to Congress (April 1989).

f. Participation and Assignment

Whether Congress opts for a physician DRG scheme, a more equitable fee schedule, or other reform of physician reimbursement, it is also likely to give considerable attention to the issues of participation and assignment. As described above, the recent interest in Congress in reforming Part B reimbursement has been clearly driven by a concern to control the costs of the program (and to a lesser extent by a concern for treating physicians more equitably), but Congress has evidenced an equally strong interest in containing the costs of the program to the beneficiary and maintaining the availability of services for the Medicare population.

One issue that is now under consideration — which would have been practically unthinkable only a decade ago — is mandatory assignment of Medicare Part B claims. The 1984 reforms took one step in that direction, but only one step, creating financial incentives for physicians to accept assignment. The results were somewhat mixed, but physicians did accept assignments at a higher rate. On the other hand, voluntary assignment, as discussed earlier, allows the physician the option of shifting the burden of cost containment from the provider to the beneficiary. If a physician DRG scheme or a new RVS is adopted with more stringent cost containment, both participation and assignment rates may drop.

Thus far, Congress has only considered, but not enacted, mandatory assignment. At least four states (Rhode Island, Connecticut, Vermont, and Massachusetts), however, have legislation requiring some level of Medicare assignment. The most comprehensive law was enacted in Massachusetts in 1985, requiring a ban on "balance billing" for Medicare patients as a condition on medical licensure. See Massachusetts Medical Society v. Dukakis, 815 F.2d 790 (1st Cir. 1987), *cert. denied,* — U.S. — (1987) (state law mandating assignment of Medicare claims did not violate federal law or constitution). Interestingly, Massachusetts Blue Shield has also required a ban on "balance billing" from physicians who participate in the state's Blue Shield program. See Kartell v. Blue Shield of Massachusetts, Inc., 749 F.2d 922 (1st Cir. 1984), *cert. denied,* 471 U.S. 1029 (1985) (ban on "balance billing" by a private third party did not violate antitrust laws). (For a discussion of *Kartell* and related cases, see Chapter 8.)

g. The Economics of Physician Reimbursement

Obviously, one concern with the manner in which physicians are reimbursed involves the extent to which the incentives for economic gain lead the physician to provide more services than necessary or more than the patient would otherwise want or need. In traditional economic terms, the problem is one of "demand creation" or "demand inducement," the extent to which a physician advises a patient to accept additional medical care beyond that which the patient would want if he or she had the information and expertise of the physician. Obviously, under any fee-for-service scheme, the physician has, in theory, an economic incentive to provide more care. Under a fee-per-diagnosis or case basis, there is an incentive to initially treat or accept a patient, but not for additional services; under a salary or capitation scheme, there is no economic incentive for treatment at all. The extent to which demand is actually induced or created, however, is a source of some controversy; and its exact role in driving increases in physician expenditures is difficult to assess. Most often the allegation is inferred from aggregate statistics on the number or distribution of physicians, physician income, utilization patterns, and so on. Nonetheless, the available indirect evidence is persuasive. For example, in one study of Medicare Part B payments in Colorado over a two year period, following increases in rates for some services and decreases in rates for others, it was found that the physicians subjected to the reduced fees responsed by increasing the intensity of their service, providing more surgical procedures, ordering more laboratory tests and the like. The study was consistent with the hypothesis — hotly denied by physicians — that a physician's services under a fee-for-service scheme will be determined, at least in part, by the physician's need to produce a certain level of income and not entirely by patient need. See Rice, The Impact of Changing Medicare Reimbursement Rates on Physician-Induced Demand, 21 Med. Care 803 (1983).

h. Physician Reimbursement and HMOs

With the growing acceptance of HMO-type insurance arrangements, the implications of reimbursement for physician services on a capitated basis have grown in importance. Alex Capron argues that the key to a capitation arrangement is that the risk of open-ended liability is shifted from the payer to the provider, either the physician or the physician's employer or contractor. When that risk is borne directly by the physician, the incentives are direct and obvious. But as is more frequently the case, when the risk is borne by the HMO, group practice, or other institution, the incentives are more complicated. Capron claims that the results can be viewed into two general categories: either the institution shifts some of the risk to the physician (for instance, through bonuses or profit sharing) or the institution retains the risk and attempts to exert far more control over the physician's behavior. Capron, supra at 725-27. See also Office of Technology Assessment, supra, 179-212. In either case, the result is a radical departure from traditional medicine.

C. Procedural Issues in Provider Reimbursement

Heckler v. Ringer

466 U.S. 602 (1984)

Justice Rehnquist delivered the opinion of the Court.

Respondents are individual Medicare claimants who raise various challenges to the policy of the Secretary of Health and Human Services (Secretary) as to the payment of Medicare benefits for a surgical procedure known as bilateral carotid body resection (BCBR). . . .

[Medicare] precludes reimbursement for any "items or services . . . which are not reasonable and necessary for the diagnosis or treatment of illness or injury." The Medicare Act authorizes the Secretary to determine what claims are covered by the Act "in accordance with the regulations prescribed by him." Judicial review of claims arising under the Medicare Act is available only after the Secretary renders a "final decision" on the claim. . . .

[T]he Secretary has provided that a "final decision" is rendered on a Medicare claim only after the individual claimant has pressed his claim through all designated levels of administrative review. First, the Medicare Act authorizes the Secretary to enter into contracts with fiscal intermediaries providing that the latter will determine whether a particular medical service is covered by Part A and if so, the amount of the reimbursable expense for that service.

If the intermediary determines that a particular service is not covered under Part A, the claimant can seek reconsideration by the Health Care Financing Administration (HCFA) in the Department of Health and Human Services. If denial of the claim is affirmed after reconsideration and if the claim exceeds $100, the claimant is entitled to a hearing before an administrative law judge (ALJ). . . . If the claim is again denied, the claimant may seek review in the Appeals Council. If the Appeals Council also denies the claim and if the claim exceeds $1000, only then may the claimant seek judicial review in federal district court of the "Secretary's final decision."

In January of 1979, the Secretary through the HCFA issued an administrative instruction to all fiscal intermediaries instructing them that no payment is to be made for Medicare claims arising out of the BCBR surgical procedure when performed to relieve respiratory distress. . . . HCFA explained that BCBR has been "shown to lack [the] general acceptance of the professional medical community." . . . It concluded that the procedure "must be considered investigational" and not "reasonable and necessary" within the meaning of the Medicare Act.

Many claimants whose BCBR claims were denied by the intermediaries as a result of the instruction sought review of the denial before ALJs, who were not bound by the Secretary's instructions to the intermediaries. Until October 1980, ALJs were consistently ruling in favor of individual BCBR claimants. . . .

In response to the rulings of the ALJs . . . on October 28, 1980, the Secretary through the HCFA issued a formal administrative ruling, intended to have binding effect on the ALJs and the Appeals Council, prohibiting them in all individual cases from ordering Medicare payments for BCBR operations occurring after that date.

The individuals named in the amended complaint, who are respondents before this Court, are four individual Medicare claimants. Their physician . . . prescribed BCBR surgery for all four respondents to relieve their pulmonary problems. Respondents Sanford Holmes, Norman Webster-Zieber, and Jean Vescio had the surgery before October 28, 1980, and all three filed a claim for reimbursement with their fiscal intermediary. At the time that the amended complaint was filed, none of the three had exhausted their administrative remedies, and thus none had received a "final decision" on their claims for benefits from the Secretary. The fourth respondent, Freeman Ringer, informally inquired of the Secretary and learned that BCBR surgery is not covered under the Medicare Act. Thus he has never had the surgery, claiming that he is unable to afford it.

The essence of their amended complaint is that the Secretary has a constitutional and statutory obligation to provide payment for BCBR surgery because overwhelmingly her ALJs have ordered payment when they have considered individual BCBR claims. According to the complaint, the Secretary's instructions to the contrary to her intermediaries violate constitutional due process and numerous statutory provisions in that they force eligible

Medicare claimants who have had BCBR surgery to pursue individual administrative appeals in order to get payment, even though ALJs overwhelmingly have determined that payment is appropriate. . . . The complaint seeks a declaration that the Secretary's refusal to find that BCBR surgery is "reasonable and necessary" under the Act is unlawful, an injunction compelling the Secretary to instruct her intermediaries to provide payment for BCBR claims, and an injunction barring the Secretary from forcing claimants to pursue individual administrative appeals in order to obtain payment.

The District Court dismissed the complaint in its entirety for lack of jurisdiction. It . . . concluded that 42 U.S.C. §405(g) with its administrative exhaustion prerequisite provides the sole avenue for judicial review. . . .

On appeal the Court of Appeals for the Ninth Circuit reversed. It concluded that the thrust of respondents' claim is that "the Secretary's presumptive rule that the BCBR operation is not reasonable and necessary was an unlawful administrative mechanism for determining awards of benefits." The Court of Appeals concluded that to the extent that respondents are seeking to invalidate the Secretary's *procedure* for determining entitlement to benefits, those claims are cognizable without the requirement of administrative exhaustion under the federal-question statute.

[T]he Court of Appeals concluded that exhaustion would be futile for respondents. [W]e now reverse.

It seems to us that it makes no sense to construe . . . [these] claims . . . as anything more than, at bottom, a claim that they should be paid for their BCBR surgery. Arguably respondents do assert objections to the Secretary's "procedure" for reaching her decision — for example, they challenge her decision to issue a generally applicable rule rather than to allow individual adjudication. [T]he relief that respondents seek to redress their supposed "procedural" objections is the invalidation of the Secretary's current policy and a "substantive" declaration from her that the expenses of BCBR surgery are reimbursible [sic] under the Medicare Act. We conclude that all aspects of respondents' claim for benefits should be channeled first into the administrative process which Congress has provided for the determination of claims for benefits. We, therefore, disagree with the Court of Appeals' . . . apparent conclusion that simply because a claim somehow can be construed as "procedural," it is cognizable in federal district court by way of federal question jurisdiction.

The third sentence of 42 U.S.C. §405(h) provides that §405(g), to the exclusion of 28 U.S.C. §1331, is the sole avenue for judicial review for all "claim[s] arising under" the Medicare Act. Thus, to be true to the language of the statute, the inquiry in determining whether §405(h) bars federal-question jurisdiction must be whether the claim "arises under" the Act, not whether it lends itself to a "substantive" rather than a "procedural" label. . . .

In Weinberger v. Salfi, we construed the "claim arising under" language quite broadly to include any claims in which "both the standing and the substantive basis for the presentation" of the claims is the Social Security

Act. . . . Under that broad test, we have no trouble concluding that all aspects of respondents Holmes', Vescio's, and Webster-Zieber's challenge to the Secretary's BCBR payment policy "aris[e] under" the Medicare Act. It is of no importance that respondents . . . sought only declaratory and injunctive relief and not an actual award of benefits as well. Following the declaration which respondents seek from the Secretary — that BCBR surgery is a covered service — only essentially ministerial details will remain before respondents would receive reimbursement. . . . Thus we hold that the Court of Appeals erred in concluding that any portion of [the beneficiaries'] claims here can be channeled into federal court by way of federal-question jurisdiction. . . .

Thus §405(g) is the only avenue for judicial review of respondents' . . . claims for benefits, and, when their complaint was filed in District Court, each had failed to satisfy the exhaustion requirement that is a prerequisite to jurisdiction under that provision. We have previously explained that the exhaustion requirement of §405(g) consists of a nonwaivable requirement that a "claim for benefits shall have been presented to the Secretary" and a waivable requirement that the administrative remedies prescribed by the Secretary be pursued fully by the claimant. All three respondents satisfied the nonwaivable requirement by presenting a claim for reimbursement, . . . but none satisfied the waivable requirement.

Respondents urge us to hold them excused from further exhaustion and to hold that the District Court could have properly exercised jurisdiction over their claims under §405(g). We have held that the Secretary herself may waive the exhaustion requirement when she deems further exhaustion futile. We have also recognized that in certain special cases, deference to the Secretary's conclusion as to the utility of pursuing the claim through administrative channels is not always appropriate . . . [for instance] where the plaintiff asserted a procedural challenge to the Secretary's denial of a pretermination hearing, a claim that was wholly "collateral" to his claim for benefits, and where he made a colorable showing that his injury could not be remedied by the retroactive payment of benefits after exhaustion of his administrative remedies.

The latter exception to exhaustion is inapplicable here where respondents do not raise a claim that is wholly "collateral" to their claim for benefits under the Act, and where they have no colorable claim that an erroneous denial of BCBR benefits in the early stages of the administrative process will injure them in a way that cannot be remedied by the later payment of benefits. And here, it cannot be said that the Secretary has in any sense waived further exhaustion. [T]he Court of Appeals concluded that the Secretary's formal ruling denying payment for BCBR claims rendered further exhaustion by respondents futile. But as we have pointed out above, the administrative ruling is not even applicable to respondents' claims because they had their surgery before October 28, 1980. We therefore agree with the Secretary that exhaustion is in no sense futile for these three respondents. . . .

Respondents also argue that there would be a presumption against them as they pursue their administrative appeals because of the very existence of the Secretary's instructions and her formal ruling and thus that exhaustion would not fully vindicate their claims. . . . In promulgating the formal ruling, the Secretary took pains to exempt from the scope of the ruling individuals in respondents' position who may have had the surgery relying on the favorable ALJ rulings. [E]xhaustion of administrative remedies is in no sense futile for these respondents, and they, therefore, must adhere to the administrative procedure which Congress has established for adjudicating their Medicare claims.

Respondent Ringer is in a separate group from the other three respondents in this case. [H]e wishes to have the operation and claims that the Secretary's refusal to allow payment for it precludes him from doing so. Because Ringer's surgery, if he ultimately chooses to have it, would occur after the effective date of the formal ruling, Ringer's claim for reimbursement, unlike that of the others, would be covered by the formal ruling. Ringer insists that . . . the only relief that will vindicate his claim is a declaration that the formal ruling, and presumably the instructions as well, are invalid and an injunction compelling the Secretary to conclude that BCBR surgery is "reasonable and necessary" within the meaning of the Medicare Act. It is only after that declaration and injunction, Ringer insists, that he will be assured of payment and thus only then that he will be able to have the operation.

[W]e see Ringer's claim as essentially one requesting the payment of benefits for BCBR surgery, a claim cognizable only under §405(g). [C]onsistent with our decision with respect to the other three respondents, we hold that §§1331 and 1361 are not available as jurisdictional bases for vindicating Ringer's claim.

Ringer's situation does differ from that of the other three respondents in one arguably significant way. Because he has not yet had the operation and thus has no reimbursable expenses, it can be argued that Ringer does not yet have a "claim" to present to the Secretary and thus that he does not have a "claim arising under" the Medicare Act so as to be subject to §405(h)'s bar to federal-question jurisdiction. . . . We find that argument superficially appealing but ultimately unavailing.

Although it is true that Ringer is not seeking the immediate payment of benefits, he is clearly seeking to establish a right to future payments should he ultimately decide to proceed with BCBR surgery. The claim for future benefits must be construed as a "claim arising under" the Medicare Act because any other construction would allow claimants substantially to undercut Congress' carefully crafted scheme for administering the Medicare Act.

If we allow claimants in Ringer's position to challenge in federal court the Secretary's determination, embodied in her rule, that BCBR surgery is not a covered service, we would be inviting them to bypass the exhaustion requirements of the Medicare Act by simply bringing declaratory judgment actions in federal court before they undergo the medical procedure in question. Congress clearly foreclosed the possibility of obtaining such advisory opinions from the Secretary herself, requiring instead that a claim could be filed for her scrutiny only after the medical service for which payment is sought has been furnished. . . . Because Ringer has not given the Secretary an opportunity to rule on a concrete claim for reimbursement, he has not satisfied the nonwaivable exhaustion requirement of §405(g). . . .

[I]n the dissent's view, if a claimant wishes to claim entitlement to benefits in advance of undergoing the procedure for which payment is sought, his claim does not "arise under" the Medicare Act and hence he is not precluded by §405(h) from resorting to federal-question jurisdiction. But that argument amounts to no more than an assertion that the substance of Ringer's claim somehow changes and "arises under" another statute simply because he has not satisfied the procedural prerequisites for jurisdiction which Congress has prescribed in §405(g).

With respect to our holding that Ringer has not satisfied the nonwaivable requirement of §405(g), the dissent adopts the remarkable view that the Secretary's promulgation of a rule regarding BCBR surgery satisfies that nonwaivable requirement. The dissent would thus open the doors of the federal courts in the first instance to everyone — those who can and those who cannot afford to pay their surgeons without reliance on Medicare — who thinks that he might be eligible to participate in the . . . program, who thinks that someday he might wish to have some kind of surgery, and who thinks that this surgery might somehow be affected by a rule that the Secretary has promulgated. Of course, it is of no great moment to the dissent that after adjudicating his claim in federal court, that individual may simply abandon his musings about having surgery. And it is of no great moment to the dissent that Congress, who surely could have provided a scheme whereby claimants could obtain declaratory judgments about their entitlement to benefits, has instead expressly set up a scheme that requires the presentation of a concrete claim to the Secretary. . . .

NOTES ON PROCEDURAL ISSUES IN PROVIDER REIMBURSEMENT

Administrative Procedures for Appeal of Reimbursement Decisions

As *Ringer* illustrates, the administrative procedures employed by both public and private third party payers in determining coverage, rates of reimbursement, and other reimbursement-related decisions can be critically important for both providers and beneficiaries. At the same time, it should be obvious that the specific legal controversies concerning administrative procedures are intricately wrapped in the complex details of the Medicaid and Medicare statutes and regulations, or of the insurance agreements and the state and federal laws that regulate them — legal bases that can and do change frequently.

Nonetheless, these controversies continually raise basic policy choices and, in the case of the public third party payers, important constitutional principles that will be called into play regardless of the reimbursement methodology or the specific administrative remedies that are employed by the various payers.

The procedures followed by the public payers are also notable in that they delegate a great deal of authority to private and quasi-private decisionmakers (for instance, fiscal intermediaries and the Provider Reimbursement Review Board play important and unique roles in determining Medicare appeals, as explained infra). Furthermore, as the *Ringer* case demonstrates, it is clear that Congress has intended to limit and, in some cases, preclude altogether, both the available administrative remedies for some kinds of decisions and the scope and availability of judicial review of administrative decisions under these programs. The administrative remedies available under private insurance programs vary from payer to payer and from state to state. For an illustration and discussion of private insurance remedies, see *Sarchett* and notes following *Sarchett* in Chapter 2.

The administrative remedies available to beneficiaries or providers under the Medicaid program also vary from state to state. Some states' insurance laws require certain procedures to be followed. Private insurance plans governed by ERISA must comply with the federal requirements. The federal Medicaid statute requires the state to outline its administrative appeals in the state plan, giving fairly broad discretion to each state in fashioning its own administrative scheme. The federal statute and regulations also require that a state allow recipients a "fair hearing" and outline other procedural protections for recipients. See 42 U.S.C. §1396a(3) (1982 and Supp. 1983-1987); 42 C.F.R. §431.200 (1987). There are virtually no substantive federal requirements for administrative appeals by providers; federal laws require only that the state specify its administrative procedures in the state plan. See 42 C.F.R. §447.253 (1987). There is even some question whether providers have standing to require states to follow those procedures that are outlined in the state's plan. See Oregon Department of Human Resources v. Coos Bay Care Center, 803 F.2d 1060 (1986), *vacated and remanded,* — U.S. — (1987). The administrative remedies provided under Medicare, as outlined below, provide the best illustration for purposes of analyzing the inherent legal and public policy issues. As noted above, these procedures are frequently amended. Already some of the rules recited in *Ringer* have been changed. For the most current authority, see 42 U.S.C. §1395ff (1982 & Supp. 1983-1987); 42 U.S.C. §1395u (1982 and Supp. 1983-1987).

Medicare Administrative Appeals

Part A

Originally, most individual decisions regarding coverage and reimbursement under Medicare Part A were made by fiscal intermediaries (FIs). FIs are private financial organizations (frequently Blue Cross) contracting with the Department of Health and Human Services (HHS), essentially to carry out the agency's administrative decisions at the local level.

Since 1982, however, much of this authority with respect to hospital services has been delegated to the Peer Review Organizations (PROs) created as part of the PPS/DRG reimbursement scheme. (See description supra.) Thus PROs now have had the authority to make a variety of initial decisions relating to Medicare Part A coverage decisions for services provided in hospitals (for instance, initial admission certification, length of stay determinations, service/procedure approvals, waiver of liability decisions, decisions whether the service is covered by Part A). The FIs retain authority for initial coverage and payment decisions for services in skilled nursing homes (SNHs) and home health services (HHSs) covered by Part A, and some hospital payment-related decisions.

A Medicare beneficiary can request that a PRO or FI reconsider a payment or coverage decision. Federal regulations allow for expedited reconsideration of a decision regarding initial admission to the facility. Providers can also request a reconsideration of a payment or coverage decision, but a provider cannot seek further administrative appeal *or* judicial review of a *coverage* decision. (See below for discussion of provider appeals of reimbursement decisions.)

The Medicare statute also precludes further administrative appeal or judicial review by either the provider *or* the beneficiary of some PRO reimbursement-related decisions under PPS/DRG. For instance, there is no further appeal in a dispute over "outlier" determinations or errors in DRG coding.

Following a reconsideration of a denial of payment or coverage, the beneficiary can request a judicial-type hearing before an administrative law judge (ALJ) from the Office of Hearings and Appeals in the Social Security Administration, if the matter in controversy is more than \$200 in the case of hospital coverage decisions, or \$100 in all other hospital-related decisions or in all SNH and HH, decisions.

Decisions of the ALJ can be further appealed to the Appeals Council within the Social Security Administration. Final administration appeal from Appeals Council decisions is to the Secretary of HHS.

A beneficiary can seek judicial review of a final agency decision if the amount in controversy is more than \$2000 in the case of hospital PRO decisions or \$1000 in the case of other agency decisions.

As illustrated in *Ringer* and its predecessor decisions, the courts have interpreted the language of the Social Security Act to strictly limit the federal question jurisdiction of the courts in "claims arising under" this statutory scheme; thus the administrative process described above has been viewed as the exclusive remedy by which a beneficiary can challenge decisions regarding reimbursement and coverage, even in cases where the challenge is to an agency rule or procedure, or in some cases where the challenge raises constitutional issues.

Following initial decisions by the FI, providers may appeal the various reimbursement decisions made under the prospective reimbursement scheme (for instance, determinations regarding prospective payment rates under Part A, total Medicare payments, assessment of facility costs, and so forth). If the amount in controversy exceeds $10,000, appeals can be made to the Provider Reimbursement Review Board (PRRB) (a quasi-independent body made up of five "experts" appointed for three year terms by the Secretary of HHS). If the amount in controversy is between $1000 and $10,000, the only administrative appeal is to the FI. Providers may not, however, appeal a decision regarding coverage *or* any of the reimbursement-related PRO decisions, such as "outlier determinations" or "waiver of liability" decisions.

After a judicial-type hearing, the final PRRB decision can be appealed to the Secretary. Final decisions of the Secretary are subject to judicial review.

Part B

The Medicare statute severely limits the administrative appeals and the judicial review of Medicare Part B decisions. Initial decisions regarding reimbursement and coverage (or waiver of liability) are made by the Part B carriers (usually private health insurance companies such as Blue Shield). Any initial decision of the carrier can be appealed by the beneficiary. Only decisions involving medical necessity can be appealed directly by the Part B provider. In either case, Part B appeals are very prescribed. Prior to 1986, in disputes involving claims between $100 and $500, a beneficiary or a provider that accepts assignment could request a "fair hearing" before a hearing officer provided by the carrier. Unless reopened by the carrier, there was no further administrative appeal *or* judicial review of these decisions beyond this hearing. Under a procedure created for the first time in 1986, in disputes involving claims for more than $500, beneficiaries have a right to a hearing before an ALJ and to subsequent judicial review in Part B matters involving claims of $1000 or more.

Judicial Review of Medicare and Medicaid Reimbursement Decisions

The *Ringer* decision raises many of the statutory and constitutional challenges that both beneficiaries and providers have frequently raised to the administrative procedures available under both Medicare and Medicaid. In particular, providers have strenuously — but largely unsuccessfully — opposed the statutory limitations on the jurisdiction of the federal courts to hear objections to the government's reimbursement-related decisions.

In Weinberger v. Salfi, 422 U.S. 749 (1975), the Supreme Court held that an applicant denied eligibility for Social Security disability payments could only appeal that determination through the administrative procedures outlined in the Social Security Act, even when the applicant's objection was to the *method* of determining eligibility and based on constitutional arguments. In *Salfi,* the agency had applied an across-the-board "duration of relationship" standard in determining who was a dependent; Salfi claimed that the standard was an unconstitutionally vague presumption. Without ruling on the merits of the argument, the Court held that the language of the Social Security Act, 42 U.S.C. §405(h) (1982 and Supp. 1983-1987), precluded independent judicial review of "finding of fact or decisions" by the agency. 422 U.S. at 760-62. The applicant's only recourse would be to pursue eligibility through the administrative procedures of the Social Security disability program and then to appeal under the limited judicial remedies provided under the statute.

The significance of this ruling lies in the resulting delay. The plaintiff must await an initial determination by the agency, an exhaustion of the various levels of appeal, and only then seek judicial review of the agency's decision and a decision on the merits of the constitutional objection to the original determination. Social Security appeals can take several years, as can appeals of Medicare or Medicaid coverage or reimbursement decisions.

Interpreting §405(h) to apply to Medicare coverage and reimbursement decisions, a number of courts have followed the lead of *Salfi* and held that both procedural and substantive objections to Medicare "findings of fact or decisions" also must be pursued exclusively through the administrative procedures outlined in the statute, even when those objections are based on constitutional grounds. See, for instance, Trinity Memorial Hospital of Cudahy, Inc., v. Associated Hospital Services, 570 F.2d 660 (7th Cir. 1977); cf. St. Louis University v. Blue Cross Hospital Services, 537 F.2d 283 (8th Cir. 1976), *cert. denied,* 429 U.S. 977. Thus both beneficiaries and providers in most circumstances must pursue their objections to various Medicare reimbursement procedures, methods of cost determination, and so on, through lengthy and costly appellate procedures, a reality that has caused continual objection from the provider community.

There are exceptions, albeit narrow, to this "exhaustion of remedies" requirement. The Supreme Court has held that where the agency waives the exhaustion requirement or where the claim is based on a constitutional argument wholly collateral to the agency's decision, §405(h) may not apply, and the federal courts may take independent jurisdiction over these issues (at least when the "nonwaivable" requirement of a filing has been satisfied). Mathews v. Eldridge, 424 U.S. 319, 320 (1976). But while *Eldridge* opened the door, however slightly, to judicial review of some agency decisions, *Eldridge* foreclosed argument on one constitutional objection to the procedures typically followed by federal agencies in administering social welfare programs.

The plaintiff in *Eldridge* was a recipient of Social Security disability benefits who was held by the agency to be no longer disabled and therefore ineligible. The administrative procedures allowed him to contest that decision, but his benefits were terminated following a notification of his initial denial and a reconsideration of his written objections, but prior to any judicial-type hearing before the agency or any other body. Eldridge argued that the termination of his benefits without a full hearing and the ensuing delay while he appealed that decision through the agency's appellate procedures could result in life-threatening hardship. Thus, even if his argument had merit, the retroactive reinstatement of his benefits might result in a somewhat different and arguably unintended "exhaustion" requirement. While the Supreme Court did find that this was a collateral constitutional objection to the administrative decision to terminate his benefits, the Court was unsympathetic to his argument that he was entitled to a pretermination hearing, and Eldridge lost on the merits.

The concern of health care providers that most closely parallels that under examination in *Eldridge* arises in situations where the determination involves the termination of the provider from Medicaid or Medicare altogether. For many facilities, Medicaid and Medicare reimbursement is an important if not necessary source of revenue. In some cases, loss of certification to participate in the program can jeopardize institutional survival. Nonetheless, the logic of *Eldridge* generally has been applied to Medicaid and Medicare provider reimbursement decisions that result in denial of participation in the program. For example, in Town Court Nursing Center v. Beal, 586 F.2d 266 (3d Cir. 1978), a nursing home terminated from the Medicaid program for alleged violations of the safety code was held not to be entitled to a pretermination hearing; the court held that so long as the administrative procedures, taken as a whole provide a minimum amount of fairness and an opportunity to contest the decision in a judicial-type hearing (eventually), the administrative scheme satisfies the requirements of procedural due process.

Other courts have applied this same logic to both hospitals and physicians who are denied participation in the federal programs. See Northlake Community Hospital v. United States, 654 F.2d 1234 (7th Cir. 1981); Varandani v. Bowen, 824 F.2d 307 (1987), *cert. denied,* — U.S. — (1988). As the court stated it in *Northlake:*

> The private interest involved in the termination of a Medicare provider agreement is less weighty than the interest of a disability claimant [citing *Eldridge*]. The provider, although it plays a virtually indispensible [sic] role in the administration of Medicare benefits, is *not* the intended beneficiary of the Medicare program. Obviously, the termination of Medicare assistance has a financial impact (potentially severe in many instances) on the institution. But a provider's financial need to be subsidized for the care of its Medicare patients is only "incidental to the purpose and design of the [Medicare] program." Thus, a terminated provider can still obtain revenue from the care of private patients. "The unfortunate reality that [the institution] will probably encounter difficulty operating at capacity is not of constitutional significance." [*Northlake*, 654 F.2d at 1242.]

The Supreme Court essentially affirmed this acceptance of the "unfortunate reality" and removed any doubt that it applied to beneficiaries as well as providers in O'Bannon v. Town Court Nursing Center, 447 U.S. 773 (1980), a severed portion of the *Town Court* case cited above. Plaintiffs in *O'Bannon* were Medicaid patients in the nursing home that was subject to decertification; they argued that they were entitled to a pretermination hearing prior to their transfer from the facility even if the nursing home was not. The Court of Appeals, while denying the argument of the institutions, had held that procedural due process required that the patients be allowed a pre-transfer hearing on the merits of the agency's decision, largely to avoid the irreversible hardship of "transfer trauma." The Supreme Court reversed, holding that Medicaid decertification of the nursing home did not affect a constitutionally protected interest of the recipient patients, and therefore the government was not required to hold a pre-transfer hearing. The Court's ruling made it clear that it assumed a priori that the Constitution did not require that the nursing home be given a pretermination hearing either.

As a result of the *Ringer, Salfi,* and *Eldridge* decisions, most Medicaid and Medicare decisions regarding determinations of cost, participation in the program, coverage of service, or almost any other decision must be exclusively pursued through the administrative appeals provided under the statute. A claim must be made, and all appellate procedures must be exhausted before seeking any judicial review. The only exceptions occur when the agency waives the exhaustion requirements (although the filing of a claim is a "non-waivable" requirement) or when the claim is based on a collateral constitutional claim. One implication of the decisions regarding pretermination hearings is that since the courts have so firmly denied that argument, a claim that the provider or beneficiary is entitled to a pretermination hearing is no longer a colorable constitutional claim and is therefore no longer a viable basis for seeking collateral review.

Obviously *Ringer* is the harshest application of the logic of these cases. See dissent by Justices Stevens, Brennan, and Marshall, 466 U.S. at 627.

Notwithstanding the implications of *Salfi, Eldridge,* and *Ringer* and these other decisions, many Medicaid and Medicare providers continue to seek independent (and expedited) judicial review of reimbursement decisions on both substantive and procedural grounds. Virtually all courts have strictly enforced the *Salfi* "exhaustion of remedies" requirement, even when the objection is based on constitutional grounds; see, for instance, Good Samaritan Medical Center v. Secretary of HHS, 776 F.2d 594 (6th Cir. 1985) (plaintiff hospitals claimed that certain DRG reimbursement methods favor urban over rural hospitals and thus violate equal protection). Only where the constitutional claim is wholly collateral has independent judicial review been allowed. See for instance, Whitney v. Heckler, discussed, p. 259.

Congress, of course, is always free to legislate expanded judicial review, and they have done so on occasion, albeit in minor ways. In 1980, for example, the Medicare legislation was amended to allow for expedited judicial review of some issues over which the PRRB lacks the authority to decide (that is, under some circumstances the PRRB is bound by the agency's regulations). See 42 U.S.C. §1395oo(f) (1982 and Supp. 1983-1987). Providers have also successfully challenged attempts by the Secretary to severely limit their ability to challenge the validity of agency regulations before the PRRB. See Bethesda Hospital Association v. Bowen, 485 U.S. 399 (1988) (provider can raise challenge in administrative review of end-of-year cost reports, even if issue is not raised before fiscal intermediary).

One area in which providers have had limited success in attacking the procedures used in reimbursement decisions and in securing independent judicial review involves reimbursement decisions under Medicare Part B. As described above, the Medicare statute on its face severely limits both administrative remedies and judicial review of Part B decisions. The constitutionality of these statutory limits has been upheld in United States v. Erika, Inc., 456 U.S. 201 (1982).

In Bowen v. Michigan Academy of Family Physicians, 476 U.S. 667 (1986), plaintiffs challenged agency regulations that allegedly required that different amounts be paid under Medicare Part B to similarly situated physicians. The agency argued that the statute precluded judicial review of the regulations. The Court denied the argument, holding that the statutory prohibition applied only to the determinations themselves, not to the methods of determination; the Court was not prepared to read the statute to preclude judicial review altogether, or to apply the language of §405(h), the basis of the *Ringer* and *Salfi* decisions, to all Part B decisions. 476 U.S. at 680. It further implied that such a reading of the statute would be unconstitutional. Id. at 681. It is clear, however, that the Court intended no modification of the original *Salfi* holding. It is also worth noting that the Court's approval of limited review of Part A decisions is based on the Court's reading of both §405(h) and other relevant language in the Medicare Part A provisions; see 42 U.S.C. §1395 (1982 and Supp. 1983-1987).

D. Cost Containment Through Health Planning and Certificate-of-Need Programs

Introductory Note: Capital Financing in the 1980s

The financing of capital expenditures and the relationship of capital financing to various reimbursement and cost containment schemes during the last three decades illustrate much about the complicated health politics of that period. These issues also provide the background for a problem of significant and continuing importance: the financing of the capital needs of hospitals and other health care providers.

At least through the 1960s, the economic and political pressures influencing capital expenditures were largely in one direction. Government was actively encouraging expansion of the hospital industry. Both private and public cost-based reimbursement schemes also provided incentives to capital spending, as did the nature of hospital services as perceived until the mid-1960s. Hospital services were constantly changing and improving; the demands of consumers and providers for access to this new technology made expansion of facilities and the purchase of the latest innovation in hospital care not only a necessity but a source of institutional and community pride. The result was a "building boom" in hospitals and other health facilities and was applauded as such.

During this period, most hospitals relied on sources of capital that reflected this enthusiastic public support for hospital growth and expansion: gifts from the public; gifts from private foundations, trusts, or other private donors; allocations from internally held trust or reserves (often funded by the generous treatment of capital costs by third party payers); and various government grants and subsidies.

At least through the mid-1960s, the vast majority of hospital capital expenditures were derived from these sources. Of particular importance were various federal programs that provided grants, loans, loan guarantees, and interest subsidies for construction and modernization of hospitals and other health facilities. Until discontinued in the early 1970s, the federal Hill-Burton program had been the single most important source of funds and loan guarantees for health facility construction and modernization for nearly thirty years. Less visible, but also significant were a series of other federal programs (and a few state programs) that provided loans, loan guarantees, and interest subsidies for health facility construction projects (for instance, the Housing and Urban Development Act of 1968 empowered the Federal Housing Administration to guarantee loans for hospital and nursing home construction).

Starting as early as the 1940s, some state governments had also indirectly subsidized health facilities construction by creating local and state public bond authorities empowered to sell tax exempt bonds and to use the proceeds for loans to hospitals and to other health facilities. In other states, nonprofit and public hospitals were empowered to directly issue their own tax exempt bonds to underwrite their capital projects.

To fully appreciate their impact, these government funding efforts must be paired with the reimbursement policies of both government and private third party payers. Until very recently, all third party payers have generously reimbursed hospitals for depreciation and other capital-related expenditures on a cost basis, even as reimbursement for service-related expenditures has become more stringent. (Somewhat ironically, third party payers under cost reimbursement generally include reimbursement for capital-related expenditures on a "presumed" cost basis, allowing depreciation and other cost-related expenditures even when the actual financing for those assets had been provided by outside sources and regardless of whether the funded depreciation is in fact retained as reserves to be used for future capital expenditures.)

Obviously, by the late 1960s the applause for the building of more and better hospitals had begun to fade. Of equal importance became the concern of both public and private policymakers for the rising costs associated with the nation's hospital expenditures, costs driven at least in part by the ever-expanding capacity of most hospitals. Health planning programs and later certificate of need programs were developed that attempted to assess the necessity of capital expenditures by hospitals. Particularly in their initial years, these programs worked somewhat at cross purposes with the various public and private programs that helped finance capital expenditures.

By the early 1970s, some successful attempts were made to coordinate private and public sources of capital financing with the decisions of various health planning programs. In 1972, Congress empowered the federal government to deny a portion of reimbursement under Medicaid and Medicare to health facilities that made capital expenditures that were not approved by state health planning programs, the so called "Section 1122" (of the original Social Security Act) program. Also during this period, many states attempted to coordinate their Hill-Burton programs and other loan and loan guarantee programs with the decisions of their certificate of need programs. In a few states, Blue Cross and other insurers attempted to do the same thing. The National Health Planning and Resource Development Act of 1974 essentially repealed the Hill-Burton program and created a new program combining certificate of need, health planning, and capital funding activities (although the authority to provide federal funds for capital projects under the new program was never implemented or funded).

The results of all this are several: as government policy with regard to reimbursement and cost containment has shifted in various ways and as other political and economic influences on hospitals and other health facilities have changed, both the nature and the sources of capital financing have changed as well. The rate of growth of hospital capital expenditures leveled off in the 1970s and declined in the 1980s. There has also been an important change in the financing sources of those expenditures. As some — but not all — government sponsored sources of capital have disappeared in the last decade, health facilities have had to rely more heavily on the remaining programs, such as tax exempt bonds and government guaranteed loans, and also to turn more often to other sources of capital, some of which are unfamiliar to institutions that have traditionally viewed themselves as nonprofit and publicly supported.

In particular, many hospitals are finding it necessary to rely on commercial institutions to finance their capital spending: private loans from banks and other financial institutions, publicly issued (taxable) bonds, and other forms of commercial paper. Without the advantage of government subsidy or without prior experience with private financial markets, many hospitals find these sources of capital inadequate or inaccessible.

Conversely, as proprietary hospitals have taken over a larger share of the industry, they have emerged with a decided edge over their public and nonprofit counterparts in the familiar world of commercial paper and private loans — a reversal of the circumstances only a decade earlier. Proprietary institutions and particularly proprietary chains can also raise capital by selling ownership shares in their institutions, an option unavailable to nonprofit or public institutions.

The shift from charitable and public sources to private, financial market sources is clearly one of the more important trends affecting hospital management and administration, and the future of the hospital as an institution. (See discussion in Chapter 8.)

In the 1980s, the needs of an individual facility for capital funding continue: even an established institution needs to acquire and maintain expensive equipment, to expand and modernize existing facilities, to respond to new technology and shifting utilization patterns, and to compete with other hospitals and other institutions. In fact, as pressure to contain costs increases, some institutions have had to rely on capital financing sources to generate working capital or even to finance short term operating costs. Experts have predicted that in the 1980s, hospitals may need to raise from $130-200 billion in capital, a reflection of both the uncertainty of these estimates and the problematic character of these expenditures.

At the same time, there continues to be considerable uncertainty with regard to the direction of public policy concerning financing and control of capital expenditures, particularly the continuation of the regulatory programs that were implemented in the 1960s and the 1970s. The Reagan Administration successfully dismantled programs that financed health planning activities and that required states to maintain certificate-of-need programs. Yet, as the article to follow describes, many states have continued their certificate-of-need programs, and public control over capital expenditures by hospitals and other institutions continues to be both a reality and a source of controversy.

For a further discussion and background, see D. Cohodes, Hospital Capital Formation in the 1980's (1986); Office of the Assistant Secretary for Planning and Evaluation, Department of Health and Human Services, Hospital Capital Expenses: A Medicare Payment Strategy for the Future (March 1986).

Simpson, State Certificate-of-Need Programs: The Current Status

75 Am. J. Pub. Health 1225, 1226-1227 (1985)

There are several reasons why states may have chosen not to follow the federal lead in ending support for certificate-of-need. First, states appear to use certificate-of-need to accomplish goals other than cost containment. A federal shift in preferred mechanisms to control Medicare and Medicaid costs away from certificate-of-need would thus not necessarily induce states to follow. States are more likely than the federal government to favor a regulatory approach to health cost containment because their ability to reform the institutional health care system through market incentives is limited. States cannot promote competition and consumer choice by altering the incentives to excess health insurance in the Internal Revenue Code, nor can they alter the terms of employee health insurance benefits without running afoul of federal law regulating employment benefits and collective bargaining agreements.

Most states have, however, modified their programs by cutting back on the number of projects reviewed. Capital expenditure thresholds have increased significantly, and after NHPRDA's compliance requirements were relaxed many states raised their thresholds above the maximum federal level. This practice appears most common among Western states, where Colorado has a $2 million capital expenditure threshold and several other states have $1 million thresholds. Only seven states have kept expenditure thresholds at pre-NHPRDA levels.

EXEMPTIONS AND STREAMLINED REVIEW

Most states have also cut back on reviews by adopting CON exemptions or by streamlining review procedures for expenditures unrelated to clinical services and other low-impact projects. The state of Washington, for example, exempts capital expenditures that will not substantially affect patient charges and that are for: communications and parking facilities; mechanical, electrical ventilation, heating, and air-conditioning systems; energy conservation systems; repairs to physical plant necessary to maintain state licensure; acquisition of data processing and other equipment; construction of facilities not to be used for direct provision of health services; land acquisition; and refinancing of existing debt. Most states provide for limited review of projects to eliminate safety hazards or to comply with licensure and accreditation requirements. Numerous states also provide for expedited review of projects such as capital expenditures not involving service or bed capacity increases, service terminations, expenditures below a threshold somewhat higher than their statutory coverage minimum, and the like. Several state statutes provide for exemption or expedited review of projects for replacement of facilities or equipment. The purpose of exemptions and streamlined review is to remove planning agencies from the business of reviewing routine transactions or minor projects which do not risk excess investment.

A number of states have adopted a new approach to certificate-of-need review of health service and new technology additions. These states cover additions of a limited number of specified new health services regardless of their capital or operating cost, and all other new services only if their costs exceed a high threshold. For example, Ohio covers additions of heart, lung, liver, and pancreas transplant programs without regard to cost and other new services only if their annual operating costs exceed $297,500. Kentucky covers health service additions with over $250,000 annual operating costs or additions regardless of cost of acute care services, open-heart surgery, cardiac catheterization, radiation therapy utilizing megavoltage equipment, end-stage renal disease services, CT (computed tomography) scanners, nuclear magnetic resonance imaging (MRI), and long-term care services. The purpose of this approach appears to be to cover without regard to expected cost the services for which non-cost containment rationales for certificate-of-need review apply, and to cover the services for which cost control is the paramount concern only if project costs exceed the threshold.

EXPANSION OF CERTIFICATE-OF-NEED

In recent years, many states have increased the regulatory scope of their CON programs. Some important ways states have done so include imposition of moratoria on certificate-of-need approvals; expansion of medical equipment coverage to outpatient, non-hospital settings; and adoption of ceilings or "caps" on the total dollar value of projects approvable in a given year.

A moratorium is simply a categorical ban on certificate-of-need review and approval of certain projects. Moratoria, both statutory and agency-adopted, have a long history of use by CON programs. They have been used to channel investment into or away from particular services, halt the spread of new technology while planners develop criteria for controlled introduction, or suspend the review process while major modifications in the state's CON program are implemented. The use of moratoria has increased in recent years, as states have sought to modify and strengthen certificate-of-need. Missouri, for example, has adopted a statutory moratorium on issuance of certificates-of-need for new skilled and intermediate care nursing facility beds extending through July 1, 1986. Mississippi has a similar moratorium in place through July 1, 1986, with an exemption for certain "swing bed" temporary conversions of acute care beds to nursing care. Minnesota and Kansas do not have certificate-of-need statutes per se, but their legislatures have adopted moratoria on all new hospital construction, bed capacity increases, and bed relocations through 1987. At least 11 other states have had moratoria in effect during 1984-85.

Some health care providers have tried to evade certificate-of-need by putting their expensive medical equipment in non-institutional settings. A decade ago this tactic led to CT scanners in physicians' offices; today MRI equipment is being located in similar settings. Several states have amended their CON laws to foreclose this tactic. Virginia, for example, covers acquisition of equipment by a physician's office which is generally and customarily associated with the provision of health services in an inpatient setting. Colorado, Connecticut, the District of Columbia, Hawaii, Iowa, Montana, New Hampshire, Rhode Island, and Wisconsin also cover equipment acquisitions in various non-inpatient settings.

A capital cap or ceiling on the total dollar value of projects approvable under certificate-of-need in a given year acts as a mechanism for controlling the total level of capital investment by health facilities and compelling health planning agencies to weigh the relative merits of disparate projects. In the presence of a cap, projects for remodeling existing facilities may compete with new construction, and a new open heart surgery service may vie with a new renal dialysis unit for limited capital funds. By contrast, under conventional CON programs only contemporaneously filed applications for similar projects are comparatively reviewed. A statutory cap is in operation in Rhode Island and Maine. The Massachusetts CON program contains an annual ceiling on increases in hospital operating costs resulting from capital expenditures.

ANTI-COMPETITIVE CERTIFICATE-OF-NEED PROVISIONS

The best CON law reflects a calculated risk that the benefits of public scrutiny of health facility projects will outweigh the program's unavoidable side effect of enfranchising existing providers. Some certificate-of-need laws are structured such that the side effects seem to overshadow the benefits. Under California's law, for example, existing hospitals may undertake capital expenditures of any value, or medical equipment acquisitions, without obtaining a certificate. On the other hand, surgical clinics must obtain a certificate-of-need for such transactions if costs exceed $1 million. New hospital and surgery clinic construction is also subject to review, leading to the conclusion that the purpose of the law is to protect existing hospitals from new competitors or low-cost alternatives to inpatient surgical care. A similar objection might be raised to the Minnesota and Kansas moratoria on new construction and bed expansion.

CON programs can also be administered in anti-competitive ways. Several years ago a state program was found to have denied a proprietary hospital's application because of a hidden preference for existing facilities. More recently, a state's criterion for approving new home health agencies — full utilization of existing agencies — was struck down by a court that found the rule to have been designed to protect existing agencies from competition. However, despite episodes like these, most states support a policy of promoting competition through the CON program whenever feasible.

NOTE: RECENT DEVELOPMENTS IN HEALTH PLANNING

Despite the opposition of the Reagan Administration, on both fiscal and ideological grounds, to a continuation of the federal health planning program, Congress reauthorized the program in 1981. The new legislation, however, reduced both the funding for the program and the scope of the planning authority. The federal requirements imposed on state programs were loosened in various ways. For instance, the threshold limits to trigger CON review were increased. The struggle continued in the ensuing years. Eventually the authorization for the program expired, but the annual appropriations for the program were continued, leaving the embattled state health planning agencies and the local Health Systems Agencies (HSAs) extant but politically and legally vulnerable. Annual appropriations were finally dropped from the FY 1988 budget. This decision may prove to be the official death knell for health planning, at least as a federally funded and mandated activity.

In addition, in October 1987, HHS cancelled all Section 1122 contracts, apparently terminating the last strand of federal support for health planning; the agency claimed it had no choice, since Congress had appropriated no funds to administer the Section 1122 program. (The statutory authority for Section 1122 programs, however, had not been repealed as of January 1988.)

As Simpson describes, during the 1980s many states opted to take advantage of the loosened federal requirements and the dwindling federal funds, and to repeal their health planning and CON programs. As of 1987, four had no CON or planning programs at all (Utah, Arizona, Texas, and Kansas). By 1988, at least 14 more were considering a repeal of their programs. Similarly, starved by the loss of federal funds, many of the local HSAs either were forced to close or drastically scale down their operations during this period.

Most states, however, continue some sort of planning program and some form of CON controls, despite the opposition of provider interests and the waning federal interest in sponsoring these programs. In fact, as Simpson points out, many states have expanded or reinforced their health planning programs during the 1980s.

Sinai Hospital of Baltimore, Inc. v. Maryland Health Resources Planning Commission

306 Md. 472, 509 A.2d 1202 (1986)

RODOWSKY, Judge.

Appellants, Sinai Hospital of Baltimore, Inc. (Sinai) and North Charles General Hospital (North Charles), appeal from a judgment of the Circuit Court for Baltimore City affirming an order of the Maryland Health Resources Planning Commission (Commission) which had denied each hospital's separate application for a certificate of need (CON) to perform open heart surgery. Sinai and North Charles argue, in essence, that the Commission failed to give controlling effect to the State Health Plan, which they contend determines need under the circumstances here. For the reasons set forth below we shall affirm.

. . . One of the Commission's duties is to adopt, at least every five years, a State Health Plan (SHP). Section 19-114(a)(2) in relevant part states that

> [t]he plan shall include:
>
> (i) A description of the components that should comprise the health care system;
>
> (ii) The goals and policies for Maryland's health care system;
>
> (iii) Identification of unmet needs, excess services, minimum access criteria, and services to be regionalized;
>
> (iv) An assessment of the financial resources required and available for the health care system; [and]
>
> (v) The methodologies, standards, and criteria for certificate of need review. . . .

We are concerned in this case with the 1983-88 SHP which consists of . . . policies and standards specifically relating to the availability, accessibility, cost, and quality of cardiac surgery (CS), and . . . establishes a need methodology for authorizing additional CS programs.

Before a person can develop, operate, or participate in certain health care projects the Commission must issue a CON. The purpose of this requirement, as explained in the SHP, is "to ensure that changes in service capacity and major expenditures for health care facilities are needed and affordable, and consistent with the Commission's policies." . . .

In September 1983, each appellant applied for a CON to conduct an open heart surgery program in the Central Maryland Health Service Area. Only Johns Hopkins, University of Maryland, and Saint Joseph hospitals offer open heart surgery programs in Central Maryland. Because both applications sought approval for similar projects in the same area, they were subject to a comparative review. . . .

The full Commission . . . voted to deny both applications. . . . The Commission found that at the three hospitals authorized for CS programs the times from registration for surgery to actual surgery were reasonable. Based largely on that finding the Commission further found that there was no present need for an additional cardiac surgery program, although the Commission recognized that the methodology adopted in the SHP predicted a need in 1986. . . .

The SHP provides a formula for estimating the future utilization of adult (age 15 and above) cardiac surgery procedures. The projections are made two calendar years into the future from the time a CON review takes place. Under the formula the most recent national use rates as issued by the National Center for Health Statistics, are multiplied by the projected population of the health service area as reported by the Department of State Planning. The existing total CS capacity of the area is then subtracted from the total number of procedures estimated to be required two years into the future, to determine whether additional services are needed. Before the Commission can certify a new program to fill the future need, it must also find that at least 350 CS procedures per year are performed in each existing program. . . . The result of the formula calculations was that 420 additional procedures would be required in 1986. . . .

In considering "present . . . utilization" in this case the Commission found that "current waiting times are reasonable when considered in light of the standard in the SHP. No additional need is currently shown when considering waiting times." The standard referred to by the Commission is thirty days from registration to surgery. The standard is based on a policy decision made by the Commission in the SHP. . . .

. . . The Commission found that waiting times did not exceed thirty days and concluded that there was no present need. This conclusion supports the Commission's order and the affirmance thereof by the circuit court.

In a nutshell the present case is one in which the Commission could have ruled as it did or it could have determined that there was a need for an additional CS program. It is the function of the Commission to decide whether or not a CON should be granted where, as here, there is substantial evidence to support either conclusion. . . .

Sinai and North Charles, however, argue that the Commission made an error of law. Appellants submit that the SHP determination of need is paramount because the legislative intent is that policy as established by the SHP controls in the grant or denial of a CON. But the comprehensive health planning statutes specify . . . that decisions on CON applications must be consistent both with the SHP and with the standards for review which the Commission established. . . . Under the statute neither . . . predominates.

The principal thrust of the appellants' argument is premised on the existence of a conflict between the need projection developed under the SHP formula and the Commission's fact-finding that there is no present need. [T]here is no conflict. The SHP deals with future need. It deals with projected need two years from the time a CON application is reviewed. Reg. 07D(2)(c) looks to available data reflecting actual utilization. The SHP neither provides a methodology for computing current need nor prohibits the Commission from establishing current need as one of the standards of review. The Commission's denial of the CON applications, therefore, was consistent with the SHP. . . .

There was substantial evidence to support the Commission's finding that there was no present need for additional CS capacity. Dr. Robert Brawley, Chief of Cardiac Surgery at St. Joseph Hospital, stated that there was no waiting list for open heart surgery at St. Joseph. . . . According to Dr. Bruce Reitz, Director of Cardiac Surgery at Johns Hopkins, overall waiting time for elective cardiac surgery at Johns Hopkins was three to four weeks. Chief of Cardiology at Sinai, Dr. Phillip Reid, stated that his most recent experience revealed that the waiting time at Johns Hopkins was two to four weeks.

Finally, in a letter dated June 1, 1984, to Dr. Robert Mahon, Vice President of Medical Affairs at St. Joseph Hospital, Morton Rapoport, Chief Executive Officer of the University of Maryland Hospital, stated that in the first five months of 1984 there was a 17 percent reduction in caseload from the same period in 1983. University of Maryland could accommodate referrals within one week. Mr. Rapoport also stated that cardiac surgery in the United States had dropped by 25 percent overall, and in some areas by 40 percent. . . .

The Commission in addition found that without being required to obtain a CON the existing programs could, and were willing to, expand to the extent of providing 220 of the 420 future needed procedures, leaving a net 1986 need of 200 procedures. The appellants also represented that within only three months of approval each could be operating its proposed CS program. The Commission reasoned in part that since a new cardiac surgery program could be initiated quickly should there be evidence of a then present need for additional open heart surgery capacity in 1986, such capacity could be added at that time. . . .

Statewide Health Coordinating Council v. General Hospitals of Humana, Inc.

280 Ark. 443, 660 S.W.2d 906, 281 Ark. 98, cert. denied, *467 U.S. 1205 (1984)*

George Rose Smith, Justice.

The principal appellee, General Hospitals of Humana, . . . is a subsidiary corporation of a parent company that owns about 90 hospitals. . . . In 1982 Humana applied to the Arkansas Health Planning & Development Agency, . . . for a certificate of need that would authorize Humana to construct and operate a 150-bed community hospital at Sherwood, in Pulaski County. The application was opposed by the Baptist Medical System, St. Vincent Infirmary, and Arkansas Blue Cross & Blue Shield. After a hearing the director of the State Agency, acting for the Agency, granted the application.

The three protestants asked for a review by an independent agency, as permitted by the State Agency's rules. The Governor appointed the Arkansas Social Services as the independent reviewing agency. A Social Services attorney conducted a hearing and upheld the award of the certificate of need. That decision was affirmed by the circuit court. The protestants present several arguments for reversal, but we need consider only one: the State Agency was not authorized to grant a certificate of need that was inconsistent with the State Health Plan. On the record that argument must be sustained. . . .

[W]e must emphasize at the outset that there is in progress a national effort to limit the construction of new hospitals — an effort initiated by

Congress, carried forward by regulations issued by the Secretary of Health and Human Services, and supported by legislation enacted by the states, which are expected to participate in the program and receive federal funds for health care. . . .

The policy of restricting hospital construction stems from Congress's belief that competition among hospitals, unlike competition in the market place, does not reduce the cost of inpatient hospital services to the consuming public. To the contrary, the testimony in the case at bar shows that such competition actually increases hospital charges. Fixed hospital costs are so great that an empty bed costs about half as much to maintain as an occupied bed. Hospitals compete not for patients but for doctors, who usually select the patient's hospital. Hospitals vie with one another in acquiring expensive equipment, with unnecessary and costly duplication of facilities. Hospital charges are apt to be paid without question by public and private health insurers. The hard fact is, as one witness stated bluntly: "The cost of hospital care is just outrageous to the consumer."

Congress has attacked the problem by attempting to limit the number of licensed hospital beds. The federal regulation . . . provides: "There should be less than four non-Federal, short-stay hospital beds for each 1000 persons in a health service area *except under extraordinary circumstances.*" . . . The Arkansas State Health Plan contains the same less-than-4-beds-per-1,000 limitation. . . .

Various different figures were given in the testimony about the number of hospital beds in the Central Arkansas area. . . . There is no question, however, but that the area, like most of the nation, is overbedded in that its licensed hospital beds already exceed the federal and state maximum of 4 beds per 1,000 persons. . . .

The State Health Plan is not inflexible. Both the federal and state law permit the maximum bed limit to be exceeded locally to meet exceptional conditions, which are specified as being (1) an unusually high proportion of persons over 65 years old, (2) seasonal population fluctuations, (3) rural areas in which, for example, a majority of the residents would otherwise be more than 30 minutes travel time from a hospital, (4) urban areas having a large number of beds compensated by fewer beds in the same metropolitan area, and (5) areas having referral hospitals attracting nonresident patients. There has been no finding that any such exceptional condition exists. . . .

Thus it is established without substantial dispute that Humana's application for a 150-bed hospital in an area already overbedded is contrary to the Central Arkansas Health Systems Plan and to the State Health Plan. . . .

Counsel for Humana do not and could not seriously argue that the proof supports the State Agency's determination. Instead, it is contended that the federal and state laws are mere guidelines, which the director of the State Agency is free to disregard if he chooses to do so. If that were true, the entire federal and state effort to confine the number of hospital beds to the target limitation would be futile, for every agency director would be free to ignore the limitation whenever he saw fit to do so. . . .

Reversed.

PURTLE, Justice, dissenting. . . .

I agree with petitioners' argument that federal law contemplates the states will on occasion issue a certificate of need which is not in strict compliance with the standards. . . .

It is obvious that we are dealing with a case of overregulation here. Governments are not authorized to act except within the confines of the power granted to them by the people. I do not believe that people intended to grant the government the power to regulate every facet of their affairs. A less narrow construction of these statutes and regulations would allow the state agency to depart from strict compliance, as it did in this case. . . . In the interest of public policy I would apply a very broad interpretation of these restrictive regulations. After all, the health, safety, and welfare of the residents of north Pulaski County will be affected by this decision.

The cost of medical care has skyrocketed within the past few years. Many poor and needy people can no longer afford even basic medical needs. It seems to me that competition will drive the cost of hospitalization down, not up as argued by respondents. Furthermore, the cost of hospitalization is not the only consideration involved here. Human lives may well be at stake in this instance; acutely ill persons who reside in northern Pulaski County may not survive the longer trip to other area hospitals. No value can be placed upon a human life but it seems to me the life of a north Pulaski County resident should be valued the same as one south of the river. As we interpret the laws where the health, safety, and welfare of people are at issue, we should insure that these rights are jealously guarded, and that our helpless citizens are protected. The least we should do in this matter is to return it to the state agency in control for a more complete development of the facts. It may well be that this certificate of need was issued for valid reasons. . . .

NOTES: JUDICIAL REVIEW OF CERTIFICATE-OF-NEED DECISIONS

Judicial Deference to Agency Discretion

Most courts have tended to apply the general principles of administrative law and have deferred to the discretion of state planning agencies in making certificate of need decisions (CON). See, for instance, Saint Joseph's Hospital & Medical Center v. Finley, 153 N.J. Super. 214, 379 A.2d 467 (1977); Matter of Certificate of Need Application, 234 Kan. 802, 676 P.2d 107 (1984). Some courts, however, have taken a more active role in reviewing CON decisions. For example, in Sturman v. Ingraham, 52 A.D.2d 882, 383

N.Y.S.2d 60 (App. Div. 1976), the state agency first determined the "need" (number of beds) in each area of the state; it then applied a rule of automatically denying all applications for CON if over 90 percent of the "need" was satisfied. The court held that the application of the quota was invalid and that "need" for a given application had to be determined on the actual circumstances of a particular area. At the other end of the spectrum, a Florida appellate court invalidated a state decision under its Section 1122 program that denied an application for a CAT scanner because the state agency had not adopted or followed any formal standards or other objective criteria for determining the "need" of this service. North Miami General Hospital v. Office of Community Medical Facilities, 355 So. 2d 1272 (Fla. Dist. Ct. App. 1978).

In West Virginia, the state attempted to forestall consideration of an application for a "mobile magnetic resonance imaging unit" by imposing a moratorium on all such applications until standards could be developed and other applications could be "batched." The state supreme court held that this violated the statutory authority of the agency. United Hospital Center v. Richardson, 328 S.E.2d 195 (W. Va. 1985). In general, however, most courts have been willing to give considerable discretion to state agencies, both in determining "need" and in fashioning the bases and methods for doing so, and have upheld state certificate-of-need decisions. See Simpson, supra, at 1228-29.

Constitutional Limits on Agency Discretion

Similarly, virtually all courts have been willing to defer to legislative discretion and have upheld the constitutionality of CON programs. See, for instance, Mount Royal Towers v. Alabama Board of Health, 61 Ala. 278, 388 So. 2d 1209 (1980); Attoma v. State Department of Social Welfare, 26 A.D. 2d 12, 270 N.Y.S.2d 167 (App. Div. 1966). The only exception has been the North Carolina Supreme Court decision in In the Matter of Certificate of Need for Aston Park Hospital, 282 N.C. 542, 193 S.E.2d 729 (1973).

The *Aston Park* decision is interesting in that it applies, under state constitutional doctrine, a notion of substantive due process that was popular in the nineteenth century but has been since rejected by the federal courts and most but not all state courts. Essentially the North Carolina court demanded that the state show that the objectives of the statute could not be achieved by the forces of competition in the hospital market place. All other courts have required only a minimal showing of a connection between cost containment (and the other objectives of CON legislation) and the scheme established by the legislation.

While it is unlikely that other courts will adopt the constitutional posture of this decision, the *Aston Park* decision set the stage for an important test of the constitutionality of *federal* authority to legislate in this area.

Immediately following the decision in *Aston Park,* Congress enacted the National Health Planning and Resources Development Act of 1974, which, among other things, conditioned receipt of federal funding for health planning and some health service programs on the establishment of a certificate of need program. North Carolina brought suit in federal court claiming that the federal government was coercing the state into violating or amending its own constitution and, as such, was interfering with the sovereignty of the state as protected by the Tenth Amendment to the federal constitution.

A three judge federal district court interpreted the federal legislation as an exercise of the federal spending authority and the certificate of need requirement as merely a condition on voluntary participation. Following an analysis not unlike that in Minnesota Association of Health Care Facilities, Inc. v. Minnesota Department of Public Welfare, discussed at p. 222, the court held that conditional spending can be invalidated on constitutional grounds only where the condition serves no legitimate interest or where the condition is not voluntary; that is, where compliance with the requirement was required by threat of sanction other than withdrawal of funding. North Carolina ex rel. Morrow v. Califano, 445 F. Supp. 532 (E.D.N.C. 1977), *aff'd mem.,* 435 U.S. 962 (1978). In other situations where federal legislation has imposed mandatory requirements on state government, the courts have indicated that the importance of state sovereignty may justify closer judicial scrutiny. See Environmental Protection Agency v. Brown, 431 U.S. 99 (1977); compare Equal Opportunity Employment Commission v. Wyoming, 460 U.S. 226 (1983).

For an examination of the federal power under conditional spending (or under the interstate commerce authority), see Wing & Silton, Constitutional Authority for Extending Federal Control Over the Delivery of Health Care, 57 N.C.L. Rev. 1423 (1979).

Curiously, following the *Aston Park* and *Califano* cases, the North Carolina legislature again passed a certificate of need statute, similar in many respects to the one ruled unconstitutional in *Aston Park.* N.C. Gen. Stat. §§131E-175 to 131E-199 (1989). As of 1989 the constitutionality of the new program has not been judicially examined.

While the prospects of further extension of the certificate of need concept are unlikely under current political circumstances, in the 1970s, some states were at least entertaining the possibilities of "decertification of need" legislation, that is, legislation giving planning agencies the authority to decide whether existing facilities were unnecessary. For a description of these programs and a discussion of the constitutionality of such authority, see Kopit, Hospital Decertification: Legitimate Regulation or a Taking of Private Property?, 1978 Utah L. Rev. 179. Government review of existing facilities does, however, arise even under existing legislation and can be tantamount to decertification in situations where, for example, capital expenditures are required for the modernization or reconstruction of existing facilities. Also, in some states facilities that are relocating or moving are required to seek certificate of need approval.

In Humana Medical Corp. v. State Health Planning & Development Agency, 460 So. 2d 1295 (Ala. Civ. App. 1984), Humana sought to transfer 31 beds from two facilities to another facility within the *same area*. The agency denied the application on the grounds that it would not foster cost containment and that there was no need for additional beds in that area. Area hospitals already had a low occupancy. The court upheld the constitutionality of the state's power to regulate relocation with only a minimal level of judicial scrutiny.

On the other hand, where the state program is viewed as a mandatory "taking," judicial scrutiny of the constitutionality of the "taking" may be more rigorous and may require, under some circumstances compensation of the property owner. See *Minnesota Association of Health Care*, at p. 222.

Certificate-of-Need as a Means to Encourage Access

As the principal cases demonstrate, many states tend to define "need" rather narrowly, treating all patients as essentially equivalent. Some states, however, have attempted to distinguish the needs of various populations based on their ability to pay. Thus a decision to grant a certificate-of-need may consider an institution's record with regard to Medicaid patients or the uninsured as demonstrative of "need." See, for instance, Chambrey v. Axelrod, 101 A.2d 610, 474 N.Y.S.2d 865 (App. Div., 3d Dept. 1984) (upholding a denial of a CON for expansion of a nursing home that restricted access for Medicaid patients); Collier Medical Center v. Department of Health & Rehabilitation Services, 462 So. 2d 83 (Fla. Dist. App. Ct. 1985) (upholding denial of CON to new hospital in order to protect revenue of existing hospitals that served indigent patients); Doctors' Hospital v. Maryland Health Resources Planning Commission, 65 Md. App. 656, 501 A.2d 1324 (1986) (CON denied to a hospital that served few indigents and Medicaid patients).

Neoconservative Criticism of Health Planning and CON

Advocates of competition have been heavily critical of health planning and CON programs. Such regulatory programs, they argue, are inevitably captured by the institutions they seek to regulate; with strong and immediate incentives to organize and to commit resources to influence health planning decisions, hospitals and other providers will overwhelm the agency bureaucracy and have a stronger influence than consumers and even organized public interest groups with a more generalized interest (and a smaller pocketbook) than the providers. Conservatives have even argued that providers may welcome some kinds of regulation — which they know they can dominate — knowing that they can influence this regulation to their advantage and to ward off new market entrants. They also argue that the regulatory strategy underlying health planning and CON programs assumes that "need" and other decisions are technical matters capable of "expert" resolution; in the neoconservative view, CON and other resource development decisions are inevitably value-based choices which should be made by market mechanisms not bureaucracies. For a good articulation of this view, see C. Havighurst, Deregulating the Health Care Industry: Planning for Competition (1982). For further discussion, see Chapter 8.

CHAPTER

IV

Medical Technology

The United States lags behind many other countries of the world in conquering infant mortality and in providing access to health care, but we are second to none in the area of "high tech" medicine. And we seem to want more and more. It is no longer just the cynic who declares that we are doing more and more for fewer and fewer people, at higher and higher cost, for less and less benefit. It is a cliché to observe that technology has a life of its own, but it is a fact that we have yet to develop an effective method to assess technology and have no methods for determining whether or not new or existing technologies are useful and appropriate for inclusion in any reasonable health insurance scheme.

We are ready to accept that our health care resources are finite but seem far less willing to accept limitations on extreme and expensive medical technologies or to begin formal rationing of these technologies. Of course, it is ironic that at the very time our technological possibilities seem infinite, our resources are recognized as limited. How much new technology can we afford? What new technologies should be added to the standard of "good medical practice," and which relegated to luxury or optional items? Should all new technologies be subjected to randomized clinical trials the way new drugs are tested? Is there such a thing as "acceptable social cost," and should new technologies be viewed from a societal as well as an individual perspective? Can cost-benefit and cost-effectiveness analysis be useful in medical technology evaluation?

In Chapter 9 we examine the most extreme and expensive medical technology ever introduced into the health care system: organ transplantation. In this chapter we view medical technology in its everyday application to health care. We begin by examining some classic works on medical technology and its proper role in medicine, noting how medical technology shapes medical practice and how practitioners decide to adopt new drugs, devices and procedures. We then explore the cost implications of medical technology with special emphasis on its central position in cost containment and rationing schemes. Next we examine how changes in medical technology affect the way courts (and others) define the standard of care, with special consideration of medical screening tests and their legal implications. Finally, we review some of the proposals for dealing with new medical technology in a more constructive and rational way.

A. The Role of Technology in Medicine

1. HOW TECHNOLOGY SHAPES MEDICAL PRACTICE

Thomas, The Technology of Medicine

285 N. Engl. J. Med. 1366-1368 (1971)

Technology assessment has become a routine exercise for the scientific enterprises on which the country is obliged to spend vast sums for its needs. Brainy committees are continually evaluating the effectiveness and cost of doing various things in space, defense, energy, transportation, and the like, to give advice about prudent investments for the future.

Somehow medicine, for all the 60-odd billion dollars that it is said to cost the nation, has not yet come in for much of this analytical treatment. It seems taken for granted that the technology of medicine simply exists, take it or leave it, and the only major technologic problem in which policy-makers are interested is how to deliver today's kind of health care, with equity, to all the people.

When, as is bound to happen sooner or later, the analysts get around to the technology of medicine itself, they will have to face the problem of measuring the relative cost and effectiveness of all the things that are done in the management of disease. They make their living at this kind of thing, and I wish them well, but I imagine they will have a bewildering time. For one thing, our methods of managing disease are constantly changing — partly under the influence of new bits of information brought in from all corners of biologic science. At the same time, a great many things are done that are not so closely related to science, some not related at all.

In fact, there are three quite different levels of technology in medicine, so unlike each other as to seem altogether different undertakings. Practitioners of medicine and the analysts will be in trouble if they are not kept separate.

1. First of all, there is a large body of what might be termed "nontechnology," impossible to measure in terms of its capacity to alter either the natural course of disease or its eventual outcome. A great deal of money is spent on this. It is valued highly by the professionals as well as the patients. It consists of what is sometimes called "supportive therapy." It tides patients over through diseases that are not, by and large, understood. It is what is

meant by the phrases "caring for" and "standing by." It is indispensable. It is not, however, a technology in any real sense, since it does not involve measures directed at the underlying mechanism of disease.

It includes the large part of any good doctor's time that is taken up with simply providing reassurance, explaining to patients who fear that they have contracted one or another lethal disease that they are, in fact, quite healthy.

It is what physicians used to be engaged in at the bedside of patients with diphtheria, meningitis, poliomyelitis, lobar pneumonia, and all the rest of the infectious diseases that have since come under control.

It is what physicians must now do for patients with intractable cancer, severe rheumatoid arthritis, multiple sclerosis, stroke, and advanced cirrhosis. One can think of at least 20 major diseases that require this kind of supportive medical care because of the absence of an effective technology. I would include a large amount of what is called mental disease, and most varieties of cancer, in this category.

The cost of this nontechnology is very high and getting higher all the time. It requires not only a great deal of time but also very hard effort and skill on the part of physicians; only the very best of doctors are good at coping with this kind of defeat. It also involves long periods of hospitalization, lots of nursing, lots of involvement of nonmedical professionals in and out of the hospital. It represents, in short, a substantial segment of today's expenditures for health.

2. At the next level up is a kind of technology best termed "halfway technology." This represents the kinds of things that must be done after the fact, in efforts to compensate for the incapacitating effects of certain diseases whose course one is unable to do very much about. It is a technology designed to make up for disease, or to postpone death.

The outstanding examples in recent years are the transplantations of hearts, kidneys, livers, and other organs, and the equally spectacular inventions of artificial organs. In the public mind, this kind of technology has come to seem like the equivalent of the high technologies of the physical sciences. The media tend to present each new procedure as though it represented a breakthrough and therapeutic triumph, instead of the makeshift that it really is.

In fact, this level of technology is, by its nature, at the same time highly sophisticated and profoundly primitive. It is the kind of thing that one must continue to do until there is a genuine understanding of the mechanisms involved in disease. In chronic glomerulonephritis, for example, a much clearer insight will be needed into the events leading to the destruction of glomeruli by the immunologic reactants that now appear to govern this disease, before one will know how to intervene intelligently to prevent the process, or turn it round. But when this level of understanding has been reached, the technology of kidney replacement will not be much needed, and should no longer pose the huge problems of logistics, cost, and ethics that it poses today.

An extremely complex and costly technology for the management of coronary heart disease has evolved, involving specialized ambulances and hospital units, all kinds of electronic gadgetry and whole platoons of new professional personnel, to deal with the end results of coronary thrombosis. Almost everything offered today for the treatment of heart disease is at this level of technology, with the transplanted and artificial hearts as ultimate examples. When enough has been learned to know what really goes wrong in heart disease, one ought to be in a position to figure out ways to prevent or reverse the process, and when this happens the current elaborate technology will probably be set to one side.

Much of what is done in the treatment of cancer, by surgery, irradiation, and chemotherapy, represents halfway technology, in the sense that these measures are directed at the existence of already established cancer cells, but not at the mechanisms by which the cells become neoplastic.

It is a characteristic of this kind of technology that it costs an enormous amount of money and requires a continuing expansion of hospital facilities. There is no end to the need for new, highly trained people to run the enterprise. And there is really no way out of this, at the present state of knowledge. If the installation of specialized coronary-care units can result in the extension of life for only a few patients with coronary disease (and there is no question that this technology is effective in a few cases), it seems to me an inevitable fact of life that as many of these as can be will be put together, and as much money as can be found will be spent. I do not see that anyone has much choice in this. The only thing that can move medicine away from this level of technology is new information, and the only imaginable source of this information is research.

3. The third type of technology is the kind that is so effective that it seems to attract the least public notice; it has come to be taken for granted. This is the genuinely decisive technology of modern medicine, exemplified best by modern methods for immunization against diphtheria, pertussis and the childhood virus diseases, and the contemporary use of antibiotics and chemotherapy for bacterial infections. The capacity to deal effectively with syphilis and tuberculosis represents a milestone in human endeavor, even though full use of this potential has not yet been made. And there are, of course, other examples: the treatment of endocrinologic disorders with appropriate hormones, the prevention of hemolytic disease of the newborn, the treatment and prevention of various nutritional disorders, and perhaps just around the corner the management of Parkinsonism and sickle-cell anemia. There are other examples, and everyone will have his favorite candidates for the list, but the truth is that there are nothing like as many as the public has been led to believe.

The point to be made about this kind of technology — the real high technology of medicine — is that it comes as the result of a genuine understanding of disease mechanisms, and when it becomes available, it is relatively inexpensive, relatively simple, and relatively easy to deliver.

Offhand, I cannot think of any important human disease for which medicine possesses the capacity to prevent or cure outright where the cost of the technology is itself a major problem. The price is never as high as the cost of managing the same diseases during the earlier stages of no-technology or halfway technology. If a case of typhoid fever had to be managed today by the best methods of 1935, it would run to a staggering expense. At, say, around 50 days of hospitalization, requiring the most demanding kind of nursing care, with the obsessive concern for details of diet that characterized the therapy of that time, with daily laboratory monitoring and, on occasion, surgical intervention for abdominal catastrophe, I should think $10,000 would be a conservative estimate for the illness, as contrasted with today's cost of a bottle of chloramphenicol and a day or two of fever. The halfway technology that was evolving for poliomyelitis in the early 1950's, just before the emergence of the basic research that made the vaccine possible, provides another illustration of the point. Do you remember Sister Kenney, and the cost of these institutes for rehabilitation, with all those ceremonially applied hot fomentations, and the debates about whether the affected limbs should be totally immobilized or kept in passive motion as frequently as possible, and the masses of statistically tormented data mobilized to support one view or the other? It is the cost of that kind of technology, and its relative effectiveness, that must be compared with the cost and effectiveness of the vaccine.

Pulmonary tuberculosis had similar episodes in its history. There was a sudden enthusiasm for the surgical removal of infected lung tissue in the early 1950s, and elaborate plans were being made for new and expensive installations for major pulmonary surgery in tuberculosis hospitals, and then INH [a tuberculosis drug] and streptomycin came along and the hospitals themselves were closed up.

It is when physicians are bogged down by their incomplete technologies, by the innumerable things they are obliged to do in medicine when they lack a clear understanding of disease mechanisms, that the deficiencies of the health-care system are most conspicuous. If I were a policy-maker, interested in saving money for health care over the long haul, I would regard it as an act of high prudence to give high priority to a lot more basic research in biologic science. This is the only way to get the full mileage that biology owes to the science of medicine, even though it seems, as used to be said in the days when the phrase still had some meaning, like asking for the moon.

S. Reiser, Medicine and the Reign of Technology

229-230 (1978)

Technologies can develop identities of their own. Human ingenuity, anxiety, and fantasy can transform technologies into independent creatures, which are supposed to operate according to unvarying automatic procedures and to produce uniformly trustworthy evidence. The numbers generated by the thermometer, the graphs drawn by the electrocardiograph, the pictures created by the X-ray machine, the images captured by the microscope, the diagnostic judgments rendered by the computer — all are generally assumed to be free of the flaws and biases that admittedly distort facts gathered by human beings through their natural senses. Such evidence, it is further assumed, is therefore the most valuable in diagnosing and treating disease. Neither belief is true. The evidence produced by such instruments, though valuable, is inevitably influenced by the human hand that operates them and the human mind that evaluates the results. Furthermore, the machines are denied complete access to a whole range of nonmeasurable facts about a human being that a physician can obtain only through his own senses — questioning, observing, making judgments.

If physicians in general come to accept a fundamentally mechanical view of human beings, in a world that is more and more enamored of technology, the prospect for the future of medicine is extremely disquieting. To counter the fears of such a prospect, a myth has arisen in contemporary medicine that the more the machines can take over the performing of medical functions, the more the doctor will have time to deal with his patient as a human being. Thus reliance on technology is supposed to improve the doctor-patient relationship, to the benefit of both.

These are illusions. Machines inexorably direct the attention of both doctor and patient to the measurable aspects of illness, but away from the "human" factors that are at least equally important. . . . So, without realizing what has happened, the physician in the last two centuries has gradually relinquished his unsatisfactory attachment to subjective evidence — what the patient says — only to substitute a devotion to technological evidence — what the machine says. He has thus exchanged one partial view of disease for another.

Notes: Technology and Science

(1) Thomas's views on the primacy of basic research continue to dominate policy discussion. His views on halfway technologies, however, have not gone completely unchallenged. James Maxwell, for example, has argued that the example of the iron lung contrasted with the polio vaccine distorts and oversimplifies history. When viewed in historical perspective, "the iron lung must be viewed as a simple ventilator, similar in its physiologic effects to modern respiratory equipment" in which context it was a "lifesaving device." Rather than being replaced by a simple vaccine, he sees its true replacement as modern mechanical ventilation equipment used in the ICU.

Maxwell characterizes the Thomas thesis as part of a "larger intellectual tradition in the history of science," which posits that "truly useful and effective technologies depend upon basic research and the creative genius of the scientist for their creation." Maxwell, The Iron Lung: Halfway Technology or Necessary Step?, 64 Milbank Mem. Fund Q. 3, 23 (1986). This is the National Institutes of Health (NIH) model. An alternative model, he notes, rejects the view that technology is the handmaiden of science, and argues instead that technology itself often is the "wellspring of scientific discovery." Id. Examples include the telescope and the steam engine. The telescope was used to discover the planets and their relationship to the earth and sun; the steam engine ultimately led to the development of the laws of thermodynamics. Examples in medicine include the X-ray, the electron microscope, and cancer chemotherapy; all of which made basic understanding of human physiology possible. In Maxwell's words: "The halfway technology concept minimizes the role of technology as a source of ideas and understanding. Science and technology are not in conflict; knowledge from these fields flows along separate tracks, proceeding from different necessities, and enjoying different serendipities. Technical change in medicine is not a single linear process, but one in which science and technology interact in complex and largely unpredictable ways." Id. at 24. And see Price, Is Technology Historically Independent of Science? The Clinical Context of Technology Assessment, 9 J. Health Policy Polit. L. 31 (1984).

(2) In late 1987, the Reagan Administration floated a proposal to convert the National Institutes of Health into a private research facility, financed primarily by the private sector. Administration officials said the move would "permit more collaboration with the biotechnology industry, increase salaries for the best scientists at the institute, and free them from bureaucratic constraints that may threaten the 'scientific pre-eminence' of the agency." Pear, Budget Plan Would Privatize National Institutes of Health, N.Y. Times, Dec. 16, 1987, at 1. In 1987 Congress had appropriated $6.2 billion for the NIH, of which about $4.4 billion was distributed in grants to researchers outside the government. The proposal generated almost no support and was dropped. Representative of scientific commentary on it are the words of Phillip Leder, Chairman of the Department of Genetics at Harvard Medical School, who said the proposal represented "an abdication of the government's responsibility to conduct research at the highest level of sophistication." Id. What is the government's "responsibility" to fund "sophisticated" research? If the government funds the development of a new medical drug or device, does this have any implications for how it should be distributed, marketed, or financed?

2. HOW PRACTITIONERS ADOPT MEDICAL TECHNOLOGY

Medical technology may be adopted for a variety of reasons. We have a highly sophisticated methodology for testing drugs, usually using a randomized clinical trial, for safety and efficacy. If so certified by the Food and Drug Administration, the drug may be labelled and sold in interstate commerce. Safety and efficacy are important, but they leave out cost altogether, whether absolute or comparative. Thus a drug may be marketed and used if it is 10 percent more effective than an existing one, even if it costs twice as much. Perhaps in no other industry (other than defense) would this indifference to price be tolerated. John McKinlay's description of how "medical innovation" works may read like a satire, but it is factually accurate. *Rutherford* illustrates the almost unconditional support the U.S. Supreme Court has shown the FDA in its determinations of safety and efficacy. The FDA also has authority to regulate medical devices in a similar manner. Outside of the drug and device arena, however, there are no established criteria for the validation and introduction of a new technology or surgical technique into general medical practice. *Rutherford* also raises a recurring issue, one at the center of the debate about experimental AIDS drugs; should terminally ill patients have the "right" to use any drug they want?

McKinlay, From "Promising Report" to "Standard Procedure": Seven Stages in the Career of a Medical Innovation

59 Milbank Mem. Fund Q. 374-411 (1981)

In 1972, in an editorial for the Annals of Thoracic Surgery, Tom Chalmers . . . provided examples of widely advocated and commonly used therapies that either had never been established to be effective by adequate clinical trials, or in a number of instances had actually been shown to be without merit. The editorial concluded with the question, "Can we learn from our mistakes of the past?" That question is as poignant today (perhaps even more so) as it was when posed by Chalmers nearly a decade ago. This paper is a response. . . . Several aspects of the career approach to the diffusion of medical innovations should be highlighted here in order to minimize misunderstandings. There is, *first,* no suggestion here that every innovation passes through each of the seven stages in the exact order in which they are discussed. . . . The concept of a career, with its seven stages, is simply a heuristic device employed to highlight particular issues and possible points of intervention. The following discussion is intended to identify the typical or usual stages in the career of an innovation — the pattern that is followed more often than not. . . .

Second, every effort is made to avoid the suggestion that the medical establishment is only self-interestedly involved in the diffusion of innovations. . . .

Third, there is obviously variation within, and between, medical specialties in the sponsorship of innovations, and the willingness to undertake proper evaluations. Spodick argues that there is a double standard in the acceptance of reports of surgical versus medical treatments, and that this arises from professional and lay attitudes. After reviewing some 70 reports in specialty journals appearing during 1971, to compare the methods used for evaluating medical versus surgical treatments for cardiovascular disease, he found that 9 of 16 qualifying studies evaluating medical treatments were controlled. None of the 49 studies of surgical intervention involved a controlled study. Cochrane considers it not unreasonable to judge the medical profession, and its specialties, by the use they have made of the RCT technique. . . . After considering psychiatry, surgery, and cardiology, he awarded the wooden spoon to obstetrics and gynecology, with the following explanation:

> The specialty missed its first opportunity in the sixties when it failed to randomize the confinement of low risk pregnant women at home and in the hospital. This was followed by a determined refusal to allow "Pap smears" to be randomized, with disastrous results for the whole world. Then having filled the emptying beds by getting nearly all pregnant women into the hospital, the obstetricians started to introduce a whole series of expensive innovations into the routines of pre- and post-natal care and delivery, without any rigorous evaluation. The list is long but the most important were induction, ultrasound, fetal monitoring and placental function tests. The specialty reached its apogee in 1976 when they produced 20 percent fewer babies at 20 percent more cost. G and O stands for gynecologists and obstetricians but it could also stand for GO ahead without evaluation!

1. THE STAGE OF THE "PROMISING REPORT" . . .

The careers of most medical innovations seem to be launched with the appearance of an enthusiastic report on some promising performance, increasingly in the mass media. One reads, almost daily, of startling "scientific" breakthroughs and new weaponry for the battle against illness and death. . . .

It is understandable that the media should seize upon these promising reports, since they are highly newsworthy for a public conditioned to expect miracle cures for the diseases that plague it. Many magazines and newspapers regularly devote a section or column to promising reports, and have a staff of medical reporters constantly looking for the latest newsworthy innovation in professional journals and through contact with the researchers directly. These promising media stories usually report activities that meet no methodological criteria whatsoever. . . .

Sometimes, after reading these isolated "promising reports" in either the media or in professional journals (or both), but usually after word-of-mouth endorsements among colleagues (one of the principal means by which physicians and researchers exchange information on innovations), someone may decide to check out the promising report on a series of cases — say, 25, or even 100. Some medical researchers seem to believe that the soundness of an inference is related to the number of observations from which it is derived, or perhaps the length of period of follow-up. This paper will argue that such reasoning is seriously flawed because, while numbers are certainly important, other equally essential methodological criteria are overlooked, and such studies still constitute only promising reports.

Clinicians sometimes do attempt exploratory or pilot studies of the *effectiveness* of an innovation at this stage. Although well intentioned, these studies are usually also severely limited and can most appropriately be included in the category of uncontrolled observational reports. . . .

2. *THE STAGE OF PROFESSIONAL AND ORGANIZATIONAL ADOPTION*

. . . During this second stage more widespread and influential support is mobilized. Here we see movement from scattered support for the innovation to its *adoption* by powerful interest groups, involving professional associations, institutional structures, and other resources. The term "adoption" is employed to distinguish the scattered support evident during the first stage from the organized commitment of institutional resources during this second stage. It denotes a unique relationship with the innovation: the act of formally accepting and taking up some activity and using it as one's own, without the idea of its having been another's — to embrace or espouse it. . . .

With regard to the adoption of innovations by medical organizations (hospitals, medical centers, health clinics), it appears that organizational and economic considerations may be more important than they are among physicians. In adopting an innovation, administrators may, of course, be simply responding to intense pressure from their medical staff. Such a response, although consistent with the requests of physicians, may be motivated by a different set of reasons. For example, the adoption of certain innovations may be viewed as an attempt to enhance a hospital's reputation in the community, thereby improving its competitive position with respect to other hospitals. Additionally, adoption may be affected by the nature of a hospital's relation with other organizations and interests (insurance companies, banks, construction companies). . . .

3. *THE STAGE OF PUBLIC ACCEPTANCE AND STATE (THIRD-PARTY) ENDORSEMENT*

Partly because of exposure to promising reports (Stage 1), but mainly as a result of professional and organizational adoption (Stage 2), a general approval (acceptance) of the innovation emerges among the public. This approval broadens its base of support and creates a constituency that can be appealed to in further advancing the career of the innovation. Public acceptance takes the form of a generalized belief that the innovation is a "good thing" and ought to be available. It is usually less well formulated and organized than the boost received from its adoption by professional and organizational interests. Having once fostered acceptance and even a demand among the public, these interests are in a position to satisfy it, while appealing to a demand that they may have created as justification for their activities with respect to the innovation. . . .

An innovation can be said to have "made it" when it eventually receives endorsement or support from the state and/or is underwritten by third parties. . . .

4. THE STAGE OF "STANDARD PROCEDURE" AND OBSERVATIONAL REPORTS

There follows a period during which the innovation (having received professional and public support and legitimation through state endorsement and third-party coverage) achieves the privileged status of a "standard procedure." For a period of time it becomes generally accepted by interested parties as the most appropriate way of proceeding with a particular problem or situation. It is probably incorrect to refer here to the activity as an "innovation" (although we shall continue to do so in this paper), since at this stage it has graduated from being just another promising performance (something new with great potential) to the position of being an established and respected activity. . . . [D]espite the resources and institutions already committed to the innovation at this midpoint in its career, it still remains without any formal evaluation. . . .

5. THE STAGE OF THE RANDOMIZED CLINICAL TRIAL (RCT)

Whether an innovation is worthwhile or not is an issue that, for many, appears to be satisfactorily settled by the sheer volume of observational reports. However, such reports never really place the issue of the *effectiveness* of an innovation beyond dispute. Byar and his colleagues have discussed the relative merits of different ways of assessing various medical treatments, and they conclude that "randomized clinical trials remain the most valuable method of evaluating the efficacy of therapies." Ten British and American statisticians have also reached the same conclusion. Although there are many understandable questions concerning RCTs, this author has yet to meet an informed researcher who doubts the inferential superiority of experimentally derived evidence. The ratio of observational reports to RCTs may be the order of 100 to 1 (as . . . was the case with aortocoronary bypass for arteriosclerotic heart disease), but there are few who would not prefer experimental results, given a choice. . . .

Sometimes the results of an RCT do show an innovation to be effective, and these are immediately seized upon by its proponents and used to advance its career. More often, however, RCTs show innovations to be either ineffective or, at best, no more effective than existing and often much cheaper alternatives. Under these circumstances it is wasteful and perhaps unethical that proper evaluations of innovations should be postponed until the penultimate stages in their career. Imagine the potential for harm that could be avoided, and the resources saved, if innovations were routinely evaluated during earlier stages in their careers — certainly well before they become "standard procedure."

6. *THE STAGE OF PROFESSIONAL DENUNCIATION . . .*

Professional denunciation often takes the form of letters to the editors of professional journals, particularly those that have the temerity to first publish the results of an RCT that question the effectiveness of some standard procedure. By mounting a write-in campaign, some interests can create the impression that there is more opposition than there actually is. At the same time, disquieting findings are often "put into context" by special editorials from "invited experts," who may attempt to reconcile the contradictory findings with their own clinical experience. These experts may also be called upon to constitute a special committee, or working party, to evaluate the results of an RCT that pose enough of a challenge to standard procedure. Attempts are made to shore up an activity, the general standing of which is being threatened by an RCT, by appointing a panel of experts, or an "advisory group," which is expected to review any available evidence and make some recommendation. . . .

7. *THE STAGE OF EROSION AND DISCREDITATION . . .*

After some period of time (often more than a decade), and ever so gradually, an erosion of support begins to set in. The enthusiastic claims made for the innovation during its earlier stages are modified somewhat; it is not as universally applicable as once thought; it is useful only for certain groups of the population, or particular types of or stages in an illness. Its career can sometimes be propped up for a while if it is combined with some other innovation or it may be relegated to the position of therapy of last resort — something to be employed after all other efforts are exhausted. Sometimes there is a scandal (e.g., thalidomide, dystilbesterol) and the innovation's career is abruptly terminated. And then, of course, people emerge who now claim to have had doubts about it all along! In these relatively rare situations the innovation may become so discredited that it is viewed as unethical to continue with it (e.g., radical mastectomy); it may eventually even be ridiculed. But scandal is not the only reason for a promising career's demise. More often it is simply eclipsed by some other rising star, and just drops out of public view. The innovation no longer enjoys public attention, little prestige is derived from association with it, cheaper alternatives become available, and so forth. Finally, it is relegated to that great dust heap called History. The slow demise of innovations is, indeed, consistent with the medical profession's resistance to change and preference for accepted procedures. Discreditation or discard usually occurs only when a *replacement* procedure becomes available.

From the above discussion it is evident that the typical career of most medical innovations is extraordinarily wasteful of scarce resources. To paraphrase Hegel, "What experience and the history of medical innovation teach is this — that the professions, hospitals, and the state never have learned anything from history, or acted on principles deduced from it." Innovation after innovation begins its slow, costly journey through the stages described only to end up — in the overwhelming majority of cases — either discarded or discredited. Is there no way of ensuring that more reliable information is available during earlier formative stages when the innovation is not yet firmly ensconced? Is there no way of temporarily curtailing the understandable, but so often premature, enthusiasm of the professions and medical organizations? Can the public and the state be encouraged to withhold their endorsement until some more reliable objective evaluation has been undertaken? How can some of the resources now consumed by wasteful observational reports be diverted into more reliable controlled experimentation? Is there some way of moving the evaluation of an innovation from the end of its career to some earlier beginning stage? Must we always remain uninformed by earlier experience and end up going through all these stages with every new innovation?

NOTE ON MCKINLAY'S SEVEN STAGES

To prevent the continuing recurrence of the "seven stages," McKinlay suggests that government should not support for general use any "service, procedure or technology, the effectiveness of which has not been, or cannot be, demonstrated." Id. at 259. In addition, he suggests that before we can develop an effective social services system, we "must determine, in some objective and independent fashion, the nature and magnitude of the human needs in our society." Id. And then (as you should be able to guess by now) "all new services must be evaluated objectively — preferably and where appropriate by RCTs — before they are introduced." Id. He also recommends that we begin immediately to do a systematic evaluation of the medical technologies currently in use, and that they be judged on the basis of effectiveness, cost efficiency, and social acceptance and equity. Is such an elaborate and systematic evaluation system feasible? How should it be funded? Who should sponsor it?

The randomized clinical trial is widely recognized as the "gold standard" for determining the efficacy of medical treatments. Nonetheless, very few medical treatments have ever been subjected to the RCT. Office of

Technology Assessment, The Impact of Randomized Clinical Trials on Health Policy and Medical Practice, Background Paper, OTA (1983). In addition to the work of Cochrane, especially his Effectiveness and Efficiency (1972), another classic piece on evaluation is Frederick Mosteller's Innovation and Evaluation, 211 Science 881 (1981). Among other things, Mosteller presents the "safe surgery dilemma":

> Information about economics, about outcome, and agreed-on ethics cannot entirely determine social policy. . . . Consider a safe surgical operation like that for appendicitis. If physicians operated whenever they saw even slight signs and symptoms, the total lives lost might be minimized. But if they operated only when the symptoms were severe, this would minimize the total number of days spent by patients recuperating. None of us want to be operated on needlessly, nor do we want to die because we have shown only mild symptoms. What should the policy be? To save the last life may require a million extra operations or hundreds of lifetimes of recuperation. This is a problem that society must settle. . . . Note that the conflict is not the usual one between society's interests and those of the individual, but is a conflict within the individual.

Even randomized clinical trials may be difficult for the medical profession to properly evaluate when large sums of money are at stake and heavy advertising is used. An example is the continuing controversy over the comparative effectiveness and safety of two drugs designed to be administered immediately after an individual experiences a heart attack: streptokinase and tissue plasminogen activator (TPA). Initial data seemed to suggest that TPA was just as effective as streptokinase at decreasing mortality and produced fewer harmful side effects. TPA sold for $2000 a dose, about ten times the cost of streptokinase. Kolata, New Drug Findings on Heart Attack Buoying Doctors, N.Y. Times, April 10, 1988, 1, 32. TPA's manufacturer, Genentech, heavily and aggressively advertised the drug, which became its "flagship product," and on its strength its stock did well. However, a series of RCTs comparing the two drugs began to show no difference in either effectiveness in preventing mortality or in frequency of harmful side effects. Which Clot-Dissolving Drug is Best? 242 Science 1505 (Dec. 16, 1988). It was also disclosed that some of the original researchers who tested TPA had stock in Genentech (not illegal, but obviously presenting conflict-of-interest problems). Okie, Drug's Tester Had Stock in Its Maker, Wash. Post, Sept. 30, 1988, at A6. In addition, hospitals testing TPA seem to have been pressured by the company to use a standardized consent form that implied TPA was new rather than "experimental." When one hospital, Boston City Hospital, refused, it was dropped from the study. Maher, Genentech: Taking Stocks, Barron's, Nov. 21, 1988, 13, 31. Genentech had to suspend production of the drug (because of surpluses) and curtail its 1988 sales projection from $500 million to less than $180 million. Fisher, Biotech Woes: A Shortage of Cash, N.Y. Times, Dec. 3, 1988, 35. Shareholders sued Genentech alleging they were misled "by inflated prospects of its tissue plasminogen activator" N.Y. Times, Oct. 17, 1988 at D2. By January, 1989, the president of Genentech had scaled back 1989 sales projections to $150 million for TPA but "said the company will continue to invest heavily in marketing to sell physicians on the merits of clot-dissolving therapy." Wall St. J., Jan. 11, 1989, at B2.

Just as the failure of a new drug to live up to expectations can have a devastating effect on the future of a drug company, the erosion of the market of an established drug can also spell doom for even a giant. SmithKline Beckman, the 8th largest U.S. drug company, with more than $6 billion in annual sales, faced a likely takeover in 1989 when sales of its major drug Tagamet (an inhibitor of stomach acid) plummeted, and the company had no new drug to make up the difference. Koenig & Smith, Drop in Tagamet Sales is Putting SmithKline in Danger of Takeover, Wall St. J., Jan 13, 1989, 1.

One question is whether stock ownership is compatible with scientific integrity. One former academic justified stock options by noting, "We academic guys work for peanuts, while companies make millions off our work." The head of the NIH, on the other hand, insists that it "looks bad"; and another scientist sold her shares in a company when she was named to head a study of their new drug: "I sold my Merck stock because I'm chairman of the trial. . . . As these trials become scrutinized, we see an economic spotlight on our activity." A pioneering TPA researcher who eventually returned his stock options to Genentech has only one regret: "I should have sent them back the day they arrived." Chase, Mixing Science, Stocks Raises Question of Bias in the Testing of Drugs, Wall St. J., Jan. 26, 1989, 1, A6.

The medical profession has only just begun to develop guidelines for financial conflict of interest in the conduct of clinical trials. Arnold Relman, editor of the New England Journal of Medicine, has argued that such guidelines are urgently needed because financial conflicts of interest "erode scientific objectivity and engender the loss of public trust." Economic Incentives in Clinical Investigation, 320 N. Engl. J. Med. 933 (1989). While agreeing that disclosure of such conflicts is required, he finds disclosure alone insufficient. Instead he argues for institutionalizing a rule such as that suggested by NIH that "participating investigators and consultants will not have financial interests in organizations or entities that produce drugs, devices, or other inventions studied in a controlled clinical trial." Id at 934, citing National Institutes of Health Guide for Grants and Contracts, 1989 at 1. Relman concludes: "It is time to take a critical look at the consequences of attempting to fuse the disparate traditions of academic clinical research and business enterprise. . . . Whatever is done should be discussed collectively and in public. Leaving arrangements to the private discretion of individual researchers and companies will surely multiply problems that are already receiving unfavorable public attention." Id. And see Healy, Campeau, Gray, et al. Conflict-of-Interest Guidelines for a Multicenter Trial of Treatment after Coronary-Artery Bypass-Graft Surgery, 320 N. Engl. J. Med. 949 (1989).

United States v. Rutherford

442 U.S. 544 (1979)

Mr. Justice MARSHALL delivered the opinion of the Court.

The question presented in this case is whether the Federal Food, Drug, and Cosmetic Act precludes terminally ill cancer patients from obtaining Laetrile, a drug not recognized as "safe and effective" within the meaning of §201(p)(1) of the Act, 52 Stat. 1041, as amended, 21 U.S.C. §321(p)(1).

I.

Section 505 of the Federal Food, Drug, and Cosmetic Act, 52 Stat. 1052, as amended, 21 U.S.C. §355, prohibits interstate distribution of any "new drug" unless the Secretary of Health, Education, and Welfare approves an application supported by substantial evidence of the drug's safety and effectiveness.[1] As defined in §201(p)(1) of the Act, 21 U.S.C. §321(p)(1), the term "new drug" includes

1. Section 505, as set forth in 21 U.S.C. §355, provides in part:

(a) . . . No person shall introduce or deliver for introduction into interstate commerce any new drug, unless an approval of an application filed pursuant to subsection (b) of this section is effective with respect to such drug.

(b) . . . Any person may file with the Secretary an application with respect to any drug subject to the provisions of subsection (a) of this section. Such person shall submit to the Secretary as a part of the application

(1) full reports of investigations which have been made to show whether or not such drug is safe for use and whether such drug is effective in use. . . .

(d) . . . If the Secretary finds . . . that

(1) the investigations . . . required to be submitted to the Secretary . . . do not include adequate tests by all methods reasonably applicable to show whether or not such drug is safe for use under the conditions prescribed, recommended, or suggested in the proposed labeling thereof;

(2) the results of such tests show that such drug is unsafe for use under such conditions or do not show that such drug is safe for use under such conditions; . . .

(4) . . . he has insufficient information to determine whether such drug is safe for use under such conditions; or

(5) . . . there is a lack of substantial evidence that the drug will have the effect it purports or is represented to have under the conditions of use prescribed, recommended, or suggested in the proposed labeling thereof; or

(6) based on a fair evaluation of all material facts, such labeling is false or misleading in any particular; he shall issue an order refusing to approve the application.

. . . As used in this subsection . . . , the term "substantial evidence" means evidence consisting of adequate and well-controlled investigations, including clinical investigations, by experts qualified by scientific training and experience to evaluate the effectiveness of the drug involved, on the basis of which it could fairly and responsibly be concluded by such experts that the drug will have the effect it purports or is represented to have under the conditions of use prescribed, recommended, or suggested in the labeling or proposed labeling thereof. . . .

(i) . . . The Secretary shall promulgate regulations for exempting from the operation of the foregoing subsections of this section drugs intended solely for investigational use by experts qualified by scientific training and experience to investigate the

> "[a]ny drug . . . not generally recognized, among experts qualified by scientific training and experience to evaluate the safety and effectiveness of drugs, as safe and effective for use under the conditions prescribed, recommended, or suggested in the labeling. . . ."

Exemptions from premarketing approval procedures are available for drugs intended solely for investigative use and drugs qualifying under either of the Act's two grandfather provisions.

In 1975, terminally ill cancer patients and their spouses brought this action to enjoin the Government from interfering with the interstate shipment and sale of Laetrile, a drug not approved for distribution under the Act. Finding that Laetrile, in proper dosages, was nontoxic and effective, the District Court ordered the Government to permit limited purchases of the drug by one of the named plaintiffs. 399 F. Supp. 1208, 1215 (W.D. Okl. 1975). On appeal by the Government, the Court of Appeals for the Tenth Circuit did not disturb the injunction. However, it instructed the District Court to remand the case to the Food and Drug Administration for determination whether Laetrile was a "new drug" under § 201 (p)(1), and, if so, whether it was exempt from premarketing approval under either of the Act's grandfather clauses. 542 F.2d 1137 (1976).

After completion of administrative hearings, the Commissioner issued his opinion on July 29, 1977. 42 Fed. Reg. 39768 (1977). He determined first that no uniform definition of Laetrile exists; rather, the term has been used generically for chemical compounds similar to, or consisting at least in part of, amygdalin, a glucoside present in the kernels or seeds of most fruits. Id. at 39770-39772. The Commissioner further found that Laetrile in its various forms constituted a "new drug" as defined in §201(p)(1) of the Act because it was not generally recognized among experts as safe and effective for its prescribed use . . . and concluded that there were no adequate well-controlled scientific studies of Laetrile's safety or effectiveness. 42 Fed. Reg. 39775-39787 (1977).

Having determined that Laetrile was a new drug, the Commissioner proceeded to consider whether it was exempt from premarketing approval under the 1938 or 1962 grandfather provisions. On the facts presented, the Commissioner found that Laetrile qualified under neither clause. See id. at 39787-39795. First, there was no showing that the drug currently known as Laetrile was identical in composition or labeling to any drug distributed before 1938. See 21 U.S.C. §321(p)(1); n. 3, supra. Nor could the Commissioner conclude from the evidence submitted that, as of October 9, 1962, Laetrile in its present chemical composition was commercially used or sold in the United States, was generally recognized by experts as safe, and was labeled for the same recommended uses as the currently marketed drug. . . .

---

safety and effectiveness of drugs. . . ."

The Secretary has delegated his approval authority to the Commissioner of the Food and Drug Administration. See 21 CFR §5.1(a)(1) (1978).

On review of the Commissioner's decision, the District Court [concluded] . . . that the record did not support the Commissioner's findings as to the 1962 grandfather provision, the District Court ruled that Laetrile was entitled to an exemption from premarketing approval requirements. Id. at 1294-1298. Alternatively, the court held that, by denying cancer patients the right to use a nontoxic substance in connection with their personal health, the Commissioner had infringed constitutionally protected privacy interests.

The Court of Appeals addressed neither the statutory nor the constitutional rulings of the District Court. Rather, the Tenth Circuit held that "the 'safety' and 'effectiveness' terms used in the statute have no reasonable application to terminally ill cancer patients." 582 F.2d 1234, 1236 (1978). Since those patients, by definition, would "die of cancer regardless of what may be done," the court concluded that there were no realistic standards against which to measure the safety and effectiveness of a drug for that class of individuals. Id. at 1237. The Court of Appeals therefore approved the District Court's injunction permitting use of Laetrile by cancer patients certified as terminally ill. However, presumably because the Commissioner had found some evidence that Laetrile was toxic when orally administered, see 42 Fed. Reg. 39786-39787 (1977), the Court of Appeals limited relief to intravenous injections for patients under a doctor's supervision. 582 F.2d at 1237. In addition, the court directed the FDA to promulgate regulations "as if" the drug had been found "'safe' and 'effective'" for terminally ill cancer patients. Ibid.

We granted certiorari, 439 U.S. 1127 (1979), and now reverse.

II.

The Federal Food, Drug, and Cosmetic Act makes no special provision for drugs used to treat terminally ill patients. By its terms, §505 of the Act requires premarketing approval for "any new drug" unless it is intended solely for investigative use or is exempt under one of the Act's grandfather provisions. . . . Exceptions to clearly delineated statutes will be implied only where essential to prevent "absurd results" or consequences obviously at variance with the policy of the enactment as a whole. . . .

A.

Nothing in the history of the 1938 Food, Drug, and Cosmetic Act, which first established procedures for review of drug safety, or of the 1962 Amendments, which added the current safety and effectiveness standards in §201(p)(1), suggests that Congress intended protection only for persons suffering from curable diseases. To the contrary, in deliberations preceding the 1938 Act, Congress expressed concern that individuals with fatal illnesses, such as cancer, should be shielded from fraudulent cures. . . .

. . . In implementing the statutory scheme, the FDA has never made exception for drugs used by the terminally ill. As this Court has often recognized, the construction of a statute by those charged with its administration is entitled to substantial deference. . . .

Unless and until Congress does so, we are reluctant to disturb a longstanding administrative policy that comports with the plain language, history, and prophylactic purpose of the Act.

B.

. . . In the Court of Appeals' view, an implied exemption from the Act was justified because the safety and effectiveness standards set forth in §201(p)(1) could have "no reasonable application" to terminally ill patients. 582 F.2d, at 1236. We disagree. Under our constitutional framework, federal courts do not sit as councils of revision, empowered to rewrite legislation in accord with their own conceptions of prudent public policy. . . .

. . . A drug is effective within the meaning of §201(p)(1) if there is general recognition among experts, founded on substantial evidence, that the drug in fact produces the results claimed for it under prescribed conditions. . . . [E]ffectiveness does not necessarily denote capacity to cure. In the treatment of any illness, terminal or otherwise, a drug is effective if it fulfills, by objective indices, its sponsor's claims of prolonged life, improved physical condition, or reduced pain. See 42 Fed. Reg. 39776-39786 (1977).

. . . So too, the concept of safety under §201(p)(1) is not without meaning for terminal patients. Few if any drugs are completely safe in the sense that they may be taken by all persons in all circumstances without risk. Thus, the Commissioner generally considers a drug safe when the expected therapeutic gain justifies the risk entailed by its use. For the terminally ill, as for anyone else, a drug is unsafe if its potential for inflicting death or physical injury is not offset by the possibility of therapeutic benefit. Indeed, the Court of Appeals implicitly acknowledged that safety considerations have relevance for terminal cancer patients by restricting authorized use of Laetrile to intravenous injections for persons under a doctor's supervision. . . .

Moreover, there is a special sense in which the relationship between drug effectiveness and safety has meaning in the context of incurable illnesses. An otherwise harmless drug can be dangerous to any patient if it does not produce its purported therapeutic effect. See 107 Cong.Rec. 5640 (1961) (comments of Sen. Kefauver). But if an individual suffering from a potentially fatal disease rejects conventional therapy in favor of a drug with no demonstrable curative properties, the consequences can be irreversible. . . .

. . . The FDA's practice also reflects the recognition, amply supported by expert medical testimony in this case, that with diseases such as cancer it is often impossible to identify a patient as terminally ill except in retrospect.[14]

14. See, e.g., id., at 39805 (statement of Dr. Peter Wiernik, Chief of the Clinical Oncology Branch of the National Cancer Institute's Baltimore Research Center) ("[N]o one can prospectively define the term 'terminal' with any accuracy. A patient can be said to be ter-

Cancers vary considerably in behavior and in responsiveness to different forms of therapy. See 42 Fed. Reg. 39777 (1977). Even critically ill individuals may have unexpected remissions and may respond to conventional treatment. Id. at 39777, 39805. Thus, as the Commissioner concluded, to exempt from the Act drugs with no proved effectiveness in the treatment of cancer "would lead to needless deaths and suffering among . . . patients characterized as 'terminal' who could actually be helped by legitimate therapy." Id. at 39805.

It bears emphasis that although the Court of Appeals' ruling was limited to Laetrile, its reasoning cannot be so readily confined. To accept the proposition that the safety and efficacy standards of the Act have no relevance for terminal patients is to deny the Commissioner's authority over all drugs, however toxic or ineffectual, for such individuals. If history is any guide, this new market would not be long overlooked. Since the turn of the century, resourceful entrepreneurs have advertised a wide variety of purportedly simple and painless cures for cancer, including liniments of turpentine, mustard, oil, eggs, and ammonia; peat moss; arrangements of colored floodlamps; pastes made from glycerin and limburger cheese; mineral tablets; and "Fountain of Youth" mixtures of spices, oil, and suet. In citing these examples, we do not, of course, intend to deprecate the sincerity of Laetrile's current proponents, or to imply any opinion on whether that drug may ultimately prove safe and effective for cancer treatment. But this historical experience does suggest why Congress could reasonably have determined to protect the terminally ill, no less than other patients, from the vast range of self-styled panaceas that inventive minds can devise.

We note finally that construing §201(p)(1) to encompass treatments for terminal diseases does not foreclose all resort to experimental cancer drugs by patients for whom conventional therapy is unavailing. Section 505(i) of the Act, 21 U.S.C. §355(i), exempts from premarketing approval drugs intended solely for investigative use if they satisfy certain preclinical testing and other criteria.[17] An application for clinical testing of Laetrile by the National Cancer Institute is now pending before the Commissioner. Brief for United States 35 n.23. That the Act makes explicit provision for carefully regulated use of certain drugs not yet demonstrated safe and effective reinforces our conclusion that no exception for terminal patients may be judicially implied.

minal only after he dies. Many patients who are critically ill respond to modern day management of cancer"); ibid. (statement of Dr. Joseph Ross, Professor of Medicine, University of California School of Medicine at Los Angeles) ("[T]he distinction of 'terminal' patients from 'non-terminal' patients may not be reliably determined and an assumption that Laetrile may be given to ['terminal'] patients with impunity may deprive such patients of therapeutic measures which could help them").

17. See n.1, supra. At present, some 300 experimental drugs are available to critically ill cancer patients at authorized institutions. See Brief for United States 34 n.23; National Cancer Institute, Extramural Clinical Trial Programs of the Division of Cancer Treatment, General Overview and Scope of Contract-Supported Activities (1979). During 1977, over 90,000 cancer patients participated in investigative programs under the auspices of the National Cancer Institute or the Veterans' Administration. Brief for United States 35 n.23.

Whether, as a policy matter, an exemption should be created is a question for legislative judgment, not judicial inference.

The judgment of the Court of Appeals is reversed, and the case is remanded for further proceedings consistent with this opinion.[18]

So ordered.

Notes on Access to Unproven Drugs

(1) Almost twenty states "legalized" Laetrile in the late 1970s in an attempt to make the drug available to dying cancer patients for whom conventional treatment was unsuccessful or unwanted. This effort was unsuccessful in bringing Laetrile to the market because of the FDA's exclusive jurisdiction over drugs in interstate commerce and the inability to "manufacture" Laetrile exclusively in any one state. Frustration, nonetheless, continues to haunt the "war on cancer" initiated by President Nixon in 1971 with the signing of the National Cancer Act, whose goal was to discover a cure for cancer by 1976 to commemorate the bicentennial. Cancer remains unconquered and feared, and oil company president Armand Hammer has announced a "March of Dimes" type program to cure cancer by the year 2000. Hammer, N.Y. Times, Jan. 16, 1989, at A17. Progress in treating most cancers has been slight, and large interest groups have built up in support of existing treatment modalities. See, for instance, Bailar & Smith, Progress Against Cancer?, 314 N. Engl. J. Med. 1226-1232 (1986); R. Moss, The Cancer Syndrome (1980). The National Cancer Institute continues to complain that insufficient numbers of cancer patients are enrolling in clinical trials and has set up an information number (800-4-cancer) for patients to ask their physicians to call about NCI-sponsored trials. Boffey, "Cancer Agency Seeks Patients for Clinical Trials," N.Y. Times, June 2, 1988, at B13, col. 3.

(2) In May, 1988, the Dallas Gay Alliance (DGA) sued Parkland Hospital because there was a long list of AIDS patients waiting to get AZT; the hospital would not make aerosol pentamidine (an experimental drug at that time) available to Parkland patients; and the hospital seemed to be limiting the number of beds available for AIDS patients. The suit asked for an immediate temporary restraining order to compel the hospital to (1) dispense AZT to all patients who qualified for and needed it; (2) deliver aerosolized pentamidine inhalation treatment to all patients who qualified for and needed it; and (3) abolish all bed controls for HIV-positive patients and allocate hospital beds to AIDS and ARC patients on the basis of need.

Judge John M. Marshall of the Dallas County District Court ruled on the request for a temporary restraining order after a brief hearing on the day it

18. Respondents urge that we consider the District Court's rulings on the constitutional and grandfather clause questions as alternative bases for sustaining the judgment below. However, since the Court of Appeals addressed neither issue, we remand the case for further consideration of respondents' claims.

was filed. He essentially gave the DGA all they requested, ordering the immediate elimination of the AZT waiting list; the immediate dispensing of AZT to qualified patients who could prove they were indigent and had a physician's prescription; the immediate delivery of "aerosolized pentamidine inhalation treatment" to all qualified patients upon prescription; and the immediate abolition of all bed controls for HIV-positive patients. The judge read a brief statement explaining his decision:

> This case presents the paradigm of AIDS cases that we will undoubtedly see in the future if a cure should not be found, that is, an AIDS victim, as the disease progresses, will descend the economic ladder into indigency so that, at the moment of greatest need, the victim has the fewest resources to meet it. To whom must the victim turn? Obviously, the public must intervene or else adopt a policy that says, "Let them die because we can't afford them." Such a result is not tolerable in a society that for over 200 years has prided itself on placing human values first.
>
> On the other hand, there should be steps taken to insure that the effective treatment to be administered be administered by competent staff under the most efficacious conditions. . . . Bed control as a means of excluding anyone from the treatment provided by a facility is not acceptable.
>
> This Court is not a physician, nor is it a hospital administrator, but it must be to some extent a voice of the conscience of the community. That voice, even when confronted with the moral background of the AIDS pheomenon, must be, and is, raised in favor of life. . . . [Dallas Gay Alliance v. Parkland Memorial Hospital, No. 88-6346-A (4th Dist. Dallas Co., May 20, 1988).]

The case was removed to federal court and dismissed one year later as moot and nonjusticiable.

Is this opinion consistent with *Rutherford*? How is AIDS different from cancer? Should terminally ill patients have a right to any drug they want? Should the answer to this question depend on whether or not they can afford to pay for the drug? AZT was the only approved treatment for AIDS. Does this mean AZT is a "necessary" treatment that must be covered by Medicaid? Should public hospitals and/or Medicaid make experimental drugs available to those unable to pay for them? Can a public hospital have a waiting list for treatment? May hospitals in such circumstances limit the number of beds for a specific condition?

(3) The AIDS epidemic forced the FDA to re-evaluate its "all or nothing" position on non-approved drugs. On May 22, 1987, the FDA issued new regulations that permit the treatment use and sale of an investigational new drug that is not otherwise approved for treatment and sale while the drug is still in clinical trials if:

> The drug is intended to treat a serious or immediately life-threatening disease;
>
> There is no comparable or satisfactory alternative drug or other therapy available to treat that stage of the disease in the intended patient population;

> The drug is under investigation in a controlled clinical trial under an IND in effect for the trial, or all clinical trials have been completed; and
>
> The sponsor of the controlled clinical trial, or all clinical trials is actively pursuing marketing approval of the IND with due diligence. [21 CFR §312.34(b).]

According to the counselor to the Under Secretary of Health and Human Services, S. Jay Plager, the purpose of the rule is to give "desperately ill patients the opportunity to decide for themselves whether they would rather take an experimental drug or die of the disease untreated." N.Y. Times, May 21, 1987, at 1. The new regulation would not, of course, apply to Laetrile, because that drug could not meet the requirements. The FDA Commissioner informed physicians that even though his agency had initiated a special category (1-AA) to "fast track" AIDS drugs at all stages of review, these new rules were needed so that "everything possible be done to make not only promising AIDS-related drugs, but also other significant therapies, available to the public as soon as we have enough data to make a reasonable judgment that the drug may be effective and that it will not cause unreasonable risk." Young, Norris, Levitt & Nightengale, The FDA's New Procedures for the Use of Investigational Drugs in Treatment, 259 J.A.M.A. 2267 (1988). Does this new rule hopelessly blur the distinction between treatment and research? Are the desperately ill in any position to give "voluntary" informed consent?

(4) As difficult as it is to justify making unproven drugs available on the basis of "compassion," it is more difficult still to justify the importation from other countries of drugs that are not approved in this country and are not seriously considered as possibly therapeutic (like Laetrile). Nonetheless, the FDA Commissioner announced in July, 1988, that the FDA would permit individuals to import unapproved drugs from abroad for personal use (not resale) via the mails. In explaining this new policy, Commissioner Frank Young said, "There is such a degree of desperation, and people are going to die, that I'm not going to be the Commissioner that robs them of hope." Boffey, F.D.A. Will Allow Patients to Import AIDS Medicines, N.Y. Times, July 25, 1988, at A15, col. 1, 2. See also Boffey, Importing AIDS Drugs: Analysis of F.D.A. Policy, N.Y. Times, July 26, 1988, at C1, col. 4. How does one distinguish hope from hype or fraud? What should the role of the FDA be in the AIDS epidemic? See Annas, Faith (Healing), Hope and Charity at the FDA: The Politics of AIDS Drug Trials, 34 Villanova L. Rev. 30 (1989).

(5) Shortly before *Rutherford* the California Supreme Court upheld the conviction of a physician and others for conspiracy to sell and prescribe an unapproved drug — Laetrile — intended for the alleviation or cure of cancer contrary to California Health and Safety Code §1701.1. Chief Justice Bird dissented, arguing that the use of Laetrile by a physician for his or her patient

was constitutionally protected by the right of privacy (an issue the U.S. Supreme Court has not yet dealt with). In her words:

> I do not question for a moment that the effective treatment of persons suffering from cancer is a matter of paramount public importance. However, we are dealing here with a disease whose causes and treatment continue to baffle the medical community. . . . Cancer is a disease with potentially fatal consequences; this makes the choice of treatment one of the more important decisions a person may ever make, touching intimately on his or her being. For this reason, I believe the right to privacy . . . prevents the state from interfering with a person's choice of treatment on the sole grounds that the person has chosen a treatment which the state considers "ineffective." . . . The right to control one's body is not restricted to the wise; it includes the "foolish" refusal of medical treatment. . . . There [also] exists in the doctor licensed to practice medicine a right, constitutional in nature, as yet ill-defined, to treat and to treat by unorthodox modalities as yet unapproved by the state board [set up to approve cancer remedies] an informed consenting patient. . . . To require the doctor to use only orthodox "state sanctioned" methods of treatment under threat of criminal penalty for variance is to invite a repetition in California of the Soviet experience with "Lysenkoism." . . . [and] raises the spector of medical stagnation at best, statism, paternalistic Big Brother at worst. It is by the alternatives to orthodoxy that medical progress has been made. A free, progressive society has an enormous stake in recognizing and protecting this right of the physician. [People v. Privitera, 23 Cal. 3d 697, 153 Cal. Rptr. 431, 591 P.2d 919 (1979).]

Is Justice Bird correct regarding the "right of privacy" in the doctor-patient relationship? Are there any boundaries to this right? Would it, for example, include the right to mutilation? (See State v. Bass, 255 N.C. 42, 120 S.E.2d 580 (1961) (physician convicted as accessory before the fact for mayhem for anesthetizing the fingers of an individual who desired to amputate them to obtain insurance proceeds.) What do you think of Justice Bird's invocation of orthodox medicine as "stagnation" and unorthodox medicine as "medical progress"?

B. The Impact of Medical Technology on Cost and Rationing

There is general agreement that the major uncontrolled cost of medical care is the cost of technology, fueled by technology's rapid change and expansion. There is a constant hope that new technologies will lessen costs, but except for Thomas's "genuinely decisive technologies," like vaccines, this has always been an illusion. Other technologies, like noninvasive diagnostic technologies (such as magnetic resonance imaging and positron emission tomography) may provide a unit of service less expensively than their predecessors, but they will be used on many more patients because of their noninvasive quality. William Schwartz has made these points, and also argued persuasively that it is not "little ticket" laboratory tests that make a major contribution to medical cost increases, but rather that "new procedures and high-technology care have been the major culprits." Little ticket items, for example, amounted to only 10 percent of hospital expenditures in 1983. Likewise, aging of the population will contribute only 0.2 percent points annually to costs between now and the year 2000, and malpractice insurance costs will contribute less than 0.1 percent. Schwartz, The Inevitable Failure of Current Cost-Containment Strategies, 257 J.A.M.A. 220 (1987). It appears we will have little choice but to establish priorities and perhaps even make "rationing" decisions. The two major tools that have been developed by economists to help us in such decisionmaking are cost-benefit and cost-effectiveness analysis.

1. ATTEMPTS TO USE COST-BENEFIT AND COST-EFFECTIVENESS ANALYSIS IN MEDICINE

Roberts, The Economics of Organ Transplants

25 Jurimetrics J. 256-273 (1985) *

There has been a great deal of recent attention in the use of formal quantitative analysis in public policy decisions. The purpose of this section is to explore the possible role of such techniques in the work of the Task Force.

In approaching this question, we must realize that no analytic technique can be any more persuasive or compelling than the assumptions on which it is based. Every method has built into it certain ethical biases. There is no purely "scientific" way to decide what "ought" to be done in any given situation. In addition, describing the consequences of alternative policies in numerical terms has both advantages and drawbacks. Making our prediction quantitative forces us to be explicit and precise in our thinking. On the other hand, there may be no practical index or readily available number that does a good job of measuring what we really care about. And it is all too easy, as an analysis progresses, to ignore that which is not measured. Hence, formal analysis can distort as well as sharpen, thus obscuring rather than clarifying the central issue.

Historically there have been two main approaches to policy analysis, although these two schools have increasingly come together in recent years. One has its roots in economics and economic efficiency. The key ethical assumption is that the purpose of all economic activity (including health care)

*Adapted from Massachusetts Task Force on Organ Transplantation, Report of the Massachusetts Task Force on Organ Transplantation (Mass. Dept. of Public Health, 1984).

is to satisfy consumer preferences. An efficient activity is one where consumers (or beneficiaries) would pay more for it than the costs of production. This follows because, in a competitive economy, the price a producer has to pay for any input will equal the market value of the output that input could produce elsewhere. The various buyers of any input will bid up its price until the cost of that input to them is equal to what they could gain by utilizing it. Now suppose that the buyers or users of some good or service would pay more for it than it costs. That must mean that the good or service in question will produce more consumer satisfaction than the outputs which its inputs might otherwise produce. Thus if, and only if, consumers are willing to pay more than the cost of producing what they consume, it is efficient to provide them with that output. This is the test that *cost-benefit analysis* uses to judge public policy.

For several reasons the Task Force believes that this approach is unlikely to be helpful to its decision making. First, any individual's willingness to pay is limited by his ability to pay (i.e., his income and wealth). Thus the views of the rich are given greater weight in the analysis. While the professional literature contains some proposals to rectify this problem, none of them are really satisfactory. The problem of economic inequality may not be quite so significant in all the applications of cost-benefit analysis, for example, in areas like water resources or transportation planning. It is, however, a decisive objection (given prevailing moral sentiments) when life-saving decisions are at issue.

Nor is the Task Force convinced that the fundamental ethical premise of cost-benefit analysis is the appropriate one for its work. We do not believe the only objective in allocating resources should be the satisfaction of current individual tastes and preferences. Instead, we are persuaded that most citizens want to serve a variety of objectives, including fairness and freedom. We believe more is at stake in transplant policy than giving people what they are willing to pay for. All of us have complicated ideas about right and wrong, and about what we want to do together as a community and a society. In formulating transplant policy, we need to consider such value concerns in a way that a strict cost-benefit approach would make impossible.

The second major approach to quantitative policy analysis is noticeably less ambitious. Called *cost-effectiveness analysis,* it simply urges us to compare the costs of alternative ways of achieving our objectives. Unlike cost-benefit analysis, which presumes to tell us what ends to seek, this approach merely helps us minimize the costs of achieving whatever ends we select. It is essentially a consistency condition, a way of cross-checking various policy options against each other. We find this approach helpful, and in subsequent sections attempt to compare the costs of organ transplantation with the costs of other life-saving procedures supported by the health care delivery system.

We emphasize, however, that such an analysis is not, in itself, sufficient for making a public policy decision. Society could quite conceivably choose to be inefficient or inconsistent in some specific case (e.g., out of a concern for fairness). Furthermore, the definition of our objectives is not a scientific, but an ethical or political act. No one can tell us from a technical perspective whether we ought to compare cost-per-life saved or cost-per-year-of-life saved. And a policy that looks good on one basis might not look good on another. Still, we believe there is a general social value in minimizing the costs of doing good things (so that as a society we can do still more good things). Also, there is a value in being direct and explicit about one's presumptions; both empirical and philosophical. We should understand the cost implications of ethical commitments we accept.

A final note on methodology. We have chosen not to consider what is perhaps the most widely used method for the economic valuing of lives, the so-called "human capital" approach. In this method lives are valued on the basis of the sum total of the current expected value of a citizen's future lifetime earnings. We believe society should view its citizens as having an intrinsic value apart from their expected contribution to the economy. . . .

Comparing the costs of organ transplantation with the costs of other kinds of life-saving medical care is easier said than done. Practically, the requisite data are typically not generated by hospital accounting records, and so are not widely available, either for organ transplants or their alternatives. More fundamentally, there are deep conceptual problems concerning what costs we count and how we count them.

We would like to know what additional real resources the health care system would utilize if we were to follow one or another policy on organ transplantation. We might also like to know who would pay for those added resources, both initially and ultimately. But it is important to stress that the long-run cost to the society (that is, the real resource costs) and its distribution might be quite different than the short-run fiscal burden. We must worry about inadvertently setting in motion a chain of events that has acceptable results for the next few years, but creates serious difficulties a few years down the road.

The most important conclusion of the analysis which follows is that *the net costs of doing transplants, from a systemwide perspective, are not fixed and given*. Instead, those costs will vary substantially, depending on how various public and private policy decisions are made. Consider, for example, two scenarios. First, suppose transplants were done by existing institutions that "made room" for the activity by utilizing existing capacity more efficiently. Alternatively, suppose one or more institutions were to use transplant activity as the reason for a major expansion of plant and equipment. The real resource costs would be much higher in the second situation than in the first. . . .

There are at least four different ways the "costs" of organ transplantation have been defined:

- bills — taken directly from hospital financial records;
- fully allocated average costs — usually based on reimbursement cost reports;

- direct costs — derived from studies of actual resource use; and
- incremental costs — which have been estimated by asking which costs would be incurred only if transplantation were performed. . . .

As to what incremental costs the state can expect, the literature makes it clear, as noted previously, that these will depend on how the system responds, and is allowed to respond. If transplantation becomes such a high-volume activity that it leads to an expansion in the states' health care system, the cost of a liver transplant per case is likely to be more than the $160,000-240,000 range allocated average cost for the first year per patient treated, the range suggested by the prior Task Force and Blue Cross. Likewise the $120,000-140,000 range suggested by the published Stanford studies and Blue Cross could prove to be an underestimate for heart transplant costs. The estimates in those studies are based on existing averages. These are likely to be well below the long-run incremental costs of adding new plant and equipment at today's all-time high, and rapidly escalating construction, equipment, and financing costs. They also contain the partially offsetting screening costs incurred and death costs avoided.

On this same basis, *if we have 70 percent survival for one year, we get costs of $230,000-340,000 per liver transplant patient alive at the end of one year and $170,000-200,000 per one-year survival for heart transplants.* If we assume a five-year average life expectancy and from $10,000 to $20,000 in annual costs after the first year, we get numbers anywhere from $35,000 to $60,000 per year of life saved by either kind of transplant program.

At the opposite end of the spectrum, the system's incremental costs could even be below the $60,000 estimated by the Liver Consortium, or the $30,000 for hearts estimated by Brigham and Women's. To do this, both individual institutions and the system as a whole would have to *give up providing other services* in order *to make room for organ transplants.* This is so even though the Brigham's total costs are almost certainly quite optimistic, since some of the costs they cite as incremental (e.g., nursing) are not incremental in the postulated circumstances.

The challenge to state health policy makers and regulators with regard to organ transplantation is thus twofold:

- First, to make sure that transplantation is, to the largest extent possible, undertaken within the limits set by existing resources, so that adding this service does not lead to an expansion of the total delivery system.
- Second, to ensure that whatever care is given up in the process is of doubtful value, that is, "gold plated" or unnecessary care, with little or no positive payoff for the patient. In that case the decision to do something else with the resources that previously produced such care (whether we use it for transplants or something else) will be much less difficult to make.

This leads to an ironic realization. Either one has to believe that there is nontrivial inefficiency in the current system, or one has to believe organ transplantation will be very costly in social and economic terms. If there is no waste today, and we add transplantation, we will either have to expand the delivery system or give up valuable services. On the other hand, there is reason to believe that the state is overbedded, particularly in Boston, that lengths of stay are too long, and that too much cost-ineffective use is currently made of intensive care and sophisticated ancillary services. The high concentration of teaching hospitals in Boston appears in part responsible for these conditions. The bright side is that current inefficiency makes possible the careful accommodation of a modest volume of transplant activity at reasonable cost, provided its introduction is carefully controlled. . . .

[Roberts concludes his piece by analysing all of the published studies on high cost medical procedures to try to place organ transplantation in the context of the current health care delivery system. These studies yield the following information: neonatal intensive care costs on the average of $8000 to $11,000 per case for broad samples of newborns, and $16,000 to $25,000 for infants weighing less than 1000 grams. Cost for intensive care for adults varies more, but no study yields average costs of more than $25,000 per patient. Since the one year mortality figure for these patients is approximately 50 percent, however, the cost per survivor rises to approximately $50,000. This compares to infants, assuming a life expectancy of 60 years, to a cost of about $1200 per year of life saved (assuming a five year survival rate for adults, the rate would be $10,000 per year of life saved). The highest non-transplant cost procedure is renal dialysis, averaging $108,000 to $209,000 per patient. Given an average life-expectancy of 8 years per patient, this is approximately $12,000 to $30,000 a year of added life. From these, and other studies, Roberts concludes:]

In summary, on both a cost-effectiveness basis (cost per year of life) and a cost-per-case basis, heart and liver transplantation is likely to be, in almost all cases, substantially more expensive than almost everything we currently do in the medical care system. There are only two exceptions to this generalization. First, if one makes optimistic assumptions, the five-year cost per case of heart transplants might be low enough to be comparable to the five-year costs of center hemodialysis. But the cost per year of life saved is noticeably higher for transplantation. Also, it is perfectly reasonable to argue that center dialysis is so much less cost effective than the alternative treatments for ESRD that it should not generally be pursued in any event. To put it crudely, the fact that we as a society make one mistake in medical care resource allocation does not justify making another, especially one even more costly from a cost-effectiveness viewpoint.

The other exception to the rule "transplants cost more" is the treatment of certain subclasses of very acutely ill individuals in intensive care. Their costs per case, however, are well below transplantation even if their costs per year are equal or above, especially if we can identify subsamples for which the mortality rates are high enough. Yet if the care of such individuals is justified on the basis of fairness, not effectiveness (as presumably it must be since it is so cost ineffective), then total cost is the relevant measure for comparative purposes. On that basis, transplants will cost two to four times as much per case as the costs of even the sickest patients in intensive care, with liver transplants looking particularly expensive.

The entire preceding discussion has focused on fully allocated average costs, often as imperfectly measured by hospital bills. The incremental costs of transplants, like those for any of these other procedures, could be noticeably less if the added volume is accommodated within existing capacity. In that case, as we have stressed repeatedly, marginal or incremental costs could be much lower than average costs. But those costs, for any procedure, will depend on how the health care system in a given area responds to the increased demand. Consequently, it seems most appropriate to compare procedures on a fully allocated average cost basis that provides an insight into the relative system burden imposed (or problem posed) by the options in question. From that perspective, heart and liver transplants are exceptionally, and uniquely, expensive.

NOTES ON COST-EFFECTIVENESS AND COST-BENEFIT ANALYSES

(1) The outcome of a cost-effectiveness analysis is often determined in advance by deciding which interventions are to be compared. Physicians David Himmelstein and Steffie Woolhandler argue that "unpopular alternatives may be subject to the most stringent comparisons, with radical innovations totally excluded from consideration. In contrast, practices that are less controversial or enjoy the support of powerful constituencies may be evaluated for efficacy but not cost or even accepted without evaluation." Free Care, Cholestyramine and Health Policy, N. Engl. J. Med. 1511 (1984). They go on to argue that narrow comparison trials can be misleading, and compare two recent trials, one of which purported to show that cholestyramine therapy was a "breakthrough" and the other that free medical care did not improve health status. Using data from these two studies, the authors compared their respective performances in reducing the risk of early death. Their analysis "suggests that free care is between 3 and 100 times as cost-effective as cholestyramine therapy in preventing death." Id. at 1513. They further concluded that the perception that cholestyramine therapy is a breakthrough and free care is not useful is "unwarranted and may be due to unrecognized bias" including the bias of physicians and drug manufacturers, and others wedded to the status quo in health care delivery. Id.

(2) It is one thing to compare technologies in terms of how many lives they each might save; it is quite another to attempt to value those lives in monetary terms. Nicholas Rescher, for example, argues:

> If lives indeed have a measurable value, then why should not some lives bear a *negative* value — the terminally ill, the severely handicapped, the parentally unwanted unborn, and so on. To put even a high price on life is to make it cheap. . . . It opens the doors to gas chambers — to mercy killing, genetic culling, and other such like projects of "social engineering." [Risk and the Social Value of Life in Quantitative Risk Assessment (J. Humber & R. Almeder eds. 1987).]

Along the same lines, technologies can be measured in terms of years saved; but those years may be of various kinds. For example, eliminating heart disease would add 11 to 12 years to average life expectancy, but only one year to average work-life expectancy, since the disease takes its highest toll on the elderly. Klarman, Applications of Cost-Benefit Analysis to Health Systems Technology in Technology and Health Care Systems in the 1980's, DHEW Pub. No. 733016 (F. Collen ed. 1973).

Examining cost-benefit analysis as a possible tool to determine how much should be spent on geriatric care, Jerry Avorn concludes that this analysis is not only useless, but discriminatory. Using the "human capital" approach, for example, in which individuals are valued on the basis of productivity, places the elderly in "a kind of double jeopardy, since mandatory retirement often forces elderly workers out of the workplace — elderly people who are then valued less because they are 'unproductive.'" Avron, Benefit and Cost Analysis in Geriatric Care: Turning Age Discrimination into Health Policy, 310 N. Engl. J. Med. 1294, 1297 (1984). Likewise, using measures such as life-years saved discriminates against the elderly who will live fewer additional years than younger patients if a medical technology is used to save their life. He concludes that cost-benefit analysis in medicine should be abandoned because "the alleged quantification is so imprecise and so laden with value judgments that such numbers are useless as ingredients in any quantitative analysis." Id. at 1299. He does, however, concede that cost-effectiveness analysis can be a "valuable tool" if used appropriately:

> Given an obvious, agreed-on clinical end point such as treating chronic renal failure . . . cost-effectiveness analysis, done well, can be an extremely useful tool to compare the efficiency of various means of achieving a particular goal. When the analysis moves beyond these topics, particularly in making judgments on the quality of a year of life with a particular disability, it loses both moral and intellectual legitimacy. Few would argue that a life with Alzheimer's disease, arthritis, and incontinence is as desirable as a life free of these afflictions. But who among us is to provide the number that quantifies this for patients as a whole? And when this is done, by what right is this "diminished utility" to be translated into public policy? [Id. at 1298-1299.]

(3) There is no one method to determine when a new technology will be covered by private insurance, Medicare, or Medicaid. Most private insurance companies rely on physician committees to give them advice about the

current standards of practice. Medicare permits local contractors to make the initial coverage decision and to refer issues that cannot be resolved to the regional office, and, if necessary, to the Health Care Financing Administration (HCFA), which may, in turn, receive guidance from the Office of Health Technology Assessment. Medicare contractors vary widely in their determinations; and there is no mechanism for Medicare to reverse a coverage decision, even if the technology has become outmoded or less effective than other approaches. Congress of the United States, Office of Technology Assessment, Federal Policies and the Medical Devices Industry 43-45 (1984). Shouldn't there at least be a uniform Medicare policy on how new technologies will be assessed and what standards must be met before they are paid for by Medicare? The most extensive technology assessment ever carried out by Medicare involved heart transplants. See Chapter 9 for a complete discussion of this assessment process.

In January, 1989, HCFA finally announced its proposed regulations on "Criteria and Procedures for Making Medical Services Coverage Decisions that Relate to Health Care Technology." 54 Fed. Reg. 4302-18, Jan. 30, 1989. The new proposals set up a mechanism for making *national* coverage decisions and for the first time include "cost-effectiveness" as an additional criterion for Medicare coverage of "medically reasonable and necessary services." In the comments to the proposal, HCFA notes that cost-effectiveness may not always be relevant: "However, if a service were to be viewed as marginal with respect to safety and effectiveness, but expensive in comparison with available covered alternatives, we think that cost-effectiveness considerations are appropriate." Id. at 4309, col. 1. Once a national coverage decision is made, all Medicare contractors would be bound by it. Some relevant portions of the proposed regulation:

> Sec. 405.380 (2) . . . a service is covered by Medicare only if the service is reasonable and necessary for the diagnosis or treatment of illness or injury . . . with reference to the following criteria . . .
>
> (i) the service is safe and effective.
>
> (ii) the service is not experimental or investigational.
>
> (iii) the service is cost-effective.
>
> (iv) the service is appropriate. . . .
>
> (3) *Cost-effectiveness.* A technology is considered cost-effective if it is:
>
> (i) Very expensive to the program, but provides significant medical benefits not otherwise available;
>
> (ii) Less costly and at least as effective as an alternative covered intervention;
>
> (iii) More effective and more costly than a covered alternative, but the added benefit is significant enough to justify the added cost; and
>
> (iv) Less effective and less costly than an existing alternative, but a viable alternative for some patients.
>
> (4) *Appropriateness.*
>
> (i) A service is considered appropriate if it is furnished in a setting commensurate with the patient's medical needs.

(ii) A service is considered appropriate if it is furnished by qualified personnel. [Id. at 4317.]

Is there any reason why these proposals should not be adopted? Would they stifle innovation and local experimentation? Do they go far enough?

2. HOW MEDICAL TECHNOLOGY CHANGES THE STANDARD OF CARE

Helling v. Carey

83 Wash. 2d 514, 519 P.2d 981 (1974)

HUNTER, J. — This case arises from a malpractice action instituted by the plaintiff (petitioner), Barbara Helling.

The plaintiff suffers from primary open angle glaucoma. Primary open angle glaucoma is essentially a condition of the eye in which there is an interference in the ease with which the nourishing fluids can flow out of the eye. Such a condition results in pressure gradually rising above the normal level to such an extent that damage is produced to the optic nerve and its fibers with resultant loss in vision. The first loss usually occurs in the periphery of the field of vision. The disease usually has few symptoms and, in the absence of a pressure test, is often undetected until the damage has become extensive and irreversible.

The defendants (respondents), Dr. Thomas F. Carey and Dr. Robert C. Laughlin, are partners who practice the medical specialty of ophthalmology. Ophthalmology involves the diagnosis and treatment of defects and diseases of the eye.

The plaintiff first consulted the defendants for myopia, nearsightedness, in 1959. At that time she was fitted with contact lenses. She next consulted the defendants in September 1963, concerning irritation caused by the contact lenses. Additional consultations occurred in October 1963; February 1967; September 1967; October 1967; May 1968; July 1968; August 1968; September 1968; and October 1968. Until the October 1968 consultation, the defendants considered the plaintiff's visual problems to be related solely to complications associated with her contact lenses. On that occasion, the defendant, Dr. Carey, tested the plaintiff's eye pressure and field of vision for the first time. This test indicated that the plaintiff had glaucoma. The plaintiff, who was then 32 years of age, had essentially lost her peripheral vision and her central vision was reduced to approximately 5 degrees vertical by 10 degrees horizontal.

Thereafter, in August of 1969, after consulting other physicians, the plaintiff filed a complaint against the defendants alleging, among other things, that she sustained severe and permanent damage to her eyes as a proximate result of the defendants' negligence. During trial, the testimony of the medical experts for both the plaintiff and the defendants established that the standards of the profession for that specialty in the same or similar circumstances do not require routine pressure tests for glaucoma upon patients under 40 years of age. The reason the pressure test for glaucoma is not given as a regular practice to patients under the age of 40 is that the disease rarely occurs in this age group. Testimony indicated, however, that the standards of the profession do require pressure tests if the patient's complaints and symptoms reveal to the physician that glaucoma should be suspected.

The trial court entered judgment for the defendants following a defense verdict. The plaintiff thereupon appealed to the Court of Appeals, which affirmed the judgment of the trial court. Helling v. Carey, 8 Wash. App. 1005 (1973). The plaintiff then petitioned this court for review, which we granted.

In her petition for review, the plaintiff's primary contention is that under the facts of this case the trial judge erred in giving certain instructions to the jury and refusing her proposed instructions defining the standard of care which the law imposes upon an ophthalmologist. As a result, the plaintiff contends, in effect, that she was unable to argue her theory of the case to the jury that the standard of care for the specialty of ophthalmology was inadequate to protect the plaintiff from the incidence of glaucoma, and that the defendants, by reason of their special ability, knowledge and information, were negligent in failing to give the pressure test to the plaintiff at an earlier point in time which, if given, would have detected her condition and enabled the defendants to have averted the resulting substantial loss in her vision.

We find this to be a unique case. The testimony of the medical experts is undisputed concerning the standards of the profession for the specialty of ophthalmology. It is not a question in this case of the defendants having any greater special ability, knowledge and information than other ophthalmologists which would require the defendants to comply with a higher duty of care than "that degree of care and skill which is expected of the average practitioner in the class to which he belongs, acting in the same or similar circumstances." Pederson v. Dumouchel, 72 Wash. 2d 73, 79, 431 P.2d 973 (1967). The issue is whether the defendants' compliance with the standard of the profession of ophthalmology, which does not require the giving of a routine pressure test to persons under 40 years of age, should insulate them from liability. . . .

The defendants argue that the standard of the profession, which does not require the giving of a routine pressure test to persons under the age of 40, is adequate to insulate the defendants from liability for negligence because the risk of glaucoma is so rare in this age group. The testimony of the defendant, Dr. Carey, however, is revealing as follows: . . .

Q. Now, Doctor, there's been some reference to the matter of taking pressure checks of persons over 40. What is the incidence of glaucoma, the statistics, with persons under 40?

A. In the instance of glaucoma under the age of 40, is less than 100 to one

> per cent. The younger you get, the less the incidence. It is thought to be in the neighborhood of one in 25,000 people or less.
>
> *Q.* How about the incidence of glaucoma in people over 40?
>
> *A.* Incidence of glaucoma over 40 gets into the two to three per cent category, and hence, that's where there is this great big difference and that's why the standards around the world has been to check pressures from 40 on.

The incidence of glaucoma in one out of 25,000 persons under the age of 40 may appear quite minimal. However, that one person, the plaintiff in this instance, is entitled to the same protection, as afforded persons over 40, essential for timely detection of the evidence of glaucoma where it can be arrested to avoid the grave and devastating result of this disease. The test is a simple pressure test, relatively inexpensive. There is no judgment factor involved, and there is no doubt that by giving the test the evidence of glaucoma can be detected. The giving of the test is harmless if the physical condition of the eye permits. The testimony indicates that although the condition of the plaintiff's eyes might have at times prevented the defendants from administering the pressure test, there is an absence of evidence in the record that the test could not have been timely given.

Justice Holmes stated in Texas & P. Ry. v. Behymer, 189 U.S. 468, 470, 47 L. Ed. 905, 23 S. Ct. 622 (1903):

> What usually is done may be evidence of what ought to be done, but what ought to be done is fixed by a standard of reasonable prudence, whether it usually is complied with or not.

In The T.J. Hooper, 60 F.2d 737 (2d Cir. 1932), Justice Hand stated on page 740:

> [I]n most cases reasonable prudence is in fact common prudence; but strictly it is never its measure; a whole calling may have unduly lagged in the adoption of new and available devices. It never may set its own tests, however persuasive be its usages. *Courts must in the end say what is required; there are precautions so imperative that even their universal disregard will not excuse their omission.* [Italics ours.]

Under the facts of this case reasonable prudence required the timely giving of the pressure test to this plaintiff. The precaution of giving this test to detect the incidence of glaucoma to patients under 40 years of age is so imperative that irrespective of its disregard by the standards of the ophthalmology profession, it is the duty of the courts to say what is required to protect patients under 40 from the damaging results of glaucoma.

We therefore hold, as a matter of law, that the reasonable standard that should have been followed under the undisputed facts of this case was the timely giving of this simple, harmless pressure test to this plaintiff and that, in failing to do so, the defendants were negligent, which proximately resulted in the blindness sustained by the plaintiff for which the defendants are liable.

There are no disputed facts to submit to the jury on the issue of the defendants' liability. Hence, a discussion of the plaintiff's proposed instructions would be inconsequential in view of our disposition of the case.

The judgment of the trial court and the decision of the Court of Appeals is reversed, and the case is remanded for a new trial on the issue of damages only.

HALE, C.J., and ROSELLINI, STAFFORD, WRIGHT, and BRACHTENBACH, J.J., concur.

UTTER, J. (concurring) — I concur in the result reached by the majority. I believe a greater duty of care could be imposed on the defendants than was established by their profession. The duty could be imposed when a disease, such as glaucoma, can be detected by a simple, well-known harmless test whose results are definitive and the disease can be successfully arrested by early detection, but where the effects of the disease are irreversible if undetected over a substantial period of time.

The difficulty with this approach is that we as judges, by using a negligence analysis, seem to be imposing a stigma of moral blame upon the doctors who, in this case, used all the precautions commonly prescribed by their profession in diagnosis and treatment. Lacking their training in this highly sophisticated profession, it seems illogical for this court to say they failed to exercise a reasonable standard of care. It seems to me we are, in reality, imposing liability, because, in choosing between an innocent plaintiff and a doctor, who acted reasonably according to his specialty but who could have prevented the full effects of this disease by administering a simple, harmless test and treatment, the plaintiff should not have to bear the risk of loss. As such, imposition of liability approaches that of strict liability. . . .

When types of problems rather than numbers of cases are examined, strict liability is applied more often than negligence as a principle which determines liability. Peck, Negligence and Liability Without Fault in Tort Law, 46 Wash. L. Rev. 225, 239 (1971). There are many similarities in this case to other cases of strict liability. Problems of proof have been a common feature in situations where strict liability is applied. Where events are not matters of common experience, a juror's ability to comprehend whether reasonable care has been followed diminishes. There are few areas as difficult for jurors to intelligently comprehend as the intricate questions of proof and standards in medical malpractice cases.

In applying strict liability there are many situations where it is imposed for conduct which can be defined with sufficient precision to insure that application of a strict liability principle will not produce miscarriages of justice in a substantial number of cases. If the activity involved is one which can be defined with sufficient precision, that definition can serve as an accounting unit to which the costs of the activity may be allocated with some certainty and precision. With this possible, strict liability serves a compensatory function in situations where the defendant is, through the use of insurance, the financially more responsible person. Peck, Negligence and Liability Without Fault in Tort Law, supra at 240-41.

If the standard of a reasonably prudent specialist is, in fact, inadequate to offer reasonable protection to the plaintiff, then liability can be imposed without fault. To do so under the narrow facts of this case does not offend my sense of justice. The pressure test to measure intraocular pressure with the Schiotz tonometer and the Goldman applanometer takes a short time, involves no damage to the patient, and consists of placing the instrument against the eyeball. An abnormally high pressure requires other tests which would either confirm or deny the existence of glaucoma. It is generally believed that from 5 to 10 years of detectable increased pressure must exist before there is permanent damage to the optic nerves.

Although the incidence of glaucoma in the age range of the plaintiff is approximately one in 25,000, this alone should not be enough to deny her a claim. Where its presence can be detected by a simple, well-known harmless test, where the results of the test are definitive, where the disease can be successfully arrested by early detection and where its effects are irreversible if undetected over a substantial period of time, liability should be imposed upon defendants even though they did not violate the standard existing within the profession of ophthalmology.

The failure of plaintiff to raise this theory at the trial and to propose instructions consistent with it should not deprive her of the right to resolve the case on this theory on appeal. Where this court has authoritatively stated the law, the parties are bound by those principles until they have been overruled. Acceptance of those principles at trial does not constitute a waiver or estop appellants from adapting their cause on appeal to such a rule as might be declared if the earlier precedent is overruled. Samuelson v. Freeman, 75 Wash. 2d 894, 900, 454 P.2d 406 (1969).

FINLEY and HAMILTON, JJ., concur with Utter, J.

Petition for rehearing denied July 31, 1974.

NOTES ON *HELLING*

(1) *Helling* is an exceptional, arguably unique, case in which the court itself decided not to be bound by "medical custom" in setting the standard of care. On the other hand, it is worth noting that, even though the court does not seem to have known it, physicians in almost every other state were routinely testing for glaucoma in the early 1970s. Thus the case could be looked at as one applying a national standard (albeit one devised by the court instead of by an expert from another jurisdiction) instead of the locality rule. See discussion of the locality rule in Chapter 5.

It should also be noted that courts have not felt bound by professional standards in setting the "duty to disclose" in informed consent. See, for instance, Cobbs v. Grant in Chapter 6.

(2) In 1975 the Washington legislature passed a statute in response to *Helling* that required the plaintiff in a malpractice action to prove "by a preponderance of the evidence that the defendant . . . failed to exercise that degree of skill, care and learning possessed by other persons in the same profession. . . ." Wash. Rev. Code §4.24.290. In Gates v. Jensen, 92 Wash. 2d 246, 595 P.2d 919 (1979) the physician did a glaucoma test (which revealed that the patient had "borderline glaucoma") but failed to dilate the patient's pupils and failed to inform the patient that her test results indicated "borderline glaucoma" or that there were two additional "simple, inexpensive and risk free" tests available to confirm or deny her glaucoma. The patient had glaucoma, and became functionally blind. The trial court refused to give a *Helling* instruction, the Court of Appeals affirmed, and the Washington Supreme Court reversed. The court concluded that the statute (Wash. Rev. Code §4.24.290) actually continued to permit use of the *Helling* rule: "The statute as passed requires physicians to exercise the skill, care and learning *possessed* by others in the same profession. This standard is much broader than the one embodied in the original bill [which used the word "practiced"] and allows ample scope for the application of the limited *Helling* rule."

Later, in a circumstance similar to *Gates,* the court refused to impose a duty of disclosure based solely on possession of information, but instead reverted to the assumption that unless the physician actually touched the patient, the only issue was the doctor's competence. Keogan v. Holy Family Hospital, 95 Wash. 2d 306, 622 P.2d 1246 (1980) (physician had obtained test results suggesting but not confirming that the patient's chest pain was caused by heart disease, but did not inform the patient of this possibility; the patient later died of a heart attack). Commenting on these cases, Marjorie Shultz has argued:

> *Gates* has been criticized as interfering with proper professional judgment, indulging in the fantasy that a patient can "correct the reasonable errors of his physician." Yet *Gates* glimpsed what *Keogan* lost sight of: Although the patient is not more competent in making judgments assessing the likelihood of a particular disease, she is more competent in deciding whether she wishes to undergo more tests and spend more money in order to be more certain about the diagnosis in her case. [Shultz, From Informed Consent to Patient Choice: A New Protected Interest, 95 Yale L.J. 219, 244 (1985).]

(3) *Helling* can be approached from an economic point of view as well, by comparing the cost of preventing one case of blindness to whatever value one puts on eyesight. Two authors, for example, suggested that if the average cost of tonometry was put at $5, and the average jury verdict for total or legal blindness was (for 1973-1977) $678,000, then it would "pay" to screen for blindness (at $5, prevention of one case would cost $125,000) as long as

screening cost less than $27. Schwartz & Komesar, Damages and Deterrence; An Economic View of Medical Malpractice, 298 N. Engl. J. Med. 1282, 1284 (1978). On the other hand, things may not be as simple as either these authors or the *Helling* court thought. Initial glaucoma screening will yield a high number (perhaps 30 to 50 for every "true positive") of incorrect or "false-positive" results which will have to be individually worked up at a cost of $100 or more each to ascertain if the patients in fact have glaucoma, because ocular tension can be temporary or can persist without adverse effects. This generally raises the cost of screening, as well as patient anxiety. In addition, this test will miss almost half of those who actually have glaucoma, and it is unclear just how effective treatment is at arresting glaucoma, since it has never been subjected to an RCT. On this basis it has been argued that "screening with tonometry does not appear to be warranted." Eddy, Sanders & Eddy, The Value of Screening for Glaucoma with Tonometry, 23 Survey of Ophthalmology 194 (1983). A more sophisticated glaucoma screening test is now used by most ophthalmologists. How should a glaucoma screening decision be made? Who should make it?

(4) Which, if any, other medical screening tests would the *Helling* court require physicians to offer to their patients on a *routine* basis? Other screening tests in medicine include the taking of blood pressure, checking glucose and cholesterol levels, electrocardiograms, mammograms, chest x-rays (now discouraged), Pap smears, and so forth. At what point does a screening test become "standard medical procedure" such that a physician should be expected to perform it routinely? Obviously some tests are indicated when the patient shows specific symptoms. Would *Helling* have been a more satisfactory case if it had been tried and decided on the basis that a physician had an obligation to perform a glaucoma screening test when the patient, regardless of age, exhibited symptoms that might indicate glaucoma? In the interplay between professional standards for giving screening tests "routinely" and informed consent, what should the physician's practice be? Is giving the patient a booklet that lists all possible screening tests and the recommendations of physician groups sufficient? What about a video tape that the patient could view prior to the scheduled appointment?

(5) Countering the movement toward routine tests to detect serious, arrestable, or treatable conditions, is the movement to contain costs by discouraging routine testing. Is it clear that some sort of priority for testing will have to be established, with some tests recommended for routine use and others discouraged? In mid-1989, for example, the U.S. Preventive Services Task Force, a group convened by HHS to study commonly employed medical tests, found insufficient support in the 2400 scientific studies they reviewed to justify routine electrocardiograms, glaucoma testing for people under 65, and universal fetal monitoring during labor. The Task Force recommended against routine mammograms for women under 50; it recommended restricting cholesterol screening to middle-aged men and others with a history of heart disease and abolishing the use of digital rectal exams for

detecting prostate cancer. Instead the Task Force urged that patients be advised to stop smoking, use seat belts, limit alcohol consumption, and reduce dietary fat intake. The chairman of the Task Force, Dr. Robert S. Lawrence, noted that expense is not the only reason to limit routine testing: "Too often, people are told they have a medical problem when they do not. They may worry needlessly, alter their lifestyles unnecessarily, take drugs they do not need or undergo more expensive and invasive testing to rule out disease." Lehman, Doctors Should Stress Good Habits, Not Costly Tests, US Panel Concludes, Boston Globe, May 3, 1989, p.3.

Truman v. Thomas

27 Cal. 3d 285, 165 Cal. Rptr. 308, 611 P.2d 902(Cal. 1980)

Bird, C. J. — This court must decide whether a physician's failure to inform a patient of the material risks of not consenting to a recommended pap smear, so that the patient might make an informed choice, may have breached the physician's duty of due care to his patient, who died from cancer of the cervix.

Respondent, Dr. Claude R. Thomas, is a family physician engaged in a general medical practice. He was first contacted in April 1963 by appellants' mother, Rena Truman, in connection with her second pregnancy. He continued to act as the primary physician for Mrs. Truman and her two children until March 1969. During this six-year period, Mrs. Truman not only sought his medical advice, but often discussed personal matters with him.

In April 1969, Mrs. Truman consulted Dr. Casey, a urologist, about a urinary tract infection which had been treated previously by Dr. Thomas. While examining Mrs. Truman, Dr. Casey discovered that she was experiencing heavy vaginal discharges and that her cervix was extremely rough. Mrs. Truman was given a prescription for the infection and advised to see a gynecologist as soon as possible. When Mrs. Truman did not make an appointment with a gynecologist, Dr. Casey made an appointment for her with a Dr. Ritter.

In October 1969, Dr. Ritter discovered that Mrs. Truman's cervix had been largely replaced by a cancerous tumor. Too far advanced to be removed by surgery, the tumor was unsuccessfully treated by other methods. Mrs. Truman died in July 1970 at the age of 30.

Appellants are Rena Truman's two children. They brought this wrongful death action against Dr. Thomas for his failure to perform a pap smear test on their mother. At the trial, expert testimony was presented which indicated that if Mrs. Truman had undergone a pap smear at any time between 1964 and 1969, the cervical tumor probably would have been discovered in time to save her life. There was disputed expert testimony that the standard of medical practice required a physician to explain to women patients that it is important to have a pap smear each year to "pick up early lesions that are treatable rather than having to deal with [more developed] tumor[s] that very often aren't treatable. . . ."[1]

Although Dr. Thomas saw Mrs. Truman frequently between 1964 and 1969, he never performed a pap smear test on her. Dr. Thomas testified that he did not "specifically" inform Mrs. Truman of the risk involved in any failure to undergo the pap smear test. Rather, "I said, 'You should have a pap smear.' We don't say by now it can be Stage Two [in the development of cervical cancer] or go through all of the different lectures about cancer. I think it is a widely known and generally accepted manner of treatment and I think the patient has a high degree of responsibility. We are not enforcers, we are advisors." However, Dr. Thomas' medical records contain no reference to any discussion or recommendation that Mrs. Truman undergo a pap smear test.

For the most part, Dr. Thomas was unable to describe specific conversations with Mrs. Truman. For example, he testified that during certain periods he "saw Rena very frequently, approximately once a week or so, and I am sure my opening remark was. 'Rena, you need a pap smear,'. . . I am sure we discussed it with her so often that she couldn't [have] fail[ed] to realize that we wanted her to have a complete examination, breast examination, ovaries, and pap smear." Dr. Thomas also testified that on at least two occasions when he performed pelvic examinations of Mrs. Truman she refused him permission to perform the test, stating she could not afford the cost. Dr. Thomas offered to defer payment, but Mrs. Truman wanted to pay cash.

Appellants argue that the failure to give a pap smear test to Mrs. Truman proximately caused her death. Two instructions requested by appellants described alternative theories under which Dr. Thomas could be held liable for this failure. First, they asked that the jury be instructed that it "is the duty of a physician to disclose to his patient all relevant information to enable the patient to make an informed decision regarding the submission to or refusal to take a diagnostic test. Failure of the physician to disclose to his patient all relevant information including the risks to the patient if the test is refused renders the physician liable for any injury legally resulting from the patient's refusal to take the test if a reasonably prudent person in the patient's position would not have refused the test if she had been adequately informed of all the significant perils." Second, they requested that the jury be informed that "as a matter of law . . . a physician who fails to perform a pap smear test on a female patient over the age of 23 and to whom the patient has entrusted her general physical care is liable for injury or death proximately caused by the failure to perform the test." Both instructions were refused.

The jury rendered a special verdict, finding Dr. Thomas free of any neg-

1. Dr. Thomas conceded at the trial that it is the accepted standard of practice for physicians in his community to recommend that women of child-bearing age undergo a pap smear each year. His records indicate that during the period in which he acted as Mrs. Truman's family physician he performed between 10 and 20 pap smears per month.

ligence that proximately caused Mrs. Truman's death. This appeal followed.

The central issue for this court is whether Dr. Thomas breached his duty of care to Mrs. Truman when he failed to inform her of the potentially fatal consequences of allowing cervical cancer to develop undetected by a pap smear.

In Cobbs v. Grant (1972) 8 Cal. 3d 229 [104 Cal. Rptr. 505, 502 P.2d 1], this court considered the scope of a physician's duty to disclose medical information to his or her patients in discussing proposed medical procedures. Certain basic characteristics of the physician-patient relationship were identified.

> "The first is that patients are generally persons unlearned in the medical sciences and therefore, except in rare cases, courts may safely assume the knowledge of patient and physician are not in parity. The second is that a person of adult years and in sound mind has the right, in the exercise of control over his own body, to determine whether or not to submit to lawful medical treatment. The third is that the patient's consent to treatment, to be effective, must be an informed consent. And the fourth is that the patient, being unlearned in medical sciences, has an abject dependence upon and trust in his physician for the information upon which he relies during the decisional process, thus raising an obligation in the physician that transcends arms-length transactions." Id., at p. 242.

In light of these factors, the court held that "as an integral part of the physician's overall obligation to the patient there is a duty of reasonable disclosure of the available choices with respect to proposed therapy and of the dangers inherently and potentially involved in each." (Id., at p. 243.) (1) The scope of a physician's duty to disclose is measured by the amount of knowledge a patient needs in order to make an informed choice. All information material to the patient's decision should be given. (Id., at p. 245.)

Material information is that which the physician knows or should know would be regarded as significant by a reasonable person in the patient's position when deciding to accept or reject the recommended medical procedure.

(2) Applying these principles, the court in *Cobbs* stated that a patient must be apprised not only of the "risks inherent in the procedure [prescribed, but also] the risks of a decision not to undergo the treatment, and the probability of a successful outcome of the treatment." (*Cobbs,* supra, 8 Cal. 3d at p. 243.) This rule applies whether the procedure involves treatment or a diagnostic test. On the one hand, a physician recommending a risk-free procedure may safely forego discussion beyond that necessary to conform to competent medical practice and to obtain the patient's consent. (See id., at pp. 244-245.) If a patient indicates that he or she is going to decline the risk-free test or treatment, then the doctor has the additional duty of advising of all material risks of which a reasonable person would want to be informed before deciding not to undergo the procedure. On the other hand, if the recommended test or

treatment is itself risky, then the physician should always explain the potential consequences of declining to follow the recommended course of action.

Nevertheless, Dr. Thomas contends that *Cobbs* does not apply to him because the duty to disclose applies only where the patient *consents* to the recommended procedure. He argues that since a physician's advice may be presumed to be founded on an expert appraisal of the patient's medical needs, no reasonable patient would fail to undertake further inquiry before rejecting such advice. Therefore, patients who reject their physician's advice should shoulder the burden of inquiry as to the possible consequences of their decision.

This argument is inconsistent with *Cobbs*. The duty to disclose was imposed in *Cobbs* so that patients might meaningfully exercise their right to make decisions about their own bodies. (*Cobbs,* supra, 8 Cal. 3d at pp. 240-241, 243.) The importance of this right should not be diminished by the manner in which it is exercised. Further, the need for disclosure is not lessened because patients reject a recommended procedure. Such a decision does not alter "what has been termed the 'fiducial qualities' of the physician-patient relationship," since patients who reject a procedure are as unskilled in the medical sciences as those who consent. (Id. at p. 246.) To now hold that patients who reject their physician's advice have the burden of inquiring as to the potential consequences of their decisions would be to contradict *Cobbs*. It must be remembered that Dr. Thomas was not engaged in an arms-length transaction with Mrs. Truman. Clearly, under *Cobbs,* he was obligated to provide her with all the information material to her decision.

Dr. Thomas next contends that, as a matter of law, he had no duty to disclose to Mrs. Truman the risk of failing to undergo a pap smear test because "the danger [is] remote and commonly appreciated to be remote." (*Cobbs,* supra, 8 Cal. 3d at p. 245.) The merit of this contention depends on whether a jury could reasonably find that knowledge of this risk was material to Mrs. Truman's decision.

The record indicates that the pap smear test is an accurate detector of cervical cancer. Although the probability that Mrs. Truman had cervical cancer was low, Dr. Thomas knew that the potential harm of failing to detect the disease at an early stage was death. This situation is not analogous to one which involves, for example, "relatively minor risks inherent in [such] common procedures" as the taking of blood samples. (*Cobbs,* supra, 8 Cal. 3d at p. 244.) These risks are not central to the decision to administer or reject the procedure. In contrast, the risk which Mrs. Truman faced from cervical cancer was not only significant, it was the principal reason why Dr. Thomas recommended that she undergo a pap smear.

Little evidence was introduced on whether this risk was commonly known. Dr. Thomas testified that the risk would be known to a reasonable person. Whether such evidence is sufficient to establish that there was no general duty to disclose this risk to patients is a question of fact for the jury. Moreover, even assuming such disclosure was not generally required, the circumstances in this case may establish that Dr. Thomas did have a duty to inform Mrs. Truman of the risks she was running by not undergoing a pap smear.

Dr. Thomas testified he never specifically informed her of the purpose of a pap smear test. There was no evidence introduced that Mrs. Truman was aware of the serious danger entailed in not undergoing the test. However, there was testimony that Mrs. Truman said she would not undergo the test on certain occasions because of its cost or because "she just didn't feel like it." Under these circumstances, a jury could reasonably conclude that Dr. Thomas had a duty to inform Mrs. Truman of the danger of refusing the test because it was not reasonable for Dr. Thomas to assume that Mrs. Truman appreciated the potentially fatal consequences of her conduct. Accordingly, this court cannot decide as a matter of law that Dr. Thomas owed absolutely no duty to Mrs. Truman to make this important disclosure that affected her life.

The instruction proposed by appellants was a modification of BAJI No. 6.11 (1975 rev.), which was adopted to describe a physician's duty of reasonable disclosure as established by this court in *Cobbs*. Appellants' instruction correctly indicated that a physician has a duty to disclose all material information to a patient. The instruction also stated that breach of this duty renders the physician liable for any "legally resulting [injury] . . . if a reasonably prudent person in the patient's position would not have refused the test if she had been adequately informed of all the significant perils."

The term "legally resulting" was defined for the jury in accordance with BAJI No. 3.75. The jury was instructed that a "proximate cause of an injury is a cause which, in natural and continuous sequence, produces the injury, and without which the injury would not have occurred." Obviously, this test could not be satisfied if the jury were to conclude that even given adequate disclosure Mrs. Truman would have refused to take the recommended test in time to save her life. Thus, the rejected instruction would have correctly indicated that satisfaction of the prudent person test for causation established in *Cobbs* was necessary but not sufficient for plaintiffs to recover. If the jury were to reasonably conclude that Mrs. Truman would have unreasonably refused a pap smear in the face of adequate disclosure, there could be no finding of proximate cause. Though awkwardly phrased, the rejected instruction accurately reflected the law and a theory of liability applicable to the facts of this case.

Refusal to give the requested instruction meant that the jury was unable to consider whether Dr. Thomas breached a duty by not disclosing the danger of failing to undergo a pap smear. Since this theory finds support in the record, it was error for the court to refuse to give the requested instruction. . . . If the jury had been given this instruction and had found in favor of the appellants, such a finding would have had support in the record before us. Reversal is therefore required. . . .

[T]he trial court refused to instruct the jury that "as a matter of law . . . a physician who fails to perform a Pap smear test on a female patient over the age of 23 and to whom the patient has entrusted her general physical care is liable for injury of death proximately caused by the failure to perform the test." In support of this instruction plaintiffs relied on the decision of the Supreme Court of Washington in Helling v. Carey (1974) 83 Wash. 2d 514 [519 P.2d 981, 67 A.L.R. 3d 175].

That decision involved a suit against two physicians specializing in opthalmology who *failed to recommend* a test for glaucoma. The court held as a matter of law that the exercise of due care required the administration of that test. That holding has no application to this case since the evidence presented showed that the physician recommended the appropriate test but failed to inform the patient of the risks entailed in refusing to follow his advice. The suggestion that a physician *must* perform a test on a patient, who is capable of deciding whether to undergo the proposed procedure, is directly contrary to the principle that it is the *patient* who must ultimately decide which medical procedures to undergo. Accordingly, the trial court did not err in refusing this instruction.

The judgment is reversed.

TOBRINER, J., MOSK, J., and NEWMAN, J., concurred.

CLARK, J. — I dissent.

The consent instruction demanded by plaintiffs will impose upon doctors the intolerable burden of having to explain diagnostic tests to healthy patients. To meet their new burden doctors will have to spend the greater part of their day not examining or treating patients, but explaining to them all information relevant to the purposes of diagnostic examinations and tests. Such burden is unreasonable, and the trial court properly refused the instruction. Further, the proposed instruction is erroneous because it is confusing. Counsel's failure to clarify the instruction at the trial court's request should preclude any claim of error. . . .

The burden of explaining the purposes of a pap smear and the potential risks in failing to submit to one may not appear to be great, but the newly imposed duty upon physicians created by today's majority opinion goes far beyond. The instruction requires disclosure of all "relevant information to enable the patient to make an informed decision regarding the submission to or refusal to take a diagnostic test." In short, it applies not only to pap smears, but to all diagnostic procedures allegedly designed to detect illness which could lead to death or serious complication if not timely treated.

Carried to its logical end, the majority decision requires physicians to explain to patients who have not had a recent general examination the intricacies of chest examinations, blood analysis, X-ray examinations, electrocardiograms, urine analyses and innumerable other procedures. In short, today's ruling mandates doctors to provide each such patient with a summary course covering most of his or her medical education. Most medical tests — like pap smears — are designed to detect illness which might prove fatal absent timely treatment. Explaining the purposes of each procedure to each such patient will obviously take hours if not days. . . .

Nothing in Cobbs v. Grant (1972) 8 Cal. 3d 229 [104 Cal. Rptr. 505, 502 P.2d 1] warrants imposition of such an onerous duty — to the contrary, that case expressly rejected any such duty. In *Cobbs,* a doctor performed risky ulcer surgery on a patient which resulted in severe complications. While the surgeon explained the nature of the operation to the patient, he did not discuss the inherent risks.

We pointed out that bodily intrusion is actionable either on the basis of battery or negligence unless the patient consents. (8 Cal. 3d at pp. 239-241.) The court reasoned that because patients ordinarily are unlearned in medical science, an adult of sound mind "in the exercise of control over his own body" has a right to determine for himself whether to submit to proposed medical treatment, and that consent to intrusion must be informed to be effective. (8 Cal. 3d at p. 242.) We held that the physician who ordinarily has superior knowledge had a "duty of reasonable disclosure of the available choices with respect to proposed therapy and of the dangers inherently and potentially involved in each." (8 Cal. 3d at pp. 242-243.)

In *Cobbs,* we expressly circumscribed the duty of the doctor, holding that a "mini-course in medical science is not required," that "there is no physician's duty to discuss the relatively minor risks inherent in common procedures, when it is common knowledge that such risks inherent in the procedure are of very low incidence," that as to common procedures "no warning" is "required as to the remote possibility of death or serious bodily harm," and that recovery would be permitted only if a "prudent person in the patient's position" adequately informed of the perils would have declined treatment. (8 Cal. 3d at pp. 244-245.)

Thus, *Cobbs* is not helpful to the majority because the duty of disclosure in that case was imposed to assure consent to the intrusion would be effective. When no intrusion takes place, no need for consent — effective or otherwise — arises. . . .

I would affirm the judgment.

RICHARDSON, J., and MANUEL, J., concurred.

NOTE ON THE PAPNICOLAOU TEST

(1) Perhaps the single most established screening test, the Pap test is nevertheless still surrounded by controversy. In 1988, after years of giving conflicting advice, the American Cancer Society, the American College of Obstetricians and Gynecologists (ACOG), the AMA, and the National Cancer Institute agreed on a uniform recommendation that women have three annual Pap smears beginning at age 18 or when they become sexually active. Thereafter, if the first three tests were all negative, then "at the discretion of their physicians" women could have the test less frequently.

Approximately 13,000 new cases of invasive cervical cancer develop annually in the U.S., with 7,000 deaths. Am. Med. News 45 (Feb. 5, 1988). Because of laboratory errors and false negatives, however, many physicians continue to recommend an annual Pap smear. It has been reported that

> some gynecologists also fear that they may be held liable if they advise a woman to wait three years between Pap tests and she subsequently develops cervical cancer. Mort Lebow of ACOG said, "Any doctor who is concerned about being sued will advise women to come in annually." Harold Kaminetzky (director of practice activities of ACOG) said about the new guidelines: "If you ask, 'How do we feel now that we have come to a compromise,' the answer is 'not as good as we used to feel.' We would like all women to have annual Pap smears, but we yielded because we think it is important that all organizations involved speak in the same voice. [Kolata, Medical Groups Reach Compromise on Frequency of Giving Pap Tests, N.Y. Times, Jan. 7, 1988 at B13]

(2) The cost/benefit analyses of Pap smears was one of the things that led to changing the recommendations on frequency of testing. One major study found that if women undergo 55 years of screening, from age 20 to 74, annual Pap smears would detect an additional 6 cancers in every 100,000 women. The cost would be $6 billion a year if every woman had the test annually; $2 billion if the test was done every three years. Should Medicaid pay for more Pap smears than are recommended by ACOG?

(3) Laboratories make frequent errors in reading Pap tests results, missing precancerous lesions in 20 to 40 percent of all cases. What should patients be told about this? What can they do about it? Bogdanich, The Pap Test Misses Much Cervical Cancer Through Labs' Errors, Wall St. J., Nov. 2, 1987, p.1 New medical technology itself may help alleviate this problem, but begs the question again of when its use should be legally required. A DNA probe for the strains of human papillomavirus (HPV) most commonly associated with cervical cancer is being developed as an adjunct (rather than a replacement) for the Pap smear. The presence of HPV is described as "circumstantial evidence of its complicity in carcinogenesis." "DNA Probes for Papillomavirus Strains Readied for Cervical Cancer Screening," 260 J.A.M.A. 2771 (1988). How should this new screening test be introduced into medical practice? Does it matter how much it costs?

3. INTRODUCING NEW SCREENING TESTS INTO MEDICAL PRACTICE

Elias & Annas, Routine Prenatal Screening

317 N. Engl. J. Med. 1407-1408 (1987)

Standards of medical practice have traditionally been set by physicians on the basis of their best judgment of what constitutes good patient care. This tradition is in danger. The structure of medical practice — factors such as cost containment, the profit motive, government regulations, fear of medical-malpractice suits, media hype, and risk-management schemes — may influence actual practice more than professional standards. Whether a prenatal screening test is offered may depend as much on the patient's health insurance and the physician's perception of possible legal liability as on the physician's view of the patient's welfare.

There is widespread ethical, legal, and medical agreement that prenatal screening must be preceded by counseling about its purposes and followed by counseling about its results and their implications. The patient's choice is the centerpiece of legitimate screening, and even when a screening test becomes "routine," what that means is not that it is routinely done, but that it is routinely made available to patients who may accept or reject it.

From the outset, screening of maternal serum alpha-fetoprotein levels to detect neural-tube defects has been controversial in the United States. In 1982, the American College of Obstetricians and Gynecologists (ACOG) took a position that we still believe is the responsible one:

> Maternal serum AFP screening should be implemented only when it can be performed within a coordinated system of care that contains all the requisite resources and facilities to provide safeguards essential for ensuring prompt, accurate diagnosis and appropriate follow through services. When such coordination and services are not possible, the risks and costs appear to outweigh the advantages and the program should not be implemented.

Nonetheless, with no stated justification other than Food and Drug Administration approval of commercial kits for the radioimmunoassay of alpha-fetoprotein, ACOG members in May 1985 received "an alert" from the College's Department of Professional Liability that stated in part: "It is . . . imperative that *every prenatal patient* be advised of the availability of this test and that your discussion about the test and the patient's decision with respect to the test be documented in the patient's chart" (emphasis added).

We (and others) have expressed the opinion that it is destructive for a professional medical association, dedicated to promoting sound medical practice, to permit its legal department to promulgate medical standards. The general rule is that "good medicine is good law" — physicians who follow "good and accepted medical standards" in their practice will be acting in a manner consistent with the general rule of "reasonable prudence" for physicians and thus will not be found negligent in a malpractice suit. If routine screening for alpha-fetoprotein has come of age, ACOG's scientific committees, not its legal-liability department, should so advise its members. The pernicious alternative is to have a health care system in which standards are set by lawyers, insurers, businessmen, and regulators, with the focus on the bottom line rather than on good patient care.

Asserting their proper leadership role, ACOG's scientific committees subsequently took the responsible course and reaffirmed their earlier stance on alpha-fetoprotein screening. ACOG will probably soon recommend that such screening be made available to all pregnant women as part of routine prenatal care.

Since 25 to 35 percent of all fetuses with Down's syndrome can also potentially be identified by alpha-fetoprotein screening, physicians will have to decide what if anything to tell patients when low levels of alpha-fetoprotein are found. ACOG has taken the position that the measurement of alpha-fetoprotein levels as a screening test for Down's syndrome is still investigational. We support this position, with the added recommendation that patients should be informed before they are screened of the reported association of low alpha-fetoprotein levels and Down's syndrome and about the test's current investigative status.

The issues involved in the use of ultrasonography to screen for Down's syndrome are similar to those involved in alpha-fetoprotein screening. In this issue of the Journal, Benacerraf et al.[8] report that in a selected group of women undergoing ultransonographic evaluation before genetic amniocentesis, they were able to identify fetuses with Down's syndrome on the basis of a thickened nuchal skin fold and relatively short femur. These investigators "would recommend amniocentesis if evidence of a thickened nuchal fold or a shortened femur was obtained sonographically in the second trimester . . . since the risk of Down's syndrome would warrant the procedure."

Does this imply that all pregnant women in the United Sates should now be screened during the second trimester for fetal Down's syndrome as well as other anomalies? The 1984 National Institutes of Health Consensus Conference on Diagnostic Ultrasound Imaging in Pregnancy concluded that "it is the consensus of the panel that ultrasound examination in pregnancy should be performed for a specific medical indication. The data on clinical efficacy and safety do not allow a recommendation for routine screening at this time." Thus, a physician should not be considered negligent for not screening all pregnant women. If and when routine screening is recommended (and its efficiency has yet to be demonstrated in a randomized clinical trial), it should be performed only with informed consent.

Even though "routine" ultrasonographic scanning is not the current standard of care in the United States, the reality is that an increasing number of women (the majority in some centers) are undergoing scanning for a wide variety of obstetrical indications. Once a patient is already undergoing scanning, are we now obliged to look specifically for a thickened nuchal skin fold and shortened femur? If so, should we follow the recommendation of Benacerraf et al. by offering amniocentesis if these findings are present? Although this report is intriguing, we urge clinicians to resist the temptation to introduce ultrasound screening for Down's syndrome into widespread practice

8. Benacerraf, Gelman, Frigoletto, Sonographic identification of second-trimester fetuses with Down's syndrome, 317 N. Engl. J. Med. 1371-1376 (1987).

before these findings are confirmed by others. Like screening for low alpha-fetoprotein levels, ultrasound screening must be considered investigational as a test for Down's syndrome. In this context, it is noteworthy that Toi et al. found that nuchal-skin thickening alone was present in a substantial proportion of chromosomally normal fetuses and that this sign could be created artificially by varying the angle of the transducer caudally from Reid's base line. This should not detract from the potential usefulness of this sign when the measurements are determined precisely and when it occurs in combination with a shortened femur. It does, however, underscore the point that serious errors can easily be made and that the skill of the sonographer is critical.

In the near future, we are likely to see the development of numerous genetic screening tests to predict disorders as widely varied as cystic fibrosis, a predisposition to cancer, Alzheimer's disease, and manic depression. If these tests are to do more good than harm, their careful validation will be essential, coupled with education of both practicing physicians and patients concerning their use. At this critical juncture, the medical profession must take the lead in ensuring that the welfare of individual patients remains the central concern in the setting of practice standards.

American College of Obstetricians and Gynecologists, Department of Professional Liability, Alert: Professional Liability Implications of AFP Tests

(May 1985)

Professional Liability Implications of AFP Tests

Now that alpha-fetoprotein (AFP) test kits have been approved by the Food and Drug Administration (FDA) and are becoming more widely available, some professional liability implications should be kept in mind.

It is now imperative that you investigate the availability of these tests in your area and familiarize yourself with the procedure, location and mechanism of the follow-up tests to screen for neural tube defects. It is equally imperative that every prenatal patient be advised of the availability of this test and that your discussion about the test and the patient's decision with respect to the test be documented in the patient's chart. This discussion should include the information you have discovered about the availability, location and mechanism of follow-up tests to screen for neural tube defects in the event of positive AFP test results.

The following ACOG publications should prove to be helpful in fully informing your patients about this test; ACOG Technical Bulletin, No. 67, October, 1982, "Prenatal Detection of Neural Tube Defects;" Patient Education Pamphlets P-010, "Neural Tube Defects," P-019, "Amniocentesis for Prenatal Diagnosis of Genetic Disorders," and P-023, "Genetic Disorders." As with all printed materials, it is important to make sure that the content described therein is commensurate with your mode of practice.

With the availability of prenatal testing for the rare but tragic circumstance of the birth of a child with a neural tube defect, it is important that patients be appropriately counseled. The physician who has fully discussed AFP tests and follow-up testing with his or her patients, who has let the patient make the decision, and who has documented it in the chart should be in the best possible defense position.

California Administrative Code, Provisions for Maternal Serum Alphaprotein Screening

Title 17, sec. 6527 (1986)

6527. CLINICIANS

(a) Clinicians shall provide or cause to be provided to all pregnant women in their care before the 140th day of gestation, or before the 126th day from conception, as estimated by medical history of clinical testing, information regarding the use and availability of prenatal screening for neural tube defects of the fetus. This information shall be in a format to be provided or approved by the Department and shall be given at the first prenatal visit and discussed with each pregnant woman.

(b) The provisions of subsection (a) shall not apply if the pregnant woman has completed more than 140 days of gestation or 126 days post conception, as estimated by the medical history or clinical testing, and this fact is entered in the medical record.

(c) Clinicians shall cause to be provided to all pregnant women who, after being provided with the information pursuant to subsection (a), voluntarily request prenatal screening for neural tube defects of the fetus, the opportunity, the circumstances of which are to be documented in the medical record, to read and sign an informed consent document in a format provided or approved by the Department [of Health Services].

(d) If the pregnant woman consents to testing, the clinician shall arrange for prenatal screening directly or by referral to another clinician by:

(1)fully and accurately completing all required specimen collection forms provided by the Department for this purpose;

(2) Collecting or arranging for the collection of an initial specimen.

(3) As soon as possible, but within 24 hours of collection, place or cause to be placed all initial and repeat specimens in the channel of transmittal to the designated AFP screening laboratory.

(e) AFP collection forms and kits supplied by the Department shall not be copied, printed, reproduced, acquired, purchased, substituted or distributed other than as specified for use in the AFP Screening Program. . . .

(g) For each woman in their care who was prenatally screened for neural tube defects of the fetus and who had an initial presumptive positive test, the clinician shall: Report on the form provided by the Department for this purpose, within 30 calendar days of the end of the pregnancy, the outcome of the pregnancy and status of each fetus, or infant resulting therefrom.

(h) The test results shall be confidential so that such information shall only be released with the knowledge and specific written consent of the woman tested. Persons authorized by the Department to conduct and monitor screening and to provide and monitor differential diagnostic followup services shall be provided information without necessity of specific written consent.

Notes on Prenatal and Neonatal Screening

(1) The complexities of all screening tests are well illustrated by MSAFP screening and include pre-test counseling, follow up to eliminate false positives, post-test counseling, and availability of effective interventions. Neural tube defects (NTDs) are genetic disorders that occur with an overall incidence of one or two for every 1000 live births in the United States. The two major types are anencephaly (lack of a brain) and spina bifida (a lesion on an incompletely closed spinal cord). Couples who have had a child with one of these conditions have a 2 to 3 percent risk of recurrence and account for 5 to 10 percent of all NTDs. The remaining 90 to 95 percent of NTDs occur in families without any prior medical history. This means that to be effective, a screening test for NTDs must be used routinely on all pregnant women. Alpha-fetoprotein is a major fetal serum protein secreted by the fetal kidneys and is normally present in amniotic fluid in measurable amounts. It may also, however, enter the amniotic fluid directly from exposed membrane surfaces on the fetus, as in anencephaly or open spina bifida. There is also an association between elevated levels of maternal serum alpha-fetoprotein (MSAFP) and NTDs; measuring second trimester concentration of MSAFP has been shown to be an effective means of identifying pregnant women who are at risk of having a fetus with an NTD.

Following counseling and the obtaining of informed consent, a blood sample is taken from the pregnant woman some time between sixteen and eighteen weeks of gestation, as calculated from the first day of the last menses. In patients who show an elevated MSAFP (approximately 5 percent of those screened), the test is repeated. If the second MSAFP level is again elevated, an ultrasonographic evaluation is advised to detect conditions other than NTDs, such as underestimation of gestational age, multiple pregnancies, fetal death or threatened spontaneous abortion, Rh disease, and certain rare congenital abnormalities that are also associated with elevated MSAFP. In less than half of this group (1 to 2 percent of the original number screened) no explanation for the elevated level is found, and an amniocentesis for amniotic fluid AFP is recommended. Approximately 5 to 10 percent of those undergoing amniocentesis show elevated AFP levels, the majority of which will be associated with NTDs. Properly administered, this series of tests detects 80 to 90 percent of all anencephalies and 63 to 90 percent of all open spina bifidas. It has also been shown that such testing may also detect 20 to 40 percent of all Down's syndrome fetuses. S. Elias & G.J. Annas, Reproductive Genetics and the Law, 106-109 (1987).

(2) "Wrongful birth" is a catch-all phrase used to describe, among other actions, those lawsuits brought by parents against physicians, testing laboratories, and others on the basis that their negligence deprived parents of their right to make an informed decision concerning pregnancy or childbirth. In prenatal diagnosis cases in which the physician neglects to inform the parents of the existence of a test applicable to their situation, or negligently performs the test, negligently fails to refer to a specialist who could perform the test, or negligently informs the couple about their risks of having an affected child, courts now almost universally permit the parents to sue their physician for depriving them of their right to make a decision about commencing or continuing a pregnancy. The rationale for permitting parents to recover damages in such a case is set forth in typical language by a Texas court:

> It is impossible for us to justify a policy which at once deprives the parents of information by which they could elect to terminate the pregnancy likely to produce a child with a defective body, a policy which in effect requires that the deficient embryo be carried to full gestation until the deficient child is born, and which policy then denies recovery from the tortfeasor of costs of treating and caring for the defects of the child. [Jacobs v. Theimer, 519 S.W.2d 846, 849 (Tex. 1975)]

See generally, Capron Tort Liability in Genetic Counseling, 79 Colum. L. Rev. 618 (1979); and President's Commission for the Study of Ethical Problems in Medicine and Biomedical and Behavioral Research, Screening and Counseling for Genetic Conditions (1983).

Although the majority of courts considering the issue have rejected it, there are a handful of states that have permitted the handicapped child to sue on its own behalf under the rubric of "wrongful life," at least where the child's impairment is so serious that a plausible argument can be made that it would have been better off had it never been born (for instance, Tay Sachs disease or polycystic kidney disease). Curlender v. Bio-Science Lab., 165 Cal. Rptr. 477 (Ct. App. 2d Dist. 1980) (Tay Sachs); Harbeson v. Parke-Davis, 656 P.2d 483 (Wash. 1983) (fetal hydanton syndrome); Procanik v. Cillo, 478 A.2d 755 (N.J. 1984) (German measles).

(3) Another group of screening tests involves newborns. By 1989, 48 states had enacted legislation governing newborn screening for a variety of disorders. Only three of these statutes clearly indicate that their screening program is voluntary, although a majority permit refusal on religious grounds. Twenty-two states require the blood sample used in screening to be obtained by the health care institution. One major issue is whether screening newborns for disorders like PKU or sickle cell disease should be mandatory or voluntary. On the one hand, to be effective for rare conditions (PKU, which if untreated can cause severe mental retardation, occurs in approximately 1 in 14,000 births) screening tests must be done for almost everyone in the reference group. On the other hand, voluntariness and free choice is a critical value in U.S. health care. Informed consent and education have always been seen as critical to the success of any mass screening effort, but we nonetheless use coercion in the newborn area. Perhaps it is time to give educated parental choice another try. As Daniel Callahan has argued: "It will mean taking the idea of free choice seriously, allowing parents to make their own choice without penalizing them socially for the choices they make. . . . Part of the very meaning of human community, I would contend, entails a willingness of society to bear the social costs of individual freedom." Callahan, Genetic Disease and Human Health, 4 Hastings Cent. Rep. 7, 9 (Aug. 1974). For an argument in favor of mandatory newborn screening, see Faden, Holtzman & Chwalaw, Parental Rights, Child Welfare and Public Health, 72 Am. J. Pub. Health 1396 (1982); and one in favor of parental choice, see Annas, Mandatory PKU Screening: The Other Side of the Looking Glass, 72 Am. J. Pub. Health 1401 (1982).

(4) The mapping and sequencing of the estimated 3 billion base pairs of the human genome (the 50,000 to 100,000 genes we are composed of) could make current genetic screening seem quaint and rudimentary. Theoretically, when the project is completed (in 10 to 20 years), one would be able to identify the gene sequences for such things as cancer, manic depression, intelligence, race, eye color, height, and so forth. Some, including the European Parliament, have urged caution in proceeding with this project because of the sad history of eugenics in the U.S. and Europe. Others, such as the Wall Street Journal, have urged full speed ahead, noting the potential great benefits to mankind and urging that solving the ethical problems before the scientific ones "is a formula for making no progress at all. . . . The Human Genome Initiative . . . may well invite attack from those who are fearful of or hostile to the future. It should also attract the active support of those willing to defend the future." Editorial, Chromosome Cartography, Wall St. J., March 16, 1989, p. A16 col.1. The genome project raises not just the screening issues currently confronted by MSAFP screening, but also issues of eugenics and defining human "normalcy." The U.S. Congress's Office of Technology Assessment illustrates how our future may be played out in its 1988 Report:

> Human mating that proceeds without the use of genetic data about the risks of transmitting diseases will produce greater mortality and medical costs than if carriers of potentially deleterious genes are alerted to their status and encouraged to mate with noncarriers or to use artificial insemination or other reproductive strategies. . . . New technologies for identifying traits and altering genes [such as embryo biopsy and gene therapy] make it possible for eugenic goals to be achieved through technological as opposed to social control. [U.S. Congress, Office of Technology Assessment, Mapping Our Genes — The Genome Projects: How Big, How Fast?, 1988 at 84.]

See also, Annas, Who's Afraid of the Human Genome?, 19 Hastings Cent. Rep. 19 (Aug. 1989), and McKusick, Mapping and Sequencing the Human Genome, 320 N. Engl. J. Med. 910 (1989). For an in-depth historical view of the role eugenics has played in Western medicine, with special attention to the U.S. influence on Nazi physicians, see R. Proctor, Racial Hygiene (1988). The Human Genome Project is biology's first megaproject. It is instructive to contrast it to two of the largest scientific projects in other areas: the Manhattan Project (physics) and the Apollo Moon Project (engineering). See R. Rhodes, The Making of the Atomic Bomb (1986), and W. McDougall, The Heavens and the Earth (1985). If one was concerned about the potential impact of mapping and sequencing the human genome on society, what steps could be taken now to help predict and channel that impact?

Notes on Birth Technology

(1) Technology does not just change what we can do, it changes how we think. Unlike many other technologies, medical technology tends to change not only the way we think about medicine, but the way in which we think about ourselves. It influences, for example, how we think about an "average life span," how we think about death and its definition, and even how we think about life itself. Some of the most spectacular examples are in the area of human reproduction. Effective contraception changed the way we viewed the roles of the sexes, as well as the way we viewed sex and reproduction. Safe and effective methods of abortion helped shape society's view on the propriety of making abortion illegal. The framework of Roe v. Wade itself is technologically based and quite unintentionally and perhaps unpredictably has been interpreted (wrongly we believe) by many as granting the postviable fetus the right not to be intentionally harmed by its mother. See discussion in Symposium on Reproductive Rights, 13 Nova. L. Rev. 319-669 (1989).

An examination of the technology used in childbirth may seem a bit far afield in a chapter on medical technology. But it is worth recalling that there are more than 4 million births in the U.S. annually; and based on 1983 data, the most recent data available, the three most common surgical procedures are related to human reproduction as well: (1) cesarean section (809,000);

(2) hysterectomy (673,000); and (3) diagnostic dilation and curettage of the uterus (632,000). In studies that count abortion as a surgical procedure (as it should be) it is the most common one performed, at approximately 1.5 million abortions annually in the U.S. Accordingly, any analysis that ignored the legal issues involved in "high-tech" human reproduction would be incomplete. It should also be noted, however, that even rare technological procedures can shape the way we think about ourselves and the proper role of the law. For example, in vitro fertilization (IVF) and embryo transfer (ET) have made it possible to separate the genetic and gestational mother and thus have made it possible for children to have five separate parents: a genetic and social father, and a genetic, gestational, and social mother. We have just begun to appreciate the effects this technology will have on our understanding of such concepts as fundamental as "motherhood," to say nothing about effects on custody, adoption, inheritance, and child support obligations. The new reproductive technologies will not be dealt with here. For two diverse views on how the law should shape their use see: Robertson, Embryos, Families and Procreative Liberty: The Legal Structure of the New Reproduction, 59 S. Cal. L. Rev. 939 (1986), and Elias & Annas, Social Policy Consideration in Noncoital Reproduction, 255 J.A.M.A. 62 (1986). On a non-technological reproductive method, surrogate motherhood, see Matter of Baby M, 537 A.2d 1227 (N.J. 1988); and symposium issue on Surrogate Motherhood, Law, Medicine & Health Care (Fall, 1988). And see generally, Office of Technology Assessment, Infertility: Medical and Social Choices (OTA-BA-358; May, 1988).

(2) It is universally acknowledged that the U.S. rate of cesarean sections is too high, perhaps twice as high as it should be, and that steps must be taken to bring it down. The rate of cesarean sections has continued to rise approximately 1 percent of total births every year in the U.S. for the past 15 years, and no change is in sight. During this time it has gone from approximately 10 percent of total births to 25 percent of total births in 1988. Among other things, the 1986 average cost of an uncomplicated cesarean was $4270, according to the Health Insurance Association of America. Electronic fetal monitoring seems to increase the number of cesarean sections and has a high false positive rate. On the other hand, it has been demonstrated that a strict hospital-based protocol can reduce the cesarean section rate to about 11 percent in a public hospital. Myers & Gleicher, A Successful Program to Lower Cesarean-Section Rates, 319 N. Engl. J. Med. 1511 (1988). Nonetheless, others continue to worry about the impact on the safety of the child, arguing that neonatologists need to be involved in any major changes in childbirth management. Battaglia, Reducing the Cesarean-Section Rate Safely, 319 N. Engl. J. Med. 1540, 1541 (1988). Whatever one's view on the proper use of fetal monitoring, there does seem to be agreement that "[t]he tools at the obstetrician's disposal for assessing fetal well being during labor are inadequate. The promise of such major technological advances as continuous electronic monitoring of the fetal heart rate and fetal-scalp blood sampling have

not been fulfilled . . . for low-risk cases, there is yet no proof of the overall value of such monitoring. . . ." Freidman, The Obstetrician's Dilemma: How Much Fetal Monitoring and Cesarean Section is Enough? , 315 N. Engl. J. Med. 641, 642 (1986). The American College of Obstetricians and Gynecologists is moving toward overturning its longstanding policy in favor of routine fetal monitoring in view of studies that show it is not useful in routine childbirth. Nonetheless, many obstetricians insist they will continue to use the monitors for medicolegal reasons. As one put it, "in the current obstetrical climate, every patient is approached as a potential litigant. . . . The insanity is that we spend our money on technology we don't need, but we don't pay for basic prenatal care for poor women, something that we know produces healthier babies." Lewin, Despite Criticism, Fetal Monitors Are Likely to Remain in Wide Use, N.Y. Times, March 27, 1988, at 24.

(3) One group of researchers report:

> The forces driving the increasing rate of cesarean childbirth in the U.S. are not well understood. Much discussion has centered around medicolegal issues. However, the 1980 consensus conference concluded that, "Although commonly cited, there is no evidence that fear of litigation and the possible consequent practice of defensive medicine is a major cause of the increased cesarean birth rate." Though formal evidence is lacking, the perception that concern about litigation tilts borderline cases toward abdominal delivery appears to have become increasingly widespread over the last six years. . . . Recently a call was made for the increased use of committee reviews of institutional cesarean birth rates. However, the American College of Obstetricians and Gynecologists survey shows that cesarean delivery rates are not lower in the presence of committee audits of cesarean deliveries. Another strategy, which 43 percent of hospitals are apparently using, is to require mandatory consultation prior to doing a primary cesarean delivery. Cesarean delivery rates adjusted for hospital size were 4 percent lower among these hospitals than in those without such a policy. [Shiono, Fielden, McNellis et al., Recent Trends in Cesarean Birth and Trial of Labor Rates in the United States, 257 J.A.M.A. 494 (1987).]

Public Citizen Health Research Group has charged that about half (455,000 of the 906,000 cesarean sections performed in 1986) of all cesarean sections performed in the U.S. are unnecessary. The group alleged that one major reason is that cesarean sections are more remunerative for obstetricians. Dr. Norbert Gleicher, chairman of OB at Mount Sinai Hospital in Chicago commented that he thought 10 percent of total was probably the right number. He thinks fetal monitoring is a main cause because: "Doctors don't know how to interpret the tracings. They overinterpret and misinterpret them." Friedman, Consumer Group Calls Half of Nation's Cesareans Unnecessary, Medical World News, Dec. 28, 1987, 70, 71. He and others advocate a procedure-neutral payment rate for deliveries. Reportedly, the Foundation Health Plan of New Mexico and an affiliate HMO in California are experimenting with a payment plan that pays approximately $1000 for a vaginal delivery; $1100 for a cesarean section, and $1,250 for a vaginal delivery following a cesarean. Id. at 70-71.

(4) At least one plaintiff's attorney has suggested that all women be given the option of having a cesarean section to avoid "unpredictable disaster." Does this idea make any sense? See Feldman & Freiman, Prophylactic Cesarean Section at Term?, 312 N. Engl. J. Med. 1264 (1985). It has also been suggested that the decision whether or not to have a cesarean section can be made just like the decision to purchase particular products: that is, as if patients and physicians were rational economic actors attempting to "maximize their utility" through voluntary transactions in which each party balances marginal economic costs against marginal health. Enthoven, Health Plan: The Only Practical Solution to the Soaring Costs of Medical Care, (1980); and Havighurst & Blumstein, Coping with Quality/Cost Trade-Offs in Medical Care: The Role of PSROs, 70 N.W.U.L. Rev. (1975).

J. Katz, The Silent World of Doctor and Patient

175-184 (1984)

The history of the treatment of breast cancer illustrates some of the problems that uncertainty about medical knowledge has posed for decision making between physicians and patients throughout the ages. I shall present its early history briefly in order to make the point that, until recently, physicians had to profess certainty about the treatment of breast cancer because they possessed neither the experimental nor the intellectual tools to distinguish between certainty and uncertainty. Every proposed treatment, however valuable or silly, found its enthusiastic adherents. If it eventually fell into disrepute because of lack of any success, it was quickly replaced by another method, touted with equal certainty. . . .

Breast cancer was probably known to the ancient Egyptians and surely was known to the Greeks, who treated it by surgery, caustic agents, and a variety of medicines — mineral, vegetable, and animal. Physicians employed many treatment modalities throughout the ages — bleeding, dieting, purging, using lead plates to compress the tumor, and applying goat dung, with each treatment being advocated in the belief that it was the best. William Clowes, physician to Queen Elizabeth I, resorted to exorcism, the laying on of royal hands, a venerable tradition dating back to Edward the Confessor whose "royal touch" was considered curative. . . .

The modern approach to treatment of breast cancer can be divided into two phases. The first began in the late 1860s, when radical surgery emerged as the treatment of choice and, until most recently, was accepted without question by the majority of physicians. Even though William S. Halsted was not the first to propose it, his surgical technique — the en bloc removal of the entire breast, the underlying chest muscles, and the lymph nodes in the armpit — a treatment which his zeal brought to preeminence, deservedly bears his name. In the United States, it was adopted by the majority of practicing surgeons. His 1894 paper, optimistically entitled, "The Results of Operations for the Cure of Cancer of the Breast Performed at The Johns Hopkins Hospital from June, 1889 to January, 1894," electrified the medical community and quickly transformed the prevailing pessimism about treatment into optimism.

How could it have been otherwise? The one-sentence opening paragraph of Halsted's paper read: "In 50 cases operated upon by what we call the complete method we have been able to trace only three local recurrences." This most remarkable achievement, never duplicated, led Halsted to conclude his paper by observing dispassionately that he could understand why, until then, many physicians had despaired of breast cancer's treatability and thus had not referred their patients to surgeons. . . .

On the basis of the most limited data, Halsted's sweeping claims about the defeat of an ancient foe were accepted by the medical community. It is true that Halsted published his results at a time when medical science was still in its infancy; however, the scientific method had already begun to exert its influence over the practice of medicine. Academic physicians in particular had become sensitized to the need not only to subject innovative treatments to carefully controlled studies but also to await confirmation of their findings by other investigators. Yet, Halsted's claims were accepted despite the fact that by that time physicians were well aware that the history of medical practices was studded with instances of harm done to patients in the darkness of deeply held, unquestioned professional beliefs. For example, the story of Benjamin Rush, a signer of the Declaration of Independence and an eminent physician of his time, was well known. Convinced of the efficacy of bloodletting and purges for the treatment of a great many medical maladies, Rush employed them with abandon during the plague epidemic, killing patients who would have survived if left untreated. Rush lived prior to the modern scientific era, but Halsted was practicing in a different age. In saying this, I do not question Halsted's considerable accomplishments. I only wish to highlight his certainty about the correctness of his recommendations. Recall that he wrote, after a long history of dismal failure to cure breast cancer, "we can state positively that cancer of the breast is a curable disease."

This episode from the age of Halsted is a not uncommon example of how hard it is for human beings to live with doubt and uncertainty and of their proclivity to embrace certainty instead. The widespread and enthusiastic acceptance of Halsted's findings by most of his fellow physicians, even after repeated failures to cure breast cancer by radical mastectomy, demonstrates how readily any awareness of uncertainty succumbs to venerable authority and orthodoxy. These powerful defenses against awareness of uncertainty continue to rule professional practices. Sir Geoffrey Keynes appreciated the commanding influence of orthodoxy and authority on professional practice.

In a remarkable paper, "Carcinoma of the Breast — The Unorthodox Views" (1954), he used words rarely spoken by a surgeon:

> Orthodoxy in surgery is like orthodoxy in other departments of the mind — it starts as a tentative belief in some particular course of action, but later begins almost to challenge comparison with a religion. It comes to be held as a passionate belief in the absolute rightness of that particular view. A dissentient view is regarded as a criminal subversion of the truth, and the holder is sometimes exposed to slander and abuse. . . . None of us have been burnt at the stake, but feelings have run pretty high. . . .

Lewis Thomas, a physician deeply committed to the practice of scientific medicine, has called attention to physicians' increasing capacity in the light of modern science to be more aware of their ignorance and uncertainty:

> The only solid piece of scientific truth about which I feel totally confident is that we are profoundly ignorant about nature. Indeed, I regard this as a major discovery of the past hundred years of biology. . . . It is this sudden confrontation with the depth and scope of ignorance that represents the most significant contribution of twentieth-century science to the human intellect. *We are, at last, facing up to it.* In earlier times, we either pretended to understand how things worked or ignored the problem or simply made up stories to fill the gaps.

Thomas may be too optimistic in his belief that professionals now do not make "up stories to fill the gaps." At least, too few face up to medicine's uncertainty. But I agree that in today's age of science the means for facing up to our ignorance exist as they never did before. Yet it is precisely this potential for greater clarity of what is known and unknown that has not been sufficiently heeded in medical practice in general, and in decision making between physicians and patients in particular.

Physicians do not have to disregard uncertainty so thoroughly. Thomas, aware of both the pitfalls and the potentialities of science, points doctors in the right direction:

> The scientific method is guesswork, the making up of stories. The difference between this and other imaginative works of the human mind is that science is then obliged to find out whether the guesses are correct, the stories true. Curiosity drives the enterprise and the open acknowledgment of ignorance. [W]e know very little about nature and we understand even less.
>
> Starting with ourselves, and the life immediately around us, we have lots of homework to do, lots of pride to swallow, lots more ignorance to face, some of it only sensed out of the corner of the eye. . . .

An appreciation of medicine's vast ignorance could make physicians more cautious about claims to have found *the* answer to the treatment of any disease, particularly during the early stages of the discovery of a new and "promising" therapy. Assuming that pride can be swallowed, such an appreciation also permits making distinctions between ignorance and knowledge. A look at a second, more recent episode in the treatment of breast cancer may clarify what I have in mind. . . . In the early 1930s, doubts began to be raised about the premise that breast cancer spreads by continuous, centrifugal permeation. Injection studies with contrast media had led to inferences that the spread of breast cancer is often discontinuous in space, that it is disseminated to outlying lymph nodes by cancer emboli and to other areas by way of blood channels. These findings were largely disregarded by practicing surgeons, however. Moreover, other studies suggested that improvements in cure rates were more a function of earlier detection than of the extensiveness of the surgical procedures employed. (It was soon learned, however, that early detection was not *the* answer either.) These and other considerations moved a few surgeons, like Sir Geoffrey Keynes of England and Oliver Cope and George Crile, Jr. of the United States, to abandon radical surgical treatments.

Their decision was aided by advances in radiation therapy which led them to combine conservative surgery with radiation treatment. Yet for a long time their voices were crying in a hostile wilderness in which mutilating surgery continued to be inflicted on countless women. Indeed, their colleagues often shunned and severely censured them for their unorthodox views. More important, the two groups divided into hostile camps, as the unusually acrimonious debates, carried on in scientific journals between Anglem, an advocate of radical surgery, and Crile, a champion of more conservative treatment, so clearly demonstrate. Anglem and Crile bombarded each other with scientific data, often interpreting the same scientific studies differently, and they unwaveringly clung to the correctness of their respective positions. Rabid convictions do not lend themselves to the admission of uncertainty. Thus it made little difference to either of them that Bernard Fisher, another authority on breast cancer, has asserted, and I believe correctly, that we simply do not know which treatment is best. Why his conclusion, so true in theory, remains so unacceptable in practice, even today, requires explanation.

If one contemplates the current status of the treatment of breast cancer, it becomes apparent that one has to think about the problem of uncertainty of medical knowledge in more discriminating ways. Since the turn of this century, we have acquired bits and pieces of knowledge about the vagaries of breast cancer and its response to treatment, as well as the intellectual and experimental tools to discriminate better between what we know, what is still conjectural, and what is still shrouded in ignorance. For example, in the 1980s we think we know that, from its beginnings, breast cancer is generally a systematic disease and that complex, as yet poorly understood host-tumor interactions affect the progression of the disease. We also seem to know that even with very early discovery and treatment, some breast cancers will lead to death sooner or later, and that others respond favorably even when treated after considerable delay. We also seem to know that surgery, from its most limited to its most extensive varieties, as well as radiation therapy, chemotherapy, hormone therapy, and immunotherapy in various combinations and permutations of their own, and with surgery have therapeutic impact. Moreover, we seem to know that biological and genetic factors have a considerable impact on breast cancer control and cure, and that therefore any of these treatments can be detrimental, most likely by interfering with delicate tumor-host balances. Despite all these and other problems, we also seem to know that some treatment is better than none.

What we do not know, however, is which treatment is best. Most likely any or all of these theories of cure will be modified or discarded over time. They attest to our vast ignorance about the big picture but they also attest to our knowing a great many significant bits and pieces about the treatment of breast cancer.

Of importance to decision making between physician and patient is the fact that, if they are so inclined, physicians now can make clearer distinctions between what they know and do not know. Thus, they can offer patients a variety of treatment options based on pieces of evidence from available clinical data. *There is no certainty about the available knowledge, but its uncertainty can be specified.* This crucial point holds true for the treatment not only of breast cancer but for many other diseases as well.

Notes on Breast Cancer

(1) It is estimated that approximately 120,000 U.S. women develop breast cancer annually, and approximately 40,000 die of the disease. Breast cancer will develop in approximately one of every 11 U.S. women, or about 9 percent. In a 1979 survey, over three-fourths of the respondent American women "thought that cancer was the greatest health concern of women today, and nearly half of them mentioned breast cancer specifically." In spite of the emphasis on early detection, "over 90 percent of all breast cancers are still detected by examination by the women themselves." Wertheimer et al., Increasing the Effort Toward Breast Cancer Detection, 255 J.A.M.A. 1311 (1986).

Since 1979, more than a dozen states have passed informed consent statutes that require that women with breast cancer be told of "all medically acceptable treatment alternatives." A 1981 study commissioned by the American College of Surgeons on the frequency of lumpectomies in Massachusetts and California (states with statutes) and New York (a state without a statute) concluded that the number of lumpectomies was directly related to informed consent statutes. Figures for wedge excisions of tumors under 1 cm. as a percentage of total were as follows: national average, 4.8 percent; Massachusetts (2 year old law), 17.9 percent; California (1 year old law) 10 percent; and New York (no law) 2 percent. Dabice & Cordes, Informed

Consent Heralds Change in Breast Treatment, Medical News, Nov. 11, 1985, 1, 4.

(2) As Katz chronicles, medical history is filled with uncertainty. But it is also filled with fashion, and it is well recognized by clinicians that both treatments and disease come into and go out of fashion, much like clothes. See, for instance, Burnum, Medical Practice a la Mode: How Medical Fashions Determine Medical Care, 317 N. Engl. J. Med. 1220 (1987):

> Diseases of fashion exert a strong influence on medical practice — on what we and the public think about disease and what is treated. These are conditions that epidemically gain the medical limelight and in their time receive an inordinate amount of media and public attention. In the 1930s people were afflicted wholesale by "an acid condition," and in the 1940s by a lack of acid, which we treated with hydrochloric acid. Hypoglycemia soon swept the country and continues to ebb and flow in popularity. Chronic mononucleosis had its day and is currently having a scientific renaissance . . . we are predisposed to diagnose, and our patients to worry about, the diseases that are in the news, popularized, and impressed on our minds. As an accompanying phenomenon, entrepreneurial specialists and clinics for the various bandwagon diseases often spring up to capitalize on medical chic: for example, whether scientifically justified or not, hundreds of osteoporosis clinics are in the offing. Cousins to diseases of fashion are media-sown disease panics; for example, fear of saccharin, of reserpine, or of coffee's causing cancer, or an obsessional dread of having colon cancer, AIDS, or Alzheimer's disease.
>
> Consider the irony: as professed scientists and proponents of Cartesian doubt, we physicians find ourselves, like lemmings, episodically and with a blind infectious enthusiasm pushing certain diseases and treatments primarily because everyone else is doing the same. This is unacceptable. . . . Which shall it be, science or fashion? Let each decide.

Since there still is no effective treatment for breast cancer, fads continue to arise. A newer development, however, is the publication of suggested treatments in the newspapers *before* their rationale is published in the medical literature. On May 21, 1988, for example, the New York Times (and other major newspapers) ran a front page story entitled Cancer Drug Therapy Urged for all after Breast Surgery. The article read in part:

> In a major change of longstanding policy, the National Cancer Institute is urging that all women who have breast cancer should have chemotherapy or hormonal therapy after the initial surgery, even if there is no evidence that the cancer has spread. The advice is based on three still unpublished studies. The institute had previously said there was no reason to administer drug therapy to most women who had surgery for early breast cancer in which there is no sign the cancer has spread to the lymph nodes. . . . In an unusual effort to reach physicians quickly, the institute sent a letter to 13,000 cancer specialists this week, rather than waiting months for data from the three studies to be published in medical journals . . . the studies used three different treatments . . .

women and their doctors still will have to decide which drug regimen to use. . . .

The original letter, drafted in haste, contained errors, and a second letter had to be sent. Is this type of "alert" reasonable? See correspondence on "The Cancer Alert," 319 N. Engl. J. Med. 948-49 (1988), and the four scientific articles and five editorials published on them in New England Journal of Medicine (Feb. 23, 1989).

(3) One of the most heated continuing controversies involves the use of mammography screening to find breast cancer. There is virtual unanimity that routine screening (once a year) by mammography together with regular breast exams and a careful physical examination will benefit women in terms of survival from breast cancer. For instance, Eddy, Hasselblad, McGivney & Hendee, The Value of Mammography Screening in Women Under Age 50 Years, 259 J.A.M.A. 1512 (1988). But it is thought that "existing evidence does not justify the conclusion that failure of an individual physician to recommend or cover mammography is bad medical practice, or constitutes malpractice." Id. and Bailar, Mammography Before Age 50 Years?, 259 J.A.M.A. 1548 (1988). What does this mean? Can it be that it is "accepted" and "recommended" medical practice to provide routine breast cancer screening to women over the age of 50, but not negligent to fail to advise women to have a mammogram who fall into this age group? What about women younger than 40? Who should make the screening decision for them? A National Cancer Institute study, for example, indicates that annual mammography can have as important a life saving benefit for women under 50 as it has demonstrated for women over 50. Brody, Study Finds Women in 40's Benefit from Mammograms, N.Y. Times, Sept. 21, 1988, at B5. See also, Controversy Over Mammography Screening, 297 Brit. Med. J. 932 (1988).

(4) As of January 1, 1986, Colorado physicians covered by the state's physician-created medical malpractice company (COPIC Insurance Co.) who are involved in breast cancer malpractice claims face surcharges up to $25,000 if they failed to observe the American Cancer Society's mammography screening guidelines in treating the patient. Failure to Diagnose Breast Cancer Hot Topic, American Medical News, Feb. 28, 1986, at 3. Is this an effective way to change physician behavior? Denver risk management consultant Robert S. Britain, M.D., notes, "We don't care if there's unanimous opinion on whether the lawsuit is good or bad. What we care about is whether we're going to lose in court, and we already know that we'll lose a case if a physician doesn't follow the ACS standards in such cases." He continues, "Doctors should get their patients to sign a note saying, 'You advised me to have a mammogram.' Whether or not they get one is their own business." (Id. at 19).

Many have argued that it would be impossible to institute large scale mammography screening in this country because of the lack of trained radiologists and technicians. For instance, Hall, Screening Mammography — Potential

Problems on the Horizon, 314 N. Engl. J. Med. 53 (1986); Skrabanek, False Premises and False Promises of Breast Cancer Screening, Lancet, Aug. 10, 1985, 316; and Witcombe, A License for Breast Cancer Screening?, 296 Brit. Med. J. 909 (1988). Nonetheless, at least four states, California, Maryland, Massachusetts and Texas require some insurance policies to cover mammograms. How should such a decision be made?

What steps should a physician who works for an HMO that will not provide mammograms for its patients consistent with the ACS guidelines take if the physician believes a mammogram is indicated?

(5) Breast cancer is a major topic of press coverage and has even been the cover story on national news magazines. U.S. News and World Report, for example, ran a cover story on "How to Beat Breast Cancer" on July 11, 1988. The article strongly supported mammography screening but admitted that when it came to treatment, little was known: "The fact is that since so much of breast cancer treatment is experimental, no one really knows the bottom line about what benefits whom. Three well-qualified doctors may suggest three completely different treatment plans. So no woman diagnosed with breast cancer can afford to let her doctor do all the deciding." (Id. at 56).

The problems of informed consent to breast cancer treatment are perhaps best explored in Marcia Lynch's poem Peau D'Orange:

We barter the difference
between black and gray
"Surgery, radiation or
death," you say and leave
the decision to me,

while I insist you are the gods
I believed in as a child.
I prayed you to pull magic
out of your black leather bags
to wave away the rattling
in my bones.

I accept your calling
my breast an orange peel,
let you lay hands on this fruit
my mother said no man
must touch. In this disease
there is no sin.

If you lift the chill
that unravels my spine,
I will send you stars,
from the Milky Way,
send them spinning down,
dancing a thousand-fold. Please
let me grow old.

(6) Men do not escape the cancer dilemmas. Testicular cancer is one of the curable ones, but the treatment men have been receiving may have been much more vigorous than required. Testicular cancer accounts for only about 1 percent of all male malignancies, but is the most common cancer among males aged 15 to 35 years. Until 1978, physicians used a two year course of chemotherapy for testicular cancer. Then a study showed that four months of treatment was just as effective. In 1988, another study showed that this could be reduced 25 percent, to just three months. This may seem trivial, but the chemotherapy is very debilitating. As Nicholas Vogelzang of the University of Chicago noted, "For a patient, the last month of chemotherapy may be devastating. . . . Being able to eliminate it may allow a much higher quality of life." The American Cancer Society estimates that 5600 U.S. males will be diagnosed with testicular cancer annually, and 350 will die of the disease. Study Finds Chemotherapy Can be Cut by 25% for Testicle Cancer, N.Y. Times, May 25, 1988, at A18.

C. Technology Assessment

As Professor John E. Wennberg has noted over and over, the same person with the same disease will be treated radically differently by physicians in different parts of the country. For example,

> A Bostonian is about twice as likely to undergo a carotid endarterectomy as a New Havenite; for coronary bypass operations the risk is the reverse. New Haven residents experience substantially higher rates for hysterectomies and back surgery, while the rates for knee and hip replacements are much greater for Bostonians. Across a wide spectrum of common acute and chronic conditions such as back pain, gastroenteritis, pneumonia, and diabetes, the incidence of hospitalization is much greater for residents of Boston than for those of New Haven, even though the populations are very similar in demographic characteristics related to the need for care. These overall differences in utilization translate into large differences in expense to third-party insurers. For example, in 1982, the Medicare program's outlays were $2647 per enrollee for Boston residents while the average expenditure in New Haven county was $1561. [The Paradox of Appropriate Care, 258 J.A.M.A. 2568 (1987).]

Which patients are getting the "right" amount of surgery and the "right" application of medical technology? How can we get physicians to agree on what "right" means, and how can patients meaningfully participate in treatment decisions?

What technologies should be available to everyone under any reasonable system of national health insurance? What technologies are so expensive that they should not be used or pursued? What technologies are so useless that they should be discarded? The general goal of technology assessment is to provide a framework for decreasing or containing health care costs while maintaining or improving the quality of health care services. The goal can be graphically pictured by dividing technologies according to their costs and medical benefits in a fourfold table:

High Cost High Benefit	Low Cost High Benefit
High Cost Low Benefit	Low Cost Low Benefit

We may easily conclude that procedures with high costs and low benefits should be eliminated (or at least not developed) and that interventions with high benefits and low costs should be pursued. Most problems are likely to arise in how to evaluate procedures in the other two boxes. Although we have flirted with potential mechanisms, there is no standard or accepted way to assess new medical technologies in the U.S. today. As previously discussed, randomized clinical trials are the only way to see if a new technology is beneficial — and in the absence of such tests, expert panels may have to be relied upon. But even RCTs cannot answer questions relating to cost.

Ultimately additional issues, such as quality of life concerns, equity of access, and impact on social values, must be considered. The free market appears to make these choices easy — just let people buy what they want. Since no one is likely to buy high-cost, low-benefit procedures, such procedures will die out. In fact, however, medical care does not respond to market incentives, and sick people, especially those who are dying, will often agree to purchase "everything" that holds out even a remote hope of benefit, no matter what the cost. See, for instance, supra A(2).

In 1976 Congress asked the Office of Technology Assessment to make recommendations about "existing medical practices to determine whether a reasonable justification should be provided before costly new medical technologies and procedures are put into general use." Perry, Technology Assessment: Continuing Uncertainty, 314 N. Engl. J. Med. 240 (1986). OTA's report made a strong case for establishing formal mechanisms for technology assessment and played a role in NIH's creation in 1977 of the consensus-development program, and the establishment of the National Center for Health Care Technology. This Center, however, was allowed to expire in 1981. A different mechanism was created in HHS (the National Center for

Health Services Research and Health Care Technology Assessment) in 1984 to do technology assessments, although funding levels have remained low. There have also been initiatives by the Institute of Medicine. The current situation is well summed up by Seymour Perry,

> [T]he possibility of a coherent system for technology assessment in this country and support for it seems uncertain [although] there appear to be wide recognition and acceptance that overall, the nation's capability for technology assessment must be strengthened if we are to make rational (both medical and economic) decisions about health care technologies, particularly in the current environment, in which there is almost an obsession with reducing health care costs and relatively little attention to the quality of health care. [Id. at 243.]

1. NATIONAL INSTITUTES OF HEALTH (NIH) CONSENSUS CONFERENCES

Perry, The NIH Consensus Development Program: A Decade Later

317 N. Engl. J. Med. 485, 486-488 (1987)

The NIH proposed the use of "technical consensus development" with respect to "the clinical significance of new findings; whether validation for safety and efficacy has been adequate, and if not, what more needs to be done; what cost, ethical or other social impacts need to be identified for caution when formal recommendations are made." For issues other than safety and efficacy, the NIH suggested that another forum be established in the Department of Health and Human Services that would address "interface consensus," and such an agency was created in November 1978, when Congress enacted legislation establishing the National Center for Health Care Technology.

The NIH Consensus Development Program began in September 1977 with the convening of a conference on breast cancer detection. . . .

The principles underlying the philosophy of the NIH Consensus Development Program and the details of its operation have been described in detail elsewhere. A key feature is the appointment of a carefully selected panel of persons thought to be without vested interest, to listen to the evidence presented at the consensus-development conference and to prepare a report on the topic under consideration, including recommendations. A draft outline of the report is presented to the audience before the end of the conference. Broad and open participation is emphasized so that all viewpoints, including those of the public, can be considered. It is a highly decentralized activity, with each institute relatively free to choose its own topics for examination. . . .

. . . There is no outside advisory apparatus, no priority-setting mechanism, and no formal relationship with Medicare affecting coverage or reimbursement.

As the program got under way in 1977, alarms were sounded by some members of the medical profession. There was concern that the recommendations promulgated at consensus-development conferences might become regulations, that they would lead to "cookbook therapy" and physicians would become "automatons," their actions directed by a small group, and that patients would no longer be viewed as individuals. The head of a major medical professional society raised the question whether consensus-development conferences should be boycotted, since participation "is an odious alternative" because consensus may be "inappropriately arrived at and nearly impossible for the individual physician to repudiate once the 'consensus' recommendations have been trumpeted to the public." There was apprehension about the "media-oriented nature" of some of the conferences and worry that the consensus-development statements could be used as evidence in lawsuits. There was also concern over the potential liability of panel members, and one medical professional society threatened to sue the NIH and the participants in a proposed conference. Finally, there was the view that the recommendations were "bland generalities" and often represented compromises forced in the effort to achieve consensus.

In the 10 years since the start of the consensus program, more than 60 conferences have been convened and the concept has become a recognized forum, although such group-judgment models have been subjected to relatively little initial study.

The results of individual conferences have been published in a wide variety of professional journals, including this one, the British Medical Journal, and the Journal of the American Medical Association. Depending on the topic, there has been major media coverage, including reports on television, in newspapers, and in women's magazines. Among the most popular topics have been breast cancer screening (1977), the treatment of primary breast cancer (1979), cesarean childbirth (1980), liver transplantation (1983), and the health implications of obesity (1985). Consensus development has attracted increasing attention in foreign countries; Sweden, the United Kingdom, Denmark, the Netherlands, Israel, and Norway have all convened similar conferences.

In spite of what appears to be general acceptance of the process, however, criticism continues both in the United States and abroad. There have been charges that data provided to some panels have been incomplete, that they have been overinterpreted or misrepresented, that recommendations have been made in the absence of supporting evidence, and that there has been bias in the selection of participants. Finally, it has been contended that consensus development may stifle research in certain instances.

In spite of the coverage in both the public media and the medical literature, awareness of the conclusions of a conference or even that one has taken place appears to be low. For example, after the conference on CT scanning of the brain (1979), only about one third of neurosurgeons or neurologists knew of the conference and less than half of these were aware of the conclusions.

Determining the effect of the recommendations emanating from a conference is difficult, but it is clear that in certain instances physicians' behavior has been affected and in others it has not. The consensus statement that probably had the greatest impact resulted from the conference on breast cancer screening (1977). At the time, the National Cancer Institute was supporting 27 breast cancer-detection demonstration projects around the country, with 280,000 women enrolled for screening. After the conference, the National Cancer Institute instructed these demonstration projects to adopt the consensus recommendations on limiting routine mammographic screening. In a short time, there appeared to be general compliance with the change in policy.

Another consensus-development conference that apparently had an important influence was the one on the treatment of primary breast cancer (1979). The panel's recommendation of a two-stage procedure — i.e., biopsy followed by surgery (if indicated) at a later date rather than while the patient was still on the table — seems to have been widely adopted. . . .

On the other hand, many of the conferences appear to have had little or no effect on the practice of medicine. After the conference on cesarean delivery (1980), there was some expectation that cesarean rates would decline, but studies have since demonstrated that the rates have continued to increase. Similarly, the conference entitled "Cervical Cancer Screening: the Pap Smear" (1980) had little effect on the use of that technique.

In my opinion, influenced no doubt by my having played a part in designing the NIH consensus-development process and having directed it during its first two years, the program has achieved a certain prominence and importance in this country and abroad, and it has had some overall influence on medical practice and in stimulating interest in technology assessment in health care. When implemented properly, it provides a unique forum in which the issues raised by modern technical advances, at least those of safety and efficacy, can be addressed, allowing open discussion and the airing of various perspectives.

Nonetheless, the NIH Consensus Development Program can be substantially improved, as the NIH itself recognizes. The first question one might ask (and it was asked at the very beginning) is whether the NIH should be engaging in this kind of assessment activity. At present, although it is deficient in some respects, the program provides the only established forum in the nation where issues raised by medical innovations can be addressed and to which the Congress and the executive branch, among others, can turn for advice about innovations that have major national implications. . . .

In any case, there are a number of deficiencies in the current process, some of which I have already alluded to. If the NIH is to spend an average of more than $90,000 on each conference then it should have a mechanism for setting priorities among the approaches to be assessed, so that the money is spent as productively as possible. The topics have not always been sufficiently important to warrant this type of evaluation or expenditure. Currently, there is a set of criteria to guide the choice of topics, but an outside advisory body would improve the selection process.

Participants and panelists at consensus-development conferences would profit from having available a comprehensive synthesis and analysis of the available literature, to avoid the criticism that panelists have not been adequately informed. Such background papers should be subjected to peer review before the conference.

There have also been charges of bias in the composition of the panel and in the selection of speakers. Although an effort has been made to improve the process of selection, it needs to include a broader search for appropriate participants. Such efforts are critical, since the validity of the results of these exercises depends to a large extent on the credentials and credibility of the panel members.

Having to deliver what is virtually a final document before the end of the conference — a requirement that usually involves a "grueling night session" — is onerous and unnecessary. As part of their commitment, panelists should understand that they will need to return within a few weeks, after they have had the opportunity to contemplate their original recommendations, to develop the final version.

There should be no effort to force consensus or compromise. One of the most frequent criticisms of the program is that minority views are submerged or obscured, contrary to the original concept. The consensus statements themselves would have more credibility if the bases for the conclusions and recommendations were validated by the citation of appropriate references.

As stipulated in the policy paper that established it, the program needs to react more promptly to advances affecting previous recommendations. A good example is breast cancer screening: developments in mammography since 1977 would be likely to prompt important changes in the recommendations made in that year.

Finally, more could be done to extend the influence of these conferences and the statements they develop. Direct mailings to target groups should be intensified; although this would add to the expense of each conference, there is little point in engaging in the consensus-development exercise if relatively few people are aware of the results. There should also be an effort to gain a hearing at meetings of relevant professional societies, where the results of a consensus conference could be presented and discussed.

NOTES ON CONSENSUS CONFERENCES AND ALTERNATIVES

(1) The NIH Consensus Conference has been called "the most visible federally mandated medical technology assessment activity in existence." Jacoby, Evidence and Consensus, 259 J.A.M.A. 3039 (1988). Nonetheless, in the only evaluation study to date, the process has been properly criticized for selection bias in the participants, too little attention to developing materials and proper questions prior to the meetings, inadequate attention to selecting speakers and topics to be presented at the meetings, too little attempt at synthesis of scientific information, too little time at the conference allotted to the actual drafting of the consensus statement, and insufficient clarity in the final product. Wortman, Vinokur & Sechrest, Do Consensus Conferences Work? A Process Evaluation of the NIH Consensus Development Program, 13 J. Health Politics Policy & Law 469 (1988). Drummond Rennie, former Associate Editor of the New England Journal of Medicine, raises a more substantive problem:

> If you wanted to know whether a new unproved clinical test or operation or a new health program was any good, how would you proceed to find out? The best way would be to set up a controlled clinical trial, comparing the new with the old in everything from morbidity to dollar cost. Such essential trials, however, are always lengthy and very expensive. . . . In the meantime, as a practicing physician you want to advise your patients prudently, and you need some help. Most of us would then compromise by asking someone whom we considered to be an expert . . . [or even by setting up a] consensus development conference. . . .
>
> Since their theoretical benefits are so obvious, why doesn't the Journal publish every one of the consensus statements? The reasons range from the feeling that our readership has heard it all before to the impression that the panel has come up with nothing useful. There are, however, other difficulties with this sort of consensus statement. As I read such statements I have the sensation that I am being provided with the bland generalities that represent the lowest common denominator of a debate — the only points on which the experts wholeheartedly agree — and that these points must be so mild, so far from the cutting edge of progress, and so well established that surely everyone must already know them. We are kept from the debate: there is little sense of doubt and disagreement in the statements; yet the debate, as we know from many panelists, is immensely stimulating and instructive to the participants. Moreover, because of the "event," the statements may be taken to embalm a set of truths — an idea that the scientists who develop these statements would be horrified to consider. This spurious stamp of approval would be very hard for the individual physician to resist, and it might have legal as well as other implications.
>
> . . . This feeling of received truth that is conveyed by consensus statements reminds us that most explorations of nature would have been stillborn if the scientists or navigators or climbers had heeded the advice of consensus panels. I fear lest these statements will act like a dead hand, discouraging thought. After

all, in the nature of things, they can rehash, codify, and grade work already done. . . . I hope that readers will take such documents for no more and no less than what they profess to be: an attempt by a panel of honest experts to reach agreement on what we think we know and what we do not know about important medical topics. [Consensus Statements, 304 N. Engl. J. Med. 665-666 (1981).]

(2) Consensus building can also be a poor substitute for RCTs. In the consensus conference on prostate cancer, for example, the chairman told a press conference: "We are dealing with a situation where data have been accumulating but they are difficult to compare and we don't have randomized controlled trials to help us. We can only offer vague guidelines." Kolata, Prostate Consensus Hampered by Lack of Data, 236 Science 1626 (1987). Nonetheless, as frustrating as the process can be, the alternative (in the absence of RCTs) is a reversion to the "McKinlay model" with "advances" being announced anecdotally in the lay press. After the conclusions of the prostate cancer consensus conference were announced (they dealt only with surgery and radiation treatments), an interview with a man said to be one of the 4000 to 8000 American men who shun surgery or radiation (of 90,000 annually who develop prostate cancer, 25,000 of whom die) was run in the Boston Globe. The man (a physician) told a urological meeting why he took a new drug instead: "I could have chosen castration but I chose leuprolide because I thought I might retain my sexual powers." Foreman, Drug Offers Choice in Treating Prostate Cancer, Boston Globe, June 7, 1988, at 18. The article implied that the drug treatment was a reasonable medical alternative, quoting one doctor who prescribes it as saying: "In our society a lot of men don't want to be castrated . . . quite literally, they would rather die." Id. The consensus study was eventually published in a relatively obscure medical journal. Perry, Blanpain, Hanft et al., The Management of Clinically Localized Prostate Cancer: Consensus Development Conference Statement, 4 Intl. J. Tech. Assessment in Health Care 463 (1988).

2. OTHER METHODS TO ASSESS TECHNOLOGY

Cost may seem easier to deal with than efficacy, because it is easier to quantify. But major problems remain. One "simple" solution has been suggested: to pick an admittedly arbitrary age cutoff for government-sponsored medical treatments that do not improve the quality of life (but "merely" prolong it). This proposal is not made just for economic reasons (although this is its primary rationale), but also as a plea to our society to stop denying death and start planning for it, and to stop "the cruel imbalance that exists between support for life-extending, high technology medicine and that less fancy medicine necessary for a decent quality of life, notably affordable long-term institutional care and decent home care." Callahan, Rethinking Health Care for the Aged, N.Y. Times, Sept. 25, 1987, at A39. In his book, Setting Limits:

Medical Goals in an Aging Society (1987), Callahan suggests three principles that should guide decisions about the appropriateness of medical technology in the elderly.

D. Callahan, Setting Limits: Medical Goals in an Aging Society

171-173 (1987)

1. *After a person has lived out a natural life span, medical care should no longer be oriented to resisting death.* — No precise chronological age can readily be set for determining when a natural life span has been achieved — biographies vary — but it would normally be expected by the late 70s or early 80s. While a person's history may not be complete — time is always open-ended — most of it will have been achieved by that stage of life. It will be a full biography, even if more details are still to be added. Death beyond that period is not now, nor should it be, typically considered premature or untimely. . . .

2. *Provision of medical care for those who have lived out a natural life span will be limited to the relief of suffering.* — Medicine is not in a position to bring meaning and significance to the lives of the old. That only they can do for themselves, with the help of the larger culture. Yet medicine can help promote the physical functioning, the mental alertness, and the emotional stability conducive to this pursuit. These remain valuable goals, even when a natural life span has been attained. The difference at that point is that death should no longer be treated by medicine as an enemy. . . .

3. *The existence of medical technologies capable of extending the lives of the elderly who have lived out a natural life span creates no presumption whatever that the technologies must be used for that purpose.* — The uses of technology are always to be subordinated to the appropriate ends of medicine: that is, to the avoidance of premature death and to the relief of suffering. The alternative is slavery to the powers of technology — they, not we, will determine our end. Medicine should in particular resist the tendency to provide to the aged the life-extending capabilities of technologies developed primarily to help younger people avoid premature and untimely death. . . .

Note: Life-Sustaining Technologies and the Elderly

As the following chart indicates, most Americans die of heart disease, with cancer being the second leading cause of death. This, of course, explains our

TABLE 4.1
Top Ten Causes of Death, Population Aged 65 and Over, United States: 1980

Rank	*Cause of Death*	*Number per 100,000 65+*	*Percent of All Deaths*
1	Heart disease	2,330	44.4
2	Malignant neoplasms	1,011	19.2
3	Cerebrovascular diseases	573	10.9
4	Pneumonia and influenza	178	3.4
5	Chronic obstructive pulmonary diseases	171	3.2
6	Atherosclerosis	110	2.1
7	Diabetes mellitus	99	1.9
8	Accidents and trauma	97	1.8
9	Nephritis and related conditions	51	1.0
10	Chronic liver disease and cirrhosis	37	0.7
All causes		5,252	100.0

Office of Technology Assessment, Life-Sustaining Technologies and the Elderly 78 (1987).

research priorities (especially in cancer) and our continued fascination with the artificial heart. See Chapter 9(c).

Limiting life sustaining technologies on the basis of age has some superficial appeal: it is a "bright line" test, benefits seem intuitively to decrease with age, and this method has been de facto used in other countries, such as Great Britain, with some success. See, for instance, H.J. Aaron & W.B. Schwartz, The Painful Prescription: Rationing Hospital Care (1984). On the other hand, as Jerry Avron has noted, such a policy would institutionalize age discrimination, and the Office of Technology Assessment of the U.S. Congress has also noted that much remains to be understood before any comprehensive policy regarding payment of bills for medical technologies used on the elderly is possible. The OTA notes among other things, for example:

> The acute care orientation in medical training and practice emphasizes cure and prolongation of life and justifies "doing everything humanly possible" to achieve these goals. This *bias to treat* appears to prevail for patients of all ages. It has been reinforced by the wide availability of life-sustaining technologies in hospitals, reluctance to consider cost as an appropriate factor in individual decisionmaking, health professionals' and institutions' fear of legal action, and the weighty uncertainties surrounding treatment decisions. Since a wrong decision is irreversible, most health professionals would choose to "err on the side of life."
>
> While withholding of treatment is resisted, withdrawal may be even more so. Despite wide agreement among ethicists and legal scholars that there is no theoretical basis for distinguishing between withholding and withdrawal of

> life-sustaining technologies, in actual practice it is frequently *easier* to withhold a life-sustaining treatment whose benefit is uncertain than later to "pull the plug," even when the patient or patient's surrogate requests this. Grief, guilt, and health professionals' feelings of failure at times prevent rational decision-making. [Office of Technology Assessment, Life-Sustaining Technologies and the Elderly 80 (1987).]

Although we like to believe otherwise, it seems accurate to conclude that the overall health of the American population has not improved greatly in this century. Specifically, although mortality from a variety of infectious diseases has declined dramatically, as well as death from coronary heart disease and stroke, the death rates for cancer continue to increase. Medical interventions continue to have relatively little impact on these declines. "The role of environmental and personal risk factors for major causes of death remains dominant. . . ." McKinlay, McKinlay & Beaglehold, A Review of the Evidence Concerning the Impact of Medical Measures on Recent Mortality and Morbidity in the United States, 19 Int. J. Health Serv. 181, 182 (1989). Perhaps most discouraging is that "morbidity changes do not necessarily parallel mortality changes." Id. Specifically, studies indicate that although life expectancy has increased over the past two decades, most of this increase has been in increased years of living with a disability:

> For example, in 1964, a man reaching the age of 45 could expect to live nearly 20 more years free of disability, and a further 7.2 years disabled. In 1985, a man of the same age had about the same number of years to live free of disability, but nearly ten years to live disabled. In other words, the gain of 2.8 years in overall life expectancy was almost entirely offset by an increase of 2.5 years of disability for men aged 45 years. . . . Gruenberg has argued that "the net effect of successful technological innovations used in disease control has been to raise the prevalence of certain diseases and disabilities by prolonging their average duration . . . the net contribution of our success has actually been to worsen the people's health." [Id. at 202.]

What are the policy implications of this finding? The authors conclude that continued focus on medicine to improve our lives is misplaced: "Profound policy implications follow from our findings. If we should subscribe to the view that we are slowly but surely eliminating one deadly disease after another, largely because of medical intervention, then we may make little commitment to social change and may even resist a reordering of social priorities. Id. at 205. But they conclude, if we recognize that medical interventions have failed to bring about an overall improvement in the health of the nation, "then we may make some commitment to social change and a reordering of those priorities." Id.

Office of Technology Assessment, Strategies for Medical Technology Assessment

7, 47 (1982)

Medical technology assessment involves numerous components and subcomponents at various stages of process. Though these do not exist as a coherent system, discussion of them is facilitated by describing a systematic framework. The multiple components of the medical technology assessment process can be conceptualized as an information flow associated with the following four stages of assessment

- *Identification.* — Monitoring technologies, determining which need to be studied, and deciding which to study.
- *Testing.* — Conducting the appropriate analyses or trials.
- *Synthesis.* — Collecting and interpreting existing information and the results of the testing stage, and, usually, making recommendations or judgments about appropriate use.
- *Dissemination.* — Providing the synthesis of information, or any other relevant information, to the appropriate parties who use medical technologies or make decisions about their use.

This four-stage process is applicable to the three classes of medical technologies mentioned earlier — namely, drugs, devices, and medical and surgical procedures. It is also applicable to any technology in any of four typical stages of development loosely defined as follows:

- *Emerging technology.* — A technology in the phase prior to adoption.
- *New technology.* — A technology in the phase of adoption.
- *Existing technology.* — A technology in general use.
- *New application of an existing technology.* — A new application of a technology in general use. [At 7.]

An important task in medical technology assessment is to identify the conflicting social values that underlie policy alternatives. This assessment task is sometimes referred to as "value analysis." In the broadest sense, the task of value analysis in examining social implications is to bring into focus the compromises that are made with society's preexisting goals, values, and institutions when choices are made between policy alternatives. Often, value analysis may simply provide a more conceptually clear understanding of policy problems by describing the complex interaction of interests within the confines of established social — economic, medical, legal, and cultural — values.

Some work has been done in the area of suggesting techniques for assessing social implications. In 1976, OTA developed an illustrative list of questions that could be asked regarding a medical technology:

- What are the implications of the technology for the patient?
- What are the implications for the patient's family?
- What are the implications for society?
- What are the implications for the medical care system?
- What are the implications for the legal and political systems?
- What are the implications for the economic system? [At 47.]

Problem: Indications for Human Growth Hormone

Until 1988, the supply of human growth hormone (derived from human pituitary glands) was very limited, and it was thus quite easy to limit its therapeutic use to rigidly-defined medical criteria (children with a documented growth hormone deficiency, who had a growth rate under the 25th percentile for age, and a plasma growth hormone concentration at a specified low rate on at least two laboratory tests). Now that synthetically produced recombinant DNA growth hormone is commercially available, there is tremendous pressure to expand the clinical use of this product. There is a "height bias" in this country, and "not only is height prized in the sports and entertainment worlds, it also has an important influence on decisions pertaining to employment and salaries, advancement in various occupations, the choice of marital partner, and politics . . . a large group of patients with short stature not due to a deficiency of growth hormone may benefit from treatment . . . the current cost of treatment is approximately $18,700 a year." Grumbach, Growth Hormone Therapy and the Short End of the Stick, 319 N. Engl. J. Med. 238 (1988).

(1) Is short stature a disease?

(2) Should human growth hormone be offered for children below the average median height? To any parent who wants a child to be an athlete? To any parent who can get a physician to prescribe it?

(3) Who, and on what basis, should decide the answers to (1) and (2)?

(4) Should human growth hormone be part of a minimum or adequate benefit package under a system of national health insurance?

(5) How would one go about doing a cost-effectiveness analysis of the use of human growth hormone?

(6) How would one go about doing "technology assessment" on the use of human growth hormone?

(7) Would any of the answers to these questions change if you were (1) a

parent, (2) a short child, (3) a state legislator, (4) the director of Medicaid, (5) the head of HCFA, or (6) a physician?

3. TECHNOLOGY AND DEATH

Blackhall, Must We Always Use CPR?

317 N. Engl. J. Med. 1281-1284 (1987)

Cardiopulmonary resuscitation (CPR) as we know it today came into being after the invention of closed-chest cardiac massage in 1960. This technique was originally developed for victims of sudden cardiac or respiratory arrest. As the introduction to one monograph on CPR, written in 1965, says, "The techniques described in this monograph are designed to resuscitate the victim of acute insult, whether it be from drowning, electrical shock, untoward effect of drugs, anesthetic accident, heart block, acute MI [myocardial infarction] or surgery." At present, however, it is standard practice to attempt CPR on any patient in the hospital who has a cardiac arrest, regardless of the underlying illness. The exceptions, of course, are patients who request not to receive such treatment. The rights of patients to refuse this intervention have been well delineated in the courts, yet despite 27 years of experience with CPR and approximately 10 years of experience with "do-not-resuscitate" (DNR) protocols, many questions concerning CPR remain, including who should be involved in decisions about DNR orders and under what circumstances such decisions should be made. Infrequently discussed (although perhaps not infrequently encountered) is the situation in which a patient wants CPR but the physician believes that it is contraindicated. In these cases, patients almost invariably remain "full code," and physicians feel obligated to provide a treatment that they have reason to believe will not be beneficial and may actually be harmful. Are they so obligated? . . .

We use CPR in the way we do for a variety of medical, historical, and psychological reasons. Although CPR was initially used selectively on patients with acute illness — mainly because those trained in its use were cardiologists, anesthesiologists, and surgeons whose patients tended to have the reversible causes of cardiac arrest described in the quotation above — the increased training of nurses and physicians in the technique and the development of "code teams" rapidly expanded the patient population undergoing CPR. The development of code protocols in hospitals, whereby CPR was promptly begun on any patient discovered to have no pulse, extended the indications for this technique to include all patients with cardiac arrest, regardless of the underlying illness. These changes were instituted to improve the chances of a response to CPR and to ensure good neurologic function in patients who did respond. They created a problem, however, because many physicians recognized that there were some patients for whom CPR was inadvisable because of terminal illness or poor quality of life. The dilemma was how to decide when not to do CPR. After many court cases and much discussion among physicians, DNR orders were developed to encourage open discussion of these issues and to allow patient participation in the decisions. Analysis of the legal and ethical aspects of such orders has focused on the issue of patient autonomy — the right of competent patients to refuse any procedure and of incompetent patients to refuse through a surrogate. Thus, although the DNR order is written by a physician, its legitimacy comes from the patient; the order signifies that the patient has refused a procedure. The development of DNR protocols has not solved all the problems associated with CPR, however. Since CPR is performed routinely in the absence of a DNR order and because physicians frequently do not offer their patients a choice between CPR and a DNR order, the decision to perform CPR is usually made without the patient's involvement. . . .

Kouwenhoven et al., in a paper that first described closed-chest cardiac massage, reported a long-term survival rate of 70 percent (14 of 20 patients). This impressive rate has never been duplicated. In 13 papers published since 1960, the rates for survival until hospital discharge ranged from 5 to 23 percent. Most papers report a survival rate of less than 15 percent, and one of the three studies with rates higher than 15 percent excluded patients with cancer, repeated arrests, or chronic illness and total dependence — all conditions associated with poor outcome. It is clear that survival after CPR is related to the underlying illness that leads to the arrest and that patients with certain conditions very rarely survive. For example, Bedell et al., in a study of 294 consecutive patients who had cardiac arrest at the Beth Israel Hospital in Boston, found that although 44 percent initially responded to CPR, only 14 percent survived until discharge. No patient with metastatic cancer survived until discharge, nor did any patient with an acute stroke, sepsis, or pneumonia. Only 2 percent of patients with severe cardiomyopathy and 2 percent of patients who had had hypotension for 24 hours survived. Only 3 percent of the patients with renal failure (defined as a blood urea nitrogen level >50 mg per deciliter) survived, and no patient who required dialysis or had oliguria for 24 hours before the cardiac arrest survived until discharge.

These dismal results only confirmed what numerous other studies had shown before — that CPR is frequently ineffective, even in patients in whom it has the best chance of succeeding: those with acute myocardial infarctions or complications due to anesthesia. It is almost never successful in patients with chronic debilitating illnesses. . . .

What I suggest is a different way of using CPR that takes into account not only the patient's autonomy but also the physician's responsibility to provide care consonant with medical reality. In cases in which CPR has been shown to be of no benefit, as in patients with metastatic cancer, it should not be considered an alternative and should not be presented as such. In these cases physicians could write DNR orders on the chart, with the following type of documentation: "This patient has a condition for which CPR has been shown not to be effective. In case of cardiopulmonary arrest, CPR should not be performed." Because there is a potential for misuse, the type of diagnosis for which such an order could be written should be strictly limited to those for which there is clear documentation of the ineffectiveness of CPR. Consensus needs to be reached, probably on the national level, about what those diagnoses are.

Many cases will not be so clear. Patients with some chronic diseases, such as renal failure, have long term survival rates after CPR that are low (usually less than 5 percent) but real. In such cases, patient autonomy is the overriding principle and informed consent for CPR should be obtained. Physicians should be strongly encouraged to discuss the preferences of their chronically ill patients with them. The discussions should include the provision of information about the chances of survival after CPR and the risks involved. If a patient's preferences have not been ascertained before cardiac arrest (and it is our responsibility as physicians to see that this seldom happens), CPR should be initiated and continued until the patient's wishes can be ascertained.

Patients who have a cardiac arrest as a result of an acute insult, such as a drug overdose, a complication of a procedure or anesthesia, or an acute myocardial infarction, make up a third category. They are the patients for whom CPR was originally designed and the patients in whom it is more frequently successful. There is usually no question about the appropriateness of CPR in these patients, and CPR should be initiated unless the patient has previously expressed a desire not to have such treatment.

CPR is a desperate technique that works relatively infrequently, and in many types of patients, virtually never. To solve the ethical dilemmas posed by CPR we must first face that medical fact. Furthermore, as we have seen, there is potential harm in CPR in that patients may be kept alive for days to weeks undergoing painful and dehumanizing procedures with no conceivable medical benefits. Because of these facts, we need to reevaluate the ways we use CPR. Too often CPR just happens, without inquiry into the patient's wishes or consideration of its chances of success. Both patient autonomy and physician responsibility are important factors in making decisions regarding CPR. In cases in which CPR has any potential for success, the principle of patient autonomy dictates the patient's right to choose or refuse such treatment. In order for patients to exercise this right, however, two conditions must be met. First, patients need to be given sufficient information concerning the likely outcome of CPR and the risks involved, so that an informed decision can be made. Second, because CPR is attempted unless patients have been asked whether they wish it and have refused it, physicians need to involve their patients earlier and more frequently in the decision to use CPR.

The issue of patient autonomy is irrelevant, however, when CPR has no potential benefit. Here, the physician's duty to provide responsible medical care precludes CPR, either as a routine process in the absence of a decision by a patient or as a response to a patient's misguided request for such treatment in the absence of adequate information. In such cases it is not the physician's responsibility to offer CPR. Both physicians and patients must come to terms with the inability of medicine to postpone death indefinitely.

NOTE ON DEATH AND TECHNOLOGY

(1) It is quite astonishing how readily new medical technologies, such as CPR, take on a "life of their own" and often seem to used for their own sake rather than for the sake of the patient. This discontinuity between medical technology and the personhood of the patient is caused by many factors, not the least of which are the "action oriented" training of physicians and a reductionist attitude that concludes that treating a body part or function is worthwhile even if it does not benefit the whole person. As Nancy Rhoden has put it:

> For example, a persistently vegetative patient's fever can be cured without regard to whether this benefits the patient as a person. . . . From the outside, one might think that doctors and hospital administrators make conscious, fully informed decisions to adopt a technology, and to make any changes that it requires. Yet to a disturbing extent, technologies adopt hospitals. New medical technologies are typically developed to solve a fairly specific problem. . . . Nevertheless, quite predictably, they are used on additional groups of patients for whom the technologies were not originally intended and may not be so beneficial. Cardiopulmonary resuscitation (CPR), for example, was initially developed to save otherwise healthy persons whose heartbeat and breathing failed following surgery, near drowning, or other unexpected catastrophic events. Needless to say, CPR's developers did not tout it as a method to prolong terminally ill patients' dying process by reviving them time and time again . . . [o]nce a technology or technique is available, a presumption arises that it should be used unless it is clearly contraindicated. This presumption often means that a technology is overused: in some hospitals virtually all deaths are attended by resuscitation efforts. [Rhoden, Litigating Life and Death, 120 Harv. L. Rev. 375, 421, 423 (1988).] See also, New York State Task Force on Life and the Law, Do Not Resuscitate Orders 5 (2d ed. 1988).

(2) The misuse of our technology is strongly related to our fear of death and a seeming quest for immortality. Political scientist Langdon Winner, for example, has suggested that the only two shared goals we now have as a society are accumulating wealth and avoiding cancer. L. Winner, The Whale and the Reactor (1986). Novelist Don Delillo has one of his characters put our three choices about death this way: you can deny it, you can put your faith in religion, or

> [y]ou could put your faith in technology. It got you here, it can get you out. This is the whole point of technology. It creates an appetite for immortality on

> the one hand. It threatens universal extinction on the other. . . . It's what we invented to conceal the terrible secret of our decaying bodies. But it's also life, isn't it? It prolongs life, it provides new organs for those that wear out. New devices, new techniques every day. Lasers, masers, ultrasound. Give yourself up to it. . . . They'll insert you in a gleaming tube, irradiate your body with the basic stuff of the universe. Light, energy, dreams. God's own goodness. [D. Delillo, White Noise 285 (1985).]

When death is seen as the ultimate enemy, the language of warfare is commonly used. As Susan Sontag has noted in the context of cancer:

> Cancer cells do not simply multiply; they are "invasive.". . . Cancer cells "colonize: from the original tumor to far sites in the body, first setting up tiny outposts ("micrometastases.") . . . Rarely are the body's "defenses" vigorous enough to obliterate a tumor. . . . Treatment also has a military flavor. Radiotherapy uses the metaphors of aerial warfare; patients are "bombarded" with toxic rays. And chemotherapy is chemical warfare, using poisons. Treatment aims to "kill" cancer cells. . . . [S. Sontag, Illness as Metaphor 65-66 (1977).]

That technology has proven uncontrollable should not surprise us. It is not only inseparable from our fear of death but also from our fear of the annihilation of our entire species. Lewis Thomas, whose essay opened this chapter, also wrote:

> Up to now, we have been living through the equivalent of an early childhood for our species. . . . We could fumble and do it wrong. Thermonuclear war is the worst case to contemplate, enough in itself to cause the crash of the species, but we have other threats to make against our lasting existence: overpopulation and crash, deforestation and crash, pollution and crash, a long list of possible bad dreams come true, the sounds, always outside the window offstage, of the destruction of the orchard. With luck we may come through. The luck will have to be incalculable, and unbelievably on our side over the next few decades. The good thought I have about this is that we are, to begin with, the most improbable of all the earth's creatures, and maybe it is not beyond hope that we are also endowed with improbable luck. [L. Thomas, The Youngest Science 248 (1983).]

What types of legal tools might help in making technology more closely related to human needs? Would it make sense to require some sort of "health care system impact statement" before Medicare adopted a technology as reimbursable? What steps could the judiciary take to discourage physicians from using technologies inappropriately, especially on terminally ill patients? See also Chapter 6.

A look back to the beginning of this century and a look forward to the next provide the two notes that aptly end this chapter: "Do not try to live forever, you will not succeed." G.B. Shaw, The Doctor's Dilemma 86 (1905).

"During a panel discussion at a science fiction convention someone in the audience asked, 'What can we expect during the next century?' . . . Writer Bruce Sterling leapt up and exclaimed, '*You're* all gonna die!'" Bryant, "Dateline 1999," Omni, Jan. 1989, at 22. (Emphasis added.)

CHAPTER

V

Quality of Care and the Law: Defining Standards and Structuring Enforcement

This chapter is about how quality of care is defined and enforced, and the role of the legal and financing systems in that process. Judicial opinions, statutes, and scholarship about law and health policy reflect at least three different models of what the law's role should be and of the definition of quality itself. The dominant model in the United States since the early twentieth century has emphasized the primacy of the medical profession, particularly in its fragmented, individual practice form. Under this view, quality of care is defined and largely enforced by the community of private practitioners; the role of the law is to authorize these physicians to play this role, and to protect them against liability and oversight imposed by lay juries, or by government agencies, hospitals, and insurance companies.

In the 1970s and 1980s, however, two other models gained greatly in importance. One, which can be termed the social contract model (and which actually encompasses a range of models reflecting different political values), sees the definition and enforcement of quality as a complex and ongoing negotiating process among all parties affected by health care delivery, including doctors, hospitals, other providers, governmental financing and regulatory agencies, legislatures, insurance companies, employers, and organized and unorganized consumers. Under this view, the role of the law is varied and flexible, depending on the context and policy goal; at times supportive of professional consensus and punitive toward those who deviate from it; at other times skeptical of professional consensus, or aware of and selective among competing professional views, and seeking through positive and negative incentives to achieve such social goals as greater patient satisfaction, better health outcomes, reduced costs and/or greater efficiency, and increased equality. The other, which can be termed the economic competition model, envisions quality of care and its enforcement as primarily a process of contract and bargaining under conditions of economic competition. Under this view, the role of the law is to maximize liberty of contract by enforcing the antitrust laws against monopolistic professional practices, reducing insurance coverage so as to heighten consumer price consciousness, and permitting bargaining regarding tort standards and remedies, thereby creating different standards of care for patients with different degrees of purchasing power.

Most of the major health law developments of this century regarding quality of care have involved a struggle between the professional and social contract models, and most of this chapter is built around that great debate.[1] Thus after an initial Section A exploring varying conceptions of quality of care (which themselves reflect these competing models), Section B turns to the core of medical malpractice law — the standard of care applicable to doctors — and traces the debate between the professionally deferential "locality rule" and the more socially protective "national standard." It is important to note that here, as elsewhere, the debate was and is not simply between the medical profession and the rest of society, but also *within* the medical profession, with doctors themselves playing an essential role in defining and enforcing more socially responsible standards. Section C focuses on analogous doctrinal developments about the legal responsibilities of hospitals to patients — about whether hospitals are simply passive workplaces for private, unorganized doctors, or whether they must have certain collective structures and responsibilities for quality of care. Again, as we shall see, the role of the law was not so much to impose an external, nonmedical vision on hospitals, but rather to attempt to empower and enforce the vision of institutional responsibility articulated by some doctors and hospitals, a vision that was also seen as consistent with the interests and expectations of the community at large.

Sections D, E, and F focus on the regulatory roles of the major institutions that define and enforce quality of care standards: hospitals (Section D); state licensing agencies and private accreditation organizations (Section E); and governmental and private payers (Section F). In each case, the institution entered the 1970s with a long tradition of deference toward the decentralized private practice of medicine, and found itself challenged to adhere to a more independent and socially-protective model. It is important to note, however, that particularly for the hospitals and payers the social values sought to be protected were not only, or even primarily, increased quality of care. For reasons explored in Chapters Two and Three, cost containment had become, and remains, the major focus of governmental and nongovernmental health policy. Section G explores the tension within the social contract model between two potentially conflicting social goals: promoting a much more sophisticated concept of quality, and reducing health care expenditures and provider incomes.

1. The economic competition model, although much less prominent in judicial opinions and other sources of law than the first two, is an important legal and policy perspective that is examined in this chapter in relation to malpractice law reform, a lower standard of care for the poor, and the tension between quality of care and cost containment.

Specific questions addressed in this chapter include the following: to what extent should the legal system enforce "national" standards of care? Should that standard be "state of the art," or something less? Should allowances be made for varying local patterns? What about such previously "unthinkable" questions — now explicitly debated by policy advocates — as whether lower standards should be applied to patients who are poor or who pay a lower price for care? To what extent is malpractice law itself part of the problem of unnecessary costs and threatened quality, and what legal reforms are desirable?

With respect to institutions, to what extent should hospitals, health maintenance organizations, and other institutions be responsible for the quality of care provided through them? How should these legal duties be defined, and to whom should they be owed — to patients themselves in civil actions? to governmental payers and state licensing agencies through administrative proceedings based on inspections by experts? How should the institutions be structured? What guidance should the legal system give to institutions and individual providers attempting to balance financial pressures and profits against the costs of delivering high quality care?

What is and should be the role of licensing agencies? What is and should be the role of payers and payers' agents (such as Peer Review Organizations, typically private nonprofit corporations controlled by doctors and under contract to the federal government to monitor the necessity and quality of care)? Are their sanction procedures fair to providers and affected patients? Might such agencies have their own duty of care to patients affected by their programs and actions? How do (or might) the larger tensions between cost containment, access, and quality of care express themselves in the law?

A chapter on the law of quality of care inevitably focuses on the lack of quality; on story after story of incompetence, insensitivity, and venality, broken occasionally by a good doctor candidly confessing error or a rural community rallying (perhaps irrationally) to protect its only doctor from regulatory punishment. It is therefore worth noting at the outset that American medicine does a lot of good at the same time that it does a lot of harm. A most dramatic reminder of this is provided by Haing Ngor, the Cambodian doctor who, after surviving four years of severe oppression at the hands of the Khmer Rouge, came to the United States and won an Academy Award for his portrayal of the similar experiences of Cambodian journalist Dith Pran in the film The Killing Fields. In his recently published memoirs, Ngor recounts three extraordinary scenes in which he was forced to watch people — including his own wife in childbirth — die needlessly, because to have revealed himself as a doctor would not have saved them and would have meant his own death. These scenes highlight the importance of the medical knowledge, competence, and fidelity that we often take for granted, and that we rightfully strive to attain in part through the law of quality of care.

A. The Concept of Quality of Care

1. INTRODUCTION TO THE CONCEPT OF QUALITY OF CARE

At first glance, the concept of quality of care in medicine may appear to be primarily a technical matter: did the doctor order the correct tests in response to the symptoms, interpret them correctly, choose the right treatment, and implement it competently? These are indeed important questions; they occupy most of medical malpractice law, and the answers are understandably largely in the hands of medical experts.

From this perspective, quality of care focuses on the identification and avoidance of medical "error", that is, of deviations by individual doctors from established professional norms. The selection from Charles Bosk's Forgive and Remember dramatically illustrates how error in this sense is defined and dealt with in the surgical service of a large teaching hospital.

However, the concept of medical error, although important and intuitively appealing, cannot exhaust the meaning or reality of quality of care. Besides the doctor there are at least two other participants in the health care process: the patient and the larger society. If the goal of medical care (and more broadly, health care) is not only technical competence by the doctor, but also promotion of the patient's well being, then even technically competent care must be evaluated in light of the patient's own treatment goals and weighing of risks and benefits. Surgery or medication that is considered technically correct by doctors might prolong a patient's life, but cause great pain, discomfort, or disability. For example, the technically correct surgery for a certain type and stage of throat cancer, in terms of maximizing years of survival, might involve removal of the vocal chords and hence inability to speak normally. Less aggressive surgery might raise the risks of recurrence of the cancer, but save the patient's ability to speak. A patient, particularly an older patient whose life expectancy is not very long in any event, might well choose the less radical surgery. If patients are not permitted and encouraged to make that choice according to their own goals and values, have they received "quality of care"? See, for answers in the negative, McNeil, Weichselbaum & Pauker, Speech and Survival: Tradeoffs between Quality and Quantity of Life in Laryngeal Cancer, 305 N. Engl. J. Med. 982 (1981) (finding that 20 percent of 37 healthy persons surveyed chose quality over quantity of life, and advocating that "treatment choices should be made on the basis of the patient's attitudes toward the quality as well as the quantity of survival"); Donabedian, The Quality of Care: How Can It Be Assessed? 243 J.A.M.A. 1743, 1744 (1988); Brook and Kosecoff, Commentary: Competition and Quality, Health Affairs, Summer 1988, at 150, 151.

There is another, perhaps more fundamental reason, why the concept of medical error by individual doctors is not, by itself, an adequate definition of quality of care. Over the past 20 years, many studies have found that hundreds of thousands of Americans annually undergo unnecessary surgery and other medical procedures, and suffer from "iatrogenic " (that is, physician-caused) injury. See, e.g., S. Law & S. Polan, Pain and Profit: The Politics of Malpractice 18-19, 61-62, 251-252 (1978); Steel et al., Iatrogenic Illness on a General Medical Service at a University Teaching Hospital, 304 N. Engl. J. Med. 638 (1981) (finding that 36 percent of patients had iatrogenic illness). A particularly careful study of three surgical procedures based on 1981 Medicare data found "substantial numbers of procedures [from 17 to 32 percent] performed for inappropriate indications," where inappropriateness was defined quite restrictively. Chassin et al., Does Inappropriate Use Explain Geographic Variations in the Use of Health Care Services? 258 J.A.M.A. 2533, 2536 (1987). Moreover, even including those procedures considered appropriate, there was wide geographic variation in the rate that these procedures were performed — ranging with respect to one procedure from 6 to 23 per 10,000 elderly, a difference of almost 400 percent. Id. at 2534. The main purpose of the study was to find out whether the higher rates of use could be explained by higher rates of inappropriate use — a hypothesis that was largely not confirmed.

The high degree of geographic variation in the rates at which procedures are performed by doctors — a topic also addressed in the selection by Dr. John Wennberg in this section — and the relatively high rate of inappropriate or unnecessary procedures strongly suggest that the problem of quality of care is not simply a matter of error or deviance by individual doctors. When thousands of physicians are making similar "errors," or even more seriously, when no one can explain why the rate of "appropriate" surgery varies by several hundred percent among seemingly similar populations, there are likely to be more general problems than individual deviations from established norms. These problems should trouble both individual patients, whose treatments are affected by unexplainable variations, and the larger society that must allocate scarce resources both within health care and to other important social needs. "[T]he larger problem of quality in medical care must also address systemic failures, poor administrative design for review of health care, inadequacies in training of physician[s], and the nature of practice incentives." Furrow, The Changing Role of the Law in Promoting Quality in Health Care: From Sanctioning Outlaws to Managing Outcomes, 26 Houston L. Rev. 147, 153 (1989). From this perspective, the focus of quality assurance must be both on serious efforts at preventing medical error and also on examining and perhaps changing hitherto unexamined practices and their structural foundations.

The new efforts to define and measure quality of care are taking place against a traditional triad of concepts: (1) inputs or structure, (2) process, and (3) outcomes. Inputs or structure refers to the resources and organizational arrangements in place to deliver care. The assumption is that more elaborate inputs — such as the number and credentials of medical personnel, the sophistication of facilities and equipment, and the existence of organizational checks such as quality review committees — will lead to high quality care. It indeed seems "unlikely that a poorly staffed, poorly equipped, and disorganized hospital could deliver optimal care. But it is only an educated guess, without any end-result verification, to conclude that a high caliber of input necessarily produces high quality care. Does the mere presence of sophisticated equipment and highly trained professionals mean that these resources are actually being used, [or used appropriately]?" C. Jacobs, T. Christoffel & N. Dixon, Measuring the Quality of Patient Care 25 (1976).

The process of care refers to the activities of physicians and other health professionals engaged in providing medical care. Examples include taking medical histories, listening carefully to patients' accounts, performing appropriate diagnostic tests, choosing the correct treatment, and implementing it competently. Although this would appear to be the formulation of quality most easy to define, measure, and verify in terms of outcomes, in fact there is a paucity of information about the efficacy of even well accepted medical procedures, and, as Wennberg's article suggests, wide variations in actual medical styles of practice. As with inputs, one has an intuitive sense that it should be possible to correlate good quality with informed medical consensus, but in fact much work remains to be done both to develop various points of consensus and to validate them.

Measuring quality via outcomes, namely changes in patients' satisfaction and health status, is the third approach. Outcomes are evidently relevant; if a hospital has a much higher than average rate of infections or deaths, that raises at least a question about its quality of care. The problem with this method is that attributing changes in outcomes to medical care requires distinguishing the effects of medical care from the effects of the many other factors — such as patients' prior health status before seeking care — that influence ultimate outcomes.

In its 1988 report, The Quality of Medical Care: Information for Consumers, the Congressional Office of Technology Assessment (OTA) concludes that

> [i]n light of the conceptual difficulties just mentioned, process and outcome measures should be regarded as complements rather than alternatives to assess quality. Process measures gain validity as quality indicators only to the extent that they have been found likely to improve patient outcomes, and outcome measures gain validity only to the extent that they have been linked to the prior medical care process. Similarly, to acquire validity as indicators of quality, structural measures must be shown to be associated with efficacious medical processes or validated outcomes. . . .
>
> . . . Reflecting this task and the points above, this report uses the following definition of quality to guide its discussion: The quality of medical care is the

degree to which the process of care increases the probability of outcomes desired by patients and reduces the probability of undesired outcomes, given the state of medical knowledge. . . .

This definition of quality also incorporates the notion that there are different levels of quality: a minimum level below which quality is unacceptable and levels of acceptable quality, including some levels in which important concerns about the quality of care remain and improvement is possible. Quality assessment and information systems take on different purposes that correspond to the different levels of quality: to identify unacceptable providers, so that they can be helped to improve and, as a last resort, be removed from practice; and to identify gradations among good quality providers, so that people can gravitate to the better ones and perhaps ultimately improve the general level of care. Since consumers vary in the importance that they attach to different aspects of care, information systems could also identify discretionary aspects of practice, so that people could act on their preferences. [Id. at 9.]

The readings that follow illustrate various aspects of quality and barriers to its achievement. The selection from Charles Bosk's sociological study, Forgive and Remember, based on months of close observation, presents how surgeons define a professional ideal of quality at a large urban teaching hospital. The article by Dr. David Hilfiker then describes some of the barriers to achieving that or any other professional ideal from the perspective of a conscientious country doctor laboring against the limits of his underfunded technology, individual knowledge, and personal stamina. The summary of the 1968 study by Duff and Hollingshead reveals other constraints in an urban medical school, in which the quality of communication between patients and doctors is directly correlated with socioeconomic class. The article by Dr. John Wennberg summarizes his research about pervasive geographic variations in doctors' use of many medical procedures. These and other broad questions about the process by which quality of care is continually defined and implemented, and by which we as a society decide how to distribute it and how much to pay for it, reappear throughout this chapter.

2. QUALITY OF CARE AS A PROFESSIONAL IDEAL

C. Bosk, Forgive and Remember: Managing Medical Failure

37-50 (1979)

A surgeon's attempts to explain preventable failure may be divided into four categories: (1) technical error, (2) judgmental error, (3) normative error, and (4) quasi-normative error. Although other interpretations of failure exist, only these four categories deal directly with the issue of physician competence and the social control of performance. Other labels are an attempt to locate responsibility in an area outside the surgeon's control, and are thus often of questionable legitimacy because of the highly developed ethic of individual responsibility among surgeons.

TECHNICAL ERRORS

When a surgeon makes a technical error, he is performing his role conscientiously, but his skills fall short of what the task requires. Technical errors are expected to happen to everyone, but rarely. They are expected to happen to everyone because surgeons understand that theirs is at best an imperfectly applied science. At times, interventions fail because techniques have been less than perfectly performed. Certain failures of technique are expected as a routine and calculable part of the work environment: they are built into training. Knots tied by the unpracticed may leave dead space for infection or may split; probes and scopes in the hands of the inexperienced may explore more of the body than desired:

> There are always complications from unfamiliar techniques. A resident may get a pneumothorax [air or gas introduced into the pleural cavity] when he taps a chest, or he may get a hematoma [a large bruise] after a procedure. If these things didn't happen to him, he wouldn't need us; he'd already be a professor of surgery. These things still happen to me but not nearly so often. They are the reason we have a training program, so housestaff can learn to do procedures without incident (Attending [that is, a senior physician]). . . .

For an error to be defined as technical, two conditions must be met. First, the error has to be speedily noticed, reported, and treated. Such a chain of events serves as a signal of the subordinate's good intentions at the same time that it allows treatment of the problem before it becomes unmanageable. The same objective condition reported immediately on one occasion and later on another will meet with a different response from attendings. Given the inevitability of problems, their speedy report underscores a houseofficer's conscientiousness and his concern for the patient; it pays tribute to the norms of clinical responsibility at the same time that events themselves mock these norms. As we shall see, a slow discovery of a technical error leads attendings to suspect that more than a technical failure was involved; they begin to think a moral lapse may have been involved as well. Moreover, quick reporting of error maximizes the possibility of routine remedies and thus minimizes for all the cost of failure. . . .

It is nevertheless important to remember that the costs of technical failure never shrink to zero, and it is the patient who always pays. The patient pays financially in increased hospital costs and pays personally in the discomfort of a complication. For subordinates, quick report of failure is one of the primary means of establishing that the error is not representative of its maker, that it signals only a momentary lapse, and that it occurred merely because of its maker's inexperience.

A second condition must be met for failure to be defined as technical; mistakes must not be frequently made by the same person. When an individual makes mistakes frequently, he cannot legitimately claim that a momentary lapse occurred. Moreover, attendings would not accept such a claim because frequent failure makes them doubt not only a subordinate's efforts but also his intentions. . . .

JUDGMENTAL ERRORS

A judgmental error occurs when an incorrect strategy of treatment is chosen. These errors are also unevenly distributed through the division of labor. Subordinates who have only little discretionary power make few and relatively minor judgmental errors. Attending surgeons in charge of devising treatment plans make the most and the most serious judgmental errors. In these cases judgment is not always incorrect in any absolute sense; the surgeon, given the clinical evidence available at the time, may have chosen an eminently reasonable course of action, but the result — a death or complication — forces the surgeon to consider whether some alternative might have been more profitably employed. Clinical results, not scientific reasoning, determine how correct judgment is. . . .

The two most common judgmental errors that attendings make are (1) overly heroic surgery and (2) the failure to operate when the situation demands. Overly heroic surgery involves the decision to operate when the patient cannot tolerate the procedure. This decision to operate is a surgeon's commitment to his skills; it is also a moral-ethical decision about what "tolerable" risk is and a decision about what the proper role of the physician is — whether he is charged with merely sustaining life or whether he may subject his patients to great risk in order to upgrade the quality of life. Needless to say, these are not easy or pleasant decisions. Consider the following:

> Mrs. Hardy is an old patient of Dr. Peters who has metastatic cancer. She has at most a few months to live. Recently her condition has worsened. Without an operation, she will probably literally vomit to death within a month. She has poor pulmonary and cardiac function; it is not clear whether she could tolerate an operation. If one is successfully performed, her life expectancy would be between three and six months — a month and a half of which would be postoperative convalescence. . . .

In this case can the surgeon justify putting a patient through the risk and trauma of surgery for such dubious rewards? But in good conscience can he stand idly by and sentence her to such an unpleasant death? An attending makes these decisions for himself. He may ask his subordinates what they would do if the decision were theirs. A favorite way of phrasing this question is, "What would you do if the patient were your mother?" After listening to his subordinates, the attending announces his decision. He need not justify this choice to other attendings. He need not explain the basis of his decision to his subordinates, although the didactic situation of surgical training encourages such explanations. To mobilize the resources necessary for action, the attending need only make up his mind. In this sense, his patients are his to do with as he wishes.

If subordinates disagree with an attending, there is very little they can do. A common tactic is to anticipate complications from a procedure and ask the attending how he intends to manage them. . . .

A second common judgmental error of attendings is the failure to establish a clear-cut plan of action for chronic problems. For most of these patients, secondary problems make operating impossible. These patients tend to linger in the hospital. They are not discharged nor are they aggressively treated. . . .

> Surgeons in general don't like theoretical or psychological problems. Things are either black or white. If they don't understand something, they try to put it out of their minds. . . . Unfortunately some patients, not a lot, die because the surgeon loses interest (Chief Resident). . . .

NORMATIVE ERRORS

A normative error occurs when a surgeon has, in the eyes of others, failed to discharge his role obligations conscientiously. Technical and judgmental errors are errors in a role; normative errors signal error in assuming a role. These errors are not distributed throughout the division of labor but are almost exclusively subordinate errors. Normative error occurs when, in the attending's judgment, a houseofficer's conduct violates the working understandings on which action rests. When a normative error occurs, the mistake renders it impossible to consider the person making it — in legal terms — a just and reasonably prudent individual. Viewed sociologically, normative errors challenge tacit background assumptions about how reality in a scene is constructed.

When spelled out, the background assumptions that govern clinical action are few, and they are drilled into the subordinate from his first clinical rotation as a medical student. The covering law for all behavior is, simply stated, "No surprises." Superordinates expect their subordinates to inform them of all changes, however small. . . .

> Dr. Arthur was concerned that a complication from the operation on Mrs. Prewitt might be a perineal nerve palsy [temporary paralysis of the foot from operative damage to the perineal nerve]. In clinic when he asked Ernest, the chief resident, and Josh, the second-year resident, about it, they both assured him that on morning rounds she was quite all right. However, her examination on afternoon rounds revealed a perineal nerve palsy. Dr. Arthur's anger was apparent as we left the room. We walked about sixty feet down the corridor before he stopped to speak: "Goddammit! I will not have this on my service.

Do you understand? I ask if the patient has a perineal nerve palsy and am assured by my housestaff that she doesn't and she damn well does. Now, this is not caused by your not being smart enough to recognize the problem. It's not your skill that is wanting here. This is a case pure and simple of your being too lazy to get off your asses and look at the patients. I will not tolerate this. Did you see this patient this morning, Ernest?" "I did — yes, I did, sir." Arthur: "And you didn't notice that she had no dorsal flexion [movement of the foot at the ankle]?" Ernest: "No, sir." "Well, what the hell were you looking at? What am I going to have to do to get this service running right? If I can't count on my housestaff to provide decent preoperative and postoperative care for my patients, then Grant and I will cancel our operations until the patients we have are under control and until we are sure that we have housestaff who can do the job. Do I make myself clear?". . .

Normative breaches are breaches of the etiquette governing the role relations between attending surgeons and housestaff. A normative error in turn carries with it the implication that a fundamental breach of etiquette governing the role relation between doctor and patient has occurred. . . . Fatigue, pressing family problems, a long queue of patients waiting to be seen, a touch of the flu — all the excuses that individuals routinely use in everyday life, are inadmissible on a surgery service. . . .

[Discussion of quasi-normative errors omitted]

3. BARRIERS TO ACHIEVING QUALITY OF CARE

a. Professional Uncertainty and Silence

D. Hilfiker, Facing Our Mistakes

310 N. Engl. J. Med. 118 (1984)

Looking at the appointment book for July 12, 1978, I notice that Barb Daily will be in today for her first prenatal examination. "Wonderful," I think, remembering my joy as I helped her deliver her first child two years ago. Barb and her husband Russ are friends, and our relationship became much closer with the shared experience of that birth. With so much exposure to disease every day in my rural family practice, I look forward to today's appointment with Barb and to the continuing relationship over the next months.

Barb seems to be in good health with all the symptoms and signs of pregnancy, but her urine pregnancy test is negative. I reassure Barb and myself that she is fine and that the test just hasn't turned positive yet. Rescheduling another test for the following week, I congratulate her on her condition and promise to get all her test results to her promptly.

But the next urine test is negative, too, which leaves me troubled. Isn't

Barb pregnant? Has she had a missed abortion? I could make sure right now, of course, by ordering an ultrasound, but the new examination is available only in Duluth, 110 miles away from our northern Minnesota village, and it is expensive. I am aware of the Dailys' modest income. Besides, by waiting a few weeks, I'll find out for sure without the ultrasound. I call Barb on the phone and tell her about the negative test, about the possible abortion, and about the necessity of a repeat appointment in a few weeks if her next menstrual period does not occur on schedule.

It is, as usual, a hectic summer, and I almost forget about Barb's situation until a month later when she returns. Still no menstrual period, no abortion. She is confused and upset, since, she says, "I feel so pregnant." I am bothered, too, especially because her uterus continues to be enlarged. Her urine test remains definitely negative.

I break the bad news to her. "I think you have a missed abortion. You were probably pregnant, but the baby appears to have died some weeks ago, before your first examination. Unfortunately, you didn't have the miscarriage to get rid of the dead tissue from the baby and the placenta. If a miscarriage does not occur within a few weeks, I'd recommend a reexamination, another pregnancy test, and if nothing shows up, a dilation and curettage to clean out the uterus."

Barb is disappointed and saddened; there are tears. Both she and Russ have sufficient background in science to understand the technical aspects of the situation, but that doesn't alleviate the sorrow. We talk in the office at some length and make an appointment for two weeks later.

When Barb returns, Russ is with her. Still no menstrual period, no miscarriage, and a negative pregnancy test. It is difficult, but it also feels right to be able to share in friends' sadness. Thoroughly reviewing the situation with both of them, I schedule the D and C for later in the week.

Friday morning, when Barb is wheeled into the operating room, we chat before she is put to sleep. The surgical nurses in our small hospital are all friends, too, so the atmosphere is warm and relaxed. After induction of anesthesia, I examine Barb's pelvis. To my hands, the uterus now seems bigger than it had two days previously, but since all the pregnancy tests were negative, the uterus couldn't have grown. I continue the operation.

But this morning there is considerably more blood than usual, and it is only with great difficulty that I am able to extract any tissue. The body parts I remove are much larger than I had expected, considering when the fetus died, and they are not the decomposing tissue I'd anticipated. These are body parts that were recently alive! I suppress the rising panic in my body and try to complete the procedure. I am unable to evacuate the uterus completely, however, and after much sweat and worry, I stop, hoping that the uterus will expel the rest within a few days.

Russ is waiting outside the operating room, so I sit with him for a few minutes, telling him that Barb is fine but that there were some problems with the procedure. Since I haven't completely thought through what has happened, I can't be very helpful in answering his questions. I leave hurriedly for the office, promising to return that afternoon to talk with them once Barb has recovered from the anesthesia.

In between seeing other patients in the office that morning, I make several rushed phone calls, trying to figure out what has happened. Despite reassurances from the pathologist that it is statistically "impossible" for four consecutive pregnancy tests to be negative during a viable pregnancy, the horrifying awareness is growing that I have probably aborted Barb's living child. I won't know for sure until several days later, when the pathology report is available. In a daze I walk over to the hospital and try to tell Russ and Barb as much as I know, without telling them all that I suspect. I tell them that there may be more tissue expelled and that I won't know for sure about the pregnancy until the next week.

I can't really face my own suspicions yet.

That weekend I receive a tearful call from Barb. She has just passed some recognizable body parts of the baby; what is she to do? The bleeding has stopped, and she feels physically well, so it is apparent that the abortion I began on Friday is now over. I schedule a time in midweek to meet with them and review the entire situation.

The pathology report confirms my worst fears: I have aborted a living fetus at about 13 weeks of age. No explanation can be found for the negative pregnancy tests. My consultation with Barb and Russ later in the week is one of the hardest things I have ever done. Fortunately, their scientific sophistication allows me to describe in some detail what I have done and what my rationale was. But nothing can obscure the hard reality: I have killed their baby.

Politely, almost meekly, Russ asks whether the ultrasound examination could not have helped us. It almost seems that he is trying to protect my feelings, trying to absolve me of some of the responsibility. "Yes," I answer, "if I had ordered the ultrasound, we would have known that the baby was alive." I cannot explain to him why I didn't recommend it.

Over the next days and weeks and months, my guilt and anger grow. I discuss the events with my partners, with our pathologist, and with obstetric specialists. Some of my mistakes are obvious: I relied too heavily on one particular test; I was not skillful in determining the size of the uterus by pelvic examination; I should have ordered the ultrasound before proceeding with the D and C. Other mistakes become apparent as we review my handling of the case. There is simply no way I can justify what I have done. To make matters worse, complications after the D and C have caused much discomfort, worry, and expense. Barb is unable to become pregnant again for two years.

As physicians our automatic response to reading about such a tragedy is to try to discover what went wrong, to analyze why the mistakes occurred, and to institute corrective measures so that such things do not happen again. This response is important, indeed necessary, and I spent hours in such a review. But it is inadequate if it does not address our own emotional and spiritual experience of the events.

Although I was as honest with the Dailys as I could be in those next months, although I told them everything they wanted to know and described to them as completely as I could what had happened, I never shared with them the agony that I underwent trying to deal with the reality of the events. I never did ask for their forgiveness. I felt somehow that they had enough sorrow without having to bear my burden as well. Somehow, I felt, it was my responsibility to deal with my guilt alone.

Everyone, of course, makes mistakes, and no one enjoys the consequences. But the potential consequences of our medical mistakes are so overwhelming that it is almost impossible for practicing physicians to deal with their errors in a psychologically healthy fashion. Most people — doctors and patients alike — harbor deep within themselves the expectation that the physician will be perfect. No one seems prepared to accept the simple fact of life that physicians, like anyone else, will make mistakes.

By the very nature of our work, we physicians daily make decisions of extreme gravity. Our work in the intensive-care unit, in the emergency room, in the surgery suite, or in the delivery room offers us hundreds of opportunities daily to miscalculate, often with drastic consequences.

And it is not only in these settings but also in the humdrum of routine daily care that a physician can blunder into tragedy. One evening, for instance, a local boy was brought to the emergency room after an apparently minor automobile accident. One leg and foot were injured, but he was otherwise fine. After examining him, I consulted by telephone with an orthopedic surgeon in Duluth, and we decided that I would try to correct what appeared on the x-ray film to be a dislocated foot. As usual, I offered the patient and his mother (who happened to be a nurse with whom I worked regularly) a choice: I could reduce the dislocation in our small hospital or they could travel to Duluth to see the specialist. I was somewhat offended when they decided they would go to Duluth. My feelings changed considerably when the surgeon called me the next morning to thank me for the referral. He reported that the patient had not had a dislocation at all but a severe posterior compartment syndrome, which had hyperflexed the foot, causing it to appear dislocated. The posterior compartment had required immediate surgery the previous night in order to save the muscles of the lower leg. I felt physically weak as I realized that his young man would have been permanently injured had his mother not decided on her own to take him to Duluth.

Although much less drastic than the threat of death or severe disability, perhaps the most frequent result of physician misjudgment is the wasting of money, often in large amounts. Every practicing physician spends thousands of dollars of patients' money every day in the costs for visits, laboratory examinations, medications, and hospitalizations. An unneeded examination, the needless admission of a patient to the hospital, even the unnecessary advice to stay home from work can waste large amounts of money — frequently, the money of people who have little to spare. One comes to feel that any decision may have important consequences. . . .

[T]he possibility of a serious mistake is present with each patient the physician sees. The inherent uncertainty of medical practice creates a situation in which errors are always possible. . . .

. . . Indeed, the closest I have ever come to involvement in a courtroom malpractice case was the result of my treatment of an apparently minor wrist injury one week after it happened: I misread a straightforward x-ray film and sent the young boy home with a diagnosis of sprain. I next heard about it five years later, when after being summoned to a hearing, I discovered that the fracture I had missed had not healed, and the patient had required extensive treatment and difficult surgery years later.

As practicing primary-care physicians, then, we work in an impossible situation. Each of the myriad decisions to be made every day has the potential for drastic consequences if it is not determined properly. And it is highly likely that sooner or later we will make the mistake that kills or seriously injures another person. How can we live with that knowledge? And after a serious mistake has been made, how can we continue in daily practice and expose ourselves again? How can we who see ourselves as healers deal with such guilt?

Painfully, almost unbelievably, we physicians are even less prepared to deal with our mistakes than the average layperson is. The climate of medical school and residency training, for instance, makes it nearly impossible to confront the emotional consequences of mistakes; it is an environment in which precision seems to predominate. In the large centers where doctors are trained, teams of physicians discuss the smallest details of cases; teaching is usually conducted to make it seem "obvious" what decisions should have been made. And when a physician does make an important mistake, it is first whispered about in the halls, as if it were a sin. Much later, a case conference is called in which experts who have had weeks to think about the situation discuss the way it should have been handled. The environment in which physicians are trained does not encourage them to talk about their mistakes or about their emotional responses to them.

Indeed, errors are rarely admitted or discussed once a physician is in private practice. I have some indication from consultants and colleagues that I am of at least average competence as a physician. The mistakes I have discussed here represent only a fraction of those of which I am aware. I assume that my colleagues at my own clinic and elsewhere are responsible for similar numbers of major and minor errors. Yet we rarely discuss them; I cannot remember a single instance in which another physician initiated a discussion of a mistake for the purpose of clarifying his or her own emotional response or deciding how to follow up.(I do not wish to imply that we don't discuss difficult cases or unfortunate results; yet these discussions are always handled so delicately in the presence of the "offending" physician that there is simply no space for confession or absolution.) . . .

If the profession has no room for its mistakes, society seems to have even more rigid expectations of its physicians. The malpractice situation in our country is symptomatic of this attitude. In what other profession are practitioners regularly sued for hundreds of thousands of dollars because of a misjudgment? A lawyer informed me I could be sued for $50,000 for misreading the x-ray film that led to the young man's unhealed fracture. I am sure the Dailys could have successfully sued me for large amounts of money, had they chosen to do so. Experienced physicians who are honest with themselves can count many potential malpractice suits against them. Even the word "malpractice" carries the implication that one has done something more than make a natural mistake; it connotes guilt and sinfulness. . . .

[T]here is no place for real confession: "This is the mistake I made; I'm sorry." How can one say that to a grieving mother, to a family that has lost a member? It simply doesn't fit into the physician-patient relationship.

Even if one were bold enough to consider such a confession, strong voices would raise objections. When I finally heard about the unhealed fracture in my young patient, I was anxious that the incident not create antagonism between me and the family, since we live in a small town and see each other frequently. I was tempted to call the family and express my apologies and the hope that a satisfactory settlement could be worked out. I mentioned that possibility to a malpractice lawyer, but he was strongly opposed, urging me not to have any contact with the family until a settlement was reached. Even if a malpractice suit is not likely, the nature of the physician-patient relationship makes such a reversal of roles "unseemly." Can I further burden an already grieving family with the complexities of my feelings, my burden?

And if confession is difficult, what are we to say about restitution? The very nature of our work means that we are dealing with elements that cannot be restored in any meaningful way. What can I offer the Dailys in restitution?

I have not been successful in dealing with the paradox. Any patient encounter can dump me back into the situation of having caused more harm than good, yet my role is to be a healer. Since there has been no permission to address the paradox openly, I lapse into neurotic behavior to deal with my anxiety and guilt. Little wonder that physicians are accused of having a God complex; little wonder that we are defensive about our judgments; little wonder that we blame the patient or the previous physician when things go wrong, that we yell at the nurses for their mistakes, that we have such high rates of alcoholism, drug addiction, and suicide.

At some point we must bring our mistakes out of the closet. We need to give ourselves permission to recognize our errors and their consequences. We need to find healthy ways to deal with our emotional responses to those errors. Our profession is difficult enough without our having to wear the yoke of perfection.

Notes and Questions

(1) Dr. Hilfiker is a graduate of the University of Minnesota medical school, and writes that he has reason to believe, based on the judgments of other doctors, that he is "of at least average competence as a physician." In a book published one year after his 1984 article, he reports that he received many letters from fellow doctors praising his courage in revealing his errors and insecurities, and reporting similar experiences of their own. See D. Hilfiker, Healing the Wounds 12 (1985).

(2) Consider one or more of the errors reported by Dr. Hilfiker. Using Bosk's categories of error, would you characterize them as "technical," "judgmental," or "normative"? Can a single mistake fall into more than one category?

(3) Dr. Hilfiker asks: "what are we to say about restitution? The very nature of our work means that we are dealing with elements that cannot be restored in any meaningful way. What can I offer the Dailys in restitution?" Although Hilfiker seems to be implying that the answer to this question is "nothing," is that answer necessarily or completely correct? For example, apparently the Dailys chose not to sue Dr. Hilfiker for the mistaken abortion. Why do you think they made that choice? Do some possible reasons suggest that Dr. Hilfiker has given, and continues to give them something that functions like "restitution?" For discussion of the potential relationship of apology to malpractice litigation, see Kellett, Healing Angry Wounds: The Roles of Apology and Mediation in Disputes Between Doctors and Patients, 1987 Mo. J. of Dispute Resolution 111, reprinted in Specialty Law Digest: Health Care, March 1989, at 7 (suggesting that apology may be particularly helpful in repairing intangible injuries such as insult, degradation, and loss of status); see also Wagatsuma & Rosett, The Implications of Apology: Law and Culture in Japan and the United States, 20 Law & Socy. Rev. 461 (1986); Annas, Malpractice in Perspective, Section (B) (4) infra (discussing importance of doctor-patient communication in reducing the number of malpractice suits).

b. Socioeconomic Class

Note: Summary of R. Duff & A. Hollingshead, Sickness and Society (1968)

In 1968, Dr. Raymond S. Duff, Chair of Pediatrics at Yale University, and Dr. August B. Hollingshead, Chair of the Sociology Department, published Sickness and Society, their seminal study of the organization of work, provision of care, and interpersonal relations at one of the nation's most prestigious university teaching hospitals. The study is unique. No other examination of the work and personal relationships in a hospital is so systematic and detailed.

The central observation of Sickness and Society is that the care people receive in the hospital and the relationships patients have with everyone who works there are stratified along socio-economic class lines. Although accommodations were then divided into three socio-economic distinctions (private, semi-private, and ward) and now are divided into two (private and semi-private), the primary mechanism of class stratification was and remains the patient/physician relationship.

Duff and Hollingshead distinguish four types of patient/physician relations. *Committed sponsorship,* the relation between the highest class patients and their doctors, involves a determined assumption of responsibility for the patient by the physician, which extends beyond the doctor's interest in the patient's disease. These physicians are specialists, to whom the patient was referred prior to hospitalization. The patients enjoy private accommodations and have limited interaction with house staff or medical students. Id. 140-145. The next highest class of patients had a relationship of *casual sponsorship* with their physicians, characterized by a focus on "the symptoms of the disease and the diagnostic and treatment procedures. " The physician "looked upon the patient as his own" and did not allow house staff to dominate care and treatment. The physician knew little of the patient's personal circumstances. Id. at 137-139. Moving down the class ladder, *semi-committee sponsorship* involved a private physician who was nominally responsible for the patient's diagnosis and treatment, but in fact house staff assumed actual responsibility for diagnosis and treatment, as well as communication with the patient. Id. at 134-137. Finally, the lowest class of patients, *committee sponsored or ward patients,* had no private physicians. The correlation between sponsorship and accommodation was exact; the committee sponsorship arrangement applied to all ward patients and to no others. Responsibility for patient care rested with a committee of housestaff and students, whose membership shifted as people rotated through their educational process. Patients were admitted to the hospital by a staff physician, from an outpatient clinic or emergency room. They were significantly more ill than other patients, and communication between patients and physicians was very poor. Id. at 127-134.

Although stratification of patients was defined primarily in terms of relations with physicians, it also affected their relations with nurses and other hospital staff. Higher status patients received more nursing care, id. at 67-68, and the house staff spent nearly as much time with private patients as they did with patients on the wards, even though they had no formal responsibility for many of the private patients and were totally responsible for care of patients on the ward. Id. at 234.

Duff and Hollingshead found that no one on the hospital staff, either doctors or nurses, knew much about the patients as people, their personal situations, mental status, or feelings about their illness. Id. at 226-228. By contrast, both nurses and doctors had consistent and accurate knowledge of the patient's social status. Id. at 231-232. The failure to know the patients as people led to high levels of misdiagnosis, particularly failure to recognize alcoholism, mental illness, and pain, in all classes of patients. Id. at 158-165. Few dying patients were informed of their prognosis, and all who were told were white men of high status. Id. at 314-318.

Lack of communication had adverse consequences upon the hospital workers as well as upon the patients. RNs felt conflicts most acutely. They felt they should do more bedside care and know their patients better, but administrative requirements of the bureaucratic structure within which they worked placed heavy demands upon their time. RNs were frustrated by the deference they were required to give to some new house staff, whose sense of their own importance exceeded their experience and knowledge. Id. at 70-77, 217-218. Although the aides and LPNs spent most time in direct patient care, and the LPNs had greatest knowledge of the patients' emotional and personal circumstances, that knowledge was not used or valued. Communication among various groups of hospital workers flowed in only one direction, from the top down. Id. at 86-87, 374-376.

Questions

After reading the above summary of Duff and Hollingshead's work, reconsider the categories of error discussed by Bosk. Do the quality of care problems found by Duff and Hollingshead fit easily within those categories? If not, why not? Does the Duff and Hollingshead study suggest a need for new categories or conceptions of "error," or more broadly conceived quality of care concepts? What should these new concepts or categories be?

c. The Decentralized Professional Tradition

Wennberg, Dealing With Medical Practice Variations: A Proposal For Action

3 Health Affairs at 6, 9-10, 12, 15, 30-31 (Summer 1984)

Why is it that the norms of medical practice can be so loose or ambiguous as to allow a wide range of professional discretion? The answer is seen in a review of the medical literature on the degree of professional consensus concerning the value of specific treatments and in the critical examination of the scientific strengths and weaknesses of the studies which support a particular viewpoint.

The procedures exhibiting the most variation are often for conditions that are part of the aging process. The controversies arise because for such conditions the natural history of the untreated or conservatively treated case is often poorly understood, and well-designed clinical trials are notably absent. Examples include hysterectomy for noncancerous conditions, prostatectomy for benign hyperplasia of the prostate, tonsillectomy for hypertrophy of the tonsil, and coronary bypass surgery for mild angina. Well-defined scientific norms simply do not exist to limit the practice options physicians select to treat these maladies. As a consequence, the opinions of individual doctors can vary substantially, based upon subjective experience. Because many of the conditions are associated with the aging process, the number of candidates that could qualify for operative intervention is sometimes upwardly limited only by the size of the population.

For example, I have observed that in Maine, by the time women reach 70 years of age in one hospital market the likelihood they have undergone a hysterectomy is 20 percent while in another market it is 70 percent. In Iowa, the chances that male residents who reach age 85 have undergone prostatectomy range from a low of 15 percent to a high of more than 60 percent in different hospital markets. In Vermont the probability that resident children will undergo a tonsillectomy has ranged from a low of 8 percent in one hospital market to a high of nearly 70 percent in another.

By contrast, the low-variation procedures derive from quite specific conditions for which there is a professional consensus on the preferred place or style of treatment. Prime examples are surgical repair of inguinal hernia and hospitalizations for hip fractures. For these conditions, practice style, at least in the United States, only plays a small part in affecting demand. As a general rule, diagnosis is not difficult. If the patient seeks medical care, variations in clinical judgments are constrained by a consensus. For inguinal hernia, the treatment is an operation. For hip fraction virtually all patients are hospitalized. The rates show little variation between hospital markets. . . .

I developed the practice style theory after it became clear to me that the variation phenomenon could not be explained adequately by traditional theories. For example, consumer or population factors do not explain much of the difference in utilization rates among local hospital markets. Household interview studies in Vermont and Manitoba, Canada compared the characteristics of residents living in high- and low-rate market areas. These studies failed to show correlations between service use rates and illness rates, insurance coverage, access to service, and other demand-related attributes of patients or populations. The variations also persist after adjustment for age, which tends to account for most illness-related differences in populations. While some variation in the use rate of specific procedures is explained by the per capita supply of facilities and physicians, most remains unexplained. For example, Noralou Roos has shown that per capita number of beds and gynecologists are virtually the same in hospital markets with low and with high per capita hysterectomy rates.

The variation phenomenon appears to be a worldwide phenomenon, not explained by incentives associated with fee-for-service medicine. The pattern of variation for common procedures is similar among fee-for-service hospital markets in Iowa, Maine, Massachusetts, Rhode Island, and Vermont; among health maintenance organizations in the United States; and among the health care regions in Canada, England, and Norway, even though obvious differences exist in the supply of surgeons, the organization and financing of services, and in the cultural and demographic characteristics of hospital market area residents. There is one common factor: physicians in each of these areas of the world read the same medical literature, participate in the same scientific traditions, and share the same scientific uncertainties concerning the value of certain procedures.

The most direct evidence for the importance of practice styles in influencing utilization rates comes from natural experiments in which practice styles change following the feedback of information to physicians on the rates in their own and neighboring market areas. Changes have been documented for hysterectomy rates in Saskatchewan, Canada and Maine; for tonsillectomy rates in Vermont and Maine; and for lens extractions in Norway. The evidence indicates that the changes occurred primarily because physicians took actions to modify their clinical policies. In one example, a letter from hospital officials speaks directly to the importance of admission policies in influencing the demand for services and documents the effect of feedback. The letter reads: "We are following up after an ongoing one-year audit (of) hysterectomies . . . (concerning) the high numbers of hysterectomies. . . . (The past experience) in no way reflects the (current) actual numbers. The department of OB/GYN has set its own goals of between 220 and 240. This past year, 229 hysterectomies were completed during that period. Also, we have met our own criteria regarding the number of hysterectomies showing normal pathology at 20 percent to 25 percent. During this one-year period, a percentage of 24.9 was reached." In the year prior to feedback, the market area served by this hospital had a rate of 118 procedures per 10,000 women which was more than double the state average. In 1981, the year the letter discusses, the rate was 58, less than half the previous rate but 25 percent higher than the 1981 state average. . . .

To understand the cost implications of the practice style factor, return to the case of hysterectomy. Over the last decade, about 2500 more hysterectomies were performed in one Maine market area, with about 35,000 women in the eligible age range, than would have been performed if the practice style of physicians located in a low-rate neighboring market had applied. At the current market value of approximately $4000 per hysterectomy, this translates into an excess of $10 million. Yet the price of hysterectomy in this high-rate market is below average. Under DRG prospective pricing plans and preferred provider strategies, the hospitals in the high-rate market will be rewarded for their "efficiency." Yet the data show that the most important determinant of variations in per capita costs, or the "bottom line" for payers, are physicians' decisions to admit patients to the hospital or to employ a specific treatment, not the decisions they or other health care providers may make that affect the efficiency of medical care as reflected in the unit price of service or the length of a hospital stay.

Since more than 85 percent of hospitalizations classified under the DRG system appear to have greater variation in per capita use rates among hospital market areas than hysterectomy, the above example is a conservative demonstration of the problems that attend unit pricing approaches to cost containment. Indeed, through the incentives they create for reducing lengths-of-stay in hospitals — thus freeing beds to allocate to new patients — cost-containment programs that focus only on the reduction of unit price may add to rather than reduce the overall costs. If hospitals that stand to lose money under the DRG system are able to improve their financial status by increasing the volume of services, then the inevitable result will be an acceleration in the rate of increase in per capita expenditures. . . .

SUMMARY

Most treatments, diagnostic tests, and surgical operations have highly variable use rates among hospital markets. One reason for the variation is professional controversies that arise because of ambiguous or incomplete scientific evidence on the value of specific services. To resolve the controversies — and to improve the opportunity for informed judgment on their use — better information on the outcome of care is needed. A second reason for the variation phenomenon is the individualistic practice styles adopted by physicians for reasons of their own or their patient's convenience or their interpretation of the requirements for "defensive"medicine. The reduction in demand for hospitalization based on these reasons offers opportunities for large savings without fear that needed services are being withheld.

NOTE: IS HIGH UTILIZATION BAD MEDICINE?

Wennberg strongly implies that geographic areas with high rates of surgical procedures are performing excess or unnecessary surgery and could lower their rates without compromising quality of care. His argument is based in part on the lack of any obvious demographic differences between high and low rate areas and in part on the fact that when doctors were informed of the variations in rates for hysterectomies and tonsillectomies in certain geographic areas, the high use areas lowered their rates dramatically without apparent ill effects on patient well being. But see Brook, Lohr, Chassin, Kosecoff, Fink & Solomon, Geographic Variations in the Use of Services: Do They Have Any Clinical Significance? Health Affairs at 63 (Summer 1984) (reviewing the literature, concluding that "no one can really say" whether geographic variations mean that high use or low use rates, or both, are appropriate, and outlining research agenda); Perrin, Homer, Berwick, Woolf, Freeman &

Wennberg, Variations in Rates of Hospitalization of Children in Three Urban Communities, 320 N. Engl. J. Med. 1183 (1989) (finding that large geographic variations among Boston, New Haven, and Rochester in the rate of hospitalizing children may be a function of unavailability of primary care services for low income families).

The 1987 study by Chassin et al., discussed in the introduction to this chapter, found a high degree of geographic variation in the use of three procedures, but did not find a clear correlation between high use and inappropriate use. The authors suggest a number of alternative explanations of variation that require further research: the largely unexplored question of "underuse" (suggesting that for certain procedures, the low use areas rather than the high use areas may be problematic); possible regional differences in disease incidence; social and cultural differences among patients that may produce differences among geographic areas in the stage of illness at which patients seek health care; and geographic differences in the role of primary care physicians and referral patterns to specialists who control utilization of many specialized procedures. See Chassin et al., supra, at 2536.

B. Defining and Enforcing Quality Through Common Law Courts: Medical Malpractice Law

1. MEDICAL MALPRACTICE LAW AND QUALITY OF CARE

When considering the concept of "quality of care," most lawyers and law students probably turn immediately, and perhaps exclusively, to the law of medical malpractice. This law consists of the principles used by judges and juries to decide whether doctors, hospitals, and other providers (and their insurance companies) must pay for the costs of particular medical errors or adverse outcomes. In theory, these decisions about liability should serve as a quality assurance system, with damage awards signaling that certain errors should be avoided, certain procedures revised, or individual practitioners monitored and disciplined. Indeed, economist Patricia M. Danzon argues that "the primary economic rationale for tort liability is deterrence [of injury-producing behavior]. In principle, the law of negligence can create an incentive structure designed to induce physicians to invest optimally in injury prevention." P. Danzon, Medical Malpractice 9 (1985). See also Bovbjerg, Medical Malpractice On Trial: Quality of Care is the Important Standard, 49 Law & Contmp. Prob. (Spring 1986) at 321.

In fact, at least until very recently, medical malpractice law has made relatively little contribution to assuring quality of care or deterring doctor-caused injuries. First, malpractice litigation is expensive, and is largely financed on the plaintiffs' side by contingent attorneys' fees. Most lawyers in private practice will thus not provide representation (or will drop the case without obtaining compensation) unless the case has a substantial dollar value. For example, a 1976 study suggested that New York lawyers generally insisted on a likely recovery of over $40,000 in order to justify litigation. The vast majority of quality of care issues are thus never even touched by the malpractice system.

Second, the malpractice system is widely perceived, particularly by doctors, as not sending reliable signals about quality of care. Medical malpractice insurance is not usually "experience rated." This means that even doctors who have been found negligent repeatedly pay the same rates as those who are never sued. See Note, The Applicability of Experience Rating to Medical Malpractice Insurance, 38 Case W. Res. L. Rev. 255 (1987) (discussing pros and cons of experience or merit rating and recent merit rating legislation in New York and Massachusetts). In addition, widespread anecdotal evidence suggests that many physicians regard malpractice judgments against their colleagues as artifacts of the legal system — of skillful plaintiffs' lawyers and emotional juries — rather than as reliable signals regarding quality of care.

Third, even if physicians with special quality of care responsibilities — hospitals' chiefs of staff, or members of state licensing boards — wish to use malpractice awards as part of a quality feedback system, they often lack (or lacked until recently) the institutional support, information, resources, and (in the case of licensing boards) legal authority to undertake effective action. See S. Law & S. Polan, Pain and Profit: The Politics of Malpractice 39-50 (1978); Law, A Consumer Perspective on Medical Malpractice, 49 Law & Contemp. Prob. (Spring 1986) at 305, 310-315.

Finally, and more fundamentally, the entire design of medical malpractice law seems ill-suited to serve as the major means for achieving quality of care. A system characterized by high administrative expenses, narrow selection of cases, vaguely worded standards of evaluation, retrospective and long-delayed judgments rendered by tribunals sharply separated from (and often despised by) the providers of care, and no coherent feedback system to hospitals, state licensing boards, and the public, seems virtually guaranteed to fail as a serious quality assurance program (while, paradoxically, perhaps having pervasive and often perverse effects). Even given these limitations, Danzon estimates that "if the number of negligent injuries is, generously, 20 percent lower than it otherwise would be because of the incentives for care created by the malpractice system, the system is worth retaining, despite its costs." P. Danzon, supra, at 226. Alternatively, one could argue that medical malpractice law may be defensible as a crude compensation system, at least in the absence of alternatives, such as comprehensive and adequately funded social insurance for health care in general and for the costs of accidental injuries. See, in addition to sources cited above, Brook, Brutoco & Williams, The Relationship

Between Medical Malpractice and Quality of Care, 1975 Duke L.J. 1197 (arguing that medical malpractice contributes relatively little to quality of care and advocating strengthening and democratizing of peer review mechanisms); Bovbjerg, supra, at 326-328 (arguing forcefully that malpractice law and insurance fail miserably as a compensation system); Annas, Katz & Trakimas, Medical Malpractice Litigation under National Health Insurance: Essential or Expendable?, 1975 Duke L.J. 1335 (exploring possible impact of various national health insurance proposals on medical malpractice litigation); Bovbjerg, The Medical Malpractice Standard of Care: HMO's and Customary Practice, 1975 Duke L.J. 1375, 1398-1399 (hereinafter cited as "HMO Standard") (arguing that malpractice standards have pervasive regulatory effects in the absence of clear professional or scientific standards of reasonableness and efficacy).

Given these limitations, we put medical malpractice law near the beginning of this chapter not because it is the most important or best means of assuring quality, but rather because historically it was one of the earliest, and for many years largely the only system of reviewing physician actions against some standard of quality of care.

2. THE ROLE OF LAW IN THE AGE OF EXPANDING MEDICAL AUTHORITY: 1860 TO 1960

As discussed in the Introduction and in Chapter 7 (regarding medical education), the social authority and internal organization of the medical profession was strengthened dramatically in the century between 1860 and 1960. Law — statutes as well as judicial decisions — provided indispensable support for these developments by granting doctors virtually unreviewable autonomy over training, operating, and financing their profession. Entry was controlled by state licensing boards, discussed in Section E infra, whose functions and composition were defined by the state medical societies. Medical education, discussed in Chapter 7, was controlled through an accreditation process operated by the medical profession and hospital industry. Appointments to hospital medical staffs, discussed in Section D infra, were in practice controlled by existing staff physicians without significant external review. As we have seen in Chapters 2 and 3, financing, until very recently, was also dominated by the interests of organized doctors and hospitals. Finally, patients who wanted to sue a doctor for damages would encounter two doctrines of medical malpractice law that effectively delegated the liability decision to the local medical profession itself.

a. THE PROFESSIONAL STANDARD DOCTRINE

As early as 1767, an English court indicated that in order to recover damages against a surgeon, a patient had to show that the doctor had violated "the usage and law of surgeons . . . the rule of the profession . . ." as testified to by other surgeons themselves. Slater v. Baker and Stapleton, 95 Eng. Rep. 860, 862 (King's Bench 1767). The effect of this professional standard of care is to accord the customary practices of doctors virtually conclusive weight as to what constitutes "reasonable care." As a practical matter, one of the most important consequences of defining the legal standard of care in terms of professional custom is to require the plaintiff, in most instances, to find an expert medical witness willing to testify that the defendant doctor violated the professional standard of care. See S. Law & S. Polan. supra at 7-8; Bovbjerg, "HMO Standard" supra, 1975 Duke L.J. at 1392-1397 (arguing that reliance on medical custom is a practical necessity, but is flawed by doctors' lack of competence to assess the social costs of medical custom and by the effects of open-ended insurance reimbursement).

Early American courts, like the English courts, defined the doctor's legal duty in terms of the "reasonable skill and diligence as are ordinarily exercised in his profession. . . ." McCandless v. McWha, 22 Pa. (10 Harris) 261, 267-268 (1853). Although one early court defined the applicable standard as that which "thoroughly educated surgeons ordinarily employ," most American courts rejected this standard as too high, and required only the standard set by the actual practices of the "average" or "ordinary" practitioner. See, for instance, Smothers v. Hanks, 34 Iowa 286 (1872).

b. The Locality Rule

Equal in importance to the professional standard was the geographic scope by which that standard was to be determined. By the 1870s and 1880s, a number of courts had ruled that a doctor practicing in a rural area or small town was

> bound to possess that skill only which physicians and surgeons of ordinary ability and skill, practicing in similar localities, with opportunities for no larger experience, ordinarily possess; and he was not bound to possess that high degree of art and skill possessed by eminent surgeons practicing in larger cities, and making a specialty of the practice of surgery. [Small v. Howard, 128 Mass. 131, 132, 35 Am. Rep. 363, 365 (1880) (trial court charge approved by state supreme court).]

Some courts required the plaintiff to prove a violation of the customary professional standard in the *particular* locality where the defendant practiced; thus, only doctors who practiced in that same community were qualified to be expert witnesses. Needless to say, finding one doctor to testify against another in a small community was often impossible. Many courts relaxed the standard enough to allow experts from the "same or similar locality," which gave rise to much uncertainty and litigation over what a "similar" locality was. See Waltz, The Rise and Gradual Fall of the Locality Rule in Medical Malpractice Litigation, 18 DePaul L. Rev. 408, 410-412 (1969). Moreover, proof of a doctor's deviation from local medical custom did not necessarily establish a breach of duty; courts permitted (and still permit) the defendant doctor to justify his actions as those of a "respectable" or "reputable" minority of medical practitioners or as a "medical judgment" about which reasonable doctors might disagree.

Although the technology of medicine and medical education has changed greatly from the late 1800s to the late 1900s, the sense of "uneven" access to resources and even knowledge remains, as the readings by Hilfiker and Duff and Hollingshead, supra, suggest. As you read the modern cases grappling with arguments for national versus local or otherwise special standards, consider whether the concerns of the nineteenth century courts retain some vitality, and if so, in what modified modern form?

3. RAISING (OR LOWERING) THE LOCAL PROFESSIONAL STANDARD OF CARE: THE THEORY OF MODERN MEDICAL MALPRACTICE LAW

The trend in medical malpractice law from roughly the 1940s to the present has been the gradual and rather piecemeal abandonment of the local professional standard of care, generally with the effect of raising the applicable standard. This has been accomplished through two major legal theories. The first, and by far the dominant, is that the medical profession itself has in effect adopted national standards and that the courts ought to enforce the profession's own view of minimally acceptable or adequate care. See, for instance, Blair v. Eblen, 461 S.W.2d 370, 373 (Ky. 1970). This view, which normally leads to raising the standard of care by allowing outside medical experts to criticize local practices, is explored in sections (a) and (b) below.

The second theory is that the professional standard itself, like customary practices generally, is "evidence" of what ought to be done, but not conclusive evidence; in the final analysis "what ought to be done is fixed by a standard of reasonable prudence, whether it is usually complied with or not." Texas & Pacific Railway v. Behymer, 189 U.S. 468, 470 (1903). The two major examples of this approach are the rare trumping of a professional cost-benefit consensus by lay decisionmakers (as in Helling v. Carey, discussed in Chapter 4 and in section (a) below) and the rise of the patient-oriented informed consent standard, discussed in section (d) and, in more detail, in Chapter 6.

Although many judges and legal commentators have celebrated the trend toward rising standards, few have been willing to address the law's de facto (and at times de jure) *lowering* of the local standard of care with respect to the poor. This topic is explored in section (e). The trend of lowering the standard of care, or of creating multiple standards of care based on ability to pay, is now assuming unprecedented importance because it is beginning to affect middle-income patients through a variety of cost-containment programs. This topic is addressed in section (f), and again at the end of the chapter.

In addition, in response to a perceived crisis in the cost and availability of medical malpractice insurance, many state legislatures have imposed procedural and substantive restrictions on medical malpractice remedies, and one state (Florida) has actually lowered the standard of care for all patients for emergency services. This topic is explored in section (4).

a. The Assault on the Locality Rule and the Concept of a National Standard

Critics of the locality rule repeatedly pointed out its two major defects: it permitted substandard practitioners to set an authoritative local "standard," and it often made it impossible for injured patients to find a medical expert willing to testify even against gross negligence. See, for instance, Walz, supra, 18 DePaul L. Rev. at 420; Pederson v. Dumouchel, 72 Wash. 2d 73, 431 P.2d 973, 977 (1967). Moreover, the stated justifications for the locality rule — the isolation and rudimentary conditions of small-town or rural medical practice — seemed increasingly untenable as medical education and hospital procedures became, or at least claimed to be, standardized under national accreditation programs. See, for instance, Shilkret v. Annapolis Emergency Hospital, 276 Md. 187, 349 A.2d 245, 249-250 (1975); Brune v. Belinkoff, 235 N. E. 2d 793 (Mass. 1968) (overruling locality rule announced in Small v. Howard, supra). By the mid-1970s, many state courts had abandoned the traditional locality rule, and now held physicians to "that degree of care and skill which is expected of a reasonably competent practitioner in the same class to which he belongs, acting in the same or similar circumstances. Under this standard, advances in the profession, availability of facilities, specialization or general practice, proximity of specialists and special facilities, together with all other relevant considerations, are to be taken into account." *Shilkret* supra, 349 A.2d at 253. Yet as late as 1983, when a very experienced Florida orthopedic surgeon testified that practically every procedure used by a defendant Mississippi physician in treating a logger's wounded leg was negligent, the Mississippi Supreme Court excluded his testimony on the ground that the Florida surgeon was not familiar with the Mississippi standard of care. See King v. Murphy, 424 So. 2d 547 (Miss. 1983). Two years later, the Mississippi Supreme Court reconsidered in depth its position on the locality rule, and explicitly discussed the tension between the concept of a national "minimum standard" and the continuing need to take local resources, if not "standards," into account.

Hall v. Hilbun

466 So. 2d 856 (Miss. 1985)

En banc.

[Dr. Hilbun, a general surgeon who had practiced for 16 years at Singing River Hospital in Jackson County, Mississippi, performed an exploratory laporatomy on Terry Hall to remove an obstruction of the small bowel. After surgery Mrs. Hall died of adult respiratory distress syndrome. Mrs. Hall's husband sued Dr. Hilbun for negligent post-operative care, focusing in particular on Dr. Hilbun's failure to ascertain his patient's condition during the evening after surgery and his failure to give appropriate instructions to the nurses. The Singing River Hospital and its administrator were also originally named as defendants, but were dismissed on "sovereign and public official immunity grounds." The nurses were never sued.

The plaintiff called Dr. S. O. Hoerr, a retired surgeon of Cleveland, Ohio, as an expert witness. Despite Dr. Hoerr's distinguished academic and practice credentials, the trial court ruled that because of the locality rule, Dr. Hoerr was not qualified to give an opinion as to whether Dr. Hilbun's post-operative regimen departed from the obligatory standard of care. As recorded through a question-and-answer proffer of testimony, Dr. Hoerr's excluded testimony was that serious complications regarding bleeding, infection, and breathing can follow abdominal surgery, and that therefore careful post-operative monitoring by the surgeon is necessary. This can be accomplished by personal observation by the surgeon, or by indirect monitoring through other physicians and nurses. If the surgeon has doubts about the capacity of the nurses, he can and should leave detailed instructions to contact him if the vital signs reach certain specified levels.

After summarizing the assumption of physician isolation underlying the traditional locality rule, the court addressed modern developments.]

2. *THE INEVITABLE ASCENDENCY OF NATIONAL STANDARDS*

. . . We would have to put our heads in the sand to ignore the "nationalization" of medical education and training. Medical school admission standards [and curricula] are similar across the country. . . . Internship and residency programs for those entering medical specialties have substantially common components. Nationally uniform standards are enforced in the case of certification of specialists. . . .

Physicians are far more mobile than they once were. [T]hey have ready access to professional and scientific journals and seminars for continuing medical education from across the country. . . .

[T]he medical centers in Memphis, Birmingham, Mobile, New Orleans and other nearby areas in adjoining states are a very real part of the Mississippi-centered universe of hospitalization, medical care and treatment, and other health related services. . . .

3. *THE COMPETENCE-BASED NATIONAL STANDARD OF CARE: HEREIN OF THE LIMITED ROLE OF LOCAL CUSTOM*

All of the above informs our understanding and articulation of the competence-based duty of care. Each physician may with reason and fairness be expected to possess or have reasonable access to such medical knowledge as is commonly possessed or reasonably available to minimally competent physicians in the same specialty or general field of practice throughout the United States, to have a realistic understanding of the limitations on his or her knowledge or competence, and, in general, to exercise minimally adequate medical judgment. Beyond that, each physician has a duty to have a practical working knowledge of the facilities, equipment, resources (including personnel in health related fields and their general level of knowledge and competence), and options (including what specialized services or facilities may be available in larger communities, e.g., Memphis, Birmingham, Jackson, New Orleans, etc.) reasonably available to him or her as well as the practical limitations on same. . . .

We recognize that customs vary within given medical communities and from one medical community to another. Conformity with established medical custom practiced by minimally competent physicians in a given area, while evidence of performance of the duty of care, may never be conclusive of such compliance. Cf. Helling v. Carey, 83 Wash. 2d 514, 519 P.2d 981 (1974). The content of the duty of care must be objectively determined by reference to the availability of medical and practical knowledge which would be brought to bear in the treatment of like or similar patients under like or similar circumstances by minimally competent physicians in the same field, given the facilities, resources and options available. The content of the duty of care may be informed by local medical custom but never subsumed by it. . . .

4. *THE RESOURCES-BASED CAVEAT TO THE NATIONAL STANDARD OF CARE*

[In the light of these considerations,] [t]he duty of care . . . takes two forms: (a) a duty to render a quality of care consonant with the level of medical and practical knowledge the physician may reasonably be expected to possess and the medical judgment he may be expected to exercise, and (b) a duty based upon the adept use of such medical facilities, services, equipment and options as are reasonably available. With respect to this second form of the duty, we regard that there remains a core of validity to the premises of the old locality rule. For reasons well known to all, the facilities, equipment, health care personnel, and other such resources reasonably available to

Mississippi's physicians vary from community to community. . . . Because of these differences in facilities, equipment, etc., ... [a] physician practicing in Noxubee County, for example, may hardly be faulted for failure to perform a CAT scan when the necessary facilities and equipment are not reasonably available. In contradistinction, objectively reasonable expectations regarding the physician's knowledge, skill, capacity for sound medical judgment and general competence are, consistent with his field of practice and the facts and circumstances in which the patient may be found, *the same everywhere*. . . .

As we deal with general principles, gray areas necessarily exist. One involves the case where needed specialized facilities and equipment are not available locally but are reasonably accessible in major medical centers — New Orleans, Jackson, Memphis. Here as elsewhere the local physician is held to minimally acceptable standards. In determining whether the physician's actions comport with his duty of care, consideration must always be given to the time factor — is the physician confronted with what reasonably appears to be a medical emergency, or does it appear likely that the patient may be transferred to an appropriate medical center without substantial risk to the health or life of the patient? Consideration must also be given to the economic factors — are the proposed transferee facilities sufficiently superior to justify the trouble and expense of transfer? Further discussion of these factors should await proper cases.

D. *Who May Qualify As Expert Medical Witness In Malpractice Case: A rule of evidence*

. . . Generally, where the expert lives or where he or she practices his or her profession has no relevance *per se* with respect to whether a person may be qualified and accepted by the court as an expert witness. . . .

[A] qualified medical expert may express an opinion regarding the conclusions . . . minimally knowledgeable and competent physicians in the same specialty or general field of practice would draw, or actions (not tied to the availability of specialized facilities or equipment not generally available) they would take.

Before the witness may go further, he must be familiarized with the facilities, resources, services and options available. This may be done in any number of ways. The witness may prior to trial have visited the facilities, etc. He may have sat in the courtroom and listened as other witnesses described the facilities. . . . [In addition], the witness [may] be made familiar with the facilities (and customs) of the medical community in question via a properly predicated and phrased hypothetical question.

Once he has become informed of the facilities, etc. available to the defendant physician, the qualified medical expert witness may express an opinion what the care duty of the defendant physician was and whether the acts or omissions of the defendant physician were in compliance with, or fell substantially short of compliance with, that duty.

At this point it is appropriate to note the earnestness with which counsel for Dr. Hilbun, no doubt purporting to speak on behalf of the medical community generally, begs for protection from the circuit-riding charlatan, the man from out of town with a briefcase. . . . We remind one and all that qualification of a medical expert witness in a malpractice action is no more a mechanical process than any other procedure in our law. Within the limits of the general rule stated above, the trial judge is necessarily called upon to exercise his sound discretion in determining whether a proffered witness is in fact qualified as an expert. . . .

Notes and Questions

(1) Recall the medical case of the boy with the injured leg and foot discussed by Dr. Hilfiker at page 390 supra. Under the *Hall* standard and your best prediction of its future development, did Dr. Hilfiker have a duty to refer his patient to the specialist in Duluth? Dr. Hilfiker writes that he offered the patient a choice: stay in the locality or travel to Duluth. Is that an adequate way for a doctor in a small community to discharge his duty under *Hall*? Would the tone and manner in which the doctor offered the choice be important?

(2) The *Hall* court cites Helling v. Carey, presented in Chapter 4. In *Helling*, the Washington Supreme Court held that a physician's compliance with the prevailing professional standard of care — that routine pressure tests for glaucoma should not be administered to persons under 40 — was not sufficient to satisfy the physician's legal duty of reasonable care, because the professional standard itself was not "reasonably prudent" from the perspective of general legal principles of reasonable care. What is the significance of the Mississippi Supreme Court's citation of *Helling*? Is the Mississippi court saying that in some circumstances local medical custom may not be reasonably prudent? If so, what kind of evidence would you as plaintiff's attorney try to introduce to establish that?

(3) According to plaintiff's expert, the nurses in *Hall* were also deficient in failing to monitor the patient and to contact the doctor, particularly after a high pulse rate was recorded. Like doctors, nurses are now generally held to a national standard of care expected of a "reasonably prudent and competent registered nurse." G. Annas, L. Glantz & B. Katz, The Rights of Doctors, Nurses, and Allied Health Professionals 28 (1981).

(4) Traditionally, hospitals, like physicians, were only held to the standard of care practiced by similar hospitals in their own locality. However, the existence of national hospital accreditation, state-wide licensure, and increasingly comprehensive state regulatory systems has convinced most state courts to reject a locality standard for hospitals and to apply a roughly uniform national standard. Thus, "a hospital is required to use that degree of care and skill which is expected of a reasonably competent hospital in the same or

similar circumstances. As in cases brought against physicians, advances in the profession, availability of special facilities and specialists, together with all other relevant considerations, are to be taken into account." Shilkret v. Annapolis Emergency Hospital Association, 276 Md. 187, 349 A.2d 245, 254 (1975). For further discussion of hospitals' duties of care, see Section C infra.

Problem: Continued Validity of the Locality Rule?

In his book Healing the Wounds, Dr. David Hilfiker describes a particularly harrowing childbirth. A woman whose pregnancy has been "wonderfully normal" and who has traveled over 50 miles to be attended by Dr. Hilfiker because he believes in natural childbirth, is in the hospital and about to give birth when the nurse listening to the fetus' heart rate suddenly notices that it has increased sharply. When the baby is born a minute or so later, it is blue, with a pulse of only 40 (instead of the normal 140), and not trying to breathe. Dr. Hilfiker and a nurse resuscitate the baby, and through a blood sample Hilfiker identifies the immediate problem as low blood sugar. Unsure of the proper concentration of glucose or how to administer it, Hilfiker calls a specialist, Dr. Mary Donaldson, at the Newborn Intensive Care Unit in Duluth. After Hilfiker describes the situation as succinctly as he can, their conversation goes as follows:

> "Did you have a fetal monitor [an electronic device for measuring fetal heartrate] on during labor?" she [Dr. Donaldson] asks. "What was the heart rate then?"
>
> "We don't have the monitor yet, Mary." How can I explain to her that our little hospital can't afford the $10,000 piece of equipment since it would be used only a few times a year? "The nurses listened, of course, but the heart rate seemed normal to them. We must have missed the decelerations in heartbeat."
>
> "Yes, I think so. You said the baby's small? Did you get an ultrasound picture during pregnancy?"
>
> "No, I didn't. The baby seemed normal size to me on examination, so I didn't get an ultrasound. I suppose I should have."
>
> "Well, it might have tipped you off that something was wrong. But then, we don't always get them down here either, and these surprises can happen. . . . I think you should get some glucose in as soon as possible to prevent brain damage."
>
> "OK," I say. "What route should we use for administration, and what dosages?"
>
> "I think an intraumbilical catheter [a plastic tube through a vein in the belly button] would be best. Just give five percent glu — "
>
> I interrupt her. "I've never put in an intraumbilical line." I feel so ignorant — one more skill, one more bit of information I should have. . . . "I'm not even sure we have the correct supplies up here."

> "Oh . . . well, then put an IV into a scalp vein and give a simple five percent glucose solution. If you can't get an IV going, you can put a gavage tube down into the baby's stomach and instill ten percent glucose; that would be better than nothing. . . . I'd suggest we come up in the ambulance and bring the baby down here for intensive care. . . ."
>
> [Jean Appleton, the head nurse] and I work unsuccessfully for fifteen minutes trying to pass an IV catheter into one of the fragile veins of the baby's scalp. I haven't had to do this since my internship five years ago and my skills have noticeably deteriorated. The small veins keep breaking. Finally we give up on the IV and put a tube in the baby's stomach. Fortunately, one of the newly recruited nurses used to work in a newborn intensive care unit. We get her out of bed . . . and she hurries to help me manage the gavage tube, since I've never done that either. . . .
>
> During the next two hours while we are waiting for the specialized neonatal transport ambulance from Duluth, the baby seems to do pretty well. I, however, am a nervous wreck! I remember vaguely that abnormal levels in blood minerals, trouble getting enough oxygen to the brain, and numerous other problems can plague [small] babies . . . but I don't have the knowledge or skills, nor does our hospital have the equipment, to do the required testing or treatment." [After a few months of complications, concern, and treatment in Duluth, the baby is pronounced fine.] [D. Hilfiker, Healing the Wounds 45-47 (1985).]

Assume, however, that the baby was permanently and seriously brain damaged because of inadequate blood sugar at and after childbirth. Assume further that you are representing Dr. Hilfiker in the subsequent malpractice suit, and that the Hall v. Hilbun opinion is the governing law. What kinds of witnesses, offering what kinds of evidence, would you expect the plaintiffs to call? What do you think the plaintiffs' strongest arguments will be? What kinds of witnesses, offering what kinds of evidence, would you call in Hilfiker's defense? What are your strongest arguments? Who do you think will prevail, and why?

b. Required and Permitted Deviations from Customary and Local Practice: Specialists, the "Best Judgment" Rule, and "Reputable Minorities"

What is the relevant professional community of the specialist, who presents himself to the public as more qualified than the ordinary practitioner? The organization of medical specialties with national standards for accrediting training programs, national examinations, and national organizations and journals has provided a strong basis for applying a national standard of care. The question was squarely posed in Robbins v. Footer, 553 F.2d 123 (D.C. Cir. 1977), in which a Washington, D.C., obstetrician was sued for negligent administration of pitocin during childbirth. One of the plaintiff's experts testified that "actual common practice" among obstetricians in Washington, D.C. was "more lax" than the national specialty standard; on this basis, the trial judge excluded testimony about the national standard and instructed the jury to apply the standards actually used among specialists in the locality. The District of Columbia Circuit Court of Appeals reversed, holding that nationally certified specialists must meet a national standard: that is, "that degree of care and skill expected of a reasonably competent practitioner in his specialty acting in the same or similar circumstances." The fact that specialists in one locality may have followed a lower standard was no defense, unless that deviation was justified by "[t]he availability of medical facilities, accessibility of professional consultation and the communication and transportation systems of the area. . . ." National standards are typically applied to specialists, even in states that retain a version of the local standard for general practitioners. See id. at 126-130; G. Annas, L. Glantz & B. Katz, supra at 247 (1981).

Reliance on local or customary practice is also not adequate where the physician knows, or has reason to know, that customary practice is problematic; in other words, the doctor has a duty to exercise his "best judgment," even if that judgment differs from the customary standard. A number of cases involving this principle arose out of the fact that in the early 1950s there was extensive debate among doctors about whether administration of high doses of oxygen to premature infants actually benefited them at all or whether it caused blindness. For example, shortly before a study conclusively showed that oxygen treatment was pointless and harmful, and hence while such treatment still remained the standard, albeit subject to debate, a pediatrician ordered four liters of oxygen per minute be administered to two premature infants, rather than the customary six liters per minute. The nurses failed to follow the four liter per minute order and administered the usual six, causing the infants' blindness. In a subsequent lawsuit the doctor was found not liable for having ordered the oxygen — since it was still the standard — but the question arose whether he might still be liable for failing to ascertain that the hospital staff had mistakenly increased the dosage. The doctor argued that since the "mistaken" dosage was still the customary standard, he should not be held liable for the mistake. The New York Court of Appeals disagreed and held that the doctor had in effect established a higher standard for himself through his own knowledge of the risks of oxygen treatment. See Toth v. Community Hospital at Glen Cove, 22 N.Y.2d 255, 292 N.Y.S.2d 440, 239 N.E.2d 368 (1968).

NOTE: OTHER DEVIATIONS FROM CUSTOMARY PRACTICE

(1) *The "best judgment" rule.* A doctor's deviation from customary practice, via the "best judgment" rule, may itself result in harm. For example, if

the nurses had followed the pediatrician's order in *Toth* to administer four liters of oxygen per minute, and if injury had resulted, would the pediatrician be liable for failing to adhere to customary practice? Most courts would be inclined *not* to hold the doctor liable in situations where, as here, the deviant procedure "had some reputable support in the profession."

As customary practices come under the increasing scrutiny of geographic variations research and other quality assessment programs discussed in section A supra, at what point should a doctor be required to use his or her "best judgment" in questioning conventional tests and treatments? One desirable and perhaps legally required way to deal with this issue is for the doctor to inform the patient of the competing perspectives, so as to enable the patient to exercise truly informed choice. See Burton v. Brooklyn Doctors Hospital, 88 A.D.2d 217, 452 N.Y.S.2d 875, 880-881 (1982) (doctor who raised premature infant's oxygen to high levels for experimental rather than therapeutic purposes liable both for violating her duty to use her best judgment, and her duty to explain to infant's parents the risks and options so as to obtain informed consent).

(2) *The "respectable minority" rule.* Courts have long recognized that medicine is a highly variable craft, and the locality rule served as doctors' main defense against their being judged by allegedly unfamiliar practices. A second defense lay in the "respectable minority" or "reputable school" rule, which permitted deviations from the dominant local custom as long as they could be supported by some "respectable" scientific argument. This doctrine was important in the nineteenth and early twentieth centuries, when numerous competing "schools" or approaches to medicine flourished, but diminished in importance as the allopathic approach became the dominant orthodoxy. However, two recent developments are likely to give this doctrine greatly increased importance: geographic variations research and cost containment programs, which tend to generate multiple standards of care. See, for instance, Bovbjerg, HMO Standard, 1975 Duke L.J. at 1409-1410.

(3) *Overriding the Profession's Cost-Benefit Consensus or Other Standard for Quality of Care.* Courts have occasionally subjected professional standards to lay or legal criteria of "reasonable prudence." The most famous recent case of this sort is Helling v. Carey, 83 Wash. 2d 514, 519 P.2d 981 (1974), discussed in Chapter 4. See also Gonzales v. Nork, Superior Ct., Sacramento Co., No.228566, Nov. 19, 1973, reprinted in part in S. Law & S. Polan, *supra,* at 215, and discussed in Section (C) (5) (d) *infra,* and informed consent doctrine discussed immediately below.

c. The Special Case of Informed Consent

Doctors have traditionally claimed that professional custom should govern not only the technical arts of diagnosis and treatment, but also the issue of how much information should be disclosed to the patient about his or her condition and about treatment alternatives. Although most states still adhere to this professional standard of informed consent, a number of jurisdictions — notably California and the District of Columbia — have adopted a patient-oriented standard. From this perspective, the doctor's legal duty to disclose is measured not by what doctors consider reasonable, but rather by what (reasonable) patients would consider relevant to making the decision. Although in theory a patient-oriented standard should increase the amount and quality of information given to patients and enhance the patient's power of self-determination, there are strong reasons to believe that legal doctrines have had little impact on patient self-determination. For a full discussion of the doctrines and the policy issues, see Chapter 6.

The concept of informed consent may be used not only to raise the standard of care, but also to lower it. Thus before the late 1950s, low income patients were traditionally "presumed" to consent, or were explicitly required to consent, to waiver of their malpractice rights, at least against charitable hospitals, thus in effect "consenting" to a subnormal standard of care. (Such presumptions and requirements were disapproved in Tunkl v. Regents of University of California, 60 Cal. 2d 92, 32 Cal. Rptr. 33, 383 P. 2d 441 (1963); see also President and Directors of Georgetown College v. Hughes, 130 F.2d 810 (D.C. Cir. 1942).) The modern era of cost containment and market competition in health care has generated numerous proposals and actual programs whereby patients in effect consent to a narrower choice of providers, a more restricted range of therapies, and less legal protection against medical malpractice. Whether and to what extent this constitutes consent to a lower standard of care, and the legal status of such consent, are explored in Subsection (f) and Section G below.

d. Permitting and Justifying a Lower Standard of Care for the Poor

American patients with little money have typically had two major problems regarding medical care: outright denial of care and separate and inferior care when it is provided. This section focuses on a particular aspect of the quality of care problem: the extent to which medical malpractice law requires a unitary standard of care for all patients, regardless of income, and the extent to which it permits and even justifies a lower standard of care for the poor.

Principles of medical ethics have long held that *once a doctor has agreed to accept a patient,* the doctor owes that patient the same duty of care and fidelity, regardless of the patient's income or social status. Indeed, a powerful image in popular culture is that of the wartime doctor who treats friend and foe alike with equal commitment. According to the various codes of medical ethics promulgated by the American Medical Association, the doctor's duty is to provide "competent medical service with compassion and respect for human dignity," AMA Principles (1980) in T. Beauchamp & J. Childress, Principles of Biomedical Ethics 331 (2d ed. 1983), and, according to the World Medical Association, "not permit considerations of religion, nationality, race, party politics or social standing to intervene between my duty and my patient." The World Medical Association Declaration of Geneva (1948, as amended, 1968), in id.

In theory, malpractice law has adopted the same unitary standard of care, but this principle has always been subject to serious tensions and inconsistencies. In response to a defendant physician's argument in 1891 that the standard of care for charity patients should only be to avoid gross negligence, a New York trial judge eloquently stated the dominant principle in a jury charge:

> Whether the patient be a pauper or a millionaire, whether he be treated gratuitously or for reward, the physician owes him precisely the same measure of duty, and the same degree of skill and care. He may decline to respond to the call of a patient unable to compensate him; but if he undertake the treatment of such a patient, he cannot defeat a suit for malpractice, nor mitigate a recovery against him, upon the principle that the skill and care required of a physician are proportioned to his expectation of pecuniary recompense. Such a rule would be of the most mischievous consequence, would make the health and life of the indigent the sport of reckless experiment and cruel indifference. [Becker v. Janinski, 15 N.Y.S. 675, 677 (N.Y. Com. Pl. 1891).]

On the other hand, the fact that attorneys for doctors continued to argue for the gross negligence standard for the poor well into the twentieth century may reflect something about doctors' (and lawyers') actual attitudes and practices.

Other features of malpractice law suggest a strong if not always acknowledged impulse toward lower standards for the poor. For example, for most of American history up to and including the present, lower income patients have received most of their care from doctors-in-training employed in hospitals and outpatient clinics, rather than from private, fee-charging physicians. Yet from the 1870s to roughly the 1960s, these hospitals were generally insulated from liability for negligence under doctrines discussed in Section C infra. Although the (often young) physicians employed by the hospitals were not immune, they may well have had few resources with which to satisfy judgments. Much care to lower income patients was thus provided without even the minimal protections of malpractice law as defined by the locality standard.

A second example of the impact of economics on the standard of care is the locality rule itself; the lower standard for general practitioners and the higher standard for specialists (who typically charge higher fees) may well reflect judicial endorsement of an implicit bargain, in which a lower price is charged for a lower permissible standard of care.

A third example of legal acquiescence in substandard care involves economic transfers from hospitals or "patient-dumping," discussed in Chapter 1. The "no duty to treat" rule announced in such cases as *Harper* and *Crews* and the distinction between the emergency room and hospital admission also found in those cases mean that hospitals can refuse to treat, or merely "stabilize" and transfer, as long as they do not actively harm the patient or make his or her condition worse. While this is an access issue, it also represents a very low standard of care, and one that is applied disproportionately to poor patients who are more likely to seek care through the emergency room.

The most serious legal failure to assure minimal standards for the poor has been with regard to conditions in public hospitals. These facilities, which provide vital services to millions of low income patients, have been repeatedly found to be in "desperately inadequate" condition, with significant breakdowns in such crucial services as emergency room, intensive care, medical records, laboratory, X-ray, infection control, and major building maintenance. For a variety of reasons — such as lack of access to the plaintiffs' bar and the low economic worth of poor people's lives in terms of money damages — malpractice law has played a remarkably small role in deterring these grossly substandard conditions. See S. Law & S. Polan, supra, at 18-20; Rosenblatt, Rationing "Normal" Health Care: The Hidden Legal Issues, 59 Tex. L. Rev. 1401, 1414-1416 (1981). Two rare examples of judicial consideration of these conditions are found in the following cases.

Boone v. Tate

Civil No. 713 (C.P. Phila. Co., Apr. 30, 1971), appeal dismissed as moot, 4 Pa. Cmwlth. 101, 286 A.2d 26 (1972)

McDevitt, J.

[In December 1970, the Mayor of Philadelphia (James Tate) ordered the dismissal of 550 employees from Philadelphia General Hospital (PGH). Patients and potential patients at PGH successfully sought a preliminary injunction against the mass dismissal, and the Mayor rescinded the dismissal order. A hearing was then held] on the merits of issuing a final injunction enjoining the Mayor from continuing to impose a freeze or other extraordinary restriction on the hiring of personnel to fill staff vacancies which, in the judgment of the PGH Trustees and staff, were necessary to provide adequate medical care. . . . [The Court's findings of fact included the following]:

3. The Mayor has the responsibility of shaping and controlling the City's fiscal policies, and the general duty of preventing the incurring of deficits in any fiscal year. . . .

13. Satisfactory hospital conditions, adequate facilities, proper care of patients, proper staffing of the hospital are the direct responsibility of the PGH's Board of Trustees. . . .

14. PGH is the only municipal hospital in the City of Philadelphia. It provides a full range of general hospital services including inpatient and outpatient care, emergency room attention, house care, and operates a School of Nursing Education and facilities for medical research.

15. A large segment of the City's population, particularly its indigent citizens, rely upon PGH as the sole available provider of a broad range of medical services.

16. PGH is, and in the foreseeable future, will continue to be, critically important and necessary to meet the daily health needs of Philadelphians.

17. City Hospitals lack the capacity to absorb the large numbers of inpatients and outpatients treated at PGH, and many refuse to admit patients who have no source of payment for hospital services. Certain hospital services, such as treatment of communicable diseases, alcoholism, drug addiction and psychiatric disorders, are provided only at PGH.

18. . . . One critical area is moderately extended inpatient care. The voluntary or independent hospital cannot and will not provide care beyond the period of immediate need for inpatient care. . . .

33. At its meeting of November 18, 1970, the Board of Trustees of Philadelphia General Hospital determined that many key positions at the Hospital remained unfilled as a result of the job freeze and that as a result of this staff shortage the Hospital had become unable to provide medically adequate patient care. . . .

38. The shortage of nursing staff in the Hospital's Pediatrics Department has required that Department to house inpatients with communicable diseases on the same floor with other inpatients. This creates a risk that these other patients and their families at home will become infected with the various contagious diseases carried by the Department's infectious patients. . . .

51. A shortage of Vector Control personnel has prevented the Hospital from bringing under control an infestation of cockroaches and mice, particularly in the Medicine Department, which infestation has created dangers of contamination. . . .

DISCUSSION

The citizens of Philadelphia have come to expect certain services will be available to them either from private or public sources. Every citizen of Philadelphia rightfully expects that adequate medical care will be available to himself, his family and those in his community.

The testimony of the nurses and doctors from PGH clearly demonstrates that patients at that hospital are not receiving *medically adequate* care because of severe staff shortages.

The City does not question the medical opinion concerning the level of medical care. It defends on the basis that the curtailment of essential City services is necessitated by the financial crisis that is confronting the City. . . .

There is no evidence that the City Officials have not acted in good faith, and abused their discretion, or acted from improper motives. . . .

The adequacy of medical care that any patient or any citizen receives is not only a function of medical skills and technology but also the financial ability of the City to supply these needs. . . .

CONCLUSIONS OF LAW

1. There is an obligation upon the City of Philadelphia to provide general hospital care.

2. Philadelphians have the right to expect that adequate medical care will be available. . . .

3. What constitutes "adequate medical care" is an administrative decision taking into account not only medical opinion and medical standards of adequate care but also the financial resources available to the City. . . .

18. Plaintiffs have not established that in the light of the financial conditions of the City . . . [that PGH patients have been deprived] of the adequate medical care they are entitled to expect. . . .

Greater Washington D.C. Area Council of Senior Citizens v. District of Columbia Government

406 F. Supp. 768 (D.D.C. 1975)

PARKER, District Judge.

This proceeding is concerned with one aspect of the failure of the District of Columbia Government to deliver adequate health services to its residents. The plaintiffs are two local senior citizens organizations and several area residents. They seek declaratory and injunctive relief, alleging that inadequate treatment and facilities are afforded at the principal City-operated health and medical facility — The District of Columbia General Hospital (D.C. General). . . .

The testimony and evidence presented focused on only eight areas of services at D.C. General: medical records, the radiology department, emergency room, nursing department, pharmacy, infection control, laboratory, and general maintenance. On the basis of the record the Court concludes that in those areas, the mission of the defendants to provide adequate services has failed; that the facilities fall far short of recognized and acceptable standards in this community; that relief is long overdue; and that the defendants should be enjoined to undertake appropriate corrective action. . . .

[The court made detailed findings regarding each department listed above. In medical records, a 1972 federal task force had found transcription backlogs of up to six years, and an annual misplacement rate of 150-200 charts. By 1975 these problems remained, and "only feeble efforts, if any" had been attempted to remedy the situation. 406 F.Supp. at 771. Even worse, the disorganization of medical records undermined efforts to provide timely diagnosis and treatment. The acute inpatient renal dialysis unit had established its own internal records department to avoid the central unit's inadequacies. The hospital's acting executive director conceded that medical records were "a critical problem." Id. In radiology there was no preventive maintenance, leading to numerous mechanical breakdowns, and after-hours staffing was completely inadequate. In the emergency room, already under court order to be staffed by physicians, lack of support staff to deal with patients who may be dangerous to themselves or others had "contributed to the death of several patients." Id. at 772. Staff shortages and inadequate management in the nursing, pharmacy, and general maintenance departments were also found by the court to seriously impair quality of care.]

DEFENDANTS' DUTY TO PROVIDE ADEQUATE MEDICAL CARE

[The hospital's] duty to provide adequate care "is measured by the degree of care, skill and diligence customarily exercised by hospitals generally in the community." Nor does the argument that the failure to carry out this obligation may stem from budgetary or political restraints preclude this Court's concern and action. . . .

> The hospital may be unable to fulfill its obligation to provide medical care for indigents without affirmative action by the legislative or executive branch, appropriating or reallocating funds for that purpose. But that is no reason for the court to refrain from declaring that the obligation exists even though persons beyond the reach of the court prevent its discharge. [Doe v. General Hospital of the District of Columbia, 140 U.S. App. D.C. 149, 434 F.2d 427, 433 (1970). . . .]

In reviewing the facts presented, the Court has carefully noted the efforts of the defendants to resolve the vexing problems which plague the Hospital. Their efforts have not been successful. Their excuse that the conditions are a product of fiscal constraints is unacceptable absent a clear demonstration that even within those constraints, timely and positive efforts have been launched by exacting, sensitive and demanding administrators. These ingredients appear to be lacking. . . .

Problem: Advocate for the Poor

(1) Assume you are attorney for the plaintiffs in Boone v. Tate. At the hearing on whether to grant the permanent injunction, assume that the trial judge says to you from the bench: "I'm very sympathetic to your clients' problems, counselor. I agree that the conditions at Philadelphia General Hospital are very bad. However, as a judge I cannot start running the budgetary process of the city government. Therefore, I have no alternative but to hold that the legally relevant standard of "adequate medical care" at PGH is "an administrative decision taking into account not only medical standards of adequate care but also the financial resources available to the City."

Given that you will not obtain the injunction against layoffs that you are seeking, can you think of a narrower ground that would justify denial of relief but not imperil the definition of adequate medical care?

(2) Assume that the trial judge did not accept your narrower ground proposed under (1) above, and issued the actual *Boone* opinion reprinted above. Assume further that some months later, you are now representing before the same judge a medical malpractice plaintiff who is suing PGH for damages for injuries caused by an adverse drug reaction that could have been avoided had the medical records system been adequate. The judge states from the bench: "Counselor, I'm sympathetic to your case. But I just ruled a few months ago that that these same conditions at PGH constituted 'adequate medical care.' Doesn't that preclude me now from allowing a jury to reach the opposite conclusion?" Can you think of a response that would allow the judge to award damages to your client without overruling *Boone?*

(3) Assume that the *Boone* case arises in 1989, after the Mississippi Supreme Court's opinion in Hall v. Hilbun, supra. Now the trial judge says to you, the plaintiffs' attorney, that he is going to deny you the injunction on the grounds of the "resources-based defense" articulated in *Hall*. Can you think of any arguments to try to persuade him that *Hall* does not mean what he seems to think it does?

Notes and Questions: Can a Lower Standard of Care for the Poor Be Justified?

(1) For two interesting perspectives on these issues, consider the debate between Professor Barry Furrow, a law professor specializing in health care delivery, and Professor E. Haavi Morreim, a philosopher specializing in medical ethics. Furrow argues that "bedside cost constraints should not be allowed as a defense in a tort suit when a doctor decides that a particular patient should forgo a treatment or test that would have been prescribed if the patient had been insured or had greater private resources." Furrow, Medical Malpractice and Cost Containment: Tightening the Screws, 36 Case W.

Res. L. Rev. 985, 988 (1986). Morreim disagrees, at least to the extent of advocating a resource based malpractice defense for doctors who practice in underfunded public hospitals.

Furrow argues that allowing a cost based defense is too dangerous for individual patients; doctors would in effect have a license to withhold beneficial care according to the individual doctor's or hospital's own cost-benefit perspective. Moreover, such a defense would have undesirable social effects, as it would reduce pressure on doctors and other staff in underfunded public hospitals to expose their inadequacies and press for political change. Id. at 1025-1026, 1032. Morreim counters that in public hospitals without sophisticated and expensive technology, (such as CT scanners or third-generation cephalosporins (an antibiotic)), substandard care will inevitably be provided. This being so, she argues that normal malpractice standards cannot induce doctors in these hospitals to practice adequate medicine, since it is beyond their capacity to do so. Moreover, she disagrees with Furrow that the pressure of malpractice liability will generate advocacy for change; on the contrary, *allowing* a cost based malpractice defense will, in her view, provide an incentive to "bring these concerns before the public." In these circumstances, not allowing a cost-based malpractice defense is morally unjustified (because it serves no useful social purpose) and may well deter doctors from serving the poor. Morreim, Commentary: Stratified Scarcity and Unfair Liability, 36 Case W. Res. L. Rev. 1033, 1050-1051 (1986); see also Morreim, Cost Containment and the Standard of Medical Care, 75 Calif. L. Rev. 1719 (1987).

(2) Unfortunately, neither Morreim nor anyone else knows much about why doctors do or do not agree to work in public hospitals or otherwise serve the poor, and what the role (if any) fear of malpractice liability plays in that decision. Given all the other difficulties and pressures of working in most public hospitals, it seems unlikely that fear of malpractice liability because of inadequate resources is a major factor in doctors' decisions. To be sure, it would be useful to have a deeper understanding of this and other factors that affect service to the poor.

(3) Note that Morreim focuses on shortages of sophisticated and expensive items — CT scanners and third-generation cephalosporins. What about the primitive deficiencies in medical records, X-rays, nursing services, and maintenance that were the subjects of the *Boone* and *Greater Washington* litigation? Leaving aside the issue of the hospital's liability (as does Morreim), should we allow a doctor to plead a resources based defense if a patient dies because his or her medical record was lost? Because a simple X-ray could not be performed? Morreim might argue that these are matters of degree — that such errors occur in the best equipped hospitals, as the *Libby Zion* case, discussed in Section E *infra,* indicates — and that in any case there is no difference in principle between an expensive treatment or diagnostic device considered "standard" for paying patients and a simple, inexpensive one. Do you agree or disagree? Why?

(4) Furrow believes that malpractice liability pressure encourages phy-

sicians to be advocates for their low income patients; Morreim is skeptical about whether that happens and if it does, whether it can be effective. In-depth empirical case studies are strongly needed to throw light on this issue. Residents (that is, salaried physicians) in public hospitals have gone on strike in New York City and San Francisco over quality of care issues; many others have testified in legislative and judicial hearings and otherwise attempted to press the system. Even if fear of malpractice liability plays a minor role in such efforts, what kind of signal would be sent to doctors if a resources based defense were allowed?

(5) Morreim argues that allowing a resources based defense would pressure doctors, hospitals, and perhaps Peer Review Organizations, discussed in Section F, to develop reasonable standards for rationed, "minimal" medical practice (although she concedes that developing such standards will be very difficult). One could argue equally and perhaps more plausibly that only *increased* pressure of malpractice liability on both doctors and hospitals because of inadequate resources will lead to such standards, which then could be pled under the "respectable minority" or modified *Hall*-type resources defense. Morreim's position — which seems to call for recognizing such a defense "in principle" before detailed standards are worked out, might well remove any pressure for their development, or at best reallocate the pressure to low visibility decisions by trial judges and juries.

(6) The core of Morreim's argument is that *given* certain limits on resources (such as no CT scanner or few sophisticated drugs), there is no reasonable alternative to delivering rationed care that will be substandard for many patients. But must such limits be accepted as "given"? The court in *Boone* answered yes, at least as a judicial matter; the court in *Greater Washington* said no. Even though the *Greater Washington* court admitted that it had no power to order increased appropriations for the hospital, it did order that existing resources be used as effectively as possible to meet proven emergency needs. That is no small matter; underfunded (and hence often demoralized) public hospitals are often seriously mismanaged *as well as* seriously underfunded. Second, the symbolic and political pressure of the court's decision might well be helpful in persuading the funding authorities to find more resources. Cf. Blake v. District of Columbia, No. 2623-80 (D.C. Super. Ct., June 30, 1981) (D.C. General Hospital permitted to lease CT scanner after losing a $240,000 malpractice verdict for causing a patient's death by failure to transfer patient to hospital equipped with CT) (unreported case discussed in Mehlman, Rationing Expensive Lifesaving Medical Treatments, 1985 Wis. L. Rev. 239, 287).

f. Competitive Theory and Alteration of Malpractice Standards

Existing medical norms have been shaped by open ended, fee-for-service reimbursement for doctors and largely open ended reasonable cost reimbursement for hospitals. Under conventional market principles, patients would not agree to diagnostic tests or medical procedures whose "value" was less than their cost. But in addition to the problem of determining the "value" of an extra margin of safety, insurance shields large numbers of patients from having to consider monetary costs. This in turn influences doctors' definitions of reasonable or high quality practice. As Randall Bovbjerg points out,

> most doctors doubtless take quite seriously their fiduciary duty to patients and would not bankrupt them in an uncertain quest for small reductions in risk. Doctors owe no fiduciary duty, however, to the insurers and government agencies that pay for the lion's share of medical [and hospital] care. . . . Providers of insured medical services can be expected to consider not whether their patients or society can afford a particular risk-reducing measure, but rather only whether their patients will receive any medical benefit. [Bovbjerg, "The Medical Malpractice Standard of Care: HMOs and Customary Practice," 1975 Duke L.J. 1375, 1395-1396.]

Competitive theory in health care — and cost containment programs more generally — are designed to change these patterns of care by financially inducing doctors to use fewer tests, fewer hospital days, and less expensive procedures and personnel. To the extent that these changes heighten the risks of nondiagnosis or other harm, they may also increase the risk of malpractice liability under existing legal/professional standards. Some of the many quality issues arising from competitive and cost containment programs are explored in Sections F and G at the end of this chapter. This section focuses on two particular proposals to solve the malpractice/competition tension by changing malpractice standards: (1) an "HMO custom" standard and (2) explicit contracting to change malpractice norms and remedies.

i. The HMO Custom Standard

In a 1975 article widely cited in the academic literature, Randall Bovbjerg sharply contrasted the risk reduction or quality of care perspective of the individual physician, reimbursed on an open ended fee-for-service basis, with the perspective of an HMO committed to serving a defined population for a fixed, prepaid sum.[1] For the individual doctor, every increase in safety or

1. A health maintenance organization (HMO) combines insurance and direct provision of health care services by agreeing to provide a specified range of services for a fixed, prepaid sum. Unlike a fee-for-service provider, the HMO is thus at financial risk if the cost of the services exceeds the fixed premium income. The HMO patient, instead of being free to choose among all private practitioners for each illness and paying a fee for each service, instead enrolls with the HMO, pays a fixed monthly premium regardless of usage, and agrees to use a limited pool of physicians. HMOs exist in many forms, notably "staff" models (physicians on salary), "group" models (physicians in group practices under contract to the HMO), and individual practice associations (IPAs) (physicians in individual practice under contract to the HMO). See generally the discussion of HMOs and other alternative delivery systems in Chapter 8.

reduction in risk for a particular patient is justified, as long as it is paid for; moreover, except in unusual situations (such as organ transplants) there is little possibility or incentive to consider the external effects of resources used by one patient on the welfare of other patients. The HMO has the opposite perspective. "The comprehensiveness and integration of their services give HMOs numerous occasions to evaluate alternatives in seeking to achieve maximum health benefits for given expenditures. . . ." Health benefits are considered not only, or even primarily, from the perspective of individual patients, but from the perspective of the enrolled population as a group.

> Thus, there might be universal agreement that a certain test improves the accuracy of a diagnosis from ninety to ninety-five percent in some moderately serious and generally treatable condition; a fee-for-service doctor would almost certainly perform such a test if it were readily available and covered by insurance, since no obvious benefit for his patient or himself could be achieved by foregoing the potential insurance payment. On the other hand, an HMO might decide that its subscribers' resources were better spent, for example, on upgrading the staff of its emergency room than on the test."

Traditional malpractice law standards, based on traditional medical practice, do not contemplate justifying an increased risk for a particular patient, or all patients, by a reduced risk or improved quality in some other aspect of health care. Bovbjerg, The Medical Malpractice Standard of Care: HMOs and Customary Practice, 1975 Duke L.J. 1375, 1379, 1390, 1391-1407.

Bovbjerg defines the resulting dilemma as follows: on the one hand, it is important to subject HMOs to potential malpractice liability, in order to guard against economically motivated underservice and unreasonably low quality of care. On the other hand, malpractice law should not be permitted to interfere "inappropriately . . . with HMOs' desirable ability to count costs in evaluating what care to provide." Id. at 1379 n.5. Bovbjerg's proposed solution to this dilemma is for the courts to recognize "HMO custom" as the appropriate standard for HMO care. Where the dispute concerns alternative procedures or approaches about whose medical efficacy doctors disagree, this would amount to a restatement of the "reputable minority" rule discussed in Section 3(b) supra. The harder case arises when an HMO foregoes a test or procedure whose medical efficacy is clear in order to improve quality in some other aspect of health care delivery. Bovbjerg admits that the courts' case by case process is not well suited to resolving these issues, nor does he begin to suggest the substantive standards by which they might be evaluated, other than "HMO custom" itself. Yet it seems unlikely that the community of HMO's will have made sufficiently similar trade-offs to establish a customary standard. Other, perhaps surmountable problems include defining an "HMO" to ensure that the financial incentives are "appropriate"; defining appropriate comparison groups of similarly situated HMOs, and amending the locality rule where necessary.

Although the tension between malpractice law and HMO policies seems powerful in theory, it has only begun to surface in litigation and the few existing cases are discussed in Section G. This may mean that there is so much waste in the fee-for-service system that HMOs are able to make profits without coming close to withholding beneficial care, at least of the sort that results in large malpractice claims. Or it may mean that the plaintiffs' malpractice bar is insensitive to the possibilities for argument along these lines. A third possibility is that mandatory arbitration provisions in many HMO enrollment contracts are effectively blocking these issues from getting to the courts. See, for instance, Madden v. Kaiser Foundation Hospitals, 17 Cal. 3d 699, 131 Cal. Rptr. 882, 552 P.2d 1178 (1976) (upholding mandatory arbitration agreement between the state as employer and HMO against a contract of adhesion challenge by injured employee barred from tort remedies); see generally Henderson, Agreements for Changing the Forum for Resolving Medical Malpractice Claims, 49 Law & Contemp. Prob. at 243 (Spring 1986); Terry, The Technical and Conceptual Flaws of Medical Malpractice Arbitration, 30 St. Louis U.L.J. 571 (1986).

ii. Altering Malpractice Standards by Contract

In addition to the article by Havighurst below, major work advocating reconceptualizing medical malpractice law in terms of contract rather than tort includes the following: Epstein, Contracting Out of the Medical Malpractice Crisis, in 20 Perspectives in Biology and Medicine 228 (1977); Epstein, Medical Malpractice: The Case for Contract, 1976 Am. B. Found. Res. J. 87; Robinson, Rethinking the Allocation of Medical Malpractice Risks Between Patients and Providers, 49 Law & Contemp. Prob. at 173 (Spring 1986).

Havighurst, Altering the Applicable Standard of Care

49 Law & Contemp. Prob. at 265, 271, 273 (Spring 1986).

[Having argued the general case for increased contracting about malpractice standards, Havighurst offers several specific contract proposals. One approach involves leaving the substantive standard of professional custom formally unchanged, but "specifying that the plaintiff has not established a prima facie case just by showing a departure from customary practice." Havighurst's proposed physician-patient contract provision of this sort is as follows:]

> The Physician warrants that he or she possesses at least the skill and knowledge of a reasonably competent medical practitioner in the Physician's specialty and undertakes to you that he or she will exercise that skill and knowledge in a reasonable and prudent manner in your case. In so doing, the Physician may sometimes depart from practices customary among other physicians. Such departures shall not be deemed to breach the foregoing undertaking, however, unless they are expressly found to have been unreasonable and imprudent; evidence to support such a finding shall consist solely of the testimony of experts knowledgeable about scientific studies bearing on the appropriateness of the actions taken and about what, in the light of all the circumstances including the cost of alternative measures, constitutes appropriate medical care. You agree that the undertaking in this paragraph fully defines the Physician's duty to you.

The advantages of this provision are that it leaves adherence to custom as a substantial (though not necessarily conclusive) defense, prevents departures from custom from being the basis for any automatic inference of negligence, and contemplates that scientific studies and cost factors will be considered before conduct is labeled negligent. The clause thus states a sound legal principle, one that is appropriate for legislative or judicial adoption. It is fair to ask how much difference such a clause would make in the outcome of cases. Although the answer probably is "not much," a jury instructed in accordance with the provision might appreciate that the issues are hard ones and not to be resolved on the basis of emotion alone. . . .

[An alternative provision is as follows]:

> ***Limitations on Your Legal Rights Against the Physician***
>
> In return for the Physician's acceptance of you as a patient on the terms provided for this agreement, you agree that, in any legal action hereafter brought by you against the Physician for any injury suffered in the course of your treatment, you will be entitled to recover damages only if such injury was the result of the Physician's gross negligence. Gross negligence is distinguishable from ordinary negligence and is characterized by willful neglect of your personal well being or reckless disregard for the consequences of some act or omission.

NOTES AND QUESTIONS

(1) What justification is there for encouraging contracts that permit recovery only for gross negligence, or otherwise substantially change legal norms and remedies? Do you have any objections to these proposals, and how do you think Havighurst would respond to them?

(2) In the first proposed contract clause, Havighurst defines "appropriate medical care" to include consideration of "the cost of alternative measures," as testified to by experts knowledgeable about how to incorporate cost considerations into judgments of appropriateness. From whose perspec-

tive are such costs being considered? Apparently not the individual patient's — because otherwise the patient herself could be consulted, and there would be no need for experts. Apparently the expert will be applying some social, professional, or market-based perspective. If that is true, should that be specified in the contract? Would patients be less likely to sign such a contract?

(3) Havighurst notes that the second clause, limiting providers' liability to damages caused by gross negligence, "would undoubtedly trouble many . . . courts." Nevertheless, he maintains that "a substantial case can be made for enforcing such an agreement." Havighurst invokes what he terms a "general rule," that "those who are not engaged in public service [such as common carriers] may properly bargain against liability for harm caused by their ordinary negligence in performance of contractual duty. . . ." 6A A. Corbin, Corbin on Contracts §1472 at 596-597 (1962). Having argued that health care should be conceived largely as a consumer good, and the doctor-patient relationship largely as one of contract, Havighurst believes that waivers of liability for negligence should be permissible. Id. at 273 n.29.

However, the "general rule" invoked by Havighurst is a matter of much dispute. The Corbin treatise itself concedes that "[t]here is much apparent conflict . . . even in the cases in which the public service is not directly involved, as to the validity of provisions for exemption from liability for harm caused by negligence." A. Corbin, supra, at 598. After stating a similar general rule, Prosser notes that "[t]he courts have refused to uphold such agreements . . . where one party is at such obvious disadvantage in bargaining power that the effect of the contract is to put him at the mercy of the other's negligence." Prosser and Keeton on The Law of Torts 482 (5th ed. 1984). There are strong arguments that patients usually fit within this doctrine, and both judicial decisions and state statutes have so concluded. See Tunkl v. Regents of University of California, 60 Cal. 2d 92, 32 Cal. Rptr. 33, 383 P.2d 441 (1963) (holding invalid a hospital exculpatory clause demanded from charitable patients); Ill. Ann. Stat. ch. 111, para. 4478 (Smith-Hurd Supp. 1985) (declaring that releases entered into prior to treatment are against public policy).

4. THE MALPRACTICE "CRISIS" AND THE POLITICS OF LEGAL CHANGE

There have been periodic assertions of "crisis" regarding medical malpractice law throughout American history, usually from physicians dismayed at what they regard as an excessive number of legal claims and excessively large judgments against them. In response to these complaints, and to concerns by Congress and other payers that they were paying for a great deal of dubiously necessary "defensive medicine" (that is, tests and services not actually needed by the patient but provided by the doctor in the belief that such services would help avoid malpractice liability), the Secretary of Health, Education and Welfare established a major Commission on Medical Malpractice in 1970 to investigate the entire system. The Commission's findings, issued in 1972, infuriated the American Medical Association by refuting the doctors' vision of a "crisis." The Commission found that there were a large number of doctor-caused injuries for which claims were never made; that 75 percent of jury verdicts were for the defendant; that malpractice insurance was available, albeit at rising premiums; that most hospitals had experienced little litigation; that defensive medicine was widely believed to exist but impossible to measure, because of difficulties in identifying services provided solely or primarily to avoid legal liability; and that state licensing agencies had little authority, staff, or inclination to discipline incompetent or "impaired" (alcoholic, drug-addicted, or mentally-ill) physicians. Indeed, the Commission's report revealed an actual or incipient "crisis" very different from the one pictured by doctors: a medical malpractice system that failed to compensate enough patients or effectively penalize the relatively small number of doctors responsible for a disproportionate share of injuries and claims.

Despite the HEW Commission's findings, by 1975 the American Medical Association found state legislatures responsive to its analysis of a "crisis" and its proposals for statutory change. The reason was an alarming rise in malpractice insurance premiums, coupled with threats or actual withdrawal of companies from the malpractice insurance market. See S. Law & S. Polan, supra, at 166 (describing premium rises of 82 and 93 percent in North Carolina and New York in 1974); see also Robinson, The Medical Malpractice Crisis of the 1970s: A Retrospective, 49 Law & Contemp. Prob. at 5, 7-9 (Spring 1986) (noting that malpractice insurance premiums increased from 1960 to 1972 by an average of 600 to 900 percent in different risk categories).

Although the reality of the crisis was now not in dispute, there was sharp debate about its nature and causes. The American Medical Association, and the insurance industry, argued that plaintiffs' lawyers, hungry for contingent fees, brought unjustified suits, and that allegedly liberalized malpractice law (such as easier qualification of expert witnesses following abandonment of the locality rule, expanded use of res ipsa loquitur, and patient-oriented informed consent) made it all too easy for lay juries to render unjustified and excessive verdicts for plaintiffs. This analysis led predictably to calls for legislative restrictions of plaintiffs' rights and remedies, including limitations on plaintiffs' attorneys' contingent fees. The American Trial Lawyers Association (ATLA), representing the plaintiffs' bar, responded that doctors had failed totally to discipline their own ranks, either through state licensing boards or through in-hospital peer review, and that existing malpractice law was one of the few protections against widespread substandard care. Predictably, the ATLA also attacked the costs generated by defense lawyers. Some independent analysts agreed that doctors had done little to deter malpractice, and also pointed to the unregulated nature of the malpractice insurance industry, in which companies set unrealistically low premiums to collect capital for investment, and then radically raised premiums or abandoned the market when investment strategies faltered. See S. Law & S. Polan, supra, at 161-195.

In theory, there are three broad reform strategies that might relieve various aspects of the perceived crisis. The most profound change would be to separate the entire system of health care financing from private markets and injury compensation from fault based tort law and adopt a social insurance system of the sort that exists in Sweden. Needless to say, this approach would face enormous political obstacles in the United States. A second change, not as large but still substantial, would be to move to a no-fault, workers compensation type model that would sharply reduce damage awards in return for faster and more comprehensive coverage. The third approach, and the one so far followed almost exclusively, has been to change one or more elements of the fault-based system. In the mid-1970s these changes largely took the form of making it more difficult for patients to recover damages. The changes included:

1. procedural and cost barriers to recovery:
   - shortened statutes of limitations
   - restriction of plaintiffs' attorneys' contingent fees
   - penalties for frivolous suits
   - restrictions on experts' qualifications
2. less financial responsibility for providers and insurance companies:
   - taking into account recoveries from collateral sources (e.g., general health insurance)
   - dollar caps on noneconomic damages, or on all damages
   - limitation of provider liability to a specified dollar amount, with patient compensation funds paying additional amounts, often subject to a maximum limit
3. alternative dispute resolution:
   - voluntary or mandatory use of pretrial screening panels or arbitration
4. minimal reform of insurance markets:
   - establishment of joint underwriting associations, in which insurance companies are required to offer medical malpractice coverage without much risk of loss or opportunity for profit
5. reduced standard of care:
   - legislative specification of professional rather than patient-oriented standard of care for informed consent
   - lower than negligence standard for emergency care

Beginning primarily in the early and mid-1980s, the states and the federal government began pursuing another set of reforms, often in conjunction with and as a quid pro quo for the first five types, directed to reforming the system of professional self regulation. These reforms can be summarized as follows:

6. reform of professional discipline and peer review:
   - legislative requirement of in-hospital peer review and risk management programs
   - required reporting of adverse actions to state licensing agency
   - immunity for peer review and other quality assurance programs

Section (a) explores one of the most controversial of the mid-1970s reforms: dollar limits on damages in medical malpractice cases. Section (b) briefly considers some of the reform directions that are being proposed and enacted in the late 1980s.

a. Dollar Limits on Malpractice Damages: Constitutional Issues

By July 1985, 17 states had enacted laws that limit the damages recoverable in medical malpractice actions. Some of these statutes apply to all components of loss (Indiana and Idaho), while others apply only to noneconomic damages (typically designated "pain and suffering," as distinct from lost earnings and medical expenses) (California). An empirical study by Patricia Danzon found that such "caps" reduced malpractice awards by 19 percent within two years of enactment. See P. Danzon, The Frequency and Severity of Medical Malpractice Claims, Rand R-2870-ICJ/HCFA, 1982, cited in U.S. General Accounting Office, Medical Malpractice: No Agreement on Problems or Solutions 19 (1986). On the other hand, a study by Frank Sloan found no statistically significant connection between damages caps and lower insurance premiums. See Sloan, State Responses to the Malpractice "Crisis" of the 1970s: An Empirical Assessment, 9 J. Health Pol. Poly. & L. 629 (1985). But see Freudenheim, Costs of Medical Malpractice Drop After 11-year Climb, N.Y. Times, June 11, 1989, 1:1.

Aside from their effects on malpractice premiums, Law and Polan argue that

> as a matter of principle, laws restricting the amounts recoverable by seriously injured patients are outrageous. The actions of many people contribute to the malpractice crisis: doctors, hospitals, lawyers, insurance companies, and perhaps patients who press frivolous claims. No one suggests that the crisis is caused by patients who suffer very serious injuries. . . . Although we all ultimately pay for soaring malpractice premiums through rising health care costs, it seems grossly unjust to impose a disproportionate share of these costs on people who are unfortunate enough to be seriously injured as a result of negligent medical treatment. [S. Law & S. Polan, supra, at 139-140.]

Of course, the AMA and other defenders of these laws argue that jury assessments of damages, particularly for noneconomic injuries, are inherently untrustworthy and must be limited by strict rules. Aside from its debatable premises and conclusions, the problem with this argument is that while some legislatures are accepting it for medical malpractice cases, many state courts, with apparent legislative acquiescence, have simultaneously expanded the power of juries to award damages for emotional and other nonphysical and noneconomic injuries in other types of torts cases, such as accidents and products liability. See Smith, Battling a Receding Tort Frontier: Constitutional Attacks on Medical Malpractice Laws, 38 Okla. L. Rev. 797 (1985). Reflecting these tensions, at least six state courts have found damages limitations to be in violation of state constitutions.

Lucas v. United States

757 S.W.2d 687 (Tex. 1988)

KILGARLIN, Justice.

[Fourteen-month-old Christopher Lucas was permanently paralyzed when an army doctor and nurse negligently injected a large overdose of antibiotics directly into one of his arteries. The treatment took place at an army hospital near El Paso, Texas. A federal district court awarded Christopher's parents $498,630 for the child's medical expenses until his majority, and Christopher himself $350,000 for his post-majority medical expenses, $600,000 for his lost earning capacity, and $1,500,000 for pain and suffering. The district court refused to apply Texas' statutory cap of $500,000 for nonmedical damages in medical malpractice cases, but the Fifth Circuit ruled that the state law cap did apply to federally operated hospitals in Texas. The Fifth Circuit certified to the Texas Supreme Court the question of whether the liability cap was consistent with the Texas Constitution.]

[Tex. Rev. Stat. Ann. art. 4590i, sec. 11.02 provides that damages against a physician or health care provider are limited to $500,000. The statutory cap does not apply to damages for the past or future expenses of necessary medical, hospital, and custodial care. Article 4590i, sec. 11.03 provides that if section 11.02 is invalidated by nonlegislative means, the liability limit shall be $150,000 for "noneconomic" losses (such as pain and suffering). The statute also states that these dollar limits shall increase or decrease depending on the consumer price index published by the federal government.]

[Article I, section 13 of the Texas Constitution provides that "All courts shall be open, and every person for an injury done him, in his lands, goods, person or reputation, shall have remedy by due course of law."] . . . [W]e . . . conclude that the [statutory] liability limits . . . are unconstitutional as applied to catastrophically damaged malpractice victims seeking a "remedy by due course of law."

Texas courts have long recognized that victims of medical negligence have a well-defined common law cause of action to sue for injuries negligently inflicted upon them. [T]he remaining inquiry is whether the restriction on Lucas' right of recovery "is unreasonable or arbitrary when balanced against the purpose and basis of the statute." We hold that the restriction is unreasonable and arbitrary. . . .

Our first concern with the statute is that the legislature has failed to provide Lucas any adequate substitute to obtain redress for his injuries. . . .

It is significant to note that in two of the jurisdictions in which damages caps were upheld, the fact that alternative remedies [in the form of patient compensation funds] were provided weighed heavily in the decisions. . . .

We also question whether the restrictions . . . are reasonable when balanced against the purposes and bases of the statute. The legislature . . . apparently did not intend to strike at frivolous malpractice suits. . . . The legislature did find that a "medical malpractice insurance crisis" had been created and that "satisfactory insurance coverage . . . [was] often not available at any price," but it then stated that "adoption of certain modifications in the medical, insurance, and legal systems . . . *may or may not have an effect* on the rates charged by insurers for medical professional liability coverage.". . . In the context of persons catastrophically injured by medical negligence, we believe it is unreasonable and arbitrary to limit their recovery in a speculative experiment to determine whether liability insurance rates will decrease. [W]e hold it is unreasonable and arbitrary for the legislature to conclude that arbitrary damages caps, applicable to all claimants no matter how seriously injured, will help assure a rational relationship between actual damages and amounts awarded. . . .

We understand the legislature's concern in attempting to solve the health care problems it perceived during the middle of the 1970s. Nevertheless, we agree with the statement by the Supreme Court of New Hampshire: "It is simply unfair and unreasonable to impose the burden of supporting the medical care industry solely upon those persons who are most severely injured and therefore most in need of compensation." Carson v. Maurer, 120 N.H. 925, 424 A.2d 825, 837 (1980). . . .

GONZALEZ, Justice, dissenting.

. . . This court has never expressly required an individual quid pro quo in the past; to do so now would unquestionably restrain the legislature's ability and duty to effect social change through legislative enactment. . . .

Legislative action withdrawing or restricting a common law remedy will be sustained if it is reasonable in substituting other remedies. . . . I believe the stated purposes for enacting the Medical Liability and Insurance Improvement Act demonstrates that the legislature acted reasonably under this standard. . . .

> [T]he medical cap . . . provides both a societal and individual quid pro quo. The benefit to society is that by reducing the awards given to those injured in excess of the caps, insurance payouts are more readily calculable. This in turn allows a predictable rate structure to be erected, thus allowing policies to be written on health care providers who otherwise could not afford the exhorbitant rates associated with policies of undeterminable risk. The resultant societal quid pro quo is the decrease in cost of medical malpractice insurance in the state of Texas and the increased availability of health care. I further suggest there is an individual quid pro quo because the caps enable health care providers to procure insurance in the first place. Without adequate coverage, it was reasonable for the Legislature to conclude that the plaintiff in a medical malpractice case would suffer damages with no recovery at all against an insolvent, judgment-proof defendant. I submit that a recovery of all medical costs and expenses, with a cap on $500,000 plus a Consumer Price Index adjustment on other damages, is better than a potential recovery of zero. . . .
>
> I acknowledge that there are serious questions surrounding the causes of the medical malpractice insurance crisis. . . . However, the findings are "legislative facts" which should be accorded great deference by this court, particularly because reasonable minds can differ as to the causes of the crisis. For us to "unfind" that there is no crisis on the state of this record is to act like a "super legislature" in violation of the separation of powers doctrine. . . .

Notes and Questions

(1) Seizing on the Texas Legislature's candid finding that it did not know whether its various tort reforms would lower malpractice insurance rates, the *Lucas* majority states that "it is unreasonable and arbitrary to limit [the] recovery [of persons catastrophically injured by medical negligence] in a speculative experiment to determine whether liability insurance rates will decrease." This is powerful rhetoric and persuasive policy, but is it good constitutional law? A great deal of what legislatures do could be described as an "experiment." For example, there is much debate about the health effects of various illegal drugs and the social utility of attempting to punish their use by criminal penalties. Yet it is hard to imagine a court striking down a federal or state drug law on the grounds that it sent people to jail on the basis of a debatable (and indeed arguably failed) "social experiment." Do you think there is anything different about Texas' experiment in limiting malpractice recoveries, and if so what?

(2) Isn't Justice Gonzalez's dissent on strong constitutional ground when he argues that under a reasonableness standard of review, the existence of a reasonable debate about a means-ends connection requires that the law be upheld? Two other state supreme courts avoided this problem by applying a heightened, "intermediate scrutiny" standard of review. See Carson v.

Maurer, 120 N.H. 925, 424 A.2d 825, 836 (1980); Smith v. Department of Insurance, 507 So.2d 1080, 1088–1089 (Fla. 1987).

(3) The *Lucas* majority seems to assume that once it had ruled that the $500,000 cap on nonmedical damages contained in sec. 11.02 was unconstitutional, there was no need to discuss the $150,000 limit on nonpecuniary damages provided by sec. 11.03. Can you think of an argument that would justify upholding sec. 11.03, even after sec. 11.02 had been struck down?

(4) Sylvia Law and Steve Polan point out that legislative abolition or major limitation of common law rights and remedies has generally occurred in two situations: where the social basis of the old right has collapsed (such as legislative abolition of a husband's common law right to sue another person for "alienation" of his wife's affection), or where the legislature has provided a new system of compensation (such as abolition of common law tort rights in connection with workers' compensation or no-fault automobile accident programs). "Never before [the malpractice changes of the mid-1970s] in American legal history has a legislature abolished the right of the most seriously injured to receive full compensation for personal injuries casused by the unreasonable conduct of another, without providing any substitute remedy." S. Law & S. Polan, supra, at 140. Is Justice Gonzalez's argument, that absent these changes, the injured party might receive nothing, a persuasive response to this point?

(5) The interaction of the federal law against patient-dumping, 42 U.S.C. § 1395dd, discussed in Chapter 1, with state medical malpractice reforms is illustrated in Reid v. Indianapolis Osteopathic Med. Hosp., 709 F. Supp. 853 (D. Ind. 1989). In this case a patient injured as a result of refusal to provide emergency care filed a federal lawsuit. The hospital argued that the suit should be dismissed because the plaintiff had not submitted the claim to a malpractice review panel as required by Indiana law, and that damages were limited to Indiana's statutory maximum of $100,000. The federal district court held that the federal statute did not incorporate, and preempted, Indiana procedural law regarding the malpractice review panel, but that the federal statute's reference to state law regarding damages did incorporate the state's statutory maximum on awards for medical malpractice.

PROBLEM: IS LOWERING THE STANDARD OF CARE CONSTITUTIONAL?

In 1988, the Florida legislature amended its Good Samaritan Act to provide that any hospital, hospital employee, or person licensed to practice medicine who provides emergency care to a patient who entered a hospital through its emergency room or trauma center "shall not be held liable for any civil damages as a result of such medical care . . . unless such damages result from providing, or failing to provide, medical care or treatment under circumstances demonstrating a reckless disregard for the consequences so as to affect the life or health of another." Fla. Stat. 768.13(2)(b)(1). "Reckless disregard" is defined as "such conduct which a health care provider knows or should know would be likely to result in injury . . . taking into account" such factors as the lack of time to obtain an appropriate medical history or consultation, the lack of prior patient-physician relationship, and the time constraints imposed by coexisting emergencies. Fla. Stat. 768.13(2)(b)(3). The Florida legislature found that this law was necessary because, inter alia, "[c]ivil lawsuits brought on behalf of medical emergency care patients are often the result of factors beyond the control of the . . . provider rendering such care, including, but not limited to . . . [lack of a prior physician-patient relationship, lack of time or ability to obtain a medical history, and the severe nature of the emergencies]." The legislature also found that "[t]he adequate delivery of medical emergency care services is a priority health care need and can have a dramatic impact in reducing civil lawsuits which ultimately result in high medical malpractice insurance premiums." 1988 Fla. Session Law Serv. Ch.88-1, sec.45 (West).

If the same law had been enacted in Texas after the *Lucas* case, and a patient seriously injured by physician negligence in the emergency room was denied recovery on the grounds that the physician error did not amount to reckless disregard, how would you predict that the Texas Supreme Court would rule? Why?

b. Directions for the Future

There appear to be three major directions for medical malpractice reform in the current political "mainstream" and at least another three involving more profound, and hence politically less immediately feasible, changes. (On the mainstream reforms, see generally Department of Health and Human Services, Report of the Task Force on Medical Liability and Malpractice (August 1987).) The first set involves a continuation of the relatively incremental reforms of the fault-based system begun in the mid-1970s, in the light of empirical research on what is likely to be effective in reducing insurance premiums. Such reforms might include scheduled damages for different types of injuries (thus allowing more flexibility than flat dollar caps, but also more predictability than currently discretionary juries); shorter statutes of limitations, combined with fines or other safeguards against provider concealment of injury; and greater reliance on experience rating. See Danzon, An Economic Analysis of the Medical Malpractice System, 1 Behav. Sci. & L. 39, 51-53 (1983). A second set of reforms would shift all or part of medical malpractice to a no-fault system, in which lower damage awards are delivered by a faster and cheaper administrative process. Virginia enacted such a law for certain birth-related neurological injuries in 1987. See Note, Innovative Tort Reform for an Endangered Specialty, 74 Va. L. Rev. 1487 (1988).

A third set of reforms currently being pursued at the state and federal levels does not focus primarily on medical malpractice law, but rather on the systems of professional licensure and hospital-based peer review, and even on particular medical settings and procedures. Thus, as discussed in sections D and E *infra*, New York, Florida, Massachusetts, and other states have recently amended their hospital licensure laws to require hospitals to carry out risk management and quality assurance programs, and to report violations of standards to state regulatory agencies. In addition, as discussed in section E, New York's Health Department has begun regulating particular settings and procedures, such as emergency rooms and cesarians. These reforms are closely related to medical malpractice law in several ways: by creating duties and immunities regarding quality assurance activities; by setting standards of care; and by reducing the amount of negligent or unnecessary care.

Among the directions considered outside the mainstream, the AMA/Specialty Society Medical Liability Project issued a proposal in January 1988 that would retain the concept of "fault" but would route all cases through state administrative agencies specializing in medical malpractice compensation. Damages would be more limited than in the current jury system, but would be higher than some of the current state dollar caps. The suggestion that the state agencies could be formed by restructuring the current state Medical Boards (with the obvious danger of doctor domination) and the reduction of the role and compensation of the plaintiffs' bar are likely to generate great political opposition.

A second direction involves reconceiving malpractice law as a branch of contract law, rather than as torts. This approach is discussed in Section (f)(ii) supra.

A third approach involves developing the themes articulated by Dr. Hilfiker at the beginning of this chapter: that doctors should share their uncertainty with patients and promote a model of true joint decisionmaking. In the following article, Professor George Annas discusses the relationship between doctor-patient communication and malpractice litigation.

G. J. Annas, Malpractice in Perspective

Medical and Health Annual 261 (A. Bernstein ed. 1987)

Doctors have been only too eager to support the mechanistic view spawned by this technological age (i.e., patients as machines, doctors as mechanics or repair persons). They have done little to try to explain the limitations of rescue medicine to their patients, and instead promote modern medical technology as something both wonderful and inevitable. . . .

As psychiatrist Jay Katz of Yale Law School has pointed out, although most medical diagnoses and treatments are filled with uncertainty, traditional medicine has stressed authoritarianism, and "power and control is maintained not only by projecting a greater sense of certainty than is warranted, but also by leaving patients in a state of uncertainty." He suggests a major effort to promote "shared decision-making" between physicians and patients. But this is not easy.

Can the authoritarian doctor and the submissive patient be brought together? And if they are brought together, can this new understanding of our mortality and the limits of medical intervention have a salutary effect on the medical malpractice crisis? The President's Commission on Bioethics suggested that the key to a new understanding is taking the legal doctrine of "informed consent" seriously. Specifically, the doctrine requires that patients, before they are asked to consent to invasive or risky medical procedures, be told (1) what the doctor proposes to do, (2) what the risks of death and bodily disability are, (3) what the benefits and the likelihood of success are, (4) what alternative treatments exist, and (5) what the major problems of recuperation are likely to be. If patients are actually given this information by their physicians, and if physicians take steps to ensure that patients actually understand it and share the decision-making burden, both doctors and patients should benefit.

The major cause of malpractice suits has consistently been described as a medically induced injury in the face of an unsatisfactory doctor-patient relationship. What little data we have suggest that patients want to know about potential risks, can handle the information well, and react more positively toward their physicians if fully informed. For example, a nationwide survey sponsored by the bioethics commission in 1981 found that 97 percent of the public believed that patients should have the right to all the available information about their condition and treatment that they wish. The president's commission also concluded that "when there is a strong pre-existing bond between patient and professional, and when the patient was prepared for the possibility of an adverse outcome, litigation is less likely." . . .

Discussion Question

Annas, Hilfiker, and many others advocate more open communication between doctor and patient, with the goal of achieving true joint decision-making and, according to Annas, less defensive medicine, malpractice and malpractice litigation. Havighurst's contracting proposals also imply more interaction between provider and patient over the terms of care. To what extent, or under what conditions, are these two proposals similar or different? Do they rest on similar or different assumptions? Are they designed to achieve similar or different kinds of communication, and similar or different policy goals?

C. Hospitals and Other Provider Institutions as Monitors of Quality of Care: the Impact of Medical Malpractice Law

What is the legal responsibility of health care institutions for the quality of the services delivered under their auspices? This section focuses primarily on how hospitals' legal duties have been defined by the evolving common law of medical malpractice, which of course itself reflects legislative, regulatory, and other social developments. Other sources of hospital duties — state licensing agencies, regulation by governmental payers, and other judicial doctrines — are considered in their own right in subsequent sections. Similar factors apply to newer kinds of health care institutions, such as nursing homes, health maintenance organizations, and home health care agencies, and they will be referred to, particularly in the sections dealing with licensing and payers.

Hospitals' legal responsibility for medical malpractice has been influenced by four major developments: (1) the changing characteristics of hospitals themselves, including their technology, financing, internal structure, and self-defined mission; (2) the hospital industry's own ideal picture of itself, embodied in the accreditation standards of the Joint Commission on Accreditation of Healthcare Organizations (JCAHO), until recently named the Joint Commission on Accreditation of Hospitals (JCAH) (and often referred to as the JCAH in this book); (3) the trend in the common law of torts toward imposing liability on corporations and other institutions under whose auspices risk-creating activities take place; and (4) the trend among payers, discussed extensively in Chapter 3, toward cost containment and increasing governmental and contractual regulation of health care delivery.

1. The Role of Law in the Age of Expanding Hospital Authority: 1876 to 1957

As discussed in the Introduction, hospitals underwent profound changes between 1850 and 1930, expanding enormously in numbers, and changing their primary mission from that of social control of the poor to being the locus of technologically advanced medical care for the whole population. Paradoxically, however, as hospitals became increasingly identified with the delivery of medical care, legal doctrines during this period held that hospitals as institutions had little control over or responsibility for the quality of doctors' and nurses' work. Three judicial concepts interacted to form the hospital's impenetrable shield: charitable immunity, the doctor as independent contractor, and the nurse as the doctor's borrowed servant. As we shall see, all three of these doctrines have been substantially eroded or entirely overruled with respect to hospitals. Nevertheless, it is difficult to understand current debates about hospitals' legal duties without some knowledge of the traditional doctrines that largely insulated hospitals from liability, and of the forces that led to their change.

a. Charitable Immunity

In McDonald v. Massachusetts General Hospital, 120 Mass. 432 (1876), the Massachusetts Supreme Judicial Court first applied the doctrine of charitable immunity to American hospitals, and its ruling was widely followed in the subsequent fifty years. McDonald, a construction worker, fractured his thigh in falling from a building and was brought to Massachusetts General Hospital, a charitable corporation supported by private and public funds that would today be described as a "private nonprofit hospital." Over McDonald's objection, a medical student set the broken bone, apparently negligently, and McDonald sued the hospital for damages. The hospital argued in defense that the doctors and medical students had direct and exclusive responsibility for the quality of patient care and that the hospital itself had none, but the Massachusetts Supreme Court chose not to rely on this ground. Rather, it held that the hospital was a "public charity," conducted for "the great public purpose" of serving the sick without compensation, and that therefore its limited funds, held in trust for its beneficiaries, should be immune from depletion by tort judgments. The corporation's only legal responsibility was to use due care in selecting its agents; apart from that, it could not be subjected to liability for any negligence by its doctors or other staff toward its beneficiaries.

The *McDonald* opinion can be easily rephrased in the modern vocabulary of risk spreading: since the bulk of the hospital's expenses were financed through philanthropy, the hospital could not spread the risk of tort losses through increased charges to patients and therefore should not be held liable in the same way as for-profit or fee-charging enterprises. But this argument begs the question of why the risk of tort losses should not be spread among philanthropic donors. In the nineteenth century the answer was probably influenced by social and legal conceptions of hierarchical charity. Hospital patients were, with rare exceptions, considered socially marginal by respectable and well-to-do citizens. Lawsuits for injuries caused by malpractice were viewed as violations of a social code that demanded gratitude and obedience in return for free services. See Vogel, Patrons, Practitioners, and Patients: The Voluntary Hospital in Mid-Victorian Boston, in Victorian America (D. Howe ed. 1976); Vogel, The Transformation of the American Hospital, 1850-1920, in Health Care in America (S. Reverby & D. Rosner, eds. 1979). Indeed, legal doctrine made that social code explicit: patients who benefited from charity by paying little or no fees were conclusively presumed to have consented to waive their right to collect damages from the hospital for negligent care. See 2 D. Louisell & H. Williams, Medical Malpractice at 17-5 (1987). The relationship of legal rights to social status was dramatic: "strangers", employees, and in some states, paying patients, often had full legal protection from negligence; only the "beneficiary" of the hospital's charity received no protection.

A similar result can be reached through the currently fashionable vocabulary of law and economics. Professor Richard Epstein argues that governmental or philanthropic funds devoted to tort judgments and medical malpractice premiums inevitably reduce resources for care for the poor. The proper question, he contends, is whether more people are harmed by being denied care altogether because of this reduction, as compared to the number harmed by being denied malpractice compensation. Epstein states that

> [i]t is hard to imagine that prominent donors to medical research would oppose use of their funds for medical malpractice litigation and damage costs if those expenditures produced any aggregate improvement in the level of overall medical care provided. . . . [The widespread desire of charitable hospitals to deny damages for negligence to the poor] is probably based on the sensible observation that a liability regime does more harm than good to its intended beneficiaries.

In the modern context, Epstein argues that federal and state Medicaid officials should be permitted to bargain with hospitals and doctors for a lower standard of care for the poor, so as to free up strained budget resources for more direct patient care. See Epstein, Market and Regulatory Approaches to Medical Malpractice, 74 Va. L. Rev. 1451, 1459-1463 (1988).

Discussion Question

Do you find Epstein's arguments convincing? Whichever way you come out on the issue, identify the two strongest arguments against Epstein's position, his likely response to those arguments, and your evaluation of the merits.

b. The Independent Contractor and Borrowed Servant Doctrines

The independent contractor and borrowed servant doctrines must be understood against the broader background of vicarious liability in tort. There are generally two ways that a hospital or any other corporate organization can be held liable for negligence: (1) directly, for its own corporate or organizational failure, and (2) vicariously, for the negligence of its employees or agents, despite the organization's own lack of fault. An example of direct or "corporate negligence" discussed in Subsection (4) infra would be the failure of the hospital's board of trustees, administration, and medical staff to review the credentials of doctors applying for permission to practice at the hospital. An example of vicarious liability would be holding the hospital liable for the negligence of a physician employee, despite all proper precautions having been taken regarding credentials, training, and supervision.

Vicarious liability has been traditionally justified by the employer's right, at least in theory, to "control" the actions of the employee. Where the employer is thought not to have a right of control — as in the case of an "independent contractor" or where the employer's own employee becomes actually subject to the control of a second employer or principal, and hence a "borrowed servant" — vicarious liability is said not to apply. Both of these principles were used by Judge Cardozo to defeat a claim of unauthorized surgery (hence battery) against a hospital in the famous case of Schloendorff v. New York Hospital, 211 N.Y. 125, 105 N.E. 92 (1914). Judge Cardozo's opinion in *Schloendorff* continues to be widely cited for its ringing statement of the principle of patient self-determination: "Every human being of adult years and sound mind has a right to determine what shall be done with his own body; and a surgeon who performs an operation without his patient's consent, commits an assault, for which he is liable in damages."Id. at 93. But Mrs. Schloendorff's suit against the *hospital* still failed, because even though she did not choose or pay the doctors, and even though they were chosen by the hospital, "[t]he wrong was not that of the hospital; it was that of physicians, who were not the defendant's servants, but were pursuing an independent calling, a profession sanctioned by a solemn oath, and safeguarded by stringent penalties. If, in serving their patient, they violated her commands, the responsibility is not the defendant [hospital's]; it is theirs. . . ." Id. at 94. Similarly, Judge Cardozo ruled that nurses, when treating a patient,

> are not acting as the servants of the hospital. . . . The superintendent is a servant of the hospital; the assistant superintendents, the orderlies, and the other members of the administrative staff are servants of the hospital. But nurses are employed to carry out the orders of the physicians, to whose authority they are subject. The hospital undertakes to procure for the patient the services of a nurse. It does not undertake through the agency of nurses to render those services itself.[Id.]

2. HOSPITALS' INSTITUTIONAL STRUCTURE AND IDEALIZED SELF-IMAGE: THE RIVAL VISIONS OF PRIVATE WORKSHOP AND COMMUNITY RESPONSIBILITY

Understanding the assumptions underlying the independent contractor and borrowed servant doctrines — and the reasons for their demise — requires some background knowledge of three related subjects: the system of staff privileges through which physicians receive permission to practice in particular hospitals, the structure of hospital governance, and the accreditation process designed and administered by the Joint Commission on Accreditation of Healthcare Organizations, formerly the Joint Commission on Accreditation of Hospitals.

Written in 1914, Judge Cardozo's *Schloendorff* opinion presents a powerful image of the nonprofit, private, or "voluntary" charitable hospital as a workshop that simply makes its facilities and equipment available to independent, individual medical and nursing practitioners. (For a collection of judicial expressions of this image, see Goldberg, The Duty of Hospitals and Medical Staffs to Regulate the Quality of Patient Care: A Legal Perspective, 14 Pac. L.J. 55, 66 n.64 (1982)). In some respects this image was not inaccurate, at least with respect to paying patients. "While certain physicians were designated to treat the poor in charity wards, the private rooms were open to the patients of almost any private physician. Thus, the typical American voluntary hospital in the late nineteenth and early twentieth centuries came to be known as having an 'open staff.'. . . There was no systematic policy in voluntary hospitals toward exercise of controls over the work of private physicians." M. Roemer & J. Friedman, Doctors in Hospitals 34 (1971). In other words, to say that a doctor was "on the hospital's staff" did *not* mean that he was an employee of the hospital; on the contrary, what it meant was that he had permission — "staff privileges" — to use the hospital's facilities for his own private, fee-generating practice of medicine. Of course, a strong contrary argument could have been made in Mrs. Schloendorff's case, because she had not selected and paid her own physician, and was relying on the hospital's designation of particular doctors to serve charitable patients. More fundamentally, what Cardozo did not mention (and perhaps did not know) was that this highly open system of individual practice was being vigorously contested within the medical profession at the time.

American hospitals faced a series of challenging and somewhat contradictory tasks in the early twentieth century. The great expansion in the number of hospitals (from 178 in 1873 to 4978 in 1923), and the numbers of doctors wanting to work in them, raised the question of who should be permitted to practice medicine in a hospital, and in particular to practice surgery. On the one hand, the American *laissez-faire* and entrepreneurial tradition precluded the European solution, which was to limit hospital practice to a small number of highly qualified doctors and relegate the rest to general office practice. On the other hand, truly wide open hospital practice threatened the economic interests and professional status of the new specialty of surgeons. Moreover, any restrictions on and organization of hospital practice had to be justified, at least at a rhetorical level, in terms of patient welfare. Finally, with the decline of the hospital's traditional missions of hierarchical charity and social control, a new legitimating image was needed to link the lucrative private practice of medicine in hospitals with broader community interests that would justify philanthropic and later governmental support.

The response to these conflicting pressures that gradually emerged in the first half of the twentieth century was, from the perspective of physicians, brilliantly successful. At the level of national ideology, the hospital standardization principles of the American College of Surgeons (ACS), formulated in 1919, were adopted by many hospitals. These standards set such goals as adequately staffed laboratories and X-ray departments, and a formal commitment that the "hospital" and its "medical staff" would be institutionally responsible for the quality of patient care, at least through careful granting of staff privileges and retrospective review by doctors of the quality of each other's work. Thus Dr. Malcolm MacEachern, a leading authority on hospital administration, advocate of hospital standards, and Director of Professional Relations of the American Hospital Association, wrote in 1935 that

> twentieth century developments have made [the distinction between public and private ownership] inaccurate, and those terms should be abandoned. With the exception of a limited number of hospitals owned by private individuals or corporations, operated for profit and admitting only pay patients, all hospitals are public in that they are directly or indirectly owned by the community and may admit free and part-pay patients as well as those who are able to pay the full cost of their care. Further than this, all hospitals have a definite relationship to the community. They must give adequate service if they are to continue to exist. . . . [These hospitals] . . . draw their support from the community, and, if they are to continue to receive that support, they must earn it by giving equally good service. [M. MacEachern, Hospital Organization and Management 35 (1935, 3rd ed. 1957).]

But although the rhetoric promised institutional responsibility and oversight of the private practice of medicine, there were no publicly accountable mechanisms of enforcement. Adherence to the standards was voluntary with each hospital, and compliance was widely resisted, not only by the less elite general practitioners, but also by most physicians who wanted to avoid bitter intra-professional disputes.

Passage of the federal Hill-Burton Act in 1946, discussed in Chapter 1, required states to enact hospital licensure laws as a condition of receiving federal funds for hospital construction; not surprisingly, the states relied heavily on the ACS standards in drafting their statutes, thereby applying them to all hospitals and backing them, at least in theory, with state regulatory enforcement. Again, however, the reality was that the states had no staff or other resources for enforcement and, more fundamentally, no desire to regulate medical practice in or out of hospitals. In 1951 the ACS standards program was succeeded by a far more powerful but still resolutely private organization, the Joint Commission on Accreditation of Hospitals (JCAH), whose governing board was (and is) composed of representatives from the two major interest groups — the American Medical Association (AMA) and American Hospital Association (AHA), as well as from a number of more specialized professional organizations. For a detailed discussion of the origins and development of the JCAH, see Jost, The Joint Commission on Accreditation of Hospitals: Private Regulation of Health Care and the Public Interest, 24 B.C.L. Rev. 835 (1983).

From physicians' perspective, the brilliant characteristic of this private regulatory apparatus was its voluntary, wholly professional, and often illusory quality. (The actual performance of the JCAHO in detecting serious hazards is examined in Section F(1)(b).) Under the JCAH standards, permission to practice in a hospital could be granted to virtually any doctor with a degree from an approved medical school. The hospital was then supposed to create various categories of staff privileges and control mechanisms to attempt to regulate the dangers of wide open, unsupervised hospital practice. As Roemer and Friedman perceptively point out, the entire American structure of accreditation standards, control committees, and legal requirements derive (paradoxically) from our primary commitment to unsupervised and — in a telling phrase — "private" practice in hospitals. (Such structures are largely absent in Europe, where hospital practice is more collective and public.) See M. Roemer & J. Friedman, supra, at 59. The highest level of staff privileges, termed "active" privileges, are given to experienced doctors who have made a commitment to focus their practice at the particular hospital. Such doctors are considered full members of the medical staff, with voting privileges and committee responsibilities. "Relatively firm standards could be applied to attainment [of this level], and to these physicians would be entrusted duties for which the hospital was legally responsible, such as service to indigent patients or various functions in administration and teaching." Id. at 43. In return, these doctors are given preferential access to scarce hospital resources, such as beds for their patients. A second category, termed "associate," is for more junior doctors who are in a probationary status. These doctors may have some committee responsibilities, but do not have a vote or participate in policymaking. A third category, termed "courtesy," simply allows doctors to treat their private patients in the hospital. This category of doctor comes closest to the model of the independent practitioner simply using the hospital as a workshop. In other words, the level of institutional involvement — and scrutiny — was often effectively voluntary with each individual doctor. Nevertheless, it is important to note that no source of hospital law — statutes, regulations, accreditation standards, or the common law — has ever suggested that hospitals have less responsibility for quality of care depending on the doctor's category of privileges. Indeed, following the Roemer and Friedman analysis above, an argument could be made that hospitals should have *more* responsibility to monitor the care of the less affiliated courtesy staff, whose credentials may be weaker than those of the active staff, and who in any case are less involved in day-to-day professional interactions.

Most doctors — whether active, associate, or courtesy staff members —

derived (and still derive) the majority of their income from the private practice of medicine. Four types of doctors represent at least partial exceptions to this rule. Anesthesiologists, radiologists, pathologists, and emergency room physicians are often termed "hospital-based physicians" because they are normally selected by the hospital, rather than by patients, and because their practices are integrally related to hospital operations. At the same time, these doctors are usually not "employees" of the hospital, have complex contracts with the hospital regarding compensation, insurance liability, time commitment to the hospital, and other matters, and may bill patients directly for their services.

3. THE COLLAPSE OF CHARITABLE IMMUNITY AND THE RISE OF RESPONDEAT SUPERIOR

Paradoxically, many of the hospitals' greatest successes in the 1930s and 1940s undermined the doctrines that insulated hospitals from legal responsibility for quality of care. The establishment of Blue Cross as the financing arm of American hospitals, discussed in Chapter 2, helped transform large numbers of formerly charity or near-charity patients into paying patients, and hospitals themselves into the "hospital industry." Once hospitals could and did charge most people for their services, they could afford to hire growing numbers of nurses, technicians, administrators, and physicians to manage their increasingly complex operations. Moreover, individual hospitals, the AHA, and the JCAH repeatedly articulated the vision of the nonprofit, voluntary hospital as a community institution that "provided" high quality care. All of these developments were inconsistent with Judge Cardozo's image of the hospital as a passive charity removed from operational responsibility.

Although the doctrine of charitable immunity for nonprofit hospitals was widely followed prior to 1942, since then 35 jurisdictions have abolished it, and only a few retain it in modified form (usually limiting damages to a specified dollar amount or to the amount of insurance coverage). See 2 D. Louisell & H. Williams, Medical Malpractice ¶17.04 (1987); Annot., 25 A.L.R. 4th 517 (1983). Two opinions were particularly influential in shaping the trend toward abrogation: President and Directors of Georgetown College v. Hughes, 130 F.2d 810 (D.C. Cir. 1942) [hereinafter *Hughes*] (written by Judge Wiley Rutledge, later a member of the United States Supreme Court), and Bing v. Thunig, 2 N.Y.2d 665, 143 N.E.2d 3, 163 N.Y.S.2d 3 (1957) [hereinafter *Bing*], in which Chief Judge Fuld of the New York Court of Appeals reversed Judge Cardozo's *Schloendorff* ruling. These opinions made three powerful arguments. First, the charitable immunity doctrine was riddled with internal contradictions; for example, fellow employees, visitors, and in some states paying patients could recover against the hospital for employees' negligence. But if the hospital could afford to compensate these claimants, and could do so without violating the terms of its trust or public function, why could it not also compensate charitable patients? Second, the conclusive presumption that nonpaying patients have "waived" their right to non-negligent care was no longer consistent with social norms; as Judge Rutledge pointed out, the charitable patient, "least of all, is able to bear the burden [of uncompensated injury]. More than all others, he has no choice. He is the last person the donor would wish to go without indemnity." *Hughes,* 130 F.2d at 827. Third, many nonprofit hospitals were now "big business," with a capacity to absorb and spread losses very different from their nineteenth-century predecessors. Indeed, this overall shift in the public's conception of the hospital led the *Bing* court to overrule *Schloendorff*'s independent contractor and borrowed servant doctrines as well. "Present-day hospitals," wrote Chief Judge Fuld, "as their manner of operation plainly demonstrates, do far more than furnish facilities for treatment. . . . Certainly, the person who avails himself of 'hospital facilities' expects that the hospital will attempt to cure him, not that its nurses or other employees will act on their own responsibility." *Bing,* 2 N.Y.2d at 666-667. Henceforth "the test should be, for [hospitals], whether charitable or profit-making, as it is for every other employer, was the person who committed the negligent injury-producing act one of its employees and, if he was, was he acting within the scope of his employment." Id.

Note: Applying Respondeat Superior: Nurses, Physician-Employees, and the Borrowed Servant Doctrine

Nurses and nonprofessional employees fit easily into the traditional respondeat superior doctrine: they are formally employees of the hospital and for the most part are subject to hospital managerial control. The obvious exception to this generalization occurs when the nurse or technician is functioning under the orders or supervision of a physician who is not himself a hospital employee. The modern trend is to recognize that *both* the hospital and the physician may be supervising the employee, and hence both may be liable for the employee's negligence. For example, Truhitte v. French Hospital, 128 Cal. App. 3d 332, 180 Cal. Rptr. 152 (1982), involved a suit for damages caused by a sponge left inside the patient's abdomen. Responsibility for insuring that all sponges were removed was shared by the surgeon and by the operating room nurses who prepared the sponges and counted them before and after the operation. Under the "captain of the ship" doctrine (which held surgeons responsible for all negligence in the operating room), the nurses would have been considered the borrowed servants of the surgeon, and the hospital would have been absolved of liability for the negligence of its employees. See Annot., 29 A.L.R. 3d 1065, 1075 (1970). But the *Truhitte* court rejected that reasoning.

> We question whether the "captain of the ship" doctrine has any remaining independent existence: the vicarious liability of a surgeon for the independent negligence of nurses and other assistants is determined in the cases under the general rules of agency. The "captain of the ship" doctrine arose from the need to assure plaintiffs a source of recovery for malpractice at a time when many hospitals enjoyed charitable immunity; other jurisdictions are moving away from a strict application of the doctrine. A theory that the surgeon directly controls all activities of whatever nature in the operating room certainly is not realistic in present day medical care. Today's hospitals hire, fire, train and provide day-to-day supervision of their nurse-employees. Fortunately, hospitals can and do implement standards and regulations governing good surgery practices and techniques and are in the best position to enforce compliance; hospitals also are in a position to insure against the risk and pass the cost to consumers. . . .
>
> The argument of the hospital in the trial court and on appeal confuses two distinct concepts: the nondelegable nature of the surgeon's duty to remove sponges, and the basis for imposing vicarious liability on the surgeon under the borrowed-servant doctrine for the independent negligence of the nurses. It is the law of California that the surgeon's duty to remove all sponges and other foreign objects from the patient's body is nondelegable. However, it does not follow that the hospital may escape liability for its independent negligence in failing to devise adequate sponge-accounting procedures or in negligently carrying out such procedures through its employee-nurses. [Truhitte v. French Hospital, 128 Cal. App.3d 351, 180 Cal. Rptr. 152 at 160-161 (1982).]

The Missouri Supreme Court reached a similar conclusion in Brickner v. Normandy Osteopathic Hospital, Inc., 746 S.W.2d 108 (Mo. 1988). The issue was whether a hospital could be held vicariously liable for the negligence of a second-year resident doctor, employed by the hospital, when performing surgery under the supervision of an attending physician, that is, a more senior doctor who was not an employee of the hospital. Echoing the *Schloendorff* opinion, the hospital argued that the second-year resident was either under the control of the attending physician, and hence a "borrowed servant," or that the resident was a physician exercising professional judgment over whom the hospital had no control. The court rejected both arguments. With respect to borrowed servants, the court held that an employee could be under the control of two masters, and that the hospital could escape liability only if it could show that it had "relinquished all control and authority . . . to the special employer." Id. at 114. Since the hospital scheduled the resident's work hours, required him to keep a log of his surgical experiences, write reports of his operations, and even question an attending physician's orders if he believed them to be erroneous, the resident was evidently under both the immediate supervision of the attending physician and the more general control of the hospital. Similarly, the fact that the resident exercised some professional judgment and was not controlled in every detail by the hospital did not mean that he was not an employee acting within the scope of his employment. See id.

Discussion Question

Why do you think it is that the *Truhhite* and *Brickner* opinions come to such different conclusions than Judge Cardozo did in *Schloendorff*? Is it because hospitals now exercise more control over nurses and employee-physicians than they did in 1914? In fact, in the early 1900's hospitals may have exercised more control in some respects; for example, doctors in training were often required to live in or near the hospital, work very long hours, and even forbidden to marry. See C. Rosenberg, The Care of Strangers (1988). Is it that the relationship of the hospital to medical practice has changed, with more explicit and substantive institutional responsibility? (Consider this question again after reading Sections D, E, and F infra.) Although the courts do not speak explicitly in these terms, do you think the competing models of quality of care outlined at the beginning of this chapter play an implicit role?

4. NON-EMPLOYEE PHYSICIANS AND THE EXPANDING CONCEPTS OF AGENCY AND NONDELEGABLE DUTY

Section 267 of the Restatement (Second) of Agency states:

> One who represents that another is his servant or other agent and thereby causes a third person justifiably to rely upon the care or skill of such apparent agent is subject to liability to the third person for harm caused by the lack of care or skill of the one appearing to be a servant or other agent as if he were such.

The comment to this section states that "[t]he mere fact that acts are done by one whom the injured party believes to be the defendant's servant is not sufficient to cause the apparent master to be liable. There must be such reliance upon the manifestation as exposes the plaintiff to the negligent conduct. The rule normally applies where the plaintiff has submitted himself to the care or protection of an apparent servant *in response to an invitation from the defendant to enter into such relations with such servant*" [emphasis supplied].

Most appellate opinions in the last decade concerning the apparent agency of hospital-based physicians have sustained hospital liability. But in theory, and at times in practice, an apparent agency claim can be thrown into question or even defeated by doubts about the patient's reliance on the hospital's "representation." The following case suggests some of the difficulties in applying the law of agency to relationships among patients, doctors, and hospitals, and the virtues of the alternative doctrine of nondelegable duty.

Jackson v. Power

743 P.2d 1376 (Alaska 1987)

[In May 1981, sixteen-year-old Brett Jackson was seriously injured when he fell from a cliff, and was airlifted to Fairbanks Memorial Hospital (FMH), the only general hospital emergency room north of Anchorage. Jackson was examined by John Power, M. D., an emergency room physician on duty at the time. Dr. Power's examination revealed extensive injuries, including gastric distension, suggesting possible internal injuries. Dr. Power ordered several tests, but did not order certain procedures that could have been used to ascertain whether there had been damage to the patient's kidneys. Jackson had, in fact, suffered damage to the renal arteries and veins which supply blood to and remove blood from the kidneys. This damage, undetected for approximately 9 to 10 hours after Jackson's arrival at FMH, ultimately caused Jackson to lose both of his kidneys.

Jackson and his mother filed suit. In their complaint they alleged negligence in the diagnosis, care and treatment Jackson received at FMH. Jackson moved for partial summary judgment seeking to hold FMH vicariously liable as a matter of law for the care rendered by Dr. Power. In support of his motion, Jackson advanced three separate theories: (1) enterprise liability; (2) apparent authority; and (3) non-delegable duty.

The trial court rejected the enterprise liability theory, and ruled that genuine issues of material fact precluded summary judgment on the two remaining theories. The Alaska Supreme Court granted Jackson's petition for review of the trial court's ruling.]

. . . Initially, it is important to clarify the exact issue that we have been asked to resolve. Jackson has conceded, for purposes of this appeal, that Dr. Power was not an employee of FMH, but an independent contractor employed by respondent Emergency Room, Inc. (ERI), and that ERI and FMH are separate legal entities. . . . Jackson also makes no claim that FMH was itself negligent in its selection, retention, or supervision of Dr. Power. Consequently, we have no occasion to consider the doctrine of corporate negligence. Jackson asks us to resolve only whether a hospital should be vicariously liable, as a matter of public policy, for the negligence or malpractice of an independent contractor/physician, committed while treating a patient in the hospital's emergency room [under the three theories stated above].

[*ENTERPRISE LIABILITY*]

Jackson . . . contends [that] if the enterprise impacts society and the negligent act occurred during an activity performed for the benefit or in the interest of the enterprise, the enterprise is liable. [Although the court notes that two courts in other states have indicated some willingness to accept this theory, and that it has been advocated by some commentators, it declines to adopt it where the negligence has been committed by a person who was not an employee of the enterprise.]

[*APPARENT AUTHORITY*]

[On this point the Alaska Supreme Court reviewed cases from other states, as well as the Restatements of Torts and Agency, and affirmed the trial court's ruling that genuine issues of material fact precluded summary judgment for the plaintiff on this theory. Among the facts noted by the court as relevant for trial were the lack of a contract between FMH and ERI, and the absence of any role by FMH employees in scheduling or monitoring the emergency room physicians. In addition, the court considered it relevant that there was a sign adjacent to the desk of the admissions clerk in the emergency room indicating that physicians from ERI were working in the emergency room, and that Jackson was not unconscious when he arrived at the hospital.]

[*NON-DELEGABLE DUTY*]

. . . Physicians, not hospitals, FMH asserts, have a duty to practice medicine non-negligently. Thus, according to FMH, a hospital cannot be held to have delegated away a duty it never had. . . .

FMH is licensed as a "general acute care hospital." As such, it is required to comply with state regulations designed to promote "safe and adequate treatment of individuals in hospitals in the interest of public health, safety and welfare." . . . These regulations provided, at the time of Jackson's accident, that an acute care hospital shall "insure that a physician is available to respond to an emergency at all times." . . . Thus, at a minimum, the law imposed a duty on FMH to provide emergency care physicians on a 24-hour basis.

FMH, however, voluntarily assumed a much broader duty. At the time of Jackson's accident, FMH was accredited by the Joint Commission on the Accreditation of Hospitals (JCAH). In order to receive and maintain accreditation, FMH had to comply with the JCAH's standards promulgated in the Accreditations Manual For Hospitals, Emergency Services. Standard I mandates that all accredited hospitals implement a well defined plan for emergency care based on community need and the capability of the hospital. The JCAH standards also mandate, among other things, that: (1) FMH's emergency room be directed by a physician member of the active medical staff (Standard II); (2) FMH's emergency room be integrated with other units and departments of the hospital (Standard III); (3) that emergency care be guided by written policies and procedures; and (4) that the quality of care be continually reviewed, evaluated and assured through establishment of quality control mechanisms (Standard V).

Additionally, FMH's own bylaws provided for the establishment and maintenance of an emergency room . . . [and] for the creation of an emergency room committee which is required among other things to:

(a) formulate rules and regulations for the continuous coverage of the emergency room; and

(b) supervise the clinical work in that department.

Based upon the above, it cannot seriously be questioned that FMH had a duty to provide emergency room services and that part of that duty was to provide physician care in its emergency room. Having so determined, we must next ascertain whether FMH's duty to provide physician care in the emergency room is non-delegable. . . .

A non-delegable duty is an established exception to the rule that an employer is not liable for the negligence of an independent contractor. [S]uch a duty "may be imposed by statute, by contract, by franchise or by charter, or by the common law. . . ." [After reviewing many particular non-delegable duties, such as those of common carriers to passengers, landlords to tenants, and so forth, the court quoted Prosser and Keeton that] "[i]t is difficult to suggest any criterion by which the non-delegable character of such duties may be determined, *other than the conclusion of the courts that the responsibility is so important to the community that the employer should not be permitted to transfer it to another.*" (Emphasis added.) [Prosser and Keeton on The Law of Torts 511-512 (5th ed. 1984).] . . .

[After discussing a recent Alaska case holding that a scheduled airline could not delegate its duty to provide safe passage to a sub-contracting carrier, the court stated that] the importance to the community of a hospital's duty to provide emergency room physicians rivals the importance of the common-carrier's duty for the safety of its passengers. We also find a close parallel between the regulatory scheme of airlines and hospitals. Undoubtedly, the operation of a hospital is one of the most regulated activities in this state. Besides the license, and certificate of need . . . a hospital must comply with state regulations promulgated to control its activities, . . . adopt a state approved risk management program "to minimize the risk of injury to patients," . . . and undergo "annual inspections and investigations" of its facilities. Failure to comply with these statutory requirements can lead to suspension or revocation of the hospital's license.

The hospital regulatory scheme and the purpose underlying it . . . manifest the legislature's recognition that it is the hospital as an institution which bears ultimate responsibility for complying with the mandates of the law. It is the hospital that is required to ensure compliance with the regulations, and thus, relevant to the instant case, it is the hospital that bears final accountability for the provision of physicians for emergency room care. We, therefore, hold that a general acute care hospital's duty to provide physicians for emergency room care is non-delegable. Thus, a hospital such as FMH may not shield itself from liability by claiming that it is not responsible for the results of negligently performed health care when the law imposes a duty on the hospital to provide that health care.

We are persuaded that the circumstances under which emergency room care is provided in a modern hospital mandate the rule we adopt today. Not only is this rule consonant with the public perception of the hospital as a multifaceted health care facility responsible for the quality of medical care and treatment rendered, it also treats tort liability in the medical arena in a manner that is consistent with the commercialization of American medicine. Finally, we simply cannot fathom why liability should depend upon the technical employment status of the emergency room physician who treats the patient. It is the hospital's duty to provide the physician, which it may do through any means at its disposal. The means employed, however, will not change the fact that the hospital will be responsible for the care rendered by physicians it has a duty to provide.

This holding is necessarily limited. We do not change the standard of care with which a physician must comply, nor do we extend the duty which we find non-delegable beyond its natural scope. Our holding does not extend to situations where the patient is treated by his or her own doctor in an emergency room provided for the convenience of the doctor. Such situations are beyond the scope of the duty assumed by an acute care hospital. Rather our holding is limited to those situations where a patient comes to the hospital, as an institution, seeking emergency room services and is treated by a physician provided by the hospital. In such situations, the hospital shall be vicariously liable for damages proximately caused by a physician's negligence or malpractice. . . .

Jackson is [thus] entitled to partial summary judgment on the issue of FMH's vicarious liability.

NOTES AND QUESTIONS

(1) The *Jackson* opinion represents an unusually comprehensive and scholarly effort to clarify the law of hospital liability for the negligence of independent contractor physicians. Nevertheless, the court's effort to distinguish sharply among different theories raises difficult questions. For example, in the nondelegable duty section, the court states that "we simply cannot fathom why liability should depend upon the technical employment status of the emergency room physician." Yet if that is so, then why does the court suggest that exactly such "technical" issues (the absence of a contract between FMH and ERI, the fact that the severely injured Jackson may have been dimly aware of an ambiguous sign and so forth) could be the basis for a jury verdict in favor of the hospital on the apparent authority theory? Similarly, it is hard to reconcile the court's strong and sophisticated endorsement of institutional responsibility derived from general statutory policy, regulations, accreditation standards, and public perception, with its implication that it might reward a hospital for *not* having a contract with its emergency room subcontractor, in apparent gross violation of the JCAH standards and the hospital's own bylaws.

(2) Many state appellate courts have ruled that hospitals are vicariously

liable for the negligence of hospital-based physicians not chosen by the patients themselves. See, for instance, Mehlman v. Powell, 378 A.2d 1121 (Md. 1977) (emergency room physician under contract to hospital found to be hospital's apparent agent; court contrasts public's expectations about gas stations, where franchising under national brand names is well known, with public's reliance on hospital as source of care and impracticality of patient inquiries about precise status of numerous members of the hospital staff); Hannola v. City of Lakewood, 68 Ohio App. 2d 61, 426 N.E.2d 1187 (1980) (court distinguishes agency and reliance doctrines in commercial context, where customer has time to read and act on disclaimers of liability, from hospital emergency room context, where patient often has no realistic opportunity to absorb or react to information about ownership and control); Beeck v. Tucson General Hospital, 18 Ariz. App. 165, 500 P.2d 1153 (1972) (court finds hospital vicariously liable for negligence of radiological technician; opinion focuses not only on the fact that the hospital furnished all the equipment for the radiology department, had entered into an exclusive contract with a particular group of radiologists, and exercised extensive control over the employment of the technicians, but also that radiology "was an inherent function of the hospital, a function without which the hospital could not properly achieve its purpose.") But see Trapp v. Cayson, 471 So. 2d 375 (Miss. 1985) (court finds that although hospital furnishes all equipment, technicians, and supplies for its radiology department, hospital does not compensate the radiologists or schedule their work; moreover, X-rays are ordered directly from the radiologists by the private physician, and particular radiologists can be requested by the patient or primary doctor. In these circumstances, radiologist is not an agent of the hospital); Walker v. Winchester Memorial Hospital, 585 F. Supp. 1328, 1331 (W.D. Va. 1984) (suggesting that fact that patient was unconscious when brought to the emergency room and for eight days thereafter casts doubt on a claim of apparent agency, but leaving the issue to the jury); Stewart v. Midani, 525 F. Supp. 843, 853 (N.D. Ga. 1981) (suggesting that "a simple notice might suffice to inform the prospective patient that the emergency room (or X-ray laboratory) is under the control of an independent contractor").

Discussion Question

Assume you are counsel to a state legislative committee considering revisions to statutes regarding hospitals and medical malpractice. The chairman poses the following questions: "Should we have a single rule of apparent agency or nondelegable duty for all hospitals in our state? Our big city hospitals look like what the JCAH has in mind; they at least have the capacity to review the work of their radiologists and emergency room doctors, although their actual review may be pretty weak. But some of our smaller rural hospitals really don't have the resources and manpower to achieve the JCAH ideal, and operate as extensions of doctors' private practices, even for radiology and the emergency room. Shouldn't we have different rules for the two types of hospitals and explicitly tell patients in the rural communities that the hospital isn't going to be responsible for what most doctors do? Maybe we should also require those doctors to carry much more than $1 million medical malpractice insurance, since injured patients wouldn't have the hospital to supplement the doctor's coverage. Alternatively, maybe we should hold the rural hospitals vicariously liable, and also require them to contract with independent peer review organizations to monitor their doctors' quality of care. What are your views?"

5. THE RISE OF CORPORATE LIABILITY

a. Introduction

Thus far our focus has been on the hospital's liability for the actions of its employees or agents engaged in the treatment of patients. We now turn to the hospital's liability for its "own" acts and omissions. Such acts can be performed not only by the board of directors and senior administrative and medical officials, but also by any employee or medical staff member whose organizational role involves carrying out a duty or function of the hospital as an institution. Three areas in particular have given rise to litigation about hospitals' direct duties to patients regarding quality of care. The first involves the hospital's duty to screen out incompetent physicians and other providers at the time of initial appointment, a duty recognized even by the *McDonald* court in 1876. Second, hospitals have been held liable for failing to respond to apparent serious errors by physicians as they occur. Third, in a related point, hospitals have been held liable for failing to monitor the performance of particular physicians, and of failing to restrict or terminate doctors with a track record of significant mistakes. (In addition, hospitals have a duty to provide adequate equipment, policies, training, and supervision to their employees, a point made in the *Truhitte* case regarding systems for counting surgical sponges.) Cutting across these particular duties are questions about the relative powers, duties, and rights of the major actors in the hospital: the doctors, nurses, administration, and governing board.

The typical structure of the private nonprofit hospital been described as a "triad" composed of the governing body, the administration or management, and the "self-governing" medical staff, and are graphically represented in Figure 5.1. According to JCAH standards, the governing body "is responsible for establishing policy, maintaining quality patient care, and providing for institutional management and planning." 1988 Accreditation Manual for Hospitals GB.1, at 47. The Medical Staff is described as having "overall responsibility for the quality of the professional services . . . as well as the responsibility of accounting therefor to the governing body." Id., MS.1 at 111.

FIGURE 5.1

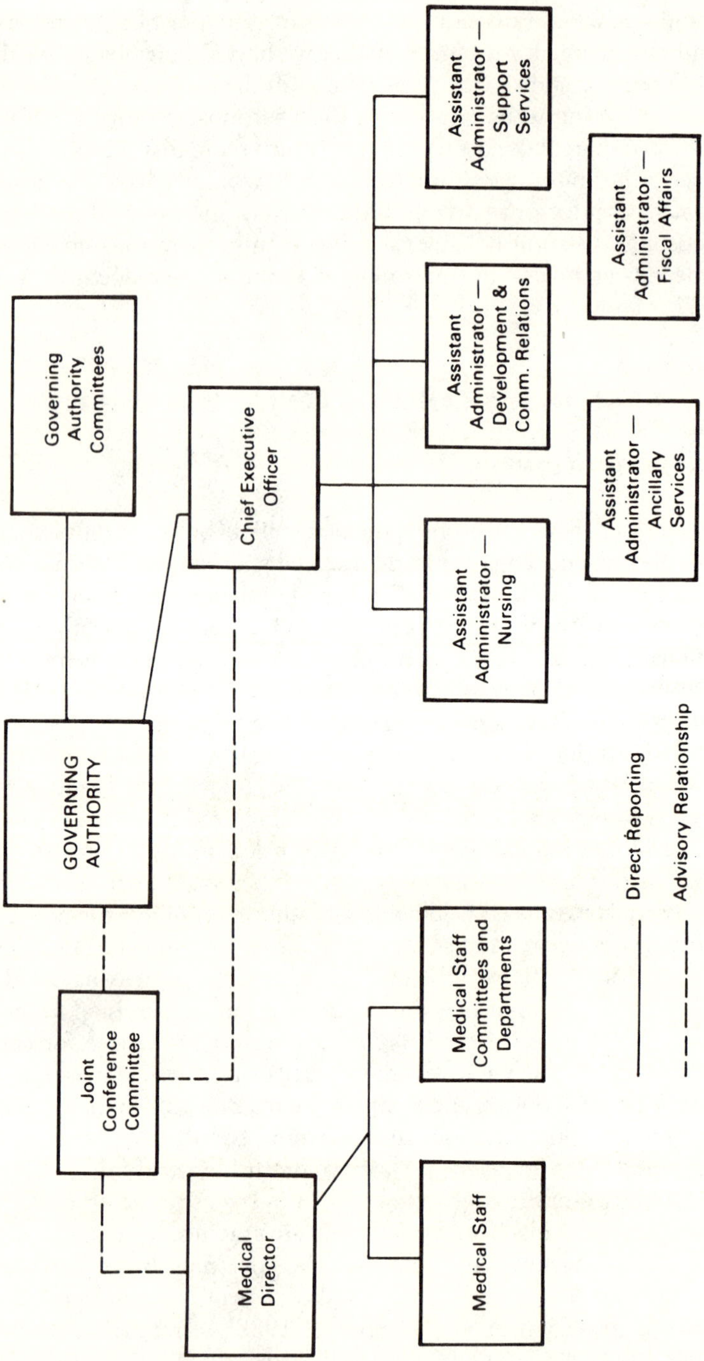

Source: J. Rakich & K. Darr, Hospital Organization and Management 26 (1983).

Accountability is said to be consistent with "a framework of self-governance" of the medical staff; Id., MS.2 at 114. Neither the governing body nor the medical staff may unilaterally amend the medical staff bylaws. See id., MS2.1, at 114. The administrator or chief executive officer is appointed by and responsible to the governing body, but has no direct authority over the Medical Staff, which has the right of direct access to the governing body. See id., GB1.10, at 48-49. These relationships are diagrammed in Figure C-1, in which no authority runs from the CEO to the Medical Staff, and indeed only a dotted line, representing an "advisory relationship," runs both ways between the Medical Director and the governing body.

Despite these tensions and ambiguities, the clear message of the JCAH standards is that according to the hospital industry and medical profession themselves, hospitals have important and specific responsibilities as institutions for the quality of care delivered under their auspices. However, as articulated by the JCAH and as expressed in actual hospital practice, these responsibilities are allocated among, and often shared by, the governing body, the medical staff, and hospital administration, and by numerous committees and joint committees. As K.J. Williams, a doctor and hospital consultant puts it, "[w]hat frequently happens is that responsibility and authority are diffused and diluted throughout committees of the medical staff rather than being pinpointed in certain officials. Accordingly, that which is everyone's business becomes no one's business. . . ." Williams, The Quandary of the Hospital Administrator in Dealing with the Medical Malpractice Problem, 55 Neb. L. Rev. 401, 407 (1976). The question for the courts has been the extent to which the accreditation standards, their analogues in state licensure laws and hospital by-laws, and more broadly the social expectations of the hospital's mission that they both define and reflect, should function not only as voluntary industry guidelines with often minimal effects, but also as legal standards for assessing hospitals' responsibility for quality of care.

b. The Hospital's Duty to Evaluate the Credentials of Physicians at the Time of Initial Appointment

Johnson v. Misericordia Community Hospital

99 Wis. 2d 708, 301 N.W.2d 156 (1981)

[Plaintiff's right thigh was permanently paralyzed by an operation negligently performed by Dr. Salinsky. Plaintiff's claim against the hospital was not based on respondeat superior, but rather on the alleged duty of care owed directly by the hospital to its patients to use reasonable care in the granting of staff privileges. Misericordia was not accredited by the Joint Commission on the Accreditation of Hospitals.]

[T]he granting of staff privileges to [unqualified physicians] would undoubtedly create an unreasonable risk of harm or injury to their patients. Therefore, . . . we hold that a hospital has a duty to exercise due care in the selection of its medical staff. . . .

[W]hether the hospital was negligent . . . depends on whether Misericordia exercised that degree of care and skill as the average hospital exercises in selecting its medical staff. . . .

The facts adduced at trial establish that had Misericordia sought information from the hospitals referred to in Salinsky's application, it would have discovered: (1) that Doctors Hospital revoked Salinsky's orthopedic privileges and required that he obtain consultation before attempting any open surgical procedure just two months before he applied for orthopedic privileges at Misericordia; (2) that he had been denied staff privileges at St. Anthony's Hospital in January of 1971; (3) that he was never on the consulting staff of New Berlin Memorial Hospital or Northwest General Hospital; [and] (4) that Mt. Sinai Hospital granted him privileges to perform simple orthopedic procedures but later reduced his rank to courtesy physician in the Department of General Practice and ultimately revoked all of his privileges for failure to use their clinical departments. . . . Additionally, Misericordia had access to the Milwaukee Circuit Court files wherein it would have discovered that seven malpractice suits had been filed against Salinsky. Given that Misericordia with due diligence must be charged with the knowledge of the foregoing facts before it appointed Salinsky to its medical staff, the dispositive issue is whether a hospital with knowledge of such facts would, in the exercise of ordinary care, have granted Salinsky orthopedic surgical privileges. [Expert testimony established that given these facts, a hospital exercising ordinary care would not have appointed Salinsky to its medical staff.] . . .

In summary, we hold that a hospital owes a duty to its patients to exercise reasonable care in the selection of its medical staff and in granting specialized privileges. [Under both JCAH standards and state hospital licensing law,] the final appointing authority resides in the hospital's governing body, . . . although it must rely on the medical staff and in particular the credentials committee (or committee of the whole) to investigate and evaluate an applicant's qualifications for the requested privileges. . . . However, this delegation of the responsibility to investigate and evaluate the professional competence of applicants for clinical privileges does not relieve the governing body of its duty to appoint only qualified physicians and surgeons to its medical staff and periodically monitor and review their competency. . . . The credentials committee (or committee of the whole) must investigate the qualifications of applicants. The facts of this case demonstrate that a hospital should, at a minimum, require completion of the application and verify the accuracy of the applicant's statements, especially in regard to his medical education, training and experience. . . . Additionally, it should: (1) solicit information from the applicant's peers, including those not referenced in his application, who are knowledgeable about his education, training, experience, health, competence and ethical character; (2) determine if the applicant is currently licensed to practice in this state and if his licensure or registration has been or is currently being challenged; and (3) inquire whether the applicant has been involved in any adverse malpractice action and whether he has experienced a loss of medical organization membership or medical privileges or membership at any other hospital. . . . The investigating committee must also evaluate the information gained through its inquiries and make a reasonable judgment as to the approval or denial of each application for staff privileges. The hospital will be charged with gaining and evaluating the knowledge that would have been acquired had it exercised ordinary care in investigating its medical staff applicants. . . .

NOTE

Although Misericordia apparently never applied for accreditation, and hence was not formally subject to the JCAH standards, many of the JCAH concepts were included in the state's licensing regulations. Moreover, the *Johnson* court was apparently willing, without explicit discussion, to look to the JCAH standards for guidance in defining "ordinary care" in the granting of staff privileges.

c. THE HOSPITAL'S DUTY TO MONITOR ONGOING TREATMENT PROVIDED BY INDEPENDENT PHYSICIANS WITH STAFF PRIVILEGES

Darling v. Charleston Community Memorial Hospital

33 Ill. 2d 326, 211 N.E. 2d 253 (1965)

SCHAEFER, Justice.

. . . On November 5, 1960, the plaintiff [Dorrence Darling II], who was 18 years old, broke his leg while playing in a college football game. He was taken to the emergency room at the defendant [Charleston Community Memorial Hospital] where Dr. Alexander, who was on emergency call that day, treated him. Dr. Alexander, with the assistance of hospital personnel, applied traction and placed the leg in a plaster cast. A heat cradle was applied to dry the cast. Not long after the application of the cast plaintiff was in great pain and his toes, which protruded from the cast, became swollen and dark in color. They eventually became cold and insensitive. On the evening of November 6, Dr. Alexander "notched" the cast around the toes, and on the afternoon of the next day he cut the cast approximately three inches up from the foot. On November 8 he split the sides of the cast with a Stryker saw; in the course of cutting the cast the plaintiff's leg was cut on both sides. Blood and other seepage were observed by the nurses and others, and there was a stench in the room, which one witness said was the worst he had smelled since World War II. The plaintiff remained in Charleston Hospital until November 19, when he was transferred to Barnes Hospital in St. Louis and placed under the care of Dr. Fred Reynolds, head of orthopedic surgery at Washington University School of Medicine and Barnes Hospital. Dr. Reynolds found that the fractured leg contained a considerable amount of dead tissue which in his opinion resulted from interference with the circulation of blood in the limb caused by swelling or hemorrhaging of the leg against the constriction of the cast. Dr. Reynolds performed several operations in a futile attempt to save the leg but ultimately it had to be amputated eight inches below the knee.

[In the subsequent lawsuit against Dr. Alexander and the hospital, Dr. Alexander paid $40,000 in settlement. The jury returned a verdict against the hospital for $150,000, which amount was reduced by the $40,000 paid by Dr. Alexander. The judgment against the hospital was affirmed by the intermediate appellate court, which summarized the evidence in a lengthy opinion, 50 Ill. App. 2d 253, 200 N.E.2d 149.]

. . . The plaintiff contends that it established that the defendant [hospital] was negligent in permitting Dr. Alexander to do orthopedic work of the kind required in this case, and not requiring him to review his operative procedures to bring them up to date; in failing, through its medical staff, to exercise adequate supervision over the case, especially since Dr. Alexander had been placed on emergency duty by the hospital, and in not requiring consultation, particularly after complications had developed. Plaintiff contends also that in a case which developed as this one did, it was the duty of the nurses to watch the protruding toes constantly for changes of color, temperature and movement, and to check circulation every 10 to 20 minutes, whereas the proof showed that these things were done only a few times a day. Plaintiff argues that it was the duty of the hospital staff to see that these procedures were followed, and that either the nurses were derelict in failing to report developments in the case to the hospital administrator, he was derelict in bringing them to the attention of the medical staff, or the staff was negligent in failing to take action. Defendant is a licensed and accredited hospital, and the plaintiff contends that the licensing regulations, accreditation standards, and its own bylaws define the hospital's duty, and that an infraction of them imposes liability for the resulting injury.

The defendant's position is stated in the following excerpts from its brief:

> It is a fundamental rule of law that only an individual properly educated and licensed, and not a corporation, may practice medicine. . . . Accordingly, a hospital is powerless under the law to forbid or command any act by a physician or surgeon in the practice of his profession. . . . A hospital is not an insurer of the patient's recovery, but only owes the patient the duty to exercise such reasonable care as his known condition requires and that degree of care, skill and diligence used by hospitals generally in that community. . . . Where the evidence shows that the hospital care was in accordance with standard practice obtaining in similar hospitals, and Plaintiff produces no evidence to the contrary, the jury cannot conclude that the opposite is true even if they disbelieve the hospital witnesses. . . . A hospital is not liable for the torts of its nurse committed while the nurse was but executing the orders of the patient's physician, unless such order is so obviously negligent as to lead any reasonable person to anticipate that substantial injury would result to the patient from the execution of such order. . . . The extent of the duty of a hospital with respect to actual medical care of a professional nature such as is furnished by a physician is to use reasonable care in selecting medical doctors. When such care in the selection of the staff is accomplished, and nothing indicates that a physician so selected is incompetent or that such incompetence should have been discovered, more cannot be expected from the hospital administration.

The basic dispute, as posed by the parties, centers upon the duty that rested upon the defendant hospital. . . .

Custom is relevant in determining the standard of care because it illustrates what is feasible, it suggests a body of knowledge of which the defendant should be aware, and it warns of the possibility of far-reaching consequences if a higher standard is required. But custom should never be conclusive. . . .

In the present case the regulations, standards, and bylaws which the plaintiff introduced into evidence, performed much the same function as did evidence of custom. This evidence aided the jury in deciding what was feasible and what the defendant knew or should have known. It did not conclusively determine the standard of care and the jury was not instructed that it did. . . .

The Standards for Hospital Accreditation, the state licensing regulations and the defendant's bylaws demonstrate that the medical profession and other responsible authorities regard it as both desirable and feasible that a hospital assume certain responsibilities for the care of the patient.

We now turn to an application of these considerations to this case. [A]n entire verdict is not to be set aside . . . if one or more of the grounds is sufficient. . . . Therefore we need not analyze all of the issues submitted to the jury. Two of them were that the defendant had negligently:

> 5. Failed to have a sufficient number of trained nurses for bedside care of all patients at all times capable of recognizing the progressive gangrenous condition of the plaintiff's right leg, and of bringing the same to the attention of the

> hospital administration and to the medical staff so that adequate consultation could have been secured and such conditions rectified; . . . 7. Failed to require consultation with or examination by members of the hospital surgical staff skilled in such treatment; or to review the treatment rendered to the plaintiff and to require consultants to be called in as needed.

We believe that the jury verdict is supportable on either of these grounds. On the basis of the evidence before it the jury could reasonably have concluded that the nurses did not test for circulation in the leg as frequently as necessary, that skilled nurses would have promptly recognized the conditions that signalled a dangerous impairment of circulation in the plaintiff's leg, and would have known that the condition would become irreversible in a matter of hours. At that point it became the nurses' duty to inform the attending physician, and if he failed to act, to advise the hospital authorities so that appropriate action might be taken. As to consultation, there is no dispute that the hospital failed to review Dr. Alexander's work or require a consultation; the only issue is whether its failure to do so was negligence. On the evidence before it the jury could reasonably have found that it was.

Notes

(1) *Darling* is widely viewed as the landmark opinion that inaugurated the doctrine of corporate liability for hospitals. For example, in a portion of the *Johnson* opinion not reproduced above, the Wisconsin Supreme Court characterizes *Darling* as "[o]ne of the leading cases introducing the concept that a hospital, as an institution, has a responsibility for the quality of medical care provided by members of its medical staff. . . ." Johnson v. Misericordia Community Hospital, 99 Wis. 2d 708, 301 N.W.2d 156, 165 (1981). For citations to other courts and commentators treating *Darling* as a landmark source of corporate negligence theory, see Hardy, When Doctrines Collide: Corporate Negligence and Respondeat Superior, 61 Tulane L. Rev. 85, 92 n.25 (1986).

(2) As the Illinois Supreme Court recognized in its *Darling* opinion, the crucial doctrinal breakthrough was its rejection of the hospital's argument that hospital duties should be defined solely by the local customary practices of similarly situated hospitals, and rather could be defined by state licensing regulations and national accreditation standards. Indeed, in an ironic moment at trial, a hospital administrator called by the defense to testify that the hospital was in compliance with customary practice, conceded on cross-examination that he agreed with the famous Dr. MacEachern that a hospital is more than just bricks and mortar and that the governing board of the hospital is responsible for the proper care of the patient, and has the power to choose the standard of medicine practiced in the hospital. *Darling,* 200 N.E.2d at 173. Thus did MacEachern's vision of the hospital as a community

corporation, discussed in Section 1(b) supra, move from often ignored rhetoric to judicially enforceable law.

NOTE: THE IDEAL OF CORPORATE RESPONSIBILITY AND THE REALITIES OF POWER

Although the *Darling* opinion is consistent with the rhetoric of JCAHO and the hospital industry that the hospital medical staff and the hospital itself are responsible in some sense for quality of care in the hospital, how consistent is this expectation with the realities of power and influence in hospitals? Is it realistic to expect nonphysician administrators and lay governing board members to overrule or even seriously question well-known senior physicians? Dr. K. J. Williams, a doctor and hospital consultant, wrote an article in 1976 detailing the hospital administrator's and governing board's lack of real power over the medical staff. See Williams, The Quandary of the Hospital Administrator in Dealing with the Medical Malpractice Problem, 55 Neb. L. Rev. 401 (1976). Although in theory the medical staff is supposed to be an "integral" part of the hospital that functions as an "organizational extension" of the governing board in assuring quality of care, in practice the medical staff strongly resists any direction or oversight from the administrator and governing board. (Indeed, even as a formal matter, JCAH standards and AHA Model Bylaws, incorporated into most hospital bylaws, restrict governing board authority by requiring any change in the medical staff (as distinct from the hospital) bylaws to be approved by both the governing board and the medical staff. See St. John's Hospital Medical Staff v. St. John Regional Medical Center, Inc., 90 S.D. 674, 245 N.W.2d 472 (1976), discussed in Section D infra.) Williams reports that hospital administrators, not to mention governing boards, are often not told of patterns of substandard physician care well known to the medical and nursing staff. Even when hospital management does find out about such problems, it must rely on the medical staff to do something about them.

The medical staff leaders in turn are often effectively disabled from acting by vague bylaws, by lack of clear standards and institutional traditions, and by rotating leadership and overlapping committees that diffuse responsibility. Williams closes his analysis of the hospital administrator's "quandary" by focusing on a case of a repeatedly incompetent physician who severely injured a teenage patient by negligently "treating" him for the wrong condition. If the hospital's mission is truly to safeguard patients' interests, Williams asks, should not the patient be told of the nature and cause of his injury? This suggestion was regarded by the hospital's governing board "as akin to asking them to commit suicide," thereby further dramatizing the tensions in the hospital's responsibility for quality of care. On proposals to require disclosure by doctors and other providers of physician-caused injuries, see Delgado &

Vogel, To Tell the Truth: Physicians' Duty to Disclose Medical Mistakes, 28 U.C.L.A.L. Rev. 52 (1980).

To point out these difficulties and realities is not to suggest that the doctrine of corporate liability be abandoned. The point is rather that seriously pursuing the goals of the corporate liability doctrine and the industry's own JCAHO standards will be a complex longterm process, in which malpractice law has played and will continue to play an important role, both in its own right and as a stimulus to other regulatory efforts discussed in Sections D, E, and F below.

d. The Hospital's Duty to Monitor the Competence of Independent Physicians with Staff Privileges

Elam v. College Park Hospital

132 Cal. App. 3d 332, 183 Cal. Rptr. 156 (1982)

Work, Associate Justice.

Elam complains Schur, a licensed podiatrist, performed negligent podiatric surgery at [College Park] Hospital [Hospital] to correct bilateral bunions and bilateral hammer toes. She was admitted to Hospital for surgery by Schur and Markarian, a medical doctor, pursuant to a hospital co-admission procedure requiring concurrence of a medical doctor before admitting a podiatric patient and the physician's assumption of responsibility for the overall medical care of that patient. . . . The surgery was performed by Schur and Cahn. [In the subsequent malpractice suit, Hospital was granted summary judgment.]

Schur was always an independent contractor with Hospital and never an employee or agent. He was never paid by Hospital, as he operated his own office and billed Elam directly. She had personally selected him for medical treatment. In June 1974, he applied for appointment to Hospital's medical staff. After verifying his Doctor of Podiatric Medicine degree, state podiatric license, and podiatric surgery privileges at Hillside and Heartland Hospitals in San Diego, Hospital's governing board granted Schur podiatric surgery privileges on April 25, 1975. Between April 25, 1975, and the date of surgery, Hospital's Medical Care Evaluation Committee . . . was responsible for evaluating and improving the quality of care rendered to patients treated at Hospital. The Committee met monthly, reviewing the medical charts of doctors and podiatrists treating patients at Hospital. On this routine basis, Schur's medical charts were reviewed along with the charts of other doctors and podiatrists. The Committee constituted a peer review mechanism designed to continually monitor, evaluate and improve the quality of medical care furnished patients at Hospital in compliance with the standards of the Joint Commission on Accreditation of Hospitals. The Committee never complained or reported to the Hospital's administration it considered or had reason to consider Schur incompetent or unqualified to practice podiatric surgery.

Elam's counsel has handled three other cases against Schur, including Perez v. Schur, . . . filed June 17, 1974; Earlywine v. Schur, . . . filed October 22, 1974; and Bailey v. Schur, . . . filed June 17, 1976. Each case involved Schur's first seeing the patient less than a week before the operation. In its answers to interrogatories, Hospital *admits it learned of the Bailey malpractice suit against Schur approximately four and one-half months before Elam's surgery*. . . .

THE DOCTRINE OF CORPORATE HOSPITAL LIABILITY

Elam . . . contends a hospital owes a duty to the patient of selecting, reviewing and supervising its staff physicians carefully. . . .

Our analysis of whether Hospital owed the disputed duty to Elam commences with the fundamental policy embodied in Civil Code section 1714, providing liability for injuries to another caused by one's failure to exercise ordinary care under the circumstances. . . . "Duty" is thus presumed, as "no . . . exception should be made unless clearly supported by public policy."

. . . We can perceive of no reason why this established duty of due care does not encompass the duty asserted by Elam; for, as a general principle, a hospital's failure to insure the competence of its medical staff through careful selection, review and supervision creates an unreasonable risk of harm to its patients.

Our conclusion accords with statutory authority recognizing hospital accountability for the quality of medical care provided and the competency of its medical staff. [The] Health and Safety Code define[s] hospital in pertinent part as "a health facility having a duly constituted governing body with overall administrative and professional responsibility. . . ." [It] . . . confers upon the board of directors of a public hospital the responsibility of its operation in accordance with "the best interests of the public health," including the power to "make and enforce all rules, regulations and by-laws necessary for the administration, government, protection and maintenance" of the hospital, and to insure that minimum standards of operation required by statute are followed. [A]lthough the medical staff is to be "self-governing," a hospital must provide procedures for selection and reappointment of the medical staff in accordance with JCAH standards, implying investigation of competency for initial appointment and periodic review of competency before reappointment. Regarding staff supervision, the hospital's duty to regulate physician conduct is implied by requiring renewal of staff privileges at least every two years (implying a periodic competency review) and the periodic review of the medical records of hospital patients. Although these reviews are conducted by medical staff "peer" committees, the governing body of the hospital is responsible for establishing the review procedures. . . .

[The] California Administrative Code, [is] even more explicit. [I]t mandates the hospital governing body "(r)equire that the medical staff establish controls that are designed to ensure the achievement and maintenance of high standards of professional ethical practices including provision that periodically all physicians may be required to demonstrate their ability to perform surgical and other procedures competently and to the satisfaction of an appropriate committee or committees of the staff.". . .

Further, our conclusion is consonant with the public's perception of the modern hospital as a multi-faceted healthcare facility responsible for the quality of medical care and treatment rendered. . . . Moreover, imposing the duty of care upon a hospital should have the "prophylactic" effect of supplying the hospital with a greater incentive to assure the competence of its medical staff and the quality of medical care rendered within its walls. . . . Indeed, the hospital is in the best position to evaluate the competence of physicians it, in its discretion, allows to perform surgery and to practice within its premises, as it constitutes the only institutional "vehicle available to coordinate the delivery of health care of reasonable quality to large numbers of people, especially in urban areas." . . .

[In the light of our holding concerning the hospital's duty to insure the competency of its staff, there were a number of triable issues of fact precluding summary judgment for the hospital.] For example, whether Hospital should have conducted an investigation through its peer review committee upon notice of the Bailey case? Whether the committee had conducted its periodic reviews of Schur in a non-negligent manner? Assuming a review was made after notice of the Bailey case, was it performed in a non-negligent manner? If it had been made in a careful and proper manner, would the committee have recommended revocation or suspension of Schur's staff privileges?

Corleto v. Shore Memorial Hospital

138 N.J. Super. 302, 350 A.2d 534 (Law Div. 1975)

Manuel H. Greenberg, J.C.C., Temporarily Assigned.

Plaintiffs' amended complaint sets forth that their decedent was subjected to malpractice on the part of defendant Dr. Josiah Calvin McCracken, Jr., while a patient in defendant hospital, leading to her death. In addition to setting forth a claim against the doctor, claim is also made against the hospital as well as the administrator, board of directors and the medical staff thereof [composed of 141 doctors] on the ground that they knew or should have known that Dr. McCracken was not competent to perform the surgical procedure on the decedent which he did, but they nevertheless permitted him to do so and allowed him to remain on the case when the situation was obviously beyond his control. . . . [Defendants have moved to dismiss the amended complaint for failure to state a claim upon which relief can be granted.]

[Dr. McCracken is not alleged to be an employee of the hospital.] [T]he moving defendants are charged with wrongdoing separate and distinct from that of Dr. McCracken, albeit that plaintiffs would obviously have to establish wrongdoing on the part of that doctor in order to prevail against the other defendants. . . .

It needs no citation of authority to state that, in general, where one is charged with liability for the negligence of another it is a good defense that the person doing the ultimate harm was an independent contractor rather than an employee of the one sought to be charged. However, certain exceptions have come to be accepted, one of which is that if a person engages an incompetent contractor he may be held liable for the ultimate damage caused by such contractor. In such case [l]iability does not attach vicariously but because of the wrongful act in placing an incompetent in a position to do harm. This, in essence, is what plaintiffs now contend. Thus, the principle of law involved herein is not at all novel, although its application to the present alleged factual situation in this State may well be. . . .

It is the position of *amicus curiae* [New Jersey Hospital Association] in its brief that the issue of Dr. McCracken's general competence to practice medicine and surgery is not appropriate for determination by a judge or jury and that this determination is within the exclusive province of the hospital and its related personnel. In other words, the contention is that matters such as the competence of a physician are purely internal affairs of the hospital and any such determinations are binding on all who might be affected thereby, or at least not susceptible of being challenged in a court of law. Reference is made to the [Hospital's] by-laws, rules and regulations of the medical staff . . . and to the [JCAH] Standards . . . all of which purportedly deal with the matter on an "intra-professional" basis. The cases cited in support of this position are cases in which the dispute generally was between the doctor and the hospital seeking to exclude him. It is one thing to say that a hospital should have the right to determine the fitness or qualifications of a physician to perform certain procedures within the hospital when the physician applies therefor; it is quite another matter to say that if the hospital makes such a determination in favor of the physician then all third parties are barred from basing a cause of action upon such determination, even though it may have been improper or, indeed, from ascertaining whether any inquiry was even made as to his qualifications. What is really asked for is an immunity from suit based upon considerations of public policy. Arguments are made to the effect that permitting this lawsuit to proceed will have a widespread impact on New Jersey hospitals and doctors; it will affect the composition of medical staffs and hospital boards; it will lead to an increase in insurance premiums, and it will perhaps have a detrimental impact on health care delivered to residents of the State.

An injured party has a common law right, where the injury is compensable, to maintain an action for damages; an immunity from suit is in derogation of this right and will be strictly construed. . . . The argument is made that the public good can best be served by not subjecting every hospital administrator, . . . trustee and medical staff member in the State to the constant threat of a lawsuit whenever it is alleged that negligence occurred in a hospital. . . . [The court doubts that this will occur, because of the expense of adding what might well be unnecessary parties, and the risk of adverse summary judgment unless there are facts to support the medical staff's and hospital's alleged negligence. As to the broader public policy effects, the court notes that the liability rule may make hospitals and medical staffs more careful, and hence improve the quality of care in the state. Given the debate over which rule would really advance public policy, the legislature should resolve it, and the court will not create an immunity.]

The medical staff of the Shore Memorial Hospital, a group of 141 doctors, named as a defendant, urges that it is not amenable to suit as an unincorporated association. . . . This argument is without merit. Plaintiffs could have named all 141 doctors individually as defendants, but to do so would serve no useful purpose. The law permitting suits against unincorporated associations is remedial legislation and is to be given as liberal an interpretation as possible, consistent with its language. . . .

For the reasons stated above the motion will be denied.

Notes

(1) *Corleto* is notable for three reasons. First, in contrast to *Elam,* there is no allegation that the hospital and its decisionmaking staff overlooked any formal actions or judgments against Dr. McCracken; rather, Dr. McCracken's disabilities were apparently so clear that the defendants should have been aware of them "by the exercise of reasonable care," and the court agrees that this is a sufficient allegation to withstand a motion to dismiss.

(2) Second, in *Darling* and many other corporate liability cases, defendants cite general tort law principles regarding independent contractors, while plaintiffs cite the JCAHO accreditation standards, state licensing standards, and hospital bylaws as the legal basis for hospital responsibility for quality of care provided by independent, nonemployee physicians. In *Corleto,* however, an interesting reversal takes place; the amicus New Jersey Hospital Association, on behalf of the defendants, cites accreditation standards and hospital bylaws to argue that staff privilege decisions are delegated to the medical staff and are to be made on a professional (rather than reasonable person) basis. Certainly the "self-governing" characteristic of the medical

staff, and the history and realities of hospital accreditation, discussed in Sections C(2) supra and D infra, lend some support to this position. The plaintiffs and the *Corleto* court respond on the basis of general tort law principles: no decisionmaker should have legal immunity to allow a known incompetent to use the decisionmaker's facilities to perform a task likely to harm others.

(3) Third, *Corleto* is famous for its holding that all 141 doctors on the hospital's medical staff may be collectively (and hence presumably individually) liable for negligent failure to restrict the activities of an incompetent staff member. Given the complexity and compartmentalization of the modern hospital, is this fair? What more facts would you want to know before deciding whether or not it was? Should liability be restricted only to the committees with formal responsibility for peer review, or is there some reasonable and important middle ground between the narrowest definition of legal responsibility (the formal committees) and the broadest (the entire medical staff)? Should a defense be allowed for doctors and other staff who attempt (by hypothesis unsuccessfully) to raise the issue of a doctor's substandard performance?

(4) In Collopy v. Newark Eye and Ear Infirmary, 27 N.J. 29, 141 A.2d 276 (1958), the New Jersey Supreme Court joined the widespread judicial trend discussed in Section (3) above and abrogated the charitable immunity doctrine for hospitals. The New Jersey legislature promptly responded with a statute limiting hospitals' liability for their own or their agents' negligence to $10,000. See N.J.S.A. 2A:53A-8 (1959). Since this limitation applies only to the hospital as an institution, it provides an obvious incentive for suits against individual directors, administrators, and members of medical staffs.

(5) Another well known, albeit unreported, case of this type is the trial court opinion in Gonzales v. Nork, Superior Ct., Sacramento Co., No. 228566 (Nov. 19, 1973), reprinted in part in S. Law & S. Polan, supra, at 215, *rev'd on other grounds,* 131 Cal. Rptr. 717 (Cal. App. 3d Dist. 1976), *court of appeal ruling rev'd,* 20 Cal. 3d 500, 143 Cal. Rptr. 240, 573 P.2d 458 (1978). Dr. Nork performed over 50 laminectomies and other complex spinal surgery for which he was unqualified for more than six years; these operations were found by the trial judge to be "either unnecessary, or bungled, or both." Having falsely told patients that they needed such surgery, and then having severely injured them, Dr. Nork proceeded to falsify medical records to protect himself. Dr. Nork's defense was that he was drug dependent, and thus unable to form the intent to defraud. The hospital argued that it had followed all applicable quality assurance procedures required by the JCAH. These procedures were not, however, designed to detect fraud of the sort perpetrated by Dr. Nork. The trial judge, B. Abbott Goldberg, ruled that even if the JCAH standards represented the industry norm, and even if the hospital had complied with them, that did not insulate the norms from judicial review, nor the hospital from liability.

Pedroza v. Bryant

101 Wn.2d 226, 677 P.2d 166 (1984)

Pearson, Justice.

The issue before us is whether a hospital may be held liable under a theory of corporate negligence for its action in granting privileges to a nonemployee doctor who allegedly commits malpractice while in private practice off the hospital premises.

In December of 1978, Maria Pedroza was in her 35th week of pregnancy and under the care of Dr. Ben Bryant. During the week of December 3 through 9, Maria became ill and exhibited the classical symptoms of pre-eclampsia (a toxemia of pregnancy), namely, hypertension, headaches, and edema of the lower extremities. Mrs. Pedroza visited Dr. Bryant's office on December 6 and 7, and telephoned him on December 8. Dr. Bryant prescribed no medicine other than bed rest and aspirin. He did not refer Mrs. Pedroza to another health care provider.

On December 9, 1978, Maria Pedroza was admitted, comatose, to defendant Skagit Valley Hospital. She was admitted to surgery, with a diagnosis of irreversible cerebral death due to intracerebral hemorrhage resulting from eclampsia. Dr. Bryant was neither the admitting nor the treating physician for this hospitalization. Indeed, the hospital had, on April 13, 1977, limited Dr. Bryant's obstetrical and newborn privileges to Class II for the years 1977 and 1978. Dr. Bryant was thus required to consult with a Class I physician on all "seriously ill patients," including pregnancies with "major medical complications" and "[l]ate or severe toxemia of pregnancy." Thus, Dr. Bryant would not have been allowed to treat Maria Pedroza for eclampsia in the hospital.

[After Maria Pedroza's death, her husband] brought a malpractice action against Dr. Bryant, and further alleged that defendant Skagit Valley Hospital was negligent in that it violated a duty of care owed Maria Pedroza to grant hospital admitting and treating privileges only to those physicians who are competent. [Defendant hospital's motion for summary judgment was granted, in part on the grounds that the theory of corporate negligence does not extend to acts done outside the hospital.]

The doctrine of corporate negligence reflects the public's perception of the modern hospital as a multifaceted health care facility responsible for the quality of medical care and treatment rendered. . . . The patient treated in such a facility receives care from a number of individuals of varying capacities and is not merely treated by a physician acting in isolation. . . .

Having adopted the doctrine of corporate negligence, we turn now to the task of defining the standard of care to which hospitals will be held. . . . Perhaps the most important of the national standards voluntarily adopted by hospitals are those promulgated by the JCAH. The JCAH standards clearly establish the institution's governing board as ultimately responsible for the overall quality of patient care provided in the hospital. The medical staff, in turn, is responsible to the governing board for the professional competence of all physicians . . . who are members of the hospital's medical staff. The standards place particular emphasis on the appointment/reappointment process, delineation of clinical privileges, and periodic appraisals of each physician staff member. In addition, the hospital is required to institute reliable and valid measures that continuously evaluate the quality of care rendered all patients. . . .

Our decision to adopt the doctrine of corporate negligence . . . does not necessarily entitle plaintiff in the case at bar to a reversal of the summary judgment against him. The alleged acts of malpractice committed by Dr. Bryant occurred entirely outside the hospital. Mrs. Pedroza was not a patient of the hospital at the time. For plaintiff to prevail, we must decide that the duty of care owed by hospitals under the corporate negligence doctrine extends not only to hospital patients, but also to patients treated by hospital staff members in those staff members' private office practices, where the hospital is not involved. . . .

Defendant argues that extending a hospital's duty of care to patients outside the hospital would require a hospital to supervise and, if necessary, limit the private medical practices of its staff members outside the hospital. Such intervention could adversely affect the delicate physician-patient relationship. Substantial administrative problems would probably result as well.

This argument appears to be based upon a misconception of the doctrine of corporate negligence. The doctrine does not impose vicarious liability on a hospital for the acts of a medical staff member. The pertinent inquiry is whether the hospital exercised reasonable care in the granting, renewal, and delineation of staff privileges. . . . Acts of malpractice committed by a staff physician outside the hospital are relevant only if the hospital has actual or constructive notice of them, and where failure to take some action as a result of such notice is negligence.

Plaintiff argues that defendant hospital's independent duty of care should extend to Maria Pedroza because she was a foreseeable plaintiff. . . . Plaintiff alleges that Maria Pedroza used Dr. Bryant's services only because Dr. Bryant possessed admitting and obstetrical privileges at defendant hospital (each of Maria Pedroza's seven children had been born at Skagit Valley Hospital), and that it was, therefore, foreseeable that the hospital's alleged negligence in the granting or renewal of Dr. Bryant's staff privileges might result in harm to his obstetrical patients. Plaintiff argues that it should make no difference whether the harm occurred in or out of the hospital, as long as the harm was foreseeable. The doctrine of corporate negligence focuses on the negligence of the hospital in failing to rescind Dr. Bryant's privileges.

The fact remains, however, that every jurisdiction that has adopted corporate negligence has based the hospital's liability on the duty owed by the hospital to its patients. . . . The hospital holds itself out to the community as a competent provider of medical care. The hospital does not hold itself out as an inspector or insurer of the private office practices of its staff members. The delineation of staff privileges by the hospital can only affect the procedures used by staff members while they are inside hospital walls. The public cannot reasonably expect anything more. . . . Extending the hospital's duty of care to those who are not its patients would be undesirable in that it would likely grant those people a windfall, as any increased hospital costs resulting from such an extension of liability would be spread among hospital patients, rather than those who would benefit from the extended liability.

Accordingly, we hold that a hospital's duty of care under the doctrine of corporate negligence extends only to those who are patients within the hospital. Defendant Skagit Valley Hospital owed no duty to Maria Pedroza under the doctrine because she was not a hospital patient when the harm occurred. The fact that she had been a patient at defendant hospital in years past does not make her a patient for purposes of this case. Each of those prior hospital-patient relationships ended upon her discharge from the hospital; they did not continue indefinitely. Since there are no allegations of negligence after Mrs. Pedroza was admitted to the hospital, we affirm the trial court's order of summary judgment.

WILLIAM H. WILLIAMS, C.J., ROSELLINI, UTTER, BRACHTENBACH, DOLLIVER, AND DIMMICK, JJ., and CUNNINGHAM, J. Pro Tem., concur.

DISCUSSION QUESTIONS

Do you find the *Pedroza* reasoning persuasive? In evaluating the opinion, what more might you want to know about the hospital's quality assurance process and about Mrs. Pedroza? For example, where do you think Mrs. Pedroza intended to have the baby? Does it matter why Mrs. Pedroza chose Dr. Bryant? (Her husband alleged that she chose him only because he had privileges at the defendant hospital, where each of her seven prior children had been born). Why, if the hospital is earning income from the hospital side of Dr. Bryant's practice, does it not have some responsibility for what he does before hospitalization, particularly with respect to childbirth, where hospitalization is the normal and expected outcome of prenatal office care? Although these facts were not alleged in the case, what if Mrs. Pedroza had been referred to Dr. Bryant by the hospital's doctor referral service or had responded to advertisements that had praised the quality of care offered by doctors on the hospital's staff? And what if a patient is treated adequately in the hospital but then receives substandard post-hospital care? Should it matter if the hospital is aware of a series of pre- or post-hospital problems?

D. Structuring the Hospital Quality Assurance Process: Substance, Procedure, and Confidentiality

Note: An Overview of Hospital-Based Quality Assurance and Peer Review

The modern hospital's efforts to assure quality of care to patients reflect the hospital's complex structure, notably the overlapping responsibilities of the administration and medical staff. Hospital administrations are increasingly turning to "risk management programs," discussed in more detail below, whose explicit function is to identify and minimize risks that can lead to legal liability and financial loss. Although the term "risk management" is sometimes used to refer to all sources of potential liability in a hospital, its main focus historically has been on risks generated by nonphysician personnel and facilities under the direct control of the hospital administration. Problems caused by physicians are supposed to be dealt with by a process of "quality assurance" or hospital-based "peer review" — that is, evaluation of doctors' work by other doctors, their peers. Quality assurance is both narrower and broader in scope than risk management; narrower in that quality assurance focuses on issues of patient care while risk management covers all safety problems, including building standards and so forth, but broader in that quality assurance is concerned with a wide range of quality-related activities, while risk management has traditionally focused on discrete "incidents" that might give rise to legal liability. Most practically, risk management is clearly organized and controlled by the hospital administration, while quality assurance or peer review is under the primary control of the medical staff, at least with regard to review of physicians.

A doctor's first post-training encounter with hospital-based peer review comes when she or he initially applies for staff privileges at a hospital. (Of course, a doctor is frequently reviewed by superiors and others during the process of medical education and training.) The doctor applicant is then supposed to be subjected to the kind of inquiry described in the *Johnson* case: the hospital's "credentials committee" should investigate the applicant's academic credentials, residency experience, and practice experience at other institutions. The credentials committee then makes a recommendation to the medical staff's executive committee, which in turn may have its decision ratified by the entire medical staff before presenting it to the governing board for final approval.

Hospitals have traditionally excluded initial applicants for staff privileges on two types of grounds: category or group characteristics and individual performance. The first does not involve any assessment of the individual practitioner's skills, but rather is based on a *category* into which the individual falls. Categorical exclusions can in turn be divided into two subgroups: negative categories (such as a ban on chiropractors), which express a judgment that all members of the category are not qualified to provide care, and functional categories (such as "closing" the medical staff or some clinical specialty), which express a judgment that the hospital does not need or cannot accommodate particular kinds of practitioners at a particular time.

The second type of exclusion does rest on a negative judgment of an individual's qualifications or performance. This basis is used for some denials of initial privileges, and overwhelmingly for revocation of already granted privileges. Finally, there are some cases that seem to fall in between the two broad types, in that they reflect both a categorical judgment about the "kind" of practice that an applicant is interested in and a judgment about the individual's personality and "ability to contribute." See Robinson v. Magovern, 521 F. Supp. 842 (W.D. Pa. 1981), *aff'd,* 688 F.2d 824 (3d Cir. 1982), *cert. denied* 458 U.S. 971 (1982), discussed later in this section.

Once a doctor has been granted staff privileges, she or he is supposed to be subject to continuing peer review through two kinds of mechanisms. First, "control committees" sponsored by the medical staff, "risk-management programs" sponsored by the hospital administration, and similar efforts under joint sponsorship are supposed to monitor continuously surgery, use of drugs, infections, and other risky phenomena or procedures. These committees and programs are supposed to identify problematic patterns, such as in drug prescriptions, and either intervene with the particular practitioner involved or refer the case to the medical staff executive committee. In urgent cases, the chief of the medical staff, chiefs of medical departments, or administrators may be authorized to suspend privileges summarily, subject to a prompt hearing before the medical staff executive committee and/or governing board.

The second mechanism involves the reappointment process. Every two years, each member of the medical staff is supposed to be re-evaluated as to health status and competence, and staff privileges must be renewed or restricted. Problems that have not been adequately identified or dealt with previously are supposed to be resolved then.

Two different lines of cases offer remarkably contrasting images of hospital-based peer review. In the corporate negligence cases, the process of granting and periodically reviewing staff privileges every two years, and other forms of in-hospital peer review, are held up by the courts as what hospitals should have been doing to protect patients from the substandard care that they actually received. In another line of cases, however, the plaintiffs are angry doctors, and the stories they tell are very different: of adverse peer review actions motivated by economic greed and personal vendettas, implemented by dubious, sometimes grossly unfair procedures. Through judicial doctrines and statutes described below, the law encourages doctors and hospitals to attain the ideal embodied in the first version, while providing some protection for doctors who might be victims of the motives portrayed in the second.

The realities of hospital-based peer review vary enormously among hospitals, depending on the institution's mission, market position, internal distribution of formal authority and actual power, and the values and interests of key individuals. This section first presents a case in which a hospital medical staff won a suit against a hospital governing board over control of medical staff organization, and summarizes a joint AHA/AMA Report that attempts to reconcile the tensions among boards, administrators, and doctors. It then explores several major legal questions that have arisen in connection with hospital-based peer review: (1) what are the state-law standards of judicial review, peer review immunity, and procedural due process? (2) what impact does the federal Health Care Quality Improvement Act, 42 U.S.C. §§11101 et seq., effective in October, 1989, have on these state-law issues and on hospital-based peer review? (3) what substantive grounds for adverse hospital action have been upheld? (4) to what extent do hospital-based peer review proceedings have a privilege of confidentiality against discovery or use in other proceedings? and (5) what is the nature and legal status of hospital risk-management programs?

1. AUTHORITY AND POWER IN THE MODERN HOSPITAL: CONFLICT AND COOPERATION BETWEEN MEDICAL STAFF AND GOVERNING BOARD

As discussed in Section (C)(5) above, the actual distribution of power in the modern hospital is a complex and delicate affair. These complexities are reflected in the hospital's formal structure. For example, there are typically two sets of bylaws: one for the hospital and one for the medical staff. According to JCAHO hospital accreditation standards, the medical staff bylaws, rules, and regulations are "adopted by the medical staff and approved by the governing body prior to becoming effective. Neither body may unilaterally amend the medical staff bylaws. . . ." 1988 Accreditation Manual for Hospitals, MS. 2.1, at 114. The medical staff is supposed to operate within a "framework of self-governance" while remaining "accountable" to the governing board. Id., MS.2, at 114. The governing board appears to have ultimate responsibility for assuring quality of care, but the medical staff also has "overall responsibility for the quality of professional services." See id., QA.1, MS.1, at 235, 111. See generally, Harris, The Internal Organization of Hospitals: Some Economic Implications, 8 Bell J. Econ. 467 (1977).

St. John's Hospital Medical Staff v. St. John Regional Medical Center, Inc.

90 S.D. 674, 245 N.W.2d 472 (1976)

MILLER, Circuit Judge.

St. John's Hospital Medical Staff (hereinafter referred to as medical staff) is an unincorporated association whose members are physicians duly licensed to practice medicine in South Dakota, holding medical staff privileges at and utilizing the facilities of the St. John Regional Medical Center, Inc., of Huron, South Dakota. St. John Regional Medical Center (hereinafter referred to as medical center) is a South Dakota corporation, incorporated under the laws regulating nonprofit corporations and is authorized to operate in the State of South Dakota. . . .

[The medical center was formed in 1947 through the merger of two previously separate hospitals. The medical staff bylaws adopted at that time contained an "Amendment Article" requiring that any change in the medical staff bylaws be approved by a two-thirds majority of the medical staff before being submitted for approval to the governing body. The medical staff bylaws also contained an "Equally Binding Article" providing that "[t]hese bylaws shall be adopted at any regular meeting of the staff and shall become effective when approved by the governing body of the hospital. They shall when adopted and approved, be equally binding on the governing body and the staff."]

These medical staff bylaws were in effect from 1947 until 1972. During that time, various amendments were made to them in accordance with the amendment procedure prescribed. In 1972, the medical center wished to make certain changes in the bylaws.[2] The attempted changes were unacceptable to the medical staff and an impasse developed. Out of this impasse springs the present lawsuit.

On November 24, 1972, the board of directors of the medical center unilaterally adopted new medical staff bylaws which were not approved by the medical staff. The medical center now insists that the medical staff is bound by the bylaws so adopted. The medical staff contends and the trial court held that the 1972 revised medical staff bylaws are null and void by reason of the fact that they were not enacted according to the provisions set out in the original 1947 medical staff bylaws.

The main issue raised in this appeal is whether the board of directors of the medical center has the power to amend the 1947 medical staff bylaws

2. E.g., one change would allow the Chief Executive Officer of the medical center to temporarily suspend the clinical privileges of a staff physician upon a determination that the action must be taken immediately in the best interests of the patient care in the medical center. Another change would require medical center approval of all officers of the medical staff. These examples are for illustrative purposes only.

without the participation and approval of the medical staff. . . . The medical center argues that the trial court erred in holding that a legal contract existed between the medical staff and the medical center by reason of the original 1947 medical staff bylaws. It raises two policy arguments in support of this contention: the power to amend the articles must be lodged in the directors in order (a) to avoid impending loss of accreditation, and (b) to avoid the possibility of independent hospital liability in some future case of malpractice. After a review of the record, we find these arguments to be without merit. The trial court specifically held that there was no evidence that the hospital would lose accreditation if it were not allowed to revise the medical staff bylaws. Further, the medical center's assertions regarding independent liability are premature. . . . We therefore decline to decide that issue.

The medical center additionally argues that the medical staff lacks the attributes of a legal entity necessary to commence this action. As stated above, the medical staff represents an unincorporated association of the individual physicians holding medical staff privileges at the medical center. . . .

[The court also holds that the 1947 medical staff bylaws constitute a contract between the medical staff and the medical center.]

It is therefore the holding of this court that the 1947 medical staff bylaws, after approval by the medical center, were binding upon the medical center and must be amended in accordance with . . . those bylaws. Therefore, the medical staff bylaws unilaterally adopted by the medical center are null and void.

NOTE: THE AMA AND AHA ATTEMPT A RESOLUTION

Although the *St. John's* case is one of the few examples of a fully litigated dispute between a hospital governing board and its medical staff, tensions between the two bodies have become so common in recent years as to lead the American Medical Association (AMA) and the American Hospital Association (AHA) to form a joint task force to promote "constructive relationships" and avoid "unnecessary conflicts and wasteful litigation." Report of the AMA/AHA Joint Task Force on Hospital-Medical Staff Relationships 3 (1985) (hereinafter AMA/AHA Report). The AMA/AHA Report stated that although much of the literature on board-staff relations focuses on adversarial legal rights, the major causes of contemporary board-staff conflict are not law-related, but rather stem from economic pressures generated by payer cost containment and competitive market conditions. In the face of ever scarcer resources, boards are having to make "hard choices," which often incur strong physician resentment. The Report strongly urged boards and staff to turn to "problem-solving" methods, including if necessary mediation by respected third parties, rather than litigation.

To encourage constructive relations, the AMA/AHA Report attempted to clarify the respective responsibilities of individual physicians, the organized medical staff, and the governing board regarding quality of care and other matters. "The hospital governing board is responsible for the conduct of the institution as an institution, including oversight of the overall quality of care provided in the hospital and the allocation of resources." Id. at 9. "Oversight of the overall quality of care" could best be understood as the highest level of a three-step process:

> (1) the fulfillment of the individual physician's individual professional responsibility to patients; (2) the assessment of the individual physician's professional performance by his or her peers acting through the medical staff; and (3) the evaluation and monitoring by the hospital governing board/administration of the efficacy and impartiality in which the organized medical staff discharges its responsibility — which comprises the institution's accountability for the medical care provided in the institution. . . . [Id. at 13-14.]

In other words, the organized medical staff has the primary responsibility for assuring quality of care among physicians, and the governing board's role is to see that the medical staff is performing its role properly.

In general, the AMA/AHA Report suggested four ways that authority could be allocated between the board and staff, with different allocations applying to different issues, as structured by the hospital and medical staff bylaws. At one end of the spectrum is what the Report termed "singular responsibility," that is, the board or staff has sole responsibility for the issue and no need to consult the other entity, even informally. Although in theory the board or staff may have this authority over certain issues — such as the board's development of the hospital bylaws — as a practical matter it is hard to imagine any major decision being taken without at least informal consultation with the other entity. A second allocation is "consultative responsibility," where one entity has ultimate responsibility for a decision, but informally seeks or receives recommendations from the other. Examples include the board's decisions regarding corporate reorganization, hospital diversification, marketing, and general allocation of financial resources. A third category is "shared responsibility," in which one entity has ultimate responsibility for a decision, but must receive input from the other entity through a formal process of consultation before making its own decision. Examples include hospital criteria for medical staff privileges, quality assurance standards and enforcement, and utilization review. The fourth category is "joint responsibility," under which neither the governing board nor the medical staff may act without concurrence from the other. Examples include development of the medical staff bylaws, including medical criteria for staff privileges, and selection of medical staff officers. Of course, exactly which allocation of authority applies to which area of decisionmaking is defined in the bylaws of each hospital and medical staff; the examples given in the Report are illustrative, not mandatory.

Problem: Counsel to the Governing Board

Assume that Charles Smith, the chair of the governing board of the hypothetical Central Hospital, also located in South Dakota, has recently hired you as the board's counsel. Smith calls you in for a private meeting and explains that he is very worried about quality of care at Central. "One of our surgeons — Ted Jones — is almost as bad as Dr. Nork. Jones is not on drugs, as far as I know, but I've been hearing reports for months of operations he's botched and how other doctors have to cover for him and try to fix his mistakes. Fortunately — or maybe unfortunately — neither he nor the hospital have been sued yet, because none of these patients seem to connect their problems with Dr. Jones. The biggest problem is that Ed White, the chief of the medical staff, is an old friend of Jones's and refuses to do anything about him. I've talked to White time and again about how we have to limit Jones's privileges or take some action, but White just shrugs it off. Now I've just heard about the South Dakota Supreme Court decision in the *St. John's* case. Our bylaws are the standard ones, just like theirs. The board has "ultimate authority" for quality of care, and we have to approve all appointments to the medical staff, but we are bound to follow the recommendations of the medical staff promptly except for "good cause." Moreover, like St. John's, our governing board can't amend the medical staff bylaws without approval from the medical staff itself. And under the current medical staff bylaws they get to choose their own chief of staff — and they've chosen Ed White! I'd really like to get a new chief of staff, get rid of Jones entirely, and try to get some new doctors on board to raise our quality of care and revitalize our sense of mission. Is there anything the board can do?"

Before advising Charles Smith, what more would you like to know about Central Hospital? its bylaws? state tort law doctrine about the corporate responsibility of hospitals? After making reasonable hypotheses about these and other relevant matters, what advice would you give Mr. Smith?

Note: Hospital Governing Boards and Consumer Participation

The governing boards of voluntary, nonprofit hospitals are supposed to reflect the constituencies vitally concerned with and affected by the hospital's mission, as well as constituencies in a position to assist with and participate in fundraising. Typically, this has been understood to mean various types of prominent citizens — business leaders, attorneys, government officials, religious leaders, and members of wealthy families, and at times persons recruited for specific expertise. But because hospital governing boards make decisions that affect not only the quality of care conceived in professional terms, but also access to care and the distribution of care among social groups, there have been periodic calls to broaden governing board membership to include traditionally excluded sectors of the population. A unique West Virginia statute, effective July 1, 1984, provides as follows:

> (a) The legislature declares that a crisis in health care costs exists, and that one important approach to deal with this crisis is to have widespread citizen participation in hospital decision-making, and that many hospitals in West Virginia exclude from their boards important categories of consumers, including small businesses, organized labor, elderly persons and lower-income consumers. The legislature further declares that non-profit hospitals receive such major revenue from public sources and are so crucial in health planning and development that it is necessary to require consumer representatives on their boards of directors. Therefore, the legislature determines that non-profit hospitals and hospitals owned by local governments should have boards of directors representative of the communities they serve. . . .
>
> (c) At least 40 percent of the boards of directors of applicable hospitals shall . . . be composed of an equal proportion of consumer representatives from each of the following four categories: small businesses, organized labor, elderly persons and persons whose income is less than the national median income. Special consideration shall be made to select women, racial minorities and handicapped persons.
>
> (d) The provisions of this section may be enforced by the director of health, or by any citizen of the county wherein any offending hospital is located, by the filing of an action at law in the circuit court of such county. [W. Va. Code 16-5B-6a.]

The American and West Virginia Hospital Associations, five individual West Virginia hospitals, and the Catholic Health Association (including several orders of nuns with hospitals in West Virginia), challenged the statute on federal and state constitutional grounds, including equal protection (contesting the exemption of for-profit and state-owned hospitals), freedom of association (particularly on behalf of the religious orders), and due process (arguing that the law had no rational connection to cost containment, would arbitrarily impair the hospitals' legal responsibility to deliver quality as well as cost-efficient care, and constituted a taking of private property). The plaintiffs also argued that the issue was preempted by federal labor law. The federal district court rejected all of these challenges, relying on a deferential standard of review, and the fact that the statute did not displace any hospital qualification standards for board membership, but rather required hospitals in applying their standards to "be sensitive to the four categories set forth in the Act. Certainly, there are individuals within those categories who would make excellent board members." American Hospital Association v. Hansbarger, 600 F. Supp. 465, 477 (N.D. W.Va. 1984), *aff'd* 783 F. 2d 1184 (4th Cir. 1986), *cert. denied sub nom.* American Hospital Association v. Heydinger, 107 S. Ct. 85 (1986).

2. JUDICIAL REVIEW OF HOSPITAL STAFF PRIVILEGE DECISIONS

Doctors and other health care providers aggrieved by hospitals' peer review decisions typically turn to two broad theories of legal relief. The first is that the hospital failed to follow applicable substantive or procedural standards, as embodied in the hospital's bylaws. Second, the aggrieved provider may allege a particular bad motive prohibited by some other body of law, such as antitrust law, civil rights law, and tort law concerning defamation. Although differing in legal theory, both types of cases often end up turning on the same issue: whether the hospital's action was demonstrably reasonable in relation to legitimate institutional objectives. However, in some contexts the two types of legal action may differ with respect to the scope of discovery, the burdens of proof and standards of review, and the availability of a factual trial, as opposed to review of the record of hospital hearings.

Until recently, very few states have had statutes explicitly authorizing judicial review of staff privilege decisions by private (and typically nonprofit) hospitals. (Publicly owned hospitals, in contrast, have always been considered governmental entities and hence subject at least to the procedural due process requirements of the federal and state constitutions.) The rule followed by most states was that in the absence of a statute to the contrary, hospital refusals to make initial appointments were not subject to judicial review, and that revocations of existing privileges would be reviewed, if at all, only on the issue of whether the hospital had followed its own bylaws. See, for instance, Jain v. Northwest Community Hospital, 67 Ill. App. 3d 911, 385 N.E.2d 108, 112 (1978) (collecting cases). Courts in four states have recently reaffirmed this traditional position. See Lakeside Community Hospital, Inc. v. Levenson, 710 P.2d 727 (Nev. 1985); Grossling v. Ford Memorial Hospital, 614 F. Supp. 1051 (E.D. Tex 1985) (applying Texas law); Hoffman v. Garden City Hospital — Osteopathic, 115 Mich. App. 773, 321 N.W.2d 810 (1982); Bello v. South Shore Hospital, 384 Mass. 770, 429 N.E.2d 1011 (1981) (distinguishing between denial of initial appointment and revocation of privileges). See also Annot., 37 A.L.R.3d 645 (1971 & Supp. 1987).

On the other hand, courts in at least seven states, including California, New York, Illinois, Ohio, and Hawaii, have followed the lead taken by the New Jersey Supreme Court in 1963 in allowing judicial review of staff privilege decisions even without explicit statutory authorization. The New Jersey court's reasoning was that "while the managing officials [of private nonprofit hospitals] may have discretionary powers in the selection of the medical staff, those powers are deeply imbedded in public aspects, and are rightly viewed, for policy reasons . . . as fiduciary powers to be exercised reasonably and for the public good." Greisman v. Newcomb Hospital, 40 N.J. 389, 192 A.2d 817, 824 (1963) (overturning hospital's categorical refusal to consider doctors of osteopathy for staff privileges). The following New Jersey Supreme

Court opinion reveals how judicial review generates substantive and procedural norms for hospital staff privilege decisions.

Nanavati v. Burdette Tomlin Memorial Hospital

107 N.J. 240, 526 A.2d 697 (1987)

POLLOCK, J.

This appeal arises out of the revocation of the staff privileges of Suketu H. Nanavati (Dr. Nanavati) as a cardiologist at Burdette Tomlin Memorial Hospital (the hospital). The Chancery Division found that the hospital had prejudged the matter, thereby depriving Dr. Nanavati of a fair hearing. After making independent findings of fact, the court permanently enjoined the revocation of Dr. Nanavati's privileges. [T]he Appellate Division affirmed the issuance of the injunction "without prejudice to the relodging of the charges against plaintiff." The court also determined that the trial court should not have made independent findings of fact. . . .

We . . . now reman[d] the matter to the hospital with the understanding that within a reasonable time it may reinstitute the proceedings against Dr. Nanavati. . . .

The background of this case is a dispute between Dr. Nanavati and Dr. Robert Sorensen, who at the time was the chief of cardiology, chairman of the Department of Medicine, and a member of the Board of Governors at the hospital. The dispute originated over the allocation of the reading of electrocardiograms (ECGs or EKGs), which, at $5 per reading, produced an annual income of approximately $75,000. Burdette Tomlin is the only hospital in Cape May County, and when he was granted staff privileges, Dr. Nanavati was the only board-certified cardiologist in the county. Before the arrival of Dr. Nanavati in 1979, Dr. Sorensen, an internist, enjoyed a virtual monopoly on reading ECGs. Dr. Nanavati was allowed to read ECGs one day each week, but when he requested an additional day, Dr. Sorensen rejected his request. The rejection stimulated Dr. Nanavati into criticizing Dr. Sorensen, who retaliated.

As the discord between the two doctors escalated, Dr. Nanavati allegedly committed a series of violations of the hospital's bylaws. [In August 1982, the medical staff executive committee voted unanimously to revoke Dr. Nanavati's medical staff privileges.] . . .

The charges against Dr. Nanavati were captioned as "Acts of Disruptive Behavior" and "Failure to Cooperate with Hospital Personnel Regarding the Use of Facilities Especially During the Summer Months and the Emergent Admissions Procedures."

Underlying these charges is the contention that Dr. Nanavati caused disruption in violation of a bylaw provision requiring a staff doctor to

> be of a temperament and disposition that will enable him to work in harmony with his colleagues on the Medical Staff; with the professional, technical, and other personnel in the hospital, and with the administration, accepting criticism without resentment and offering it in a spirit and manner that is constructive and devoid of offense and malice. . . .

The further allegation is that Dr. Nanavati violated a bylaw provision that a staff member "must enjoy the reputation of being an ethical and conscientious practitioner and must strictly abide by the Code of Ethics. . . ." At no time has the hospital questioned Dr. Nanavati's technical competence. . . .

After finding that the hospital proceedings were unfair, the Chancery Division independently reviewed the record by a preponderance-of-the-evidence standard. The court determined that Dr. Nanavati's staff privileges should not be revoked on the ground of disharmony, absent a showing of actual interference with patient care, and concluded that the record did not support any such showing. Consequently, the court issued a permanent injunction against revocation of his privileges.

Although the Appellate Division affirmed the trial court's finding that the hospital proceedings were invalid, it disagreed with other portions of the trial court's opinion and held that the trial court, in reviewing the revocation of hospital staff privileges, should not have made independent findings of fact, but should have determined whether the hospital's decision was supported by sufficient credible evidence. In addition, the Appellate Division ruled that mere disharmony, although an insufficient ground by itself, is a relevant consideration in revocation proceedings. . . .

Both doctors and their patients can suffer if otherwise qualified doctors are wrongly denied staff privileges. Hence, we have not hesitated to invalidate unreasonable restrictions on staff privileges. . . . Furthermore, hospitals must follow fair procedures when considering staff privileges, and may not arbitrarily foreclose otherwise qualified doctors from their staffs. . . .

[C]ourts should sustain a hospital's standard for granting staff privileges if that standard is rationally related to the delivery of health care. A decision is so related if it advances the interests of the public, particularly patients; the hospital; or those who are essential to the hospital's operations, such as doctors and nurses.

Although not quite so deferential when reviewing decisions denying staff privileges, courts still apply a relaxed standard of review to those decisions. . . . The test for judicial review of such a decision is whether it is supported by "sufficient reliable evidence, even though of a hearsay nature, to justify the result." . . .

[H]ospitals . . . regularly function in a crisis atmosphere. Emergencies arise not only in emergency rooms, but throughout the hospital: in intensive care units, operating rooms, and patient rooms. In so intense a setting, flaring tempers, harsh words, and bruised feelings are to be expected. Nonetheless, if a hospital is to care for its patients, the staff, particularly doctors and nurses, must work together. . . . As important as cooperation is to other corporations, it is even more critical in a modern hospital, where no single doctor cares for all the needs of any one patient. Hospital doctors depend on their colleagues, nurses, technicians, and other employees for total patient care. Just how to bring about the necessary cooperation among them is a matter best left to hospital authorities: the medical staff, hospital committees, and the governing body. . . .

In evaluating a physician for staff membership, a hospital may consider not only his or her technical skills, but also his or her ability to work with others. . . . Consequently, a hospital may adopt a bylaw providing that the inability of a doctor to work with nurses and other doctors is a ground for denying or terminating staff privileges. . . .

[A]llegations of "disharmony" [should never] be used as a ruse to deny or terminate staff privileges because of a doctor's race, religion, color, or gender. Likewise, a doctor should not be cut off from staff membership merely because he or she has criticized hospital practices and other doctors. . . . Constructive criticism of an incompetent physician, like criticism of an unsafe or inefficient hospital practice, protects both the public and the hospital. So strong is the public interest in open communication involving "matters directly affecting the quality of health care" that otherwise defamatory statements by one staff physician about another may be privileged. . . .

When a doctor's conduct actually interferes with patient care, the disruption justifies ending his or her privileges. . . . A hospital need not wait for a disruptive doctor to harm a patient before terminating his or her privileges. Nonetheless, more should be required than general complaints of a physician's inability to cooperate with others. To constitute disruptive behavior meriting termination of staff privileges, hospital authorities should present concrete evidence of specific instances of misbehavior, such as unjustified altercations with other doctors or nurses, violations of hospital routines or rules, breaches of professional standards, or the commission of some other act that will adversely affect health care delivery. . . .

Because it found that the Board of Governors had improperly prejudged the issue, the Chancery Division reversed the revocation of Dr. Nanavati's privileges. In light of the length of the proceedings before the hospital authorities and the court, however, the Chancery Division tried to bring the matter to a close. The court reasoned that the crucial questions were primarily legal, rather than factual, and that "the administrative remedy [sic] certainly would be futile." Consequently, the court made independent findings of fact based largely on the record made in the tainted hospital proceeding.

Notwithstanding the Chancery Division's conclusion about the futility of further hospital proceedings, we are satisfied that the appropriate judicial response is to permit the hospital, if it so elects, to reinstate the disciplinary proceedings. . . . We base that conclusion on the fact that since the Board of Governors voted to terminate Dr. Nanavati's staff privileges, the majority of its members have been replaced. Only six of the former members remain on the Board. If Dr. Nanavati fears that he will not receive a fair hearing from the hospital authorities, he may move before the Chancery Division to transfer the proceedings to an impartial forum. That court, if it finds that Dr. Nanavati cannot receive a fair hearing, may transfer the matter to an alternative forum such as an arbitrator or panel of arbitrators. Obviously, if the parties can agree on a forum, the court should give great weight to their agreement. In designating any such forum, the court should consider the specialized knowledge of the practice of medicine and of hospital administration that is required to make decisions concerning staff privileges. Failing all else, and as a last resort, the court may conduct a plenary hearing on the charges against Dr. Nanavati.

The judgment of the Appellate Division is affirmed as modified, and the case is remanded to the hospital.

NOTES AND QUESTIONS

(1) Most of the New Jersey Supreme Court's staff privilege decisions have dealt with challenges to hospital rules themselves (such as categorical exclusion of osteopaths, closure of the medical staff except to new associates of existing medical practices), rather than, as in *Nanavati,* disputes about the rules' application in particular cases. Is the first type of case more appropriate for judicial review — in terms of the facts and values at issue — than the second? More justified?

(2) The facts and proceedings in *Nanavati* — not set out in detail in the New Jersey Supreme Court's opinion — present what might be considered a "worst case" scenario for judicial review, or indeed for any type of objective decisionmaking process. A foreign-born specialist arrives in a small New Jersey community. He immediately and apparently abrasively demands a larger share of power and income than he was initially granted. When the long established local doctor refuses to concede, the newcomer publicly accuses him of incompetence. The newcomer is then charged with "disruptive behavior" and "failure to cooperate with hospital personnel" and is given an unfair hearing before the hospital board. See Nanavati v. Burdette Tomlin Memorial Hospital, 645 F. Supp. 1217, 1219-1220 (D.N.J. 1986).

To the external lay observer, fault and justified grievance appear to lie on both sides, and it is extremely difficult to assess the precise balance of blame. Was Dr. Nanavati treated fairly in terms of income and power, considering his specialty qualification and comparing him to other, nonforeign newcomers in comparable communities? The number of examples is so small, and the personal and market factors involved so various, that it is probably impossible to come up with a general standard. Was Dr. Sorensen truly incompetent and endangering his patients? Even if so, was talking to the newspapers the right way to raise the issue, at least in the first instance? (On the inadequacies of the formal state disciplinary process in this regard, see Section E infra.) Given all the bitterness that has occurred, is a fair hospital hearing truly possible, even before a reconstituted board? Compare New York Public Health Law §2801-b (McKinney 1985 & 1987 Supp.) (authorizing doctors and other providers aggrieved by hospital staff privilege decisions to file complaints with the New York public health council).

(3) Assuming that an objective forum could be found, what should it consider? As a matter of policy, should the focus of the hearing be on exactly what happened in the early 1980s and who is to blame for what, or rather on the current needs of the hospital and its patients and whether Dr. Nanavati is capable of meeting them, given the necessity of working with others and all that has come before? Does the New Jersey Supreme Court's *Nanavati* opinion permit the hospital to hold a "future-oriented" hearing (albeit with reference to the past), or does it require an exclusive focus on past events?

Problem: Counsel to the Hospital on a Staff-Privilege Case

Assume you are counsel to Burdette Tomlin Memorial Hospital. After the court's decision in *Nanavati,* your client (the hospital) is trying to decide whether to attempt to revoke Dr. Nanavati's privileges again. How would you explain the court's holding to your client? In particular, is it clear which party has the burden of production and ultimate persuasion as to which issues? If the hospital wished to start the revocation process again, what would you advise them to do, not only as to the forum, but also as to type of evidence needed? If your advice were asked about whether to start the revocation process again, how would you respond? What other information would you need in order to respond?

Note: Availability of Independent Judicial Factfinding

When hospitals deny privileges on grounds of individual performance, there is usually some sort of a hospital hearing and record; indeed, the New Jersey and California courts have required an aggrieved physician to exhaust internal hospital remedies before seeking any kind of judicial review. See Zoneraich v. Overlook Hospital, 212 N.J. Super. 83, 514 A.2d 53 (App. Div. 1986); Westlake Community Hospital v. Superior Court of L.A. County, 17 Cal. 3d 465, 131 Cal. Rptr. 90, 551 P.2d 410 (1976). Judicial review is normally limited to the record before the hospital decisionmakers, and if the hospital's decision is affirmed — as it is likely to be in states using deferential standards — the doctrine of collateral estoppel or preclusive effect will likely block the aggrieved doctor from pursuing other state-law actions based on tort, contract, or state antitrust law. See *Zoneraich* supra. Federal antitrust claims, however, are often treated quite differently, as discussed in Chapter 8. Moreover, where the hospital has denied privileges on categorical grounds (such as excluding all podiatrists, or declaring the medical staff "full," or granting anesthesia privileges to only one group of doctors through an exclusive contract), there is usually no hospital hearing or record, and a judicial trial of facts is typically held.

NOTE: STATE-LAW IMMUNITY OR PRIVILEGE FOR HOSPITAL-BASED PEER REVIEW

At common law, false statements that tend to injure a person's reputation or business relationships — which might well occur in the course of hospital peer review — would be considered defamatory per se, with both malice and injury presumed. But peer review participants would probably be protected by a common law privilege granted to

> communication[s] . . . made in good faith on any subject matter in which the person communicating has an interest, or in reference to which he has a right or duty, if made to a person having a corresponding interest or duty on a privileged occasion and in a manner . . . fairly warranted by the . . . duty, right or interest. . . . The privilege arises from the necessity of full and unrestrained communication concerning [the] matter. . . . [Mayfield v. Gleichert, 484 S.W.2d 619, 625 (Tex. Ct. Civ. App. 1972) (applying qualified privilege to written report of physician misconduct from department head to hospital medical staff).]

The effect of the privilege is to eliminate the presumption of malice and require the plaintiff to prove actual malice, meaning knowledge of falsity or reckless disregard of the truth. The privilege is typically termed "conditional" or "qualified," because it can be defeated by a showing of "bad faith." In some circumstances, such as when the hospital proceedings are considered quasi-judicial or when the physician has requested the disclosure, the privilege can be deemed "absolute." See Southwick & Slee, Quality Assurance in Health Care, 5 J. Leg. Med. 343, 382-386 (1984).

At least 35 states have also enacted statutes granting immunity from damages for good faith hospital-based peer review. See Note, The Legal Liability of Medical Peer Review Participants for Revocation of Hospital Staff Privileges, 28 Drake L. Rev. 692, 694, n.11 (1978–1979) (citing statutes). These statutes vary greatly in how they define the activity or entity that qualifies for the immunity, with some referring to hospital-based medical review committees, others including any "review organization," and still others encompassing all proceedings that "resemble" judicial proceedings. The degree of protection also varies, with most granting qualified immunity based on "good faith," while some have been interpreted in more absolute terms. The concept of immunity is of course broader than that of privilege; while the latter only provides some protection for communications against defamation claims, the former provides wider protection against all types of civil actions.

NOTE: STATE-LAW PROCEDURAL REQUIREMENTS FOR STAFF PRIVILEGE DECISIONS

Standards for what constitutes procedural fairness under state law vary considerably. Publicly owned hospitals are held to federal and state constitutional standards of procedural due process and therefore are likely to have to provide adequate notice of the charges, opportunity to call and cross-examine witnesses, opportunity for assistance of counsel, and a hearing before an impartial tribunal. Nongovernmental hospitals have been traditionally held to less demanding standards. At a minimum, hospitals are required to comply with the procedural requirements of their own bylaws. Unfortunately, the JCAHO does not offer much specific guidance on procedural fairness, requiring only that there be "fair-hearing and appellate review mechanisms." JCAHO, Accreditation Manual for Hospitals 114, MS 2.4 (1988). Many state courts have held that physicians facing termination of staff privileges are entitled to "fundamentally fair procedures," which usually include notice and the opportunity to be heard before an unbiased tribunal. Courts have traditionally given hospitals much latitude within the broad bounds of fundamental fairness, allowing the tribunal members to have had at least some prior knowledge of the case, not requiring rules of evidence or other formal hearing procedures, and not requiring (but permitting) assistance of counsel. However, state diversity and latitude on these issues may end as a result of the federal Health Care Quality Improvement Act of 1986, 42 U.S.C. 11101 et seq., discussed in the next section.

3. FEDERAL AND STATE STATUTES ON HOSPITAL-BASED PEER REVIEW

Until very recently, the law of hospital-based peer review was fashioned largely by state courts, with some assistance from state statutes on specific subjects such as peer review immunity and confidentiality (discussed in section (6) below). In the mid-1980s, however, in response to increased concern about the medical malpractice insurance crisis and apparent legal threats to peer review, Congress and some states passed more comprehensive legislation in an attempt to strengthen hospital-based quality assurance.

a. The Federal Health Care Quality Improvement Act of 1986, P.L. 99-660, 42 U.S.C. 11101 et seq.

The event that precipitated Congressional action in this area was a federal jury award in 1985 of $2.2 million in antitrust damages in favor of an Oregon physician who claimed — with much justification — that peer review sanctions against him were part of a conspiracy to monopolize medical practice. See Patrick v. Burget, 108 S. Ct. 1658 (1988), discussed in Chapter 8. Although the facts in *Patrick* may have justified relief, several national medical and hospital organizations argued that federal antitrust and state-law liability threatened good faith peer review, and Congress responded to their concerns by enacting the Health Care Quality Improvement Act of 1986.

Iglehart, Congress Moves to Bolster Peer Review: The Health Care Quality Improvement Act of 1986

316 N. Engl. J. Med. 960 (1987).

[T]he law creates new requirements to which hospitals and physicians must adhere if they want to gain the full benefit of its provisions regarding immunity. Two different types of immunity are provided by the law. One is for persons who provide information (e.g., witnesses and people who give tips) to professional review bodies that are part of such entities as hospitals, health maintenance organizations, group medical practices, and professional societies. The other is for persons and organizations involved in taking actions against physicians on the basis of professional review.

Specifically, the act stipulates that any person who provides information to a professional review body regarding the competence or professional conduct of a physician shall be immune from liability in the form of damages under any federal or state law, unless the information provided is false and the person providing it knew that it was false. This immunity is not contingent on the propriety of the behavior of the peer-review body.

Professional review bodies and persons who assist them are also protected from damage suits if the review activities were undertaken (1) in the reasonable belief that the action would further the provision of good-quality health care, (2) after a reasonable effort to ascertain the facts of the matter, (3) after adequate notice and hearing procedures had been afforded to the physician involved, and (4) in the reasonable belief that the action was warranted by the facts known. The law creates a presumption that these four standards have been met and requires a physician who has been disciplined to prove otherwise.

The law specifies procedures that, if followed, satisfy the requirement of adequate notice and hearing procedures. These procedures are essentially the "due process" proceedings that hospitals commonly follow in cases in which a physician is accused of misconduct. One noteworthy requirement is that if the physician whose conduct is in question requests a hearing, it must be held by a person who is not in direct economic competition with the physician. However, a competing physician may provide evidence to the peer-review body.

The law also provides additional protection by allowing defendants in suits challenging the actions of professional review boards to recover attorneys' fees and other defense costs if they substantially prevail in the action. Immunity provided for professional review activities is not absolute, however. The new protections do not apply to actions for damages brought under federal or state civil rights laws, injunctions or declaratory judgments, actions by government agencies, or criminal proceedings. The immunity also does not apply in the case of actions brought by nonphysician practitioners, such as chiropractors, nurses, or podiatrists, who are challenging disciplinary actions taken against them. The American Nurses Association was particularly active in opposing immunity for physicians in cases brought by or against nurses in the hospital setting.

The new immunity provisions have gone into effect in suits brought under federal law that are based on actions taken by professional review boards after November 14, 1986, the date when [President] Reagan signed the measure into law. They will also apply to actions brought under state law in most cases after October 14, 1989. However, the immunity provisions will apply to state court suits before 1989 only if the state accepts the new law. The state can also reject it by explicitly rejecting the immunity provisions, but if it takes no action before 1989, these provisions automatically apply to state lawsuits as well.

To balance the new protections, Congress created substantial new reporting requirements designed, as [Congressman Henry] Waxman explained last July 15 at his subcommittee's only hearing on the measure, to prevent "incompetent doctors from jumping from hospital to hospital or state to state." Under these requirements, insurers, self-insured companies, and other organizations that make payments in settlement or satisfaction of a judgment or claim in a medical malpractice action must report monthly to a clearinghouse the names of the practitioners involved, the amounts of the payments, and descriptions of the acts or omissions that led to the claims. Failure to report could lead to a fine of up to $10,000 for each such payment.

Settlements of all amounts must be reported. One of the issues raised in the debate on the legislation was whether there should be a minimum threshold (both $10,000 and $25,000 were discussed) below which organizations would not have to report settlements of claims or judgments. In the end, Congress decreed that all payments of any amount must be reported, but it directed the DHHS to study whether this requirement is necessary and to report on its findings.

In addition, each state board of medical examiners is required to report to the clearinghouse instances in which it revokes or suspends a physician's license or censures, reprimands, or places a physician on probation for reasons relating to professional competence or conduct; the board must also report cases in which licenses are voluntarily surrendered and the acts or omissions that led to such actions. If a state board fails to provide such information to the clearinghouse, the DHHS secretary can designate another qualified organization to report the information.

Every health care organization (including hospitals, health maintenance organizations, and group medical practices) that follows a formal professional review process and that restricts the clinical privileges of a physician for a period longer than 30 days or accepts the surrender of a physician's clinical privileges while that doctor is facing an investigation must report this information to the state board of medical examiners. The board, in turn, must report this information to the clearinghouse. The law also requires the reporting of decisions based on professional review undertaken by professional societies with respect to membership, if the society wants to take advantage of immunity with respect to such decisions.

The law not only stipulates the extensive reporting of the activities of physicians who are disciplined, but it also requires that hospitals request information from the clearinghouse at the time a physician applies to be on the medical staff (as a courtesy or other appointment) or for clinical privileges at the hospital. The clearinghouse must also be checked by a hospital once every two years for information concerning any physician who is on its medical staff. If a hospital fails to obtain such information, the hospital will be presumed in any medical malpractice action to have knowledge of the information contained in the clearinghouse.

Physicians have the right to review information about themselves that is contained in the clearinghouse, and the clearinghouse must establish procedures for verifying disputed information. The clearinghouse will, on request, provide information about a physician to state licensing boards, hospitals, and other health-care organizations that have entered or may be entering into a relationship of employment or affiliation with the physician in question. Information reported to the clearinghouse is to be confidential and will be disclosed only as authorized by the law. Violation of the confidentiality requirement carries a civil penalty of $10,000. . . .

Notes and Questions

(1) As originally enacted in 1986, the Health Care Quality Improvement Act (HCQIA) seemed to imply that malpractice plaintiffs might have access to the national data bank of reported information. Public Law 100-177, enacted in December 1987, amended 42 U.S.C. §11137(b) to make it clear that information identifying particular physicians would only be disclosed

with respect to professional review activity, or, in pertinent part, "as necessary to carry out subsections (b) and (c) of section 11135 of this title." Under section 11135(b), a hospital that fails to request information from the National Data Bank about a physician being considered or reconsidered for staff privileges is presumed to know that information. On March 21, 1988, the Secretary issued proposed regulations that granted access to National Data Bank information to hospitals, providers requesting information about themselves, and to attorneys or patients who have filed a medical malpractice claim against a hospital and who request information about a practitioner who is also named in the lawsuit. The information will be disclosed to the attorney only "upon the submission of evidence that the hospital failed to obtain information . . . as required [by the Act]" and may be used only in litigation against the hospital. Proposed 45 C.F.R. §60.10(a)(4), 53 Fed. Reg. 9270 (1988).

(2) In addition to its immunity provisions, the HCQIA attempts to deter lawsuits attacking peer review through §11113, which requires courts to award attorney's fees in cases in which the defendant "substantially prevails," and in which the claim was "frivolous, unreasonable, without foundation, or in bad faith." Given the close and potentially competitive working relationships among doctors at a hospital and the historic informality of hospital proceedings, how likely do you think it is that attorney's fees would be assessed against unsuccessful physician plaintiffs under this provision? See 1988 Fla. Sess. Law Serv. Ch. 88-1, §3 (West), amending Fla. Stat. §395.0115(8)(a) (awarding attorney's fees to defendants prevailing against physician-plaintiffs in cases arising out of peer review action without regard to reasonableness of plaintiff's claim).

(3) Although the HCQIA is clearly intended to reduce the incidence of malpractice, its most immediate impact may be to increase the amount of malpractice litigation, if doctors refuse to settle cases and insist on full litigation in an effort to avoid a report to the Secretary.

b. State Legislation on Hospital-Based Peer Review

Two states — Florida and New York — have enacted what can be termed a "third wave" of medical malpractice law reform. Although some of this legislation continues the trend, established by reforms in the mid-1970s and early 1980s, of reducing plaintiffs' rights and remedies, much of it tries to support major changes already underway in the medical profession's approach to quality assurance. The provisions dealing with staff privileges and hospital-based review are discussed here; other provisions dealing with risk management and state licensing of physicians are discussed in sections (D)(5) and (E)(2) below.

Florida now requires hospitals, as a condition of state licensure, to establish a written and binding peer review process whose purpose must be the improvement of patient care. The process must include a mechanism for identifying and avoiding conflicts of interest on the part of peer review panel members, and a process for responding to oversight by the new state Division of Medical Quality Assurance of the Department of Professional Regulation. Grounds for hospital discipline are specified as: incompetence, habitual use of intoxicants or drugs, mental or physical impairment, having been found liable for medical negligence, having one or more settlements exceeding $10,000 based on medical negligence, any other medical negligence, and failure to comply with the policies or directives of the hospital's risk management or quality assurance programs. When a reasonable belief exists that a staff member or physician with staff privileges may be subject to discipline on these grounds, the hospital must investigate and, if grounds are found, must respond with a sanction ranging from revocation of privileges to required education and counseling. Final disciplinary actions against physicians must be reported to the state Division of Medical Quality Assurance, which must investigate to determine if licensure sanctions should also be applied. See Ch.88-1, §3, 1988 Fla. Sess. Law Serv. 6 (West 1988), amending Florida Statutes §395.0115. New York's statute contains similar provisions, including a requirement that hospitals maintain detailed files on the credentials and performance of each physician, dentist, and podiatrist, and establish a procedure for "prompt resolution of grievances by patients" that may result in claims of malpractice. N.Y. Pub. Health L. §2805-j (McKinney Supp. 1987).

In addition, the Florida statute provides that "[t]here shall be no monetary liability on the part of, and no cause of action for damages shall arise against, any licensed facility, its governing body, . . . peer review panels, medical staff, . . . or . . . witnesses . . . or any other person for any action taken without intentional fraud in carrying out the provisions of this section." Ch.88-1, §3, 1988 Fla. Sess. Law Serv. 7 (West 1988), amending Fla. Stat. §395.0115(5). As indicated above, the law also provides for award of attorney's fees to a defendant prevailing against a physician-plaintiff in a case arising out of a peer review action without regard to reasonableness of the plaintiff's claim. Id., Fla. Stat. §395.0115(8)(a).

Discussion Questions

(1) In what ways does the Florida statute go further than the federal HCQIA in requiring or encouraging hospital-based peer review? Which approach is preferable? Why?

(2) Read literally, the civil immunity provision in Fla. Stat. §395.0115(5) quoted above threatens to wipe out or at least substantially restrict the doctrine of corporate negligence as articulated in Section C(4) supra. Do you see why? Do you think that was the intent of the Florida

legislature? As counsel to the appropriate legislative committee, how would you redraft §395.0115(5) so as to preserve the legislature's apparent goals without compromising the doctrine of corporate negligence developed by *Darling* and its progeny?

4. SUBSTANTIVE GROUNDS FOR ADVERSE HOSPITAL ACTION

a. NEGATIVE CATEGORICAL EXCLUSIONS: RACE AND NON-M.D. PROVIDERS

With respect to negative categories, courts on their own have played a relatively limited role. To be sure, one major traditional negative category — exclusion of black and other minority practitioners — has been ruled illegal, first by the federal courts on equal protection grounds (with the help of greatly expanded "state action" doctrine in the case of private nonprofit hospitals) and then by Titles VI and VII of the 1964 Civil Rights Act, which respectively prohibit discrimination on grounds of race, color, or national origin in federally-funded activities, and discrimination on grounds of (among others) race in employment. See Simkins v. Moses H. Cone Memorial Hospital, 323 F.2d 959 (4th Cir. 1963) (granting injunction prohibiting racial discrimination in staff privilege decisions by private nonprofit hospitals and holding "separate but equal" provision of the federal Hill-Burton Act, 42 U.S.C. §291e(f) (1963) unconstitutional); Titles VI and VII of the 1964 Civil Rights Act, 42 U.S.C. §§2000d, 2000e (1982); but see Diggs v. Harris Hospital — Methodist Inc., 847 F.2d 270 (5th Cir. 1988) (neither staff privileges nor doctor-patient relationship is "employment" under Title VII, hence challenge to staff privilege termination on racial discrimination grounds dismissed). In addition, as noted above, the New Jersey Supreme Court's landmark 1963 *Greisman* opinion ruled invalid on state common law grounds the widespread hospital categorical exclusion of doctors of osteopathy.

For the most part, however, hospital categorical exclusions have been ruled illegal not by the courts, but by state legislation prohibiting particular categorical exclusions. See, for instance, Shaw v. Hospital Authority of Cobb County, 614 F.2d 946 (5th Cir. 1980) (upholding a public hospital bylaw categorically excluding podiatrists against federal constitutional challenges); Calif. Health & Safety Code §1316 (1979) (prohibiting categorical exclusion of osteopaths and podiatrists); N.Y. Pub. Health Law §2801-b (McKinney 1985 & 1987 Supp.) (prohibiting categorical exclusion of physicians, podiatrists, optometrists, and dentists); D.C. Code Ann. §32-1307(c)(1986) (prohibiting categorical exclusion of certified nurse midwives, nurse anesthetists, nurse practitioners, and psychologists). Antitrust law, further discussed in Chapter 8, has played some role in these developments, particularly in persuading the JCAHO to drop its requirement that only individuals "fully licensed to practice medicine" were eligible for staff privileges. See Note, Health Professionals' Access to Hospitals: A Retrospective and Prospective Analysis, 34 Vand. L. Rev. 1161, 1190 (1981).

b. Functional Categorical Exclusions

A functional categorical exclusion occurs where a hospital purports not to make any judgment about an individual practitioner's capabilities, but rather denies privileges on assertedly neutral, functional grounds. The two most typical reasons are: (1) that the hospital staff is "full" — that is that the facilities and staff cannot support more services of the type that the applicant wishes to provide; and (2) that the hospital wishes to grant a particular group of doctors a monopoly over certain functions, typically the hospital-based practices of anesthesiology, pathology, and radiology.

In defending these hospital policies against legal attack, hospitals must show that they are rationally related to legitimate institutional goals. In contrast to hospital actions based on individual performance, which, at least in some states must rest on "sufficient reliable evidence, including hearsay . . . ," actions based on broad policies (such as staff closure) need only be "reached in the normal and regular course of conducting . . . affairs . . . and [be] based on adequate information, regardless of form, origin, or authorship, that is generally considered reasonable and reliable by professional persons responsibly involved in the health care field." Desai v. St. Barnabas Medical Center, 103 N.J. 79, 510 A.2d 662, 669 (1986). Thus a New Jersey hospital convinced the state supreme court that the primary function of its new satellite facility was to treat urgent and emergency cases, thereby providing a "rational basis" for closure of surgical appointments until the pattern of usage became clear. Guerrero v. Burlington County Memorial Hospital, 70 N.J. 344, 360 A.2d 334, 341 (1976). Similarly, expert testimony persuaded New Jersey courts that because surgeons control patient usage of anesthesia services, an exclusive contract between a hospital and a particular group of anesthesiologists was a reasonable way to avoid undue accumulation of power by surgeons and resulting tensions and disruption of service. Belmar v. Cipolla, 96 N.J. 199, 475 A.2d 533, 539-540 (1984). (For the antitrust aspects of the exclusive contracting issue, see Chapter 8.)

In both *Guerrero* and *Belmar,* the courts emphasized that they would intervene if exclusions were "motivated by a desire to exclude newcomers in order to maintain the status quo of the staff. . . ." *Guerrero,* 360 A.2d at 341. Thus a hospital policy closing its staff except to newcomers joining one of the hospital's existing medical practices was found to "arbitrarily discriminat[e] against qualified applicants. . . " The hospital's argument that this exception improved public health by increasing coverage among the partnership, without increasing the patient load in the crowded facility, was dismissed as "pure supposition." *Desai,* 510 A.2d at 671, 670. See also Berman v. Valley Hospital, 103 N.J. 100, 510 A.2d 673 (1986) (rejecting exclusion of nonaffiliated doctors who had practiced in area for more than two years; asserted health rationales lack any empirical or academic support, therefore do not mitigate discriminatory and exclusionary impact).

c. Individual Performance: Medical Incompetence, Inability to Work With Others, and Other Risk-Creating Grounds

i. Medical Incompetence

Protecting patients from medical incompetence is clearly the central justification for hospital-based peer review, and therefore hospitals do and should have the authority to deny, restrict, suspend, and revoke staff privileges on that ground. Serious risks to patient well being can justify summary suspension, as long as a post-suspension hearing is held within a reasonable time. See Woodbury v. McKinnon, 447 F.2d 839 (5th Cir. 1971). Revocations are normally based on a pattern of substandard care, and a doctor's periodic reappointment to the medical staff does not preclude the hospital from relying on incidents preceding the reappointment. Miller v. Indiana Hospital, 419 A.2d 1191, 1194 (Pa. Super. 1980) (proper for hospital to rely on prior misconduct "which may not have been so egregious in any one year as to warrant denial of reappointment, but the cumulative effect of which called for [the doctor's] dismissal from the staff"). However, a single incident of substandard care, if sufficiently serious, can also justify termination of privileges. Storrs v. Lutheran Hospitals and Homes Society of America, 661 P.2d 632 (Alaska 1983). Finally, "impairment" — disabilities caused by drugs, alcohol, and age — is a permissible basis for revocation. Theissen v. Watonga Municipal Hospital Board, 550 P.2d 938 (Okla. 1976). See generally Hollowell, Medical Staff Credentialling, 15 Legal Aspects of Med. Prac. (Sept. 1987) at 1.

ii. Inability to Work With Others and Other Risk-related Grounds

Revocation of privileges because of "inability to work with others" or similar grounds is troublesome and controversial. As in *Nanavati,* supra, modern decisions require the hospital to show specific physician behaviors that create the kind of disharmony that presents a "realistic and specific threat to the quality of medical care." Miller v. Eisenhower Medical Center, 27 Cal.3d 614, 166 Cal. Rptr. 826, 614 P.2d 258, 269 (1980).

Physicians' staff privileges are occasionally revoked not because of specific instances of substandard care, but because of other behavior that creates a reasonable concern for patient well being or hospital liability. See Miller v. National Medical Hospital of Monterey Park, 124 Cal. App. 3d 81, 177 Cal. Rptr. 119 (1981) (doctor's conviction of conspiracy to murder his wife); Holmes v. Hoemako Hospital, 117 Ariz. 403, 573 P.2d 477 (1977) (refusal to carry malpractice insurance).

d. "Economic Performance" and Staff Privileges

As Chapters 3 and 8 make clear, hospitals are under increasing pressure from cost containment programs, market competition, and other forces to lower costs, increase efficiency, maximize revenue, and defend and expand their "market share." To what extent may hospitals encourage and even require doctors to promote these institutional objectives in the doctors' patterns of practice and patient care, and penalize them if they do not? These questions have barely been touched on by courts or legislatures, but they represent the potential cutting edge of staff privilege law in the age of cost containment and entrepreneurial hospital management.

i. Hospitals' Duties and Doctors' Economic Costs

Issues regarding a doctor's economic performance can be seen as arising in three different contexts. The first, not necessarily linked to cost containment, occurs when public policy requires the hospital to take certain actions with economic consequences, which actions can only be performed by doctors who themselves are not under a similar duty. The clearest example is the federal regulatory requirement that hospitals that have accepted federal construction funds under the Hill-Burton Act assure that their facilities are actually available to Medicaid recipients and, at least with respect to emergencies, all low income people. See 42 C.F.R. §124.603 (1987), discussed in Chapter 1. Aside from hospital bylaws, individual doctors are not themselves required to accept Medicaid patients, or to treat any particular patient, even in an emergency. But in order to fulfill its own regulatory duties, a hospital may condition its staff privileges on doctors' accepting low-income patients or rendering other service, and may revoke privileges for refusal to satisfy that condition. See Clair v. Centre Community Hospital, 317 Pa. Super. 25, 463 A.2d 1065 (1983), discussed in Chapter 1.

ii. Hospitals' Institutional Objectives and Doctors' Patterns of Practice

A second dimension of economic performance, often combined with non-economic considerations, arises when a hospital seeks institutional objectives through means that deny staff privileges to competent physicians, or attempts to regulate where or through whom certain procedures are performed. The most familiar example of this problem is exclusive contracting for hospital-based physicians, under which a hospital will require, for instance, all anesthesiology services to be performed by a particular group of doctors and will deny privileges to other anesthesiologists regardless of competence. Despite numerous legal challenges to this practice on state and federal grounds, the courts have uniformly upheld it because it contributes to important institutional objectives such as availability of services, efficiency of scheduling, familiarity with equipment, maintenance of quality, and performance of administrative and educational functions. See, for instance, Adler v. Montefiore Hospital Association of Western Pennsylvania, 453 Pa. 60, 311 A.2d 634 (1973), *cert. denied* 414 U.S. 1131 (1974); Belmar v. Cipolla, 96 N.J. 199, 475 A.2d 533 (1984); see also Jefferson Parish Hospital District No. 2 v. Hyde, 466 U.S. 2 (1984) (upholding exclusive anesthesiology contract against federal antitrust challenge), discussed in Chapter 8. Similarly, a hospital policy prohibiting neurologists on its medical staff from transporting hospital patients to their own privately owned CAT scanner, and requiring them to use the hospital's scanner, was upheld as a reasonable effort "to deal with the . . . complex task of providing comprehensive medical services to the citizens of [the] state." Cobb County — Kennestone Hospital Authority v. Prince, 242 Ga. 139, 249 S.E.2d 581 (1978).

Another, more complex version of this issue arises when a hospital has adopted an institutional strategy to develop itself along certain lines, emphasizing certain kinds and styles of practice. May a hospital then deny privileges to a competent doctor whose style or pattern does not fit the desired economic-institutional mold? A fascinating (and to our knowledge the only) case addressing this issue is Robinson v. Magovern, 521 F. Supp. 842 (W.D. Pa. 1981), *aff'd* 688 F.2d 824 (3d Cir. 1982), *cert. denied,* 459 U.S. 971 (1982) (hereinafter *Robinson*). This case arose when Dr. Robinson, a thoracic (open-heart) surgeon with good academic credentials but debatable practice experience, was denied staff privileges at Allegheny General Hospital in Pittsburgh on three major grounds. First, Dr. Robinson's pattern of practicing at several hospitals, and refusing to make a major commitment to Allegheny General, was said to "prevent him from adequately covering his heart patients at Allegheny General." *Robinson,* 521 F. Supp. at 915. Second, Dr. Robinson was said not to have the ability or the interest to contribute to the hospital's research and educational programs, for instance, by doing research or joining the medical school faculty. Third, the medical staff had serious doubts about Dr. Robinson's ability to function harmoniously with his fellow doctors, residents, and support personnel. Id. These reasons were important to Allegheny General not only on general grounds of high quality patient care, but also because of the hospital's specific institutional objectives and competitive strategy. Dr. Robinson challenged the legitimacy of those objectives and of the specific criteria applied to his application by suing the hospital and Dr. Magovern, the head of the surgical department and chief thoracic surgeon, on federal antitrust and analogous state-law grounds.

To determine whether the hospital's objectives and criteria imposed an unreasonable restraint on competition or trade, Judge Cohill undertook exhaustive analyses of the hospital industry, the specialized market in open heart surgery, and the institutional development of Allegheny General. He determined that Allegheny General was a "regional referral" or "secondary teaching" hospital, midway between community hospitals offering basic health services and major teaching hospitals. Hospitals such as Allegheny General provide both basic health care to their immediate areas and advanced care units in some subspecialities for patients from larger, regional areas. Id. at 857-858. In the late 1960s, Allegheny General sought to reverse an era of financial decline and low morale by developing its educational and research programs in particular specialties, notably cancer and heart disease. Id. at 859-860. Under Dr. Magovern's leadership, the open heart surgery department "greatly expanded its research activities, and . . . developed a reputation for providing secondary and tertiary level patients with high quality, innovative care. [These] achievements . . . have attracted a large volume of patients to Allegheny General. . . ." Id. at 862-863.

Against this background, Judge Cohill concluded that the hospital's highly selective criteria for granting staff privileges — such as the insistence that physicians have an active interest in research, be eligible for appointment to a medical school faculty, and be willing to concentrate their practices at Allegheny General — were related to legitimate hospital objectives. Moreover, while these criteria did have some anticompetitive effects — such as excluding competent doctors who did not wish to do research or make a primary commitment to Allegheny General — these effects were outweighed in the court's view by the procompetitive effects of enhancing Allegheny General's ability to compete and by raising the prevailing level of patient care. Id. at 919. Finally, the hospital's policies and market share did not preclude Dr. Robinson from practicing at other hospitals in the area or even from receiving referrals from doctors at Allegheny General. For these reasons, and others, Judge Cohill found against Dr. Robinson on all of his federal and state claims.

Robinson v. Magovern reflects unusually strong facts in the hospital's favor. The hospital had hired a consulting firm in the late 1960s, had formally adopted explicit institutional objectives and a competitive strategy, and had implemented that strategy by hiring strong administrators and department chairs. In other words, the hospital could credibly claim that its selective, exclusionary staff privilege criteria were not simply serving to protect the power and income of established doctors, but were rather designed to heighten the research and educational reputation of the hospital and hence its competitive position. Moreover, Dr. Robinson had a history of personality conflict and rigidity that might have justified denial even without special institutional objectives. The lesson of *Robinson* thus cuts two ways; hospitals may be able to justify exclusion on the basis of special institutional and competitive objectives, but (perhaps) not if all that is taking place is the dressing up of traditional private practice in the rhetoric of high quality care.

iii. Maximizing Hospital Income in an Era of Cost Containment

What if a hospital cannot link its economic objectives to the respectable goals of expanded research and education, but rather simply wants to maximize its income by encouraging doctors to change their practice styles? This third dimension of economic performance is one of the great potential contemporary issues of staff privilege law and will be taken up in Section G below, after more detailed discussion of the role of payers and their agents in the processes of cost containment and quality assurance.

5. THE EVOLUTION OF RISK MANAGEMENT PROGRAMS

As discussed at the beginning of Section D, the term "risk management" has been historically associated with areas under the direct control of the hospital administration — notably nursing, pharmacy, the work of numerous technicians, food service, and building maintenance. Risk management programs were (and are) designed to investigate "incidents" that might lead to a claim or legal liability. The purpose of the incident investigation is to help the hospital administration decide how to respond to a claim (for instance by settlement or litigation), lay the basis for a legal defense if necessary, and identify problems in management or employee performance that need correction. An example of an incident investigation is provided in the excerpt from the article by Patricia Blake below.

Despite these important functions, risk management has traditionally been something of a stepchild in the world of hospital administration, and the Blake article suggests some obvious reasons why. As Blake points out, the "proximate cause" of the "incident" — a patient receiving the wrong kind of transfused blood — lay not simply in a mistake by a nurse's aide, but also in the attitude and competence of a registered nurse and in broader problems of patient classification and nurse staffing patterns. Criticizing one low-level employee's performance is one thing; raising more systematic problems, reflecting on the work of higher-level employees, is another. Not surprisingly, the risk-management function was (and is) often assigned to a middle-level administrative employee with little capacity to highlight major problems or challenge established authority. Indeed, so threatening is the idea of serious administrative review of quality of care that the work of doctors was (and is) not even included, sometimes formally, and almost always practically, in the scope of the risk management program.

These historic patterns are now undergoing change. As doctors and hospitals continue to complain to state legislatures and Congress about soaring malpractice insurance premiums, the response has been in part to require providers to put their own house in order. At least seven states — Alaska, Florida, Kansas, Massachusetts, Maryland, New York, and Rhode Island — now require hospitals to have risk management programs as a condition of state licensure. The Florida statute discussed in Section (3) above defines risk management in detail, requires investigation of all "adverse incidents causing injury to patients," including those generated by physicians, and immediate reports to the state Department of Professional Regulation of all incidents involving the death of a patient, severe brain or spinal damage to a patient, a surgical procedure being performed on the wrong patient, or a surgical procedure unrelated to the patient's diagnosis or medical needs. Fla. Stat. §395.041.

The effect of these statutes is to bridge the historic gap between administration based risk management and medical staff based quality assurance, and to link more closely internal hospital quality control to state licensure of hospitals and physicians (discussed in Section E below). The JCAHO is moving in a similar direction, with its new requirement, effective January 1, 1989, that there be "operational linkages between the risk management functions related to the clinical aspects of patient care and safety and quality assurance functions." JCAHO, 8 Joint Commission Perspectives No. 112 (January/February 1988) at 7 et seq., quoted in M. Macdonald, K. Meyer & B. Essig. Health Care Law: A Practical Guide §12.03 at 12-8 (1988 ed.)

The major legal issue regarding risk management has been whether incident reports are discoverable by malpractice plaintiffs suing doctors and hospitals, a topic covered in Section (6) immediately following. As risk management becomes increasingly related to patient care, one can expect claims of negligently designed or implemented risk management to emerge as part of the doctrine of corporate negligence for hospitals. In this connection, consider Fla. Stat. §395.041(10), which provides that "[t]here shall be no monetary liability on the part of, and no cause of action for damages shall arise against, any [certified] risk manager . . . for the implementation and oversight of [a] risk management program . . . as required by this section, for any act or proceeding undertaken or performed within the scope of the functions of such risk management program if the risk manager acts without intentional fraud." Like the Florida peer review immunity provision discussed above, does this provide too much immunity, especially with respect to claims by patients? Does it immunize the hospital? Should it?

Blake, Incident Investigation, A Complete Guide

15 Nursing Management 39, 40-41 (Nov. 1984)

One morning, the head nurse of a 25-bed surgical ICU finds, on her desk, an incident report entitled "Hemolytic Transfusion Reaction." "Because of the usual extreme shortage of *qualified* nurses on our station, I was forced to have an aide help me check blood for a patient who was massively GI bleeding. She made a mistake: the patient received the wrong unit of blood and had a transfusion reaction. I stopped the blood stat as soon as I assessed what was happening. This would never have happened if our head nurse knew how to schedule nurses for the intensive care unit and didn't ask nurses to work doubles all the time." Signed: Betty Jones, RN.

Ms. Jones, an RN with eight years of critical care experience, has worked on the surgical ICU for nine months. She tends to defy authority and has been openly hostile and aggressive towards the head nurse during station staff meetings. She also tends to belittle and intimidate newly hired, inexperienced RNs and often "flaunts her knowledge." Two RNs on the station have specifically requested that they not be scheduled to work with her because of her aggressive and abrasive personality and her unwillingness to accept help from others.

Betty has had two disciplinary conferences with the head nurse of the unit regarding these tendencies, their effect on co-workers, and the necessity to modify her behavior and work cooperatively with her peers in a stressful environment.

THE FACTS

Investigation revealed the following facts. On the day that the incident occurred, Betty was scheduled to work the 7:00 a.m. to 3:00 p.m. shift. Betty was asked to double and to work the 3:00 p.m. to 11:00 p.m. shift and was assigned three stable post-operative patients. At 5:00 p.m., she was informed that she would be assigned a fourth patient who had had a cardiopulmonary arrest in the operating room.

Forty-five minutes after this patient arrived in an unstable condition on the unit, one of the other patients began to GI bleed, and required rapid administration of several units of blood. The nurse's aide stated that when she delivered the third unit of blood from the blood bank to Betty, Betty told her to check the third unit with her. The aide stated that she informed Betty that she had never done this and did not know how to do it. Betty responded by saying "Just look at these numbers on this label and make sure they are the same as what I am reading out loud." Betty stated that she asked the aide to check the blood with her because no one else was available to do so, because of the acuity of the patient, and because of the work load and fast pace of the unit at that time.

Fifteen minutes after the infusion of the third unit of blood was begun, the patient exhibited the following symptoms: a rectal temperature of 104°F (previous rectal temperature had been 101°F), chills, a flushed face, respirations which were slightly more rapid than they had been, systolic blood pressure of 86 mm Hg (previous pressure had been 100 mm Hg), and a pulse rate of 140 (previous rate had been 110). Betty stopped the transfusion immediately and rechecked the blood slip with the unit of blood and the patient to determine if an error had been made and found that there was an error. She assessed that the patient was most likely having a hemolytic transfusion reaction and immediately informed a critical care resident. The critical care resident and the charge nurse informed the head nurse that they were on the station with another patient, but could have easily and quickly been summoned to check the unit of blood with Betty.

CAUSES AND EFFECTS

After analyzing these facts, the head nurse determined that the proximate cause of this incident was that pressure from the immediate tasks obscured the full scope of Betty's responsibilities. Applying the principles previously discussed, the head nurse defined the following potential primary causes:

1. Inadequate staffing for the acuity of the patients.
2. Inadequate development or enforcement of a policy for staffing for changes in the acuity levels of patients.
3. Inadequate development of a staff nurse.

In the last step in the incident investigation, the head nurse decided to take these measures to correct the situation:

1. Review her past disciplinary conferences with Betty with her supervisor, and discuss her current assessment of Betty's work habits and ability to work cooperatively with her peers.
2. Schedule another disciplinary conference with Betty Jones since she did make an error of judgment and did not follow the established policy and procedure for checking blood.
3. Review the patient acuity classification system and the staffing patterns for the unit with particular emphasis placed on the frequency of double-shifts and double-backs for the staff.
4. Schedule a meeting with the other head nurses and supervisors to determine the extent of the staffing shortage problem and to discuss the advantages and disadvantages of developing an internal float pool,

utilizing external nursing pools, and/or closing patient beds when necessary.

6. CONFIDENTIALITY OF PEER REVIEW AND RISK MANAGEMENT RECORDS

Hospital-based peer review and risk management programs have historically been uneven in providing patients much protection against incompetent physicians and substandard care. As recently as 1965, the administrator of the defendant hospital in the *Darling* case could testify that it was not his responsibility to be concerned about the competence of physicians with staff privileges. Cases such as Johnson v. Misericordia Community Hospital, discussed in Section C supra, revealed that some hospitals did not even minimally comply with industry norms and elementary standards of reasonable care. Moreover, Gonzales v. Nork, discussed in Section B(3)(c) supra, displayed grave weaknesses in the industry norms themselves, as expressed in the JCAHO standards for hospital-based quality assurance. As an excellent health law book written "for the health care industry" by experienced in-house hospital counsel puts it,

> Initially, the JCAHO [standards of hospital accreditation] emphasized the performance of studies [by the hospital quality assurance process,] which often did not focus on the critical elements of patient care and did not identify important patient care deficiencies. Usually, JCAHO reviewers would focus merely on the number of studies done and whether the institution had adopted a written quality assurance plan. The problem-oriented approach then began to emerge. But again, the problems that often were identified were not serious patient care problems and frequently were administrative. Moreover, quality assurance efforts were often undertaken only on a periodic basis and JCAHO studies tended to concentrate on . . . the number of problems identified rather than on the comprehensiveness and quality of the program. [The JCAHO approach has now changed and requires continuous and systematic monitoring of all important aspects of patient care.] [M. Macdonald, K. Meyer, & B. Essig, Health Care Law: A Practical Guide §12.03[2] at 12-10 to 11 (1988 ed.).]

Spokespersons for the JCAHO itself concede that before the 1970s, the quality assurance component of hospital accreditation was "informal and subjective," and that the "medical audit" methodology of the 1970s led, "in too many cases," to "paper exercises," that "compromised" the quality assurance effort. Roberts, Coale & Redman, A History of the Joint Commission on Accreditation of Hospitals, 258 J.A.M.A. 936, 939, 940 (1987) (also noting that beginning in 1979, the JCAH has "directed hospitals to develop a hospital-wide program that integrates all quality assessment activities"). Given this background, it is not surprising that until very recently, the main external pressure on hospitals to perform serious quality assurance came from malpractice suits and the evolving doctrines of corporate negligence and ostensible agency discussed in Section C.

It is thus a matter of some irony and much concern that while many state courts have been enlarging hospitals' duties to monitor and assure quality of patient care, many state legislatures have been undercutting those duties by enacting statutes granting sweeping immunity from liability and discovery to participants in the peer review process. The impetus for such legislation is understandable. Given the great sensitivity of intra-professional criticism, the impact on a doctor's reputation, the need for harmonious working relations, and the tendency of doctors to litigate against critical peers, a strong argument can be made that if it is to exist at all, hospital-based peer review must be confidential to some extent and must enjoy some protection against litigation by the physicians under investigation. On the other hand, given the long history of weak performance by hospital-based peer review, and the historic role of malpractice litigation in strengthening that process, it seems premature to insulate completely hospital-based peer review from judicial oversight, particularly on behalf of injured patients. Yet such insulation now appears to be widespread.

Consider the 1982 *Elam* case, discussed in Section C supra. In that case, the plaintiff's attorney happened to represent several other patients in suits against the defendant podiatrist, and therefore the attorney knew from his own experience that the defendant hospital's counsel was aware of serious allegations and findings against the podiatrist before the date of Elam's surgery. Given these facts, the California intermediate appeals court remanded the case for trial on whether the hospital's peer review committee had conducted reviews of the defendant podiatrist in a non-negligent manner. But California Evidence Code §1157, enacted in 1968 at the urging of the California Medical Association and California Hospital Association, prohibits discovery of the "proceedings" and "records" of "organized committees of medical [and other provider] staffs in hospitals having the responsibility of evaluation and improvement of the quality of care rendered in the hospital. . . ." Id. The statute also provides that "no person in attendance at a meeting of any such committee shall be required to testify as to what transpired thereat." Id. The statute further contains a revealing exception: the prohibitions on discovery and testimony do not apply, or apply only partially, to physicians attempting to use peer review proceedings to defend themselves in malpractice suits, or to challenge denial of staff privileges.

In short, Evidence Code §1157 bars Elam from discovering the records needed to try the issue remanded by the appellate court. Indeed, except for the plaintiff's attorney's fortuitous knowledge, it seems unlikely that the case would have gone even that far. For the subsequent efforts of California plaintiffs' attorneys and judges to "get around" §1157 and pursue *Elam*-type actions, see Note, Anatomy of the Conflict Between Hospital Medical Staff Peer Review Confidentiality and Medical Malpractice Plaintiff Recovery: A

Case for Legislative Amendment, 24 Santa Clara L. Rev. 661, 680-683 (1984).

The content of state statutes varies enormously, with some protecting only narrowly defined named committees or types of documents, while others grant sweeping discovery immunity to all "medical review boards" of virtually any description. See Holbrook & Dunn, Medical Malpractice Litigation: The Discoverability and Use of Hospitals' Quality Assurance Committee Records, 16 Wash. L.J. 54, 74-75 (1976). But in many states legislation similar to that in California severely limits patients' ability to pursue their rights to quality assurance by hospitals. See, for instance, Coburn v. Seda, 101 Wn. 2d 270, 677 P.2d 173 (1984); Goldberg, The Peer Review Privilege: A Law in Search of a Valid Policy, 10 Am. J.L. Med. 151 (1984). Indeed, in some states the discovery immunity is so sweeping that it has been held to extinguish doctors' substantive rights as well. See Holly v. Auld, 450 So. 2d 217 (Fla. 1984) (holding that statutory prohibition on discovery of proceedings and records of medical review committees applies to doctor's defamation action against members of and witnesses to a hospital credentials committee, thereby effectively extinguishing doctor's right to sue for defamation in this context).

The policy reasons cited in support of these results are not persuasive. The most common argument is that without discovery immunity for all committee proceedings against all patient actions, peer review would not take place; doctors would refuse to make critical comments if they believed that these comments would be used in patient litigation against the doctor being reviewed. Such a result would then diminish the quality of patient care, by allowing substandard doctors to work unchecked. But as former Judge B. Abbott Goldberg — the trial judge in Gonzales v. Nork — points out, this argument is self-contradictory: the goal of protecting patients is achieved by denying patients a crucial means of protecting themselves. See Goldberg, supra, 10 Am. J. L. Med. at 155-156. At the same time, the prospect of being subject to discovery by their fellow-doctors — often and, in our view, correctly permitted by the statutes — does not apparently deter peer review committee members from carrying out their duties.

Clearly there is some middle ground between no confidentiality at all and sweeping blockage of patient (and in some states physician) actions. Exceptions to a discovery privilege could be provided for patient actions against the hospital for negligent quality assurance (as in *Elam*) or in cases in which the patient has no other way of proving hospital or physician negligence. Individual participants in peer review could still be protected by qualified liability immunity statutes, leaving actions against the hospital still available to provide pressure for serious peer review. Such pressure seems essential in the light of history; it seems far too early to turn over the hospital-based quality assurance process to the impulses of doctors and state agencies, unchecked by any independent patient and judicial oversight.

Risk management reports have traditionally not been accorded the same kind of common law or statutory public policy privilege as peer review. The reasons are obvious: risk management was not thought to be as integrally connected to improving patient care, and risk managers, as hospital administrative employees, could threaten less credibly than independent doctors not to participate. On the other hand, the connection of risk management to insurance and legal defense opened up the "attorney work product" argument for resisting discovery. Interestingly, the same Florida statute that requires hospitals to establish risk management programs and grants sweeping liability immunity to risk managers themselves, carefully classifies risk management incident reports as "the work papers of the attorney defending" the hospital, and "shall be subject to discovery, but shall not be admissible as evidence in court. . . ." Fla. Stat. Ann. §395.041(4) (West, 1986). If risk management programs indeed begin to merge with the quality assurance process, there may be increased pressure in both directions: to expand immunity by prohibiting all discovery, and to contract immunity by permitting admission of evidence regarding a negligently implemented program.

E. LICENSING AGENCIES AS MONITORS OF QUALITY OF CARE

In order to provide health care on a legal basis, both individuals and institutions must have a license from the state. For individuals, obtaining a license means attending approved educational and training programs and passing examinations, often requiring great time and expense. For institutions, such as hospitals, nursing homes, health maintenance organizations, and home health agencies, licenses involve numerous requirements regarding organizational structure, staffing, services, building construction standards, and financial solvency. The usual justification for imposing these requirements on individuals and institutions is protection of the public from unqualified providers and substandard quality of care. Licensure is said to protect the public through two main mechanisms: excluding the unqualified, and regulating or monitoring the conduct of the licensees. The exclusionary mechanism raises obvious issues of interprofessional rivalry that are explored in Chapter 7. This section focuses on the licensing agencies' regulatory role.

In performing this role, state licensing agencies are heavily influenced by the standard norms and practices of the professions and industries they regulate. Most licensing programs — whether of individual providers or institutions — assume that adequate professional and industry standards exist, and that the task of quality assurance under licensure is to identify and deal with relatively rare cases of individual provider deviation from those norms. As we shall see, licensing agencies have performed even this limited but important role very badly, and most contemporary reform efforts are designed to improve this kind of enforcement.

A second approach to quality assurance, exemplified in Dr. Ernest Codman's efforts to evaluate surgical outcomes in the early twentieth century, and geographic variations research in the 1970s and 1980s, takes nothing for granted and asks: do our "standard" practices and organizational patterns actually advance or undermine quality of care, as defined and measured as carefully and comprehensively as we can? In a few instances, some state licensing agencies have made efforts to implement this approach of questioning existing norms and their structural foundations.

1. THE HISTORIC GAP BETWEEN LICENSURE AND QUALITY OF CARE

NOTE: LICENSURE, QUALITY OF CARE, AND PROFESSIONAL POWER

Medical licensure laws existed in the colonial and early republican eras, but they were ineffective because they generally contained no standards for education, no penalties for unlicensed practice, and no powers to discipline licensed practitioners. See P. Starr, The Social Transformation of American Medicine 44-45 (1982). After a widespread trend toward repeal or nonenforcement of these laws in the 1830-1850 period, states began to re-enact medical licensure laws in the late nineteenth century. The new wave of licensure laws succeeded brilliantly in equating "quality of care" with the power and autonomy of organized medicine. Licensure laws were formally enacted by state legislatures, but actually delegated power to the private medical societies by allowing only graduates of medical schools approved by the AMA to sit for the licensing examination and by appointing only or almost only physicians nominated by the medical societies to the licensing boards themselves.

The equation of quality of care with organizational power can be seen most clearly in the text of the medical licensure laws themselves. It may come as a shock to many members of the general public (including lawyers) to learn that until quite recently, professional incompetence, negligence, even gross negligence, were not explicit grounds for discipline or license revocation. See Kansas State Board of Healing Arts v. Foote, 436 P.2d 828 (Kan. 1968); R. Derbyshire, Medical Licensure and Discipline in the United States 87 (1969) (in 1965, only 18 states provided for licensure action because of physical or professional incompetence). The primary obligation imposed by the licensure laws was adherence to the norms of the medical profession itself. These norms were not concerned with quality of care in explicit terms, but rather with loyalty to the profession and protection of its good name. Thus a typical medical licensure act of the early 1960s provided for license suspension or revocation when a physician: (1) had been adjudicated insane; (2) habitually used intoxicants; (3) had practiced criminal abortion or had been convicted of a crime involving moral turpitude; (4) had advertised fraudulently; (5) had misrepresented his credentials to the licensing board; or (6) had employed unlicensed persons to do work reserved for licensed practitioners. See N.J. Stat. Ann. 45:9-16 (1961), reprinted in State Board of Medical Examiners v. Weiner, 68 N.J. Super. 468, 172 A.2d 661 (1961). To be sure, revoking the licenses of doctors who had become insane or habitually intoxicated, or who allowed unlicensed employees to practice medicine, would probably prevent some incompetent care. But the focus of the regulatory licensure mechanism was not quality of care itself, but only the risk of poor quality when caused by certain specified conditions that were associated with disloyalty or gross personal (as distinct from professional) incompetence. The tension between the general justification for licensure and its specific regulatory mechanisms is explored in the following case.

Raymond v. Board of Registration in Medicine

387 Mass. 708, 443 N.E. 2d 391 (1982)

O'CONNOR, Justice

. . . The board [of registration in medicine] commenced an adjudicatory proceeding against Raymond . . . alleging in material part: [that Raymond had sold under "clandestine circumstances" two automatic submachine guns and four pistols . . . had [illegally] . . . sold five unregistered pistols . . . [and] had been convicted [in federal court] of knowing possession of two unregistered automatic submachine guns, each equipped with a silencer. . . .

General Laws c.112, §5 . . . provides that the board may revoke the [license] of a physician upon proof that the physician "(g) has been convicted of a criminal offense which reasonably calls into question his ability to practice medicine." Section 5 further provides that "[t]he board shall, after proper notice and hearing, adopt rules and regulations governing the practice of medicine in order to promote the public health, welfare, and safety and nothing in this section shall be construed to limit this general power of the board." . . . [P]ursuant to the authority vested in it . . . the board promulgated a rule making conviction of any crime a basis for discipline. . . .

[After holding that the phrase "reasonably calls into question his ability to practice medicine" in §5(g) does not invalidate the board regulation providing for discipline for conviction of "any crime," the court goes on to state that] Raymond could be disciplined for his criminal conviction under c.112, §5, as well as under the board's regulations. Section 5(g) provides that a physician is subject to discipline if he is convicted of a crime which reasonably calls into question his ability to practice medicine. The board correctly found that Raymond's conviction reasonably called into question his ability to practice medicine. To be sure, the conviction did not arise out of Raymond's medical practice. That is not essential, however. The ability to practice medicine requires not only technical competence, but also the unswerving dedication to employ it to preserve life, restore health, and alleviate suffering. See . . . Lawrence v. Board of Registration in Medicine, 239 Mass. 424, 428-429, 132 N.E. 174 (1921) ("Mere intellectual power and scientific achievement without uprightness of character may be more harmful than ignorance. Highly trained intelligence combined with disregard of the fundamental virtues is a menace"). It is difficult to conceive of an attitude more antithetical to a commitment to preserve life, alleviate suffering, and restore health, than the mentality demonstrated by knowing possession of unregistered automatic submachine guns. . . .

The board's second and third grounds for revoking Raymond's license were that he lacked good moral character and that his conduct undermined the confidence of the public in the integrity of the medical profession. [The court holds that the board had authority to apply these standards in individual disciplinary proceedings even though they are not expressly stated in the statute as standards for discipline, nor were they adopted by the board through formal rulemaking.]

Raymond contends that these are proper disciplinary grounds only if the offensive conduct occurs in the course of, or is "related to," the practice of medicine. This is the same argument that he advances against the board's authority to adopt a rule making conviction of any crime a basis for discipline, and it fails for the reasons stated in our discussion of that issue. Disciplining physicians for lack of good moral character, and for conduct that undermines public confidence in the integrity of the profession, is reasonably related to promotion of the public health, welfare, and safety. A physician's bad moral character may reasonably call into question his ability to practice medicine. In addition, conduct such as Raymond's, some of which led to criminal conviction, undermines the public's confidence in the integrity of the medical profession. The board has the authority to protect the image of the profession.

Discussion Questions

Are you persuaded by the court's reasoning in the *Raymond* case? Would it change your view if you knew something more about Dr. Raymond's medical skills — for example, if he were an excellent practitioner? What if his connection with weapons was for a political cause — the Irish Republican Army, for example? Even if you agree with the court's reasoning in this case, does the breadth of the board's authority disturb you? What if the board attempted to revoke a medical license for the crime of civil disobedience while protesting apartheid in South Africa, or the construction of a nuclear power plant?

2. CONTEMPORARY EFFORTS AT REFORM

a. State Efforts to Discipline Substandard Doctors

Although the asserted justification of medical licensure is to promote quality of care, or at least to prevent grossly substandard care, in most states virtually the only technique used to achieve this is the initial granting or denial of the license itself. (Even this safeguard has not proved to be impenetrable; a Congressional subcommittee reported in June 1988 that probably over 10,000 people in the United States possessed fraudulent medical degrees. "U.S. Spotlight on Fake Doctors," *N.Y. Times,* June 19, 1988, at 36:1.) Once the license is granted, virtually no effort is made by the state licensing agency to monitor or enforce any standard of quality or competence. For example, most experts estimate that at least five percent of physicians are seriously incompetent, or impaired by alcoholism, drug addiction, and other major disabilities. In the early 1980s this percentage constituted 22,500 doctors. Yet in 1981 the number of disciplinary actions against physicians nationwide had sharply risen to 568, a rate of 0.14 percent. In 1986 there were a total of 2302 disciplinary actions of all types, including 458 license revocations.

In a few states, this is beginning to change. Every major study of malpractice and quality over the past twenty years — such as the HEW Secretary's Commission on Medical Malpractice (1972) and a study by the U.S. General Accounting Office in 1986 — has deplored the pathetic legal and organizational weaknesses of the state licensing boards and has strongly recommended change. A number of states have begun to take action. In 1988, Florida established in the Department of Professional Regulation a new "Division of Medical Quality Assurance," headed by a new deputy assistant secretary. The function of this new division is clearly to professionalize the work of regulating the medical profession; to take it out of the exclusive hands of the practitioners and "concentrate sufficient resources and efforts . . . as are necessary to meet the challenge of identifying those physicians who are not providing adequate medical care in order to take forceful corrective measures. . . ." 1988 Fla. Sess. Law Serv., Ch. 88-1, §2 (West), amending Fla. Stat. §20.30(c). As discussed above, the 1988 Florida law enacted and reinforced numerous requirements that hospitals closely monitor their medical staffs under the supervision of the new Division, and report to the Division all major incidents of substandard care.

On the other hand, the results of *not* breaking with the passive tradition are clear. In October 1987 the New Jersey State Commission on Investigation — an independent investigative agency of state government — released a devastating report on impaired and incompetent physicians. Its case studies included the story of a hospital chief executive officer who attempted, in May 1985, to report to the state medical licensing board that a cardiologist on his hospital's staff had engaged in "an appalling litany of sexual indignities inflicted on anesthetized patients." The CEO was referred to a private medical society counseling service for impaired physicians, and no one at that service, at the hospital, or at the licensing agency took effective responsibility for investigation or discipline. The doctor was still practicing in December 1985, despite what the Report terms the "obvious threat to patients." Cf. O'Kane v. Board of Registered Nursing, Board of Quality Assurance, No. 19616 (3d App. Dist. Cal., Jan. 27, 1981) (can medical and nursing licensure boards discipline practitioners for failing to report physician who commits sexual indignities on unconscious patients?), discussed in Comment, The Impaired Physician: An Old Problem Creates the Need for New Legislation, 26 St. Louis U.L.J. 727, 743-746 (1982) (advocating mandatory reporting laws, liability for nonreporting, and doctor-patient privilege for treatment for impaired providers). See also Copithorne v. Framingham Union Hospital, 401 Mass. 860, 520 N.E.2d 139 (1988) (hospital may be held liable for damages to sexually assaulted patient for negligently continuing physician's staff privileges after receiving actual notice of prior incidents in which physician sexually assaulted patients); but see Foster v. The Greenville County Medical Society, 367 S.E.2d 468 (S.C. App. 1988) (medical society has no duty to patients allegedly injured by alcoholic physician to investigate or act on prior complaints of doctor's alcoholism); cf. State v. Joint Commission on Accreditation of Hospitals, 470 So. 2d 169 (La. App. 1985) (private national hospital accreditation commission owes no tort or contract duties to renal dialysis patients injured by contaminated water undiscovered in accreditation survey).

Like many states, New Jersey's laws regarding reporting of substandard care and impaired physicians have serious limitations. Mandatory reporting applies only to formal actions by hospitals and insurance companies, leaving much room for evasion via informal settlements. Individual providers are granted immunity against civil damages for voluntary reporting, but that has not been effective; the licensure board believes that it is aware of only a tiny fraction of the estimated 10 to 15 percent of impaired physicians.

If state licensure agencies are to play a serious role in identifying and disciplining substandard physicians, they must be given considerably increased staff, resources, governmental status, legal authority, and independence from practicing doctors. Moreover, state laws must be made consistent with the federal HCQIA, or even stronger, as in Florida, to require reporting of all events that signal significant substandard care.

More audacious still is the proposal in New York to go beyond a complaint or report driven system and require all physicians to be relicensed every nine years. Physicians would be "offered a choice of taking an examination, undergoing a peer review, or having their patient records evaluated." Lambert, New York Panel Urges Re-testing of all Physicians, N.Y. Times, Feb. 26, 1988, at A:1. Specialty re-certification, already required in some specialties every seven to ten years, would also satisfy the licensure requirement. "We would try to weed out the worst ones," said Martin Barell, Chancellor of the State Board of Regents. "This move to review physicians results from what medical critics say is the profession's lack of self-policing and the reluctance of physicians to criticize or act against deficient colleagues." Id.

b. State Licensure Efforts to Enforce Structural Reforms to Enhance Quality

As suggested at the beginning of this section, most licensing programs accept professional and industry norms as adequate and seek to police gross individual deviance from them. Occasionally, however, events highlight the need for questioning the norms themselves.

Note: The Libby Zion Case

The most well known recent story of this sort is that of Libby Zion. Ms. Zion, an 18-year-old college student and daughter of attorney and former journalist Sidney Zion, entered the emergency room of New York Hospital, a well known teaching hospital, late Sunday night, March 4, 1984, on the advice of her family physician, an attending physician at the hospital. She had a fever of 103, was agitated, had recently had a tooth extracted and an ear infection, and was under psychiatric care. She had taken several kinds of drugs over the past few days, including phenelzine (Nardil), an antidepressant. At the hospital she was examined by Dr. Gregg Stone, a second-year resident, and by Dr. Luise Weinstein, a first-year intern, who conferred by telephone with the referring physician, entered a tentative diagnosis of "viral syndrome with hysterical symptoms," and admitted her to the hospital at 2:00 A.M. In addition to ordering blood, urine, and stool cultures, and discontinuance of phenelzine, Dr. Stone ordered 25 mg. of meperidine (Demerol) to be given for agitation and shivering. The Demerol was administered at 3:30 A.M., after which the young doctors left the floor to care for other patients.

When Ms. Zion became more restless and confused, and began thrashing about in bed, the nurses notified Dr. Weinstein, who by phone ordered physical restraints and 1 mg. of haloperidol. Between 4:30 and 6:00 A.M. Ms. Zion showed some improvement, but at 6:30 A.M. she became more agitated and her fever was recorded at 108. Dr. Weinstein was again informed, but before she could reach the room, Ms. Zion went into respiratory arrest and could not be resuscitated. See Asch & Parker, The Libby Zion Case, 318 N. Engl. J. Med. 771 (1988); Farber, Who Killed Libby Zion? Vanity Fair, Dec. 1988, at 190; Margolick, New York Hospital and 4 Doctors Sued in Death of Patient, N.Y. Times, Aug. 27, 1985, at B18:1.

Why did Libby Zion die? After an exhaustive autopsy, a grand jury investigation report, Health Department investigation of the hospital, and a lengthy disciplinary hearing on the conduct of doctors Stone and Weinstein, there is no clear consensus. What is clear is that Demerol should not be given to patients who have been taking Nardil. The 1983 Physician's Desk Reference entry on Nardil warns that "death has been reported in patients who received [Demerol] concomitantly." Dr. Weinstein testified at the disciplinary hearing that she read the entry on Nardil on the night of March 4-5 after learning that Ms. Zion had been taking it, but did not see the sentence warning against the use of Demerol. She did not read the entry on Demerol, which contained an even stronger warning about Nardil, because she felt she understood Demerol thoroughly. See Farber, supra, at 222.

These facts, although tragic, can be easily confined within the individual deviance model of quality of care by focusing on the particular actions and inactions of the four doctors involved that night in Ms. Zion's care (Dr. Sherman, her family physician; Dr. Stone; Dr. Weinstein; and another resident who also examined her). Indeed, Ms. Zion's father, Sidney Zion, has filed a malpractice action against the four doctors alleging that her death was caused by the Demerol prescription and the failure to know that it was contraindicated with Nardil. See Margolick, supra. What is fascinating about the Libby Zion case is how it has also led to a wide-ranging examination of the conditions of practice in large teaching hospitals.

According to Tom Wicker, a columnist for the New York Times and former colleague of Sidney Zion's, Mr. Zion had no intention of quietly settling his malpractice suit, "not only because he wants those responsible for his daughter's death to be *held* responsible but because the case has convinced him that the public needs to know more about the competence and integrity of doctors and hospitals." Wicker, Doctors in the Dock?, N.Y. Times, Dec. 27, 1985, at A17:1. Mr. Zion persuaded Robert Morgenthau, the District Attorney for New York County, to empanel a grand jury to investigate Libby Zion's death. Although the grand jury did not return a criminal indictment, it issued a lengthy report that "was, in effect, an indictment of American graduate medical education." Asch & Parker, supra, at 772. In other words, the grand jury found that Libby Zion's death was not only the probable result of individual errors, but also the result of a flawed system of care. Its report recommended that the state Health Department promulgate regulations embodying the following systemic reforms: staffing of emergency rooms in Level One hospitals (those with 24-hour comprehensive emergency services) with doctors with at least three years of post-graduate training and who are specifically trained to provide emergency care; requiring in-person supervision of residents and interns by doctors who have completed at least a three-year residency program; limiting the consecutive working hours of interns and junior residents; specifying when physical restraints could be used, and standardizing care for patients in restraints; and conducting a feasibility study of whether a computerized system of checking for contraindicated drug combinations should be required in Level One hospitals. See New York Supreme Court, New York County, Report of the Fourth Grand Jury for the April/May Term of 1986, reprinted in N.Y. State Dept. of Health, Final Report of the New York State Ad Hoc Advisory Committee on Emergency Services (October 1987) (hereinafter Final Report), and summarized in Asch & Parker, supra, at 772-773.

The grand jury report was not alone in suggesting the need for systemic reforms. A sociological study of house officers published in 1986 "suggested that long work hours and other intense pressures of clinical training condition physicians to view patients as enemies. . . ." Asch & Parker, supra, at 773, citing T. Mizrahi, Getting Rid of Patients: Contraindications in the Socialization of Physicians (1986). Andrew Stein, the New York City Council President, published a Health Department study suggesting that mistakes were to blame for many New York City hospital deaths. The Committee of Interns and Residents, a union of about 5000 residents working in public hospitals in New York, New Jersey, and the District of Columbia, strongly supported a 16-hour limit on work shifts and other work load restrictions. See Asch & Parker, supra, at 773-774. Not surprisingly, the major media in New York City, including the New York Times, gave unprecedented coverage to these issues and advocated reforms.

In response to these influences, Dr. David Axelrod, the New York State Health Commissioner, appointed an Ad Hoc Advisory Committee on Emergency Care. The Committee endorsed the grand jury's five recommendations, and ultimately recommended, among other items, 12-hour work shift limits in emergency rooms and some limits (including 80 hours per week) in nonemergency work shifts. The Committee's recommendations were incorporated into New York State hospital licensing regulations, effective January 1, 1989. See N.Y. Admin. Code tit.10, §405 (1989).

The new rules will cost money to implement. The New York City Health and Hospital Corporation — the public hospital system — estimated $42 million, compared to a total annual budget of $24 billion. See Daley, Work-Hour Curbs Await Hospitals, N.Y. Times, June 19, 1988, at 22:1 (also reporting that the Health Commissioner announced that he would allow reimbursement rate increases to cover the cost of the new rules). Whether this is perceived as a great deal of money depends on how it compares to overall hospital expenditures and on whether it is perceived as saving money in terms of better care, fewer errors, and lower costs associated with those errors, including treatment and malpractice liability, not to mention the hard-to-quantify longterm benefits of encouraging young doctors not to see their patients as enemies.

The Libby Zion case shows how a particular incident of alleged malpractice can also be perceived as a systemic problem, and how a state licensing agency, under certain political conditions, can be motivated to address it. Another major political condition, of course, is the escalating cost of health care. Indeed, unlike most states, New York's Health Department is deeply involved in hospital rate regulation as well as in quality assurance through hospital and professional licensing. It is perhaps for this reason that New York has recently "begun the first statewide program in the nation to reduce the rate of cesarian births" by asking hospitals "to keep records explaining in detail why each cesarian section was performed, and by convening an expert committee to review cases and establish standards. Kolata, New York Seeks to Reduce Rate of Cesarian Births," N.Y. Times, Jan. 27, 1989, at A1:2. By inventing this creative role for state licensure agencies, the New York Health Department is challenging the dominant model of decentralized, private practitioner control over quality and resource allocation, and articulating, with the support of a significant portion of the medical profession, a version of the social contract model discussed at the beginning of this chapter.

F. Payers as Monitors of Quality of Care: The Ambiguous Wakening of the Sleeping Giant

"The federal and state governments are the largest purchasers of health care in the United States. Through medicare, medicaid, and other government programs, they purchase 53 percent of hospital care, 48 percent of nursing home care, and 29 percent of physician services. Obviously, this considerable purchasing power could have an effect if directed toward improving the quality of health care received by beneficiaries." Jost, The Necessary and Proper Role of Regulation to Assure the Quality of Health Care, 25 Houston L. Rev. 525, 589-590 (1988). The major nongovernmental health insurers — Blue Cross, Blue Shield, and large commercial companies — also have a significant market share and potentially large influence on quality. Payers can enforce quality-based standards regarding training, institutional resources, and performance through three main devices: (1) excluding providers from program participation and hence from any reimbursement; (2) denying reimbursement for particular services because they fail to meet quality criteria; and (3) imposing other sanctions, such as monetary or monitoring penalties, as allowed by regulation or contract.

In addition, payers can use positive incentives, such as higher prices or bonus payments for providers who satisfy specified quality criteria, and some such efforts have recently begun. See Iglehart, Competition and the Pursuit of Quality: A Conversation with Walter McClure, Health Affairs at 79 (Spring 1988); Carlsen, HMOs try new doctor-incentive: quality-care bonuses, HealthWeek, Aug. 8, 1988, at 22, col.1.

Given the medical profession's long history of hostility to external (or, for that matter, serious internal) review, it is not surprising that for many years, payers remained sleeping giants on the issue of quality. Indeed, one of the primary purposes of the formation of Blue Cross and Blue Shield in the 1930s and 1940s was to foreclose other financing options (governmental, corporate, or labor), and to insist that all licensed physicians and hospitals were to be reimbursed without serious quality review. See S. Law, Blue Cross: What Went Wrong? (2nd ed. 1976). As discussed below, the Medicare and Medicaid programs took a similarly passive approach toward quality at their inception in 1965.

In the 1970s and 1980s, the major governmental institutions involved in financing and regulating health care — Congress and the Health Care Financing Administration (HCFA), and state legislatures and health departments — became much more actively involved in quality of care, although often frustrated by bureaucratic inertia and political stalemate. There were two major reasons for this shift. First, the longstanding pattern of unsafe conditions and substandard care in nursing homes resulted in a series of tragic fires and dramatic financial scandals that, together with sharply escalating expenditures, made the issue of governmental quality regulation difficult to ignore. A second, related reason was the huge increase in overall expenditures for all types of health care, discussed in detail in Chapters 2 and 3. Efforts to contain these costs by both governmental and nongovernmental payers have led to major changes in methods of reimbursement and utilization review, which in turn have raised new concerns about quality of care. The awakening of the sleeping power of payers to affect quality of care has thus been ambiguous, because of the payers' double goals: to contain costs while, at least in theory, not compromising quality of care.

This section first examines the long struggle that has taken place in Congress, the executive branch, and the courts, with the active participation of the nursing home industry and patient advocates, about the role of the federal financing agency (HCFA) and the state licensing agencies regarding nursing home quality of care. It then considers a similarly complex relationship between HCFA and the JCAHO regarding quality standards for hospitals. Finally, this section examines the emerging quality regulation role of Peer Review Organizations (PROs), HCFA's agents in monitoring both quality and appropriateness of care.

This section, 5(F), focuses on two major legal questions: (1) the federal financing agency's own legal responsibility and authority to monitor quality of care, and the extent to which it can delegate that function to other organizations; and (2) the legal structure and limits of one of HCFA's major quality enforcement tools, the PRO program. However, as noted above, both governmental and nongovernmental payers' policies and actions have also been devoted to a different goal: reducing the costs of care or at least the expenditures by each particular payer. The final section of this chapter, 5(G), focuses on one of the most urgent and important frontier issues in health law: the legality of cost containment efforts that may threaten quality of care.

1. DECIDING WHOM TO REIMBURSE: MEDICARE AND MEDICAID CERTIFICATION

a. Federal Financing and Nursing Home Quality of Care

Note: The Structure of Nursing Home Regulation

There are about 15,000 nursing homes in the United States, with a total of about 1.5 million beds, that are certified to be reimbursed by the Medicare and/or Medicaid programs. They are classified into two types by federal regulations: skilled nursing facilities (SNFs), which are required to be staffed and equipped to provide skilled nursing care, and intermediate care facilities (ICFs), which are supposed to serve residents requiring less nursing and more personal service care. About 70 percent of the certified homes are operated on a for-profit basis, 22 percent by nonprofit organizations, and 8 percent by government. Private insurance for longterm care is rare and expensive. Low income patients may enter nursing homes already eligible for Medicaid, which reimburses the nursing home for their care. Many other patients enter on a self-pay basis and exhaust their resources in one or two years, thereby "spending down" to Medicaid eligibility. Medicare pays for some long-term care that occurs after a hospitalization.

The financing and regulation of the nursing home industry has always been heavily affected by a complex mixture of federal and state authority. State licensing of nursing homes was stimulated in the 1950s by requirements in the federal Social Security and Hill-Burton statutes that made federal funds contingent on the existence of state licensure standards. Not surprisingly, these standards were modeled on hospital licensure and JCAH standards, which focused on such structural features as physical plant and the numbers and type of staff. After 1965, nursing homes also had to be "certified" as satisfying federal "Conditions of Participation" in order to be reimbursed by Medicare and later by Medicaid. These standards too followed the hospital/JCAH model and focused on the physical and staffing structure of facilities and the existence of written policies. See Butler, Assuring the Quality of Care and Life in Nursing Homes: The Dilemma of Enforcement, 57

N.C.L. Rev. 1317, 1319-1325 (1979); B. Vladeck, Unloving Care: The Nursing Home Tragedy 147-157 (1980). Moreover, the federal government contracts with state agencies — typically state health departments who also conduct state licensure surveys — to determine compliance by individual facilities with the federal Conditions of Participation and other features of the federally regulated state medicaid plan.

Despite page after page of government regulations regulating such important matters as minimum square footage per bed and maximum hours between meals, many studies of nursing home care, particularly in the 1970s, identified "both grossly inadequate care and abuse of residents." Institute of Medicine, Improving the Quality of Care in Nursing Homes 3 (1986). The following case, filed in 1975 but not tried until 1982, focused blame for this situation on the federal government's failure to inform itself, through state agency surveys, of the actual conditions in nursing homes that were most relevant to patient care.

Estate of Smith v. Heckler

747 F.2d 583 (10th Cir. 1984)

McKay, Circuit Judge.

Plaintiffs, seeking relief under 42 U.S.C. §1983 (1982), brought this class action on behalf of medicaid recipients residing in nursing homes in Colorado. They alleged that the Secretary of Health and Human Services (Secretary) has a statutory duty under Title XIX of the Social Security Act, 42 U.S.C. §§1396-1396n (1982), commonly known as the Medicaid Act, to develop and implement a system of nursing home review and enforcement designed to ensure that medicaid recipients residing in medicaid certified nursing homes actually receive the optimal medical and psychosocial care that they are entitled to under the Act. The plaintiffs contended that the enforcement system developed by the Secretary is "facility oriented," not "patient oriented" and thereby fails to meet the statutory mandate. . . .

[The plaintiffs] presented evidence of the lack of adequate medical care and of the widespread knowledge that care is inadequate. Indeed, the district court concluded that care and life in some nursing homes is so bad that the homes "could be characterized as orphanages for the aged." . . .

To receive [federal] funding under the Medicaid Act, a state must submit to . . . and have approved by the Secretary a plan for medical assistance which meets the requirements of 42 U.S.C. §1396a(a). . . .

[Among those requirements,] the state agency is responsible for establishing and maintaining health standards for institutions where the recipients of the medical assistance under the plan receive care or services. The plan must include descriptions of the standards and methods the state will use to assure that medical or remedial care services provided to the recipients "are of high quality." . . .

[Federal law sets out numerous quality of care topics that the state agency must address through federally regulated but state defined standards and inspections. In addition to these state plan requirements, set out in the statute,] [t]he key requirement for purposes of this lawsuit is that a skilled nursing facility must meet "such other conditions relating to the health and safety of individuals who are furnished services in such institution or relating to the physical facilities thereof as the Secretary may find necessary. . . ." §1395x(j)(15). . . .

While the state has the initial responsibility for determining whether institutions are meeting the conditions of participation [in the Medicaid program], §1396a(a)(33)(B) gives the Secretary the authority to "look behind" the state's determination of facility compliance, and make an independent and binding determination of whether institutions meet the requirements for participation in the state Medicaid plan. Thus, the state is responsible for conducting the review of facilities to determine whether they comply with the state plan. In conducting the review, however, the states must use federal standards, forms, methods, and procedures. 42 C.F.R. §431.610(f)(1) (1983). From 1972 through 1980, Congress required the Secretary to reimburse the states for all necessary costs of inspecting longterm care facilities. In 1980, Congress reduced the rate of reimbursement to 75 percent of such costs.

The Secretary "shall approve" any plan which fulfills the requirements of §1396a(a). . . . If after approving a state plan, the Secretary determines that the plan has been so changed that it no longer complies with §1396a(a), or that it complies on paper but not in its actual administration, the Secretary is required to terminate payments to the state, effectively disapproving the plan.

Congress gave the Secretary a general mandate to promulgate rules and regulations necessary to the efficient administration of the functions with which the Secretary is charged by the Act. 42 U.S.C. §1302 (1982). Pursuant to this mandate the Secretary has promulgated standards for the care to be provided by [nursing homes] . . . [and] a procedure for determining whether state plans comply with the standards set out in the regulations. This enforcement mechanism is known as the "survey/certification" inspection system. Under this system, the states conduct reviews of nursing homes. . . . The Secretary then determines, on the basis of the survey results, whether the nursing home surveyed is eligible for certification and, thus, eligible for Medicaid funds. The states must use federal standards, forms, methods, and procedures in conducting the survey. . . .

Plaintiffs contend that the statutory requirements regarding the content of state plans create a correlative entitlement for Medicaid recipients to quality care. They argue that the Secretary has an enforcement obligation to insure compliance with the approved state plan. More specifically, plaintiffs argue that the Secretary has a statutory duty to develop an enforcement system whereby to receive medicaid funds states would be forced to use a patient care management system. Such a system would ensure, through the review process of §1396a(a)(33), that Medicaid recipients residing in nursing homes certified for Medicaid participation are "actually, continuously receiving their Medicaid entitlements to optimal medical and psychosocial care in a safe, sanitary, rehabilitatively supportive, accessible, personalized environment and in a context of full civil liberties as a condition of such facilities' receipt of Federal and State financial reimbursement from the Medicaid Program."

The plaintiffs do not challenge the substantive medical standards, or "conditions of participation," which have been adopted by the Secretary and which states must satisfy to have their plans approved. See 42 C.F.R. §405.1101-.1137. Rather, plaintiffs challenge the enforcement mechanism the Secretary has established. The plaintiffs contend that the federal forms, form SSA-1569 in particular, which states are required to use, evaluate only the physical facilities and theoretical capability to render quality care. They claim that the surveys assess the care provided almost totally on the basis of the records, documentation, and written policies of the facility being reviewed. Further, out of the 541 questions contained in the Secretary's form SSA-1569, which must be answered by state survey and certification inspection teams, only 30 are "even marginally related to patient care or might require any patient observation. . . ." Plaintiffs contend that the enforcement mechanism's focus on the facility, rather than on the care actually provided in the facility, results only in "paper compliance" with the substantive standards of the Act. Thus, plaintiffs contend, the Secretary has violated her statutory duty to assure that federal Medicaid monies are paid only to facilities which meet the substantive standards of the Act — facilities which actually provide high quality medical, rehabilitative and psychosocial care to resident Medicaid recipients. . . .

After hearing the evidence, the district court found the type of patient care management system advocated by plaintiffs clearly feasible. . . . However, the court concluded that the failure to implement and require the use of a "patient oriented" system is not a violation of the Secretary's statutory duty. The essence of the district court's holding was that the State of Colorado, not the federal government, is responsible for developing and enforcing standards which would assure high quality care in nursing homes and, thus, the State of Colorado, not the federal government, should have been the defendant in this case. [557 F. Supp. at 295-297]

[The District Court based its conclusion on the Medicaid statute's allocation to the state of responsibility for defining quality standards and methods of assuring compliance, including compliance with the federally defined conditions of participation, the state's authority to license nursing homes and the various professions involved in running them, and the lack of mandatory language in the federal statute requiring the Secretary to override state decisions or to adopt particular survey techniques. In this vein, the district court concluded that the "look behind" provision of §1396a(a)(33)(B), authorizing the Secretary to reject a survey/certification performed by the state agency and substitute her own independent and binding determination, is "nothing more than permitted authority to intervene for the purpose of protecting the public funds used to reimburse the state."]

(1) After carefully reviewing the statutory scheme of the Medicaid Act, the legislative history, and the district court's opinion, we conclude that the district court improperly defined the Secretary's duty under the statute. The federal government has more than a passive role in handing out money to the states. The district court erred in finding that the burden of enforcing the substantive provisions of the Medicaid Act is on the states. The Secretary of Health and Human Services has a duty to establish a system to adequately inform herself as to whether the facilities receiving federal money are satisfying the requirements of the Act. These requirements include providing high quality patient care. This duty to be adequately informed is not only a duty to be informed at the time a facility is originally certified, but is a duty of continued supervision.

Nothing in the Medicaid Act indicates that Congress intended the physical facilities to be the end product. Rather, the purpose of the Act is to provide medical assistance and rehabilitative services. The Act repeatedly focuses on the care to be provided, with facilities being only part of that care. . . .

While the district court correctly noted that it is the state which develops specific standards and actually conducts the inspection, there is nothing in the Act to indicate that the state function relieves the Secretary of all responsibility to ensure that the purposes of the Act are being accomplished. The Secretary, not the states, determines which facilities are eligible for federal funds. . . .

It would be anomalous to hold that the Secretary has a duty to determine whether a state plan meets the standards of the Act while holding that the Secretary can certify facilities without informing herself as to whether the facilities actually perform the functions required by the state plan. The Secretary has a duty to ensure more than paper compliance. The federal responsibility is particularly evident in the "look behind" provision. 42 U.S.C. §1396a(a)(33)(B) (1982). We do not read the Secretary's "look behind" authority as being "nothing more than permitted authority . . . ," 557 F. Supp. [at] 296, as the district court found. Rather, we find that the purpose of that section is to assure that compliance is not merely facial, but substantive. . . .

Having determined that the purpose and the focus of the Act is to provide high quality medical care, we conclude that by promulgating a facility oriented enforcement system the Secretary has failed to follow that focus and such failure is arbitrary and capricious. . . .

Notes and Questions

(1) When *Estate of Smith* was originally filed in 1975, the defendants included the Colorado departments of health and social services, as well as the Secretary of HEW and a particular Colorado nursing home. In 1978, the plaintiffs — a class comprising all Medicaid recipients residing in the named nursing home — stipulated to a dismissal of the claims against the state defendants, in return for which the state parties agreed to file their own complaint against HEW "seeking a redesign of the federal Medicaid nursing home enforcement system so that the system is premised on resident assessment." In re Estate of Smith, 557 F. Supp. 289, 291 (D. Colo. 1983).

In ruling against the state as well as the individual plaintiffs, the District Court stated, in addition to the statutory arguments noted above, that "Colorado officials understand that the state can cause improvement in the conditions in the nursing homes which the state licenses and regulates. It is also apparent that what is lacking is the resolve to dedicate the necessary resources to this task. It would appear easier to seek a declaration of subservience to the national government to avoid the expenditure of state funds, as well as the responsibility for lack of enforcement. In short, to substitute feudalism for federalism." Id. at 298.

Assume that the Secretary of HHS (formerly HEW) decides to appeal the Tenth Circuit's decision to the United States Supreme Court, and writes a brief relying heavily on this argument. As attorney for the state, how would you respond? Would your answer be any different if you were attorney for the nursing home residents?

(2) The statutory and administrative pattern so evident in *Estate of Smith* characterizes much health care reform legislation: the statement in general terms of apparently serious legal standards to protect patients or other politically weak social interests and then the apparent delegation of further definition and enforcement of those standards to the discretion of federal and state agencies, with no clear patient remedies for nonenforcement. Faced with a variety of pressures against enforcement — lack of funding and resources, lack of expertise, the political power and cultural prestige of the regulated industry or profession, and the undeniable difficulty of defining and achieving quality of care, particularly in nursing homes, the agencies will often fail to "operationalize" the pro-patient statutory norms in exactly the way revealed in *Estate of Smith*. See Rosenblatt, Health Care Reform and Administrative Law: A Structural Approach, 88 Yale L.J. 243, 247-250 and passim (1978) (discussing Hill-Burton Act, Medicaid coverage and recipient participation provisions, and the Health Planning Act); Butler, supra, at 1327-1330. "The courts then face a choice of either legitimizing the gap between general statutory goals and specific agency practices or attempting to bring agency and provider performance into line with what appears to be national health policy. Such decisions are made enormously difficult by the

ambiguity of the congressional mandate: was Congress "serious" about the statute's general substantive goals, or was its "real" intent better expressed in its silences and omissions, which, according to the agencies, justify passivity and nonenforcement." Rosenblatt, supra, at 250.

Judges approaching these cases from a "social contract" model tend to try to enforce the general statutory norms, as did the Tenth Circuit in *Estate of Smith,* while judges relying on models that favor professional, industry, and agency discretion — such as the district court in *Estate of Smith* — refuse to find enforceable patient rights unless they are extremely clearly stated in mandatory statutory terms. From the mid-1960s to the mid-1970s, the dominant judicial trend in many doctrinal contexts — for instance, standing, private rights of action, and administrative law — was toward enforcement of pro-patient statutory norms. See Rosenblatt, supra, at 254-264 and passim. Since then, however, the trend in the federal courts had swung sharply the other way, with even statutory provisions labeled "patients' bill of rights" being interpreted as nonenforceable. See Pennhurst State School and Hospital v. Halderman, 451 U.S. 1 (1981).

(3) For an example of this alternative judicial trend, consider Stewart v. Bernstein, 769 F.2d 1088 (5th Cir. 1985). Stella Stewart was involuntarily transferred from a nursing home on three days notice, and without alternative arrangements to meet her needs, in violation of, inter alia, a federal regulation requiring consultation with the resident and family at least five days before discharge and use of casework or other services to "insure that adequate arrangements are made to meet the resident's needs through other resources," 42 C.F.R. §405.307(b) (1987), and a provision titled "Residents' bill of rights," 42 C.F.R. §442.311 (1987). But the Fifth Circuit dismissed Stewart's federal claim for damages and declaratory and injunctive relief against the nursing home on the grounds that Congress had not created a federal private right action against nursing homes to enforce the standards in the Medicaid Act; those standards were not, in effect, rights enforceable by individuals, but rather standards to be enforced by the federal and state agencies. Stewart's claim against the state agency, for failing to have policies and procedures to monitor and enforce compliance with the federal standards, was dismissed on several grounds: that the state was not responsible for an individual nursing home's violation of the regulations and that Stevens lacked standing because she could not show that ordering the state to revise its regulatory process would actually protect her against similar violations by individual homes in the future. Expressing a view similar to that of the district court in *Estate of Smith,* the Fifth Circuit stated that Stevens' remedies lay in state law derived from licensing standards and from the nursing home's contract with the state agency. For judicial recognition of state-law causes of action to enforce federal regulatory standards incorporated into nursing home contracts, see, for instance, Fuzie v. Manor Care, Inc., 461 F. Supp. 689 (N.D. Ohio 1977). Some state statutes and/or courts allow private rights

of action to enforce state regulatory standards. See, for instance, Stiffelman v. Abrams, 655 S.W.2d 522 (Mo. 1983); see generally S. Johnson, N. Terry & M. Wolff, Nursing Homes and the Law: State Regulation and Private Litigation §§1-21 to 1-28 (1985).

(4) The *Estate of Smith* litigation must also be seen against the background of a long series of struggles in the 1970s and 1980s between the usually Democratic majority in Congress and the usually Republican Presidency over health policy in general and nursing home policy in particular. Put simply, Congressional Democrats such as Senator Frank Moss were assiduous in exposing substandard conditions in nursing homes and pressing for greater federal and state regulation to protect patients, while Republican Administrations, notably those of Nixon and Reagan, resisted such efforts and, at the urging of the nursing home industry, wanted to reduce the extent of federal regulation. See B. Vladeck, supra, at 59-67; Institute of Medicine, supra, at 245-249. Indeed, in direct response to what it apparently regarded as the district court's mistaken interpretation of the statute in *Estate of Smith,* Congress amended the Medicaid Act to clearly impose on the Secretary of HHS a duty to assure that Medicaid patients in nursing homes receive high quality care. See Tax Reform Act of 1984, Pub. L. No. 98-369 (1984), discussed at 747 F.2d at 590 n.3.

(5) In response to the Tenth Circuit's opinion in *Estate of Smith,* HHS/HCFA revised the survey process in patient-oriented terms, using a system known as PaCS (for Patient Care and Services). While the Institute of Medicine Report termed PaCS "a significant improvement over the traditional survey process," it noted that several major problems remained unresolved by HCFA, including failure to revise the substantive standards that the survey was supposed to enforce, and failure to develop guidelines and databases to make the survey process truly reliable. Institute of Medicine, supra, at 130-132.

(6) Faced with a 1982 HCFA proposal to weaken federal regulation of nursing homes, Congress ordered HCFA to defer the proposed changes until a special committee of the Institute of Medicine (IOM) could study the problem of nursing home quality and make recommendations. The IOM study, published in 1986, in turn became the basis for the nursing home provisions of the Omnibus Budget Reconciliation Act of 1987, Pub.L. No. 100-203, §§4201-18. In this legislation Congress specified detailed requirements for nurse staffing, training, and data relating to quality of care, specified a redesigned, patient-oriented survey process, and required the HHS to conduct on site validation of the state surveys for at least 5 percent of the facilities surveyed by the states each year. See House Energy and Commerce Committee, Omnibus Budget Reconciliation Act of 1987, Jan. 5, 1988, reprinted in CCH Medicare-Medicaid Guide ¶36,784. HHS/HCFA began issuing new final rules regarding nursing home Conditions of Participation in February 1989, see 54 Fed. Reg. 5316 (2/2/89), albeit at a slower rate than demanded

by timetables set forth in the new legislation. See Tolchin, New Rules Issued on Patients' Care in Nursing Homes, N.Y. Times, Jan. 31, 1989, at A1:4.

b. Medicare Conditions of Participation for Hospitals

Like nursing homes, hospitals are supposed to meet at least minimum standards of quality, embodied in federal "Conditions of Participation," in order to participate in and be reimbursed under the Medicare program. Since Medicare is an exclusively federal program, the problems of divided federal/state authority that arose with respect to Medicaid and nursing homes should not in theory exist. However, the hospital industry was sufficiently powerful to create another problem of divided authority: between HHS and the industry's own private standard setting organization, the JCAHO. Moreover, for hospitals not accredited by the JCAHO, HHS has contracted with state health departments to survey compliance with federal standards, thereby creating some of the same problems examined in *Estate of Smith.*

In the original 1965 Medicare Act, the federal conditions of participation were modeled on, and were not permitted to be higher than, the structure-focused "hospital model" embodied in the JCAHO accreditation standards. Moreover, any institution accredited by the JCAHO was automatically and conclusively presumed to satisfy the statutory requirements, except for the utilization review standard which was not then included in the JCAHO process. But as the selection from Macdonald et al. in Section C(6) supra suggests, the JCAHO standards are not designed to focus on the realities of patient care (although they are now undergoing revision to become outcome-oriented by the early 1990s). Like the standards and survey process at issue in *Estate of Smith,* they focus on the institution's "capacity" for adequate care, rather than on whether it is actually being delivered. Vaguely worded standards, advance notification of inspections, and refusal to release any findings to the public further weaken the JCAHO as a regulatory agency. Indeed, in October 1988 the Wall St. Journal described several hospitals with long histories of substandard, life-endangering care that had been re-accredited by the JCAHO and whose problems had come to light only when patients or staff had complained to governmental agencies. See Bogdanich, Prized by Hospitals, Accreditation Hides Perils Patients Face, Wall St. J., Oct. 12, 1988, at 1:6.

The major legal issue raised with respect to the JCAHO regulatory role has been whether Congress has unconstitutionally delegated governmental authority to the private JCAHO. Cases brought by elderly patients in the early 1970s challenged continued accreditation and hence certification of grossly inadequate public hospitals. Although these cases never went to trial, Congress responded in 1972 to the charges of unconstitutionality and inadequacy by increasing the Secretary's authority in several respects, notably by requiring the Secretary to survey (typically through state agencies) three percent of the JCAH-accredited hospitals to validate compliance with the Conditions of Participation. Unfortunately, this formal expansion of the Secretary's power has not led to significant improvements; a 1979 GAO Report remained highly critical of the entire process and found the validation surveys to be largely meaningless because the JCAH and state bureaucracies could not agree on standards or procedures. At the same time, the Secretary's formal power has served to insulate the JCAHO's regulatory role from legal challenge. See Cospito v. Heckler, 742 F.2d 72, 87-89 (3rd Cir. 1984) (upholding JCAH revocation of the accreditation of Trenton Psychiatric Hospital, and automatic HEW termination of the health care and Social Security benefits of the patients, even though they were involuntarily committed and not free, under state law, to find alternative sources of care, on the grounds that the Medicare statute in theory allows HEW to make its own determination of whether the hospital should be permitted to participate in Medicare and hence whether the patients would receive their benefits). But see id. at 91 (pointing out that HEW had never in fact exercised its (debatable) independent authority, and arguing that "courts should not permit Congress to delegate to private bodies, that are not required by statute to listen to affected parties in making their regulations, and whose regulations are not subject to review under . . . any . . . federal or state statute, the right to take actions in areas of traditional public law that seriously affect individuals' rights, especially those of perhaps the most powerless group in this nation: the elderly handicapped. . . .") (Becker, J., dissenting).

In June 1986, HCFA published the first substantial revision in 20 years of the Conditions of Participation. See 51 Fed. Reg. 22010 (June 17, 1986), amending 42 C.F.R. Part 482. Major changes included new requirements that hospitals establish hospital-wide quality assurance programs that would include discharge planning and document remedial actions and their outcomes. Id. at 22015-16, 42 C.F.R. sec. 482.21. At the same time, following the Reagan Administration's general preference for deregulation, HCFA deleted many detailed requirements regarding staff credentials and organizational structure, replacing them with general language about "expected outcomes." Id. at 22011. Some of these changes were undoubtedly appropriate; many of the detailed organizational requirements derived from the discredited JCAHO tradition of formal compliance with organizational norms. On the other hand, eliminating staff credential requirements raised the possibility of hospitals attempting to fulfill complex tasks (such as discharge planning) with less than fully qualified personnel.

2. PEER REVIEW ORGANIZATIONS (PROs): THE PAYER'S DOCTOR-AGENTS AS REGULATORS OF QUALITY OF CARE

Peer Review Organizations (PROs), established by federal statute in 1982, are nonprofit corporations staffed by physicians and nurses whose function is to review the medical necessity, quality, and appropriate institutional level of care provided under the Medicare program. Although in formal terms PROs are not governmental agencies, they are entirely creatures of federal statutes, regulations, and guidelines, and of the detailed contracts between each PRO and the federal Health Care Financing Administration (HCFA). In their initial operation, PROs focused primarily on saving Medicare money by deterring unnecessary hospitalization and by policing the DRG reimbursement system. After 1985, however, in response to Congressional and consumer concern about the negative impact of DRG reimbursement on quality of care, PROs shifted more of their attention to quality issues. These recent developments have taken place against a complex historical background; PROs represent the third phase of a long federal effort to induce doctors, or at least a significant number of them, to act as agents of the payer (Medicare) to achieve cost containment and quality goals.

a. Historical Background, Composition, and Function of PROs

As Chapters 2 and 3 make plain, Medicare's original open-ended, cost-based and procedure-based reimbursement system provided enormous financial incentives to doctors and hospitals to hospitalize patients and to keep them in the hospital as long as possible. Recognizing this danger at least in theory, Congress insisted on going beyond the hospital industry's own quality standards in one respect: requiring all hospitals, as a condition of participation in Medicare, to establish "utilization review" (UR) committees composed of physicians. These committees were supposed to review the medical necessity of hospitalization, length of stay, and professional services on a retrospective basis for a sample of short-stay cases, and on a concurrent basis (that is, while services were still being delivered) for all hospital stays of "extended duration." See 42 U.S.C. §§1395x(k)(1), (3); S. Law, Blue Cross: What Went Wrong? 118-120 (2d ed. 1976); J. Feder, Medicare: The Politics of Federal Hospital Insurance 33 (1977). The UR committees were required to consult with the treating physician regarding the necessity of extended stays, but if they disagreed with him, they were required to notify the doctor, the hospital, and the patient that continued hospitalization was no longer necessary. Medicare payments could be made for only four days after such notice was given, to give the patient time to make alternative arrangements for care. See S. Law, supra, at 119-120.

While some aspects of the UR program related to quality of care, the main thrust of the effort was to save money by denying payment for unnecessary hospitalization. When, not surprisingly, in-hospital committees failed to perform this function, HEW quietly authorized Blue Cross, which functioned as the fiscal intermediary for Medicare, to deny payment retrospectively for services it deemed "custodial" (rather than skilled nursing) care. See S. Law, supra, at 121-130 (analyzing in detail the role of Blue Cross in carrying out Medicare UR from 1968-1972). Thus the term "utilization review" became associated with cost containment and denial of payment by the payer's agent on the basis of (often undisclosed) criteria of "necessity," while "quality assurance" (QA) or "medical audit" (MA) remained a more ad hoc and educational function, itself often without clear standards or enforcement, under physician and hospital control.

Clearly dissatisfied with the performance of the UR program, Congress amended the Social Security Act of 1972 to establish Professional Standards Review Organizations (PSROs). The explicit purpose of this new program was to transfer the UR function from Blue Cross to regional (that is, multicounty) organizations controlled by state and local medical societies, who were supposed to establish various standards to be used by revived in-hospital UR committees now operating under PSRO surveillance, and by the PSROs themselves. See J. Feder, supra, at 43-45. Although PSROs were clearly supposed to perform UR functions, the program attempted to induce physician participation and compliance by emphasizing quality assurance and educational goals. See id.; Havighurst & Blumstein, Coping with Quality/Cost Trade-offs: The Role of PSROs, 70 N.W.U.L. Rev. 6, 38-45 (1975).

Given the PSROs' multiple and inconsistent functions, their local character, and their lack of a clear national mandate and quantifiable goals, it is not surprising that Havighurst and Blumstein's 1975 prediction was largely vindicated: the PSROs were generally unable to "achieve more than minor improvements over 'business as usual.'" Id. at 68. Congress reacted in 1982 by transforming PSROs into Peer Review Organizations (PROs). These new organizations have some of the same programmatic functions as the PSROs: to determine whether services paid for by Medicare are reasonable and medically necessary, whether the quality of such services meets professionally recognized standards of care, and whether inpatient services could have been provided at a more economical level of care. See Social Security Act §1154(a), 42 U.S.C. §1320c-3(a). Like the PSROs, the PROs and persons relying on their standards and decisions are granted civil immunity for actions taken with due care. See 42 U.S.C. §1320c-6. Moreover, 43 of the 54 new PROs are former PSROs for all or part of the area served. However, the new program differs from the old in several major respects. First, the geographic areas for each PRO are much larger, now typically covering an entire state rather than several counties. Second, the degree of required physician sponsorship or support is much lower, thereby weakening the influence of the profession as a whole. Third, the contracts between HHS and the nongovernmental PROs contain highly specific and quantified objectives. Fourth, the PRO law explicitly requires health care practitioners and institutions to provide care that meets standards of necessity, quality, and efficiency, and grants the PROs and the Secretary of HHS important new powers to enforce these provisions. See Social Security Act §1156, 42 U.S.C. §1320c-5.

Finally, and most importantly, the mission of the PROs was heavily affected by the adoption of Medicare's prospective payment system (PPS), based on Diagnosis Related Groups (DRGs), in 1983. To the original 1982 PRO mandate Congress added several new functions in the nature of what might be termed "DRG police." First, PROs are to validate the diagnostic and procedural information that is used to determine a patient's DRG, and hence the hospital's reimbursement; without such validation, hospitals could inflate the seriousness of a patient's condition, a process colloquially known as "DRG creep." Second, PROs are to guard against "churning" — multiple discharges and admissions of the same patient — by reviewing the appropriateness of admissions and discharges. Third, PROs are to review the appropriateness of care for which outlier payments are sought, to counteract the hospital's financial incentive to extend the stay of difficult cases into the outlier zone. Fourth, PROs now have a general mandate to review "the completeness, adequacy, and quality of care provided," to guard against the general financial incentive provided by DRGs to reduce the resources devoted to patient care. See Social Security Act 42 U.S.C. §1395cc(a)(1)(F)(i).

b. The PRO Sanction Process

Note: The Sources of PRO Authority to Regulate Quality of Care

The PROs' substantive authority to review the quality of care reimbursed by Medicare and their enforcement or sanctioning powers, derive from three separate statutory provisions. First, under §1154 of the Social Security Act, 42 U.S.C. 1320c-3, PROs are to review, in addition to the reasonableness and medical necessity of services, §1154(a)(1)(A), and the appropriate level of care (such as hospital or nursing home), §1154(a)(1)(C), whether "the quality of such services meets professionally recognized standards of care." Section 1154(a)(1)(B). As originally enacted in 1982, the legislation authorized PROs to deny Medicare payment for services found to be in violation of Sections (A) and (C), but contained no such authorization to deny payment for services found to be of substandard quality under Section (B). Effective April, 1986, however, Congress amended the statute to authorize PROs to deny payment on quality grounds "on the basis of criteria which are consistent with guidelines established by the Secretary [of HHS]." Section 9403 of the Consolidated Omnibus Budget Reconciliation Act of 1985, Pub. L. 99-272, amending Social Security Act sec.1154(a)(2).

In January 1989, HCFA issued proposed rules embodying such guidelines for inpatient hospital care, under which the PROs are to develop written criteria to assess substandard quality with respect to dozens of clinically significant matters. See 54 Fed. Reg. 1956 (1/18/89). For example, for hospital admissions for acute medical conditions, the PROs are to develop criteria to evaluate the adequacy of the initial assessment of respiratory function, cardiac function, neurologic function, and so forth; the determination of proper drug doses, and consideration of drug interactions. Medicare payment will be denied where substandard care results in "an actual, significant, adverse effect on the beneficiary," that is, unnecessarily prolonged treatment, medical complications, readmission to the hospital, impairment, disability, or death, or presents "an imminent danger to the health, safety, or well being of the beneficiary." Care involving less serious breaches of quality standards will still be paid for, but intervention will be pursued through other procedures, such as education, intensified review, and, if appropriate, sanctions. (These interventions may also be pursued in addition to denial of payment.) Id. at 1958. Also of great significance, the PRO will notify the beneficiary in writing if Medicare payment has been denied on quality grounds. Finally, the statute prohibits providers from charging Medicare beneficiaries for services denied reimbursement on quality grounds.

Any beneficiary or provider dissatisfied with a PRO denial of payment under §1154 may request reconsideration by the PRO. In addition, beneficiaries (but not providers) have a right to a hearing before an administrative law judge (ALJ) of the Social Security Administration's Office of Hearings and Appeals, if the matter in controversy is $200 or more, and to judicial review of the ALJ's decision if the matter in controversy is $2000 or more. Social Security Act §1155, 42 U.S.C. §1320c-4.

Second, as noted above, PROs have a specific mandate under Social Security Act §1866 to detect and punish what HHS manuals refer to as "circumvention of PPS and substandard quality of care." See Medicare Hospital Manual §195, and Peer Review Organization Manual §3000, reprinted in 2 CCH Medicare-Medicaid Guide ¶12,872.09 at 5255-2. For example, if a PRO finds a premature hospital discharge that results in the subsequent readmission of the patient to the same hospital or readmission for care that could have been provided during the first admission, the PRO must deny reimbursement for the second admission. In addition, depending on the frequency of the violations and the severity of any health effects, the PRO may (or must) review 100 percent of the physician's or hospital's discharges, and develop a sanction recommendation for monetary fines or program suspension or exclusion under Social Security Act §1156, discussed immediately below.

Third, Social Security Act §1156, 42 U.S.C. §1320c-5, defines a new federal statutory duty of providers to deliver care "of a quality which meets professionally recognized standards of health care," and authorizes the PROs to enforce this duty through sanctions — program exclusion and monetary penalties — directed at the provider. Thus while PROs have, at least at present, only limited authority to deny Medicare *payment* for substandard care, they have extensive authority to punish providers for delivering such care. The PROs' exercise of their sanctioning authority has generated most of the litigation under the statute, focusing primarily on two issues: procedural due process protections for doctors charged with quality violations and substantive fairness for rural practitioners sanctioned for violating statewide or national standards.

Note: PRO Sanctions in Operation

There were nearly 30 million hospital discharges of Medicare patients between October 1, 1983, when DRG-based reimbursement came into effect, and the end of 1986. During this period, approximately 6500 discharges involving 2500 providers were identified by PROs as having potential quality of care or utilization problems. Twenty percent of these cases — approximately 1300 — represented potential "gross and flagrant" violations of the statutory standards. See Testimony of Richard P. Kusserow, Inspector General of Department of Health and Human Services before the Subcommittee on Intergovernmental Relations and Human Resources of the House Committee on Government Operations, October 20, 1987, at 52. If 1300 cases seems like a tiny percentage of 30 million discharges, recall that 1300 represents an enormous increase in quality-based professional review compared with the activities of the state licensing boards discussed in Section E above.

The vast majority of cases involving potential quality and utilization problems have been resolved at the PRO level, in which, if the PRO finds a violation, the provider agrees to a corrective action plan. Cases not resolved at this level are referred to HHS's Office of the Inspector General (OIG) for independent review and imposition of any sanctions. Through September, 1987, 138 cases have been referred by the PROs to OIG. Of this number, 54 resulted in the exclusion of the provider (53 physicians, 1 facility). In an additional 25 cases, monetary penalties were imposed (24 physicians, 1 facility). Sixty-two of these 79 cases, or 78 percent, involved "gross and flagrant" violations of statutory standards. See id. at 53. One example involved a hospital discharge of a 78-year-old patient with multiple health problems who was not medically stable to a home situation in which often no one else was present; the patient was readmitted two days after discharge and died three days thereafter from pneumonia. A second example involved a patient with known cardiovascular disease and numerous other conditions contraindicating surgery; nevertheless, minor elective nasal surgery was performed, and the patient died shortly thereafter. See id. at 53-54.

Although in these cases sanctions seem to be justified, the PRO sanction process has generated sharp opposition from some rural communities and from organized medicine. Many of the physicians subject to sanctions practice in rural areas, and some of these communities fear that the PROs, representing the views of urban doctors, are depriving rural patients of their only sources of medical care. See Reinhold, Quality Care Reviews Hurting Rural Doctors, N.Y. Times, March 24, 1987, at A1:3. Indeed, when the California PRO recommended a two-year exclusion against a rural surgeon who delegated post-operative care to primary care physicians, the surgeon won an injunction against the exclusion on the grounds that the statute and regulations required the PRO at least to consider varying statewide standards in the light of local conditions. See Greene v. Bowen, 639 F.Supp. 554 (E.D. Cal. 1986).

The objection of most sanctioned doctors, and of organized medicine, has been directed at the procedures of the sanction process. As the following *Doyle* case makes clear, doctors resisting a proposed sanction have a right to notice and an informal hearing before the PRO, and to submit written material to the OIG, but have no access to a formal adversarial hearing before an ALJ until *after* they have been excluded from the Medicare program and that fact has been made known to other providers and to the public at large through newspaper advertisements.

Doyle v. Secretary of Health and Human Services

848 F.2d 296 (1st Cir. 1988)

BREYER, Circuit Judge.

On December 31, 1986, the Inspector General of the Department of Health and Human Services ("HHS") entered an order forbidding Dr. Robert Doyle, the plaintiff in this case, from receiving reimbursement for treatment of Medicare patients for at least five years. In doing so, the Inspector General accepted a recommendation of a Maine peer review organization ("PRO") that he impose this serious sanction because Dr. Doyle "grossly and flagrantly violated" his obligation to provide medical care "of a quality which meets professionally recognized standards of health care," . . . in particular by improperly treating three patients. . . .

[Under the statute and regulations], [i]f a PRO "identifies" a "substantial violation" of professional health care standards in "a substantial number" of a doctor's "cases," or a "violation" that is "gross and flagrant," it is to notify the doctor in writing. The doctor must have a chance to submit information to the PRO or to meet with it to review its initial finding, or both. If the PRO still believes the doctor has violated Medicare standards, it will submit a report and a sanction recommendation to HHS's Inspector General. The PRO must send a copy of the report and recommendation to the doctor. The doctor may submit additional material to the Inspector General. The Inspector General will then decide whether to apply a sanction. He must notify the doctor of the sanction decision. If he imposes a sanction, it will take effect two weeks after notification. At that time, the Inspector General must also notify members of the medical community (hospitals, medical societies, etc.) and publish notice in the newspaper.

The statutes and the regulations provide further administrative remedies for a doctor whom the Inspector General sanctions. The doctor is entitled to a hearing before an Administrative Law Judge (ALJ). The doctor may appeal an adverse ALJ decision to the Secretary's Appeals Council. . . . And, he can obtain judicial review of the final decision of the Secretary. See generally 42 U.S.C. §§1320c-1 through 13; 42 C.F.R. §§1004.30-130. . . .

The relevant facts here are as follows:

(1) A private company called Health Care Review, Inc., ("HCRI") is under contract with HHS to run the peer review system in Maine. It employs nurses who examine medical charts of 25 percent to 30 percent of Maine's Medicare patients. If he or she finds a possible problem, the reviewing nurse alerts a doctor, who may refer the matter to a Quality Review Committee (four doctors), which may refer the matter to the Maine advisory Committee (six doctors), which may make recommendations to the Inspector General.

(2) HCRI followed this process in respect to Dr. Doyle. The Quality Review Committee found seven instances in which Dr. Doyle may have committed a sanctionable offense. The Maine Advisory Committee, after hearing from Dr. Doyle, unanimously found there was a "gross and flagrant" violation in three instances, and recommended a five-year exclusion from the Medicare program. After reviewing Dr. Doyle's further submissions, the Inspector General adopted that recommendation.

(3) At this point, during the two weeks before the sanction would take effect, Dr. Doyle brought his suit in district court. . . . After hearing evidence about how the Maine Advisory Committee had conducted its deliberations, the court concluded that the committee had not properly applied the factors listed in a particular HHS regulation. That regulation says: The PRO's specific recommendation must be based on a consideration of:

> (a) The type of the offense involved;
> (b) The severity of the offense;
> (c) The deterrent value;
> (d) The practitioner's or other person's previous sanction record;

(e) The availability of alternative sources of services in the community; and
(f) Any other factors that the PRO considers relevant (for example, the duration of the problem).

42 C.F.R. §1004.80 (1987). (At the time of Dr. Doyle's sanction, the fifth factor, availability of alternative sources of services in the community, was not part of the list. 42 C.F.R. §474.6 (1985), amended 1986.) For this reason, the court enjoined "enforcement and publication" of plaintiff's five-year exclusion. The court ordered a new meeting of the Maine Advisory Committee to reconsider its sanction recommendation, this time on the basis of the factors in §1004.80.

The Secretary argues that the district court could not legally issue an injunction because Dr. Doyle came to court before exhausting his administrative remedies. We believe the Secretary is right. . . . In the Medicare area, Congress has elevated the ordinary administrative "common law" principle of exhaustion into a statutory requirement. The Medicare statute allows judicial review only after a "final decision by the Secretary." . . .

In this instance, Dr. Doyle's claim has "been presented" to the Secretary; indeed one of the Secretary's administrators, the Inspector General, has imposed the very sanction about which Dr. Doyle complains. Dr. Doyle, however, has not "exhausted" the Department's administrative appeals; and, there is no "final" decision of the Secretary because the Secretary has not "waived" exhaustion.

Dr. Doyle argues that his claim fits within a narrow exception to the exhaustion rule, an exception where courts have found the agency must waive exhaustion. That exception applies to an "entirely collateral" matter where the agency has deprived an individual of something important and "full relief cannot be obtained" later from the agency. . . . In our view, however, Dr. Doyle's case does not fall within this exception.

To understand why, one must first understand the policy basis of an exhaustion rule:

> [Exhaustion] allows the agency to develop a factual record, to apply its expertise to a problem, to exercise its discretion, and to correct its own mistakes, all before a court will intervene. Insofar as specialized administrative understanding is important, the doctrine thereby promotes accurate results, not only at the agency level, but also by allowing more informed judicial review. By limiting judicial interruption of agency proceedings, the doctrine can encourage expeditious decision making. Insofar as Congress has provided that an agency will decide a matter in the first instance, to apply the doctrine normally furthers specific Congressional intent. And, as a general matter, the doctrine promotes a sensible division of tasks between the agency and the court: litigants are discouraged from weakening the position of the agency by flouting its processes, while court resources are reserved for dealing primarily with those matters which could not be resolved administratively. Thus, the doctrine serves the interests of accuracy, efficiency, agency autonomy and judicial economy. . . .

Given these policy principles, one can understand why, for example, when a plaintiff attacks the lawfulness of an important "systemwide" agency policy (say, a constitutional challenge to a policy disqualifying a large class of potential Social Security recipients), the Supreme Court has held that the agency must waive its exhaustion requirements. In that sort of case exhaustion serves little purpose; the agency's policy is well-established and unlikely to change; agency expertise is not particularly likely to help the court; and, at the same time, to insist upon exhaustion of agency procedures might well physically harm a plaintiff needing benefits. . . . Where the plaintiff's claims, however, raise issues where the agency's expertise may be helpful, or attack policies to which the agency is less firmly attached, or seem more closely confined to the facts of a particular case, exhaustion is required. . . .

The case before us is one that falls within the rule, not the exception. Dr. Doyle's case involves one plaintiff, not a class. In Dr. Doyle's case, agency expertise can help the court evaluate whether or not the Advisory Committee recommendation was "based on a consideration of" the relevant factors, because the agency (HHS) is likely better to understand (1) how a PRO does, or should, go about considering those factors, (2) how HHS, which wrote the regulation, interprets the word "consideration,". . . and (3) whether, given the statute, rules, and regulations, any PRO deviation from the regulation's norm made a significant difference to Dr. Doyle. There is no reason here to think the agency has a closed mind on these matters. It is not wedded to a particular long-standing policy that is under attack. . . . If the PRO has made a mistake in applying the agency's rules, the agency will likely correct it. . . .

Dr. Doyle cross-appeals from the district court's rejection of his claims that the Inspector General's decision violated the Constitution. Since all parties wish us to hear the merits of these arguments, and the Secretary, at oral argument, expressly waived any exhaustion requirement, we shall do so. . . .

(1) Dr. Doyle argues that the relevant statute's terms, punishing those who "grossly and flagrantly violated" the "obligation" to "assure services . . . of a quality which meets professionally recognized standards of health care,". . . are so vague that the Constitution's Due Process Clause prohibits Congress from using the statute to deprive him of part of his income. . . .

Other courts, holding this provision constitutional, have done so in part because "[t]he definition of adequate medical care cannot be boiled down to a precise mathematical formula; it must be grounded in what, from time to time, other health professionals consider to be acceptable standards of medical care.". . . To the medical profession, which will administer this standard, it has reasonably clear meaning.

(2) Dr. Doyle argues that the procedure that HHS uses to decide whether, and how, to institute a sanction is constitutionally inadequate. In particular, he says that the Constitution entitles him to a full evidentiary hearing before the Inspector General imposes a sanction.

Even if we assume, however, for the sake of argument, that Dr. Doyle's injury amounts to a deprivation of "liberty" or "property," within the terms of the Fifth Amendment, . . . we must still reject his argument, for HHS provides Dr. Doyle with all of the "process" that is constitutionally "due." . . . [Repetition of agency procedures noted at beginning of opinion omitted.] While a full, formal, courtroom-type evidentiary hearing prior to the Inspector General's imposition of a sanction might offer still more protection against one kind of agency mistake (wrongly sanctioning a doctor), it would offer Medicare patients less protection against another equally important kind of mistake (failing to warn patients against a doctor whose services are seriously deficient). Under the Constitution, the agency should, and does, have leeway to balance these two risks. And, the procedural result of that balancing here is reasonable. . . .

(3) Dr. Doyle claims that the PRO's recommendation deprived him of "property" or "liberty" without due process of law because the PRO was "biased" against him. Insofar as this argument rests upon the PRO's dual role as prosecutor and judge, the Supreme Court has explicitly rejected it. Withrow v. Larkin, 421 U.S. 35 (1975). Insofar as it rests on his claim that the Committee decided against him because it was "under pressure" to find a "victim" and impose a sanction, the district court rejected it as a matter of fact. Similarly, the court found that the Committee's recommendation did not rest on any personal bias against Dr. Doyle growing out of his attacks on the Committee. . . .

The part of the judgment of the district court upholding the constitutionality of the Secretary's sanction decision is affirmed. The part of the judgment of the district court declaring the Secretary's sanction decision an invalid violation of agency regulations and enjoining further agency action is reversed.

Notes and Questions

(1) As Judge Breyer points out, one of Dr. Doyle's claims was that he had been deprived of liberty or property without due process of law because the Maine PRO (HCRI) was biased against him due to Doyle's prior criticism of HCRI. The district court summarized the evidence on this point as follows:

> Dr. Doyle is the first physician ever sanctioned by HCRI, and in fact is the first physician to be sanctioned by any peer review organization in all of New England. Although it falls far short of being substantive proof of any impropriety, the Court is nevertheless given some pause by the fact that the first physician to be sanctioned by HCRI is someone who is well known to that organization and who has been one of the most vocal critics of its operations in Maine. The Court is particularly troubled by the testimony of former HCRI Medical Director Michael Lacombe that when HCRI Vice President Edward Lynch was

> told that Doyle's opposition was making it difficult to recruit physician reviewers in Bridgton, Lynch suggested doing a review of every Medicare patient treated by Dr. Doyle so as to make him "feel the heat." Although this complete review never took place, . . . it is clear that Lynch and perhaps other HCRI administrators considered Doyle to be a thorn in their sides. . . . Doyle v. Bowen, 660 F. Supp. 1484, 1488-1489 (D. Me. 1987), *aff'd in pertinent part,* 848 F.2d 296 (1st Cir. 1988).

The district court ultimately found that although HCRI had audited Dr. Doyle's practice at a higher-than-average rate, there was no proof that this audit was not based on neutral criteria, such as the types of diagnoses involved. The district court also stressed the apparent neutrality and unanimity of the multi-layer review process.

(a) In the light of Judge Breyer's opinion, should Dr. Doyle's claim of PRO bias against him for prior criticism be considered a "collateral issue" not subject to the normal requirement of exhaustion of administrative remedies?

(b) If your answer to question (a) is negative — that is, if you insist that Dr. Doyle first present his claim of bias through the administrative process — does that affect your answer to the question of whether an ALJ hearing is constitutionally required before sanctions can be imposed?

(c) Whoever hears the bias claim, should the burden of proof be shifted if the accused doctor can make out a prima facie case? The district court apparently placed the burden on Dr. Doyle to prove by a preponderance of the evidence that the PRO had targeted him for an illegitimate reason, and ultimately ruled that Dr. Doyle had not carried that burden. But do the facts summarized by the district court above make out at least a prima facie case of bias, justifying shifting the burden to the PRO to explain the neutral criteria that led to the selection of Dr. Doyle as the first object of sanctions?

(2) In developing the Omnibus Budget Reconciliation Act of 1987, P.L. 100-203 (herinafter OBRA 1987), the House of Representatives passed a provision that attempted to balance physicians' strong desire for a formal evidentiary hearing before sanctions were imposed with the strong opposition of HHS and PROs to such a provision as endangering patient care. The House bill provided that "before an exclusion took effect, the provider would be entitled to a decision by an administrative law judge as to whether patients would be at serious risk if the provider were to continue furnishing services during the review process." H.R. Rep. 100-391, at 427. In other words, a provider would be entitled to a limited pre-sanction hearing before an ALJ on whether sanctions could be postponed until after a full hearing on the merits without posing a "serious risk" to patients. The Senate had passed no comparable provision, and the conferees accepted the House version but limited it to providers located in rural areas with health manpower shortages or in counties with fewer than 70,000 people. See Joint Explanatory Statement of the Committee of Conference at 664-665; Social Security Act §1156(b)

(5), 42 U.S.C. §1320c-5(b)(5), set out above. Since the amendment grants retroactive relief to doctors who received their exclusion notices up to 365 days before the effective date of the act (December 22, 1987), Dr. Doyle would apparently be entitled to a limited ALJ hearing if he qualified as a rural practitioner.

G. Cost Containment and Quality of Care

"Cost containment" takes many forms in contemporary American health care delivery. What most of them have in common is attempting to change provider behavior developed under the previously dominant, and still existing, fee-for-service and cost-based reimbursement. In abstract terms, there are two major techniques of cost containment. The first is retrospective, concurrent, or prospective review of the "appropriateness" or "necessity" of services: for instance, is this hospital admission, length of stay, or test medically justified, and hence worth paying for? The second technique relies on financial incentives; it does not review particular services, but says to the provider, in one way or another: if you hospitalize this patient, or order a certain test, or refer the patient to a specialist, it will cost you, the provider, money. These techniques can be used separately or — as in the case of Medicare DRGs and PROs — together. Both are designed to induce the provider to charge the payer less than under previous reimbursement systems.

Cost containment is often discussed, particularly by doctors, as if it is obviously inconsistent with high quality care. This is clearly not so. The disturbing statistics discussed at the beginning of this chapter regarding unnecessary surgery represent enormous human and financial costs and, most likely, low quality care. If financial incentives could induce physicians to lower the rates of inappropriate procedures found by Chassin et al., that would simultaneously contain costs and *raise* quality. It is also true, of course, that cost containment can lead to substandard care. Indeed, as the material in Section B on the poor, and in Chapter 1 on access, dramatically reveal, the traditional "cost containment" practiced with respect to the poor in many public and private hospitals has had exactly that result. What is different in the 1980s is that the pressures of cost containment have reached beyond charity hospitals and emergency rooms to general health care for middle-class Americans. For that reason, the quality of care problems of cost containment are now considered legitimate and pressing.

This chapter considers these problems in four contexts: (1) application of malpractice norms to utilization review programs, notably one operated by a state Medicaid program; (2) application of malpractice norms to financial incentive programs, notably HMOs; (3) application of the law regarding hospital staff privilege decisions to economic factors; and (4) the structure of market competition in relation to quality of care.

1. MALPRACTICE NORMS AND UTILIZATION REVIEW

a. Governmental Utilization Review Programs

Wickline v. State of California

228 Cal. Rptr. 661 (Cal. App. 1986), petition for review dismissed, *239 Cal. Rptr. 805, 741 P.2d 613 (1987)*

Rowen, Associate Justice.

. . . Principally, this matter concerns itself with the legal responsibility that a third party payor, in this case, the State of California, has for harm caused to a patient when a cost containment program is applied in a manner which is alleged to have affected the implementation of the treating physician's medical judgment.

The plaintiff, respondent herein, Lois J. Wickline (plaintiff or Wickline) sued defendant, appellant herein, State of California (State or Medi-Cal). The essence of the plaintiff's claim is [that state employees negligently terminated Wickline's eligibility for medical assistance, causing her to be discharged prematurely from Van Nuys Community Hospital. As a result of this premature discharge, plaintiff suffered a complete occlusion of the right infra-renoaorta, necessitating an amputation of plaintiff's right leg.]

I

Responding to concerns about the escalating cost of health care, public and private payors have in recent years experimented with a variety of cost containment mechanisms. We deal here with one of those programs: the prospective utilization review process.

At the outset, this court recognizes that this case appears to be the first attempt to tie a health care payor into the medical malpractice causation chain and that it, therefore, deals with issues of profound importance to the health care community and to the general public. . . .

Traditionally, quality assurance activities, including utilization review programs, were performed primarily within the hospital setting under the general control of the medical staff. The principal focus of such quality assurance review schema was to prevent overutilization. . . .

Early cost containment programs utilized the retrospective utilization review process. In that system the third party payor reviewed the patient's chart after the fact to determine whether the treatment provided was medically necessary. If, in the judgment of the utilization reviewer, it was not, the health care provider's claim for payment was denied.

In the cost containment program in issue in this case, prospective utilization review, authority for the rendering of health care services must be obtained before medical care is rendered. Its purpose is to promote the well recognized public interest in controlling health care costs by reducing unnecessary services while still intending to assure that appropriate medical and hospital services are provided to the patient in need. However, such a cost containment strategy creates new and added pressures on the quality assurance portion of the utilization review mechanism. The stakes, the risks at issue, are much higher when a prospective cost containment review process is utilized than when a retrospective review process is used.

A mistaken conclusion about medical necessity following retrospective review will result in the wrongful withholding of payment. An erroneous decision in a prospective review process, on the other hand, in practical consequences, results in the withholding of necessary care, potentially leading to a patient's permanent disability or death.

II

[Wickline was diagnosed by Dr. Polonsky, a specialist in vascular surgery, as having . . . [an] obstruction of the terminal aorta. . . . Dr. Polonsky concluded that it was necessary to remove a part of the plaintiff's artery and insert a synthetic (Teflon) graft in its place. . . . After receiving authorization from Medi-Cal for the operation and 10 days of hospitalization, Dr. Polonsky performed the surgery on January 7, 1977.]

Later that same day Dr. Polonsky was notified that Wickline was experiencing circulatory problems in her right leg. He concluded that a clot had formed in the graft. As a result, Wickline was taken back into surgery, the incision in her right groin was reopened, the clot removed, and the graft was resewn. [After further pain and spasms in Wickline's lower leg vessels] Dr. Polonsky performed a lumbar sympathectomy.

A lumbar sympathectomy is a major operation in which a section of the chain of nerves that lie on each side of the spinal column is removed. . . . Dr. Polonsky was assisted in all three surgeries by Dr. Leonard Kovner . . . a board certified specialist in the field of general surgery and the chief of surgery at Van Nuys. Dr. Daniels was [also present for some of the surgery.] . . .

On or about January 16, 1977, Dr. Polonsky concluded that "it was medically necessary" that plaintiff remain in the hospital for an additional eight days beyond her then scheduled discharge date. Drs. Kovner and Daniels concurred in Dr. Polonsky's opinion.

Dr. Polonsky cited many reasons for his feeling that it was medically necessary for plaintiff to remain in an acute care hospital for an additional eight days, such as the danger of infection and/or clotting. His principal reason, however, was that he felt that he was going to be able to save both of Wickline's legs and wanted her to remain in the hospital where he could observe her and be immediately available, along with the hospital staff, to treat her if an emergency should occur.

In order to secure an extension of Wickline's hospital stay, it was necessary to complete and present to Medi-Cal a form called "Request for Extension of Stay in Hospital," commonly referred to as an "MC-180" or "180." It is the hospital's responsibility to prepare the 180 form. The hospital must secure necessary information about the patient from the responsible physician. It then submits the 180 form to Medi-Cal's representative and obtains appropriate authorization for the hospital stay extension.

The physician's responsibility in the preparation of the 180 form is to furnish (to the hospital's representative) the patient's diagnosis, significant history, clinical status, and treatment plan in sufficient detail to permit a reasonable, professional evaluation by Medi-Cal's representative, either the "on-site nurse" or/and the Medi-Cal Consultant, a doctor employed by the State for just such purpose.

The Medi-Cal Consultant's responsibility is to review requests submitted by private physicians on behalf of their patients for hospital treatment they believe necessary and to review requests for extensions of hospital time submitted on behalf of hospitalized patients. The Medi-Cal Consultant is not permitted to approve the request unless the information furnished is timely, complete, and indicates the medical necessity of the requested treatment.

At Van Nuys, Patricia N. Spears (Spears), an employee of the hospital and a registered nurse, had the responsibility for completing 180 forms. In this case, as requested by Dr. Polonsky, Spears filled out Wickline's 180 form and then presented it to Dr. Daniels, as plaintiff's attending physician, to sign, which he did, in compliance with Dr. Polonsky's recommendation. All of the physicians who testified agreed that the 180 form prepared by Spears was complete, accurate, and adequate for all purposes in issue in this matter.

Doris A. Futerman (Futerman), a registered nurse, was, at that time, employed by Medi-Cal as a Health Care Service Nurse, commonly referred to as an "on-site nurse." As such, her primary duties were to contact, daily, a group of hospitals assigned to her to review requests for extensions of hospital stays prepared on behalf of patients in those particular hospitals. Van Nuys was one of the hospitals to which she was assigned.

Futerman had the authority, after reviewing a 180 form, to approve the requested extension of time without calling a Medi-Cal Consultant. She could not, however, either reject the request outright or authorize a lesser number of days then requested. If, for any reason, she felt she could not approve the extension of time in the hospital as requested, she was required to contact a Medi-Cal Consultant and that physician would make the ultimate decision on the request.

Futerman, after reviewing Wickline's 180 form, felt that she could not approve the requested eight-day extension of acute care hospitalization. While conceding that the information provided might justify some additional time beyond the scheduled discharge date, nothing in Wickline's case, in Futerman's opinion, would have warranted the entire eight additional days requested and, for those reasons, she telephoned the Medi-Cal Consultant. She reached Dr. William S. Glassman (Dr. Glassman), one of the Medi-Cal Consultants on duty at the time in Medi-Cal's Los Angeles office. The Medi-Cal Consultant selection occurred randomly. As was the practice, whichever Medi-Cal Consultant was available at the moment took the next call that came into the office.

Dr. Glassman was board certified in general surgery and had practiced in that field until 1975 when he became employed by the Department of Health of the State of California as a Medi-Cal Consultant I. At the time of trial Dr. Glassman was not employed by the State and attempts to personally serve him with a subpoena to appear as a witness in this case were without success. Without objection from the State, Dr. Glassman's testimony was taken at trial by the reading of his deposition in open court.

After speaking with Futerman on the telephone, Dr. Glassman rejected Wickline's treating physician's request for an eight-day hospital extension and, instead, authorized an additional four days of hospital stay beyond the originally scheduled discharge date.

Dr. Glassman testified that since the initial request for extension of hospital stay is made to him by way of a telephone call from the on-site nurse, he does not actually see the 180 form itself until after he has acted on it, when it is forwarded to him for his signature. While there are appropriate places provided on the 180 form to indicate what the on-site nurse's recommendation is and the reason given for disapproval of the requested hospital stay extension by the Medi-Cal Consultant, both of those places were left blank on Wickline's 180 form. Dr. Glassman could not recall why he granted a four-day extension rather than the eight days requested by plaintiff's treating physician.

Neither Futerman nor Dr. Glassman had any specific recollection of the Wickline case. Each testified based upon their ordinary practice and procedure except where requested to state their opinion based on information provided to them at the time their respective testimony was taken as, for example, regarding information appearing on Wickline's 180 form.

After review of Wickline's 180 form, Dr. Glassman testified that the factors that led him to authorize four days, rather than the requested eight days, was that there was no information about the patient's temperature which he, thereupon, assumed was normal; nothing was mentioned about the patient's diet, which he then presumed was not a problem; nor was there any information about Wickline's bowel function, which Dr. Glassman then presumed was functioning satisfactorily. Further, the fact that the 180 form noted that Wickline was able to ambulate with help and that whirlpool treatments were to begin that day caused Dr. Glassman to presume that the patient was progressing satisfactorily and was not seriously or critically ill.

Dr. Glassman testified that he had no recollection of reviewing any documentary information available to him before rejecting the requested eight-day extension and authorizing four days instead. Initial treatment authorization requests, form MC-161, which had to be completed by the plaintiff's physician in order to obtain prior authorization from Medi-Cal for her initial hospitalization was, according to the State's own witness, Dr. Harry Kaufman (Dr. Kaufman), the chief Medi-Cal Consultant at the Los Angeles field office (and Dr. Glassman's supervisor), always supported by documentation submitted by the physician before such authorization was granted. Therefore, such material was apparently available to Dr. Glassman for review before he acted.

Further, it is reasonable to conclude from the record that Dr. Glassman did not consult with a specialist in peripheral vascular surgery before making his decision. Such specialists were employed by Medi-Cal, according to Dr. Kaufman, and were made available to Medi-Cal Consultants to confer with for special information and guidance in areas beyond the Medi-Cal Consultants' own general knowledge, training, and experience.

In essence, respondent argues, Dr. Glassman based his decision on signs and symptoms such as temperature, diet, and bowel movements, which were basically irrelevant to the plaintiff's circulatory condition for which she was being treated and did not concern himself with those symptoms and signs which an ordinary prudent physician would consider to be pertinent with regard to the type of medical condition presented by Wickline.

Complying with the limited extension of time authorized by Medi-Cal, Wickline was discharged from Van Nuys on January 21, 1977. Drs. Polonsky and Daniels each wrote discharge orders. At the time of her discharge, each of plaintiff's three treating physicians were aware that the Medi-Cal Consultant had approved only four of the requested eight-day hospital stay extension. While all three doctors were aware that they could attempt to obtain a further extension of Wickline's hospital stay by telephoning the Medi-Cal Consultant to request such an extension, none of them did so.

Dr. Polonsky, the senior man on the Wickline matter, and the specialist brought in specifically to treat Wickline's condition, was acknowledged by his associates as the doctor with primary responsibility in making decisions regarding her case. It would appear that both Drs. Daniels and Kovner, observing nothing that looked threatening to the patient, deferred to Dr. Polonsky and allowed Wickline to be discharged at the expiration of the period authorized by Dr. Glassman, the Medi-Cal Consultant.

At trial, Dr. Polonsky testified that in the time that had passed since the first extension request had been communicated to Medi-Cal, on January 16th or 17th, and the time of her scheduled discharge on January 21, 1977, Wickline's condition had neither deteriorated nor become critical. In Dr. Polonsky's opinion no new symptom had presented itself, and no additional factors had occurred since the original request was made to have formed the basis for a change in the Medi-Cal Consultant's attitude regarding Wickline's situation. In addition, he stated that at the time of Wickline's discharge it did not appear that her leg was in any danger.

Dr. Polonsky testified that at the time in issue he felt that Medi-Cal Consultants had the State's interest more in mind than the patient's welfare and that that belief influenced his decision not to request a second extension of Wickline's hospital stay. In addition, he felt that Medi-Cal had the power to tell him, as a treating doctor, when a patient must be discharged from the hospital. Therefore, while still of the subjective, non-communicated, opinion that Wickline was seriously ill and that the danger to her was not over, Dr. Polonsky discharged her from the hospital on January 21, 1977. He testified that had Wickline's condition, in his medical judgment, been critical or in a deteriorating condition on January 21, he would have made some effort to keep her in the hospital beyond that day, even if denied authority by Medi-Cal and even if he had to pay her hospital bill himself.

Dr. Daniels testified that he believed it was medically proper to discharge Wickline from the hospital on January 21, 1977. Dr. Kovner testified that while he did not recall whether or not he saw Wickline on January 21, as he was given credit for doing in a nurse's note in the hospital record, he did see her on January 19, 1977, and from his knowledge of her case he had no objection to her discharge from the hospital. Dr. Kovner stated that if he had seen (on the day of her discharge) "a grossly infected wound, that in any way looked threatening to the patient," he would have done whatever was necessary to take measures to continue her hospitalization.

All of the medical witnesses who testified at trial agreed that Dr. Polonsky was acting within the standards of practice of the medical community in discharging Wickline on January 21, 1977. . . .

Had the eight-day extension requested on Wickline's behalf been granted by Medi-Cal, she would have remained in the hospital through the morning hours of January 25, 1977. In Dr. Polonsky's medical opinion, based upon hypothetical questions derived from Wickline's recollection of her course subsequent to her discharge from the hospital, had she been at Van Nuys on January 22, 23 or 24, he would have observed her leg change color, would have formed the opinion that she had clotted and would have taken her back into surgery and reopened the graft to remove the clot again, not an uncommon procedure in this type of case. As previously stated, he had performed a similar procedure on the first day of surgery, January 7, 1977. In addition thereto, Dr. Polonsky testified that had Wickline developed an infection while she was in the hospital, it could have been controlled with the vigorous use of antibiotics.

In Dr. Polonsky's opinion, to a reasonable medical certainty, had Wickline remained in the hospital for the eight additional days, as originally requested by him and her other treating doctors, she would not have suffered the loss of her leg. . . .

Dr. Polonsky testified that in his medical opinion, the Medi-Cal Consultant's rejection of the requested eight-day extension of acute care hospitalization and his authorization of a four-day extension in its place did not conform to the usual medical standards as they existed in 1977. He stated that, in accordance with those standards, a physician would not be permitted to make decisions regarding the care of a patient without either first seeing the patient, reviewing the patient's chart or discussing the patient's condition with her treating physician or physicians.

III

From the facts thus presented, appellant takes the position that it was not negligent as a matter of law. Appellant contends that the decision to discharge was made by each of the plaintiff's three doctors, was based upon the prevailing standards of practice, and was justified by her condition at the time of her discharge. It argues that Medi-Cal had no part in the plaintiff's hospital discharge and therefore was not liable even if the decision to do so was erroneously made by her doctors. . . .

"All persons are required to use ordinary care to prevent others being injured as a result of their conduct." And, "in the absence of statutory provision declaring an exception to the fundamental principle enunciated by section 1714 of the Civil Code, no such exception should be made unless clearly supported by public policy." . . .

"A departure from this fundamental principle involves the balancing of a number of considerations; the major ones are the foreseeability for harm to the plaintiff, the degree of certainty that the plaintiff suffered injury, the closeness of the connection between the defendant's conduct and the injury suffered, the moral blame attached to the defendant's conduct, the policy of preventing future harm, the extent of the burden to the defendant and consequences to the community of imposing a duty to exercise care with resulting liability for breach, and the availability, cost, and prevalence of insurance for the risk involved.". . .

Applying those standards to the facts in issue in this matter causes this court to conclude that appellant's contentions are well taken and that it is absolved from liability in this case as a matter of law. . . .

Dr. Kaufman, the chief Medi-Cal Consultant for the Los Angeles field office, was called to testify on behalf of the defendant. He testified that in January 1977, the criteria, or standard, which governed a Medi-Cal Consultant in acting on a request to consider an extension of time was founded on title 22 of the California Administrative Code. That standard was "the medical necessity" for the length and level of care requested. That, Dr. Kaufman contended, was determined by the Medi-Cal Consultant from the information provided him in the 180 form. The Medi-Cal Consultant's decision required the exercise of medical judgment and, in doing so, the Medi-Cal Consultant would utilize the skill, knowledge, training, and experience he had acquired in the medical field.

Dr. Kaufman supported Dr. Glassman's decision. He testified, based upon his examination of the MC-180 form in issue in this matter, that Dr. Glassman's four-day hospital stay extension authorization was ample to meet the plaintiff's medically necessary needs at that point in time. Further, in Dr. Kaufman's opinion, there was no need for Dr. Glassman to seek information beyond that which was contained in Wickline's 180 form.

Dr. Kaufman testified that it was the practice in the Los Angeles Medi-Cal office for Medi-Cal consultants not to review other information that might be available, such as the TAR 160 form (request for authorization for initial hospitalization), unless called by the patient's physician and requested to do so and, instead, to rely only on the information contained in the MC-180 form. Dr. Kaufman also stated that Medi-Cal Consultants did not initiate telephone calls to patient's treating doctors because of the volume of work they already had in meeting their prescribed responsibilities. Dr. Kaufman testified that any fact relating to the patient's care and treatment that was not shown on the 180 form was of no significance.

As to the principal issue before this court, i.e., who bears responsibility for allowing a patient to be discharged from the hospital, her treating physicians or the health care payer, each side's medical expert witnesses agreed that, in accordance with the standards of medical practice as it existed in January 1977, it was for the patient's treating physician to decide the course of treatment that was medically necessary to treat the ailment. It was also that physician's responsibility to determine whether or not acute care hospitalization was required and for how long. Finally, it was agreed that the patient's physician is in a better position than the Medi-Cal Consultant to determine the number of days medically necessary for any required hospital care. The decision to discharge is, therefore, the responsibility of the patient's own treating doctor.

Dr. Kaufman testified that if, on January 21, the date of the plaintiff's discharge from Van Nuys, any one of her three treating doctors had decided that in his medical judgment it was necessary to keep Wickline in the hospital for a longer period of time, they, or any of them, should have filed another request for extension of stay in the hospital, that Medi-Cal would expect those physicians to make such a request if they felt it was indicated, and upon receipt of such a request further consideration of an additional extension of hospital time would have been given.

Title 22 of the California Administrative Code section 51110, provided, in pertinent part, at the relevant time in issue here, that: "The determination of need for acute care shall be made in accordance with the usual standards of medical practice in the community."

The patient who requires treatment and who is harmed when care which should have been provided is not provided should recover for the injuries suffered from all those responsible for the deprivation of such care, including, when appropriate, health care payors. Third party payors of health care services can be held legally accountable when medically inappropriate decisions result from defects in the design or implementation of cost containment mechanisms as, for example, when appeals made on a patient's behalf for medical or hospital care are arbitrarily ignored or unreasonably disregarded or overridden. However, the physician who complies without protest with the limitations imposed by a third party payor, when his medical judgment dictates otherwise, cannot avoid his ultimate responsibility for his patient's care. He cannot point to the health care payor as the liability scapegoat when the consequences of his own determinative medical decisions go sour.

There is little doubt that Dr. Polonsky was intimidated by the Medi-Cal program but he was not paralyzed by Dr. Glassman's response nor rendered powerless to act appropriately if other action was required under the circumstances. If, in his medical judgment, it was in his patient's best interest that she remain in the acute care hospital setting for an additional four days beyond the extended time period originally authorized by Medi-Cal, Dr. Polonsky should have made some effort to keep Wickline there. He himself acknowledged that responsibility to his patient. It was his medical judgment, however, that Wickline could be discharged when she was. All the plaintiff's treating physicians concurred, and all the doctors who testified at trial, for either plaintiff or defendant, agreed that Dr. Polonsky's medical decision to discharge Wickline met the standard of care applicable at the time. Medi-Cal was not a party to that medical decision and therefore cannot be held to share in the harm resulting if such decision was negligently made.

In addition thereto, while Medi-Cal played a part in the scenario before us, in that it was the resource for the funds to pay for the treatment sought, and its input regarding the nature and length of hospital care to be provided was of paramount importance, Medi-Cal did not override the medical judgment of Wickline's treating physicians at the time of her discharge. It was given no opportunity to do so. Therefore, there can be no viable cause of action against it for the consequences of that discharge decision.

The California Legislature's intent, in enacting the Medi-Cal Act, was to provide "mainstream" medical care to the indigent. (California Medical Assn. v. Brian (1973) 30 Cal. App. 3d 637, 642, 106 Cal. Rptr. 553.) The Legislature had expressly declared that Medi-Cal recipients should be able "whenever possible and feasible . . . , to the extent practical, . . . to secure health care in the same manner employed by the public generally, and without discrimination or segregation based purely on their economic disability." (Welf. & Inst. Code, §14000.) . . . [Hospitalization is covered by Medi-Cal subject to prior authorization of medical necessity.]

In the case before us, the Medi-Cal Consultant's decision, vis-à-vis the request to extend Wickline's hospital stay, was in accord with then existing statutory law.

V

This court appreciates that what is at issue here is the effect of cost containment programs upon the professional judgment of physicians to prescribe hospital treatment for patients requiring the same. While we recognize, realistically, that cost consciousness has become a permanent feature of the health care system, it is essential that cost limitation programs not be permitted to corrupt medical judgment. We have concluded, from the facts in issue here, that in this case it did not. . . .

The judgment is reversed.

NOTES AND QUESTIONS

(1) Cases such as *Wickline* are not entirely unprecedented. The defendant state Medicaid agency (Medi-Cal) is a payer, and as such can be analogized to Blue Cross-Blue Shield and other insurance companies. As we have seen in Chapter 2, insurance companies have been held liable for breach of contract and for the quasi-tort like action of "bad faith breach of contract," when they have refused to pay claims. As the *Wickline* court points out, when such cases involve only retrospective denial, treatment has already been received, and the only issue is normally who will pay for it. However, as the *Siegel* and Medicare custodial care cases indicate, sometimes these denials are in cases involving treatment for chronic conditions, in which the payer's decision can affect the provision of care. What makes *Wickline* somewhat different is that it applies prospective cost contraints to inpatient hospital care — indeed to major surgery — which raises the health risks and makes a causation claim against the payer more plausible.

(2) The dilemma anticipated by the academic literature is whether a cost containment program can effectively revise downward the standard of care or available legal remedies. In *Wickline* no one attempted to defend the discharge as justified, economizing medicine; rather, the dispute was about who was responsible for what seemed even at the time to have been a questionable decision (despite testimony that it was consistent with the prevailing standard of care). The two major protagonists in the case — Medi-Cal and Dr. Polonsky — take diametrically opposite positions regarding responsibility and liability. The state argues, naturally enough, that it is simply the payer, with no asserted or actual responsibility for medical decisions. Dr. Polonsky argues that Medi-Cal has the effective power to tell him when the patient must be discharged. Can you evaluate these competing arguments on the basis of the facts presented in the opinion? What more facts would you want to know in order to decide how the lines of influence and responsibility actually run? Is it possible that this should not be treated as an either/or question, but rather that both could be held liable (as well as other potential defendants)? Of course, Dr. Polonsky was not a defendant; only the state was sued. If you were Mrs. Wickline's attorney, what other possible defendants might you have suggested to her? Why?

(3) In a crucial sentence, the *Wickline* opinion states that "[t]hird party payors of health care services can be held legally accountable when medically inappropriate decisions result from defects in the design or implementation

of cost containment mechanisms as, for example, when appeals made on a patient's behalf for medical or hospital care are arbitrarily ignored or unreasonably disregarded or overridden." The examples given — that is, arbitrarily ignored appeals — suggest that the treating physician remains legally responsible for quality of care unless the state agency acts unreasonably in a particular case. But should the concept of a "defect in the *design*" of a cost containment program (emphasis supplied) be limited to these examples? Is such a limitation consistent with the first part of the *Wickline* opinion, in which the court stresses the unique dangers of prospective utilization review? Should the state agency have an affirmative duty to educate its own employees, doctors, and hospital personnel about how to operate the system so as to avoid major quality of care problems? To at least monitor the impact of its program on quality of care? What duty should the hospital and its staff have for the operation of the program? Put another way, can you imagine facts that might justify holding both Dr. Polonsky and the state agency (and perhaps the hospital as well) liable for Mrs. Wickline's injuries?

b. Nongovernmental Utilization Review Programs

The *Wickline* court drew on a number of sources of law for the principle that a state utilization review program owes a duty of reasonable care to the patients affected: California Civil Code §1714, imposing a duty of "ordinary care" on all persons; California Welfare & Institutions Code §14000, providing for equality of medical care for Medi-Cal recipients with that received by the public generally, "whenever possible and feasible"; and regulations stating that "the usual standards of medical practice" should apply to determinations of need for acute care under Medi-Cal. Of course, as discussed in Section D, with respect to hospital-based peer review, and in Section F with respect to payers and PROs, federal and state immunity statutes provide varying and often considerable protection to the individual doctors, nurses, and others engaged in implementing utilization review, and in some instances to the institutional bodies as well.

Private entities also use utilization review. Insurance companies and self-funded health benefit plans hire or contract for services from doctors, nurses, and specialized utilization review companies to review the medical necessity of services for which claims are being made. For example, a utilization review company under contract to a large employer would develop and apply standards regarding length of hospital stay for various diagnoses; if a hospital submitted a bill for a length of stay that appeared to be excessively long for a patient with a particular diagnosis, the utilization review company would request special justification for the excess days and could recommend refusal to pay for them.

Until relatively recently, one would have thought that these activities were subject to general state law regarding torts, contracts, and insurance, and to any statutes specifically addressing them. However, the 1974 enactment of the federal Employee Retirement Income Security Act (ERISA), 29 U.S.C. §1001 et seq. and its subsequent interpretation by the courts raise the likely possibility that state law has been largely pre-empted in this field, without any significant federal law to replace it.

NOTE: ERISA AND UTILIZATION REVIEW

ERISA was adopted primarily to address the plight of workers denied expected pension benefits. Its central provisions require that employer-sponsored pension plans meet substantive federal standards regulating funding, participation, vesting, benefit accrual, and disclosure of information. As Metropolitan Life Insurance Co. v. Massachusetts, 471 U.S. 724 (1985), discussed in Chapter 2, makes clear, ERISA also covers "employee welfare benefit plans" that provide, inter alia, medical and hospital benefits, but does not set substantive standards for such plans. Despite this lack of federal regulation of employee welfare benefit plans, ERISA contains a broad provision pre-empting all state laws that "relate to any employee benefit plan. . .", 29 U.S.C. §1144(a) (1982), albeit subject to certain exceptions. (An "employee benefit plan" is elsewhere defined as an employee welfare benefit plan or an employee pension benefit plan or both, 29 U.S.C. §1002(3) (1982).)

Since a great many Americans obtain health care benefits through their employment, it is likely that an attempt to apply state medical malpractice law — as in *Wickline* — to private utilization review programs would be met with the argument that state medical malpractice law has been pre-empted by ERISA with respect to employee benefit plans. The Supreme Court has clearly held that application of state common law tort remedies to employee benefit plans constitutes state law "relating to" such plans and therefore comes within the reach of the pre-emption provision. Pilot Life Insurance Co. v. Dedeaux, 107 S. Ct. 1549, 1553 (1987). Morever, the one major relevant exception to the pre-emption provision — the insurance law saving clause discussed in *Metropolitan Life* — is unlikely to be helpful in this context, because the Supreme Court has held that general state tort law as applied to an insured employee benefit plan does not constitute a law "which regulates insurance" and therefore is not exempt from ERISA pre-emption. *Pilot Life,* supra, at 1553-1558. The exclusive remedy is thus likely to be a contract enforcement action under §502 of ERISA, 29 U.S.C. §1132, which limits relief to declaratory judgments, injuctions, and recovery of accrued benefits due, thus precluding punitive and even compensatory damages. See id. at 1556. Needless to say, these interpretations do not augur well for *Wickline*-type challenges against private utilization review programs, although it is possible to conceive of employee benefit contracts that might provide a basis for interesting injunctive relief. In addition, much may depend on exactly how the utilization review program is structured: for instance, whether it is part of an insurance company's administration of the benefit plan. For further discussion of ERISA and utilization review, see Blum, An Analysis of Legal Liability in Health Care Utilization Review and Case Management, 26 Houston L. Rev. 191 (1989).

Alternatively, states that wished to regulate nongovernmental utilization review could enact legislation specifically designed to that end, framed as a law regulating insurance to attempt to come within ERISA's insurance law saving clause. (See analogous discussion of state regulation of HMO financial incentives in Section 2 below.) Would such a tactic be successful? The Supreme Court has articulated a three-part test for determining whether a state law falls into the saving clause:

> [*F*]*irst,* whether the practice [regulated by the law] has the effect of transferring or spreading a policyholder's risk; *second,* whether the practice is an integral part of the policy relationship between the insurer and the insured; and *third,* whether the practice is limited to entities within the insurance industry. [Union Labor Life Insurance Co. v. Pireno, 458 U.S. 119, 129 (1982), quoted in *Pilot Life,* supra, at 1553-1554.]

As applied to utilization review by insurance companies involved in employee benefit plans, all three factors are debatable, particularly the third. Moreover, however the Supreme Court ruled on such a law, the law would clearly be pre-empted with respect to self-insured employee benefit plans, thereby creating a further incentive for employers to turn away from the traditional insurance market. Of course, Congress itself could regulate employment-based utilization review by amending ERISA, perhaps using standards currently under development with respect to Medicare and Medicaid HMO financial incentives discussed in Section 2 below.

2. MALPRACTICE NORMS AND HMO FINANCIAL INCENTIVES

Health maintenance organizations (HMOs) are clearly a major phenomenon in contemporary American health care delivery. After 40 years of holding a minor and largely static market share, they have expanded enormously in the 1980s, increasing from 10.8 million enrollees in 1982 to 29.3 million enrollees in 1987. See Gruber, Shadle & Polich, From Movement to Industry: The Growth of HMOs, 7 Health Affairs 197, 198 (Summer 1988). The historical, organizational, and legal context of HMO development is explored primarily in Chapter 8, Section B, with additional material in the Introduction and in Section B of this chapter. This section focuses on a particular issue at the heart of the cost containment/quality of care tension: do HMOs owe a duty of reasonable care (including disclosure) to their enrollees in designing and administering the financial incentives applied to the providers who deliver services?

Several sources of law apply to HMOs. If an HMO wishes to be eligible for federal loans and other subsidies, and to obtain federally required access to the employee health insurance market, it must comply with the provisions of the federal Health Maintenance Organization Act, 42 U.S.C. §§300 et seq., discussed in Chapter 8. HMOs are also licensed by the states and must comply with various requirements to obtain contracts under Medicare and Medicaid. For the most part, however, these sources of law focus on such matters as benefit coverage, open enrollment periods, disenrollment and grievance procedures, marketing, and financial solvency. With rare exceptions, they do not address what is coming to be seen as a central policy issue with regard to HMOs and quality of care: the details of the financial relationship between the HMO and the primary care physician, that is, the doctor who sees the patient in the first instance and who is responsible for ordering laboratory tests, referring to specialists, and deciding on hospitalization.

HMOs are organized in a variety of ways and use a variety of financial techniques to motivate physicians to economize.

> . . . There are four organizational models of HMOs: the staff model (the HMO delivers health services through physicians who are employed and controlled directly by the HMO), the group model (the HMO contracts with an independent, group practice), the network model (the HMO contracts with two or more independent group practices), and the individual practice association (IPA) model (the HMO contracts predominantly with physicians in independent practice). Each of these types of HMO may use one or more of three methods of paying its practitioners: salary, fee-for-service, or capitation.
>
> In a typical HMO, after an administrative percentage is deducted, the premium is divided into various special-purpose funds, adjusted for age and sex, to pay for the services of primary care physicians, specialists, and hospitals and for outpatient laboratory tests. The primary care fund is used to pay the primary care physicians, although a percentage of their payment is often withheld until the status of the other funds is determined at the end of the year. If there is a surplus, the HMO may return the withheld amount to the primary care physicians; if there is a deficit, the withheld funds may be retained by the HMO. HMOs may share part or all of any surpluses in these funds with the primary care physicians as bonuses. Similarly, HMOs may penalize physicians for deficits beyond the withheld amount. The penalties and rewards may be based on the experience of individual practitioners or a pool of providers. Variations on this model include plans that do not use separate funds, withholding, or bonuses (such as many staff-model HMOs), plans in which two or more of the special-purpose funds are combined, and plans in which the penalty or bonus is based on part, rather than all, of the funds. [Hillman, Financial Incentives for Physicians in HMOs: Is There a Conflict of Interest?, 317 N. Engl. J. Med. 1743, 1744 (1987).]

As this summary suggests, four factors are particularly important in structuring the financial relationship between the HMO and the primary care physician. The first is the general form of compensation: salary, fee-for-service, or capitation (a fixed amount per month per patient enrolled, regardless of patient use of services). The second is the percentage of physician compensation at risk. This risk depends on the cost experience of the reserve or specialized funds, such as for laboratory, specialists, and hospitalization. The third is the size of the physician and patient pool in relation to which the cost experience is determined: for instance, each physician and his or her patients, or a larger pool of physicians and patients. The fourth is the time frame in which costs are measured, such as monthly, quarterly, or yearly. The last three factors effectively determine the strength of the financial incentive for any individual physician. Suppose that a system measures the laboratory, specialist, and hospitalization costs generated by each primary care physician each month and penalizes the physician by a significant percentage (such as 50 percent of the standard capitation fee). Such a system does not spread the risk of a high cost illness over a large group of patients or over time and would seem to generate strong pressures on the physician to withhold services (or, perhaps, to attempt to transfer the "expensive" patient to another provider). See General Accounting Office, Medicare: Physician Incentive Payments by Prepaid Health Plans Could Lower Quality of Care, GAO/HRD-89-29 (Dec. 12, 1988).

Legal involvement in these questions is in its infancy but is likely to grow significantly. The first, and as of May 1989, only reported judicial opinion on the subject touches only briefly on the issues and does not constitute a significant precedent. See Pulvers v. Kaiser Foundation Health Plan, 99 Cal. App. 3d 560, 160 Cal. Rptr. 392 (1980) (in suit against HMO, alleging negligently delayed biopsy as cause of patient's death, jury refused to find negligence on part of treating physician, and court dismissed claim of HMO fraudulent concealment of physician financial incentives on the grounds that such incentives were recommended by professional organizations and "required" (sic) by the federal HMO Act of 1973, 42 U.S.C. §300e).

A more carefully litigated malpractice claim against an HMO financial incentive system would likely be taken more seriously by the courts in 1989. The degree of concern by physicians and policymakers about HMO (and similar) financial incentives is far greater and better grounded in 1989 than it was in 1980. For example, in July 1986 the General Accounting Office reported to Congress that certain financial incentive plans offered to physicians by hospitals could have detrimental effects on the quality of care provided to Medicare patients. Of particular concern was a plan used by Paracelsus Healthcare Corporation, under which each month, hospital charges for Medicare patients admitted by each physician were compared with the prospective payments that the hospital received from Medicare for those patients. If this comparison showed a financial surplus for the hospital, the physician received a percentage of it, without any quality control mechanisms to prevent or identify abuses. See General Accounting Office, Medicare: Physician Incentive Payments by Hospitals Could Lead to Abuse (GAO/HRD-86-103, July 22, 1986).

In response to this potentially strong financial incentive on individual physicians to reduce laboratory tests, hospital length of stay, and other services to patients, Congress enacted §9313 of the Omnibus Budget Reconciliation Act of 1986 [OBRA 1986], Pub. L. 99-509. Effective April 21, 1987, this statute prohibits hospitals participating in Medicare from making "a payment, directly or indirectly, to a physician as an inducement to reduce or limit services provided" to Medicare and Medicaid beneficiaries. Pub. L. 99-509, §9313(c)(1), 100 Stat. 2003, codified at 42 U.S.C. §1320a-7a(b). The prohibition also applies to an HMO or other entity with a risk sharing contract with Medicare or Medicaid, but the effective date of the HMO prohibition has been delayed until April 1, 1990, to give Congress time to consider a statutorily required (but overdue) report from the Secretary of HHS evaluating the potential of HMO financial incentives "to reduce or limit services in a medically inappropriate manner," Pub. L. 99-509, §9313(c)(3). See also Iglehart, Second Thoughts About HMOs for Medicare Patients, 316 N. Engl. J. Med. 1487, 1490 (1987). But see Hall, Institutional Control of Physician Behavior: Legal Barriers to Health Care Cost Containment, 137 U. Pa. L. Rev. 431, 499-502 (1988) (criticizing the incentive payment prohibition as hypocritical, poorly conceived posturing, because: (i) Congress itself uses incentive payments to reduce services through DRGs and HMO contracts; (ii) the prohibition applies only to payments or positive incentives, and not to equally problematic penalties; and (iii) it is not seriously conceivable that Congress will actually enforce the flat prohibition against HMOs, because such a ban "would destroy or radically alter the [HMO] industry." Id. at 501 n.247).

In addition, OBRA 1986 contained a number of other provisions designed to improve quality of care in prepaid programs or to protect beneficiaries, including a requirement that Medicare HMOs and state Medicaid agencies contract with PROs to assess quality of care in at-risk health plans, and imposing civil penalties on HMOs for failure to furnish medically necessary services to Medicare and Medicaid enrollees. See 42 U.S.C. §§1395mm (i)(7)(A), (6) [Medicare]; 1396b(m)(6)(B)(iv), 5(a) [Medicaid] (Supp. V 1987). See generally House Committee on Energy & Comm., Subcommittee on Health & Environment, Medicaid Source Book: Background Data and Analysis 150-152 (Comm. Print 100-A, Nov. 1988).

The concerns underlying these legislative developments are also coming to the attention of the plaintiffs' malpractice bar. The following excerpt draws attention to several important issues.

> When Kelly Anne Sweede's gynecologist examined a lump in her breast and recommended that she undergo a biopsy to test for malignancy, Sweede passed

> that along to her HMO physician. Under her health coverage plan, she needed his permission to receive the procedure.
>
> But the physician instead ordered a mammogram, less expensive to perform than a biopsy, and the results were negative.
>
> Now, three years later, Sweede, 24, of Wilmington, [Del.,] is dying of breast cancer.
>
> In addition to suing her physician for failing to diagnose the cancer, she is suing her health maintenance organization, Cigna Healthplan of Delaware Inc., contending that the missed diagnosis was caused in part by an incentive system that rewarded her physician financially for keeping down referrals to specialists. [Hallowell, Challenging the HMO system of incentives, Philadelphia Inquirer, Mar. 28, 1989, at 1-B:2.]

In response to Sweede's complaint, the HMO claimed that ERISA pre-empted the application of state tort law to HMO financial incentives, because Sweede's coverage was part of an employee benefits plan. Although the case was settled before trial, it seems very likely that both the substantive tort issues and the ERISA pre-emption issue will be decided in some subsequent case. Telephone interview with Randall E. Robbins, Esq., attorney for Kelly Anne Sweede, May 15, 1989.

Problem: Medical Malpractice Law and HMO Financial Incentives

Assume you are an associate in a firm representing a patient in the same circumstances as Kelly Anne Sweede. Your senior partner has asked you to answer the following questions:

1. What do we have to find out in discovery about the HMO's financial incentives with respect to primary care physicians?
2. What do we have to find out about the HMO physicians' patterns of treatment?
3. What kind of expert testimony do we need, making what points?
4. What is our best response to the argument that ERISA preempts application of state tort law to employment-based HMO financial incentives?

Notes and Questions: State Legislative Responses to HMO Financial Incentives

Massachusetts House Bill No. 2777 (Jan. 1987), which has not been enacted, would amend the state's insurance law to provide that "[e]very policy or contract of health insurance," including commercial indemnity plans, Blue Cross and Blue Shield plans, HMO contracts, and employee benefit plans "to the extent permitted under federal law," shall "disclose in a clear, concise, complete, explicit, and understandable manner," inter alia, the method of payment of providers, and the financial obligations and risks imposed upon providers, including the explicit and implicit financial incentives and disincentives on both providers and consumers with respect to the use or non-use of various health care resources. See also Levinson, Toward Full Disclosure of Referral Restrictions and Financial Incentives by Prepaid Health Plans, 317 N. Engl. J. Med. 1729 (1987) (arguing that even though effects of varying incentives are unclear, consumers should have a right to accurate information about how health benefits will actually be distributed, and the right to make their own decisions about the relative costs and benefits of prepaid versus fee-for-service care).

What do you think the effect of such legislation would be? According to one review of the literature, consumers may equate quantity of care with technical quality, and vice-versa, even though the relationship is not always valid. Davies & Ware, Involving Consumers in Quality of Care Assessment, 7 Health Affairs at 33, 36-37 (Spring 1988). If this is true, mandatory disclosure might create consumer pressure for unnecessary services and unnecessarily expensive financial incentives. On the other hand, as the discussion on geographic variations in Section A makes plain, physicians themselves are often not sure about the relationship between quantity and quality. For this reason, and others (such as the fact that consumer judgments about technical care usually agree with those of physicians, and the necessity of consumer views on inter-personal aspects of care), Davies and Ware argue that consumer views should be an important component of quality assessment programs.

Would mandatory disclosure be effective? In the wake of the *Sweede* case, state Representative Amick introduced a bill in the Delaware legislature prohibiting health insurance contracts from containing "any incentive provisions or any other provision which forces a physician to make a decision which is against the physicians [sic] pecuniary self-interest but are [sic] in the patient's best interest." H.R. Bill No. 100, 135th Gen. Assem. (Del., Jan. 1989). Amick stated that disclosure would be inadequate, "because disclosure then 'becomes merely a part of the fine print in the contract' that is forgotten." Hallowell, supra. If you were representing the HMO industry, what policy and legal arguments would you make to the legislature about this bill? If you were representing a consumer coalition that supported the bill's general aims, in what ways would you try to improve it?

In addition to the federal legislation regarding HMO contracts with Medicare and Medicaid noted above, there is also a significant history of state statutes and regulations (often combined with federal administrative action) regarding at-risk contracts under Medicaid. See generally Schneider & Stern, Health Maintenance Organizations and the Poor: Problems and Prospects, 70 N.W.U.L. Rev. 90, 124-138 (1975) (detailing California legislative response to prepaid health contracting problems in the early 1970s); Rosenblatt, Medicaid Primary Care Case Management, The Doctor-Patient Relationship, and the Politics of Privatization, 36 Case W. Res. L. Rev. 915,

949-959 (1986) (detailing federal and state administrative action and inaction regarding quality of care and Medicaid prepaid health plans).

This section has focused on ways that HMOs financially reward or penalize physicians for the impact of their decisions on the costs of health care services for enrollees. Such rewards and penalties may threaten quality care, although the definition of quality and patterns of causation are far from clear. Given this uncertainty, some HMOs try to counteract the unknown but plausible threats to quality by also financially rewarding or penalizing physicians in relation to quality of care standards. In other words, the system is designed to foster not just "economizing," but economizing that is consistent with concrete standards of quality of care. These efforts resemble other proposals about how to structure competition in ways that promote rather than undermine quality of care, discussed in Section 4 below.

3. MAXIMIZING HOSPITAL INCOME IN AN ERA OF COST CONTAINMENT: PHYSICIANS' "ECONOMIC PERFORMANCE" AND HOSPITAL STAFF-PRIVILEGE DECISIONS

When Medicare DRG reimbursement began in 1983, many observers believed that hospitals and/or medical staffs would begin extensive economic monitoring of physician behavior, and to some extent this has occurred. See Omenn & Conrad, Implications of DRGs for Clinicians, 311 N. Engl. J. Med. 1314, 1315 (1984) (predicting that hospitals and medical staffs "could make individual physicians accountable for certain cost-influencing variables within their control."); Cantrell & Flick, supra, at 48-50 (reporting amendment of hospital bylaws to consider economic efficiency criteria such as average length of stay, average charges per admission, number of reimbursement denials, number of bad debts generated, and adverse malpractice suits), cited in Hall, supra, at 518 n.316. Such efforts often require structural reorganization of hospitals away from the traditional model of deference to the autonomous private practitioner. Glandon and Morrisey suggest a continuum of increasingly collective structures beginning with "shared common interest" (that is, educational informational efforts to persuade physicians to practice in ways that economically benefit the hospital); moving to "joint venture" (formal sharing of power to set standards and divide profits); "limited access" to the medical staff (conditioned on economically appropriate practice patterns); and, ultimately, employment of physicians by the hospital, with the advantages and costs of direct managerial control. See Glandon & Morrisey, Redefining the Hospital-Physician Relationship Under Prospective Payment, 23 Inquiry 166 (1986).

Law professor Mark Hall argues that physicians will be able to resist all of these efforts with the assistance of legal doctrines supportive of professional autonomy. Hospital efforts to mandate practice protocols may run afoul of medical practice statutes and other doctrines protecting individual doctors from lay or institutional control. See Hall, Institutional Control of Physician Behavior: Legal Barriers to Health Care Cost Containment, 137 U. Pa. L. Rev. 431, 449-479 (1988). Financial incentives encounter obstacles from the Medicare/Medicaid Fraud and Abuse statute, 42 U.S.C. §1395nn(b) (1982) and analogous state statutes prohibiting fee splitting and "kickbacks," and from the Medicare/Medicaid prohibition on hospital incentive payments to physicians, 42 U.S.C. §1320a-7a (West Supp. 1988) discussed in Section 2 above. See id. at 488-504. Use of economic performance criteria in granting staff privileges may be vetoed by doctors themselves, because, as in the *St. John's* case in Section D above, governing boards are not permitted to unilaterally change medical staff bylaws. Id. at 527. Hall concedes that many judicial opinions have upheld hospital denial of staff privileges based at least in part on efficiency grounds; see, for instance, Knapp v. Palos Community Hospital, 125 Ill. App. 3d 244, 251, 465 N.E.2d 554, 560 (1984) (upholding exclusion based in part on physician's 50 percent longer hospitalizations and 31 percent higher costs than the norm), and cases discussed in Sections D(4)(b) and (d), supra. But these opinions always stress quality as well as efficiency concerns, and as Hall correctly points out, "no case cleanly supports the exclusion of physicians because of factors wholly unrelated to quality of care, much less opposed to quality." Id. at 525. Hall regards this as a defect in the law, as a surrender to "a professional libertarian credo" under which "our health care cost containment policy is doomed to failure, or at least to mediocrity." Id. at 536.

Hall's underlying theme is that if cost containment is to work, doctors must be able to retain some of the reduced costs as profit. This is the foundation principle of HMOs, and if it is accepted in that context, why not in the hospital staff-privilege context as well? He concedes that consumers may be more aware of these incentives in the HMO context than in the context of general hospital practice, but he argues that this can be cured by disclosure of the new hospital rules. See id. at 501 n.249. Are you persuaded? Can you think of other reasons why hospitals are not the same as HMOs? Are all reductions in services equivalent to increases in "efficiency"? Even if you agree that hospitals should be able to offer some financial inducements or to take economic performance into account to some extent, do you agree with Hall's support for the Paracelsus Hospital DRG incentive plan described in Section 2 above, under which the doctor gets a percentage of the hospital's DRG surplus on his particular patients on a monthly basis, apparently without any special controls for quality of care? Compare Welch, Prospective Payment to Medical Staffs: A Proposal, 8 Health Affairs at 34 (Spring 1989) (arguing that current system gives physician no financial incentive to control costs, but that fixed payments to a single physician create incentives so strong as to threaten quality of care; appropriate middle ground is to direct prospective payments to hospital medical staff as a whole, who would then divide surplus according to productivity formulas as is now done by medical school-based practices).

4. THE STRUCTURE OF MARKET COMPETITION AND THE QUALITY OF CARE

Market competition advocates, such as Professor Hall, often write as if there were only two models of quality of care and, more broadly, of health care delivery: one that grants virtually unreviewable power to the medical profession and another that accords virtually absolute authority to the outcomes of unregulated economic transactions. In this second model, market competition is supposed to make providers and consumers price conscious, and such knowledge will lead to rational decisions about which health care services are truly "worth" their costs, thus improving both the efficiency and quality of care. See generally Havighurst and Blumstein, Coping with Quality/Cost Trade-offs in Medical Care: The Role of PSROs, 70 N.W.U.L. Rev. 6, 15-20 (1975).

Critics of market competition have long argued that this scenario is seriously flawed: that neither providers nor consumers have accurate information about costs and benefits; that profits can and will be made not by the difficult road of improving efficiency and quality, but by the easy roads of market segmentation (that is, insuring the healthy) and unreliable service reductions; that medical malpractice law cannot function adequately to protect against underservice, particularly since some market competition advocates also want to reduce the standard of care through bargaining; and that lower-income market participants will suffer grievously, while higher-income patients exempt themselves from market discipline as much as possible through insurance. See, for instance, Rosenblatt, Health Care, Markets, and Democratic Values, 34 Vand. L. Rev. 1067 (1981); Rosenblatt, Rationing "Normal" Health Care: The Hidden Legal Issues, 59 Tex. L. Rev. 1401 (1981); Vladeck, The Market v. Regulation: The Case for Regulation, 59 Milbank Mem. Fund Q. 209 (1981), discussed in Chapter 8. In making these points, the market competition critics have not at all endorsed the medical professional model, but rather have called for a middle ground embodying one or another version of the social contract model discussed at the beginning of this chapter. See Rosenblatt, supra, at 1069; Vladeck, supra at 218-222.

A fascinating development in the last few years has been the emergence of social contract perspectives *among* advocates of market competition. The earliest and most prominent example is Alain Enthoven, whose "Consumer Choice Health Plan" is set forth in Chapter 8. Enthoven proposes both wide ranging tax incentives and subsidies to create market competition in health care, and extensive government regulation to insure that the competition is "socially desirable." A. Enthoven, Health Plan 126 (1980). These regulations would include government-supervised open enrollment periods, community rating of premiums, and mandated benefit packages (including catastrophic expense protection), which Enthoven says are necessary "to ensure that all health plans are competing to provide good-quality comprehensive care at a reasonable cost," rather than profiting from preferred risk selection and inadequate coverage. Id. at 72.

Writing in 1988, Enthoven concedes that "[a] competitive market will not automatically produce high-quality care, especially to the extent the market is characterized by poor information about quality. Suppliers to a competitive market seek to produce what the purchasers want. If the purchasers do not measure and demand high-quality care, there is little reason to expect they will get it." Enthoven, Managed Competition: An Agenda for Action, 7 Health Affairs at 25, 33 (Summer 1988). Walter McClure, who, along with Paul Ellwood, was one of the pioneering advocates of market competition in health care in the early 1970s, puts it even more bluntly: if group purchasers (such as employers, Medicare, and Medicaid) do not give their beneficiaries the right information and incentives, "[t]he market will necessarily be unsound, and these comprehensive [health] plans will compete on all the wrong things — creaming, image, fluff, quality-cutting, price-following, cost-raising behavior — all that bad stuff that too many providers and plans still compete over, because too few purchasers buy correctly yet." Put another way, "cheap care may well drive out good care, unless quality providers give purchasers the tools to identify objectively the quality provider." Iglehart, Competition and the Pursuit of Quality: A Conversation with Walter McClure, 7 Health Affairs at 79, 81, 85 (Spring 1988).

McClure and his associates are engaged in an interesting effort to define and implement what he terms a "buy-right" strategy of health care competition. The basic buy-right principle is that group purchasers should reward efficient, high-quality providers with patients. This requires two mechanisms: a technology for measuring and comparing quality and efficiency ("the Q & E problem"), and a system of incentives to induce individual beneficiaries to choose the high-quality providers ("the incentive benefits problem"). McClure's solution to the Q & E problem is persuade purchasers and providers in a single city or other sensibly defined local region to adopt a single Q & E system provided by one of the existing major, "qualified" vendors of Q & E technology. Such technology establishes a uniform data reporting system and criteria for measuring quality and efficiency. After a trial period in which defects are identified and corrected, and all providers learn how to use the new technology and adjust their practices if necessary, group purchasers will begin getting provider-specific ratings on quality and efficiency. They would then pass that information along to consumers (plan beneficiaries), who would also be given financial incentives to choose the higher rated providers.

McClure concedes that Q & E technology is currently at the "Model T" stage, but he believes it is good enough to start with and that development of buy-right markets would stimulate enormous growth of the "quality assessment industry." The real barrier to the buy-right strategy is the need for a social contract, at least at the local level. When McClure and his associates tried to persuade individual purchasers and providers to adopt their plan, they discovered that the economic and political costs were too great for a single purchaser or small group of purchasers to begin. Only when consensus is reached among all or almost all of the relevant actors can the costs and risks be spread, and the chances of success improved. Id. at 84-87. Brook and Kosecoff go further along the line and argue that only government investment of $50 million to $200 million over the next five years, together with systematic assessment of consumer values and political preferences, can provide a basis for developing a serious quality assessment system. Brook & Kosecoff, Commentary: Competition and Quality, 7 Health Affairs at 150, 157 (Summer 1988).

H. Conclusion

The law of quality of care, like other areas of health law, is in great flux, responding to numerous competing forces and to at least three models of quality of care law. The medical professional model, granting legal and social authority to the individual practicing physician to define and implement quality standards, is clearly on the defensive, although retaining considerable influence. Individual practitioners are now subject to national standards, and the responsibility for implementing those standards lies not only with the common law courts, but also increasingly with hospitals and other institutional providers, licensing and accreditation agencies, and payers and their agents, such as PROs and utilization review companies. These developments reflect the emergence of a social contract model of the law of quality of care, in which quality standards and their enforcement are seen as a matter of political and social choice regarding such profoundly important issues as quality and quantity of life, the dynamics of the doctor-patient relationship, the allocation of health care resources, and more general social resource allocation. At the same time, there is fierce debate over the content of the social contract, with some advocating an unregulated market competition version and others seeking a range of goals including efficiency, quality, individual autonomy, and equality. This debate and its outcome will both shape, and be shaped by, the law of quality care.

CHAPTER VI
Patient Rights

With all of the emphasis on access, quality, and cost, it is easy to lose sight of the individual patient. Hospitals serve many constituencies, and patients are only one of them. Because the hospital is a frightening, alien, and alienating environment for patients, and because the doctor-patient relationship is often skewed in favor of the doctor, the law's direction, at least over the past two decades, has been toward giving the patient more authority over decisions that directly affect the patient's mind and body.

Movement in this direction has occurred by articulating the doctrine of informed consent, giving patients the right to refuse treatment in almost all circumstances, and attempting to humanize the hospital environment through various strategies, such as statements of patient rights. The law works best in the medical arena when it promotes the rights of patients in a way that enhances their autonomy in the doctor-patient relationship and supports the supposition that decisions made in this confidential, voluntary, and informed relationship can be carried out without governmental or institutional interference (at least so long as they do not violate important public policy). The reasonable goal is to forge a doctor-patient relationship that is a true partnership in decision making. Because they enhance a doctor-patient partnership, patient rights become central to all medical decisionmaking, and defining and promoting patient rights in the hospital setting becomes a matter of critical importance to both physicians and patients.

Patients see many different doctors in the hospital. Even if they have a good relationship with their family physician, patients will encounter many specialists for the first time. Drugs and machines have made medicine more powerful, and this makes autonomy even more important. It is not true, for example, that all patients want to be treated like children and want their physician-parent to make decisions for them. The patient rights movement can best be understood as a reaction against the arbitrary exercise of authority by doctors and hospitals and is ultimately about power and control.

Literature from around the world informs us that many physicians cannot understand why patients seem to take autonomy so seriously, when the physicians "know" that fighting death and disease, and teaching others to fight it, is so much more important. In Aleksander Solzhenitsyn's The Cancer

Ward (1968), for example, a patient, Oleg Kostoglotov, discovers he has been receiving hormone therapy for cancer without his knowledge:

> By some right — it doesn't occur to them to question the right — they are deciding for me, without me, on a terrible treatment, hormone therapy. This is like a red hot iron which, once it touches you, leaves you maimed for life. *But it appears so ordinary in the ordinary life of the hospital.* [at 346.] [Emphasis added.]

Oleg understands fully that his physicians believe the treatment is absolutely necessary if he is to survive. But he also understands much more fully than they that there are fates worse than death:

> What, after all, is the highest price one should pay for life? *How much should one pay, how much is too much?* . . . — to save one's life at the cost of surrendering everything that gives it color, flavor and sparkle. To get a life of digestion, breathing, muscular and mental activity, and nothing more? To become a walking husk of a man — isn't that an exorbitant price? [Id.] [Emphasis added.]

Most Americans believe they should be active participants in medical treatment decisions and retain the right to refuse *any* medical intervention. Nonetheless, we know it will be extremely difficult to ensure that our human rights are honored in the hospital. Larry McMurtry's description of Emma's feelings on being hospitalized for cancer in Terms of Endearment (1975), conveys this almost universal fear of dehumanization:

> From that day, that moment almost, she felt her life pass from her own hands and the erring but personal hands of those who loved her into hands of strangers — and not even doctors, really, but technicians: nurses, attendants, laboratories, chemicals, machines. [Id. At 356.]

This is powerful imagery, powerful primarily because of its accuracy. Does it really have to be like this? Must doctors continue to train doctors to ignore the person and concentrate exclusively on the body? Must we really choose between expert technicians and humane caretakers? Can we really expect no better when we deliver ourselves "into the hands of strangers"? This chapter explores these questions. The law is important. But patient rights are often more a matter of informal agreement, hospital custom, and the ethical sensibilities of providers, than of explicit legal rule. And medical professionals tend to view the law as alien and threatening, and lawyers as predators to be avoided at almost all costs. Although legal developments and trends are the central foci of these materials, the law is only one piece of the whole: it sets a floor by defining duty. Ethics calls upon physicians and nurses to do not just what is legal, but what is "right." Communication, interpersonal relationships, expectations of all parties, and ethical standards all influence change and reform, and will strongly influence how legal changes actually affect real people.

A. Hospital Policies and Practices Regarding Patient Rights

1. OVERVIEW

Hospitals have historically been rigid, hierarchical institutions; although it is only recently, with the advent of technologically sophisticated medicine, that physicians have been at the top of the hierarchy. Patients, on the other hand, have always been at the bottom. At the end of the nineteenth century, for example, it was not uncommon to compare hospitals to prisons and patients to prisoners. Cleveland's Lakeside Hospital, for example, warned that:

> Patients admitted to the Hospital are forbidden to use profane or indecent language; to express immoral or infidel sentiments; to play cards or any other game for money; to smoke tobacco in the house, or to procure for themselves or others any intoxicating liquors. [Quoted in C.E. Rosenberg, The Care of Strangers 265 (1987).]

"Patients were — almost literally — incarcerated and required to apply for passes should they choose to leave the hospital grounds . . . Catholic hospitals may have seemed less threatening to immigrant clients than their Protestant peers, but they could be equally paternalistic in their regulations." Id.

Annas, The Hospital: A Human Rights Wasteland

4 Civ. Lib. Rev. 9-11 (1974)

Civil libertarians have little difficulty appreciating the plight of prisoners or mental patients. But tell the average civil libertarian that there are significant and unnecessary restrictions on the individual rights and liberties of patients in general hospitals, and you are likely to encounter a blank stare. There are a number of reasons for this lack of attention to hospitals. One is the general misconception that the problems are minor, or that certain temporary restrictions on individuals are essential if hospitals are to treat sick people properly. An unconscious desire not to perceive ourselves as being at risk may be another reason. Civil rights lawyers seldom seriously think they will ever be either prisoners or mental patients. But almost all of them — and us —

have been hospital patients at least once, however, and it is predictable that each of us will be a hospital patient an average of seven times during our lives. By not dealing with the issue, perhaps we are seeking to avoid thinking about our own future hospitalization — an event which is almost always traumatic and undesired.

Other than the fact that the average length of a hospital stay is about eight days, there are probably more similarities than differences among prisoners, mental patients, and general hospital patients. While no social stigmatization attaches to admission, the patient, for example, almost never comes to the hospital voluntarily. Some outside force, usually an illness or injury, has made admission mandatory. Unless the patient comes in through the emergency room, a doctor is likely to have ordered the admission and chosen the particular hospital. Upon arriving the patient is made to sign a variety of forms which generally are explained only with the assurance that they are routine. The patient then is separated from accompanying friends or relatives and escorted to a preassigned room. The patient's clothes are replaced with a johnnie — a one-piece garment designed for the convenience of the hospital staff in testing and treating the patient. The patient is given a plastic wristband with a number written on it — a number that becomes more important than his or her name. The patient is confined to a bed and may even have to await permission to use the toilet. Medication and food may be prescribed without consulting the patient; and nurses, students, aides, and physicians may enter the patient's room without knocking and submit the patient to all manner of examination and treatment without explanation. Moreover, all of this will be carefully recorded in a written record which the patient generally is not allowed to see, but which is available to all who see the patient and probably to anyone on the hospital staff, as well as to medical researchers and insurance companies. Unless the patient is in an expensive private room, visiting hours are restricted, as is access to the outside by means of the telephone.

The experience tends to intimidate and disorient the patient and discourages any assertion of individual rights. While medical care in the past was a one-to-one relationship involving only the patient and physician, in the modern hospital one patient is treated by a team in a large, unfamiliar, institutional setting. Because of this, the institution-patient relationship becomes at least as important as the doctor-patient relationship.

Those interested in the rights of women, children, and the poor should also be able to identify many problems in the hospital. Patients are asked to behave like children, investing in the physician and staff the faith they once had in their parents. Women are often treated as more neurotic and emotional than men, and thus frequently deprived of information concerning treatment alternatives and possible complications because it might "upset" them unduly. To suit their convenience, hospital staffs often separate children from their parents, ignoring their physical and emotional needs. Finally, the source of payment often may determine the quality and type of care, as well as the manner in which it is administered. And hospitals, which have become major financial enterprises, may view their primary functions as research and education rather than patient care.

Why hasn't the voice of the consumer risen up in effective protest to demand changes in the more dehumanizing practices of hospitals? First, the average length of stay of about a week makes formation of an in-patient consumer group impossible. Second, most patients in hospitals are simply too sick to assert their personal rights. Indeed they may be more than willing to forgo them if they believe that this will speed up their treatment and return home. Third, healthy individuals do not see the issue as one which is as vital to their lives as others which affect them daily, such as housing, education, and racial discrimination. Finally, there is the great difficulty outsiders have in understanding what the institution called a hospital is all about.

Hospitals as we now know them are a product of only the past three or four decades. Before the turn of this century it was unlikely that going to a hospital (or almshouse or pesthouse, as they were more often termed) would do one any good — most people went to them only because they were poor and dying or had an incurable condition. The only recorded hospital patients' rights measure before this century was instituted in France in 1793 by the National Convention of the French Revolution. It decreed that there should be only one patient in a bed (as opposed to the usual two to eight) and that beds should be at least three feet apart. A cynic could argue that we haven't come very far since 1793.

As drugs and surgery replaced the purging and bleeding of the nineteenth and early twentieth centuries, and as medical education and specialty medicine progressed, the hospital gradually became the center of medical research. States and localities set up hospitals for their citizens, following the lead of private charities and nonprofit corporations. Perhaps the most significant development was the teaching hospital. Usually a large, general hospital in which medical students, interns, and residents are trained under the direction of experienced physicians on the faculty of a medical school, it is here that most medical research takes place, most medical advances are initiated, and where the best medical techniques available are most likely to be found.

It is also likely that in the teaching hospitals the least attention is paid to patient rights. But rights problems exist to some extent in all hospitals. The physician-director of Boston's Beth Israel Hospital has described the patient's dilemma in a modern hospital in the following terms:

> Having evolved from a shelter for wayfarers and then a place for the sick poor to die in a therapeutic community where scientific medicine can bring about diagnosis and healing, today's hospital stands increasingly to become a jungle, whose pathways to the uninitiated are poorly marked and fraught with danger, the same pathways which, as they become overgrown by the teeming hospital environment, may be poorly perceived and even invisible from above.

The argument for enhanced patient rights is based on two fundamental premises: (1) the American medical consumer possesses certain interests, many of which may properly be described as rights, that are not automatically forfeited by entering into a relationship with a doctor or a health care facility; and (2) most doctors and health care facilities fail to recognize the existence of these interests and rights, fail to provide for their protection or assertion, and frequently limit their exercise without recourse.

P. Starr, The Social Transformation of American Medicine

388-393 (1982)

. . . Recognized rights in health care, such as informed consent, obligate doctors and hospitals to share more information and authority with their patients. Thus the new health rights movement [of the 1970s] went beyond traditional demands for more medical care and challenged the distribution of power and expertise. These efforts, like the attempts to enlarge entitlements to services, met some success in the courts. Indeed, few other developments so well illustrate the decline of professional sovereignty in the 1970s as the increased tendency of the courts to view the doctor-patient relationship as a partnership in decision making rather than a doctors' monopoly. . . .

. . . Since the Progressive era . . . reformers had assumed that professionals, including physicians, would act in the interests of the dependent; consequently, they were willing to give them wide discretion in institutions such as prisons and hospitals. By the 1970s, reformers had become intensely skeptical of professionals and the benevolent institutions they supervised. From this distrust emerged a variety of legal safeguards aimed at limiting professional autonomy and power. A related movement also developed to "deinstitutionalize" the dependent and "demedicalize" critical life events, such as childbirth and dying. The interest in hospices and home births derived, at least in part, from a desire to escape professional dominance as well as the desensitizing environment of the hospital. In the view of its critics, the hospital had become a zone of medical domination, and the only escape was to remove the "patient" to a setting where medical authority would be secondary. . . .

M. Konner, Becoming a Doctor

364-365 (1987)

. . . I have developed the impatience with ethical discussions characteristic of most house officers. It isn't that I don't consider them important, it's just that I don't consider them my job. I follow the rules laid down by the hospital — meaning, the rules laid down by society. Tell me in plain English what the Do Not Resuscitate order means and exactly whom it applies to, and I will carry it out. Tell me which fetuses you want saved and which thrown away; to the best of my technical ability, I will comply. Tell me what sort of craziness warrants involuntary commitment and I will know which patients to keep off the street. Tell me the rules — define them as strictly as you can — for taking the heart out of patient A and putting it into patient B, and I will go on with that dazzling technical miracle; I won't have pangs of conscience, which I really don't need and which only make my work harder. . . .

[T]he stress of clinical training alienates the doctor from the patient, [so] that in a real sense the patient becomes the enemy. (*Goddamit, did she blow her I.V. again? Jesus Christ, did he spike a temp?*) At first I believed that this was an inadvertent and unfortunate concomitant of medical training, but I now think that it is intrinsic. Not only stress and sleeplessness but the sense of the patient as the cause of one's distress contributes to the doctor's detachment. This detachment is not just objective but downright negative. To cut and puncture a person, to take his or her life in your hands, to pound the chest until ribs break, to decide upon drastic action without being able to ask permission, to render a judgment about whether care should continue or stop — these and a thousand other things may require something stronger than objectivity. They may actually require a measure of dislike.

In the end, we all — doctors, patients, hospital staff — have a sense that the doctors are doctors, and can be allowed to do what they do, *because of* the rigors of the training. Because we view it as painful, stressful, life-distorting, and terribly long, we allow it to justify the remarkable power we give the doctor over us. The doctor has paid for the power with suffering.

Annas, The Emerging Stowaway: Patients Rights in the 1980s

10 Law, Med. & Health Care 32-35 (1982)

Related to the general attack on rights is an attack on the patient population itself. The notion is that the major problems with the health care delivery system are not problems with providers, but with patients. We eat too much, smoke too much, don't exercise, take too many risks, etc., and so what do we expect when we get sick? Not only must the American health care enterprise deal with a bad class of patients, but now they want some say in what kind of care is provided! As Lewis Thomas has put it in a related vein: this is becoming "folk doctrine about disease. You become ill because of not living right. If you get cancer it is, somehow or other, your own fault. If you didn't cause it by smoking or drinking, or eating the wrong things, it came from allowing yourself to persist with the wrong kind of personality in the wrong environment."

This attitude would be humorous if it were not so pervasive and did not affect patient care so profoundly. Martha Lear has given us some excellent and telling examples in her deeply moving book, Heartsounds, that chronicles the final four years of her physician-husband who goes through eight operations and eleven hospitalizations during that period. Together they identify the "it's your fault ploy" which means that no matter what goes wrong in the hospital setting, it is the fault of the patient, not the health care system:

> Why did the operation take so long?
> Because you lost so much blood.
> *Not:* Because the surgeon blew it.
>
> Why do you keep making these tests?
> Because you have a very stubborn infection.
> *Not:* Because I can't diagnose your case.
>
> Why did I get sick again?
> Because you were very weak.
> *Not:* Because I did not treat you competently the first time.

Dr. Lear is constantly asking himself if he treated patients that way, and usually admits that he did. He suggests that every physician spend at least a week per year in a hospital bed: "That would change some things in a hurry."

Since patients *do* have rights and *do* want to exercise them, and since the major attacks on the notion of patients rights have been based on sloppy studies and false premises, the patients rights movement is likely to gain momentum. Indeed, the 1970s can be most properly viewed as a decade in which the existence of patients rights became legitimized through basic education of the health care providers. The 1980s should be a decade in which the primary thrust is to work on ways to directly enhance the status of patients in the hospital as a means of humanizing the hospital environment so that patients can have a greater voice in how they are treated.

I suggest the following five point agenda for the '80s:

Patient Rights Agenda

1. No Routine Procedures
2. Open Access to Medical Records
3. Twenty-Four-Hour-a-Day Visitor Rights
4. Full Experience Disclosure
5. Effective Patient Advocate

(1) No Routine Procedures. It is common for nurses and others to respond to the question, "Why is this being done?" with, "Don't worry, it's routine." This should not be an acceptable response. No procedure should *ever* be performed on a patient because it is routine; it should only be performed because it is *specifically* indicated for a patient. Thus routine admission tests, routine use of johnnies, routine use of wheelchairs for in-hospital transportation, routine use of sleeping pills, to name a few notable examples, should be abolished. Use of these procedures means patients are treated as fungible robots rather than as individual human beings. Moreover, these procedures are often demeaning and unnecessary.

(2) Open Access to Medical Records. While currently provided for by federal law and many state statutes and regulations, open access to medical records by patients remains difficult, and a patient often asserts his right to see his record at the peril of being labeled "distrustful" or a "trouble-maker." The information in the hospital chart is about the patient and properly belongs to the patient. The patient must have access to it, both to enhance his own decision-making ability and to make it clear that the hospital is an "open" institution that is not trying to hide things from the patient. Surely if hospital personnel make decisions about the patient on the basis of information in the chart, the patient also deserves access to the information.

(3) Twenty-Four-Hour-a-Day Visitor Rights. One of the most important ways both to humanize the hospital and to enhance patient autonomy is to assure the patient that at least one person of the patient's choice has unlimited access to the patient at any time of the day or night. This person should also be permitted to stay with the patient during any procedure (e.g., childbirth or induction of anesthesia) as long as the person does not interfere with the care of other patients.

(4) Full Experience Disclosure. The most important gain of the past decade has been the almost universal acknowledgment of the need for the patient's informed consent. Nevertheless, some information that is material to the patient's decision is still withheld: the experience of the person doing the procedure. Patients have a right to know if the person asking permission to draw blood, take blood gases, do a bone marrow aspiration, or do a spinal tap has ever performed the procedure before, and if so, what the person's complication rate is. This applies not only to medical students and student nurses, but also to board certified surgeons. We all do things for the first time, and not every patient wants to take such an active role in education.

(5) An Effective Patient Advocate. While a patient bill of rights is necessary, it is not sufficient. Rights are not self-actualizing. Patients are sick and desire relief from pain and discomfort more than they demonstrate a desire to exercise their rights; they are also anxious, and may hold back complaints for fear of retaliation. It is critical that patients have access to a person whose job it is to work *for the patient* to help the patient exercise the rights outlined in the institution's bill of rights. This person should be a member of all major hospital committees that deal with patient care, have authority to obtain

medical records for patients, call consultants, launch complaints directly with all members of the hospital, medical, nursing, and administrative staff, and be able to delay discharges. While there appear to be some successful "patient representatives" hired by hospitals, it is not accurate to give them this title since they must represent their employer, the hospital. It is likely that ultimately effective representation can only be obtained by someone who is hired by a consumer group or governmental agency outside the hospital in which the representative works.

Notes on Hospital Patients

(1) Paul Starr's book provides an excellent historical perspective on modern medicine, and students are encouraged to read the entire volume. Charles Rosenberg's, The Care of Strangers (1988) is recommended as well, especially for those trying to understand the evolution of the hospital. Melvin Konner was a young professor of anthropology before he decided to go to medical school. His book chronicles his experiences and reflections on the third year of medical school. Following graduation, Konner decided to return to anthropology, but still writes regularly on medical topics. The first piece by George Annas was written just before the publication of The Rights of Hospital Patients (1975), the second at the beginning of the 80s. The second edition of The Rights of Hospital Patients, retitled The Rights of Patients, was published in 1989.

(2) In many ways, the hospital is like any large bureaucratic organization, in that its members are its main constituency, and its rules are developed for the primary purpose of keeping the organization running smoothly. Standardization and depersonalization are recognized and even promoted by the rationalization that the results are ultimately beneficial to the patients. Autonomy and individual choice are curtailed by protocols and the use of "routine procedures," through which the patient becomes treated as a nonperson. Information is routinely withheld to diminish the patient's ability to interact or question medical decisions.

In a study of how patients think they should behave in the hospital, and how the nurses and medical staff think they should behave, Judith Lorber drew a sample of patients who had undergone surgical procedures ranging from "routine" (33 herniorrhaphies) to "very serious" (35 gastric, colon, and abdominoperineal resections). A total of 103 patients of various ages and backgrounds were studied, as were the evaluation of these patients by the nurses and doctors. Lorber summarizes her conclusions from this study:

> In sum, doctors and nurses expect to carry out their work by well-established routines, with a minimum of interruption from patients. Those patients who make no trouble at all, who do not interrupt the smoothness of medical routines, are likely to be considered *good* patients by the medical staff. . . . Doc-

tors and nurses tend to consider *average* patients those whose complaints are medically warranted, who respond to established routines for handling such complaints, and who therefore take up the expected amount of time for their type of illness. . . . *Problem* patients are of two kinds. Those who are seriously ill, and who complain a great deal, are very emotional, anxious, and need a lot of reassurance, encouragement, and attention from the staff are problematic, but "forgivable" because the situation is not of their own making. In this study, they were often given the time and attention they demanded, particularly if they were grateful for it. Nonetheless, the extraordinary amount of time and attention they took up made them "problem patients." (Conversely, seriously ill patients who were extraordinarily cheerful, cooperative, uncomplaining, and objective about their illness were considered *great* patients and talked about after discharge as "ideal.") Patients who are *not* seriously ill in the staff's eyes, but who nevertheless act as if they are by complaining, crying, and refusing to cooperate with medical routines, are the most soundly condemned by the staff. Such problem patients, in this study, were tranquilized, sometimes discharged early, and, in one case, referred to a psychiatrist — types of response to wilfully troublesome patients other researchers have also found.

Thus, the consequences of deliberate deviance in the general hospital can be medical neglect or a stigmatizing label, while [the reward for] conformity to good-patient norms is usually a return home with only a surgical scar. [Lorber, Good Patients and Problem Patients: Conformity and Deviance in a General Hospital in Patients, Physicians and Illness 202, 216 (E. Jaco, ed. 3d ed. 1979).]

(3) Some physicians and commentators challenge the paradigm of "patient rights" as inappropriate to the doctor-patient relationship. Eric Cassell, The Healer's Art 26-35, 140-144 (1976), describes the doctor-patient relation in the following terms.

In health we know we are alive by our connectedness to the world. When we are totally disconnected, we are dead. . . . As illness deepens, connections are increasingly cut off by the symptoms of sickness and by the forced withdrawal from society caused by sickness. . . . Along with his loss of connectedness to the world, the sick person suffers a loss of his sense of indestructibility. When healthy, each of us takes his body for granted and prizes his body image. Even though we may not like its appearance, we value its intactness, its readiness to do and go. . . .

The image of omnipotence is an essential component of the healer. . . . So the doctor's life experience strengthens his already strong sense of omnipotence. His patient needs it. We saw how illness puts cracks in the essential shield of omnipotence all of us have and how damaging it is to lose the sense of omnipotence, how insecure we are when our frailty becomes known to us — who will put Humpty Dumpty together again? The doctor's feeling of omnipotence is thus essential to his role. His posture of omnipotence may annoy the healthy and infuriate the nurses — but how important it is for the sick. The patient borrows it, clothes his nakedness in it until such time as his own becomes whole again — as it does during the process of recovery from illness. . . .

> Just as the doctor's sense of omnipotence is used by both the doctor and the patient to shield the patient from the nakedness of his frailty, so too is the physician's connectedness a powerful tool in healing. . . . The patient, withdrawn deeper and deeper into himself as his sickness worsens, is protected from falling off the world by the reassuring hand of his doctor. . . .

Similarly, Professor Robert Burt argues that patients' interests are not met by reading them a bill of rights and imposing upon them the responsibility for choice. Rather patients need physicians who will enter into a relationship of dialogue and connection with them. Particularly, a patient confronted with the shock and pain of a disfiguring and disabling injury needs paternalistic help to accept his situation and be drawn back into a human community. See Taking Care of Strangers (1979).

Many commentators have observed that a model of "partnership" decision making is inevitably phoney. Physicians can always present "choices" in ways that coerce the patient to do that which the physician believes is correct, even if another doctor would have made another choice. The law, rather than encouraging a hypocritical model of patient responsibility for decision, that implicitly allows the doctor to distance himself from the patient, should place decision making responsibility on the physician and require that he or she exercise a fiduciary responsibility to do that which he or she would do if the patient were a beloved parent or spouse.

Finally, some critics believe that fundamental change in the provider-patient relationship (to make it more responsive and equitable) is possible only after there is a basic change in our social structure. The argument is that the health system is primarily a mirror of the larger social, political, and economic system of which it is a part, and that changes in health care policy and practices will come only from changes in that larger system. Problems of equity and access are thus viewed not as problems of physician discrimination or hospital policy but as problems of poverty, social class, race, and geographic location.

good point

2. HOSPITAL POLICIES AND LEGISLATION

Hospitals are not completely oblivious to patient rights and are increasingly recognizing that it makes good business sense to treat patients like consumers, even if hospitals are not yet prepared to treat them like partners in decision making. Both the Joint Commission on Accreditation of Healthcare Organizations (JCAH) and the American Hospital Association promulgated statements on patients rights in 1970 and 1972 respectively. The JCAH has updated their statement, but the AHA said in 1986 that their statement remained sufficient.

In addition, the following states have enacted patient bills of rights by statute, regulation, or resolution: California, Colorado, Illinois, Kentucky,

Maryland, Massachusetts, Michigan, Minnesota, Pennsylvania, New York, and Rhode Island. These documents are primarily a restatement of common law. Their primary characteristic is often vagueness. In this regard, nursing home patients have fared somewhat better. See Note, Nursing Home Patients' Rights in Massachusetts: Current Protection and Recommendations for Improving, 6 Am. J. L. Med. 315 (1980); Mulholland, The Corporate Responsibility of the Community Hospital, 17 Toledo L. Rev. 343 (1986); and G. J. Annas, The Rights of Patients (1989).

Joint Commission on the Accreditation of Healthcare Organizations, Accreditation Manual for Hospitals

xi-xiii (1988)

Access to Care

Individuals shall be accorded impartial access to treatment or accommodations that are available or medically indicated, regardless of race, creed, sex, national origin, or sources of payment for care.

Respect and Dignity

The patient has the right to considerate, respectful care at all times and under all circumstances, with recognition of his personal dignity.

Identity

The patient has the right to know the identity and professional status of individuals providing service to him and to know which physician or other practitioner is primarily responsible for his care. Participation by patients in clinical training programs or in the gathering of data for research purposes should be voluntary. . . .

Refusal of Treatment

The patient may refuse treatment to the extent permitted by law.

American Hospital Association, A Patient's Bill of Rights

(1973)

1) The patient has the right to considerate and respectful care.

2) The patient has the right to obtain from his physician complete current information concerning his diagnosis, treatment, and prognosis in terms the patient can be reasonably expected to understand. When it is not

medically advisable to give such information to the patient, the information should be made available to an appropriate person in his behalf. He has the right to know, by name, the physician responsible for coordinating his care.

3) The patient has the right to receive from his physician information necessary to give informed consent prior to the start of any procedure and/or treatment. Except in emergencies, such information for informed consent should include but not necessarily be limited to the specific procedure and/or treatment, the medically significant risks involved, and the probable duration of incapacitation. Where medically significant alternatives for care or treatment exist, or when the patient requests information concerning medical alternatives, the patient has the right to such information. The patient also has the right to know the name of the person responsible for the procedures and/or treatment.

4) The patient has the right to refuse treatment to the extent permitted by law and to be informed of the medical consequences of his action.

5) The patient has the right to every consideration of his privacy concerning his own medical care program. Case discussion, consultation, examination, and treatment are confidential and should be conducted discreetly. Those not directly involved in his care must have the permission of the patient to be present.

6) The patient has the right to expect that all communications and records pertaining to his care should be treated as confidential.

7) The patient has the right to expect that within its capacity a hospital must make reasonable response to the request of a patient for services. The hospital must provide evaluation, service, and/or referral as indicated by the urgency of the case. When medically permissible, a patient may be transferred to another facility only after he has received complete information and explanation concerning the needs for and alternatives to such a transfer. The institution to which the patient is to be transferred must first have accepted the patient for transfer.

8) The patient has the right to obtain information as to any relationship of his hospital to other health care and educational institutions insofar as his care is concerned. The patient has the right to obtain information as to the existence of any professional relationships among individuals, by name, who are treating him.

9) The patient has the right to be advised if the hospital proposes to engage in or perform human experimentation affecting his care or treatment. The patient has the right to refuse to participate in such research projects.

10) The patient has the right to expect reasonable continuity of care. He has the right to know in advance what appointment times and physicians are available and where. The patient has the right to expect that the hospital will provide a mechanism whereby he is informed by his physician or a delegate of the physician of the patient's continuing health care requirements following discharge.

11) The patient has the right to examine and receive an explanation of his bill regardless of source of payment.

12) The patient has the right to know what hospital rules and regulations apply to his conduct as a patient.

NOTE ON BILLS OF RIGHTS, PATIENT REPRESENTATIVES, AND PATIENT ADVOCATES

We have come to accept the proposition that it is useful and protective to enunciate the rights of individuals specifically. On the other hand, as the framers of the Constitution recognized (when they rejected the inclusion of a "Bill of Rights" in the original document), there are problems with any explicit statement of rights. First, what is the source of the rights in question? Does a bill of rights prepared by a hospital mean that we would really permit hospital administrators to define the rights of their patients? Does this mean that patient rights are not human rights, but exist only by the grace of the hospital administration? And what of the list itself? Is it all inclusive, such that any "right" not mentioned does not exist? And finally, what purpose could such a listing have if there is not an effective way to exercise the rights specified in the document?

The issue that has proven most intractable is that of an effective enforcement mechanism. Early efforts by the hospitals centered around the development of a "patient representative," and many hospitals still have individuals with this title. Although there are dedicated patient representatives in some major hospitals today, the problems that initially prevented them from being effective guardians of patient rights continue today. First, their title is inaccurate: they do not (and cannot) represent the patient; they are employed by and represent the hospital. They are "hospital representatives." This does not necessarily mean they are useless but does create a potential conflict of interest that can limit their ability to represent the patient. Secondly, their job description is often limited to nonmedical housekeeping matters, and most have no authority to review medical records, require consultation, or postpone discharge. As one hospital administrator described his model program, patient representatives deal only with "nonmedical and nonnursing matters that have to do with patient comfort and convenience, such as a room improperly cleaned or a misplaced dietary tray."

To have any chance to be a real "patient advocate" the individual must have authority to get involved with what brought the patient to the hospital in the first place: medical care and treatment. This requires that the advocate have authority to exercise, at the patient's direction, powers that belong to the patient; and that the advocate be an active member of all hospital committee monitoring quality of care. The advocate should also report directly to the hospital administrator, or the advocate's authority will not be sufficient to deal with members of the medical staff. See Annas & Healey, The Patient Rights Advocate: Redefining the Doctor-Patient Relationship in the Hospital Context, 27 Vand. L. Rev. 243 (1974).

The National Society of Patient Representatives (an American Hospital Association organization) conducted a comprehensive membership survey in 1982. Information from this survey showed that 90.5 percent of the society's members are female, at least 53 percent of those responding hold baccalaureate or master's degrees, and 75 percent have been in the field for fewer than five years; 95 percent have access to medical records; 31 percent enter information in the medical record; 55.6 percent have access to hospital legal counsel; 51.3 percent review incident reports; and 61.7 percent are in a state that has either regulations or legislation on patient rights. A.H.A., Patient Representatives in Contemporary Health Care 61 (1985).

Currently the two most widely used and potentially effective routes through which patients can launch complaints against health care providers regarding their in-hospital stay are "ethics committees" and the developing "risk management" coordinators. Although neither was developed specifically to deal with patient complaints, their expertise could make them useful allies for patients with problems. Ultimately patient advocates will probably have to be employed by independent agencies, such as a National Health Agency (under some form of national health insurance), the state's Attorney General's office, or the state's Department of Public Health. The Ombudsmen Offices some states have established to deal with nursing home complaints may provide a useful model as well.

The role lawyers should play in all this remains controversial. Probably typical of the view of patient representatives is that of a 25-year veteran of public relations/patient representative work, Fredonia French Jacques, who has argued: "While counsel of the hospital attorney can be useful, the attorney should avoid personal involvement as long as possible and should not exercise personal authority in areas of human relations. To put a lawyer in overall charge or risk management would be analogous to putting an undertaker in charge of the hospital intensive care unit." F. Jacques, Verdict Pending: A Patient Representative's Intervention 236 (1983). Nonetheless, many risk management programs are run by attorneys (probably on the theory that they are best able to determine which incidents may lead to litigation). In the area of ethics committees, it has been argued that in order to ensure procedural fairness, the chairman must either be a lawyer or have the advice of one. Annas, Ethics Committees in Neonatal Care: Substantive Protection or Procedural Diversion?, 74 Am. J. Public Health 843, 845 (1984). It has also been suggested that there are at least three roles for lawyers in ethics committees: (1) as a chair or member; (2) legal counsel to the committee to provide legal advice; and (3)nonvoting attendance by the hospital's legal counsel to represent the interests of the hospital. A.H.A. Special Committee on

Biomedical Ethics, Values in Conflict: Resolving Ethical Issues in Hospital Care 87-99 (1985).

B. Privacy and Confidentiality

1. CONFIDENTIALITY OF MEDICAL INFORMATION

Horne v. Patton

287 So. 2d 824 (Ala. 1974)

BLOODWORTH, Justice.

Plaintiff Larry Horne comes here on a voluntary nonsuit assigning as error the trial court's ruling in sustaining defendant's demurrer to his complaint.

This case is alleged to have arisen out of the disclosure by Dr. Patton, defendant herein, to plaintiff's employer of certain information acquired in the course of a doctor-patient relationship between plaintiff Horne and defendant doctor, contrary to the expressed instructions of patient Horne. . . .

Count I of the amended complaint alleges in substance that defendant is a medical doctor, that plaintiff was a patient of defendant doctor for valuable consideration, that plaintiff instructed defendant doctor not to release any medical information regarding plaintiff to plaintiff's employer, and that defendant doctor proceeded to release full medical information to plaintiff's employer without plaintiff's authorization. Count I further alleges that the doctor-patient relationship between plaintiff and defendant was a confidential relationship which created a fiduciary duty from the defendant-doctor to the plaintiff-patient, that the unauthorized release of said information breached said fiduciary duty, moreover that said disclosure violated the Hippocratic Oath which defendant had taken and therefore constitutes unprofessional conduct. Plaintiff avers that as a direct and proximate result of the release of said information, plaintiff was dismissed from his employment.

Count II alleges the same basic facts but avers that the release of said information was an unlawful and wrongful invasion of the plaintiff's privacy.

Count III alleges, in substance, that plaintiff entered into a physician-patient contractual relationship for a consideration with the defendant, whereby through common custom and practice, impliedly, if not expressly, defendant agreed to keep confidential personal information given to him by his patient. . . .

COUNT I

Whether or not there is a confidential relationship between doctor and patient which imposes a duty on the doctor not to freely disclose information obtained from his patients in the course of treatment is a question of first impression in this state. The question has received only a limited consideration in other jurisdictions, and its resolution has been varied. Those states which have enacted a doctor-patient testimonial privilege statute have been almost uniform in allowing a cause of action for unauthorized disclosure.

Alabama, however, has not enacted such a privilege statute. In reviewing cases from other states which also do not have a doctor-patient testimonial privilege, the jurisdictions are split about evenly on this issue. After a careful consideration of this issue, it appears that the sounder legal position recognizes at least a qualified duty on the part of a doctor not to reveal confidences obtained through the doctor-patient relationship.

In the case of Hague v. Williams, 37 N.J. 328, 181 A.2d 345 (1962), the Supreme Court of New Jersey considered the question as to whether an action will lie for unauthorized disclosure by a doctor of information obtained in the doctor-patient relationship. The case arose in the context of a disclosure by a physician of the medical history of a deceased patient to the patient's life insurers. After carefully noting that New Jersey, unlike several other states which had previously recognized such a cause of action, did not recognize a doctor-patient testimonial privilege, the New Jersey court went on to distinguish testimonial and non-testimonial disclosure. The court found a confidential relationship between doctor and patient giving rise to a general duty not to make non-testimonial disclosures of information obtained through the doctor-patient relationship. The court stated the duty as follows: . . .

> A patient should be entitled to freely disclose his symptoms and condition to his doctor in order to receive proper treatment without fear that those facts may become public property. Only thus can the purpose of the relationship be fulfilled. . . . *We conclude, therefore, that ordinarily a physician receives information relating to a patient's health in a confidential capacity and should not disclose such information without the patient's consent, except where the public interest or the private interest of the patient so demands.* Without delineating the precise outer contours of the exceptions, it may generally be said that disclosure may, under such compelling circumstances, be made to a person with a legitimate interest in the patient's health. . . . (Emphasis added.) . . .

Furthermore, decisions from states with testimonial privilege statutes are not necessarily inapposite. Where the tort duty is based upon breach of the statute or the public policy expressed by the statute, this may be true. However, whether or not testimony may be barred at trial does not necessarily control the issue of liability for unauthorized extra-judicial disclosures by a doctor.

This was recognized by the Supreme Court of Nebraska in the case of

Simonsen v. Swenson, 104 Neb. 224, 177 N.W. 831 (1920). There the court, after noting that Nebraska had a testimonial privilege statute, stated that such statute did not apply to non-testimonial disclosures and therefore had no bearing upon the case at hand involving extra-judicial disclosures. In seeking a source of a duty of secrecy on the part of the defendant doctor, the court pointed to a licensing provision that included "betrayal of a professional secret to the detriment of a patient" as unprofessional conduct. . . .

It should be noted that Alabama has a very similar statute which gives the state licensing board for the healing arts the power and imposes on it the duty of suspending or revoking a doctor's license who wilfully betrays a professional secret. Title 46, §257(21), Code of Alabama 1940, as last amended, reads as follows:

> The state licensing board for the healing arts shall have the power and it is its duty to suspend for a specified time, to be determined in the discretion of the board, or revoke any license to practice the healing arts or any branch thereof in the state of Alabama whenever the licensee shall be found guilty of any of the following acts or offenses. . . .
>
> (14) Wilful betrayal of a professional secret;

Moreover, the established ethical code of the medical profession itself unequivocally recognizes the confidential nature of the doctor-patient relationship. Each physician upon entering the profession takes the Hippocratic Oath. One portion of that required pledge reads as follows: "Whatever in connection with my professional practice, or not in connection with it, I see or hear, in the life of men, which ought not be spoken of abroad, I will not divulge, as reckoning that all such should be kept secret." This pledge has been reaffirmed in the Principles of Medical Ethics promulgated by the American Medical Association in Principle 9, viz:

> "A physician may not reveal the confidences entrusted to him in the course of medical attendance, or the deficiencies he may observe in the character of patients, unless he is required to do so by law or unless it becomes necessary in order to protect the welfare of the individual or of the community." American Medical Association, Principles of Medical Ethics, 1957, §9 (Published by AMA).

When the wording of Alabama's state licensing statute is considered alongside the accepted precepts of the medical profession itself, it would seem to establish clearly that public policy in Alabama requires that information obtained by a physician in the course of a doctor-patient relationship be maintained in confidence, unless public interest or the private interest of the patient demands otherwise. Is it not important that patients seeking medical attention be able to freely divulge information about themselves to their attending physician without fear that the information so revealed will be frivolously disclosed? As the New Jersey Supreme Court so aptly pointed out, what policy would be served by according the physician the right to gossip about a patient's health. . . .

The trial court erred in sustaining the demurrer to Count I.

COUNT II

The gravamen of Count II is that defendant's release to plaintiff's employer of information concerning plaintiff's health constituted an invasion of plaintiff's privacy.

This court has recognized the right of a person to be free from unwarranted publicity or unwarranted appropriation or exploitation of one's personality, publicization of one's private affairs with which the public has no legitimate concern, or the wrongful intrusion of one's private activities in such manner as to outrage or cause mental suffering, shame, or humiliation to a person of ordinary sensibilities. . . .

As a federal district court so aptly stated in Hammonds v. Aetna Casualty & Surety Co., 243 F. Supp. 793 (N.D. Ohio, 1965), involving disclosure of medical information concerning the patient to the patient's insurer:

> When a patient seeks out a doctor and retains him, he must admit him to the most private part of the material domain of man. Nothing material is more important or more intimate to man than the health of his mind and body. Since the layman is unfamiliar with the road to recovery, he cannot sift the circumstances of his life and habits to determine what is information pertinent to his health. As a consequence, he must disclose all information in his consultations with his doctor — even that which is embarrassing, disgraceful, or incriminating. To promote full disclosure, the medical profession extends the promise of secrecy referred to above. The candor which this promise elicits is necessary to the effective pursuit of health; there can be no reticence, no reservation, no reluctance when patients discuss their problems with their doctors. But the disclosure is certainly intended to be private. If a doctor should reveal any of these confidences, he surely effects an invasion of the privacy of his patient. We are of the opinion that the preservation of the patient's privacy is no mere ethical duty upon the part of the doctor; there is a legal duty as well. The unauthorized revelation of medical secrets, or *any* confidential communication given in the course of treatment, is tortious conduct which may be the basis for an action in damages.

Unauthorized disclosure of intimate details of a patient's health may amount to unwarranted publicization of one's private affairs with which the public has no legitimate concern such as to cause outrage, mental suffering, shame or humiliation to a person of ordinary sensibilities. Nor can it be said that an employer is necessarily a person who has a legitimate interest in knowing each and every detail of an employee's health. Certainly, there are many ailments about which a patient might consult his private physician which have no bearing or effect on one's employment. If the defendant doctor in the instant case had a legitimate reason for making this disclosure under the particular facts of this case, then this is a matter of defense.

The trial court erred in sustaining the demurrer to Count II.

COUNT III

The gravamen of Count III is that the alleged disclosure breached an implied contract to keep confidential all personal information given to defendant doctor by his patient. . . .

We have not been cited to, nor have we found in our research, any case in which a cause of action for the breach of an implied contract of confidentiality on the part of the doctor has been rejected. Moreover, public knowledge of the ethical standards of the medical profession or widespread acquaintance with the Hippocratic Oath's secrecy provision or the AMA's Principles of Ethics or Alabama's medical licensing requirements of secrecy (which is a common provision in many states) singly or together may well be sufficient justification for reasonable expectation on a patient's part that the physician has promised to keep confidential all information given by the patient.

Again, of course, any confidentiality between patient and physician is subject to the exceptions already noted where the supervening interests of society or the private interests of the patient intervene. These are matters of defense.

The trial court erred in sustaining demurrer to Count III.

The judgment of the trial court is therefore due to be reversed and remanded.

Reversed and remanded.

HEFLIN, C. J. and HARWOOD and JONES, JJ., concur.

MERRILL, MADDOX, and FAULKNER, JJ., concur in the result.

MCCALL, Justice (dissenting).

The prime issue is whether or not the trial court erred in sustaining the demurrer. In general, the complaint charges that the defendant wrongfully disclosed to the plaintiff's employer that the plaintiff suffered from a longstanding nervous condition with feelings of anxiety and insecurity. The verity of this medical opinion is not denied. The complaint does not charge that the defendant gave general circulation to this information as mentioned in Alexander v. Knight, 197 Pa. Super. 79, 177 A.2d 142, cited in the above opinion, or that the defendant spoke it abroad (in wide circulation). Nor does the complaint charge that the defendant frivolously disclosed or gossiped about the defendant's health as the opinion intimates. We are not writing to such issues. Those circumstances alluded to in cited cases are not the averments in this case. . . .

It is important to observe that the information allegedly revealed by the physician in the present complaint did not constitute gossiping about his patient's health or a frivolous disclosure of information, as the court alluded to in Hague v. Williams, 37 N.J. 328, 181 A.2d 345.

In Hague v. Williams, supra, the court said: "This is not to say that the patient enjoys an absolute right, but rather that he possesses a limited right against such disclosure, subject to exceptions prompted by the supervening interest of society. . . ."

The court held that where the public interest or the private interest of a patient so demands, disclosure may be made to a person with a legitimate interest in the patient's health, and, where in the course of examining an infant patient the physician became aware of a pathological heart condition, the physician was not barred from disclosing such condition to an insurer to whom the parents had applied for life insurance on the infant, the court holding that when the parents made a claim for insurance, they lost any rights to nondisclosure that they may have had. *Hague,* supra, p. 349. In my opinion the overriding competing interest and responsibility of an employer for the welfare of all of his employees, to the public who come to his establishment and who buy his merchandise, and to the furtherance of his own business venture, should entitle him to be free from the shackles of secrecy that would prevent a physician from disclosing to the employer critical information concerning the physical or mental condition of his employees.

Notes on Confidentiality

(1) Suits for breach of confidentiality are rare, probably because they require further publication of the information the individual wants to keep secret. Suits against hospitals are almost nonexistent. Most cases, like Horn v. Patton, involve physician disclosures made to employers, insurance companies, or to a spouse (usually in a divorce or custody action). In Curry v. Corn, 227 N.Y.S.2d 470 (1966), for example, the physician disclosed information to his patient's husband who was contemplating a divorce action. In Schaffer v. Spicer, 215 N.W.2d 134 (S.D. 1974), the wife's psychiatrist disclosed information to the husband's attorney to aid him in a child custody case. Representative of insurance cases are Hague v. Williams, 181 A.2d 345 (N.J. 1962), where the pediatrician of an infant informed a life insurance company of a congenital heart defect about which he had not informed the child's parents, and Hammond's v. Aetna, 243 F. Supp. 793 (N.D. Ohio 1965), where the physician revealed information to an insurance company when the insurance company falsely represented to him that his patient was suing him for malpractice. Other cases involving reporting to employers in-

clude Beatty v. Baston, 13 Ohio L. Abs. 481 (Ohio App. 1932), where the physician revealed to a patient's employer during a worker compensation action that the patient had venereal disease, and Clark v. Geraci, 208 N.Y.S.2d 564 (S. Ct. N.Y. 1960), where a civilian employee of the Air Force asked his doctor to make an incomplete disclosure to his employer to explain absences, but the doctor made a complete disclosure, including the patient's alcoholism.

(2) Confidentiality, of course, does not apply to disclosure to the patient, and the courts have consistently ruled that patients have the right of access to their medical records. Many states also have statutes or regulations that provide for direct patient access to medical records. See generally G. J. Annas, The Rights of Patients 160-174 (1989); Privacy Protection Study Commission, Personal Privacy in an Information Society (1977), and Health Law Center, Hospital Law Manual 78-107 (1988). *Sometimes* an exception is made for psychiatric records. For instance, Wallace v. University Hospitals, 164 N.E.2d 917, *aff'd and modified,* 170 N.E.2d 261 (Ohio Ct. App. 1960), *motion to dismiss granted,* 171 Ohio St. 487, 172 N.E.2d 459 (1961), involved a patient whose lawyer wanted her records to determine if filing of a malpractice action was indicated. In another case, where an insurance company sought access with patient authorization, the court said that the hospital is only the custodian of the record and the patient has a property right in it sufficient to allow access to it and to copy it without resort to litigation. Pyramid Life Insurance Co. v. Masonic Hospital, 191 F. Supp. 51 (W.D. Okla. 1961). A New York court has also held that a hospital cannot withhold a patient's medical record for the purposes of concealing the identity of a physician who may have committed malpractice on the patient. Matter of Weiss, 47 N.Y.S.2d 455 (1955).

In a District of Columbia case, a dispensary and a private physician were ordered to hand over medical records to a surviving son even though the statute of limitations for a wrongful death action had expired. The court specifically rejected the argument that the filing of a lawsuit should be a prerequisite to access: "We are unwilling to hold that one to whom a duty to disclose medical data is already owed is compelled by the rule of reasonable diligence to engage in legal proceedings to attain a loftier status." Emmet v. Eastern Dispensary & Casualty Hospital, 396 F.2d 931 (U.S. App. D.C. 1967). This case was followed in an Illinois case: "It is our opinion that the 'fiduciary qualities of the physician-patient relationship' require the disclosure of medical data to a patient or his agent on request. . . ." Cannell v. Medical and Surgical Clinic, 315 N.E.2d 278 (Ill. App. 1974). On Mental health records, see Morris v. Houster, 377 S.W.2d 841 (Tex. Civ. App. 1964) (access granted); and Gotkin v. Miller, 514 F.2d 125, 130 (1975) (access denied). Alberts v. Devine, 479 N.E.2d 113 (Mass. 1985), involved disclosure of psychiatric information to a minister's superiors that resulted in his not being reappointed. And see, Note, Breach of Confidence: An Emerging Tort, 82 Columbia L. Rev. 1426 (1982).

2. CONFIDENTIALITY AND THE DUTY TO WARN

Tarasoff v. Regents of University of California

17 Cal. 3d 424, 551 P.2d 334 (1976)

TOBRINER, Justice.

On October 27, 1969, Prosenjit Poddar killed Tatiana Tarasoff. Plaintiffs, Tatiana's parents, allege that two months earlier Poddar confided his intention to kill Tatiana to Dr. Lawrence Moore, a psychologist employed by the Cowell Memorial Hospital at the University of California at Berkeley. They allege that on Moore's request, the campus police briefly detained Poddar, but released him when he appeared rational. They further claim that Dr. Harvey Powelson, Moore's superior, then directed that no further action be taken to detain Poddar. No one warned plaintiffs of Tatiana's peril.

Concluding that these facts set forth causes of action against neither therapists and policemen involved, nor against the Regents of the University of California as their employer, the superior court sustained defendants' demurrers to plaintiffs' second amended complaints without leave to amend. This appeal ensued.

Plaintiffs' complaints predicate liability on two grounds: defendants' failure to warn plaintiffs of the impending danger and their failure to bring about Poddar's confinement pursuant to the Lanterman-Petris-Short Act (Welf. & Inst. Code, §5000ff.). Defendants, in turn, assert that they owed no duty of reasonable care to Tatiana and that they are immune from suit under the California Tort Claims Act of 1963 (Gov. Code, §810ff.). . . .

Plaintiffs, Tatiana's mother and father, filed separate but virtually identical second amended complaints. The issue before us on this appeal is whether those complaints now state, or can be amended to state, causes of action against defendants. We therefore begin by setting forth the pertinent allegations of the complaints.

Plaintiffs' first cause of action, entitled "Failure to Detain a Dangerous Patient," alleges that on August 20, 1969, Poddar was a voluntary outpatient receiving therapy at Cowell Memorial Hospital. Poddar informed Moore, his therapist, that he was going to kill an unnamed girl, readily identifiable as Tatiana, when she returned home from spending the summer in Brazil. Moore, with the concurrence of Dr. Gold, who had initially examined Poddar, and Dr. Yandell, assistant to the director of the department of psychiatry, decided that Poddar should be committed for observation in a mental hospital. Moore orally notified Officers Atkinson and Teel of the campus police that he would request commitment. He then sent a letter to Police Chief William Beall requesting the assistance of the police department in securing Poddar's confinement.

Officers Atkinson, Brownrigg, and Halleran took Poddar into custody, but, satisfied that Poddar was rational, released him on his promise to stay away from Tatiana. Powelson, director of the department of psychiatry at Cowell Memorial Hospital, then asked the police to return Moore's letter, directed that all copies of the letter and notes that Moore had taken as therapist be destroyed, and "ordered no action to place Prosenjit Poddar in 72-hour treatment and evaluation facility."

Plaintiffs' second cause of action, entitled "Failure to Warn of a Dangerous Patient," incorporates the allegations of the first cause of action, but adds the assertion that defendants negligently permitted Poddar to be released from police custody without "notifying the parents of Tatiana Tarasoff that their daughter was in grave danger from Posenjit Poddar." Poddar persuaded Tatiana's brother to share an apartment with him near Tatiana's residence; shortly after her return from Brazil, Poddar went to her residence and killed her. . . .

[Plaintiff's first cause of action is barred by governmental immunity.]

The second cause of action can be amended to allege that Tatiana's death proximately resulted from defendants' negligent failure to warn Tatiana or others likely to apprise her of her danger. Plaintiffs contend that as amended, such allegations of negligence and proximate causation, with resulting damages, establish a cause of action. Defendants, however, contend that in the circumstances of the present case they owed no duty of care to Tatiana or her parents and that, in the absence of such duty, they were free to act in careless disregard of Tatiana's life and safety.

. . . In analyzing this issue, we bear in mind that legal duties are not discoverable facts of nature, but merely conclusory expressions that, in cases of a particular type, liability should be imposed for damage done. As stated in Dillon v. Legg (1968) 68 Cal. 2d 728, 734, 69 Cal. Rptr. 72, 76, 441 P.2d 912, 916: "The assertion that liability must . . . be denied because defendant bears no 'duty' to plaintiff 'begs the essential question — whether the plaintiff's interests are entitled to legal protection against the defendant's conduct. . . .[Duty] is not sacrosanct in itself, but only an expression of the sum total of those considerations of policy which lead the law to say that the particular plaintiff is entitled to protection.' (Prosser, Law of Torts [3d. ed. 1964] at pp. 332-333.)"

In the landmark case of Rowland v. Christian (1968) 69 Cal. 2d 108, 70 Cal. Rptr. 97, 443 P.2d 561, Justice Peters recognized that liability should be imposed "for an injury occasioned to another by his want of ordinary care or skill" as expressed in §1714 of the Civil Code. Thus, Justice Peters, quoting from Heaven v. Pender (1883) 11 Q.B.D. 503, 509 stated: "'whenever one person is by circumstances placed in such a position with regard to another . . . that if he did not use ordinary care and skill in his own conduct . . . he would cause danger of injury to the person or property of the other, a duty arises to use ordinary care and skill to avoid such danger.'"

. . . We depart from "this fundamental principle" only upon the "balancing of a number of considerations"; major ones "are the foreseeability of harm to the plaintiff, the degree of certainty that the plaintiff suffered injury, the closeness of the connection between the defendant's conduct and the injury suffered, the moral blame attached to the defendant's conduct, the policy of preventing future harm, the extent of the burden to the defendant and consequences to the community of imposing a duty to exercise care with resulting liability for breach, and the availability, cost and prevalence of insurance for the risk involved."

The most important of these considerations in establishing duty is foreseeability. As a general principle, a "defendant owes a duty of care to all persons who are foreseeably endangered by his conduct, with respect to all risks which make the conduct unreasonably dangerous."

. . . As we shall explain, however, when the avoidance of foreseeable harm requires a defendant to control the conduct of another person, or to warn of such conduct, the common law has traditionally imposed liability only if the defendant bears some special relationship to the dangerous person or to the potential victim. Since the relationship between a therapist and his patient satisfies this requirement, we need not here decide whether foreseeability alone is sufficient to create a duty to exercise reasonable care to protect a potential victim of another's conduct.

. . . Although, as we have stated above, under the common law, as a general rule, one person owed no duty to control the conduct of another, nor to warn those endangered by such conduct (Rest. 2d Torts, supra, §314, com. c.; Prosser, Law of Torts (4th ed. 1971) §56, p. 341), the courts have carved out an exception to this rule in cases in which the defendant stands in some special relationship to either the person whose conduct needs to be controlled or in a relationship to the foreseeable victim of that conduct (see Rest. 2d Torts, supra, §§315-320). Applying this exception to the present case, we note that a relationship of defendant therapists to either Tatiana or Poddar will suffice to establish a duty of care; as explained in §315 of the Restatement Second of Torts, a duty of care may arise from either "(a) a special relation . . . between the actor and the third person which imposes a duty upon the actor to control the third person's conduct, or (b) a special relation . . . between the actor and the other which gives to the other a right of protection."

. . . Although plaintiffs' pleadings assert no special relation between Tatiana and defendant therapists, they establish as between Poddar and defendant therapists the special relation that arises between a patient and his doctor or psychotherapist. Such a relationship may support affirmative duties for the benefit of third persons. Thus, for example, a hospital must exercise reasonable care to control the behavior of a patient which may endanger other persons. A doctor must also warn a patient if the patient's condition or medication renders certain conduct, such as driving a car, dangerous to others.

. . . Although the California decisions that recognize this duty have involved cases in which the defendant stood in a special relationship *both* to the victim and to the person whose conduct created the danger, we do not think that the duty should logically be constricted to such situations. Decisions of other jurisdictions hold that the single relationship of a doctor to his patient is sufficient to support the duty to exercise reasonable care to protect others against dangers emanating from the patient's illness. The courts hold that a doctor is liable to persons infected by his patient if he negligently fails to diagnose a contagious disease (Hofmann v. Blackmon (Fla. App. 1970) 241 So. 2d 752), or, having diagnosed the illness, fails to warn members of the patient's family (Wojcik v. Aluminum Co. of America (1959) 18 Misc. 2d 740, 183 N.Y.S.2d 351, 357-358; Davis v. Rodman (1921) 147 Ark. 385, 227 S.W. 612; Skillings v. Allen (1919) 143 Minn. 323, 173 N.W. 663; see also Jones v. Stanko (1928) 118 Ohio St. 147, 160 N.E. 456).

Since it involved a dangerous mental patient, the decision in Merchants Nat. Bank & Trust Co. of Fargo v. United States (D.N.D.1967) 272 F. Supp.-409 comes closer to the issue. The Veterans Administration arranged for the patient to work on a local farm, but did not inform the farmer of the man's background. The farmer consequently permitted the patient to come and go freely during nonworking hours; the patient borrowed a car, drove to his wife's residence and killed her. Notwithstanding the lack of any "special relationship" between the Veterans Administration and the wife, the court found the Veterans Administration liable for the wrongful death of the wife.

In their summary of the relevant rulings Fleming and Maximov conclude that the "case law should dispel any notion that to impose on the therapists a duty to take precautions for the safety of persons threatened by a patient, where due care so requires, is in any way opposed to contemporary ground rules on the duty relationship. On the contrary, there now seems to be sufficient authority to support the conclusion that by entering into a doctor-patient relationship the therapist becomes sufficiently involved to assume some responsibility for the safety, not only of the patient himself, but also of any third person whom the doctor knows to be threatened by the patient." (Fleming & Maximov, The Patient or His Victim: The Therapist's Dilemma (1974) 62 Cal. L. Rev. 1025, 1030.)

Defendants contend, however, that imposition of a duty to exercise reasonable care to protect third persons is unworkable because therapists cannot accurately predict whether or not a patient will resort to violence. In support of this argument amicus representing the American Psychiatric Association and other professional societies cites numerous articles which indicate that therapists, in the present state of the art, are unable reliably to predict violent acts; their forecasts, amicus claims, tend consistently to overpredict violence, and indeed are more often wrong than right. Since predictions of violence are often erroneous, amicus concludes, the courts should not render rulings that predicate the liability of therapists upon the validity of such predictions.

The role of the psychiatrist, who is indeed a practitioner of medicine, and that of the psychologist who performs an allied function, are like that of the physician who must conform to the standards of the profession and who must often make diagnoses and predictions based upon such evaluations. Thus the judgment of the therapist in diagnosing emotional disorders and in predicting whether a patient presents a serious danger of violence is comparable to the judgment which doctors and professionals must regularly render under accepted rules of responsibility.

. . . We recognize the difficulty that a therapist encounters in attempting to forecast whether a patient presents a serious danger of violence. Obviously we do not require that the therapist, in making that determination, render a perfect performance; the therapist need only exercise "that reasonable degree of skill, knowledge, and care ordinarily possessed and exercised by members of [that professional specialty] under similar circumstances."

. . . Within the broad range of reasonable practice and treatment in which professional opinion and judgment may differ, the therapist is free to exercise his or her own best judgment without liability; proof, aided by hindsight, that he or she judged wrongly is insufficient to establish negligence.

In the instant case, however, the pleadings do not raise any question as to failure of defendant therapists to predict that Poddar presented a serious danger of violence. On the contrary, the present complaints allege that defendant therapists did in fact predict that Poddar would kill, but were negligent in failing to warn.

. . . Amicus contends, however, that even when a therapist does in fact predict that a patient poses a serious danger of violence to others, the therapist should be absolved of any responsibility for failing to act to protect the potential victim. In our view, however, once a therapist does in fact determine, or under applicable professional standards reasonably should have determined, that a patient poses a serious danger of violence to others, he bears a duty to exercise reasonable care to protect the foreseeable victim of that danger. While the discharge of this duty of due care will necessarily vary with the facts of each case, in each instance the adequacy of the therapist's conduct must be measured against the traditional negligence standard of the rendition of reasonable care under the circumstances. (Accord Cobbs v. Grant (1972) 8 Cal. 3d 229, 243, 104 Cal. Rptr. 505, 502, P.2d 1.) As explained in Fleming and Maximov, The Patient or His Victim: The Therapist's Dilemma (1974) 62 Cal. L. Rev. 1025, 1067: ". . . the ultimate question of resolving the tension between the conflicting interests of patient and potential victim is one of social policy, not professional expertise. . . . In sum, the therapist owes a legal duty not only to his patient, but also to his patient's would-be victim and is subject in both respects to scrutiny by judge and jury."

. . . Contrary to the assertion of amicus, this conclusion is not inconsistent with our recent decision in People v. Burnick, supra, 14 Cal. 3d 306, 121 Cal. Rptr. 488, 535 P.2d 352. Taking note of the uncertain character of therapeutic prediction, we held in *Burnick* that a person cannot be committed as a mentally disordered sex offender unless found to be such by proof beyond a reasonable doubt. (14 Cal. 3d at p. 328, 121 Cal. Rptr. 488, 535

P.2d 352.) The issue in the present context, however, is not whether the patient should be incarcerated, but whether the therapist should take any steps at all to protect the threatened victim; some of the alternatives open to the therapist, such as warning the victim, will not result in the drastic consequences of depriving the patient of his liberty. Weighing the uncertain and conjectural character of the alleged damage done the patient by such a warning against the peril to the victim's life, we conclude that professional inaccuracy in predicting violence cannot negate the therapist's duty to protect the threatened victim.

The risk that unnecessary warnings may be given is a reasonable price to pay for the lives of possible victims that may be saved. We would hesitate to hold that the therapist who is aware that his patient expects to attempt to assassinate the President of the United States would not be obligated to warn the authorities because the therapist cannot predict with accuracy that his patient will commit the crime.

Defendants further argue that free and open communication is essential to psychotherapy (see In re Lifschutz (1970) 2 Cal. 3d 415, 431-434, 85 Cal. Rptr. 829, 467 P.2d 557); that "Unless a patient . . . is assured that . . . information [revealed by him] can and will be held in utmost confidence, he will be reluctant to make the full disclosure upon which diagnosis and treatment . . . depends." (Sen. Com. on Judiciary, comment on Evid. Code, §1014.) The giving of a warning, defendants contend, constitutes a breach of trust which entails the revelation of confidential communications.

. . . We recognize the public interest in supporting effective treatment of mental illness and in protecting the rights of patients to privacy . . . and the consequent public importance of safeguarding the confidential character of psychotherapeutic communication. Against this interest, however, we must weigh the public interest in safety from violent assault. The Legislature has undertaken the difficult task of balancing the countervailing concerns. In Evidence Code §1014, it established a broad rule of privilege to protect confidential communications between patient and psychotherapist. In Evidence Code §1024, the Legislature created a specific and limited exception to the psychotherapist-patient privilege: "There is no privilege . . . if the psychotherapist has reasonable cause to believe that the patient is in such mental or emotional condition as to be dangerous to himself or to the person or property of another and that disclosure of the communication is necessary to prevent the threatened danger."

. . . We realize that the open and confidential character of psychotherapeutic dialogue encourages patients to express threats of violence, few of which are ever executed. Certainly a therapist should not be encouraged routinely to reveal such threats; such disclosures could seriously disrupt the patient's relationship with his therapist and with the persons threatened. To the contrary, the therapist's obligations to his patient require that he not disclose a confidence unless such disclosure is necessary to avert danger to others, and even then that he do so discreetly, and in a fashion that would preserve the privacy of his patient to the fullest extent compatible with the prevention of the threatened danger. . . .

The revelation of a communication under the above circumstances is not a breach of trust or a violation of professional ethics; as stated in the Principles of Medical Ethics of the American Medical Association (1957), section 9: "A physician may not reveal the confidence entrusted to him in the course of medical attendance . . . *unless he is required to do so by law or unless it becomes necessary in order to protect the welfare of the individual or of the community.*" (Emphasis added.) We conclude that the public policy favoring protection of the confidential character of patient-psychotherapist communications must yield to the extent to which disclosure is essential to avert danger to others. The protective privilege ends where the public peril begins.

. . . Our current crowded and computerized society compels the interdependence of its members. In this risk-infested society we can hardly tolerate the further exposure to danger that would result from a concealed knowledge of the therapist that his patient was lethal. If the exercise of reasonable care to protect the threatened victim requires the therapist to warn the endangered party or those who can reasonably be expected to notify him, we see no sufficient societal interest that would protect and justify concealment. The containment of such risks lies in the public interest. For the foregoing reasons, we find that plaintiffs' complaints can be amended to state a cause of action against defendants Moore, Powelson, Gold, and Yandell and against the Regents as their employer, for breach of a duty to exercise reasonable care to protect Tatiana.

. . . Finally, we reject the contention of the dissent that the provisions of the Lanterman-Petris-Short Act which govern the release of confidential information (Welf. & Inst. Code, §§5328-5328.9) prevented defendant therapists from warning Tatiana. The dissent's contention rests on the assertion that Dr. Moore's letter to the campus police constituted an "application in writing" within the meaning of Welfare and Institutions Code §5150, and thus initiates proceedings under the Lanterman-Petris-Short Act. A closer look at the terms of §5150, however, will demonstrate that it is inapplicable to the present case.

. . . The judgment of the superior court in favor of defendants Gold, Moore, Powelson, Yandell, and the Regents of the University of California is reversed, and the cause remanded for further proceedings consistent with the views expressed herein.

WRIGHT, C. J., and SULLIVAN and RICHARDSON, JJ., concur.

MOSK, Justice (concurring and dissenting).

I concur in the result in this instance only because the complaints allege that defendant therapists did in fact predict that Poddar would kill and were therefore negligent in failing to warn of that danger. Thus the issue here is very narrow: we are not concerned with whether the therapists, pursuant to the standards of their profession, "should have" predicted potential violence; they allegedly did so in actuality. Under these limited circumstances I agree that a cause of action can be stated.

Whether plaintiffs can ultimately prevail is problematical at best. As the complaints admit, the therapists *did* notify the police that Poddar was planning to kill a girl identifiable as Tatiana. While I doubt that more should be required, this issue may be raised in defense and its determination is a question of fact.

I cannot concur, however, in the majority's rule that a therapist may be held liable for failing to predict his patient's tendency to violence if other practitioners, pursuant to the "standards of the profession," would have done so. The question is, what standards? Defendants and a responsible amicus curiae, supported by an impressive body of literature discussed at length in our recent opinion in People v. Burnick (1975) 14 Cal. 3d 306, 121 Cal. Rptr. 488, 535 P.2d 352, demonstrate that psychiatric predictions of violence are inherently unreliable. . . .

CLARK, Justice (dissenting).

Until today's majority opinion, both legal and medical authorities have agreed that confidentiality is essential to effectively treat the mentally ill, and that imposing a duty on doctors to disclose patient threats to potential victims would greatly impair treatment. Further, recognizing that effective treatment and society's safety are necessarily intertwined, the Legislature has already decided effective and confidential treatment is preferred over imposition of a duty to warn.

The issue whether effective treatment for the mentally ill should be sacrificed to a system of warnings is, in my opinion, properly one for the Legislature, and we are bound by its judgment. Moreover, even in the absence of clear legislative direction, we must reach the same conclusion because imposing the majority's new duty is certain to result in a net increase in violence.

The majority rejects the balance achieved by the Legislature's Lanterman-Petris-Short Act. (Welf. & Inst. code, §5000 et seq., hereafter the act.) In addition, the majority fails to recognize that, even absent the act, overwhelming policy considerations mandate against sacrificing fundamental patient interests without gaining a corresponding increase in public benefit. . . .

Policy generally determines duty. (Dillon v. Legg (1968) 68 Cal. 2d 728, 734, 69 Cal. Rptr. 72, 441 P.2d 912.) Principal policy considerations include foreseeability of harm, certainty of the plaintiff's injury, proximity of the defendant's conduct to the plaintiff's injury, moral blame attributable to defendant's conduct, prevention of future harm, burden on the defendant, and consequences to the community. . . .

Overwhelming policy considerations weigh against imposing a duty on psychotherapists to warn a potential victim against harm. While offering virtually no benefit to society, such a duty will frustrate psychiatric treatment, invade fundamental patient rights, and increase violence.

The importance of psychiatric treatment and its need for confidentiality have been recognized by this court. (In re Lifschutz (1970) 2 Cal. 3d 415, 421-422, 85 Cal. Rptr. 829, 467 P.2d 557.) "It is clearly recognized that the very practice of psychiatry vitally depends upon the reputation in the community that the psychiatrist will not tell." (Slovenko, Psychiatry and a Second Look at the Medical Privilege (1960) 6 Wayne L. Rev. 175, 188.)

Assurance of confidentiality is important for three reasons.

Deterrence from Treatment

First, without substantial assurance of confidentiality, those requiring treatment will be deterred from seeking assistance. . . .

Full Disclosure

Second, the guarantee of confidentiality is essential in eliciting the full disclosure necessary for effective treatment. . . .

Successful Treatment

Third, even if the patient fully discloses his thoughts, assurance that the confidential relationship will not be breached is necessary to maintain his trust in his psychiatrist — the very means by which treatment is effected. "[T]he essence of much psychotherapy is the contribution of trust in the external world and ultimately in the self, modelled upon the trusting relationship established during therapy." (Dawidoff, The Malpractice of Psychiatrists, 1966 Duke L.J. 696, 704.) Patients will be helped only if they can form a trusting relationship with the psychiatrist. . . .

Given the importance of confidentiality to the practice of psychiatry, it becomes clear the duty to warn imposed by the majority will cripple the use and effectiveness of psychiatry. Many people, potentially violent — yet susceptible to treatment — will be deterred from seeking it; those seeking it will be inhibited from making revelations necessary to effective treatment; and, forcing the psychiatrist to violate the patient's trust will destroy the interpersonal relationship by which treatment is effected.

Violence and Civil Commitment

By imposing a duty to warn, the majority contributes to the danger to society of violence by the mentally ill and greatly increases the risk of civil commitment — the total deprivation of liberty — of those who should not be confined. The impairment of treatment and risk of improper commitment resulting from the new duty to warn will not be limited to a few patients but will extend to a large number of the mentally ill. Although under existing psychiatric procedures only a relatively few receiving treatment will ever present a risk of violence, the number making threats is huge, and it is the latter group — not just the former — whose treatment will be impaired and whose risk of commitment will be increased.

Both the legal and psychiatric communities recognize that the process of determining potential violence in a patient is far from exact, being fraught with complexity and uncertainty. . . .

This predictive uncertainty means that the number of disclosures will necessarily be large. As noted above, psychiatric patients are encouraged to discuss all thoughts of violence, and they often express such thoughts. However, unlike this court, the psychiatrist does not enjoy the benefit of overwhelming hindsight in seeing which few, if any, of his patients will ultimately become violent. Now, confronted by the majority's new duty, the psychiatrist must instantaneously calculate potential violence from each patient on each visit. The difficulties researchers have encountered in accurately predicting violence will be heightened for the practicing psychiatrist dealing for brief periods in his office with heretofore nonviolent patients. And, given the decision not to warn or commit must always be made at the psychiatrist's civil peril, one can expect most doubts will be resolved in favor of the psychiatrist protecting himself.

Neither alternative open to the psychiatrist seeking to protect himself is in the public interest. The warning itself is an impairment of the psychiatrist's ability to treat, depriving many patients of adequate treatment. It is to be expected that after disclosing their threats, a significant number of patients, who would not become violent if treated according to existing practices, will engage in violent conduct as a result of unsuccessful treatment. In short, the majority's duty to warn will not only impair treatment of many who would never become violent but worse, will result in a net increase in violence.

The second alternative open to the psychiatrist is to commit his patient rather than to warn. Even in the absence of threat of civil liability, the doubts of psychiatrists as to the seriousness of patient threats have led psychiatrists to overcommit to mental institutions. This overcommitment has been authoritatively documented in both legal and psychiatric studies. . . .

Given the incentive to commit created by the majority's duty, this already serious situation will be worsened, contrary to Chief Justice Wright's admonition "that liberty is no less precious because forfeited in a civil proceeding than when taken as a consequence of a criminal conviction." . . .

The tragedy of Tatiana Tarasoff has led the majority to disregard the clear legislative mandate of the Lanterman-Petris-Short Act. Worse, the majority impedes medical treatment, resulting in increased violence from — and deprivation of liberty to — the mentally ill.

We should accept legislative and medical judgment, relying upon effective treatment rather than on indiscriminate warning.

The judgment should be affirmed.

McComb, J., concurs.

Notes on *Tarasoff*

(1) The "facts" in the *Tarasoff* case are set forth somewhat more graphically in the criminal case against Poddar. Therein it is noted that Poddar was a member of the Harijan ("untouchable") caste in Bengal, India. He met Tatiana Tarasoff in the fall of 1968, and saw her weekly. On New Year's Eve she kissed him, an act he interpreted as a recognition of a serious relationship. Upon learning this, Tanya let him know she was involved with other men and not interested in an intimate relationship with him. This caused him a severe emotional crisis that persisted throughout the spring and into the summer of 1969. During this time period he saw Tanya on occasion and tape recorded their conversations so he could determine why she did not love him. After she went to South America for the summer of 1969 he began to improve and sought psychological assistance (the extent of which is described in the civil case opinion). On October 29, 1969, he went to Tanya's home to speak to her. She was not home, and her mother told him to leave. He later returned, armed with a pellet gun and kitchen knife, and found Tanya alone. She refused to speak with him, and screamed when he persisted. He shot her with the pellet gun. "She ran from the house, was pursued, caught, and repeatedly and fatally stabbed by the defendant. He then returned to Tanya's home and called the police." People v. Poddar, 111 Cal. Rptr. 910, 518 P.2d 342, 345 (1974).

Poddar's conviction of second degree murder was reversed on appeal on the basis that the jury should have been instructed on California's diminished capacity rule. By 1976, he had been released from prison, had returned to India, and was reportedly happily married. Stone, The *Tarasoff* Decisions: Suing Psychotherapists to Safeguard Society, 90 Harv. L. Rev. 358 (1976).

The 1976 opinion was a rehearing of a 1974 opinion in the same case, which arrived at the same result. Tarasoff v. Regents of University of California, 529 P.2d 553, 111 Cal. Rptr. 910 (1974). Although many psychiatrists, like Alan Stone, predicted a drastic increase in the number of warnings after *Tarasoff,* "there is only very tenuous evidence to suggest that any increase in frequency of warnings has occurred." Note, Where the Public Peril Begins: A Survey of Psychotherapists to Determine the Effects of *Tarasoff,* 31 Stan. L. Rev. 165, 179 (1978). On the other hand, among those who did warn, a greater percentage reported warning the intended victim directly after *Tarasoff* (rather than family or police). (Id. at 180.) Whom should warnings be directed to? Since psychiatrists and other therapists had the *option* to warn prior to the decision, could *Tarasoff* actually change the nature of the therapist-patient relationship from the patient's perspective? There are many times when physicians have a statutory obligation to report a patient's condition to public authorities, such as in cases of child abuse or neglect. See, for instance, Landeros v. Flood, 123 Cal. Rptr. 713 (App. Ct. 1975).

(2) *Tarasoff* remains a controversial opinion within the psychiatric

profession. There are exceptions, but it has generally been followed by courts in other jurisdictions. (Duty to warn found: McIntosh v. Milano, 403 A.2d 550 (N.J. Super. 1979); Bradley Center v. Wessner, 287 S.E.2d 716 (Ga. Ct. App. 1982); Williams v. U.S., 450 F. Supp. 1040 (D.S.D. 1978); Bardoni v. Kim, 390 N.W.2d 218 (Mich. 1986); Davis v. Lhim, 355 N.W.2d 481 (Mich. 1983); Lipari v. Sears & Roebuck, 497 F. Supp. 185 (Neb. 1980). Duty to warn not found: Furi v. Spring Grove State Hospital, 454 A.2d 414 (Md. 1983); Cooke v. Berlin, 735 P.2d 830 (Az. 1987); Hinkelman v. Borgess Medical Center, 403 N.W.2d 547 (Mich. 1987).)

There is no common law duty to protect or warn third parties. But courts have often recognized "special relationships" such as parent-child, employer-employee, and now therapist-patient, that might impose such a duty. The parent, employer, or therapist, by virtue of his position of control, owes a duty not only to the child, employee or patient, but also to those third parties who may foreseeably be affected by the child, employee or patient. Protection, commitment, warnings, or notification may all be "reasonable precautions" depending upon the circumstances. If the therapist had notified the city police instead of the campus police, would *Tarasoff* have been decided differently? Under *Tarasoff,* under what circumstances might a physician who diagnoses an individual infected with HIV (the AIDS virus) have an obligation to notify the individual's spouse of the infection? See generally, Note, Psychiatrists' Liability to Third Parties for Harmful Acts Committed by Dangerous Patients, 64 N.C.L. Rev. 1534 (1986).

Problem

You are counsel for the state medical society, and in this capacity you have been asked to prepare a memo advising the medical society on what actions its members must take to warn third parties (including sexual partners, spouses, and those with whom your patient shares needles used for IV injections) who may be at risk of becoming infected with HIV from your patient, who has tested positive for HIV. The medical society members are especially concerned about legal liability for disclosing this information, and legal liability for not disclosing it. They also want to know if you think that a statute would help protect them, and if so, what that statute should say.

The following materials have been provided to you to give you a start in thinking about this problem:

Testing for the HIV

Voluntary testing for people in high risk groups is controversial. Many people at risk do not wish to be tested. They fear that positive results will be discovered by employers or insurers and negative action will be taken against them. Others avoid testing because if the virus is discovered, no productive behavioral changes are possible. Even if the test results are negative, people in high risks groups are advised to continue practicing safe sex. Negative test results might produce a false sense of security.

Others strongly encourage voluntary testing, to aid in the epidemiologic study of AIDS, to encourage behavior change, and to identify individuals for early medical monitoring. The Report of the Presidential Commission on the Human Immunodeficiency Virus Epidemic (1988) identifies many barriers to voluntary testing. The law provides insufficient protection of both the confidentiality of test results and freedom from discrimination. Access to voluntary testing is limited, with long waiting periods in urban areas and lack of testing facilities in rural areas. Many private physicians do not offer HIV antibody tests. This places increased demands on public testing and counseling centers, which do not have adequate funding to provide services to meet demand. Id. at 74. What type of effective medical intervention, if any, would justify a policy of encouraging or requiring the screening of various populations for HIV? The costs of large-scale screening and early intervention have been estimated at $5 billion. Arno, Shenson, Siegel, Franks, and Lee, Economic and Policy Implications of Early Intervention in HIV Disease, 262 J.A.M.A. 1493 (1989).

Notifying Public Authorities

All states require that cases of AIDS be reported to public health departments and that this information be kept confidential. Some, such as Montana, allow information to be reported anonymously. In Whalen v. Roe, 429 U.S. 589 (1977), the Supreme Court upheld a New York law requiring pharmacists to report the names and addresses of people obtaining certain prescription drugs. The Court found that so long as the state provides statutory and regulatory safeguards to assure the confidentiality of information, the mandatory reporting requirement did not impermissibly infringe upon individual privacy.

Contact tracing

Contact tracing, a process whereby an infected person is required to reveal the names of sexual or drug partners so that they can be contacted by public health officials, is widely debated. Contact tracing has been encouraged, and sometimes required, in treating venereal disease. Since gonorrhea and syphilis can be treated, contact tracing has obvious benefit. Nonetheless, it is not clear whether mandatory contact tracing for venereal disease produces a benefit, since reporting requirements are easily evaded. In the absence of effective treatment for HIV infection, it is not clear what function is served by contact tracing for HIV infection. Further, in groups where rates of infection are high, contact tracing could lead an investigator to every member of the risk group and would be both expensive and futile. Contact tracing is most appropriate for groups in which the incidence of infection is low and physicians or public health officials have good reason to believe that the infected person will not notify partners who are at risk of contagion. Because of these difficulties, the National Institute of Medicine, Academy of Science recommends against mandatory contact tracing. Confronting AIDS — Update 1988, 11.

The President's Commission, recognizing that contact tracing requires substantial public health resources, suggests that "[p]artner notification should begin with the partners of the following persons: hemophiliacs, persons who have received contaminated blood . . . , rejected military applicants, bisexual males, intravenous drug abusers, persons with multiple sex partners, persons with anonymous sex partners, infected prison inmates." President's AIDS Commission at 76.

3. PRIVACY IN THE HOSPITAL

Estate of Berthiaume v. Pratt

365 A.2d 792 (Me. 1976)

POMEROY, Justice.

The appellant, as administratrix, based her claim of right to damages on an alleged invasion of her late husband's "right to privacy" and on an alleged assault and battery of him. At the close of the evidence produced at trial, a justice of the Superior Court granted defendant's motion for a directed verdict. Rule 50, M.R. Civ. P.

Appellant's seasonable appeal brings the case to this court.

The appellee is a physician and surgeon practicing in Waterville, Maine. It was established at trial without contradiction that the deceased, Henry Berthiaume, was suffering from a cancer of his larynx. Appellee, an otolaryngologist, had treated him twice surgically. A laryngectomy was performed; and later, because of a tumor which had appeared in his neck, a radical neck dissection on one side was done. No complaint is made with respect to the surgical interventions.

During the period appellee was serving Mr. Berthiaume as a surgeon, many photographs of Berthiaume had been taken by appellee or under his direction. The jury was told that the sole use to which these photographs were to be put was to make the medical record for the appellee's use. There is nothing in the case to suggest that the photographs were to be shown to students for teaching purposes or were to be used as illustrative photographs in any text books or papers. The only persons to whom the photographs were available were those members of appellee's staff and the appropriate hospital personnel who had duties to perform with respect to medical records.

Although at no time did the appellee receive any written consent for the taking of photographs from Berthiaume or any members of his family, it was appellee's testimony that Berthiaume had always consented to having such photographs made.

At all times material hereto Mr. Berthiaume was the patient of a physician other than appellee. Such other physician had referred the patient to appellee for surgery. On September 2, 1970, appellee saw the patient for the last time for the purpose of treatment or diagnosis. The incident which gave rise to this lawsuit occurred on September 23, 1970.

It was also on that day Mr. Berthiaume died.

Although appellee disputed the evidence appellant produced at trial in many material respects, the jury could have concluded from the evidence that shortly before Mr. Berthiaume died on the 23rd, the appellee and a nurse appeared in his hospital room. In the presence of Mrs. Berthiaume and a visitor of the patient in the next bed, either Dr. Pratt or the nurse, at his direction, raised the dying Mr. Berthiaume's head and placed some blue operating room toweling under his head and beside him on the bed. The appellee testified that this blue toweling was placed there for the purpose of obtaining a color contrast for the photographs which he proposed to take. He then proceeded to take several photographs of Mr. Berthiaume.

The jury could have concluded from the testimony that Mr. Berthiaume protested the taking of pictures by raising a clenched fist and moving his head in an attempt to remove his head from the camera's range. The appellee himself testified that before taking the pictures he had been told by Mrs. Berthiaume when he talked with her in the corridor before entering the room that she "didn't think that Henry wanted his picture taken."

It is the raising of the deceased's head in order to put the operating room towels under and around him that appellant claims was an assault and battery. It is the taking of the pictures of the dying Mr. Berthiaume that appellant claims constituted the actionable invasion of Mr. Berthiaume's right to privacy.

At the close of all the evidence, the presiding justice, acting on a motion seeking such action, directed a verdict for the defendant, as he is permitted to do under the provisions of Rule 50(a), M.R. Civ. P. This seasonably filed appeal followed.

We sustain the appeal.

The announced rationale of the presiding justice for the action taken may best be summed up by quoting two statements he made when he explained to the jury why he was withdrawing the case from their consideration and directing a verdict. At one point, while addressing the jury, he said: "The mere fact the taking of pictures, under the best circumstances, in other words, assuming that the pictures were taken without consent as the plaintiff-administratrix complains, the mere taking of pictures is not an invasion of privacy. There is no proof they were published; no proof they were used for any purpose other than their intended use in the record-keeping process by the doctor in the care of the patient that he had."

Later, while addressing the jury, he said:

> The law says in the course of his treating a patient, the doctor has the right to lay his hand on you in order to provide you with treatment for which you have sought his advice, and his attention and care and treatment.
>
> Although the taking of pictures is not necessarily a treatment, it is part of the overall medical care, an association, a relationship between the doctor and the patient, and as the doctor has testified, I think medical science must have some information in its effort to track down and search for a cure. . . .

. . . By our decision in this case we join a majority of the jurisdictions in the country in recognizing a "right to privacy." We also declare it to be the rule in Maine that a violation of this legally protected right is an actionable tort. . . .

. . . In this case we are concerned only with a claimed intrusion upon the plaintiff's intestate's physical and mental solitude or seclusion. The jury had a right to conclude from the evidence that plaintiff's intestate was dying. It could have concluded he desired not to be photographed in his hospital bed in such condition and that he manifested such desire by his physical motions. The jury should have been instructed, if it found these facts, that the taking of pictures without decedent's consent or over his objection was an invasion of his legally protected right to privacy, which invasion was an actionable tort for which money damages could be recovered.

Instead, a directed verdict for the defendant was entered, obviously premised on the presiding justice's announced incorrect conclusion that the taking of pictures without consent did not constitute an invasion of privacy and the further erroneous conclusion that no tort was committed in the absence of "proof they [the photographs] were published."

Another claimed basis for appellant's assertion that a right to recover damages was demonstrated by the evidence is the allegations in her complaint sounding in the tort of assault and battery. As earlier indicated, the presiding justice announced as his conclusion that consent to a battery is implied from the existence of a physician-patient relationship. While we do not acknowledge the correctness of this pronouncement by the justice presiding because in our view it is so broad as to be inaccurate, even if the statement were true, the action taken by the presiding justice was not legally justified. It was based on a major premise that a physician-patient relationship existed at the time of the actions complained of. The jury had not yet had the opportunity to decide if such a relationship had been established. The evidence in the case at the time of the justice's action clearly established that plaintiff's intestate was under the care of another physician. The patient had been referred to appellee for surgery on two occasions. The only other occasion for direct contact with the patient occurred substantially before the alleged invasion of the right to privacy when appellee examined plaintiff's intestate preliminarily to giving his opinion to the attending physician only as to the advisability of proposed therapy. There is nothing to suggest that the appellee's visit to plaintiff's intestate's room on the day of the alleged invasion of privacy was for any purpose relating to the *treatment* of the patient. Appellee acknowledges that his sole purpose in going to the Berthiaume hospital room and the taking of pictures was to conclude the making of a photographic record to complete appellee's record of the case. From the evidence, then, it is apparent that the jury had a right to conclude that the physician-patient relationship once existing between Dr. Pratt and Henry Berthiaume, the deceased, had terminated.

. . . As to the claimed assault and battery, on the state of the evidence, the jury should have been permitted to consider the evidence and return a verdict in accordance with its fact finding. It should have been instructed that consent to a touching of the body of a patient may be implied from the patient's consent to enter into a physician-patient relationship whenever such touching is reasonably necessary for the diagnosis and treatment of the patient's ailments while the physician-patient relationship continues. Quite obviously also, there would be no actionable assault and battery if the touching was expressly consented to. Absent express consent by the patient or one authorized to give consent on the patient's behalf, or absent consent implied from the circumstances, including the physician-patient relationship, the touching of the patient in the manner described by the evidence in this case would constitute assault and battery if it was part of an undertaking which, in legal effect, was an invasion of plaintiff's intestate's "right to be let alone."

It has been urged upon us that great benefit inures to medical science from the taking and preservation of photographs. The evidence discloses that the appellee had taken photographs at various stages during the course of Berthiaume's fatal illness and had made these photographs a part of appellee's medical record of the case. It is argued that by looking at Berthiaume's photographs appellee would be better able to evaluate and predict the progress of a malignancy of the same type and nature in other patients similarly afflicted. We are urged to declare as a matter of law that it was the physician's right to complete the photographic record by capturing on film Berthiaume's appearance in his final dying hours, even without the patients's consent or over his objections. This we are unwilling to do.

We recognize the benefit to the science of medicine which comes from the making of photographs of the treatment and of medical abnormalities found in patients. However, we agree with the reasoning expressed by Alessandroni, J., sitting in the Court of Common Pleas in Pennsylvania, when in writing of a fact situation almost identical to that now before us, he said in Clayman v. Bernstein, 38 Pa. D. & C. 543 (1940):

> The court recognized that an individual has the right to decide whether that which is his shall be given to the public.

> . . . The facial characteristics or peculiar cast of one's features, whether normal or distorted, belong to the individual and may not be reproduced without his permission. Even the photographer who is authorized to take a portrait is not justified in making or retaining additional copies for himself. . . .
>
> . . . Plaintiff's picture was taken without her authority or consent. Her right to decide whether her facial characteristics should be recorded for another's benefit or by reason of another's capriciousness has been violated. The scope of the authorization defines the extent of the acts necessary to constitute a violation. If plaintiff had consented to have her photograph taken only for defendant's private files certainly he would have no right to exhibit it to others without her permission. Can it be said that his rights are equally extensive when even that limited consent has not been given? Id., at 546-547. . . .

Appeal sustained.
New trial ordered.
All Justices concurring.

C. Informed Consent

1. CONSENT TO THERAPY

Cobbs v. Grant

8 Cal. 3d 229, 104 Cal. Rptr. 505, 502 P.2d 1 (1972)

Mosk, J. — This medical malpractice case involves two issues: first, whether there was sufficient evidence of negligence in the performing of surgery to sustain a jury verdict for plaintiff; second, whether, under plaintiff's alternative theory, the instructions to the jury adequately set forth the nature of a medical doctor's duty to obtain the informed consent of a patient before undertaking treatment. We conclude there was insufficient evidence to support the jury's verdict under the theory that defendant was negligent during the operation. Since there was a general verdict and we are unable to ascertain upon which of the two concepts the jury relied, we must reverse the judgment and remand for a new trial. To assist the trial court upon remand we analyze the doctor's duty to obtain the patient's informed consent and suggest principles for guidance in drafting new instructions on this question.

Plaintiff was admitted to the hospital in August 1964 for treatment of a duodenal ulcer. He was given a series of tests to ascertain the severity of his condition and, though administered medication to ease his discomfort, he continued to complain of lower abdominal pain and nausea. His family physician, Dr. Jerome Sands, concluding that surgery was indicated, discussed prospective surgery with plaintiff and advised him in general terms of the risks of undergoing a general anesthetic. Dr. Sands called in defendant, Dr. Dudley F. P. Grant, a surgeon, who after examining plaintiff, agreed with Dr. Sands that plaintiff had an intractable peptic duodenal ulcer and that surgery was indicated. Although Dr. Grant explained the nature of the operation to plaintiff, he did not discuss any of the inherent risks of the surgery.

A two-hour operation was performed the next day, in the course of which the presence of a small ulcer was confirmed. Following the surgery the ulcer disappeared. Plaintiff's recovery appeared to be uneventful, and he was permitted to go home eight days later. However, the day after he returned home, plaintiff began to experience intense pain in his abdomen. He immediately called Dr. Sands who advised him to return to the hospital. Two hours after his readmission plaintiff went into shock and emergency surgery was performed. It was discovered plaintiff was bleeding internally as a result of a severed artery at the hilum of his spleen. Because of the seriousness of the hemorrhaging and since the spleen of an adult may be removed without adverse effects, defendant decided to remove the spleen. Injuries to the spleen that compel a subsequent operation are a risk inherent in the type of surgery performed on plaintiff and occur in approximately 5 percent of such operations.

After removal of his spleen, plaintiff recuperated for two weeks in the hospital. A month after discharge he was readmitted because of sharp pains in his stomach. X-rays disclosed plaintiff was developing a gastric ulcer. The evolution of a new ulcer is another risk inherent in surgery performed to relieve a duodenal ulcer. Dr. Sands initially decided to attempt to treat this nascent gastric ulcer with antacids and a strict diet. However, some four months later plaintiff was again hospitalized when the gastric ulcer continued to deteriorate and he experienced severe pain. When plaintiff began to vomit blood the defendant and Dr. Sands concluded that a third operation was indicated: a gastrectomy with removal of 50 percent of plaintiff's stomach to reduce its acid-producing capacity. Some time after the surgery, plaintiff was discharged, but subsequently had to be hospitalized yet again when he began to bleed internally due to the premature absorption of a suture, another inherent risk of surgery. After plaintiff was hospitalized, the bleeding began to abate and a week later he was finally discharged.

Plaintiff brought this malpractice suit against his surgeon, Dr. Grant. The action was consolidated for trial with a similar action against the hospital. The jury returned a general verdict against the hospital in the amount of $45,000. This judgment has been satisfied. The jury also returned a general verdict against defendant Grant in the amount of $23,800. He appeals.

The jury could have found for plaintiff either by determining that defendant negligently performed the operation or on the theory that defendant's failure to disclose the inherent risks of the initial surgery vitiated plaintiff's consent to operate. Defendant attacks both possible grounds of the verdict.

He contends, first, there was insufficient evidence to sustain a verdict of negligence, and, second, the court committed prejudicial error in its instruction to the jury on the issue of informed consent.

Defendant's attack on the sufficiency of the evidence relates to the state of the medical testimony. Three experts testified at the trial: defendant, Dr. Sands, and defendant's expert, Dr. Yates. No expert witness was produced by plaintiff. The three experts were consistent in the opinion that the decision to operate as well as the actual procedure evidenced due care. Thus defendant insists that if experts unanimously opine that the defendant exercised due care, the jury may not substitute its judgment and find negligence. . . .

. . . We are convinced there is not substantial evidence to support a jury verdict on the issue of defendant's liability on the theory that he was negligent either when he decided to operate or in performing the surgery. . . . We therefore reverse the judgment.

Since the question of informed consent is likely to arise on retrial, we address ourselves to that issue. (Code Civ. Proc., §43.) In giving its instruction the trial court relied upon Berkey v. Anderson (1969) 1 Cal. App. 3d 790, 803, [82 Cal. Rptr. 67], a case in which it was held that if the defendant failed to make a sufficient disclosure of the risks inherent in the operation, he was guilty of a "technical battery.". . . While a battery instruction may have been warranted under the facts alleged in *Berkey,* in the case before us the instruction should have been framed in terms of negligence. . . .

. . . Where a doctor obtains consent of the patient to perform one type of treatment and subsequently performs a substantially different treatment for which consent was not obtained, there is a clear case of battery. . . .

However, when an undisclosed potential complication results, the occurrence of which was not an integral part of the treatment procedure but merely a known risk, the courts are divided on the issue of whether this should be deemed to be a battery or negligence. . . .

Dean Prosser surveyed the decisions in this area and concluded, "The earliest cases treated this as a matter of vitiating the consent, so that there was liability for battery. Beginning with a decision in Kansas in 1960 [Natanson v. Kline (1960) supra, 187 Kan. 186], it began to be recognized that this was really a matter of the standard of professional conduct. [T]he prevailing view now is that the action . . . is in reality one for negligence in failing to conform to the proper standard. . . ." (Fns. omitted; Prosser on Torts (4th ed. 1971) pp. 165-166.)

Although this is a close question, either prong of which is supportable by authority, the trend appears to be towards categorizing failure to obtain informed consent as negligence. That this result now appears with growing frequency is of more than academic interest; it reflects an appreciation of the several significant consequences of favoring negligence over a battery theory. As will be discussed infra, most jurisdictions have permitted a doctor in an informed consent action to interpose a defense that the disclosure he omitted to make was not required within his medical community. However, expert opinion as to community standard is not required in a battery count, in which the patient must merely prove failure to give informed consent and a mere touching absent consent. Moreover a doctor could be held liable for punitive damages under a battery count, and if held liable for the intentional tort of battery he might not be covered by his malpractice insurance. (Comment, Informed Consent in Medical Malpractice (1967) 55 Cal. L. Rev. 1396.) Additionally, in some jurisdictions the patient has a longer statute of limitations if he sues in negligence.

We agree with the majority trend. The battery theory should be reserved for those circumstances when a doctor performs an operation to which the patient has not consented. When the patient gives permission to perform one type of treatment and the doctor performs another, the requisite element of deliberate intent to deviate from the consent given is present. However, when the patient consents to certain treatment and the doctor performs that treatment but an undisclosed inherent complication with a low probability occurs, no intentional deviation from the consent given appears; rather, the doctor in obtaining consent may have failed to meet his due care duty to disclose pertinent information. In that situation the action should be pleaded in negligence.

The facts of this case constitute a classic illustration of an action that sounds in negligence. Defendant performed the identical operation to which plaintiff had consented. The spleen injury, development of the gastric ulcer, gastrectomy and internal bleeding as a result of the premature absorption of a suture, were all links in a chain of low probability events inherent in the initial operation.

Since this is an appropriate case for the application of a negligence theory, it remains for us to determine if the standard of care described in the jury instruction on this subject properly delineates defendant's duty to inform plaintiff of the inherent risks of the surgery. In pertinent part, the court gave the following instruction: "A physician's duty to disclose is not governed by the standard practice in the community; rather it is a duty imposed by law. A physician violates his duty to his patient and subjects himself to liability if he withholds any facts which are necessary to form the basis of an intelligent consent by the patient to the proposed treatment."

Defendant raises two objections to the foregoing instruction. First, he points out that the majority of the California cases have measured the duty to disclose not in terms of an absolute, but as a duty to reveal such information as would be disclosed by a doctor in good standing within the medical community. . . .

. . . Defendant's second contention is that this near unanimity reflects strong policy reasons for vesting in the medical community the unquestioned discretion to determine if the withholding of information by a doctor from his patient is justified at the time the patient weighs the risks of the treatment against the risks of refusing treatment.

The thesis that medical doctors are invested with discretion to withhold information from their patients has been frequently ventilated in both legal and medical literature. . . .

. . . Despite what defendant characterizes as the prevailing rule, it has never been unequivocally adopted by an authoritative source. Therefore we probe anew into the rationale which purportedly justifies, in accordance with medical rather than legal standards, the withholding of information from a patient.

Preliminarily we employ several postulates. The first is that patients are generally persons unlearned in the medical sciences and therefore, except in rare cases, courts may safely assume the knowledge of patient and physician are not in parity. The second is that a person of adult years and in sound mind has the right, in the exercise of control over his own body, to determine whether or not to submit to lawful medical treatment. The third is that the patient's consent to treatment, to be effective, must be an informed consent. And the fourth is that the patient, being unlearned in medical sciences, has an abject dependence upon and trust in his physician for the information upon which he relies during the decisional process, thus raising an obligation in the physician that transcends arms-length transactions. . . .

From the foregoing axiomatic ingredients emerges a necessity, and a resultant requirement, for divulgence by the physician to his patient of all information relevant to a meaningful decisional process. In many instances, to the physician, whose training and experience enable a self-satisfying evaluation, the particular treatment which should be undertaken may seem evident, but it is the prerogative of the patient, not the physician, to determine for himself the direction in which he believes his interests lie. . . . To enable the patient to chart his course knowledgeably, reasonable familiarity with the therapeutic alternatives and their hazards becomes essential.

Therefore, we hold, as an integral part of the physician's overall obligation to the patient there is a duty of reasonable disclosure of the available choices with respect to proposed therapy and of the dangers inherently and potentially involved in each.

A concomitant issue is the yardstick to be applied in determining reasonableness of disclosure. This defendant and the majority of courts have related the duty to the custom of physicians practicing in the community. . . . The majority rule is needlessly overbroad. Even if there can be said to be a medical community standard as to the disclosure requirement for any prescribed treatment, it appears so nebulous that doctors become, in effect, vested with virtual absolute discretion. . . . The court in Canterbury v. Spence, supra, 464 F.2d 772, 784, bluntly observed: "Nor can we ignore the fact that to bind the disclosure obligation to medical usage is to arrogate the decision on revelation to the physician alone. Respect for the patient's right of self-determination on particular therapy demands a standard set by law for physicians rather than one which physicians may or may not impose upon themselves."

Unlimited discretion in the physician is irreconcilable with the basic right of the patient to make the ultimate informed decision regarding the course of treatment to which he knowledgeably consents to be subjected.

A medical doctor, being the expert, appreciates the risks inherent in the procedure he is prescribing, the risks of a decision not to undergo the treatment, and the probability of a successful outcome of the treatment. But once this information has been disclosed, that aspect of the doctor's expert function has been performed. The weighing of these risks against the individual subjective fears and hopes of the patient is not an expert skill. Such evaluation and decision is a nonmedical judgment reserved to the patient alone. . . . A patient should be denied the opportunity to weigh the risks only where it is evident he cannot evaluate the data, as for example, where there is an emergency or the patient is a child or incompetent. For this reason the law provides that in an emergency consent is implied . . . and if the patient is a minor or incompetent, the authority to consent is transferred to the patient's legal guardian or closest available relative. . . . In all cases other than the foregoing, the decision whether or not to undertake treatment is vested in the party most directly affected: the patient. . . .

The scope of the disclosure required of physicians defies simple definition. Some courts have spoken of "full disclosure" . . . but such facile expressions obscure common practicalities. Two qualifications to a requirement of "full disclosure" need little explication. First, the patient's interest in information does not extend to a lengthy polysyllabic discourse on all possible complications. A mini-course in medical science is not required; the patient is concerned with the risk of death or bodily harm, and problems of recuperation. Second, there is no physician's duty to discuss the relatively minor risks inherent in common procedures, when it is common knowledge that such risks inherent in the procedure are of very low incidence.[2] When there is a common procedure a doctor must, of course, make such inquiries as are required to determine if for the particular patient the treatment under consideration is contraindicated—for example, to determine if the patient has had adverse reactions to medication; but no warning beyond such inquiries is required as to the remote possibility of death or serious bodily harm.

. . . However, when there is a more complicated procedure, as the surgery in the case before us, the jury should be instructed that when a given procedure inherently involves a known risk of death or serious bodily harm, a medical doctor has a duty to disclose to his patient the potential of death or serious harm, and to explain in lay terms the complications that might possibly occur. Beyond the foregoing minimal disclosure, a doctor must also reveal to his patient such additional information as a skilled practitioner of good standing would provide under similar circumstances.

2. For example, the risks inherent in the simple process of taking a common blood sample are said to include hematoma, dermatitis, cellulitis, abscess, osteomyelitis, septicemia, endocarditis, thrombophlebitis, pulmonary embolism and death, to mention a few. (Harrison, Principles of Internal Medicine (5th ed. 1966) pp. 726, 1492, 1510-1514.)

. . . In sum, the patient's right of self-decision is the measure of the physician's duty to reveal. That right can be effectively exercised only if the patient possesses adequate information to enable an intelligent choice. The scope of the physician's communications to the patient, then, must be measured by the patient's need, and that need is whatever information is material to the decision. Thus the test for determining whether a potential peril must be divulged is its materiality to the patient's decision. (Canterbury v. Spence, supra, 464 F.2d 772, 786.)

We point out, for guidance on retrial, an additional problem which suggests itself. . . . There must be a causal relationship between the physician's failure to inform and the injury to the plaintiff. Such causal connection arises only if it is established that had revelation been made consent to treatment would not have been given. Here the record discloses no testimony that had plaintiff been informed of the risks of surgery he would not have consented to the operation.

The patient-plaintiff may testify on this subject but the issue extends beyond his credibility. Since at the time of trial the uncommunicated hazard has materialized, it would be surprising if the patient-plaintiff did not claim that had he been informed of the dangers he would have declined treatment. Subjectively he may believe so, with the 20/20 vision of hindsight, but we doubt that justice will be served by placing the physician in jeopardy of the patient's bitterness and disillusionment. Thus an objective test is preferable: i.e., what would a prudent person in the patient's position have decided if adequately informed of all significant perils. (Canterbury v. Spence, supra, 464 F.2d 772, 791.)

. . . The burden of going forward with evidence of nondisclosure rests on the plaintiff. Once such evidence has been produced, then the burden of going forward with evidence pertaining to justification for failure to disclose shifts to the physician.

. . .Whenever appropriate, the court should instruct the jury on the defenses available to a doctor who has failed to make the disclosure required by law. Thus, a medical doctor need not make disclosure of risks when the patient requests that he not be so informed. (See discussion of waiver: Hagman, The Medical Patient's Right to Know, supra, 17 U.C.L.A.L. Rev. 758, 785.) Such a disclosure need not be made if the procedure is simple and the danger remote and commonly appreciated to be remote. A disclosure need not be made beyond that required within the medical community when a doctor can prove by a preponderance of the evidence he relied upon facts which would demonstrate to a reasonable man the disclosure would have so seriously upset the patient that the patient would not have been able to dispassionately weigh the risks of refusing to undergo the recommended treatment. (E.g., see discussion of informing the dying patient: Hagman, The Medical Patient's Right to Know, supra, 17 U.C.L.A.L. Rev. 758, 778.) Any defense, of course, must be consistent with what has been termed the "fiducial qualities" of the physician-patient relationship. (Emmett v. Eastern

Dispensary and Casualty Hospital (1967) 396 F.2d 931, 935 [130 App. D.C. 50].)

The judgment is reversed.

SULLIVAN, Acting C. J., MCCOMB, J., PETERS, J., TOBRINER, J., and BURKE, J. concurred.

NOTES ON INFORMED CONSENT

(1) According to the President's Commission for the Study of Ethical Problems in Medicine and Biomedical and Behavioral Research, "Although the informed consent doctrine has substantial foundations in law, it is essentially an ethical imperative." Making Health Care Decisions 2 (1982). The Commission surveyed both the public and physicians on their attitudes toward informed consent. Among its findings, "Regardless of race, income, education, age, or gender, the vast majority of people surveyed by the Commission felt that patients have a right to information and ought to participate in decisions regarding their health care." Id. at 17. More than 80 percent of patients and 90 percent of physicians believe physicians should initiate the informed consent discussion. Id. at 79. And more than three-quarters of physicians and the public think physicians should initiate discussions about uncertainty in medical treatment and outcomes. Id. at 88. On the other hand, most physicians report that they sometimes withhold information from patients for the following reasons: the family asks doctor not to tell; the patient tells doctor not to tell; the information might lead patient not to accept treatment recommendation. Id. at 97-99. Finally, 76 percent of physicians and 88 percent of the public think informed consent should be protected by law. Id. at 105. As a practical matter, it is sometimes difficult to know what is being communicated and what the patient wants to have communicated. The following is a transcript of an informed consent discussion concerning cardiac catheterization. What do you think about it? If the doctor asked you to comment on his remarks, what would you tell him about how to act toward the next similar patient?

Having explained why the procedure should be done and what information it would provide, the physician went on to describe how it was done and what it would feel like, including that the patient would feel very hot for about 20 seconds.

Patient: Oh, seconds only, that's all right. But I do want this explanation because I knew I would get this for 25 years. I guess I've heard a lot of things about it. Friends of mine have had it and so forth.

Doctor: Yes, some people like it and some people say it's the worse thing that happened to them in their lives. I think I ought to tell you that there's some possibility that we may have to do a transeptum catheterization [and he explained what this consisted of]. There's some potential risks. I think you will find they are terrifying, but I want you to remember we weigh the risks both of doing it and not doing it before we recommend it to you.

Patient: Maybe you shouldn't tell me until tomorrow.

Doctor: Well, I could wait until tomorrow, but I do have to tell you this. I want you to know the risk is low. We are talking about a one in a thousand chance of a major risk. There's some minor ones, too. But they can all be dealt with. Some of the major ones can, too, but they're not very likely. Here are some of them. First of all we have to go into the vessel, and we can injure the vessel, and that can sometimes require surgery, which can be difficult in its own right. The second one is that you might have hardening of the arteries already, and some sort of blockage could result from pushing through them. This can require surgery also to make it better, and even so there's a low risk of a heart attack or of stroke from it. Then another thing is that some people are allergic to the dye, and this can put somebody into shock, and usually we can treat that with medicine, but it's quite serious. Another thing it can do is it can cause an irregular heartbeat, and you can even need an electric shock because it can cause your heart to stop. But of course you would be asleep then, and you wouldn't feel it. Another thing is that if we need to do the transeptal catheterization, that can cause a puncture of the heart and bleeding. The blood can get between the heart and the sac around it, and then we would have to drain that. One of the minor risks is that you can have a hematoma around where we put in the catheter. That's not much of a real problem, but you can get black and blue, and that happens because of the Heparin we put in to prevent the clotting I talked about earlier.

Patient: You know, I can't remember any of that stuff.

Doctor: Well, I know it's scary, but I want you to understand that it's my feeling that it is a higher risk not to have it done. But of course ultimately it's your decision, not mine.

Patient: Do you do this often?

Doctor: Yeah, this is a big center for that sort of thing, for valve replacements, and we see a lot of these.

Patient: You see it's all new to me.

Doctor: And one other thing is that you're going to have to sign a consent form. The nurse'll bring that in later tonight.

Patient: Well, you have to do it because it's the best procedure.[Id. at 81-82.]

(2) Historically, "Disclosure and consent, except in the most rudimentary fashion, are obligations alien to medical thinking and practice." J. Katz, The Silent World of Doctor and Patient 1 (1984). As Jay Katz has persuasively documented, "Traditional professional notions of trust are based on the wrong model. The trust relationship that doctors prefer in interactions

with their patients mirrors the one that prevailed at the first stage of the parent-child interaction." Id. at 100. This model calls for absolute trust on the part of the child toward its parent's actions; just as physicians have traditionally called for "unquestioning compliance, unilateral trust, and verbal silence." Treated as helpless and incompetent children by their physicians, patients tend to take on the role. Id. at 100-101. The "new model" of the doctor-patient relationship, one that *demands* conversation and shared decision-making, rests on a number of assumptions: (1) there is no single right decision for how the life of health and illness should be lived; (2) physicians and patients bring their own vulnerabilities to the decisionmaking process; (3) both need to relate to one another as equals and unequals (physicians know more about disease; patients more about their own needs); and (4) all human conduct is influenced by rational and irrational expectations. Id. at 102. Katz summarizes his powerful psychoanalytic analysis of the doctor-patient relationship as follows:

> Ultimately disclosure and consent seek to pierce the isolation, to eliminate the feelings of abandonment, and to reverse the lack of control that patients now experience so often in their interactions with physicians. . . . Thus, the idea of informed consent is grounded not only in the principle of self-determination but in good therapeutic management as well, for relief of suffering requires doctor's presence in the full sense of the word. What is therapeutic for citizens turns out to be equally therapeutic for patients. Perhaps the ancient debate to the contrary can now finally be laid to rest. Id. at 208.

(3) Cases like *Cobbs,* and its immediate predecessor Canterbury v. Spence, 464 F.2d 772 (D.C. App. 1972), adopt a patient-centered view of the "duty to disclose" that requires disclosures of that information "material" to a patient's decision to accept or reject the proposed therapy. Unfortunately for the patient, both courts also adopted an "objective" rather than a subjective *causation* standard, so that it was unimportant whether or not the patient himself would have rejected the treatment had he been properly informed: the relevant test was whether a "prudent person in the patient's position" would have rejected the treatment. This helps explain why neither the plaintiff in *Cobbs* nor in *Canterbury* collected a penny from either physician for their failure to disclose. Note, however, that in *Cobbs* the hospital paid up rather than pursue the appeal, and that the role of hospitals in enforcing informed consent protocols on their staff physicians remains uncertain.

If informed consent is really about individual self-determination, the jury must be able to decide in favor of the plaintiff if they believe the plaintiff would have rejected the proposed therapy, regardless of what a reasonable person would have done. Although the logic of this conclusion seems unassailable, courts have been reluctant to put teeth into the informed consent doctrine by adopting the subjective causation standard. Indeed, only two courts have gone this route to date. Scott v. Bradford, 606 P.2d 554 (Okla. 1979) (rejecting the *Canterbury* standard of causation as "backtracking on its own theory of self-determination"); and McPherson v. Ellis, 305 N.C. 255, 287 S.E.2d 892 (1982) (noting that the objective standard gives "no consideration to the peculiar quirks and idiosyncracies of the individual"). See generally R. Faden & T. Beauchamp, A History and Theory of Informed Consent (1986); C. Lidz et al., Informed Consent: A Study of Decisionmaking in Psychiatry (1984).

(4) The ability of courts to fashion a subjective standard for causation is limited by legislation. Almost half of the states have passed statutes that define both the physician's disclosure obligations and adopt the objective standard of causation. One of these is North Carolina, making its pre-statutory decision in *McPherson* of little practical value. Prior to 1975, few states had any laws on informed consent. However, in 1975 and 1976, in response to the "medical malpractice crisis," at least 18 states enacted statutes that either defined or restricted the application of the doctrine, and about another 10 have done so since. About half the statutes provide that a patient's signature on a consent form is conclusive evidence that the information was provided to the patient and that the consent was valid. Florida's statute, for example, provides that the signed consent form shall be "conclusively presumed to be valid consent." Fla. Stat. Ann. §768.132(3) (a). New York passed what is probably the country's most anti-patient informed consent act, even though prior to its enactment only one case in New York's history involving informed consent as the cause of action had ever resulted in a payment to the plaintiff. N.Y. Pub. Health L. §2805-d. See generally, S. Law & S. Polan, Pain and Profit (1978), and G.J. Annas, L.H. Glantz & B.F. Katz, Informed Consent to Human Experimentation 38-42 (1977). The Texas statute is discussed in Barclay v. Campbell, 704 S.W.2d 8 (Tx. 1986).

(5) Some physicians have advocated using informed consent educationally and have recognized that information sharing can powerfully and positively affect a doctor-patient alliance or partnership to their mutual benefit. Drummond Rennie, for example, advised physicians in a New England Journal of Medicine editorial to do more than just "improve consent forms" that "are regarded by most patients as legal documents to protect the physician." Instead,

> Physicians should accept education of the patient through the process of consent as a worthwhile therapeutic goal. To deny the possibility of informed consent is to ensure that it will never be achieved — an attitude that is immoral and, in hospitals and states that have adopted the Patients Bill of Rights, illegal. This means that the physician must reject the paternalistic role in favor of the role of counselor and advocate, attempting to give patients equality in the covenant by educating them to make informed decisions. [Informed Consent by "Well-Nigh Abject" Adults, 32 N. Engl. J. Med. 971, 918 (1980).]

And see Mariner, Informed Consent in the Post-Modern Era, Law & Soc. Inquiry 301 (1988).

(6) Since both the courts and the state legislatures have tended to narrow the doctrine of informed consent to a disclosure requirement that can be functionally defined by the "reasonably prudent patient's need to know," some have suggested that we need to develop a new cause of action. This action has been variously described, but it would put an affirmative burden on physicians to share decisionmaking with the patient and would provide penalties for failure to comply, even if one of the nondisclosed risks did not materialize. For example, Alan Weisbard suggests establishing a patient's right to participate in medical decisionmaking on an informed, understanding and voluntary basis. Damages would be awarded by a tribunal for "dignitary harms on the basis of a statutory schedule . . . without any requirement that the patient allege or prove physical injury." Informed Consent: The Law's Uneasy Compromise with Ethical Theory, 65 Neb. L. Rev. 749, 763 (1986). See also Schultz, From Informed Consent to Patient Choice: A New Protected Interest, 95 Yale L. J. 219 (1985), which discusses the advantages of creating an affirmative duty on physicians to protect "patient choice." Shultz argues that the fiduciary nature of the doctor-patient relationship is an evolving one that changes as patients demand more active participation in decisionmaking. "In the wake of such redefinition, the nature of fiduciary obligation must also change to stress more advising and less deciding." Id. at 279.

A more direct approach is the suggestion by Marshall Kapp that individual and institutional health care providers not be paid by insurers unless a signed consent form for the procedure is in the patient's chart. Kapp, Enforcing Patient Preferences: Linking Payment for Medical Care to Informed Consent, 261 J.A.M.A. 1935 (1989). What are the advantages and disadvantages of this proposal? See Faden, Enforcing Informed Consent Requirements: Form or Substance? 261 J.A.M.A. 1948 (1989). And see generally R. Faden & T. Beauchamp, A History and Theory of Informed Consent (1986).

D. Human Experimentation and Research

1. HUMAN EXPERIMENTATION AND INFORMED CONSENT

The history of medical progress is to a large extent the history of human experimentation. Few wish to halt the practice of experimentation on humans altogether. Nonetheless, there is a growing awareness that individual rights have often been trampled in the process and that steps must be taken to protect patients from overzealous researchers.

There has been a history of unconscionable abuse, most notable in the Nazi experiments during World War II, but including some notorious experiments in the U.S. as well (such as the Jewish Chronic Disease Hospital case, in which aged and debilitated patients were injected with cancer cells without their knowledge to test their immunity reaction, and the Tuskegee Syphilis study, in which black males were not treated for this disease so that its "natural history" could be studied). In response, various regulatory mechanisms have been developed to protect the rights and welfare of subjects. To protect the subject's welfare, legitimate experimentation requires a sound hypothesis, based on prior research (usually with animals), reason to expect beneficial results (for society, if not for the subject), a competent researcher, and prior review by a competent panel. To protect the subject's rights, legitimate experimentation requires the voluntary, competent, informed, and understanding consent of the subject. The most important question in human experimentation is whether the experiment should be done at all. Only after this determination has been made, is it even justifiable to ask the subject to participate. Put another way, informed consent is a necessary, but not sufficient condition for legitimate experimentation.

Indictment, U.S. v. Brandt, Trials of War Criminals, Before Nuernberg Military Tribunals Under Control Council Law No. 10.

Vol. I, 38-48 (1949)

Defendants did commit war crimes and crimes against humanity . . . involving medical experiments without the subjects' consent . . . including the following:

High-Altitude Experiments. From about March 1942 to about August 1942 experiments were conducted at the Dachau concentration camp, for the benefit of the German Air Force, to investigate the limits of human endurance and existence at extremely high altitudes. . . . The experimental subjects were placed in a low-pressure chamber and thereafter the simulated altitude therein was raised. Many victims died as a result of these experiments and others suffered grave injury, torture, and ill-treatment. . . .

Freezing Experiments. From about August 1942 to about May 1943 experiments were conducted at the Dachau concentration camp, primarily for the benefit of the German Air Force, to investigate the most effective means of treating persons who had been severely chilled or frozen. In one series of experiments the subjects were forced to remain in a tank of ice water for periods up to 3 hours. . . . In another series of experiments, the subjects were kept naked outdoors for many hours at temperatures below freezing. . . .

Sulfanilamide Experiments. From about July 1942 to about September 1943 experiments to investigate the effectiveness of sulfanilamide were conducted at the Ravensbrueck concentration camp for the benefit of the German Armed Forces. Wounds deliberately inflicted on the experimental subjects were injected with bacteria such as streptococcus, gas gangrene, and tetanus. Circulation of blood was interrupted by tying off blood vessels at both ends of the wound to create a condition similar to that of a battlefield wound. Infection was aggravated by forcing wood shavings and ground glass into the wounds. The infection was treated with sulfanilamide and other drugs to determine their effectiveness. . . .

Experiments with Poison. In or about December 1943, and in or about October 1944, experiments were conducted at the Buchenwald concentration camp to investigate the effect of various poisons upon human beings. The poisons were secretly administered to experimental subjects in their food. The victims died as a result of the poison or were killed immediately in order to permit autopsies.

Kaimowitz v. Department of Mental Health for the State of Michigan

No. 73-19434-AW (Mich. Cir. Ct., Wayne County, July 10, 1973)

This case came to this Court originally on a complaint for Writ of Habeas Corpus brought by Plaintiff Kaimowitz on behalf of John Doe and the Medical Committee for Human Rights, alleging that John Doe was being illegally detained in the Lafayette Clinic for the purpose of experimental psychosurgery.

John Doe had been committed by the Kalamazoo County Circuit Court on January 11, 1955, to the Ionia State Hospital as a Criminal Sexual Psychopath, without a trial of criminal charges, under the terms of the then existing Criminal Sexual Psychopathic law. He had been charged with the murder and subsequent rape of a student nurse at the Kalamazoo State Hospital while he was confined there as a mental patient.

In 1972, Drs. Ernst Rodin and Jacques Gottlieb of the Lafayette Clinic, a facility of the Michigan Department of Mental Health, had filed a proposal "For the Study of Treatment of Uncontrollable Aggression."

This was funded by the Legislature of the State of Michigan for the fiscal year 1972. After more than 17 years at the Ionia State Hospital, John Doe was transferred to the Lafayette Clinic in November of 1972 as a suitable research subject for the Clinic's study of uncontrollable aggression.

Under the terms of the study, 24 criminal sexual psychopaths in the State's mental health system were to be subjects of experiment. The experiment was to compare the effect of surgery on the amygdaloid portion of the limbic system of the brain with the effect of the drug cyproterone acetate on the male hormone flow. The comparison was intended to show which, if either, could be used in controlling aggression of males in an institutional setting, and to afford lasting permanent relief from such aggression to the patient.

Substantial difficulties were encountered in locating a suitable patient population for the surgical procedures and a matched control group for the treatment by the antiandrogen drug. As a matter of fact, it was concluded that John Doe was the only known appropriate candidate available within the state mental health system for the surgical experiment.

John Doe signed an "informed consent" form to become an experimental subject prior to his transfer from the Ionia State Hospital. He had obtained signatures from his parents giving consent for the experimental and innovative surgical procedures to be performed on his brain, and two separate three-man review committees were established by Dr. Rodin to review the scientific worthiness of the study and the validity of the consent obtained from Doe.

The Scientific Review Committee, headed by Dr. Ellito Luby, approved of the procedure, and the Human Rights Review Committee, consisting of Ralph Slovenko, a Professor of Law and Psychiatry at Wayne State University, Monsignor Clifford Sawher, and Frank Morgan, a Certified Public Accountant, gave their approval to the procedure. Even though no experimental subjects were found to be available in the state mental health system other than John Doe, Dr. Rodin prepared to proceed with the experiment on Doe, and depth electrodes were to be inserted into his brain on or about January 15, 1973.

Early in January 1973, Plaintiff Kaimowitz became aware of the work being contemplated on John Doe and made his concern known to the Detroit Free Press. Considerable newspaper publicity ensued and this action was filed shortly thereafter.

With the rush of publicity on the filing of the original suit, funds for the research project were stopped by Dr. Gordon Yudashkin, Director of the Department of Mental Health, and the investigators, Drs. Gottlieb and Rodin, dropped their plans to pursue the research set out in the proposal. They reaffirmed at the trial, however, their belief in the scientific, medical, and ethical soundness of the proposal.

Upon the request of counsel, a Three-Judge Court was empanelled . . . the constitutionality of the detention of John Doe was considered by the Court, and on March 23, 1973 . . . the Court directed his release . . . and the Court on March 15, 1973, rendered an oral opinion holding that the matter was not moot. . . .

The issue [is as follows]: After failure of established therapies, may an adult or a legally appointed guardian, if the adult is involuntarily detained, at a facility within the jurisdiction of the State Department of Mental Health give legally adequate consent to an innovative or experimental surgical procedure on the brain, if there is demonstrable physical abnormality of the brain, and the procedure is designed to ameliorate behavior, which is either personally tormenting to the patient, or so profoundly disruptive that the patient cannot safely live, or live with others? . . . The psychosurgery we are concerned with encompasses only experimental psychosurgery where there are demonstrable physical abnormalities in the brain. . . .

We start with the indisputable medical fact that no significant activity in the brain occurs in isolation without correlated activity in other parts of the brain. Psychosurgery should never be undertaken upon involuntarily committed populations, when there is a high-risk low-benefits ratio as demonstrated in this case. This is because of the impossibility of obtaining truly informed consent from such populations. The reasons such informed consent cannot be obtained are set forth in detail subsequently in this Opinion. [W]e deal here not only with legal and medical issues, but with ethical and social issues as well.

Is brain function related to abnormal aggressive behavior? This, fundamentally, is what the case is about. . . .

The Court does not in any way desire to impede medical progress. We are much concerned with violence and the possible effect of brain disease on violence. Much research on the brain is necessary and must be carried on, but when it takes the form of psychosurgery, it cannot be undertaken on involuntary detained populations. Other avenues of research must be utilized and developed.

Although extensive psychosurgery has been performed in the United States and throughout the world in recent years to attempt change of objectionable behavior, there is no medically recognized syndrome for aggression and objectionable behavior associated with the nonorganic brain abnormality. [O]n this record there is no scientific basis for establishing that the removal or destruction of an area of the limbic brain would have any direct therapeutic effect in controlling aggressivity or improving tormenting personal behavior absent the showing of a well defined clinical syndrome such as epilepsy.

To advance scientific knowledge, it is true that doctors may desire to experiment on human beings, but the need for scientific inquiry must be reconciled with the inviolability which our society provides for a person's mind and body. Under a free government, one of a person's greatest rights is the right to inviolability of his person, and it is axiomatic that this right necessarily forbids the physician or surgeon from violating, without permission, the bodily integrity of his patient.

Generally, individuals are allowed free choice about whether to undergo experimental medical procedures. But the State has the power to modify this free choice concerning experimental medical procedures when it cannot be freely given, or when the result would be contrary to public policy. For example, it is obvious that a person may not consent to acts that will constitute murder, manslaughter, or mayhem upon himself. In short, there are times when the State for good reason should withhold a person's ability to consent to certain medical procedures.

It is elementary tort law that consent is the mechanism by which the patient grants the physician the power to act, and which protects the patient against unauthorized invasions of his person. This requirement protects one of society's most fundamental values, the inviolability of the individual. An operation performed upon a patient without his informed consent is the tort of battery, and a doctor and a hospital have no right to impose compulsory medical treatment against the patient's will. These elementary statements of tort law need no citation.

Jay Katz, in his outstanding book Experimentation with Human Beings (Russell Sage Foundation, N.Y., 1972) points out on page 523 that the concept of informed consent has been accepted as a cardinal principle for judging the propriety of research with human beings.

He points out that in the experimental setting, informed consent serves multiple purposes. He states:

> Most clearly, requiring informed consent serves society's desire to respect each individual's autonomy, and his right to make choices concerning his own life.
>
> Second, providing a subject with information about an experiment will encourage him to be an active partner and the process may also increase the rationality of the experimentation process.
>
> Thirdly, securing informed consent protects the experimentation process by encouraging the investigator to question the value of the proposed project and the adequacy of the measures he has taken to protect subjects, by reducing civil and criminal liability for nonnegligent injury to the subjects, and by diminishing adverse public reaction to an experiment.
>
> Finally, informed consent may serve the function of increasing society's awareness about human research. . . . [Id. at 523-524.]

It is obvious that there must be close scrutiny of the adequacy of the consent when an experiment, as in this case, is dangerous, intrusive, irreversible, and of uncertain benefit to the patient and society.

Counsel for Drs. Rodin and Gottlieb argues that anyone who has ever been treated by a doctor for any relatively serious illness is likely to acknowledge that a competent doctor can get almost any patient to consent to almost anything. Counsel claims this is true because patients do not want to make decisions about complex medical matters and because there is the general problem of avoiding decision making in stress situations, characteristic of all human beings.

He further argues that a patient is always under duress when hospitalized and that in a hospital or institutional setting there is no such thing as a volunteer. Dr. Ingelfinger in Volume 287, page 466 of the New England Journal of Medicine (August 31, 1972) states:

> The process of obtaining "informed consent" with all its regulations and conditions, is no more than an elaborate ritual, a device that when the subject is uneducated and uncomprehending, confers no more than the semblance of propriety on human experimentation. The subject's only real protection, the public as well as the medical profession must recognize, depends on the conscience and compassion of the investigator and his peers.

Everything defendants' counsel argues militates against the obtaining of informed consent from involuntarily detained mental patients. If, as he agrees, truly informed consent cannot be given for regular surgical procedures by noninstitutionalized persons, then certainly an adequate informed consent cannot be given by the involuntarily detained mental patient.

We do not agree that a truly informed consent cannot be given for a regular surgical procedure by a patient, institutionalized or not. The law has long recognized that such valid consent can be given. But we do hold that informed consent cannot be given by an involuntarily detained mental patient for experimental psychosurgery for the reason set forth below.

The Michigan Supreme Court has considered in a tort case the problems of experimentation with humans. In Norter v. Koch, 272 Mich. 273, 261 N.W. 762 (1935), the issue turned on whether the doctor had taken proper diagnostic steps before prescribing an experimental treatment for cancer. Discussing medical experimentation, the Court said at page 282:

> We recognize the fact that if the general practice of medicine and surgery is to progress, there must be a certain amount of experimentation carried on; but such experiments must be done with the knowledge and consent of the patient or those responsible for him, and *must not vary too radically from the accepted method of procedure*. (Emphasis added.)

This means that the physician cannot experiment without restraint or restriction. He must consider first of all the welfare of his patient. This concept is universally accepted by the medical profession, the legal profession, and responsible persons who have thought and written on the matter.

Furthermore, he must weigh the risk of the patient against the benefit to be obtained by trying something new. The risk-benefit ratio is an important ratio in considering any experimental surgery upon a human being. The risk must always be relatively low, in the non-life threatening situation to justify human experimentation.

Informed consent is a requirement of variable demands. Being certain that a patient has consented adequately to an operation, for example, is much more important when doctors are going to undertake an experimental, dangerous, and intrusive procedure than, for example, when they are going to remove an appendix. When a procedure is experimental, dangerous, and intrusive, special safeguards are necessary. The risk benefit ratio must be carefully considered and the question of consent thoroughly explored.

To be legally adequate, a subject's informed consent must be competent, knowing and voluntary.

In considering consent for experimentation, the ten principles known as the Nuremberg Code give guidance. They are found in the judgment of the Court in United States v. Karl Brandt.

> Certain basic principles must be observed in order to satisfy moral, ethical and legal concepts:
>
> 1) The voluntary consent of the human subject is absolutely essential.
>
> This means that the person involved should have legal capacity to give consent: should be so situated as to be able to exercise free power of choice, without the intervention of any element of force, fraud, deceit, duress, overreaching, or other ulterior form of constraint or coercion: and should have sufficient knowledge and comprehension to enable him to make an understanding and enlightened decision. This latter element requires that before the acceptance of an affirmative decision by the experimental subject there should be made known to him the nature, duration and purpose of the experiment: the methods and means by which it is to be conducted: all inconveniences and hazards reasonably to be expected: and the effects upon his health or person which may possibly come from his participation in the experiment. The duty and responsibility for ascertaining the quality of the consent rests upon each individual who initiates, directs, or engages in the experiment. It is a personal duty and responsibility which may not be delegated to another with impunity.
>
> 2) The experiment should be such as to yield fruitful results for the good of society, unprocurable by other methods or means of study, and not random and unnecessary in nature.
>
> 3) The experiment should be so designed and based on the results of animal experimentation and a knowledge of the natural history of the disease or other problem under study that the anticipated results will justify the performance of the experiment.
>
> 4) The experiment should be so conducted as to avoid all unnecessary physical and mental suffering and injury.
>
> 5) No experiment should be so conducted where there is a prior reason to believe that death or disabling injury will occur: except, perhaps, in those experiments where the experimental physicians also serve as subjects.
>
> 6) The degree of risk to be taken should *never* exceed that determined by the humanitarian importance of the problem to be solved by the experiment.
>
> 7) Proper preparations should be made and adequate facilities provided to protect the experimental subject against even remote possibilities of injury, disability, or death.
>
> 8) The experiment should be conducted only by scientifically qualified persons. The highest degree of skill and care should be required through all stages of the experiment of those who conduct or engage in the experiment.
>
> 9) During the course of the experiment the human subject should be at liberty to bring the experiment to an end if he has reached the physical or mental state where continuation of the experiment seems to him to be impossible.
>
> 10) During the course of the experiment the scientist in charge must be

> prepared to terminate the experiment at any stage, if he has probable cause to believe, in the exercise of the good faith, superior skill, and careful judgment required of him that a continuation of the experiment is likely to result in injury, disability, or death to the experimental subject.

In the Nuremberg Judgment, the elements of what must guide us in decision are found. The involuntarily detained mental patient must have legal capacity to give consent. He must be so situated as to be able to exercise free power of choice, without any element of force, fraud, deceit, duress, overreaching, or other ulterior form of restraint or coercion. He must have sufficient knowledge and comprehension of the subject matter to enable him to make an understanding decision. The decision must be a totally voluntary one on his part.

We must first look to the competency of the involuntarily detained mental patient to consent. Competency requires the ability of the subject to understand rationally the nature of the procedure, its risks, and other relevant information. The standard governing required disclosures by a doctor is what a reasonable patient needs to know in order to make an intelligent decision. . . .

Although an involuntarily detained mental patient may have a sufficient I.Q. to intellectually comprehend his circumstances . . . the very nature of his incarceration diminishes the capacity to consent to psychosurgery. He is particularly vulnerable as a result of his mental condition, the deprivation stemming from involuntary confinement, and the effects of the phenomenon of "institutionalization." . . . In the routine of institutional life, most decisions are made for patients. For example, John Doe testified how extraordinary it was for him to be approached by Dr. Yudashkin about the possible submission to psychosurgery, and how unusual it was to be consulted by a physician about his preference. Institutionalization tends to strip the individual of the support which permits him to maintain his sense of self-worth and the value of his own physical and mental integrity. An involuntarily confined mental patient clearly has diminished capacity for making a decision about irreversible experimental psychosurgery.

Equally great problems are found when the involuntarily detained mental patient is incompetent, and consent is sought from a guardian or parent. Although guardian or parental consent may be legally adequate when arising out of traditional circumstances, it is legally ineffective in the psychosurgery situation. The guardian or parent cannot do that which the patient, absent a guardian, would be legally unable to do.

The second element of an informed consent is knowledge of the risk involved and the procedures to be undertaken. It was obvious from the record made in this case that the facts surrounding experimental brain surgery are profoundly uncertain, and the lack of knowledge on the subject makes a knowledgeable consent to psychosurgery literally impossible.

We turn now to the third element of an informed consent, that of voluntariness. It is obvious that the most important thing to a large number of involuntarily detained mental patients incarcerated for an unknown length of time, is freedom.

The Nuremberg standards require that the experimental subjects be so situated as to exercise free power of choice without the intervention of any element of force, fraud, deceit, duress, overreaching, or other *ulterior form of constraint or coercion.* It is impossible for an involuntarily detained mental patient to be free of ulterior forms of restraint or coercion when his very release from the institution may depend upon his cooperating with the institutional authorities and giving consent to experimental surgery.

The privileges of an involuntarily detained patient and the rights he exercises in the institution are within the control of the institutional authorities. As was pointed out in the testimony of John Doe, such minor things as the right to have a lamp in his room, or the right to have grounds privileges to go for a picnic with his family assumed major proportion. For 17 years he lived completely under the control of the hospital. Nearly every important aspect of his life was decided without any opportunity on his part to participate in the decision-making process.

The involuntarily detained mental patient is in an inherently coercive atmosphere even though no direct pressures may be placed upon him. He finds himself stripped of customary amenities and defenses. Free movement is restricted. He becomes a part of communal living subject to the control of the institutional authorities. . . .

Involuntarily confined mental patients live in an inherently coercive institutional environment. Indirect and subtle psychological coercion has a profound effect upon the patient population. Involuntarily confined patients cannot reason as equals with the doctors and administrators over whether they should undergo psychosurgery. They are not able to voluntarily give informed consent because of the inherent inequality in their position.

We therefore conclude that involuntarily detained mental patients cannot give informed and adequate consent to experimental psychosurgical procedures on the brain.

The three basic elements of informed consent — competency, knowledge, and voluntariness — cannot be ascertained with a degree of reliability warranting resort to use of such an invasive procedure. . . .

For the reasons given, we conclude that the answer to . . . [the] question . . . posed for decision is no.

NOTES ON *KAIMOWITZ*

(1) The complete "Informed Consent" form signed by John Doe is as follows:

> Since conventional treatment efforts over a period of several years have not enabled me to control my outbursts of rage and anti-social behavior, I submit an application to be a subject in a research project which may offer me a form of effective therapy. This therapy is based upon the idea that episodes of anti-social rage and sexuality might be triggered by a disturbance in certain portions of my brain. I understand that in order to be certain that a significant brain disturbance exists, which might relate to my anti-social behavior, an initial operation will have to be performed. This procedure consists of placing fine wires into my brain, which will record the electrical activity from those structures which play a part in anger and sexuality. These electrical waves can then be studied to determine the presence of an abnormality.
>
> In addition electrical stimulation with weak currents passed through these wires will be done in order to find out if one or several points in the brain can trigger my episodes of violence or unlawful sexuality. In other words, this stimulation may cause me to want to commit an aggressive or sexual act, but every effort will be made to have a sufficient number of people present to control me. If the brain disturbance is limited to a small area, I understand that the investigators will destroy this part of my brain with an electrical current. If the abnormality comes from a larger part of my brain, I agree that it should be surgically removed, if the doctors determine that it should be surgically removed, if the doctors determine that it can be done so, without risk of side effects. Should the electrical activity from the part of my brain into which the wires have been placed reveal that there is no significant abnormality, the wires will simply be withdrawn.
>
> I realize that any operation on the brain carries a number of risks which may be slight but could be potentially serious. These risks include infection, bleeding, temporary or permanent weakness or paralysis of one or more of my legs or arms, difficulties with speech and thinking, as well as the ability to feel, touch, pain, and temperature. Under extraordinary circumstances, it is also possible that I might not survive the operation.
>
> Fully aware of the risks detailed in the paragraphs above, I authorize the physicians of Lafayette Clinic and Providence Hospital to perform the procedures as outlined above.

(2) After his release in March 1973, Doe worked for a few months as a silk screener in Detroit, and then returned to his home town of Kalamazoo, where he enrolled at Valley College. Shortly thereafter he was apprehended stealing a woman's girdle from a local department store. After he was booked, he was searched and found to be wearing nineteen pairs of women's underpants and ten slips. He entered a plea of guilty to the shoplifting charge and was sentenced to 32 months to four years.

While in custody, Doe confessed to the crime that had occurred more than 21 years earlier. At the trial held early in 1976, Doe pleaded innocent, with a defense of insanity. The jury, however, did not accept the defense, and found him guilty of murder in the second degree. Now in his mid-40s, he was sentenced in April 1976 to life imprisonment, with credit for the eighteen years he had already spent in institutions.

Note on Psychosurgery

Psychosurgery has been perhaps *the* most controversial experimental procedure in medical history. Egas Moniz, a Portuguese neurosurgeon, won the Nobel Prize in 1942 for the development of prefrontal lobotomy with its calming effects on otherwise unmanageable patients. The procedure was introduced into the U.S. by Walter Freeman and James Watts in the early 1940s, and more than 50,000 World War II veterans underwent prefrontal lobotomy in the U.S. after the war. In the early 1950s, with the introduction of the major tranquilizers, prefrontal lobotomy fell out of favor. By the 1960s, however, some surgeons were experimenting with selective destruction of specific areas of the brain for behavior modification. Two such physicians, Vernon Mark and Frank Ervin suggested that dangerous behavior could be predicted and prevented by operating on defective brains. V. Mark & F. Ervin, Violence and the Brain (1970). Psychiatrist Peter Breggin started a political campaign against psychosurgery as unscientific and destructive. In 1974, when Congress passed the National Research Act, it set up a National Commission to study and make recommendations on various aspects of human experimentation. The only specific procedure it required the Commission to study was psychosurgery. The Commission decided not to ban psychosurgery, but rather to develop an elaborate system of procedural safeguards. The Commission's primary recommendation was:

> (1) Until the safety and efficacy of any psychosurgical procedure have been demonstrated, such procedure should be performed only at an institution with an institutional review board (IRB) approved by DHEW specifically for reviewing proposed psychosurgery, and only after such IRB has determined that: (A) the surgeon has the competence to perform the procedure; (B) it is appropriate, based upon sufficient assessment of the patient, to perform the procedure on that patient; (C) adequate pre- and postoperative evaluations will be performed; and (D) the patient has given informed consent. . . . [Psychosurgery: Report and Recommendations 57 (1977).]

If there is any reason to call the patient's consent into question, more elaborate procedural safeguards, including a court hearing for prisoners, involuntarily committed mental patients, and children are also required.

The Commission's statistics indicated that during the years 1971-1973, about 500 psychosurgical procedures were performed annually in the United States by about 140 neurosurgeons. The Commission looked only at 61 cases of 4 surgeons who volunteered their cases for study. Most forms of psychosurgery were not seen at all; and since, in the '70s malpractice climate, surgeons could not be expected to volunteer their failures or worst cases for study, one is skeptical of those that were seen. National Commission for the Protection of Human Subjects of Biomedical and Behavioral Research, Report and Recommendations on Psychosurgery, DHEW Pub. No. (OS)

77-0001 (1977). See also, Psychosurgery (symposium issue), 54 B.U.L. Rev. 215-353 (1974).

In the late '80s physicians began to suggest that instead of cutting areas of the brain out, it might be useful in some cases to "implant" parts of the brains of others into a diseased individual's brain. Fetal brain "transplants" for Parkinson's disease was the first suggested target. See Sladek & Shoulson, Neural Transplantation: A Call for Patience Rather than Patients, 240 Science 1386 (1988). And see discussion in Chapter 9 at 880. There is a natural tendency in the U.S. not to prohibit physicians from doing anything they believe might benefit a patient or other patients in the future (at least with the patient's consent). When the procedure seems extreme or "experimental," we often require prior review by a committee before it can be used on humans. But are there procedures that "work" that nonetheless should not be performed on a human being? For example, what if the psychosurgery suggested for John Doe was 100 percent effective in eliminating aggressiveness, should it then be used on prisoners? What about castration of child molesters? And in the noncriminal context, are there limits on what society should permit doctors and patients to agree on between themselves?

Psychosurgery is the subject of Michael Crichton's novel, The Terminal Man (1972), and the social policy issues raised by effectively removing violent tendencies from individuals is the subject of Anthony Burgess's novel (and the motion picture of the same name) A Clockwork Orange (1962). Psychosurgery is also used as the ultimate form of punishment in Ken Kesey's, One Flew Over the Cuckoo's Nest (1962).

Note on the Nuremberg Code

The Nuremberg Code, formulated by three U.S. judges at the "Doctors' Trial" in 1947, is based on a type of natural law reasoning. In the court's words, "All agree . . . that certain basic principles must be observed in order to satisfy moral, ethical, and legal concepts." The Code was adopted by the U.S. Army in 1954, and was used as the basis for human experimentation regulations by the Dept. of Health and Human Services (then DHEW) in 1966. It remains today "the most comprehensive statement on the law of informed consent to human experimentation." G.J. Annas, L.H. Glantz & B.F. Katz, Informed Consent to Human Experimentation 6-10 (1977). Sixteen of the twenty-three defendants were found guilty of war crimes and crimes against humanity. Seven were sentenced to death by hanging, the others to terms of imprisonment of ten years to life. See generally Trials of War Criminals Before Nuernberg Military Tribunals under Control Council Law No. 10, vols. 1 & 2 (1949); Bassiouni, Baffes & Evrard, An Appraisal of Human Experimentation in International Law and Practice: The Need for International Regulation of Human Experimentation, 72 J. Crim. L. & Criminology 1597 (1981); and J. Katz, Experimentation with Human Beings 292-306 (1972).

Even though Congress has not ratified or adopted the Nuremberg Code, it would seem that it should apply, as the *Kaimowitz* court assumed it did, to actions taken in the U.S. Nevertheless, when the U.S. Supreme Court had the opportunity to so rule in 1987, it ruled that the Code was *not* binding on the U.S. Military. The case involved a soldier who had secretly been given LSD in 1958. The drug produced damaging psychological effects, but the subject was not even told of the experiment until 1975, when the Army sent him a letter asking him to be cooperative in a "follow-up" study. He brought suit against the Army for unlawful experimentation. The Court, however, concluded, in a 5 to 4 decision, that involuntary participation in human experimentation was no exception to the rule that a serviceman could not sue the U.S. Government for injuries which "arise out of or are in the course of activity incident to service." Four dissenting judges based their disapproval on the Nuremberg Code, which they argued applied not only to civilians, but the military as well. U.S. v. Stanley, 483 U.S. 669 (1987).

The involvement of physicians in the "medical experiments" in the concentration camps is analyzed, based on personal interviews of some of the physicians involved, by Robert Jay Lifton in his The Nazi Doctors: Medical Killing and the Psychology of Genocide (1986). As Lifton describes his work: "What I have tried to chart is a particular sequence of human actions, involved in a particular form of mass murder and genocide — that of medicalized killing. My witness is to the fact that doctors killed and did so in the name of healing, and includes questions of how, in what way, and why." Id. at 503. Lifton posits a form of psychological "doubling" that permitted the Nazi physicians to view themselves as technicians involved in healing the state's "illness." "Perhaps the single greatest key to the medical function of the Auschwitz self was the technicizing of everything. That self could divest itself from immediate ethical concerns by concentrating only on the 'purely technical' or 'purely professional.' Demonstrating 'humanity' meant killing with technical efficiency." Id at 453. For an insightful historical perspective, see R. Proctor, Racial Hygiene (1988).

Because it was based on such medical horrors, seen as exceptional and not likely to recur, many physicians found the Nuremberg Code's consent provisions too strict. Through the World Medical Association, formed immediately after World War II, this group developed the Helsinki Declaration, which, among other things permitted proxy consent to human experimentation for children and others unable to consent for themselves. In the words of Dr. Henry Beecher: "The Nuremberg Code presents a rigid act of legalistic demands. . . . The Declaration of Helsinki, on the other hand, presents a set of guides. It is an ethical as opposed to a legalistic document and is thus a more broadly useful instrument than the one formulated at Nuremberg. . . . Until recently the Western World was threatened with the imposition of the Nuremberg Code as a Western Credo. With the Declaration of Helsinki, this danger is apparently now past." Quoted in Regshauge, The Place for International Standards in Conducting Research for Humans, 55 Bull. World Health Org. 133, 135 (1977 Supp.).

The Helsinki Declaration, first promulgated in 1964, and amended in 1975, provides, among other things, "In the case of legal incompetence, informed consent should be obtained from the legal guardian in accordance with national legislation. Where physical or mental incapacity makes it impossible to obtain informed consent, or when the subject is a minor, permission from the responsible relative replaces that of the subject in accordance with national legislation." (I. 11.) See Clegg, Human Experimentation, 7 World Med. J. 77 (1960); and Belsey, Patients, Doctors and Experimentation: Doubts about the Declaration of Helsinki, 4 J. Med. Ethics 182 (1978).

2. REGULATORY MECHANISMS TO PROTECT SUBJECTS OF HUMAN EXPERIMENTATION

Note on Institutional Review Boards (IRBs)

To supplement the vague practice guidelines on performing research and obtaining informed consent, first individual institutions, and later the federal government, began to require medical investigators to submit their research protocols, complete with informed consent procedures and forms, to an in-house peer review group, termed an Institutional Review Board, or IRB. Federal regulations, most recently promulgated in 1981, require that each such IRB have at least five members; all members cannot be from the same profession or members of the same sex; at least one member must be from a nonscientific area (law, for example); and at least one member must not be affiliated with the institution. 45 C.F.R. §46.107. The criteria for IRB approval of research are as follows:

§46.111 Criteria for IRB approval of research.

(a) In order to approve research covered by these regulations the IRB shall determine that all of the following requirements are satisfied:

(1) Risks to subjects are minimized: (i) By using procedures which are consistent with sound research design and which do not unnecessarily expose subjects to risk, and (ii) whenever appropriate, by using procedures already being performed on the subjects for diagnostic or treatment purposes.

(2) Risks to subjects are reasonable in relation to anticipated benefits, if any, to subjects, and the importance of the knowledge that may reasonably be expected to result. In evaluating risks and benefits, the IRB should consider only those risks and benefits that may result from the research (as distinguished from risks and benefits of therapies subjects would receive even if not participating in the research). The IRB should not consider possible

long-range effects of applying knowledge gained in the research (for example, the possible effects of the research on public policy) as among those research risks that fall within the purview of its responsibility.

(3) Selection of subjects is equitable. In making this assessment the IRB should take into account the purposes of the research and the setting in which the research will be conducted.

(4) Informed consent will be sought from each prospective subject or the subject's legally authorized representative, in accordance with, and to the extent required by §46.116.

(5) Informed consent will be appropriately documented, in accordance with, and to the extent required by §46.117.

(6) Where appropriate, the research plan makes adequate provision for monitoring the data collected to insure the safety of subjects.

(7) Where appropriate, there are adequate provisions to protect the privacy of subjects and to maintain the confidentiality of data.

(b) Where some or all of the subjects are likely to be vulnerable to coercion or undue influence, such as persons with acute or severe physical or mental illness, or persons who are economically or educationally disadvantaged, appropriate additional safeguards have been included in the study to protect the rights and welfare of these subjects. . . .

§46.116 General requirements for informed consent.

Except as provided elsewhere in this or other subparts, no investigator may involve a human being as a subject in research covered by these regulations unless the investigator has obtained the legally effective informed consent of the subject or the subject's legally authorized representative. An investigator shall seek such consent only under circumstances that provide the prospective subject or the representative sufficient opportunity to consider whether or not to participate and that minimize the possibility of coercion or undue influence. The information that is given to the subject or the representative shall be in language understandable to the subject or the representative. No informed consent, whether oral or written, may include any exculpatory language through which the subject or the representative is made to waive or appear to waive any of the subject's legal rights, or releases or appears to release the investigator, the sponsor, the institution or its agents from liability for negligence.

(a) Basic elements of informed consent. Except as provided in paragraph (c) or (d) of this section, in seeking informed consent the following information shall be provided to each subject:

(1) A statement that the study involves research, an explanation of the purposes of the research and the expected duration of the subject's participation, a description of the procedures to be followed, and identification of any procedures which are experimental;

(2) A description of any reasonably foreseeable risks or discomforts to the subject;

(3) A description of any benefits to the subject or to others which may reasonably be expected from the research;

(4) A disclosure of appropriate alternative procedures or courses of treatment, if any, that might be advantageous to the subject;

(5) A statement describing the extent, if any, to which confidentiality of records identifying the subject will be maintained;

(6) For research involving more than minimal risk, an explanation as to whether any compensation and an explanation as to whether any medical treatments are available if injury occurs and, if so, what they consist of, or where further information may be obtained.

(7) An explanation of whom to contact for answers to pertinent questions about the research and research subjects' rights, and whom to contact in the event of a research-related injury to the subject; and

(8) A statement that participation is voluntary, refusal to participate will involve no penalty or loss of benefits to which the subject is otherwise entitled, and the subject may discontinue participation at any time without penalty or loss of benefits to which the subject is otherwise entitled.

(b) Additional elements of informed consent. When appropriate, one or more of the following elements of information shall also be provided to each subject:

(1) A statement that the particular treatment or procedure may involve risks to the subject (or to the embryo or fetus, if the subject is or may become pregnant) which are currently unforeseeable;

(2) Anticipated circumstances under which the subject's participation may be terminated by the investigator without regard to the subject's consent;

(3) Any additional costs to the subject that may result from participation in the research;

(4) The consequences of a subject's decision to withdraw from the research and procedures for orderly termination of participation by the subject;

(5) A statement that significant new findings developed during the course of the research which may relate to the subject's willingness to continue participation will be provided to the subject; and

(6) The approximate number of subjects involved in the study.

(c) An IRB may approve a consent procedure which does not include, or which alters, some or all of the elements of informed consent set forth above, or waive the requirement to obtain informed consent provided the IRB finds and documents that:

(1) The research or demonstration project is to be conducted by or subject to the approval of state or local government officials and is designed to study, evaluate, or otherwise examine: (i) programs under the Social Security Act, or other public benefit or service programs; (ii) procedures for obtaining benefits or services under those programs; (iii) possible changes in or alternatives to those programs or procedures; or (iv) possible changes in methods or levels of payment for benefits or services under those programs; and

(2) The research could not practicably be carried out without the waiver or alteration.

(d) An IRB may approve a consent procedure which does not include, or which alters, some or all of the elements of informed consent set forth above, or waive the requirements to obtain informed consent provided the IRB finds and documents that:

(1) The research involves no more than minimal risk to the subjects;

(2) The waiver or alteration will not adversely affect the rights and welfare of the subjects;

(3) The research could not practicably be carried out without the waiver or alteration; and

(4) Whenever appropriate, the subjects will be provided with additional pertinent information after participation.

(e) The informed consent requirements in these regulations are not intended to preempt any applicable federal, state, or local laws which require additional information to be disclosed in order for informed consent to be legally effective.

(f) Nothing in these regulations is intended to limit the authority of a physician to provide emergency medical care, to the extent the physician is permitted to do so under applicable federal, state, or local law.

For more on IRBs, see R. Levine, Ethics and Regulation of Clinical Research, (2d ed. 1986); National Commission for the Protection of Human Subjects of Biomedical and Behavioral Research, Institutional Review Boards: Report and Recommendations. (DHEW); and R. Veatch, The Patient as Partner (1987). IRBs tend to focus on the content of the consent form and overlook the central issue in human experimentation: "whether the experiment ought to be done at all." Fletcher, The Evolution of the Ethics of Informed Consent (in) Research Ethics (K. Berg & K.E. Tranoy eds. 1983).

Additional procedures for special populations that are considered especially vulnerable to exploitation are also included in the regulations. Ironically, the children's regulations permit research on them that would not be permitted on adults.

E. The Right to Refuse Treatment and the "Right to Die"

1. THE RIGHT TO REFUSE TREATMENT

In the Matter of Karen Quinlan

70 N.J. 10, 335 A.2d 647, cert. den., *429 U.S. 922 (1976)*

HUGHES, C.J.

The central figure in this tragic case is Karen Ann Quinlan, a New Jersey resident. At the age of 22, she lies in a debilitated and allegedly moribund state at Saint Clare's Hospital in Denville, New Jersey. The litigation has to do, in final analysis, with her life, — its continuance or cessation, — and the responsibilities, rights, and duties, with regard to any fateful decision concerning it, of her family, her guardian, her doctors, the hospital, the State through its law enforcement authorities, and finally the courts of justice.

[Joseph Quinlan, Karen's father, had sought appointment as her guardian with express authority to authorize the discontinuance of all extraordinary medical procedures. The lower court rejected his petition, primarily on the basis of physician testimony that "Karen cannot now survive without the assistance of the respirator" and the opinion "not only of the treating physicians but also of several qualified experts who testified that removal from the respirator would not conform to medical practices, standards and traditions." It was also the medical consensus that Karen, "in addition to being comatose is in a chronic and persistent 'vegetative' state, having no awareness of anything or anyone around her and existing at a primitive reflex level."

She was reduced to this state having ceased breathing "for reasons still unclear . . . for at least two fifteen minute periods . . . on the night of April 15, 1975."

The court made the following factual findings: "Severe brain and associate damage, albeit of uncertain origin, has left Karen in a chronic and persistent vegetative state. No form of treatment which can cure or improve that condition is known or available . . . she can *never* be restored to a cognitive or sapient state. . . . Her life is sustained by the respirator and tubal feeding, and removal from the respirator would cause her death soon. . . ."

The Quinlans are Catholic, and the court summarizes the position of the Catholic Church on "extraordinary treatment"; but only "in the aspect of its impact upon the conscience, motivation and purpose of the intended guardian, Joseph Quinlan, and not as a precedent in terms of civil law." This discussion, as well as the court's discussion of brain death, free exercise of religion, and cruel and unusual punishment, has been omitted.]

It is the issue of the constitutional right of privacy that has given us most concern, in the exceptional circumstances of this case. Here a loving parent, *qua* parent and raising the rights of his incompetent and profoundly damaged daughter, probably irreversibly doomed to no more than a biologically vegetative remnant of life, is before the court. He seeks authorization to abandon specialized technological procedures which can only maintain for a time a body having no potential for resumption or continuance of other than a "vegetative" existence.

We have no doubt, in these unhappy circumstances, that if Karen were herself miraculously lucid for an interval (not altering the existing prognosis of the condition to which she would soon return) and perceptive of her irreversible condition, she could effectively decide upon discontinuance of the life-support apparatus, even if it meant the prospect of natural death. To this extent we may distinguish *Heston,* supra, which concerned a severely injured young woman (Delores Heston), whose life depended on surgery and blood transfusion; and who was in such extreme shock that she was unable to express an informed choice (although the Court apparently considered the case as if the patient's own religious decision to resist transfusion were at stake), but most importantly a patient apparently salvable to long life and vibrant health; — a situation not at all like the present case.

We have no hesitancy in deciding, in the instant diametrically opposite case, that no external compelling interest of the State could compel Karen to endure the unendurable, only to vegetate a few measurable months with no realistic possibility of returning to any semblance of cognitive or sapient life. We perceive no thread of logic distinguishing between such a choice on Karen's part and a similar choice which, under the evidence in this case, could be made by a competent patient terminally ill, riddled by cancer and suffering great pain; such a patient would not be resuscitated or put on a respirator in the example described by Dr. Korein, and *a fortiori* would not be kept *against his will* on a respirator.

Although the Constitution does not explicitly mention a right of privacy, Supreme Court decisions have recognized that a right of personal privacy exists and that certain areas of privacy are guaranteed under the Constitution. . . .

. . . The Court has interdicted judicial intrusion into many aspects of personal decision, sometimes basing this restraint upon the conception of a limitation of judicial interest and responsibility, such as with regard to contraception and its relationship to family life and decision. Griswold v. Connecticut, 381 U.S. 479 (1965).

. . . The Court in *Griswold* found the unwritten constitutional right of privacy to exist in the penumbra of specific guarantees of the Bill of Rights "formed by emanations from those guarantees that help give them life and substance." 381 U.S. at 484. Presumably this right is broad enough to encompass a patient's decision to decline medical treatment under certain circumstances, in much the same way as it is broad enough to encompass a woman's decision to terminate pregnancy under certain conditions. Roe v. Wade, 410 U.S. 113 (1973).

Nor is such right of privacy forgotten in the New Jersey Constitution. N.J. Const. (1947), Art. I, par. 1.

. . . The claimed interests of the State in this case are essentially the preservation and sanctity of human life and defense of the right of the physician to administer medical treatment according to his best judgment. In this case the doctors say that removing Karen from the respirator will conflict with their professional judgment. The plaintiff answers that Karen's present treatment serves only a maintenance function; that the respirator cannot cure or improve her condition but at best can only prolong her inevitable slow deterioration and death; and that the interests of the patient, as seen by her surrogate, the guardian, must be evaluated by the court as predominant, even in the face of an opinion *contra* by the present attending physicians. Plaintiff's distinction is significant. The nature of Karen's care and the realistic chances of her recovery are quite unlike those of the patients discussed in many of the cases where treatments were ordered. In many of those cases the medical procedure required (usually a transfusion) constituted a minimal bodily invasion and the chances of recovery and return to functioning life were very good. We think that the State's interest *contra* weakens and the individual's right to privacy grows as the degree of bodily invasion increases and the prognosis dims. Ultimately there comes a point at which the individual's rights overcome the State interest. It is for that reason that we believe Karen's choice, if she were competent to make it, would be vindicated by the law. Her prognosis is extremely poor, — she will never resume cognitive life. And the bodily invasion is very great, — she requires 24 hour intensive nursing care, antibiotics, the assistance of a respirator, a catheter, and feeding tube.

. . . Our affirmation of Karen's independent right of choice, however, would ordinarily be based upon her competency to assert it. The sad truth, however, is that she is grossly incompetent, and we cannot discern her supposed choice based on the testimony of her previous conversations with friends, where such testimony is without sufficient probative weight. 137 N.J. Super. at 260, 348 A.2d 801. Nevertheless we have concluded that Karen's right of privacy may be asserted on her behalf by her guardian under the peculiar circumstances here present.

If a putative decision by Karen to permit this non-cognitive, vegetative existence to terminate by natural forces is regarded as a valuable incident of her right of privacy, as we believe it to be, then it should not be discarded solely on the basis that her condition prevents her conscious exercise of the choice. The only practical way to prevent destruction of the right is to permit the guardian and family of Karen to render their best judgment, subject to the qualifications hereinafter stated, as to whether she would exercise it in these circumstances. If their conclusion is in the affirmative this decision should be accepted by a society the overwhelming majority of whose members would, we think, in similar circumstances, exercise such a choice in the same way for themselves or for those closest to them. It is for this reason that we determine that Karen's right of privacy may be asserted in her behalf, in this respect, by her guardian and family under the particular circumstances presented by this record.

. . . Regarding Mr. Quinlan's right of privacy, we agree with Judge Muir's conclusion that there is no parental constitutional right that would entitle him to a grant of relief in propria persona. Id. at 266, 348 A.2d 801. Insofar as a parental right of privacy has been recognized, it has been in the context of determining the rearing of infants and, as Judge Muir put it, involved "continuing life styles."

. . . Karen Quinlan is a 22 year old adult. Her right of privacy in respect of the matter before the Court is to be vindicated by Mr. Quinlan as guardian, as hereinabove determined.

Having declared the substantive legal basis upon which plaintiff's rights as representative of Karen must be deemed predicated, we face and respond to the assertion on behalf of defendants that our premise unwarrantably offends prevailing medical standards. We thus turn to consideration of the medical decision supporting the determination made below, conscious of the paucity of pre-existing legislative and judicial guidance as to the rights and liabilities therein involved. . . .

Perhaps the confusion stems from mention by some courts of statutory or common law condemnation of suicide as demonstrating the state's interest in the preservation of life. We would see, however, a real distinction between the self-infliction of deadly harm and a self-determination against artificial life support or radical surgery, for instance, in the face of irreversible, painful, and certain imminent death. The contrasting situations mentioned are analogous to those continually faced by the medical profession. When does the institution of life-sustaining procedures, ordinarily mandatory, become the subject of medical discretion in the context of administration to persons in extremis? And when does the withdrawal of such procedures, from such persons already supported by them, come within the orbit of medical discretion? When does a determination as to either of the foregoing contingencies court the hazard of civil or criminal liability on the part of the physician or institution involved? . . .

. . . Determinations as to these must, in the ultimate, be responsive not only to the concepts of medicine but also to the common moral judgment of the community at large. In the latter respect the Court has a nondelegable judicial responsibility.

Put in another way, the law, equity, and justice must not themselves quail and be helpless in the face of modern technological marvels presenting questions hitherto unthought of. Where a Karen Quinlan, or a parent, or a doctor, or a hospital, or a State seeks the process and response of a court, it must answer with its most informed conception of justice in the previously unexplored circumstances presented to it. That is its obligation and we are here fulfilling it, for the actors and those having an interest in the matter should not go without remedy.

Courts in the exercise of their parens patriae responsibility to protect those under disability have sometimes implemented medical decisions and authorized their carrying out under the doctrine of "substituted judgment.". . .

The medical obligation is related to standards and practice prevailing in the profession. The physicians in charge of the case, as noted above, declined to withdraw the respirator. That decision was consistent with the proofs below as to the then existing medical standards and practices.

Under the law as it then stood, Judge Muir was correct in declining to authorize withdrawal of the respirator.

However, in relation to the matter of the declaratory relief sought by plaintiff as representative of Karen's interests, we are required to reevaluate the applicability of the medical standards projected in the court below. The question is whether there is such internal consistency and rationality in the application of such standards as should warrant their constituting an ineluctable bar to the effectuation of substantive relief for plaintiff at the hands of the court. We have concluded not. . . .

In regard to the foregoing it is pertinent that we consider the impact on the standards both of the civil and criminal law as to medical liability and the new technological means of sustaining life irreversibly damaged.

The modern proliferation of substantial malpractice litigation and the less frequent but even more unnerving possibility of criminal sanctions would seem, for it is beyond human nature to suppose otherwise, to have bearing on the practice and standards as they exist. The brooding presence of such possible liability, it was testified here, had no part in the decision of the treating physicians. As did Judge Muir, we afford this testimony full credence. But we cannot believe that the stated factor has not had a strong influence on the standards, as the literature on the subject plainly reveals. . . .

We glean from the record here that physicians distinguish between curing the ill and comforting and easing the dying; that they refuse to treat the curable as if they were dying or ought to die, and that they have sometimes refused to treat the hopeless and dying as if they were curable. . . .

. . . For those possibly curable, such devices are of great value, and, as ordinary medical procedures, are essential. Consequently, as pointed out by Dr. Diamond, they are necessary because of the ethic of medical practice. But in light of the situation in the present case (while the record here is somewhat hazy in distinguishing between "ordinary" and "extraordinary" measures), one would have to think that the use of the same respirator or like support could be considered "ordinary" in the context of the possibly curable patient but "extraordinary" in the context of the forced sustaining by cardio-respiratory processes of an irreversibly doomed patient. And this dilemma is sharpened in the face of the malpractice and criminal action threat which we have mentioned.

We would hesitate, in this imperfect world, to propose as to physicians that type of immunity which from the early common law has surrounded judges and grand jurors . . . so that they might without fear of personal retaliation perform their judicial duties with independent objectivity. . . .

Nevertheless, there must be a way to free physicians, in the pursuit of their healing vocation, from possible contamination by self-interest or self-protection concerns which would inhibit their independent medical judgments for the well-being of their dying patients. We would hope that this opinion might be serviceable to some degree in ameliorating the professional problems under discussion.

A technique aimed at the underlying difficulty (though in a somewhat broader context) is described by Dr. Karen Teel, a pediatrician and a director of Pediatric Education, who writes in the Baylor Law Review under the title "The Physician's Dilemma: A Doctor's View: What The Law Should Be." Dr. Teel recalls:

> Physicians, by virtue of their responsibility for medical judgments are, partly by choice and partly by default, charged with the responsibility of making eth-

ical judgments which we are sometimes ill-equipped to make. We are not always morally and legally authorized to make them. . . .

I suggest that it would be more appropriate to provide a regular forum for more input and dialogue in individual situations and to allow the responsibility of these judgments to be shared. Many hospitals have established an Ethics Committee composed of physicians, social workers, attorneys, and theologians, . . . which serves to review the individual circumstances of ethical dilemma and which has provided much in the way of assistance and safeguards for patients and their medical caretakers.

The concept of an Ethics Committee which has this kind of organization and is readily accessible to those persons rendering medical care to patients, would be, I think, the most promising direction for further study at this point. . . .

. . . [This would allow] some much needed dialogue regarding these issues and [force] the point of exploring all of the options for a particular patient. It diffuses the responsibility for making these judgments. Many physicians, in many circumstances, would welcome this sharing of responsibility. I believe that such an entity could lend itself well to an assumption of a legal status which would allow courses of action not now undertaken because of the concern for liability. [27 Baylor L. Rev. 6, 8-9 (1975).]

The most appealing factor in the technique suggested by Dr. Teel seems to us to be the diffusion of professional responsibility for decision, comparable in a way to the value of multi-judge courts in finally resolving on appeal difficult questions of law. . . .

. . . We consider that a practice of applying to a court to confirm such decisions would generally be inappropriate, not only because that would be a gratuitous encroachment upon the medical profession's field of competence, but because it would be impossibly cumbersome. Such a requirement is distinguishable from the judicial overview traditionally required in other matters such as the adjudication and commitment of mental incompetents. This is not to say that in the case of an otherwise justiciable controversy access to the courts would be foreclosed; we speak rather of a general practice and procedure. . . .

If there could be created not necessarily this particular system but some reasonable counterpart, we would have no doubt that such decisions, thus determined to be in accordance with medical practice and prevailing standards, would be accepted by society and by the courts, at least in cases comparable to that of Karen Quinlan.

The evidence in this case convinces us that the focal point of decision should be the prognosis as to the reasonable possibility of return to cognitive and sapient life, as distinguished from the forced continuance of that biological vegetative existence to which Karen seems to be doomed.

. . . In summary of the present Point of this opinion, we conclude that the state of the pertinent medical standards and practices which guided the attending physicians in this matter is not such as would justify this Court in deeming itself bound or controlled thereby in responding to the case for declaratory relief established by the parties on the record before us.

. . . Having concluded that there is a right of privacy that might permit termination of treatment in the circumstances of this case, we turn to consider the relationship of the exercise of that right to the criminal law. We are aware that such termination of treatment would accelerate Karen's death. The County Prosecutor and the Attorney General maintain that there would be criminal liability for such acceleration. Under the statutes of this State, the unlawful killing of another human being is criminal homicide. N.J.S.A. 2A:113-1, 2, 5. We conclude that there would be no criminal homicide in the circumstances of this case. We believe first, that the ensuing death would not be homicide but rather expiration from existing natural causes. Secondly, even if it were to be regarded as homicide, it would not be unlawful.

These conclusions rest upon definitional and constitutional bases. The termination of treatment pursuant to the right of privacy is, within the limitations of this case, ipso facto lawful. Thus, a death resulting from such an act would not come within the scope of the homicide statutes proscribing only the unlawful killing of another. There is a real and in this case determinative distinction between the unlawful taking of the life of another and the ending of artificial life-support systems as a matter of self-determination.

. . . Furthermore, the exercise of a constitutional right such as we have here found is protected from criminal prosecution. See Stanley v. Georgia, supra, 394 U.S. at 559. We do not question the State's undoubted power to punish the taking of human life, but that power does not encompass individuals terminating medical treatment pursuant to their right of privacy. See id. at 568. The constitutional protection extends to third parties whose action is necessary to effectuate the exercise of that right where the individuals themselves would not be subject to prosecution or the third parties are charged as accessories to an act which could not be a crime. . . .

Superintendent of Belchertown State School v. Saikewicz

373 Mass. 728, 370 N.E.2d 417 (1977)

Liacos, Justice.

On April 26, 1976, William E. Jones, superintendent of the Belchertown State School (a facility of the Massachusetts Department of Mental Health), and Paul R. Rogers, a staff attorney at the school, petitioned the Probate Court for Hampshire County for the appointment of a guardian of Joseph Saikewicz, a resident of the State school. Simultaneously they filed a motion for the immediate appointment of a guardian ad litem, with authority to make the necessary decisions concerning the care and treatment of Saikewicz, who was suffering with acute myeloblastic monocytic leukemia. The petition alleged that Saikewicz was a mentally retarded person in urgent need of medical treatment and that he was a person with disability incapable of giving informed consent for such treatment.

On May 5, 1976, the probate judge appointed a guardian ad litem. On May 6, 1976, the guardian ad litem filed a report with the court. The guardian ad litem's report indicated that Saikewicz's illness was an incurable one, and that although chemotherapy was the medically indicated course of treatment it would cause Saikewicz significant adverse side effects and discomfort. The guardian ad litem concluded that these factors, as well as the inability of the ward to understand the treatment to which he would be subjected and the fear and pain he would suffer as a result, outweighed the limited prospect of any benefit from such treatment, namely, the possibility of some uncertain but limited extension of life. He therefore recommended "that not treating Mr. Saikewicz would be in his best interests."...

... After hearing the evidence, the judge entered findings of fact and an order that in essence agreed with the recommendation of the guardian ad litem. The decision of the judge appears to be based in part on the testimony of Saikewicz's two attending physicians who recommended against chemotherapy. The judge then reported to the Appeals Court the two questions set forth in the margin.[2]

... On July 9, 1976, this court issued an order answering the questions reported in the affirmative with the notation "rescript and opinion . . . will follow."[3] We now issue that opinion.

The judge below found that Joseph Saikewicz, at the time the matter arose, was 67 years old, with an I.Q. of ten and a mental age of approximately two years and eight months. He was profoundly mentally retarded. The record discloses that, apart from his leukemic condition, Saikewicz enjoyed generally good health. He was physically strong and well built, nutritionally nourished, and ambulatory. He was not, however, able to communicate verbally — resorting to gestures and grunts to make his wishes known to others and responding only to gestures or physical contacts. In the course of treat-

2. "(1) Does the Probate Court under its general or any special jurisdiction have the authority to order, in circumstances it deems appropriate, the withholding of medical treatment from a person even though such withholding of treatment might contribute to a shortening of the life of such person?

"(2) On the facts reported in this case, is the Court correct in ordering that no treatment be administered to said Joseph Saikewicz now or at any time for his condition of acute myeloblastic monocetic leukemia except by further order of the Court?"

3. After briefly reviewing the facts of the case, we stated in that order: "Upon consideration, based upon the findings of the probate judge, we answer the first question in the affirmative, and a majority of the Court answer the second question in the affirmative. However, we emphasize that upon receiving evidence of a significant change either in the medical condition of Saikewicz or in the medical treatment available to him for successful treatment of his condition, the probate judge may issue a further order."

ment for various medical conditions arising during Saikewicz's residency at the school, he had been unable to respond intelligently to inquiries such as whether he was experiencing pain. It was the opinion of a consulting psychologist, not contested by the other experts relied on by the judge below, that Saikewicz was not aware of dangers and was disoriented outside his immediate environment. As a result of his condition, Saikewicz had lived in State institutions since 1923 and had resided at the Belchertown State School since 1928. Two of his sisters, the only members of his family who could be located, were notified of his condition and of the hearing, but they preferred not to attend or otherwise become involved.

On April 19, 1976, Saikewicz was diagnosed as suffering from acute myeloblastic monocytic leukemia.

Chemotherapy, as was testified to at the hearing in the Probate Court, involves the administration of drugs over several weeks, the purpose of which is to kill the leukemia cells. This treatment unfortunately affects normal cells as well. One expert testified that the end result, in effect, is to destroy the living vitality of the bone marrow. Because of this effect, the patient becomes very anemic and may bleed or suffer infections — a condition which requires a number of blood transfusions. In this sense, the patient immediately becomes much "sicker" with the commencement of chemotherapy, and there is a possibility that infections during the initial period of severe anemia will prove fatal. Moreover, while most patients survive chemotherapy, remission of the leukemia is achieved in only thirty to fifty per cent of the cases. Remission is meant here as a temporary return to normal as measured by clinical and laboratory means. If remission does occur, it typically lasts for between two and thirteen months although longer periods of remission are possible. Estimates of the effectiveness of chemotherapy are complicated in cases, such as the one presented here, in which the patient's age becomes a factor. According to the medical testimony before the court below, persons over age sixty have more difficulty tolerating chemotherapy and the treatment is likely to be less successful than in younger patients. This prognosis may be compared with the doctors' estimates that, left untreated, a patient in Saikewicz's condition would live for a matter of weeks or, perhaps, several months. According to the testimony, a decision to allow the disease to run its natural course would not result in pain for the patient, and death would probably come without discomfort.

. . . Among these side effects are severe nausea, bladder irritation, numbness and tingling of the extremities, and loss of hair.

. . . The judge below found "5. That the majority of persons suffering from leukemia who are faced with a choice of receiving or foregoing such chemotherapy, and who are able to make an informed judgment thereon, choose to receive treatment in spite of its toxic side effects and risks of failure." . . .

Balancing these various factors, the judge concluded that the following considerations weighed *against* administering chemotherapy to Saikewicz: "(1) his age, (2) his inability to cooperate with the treatment, (3) probable adverse side effects of treatment, (4) low chance of producing remission, (5) the certainty that treatment will cause immediate suffering, and (6) the quality of life possible for him even if the treatment does bring about remission."

The following considerations were determined to weigh in *favor* of chemotherapy: "(1) the chance that his life may be lengthened thereby, and (2) the fact that most people in his situation when given a chance to do so elect to take the gamble of treatment."

Concluding that, in this case, the negative factors of treatment exceeded the benefits, the probate judge ordered on May 13, 1976, that no treatment be administered to Saikewicz for his condition of acute myeloblastic monocytic leukemia except by further order of the court. The judge further ordered that all reasonable and necessary supportive measures be taken, medical or otherwise, to safeguard the well-being of Saikewicz in all other respects and to reduce as far as possible any suffering or discomfort which he might experience.

It is within this factual context that we issued our order of July 9, 1976.

Saikewicz died on September 4, 1976, at the Belchertown State School hospital. Death was due to bronchial pneumonia, a complication of the leukemia. Saikewicz died without pain or discomfort. . . . There is implicit recognition in the law of the Commonwealth, as elsewhere, that a person has a strong interest in being free from nonconsensual invasion of his bodily integrity. . . . In short, the law recognizes the individual interest in preserving "the inviolability of his person." Pratt v. Davis, 118 Ill. App. 161, 166 (1905), *aff'd,* 224 Ill. 300, 79 N.E. 562 (1906). One means by which the law has developed in a manner consistent with the protection of this interest is through the development of the doctrine of informed consent. . . . Of even broader import, but arising from the same regard for human dignity and self-determination, is the unwritten constitutional right of privacy found in the penumbra of specific guaranties of the Bill of Rights. . . . As distilled from the cases, the State has claimed interest in: (1) the preservation of life; (2) the protection of the interests of innocent third parties; (3) the prevention of suicide; and (4) maintaining the ethical integrity of the medical profession. . . . It is clear that the most significant of the asserted State interests is that of the preservation of human life. Recognition of such an interest, however, does not necessarily resolve the problem where the affliction or disease clearly indicates that life will soon, and inevitably, be extinguished. The interest of the State in prolonging a life must be reconciled with the interest of an individual to reject the traumatic cost of that prolongation. . . . The constitutional right to privacy, as we conceive it, is an expression of the sanctity of individual free choice and self-determination as fundamental constituents of life. The value of life as so perceived is lessened not by a decision to refuse treatment, but by the failure to allow a competent human being the right of choice. . . .

The last State interest requiring discussion[11] is that of the maintenance of

11. The interest in protecting against suicide seems to require little if any discussion. In

the ethical integrity of the medical profession as well as allowing hospitals the full opportunity to care for people under their control. . . . It is not necessary to deny a right of self-determination to a patient in order to recognize the interests of doctors, hospitals, and medical personnel in attendance on the patients. Also, if the doctrines of informed consent and right of privacy have as their foundations the right to bodily integrity . . . and control of one's own fate, then those rights are superior to the institutional considerations.[12]

. . . The question what legal standards govern the decision whether to administer potentially life-prolonging treatment to an incompetent person encompasses two distinct and important subissues. First, does a choice exist? That is, is it the unvarying responsibility of the State to order medical treatment in all circumstances involving the care of an incompetent person? Second, if a choice does exist under certain conditions, what considerations enter into the decision-making process?

We think that principles of equality and respect for all individuals require the conclusion that a choice exists. For reasons discussed at some length in subsection A, supra, we recognize a general right in all persons to refuse medical treatment in appropriate circumstances. The recognition of that right must extend to the case of an incompetent, as well as a competent, patient because the value of human dignity extends to both. . . .

. . . The "best interests" of an incompetent person are not necessarily served by imposing on such persons results not mandated as to competent persons similarly situated. . . . Nor do statistical factors indicating that a majority of competent persons similarly situated choose treatment resolve the issue. The significant decisions of life are more complex than statistical determinations. Individual choice is determined not by the vote of the majority but by the complexities of the singular situation viewed from the unique perspective of the person called on to make the decision. To presume that the incompetent person must always be subjected to what many rational and intelligent persons may decline is to downgrade the status of the incompetent person by placing a lesser value on his intrinsic human worth and vitality. . . .

. . . Evidence that most people choose to accept the rigors of chemotherapy has no direct bearing on the likely choice that Joseph Saikewicz would have made. Unlike most people, Saikewicz had no capacity to understand his present situation or his prognosis. The guardian ad litem gave expression to this important distinction in coming to grips with this "most troubling aspect" of withholding treatment from Saikewicz: "If he is treated with toxic

---

the case of the competent adult's refusing medical treatment such an act does not necessarily constitute suicide since (1) in refusing treatment the patient may not have the specific intent to die, and (2) even if he did, to the extent that the cause of death was from natural causes the patient did not set the death producing agent in motion with the intent of causing his own death. Byrn, supra at 17-18. Cantor, supra at 255. Furthermore, the underlying State interest in this area lies in the prevention of irrational self-destruction. What we consider here is a competent, rational decision to refuse treatment when death is inevitable and the treatment offers no hope of cure or preservation of life. There is no connection between the conduct here in issue and any State concern to prevent suicide. Cantor, supra at 258.

12. Any threats of civil liability may be removed by a valid giving or withholding of consent by an informed patient.

drugs he will be involuntarily immersed in a state of painful suffering, the reason for which he will never understand. Patients who request treatment know the risks involved and can appreciate the painful side-effects when they arrive. They know the reason for the pain and their hope makes it tolerable." To make a worthwhile comparison, one would have to ask whether a majority of people would choose chemotherapy if they were told merely that something outside of their previous experience was going to be done to them, that this something would cause them pain and discomfort, that they would be removed to strange surroundings and possibly restrained for extended periods of time, and that the advantages of this course of action were measured by concepts of time and mortality beyond their ability to comprehend. . . .

. . . We believe that both the guardian ad litem in his recommendation and the judge in his decision should have attempted (as they did) to ascertain the incompetent person's actual interests and preferences. In short, the decision in cases such as this should be that which would be made by the incompetent person, if that person were competent, but taking into account the present and future incompetency of the individual as one of the factors which would necessarily enter into the decision-making process of the competent person. Having recognized the right of a competent person to make for himself the same decision as the court made in this case, the question is, do the facts on the record support the proposition that Saikewicz himself would have made the decision under the standard set forth. We believe they do. . . . The judge heard testimony that Saikewicz would have no comprehension of the reasons for the severe disruption of his formerly secure and stable environment occasioned by the chemotherapy. He therefore would experience fear without the understanding from which other patients draw strength. The inability to anticipate and prepare for the severe side effects of the drugs leaves room only for confusion and disorientation. The possibility that such a naturally uncooperative patient would have to be physically restrained to allow the slow intravenous administration of drugs could only compound his pain and fear, as well as possibly jeopardize the ability of his body to withstand the toxic effects of the drugs.

. . . The sixth factor identified by the judge as weighing against chemotherapy was "the quality of life possible for him even if the treatment does bring about remission." To the extent that this formulation equates the value of life with any measure of the quality of life, we firmly reject it. A reading of the entire record clearly reveals, however, the judge's concern that special care be taken to respect the dignity and worth of Saikewicz's life precisely because of his vulnerable position. . . .

We turn now to a consideration of the procedures appropriate for reaching a decision where a person allegedly incompetent is in a position in which a decision as to the giving or withholding of life-prolonging treatment must be made. The Probate Court is the proper forum in which to determine the need for the appointment of a guardian or a guardian ad litem. It is also the proper tribunal to determine the best interests of a ward. . . .

The course of proceedings in such a case is readily determined by reference to the applicable statutes. The first step is to petition the court for the appointment of a guardian. (G.L. c. 201, §6A) or a temporary guardian (G.L. c. 201, §14). . . . [I]t will often be desirable to appoint a guardian ad litem, sua sponte or on motion, to represent the interests of the person. Moreover, we think it appropriate, and highly desirable, in cases such as the one before us to charge the guardian ad litem with an additional responsibility to be discharged if there is a finding of incompetency. This will be the responsibility of presenting to the judge, after as thorough an investigation as time will permit, all reasonable arguments in favor of administering treatment to prolong the life of the individual involved. This will ensure that all viewpoints and alternatives will be aggressively pursued and examined at the subsequent hearing where it will be determined whether treatment should or should not be allowed. . . .

. . . Commensurate with the powers of the Probate Court already described, the probate judge may, at any step in these proceedings, avail himself or herself of the additional advice or knowledge of any person or group. We note here that many health care institutions have developed medical ethics committees or panels to consider many of the issues touched on here. Consideration of the findings and advice of such groups as well as the testimony of the attending physicians and other medical experts ordinarily would be of great assistance to a probate judge faced with such a difficult decision. We believe it desirable for a judge to consider such views wherever available and useful to the court. We do not believe, however, that this option should be transformed by us into a required procedure. We take a dim view of any attempt to shift the ultimate decision-making responsibility away from the duly established courts of proper jurisdiction to any committee, panel or group, ad hoc or permanent. Thus, we reject the approach adopted by the New Jersey Supreme Court in the *Quinlan* case of entrusting the decision whether to continue artificial life support to the patient's guardian, family, attending doctors, and hospital "ethics committee."[20] 70 N.J. at 55, 355 A.2d 647, 671. One rationale for such a delegation was expressed by the lower court judge in the *Quinlan* case, and quoted by the New Jersey Su-

20. Specifically, the court held that

> upon the concurrence of the guardian and family of Karen, should the responsible attending physicians conclude that there is no reasonable possibility of Karen's ever emerging from her present comatose condition to a cognitive, sapient state and that the life-support apparatus now being administered to Karen should be discontinued, they shall consult with the hospital 'Ethics Committee' or like body of the institution in which Karen is then hospitalized. If that consultative body agrees that there is no reasonable possibility of Karen's ever emerging from her present comatose condition to a cognitive, sapient state, the present life-support system may be withdrawn and said action shall be without any civil or criminal liability therefor on the part of any participant, whether guardian, physician, hospital or others.
>
> By the above ruling we do not intend to be understood as implying that a proceeding for judicial declaratory relief is necessarily required for the implementation of comparable decisions in the field of medical practice.

In re Quinlan, 70 N.J. at 55, 355 A.2d at 672.

preme Court: "The nature, extent and duration of care by societal standards is the responsibility of a physician. The morality and conscience of our society places this responsibility in the hands of the physician. What justification is there to remove it from the control of the medical profession and place it in the hands of the courts?" Id. at 44, 355 A.2d at 665. For its part, the New Jersey Supreme Court concluded that

> a practice of applying to a court to confirm such decisions would generally be inappropriate, not only because that would be a gratuitous encroachment upon the medical profession's field of competence, but because it would be impossibly cumbersome. Such a requirement is distinguishable from the judicial overview traditionally required in other matters such as the adjudication and commitment of mental incompetents. This is not to say that in the case of an otherwise justiciable controversy access to the courts would be foreclosed; we speak rather of a general practice and procedure. [Id. at 50, 355 A.2d at 669.]

We do not view the judicial resolution of this most difficult and awesome question — whether potentially life-prolonging treatment should be withheld from a person incapable of making his own decision — as constituting a "gratuitous encroachment" on the domain of medical expertise. Rather, such questions of life and death seem to us to require the process of detached but passionate investigation and decision that forms the ideal on which the judicial branch of government was created. Achieving this ideal is our responsibility and that of the lower court, and is not to be entrusted to any other group purporting to represent the "morality and conscience of our society," no matter how highly motivated or impressively constituted.

Finding no State interest sufficient to counterbalance a patient's decision to decline life-prolonging medical treatment in the circumstances of this case, we conclude that the patient's right to privacy and self-determination is entitled to enforcement. Because of this conclusion, and in view of the position of equality of an incompetent person in Joseph Saikewicz's position, we conclude that the probate judge acted appropriately in this case. For these reasons we issued our order of July 9, 1976, and responded as we did to the questions of the probate judge.

NOTES ON *QUINLAN* & *SAIKEWICZ*

(1) *Quinlan* and *Saikewicz* are the first, and still the most important, cases to deal with the constitutional rights of individuals to refuse treatment. These cases are constructed on the premise that competent individuals have the constitutional right to accept or reject medical treatment under the right of privacy. Although many other courts have followed this logic in cases involving *incompetent* patients, it has yet to be applied to a more garden variety informed consent case. The logic of these cases, however, must eventually be

tied to informed consent, when it will be seen as difficult, if not impossible, to justify the denial of risk and alternative treatment information to competent patients for *any* reason (since there are no "compelling state interests" involved in denying competent patients information about their condition and the treatment options available). The U.S. Supreme Court may consider the application of privacy to medical decision making outside of reproduction in the case of Nancy Cruzan (see infra 646), but even if it refuses to find it applicable, state constitutions in many states would still recognize informed medical decision making as constitutionally protected, and, of course, there is also a common law right to refuse treatment.

(2) Even though their constitutional analyses and the application of principles involving competent patients to incompetent patients is almost exactly the same, these cases have been widely perceived as polar extremes because of the *Saikewicz* court's comments on "ethics committees" at the end of the opinion. Both the legal columnist and the editor of the New England Journal of Medicine, for example, interpreted *Saikewicz* as requiring that "all decisions on either removal of life-support systems or continuation of life-extending therapy in otherwise dying patients who are incompetent . . . must go before a Probate Court for approval." Curran, The Saikewicz Decision, 298 N. Engl. J. Med. 499 (1978). In a companion editorial, editor Arnold Relman concluded that the opinion showed that the judges had a "total distrust of physicians' judgments" and that their "astonishing opinion can only be viewed as a resounding vote of 'no confidence' in the ability of physicians and families to act in the best interests of the incapable patient suffering from a terminal illness." Relman, The Saikewicz Decision: Judges as Physicians, 298 N. Engl. J. Med. 508, 509 (1978). Relman urged judges in other jurisdictions to reject the *Saikewicz* approach and adopt the *Quinlan* model as well, adding that those who disagreed should take a "guided visit to a large acute-care hospital." Id. at 509. These articles were very persuasive in the medical community, and framed a debate that continues today over the role of the courts in making or approving decisions to withdraw treatment from incompetent patients. It is worth asking what the law in Massachusetts was prior to *Saikewicz*. Also, in what sense could there ever be a requirement to seek prior judicial approval of a patient's consent or refusal of consent before it is acted upon? It should be emphasized that the law in Massachusetts is settled. The Supreme Judicial Court has since unequivocally ruled that there never was any requirement of prior judicial review in refusal of treatment cases. In re Spring, 380 Mass. 629, 405 N.E.2d 115 (1980). See generally, Annas, Reconciling *Quinlan* and *Saikewicz,* 4 Am. J.L. Med. 367 (1979); and Rhoden, Litigating Life and Death, 102 Harv. L. Rev. 375 (1988).

(3) Consider how the New Jersey court would have decided the case of Joseph Saikewicz and how the Massachusetts court would have decided the case of Karen Ann Quinlan. Each court has had the chance to revisit these issues twice since these opinions were written. The New Jersey court's "ethics

committee" has evolved into a medical consultation of two physicians, other than the attending physician, to confirm the prognosis. In its first case after Quinlan, In re Conroy, 486 A.2d 1209 (N.J. 1985), the court held that tube feeding could be withdrawn from an elderly, incompetent nursing home resident only if there was clear and convincing evidence that this was what the patient wanted or, if the patient's wishes were unknown, that such a decision was in the patient's best interest because the patient was suffering severe pain. The court termed this pain-centered test a "pure best interests" test, and also fashioned a "limited objective" best interests test. Under this test treatment could be terminated if "there is some trustworthy evidence that the patient would have refused treatment, and . . . it is clear that the burdens of the patient's continued life with the treatment outweigh the benefits of that life for him." Id. Withdrawal must be overseen and approved of by the state's Ombudsman for the Institutionalized Elderly, who is to investigate each case as a possible case of elder abuse. Because of this procedure as of June, 1989, *no* nursing home patient had been able to refuse life-sustaining treatment in New Jersey since *Conroy,* because the Ombudsman would not approve discontinuation of treatment.

In 1987, the New Jersey court decided three cases; two involving individuals in persistent vegetative states (like *Quinlan*), and its first involving a competent individual, who was suffering from amyotrophic lateral sclerosis (ALS), commonly known as Lou Gehrig's disease. In all three the court reaffirmed the patient's constitutional and common law right to refuse treatment, and judicially accepted the usefulness of living wills and durable powers of attorney in making decisions for previously competent patients. The court also held that in cases in which the wishes of the patient could not be ascertained by clear and convincing evidence the family of the patient should be permitted to make a substituted judgment without being required to go to court to seek a formal designation as legal guardian. The protection for the patient against unjustified withdrawal of treatment was to come in a "requirement" that two physicians, other than the attending physician, examine the patient and concur either that the patient is competent (in which case the patient's decision rules) or, if incompetent, to confirm the diagnosis and prognosis. Matter of Farrell, 108 N.J. 335, 529 A.2d 404 (1987) (competent individual dying of A.L.S. at home has the right to demand mechanical ventilator be removed); Matter of Peter by Johanning, 108 N.J. 365, 529 A.2d 419 (1987) (elderly nursing home patient in persistent vegetative state has right to have tube feeding discontinued if this was her wish by clear and convincing evidence); and Matter of Jobes, 108 N.J. 394, 529 A.2d 434 (1987) (nonelderly nursing home patient in a persistent vegetative state can have tube feeding discontinued, even in the absence of clear and convincing evidence of her wishes, if the family concludes that this is in the patient's best interest). See Moore, "Two Steps Forward, One Step Back": An Analysis of New Jersey's Latest "Right to Die" Decisions, 19 Rutgers L.J. 955 (1988); and N. Cantor, Legal Frontiers of Death and Dying (1987).

The Massachusetts line of cases has not relied on physicians as required consultants, or "ethics committees," or prognosis committees, to grant legal immunity and to "bless" the decisions of others. Rather it has consistently ruled that once the individual's own preferences are determined, they should be followed. This was the ruling in the case of an elderly gentleman in a nursing home who required kidney dialysis to continue to live (In re Spring, 380 Mass. 629, 405 N.E.2d 115 (1980)); and in the case of an individual in a persistent vegetative state who, like Peter and Jobes, required tube feeding to continue to live (Brophy v. N.E. Sinai Hospital, 398 Mass. 417, 497 N.E.2d 626 (1986)).

(4) In 1988, in the case of Nancy Cruzan, Missouri broke with the "trend" in the law toward granting family petitions to remove artificial life support systems on the basis of either substituted judgment or best interests. Although in a persistent vegetative state, and even though she had expressed her desire not to be kept alive by artificial means prior to the automobile accident that left her in a permanent coma, the petition of her family to remove her feeding tube was denied by the Missouri Supreme Court (in a 4 to 3 opinion that reversed a decision in favor of removal by the trial court) on the basis that there was insufficient evidence of Nancy's wishes, that withdrawal of artificial feeding would be "killing"; and that the state had a compelling interest in maintaining the lives of individuals like Nancy, since at least some of them would want to live. The case dismissed prior opinions from other states, as not well reasoned, but the court provided almost no analysis to support its radical departure from decisions in other jurisdictions. Ultimately the case seems to have been about Missouri's 1986 abortion statute, which the court cites with approval as setting for the state's interest in life (including "unborn" children "from the moment of conception"). The court emphasizes that the state of Missouri must protect the life of premature children requiring "artificial life supports" and seems unable (or unwilling) to distinguish the case of an adult kept alive on "artificial life support" from an embryo or a premature infant so maintained. Missouri's interest, according to the court, is in "the right to life of all humans." It is thus perfectly fitting that on July 3, 1989, the same day the Court decided *Webster* (see infra p. 953) that it granted certiorari in *Cruzan*. This will be the first right to refuse treatment case ever heard by the Court. It is also an especially difficult one because the facts remain unclear. Assume that Nancy Cruzan has the same prognosis as Karen Ann Quinlan but requires only tube feeding to continue to survive. Assume further that her parents are convinced that she would not want to be artificially maintained indefinitely in a permanent coma, and want her tube feeding discontinued so that she can die. How should the Court articulate Nancy's constitutional rights? Are any of these rights fundamental? If so, can the state demonstrate a conpelling interest to continue artificial feeding against her wishes or the wishes of her parents? Cruzan v. Harmon, 760 S.W.2d 408 (Mo. 1988). See Annas, The Insane Root Takes Reason Prisoner, 19 Hastings Cent. Rep. 29 (Jan. 1989).

Lane v. Candura

376 N.E.2d 1232 (Mass. App. 1978)

BY THE COURT.

This case concerns a 77-year old widow, Mrs. Rosaria Candura, of Arlington, who is presently a patient at the Symmes Hospital in Arlington suffering from gangrene in the right foot and lower leg. Her attending physicians recommended in April that the leg be amputated without delay. After some vacillation, she refused to consent to the operation, and she persists in that refusal. Her daughter, Grace R. Lane of Medford, filed a petition in the Probate Court for Middlesex County seeking appointment of herself as temporary guardian with authority to consent to the operation on behalf of her mother. An order and a judgment were entered in the Probate Court to that effect, from which the guardian ad litem appointed to represent Mrs. Candura has appealed.

We hold that Mrs. Candura has the right under the law to refuse to submit either to medical treatment or a surgical operation, that on the evidence and findings in this case the decision is one that she may determine for herself, and that therefore her leg may not be amputated unless she consents to that course of action.

The right of a person in most circumstances to decline treatment is clearly recognized in the important recent case of Superintendent of Belchertown State Sch. v. Saikewicz, 370 N.E.2d 417 (1977). "The constitutional right to privacy, as we conceive it, is an expression of the sanctity of individual free choice and self-determination as fundamental constituents of life. The value of life as so perceived is lessened not by a decision to refuse treatment, but by the failure to allow a competent human being the right of choice." 370 N.E.2d at 426. Although the *Saikewicz* case also recognizes certain countervailing interests of the State, which may in some cases outweigh the right of a competent individual to refuse life saving or life prolonging treatment, the case before us does not involve factors which would bring it within those lines of cases and thus warrant a court's overriding the will of a competent person.

The principal question arising on the record before us, therefore, is whether Mrs. Candura has the legally requisite competence of mind and will to make the choice for herself. We look first to the findings of fact made by the judge who heard the testimony, including that of Mrs. Candura herself. His decision does not include a clear-cut finding that Mrs. Candura lacks the requisite legal competence. The nearest approach to such a finding is contained in the following passage from his decision:

> It is fair to conclude — without necessarily finding that the ward is mentally ill for all purposes — that she is incapable of making a rational and competent

> choice to undergo or reject the proposed surgery to her right leg. To this extent, at least, her behavior is irrational. She has closed her mind to the entire issue to the extent that the Court cannot conclude that her decision to reject further treatment is rational and informed. . . . In the absence of substantial evidence that the ward has come to her current position as a result of a rational process after careful consideration of the medical alternatives, the Court finds that her confused mental condition resulting from her underlying senility and depression warrants the exercise of the jurisdiction of this Court and the application of a substitute choice for the ward as enunciated in the [*Saikewicz*] case. . . .

In context, the quoted passage means only that, given some indications of a degree of senility and confusion on some subjects, the judge was not satisfied that Mrs. Candura arrived at her decision in a rational manner, i.e., "after careful consideration of the medical alternatives." We do not think that the passage can be construed as a finding of legal incompetence, and we do not think that the evidence in the case would have warranted such a finding.

The facts found by the judge or established by uncontradicted evidence are as follows. Mrs. Candura was born in Italy, emigrated to the United States in 1918, was married, and had a daughter and three sons. She lost her husband in 1976 and has been depressed and unhappy since that time. Her relationship with her children is marked by a considerable degree of conflict. She lived in her own home until her hospitalization in November, 1977. In 1974 she had an infection in a toe on her right foot which became gangrenous. It was discovered at that time she was diabetic. The toe was amputated. In 1977 she bruised her right leg while getting into a bus. The bruise developed into gangrene which resulted in an operation in November, 1977, in which a portion of her foot was amputated. At that time an arterial bypass was done to decrease the likelihood that gangrene would recur. She went from the hospital to a rehabilitation center, where she remained until April. She then returned to the hospital and was found to have gangrene in the remainder of the foot. She originally agreed to amputation of the leg, but she withdrew her consent on the morning scheduled for the operation. She was discharged on April 21 and went to her daughter's home but returned to the Symmes Hospital after a few days. Around May 9, responding to the persuasion of a doctor who has known Mrs. Candura for many years, she consented to the operation, but soon thereafter she reiterated her refusal. She has discussed with some persons the reasons for her decision: that she has been unhappy since the death of her husband; that she does not wish to be a burden to her children; that she does not believe that the operation will cure her; that she does not wish to live as an invalid or in a nursing home; and that she does not fear death but welcomes it. She is discouraged by the failure of the earlier operations to arrest the advance of the gangrene. She tends to be stubborn and somewhat irrascible. In her own testimony before the judge she expressed a desire to get well but indicated that she was resigned to death and was adamantly against the operation. Her testimony (corroborated by that of several of the witnesses) showed that she is lucid on some matters and confused on others. Her train of thought sometimes wanders. Her conception of time is distorted. She is hostile to certain doctors. She is on occasion defensive and sometimes combative in her responses to questioning. But she has exhibited a high degree of awareness and acuity. When responding to questions concerning the proposed operation, she has made it clear that she does not wish to have the operation even though that decision will in all likelihood lead shortly to her death. We find no indication in any of the testimony that that is not a choice with full appreciation of the consequences. The most that is shown is that the decision involves strong, emotional factors, that she does not choose to discuss the decision with certain persons, and that occasionally her resolve against giving consent weakens.

. . . We start with the proposition that, in a proceeding for the appointment of a guardian under G. L. c. 201, §6A or §14 (permanent and temporary guardianships, respectively), the burden is on the petitioner to prove that the proposed ward is incompetent. *Willett v. Willett,* 333 Mass. 323, 324, 130 N.E.2d 582 (1955). A person is presumed to be competent unless shown by the evidence not to be competent. . . .

. . . Such evidence is lacking in this case. We recognize that Dr. Kelley, one of two psychiatrists who testified, did state that in his opinion Mrs. Candura was incompetent to make a rational choice whether to consent to the operation. His opinion appears to have been based upon (1) his inference from her unwillingness to discuss the problem with him that she was unable to face up to the problem or to understand that her refusal constituted a choice; (2) his characterization of "an unwilling[ness], for whatever reason, to consent to life saving treatment . . . as suicidal;" and (3) a possibility, not established by evidence as a reasonable probability, that her mind might be impaired by toxicity caused by the gangrenous condition.[5] His testimony, read closely, and in the context of the questions put to him, indicates that his opinion is not one of incompetency in the legal sense, but rather that her ability to make a rational choice (by which he means the *medically* rational choice) is impaired by the confusion existing in her mind by virtue of her consideration of irrational and emotional factors.

A careful analysis of the evidence in this case, including the superficially

5. Another psychiatrist, Dr. Zeckel, who is apparently an associate of Dr. Kelley, and who offered an opinion that Mrs. Candura was competent, has been successful in eliciting from her the factors contributing to her choice. When asked to explain why his opinion differed from that of Dr. Kelley, Dr. Zeckel answered, "I think it is just a personal philosophy type of thing where I believe the person[s] themselves ought to be given the benefit of the doubt as to what they want to do with their lives, whereas, Dr. Kelley, I guess, is more protective. I can't really speak for him but his general philosophy is different from mine." Dr. Kelley stated, at one point in his testimony, "You know, it comes down really to a philosophical [difference], I hope there is no psychiatric argument in this case. It's the right of a patient to decide they want to die and I spend all my life trying to keep people alive so I take quite a different view."

conflicting psychiatric testimony, indicates that there is no real conflict as to the underlying facts. Certainly, the evidence presents no issue of credibility. The principal question is whether the facts established by the evidence justify a conclusion of legal incompetence. The panel are unanimous in the opinion that they do not.

. . . The decision of the judge, as well as the opinion of Dr. Kelley, predicates the necessity for the appointment of a guardian chiefly on the irrationality (in medical terms) of Mrs. Candura's decision to reject the amputation. Until she changed her original decision and withdrew her consent to the amputation, her competence was not questioned. But the irrationality of her decision does not justify a conclusion that Mrs. Candura is incompetent in the legal sense. The law protects her right to make her own decision to accept or reject treatment, whether that decision is wise or unwise. Compare In re Estate of Brooks, 32 Ill. 2d 361, 205 N.E.2d 435 (1965).

Similarly, the fact that she has vacillated in her resolve not to submit to the operation does not justify a conclusion that her capacity to make the decision is impaired to the point of legal incompetence. Indeed, her reaction may be readily understandable in the light of her prior surgical experience and the prospect of living the remainder of her life nonambulatory. Senile symptoms, in the abstract, may, of course, justify a finding of incompetence, but the inquiry must be more particular. What is lacking in this case is evidence that Mrs. Candura's areas of forgetfulness and confusion cause, or relate in any way to, impairment of her ability to understand that in rejecting the amputation she is, in effect, choosing death over life. This is not a case, therefore, like In the Matter of Northern, Tenn. App. (1978), in which the ward elected both to live and to reject an amputation operation, not appreciating that she must choose. Rather, this case is like In the Matter of Quackenbush, 156 N.J. Super. 282, 383 A.2d 785 (Morris County Ct. 1978), in which an elderly person, although subject (like Mrs. Candura) to fluctuations in mental lucidity and to occasional losses of his train of thought, was held to be competent to reject a proposed operation to amputate gangrenous legs because he was capable of appreciating the nature and consequences of his decision. . . .

Mrs. Candura's decision may be regarded by most as unfortunate, but on the record in this case it is not the uninformed decision of a person incapable of appreciating the nature and consequences of her act. We cannot anticipate whether she will reconsider and will consent to the operation, but we are all of the opinion that the operation may not be forced on her against her will.

The order appointing a temporary guardian and the judgment authorizing the temporary guardian to consent to the operation are reversed, and a new judgment is to enter dismissing the petition.

So ordered.

NOTES ON COMPETENCE

(1) A variety of approaches have been suggested to determine competence. The President's Commission for the Study of Ethical Problems in Medicine and Biomedical and Behavior Research (1982) identified three: outcome, status, and function. Under the *outcome approach*, actual decisions by patients which do not reflect community values are used as evidence of incompetence. Under the *status approach*, an individual's competence is based solely on physical or mental status (that is, consciousness, age, mental or physical diagnosis). The *functioning approach* focuses on the individual's actual understanding and processes in decision making situations.

Most commentators have assumed that the functioning approach is correct and have tried to better define the attributes needed to function competently. One philosopher has suggested, for example, that we can require any one of four increasingly strict standards: (1) free action, which involves a voluntary and intentional choice; (2) authentic decision, which is a decision that reflects the individual's values; (3) effective deliberation, which is an evaluation of the specific alternatives and their consequences; and (4) moral reflection, which is, in addition to effective deliberation, reflections on and acceptance of the moral values upon which the decision is based. Miller, Autonomy and Refusal of Lifesaving Treatment, 11 Hastings Cent. Rep. 22 (June 1981).

(2) The Mary Northern case referred to in *Candura* is similar, although in that case the court found the 72-year-old woman incompetent to consent to or refuse amputation. Department of Human Services v. Northern, 563 S.W.2d 197 (Tenn. Ct. App. 1978). As a result of frostbite, both of Mary Northern's feet were necrotic. They were coal black in color, "shriveled, rotting and stinking." According to the testimony, Ms. Northern was perfectly lucid and understood everything *other than* the condition of her feet. She believed her feet would heal without surgery, and refused to consider the possibility that she might die without the amputation. Because she would not explicitly acknowledge that she would rather die than have her feet amputated (she responded "possibly" when that question was put to her), the court determined that she was refusing to make a choice, and was "mentally incapable of comprehending the facts which constitute" the danger to her life. The court used the following definition to find her incompetent:

> Capacity means mental ability to make a rational decision, which includes the ability to perceive, appreciate all relevant facts and to reach a rational judgment upon such facts. [Id. at 209]

The court did not adopt the "outcome test," that is, it did not object to her refusal per se. Rather it was her capacity to make an informed decision that the court objected to: "On the subjects of death and amputation of her feet, her comprehension is blocked, blinded or dimmed to the extent that she is *incapable of recognizing facts which would be obvious to a person of normal percep-*

tion [emphasis added]." Id. The major fact Ms. Northern was consistently incapable of recognizing was that her feet were "dead, black, shriveled, rotting and stinking." As Judge Drowota wrote in a concurring opinion:

> If this court could in good faith find that she perceived as facts that her feet *do* look and smell as they do, and that her doctors are telling her that she needs surgery to save her life, we would not interfere with whatever decision she made regardless of how much it conflicted with the substance of her medical advice or with what we ourselves might have chosen. [Id. at 214]

(3) The judicial test of competence is based on an individual's capacity to understand and appreciate the nature and consequences of one's decisions. It can be restated in the medical care context by saying that if an individual understands and appreciates the information needed to give an informed consent, then that individual is competent both to consent and to refuse consent, assuming, of course, that the decision is made freely and voluntarily. The type and quantity of information that must be understood and appreciated will vary with the actual treatment options and with the risks and alternatives that face the patient, but not with the status of the patient (status test) or the actual decision made by the patient (outcome test). Annas & Densberger, Competence to Refuse Medical Treatment, 15 Toledo L. Rev. 561 (1984). Use of the "outcome approach" by physicians, as in the *Candura* case, is probably the rule rather than the exception. Typically, competence is questioned only when a patient refuses to consent to a recommended treatment or chooses a course different from the one the doctor finds most reasonable. President's Commission for the Study of Ethical Problems in Medicine and Biomedical and Behavioral Research, Making Health Care Decisions, 62 (1982). See also Meisel, The "Exceptions" to the Informed Consent Doctrine: Striking a Balance between Competing Values in Medical Decisionmaking, 1979 Wis. L. Rev. 413; Green, Judicial Tests of Mental Incompetency, 6 Mo. L. Rev. 141 (1941); C. Culver & B. Gert, Philosophy in Medicine (1982); and Appelbaum & Grisso, Assessing Patients' Capacities to Consent to Treatment, 319 N. Engl. J. Med. 1635 (1988).

(4) It follows from this discussion that when an individual is no longer competent (for example, in a coma or a state of severe dementia) the individual is no longer capable of making treatment decisions. Thus, someone else will have to make them on the individual's behalf. To enable individuals to continue to have some influence over these decisions, two mechanisms have been suggested: the "living will" and the durable power of attorney. In the living will (living because it takes effect while the individual is still alive) the individual sets forth what he or she would like done in certain circumstances. For example, no artificial feeding or mechanical ventilation if I'm in a persistent vegetative state (like Karen Quinlan); no "extraordinary care," and so forth. It is often *very* difficult to interpret the terms of these documents. If you have not already done so, you should try to write your own "living will,"

both for your own sake and the sake of your relatives who would be asked to make decisions for you. Ask friends to read it to see if they understand what you want done and not done.

Because of the inherent difficulties and ambiguities in written treatment directives, modern commentators suggest that such a document be supplemented by a "durable power of attorney." Ordinary powers of attorney terminate with the competence of the principal. A "durable" power of attorney, on the other hand, survives incompetence. Indeed, for health care, such powers of attorney generally have "springing" power, that is, they only become effective ("springing" into effect) when the principal becomes incompetent. Thereafter, the agent or attorney is given authority to make treatment decisions consistent with the instructions of the principal. This mechanism not only is a method to "fill in the gaps" of a written directive, but also gives the physician someone to talk to with legal authority to make decisions. It is important to designate your agent as your guardian as well, since in the event a guardian is appointed for you, the guardian has the authority (just as you would as principal) to discharge the agent appointed under a durable power of attorney. See G.J. Annas, The Rights of Patients (1989); New York State Task Force on Life and Law, Life-Sustaining Treatment: Making Decisions and Appointing a Health Care Agent (1987); Congress of the U.S., Office of Technology Assessment, Losing a Million Minds: Confronting the Tragedy of Alzheimer's Disease and Other Dementias, OTA-BA-323 (1987); Society for the Right to Die, Handbook of Living Will Laws (published and updated annually); and President's Commission for the Study of Ethical Problems in Medicine and Biomedical and Behavioral Research, Deciding to Forego Life-Sustaining Treatment (1983). For suggested model legislation see: NY Task Force, supra, and Annas & Glantz, The Right of Elderly Patients to Refuse Life-sustaining Treatment, 64 Milbank Mem. Fund Q. 95, 150-160 (Supp. 2 1986).

In 1988, the New York Court of Appeals issued an extremely narrow opinion requiring that prior directives precisely predict the disease and manner of death, as well as the specific method used to maintain life, before a court would honor an individual's living will. Mary O'Connor had said on many occasions that she would "never want any sort of intervention, any sort of life support system." In the matter of Mary O'Connor, 72 N.Y.2d 517 (1988), discussed in Annas, Precatory Prediction and Mindless Mimicry, 18 Hastings Cent. Rep. 31 (Dec. 1988). Nonetheless, the court found these statements not clear and convincing evidence of her wishes because they were made in the context of her husband and brother dying of cancer, and she was dying of cardiovascular collapse, and had not mentioned specifically that she wanted to be starved to death. In the court's words:

> Her statements with respect to declining artificial means of life support were generally prompted by her experience with persons suffering terminal illnesses, particularly cancer. However, Mrs. O'Connor does not have a terminal illness,

> except in the sense that she is aged and infirm. . . . She is simply an elderly person who as a result of several strokes suffers certain disabilities, including an inability to feed herself or eat in a normal manner. [72 N.Y.2d at 533.]

The court also opined that even if Mrs. O'Connor had previously expressed her wishes not to have artificial feeding, "there always exists the possibility that, despite his or her clear expression in the past, the patient has since changed his or her mind." Id. at 530. Even though the petition of Mary O'Connor's daughters was denied, the New York Court of Appeals did say that had she designated another individual to make health care decisions for her through the state's durable power of attorney statute, that person *would* have been authorized to refuse continued artificial feeding on Mary O'Connor's behalf. Thus, in New York, the durable power of attorney is currently the only effective way to refuse artificial life-support in advance. Id. at 528, n. 2. On the concept of someone who has lost his mind, changing it, see Dresser, Life, Death and Incompetent Patients, 28 Ariz. L. Rev. 373 (1986).

2. THE "RIGHT TO DIE"

Elizabeth Bouvia v. Riverside General Hospital

No. 159780, Riverside Co., Cal. (Sup. Ct. Dec. 19, 1983)

HEWS, J.

Elizabeth Bouvia, an articulate, severely handicapped young woman asserts in this application for permanent injunction that the Defendants County of Riverside, Riverside General Hospital and its staff will unless restrained and enjoined by order of this Court administer health care against her will or will cause her transfer or discharge from Riverside General Hospital. . . . She further asks the Court specifically to enjoin the Defendants from administering any health care without her consent. She does not wish to accept any fluid, food or other nutrients or sustenance. There is to be no installation by insertion, cannulation or surgical operation any intravenous nasogastric or gastrostomy, intubation or tubing to sustain her. . . .

She asked for pain medication and hygienic care until her ultimate death occurs. In essence, the Plaintiff claims that she has a right to determine when and how her life shall end and that society has an obligation to honor and to assist her in achieving that individual right.

The Defendants assert that the Plaintiff does not have this right to end her life by virtue of any statutory, constitutional, ethical, or moral theory. . . . Defendants further assert that the order sought by Plaintiff would have a devastating effect on the medical staff, administration, and patients at Riverside General Hospital. It would violate medical ethics. . . .

From the evidence presented, the Court finds that the following facts, among others, have been established: that the Plaintiff, Elizabeth Bouvia, has since birth suffered from cerebral palsy. This has left her with virtually no motor function in any of her limbs or other skeletal muscles; that she retains some slight control of her right hand sufficient to operate the mechanical control of an electrically powered wheelchair; that she maintains enough voluntary control of the muscles of her mouth, face, and throat structures so that she can eat a normal diet when essentially fed by someone else; and that she can talk with only a very slight speech impediment. . . . [S]he experiences a fairly constant degree of pain and discomfort from her inability to change her own position, from the muscle contractures and increased spasticity that affects her limbs, and from the arthritis which her bodily distortions have caused.

The Court further finds that Plaintiff is physically unable to take her own life; further, that though afflicted in her body, Plaintiff's mind and intellect are totally unaffected and are quite normal; that Plaintiff has been able to live independently with constant attendants and has even earned a Bachelor of Science Degree in social work from San Diego State University; that Plaintiff was married in San Diego to Richard Bouvia in August of 1982 and lived with him from there, and in July of 1983 she moved with her husband to the residence of her father in Oregon; that mid-August 1983 Plaintiff's husband left her.

The Court further finds that in early September 1983 Plaintiff requested and received transportation services from her father who brought her by automobile to Riverside County. On September 3rd Plaintiff directed her father to take her to the emergency department of Riverside General Hospital where she arranged for a voluntary psychiatric admission. She's disclosed her intent to discontinue sufficient caloric intake so that she would eventually succumb to starvation following her admission. The Plaintiff's life is not in a terminal state, and her death is not imminent as a result of her disability; that cerebral palsy in itself is not of a progressive nature.

The Court is convinced that Plaintiff has made her own decision to forego further feedings and will vigorously resist any feedings forced upon her. This decision was made by her after careful and mature deliberation of the alternatives, consequences and irreversibility of her decision. The Court further finds that her decision was rational and that Plaintiff is mentally competent to make decisions affecting her life; that her decision was primarily reached because of the nature and extent of her physical disability and that her dependence on others to maintain her person in all areas of physical activity and not from other experiences, such as, a failed marriage, non-employment, failure to procreate or termination of her education.

The Court is convinced that the Plaintiff is sincere in her desire to terminate her life and that she no longer desires to live. The Court is also convinced that all counsel want her to live, and they hope that she might change her mind. . . .

Further factual findings are made that Riverside General Hospital is an acute-care, limited-stay hospital; that if the Court were to follow her desires, the decision would have a profound effect on the medical staff, nurses and administration at Riverside General Hospital; that the medical and nursing staff attending to the Plaintiff fully believed that they would be subject to possible criminal, civil and license revocation proceedings if they were to honor the Plaintiff's wishes, even under the Court Order. The Court is also convinced that such an order would have a devastating effect on other patients within Riverside General Hospital and other physically handicapped persons who are similarly situated in this nation.

During the hearing, Plaintiff's decision to end her life has been called various things: the right to self-determination, the right of privacy, the right to determine the quality of one's life, the right to control one's own life and own body, the right to be let alone, the right to determine one's own future, the right to be protected from force feeding, the right to escape a useless body, freedom of choice, the acceptance of death, self-starvation, self-destruction, suicide, voluntary euthanasia and, finally, the right to die with dignity. All of the terms have some significance. The Court has determined that the ultimate issue is whether or not a severely handicapped, mentally competent person who is otherwise physically healthy and not terminally ill has the right to end her life with the assistance of society.

The Court concludes that she does not. The equitable powers of this Court may not be invoked for such a purpose. The Court bases this decision entirely on the constitutional issue presented, the unwritten right of privacy and self-determination recognized under the First, Fourth, Fifth and Fourteenth Amendments of the United States Constitution and Article 1, Section 1 of the California Constitution.

The Court concludes that the Plaintiff in this instance does have a fundamental or preferred right to terminate her own life and to terminate medical intervention but that this right has been overcome by the strong interests of the State and society. Preservation of life is the strongest State interest involved. Our society values life. The Plaintiff is not terminal, and her life will be preserved by this decision. None of the parties have cited any legal precedence which approves the proposition that a non-terminal person with a life expectancy of 15 to 20 years who has a disabling but non-progressive physical condition should be allowed to terminate life because of the sincere desire to do so by reason of the disability.

Next are the interests of the third parties involved in this case. The third parties here include other patients in the hospital, other persons similarly situated who suffer from chronic disabling diseases and health care professionals employed by Riverside General Hospital who would have to assist in the Plaintiff's death.

The next interest of society the Court has considered is the prevention of suicide. Suicide is defined as "the deliberate termination of one's existence while in possession and enjoyment of one's mental faculties" or "the deliberate and intentional destruction of one's own life by a person of years of discretion and sound mind." Plaintiff's cerebral palsy is not self-induced; however, her contemplated self-starvation with the assistance of society would be. Cerebral palsy is not terminal. Self-starvation is terminal. Self-starvation by the Plaintiff who is competent would constitute suicide. By not issuing the requested order, the State will be protecting the Plaintiff from suicide.

The California Natural Death Act authorizes persons to direct that further medical care be ceased following diagnosis of death as imminent whether or not life-sustaining procedures are authorized. The Act further does not permit any affirmative act or omission to end life other than to permit the natural process of dying. Plaintiff is not a qualified patient under this Act, and her death as proposed would not be natural. Logically, it would be the result of suicide.

Lastly, the Court has considered the State's interest in the maintenance of the integrity of the medical profession. Prevailing medical ethical standards do not without exception demand that all efforts toward life prolongation be made in all circumstances. It is recognized that the dying are often in need of comfort more than treatment; however once again, the Court comes back to the established fact that Plaintiff in this case is not dying and is not terminal. The established ethics of the medical profession clearly outweigh and overcome her own rights of self-determination. All four factors of State interest clearly overcome the Plaintiff's right of privacy of self-determination under the facts established to be true in this case. . . .

Whether or not forcing nutrients is termed medical treatment or sustaining one's life is not important under the factual situation presented here in this case. Forced feeding, however invasive, would be administered for the purpose of saving the life of an otherwise non-terminal patient and should be permitted. There is no other reasonable option. Saving her life would be paramount. . . .

The Court is aware that there are no easy solutions in this area of law, ethics, or morality. We all earnestly hope that this young woman will realize that there is hope in life and that now because of the action taken by her she can be a symbol of hope to others similarly situated if she changes her purpose. However, the Court cannot allow her to end her life in this manner. She does have the right to terminate her existence but not while she is non-terminal with the assistance of society.

An injunction should not be granted, for the harm which will occur via the injunction is greater than the harm that it is designed to avoid. . . .

NOTE ON ELIZABETH BOUVIA

Ms. Bouvia was force fed with a nasogastric tube as a result of this decision. Since she refused to cooperate, and even though she has only the use of her neck and head, and partial use of one hand, she had to be restrained by three to four hospital employees to insert the tube each day. After about a month of this "treatment" she checked out and went to Mexico with friends where, she had been told, she could refuse treatment in a health care setting. This turned out not to be possible. Upon returning to California, she was admitted to a private longterm care facility on the condition that she would not refuse nutrition there. She stayed there for more than a year before being transferred to L.A. County Hospital for placement of a morphine pump for pain relief. She was thereafter transferred to High Desert Hospital, where the staff decided to attempt to force feed her again because they believed she was losing weight on her current feeding and was planning to starve herself to death slowly. Ms. Bouvia objected, but a nasogastric tube was inserted against her will. She then sued the hospital to have it removed. The trial court refused her request, but this order was overturned on appeal. Among other things, the appeals court noted:

> At bench the trial court concluded that with sufficient feeding petitioner could live an additional 15 to 20 years; therefore, the preservation of petitioner's life for that period outweighed her right to decide. In so holding the trial court mistakenly attached undue importance to the *amount of time* possibly available to petitioner, and failed to give equal weight and consideration for the *quality* of that life; an equal, if not more significant consideration . . . who shall say what the minimum amount of available life must be? . . . Here Elizabeth Bouvia's decision to forego medical treatment or life-support through a mechanical means belongs to her. It is not a medical decision for her physicians to make. Neither is it a legal question whose soundness is to be resolved by lawyers or judges. It is a moral and philosophical decision that, being a competent adult, is her's alone. . . . It is incongruous, if not monstrous, for medical practitioners to assert their right to preserve a life that someone else must live, or, more accurately, endure, for "15 to 20 years." We cannot conceive it to be the policy of this state to inflict such an ordeal upon anyone. [Bouvia v. Superior Court, 179 Cal. App. 3d 1127, 225 Cal. Rptr. 297 (1986).]

In a concurring opinion, Judge Compton argued that "The right to die is an integral part of our right to control our own destinies so long as the rights of others are not affected. That right should, in my opinion, include the ability to enlist assistance from others, including the medical profession, in making death as painless and quick as possible." Id. at 1147. See generally on the Bouvia saga, G.J. Annas, Judging Medicine 290-301 (1988).

As of 1989, Ms. Bouvia was still alive and being treated (with her consent) at L.A. County Medical Center, to which she had been returned following her stay at High Desert Hospital. What obligations does society owe Ms. Bouvia? What, if anything, does she owe society? In what sense is "*Bouvia II*" different from "*Bouvia I*"? Are they both about the "right to commit suicide"? the right to die? How do these two concepts differ? Does it matter? Should the law force physicians and nurses to participate in the "care" of Ms. Bouvia if they don't want to?

Notes on Refusing Nutrition and CPR

(1) The issue of whether food and water should be treated like any other medical intervention remains controversial in some circles. See, for instance, May et al., Feeding and Hydrating the Permanently Unconscious and Other Vulnerable Persons, 3 Issues in L. Med. 203 (1987); and By No Extraordinary Means (J. Lynn ed. 1987). In what sense is artificial feeding like artificial (or mechanical) ventilation? How is it different? Is it correct to term death by refusal of artificial nutrition "starving to death"?

(2) Appeals courts have universally considered artificial feeding a form of medical treatment that can be refused like any other medical treatment, although some courts have demanded specific evidence of intent to refuse nutrition (not just "artificial life support") itself. The vast majority of cases on nutrition have dealt with the permanently unconscious — patients in "persistent vegetative states" like Karen Ann Quinlan. Perhaps the best known case is that of Paul Brophy, a 43-year-old firefighter in a persistent vegetative state who was kept alive by a gastrostomy tube (stomach tube) that everyone conceded he would not want. In a 4 to 3 opinion, the Massachusetts Supreme Judicial Court overruled a lower court decision that said that removal of the tube was against medical ethics. The SJC said it was for the patient to make decisions regarding the "individual's quality of life." Brophy v. New England Sinai Hospital, 497 N.E.2d 626 (Mass. 1986). It further found tube feeding like any other medical intervention, and use of a gastrostomy tube "intrusive as a matter of law." Nonetheless, the court did not require the attending physician (who had objected to removing the tube) to remove the tube, but only required him to assist the family in transferring him to another facility that would honor his wishes. Brophy was transferred shortly thereafter and died peacefully 8 days after feeding was discontinued. Accord, In re Hilda Peter and Nancy Jobes, 529 A.2d 404 (N.J. 1987); In re Joseph Gardner, 534 A.2d 947 (Me. 1987); Gray v. Romeo, 697 F. Supp 580 (D.R.I. 1988). Should physicians who place feeding tubes be required to remove them upon request? See In the Matter of Beverly Requena, 213 N.J. Super. 443 (1986). The American Medical Association supports the conclusion of these cases:

> The social commitment of the physician is to sustain life and relieve suffering. Where the performance of one duty conflicts with the other, the choice of the patient, or his family or legal representative if the patient is incompetent to act in his own behalf, should prevail. In the absence of the patient's choice or an authorized proxy, the physician must act in the best interest of the patient.
>
> For humane reasons, with informed consent, *a physician may do what is medically necessary to alleviate severe pain,* or cease or omit treatment to permit a terminally ill patient whose death is imminent to die. *However, he should not intentionally cause death.* In deciding whether the administration of potentially life-prolonging medical treatment is in the best interest of the patient who is

competent to act in his own behalf, the physician should determine what the possibility is for extending life under humane and comfortable conditions and what the prior expressed wishes of the patient and attitudes of the family or those who have responsibility for the custody of the patient.

Even if death is not imminent but a patient's coma is beyond doubt irreversible and there are adequate safeguards to confirm the accuracy of the diagnosis and with the concurrence of those who have responsibility for the care of the patient, it is not unethical to discontinue all means of life-prolonging medical treatment.

Life-prolonging medical treatment includes medication and artificially or technologically supplied respiration, nutrition, or hydration. In treating a terminally ill or irreversibly comatose patient, the physician should determine whether the benefits of treatment outweigh its burdens. At all times, the dignity of the patient should be maintained. [AMA Council on Ethical and Judicial Affairs (1987).]

(3) It is now overwhelmingly clear that patients have the legal right to refuse any medical intervention. Nonetheless, great conflict and confusion continue in the area of cardiopulmonary resuscitation (CPR). A philosopher and a physician have suggested (as have others) that in some circumstances, such as those in which CPR will be "futile" and is thus not medically indicated, physicians may withhold it or write a DNR order (do not resuscitate) *without* discussing this with the patient or family:

Patients or families who demand CPR when it will almost certainly be futile almost always do so because of denial of the prospect of death, magical thinking about the miracles of modern medicine, or benign television images of CPR. The physician who offers CPR under these conditions only supports these natural defense mechanisms and suggests, moreover — regardless of what he or she might say to the contrary — that CPR does offer something of value. Under these conditions, the patient's choice of CPR will be based on a misunderstanding of its benefits, and therefore will frustrate the pursuit of autonomy rather than serve it. [Tomlinson & Brody, Ethics and Communication in Do-Not-Resuscitate Orders, 318 N. Engl. J. Med. 43 (1988).]

Are Tomlinson and Brody correct? Compare New York law which requires that CPR be performed unless the patient or the patient's legal representative has agreed that it should not be. 1987 N.Y. Laws 818; N.Y. Pub. Health Law article 29-B. And see Chapter 4 (c) on CPR at pp. 371-374.

Anon., It's Over, Debbie

259 J.A.M.A. 272 (1988)

The call came in the middle of the night. As a gynecology resident rotating through a large, private hospital, I had come to detest telephone calls, because invariably I would be up for several hours and would not feel good the next day. However, duty called, so I answered the phone. A nurse informed me that a patient was having difficulty getting rest, could I please see her. She was on 3 North. That was the gynecologiconcology unit, not my usual duty station. As I trudged along, bumping sleepily against walls and corners and not believing I was up again, I tried to imagine what I might find at the end of my walk. Maybe an elderly woman with an anxiety reaction, or perhaps something particularly horrible.

I grabbed the chart from the nurses station on my way to the patient's room, and the nurse gave me some hurried details: 20-year-old girl named Debbie was dying of ovarian cancer. She was having unrelenting vomiting apparently as the result of an alcohol drip administered for sedation. Hmmm, I thought. Very sad. As I approached the room I could hear loud, labored breathing. I entered and saw an emaciated, dark-haired woman who appeared much older than 20. She was receiving nasal oxygen, had an IV, and was sitting in bed suffering from what was obviously severe air hunger. The chart noted her weight at 80 pounds. A second woman, also dark-haired but of middle age, stood at her right, holding her hand. Both looked up as I entered. The room seemed filled with the patient's desperate effort to survive. Her eyes were hollow, and she had suprasternal and intercostal retractions with her rapid inspirations. She had not eaten or slept in two days. She had not responded to chemotherapy and was being given supportive care only. It was a gallows scene, a cruel mockery of her youth and unfulfilled potential. Her only words to me were, "Let's get this over with."

I retreated with my thoughts to the nurses station. The patient was tired and needed rest. I could not give her health, but I could give her rest. I asked the nurse to draw 20 mg of morphine sulfate into a syringe. Enough, I thought, to do the job. I took the syringe into the room and told the two women I was going to give Debbie something that would let her rest and to say good-bye. Debbie looked at the syringe, then laid her head on the pillow with her eyes open, watching what was left of the world. I injected the morphine intravenously and watched to see if my calculations on its effects would be correct. Within seconds her breathing slowed to a normal rate, her eyes closed, and her features softened as she seemed restful at last. The older woman stroked the hair of the now-sleeping patient. I waited for the inevitable next effect of depressing the respiratory drive. With clocklike certainty, within four minutes the breathing rate slowed even more, then became irregular, then ceased. The dark-haired woman stood erect and seemed relieved.

It's over, Debbie.

NOTES ON EUTHANASIA

(1) The "Debbie" piece became the subject of national news stories in the press and on network television. The journal received over 150 letters on the column which ran four to one against the actions of the physician and three to one against the journal for publishing the piece. Lundberg, It's Over Debbie and the Euthanasia Debate, 259 J.A.M.A. 2142 (1988). The journal also printed two strong editorials. One argued that doctors must *never* kill (Gaylin et al., Doctors Must Not Kill, 259 J.A.M.A. 2139 (1988)); the other that "there has always been a place, albeit carefully restricted to a limited range of cases, for voluntary euthanasia" (Vaux, Debbie's Dying: Mercy Killing and the Good Death, 259 J.A.M.A. 2140).

Is there a role for "mercy killing" in medicine? Should terminally ill patients in severe pain be permitted to ask their physician to help them to die (for instance, by a lethal injection)? An attempt by the Hemlock Society to put this question on the California ballot failed in 1988 because of a lack of signatures. But the proposal will come up again unless physicians become more adept at pain management. How would you vote on this issue? Why?

Public opinion polls show an overwhelming majority of the public (74 percent) and almost all physicians (88 percent) agree with the proposition that patients in severe pain should have all the medications they need to ease the pain, even if this might shorten their lives. On the other hand, only a bare majority of the public (57 percent) and a minority of physicians (30 percent) think it would be right to actually end the life of a terminally ill patient in severe pain upon request of the patient. Louis Harris Poll, June, 1987.

In 1989 a group of twelve physicians convened by the Society for the Right to Die published their recommendations on "The Physician's Responsibility toward Hopelessly Ill Patients: A Second Look" in 320 N. Engl. J. Med. 844 (1989). The group made a number of very important observations for all concerned with the treatment of patients near death. The first was that the primary issues in caring for seriously ill patients are medical, not legal. Acknowledging that "health professionals have also become much more aware of patients' rights," the group nonetheless accurately observed: "There is a large gap between what the courts now allow with respect to withdrawal of treatment and what physicians actually do. All too frequently, physicians are reluctant to withdraw aggressive treatment from hopelessly ill patients, despite clear legal precedent." Id. at 845. The group also underlined the centrality of pain relief, noting that few physicians actually understand how to control pain and that the fears of dying patients regarding isolation and pain are entirely justified. They accordingly urge physicians to use as much pain medication as needed to produce a pain-free state, noting, "To allow a patient to experience unbearable pain or suffering is unethical medical practice." Id. at 847. They go on to properly conclude: "To withhold any necessary measure of pain relief in a hopelessly ill person out of fear of depressing respiration or of possible legal repercussions is unjustifiable. Good medical practice is the best protection against legal liability." Id. Perhaps the physicians should have ended their article here. Nonetheless, they continued on to discuss assisted suicide and euthanasia.

Ten of the twelve, understanding that assisted suicide is a crime, nonetheless concluded that "it is not immoral for a physician to assist in the rational suicide of a terminally ill person." Id. at 848. As to taking active steps to end a patient's life (for instance, those patients unable to commit suicide, with or without assistance), the group described the Dutch situation in which it is permissible to administer a lethal dose of a drug (usually a short-acting barbiturate, followed by a paralyzing agent) in those cases in which the patient consents, and comfort in the dying process cannot be maintained otherwise. This occurs 5,000 to 10,000 times a year in the Netherlands. The group took no position, for or against, active euthanasia in the U.S., noting only that "the majority of physicians in the United States do not favor the Dutch position," that the prospect of criminal prosecution deters even the hardiest advocates of euthanasia among physicians," and that "the medical profession and the public will continue to debate the role euthanasia may have in the treatment of the terminally or hopelessly ill patient." Id. 849.

Set forth the three most powerful arguments in favor of granting physicians the right to end the life of a competent, terminally ill adult, in severe pain, upon request. What are the counter arguments? If one wanted to permit active euthanasia in the U.S. under certain circumstances, what would those circumstances be? Should they be spelled out in a statute? Should such "mercy killings" be supervised by the courts, administrative agencies, or the medical profession itself? What are the differences between giving a patient a lethal injection for the purpose of ending the patient's suffering, and giving the patient enough pain medication to relieve his suffering, knowing that this might end his life?

Problem: Baby Doe

On April 15, 1982, a Down syndrome child was born in Bloomington, Indiana. At the age of six days, following a court-approved decision that routine life-saving surgery be withheld, the child died of starvation. The child had a tracheoesophageal fistula (a defect that made it impossible for the child to eat, but which was relatively easy to repair surgically) that was not repaired. Because it could not eat without the operation, and because the parents refused to have the operation performed, the child was instead medicated with phenobarbital and morphine to keep it comfortable until the child starved to death. The lower court, which approved the withholding of treatment, did so on the basis that the judge believed that if there was a dispute among physicians about the appropriate treatment, then the parents should have the right to decide which alternative, including no treatment if this was one, to pursue.

1. Was the lower court judge correct in this decision?
2. What is the proper standard for a judge to apply in making a treatment or nontreatment decision for an infant or young child?
3. When, if ever, should physicians seek a court order to overrule the decision of parents not to treat their handicapped or terminally ill child?
4. Draft a state statute that you believe would prevent cases like Baby Doe from recurring, but would still permit parents and physicians to withhold medical treatment that merely served to prolong death or intense suffering.

In thinking about this question it should be helpful to know that in 1983 the federal government sought to "solve" this problem by setting up a "Baby Doe Hotline" and requiring notices to be posted in all hospital delivery rooms and nurseries to the effect that "any person having knowledge that a handicapped infant is being discriminatorily denied food or customary medical care should immediately contact [the Handicapped Infant Hotline in Washington, D.C.]" which would then dispatch a federal team to investigate the allegation. After years of litigation, the U.S. Supreme Court ultimately ruled that the U.S. Department of Health and Human Services (HHS) which promulgated the regulations, had no congressional authority to enforce them. Bowen v. American Hospital Association, 476 U.S 610 (1986). In the meantime, Congress passed the Child Abuse Amendments of 1984, which required states receiving federal assistance for child abuse and neglect programs to take steps to protect handicapped infants. Among the provisions of the law was a clause that provided that treatment may be withheld if:

1. The infant is chronically and irreversibly comatose;
2. The provision of such treatment would merely prolong dying; not be effective in ameliorating or correcting all of the infant's life-threatening conditions; or otherwise futile in terms of survival of the infant; or
3. The provision of such treatment would be virtually futile in terms of the survival of the infant and the treatment itself under such circumstances would be inhumane.

Whether one of the exceptions apply is to be determined solely on the basis of "reasonable medical judgment," which later HHS regulations (promulgated under the statute) defined as "medical judgment that would be made by a reasonably prudent physician, knowledgeable about the case and the treatment possibilities with respect to the medical condition involved." It should be noted that this definition answers the question of whether nutrition and hydration can ever be withheld from an infant. The answer is that they can be withheld if they are not "appropriate" in the attending physician's "reasonable medical judgment." For more on Baby Doe see S. Elias & G. J. Annas, Reproductive Genetics and the Law 168-194 (1987); U.S. Commission on Civil Rights, Medical Discrimination Against Children with Disabilities (1989). Helga Kuhse and Peter Singer have argued that there should be a period of time after birth, perhaps 28 days, during which the child can be legally killed if it is severely handicapped. They propose that the decision should be made by the parents and physician, with the oversight of a hospital review committee. They base their proposal primarily on two rationales: (1) there is no moral justification for distinguishing between killing and letting die; and (2) focusing just on the best interests of the child neglects other important interests, such as those of parents, other children, potential future children, and society. H. Kuhse & P. Singer, Should the Baby Live? (1985).

(2) The AIDS epidemic has raised anew the issue of euthanasia. Patients with AIDS often require long term institutional care, which is scarce and expensive. It has been suggested that because most AIDS patients are gay or from minority groups, that such authoritarian care facilities may be hostile to them and actually encourage them to refuse treatment or kill themselves:

> It is reasonable, in such an atmosphere, to consider that HIV-infected will come to understand that it would be wise to exercise the right to refuse care. It need not be mandated. No legislation need even articulate such an unthinkable policy. But euthanasia can become a social reality, first for the HIV-infected, then for others who are institutionally bound, through a social unwillingness to develop other forms of health care services, ones which do not trample upon one's sense of personhood. [Schulman, AIDS Discrimination: Its Nature and Function, 12 Nova L. Rev. 1113, 1137 (1988).]

It should also be noted that although we generally frown on someone who wants to end his life, we applaud those who volunteer for experiments that will almost surely end their lives. See discussion of artificial heart experiments, chapter 9(C) pp. 900-921.

(3) Our reactions to both AIDS and the artificial heart speak to our utter inability to come to grips with death. Two of our most famous cultural artifacts concerning man's quest for immortality, Dracula and Frankenstein, speak eloquently of it. In Bram Stoker's novel of the immortal undead, Dracula, Mina Harker, who is slowly turning into a vampire, declares her "living will" to her husband in terms that make it clear that to her becoming a vampire (with its assurance of immortality) is itself a fate worse than death. She tells her husband the time for him to end her life will come:

> When you shall be convinced that I am so changed that it is better that I die that I may live. When I am thus dead in the flesh, then you will, without a moment's delay, drive a stake through me and cut off my head; or do whatever else may be wanting to give me rest! [B. Stoker, Dracula 393 (1897).]

Later, Dr. Seward, the vampire hunter, writes in his diary: "If this change should come, it would be necessary to take steps! . . . We should neither of us shrink from the task — awful though it be to contemplate. 'Euthanasia' is an excellent and comforting word! I am grateful to whoever invented it.'" Id. at 399.

In Mary Shelley's Frankenstein (1816), the central issue is not cheating immortality, but creating it by bringing the dead to life. Dr. Frankenstein explains his ambition:

> Life and death appeared to me ideal bounds, which I should first break through, and pour a torrent of light into our dark world. A new species would bless me as its creator and source; many happy and excellent natures would owe their being to me. No father could claim the gratitude of his child so completely as I should deserve theirs. Pursuing these reflections, I thought that if I could bestow animation upon lifeless matter, I might in process of time (although I now found it impossible) renew life where death had apparently devoted the body to corruption. [Id. at 52-53.]

George Bernard Shaw's injunction in his preface to The Doctor's Dilemma 86 (1905) is an apt note on which to end this chapter: "Do not try to live forever. You will not succeed."

CHAPTER

VII

Medical Personnel

Health care work is shaped by many complex and interrelated institutions and bodies of law: public licensing, private accreditation, educational programs, labor organizations and law, and antidiscrimination principles. Dozens of different categories of health care workers are licensed by the state. In addition, a variety of private professional organizations certify the competence and quality of individuals, organizations, and educational programs. Both state licensing authorities and private institutions often rely on these "private" accreditation determinations. Further, educational institutions — themselves licensed and accredited — play a semi-autonomous role in licensing and accrediting individual workers.

The first section of this chapter examines licensing and accreditation of health workers and the institutions that train them. It explores the powers and limitations conferred by a state license to practice, and examines the rights of individuals denied a state license or "private" accreditation or professional association membership. Chapter 5 discusses the use of state licensing to encourage quality medical care.

Section B describes the institutions that train and inculcate health care personnel, with particular attention to the overall supply of personnel, the patterns of financing the training of medical personnel, and the complex interrelationship between professional education, patient care and research.

Section C examines some legal issues that arise when health care workers attempt to form unions. Finally, Section D briefly considers the application of the antidiscrimination laws in the medical context.

As hospitals have become increasingly complex, an elaborate division of labor has evolved. Gone are the days when hospitals were staffed by doctors, nurses, and a large number of unskilled workers performing relatively undifferentiated tasks. Work has become specialized and subdivided into narrow functional responsibilities. A typical hospital budget in the late 1980s lists over 200 job categories, including 50 types of service and maintenance workers, 50 varieties of clerical workers, 40 categories of technical employees, and 35 different types of supervisors. Moreover, this listing understates the actual specialization of hospital employees, since similar payroll titles often include jobs with different functions, as when a "laboratory technician" title encompasses specialists in hematology, cytology, and urinalysis. Despite this diversity of hospital workers, this chapter focuses primarily on physicians and nurses.

A. Licensing and Credentialing Medical Personnel

M. Friedman, Capitalism and Freedom

Chapter 9, Occupational Licensure, 139-160 (1962)

The overthrow of the medieval guild system was an indispensable early step in the rise of freedom in the Western world. It was a sign of the triumph of liberal ideas, and widely recognized as such, that by the mid-nineteenth century, in Britain, the United States, and to a lesser extent on the continent of Europe, men could pursue whatever trade or occupation they wished without the by-your-leave of any governmental or quasi-governmental authority. In more recent decades, there has been a retrogression, an increasing tendency for particular occupations to be restricted to individuals licensed to practice them by the state.

Licensure is a special case of a much more general and exceedingly widespread phenomenon, namely, edicts that individuals may not engage in particular economic activities except under conditions laid down by a constituted authority of the state. Medieval guilds were a particular example of an explicit system for specifying which individuals should be permitted to follow particular pursuits.

Occupational licensure is by now very widespread. According to Walter Gellhorn, who has written the best brief survey I know, "By 1952 more than 80 separate occupations exclusive of 'owner-businesses,' like restaurants and taxicab companies, had been licensed by state law; and in addition to the state laws there are municipal ordinances in abundance, not to mention the federal statutes that require the licensing of such diverse occupations as radio operators and stockyard commission agents." . . . In the arguments that seek to persuade legislatures to enact such licensure provisions, the justification is always said to be the necessity of protecting the public interest. However, the pressure on the legislature to license an occupation rarely comes from the members of the public who have been mulcted or in other ways abused by members of the occupation. On the contrary, the pressure invariably comes from members of the occupation itself. Of course, they are more aware than others of how much they exploit the customer and so perhaps they can lay claim to expert knowledge.

Similarly, the arrangements made for licensure almost invariably involve control by members of the occupation which is to be licensed. Again, this is in some ways quite natural. If the occupation of plumbing is to be restricted to those who have the requisite capacity and skills to provide good service for their customers, clearly only plumbers are capable of judging who should be licensed. . . .

Licensure therefore frequently establishes essentially the medieval guild kind of regulation in which the state assigns power to the members of the profession. In practice, the considerations taken into account in determining who shall get a license often involve matters that, so far as a layman can see, have no relation whatsoever to professional competence. This is not surprising. If a few individuals are going to decide whether other individuals may pursue an occupation, all sorts of irrelevant considerations are likely to enter. . . .

Before discussing the advantages and disadvantages of licensing, it is worth noting why we have it and what general political problem is revealed by the tendency for such special legislation to be enacted. . . . Surely the explanation is different; it is that a producer group tends to be more concentrated politically than a consumer group.

. . . Each of us is a producer and also a consumer. However, we are much more specialized and devote a much larger fraction of our attention to our activity as a producer than as a consumer. We consume literally thousands if not millions of items. The result is that people in the same trade, like barbers or physicians, all have an intense interest in the specific problems of this trade and are willing to devote considerable energy to doing something about them. On the other hand, those of us who use barbers at all, get barbered infrequently and spend only a minor fraction of our income in barber shops. Our interest is casual. Hardly any of us are willing to devote much time going to the legislature in order to testify against the iniquity of restricting the practice of barbering.

The only way that I can see to offset special producer groups is to establish a general presumption against the state undertaking certain kinds of activities. Only if there is a general recognition that governmental activities should be severely limited with respect to a class of cases, can the burden of proof be put strongly enough on those who would depart from this general presumption to give a reasonable hope of limiting the spread of special measures to further special interests. . . .

MEDICAL LICENSURE

The medical profession is one in which practice of the profession has for a long time been restricted to people with licenses. Offhand, the question, "Ought we to let incompetent physicians practice?" seems to admit of only a negative answer. But I want to urge that second thought may give pause.

In the first place, licensure is the key to the control that the medical profession can exercise over the number of physicians. To understand why this is so requires some discussion of the structure of the medical profession. The American Medical Association is perhaps the strongest trade union in the United States. The essence of the power of a trade union is its power to restrict the number who may engage in a particular occupation. This restriction may be exercised indirectly by being able to enforce a wage rate higher than would otherwise prevail. If such a wage rate can be enforced, it will reduce the number of people who can get jobs and thus indirectly the number of people pursuing the occupation. This technique of restriction has disadvantages. There is always a dissatisfied fringe of people who are trying to get into the occupation. A trade union is much better off if it can limit directly the number of people who enter the occupation — who ever try to get jobs in it. The disgruntled and dissatisfied are excluded at the outset, and the union does not have to worry about them.

The American Medical Association is in this position. It is a trade union that can limit the number of people who can enter. How can it do this? The essential control is at the stage of admission to medical school. The Council on Medical Education and Hospitals of the American Medical Association approves medical schools. In order for a medical school to get and stay on its list of approved schools it has to meet the standards of the Council. . . .

Why does the Council's approval matter so much? If it abuses its power, why don't unapproved medical schools arise? The answer is that in almost every state in the United States, a person must be licensed to practice medicine, and to get the license, he must be a graduate of an approved school. In almost every state, the list of approved schools is identical with the list of schools approved by the Council on Medical Education and Hospitals of the American Medical Association. That is why the licensure provision is the key to the effective control of admission. It has a dual effect. On the one hand, the members of the licensure commission are always physicians and hence have some control at the step at which men apply for a license. This control is more limited in effectiveness than control at the medical school level.

Control over admission to medical school and later licensure enables the profession to limit entry in two ways. The obvious one is simply by turning down many applicants. The less obvious, but probably far more important one, is by establishing standards for admission and licensure that make entry so difficult as to discourage young people from ever trying to get admission. Though most state laws require only two years of college prior to medical school, nearly 100 per cent of the entrants have had four years of college. . . .

. . . [When medical leaders] explicitly comment on the desirability of limiting numbers to raise incomes they will always justify the policy on the grounds that if "too" many people are let in, this will lower their incomes so that they will be driven to resort to unethical practices in order to earn a "proper" income. The only way, they argue, in which ethical practices can be maintained is by keeping people at a standard of income which is adequate to the merits and needs of the medical profession.

. . . It is extraordinary that leaders of medicine should proclaim publicly that they and their colleagues must be paid to be ethical. And if it were so, I doubt that the price would have any limit. . . .

Control of entry is explicitly rationalized along these lines only at times like the Great Depression when there is much unemployment and relatively low incomes. In ordinary times, the rationalization for restriction is different. It is that the members of the medical profession want to raise what they regard as the standards of "quality" of the profession. The defect in this rationalization is a common one, and one that is destructive of a proper understanding of the operation of an economic system, namely, the failure to distinguish between technical efficiency and economic efficiency.

A story about lawyers will perhaps illustrate the point. At a meeting of lawyers at which problems of admission were being discussed, a colleague of mine, arguing against restrictive admission standards, used an analogy from the automobile industry. Would it not, he said, be absurd if the automobile industry were to argue that no one should drive a low quality car and therefore that no automobile manufacturer should be permitted to produce a car that did not come up to the Cadillac standard. One member of the audience rose and approved the analogy, saying that, of course, the country cannot afford anything but Cadillac lawyers! This tends to be the professional attitude. The members look solely at technical standards of performance, and argue in effect that we must have only first-rate physicians even if this means that some people get no medical service — though of course they never put it that way. Nonetheless, the view that people should get only the "optimum" medical service always lead to a restrictive policy, a policy that keeps down the number of physicians.

. . . I am myself persuaded that licensure has reduced both the quantity and quality of medical practice; that it has reduced the opportunities available to people who would like to be physicians, forcing them to pursue occupations they regard as less attractive; that it has forced the public to pay more for less satisfactory medical service, and that it has retarded technological development both in medicine itself and in the organization of medical practice. I conclude that licensure should be eliminated as a requirement for the practice of medicine.

When all this is said, many a reader, I suspect, like many a person with whom I have discussed these issues, will say, "But still, how else would I get any evidence on the quality of a physician. Granted all that you say about costs, is not licensure the only way of providing the public with some assurance of at least minimum quality?" The answer is partly that people do not now choose physicians by picking names at random from a list of licensed physicians; partly, that a man's ability to pass an examination twenty or thirty years earlier is hardly assurance of quality now; hence, licensure is not now the main or even a major source of assurance of at least minimum quality. But the major answer is very different. It is that the question itself reveals the tyranny of the status quo and the poverty of our imagination in fields in which we are laymen, and even in those in which we have some competence, by comparison with the fertility of the market. Let me illustrate by speculating on how medicine might have developed and what assurances of quality would have emerged, if the profession had not exerted monopoly power.

Suppose that anyone had been free to practice medicine without restriction except for legal and financial responsibility for any harm done to others through fraud and negligence. . . . Group practice in conjunction with hospitals would have grown enormously. Instead of individual practice plus large institutional hospitals conducted by governments or eleemosynary institutions, there might have developed medical partnerships or corporations — medical teams. These would have provided central diagnostic and treatment facilities, including hospital facilities. . . .

These medical teams — department stores of medicine, if you will — would be intermediaries between the patients and the physician. Being long-lived and immobile, they would have a great interest in establishing a reputation for reliability and quality. For the same reason, consumers would get to know their reputation. They would have the specialized skill to judge the quality of physicians; indeed, they would be the agent of the consumer in doing so, as the department store is now for many a product. In addition, they could organize medical care efficiently, combining medical men of different degrees of skill and training, using technicians with limited training for tasks for which they were suited, and reserving highly skilled and competent specialists for the tasks they alone could perform. . . .

Of course, not all medical practice would be done through such teams. Individual private practice would continue, just as the small store with a limited clientele exists alongside the department store, the individual lawyer alongside the great many-partnered firm. Men would establish individual reputations and some patients would prefer the privacy and intimacy of the individual practitioner. Some areas would be too small to be served by medical teams. And so on.

1. LICENSING AND PROFESSIONALISM: HISTORY AND THEORY

Although as a formal matter medical personnel and schools are licensed and regulated by state agencies, powerful private national organizations exert significant influence and produce a large degree of nationwide uniformity. The Federation of State Medical Boards, a voluntary association formed in 1912, prepares examinations used to license doctors in every state. While 126 medical schools are licensed by individual states, they are also accredited by the Council on Medical Education, a joint venture of the American Medical Association and the American Association of Medical Colleges (AAMC). Over

5000 residency programs, in 1700 hospitals provide the graduate clinical medical education prerequisite to certification by one of 24 national specialty boards. Traditionally the state has played little role in granting board certification or regulating graduate medical education. Rather, the individual specialty boards set and enforce standards for both residency training programs and board certification of individuals.

a. Critiques of Licensing and Accreditation

These venerable institutions have been criticized sharply from across the political spectrum. Milton Friedman rejects licensing from a free market framework. From a radical left-libertarian perspective, Ivan Illich, in his provocative book, Medical Nemesis (1976), argues that licensing has been used to create a fraudulent and immobilizing "medical clergy" with a "monopoly on deciding what constitutes disease, who is sick, and what ought to be done to him or her." Id. at 249. From a liberal orientation, Victor Fuchs criticizes state licensing as chronically ineffectual and irrelevant to any useful social purpose. Who Shall Live: Health, Economics and Social Choice (1974). He urges that "a reasonable compromise between the existing restrictive system and complete laissez-faire would be *institutional licensure,* which would restrict care to institutions and organizations that met licensure standards, while permitting them considerable freedom and flexibility in the use of personnel." Id. at 61.

A more radical, communitarian, change-oriented defense of state licensing of medical personnel rests on the perception that often isolated individuals can not exercise the "choice" advocated by Friedman from the right and by Illich from the left. Social, collective, or community effort is required to structure the services available for individual choice. State controlled licensing structures, for all their problems, are more open to democratic control, than either the "market" or elite professional credentialing mechanisms for structuring individual choice. For example, the expanded role of the nurse practitioner, described in *Sermchief,* infra, was defined through state regulation. How could market transactions or professional credentialing generate similar changes?

Despite criticisms, licensing and professional credentialing persist. Economist Kenneth Arrow defends these structures against the free market challenge, observing that "the general uncertainty about the prospects of medical treatment is socially handled by rigid entry requirements. These are designed to reduce the uncertainty in the mind of the consumer as to the quality insofar as this is possible. . . ." Uncertainty and the Economics of Medical Care, 53 Am. Econ. Rev. 941, 966 (1963). See also Leffler, Physician Licensure: Competition and Monopoly in American Medicine, 21 J.L. & Econ. 165 (1978).

b. Concepts of Professionalism

The concept of "professionalism," rooted in the ideas of the late 19th century, is perhaps even more powerfully influential than the enduring public and private organizational structures of licensing and accreditation. Sociological literature identifies professionals as people who 1) provide human services to clients rather than sell goods to customers and 2) are trained in a complex body of knowledge through an extensive educational process. The intense human importance of professional services and the sophistication of the professional's knowledge and expertise preclude control of cost or quality through traditional bureaucratic or market mechanisms. A core mission of professional education is to inculcate values to encourage self-criticism, single-minded devotion to an individual client, and an ethic of public service. See E. Friedson, Professional Dominance: The Social Structure of Medical Care (1970) at 81-104. T. Parsons, Introduction in M. Weber, The Theory of Social and Economic Organization (1947) at 59 et. seq.

It is easy enough to understand the difficulty of using market or bureaucratic mechanisms to determine the need for, quality, or cost of professional services. It is less clear that professional ethics provide a strong substitute to assure that professional services are of high quality, reasonable cost, and responsibility to the needs of clients and patients. In the language of the street, a professional license may be a license to steal. Friedson observes that several consequences flow from defining a social problem as "medical," and subject to the control of medical professionals. First, the problem is certified as demanding concern and solution. Second, the problem comes under the control of physicians, whether or not they have an interest or knowledge to solve it.

c. "The Corporate Practice of Medicine"

For most of the twentieth century, state law provided strong protection for physician monopoly over professional medical services. Most states interpreted physician licensing laws to prohibit corporations from employing physicians. So, for example, in the early 1970s, a group of Mexican Americans in San Antonio, Texas created a nonprofit corporation for the purpose of hiring physicians to serve people who had no other access to medical care. The Texas Medical Society objected, arguing state law barred physicians from working for a salary paid by an organization controlled by lay people. The consumer group sought to establish a constitutional right to organize a clinic controlled by the community it served. The courts upheld the ban on the corporate practice of medicine, saying, "By their very nature, the medical and legal professions are complex, esoteric disciplines, the practice or administration of which by the ignorant or untrained, historically and inevitably leads to the exploitation of a naive public." Garcia v. Texas State Board of Medical

Examiners, 384 F. Supp. 434, 438 (W.D. Tex. 1974), *aff'd,* 421 U.S. 995.

By the late twentieth century a very large proportion of physicians were salaried employees of a variety of organizations. Generally, the laws restricting corporate practice are simply ignored. "Nevertheless, the existence of corporate practice laws in many states threatens innovations in medical practice. [C]orporate practice laws are 'legal land-mines,' . . . half-buried on a field fast being built up with new forms of health organizations. Individuals attempting to establish new modes of health care delivery occasionally detonate a corporate practice land-mine." Note, The Corporate Practice of Medicine Doctrine: An Anachronism in the Modern Health Care Industry, 40 Vand. L. Rev. 445 (1987).

If the absolute prohibition on salaried practice of medicine is discarded, is there a need for other rules or mechanisms to assure that the physician's first loyalty will be to her patient rather than to the corporation that pays her? What form might that take?

2. THE POWERS AND LIMITS OF THE LICENSE TO PRACTICE

Sermchief v. Gonzales

680 S.W.2d 683 (Mo.1983)
En banc

This is a petition for a declaratory judgment and injunction brought by two nurses and five physicians employed by the East Missouri Action Agency (Agency) wherein the plaintiff-appellants ask the Court to declare that the practices of the Agency nurses are authorized under the nursing law of this state, §335.016.8, RSMo 1978 and that such practices do not constitute the unauthorized practice of medicine. . . . The holding below was against appellants. . . . We reverse.

The facts are simple and for the most part undisputed. The Agency is a federally tax exempt Missouri not-for-profit corporation that maintains offices in [four communities]. [It] provides medical services to the general public in fields of family planning, obstetrics and gynecology. . . . Some thirty-five hundred persons utilized these services during the year prior to trial. The Agency is funded from federal grants, Medicaid reimbursements, and patient fees. The programs are directed toward the lower income segment of the population. . . .

Appellant nurses . . . are duly licensed professional nurses in Missouri pursuant to the provisions of Chapter 335 and are employed by the Agency. Both nurses have had post-graduate special training in the field of obstetrics and gynecology. Appellant physicians are also employees of the Agency and duly licensed to practice medicine. . . . Respondents are the . . . Missouri

State Board of Registration for the Healing Arts (Board) . . . charged with the enforcement . . . of [the Act].

The services routinely provided by the nurses and complained of by the Board included, among others, the taking of history; breast and pelvic examinations; laboratory testing of Papanicolaou (PAP) smears, gonorrhea cultures, and blood serology; the providing of and giving of information about contraceptives . . . ; the dispensing of certain designated medications; and counseling services and community education. If the nurses determined the possibility of a condition designated in the standing orders or protocols that would contraindicate the use of contraceptives until further examination and evaluation, they would refer the patients to one of the Agency physicians. No act by either nurse is alleged to have caused injury or damage to any person. All acts by the nurses were done pursuant to written standing orders and protocols signed by appellant physicians. The standing orders and protocols were directed to specifically named nurses and were not identical for all nurses.

The statutes involved [provide]:

> It shall be unlawful for any person not now a registered physician within the meaning of the law to practice medicine or surgery in any of its departments, or to profess to cure and attempt to treat the sick and others afflicted with bodily or mental infirmities, or engage in the practice of midwifery in this state, except as herein provided. Section 334.010.
>
> This chapter does not apply to . . . nurses licensed and lawfully practicing their profession within the provisions of Chapter 335. . . .
>
> Definitions. — . . . [T]he following words and terms shall have the meanings indicated: . . .
>
> (8) "Professional nursing" is the performance for compensation of any act which requires substantial specialized education, judgment and skill based on knowledge and application of principles derived from the biological, physical, social and nursing sciences, including, but not limited to:
>
> (a) Responsibility for the teaching of health care and the prevention of illness to the patient and his family; or
>
> (b) Assessment, nursing diagnosis, nursing care, and counsel of persons who are ill, injured or experiencing alterations in normal health processes; or
>
> (c) The administration of medications and treatments as prescribed by a person licensed in this state to prescribe such medications and treatments; or
>
> (d) The coordination and assistance in the delivery of a plan of health care with all members of the health team; or
>
> (e) The teaching and supervision of other persons in the performance of any of the foregoing. Section 335.016.8(a)-(e).

At the time of enactment of the Nursing Practice Act of 1975, the following statutes were repealed:

> 2. A person practices professional nursing who for compensation or personal profit performs, *under the supervision and direction of a practitioner authorized to sign birth and death certificates,* any professional services requiring the application of principles of the biological, physical or social sciences and nursing skills in the care of the sick, in the prevention of disease or in the conservation of health. . . .
>
> Nothing contained in this chapter shall be construed as conferring any authority on any person to practice medicine or osteopathy or to undertake the treatment or cure of disease. Section 335.190, RSMo 1969.

The parties on both sides request that in construing these statutes we define and draw that thin and elusive line that separates the practice of medicine and the practice of professional nursing in modern day delivery of health services. A response to this invitation, in our opinion, would result in an avalanche of both medical and nursing malpractice suits alleging infringement of that line and would hinder rather than help with the delivery of health services to the general public. Our consideration will be limited to the narrow question of whether the acts of these nurses were permissible under §335. . . .

The legislature substantially revised the law affecting the nursing profession with enactment of the Nursing Practice Act of 1975.[5] Perhaps the most significant feature of the Act was the redefinition of the term "professional nursing." . . . Even a facile reading of that section reveals a manifest legislative desire to expand the scope of authorized nursing practices. Every witness at trial testified that the new definition of professional nursing is a broader definition than that in the former statute. . . . Most apparent is the elimination of the requirement that a physician directly supervise nursing functions. Equally significant is the legislature's formulation of an open-ended definition of professional nursing. The earlier statute limited nursing practice to "services . . . in the care of the sick, in the prevention of disease, or in the conservation of health." . . . The 1975 Act not only describes a much broader spectrum of nursing functions, it qualifies this description with the phrase "including, but not limited to." We believe this phrase evidences an intent to avoid statutory constraints on the evolution of new functions for nurses delivering health services. Under §335.016.8, a nurse may be permitted to assume responsibilities heretofore not considered to be within the field of

5. The impetus for the legislation was the ongoing expansion of nursing responsibilities. Several national commissions investigated the causes of and the implications of this phenomenon during the early 1970s. One committee concluded: "Professional nursing . . . is in a period of rapid and progressive change in response to the growth of biomedical knowledge, changes in patterns of demand for health services, and the evolution of professional relationships among nurses, physicians and other health professions." . . . The broadening of nursing roles necessitated altering existing nursing practice laws to reflect the changes in a nurse's professional duties. At the time the Missouri legislature acted, 30 states had amended their laws regulating the nursing profession. See Comment, Interpreting Missouri's Nursing Practice Act, 26 St. Louis U.L.J. 931, 931 n.1 (1982). Forty states currently have broadened nursing practice statutes. . . .

professional nursing so long as those responsibilities are consistent with her or his "specialized education, judgment and skill based on knowledge and application of principles derived from the biological, physical, social and nursing sciences." . . . The acts of the nurses herein clearly fall within this legislative standard. All acts were performed pursuant to standing orders and protocols approved by physicians. Physician-prepared standing orders and protocols for nurses and other para-medical personnel were so well established and accepted at the time of the adoption of the statute that the legislature could not have been unaware of the use of such practices. We see nothing in the statute purporting to limit or restrict their continued use.

Respondents made no challenge of the nurses' level of training nor the degree of their skill. They challenge only the legal right of the nurses to undertake these acts. We believe the acts of the nurses are precisely the types of acts the legislature contemplated when it granted nurses the right to make assessments and nursing diagnoses. There can be no question that a nurse undertakes only a nursing diagnosis, as opposed to a medical diagnosis, when she or he finds or fails to find symptoms described by physicians in standing orders and protocols for the purpose of administering courses of treatment prescribed by the physician in such orders and protocols.

The broadening of the field of practice of the nursing profession authorized by the legislature and here recognized by the Court carries with it the profession's responsibility for continuing high educational standards and the individual nurse's responsibility to conduct herself or himself in a professional manner. The hallmark of the professional is knowing the limits of one's professional knowledge. The nurse, either upon reaching the limit of her or his knowledge or upon reaching the limits prescribed for the nurse by the physician's standing orders and protocols, should refer the patient to the physician. There is no evidence that the assessments and diagnoses made by the nurses in this case exceeded such limits. . . .

3. THE LEGAL AUTHORITY OF LICENSED MEDICAL WORKERS

a. Changing Definitions of the Practice of Medicine and Nursing

State medical practice acts define the practice of medicine broadly and indeterminately, prohibiting anyone but licensed physicians from practicing medicine. Licensing laws allow any physician to perform any medical procedure and, for example, do not prohibit a dermatologist from performing brain surgery. As a practical matter, physician practice is limited by patient consent, fear of malpractice, and by the ability to obtain hospital staff privileges. Hospital staff privileges are, in turn, often limited by the hospital's sense of its own mission, the determinations of private accrediting organizations and the boards of the various medical specialties, and the hospital's fear of malpractice liability. See Chapter 5.

The definition of the "practice of nursing" became important in the 1930s, when organized nurses sought legislation to require that "all those who nurse for hire" be licensed. One traditional definition of the "practice of nursing," promulgated by the American Nurses Association in 1955 and adopted by 21 states, says:

> The practice of professional nursing means the performance for compensation of any acts in the observation, care, and counsel of the ill, injured, or infirm, or in the maintenance of health or prevention of illness of others, or in the supervision and teaching of other personnel, or the administration of medications and treatments as prescribed by a licensed physician or dentist; requiring substantial specialized judgment and skill and based on knowledge and application of the principles of biological, physical, and social science. The foregoing shall not be deemed to include acts of diagnosis or prescription of therapeutic or corrective measures. [A.N.A. Board Approves a Definition of Nursing Practice, 55 Am. J. Nursing 1474 (1955).]

The disclaimer that nursing did not include "acts of diagnosis or the prescription of therapeutic measures" created problems. Does a nurse violate such an act when she decides to start an intravenous fluid, or uses a defibrillator, or performs cardiopulmonary resuscitation? Doctors, nurses, and hospital administrators sought to allow some nurses to institute all of these procedures. In the 1960s, many state medical and nursing associations developed joint statements specifying the circumstances in which nurses could do particular tasks that might otherwise be thought to violate the nurse practice acts. Since the 1970s, 35 states have adopted legislation specifically authorizing the state nursing and medical regulatory boards to adopt such joint statements. See discussion, B. Bullough, The Current Phase in the Development of Nurse Practice Acts, 28 St. Louis L. Rev. 365, 374-376, 381 (1984).

In the 1970s, several factors led many groups to seek further changes in the legal definitions of nursing. First, growing medical understanding and new treatments motivated doctors, nurses, and hospitals to seek expansion of nurses' work. For example, new treatment regimens for cardiac arrhythmias could be performed efficiently and economically by trained nurses. Second, military corpsmen returning from Viet Nam had both the medical expertise and the political clout to persuade state legislatures to allow physicians to delegate a broader range of medical tasks to a new category of worker, the "physician assistant" or PA. Third, increased feminist consciousness led nurses, many of whom had received more intensive training than the male PAs, to seek similar authority. Chronic shortages of primary care givers, particularly in rural and low income areas, encouraged legal changes to allow nurses and other workers to provide a broader range of medical care. In the 1970s, all but a handful of states adopted laws to allow nurses, or other specified categories of medical care personnel, to provide a broader range of diagnosis and treatment. Some states, such as New York and Missouri, modified the general definition of nursing practice, while others, such as California and Colorado, recognized new categories of medical providers such as nurse practitioners.

The American Nurses Association opposes certification or other separate legislative identity for nurse specialists. Rather, the ANA seeks to follow the physicians' example of generalist licensing, under which every physician is legally free to do anything within the broad definition of medical practice. The ANA asserts that, "It is the function of the professional association to establish the scope and desirable qualifications required for each area of practice, and to certify individuals as competent to engage in specific areas of nursing practice." ANA, The Nursing Practice Act: Suggested State Legislation 3 (1981).

Nonetheless, all but ten states now provide for state certification of nurse specialists, most commonly including nurse practitioners, clinical specialists, anesthesiologists, and midwives. See Appendix to Bullough, supra, at 393-395. Nurse-midwives and nurse-anesthesiologists are the oldest nurse specialists. Since 1931, the American Association of Nurse Anesthetists has provided a certification to nurses that meet its requirements, though few states require special licensing or certification for such work. Since 1955, the American Academy of Nurse Midwifery has certified nurses who meet its requirements.

The volume of service provided by nurse practitioners mushroomed in the 1970s and 1980s, particularly in rural areas, group health programs, and on the West Coast. Several studies demonstrate that nurse practitioners provide primary care that is as good, or better, than that provided by physicians. Many barriers inhibit expansion of nurse practitioner services. Some insurers refuse to provide reimbursement. Other insurers provide reimbursement but seek to use nurse practitioners as a more economical alternative to physicians, while nurse practitioners seek to be paid rates comparable to those paid physicians for similar services. Some nurse practitioners have poor access to medical support or referral coverage. Spitzer, The Nurse Practitioner Revisited: Slow Death of a Good Idea, 310 N. Engl. J. Med. 1049 (1984).

b. Midwifery

Some of the most controversial issues of authorized nurse practice have involved childbirth and reproductive health services. Early in the twentieth century, most Americans were born at home with the help of a midwife.

Chapter 10 describes the history of midwifery in the United States in more detail.

Two types of midwives practice in the United States today: nurse midwives and independent or lay midwives. Nurse midwives are registered nurses who have graduated from a recognized school of nurse-midwifery and meet other qualifications for licensing. They are legally recognized in every state, though in many states are prohibited from practicing outside of a hospital or licensed clinic. Nurse-midwives who violate proscribed restrictions may lose their license. Lay midwives are sometimes registered nurses or have other formal training, but do not qualify under state licensing requirements to become nurse-midwives. Many states which adopted licensing provisions for nurse-midwives in recent years simultaneously repealed laws authorizing the licensing of lay midwives. About one-third of the states prohibit lay midwifery, one-third expressly provide for licensing or registration of lay midwives, and the remainder have no legislation specifically permitting or prohibiting lay midwifery. See Evenson, Midwives: Survival of An Ancient Profession, 7 Women's Rts. L. Rep. 313 (1983); and Note, Choice in Childbirth: Parents, Lay Midwives, and Statutory Regulation, 30 St. Louis U.L.J. 985 (1986).

Leigh v. Board of Registration in Nursing, 395 Mass. 670, 481 N.E.2d 1347 (1985), upheld the suspension of the license of a registered nurse, who was not certified as a nurse-midwife, but nonetheless delivered babies at home as a "lay midwife." Massachusetts law prohibits certified nurse-midwives from participating in home births, but allows lay people to do so. By contrast, Leggett v. Tennessee Board of Nursing, 612 S.W.2d 476 (Tenn. Ct. App. 1980), reversed a nursing board decision suspending the license of a nurse who helped women have babies at home. The court observed that lay people were not prohibited from working as midwives and questioned whether the legislature, much less the nursing board, could "constitutionally enact such a discriminatory rule. . . ." Id. at 480.

> Since midwifery is excluded from the practice of medicine, one performing within the scope of midwifery cannot be considered to be managing the medical aspects of a patient's care. [T]here were no ground for the Board to conclude that appellee was any less fit to serve as a Registered Nurse merely because she saw fit to serve as a midwife from time to time. If this were not true, a nurse could lose her license for serving occasionally as a secretary or a receptionist. . . .
>
> No one questions that in an emergency a mother and infant are better off in a hospital with a certified nurse-midwife or a physician. But given that some couples will continue to decide on home deliveries, the Board's decision overlooks the fact that certified nurse-midwives cannot participate in home deliveries.
>
> The Board's decision if allowed to stand would mean that anyone except licensed nurses could act as midwives. This is contrary to the goal of promoting public health. [Id. at 480-481.]

Bowland v. Municipal Court for Santa Cruz, 18 Cal. 3d 479, 134 Cal. 630, 638 (1976), upheld the conviction of five lay midwives for unauthorized practice of medicine for assisting in home births. California authorizes the licensing of nurse-midwives, and the court reasoned that, by implication, the legislature had prohibited unlicensed people from assisting with child birth.

The American College of Obstetricians and Gynecologists (ACOG) considers home birth as tantamount to child abuse; some hospitals withdraw staff privileges from doctors who help a woman to give birth at home. See G. Annas, Homebirth: Autonomy v. Safety, Hastings Cent. Rep. at 19 (Aug. 1978).

c. Licensing As a Restraint on Unconventional Practitioners and Treatments

Threat of license revocation deters treatments disapproved by the mainstream of the medical profession. In the mid-1970s, the AMA urged state licensing boards to prohibit acupuncture except when done in a research setting by, or under the direct supervision of, a physician. The Texas medical licensing board adopted such a rule. Consumers protested that no physician in the state was competent to provide or supervise the service, even though there were trained acupuncturists. Andrews v. Ballard, 498 F. Supp. 1038 (S.D. Tex. 1980), held that this rule, effectively denying Texas consumers access to acupuncture service, unreasonably burdened patients' constitutional right to choose among medical therapies. See also Rogers v. State Board of Medical Examiners, 371 So. 2d 1037 (Fla. Ct. App. 1979), *aff'd,* 387 So. 2d 937 (Fla. 1980), holding that the Florida constitution prohibits the state medical board from suspending the licence of a physician who prescribed vitamin therapy for arteriosclerosis. The court found that the treatment was safe, though probably ineffective, and that the physician had fully informed his patients of the facts known about it.

States have broad discretion to determine whether or not to license people who practice particular forms of therapy. For example, while a few states license naturopathic healers, most do not, and no federal constitutional provision requires that states recognize naturopathy as a discipline distinct from orthodox medical practice. See Idaho Association of Naturopathic Physicians, Inc. v. FDA, 582 F.2d 849 (4th Cir. 1978), *cert. denied,* 440 U.S. 976 (1979) and Beck v. McLeod, 240 F. Supp. 708 (E.D.S.C. 1965), *aff'd,* 382 U.S. 454 (1966).

State boards that license unconventional healers are sometimes held to have exceeded their legal authority. State ex rel. Iowa Department of Health v. Van Wyk, 320 N.W.2d 599 (Iowa 1982), struck down a state Board of Chiropractic Examiners regulation that sought to authorize chiropractors to perform acupuncture, withdraw blood specimens, and give advice on diet and nutrition. The court held that the Board had exceeded its statutory authority. Board of Optometry v. Florida Medical Association, Inc. 463 So. 2d 1213 (Fla. Ct. App. 1985), held that the Optometry Board exceeded its authority when it authorized optometrists to prescribe certain drugs.

d. Licensure as a Vehicle for Promoting Specific Social Policies

Medical licensure is usually seen as a means to promote particular concepts of technical, medical competence. See Chapter 5. It sometimes also promotes more general social policy. The lines between medical competence and social welfare are, of course, not always sharp.

For example, Massachusetts requires, as a condition of physician licensing, that doctors accept assignment of Medicare claims. Massachusetts Medical Society v. Dukakis, 637 F. Supp. 684 (D. Mass. 1986), *cert. denied,* 108 S. Ct. 229 (1987), held that the requirement is constitutional and consistent with the federal Medicare law. As another example, when consumer advocates were added to the California Medical Licensing Board, they promoted a rule that graduates of California medical schools cannot be licensed unless they have received minimal training in human sexuality. The California legislature, approving this requirement, noted that physicians knew less about this vital subject than ordinary lay people. See discussion, S. Law & S. Polan, Pain and Profit: The Politics of Malpractice, 187 (1978); and H. Lief & A. Karlen, Sex Education in Medicine (1976).

e. Licensing and Malpractice Liability

In a malpractice case should evidence that a practitioner was not licensed be regarded as per se evidence of negligence, as some evidence of negligence, or as irrelevant? With health care practitioners, as with automobile drivers, most courts exclude evidence about lack of a license as irrelevant and prejudicial. See, for instance Leahy v. Kenosha Memorial Hospital, 118 Wis. 2d 441, 348 N.W.2d 607 (Ct. App. 1984). But see Central Anesthesia Associates v. Worthy, 173 Ga. App. 150, 325 S.E.2d 819 (1984), *aff'd,* 254 Ga. 728, 333 S.E.2d 829 (1985), holding that violation of a licensing statute is negligence per se, since, if the unlicensed person had not been practicing, "it is possible that no injury or at least lesser injury would have resulted. . . ." Id. at 823. See discussion, Note, Nurse Malpractice in North Carolina: The Standard of Care, 65 N.C.L. Rev. 579 (1987).

4. PRACTITIONERS' CONSTITUTIONAL RIGHTS IN RELATION TO LICENSING AND PRIVATE CREDENTIALING

Treister v. American Academy of Orthopaedic Surgeons

78 Ill. App. 3d 746, 396 N.E.2d 1225 (App. Ct. 1979)

The plaintiff asserts that the American Academy of Orthopaedic Surgeons, . . . admits board-certified orthopaedic surgeons to fellowship and membership in the academy on the basis of standards and rules adopted by the academy and published in their by-laws. The plaintiff claims that active fellowship in the academy is a factor relied upon by hospitals in the granting of orthopaedic surgical privileges, by insurance companies in the establishment of malpractice rates, by courts in determining the expertise of an orthopaedic surgeon whose testimony is offered as expert, and by young physicians selecting a clinic in which to practice. The plaintiff characterizes membership in the academy as "a practical necessity for an orthopaedic surgeon who wishes to realize maximum potential achievement and recognition in his specialty."

In November 1974, the plaintiff applied for membership in the academy by submitting an application form. . . . In 1976 the plaintiff was interviewed by Dr. Louis Kolb, who informed him that there was adverse information in the plaintiff's file. Dr. Kolb predicted that this information would result in the rejection of his application. . . . Dr. Kolb . . . denied the plaintiff's request that he further specify the nature of the charges and that he identify the persons making the charges. In addition, Dr. Kolb refused to cite any authority for denying the plaintiff's request to see his file and to be informed of the charges and the identity of his accusers.

The plaintiff . . . wrote a letter to the academy attempting to rebut the charges as well as possible under the circumstances and requesting all available appeal rights and the right to be represented by counsel. [In 1976 the academy notified plaintiff that] . . . his application had been rejected, that the matter was closed and that he could not reapply for admission for three years.

The plaintiff claims that the procedures followed by the academy in rejecting his application violate the academy's by-laws. . . . The plaintiff claims that he meets every requirement for active fellowship except for election by two-thirds of the board of directors. The plaintiff, therefore, concludes that the procedure followed by the academy in rejecting his application was fundamentally unfair and that the rejection is void as a matter of common law.

[P]laintiff asks for a declaration that he is entitled to be informed of any charges against him; to be informed of the identity of his accusers; to have a fair hearing before an impartial adjudicator, and to have conclusions of fact fairly supported by evidence of record. . . . [He also asserts] . . . that "[B]ecause of the relationship between the academy, the American Medical Association, the hospitals of the State of Illinois, and the State of Illinois itself, rejection of Plaintiff's application is State action," [that deprives] . . . him of his liberty or property without due process of law. . . .

The academy . . . maintains that the traditional rule is that judicial review is not available to examine a decision by a private professional association to reject an application for initial membership. . . .The plaintiff contends that in recent years courts have decided that an applicant to professional associations has a right to a fair hearing on his application and to reasonable standards for admission. . . .

In 1961 the Supreme Court of New Jersey decided Falcone v. Middlesex County Medical Society, 34 N.J. 582, 170 A.2d 791, wherein it affirmed an order of the trial court directing the Middlesex County Medical Society to admit the plaintiff to full membership. The society's rejection of the plaintiff's application was based on an unwritten membership requirement which the court characterized as patently arbitrary and unreasonable. In *Falcone,* the evidence revealed that the local hospitals required all their staff physicians to be members of the society, and that the society's refusal to admit the plaintiff to membership had serious adverse economic and professional effects on him. The court, in arriving at its decision to permit judicial review as a matter of policy, stated:

> When courts originally declined to scrutinize admission practices of membership associations they were dealing with social clubs, religious organizations, and fraternal associations. Here the policies against judicial intervention were strong and there were no significant countervailing policies. When the courts were later called upon to deal with trade and professional associations exercising virtually monopolistic control, different factors were involved. The intimate personal relationships which pervaded . . . [these] organizations were hardly in evidence and the individual's opportunity of earning a livelihood and serving society in his chosen trade or profession appeared as the controlling policy consideration. [I]n a case presenting sufficiently compelling factual and policy considerations, judicial relief will be available to compel admission to membership. . . .

Undoubtedly, the court's decision was influenced by the society's virtual monopoly over the use of local hospital facilities and the fact that the plaintiff could not successfully continue his practice of surgery and obstetrics without the use of these facilities. . . .

In Pinsker v. Pacific Coast Society of Orthodontists (1969), 1 Cal. 3d 160, 81 Cal. Rptr. 623, 460 P.2d 495, the plaintiff argued that exclusion from several dental organizations would deprive him of educational, financial, and professional advantages. The California Supreme Court held that an applicant for membership has a judicially enforceable right to have his application considered in a manner comporting with the fundamentals of due process, including the showing of cause for rejection. The court stated:

> Because of the unique position in the field of orthodontics occupied by defendant AAO and its constituent organizations, membership therein, although not economically necessary in the strict sense of the word . . . , would appear to be a practical necessity for a dentist who wishes not only to make a good living as an orthodontist but also to realize maximum potential achievement and recognition in such specialty. . . .

On remand the defendants presented their reason for denying membership to the plaintiff. However, the plaintiff was not permitted to respond to the charges. The case again reached the State Supreme Court wherein it held that whenever a private association is legally required to refrain from arbitrary action, the association's action must be both substantively rational and procedurally fair. (Pinsker v. Pacific Coast Society of Orthodontists (1974), 12 Cal. 3d 541, 116 Cal. Rptr. 245, 526 P.2d 253.) The court also declared that "fair procedure" requires that before denial of the application, the applicant must be notified of the reason for the proposed rejection and given a fair opportunity to defend himself.

. . . [Illinois cases draw a distinction between expulsion and exclusion.] Although Illinois courts will require a hospital to follow its by-laws in revoking a physician's staff privileges . . . they will not review the denial of an application for appointment to the medical staff. . . .

In determining whether we should permit judicial review of the denial of the plaintiff's membership application, we must weigh the importance of two values which are in conflict in this situation. On the one hand, we recognize the necessity of judicial restraint from interfering with or regulating the affairs and decisions of a private, voluntary association. However, we also find it unconscionable that a private association could deprive an individual of the right to pursue his or her profession because of a personality conflict, his or her race or religion, or, as the plaintiff suggests in his brief, testimony on behalf of plaintiffs in malpractice actions.

Balancing these two interests, we hold that our courts can review the application procedures of a private association when membership in the organization is an economic necessity. We approve of the opinions . . . which hold that a medical society cannot arbitrarily deny membership to an applicant when the society controls access to local hospital facilities and thus can deprive the applicant of his ability to practice medicine. We find, however, that the plaintiff has not alleged that membership in the American Academy of Orthopaedic Surgeons is an economic necessity. Membership is not a requisite to hospital staff privileges as evidenced by the fact that the plaintiff is a member of the attending staff at seven Chicago hospitals. In addition, the plaintiff was board-certified and licensed by the State without academy membership.

The plaintiff's complaint alleges that membership in the academy is a "practical necessity . . . to realize maximum potential achievement and recognition in [his] specialty," language used by the California Supreme Court in *Pinsker.* We refrain from following *Pinsker,* however, because such a holding would result in complaints for judicial review of every application rejection by a voluntary association since membership in most organizations results in some professional or economic benefits. . . . (See Blatt v. University of Southern California (1970), 5 Cal. App. 3d 935, 85 Cal. Rptr. 601, plaintiff sought to compel membership in the Order of the Coif, a national honorary legal society.)

Although in this case we sympathize with the plaintiff's frustration with the academy's refusal to give him the courtesy of an explanation of the denial of his application, we believe the courts must refrain from interfering in the affairs of a private association absent a showing of economic necessity. . . .

SIMON, Presiding Justice, dissenting:

Dr. Treister is entitled to more from this court than sympathy. . . . The Academy is not simply a private body, accepting and rejecting applicants according to its private needs and desires. . . . Rather, it aspires to a more exalted function, as guardian of the profession and of the public generally. . . . The Academy holds itself out as the sole legitimate organization of its kind in the profession, and is widely recognized as such. It is a monopoly; and it is affiliated with the A.M.A., itself a monopoly, and no doubt with many local groups. No one who chooses (and, unsuspecting, trains, and practices) to become an orthopaedic surgeon in the United States or Canada can escape its jurisdiction. Indirectly, therefore, the public health is at stake. The power of such an association, tinged with a public stature or purpose . . . , almost a private, specialized government, should not be unbridled, but should be viewed judicially as a fiduciary power to be exercised in a reasonable and lawful manner. . . .

The majority underrates the Academy's capacity to harm Dr. Treister. It is true that he has so far done quite well without Academy membership; but that is because until recently his inexperience has made him obviously unripe for membership, so that his nonmembership has been perceived as routine, temporary, and insignificant. From now on, things will be different. [H]ospitals and insurance companies rely on Academy membership. [They] know that almost all Board-certified orthopaedic surgeons become members of the Academy two years after Board certification. A questionnaire or application form filled out by an orthopaedic surgeon who has not been admitted to Academy membership two years after this certification raises serious questions and can substantially impair the practitioner's career. The revelation that Dr. Treister has been rejected by the Academy is going to "red-flag" every application for staff privileges or insurance that he will ever make. . . .

The more subtle effects of rejection could prove even more crippling. . . . Because a single patient is likely to see an orthopaedic surgeon only rarely over the course of a lifetime, while he might see an internist many times, the surgeon is peculiarly dependent on referrals. Referring doctors often use Academy membership to verify their impression of specialists, and may even find a doctor for a referral by examining the Academy membership list. . . . Dr. Treister may some day desire privileges at new hospitals, which will be influenced by his rejection.

The majority's fear that there will be no way to draw the line if we allow relief to Dr. Treister is therefore unfounded. [T]he fact that the *Blatt* court did hold for the Order of the Coif in California under the *Pinsker* standard shows that distinctions can be made. Of course there will be more cases until the law is firmly settled; but that is a commonplace of the common law method.

On the other side of the balance, the Academy's legitimate interest is lighter than the majority supposes. It is important to note how modest is Dr. Treister's prayer for relief. He does not seek to compel the Academy to admit him to membership. He asks only that it consider his application fairly, in accordance with its own bylaws and the principles of ethics established by the . . . [AMA]. There should be nothing directly offensive to the Academy about doing in fact what it publicly professes to do.

After his defeat in the state courts, Dr. Treister and a colleague with a similar complaint, filed an antitrust claim in the federal courts. Preliminary skirmishes over discovery consumed six years and generated four district and circuit court opinions. Marrese v. American Academy of Orthopaedic Surgeons, 470 U.S. 373 (1985), held that the question whether the antitrust claim was precluded by the state adjudication should be resolved under state law. On remand, the federal district court held that state res judicata principles did not preclude the federal claim. 628 F. Supp. 918 (N.D. Ind. 1986). For further discussion of the antitrust claims see Chapter 7, Sec. D-3-c.

5. PRACTITIONERS' CONSTITUTIONAL RIGHTS IN RELATION TO LICENSING AND PRIVATE CREDENTIALING

a. Liberty to Practice vs. State Power to Regulate

Under the police power, states have broad authority to set licensing requirements for physicians and other health workers. In 1889, the Supreme Court rejected the claim of an eclectic practitioner who argued that a statute requiring that physicians graduate from a "reputable" medical college denied him the right to practice his calling and deprived him of liberty without due process of law. Dent v. West Virginia, 129 U.S. 114 (1889).

b. Limits on State Freedom to Delegate Public Power to Private Organizations

Many state licensing laws give professional organizations a large role in determining who should practice. Indeed, the power to control who is entitled to work is considered the hallmark of a true profession. The U.S. constitution allows states broad latitude to delegate power to professional organizations. Upholding a Texas requirement that members of the state optometry board be designated by a particular professional association, the Supreme Court said, "Unless a classification trammels fundamental personal rights or is drawn upon inherently suspect distinctions such as race, religion, or alienage, our decisions presume the constitutionality of the statutory discriminations and require only that the classification challenged be rationally related to a legitimate state interest." Friedman v. Rogers, 440 U.S. 1, 17 (1979).

Most state constitutions do not restrain legislative decisions to delegate licensing authority to private professional organizations. See, for instance, Clark v. State ex rel. Mississippi State Med. Association, 381 So. 2d 1046 (1980). A few states courts have held that laws that delegate licensing power to private professional organizations violate state constitutions. The New Jersey Supreme Court invalidated a law that empowered the state medical society to approve the trustees of Blue Shield organizations. The court explained:

> a power to determine who shall have the right to engage in an otherwise lawful enterprise may not validly be delegated by the Legislature to a private body which, unlike a public official, is not subject to public accountability, at least where the exercise of such power is not accompanied by adequate legislative standards or safeguards whereby an applicant may be protected against arbitrary or self-motivated action on the part of such private body. [Group Health Insurance v. Howell, 40 N.J. 436, 445, 193 A.2d 103 (1963).]

See United Chiropractors of Washington, Inc. v. State, 90 Wash. 2d 1, 578 P.2d 38 (1978) (similar challenge to a statute that gave each of two chiropractic associations power to appoint three of the seven members of the state licensing board). Commonwealth ex rel. Kane v. McKechnie, 467 Pa. 430, 358 A.2d 419 (1976), found that a requirement that the president of the state dental society automatically served on the state dental board violated the Pennsylvania constitution.

c. The State must meet Constitutional Guarantees of Due Process when it Suspends or Denies a Practitioners' License

The due process clauses of the fifth and fourteenth Amendments prohibit the federal and state governments from depriving citizens of liberty or property without due process of law. These provisions reflect both a distrust of governmental power and a recognition that individual liberty requires protection of the material base necessary to survival and the exercise of all other freedoms. While traditionally "property" took the form of land and personal material possessions, in modern society people increasingly depend upon more complex forms of property — including licenses to practice a profession, government entitlements, pensions and insurance. See C. Reich, The New Property, 73 Yale L.J. 733 (1964). Since 1971, the Supreme Court has recognized that the due process guarantee applies to government entitlements and largess, as well as to more traditional forms of property. Goldberg v. Kelly, 397 U.S. 254 (1970). Basic respect for individual dignity and liberty demands that before an important benefit, entitlement, license, or franchise can be denied, the individual must be told the basis for the adverse government action and be afforded an opportunity to object.

i. Notice of Charges

"Unprofessional conduct" is a common ground for suspending licenses. Generally courts have rejected the claim that this standard is unconstitutionally vague, at least when it is applied to conduct widely recognized as unprofessional. So, for example, Ward v. Oregon State Board of Nursing, 226 Or. 128, 510 P.2d 554 (1973), upheld revocation of a nurse's license for unprofessional conduct when she helped her daughter work as a registered nurse, knowing that her daughter was not in fact a nurse. But Tuma v. Board of Nursing, 100 Idaho 74, 593 P2d 711 (1979), reversed a six month suspension for "unprofessional conduct" when a nurse discussed laetrile treatment with a terminally ill cancer patient, without the physician's permission. The court suggested that the board might legitimately have prohibited this conduct by a specific rule, but held that the ban on unprofessional conduct did not give nurses sufficient warning that the conduct was prohibited.

ii. Right to be Heard by an Impartial Decision-Maker

Practitioners have a right to a fair and impartial hearing in any disciplinary proceeding that may result in state deprivation of important liberty or property interests. In Gibson v. Berryhill, 411 U.S. 564 (1973), the Court held that an optometry board composed entirely of members of an association that regarded for-profit corporations as unethical could not fairly adjudicate a claim against an optometrist working with such a corporation. See also Wall v. American Optometric Association, Inc., 379 F. Supp. 175 (N.D. Ga.), *summarily aff'd, sub nom.* Wall v. Hardwick, 419 U.S. 888 (1974).

However, Withrow v. Larkin, 421 U.S. 35 (1975), upheld a Wisconsin procedure under which a state board composed of physicians investigated allegations of physician misconduct, prosecuted complaints, adjudicated misconduct, and determined the penalty to be imposed. A Washington court held that such a process met state due process norms. Matter of Johnston, 99 Wash. 2d 466, 633 P.2d 457 (1983). Is there any justification for allowing physicians to avoid the traditional requirement of separation of prosecutorial and adjudicatory functions?

d. Due Process and Private Associations

Decisions of "private" credentialing and professional associations have a large impact on individual opportunities to practice. A physician's ability to obtain hospital staff privileges often depend upon board certification. Eligibility to serve on a state licensing board is often tied to membership in a particular professional association. Rightly or wrongly, certification and professional society membership signal skill, training, and character both to other medical care professionals and to consumers.

Nonetheless, as the decision in *Treister* suggests courts have been reluctant to extend the due process standards applicable to official state bodies to the actions of private associations denying individuals membership or credentials. Classic liberal political theory draws a sharp distinction between public power and concentrated private power, seeing the former as dangerous to individual liberty and the latter as benign. Furthermore, people who place great faith in markets argue that private organizations should be free to compete, untrammeled by external requirements that they treat people with the basic fairness demanded by due process. For a vigorous argument for expanded judicial scrutiny of the fairness of the decisions of "private" organizations see, Note, Exclusion from Private Associations, 74 Yale L.J. 1313 (1965). For a critique of the trend toward greater public accountability of private groups, see Note, Judicial Intervention in Admissions Decisions of Private Professional Associations, 49 U. Chi. L. Rev. 840 (1982).

B. Educating Medical Personnel

1. THE ORGANIZATION OF MEDICAL AND NURSING EDUCATION AND SUPPLY OF DOCTORS AND NURSES

K. Ludmerer, Learning To Heal: The Development of American Medical Education

3-7, 166-189, 235-242, 245-254 (1985)

A century ago, being a medical student in America was easy. No one worried about admission, for entrance requirements were lower than they were for a good high school. Instruction was superficial and brief. The terms lasted only sixteen weeks, and after the second term the M.D. degree was automatically given, regardless of a student's academic performance. Teaching was by lecture alone. Thus, students were spared the onerous chores of attending laboratories, clinics, and hospital wards. Indeed, except for the enterprising and affluent few who would bribe patients into submitting to an examination, students would often graduate without ever having touched a patient.

If this mode of medical teaching seems foreign to contemporary eyes, the organization and structure of the medical school are equally unrecognizable. In the post-Civil War era the typical faculty consisted of only seven or eight instructors. The schools were owned by the professors, who operated them for profit. For that reason medical schools were called "proprietary schools." Medical teaching was a part-time activity, a side business to one's private practice. Since laboratories and hospital facilities were not utilized in medical education, only modest resources were needed to run a medical school. A second floor above a corner drug store would do; a school that had a building of its own was richly endowed. Very few schools had university affiliations or were connected with teaching hospitals, and medical research was almost nonexistent.

American medical education has changed dramatically in the last century. Medical training has ceased to be a casual and superficial experience. Quite the contrary — it has become arduous, long, and demanding. Students are no longer taught by lectures alone. Instead, through laboratory instruction and clinical clerkships, they are made active participants in their own learning process. The schools — with their immense plants, sophisticated laboratories, capacious teaching hospitals, and large, full-time faculties — have become factories for the production of well-trained doctors and the pursuit of medical research. American medical education, once subservient to European medical education, has become the best in the world. . . .

Learning to heal, like every other type of learning, is profoundly influenced by the institutional framework in which instruction is carried out. For the new educational ideals to be implemented, an institutional revolution was required as well: the proprietary school had to be abandoned, and in its place had to be created the modern university medical school. Between 1885 and 1925 this transition occurred. Large sums of money were raised, new laboratories and facilities were constructed, teaching hospitals were acquired, an army of full-time faculty was assembled, and a bureaucratic administrative structure appeared. By the 1920s medical schools had assumed a corporate form. The result was a system of medical education that has been constant for the past sixty years, even though there have been many changes in the content of medical knowledge and the patterns of medical practice.

These changes in medical education were interrelated with changes in the medical profession. Before the Civil War, there were only private practitioners in America, and all medical teaching was provided by practitioners as a sideline to their medical practices. In the mid-nineteenth century, this situation began to change. As the growth of medical knowledge accelerated, the production, assessment, and transmission of knowledge became a full-time activity. Accordingly, a new class of doctors — the full-time professor — took responsibility for those functions. By the late nineteenth century, academic medicine was a powerful force on the American medical scene, and the medical scholar had assumed an identity distinct from that of the ordinary practitioner. . . .

The dominance of academic physicians in these events explains two of the most conspicuous features of the development of American medical education: the rise of medical research, and the movement of medical education to the universities. Academic physicians were medical scholars. They not only wanted to have full-time careers in medical teaching; they wanted to advance medical knowledge, just as medical professors in Germany were doing. Ultimately, research became as much a function of the modern medical school as good teaching was — some would say it even became the primary function. In America the natural milieu for advanced scholarship was the university. As medical scientists struggled to professionalize their field, their greatest allies were university presidents, who saw that the prestige of their respective universities would be enhanced if they controlled strong medical schools. The rise of academic medicine, the development of American medical research, and the movement of medical education into the universities proceeded hand-in-hand.

Contrary to popular perception, neither Abraham Flexner nor the American Medical Association (AMA) participated in the creation of modern American medical education. Both played important roles in its later development, but by that time the conceptual revolution in how medicine should be taught had already taken place and the university medical school had already appeared. Nevertheless, both Flexner and the AMA profoundly influenced the final form that the system took. Each insisted that only research-oriented university schools should be permitted to exist. In their minds, there was no room for "practical" schools — schools run by private practitioners where up-to-date teaching methods were employed but research was not promoted. . . . The enthronement of research and the elimination of the "practical" schools represented but two of the innumerable choices that were made, choices that were made not only by academic physicians and university leaders, but by the public as well. Research would not have prospered had the public not been willing to help finance its medical schools; "practical" schools would not have been eliminated had the public not supported the state licensing laws that exterminated them. . . .

STATE LICENSING AND THE RISE OF THE AMA

At the time of the Flexner report of 1910, the era of the proprietary medical school in America was already rapidly coming to an end. From 1906, the peak year, to 1910, the number of medical schools had fallen from 162 to 131, and more closures were on the way. Of the schools in existence in 1910, 37 had total enrollments of fewer than 50 students apiece, and 66 had enrollments of fewer than 100 students. Students were staying away from proprietary schools, which had ceased to be profitable ventures.

Nevertheless, medical schools of low quality still existed in 1910 because of the absence of strong licensing laws. Since the 1870s, licensing boards had been established in most states to certify medical schools and examine applicants for the license to practice, but in general the boards were weak and ineffective, and a few were even corrupt. . . .

. . . As a result, few checks existed on who was allowed to practice medicine. As late as 1906, thirteen states still granted medical licenses to nongraduates. For the situation to be corrected, strong laws had to be enforced, and in every state, not just in some states, because graduates of weak schools could migrate to states with less exacting requirements. Without effective licensing laws, physicians who still thought they could operate medical schools for profit were free to try.

In the wake of the Flexner report, an aroused public was finally ready to demand that state boards take their duties seriously. . . .

. . . In every state over the next several years, tough new laws were passed or existing laws strengthened. As one requirement of the laws, state boards passed judgment upon the medical schools of the country, and only graduates of "approved" medical schools were permitted to apply for the license to practice medicine. This requirement quickly brought about the demise of weak schools that failed to elevate their standards. Some of these schools were fraudulent; others were well intentioned but lacking in resources. The result, however, was the same for all: they were decapitated by legislative ax.

The enactment of licensing laws was not accomplished painlessly. Many persons, including many who recognized the merits of a scientific medical education, anguished over the thought that governmental regulation would abridge individual freedom. Although recognizing the need for well-trained doctors, they still respected the right of anyone who wished to operate a medical school or of anyone who so desired to practice medicine. . . .

Nevertheless, by the early 1900s broad historical forces were inexorably operating in behalf of rigorous licensing legislation. The country had become vastly more complex since the days of the founding fathers. For decades, the classic concept of laissez-faire had been giving way to the idea that the state and federal governments should take more active roles in the regulation of society's affairs. The creation of a system of tough, universally enforced state licensing laws reflected this changing view toward the responsibilities of government.

. . . Because the layman had little ability to distinguish among those with medical licenses, and because the medical profession privately had not succeeded in eliminating the inferior schools, society had only one choice: to assume that responsibility itself. . . . In short, Flexner and Pritchett maintained, the private freedoms lost were less important than the public benefits gained. This was the same justification as that given for the entry of the state into many other spheres of activity at this time.

Acceptance of this new role of government was made easier by the fact that state licensing offered a political solution compatible with the prevailing political ethic of the period. Reformers argued that control of licensing boards should be in the hands of responsible medical educators. State boards should no longer be viewed as political payoffs but should be administered, to use Flexner's words, by "trained experts."

. . . The Association of American Medical Colleges (AAMC) worked with licensing boards in each of the states, as well as with the Federation of State Medical Boards and the National Board of Medical Examiners. However, the strongest voice was that of the Council on Medical Education of the AMA, whose power in this area was profound. In the period following 1910, judgments by the council regarding the educational merits of the country's medical schools came to have the force of law. State boards decided whether to honor or reject a school's diploma based on the council's assessment of the school's qualifications.

The AMA of the early 1900s was a much different organization from the AMA of the nineteenth century, which had been a weak, ineffectual, provincial society. Based on a scheme of reorganization in which membership in a county society brought with it membership in the state and national organizations, membership in the AMA rose from 8401 in 1900 to 70,146 in 1910. Contrary to its conservative image of the present, the AMA between 1900 and 1920 supported many liberal causes, including pure food and drug legislation, more extensive public health measures, a federal health department, and compulsory health insurance. In addition, the AMA for the first two decades of the century provided a vehicle for collaboration between practitioners and professors. Indeed, during that time, a number of university medical teachers served as presidents of the organization. This situation prevailed until the 1920s, when professors and practitioners went their separate ways, with academic influence in the AMA remaining only in the university-dominated Council on Medical Education. Thereafter the AMA retained the ascendancy in political and economic affairs of concern to practitioners but not in matters of education and research.

The AMA's role in the development of American medical education is long overdue for critical evaluation. Conventional wisdom — firmly entrenched in the literature of history, sociology, political science, and medicine — deems the AMA the chief architect of reform. But this mythical view receives no confirmation from the historical facts. . . .

. . . By [1909] the outline of the country's present system of medical education was already firmly in place. The new educational concepts had been enunciated and accepted by the profession at large; universities had usurped control of medical education from the proprietary schools; the educational system had grown enormously and was producing medical students with much better preparation than before; a German-influenced academic elite had established themselves as the leaders of educational reform; and the circumstances had become ripe for an outpouring of medical philanthropy. All this had occurred without any direct contribution from the AMA. . . .

It is also difficult to assign the AMA an exclusive role in the developments that occurred after 1910. The final events in creating the modern medical school — the acquisition of reliable sources of funds; the maturation of academic medicine; and the rise of the teaching hospital — proceeded for the most part independently of the AMA. Although the AMA supported those developments and worked vigorously in their behalf, many organizations and persons besides the AMA, as previously discussed, played even larger roles, and public sentiment also shifted firmly in favor of those causes. Indeed, the system that resulted was not entirely what the AMA wished. Had the AMA got its way, strict full-time positions in the clinical departments would never have been created.

It would be a grave mistake, however, to view the AMA as an insignificant agency. It served medical education in many ways, its most important contribution occurring after 1910 as it helped procure strong state licensing laws. Between 1910 and 1930, its power in this arena was awesome. The AMA could think of the problems of medical education in a national way that even the strongest schools, concerned with their own particular problems, could not. Well organized, well financed, highly respected, and exceptionally adroit in the use of public relations, the AMA became the strongest force for state licensing. Herein lay its great impact on the reform of medical education. It was a role that was profound, even if much more circumscribed than commonly realized.

Licensing laws had a dual effect on American medical education. They brought about the death of the proprietary school, and they also helped standardize medical education at the university schools that remained. In establishing legal requirements, licensing boards followed guidelines prepared by the AMA and AAMC. In this way, medical educators collectively influenced the boards; few of them disagreed with the general principles incorporated into the state laws. Once licensing laws were established, however, schools had to yield to the dictates of the state boards. Even if a school strongly disagreed with the particulars of a state law — or merely thought a particular detail was foolish — it had no choice but to submit. Medical schools thus became bound by the rules of the larger system they had helped create.

Standardization was much needed. In the early twentieth century, demand for physicians' services had been rapidly growing. The successes of scientific medicine and the attendant publicity they had received made the public eager to have doctors readily available. At the same time, society had become much more mobile. With increasing regularity, doctors were practicing in areas other than where they had been trained. This posed a problem: how was the public to know which physicians it could trust? Before the new state licensing laws were passed, the public knew for certain the quality only of physicians who had attended local schools. . . .

The new licensing laws solved this problem. A medical license now certified a doctor's credentials to a public that might not be familiar with his place of training. Standardization thus allowed doctors to be distributed safely and efficiently to the expanding national market. A doctor trained at any school could now practice almost anywhere in the country with the public's confidence. . . .

a. Organization of Medical Education

In 1986, 126 U.S. medical schools offered four year programs training 66,604 medical students. Between 1960 and 1980, the annual number of medical school graduates in the U.S. doubled, and 40 new schools were created. All schools are affiliated with a university and accredited by the Liaison Committee on Graduate Medical Education, a private credentialing organization supported by the AMA and the American Association of Medical Colleges.

To become a doctor, college graduates must complete a four year program of basic sciences and clinical education. Since the 1960s, specialization has become the norm. Most states require that medical school graduates complete a one-year internship before they can be licensed. All but a handful of medical school graduates go on to receive specialty training in a residency program. This practice-oriented graduate medical education (GME) is far more decentralized and diverse than undergraduate medical education. About 5000 residency programs, in more than 1700 hospitals and health care facilities in the U.S., are accredited by 24 separate specialty review committees. About half of all residents receive training in a major medical center hospital associated with a medical school, but even in these institutions, the program in each specialty is independent. Current information on enrollment in medical schools and residency programs is published each year in the September volume of the Journal of the American Medical Association. See J. Schofield, New and Expanded Medical Schools, Mid-Century to the 1980s (1984).

i. The Aggregate Supply of Physicians

In the decades following World War II, most analysts perceived that there were not enough physicians. In 1966, the Surgeon General lamented, "We shall never have all the physician manpower we need." E. Ginzberg, A Hard Look at Cost Containment, 316 N. Engl. J. Med. 1151 (1987). Congress provided capitation grants to encourage medical schools to expand their enrollment. Many states provided funds to create new medical schools. Congress also changed the immigration laws to allow foreign trained doctors to settle in the United States. From 1967 to 1980, the ratio of actively practicing doctors to the rest of the population rose by over 50 percent. Between 1970 and 1986, the number of physicians per 100,000 population increased from 148 to 220. Id. at 1152.

These programs were so successful in increasing the number of physicians that in 1980 a prestigious national commission reported that by 1990 the nation would have a very large excess of physicians, particularly in surgical specialties and cardiology. Report of the Graduate Medical Education National Advisory Committee [GEMENAC] to the Secretary (1980). GEMENAC found these surpluses disturbing. An oversupply of physicians can lead to provision of marginally useful services, which can be dangerous and are certainly costly. In many specialties a surplus of physicians means that critical skills diminish when they are not used. See Chapter 5.

GEMENAC thus made these recommendations that medical schools voluntarily decrease enrollment; that specialty boards restrain themselves from certifying increased residency positions; and that the federal government enforce the law ending immigration preference for foreign doctors that had been adopted by Congress in 1976. By 1987 each of these measures — and a decline in the numbers of people applying to medical school — had a marginal effect in reducing the number of physicians being trained.

GEMENAC underscored that too many physicians are trained as specialists, particularly in the surgical specialties, and too few are trained to provide ordinary primary care. The reasons for these phenomena are well understood. Specialists, particularly surgeons, earn much more than family practitioners or other doctors providing primary care. See Chapter 3. In the 1980s, many people proposed restrictions on funding for the education of residents in overpopulated specialties. Robert Heyssel, a member of the Commonwealth Task Force on Graduate Medical Education proposes that residents be paid only for three years of post-graduate training, thereafter either assuming the cost of specialty training themselves, or finding an alternative funding source. Three years is sufficient for board-certification in family medicine, internal medicine, and pediatrics, but not in surgery and its subspecialties or the medical subspecialties. Constrained Resources in Medical Education and Research, 3 Health Affairs 110 (Winter, 1984). Then Senator Daniel Quayle proposed that in order to qualify for Medicare reimbursement of residents' salaries, teaching hospitals must offer 70 percent of their residencies in primary care. 131 Cong. Rec. S963-S965 (daily ed., Jan. 31, 1985).

Some analysts challenge the methodology used in the GEMENAC study, and assert that changes since 1980 require reevaluation of its projections. For example, Jacobson & Rimm, The Projected Physician Surplus Reevaluated, 5 Health Affairs 48 (Winter 1986), argue that GEMENAC's projections of excess physicians are overstated. Enrollment in U.S. medical schools declined in the 1980s. Fewer foreign medical graduates are entering U.S. practice. More women are entering medical practice and work fewer hours than men, who are also reducing their work hours. However, these refinements produce only marginal variations in the conclusions offered by GEMENAC.

Other analysts challenge GEMENAC's claim that an excess of physicians, particularly in the surgical specialties, will increase medical costs and diminish the quality of services provided. For example, some argue that future medical needs are inherently unpredictable and since it takes a long time to train a doctor, it is preferable to have too many doctors than too few. See, for instance, Harris, How Many Doctors are Enough? 5 Health Affairs 73 (Winter 1986). Harris points to AIDS and to rising rates of organ transplants and cesarean deliveries as medical "needs" that GEMENAC did not anticipate. Others assert that a surplus of physicians would encourage doctors to provide needed public health services, to participate in innovative health programs, or to serve the Third World through creation of a doctors' Peace Corp. Hanft, The Need for More Physicians, 6 Health Affairs 69 (Summer 1987).

Yet others argue that even if the GEMENAC projections are reasonably accurate they do not justify collective public or private actions to reduce the numbers of doctors trained or to encourage them to train for work in specialties where physician services are more needed. Both neoclassical economists and the American Medical Association claim that the free market allows patients, medical schools, and potential medical students to define social preferences for medical care through market transactions. Think about the ways in which free market transactions might regulate the supply of physicians, or fail to do so.

ii. Foreign Medical School Graduates

One consequence of the focus on acute care in U.S. medical education is that we increasingly rely upon graduates of foreign medical schools to provide services that are not attractive to graduates of U.S. schools. In 1972, 46 percent of all new medical licensees in the U.S. were graduates of foreign medical colleges. By 1985, slightly more than 20 percent of the physicians practicing in the United States had graduated from a foreign medical school. The numbers of newly licensed physicians who had trained abroad peaked in the early 1970s, when Congress restricted the immigration preference for foreign doctors seeking to study and work in the U.S. Since that time the number of foreign-born doctors entering practice here has declined significantly. Mick & Worobey, Foreign Medical Graduates in the 1980's: Trends in Specialization, 74 Am. J. Pub. Health 698 (1984).

However, in the mid-1970s, several U.S.-based entrepreneurs created over a dozen profit-making medical schools in Mexico and the Caribbean to respond to the needs of many U.S. college graduates who were disappointed by their inability to gain admission to a U.S. medical school. Grenada, Antigua, Dominica, the Dominican Republic, and other nations authorized these off-shore schools to bestow medical degrees. Because students of the off-shore schools are U.S. citizens, they are free to return home and seek to join a residency program, to be licensed, and to practice as a physician. By the 1980s, there were almost 7000 U.S. foreign medical graduates (US-FMGs) in residency training in the U.S., more U.S. graduates of foreign medical schools than foreign FMGs.

Neither state licensing authorities nor the private educational credentialing organizations inspect or certify foreign medical schools. Until 1984, state licensing agencies administered a written exam — the ECFMG — for foreign medical graduates seeking to be licensed in the various states. Even though fewer than 40 percent of those who took the test passed it, it was widely criticized as far less rigorous than the licensing exam required of people trained in U.S. medical schools. In 1984, the National Board of Medical Examiners developed a new test for graduates of foreign medical schools — the Foreign Medical Examinations in the Medical Sciences (FMGEMS). The new test is more comparable to that taken by graduates of U.S. schools. In 1984, only 17 percent of those taking the new test passed it; in 1985, the percent fell to 13 percent. Board pass rates among U.S. FMGs have always been significantly lower than the pass rates of alien FMGs. In 1984 and 1985, only three percent of the U.S. citizens trained in the off-shore medical schools were able to pass the licensing exam.

These figures confirm extensive anecdotal information that the quality of education provided in off-shore medical schools is not good. These poorly trained students then return to the U.S. to train in the least demanding residency programs. Then, if they can manage to pass the written exam, they become fully licensed physicians.

Concerns about the quality of care provided by graduates, as well as an oversupply of physicians, led the New York State Commission on Graduate Medical Education to recommend strong measures to discourage teaching hospitals from utilizing graduates of such schools. It urged that New York residency programs be prohibited from offering them training, unless the off-shore school submitted to inspection and approval by the State Education Department, and that a graduate of a foreign medical school be required to pass the FMGEMS within three attempts before being eligible for a residency in New York. Report of the New York State Commission on Graduate Medical Education 27 (1986).

These recommendations were opposed by administrators of some programs, who argued that the FMGs provided essential care to patients whom graduates of U.S. medical schools were not willing to serve. They were also challenged by the U.S. students in off-shore medical schools, and their parents, who argued that standardized tests were not a reliable measure of practical skill and that students had a "right" to pursue their chosen calling. Should a state licensing agency approve foreign medical schools whose graduates seek to train and practice here? Only those that train U.S. citizens, or those that operate on a for-profit basis?

b. Organization of Nursing Education

C. Rosenberg, Healing Hands: Nursing in the Hospital, in The Care of Strangers: The Rise of America's Hospital System

213-236, 334 (1987)

NURSING BEFORE NURSES

In 1849, nurses at Massachusetts General Hospital worked from five in the morning to nine in the evening. Before leaving duty, they communicated any special orders from the house staff to the "watchers" responsible for the wards at night. Ordinarily, one such watcher ministered to twenty patients; the pay was fifty cents for women and a dollar for men. Males were "not generally appointed."

Hospital nursing was long, hard work. It was performed by both men and women and conformed in organization to a ward structure in which at least a score of patients normally occupied the same large room. Nurses lived in the hospital, often in odd cubicles tucked in attics, in basements, or, at times, immediately adjacent to the ward. Antebellum nurses were by no means recruited from among the depraved and infirm alone. Although they often learned on the job, many ward nurses were highly skilled, enjoyed long tenures, and exercised considerable responsibility. They dressed wounds, administered drugs and enemas, prepared special diets, as well as scrubbed, dusted, and made beds. Ward nurses supervised the work of one or more assistants as well as the casual, if often indispensable, efforts of convalescent patients.

The size of the ward dictated nursing's organizational structure; there was too much work for one nurse and too little money for more than one, but someone had to be in charge. Contemporary mores and the sexual segregation of wards also implied that men nurse men and women nurse women.

Nursing was a more dignified occupation in private than almshouse hospitals; almshouse nurses had often begun as "inmates," but even as they gradually progressed from convalescent helper to assistant nurse to ward nurse, they never escaped inmate status. In every hospital, however, a traditional paternalism guaranteed that employees would be treated as minors in need of control. Both paternalism and the need to ensure stability in the ward's supervisory structure encouraged trustees to reward long-term employees. At the New York Hospital, for example, wages were increased 50 percent after "a faithful service" of five years, another 33 1/3 percent after ten years, and after twenty years an annuity of $25 and " . . . in case of need, . . . support in the hospital during life. . . ."

The line between nursing and domestic service could hardly be drawn in the mid-nineteenth century. Male and female nurses worked with their hands and ministered to their patients' most basic needs. Emptying bedpans, cleaning and cooking, changing sheets, and removing vomit and bloodstains were all tasks that guaranteed a humble status in this class-conscious society. And in many cases, nurses had in fact risen from more humble service jobs in the hospital. But the lack of secure and stable work — especially for women — guaranteed that at least some hard-working Americans would trade the freedom (and better, if less predictable, pay) of the noninstitutional labor market for the more secure, if paternalistic, world of nursing. Others moved back and forth between work outside and inside the hospital's walls.

Thus the inconsistency of many late nineteenth- and early twentieth-century accounts of hospital nursing; their authors were well aware that some mid-nineteenth-century nurses had been responsible, stable, and dedicated, even if others had been casual, filthy, and unreliable. "Of the evils of the old system," a chronicler of New York's Charity Hospital wrote in 1904, "no one of the present day can form the slightest conception. Helpers of every degree of unfitness and immorality had been employed to care for the sick." Most nurses and servants were, in fact, workhouse prisoners who remained after serving their terms, "receiving no wages but a pretty liberal allowance of whiskey. . . ." Yet many of these unpromising recruits, he conceded, "although uneducated in nursing, illiterate and even depraved, did faithful service as far as their ability permitted. No nobler character ever existed than old John Collingan, head nurse in the fever pavilion — a man whose self forgetfulness and never ceasing kindness to those under his charge brought many a desperate case of typhoid fever to a favorable termination. Although an ignorant Irish peasant, he was by instinct a gentleman and a born nurse, with the tenderness of a woman and the motives of a saint."

It was into a well-established world of hospital work and authority that the Nightingale movement intruded with the promise that it would create a more intelligent, skilled, and reliable nursing corps, as well as a new level of order and efficiency predicated on the existence of these trained nurses. . . .

The 1850s were a period of heightening interest in nurse training. The Crimean War and consequent prominence of Florence Nightingale had made American as well as English philanthropists and physicians conscious of nursing and the hospital as fields ripe for reform. . . .

It seemed obvious to most contemporaries that women were better suited than men to nursing; their innate sensitivity would bring warmth and reassurance to the patient as it brought cleanliness and order to the ward. This was as well a generation when much social activism reflected and was motivated by a secularized evangelicalism; lives were not to be wasted but dedicated to morally appropriate vocations. Such justifications were particularly important to that minority of respectable women who sought a socially acceptable sphere of activity outside the home. . . .

This complex of ideas regarding social activism and women's appropriate role was also consistent with many aspects of mid-nineteenth-century medical thought. An increasing skepticism toward much of conventional therapeutics (or at least the tendency to see such interventions as merely supportive of the body's natural healing processes) logically emphasized the importance of nursing — along with diet, cleanliness, and rest. . . .

The Nightingale movement also mobilized these views in justifying an autonomous female role in the hospital. As she originally conceived it, the nursing superintendent, a woman of class and breeding, would control nursing in the hospital, subordinate only to the institution's governing board. The prerogatives of female sensibility and class identity helped legitimate such novel demands. But this was only a part of Nightingale's argument; she assumed that femininity in itself did not guarantee nursing competence. Technical instruction was required. The knowledge needed to manage a ward or hospital does not "come by inspiration," she argued caustically, "to the lady disappointed in love nor to the poor workhouse drudge hard up for a livelihood." The Nightingale program wedded intuitive moral capacity and intellect, piety and efficiency, and promised hospital trustees and administrators a stable and relatively inexpensive labor force along with improved internal discipline and lower mortalities. It constituted a powerful and well-calculated appeal for public and medical support.

Not surprisingly this aggressive demand for hospital-based nurse training mobilized opposition as well as support. Many English hospital physicians . . . were particularly unhospitable to the notion that a female nursing superintendent should enjoy direct access to a hospital's governing board.

The demand for trained nurses and attempts to provide a supply of such women in fact antedated by a generation the founding of America's first three nursing schools in 1873. . . .

. . . The number of nurse training schools grew steadily in the 1880s and 1890s, and by century's end they had become a necessary part of every large and not a few small hospitals. . . .

Perhaps most important was the role of nursing schools in the hospitals' political economy. Nursing students provided a relatively inexpensive, stable, and disciplined workforce. It was a stability based not on the long-time service of particular individuals, but on the continued viability of the school itself. . . .

It is true that almost every nursing school paid its students a modest sum (after they left probationer status), ostensibly for uniforms and books. This was typically ten dollars the first year and twelve during the second of the training school's two-year program. But this expenditure guaranteed the service of young women who worked a minimum of sixty and, more frequently, seventy hours a week on the wards — and who accepted a discipline that could not easily have been imposed on an equal number of men. Not only the ingrained assumptions of paternalism and female deference, but the threat of expulsion (and thus denial of the school's diploma and the livelihood it promised) provided a leverage more than adequate to discourage potential defiance by the great majority of student nurses. . . .

Education and the credential it legitimated had become both inducement and part payment for a key segment of the hospital's labor force. This was an economic logic too compelling to be ignored. Both hospitals and prospective nurses were capital poor; it was only natural for the two parties to barter: work for diplomas. Even hospitals far too small to offer adequate training hastened to establish nursing schools, for training schools guaranteed small-town institutions a cheap and reliable labor supply. "Schools" with a student body of as few as four or five were established without a second thought. Community hospitals almost always operated with minuscule budgets and sought inevitably to save dollars and pennies wherever they could. In many such hospitals, indeed, student nurses not only provided unpaid labor, but became a source of much needed income when sent out on private duty assignments (usually, but not always, during their second year). Their fees were, of course, paid to the hospital. . . .

If the training school was functional to the hospital, it was equally so to the women who were its products (and in some sense its victims). The options for dignified employment were few for women in postbellum America; nursing and teaching were two exceptions, soon to be joined by office and sales work. And among these choices, nursing boasted the conspicuous advantage of allowing the prospective nurse to contribute her labor as the cost of entering a credentialed vocation. . . .

Despite early hopes of attracting middle-class women, however, the majority of student nurses at even the most selective schools were not recruited from middle- or upper middle-class families. Many in fact hailed from farms or small towns; a good many were women "on their own" who had tried other work before settling on nursing. Nevertheless, a minority of women from better social backgrounds did enter nurse training during the first half century of American nursing. . . .

The great bulk of nurse training consisted of manual skills taught by example at the bedside. Abstract learning hindered as much as helped. Worcester's Memorial Hospital described the instruction provided its nursing students in 1895; it included the dressing of burns, blisters, and wounds, the application of leeches, minor dressings, and fomentations, the administration of enemas and baths. Nurses were taught to pass catheters, manage helpless patients so as to prevent bedsores, manufacture bandages, apply splints and bandages — as well as to observe and report their patients' symptoms. Although much was said of the need to separate nursing from domestic service, the great majority of what the student nurse actually did during her long hours on the ward might as well have come under the latter heading. Students changed beds, folded and arranged laundry, swept and scrubbed, waited on patients, and bathed them, while gradually learning to change dressings, administer drugs, and take temperatures.

Discipline was severe and unremitting; it was in fact the fundamental training school subject matter. Nurses knew that their rooms might be inspected at any time of the night or day, that impertinence or carelessness might lead to immediate dismissal, that even talking with a house officer might incur the same penalty. . . .

. . . An undue familiarity with ward patients could also bring reprimand or even dismissal.

. . . Paternalism (or maternalism in this case) never questioned its right to control every aspect of the nurse's life and work; it was in fact a necessary aspect of the responsibility that came with status.

. . . Contemporaries doubted neither the practical advantages nor the morally appropriate nature of such authoritarian — and dubiously educational — relationships. Although some administrators questioned the hours and arduousness of nurse training, few challenged the structured subordination within which that work was performed.

Nevertheless, increasingly egregious flaws in the world of nurse training were soon to become the agenda for a thoroughgoing reform program. An energetic and ambitious core of nursing superintendents, with the aid of like-thinking medical men, called for a recasting of nurse training, an improvement reflecting in attenuated form the parallel movement for reform in medical education. The intellectual content of nurse training was to be made more demanding, while as a necessary prerequisite, hours of ward work were to be curtailed and the course lengthened from two to three years.

The relationship between nursing and medicine was particularly problematic. Yet the fortunes of the two groups were indissolubly related; medicine's ever increasing authority did help legitimate the social claims of nursing, and individual physicians were in many cases advocates of nurse training and appreciative of the newly trained nurses' clinical skills. Nevertheless, the nature of their relationship presumed the subordination of nursing — in the hospital and in patient care generally.

The feminization of nursing promised at first an ambiguous equity for medical men. While women could hardly be expected to master the physician's cognitive skills and challenge that aspect of his authority, they could marshal a different kind of authority, that based on their peculiar capacity to function in a sphere of emotion and empathy less amenable to man's more analytic capacities. Especially when these attributes were united with high social status, the nursing superintendent promised to be a tenacious antagonist. But such fears were generally short lived.

Not surprisingly, medical fears that trained nurses would prove restless in their subordination proved to have little basis in reality. Nevertheless, even sympathetic physicians were reluctant to expand the intellectual content of nurse education — perhaps the central demand of early twentieth-century nursing reform.

Upgrading the intellectual content of nurse training not only implied potential conflicts of authority, it conflicted directly with the hospital's labor requirements. A student in the lecture room or laboratory was not available to make beds, empty bedpans, and change dressings (or to be sent out on private duty). Such frills as physiology, pathology, or anatomy were in any case hardly appropriate to the better performance of such humble duties. . . .

By the First World War, however, nursing reformers could claim that many of their educational goals had been attained. . . .

No single change transformed the hospital's day-to-day workings more than the acceptance of trained nurses and nurse training schools, which brought a disciplined corps of would-be professionals into wards previously dominated by the values and attitudes of working-class patients (and attendants originally recruited from the same strata of society). In a period when few careers were open to women, trained nursing attracted a far greater variety of women, many of them rural and only a minority from the urban working class. Professional ambition and social origin set these first generations of credentialed nurses apart from the ward's accustomed occupants as much as any specific aspect of their schooling.

c. Organization of Nursing Education

Until the 1930s, nearly all nurses were trained in the hospital-based apprenticeship programs. Graduate nurses worked in private practice and found patients through nurse referral services or worked with the then more extensive public health programs. See Nursing History: New Perspectives, New Possibilities (E. Lagemann ed. 1983).

During the Depression, several factors motivated hospitals to hire paid staff nurses. Even though student nurses provided free labor, many hospitals could no longer afford necessary room, board, laundry, and administrative services. Private patients, who had previously retained private duty graduate nurses, were less able to do so. Organized nursing's press for greater education made the apprentice nurse a less economical source of labor. Finally, nurse historian Barbara Melosh argues that the increased bureaucratization of hospital work encouraged development of a paid nursing staff.

> [Professional administrators increasingly came to run hospitals and] introduced rationalization to the hospital, drawing parallels between hospital care and industrial production. . . . Long dominated by deals of stewardship, hospital management was entering into a realm of special expertise constructed by the "science" of efficiency. . . . A workforce comprised of student-apprentices and freelance special nurses did not facilitate the flexible personnel management that rationalizers strove to produce in other industries. . . . Although students could be summarily dismissed for poor work or insubordination, the workforce could not be increased or decreased at will to accommodate fluctuating needs. Meanwhile, hospital managers had to rely on notoriously independent special nurses to supply the extra amenities that private patients demanded, or to cover acute care that was beyond the abilities of partly trained students. [B. Melosh, "The Physician's Hand": Work Culture and Conflict in American Nursing 160, 165 (1982).]

Between 1929 and 1937, the numbers of nurses employed by hospitals increased from 4000 to 27,000. Melosh, supra, at 168. Most nurses were still educated in hospital-based training programs, but the student nurses ceased to be the core of the workforce.

Registered nurses sought to follow the model of the medical profession and gain control over the practice of nursing. Initial statutes, adopted in the early twentieth century, provided for the "registration" of nurses meeting prescribed qualifications, but allowed unregistered nurses to practice. Professional nurses, seeking stronger educational requirements and mandatory licensing, were often supported by elite physicians and medical educators desiring a more stable and qualified workforce, and able to administer an educational program meeting more demanding standards. Nurses with less training, and hospitals with fewer resources, opposed mandatory licensing and more rigorous educational requirements. See N. Tomes, The Silent Battle: Nurse Registration in New York State, 1903-1920 in Nursing History: New Perspectives, New Possibilities (E. Lagemann ed. 1983).

As hospital work became more complex, differentiated, and bureaucratized, ordinary bedside care was increasingly delegated to aides and unlicensed nurses. RNs both appreciated relief from the drudgery of routine tasks and feared that their jobs were threatened by the lower paid, less trained workers. Acute nursing shortages during World War II forced the leadership of organized nursing to accept auxiliary nurses as an official part of the nursing workforce. By the 1950s, every state licensed practical nurses (LPNs). The American Nurses Association (ANA) persuaded state legislatures to give RNs control of the LPNs certification and the definition of their work.

At the end of World War II, 80 percent of nurses were trained in hospital schools. The proportion of nurses with bachelors degrees increased to about 30 percent by the late 1960s and has since remained relatively stable. During the 1950s, community colleges began to offer associate degrees in nursing. About half of today's registered nurses are trained in such programs. The remaining 20 percent of RNs are now trained in hospital based diploma schools. Vaughn, Educational Preparation for Nursing — 1982, 4 Nursing & Health Care 460, 461, table 1 (1983).

LPNs complete a one year formal training program at an approved community college, vocational school, or hospital. For current data see Facts About Nursing, published annually by the ANA, or the Nursing Data Book published by the National League for Nursing. Below the LPNs, at the bottom of the hierarchy of patient care workers are aides and orderlies. Since World War II, the Red Cross has sponsored a training program for these workers, who are not licensed and are generally trained, for four to ten weeks, by hospitals at which they work.

Divisions of labor between RNs, LPNs, and aides are not always clear. An increasing proportion of direct bedside care is done by LPNs and aides. Between 1941 and 1951, the proportion of such care provided by RNs declined from 70 percent to 40 percent. D. Yett, An Economic Analysis of the Nurse Shortage, 1-14 (1975). Nurses are versatile hospital employees. Their broad training enables them to substitute for LPNs, aides, medical social workers, therapists, and, in many contexts, for physicians.

i. The Perennial Nurse Shortage

Since World II, American hospitals have never been able to hire the number of nurses they seek, except for brief periods in the early 1970s and the early 1980s. From 1941 to 1980, nurse vacancy rates have averaged about 14 percent, reaching a high of 23.3 percent in 1961 and lows of about 9 percent in 1971 and 1981. L. Aiken, The Nurse Labor Market, 1 Health Affairs 30 (Fall 1982). In 1988, a National Commission on Nursing, appointed by the federal Department of Health and Human Services, reported that 175,000 to 200,000 registered nurses were needed in hospitals, nursing homes and other care centers. A substantial proportion of institutions have closed units or curtailed services because of shortages. S. Rich, "Pervasive" Shortage of Registered Nurses Reported, Washington Post, A-3, Dec. 13, 1988.

Aikin argues that the nurse shortages can be explained largely by inadequate compensation. Nurses' work levels are sensitive to pay. Nurses can choose to work full or part time. Almost half of the 1.7 million registered nurses have children at home. Their income, after taxes, must finance child care and substitute homemaker services. When salaries are low, many nurses prefer part-time work. So from 1972 to 1980, when nurses' incomes failed to keep pace with other comparable groups, the proportion of RNs working part-time increased from 18 percent to 25 percent. Nurses have one of the highest labor force participation rates of predominantly female occupations. In 1980, almost 77 percent of licensed nurses were employed, with fewer than 5 percent working in nonhealth-related jobs. Aikin, supra, at 35.

Nurse shortages have persisted despite large expansion of the number of nurses being trained. Increased intensity of hospital care generates greater need for nurses. Nurse shortages do not affect all hospitals equally. Public hospitals and large urban general hospitals experience the greatest shortages. In smaller community hospitals vacancies are often limited to unpopular hours. Aikin, supra, at 30.

Two factors are key in understanding the nurse shortage. First, and most important, when nurse compensation falls, relative to the cost of living and to wages for other female dominated occupations, more nurses are apt to choose part-time work. Second, nurses are sensitive to issues of status, particularly in relation to other health care personnel. Between 1945 and 1980 the gap between nurses' incomes and those of physicians increased dramatically from a ratio of 1:3 to more than 1:5. The income gap between nurses and allied nursing personnel gradually narrowed so that by 1979, nurses' salaries were less than 30 percent higher than those of aides. Aikin, supra at 34-35.

The 1988 national Commission on Nursing recommends:

— increasing pay for nurses, rewarding "experience, performance, education and demonstrated leadership," through increased Medicare payments for this purpose.
— preserving RNs' time for direct care by getting providers of medical services to hire other, less skilled personnel for functions not requiring RN skills.
— improving staffing patterns and using more automated information systems and labor saving technologies.
— giving nurses a bigger say in policy-making in regulatory and accreditation bodies, as well as within hospitals, nursing homes and other units providing care. Washington Post, supra.

Susan Reverby argues that the nursing shortage is one manifestation of a broader cultural failing to value caring work. Nursing's "crucial dilemma," she maintains, is "the dichotomy between the duty and the desire to care for others and the right to control and define their activity." Resolution requires confrontation of "the failure of our society to create the conditions under which the desire to care can be valued." Ordered to Care: The Dilemma of American Nursing, 1850-1945, at 2 and 7, (1988).

ii. The Debate About Educational Qualifications for Licensed Registered Nurses

Throughout its history, the organized nursing profession has sought to enhance the prestige and responsibility of nurses through education. Since 1974 the ANA and some of its state affiliates have sought to amend state licensing laws to require that registered nurses possess a bachelors degree.

Such a requirement would have a dramatic impact, since less than one-third of current nursing graduates train in a bachelors program, while half obtain associate degrees in two year programs at community colleges and about one fifth train in diploma schools in hospitals. Vaughn, Educational Preparation for Nursing — 1982, 4 Nursing & Health Care 460, 461, table 1 (1983).

Proponents argue that heightened educational requirements are essential if nursing is to be recognized as a full profession and if nurses are to be accorded respect and responsibility. People with associate degrees could be re-certified as licensed practical nurses, and some versions of the proposal would allow currently licensed RNs to retain that status. Opponents argued that the proposal demeans the knowledge and skills of nurses with less elite academic credentials and is insensitive to the needs of nurses from lower class backgrounds. See, for instance, B. Melosh, supra and A. Dolan, The New York State Nurses Association : Who Needs It? 2 J. Health Poly. Pol. & L. 508 (1977). Bullough, supra, surmises that the effort to require a bachelors degree for nurses will be mooted by the growing trends toward state certification of nurse specialists which often require a masters degree.

Periodically, the AMA responds to the continuing difficulty of recruiting nurses by proposing a new category of health care worker — a registered care technologist — trained quickly to do specialized patient care tasks. Nurses oppose such proposals, noting that hospital patients are, increasingly, acutely ill and need broadly trained people to care for them. They maintain that what is needed is "a higher ratio of workers who support and free up nurses to do nursing by replacing them in all non-nursing activities on all shifts — aides and assistants, secretaries, . . . mid-level managers, and so on. . . ." C. Fagin, Why the Quick Fix Won't Fix Today's Nurse Shortage, 24 Inquiry 309 (1988).

2. MEDICAL SCHOOL GOVERNANCE AND FINANCING

a. The Costs of Medical Education

It is impossible to determine the precise costs of medical education because of the complex institutional arrangements and multiple roles played by individuals involved in graduate and undergraduate medical education. Some patterns are, however, clear.

- Patient care revenues provide most of the resources to support graduate medical education and a substantial portion of the support for undergraduate medical schools. This money, paid to physicians and hospitals, is not ordinarily reflected in medical school budgets.
- Tuition, which once provided the major financial support for medical

schools, paid only 20 percent of the cost of private medical schools by 1940. By 1970, tuition income had fallen to 4.8 percent of private medical school revenues.

- From 1950 to 1970 federal research contracts to medical schools mushroomed, so that by 1970 private schools received 63.2 percent of their revenues from federal research grants. Since then funds for research have declined.
- From 1940 to 1980, private medical schools' income from endowment, gifts and grants fell from 41 percent to 2.1 percent. This is an even less significant resource for public schools.
- Federal laws adopted in 1968 and 1971 provided capitation to medical schools that increased their enrollment. These subsidies had their desired effect and have now been eliminated.
- From 1960 to 1980 forty new medical schools were created. All but two are publicly owned and were founded with substantial state, and sometimes federal, subsidy.

See generally, J. Schofield, New and Expanded Medical Schools, Mid-Century to the 1980s, Chapters 2 and 6 (1984). See generally, J. Hadley, Medical Education Financing (1980).

b. Medical School Governance

Patient care revenues provide a primary source of funding for medical education. Under public and private insurance programs these payments are not made directly to the medical schools, but rather to either hospitals or to physicians and physician groups or departments. Thus, the university presidents, medical school deans, and university hospital administrators, who hold formal positions of leadership and responsibility in medical education, do not necessarily have control over a major portion of the schools' financial resources. J. R. Schofield, who worked for 35 years as a medical school dean and official of the American Association of Medical Colleges (AAMC), observes that many schools are

> a federation of departmental baronies, each jealously and aggressively defended by the powerful baron of that particular discipline. Under these circumstances, the dean has limited powers; like the monarch of the United Kingdom, the dean reigns but does not rule. . . . A dean who enters this type of arena expecting to function as a football quarterback may quickly discover not only that the principal players often fail to respond when he calls the signals for a play but that he never quite manages to get his hands on the ball. . . . [Schofield, supra at 74.]

Similarly, an AAMC survey of medical school deans, hospital directors and faculty members reveals that they all perceive that real power rests in the hands of those who head medical school departments, or who serve as chiefs of service in university affiliated hospitals. Often these roles are filled by the same people. M. P. Wilson, C. R. McLaughlin, Leadership and Management in Academic Medicine at 121 (1985).

These generalizations are not controversial, though the details of medical school organization and governance vary from time to time and place to place. The article that follows describes governance struggles within one medical school at a particular moment in history.

E. V. Sparer, Medical School Accountability in the Public Hospital

14-26 (1974)

Among American medical school clinical faculties, there are a variety of income generating organizations. At the University of Pennsylvania Medical School, there are two basic types of such organizations. The first we shall label the "old style" proprietary organization, and the second is called "the new style group practice."

How do these forms of group practice differ from each other? What happens to the income generated by each? What concerns and interests does each form of enterprise generate? What is the relation, if any, between these interests and the academic and public goals of the medical school?

THE OLD STYLE PROPRIETARY ORGANIZATION

. . . This type of organization, prior to 1971, was the dominant form for practice in the U. of P. Medical School, as well as in many other schools throughout the country. . . . At the present time, it is still the organizational form of practice in several departments of the medical school. . . .

The Department of Surgery is perhaps the most powerful of these old-style proprietary departments. A partnership established many years ago by I.S. Ravdin, then Chairman of the Department and later University Vice-President for Medical Affairs, has over the course of years expanded to twelve members. The majority of departmental clinicians are employed by these twelve. What the arrangements are between the twelve and the rest of the department, how much income is received individually, how much by the Department, is not known to the University. A highly placed official in the medical school stated that "surprising" types of fringe benefits are awarded to certain partners. For example, cars for personal use are rented. The partners do not belong to the University TIAA-CREF retirement plan, or comparable retirement plans. Salary equivalents, nursing home maintenance and such have been worked out for some members on a grander if unclear scale.

The owners do not account for their practices to the University or school. How much money is generated, how much is profit, to whom the money is distributed, what the "fringe" benefits are, are unknown to the University — only the owners and the Internal Revenue Service are informed on such matters. The owners, over the course of the recent reform administration in the medical school, bitterly and successfully resisted the ex-Dean's efforts to force an accounting. Because the books — or "black box," as termed by some — of these departments are closed to the University, the University refuses to provide department members the cheaper malpractice insurance it is able to purchase.

The school does pay a "teaching" budget to the department for teaching efforts, as distinguished from patient care efforts. The teaching budget payments come from tuition, departmental endowments, and government capitation grants. No very accurate basis for calculating the amounts warranted by the teaching effort appears to exist. . . . Personal income to the Department members — whatever its actual amount — is to a major extent based on patient care income. . . .

The clinical organizations of other departments, such as Radiology and Ophthalmology, are organized on a solo proprietor basis. The sole proprietors in these departments are also the chairmen. By owning the income generated by the clinical work of the department, and disbursing it under private arrangements to himself and his departmental clinician employees, the sole proprietors in these departments are in a position of far greater power than the ordinary chairman. . . .

These private enterprises within the school and medical center, however, by the very nature of their organization, are geared to obtaining . . . the business of the largest number of well-to-do, and comparatively well-to-do patients to whom they can appropriately offer their services for fees. . . . As with the individual fee-for-service practitioners generally, the faculty members of these departments by and large offer specialist and not comprehensive care to their patients (especially their poorer patients).

THE NEW STYLE GROUP PRACTICE

The leading example of Penn's new style group practices is the Pennsylvania Medical Group. [I]t was the path maker for such groups. In the past three years, several other departments have followed Medicine's lead, even though their creation met with sharp opposition. Several general considerations made the development of the new group form . . . consistent with important needs of the medical school.

The advent of Medicare and Medicaid in 1966 was a significant catalytic agent in undermining the dual-track system of delivering care in hospitals.

[I]f a patient is characterized as a "ward" or "service" patient rather than as a "private" patient, fee reimbursement to the individual or group physician cannot be obtained from Medicare or Medicaid. Rather, the hospital in which the services are given receives an added payment as part of the "reasonable costs" of the hospital which are reimbursed. (In either situation, the salaries of the residents and interns are charged as hospital costs.) Depending upon a variety of factors, the fee paid to an attending doctor of a "private" patient may be significantly larger than the payment added to the hospital's "reasonable costs" charge if the patient is "ward" or "service." Thus the characterization of the patient is critical for determining *to whom* the reimbursement payment is given and the actual amount of reimbursement received for the services of the doctor in charge of the patient. [T]he tests of the "private" patient-doctor relationship have become increasingly difficult for the old-style private enterprise department to meet with regard to the former "charity" group of patients insured under the new laws.

In addition to the impact of Medicare and Medicaid, some University practitioners have argued, persuasively we believe, that the sheer explosion of medical knowledge has made it more and more difficult for an individual practitioner to keep up with both a busy practice and his continued education. Group work, team activity, is often the necessary order of the day. This would appear especially true when the practitioner is also a teacher — when time out of practice is needed for reflection, for research, and for talking out problems with students. Finally, a group practice, where decisions are jointly made in an environment stressing academic goals and considerations, would appear more suited to experimentation in different and new forms of health care delivery — including ambulatory care — than would an old style proprietary practice where teaching is almost incidental to the making of money.

In many ways, the new style group practice meets these new needs in a far more effective manner than the old style proprietary organization. . . . The group can arrange relief from the time demands of practice, to allow whatever educational and research time is deemed appropriate. Medicare and Medicaid patients who seek the Group's services without a previously identified physician are assigned "an attending physician" from the Group, who utilizes his team assistants (including residents and interns) but retains and presumably exercises the personal role and responsibility that allows him to be dubbed the "private" physician of the patient. Under the old style system, such patients are assigned to hospital house staff, and thus considered "ward" or "service" patients. The Group's teams function similarly for *all* patients, according to the Department, regardless of Medicaid status. . . . The new Group . . . is better rationalized to meet modern knowledge acquirement and teaching demands. . . . In addition, the Medical Group is University audited. . . . The Group's books are not secret to the University; its plan for the distribution of its income is known — and the actual distribution of its income is known to the University.

CONTROL AND DISTRIBUTION OF CLINICALLY GENERATED INCOME

[T]he huge majority of the Group are "full-time group members," *i.e.*, they are compensated entirely by salary, have their office in HUP, and their private patients pay their fees to the Department Group. . . . Their fees go to the Department, their salary, derived "fully" from the Department, is made up of three elements:

(1) *The academic component.* This is set according to the rank, seniority and teaching-research role of the member. [I]t is derived from unrestricted endowment funds, the Dean's office funds, etc.
(2) *The Standard Practice Component* (SPI). The significance of this part of the salary depends upon how heavily involved in clinical work the member is. It can constitute the principal part of the member's salary. Its amount is specified by the Chairman of the Department each year, after negotiation with the member. . . .
(3) *The Bonus.* Insofar as the full-time member's practice nets the Group more than his SPI, a bonus is paid. The current bonus consists of 40% of gross earnings received after the member's net earnings have equalled his SPI. The Medical Group member's personal income . . . is dependent on the fees he generated for the Group in his practice. . . . The Medical Group member is unlike the old style proprietary entrepreneur in many ways, but he is nevertheless a type of entrepreneur. . . .

THE ACADEMIC STRESS WITHIN THE MEDICAL GROUP

Does this interest of the new style group member (and old style proprietor) conflict with legitimate and important academic and public service goals of the school? . . . From the beginning, Chairman of the Department of Medicine, Arnold Relman, has insisted that the Group and Department, in its hiring practices:

> increasingly rely on physicians who are committed to academic careers, have a talent for teaching, and have the time to devote to scholarly activity. Such is not the case with most busy practicing physicians in the community, for they have obviously chosen a different way of professional life.

In setting the SPI and academic components of the salary and in determining the amount of time away from clinical work, two other objectives are considered. As Relman and apparently the Group as a whole believe, the clinician should not make an income which is excessively more than is paid to the basic science researcher. [T]he Medical Group strives for a balance in which the Group clinician's income is somewhere between that of the basic science researcher's and the non-University practitioner.

The academic stress of the Group has incorporated a concern for the development of new means of health care as well. For example: the increase in use of ambulatory facilities and the need to break down the past emphasis on outpatient clinic fragmentation by specialties have led to the creation of a new walk-in clinic in which general medical care is offered. At this same clinic, nurse practitioners [provide] . . . follow-up care. . . .

The new style groups are organized on *departmental* lines. The fees generated by the Group go to the Department — and not the School. Income from the Group cannot be used by the School to aid poorer departments. It cannot be used by the School to sponsor health care delivery, research or education efforts outside the Department. Since the same is true for other departmental group-generated income, the *intra* — rather than inter-departmental form of the Group militates against the development of comprehensive care efforts by the School, the aid of weaker departments or sections of the Center, and — in general — a medical school-wide, medical center-wide patient care policy.

c. Medical Schools and Teaching Hospitals

In 1980, 73 teaching hospitals were owned by the 126 medical schools and/or their sponsoring universities. Medical schools that do not own a hospital rely on partnerships with major teaching hospitals. No medical school can offer the full spectrum of educational programs in a single teaching hospital. Recent decades have seen an enormous increase in the number and kinds of affiliation agreements between medical schools and teaching hospitals. Hospitals seek affiliation agreements to improve patient care and to recruit young doctors as residents. Medical schools seek these affiliations to provide clinical experience to increased numbers of students. These contractual arrangements define the rights and responsibilities of medical schools and teaching hospitals and are rarely the subject of litigation or regulatory scrutiny.

Public hospitals have traditionally been a primary locus of medical education. Service in such hospitals is attractive to students and residents because they often provide opportunities to treat challenging illnesses, with a minimum of supervision.

Until the 1960s, arrangements between public hospitals and medical schools were informal. The schools provided supervisory physicians, who often served on a voluntary basis, and the public hospital provided a source of "teaching material," that is, patients, in a setting subsidized and maintained by local government. There were often conflicts between local political leadership, who sought humane, respectful treatment for patients, and the leadership of the medical schools, who were more interested in organizing teaching and care in an efficient, effective way. In some instances, these conflicts motivated medical schools to create their own hospitals. The American Health Empire (B. and J. Ehrenreich eds. 1971).

In the 1960s, cities entered into formal contractual relations with medical schools. Under these affiliation contracts, the schools agree to provide leadership and staffing for the public hospital in exchange for payments from local government. Often, localities are unable to supervise performance under the contracts. Moreover, a person who is the chair of a department in both a public and university hospital often gives his first loyalty to the university hospital, and the public hospital consequently suffers from an absence of aggressive, creative leadership. In the most extreme form, medical school leadership with such dual loyalty can siphon well reimbursed services to the university hospital, leaving only the unreimbursed, difficult and unattractive services to the public hospital. This pattern was an important part of the destruction of several public hospitals during the 1980s. The Sparer study quoted above goes on to describe this phenomenon in Philadelphia. The classic study of affiliation arrangements in New York is R. Burlage, Institute for Policy Studies, New York City's Municipal Hospitals: A Policy Review (1967).

As we saw in Chapter 5, the care people receive in the hospital, and the relationships patients have with everyone who works there, varies with the nature of the patient/physician relationship, that is, whether the patient has an established relation with a private physician, is treated solely by interns and residents, or is somewhere between.

Patterns of treatment in public teaching hospitals replicate the entire range of arrangements described by Duff and Hollingshead. A public hospital that is the only major teaching hospital in the area provides various patterns of care to all classes of people. Other public hospitals serve only the poor and treat all patients under committee sponsorship. This pattern is most common at hospitals such as Cook County in Chicago or Bellevue in New York City, at which attending, supervising physicians have easy access to a private hospital where they treat private, sponsored patients. Finally, some public teaching hospitals seek to assign all patients to an individual physician when they first seek care, and to maintain those relations over time. These relations are closer to those described by Duff and Hollingshead as casual or subcommittee sponsorship. See C. Schmidt, et al., A Practice Plan in a Municipal Teaching Hospital: A Model for the Funding of Clinical Faculty, 304 N. Engl. J. Med. 263 (1981).

d. Patient Care Reimbursement in a Teaching Context

Medicare, Medicaid and private insurance provide two distinct forms of reimbursement for physician services delivered in a teaching setting. First, a teaching hospital is paid for salaries and stipends that it pays to supervising physicians and to interns and residents (housestaff) and for the indirect costs of supporting such services. Under Medicare this is a Part A payment. Second, a physician is entitled to payment, on a fee-for-service basis, for care provided. Under Medicare, this is a Part B payment. These two forms of reimbursement are fundamentally different. Cost based payments for salaried physicians are generally lower than fee-for-service payments. Further, cost based payments go to the hospital employer, while fee-for-service payments go to the individual physician. As Sparer notes, in "new style" medical groups, individual physicians contract to turn their fee-for-service reimbursement over to the group. Insurers have no concern about the arrangements that individual physicians make about the disposition of income received from the insurance company or from Medicare.

i. Payments to Hospitals: Part A

Prior to the adoption of DRG based reimbursement, Medicare, following the pattern of Blue Cross, paid hospitals on a reasonable-cost basis for the on-budget costs of patient care services provided through graduate medical education programs, including the costs of interns and residents, and the costs of salaries paid to physicians who supervised them. The amounts paid varied widely from hospital to hospital and from specialty to specialty.

The 1983 DRG legislation provided that the direct costs of the salaries of interns and residents would continue to be paid on a reasonable-cost basis, and the indirect hospital costs of providing such services were paid on a formula that accounted for DRG revenue, bed size, and numbers of interns and residents. The adjustment was intentionally set at a high level, as a means of ensuring that teaching hospitals, which often treat patients who are more acutely ill, would not be injured by inadequate DRG rates. Staff of the House Committee on Ways and Means, 98th Cong., 2d Sess Proceedings of the Conference on the Future of Medicare (Comm. Print 1984) at 91. The measure was intended as a temporary stop gap.

COBRA, in 1985, and OBRA, in 1986, developed a new approach to Medicare payment for hospitals' graduate medical education costs that was implemented through regulations issued in 1988. 53 Fed. Reg. 36589 (Sept. 21, 1988). The law requires calculation of hospital-specific, approved per resident amounts for each provider, to be based upon the provider's allowable costs for its cost reporting period beginning during federal fiscal year 1984. The formula for computing the Medicare payment, based on the per resident amount, does not appear controversial. However, the procedures for determining the base rate is. The preamble to the regulation notes, "[W]e would like to learn why the range of per resident for the [graduate medical education] GME base year varies from below $10,000 to over $100,000 per resident. Some of this difference can be explained by differing practices concerning fee-for-service billing by teaching physicians; however, we believe . . . that misclassification of costs and questionable physician allocation agreements are contributory factors." Id. at 36593. The regulations instruct intermediaries to reexamine base period costs and to recoup overpayments in specified circumstances.

ii. Payments to Physicians: Part B

Traditionally, the nature of care provided in a teaching hospital varies dramatically depending upon whether the patient is admitted as a "private patient" under the care of an individual supervising physician or as a "house patient" under the care of a committee of residents. See Chapter 5. Medicare sought to change this pattern by providing all elderly patients access to mainstream medical care. One Massachusetts doctor, who took this aspiration to heart, advised patients that he saw in the hospital's outpatient clinic to see him in his private office prior to hospitalization so that they could be admitted as "private patients." The medical school ordered him to stop, and dismissed him when he refused to do so. He sought redress in the federal court, and lost. Meyer v. Mass. Eye and Ear Infirmary, 330 F. Supp. 1328 (D. Mass. 1971).

In the early 1970s, Medicare administrators discovered that some supervisory physicians were claiming fee-for-service payments for care that had actually been provided by house staff. The pattern was seen as problematic, though the "problem" has been characterized in at least three different ways.

* Individuals eligible for Medicare and Medicaid are entitled to receive services from fully qualified physicians. Financial incentives should be used to assure that program beneficiaries are integrated into the medical mainstream.
* Physicians are double dipping. The same service is reimbursed twice, once as a cost based payment for the resident's salary and second as a fee-for-service payment to the supervising doctor.
* Different classes of Medicare beneficiaries should receive different services under the same universal insurance program. High status Medicare beneficiaries are entitled to payments to their private physician on a fee-for-service basis and also to a subsidy for the salary of the house staff who aid that physician. But since housestaff actually care for low status Medicare beneficiaries, only housestaff should be paid, through a cost-based payment to the hospital that pays their salary.

From 1969 to 1972, HEW and Congress treated the problem as one of providing incentives to assure that beneficiaries actually received the care from fully trained physicians, to which they were entitled, and for which Congress was willing to pay. Ever escalating requirements sought to assure that supervising physicians actually provided care. See Bureau of Health Insurance Intermediary Letter 371 (1969) and Social Security Amendments of 1972, Pub. L. 92-603, §227, 86 Stat. 1329.

These provisions provided powerful incentives for teaching physicians to organize themselves into the "new style" groups described by Sparer, so that they would be better able to meet the escalating standards for establishing that the supervising physician had the sort of individual relationship with a patient that would qualify him or her for fee-for-service reimbursement. The provisions were less successful in motivating supervising physicians to actually provide care. Both faculty physicians and the residents whom they supervised want residents to assume substantial responsibility for the care of most patients. The 1969 regulations, requiring supervising physicians to certify that they personally provided care, motivated physicians to shade the truth or, sometimes, to lie. See General Accounting Office, Report to the Congress, Need for More Explicit Teaching Physician Documentation Requirements (Jan. 21, 1986).

Regulations implementing the 1972 Amendment adopted the third characterization of the "problem" and sought to distinguish between low and high status patients. The regulations would have denied fee-for-service payment to teaching physicians who supervised the care of lower class patients, or who worked in hospitals that had traditionally provided a large volume of care for which the individual patient was unable to pay. See proposed amendments to 20 C.F.R. §405.402, 38 Fed. Reg. 17211-12 (1973). The American Association of Medical Colleges strongly opposed this approach. For almost two decades, the regulations implementing the 1972 Amendments have remained suspended, pending further study by the AAMC and the Congress. See also Medical Education Financing: Policy Analyses and Options for the 1980s (J. Hadley ed. 1980) and J. Hadley, Medicaid Reimbursement of Teaching Hospitals, 7 J. Health Poly, Pol. & L. 914 (1983).

e. The Tilt Toward Acute Care and Efforts to Counteract It

Almost all clinical medical education takes place in acute care hospitals. Many policy and academic analysts argue that such education fails to train practitioners to provide the routine and chronic care that most patients need. For example, in 1988, a national commission organized by the New York Academy of Medicine found that medical schools are producing too many specialists and insufficient doctors to provide primary care. The panel recommended that medical students be required to perform some community service and to work outside of hospitals. It also urges that medical schools, as opposed to teaching hospitals and research programs, be given greater responsibility for organizing and coordinating medical education. N.Y. Academy of Medicine, Clinical Education and the Doctor of Tomorrow (1988), reported in "Panel Urges Vast Changes in Medical Schools," N.Y. Times at A-39, Nov. 13, 1988. Dr. Thomas H. Meikle, panel member and former dean of Cornell Medical school observed that similar recommendations had been issued in the past. But, he said that this report is unusual in that it is "aimed not just at medical school faculty and deans — who have very little reason to change and significant reasons not to change — but also to state and federal policy makers, regulatory agencies, accrediting and certifying boards and professional medical organizations." D. Colburn, Kinder, Gentler Doctors; Expert Panel Calls for Adding Public Service Requirement to Medical Schools, Wash. Post, Z-11, Nov. 15, 1988. How, realistically, can state and federal public officials respond to such a call for action? Should they?

The continuing need for doctors to provide primary care services, particularly in rural and low income communities, has provided a prime impetus for several forms of state and federal financial support for medical education: direct state grants to fund new medical schools; capitation grants to schools that increase enrollment; and grants and subsidized loans to students who agree that they will practice in an area with unmet need after graduation.

General aid — capitation grants to medical schools and funding for new medical schools — has not been effective in encouraging doctors to provide primary care services or to work in geographic areas where their services are most needed. New, state sponsored, medical schools tend to replicate the programs and values of the older, established institutions. Basic patterns of physician reimbursement — paying more for specialty service than for primary care, and more for services provided in urban areas than for those delivered in a rural or low income neighborhood — mean that simply producing more doctors does not necessarily encourage doctors to practice where their services are most needed.

From 1972 until 1987, the National Health Service Corps program provided generous grants and subsidized loans to medical students who agreed to work in an area of particular need, after they graduated. Often this program was also not effective. Graduates could "buy out" of their obligations, on terms that made it financially attractive to do so. For many years, there was little effort to enforce the service obligations. See B. Ensminger & W. Bernstein, It's Time to Fund Physician Shortage Programs by Abandoning Unrestricted State Subsidies to Medical Schools, 8 J. Health Poly Pol. & L. 221 (1983).

In the 1980s, the federal government commenced vigorous enforcement of damage provisions, requiring that physicians who do not meet service obligations attached to educational grants repay the government three times the value of the loan. See, for instance, United States v. Swanson, 618 F. Supp. 1231 (E. D. Mich. 1985) (rejecting a variety of challenges to the treble damage penalty).

Young physicians who were motivated to work in underserved areas were able to do so because of the National Health Service Corp program. Between

1972 and 1988, 13,600 young doctors worked in areas of need, in exchange for forgiveness of their educational loans and subsidies. In 1985, 1500 Health Service Corp doctors were placed in community health centers in poor communities. When Congress abolished the program, poor communities that had come to rely upon these physicians, were unable to find replacements. M. Tolchin, Curbs on Tuition for Doctors Raising Fear for Care of Poor, N.Y. Times, A-14, July 25, 1988.

C. The Union Movement in Medical Work

1. PATTERNS OF UNIONIZATION IN HEALTH CARE

During the Great Depression, millions of workers sought to improve wages and working conditions through collective action, which often took the form of public protest and direct confrontation with employers. Many employers refused to recognize unions. In response, Congress adopted the National Labor Relations Act of 1935 (NLRA) to discourage workplace strife and disruption by providing a framework for legally protected negotiation between employers and organized employees.

Public employees were excluded from the protection of the original NLRA, and the 1947 Taft-Hartley Amendments excluded nonprofit hospital workers. Congress did not protect hospital workers' right to unionize because hospitals provide an essential public service that many people believed should not face the risk of disruption by strikes. Further, many hospitals depended on the low or unpaid labor of students, volunteers, and unskilled workers, many of whom are women.

Even without the protection of the federal labor law, some hospital workers sought to form unions. Five groups have dominated the organization of hospital workers involved in direct patient care: the Service Employees International Union (SEIU); the American Federation of State, County and Municipal Employees (AFSCME); District Council 1199 of the Retail, Wholesale and Department Store Workers (1199); the American Nurses Association (ANA); and the Physicians National Housestaff Association (PNHA). Other unions, such as Teamsters and skilled trades, have organized workers, such as guards and maintenance employees, whose work is not unique to hospitals.

The SEIU has the longest history and the largest membership in the hospital industry. Its first hospital-based bargaining unit was organized at San Francisco General Hospital in the mid-1930s. SEIU's greatest strength is on the west coast and the upper midwest. In Chicago, in 1966, SEIU joined forces with the Teamsters to create a local group that organized over 7000 professional and nonprofessional workers in 23 hospitals.

AFSCME began as the representative of workers in state mental hospitals. During the 1960s, AFSCME and the Teamsters competed for the right to represent the public workers in New York City hospitals. AFSCME won and District Council 37, its New York affiliate, became the representative of 18,000 public hospitals and a leader among the unions representing hospital workers.

District Council 1199 was a small union representing pharmacists and drug store employees in New York City until 1957, when the union began to organize nonprofessional workers in New York's voluntary hospitals. In a three-month period, 6000 workers, some of whom earned less than $30 for a 48 hour week, joined the union. In the late 1950s, the union conducted several prolonged strikes against hospitals that refused to bargain with it, and in 1963 the New York legislature established a framework for collective bargaining. Most of 1199's members are in New York City, but it has also organized hospital and nursing home workers in Ohio, Massachusetts, and other states. On the history of the unionization of hospital workers see R. Miller, Hospitals, in Collective Bargaining: Contemporary American Experience, 394-409 (G. Somers ed. 1980).

In the late 1950s, when 1199 began organizing nonprofessional workers in New York's voluntary hospitals, interns earned $71 a month and residents $105. In 1958, the Committee of Interns and Residents (CIR) organized and negotiated for the housestaff of both public and voluntary hospitals. During the 1960s, local housestaff organizations were formed in public hospitals in many cities, including, Los Angeles, Boston, and the District of Columbia. From 1972 until 1981, the Physician's National Housestaff Association (PNHA) served as a national coalition of local groups representing housestaff physicians. Hospitals resisted the organization of housestaff and these groups frequently had to strike to obtain recognition. While traditional issues of wages, fringe benefits, and hours were important to these organizations, they also sought improvements in funding, staff, and organization of the hospitals in which they worked. See Harmon, Intern and Resident Organizations in the United States: 1934-1977, 56 Milbank Mem. Fund Q. 500 (1978).

In the 1980s, the state chapters of the American Nurses Association represented more unionized nurses than any other group. For most of this century, the ANA had rejected unionization as inconsistent with the professional status it sought for nurses. But, in the 1940s, the California chapter responded to AFL and CIO efforts to organize hospital nurses. Since then, state nurses associations have sought to organize and represent unionized nurses, although as the materials below illustrate, they have confronted significant legal obstacles.

In 1974 Congress amended the NLRA to include all health care institutions and their employees. Pub. L. No. 93-360, 88 Stat. 395, codified as amended at 29 U.S.C. §151-158 (Supp., 1988). Union drives had publicized the poor wages and conditions of health care workers. Further, without a legal structure for bargaining, many hospital administrators refused to recognize or bargain with unions, unless the workers struck or engaged in other disruptive actions.

The 1974 Amendments include several provisions applicable specifically to the health care industry. Section 8(d) (B-C), at 29 U.S.C. §158 (Supp. 1988) requires any labor organization involved in an initial contract dispute to give 30 days notice to state or federal mediation agencies, and to engage in mediation, before any work action is taken. Section 8(g) requires labor organizations to give affected employers ten days notice before they engage in any "strike, picketing or other concerted refusal to work."

The 1970s, immediately before and after the enactment of the 1974 Amendments, saw a short lived spurt in the unionization of hospital workers. Apart from that, since the early 1960s, there has been a slow but steady growth in the number of hospitals that bargain collectively with some of their workers.

Percentage of all American Hospitals with any Union Contract

Year	Percentage
1961	3.2
1967	8.2
1970	15.7
1973	19.9
1975	22.8
1976	23.3
1977	23.5
1980	27.4

Thus most American hospitals have no unionized workers. Further, many hospitals included in these figures have a contract with only one union representing a small group of their workers. Large nonreligious hospitals, located in the west or the northwest are most likely to be unionized. According to the American Hospital Association, in 1987 approximately 20 percent of the hospital work force was unionized. Unionization has a significant impact increasing wage levels an average of 8 to 12 percent, and that impact grows over time. See Becker, Sloan & Steinwald, Union Activity in Hospitals: Past, Present, and Future, 3 Health Care Fin. Rev. 1 (1982). J. Delany, Patterns of Unions' Successes in Hospital Elections, 61 Hosp. Prog. 36 (1980). Feldman & Scheffler, The Union Impact on Hospital Wages and Fringe Benefits, 35 Indus. and Lab. Rel. Rev. 196 (1982).

Home health care workers are the most recent group to be unionized. In 1987, in New York City 50,000 home health care workers cared for people who were needy and sick. They were paid $4.15 an hour, had no overtime, no health insurance, no pension, and no job security. A coalition of three unions, the Archdiocese of the City of New York, and Jesse Jackson persuaded state and city officials to recognize a union, increase basic wages to $5.90 an hour, provide additional pay to those who worked 24 hours or on weekends and holidays, and to establish a health insurance plan for workers. The issues of pensions, job security, and overtime pay were deferred. See B. Caress, Home is Where the Patients Are: New York's Home Care Workers' Contract Victory, 18 Health PAC Bull. 4 (1988).

Obviously, labor law in the health care context raises a broad range of issues. The materials that follow address three problems that have been particularly vexing, as matters of legal practice and of public policy. The materials first examine the rules that determine how hospital bargaining units are constituted. Second, nurses and doctors, as professional workers, do not fit easily into the concepts of labor/management relations developed in the profit-making industrial context. These workers have faced formidable legal obstacles in their efforts to organize and bargain collectively. Finally, a note discusses the issues on which unions and hospitals are required to bargain. In the traditional industrial setting, "management" has a strong interest in exercising exclusive control over definition of the objectives of the enterprise and the organization of work, while labor's legitimate interests are confined to "wages, hours, and working conditions." This model does not easily capture the complexity of human service organizations dominated by professional workers.

2. COMMUNITIES OF INTEREST AMONG HOSPITAL WORKERS

International Brotherhood of Electrical Workers, Local Union 474 v. NLRB

814 F.2d 697 (D.C. Cir. 1987)

In this petition the union challenges the decision of the National Labor Relations Board dismissing an unfair labor practice complaint charging the hospital with an unlawful refusal to bargain.

Section 7 of the National Labor Relations Act provides that "[e]mployees shall have the right to self-organization, to form, join or assist labor organizations [and] to bargain collectively. . . ." Under the Act, one way for a union to gain recognition for purposes of collective bargaining is to petition the Board for a certification election among employees in an appropriate bargaining unit. NLRA, section 9. Under section 9 the Board must determine whether an "employer unit, craft unit, plant unit, or subdivision thereof" constitutes an "appropriate" employee unit for collective bargaining. Section 9(b) defines a "unit appropriate for the purposes of collective bargaining" as one which assure[s] to the employees the fullest freedom in exercising the rights guaranteed by . . . [the] Act." Under this test, the Board has followed a long-standing policy of holding that "employees with similar interests shall be placed in the same bargaining unit. This factor of mutuality of interest, together with the history of collective bargaining in the particular . . . industry involved is given great weight by the Board in deciding any unit controversy. . . ."

In 1974, Congress amended the Act to cover nonprofit health-care institutions. . . . The 1974 Amendments

> reflected Congress' judgment that hospital care would be improved by extending the protection of the Act to nonprofit health-care employees. Congress found that wages were low and working conditions poor in the health-care industry, and that as a result, employee morale was low and employment turnover high. Congress determined that the extension of organizational and collective-bargaining rights would ameliorate these conditions and elevate the standard of patient care.

In extending the Act to nonprofit health-care employees, Congress recognized the potential for interruptions in patient care. It therefore enacted special provisions that lengthen the strike notice period and require federal mediation. . . . Congress, however, did not adopt a provision . . . which would have limited the number of bargaining units in nonprofit health-care institutions to four (professional, technical, clerical, and service and maintenance) unless the employer and the union agreed otherwise.

Instead, both the House and the Senate Committee Reports contain language . . . that, "Due consideration should be given by the Board to preventing proliferation of bargaining units in the health care industry." . . .

The Board interpreted the Amendments not to preclude it from applying traditional community-of-interest criteria to determine appropriate bargaining units in the health-care industry. In one of its first decisions subsequent to the Amendments, the Board recognized that "the principal thrust of the legislative history of the health care amendments . . . admonishes the Board to avoid undue proliferation of bargaining units." . . . According to the Board, nothing in the legislative history indicates anything other than, that by refusing to amend section 9, "Congress, in the final analysis, left the matter of determination of appropriate units to the Board."

On September 28, 1979, the union requested certification of a bargaining unit of maintenance department employees of St. Francis Hospital. The hospital refused to recognize a unit that did not include both service and maintenance employees. After a hearing the Regional Director certified a unit that was slightly broader than that proposed by the Union, but that did not include any service department positions. The Hospital appealed to the Board. In St. Francis I the Board announced a new two-tier standard that balances "long-established community-of-interest criteria . . . against the legislative concern about over-proliferation of health-care bargaining units."

Under St. Francis I the Board would first consider whether the proposed unit falls into one of seven "groups of employees commonly found in a health care institution: physicians, registered nurses, other professional employees, technical employees, business office clerical employees, service and maintenance employees and skilled maintenance employees." Only if the proposed unit is broad enough to constitute one of these seven groups will the Board then apply "traditional unit principles to determine whether the specific employees involved do, in fact, display the requisite community of interest to warrant separate representation."

With respect to the bargaining unit at issue, the Board observed in St. Francis I that the Hospital's maintenance employees "possess overall greater skills and experience than are required for the service employees." Concluding that the unit constituted a group of "skilled maintenance employees," the Board then applied a traditional community-of-interest analysis. It noted that

> [t]he maintenance employees in this case . . . report to separate locations at the beginning of their work shifts, are administered separately from the service department, [and] are separately supervised. . . . They share no duties with the service departments. They are responsible for a variety of maintenance-related functions without being functionally integrated with other hospital departments.

The Board upheld the Regional Director's unit determination and ordered an election.

[T]he maintenance unit elected IBEW as its representative. The Hospital, however, refused to bargain. . . . Over one year later, the Board vacated its St. Francis I decision.

In St. Francis II, the Board "reconsidered" its earlier action. . . . It rejected the two-tier analysis of St. Francis I in favor of a disparity-of-interest standard. This standard requires "sharper than usual differences (or 'disparities') between the wages, hours and working conditions, etc., of the requested employees and those in an overall professional or nonprofessional unit."

Noting that the maintenance unit in this case included "lesser skilled individuals, who work closely with and share the same basic terms and conditions as the much larger group of service employees," the Board determined that the present record failed to demonstrate the requisite disparity-of-interest to justify separate representation. . . .

Normally, a bargaining unit determination by the Board will stand unless arbitrary and without substantial support. . . . This court cannot, however, sustain a unit determination by the Board "where it is based not on the agency's own judgment but on an erroneous view of the law." . . .

We believe that the Board, however, misconstrued the law. The 1974 Amendments in no way require the Board to apply a disparity-of-interest standard when determining appropriate bargaining units in nonprofit health-care institutions. Congress did not modify section 9 in any way when it amended the Act in 1974. . . .

The disparity-of-interest standard appears to represent a radical departure from traditional community-of-interest criteria applied by the Board to determine appropriate bargaining units in all other industries covered by the Act. . . . The disparity-of-interest standard presumes that only two appropriate bargaining units exist — professionals and nonprofessionals. Moreover, the standard places the burden on the employees to rebut this wall-to-wall units presumption. The Board in St. Francis II completely fails to address how this radical new standard will effectuate the supposed rights of health-care employees under the Act.

Because the Board improperly interpreted the 1974 Amendments to the Act as mandating the disparity-of-interest standard and compelling a presumption of only two appropriate units in the health-care industry, its decision has no basis in the law. Accordingly, we remand the case to the Board for reconsideration of whether the Hospital's maintenance employees constitute a "unit appropriate for the purposes of collective bargaining" under section 9 of the NLRA.

a. Why Does the Unit Determination Issue matter?

The structure of bargaining units has an important influence on union organizing and collective bargaining. Union organizers prefer smaller, more homogeneous, units. It is not simply that fewer people must be organized, but, more fundamentally, that it is easier to form a cohesive organization of workers who know each other, work together, do similar jobs, and have comparable skills and backgrounds. In many hospitals, distinct groups of workers are racially segregated: for instance, business office clericals may be predominantly white, while service and maintenance workers are predominantly black and hispanic. Patient-care staff provide 24-hour-a-day care and are concerned with issues arising from that staffing pattern, while other hospital employees work ordinary business hours.

Even workers involved in direct patient care often have distinct concerns. For such workers

> "[p]rofessional issues" such as staffing (nurse/patient ratio), availability of future professional educational opportunities, in service instruction, and better equipment rank high on the list of negotiating priorities. [W]hen employees with different professional goals are required to engage in a common collective bargaining process, the professional goals of both groups are submerged in favor of economic objectives, which are the only types of issues that allow a consensus to emerge. Lacking consensus, the employees also lack the bargain-

ing strength to enforce their demands on management. [W. Donahue, The *St. Francis II* Disparity of Interests Test — Is it Necessary? 9 West. N. Eng. L. Rev. 303, 322 (1987).]

Hospital administrators, by contrast, insist that if workers are to be organized, they must form larger units. Again, it is not simply that larger units are more difficult to organize. Administrators fear that undue proliferation of bargaining units could result in work jurisdiction disputes, interference with health care teamwork, and excessive administrative costs entailed in bargaining with a large number of units. Administrators express particular concern that a larger number of unions increases the risk that a strike by any one of the unions might disrupt patient care in the entire hospital. See D. Dyleski-Najjar, Professional Unions in the Health Care Industry: The Impact of *St. Francis II* and the *North Shore University Hospital,* 17 Loy. U. Chi. L.J. 383, 407-425 (1986).

Union people respond to these concerns, observing that while health care teamwork is a fine ideal that has been advocated for many years, it is not a practice that has in fact often been adopted. Further, Section 8 of the 1974 Amendments deals with the risk that strikes might disrupt essential hospital services; the section demands that unions provide advance notice of intent to strike and submit to mediation prior to any strike activity. Finally, in the hospital labor market, unlike construction or other industries, workers do not commonly respect the picket lines of other unions.

More generally, administrators oppose unions and use unit determination contests as a means to forestall them. The factors motivating hospital opposition to unions are not clear. Perhaps it is because both physicians and reimbursement authorities sharply constrain the formal authority of administrators; workers' claims to participation and voice may be seen as simply one too many complication in administrators' lives. Whatever the reasons, administrators have vigorously resisted unionization. In 1981, Congress responded to evidence that Medicare paid hospitals $30 million a year for anti-union consultants, and barred Medicare reimbursement for that purpose. Medicare and other insurers continue to finance hospitals' legal costs involved in resisting unionization. See discussion, 53 Fed. Reg. 33910 (1988).

b. Shifting Standards in the NLRB and the Courts

As the main case indicates, from 1974 until the mid 1980s, the Board certified units of workers who could establish that they shared a common "community of interest." By 1977, the Board had recognized eight appropriate units that could organize for collective bargaining purposes in health care institutions: 1) registered nurses, 2) physicians, 3) professionals except for registered nurses and physicians, 4) technical employees, 5) skilled maintenance employees, 6) business office clerical employees, 7) guards, and 8) other nonprofessional employees. Many courts criticized and reversed these determinations, holding that the Board had failed to give sufficient weight to the congressional admonition against undue proliferation of bargaining units. See M. Stapp, Ten Years After: A Legal Framework of Collective Bargaining in the Hospital Industry, 2 Hofstra Lab. L.J. 63 (1984). In the 1980s, Board members appointed by Ronald Reagan insisted upon wider, larger bargaining units. See also Sebris & McDonald, Bargaining Unit Determination Case Trends of the NLRB, 37 Lab L.J. 378, 382 (1986).

c. The Impact of Uncertainty: Ways of Knowing Facts and Making Law

Traditionally, the NLRB has not engaged in any type of rule making, informal or formal, but has rather established rules in the adjudication of individual cases. One explanation for this preference is that adjudication is less likely to expose the Board to the political controversy, which a rule making procedure would engender. See Note, NLRB Rule-making: Political Reality Versus Procedural Fairness, 89 Yale L.J. 982 (1980).

The "community of interest" standard applied in the 1970s, produced relatively stable unit determination principles allowing the eight units described above. The "disparity of interest" standard produced conflicting unit determinations in particular cases and before different courts.

In 1987, the Board issued proposed rules specifying which bargaining units would be found appropriate in various types of health care facilities. The Board conceded, "it is now no closer to successfully defining appropriate bargaining units in the health care industry than it was in 1974." Notice of Proposed Rule Making, Collective Bargaining Units in the Health Care Industry, 52 Fed. Reg. 25142 (July 2, 1987). The Board also acknowledged that it lacked an empirical basis upon which to determine what sorts of bargaining units might produce the "undue proliferation of bargaining units" that Congress sought to avoid. The proposed rules would have recognized six bargaining units in hospitals with more than 100 beds (registered nurses, physicians, other professionals, technical employees, all service, maintenance and clerical employees except for guards, and guards). In smaller hospitals and nursing homes the Board would recognize only four units, by requiring that all professional workers be included within a single unit. Id. at 25147.

In commenting on these proposed rules, organized labor was most critical of the notion that all service, maintenance, and clerical employees must be organized in a single bargaining unit. They demonstrated that business office clericals, patient-service workers, and skilled maintenance workers all operate in distinct internal and external labor markets, have little daily contact, and have fundamentally different interests in unionization. Union witnesses also presented information showing that unionized hospital workers strike far less often than workers in other areas and that workers organized into large bargaining units are more likely to strike than those who are organized in smaller units. They emphasized that wage rates are more influenced by markets external to the hospital than by comparisons amongst hospital workers. See BNA, Daily Labor Report, A-1 and A-11 (Oct. 26, 1987), summarizing testimony on proposed regulations.

Hospital representatives, on the other hand, argued that the Board should recognize only three bargaining units — all professionals, all nonprofessionals, and guards. The hospitals asserted that smaller unions would lead to more strikes and "whipsaw" negotiation in which each group attempted to obtain as much as, or more, than others. The hospitals also urged the Board to avoid promulgating unit determination rules and to continue the process of ad hoc determination that would recognize the allegedly unique circumstances of each hospital. Id.

The regulations adopted by the Board in 1988 reject the view that unit determination issues can be resolved in relation to a "principle," whether "community" or "disparity" of interests. Rather, on the basis of extensive empirical evidence gathered through public hearings and factual submissions, the Board defined as appropriate the eight specific bargaining units that had been recognized prior to the *St. Francis II* decision. Further, the Board ruled that the same rules should apply to all acute care hospitals of whatever size. Finally, the Board declined to issue any rules governing unit determinations in the nursing home context, recognizing that the evidence before it did not provide sufficient basis for such rules. NLRB, Collective-Bargaining Units in the Health Care Industry, 54 Fed. Reg. 16336 (April 21, 1989), amending 29 C.F.R. §103.30.

d. Geographical Scope of Bargaining Units

Generally the NLRB allows a union to organize a bargaining unit in a single plant or store of a multi-facility corporation. Hospitals and nursing homes are increasingly integrated into multi-institutional structures. Health care employers have sought to invoke the Congressional admonition against undue proliferation to require that unions organize workers in all facilities in a state or region. The NLRB usually certifies bargaining units in a single facility. The Congressional concern about proliferation was directed to various types of health care workers, not to workers in diverse facilities. In *Manor Healthcare Inc.*, 285 NLRB 31 (1987), the Board rejected a multi-facility nursing home corporation's claim that workers in all of their Baltimore area homes should be organized in a single unit. The Board found that "[a]lthough there is a certain degree of administrative centralization, there is an almost complete lack of functional integration. Patient care proceeds independently at each facility and all day-to-day labor matters are administered within the separate facilities, albeit under guidelines established by corporate officials and subject to their review." Id. at 35.

3. LEGAL IMPEDIMENTS TO THE UNIONIZATION OF DOCTORS

Cedars-Sinai Medical Center v. Cedars-Sinai Housestaff

223 NLRB 251 (1976)

(1) Cedars-Sinai Medical Center is a private nonprofit California corporation engaged in the operation of a medical center, including acute general hospitals, in the Los Angeles area.

(2) The Employer contends that the Petitioner is not a labor organization within the meaning of Section 2(5) of the Act. The Petitioner's constitution states its purpose is to unite the Employer's interns and residents for the attainment of their collective goals including, inter alia, contract negotiations pertaining to salaries and working conditions. As we find hereinafter that the interns, residents, and clinical fellows are not "employees" within the meaning of the Act, and the record shows that Petitioner is composed solely and exclusively of interns, residents, and clinical fellows at Cedars-Sinai, we find . . . that the Petitioner is not a labor organization within the meaning of the Act.

(3) . . . The Petitioner seeks to represent a unit of interns, residents, and clinical fellows. The Employer contends that such a unit is inappropriate because, [they] . . . are students, not employees. We find merit in the Employer's position [and] . . . conclude that the interns, residents, and clinical fellows in the petitioned-for unit are not "employees" within the meaning of Section 2(3) of the Act. The record shows that the medical education and training of a physician involves a progression from classroom and laboratory education in the basic and clinical sciences, through an internship, and usually then to a period of more advanced training in a specialty or subspecialty of medicine. It is the purpose of internship and residency programs to put into practice the principles of preventive medicine, diagnosis, therapy, and management of patients that the medical school graduate learned in medical school.

An intern is a medical school graduate serving his first period of graduate medical training in a hospital. Most states, including California, require an internship of one year to qualify for the examination to practice medicine. A resident is a physician who has completed an internship and serves a period of more advanced training, lasting from one to five years, in a specialty. A clinical fellow is a physician who has completed an internship and a residency and is taking an educational postgraduate program to qualify for certification in an identifiable subspecialty of medicine. The term "housestaff" is commonly used by medical and hospital personnel, and will be used in this Decision, when referring collectively to interns, residents, and clinical fellows. Graduate medical education and training programs to qualify for licensing and for certification in a specialty or subspecialty are governed by national medical organizations, . . . and by state licensing authorities. The standards for internships and residencies are contained in "Essentials of an Approved Internship" and "Essentials of Approved Residencies," . . . prepared by the Council on Medical Education and approved by the American Medical Association. The programs are carried out in hospitals that are accredited by these various bodies and that in many instances have affiliation agreements with approved medical schools. . . .

Cedars-Sinai offers internships and residencies in [several fields]. . . . Its programs are fully accredited by the Council on Medical Education of the American Medical Association and by the various specialty boards. Cedars-Sinai has affiliation agreements with the UCLA Medical School. [C]ertain of its approximately 1000 voluntary attending staff physicians who participate in the teaching program also hold UCLA appointments. The medical staff, but not the housestaff, has admission privileges at Cedars-Sinai.

. . . The placement of graduating medical students at Cedars-Sinai is governed by the National Intern and Resident Matching Program. This program is designed to place graduating medical students with a preferred graduate training institution. Both the students and the hospitals register with the National Matching Program by signing an agreement that they will be bound by the matching results. The procedure is for a graduating medical student to make out a preference list of positions. . . . The hospitals make out a ranking list of their student applicants. The entire basis for matching decisions is the student-ranking list in combination with the hospital list. . . .

The activities of interns, residents, and clinical fellows while in graduate programs such as those operated by Cedars-Sinai are prescribed by the accrediting bodies. . . . The training programs consist of patient care activities coordinated with a variety of teaching and educational activities designed to develop the student's clinical judgment and proficiency in clinical skills. . . . These patient-care activities, an integral part of a physician's educational training, are coordinated with a variety of teaching and educational activities, such as grand rounds, teaching rounds, laboratory instruction, seminars, and lectures. . . . During their training at Cedars-Sinai, members of the housestaff receive an annual stipend. . . . The amount of the stipend is not determined by the nature of the services rendered or by the number of hours spent in patient care. . . . The "Essentials" characterize the stipend as a scholarship for graduate study. The housestaff also receives a variety of fringe benefits, such as medical and dental care, an annual vacation and paid holidays, uniforms, meals while on duty, and malpractice insurance. They are not eligible for Cedars-Sinai's retirement plan. Discipline is administered by a housestaff committee.

The tenure of interns and residents at Cedars-Sinai is closely related to the length of the program which each individual pursues. [T]he average stay of interns and residents at Cedars-Sinai is less than 2 years. . . . Only a few interns, residents, or clinical fellows can expect to, or do, remain to establish an employment relationship with Cedars-Sinai.

[W]e do not find here that students and employees are antithetical entities or mutually exclusive categories under the Act. Instead, we find that the interns, residents, and clinical fellows who filed the petition herein are primarily engaged in graduate educational training at Cedars-Sinai. It is the educational relationship that exists between the housestaff and Cedars-Sinai (a teaching hospital) which leads us to conclude that the housestaff are students rather than employees, i.e., that the housestaff's relationship with Cedars-Sinai is an educational rather than an employment relationship. . . .

Member FANNING, dissenting:

[T]he issue in these cases is not how to exploit semantic distinctions between the terms "students" and "employees." One does not, necessarily, exclude the other and, indeed, this Board has included "students" in bargaining units in numerous cases and has authorized elections in which the voting group was composed exclusively of "students." The touchstone has always been whether the "students" were also employees. [T]he issues before us are simply stated. Are those doctors commonly denominated "housestaff" entitled to bargain collectively under the auspices of our statute . . . ?

Section 2(3) of the Act states that the term "employee" is meant to "include any employee . . . unless the Act explicitly states otherwise," and proceeds to explicitly state those excluded from the definition, e.g., agricultural laborers, domestic servants, et al. "Students" are not among those exclusions. Recognition of an underlying Federal policy which seeks to draw a line between labor and management has further led to the exclusion, on such policy grounds, of two additional classes of "employees," namely, confidential and managerial employees. That is all. Since the statutory exclusions do not mention and the policy underlying the nonstatutory exclusions does not reach "students," the relationship between "student" and "employee" cannot be said to be mutually exclusive. . . .

If we posit that Section 2(3)'s usage of the term "employee" is no broader than the common law's, housestaff officers, are, beyond doubt, employees within the meaning of the Act.

The term "employee" is the outgrowth of the common law concept of the "servant." At common law, a servant was a "person employed to perform services in the affairs of another and who with respect to the physical conduct in the performance of the services is subject to the other's control or right of control." [T]he conventional meaning of the word implies someone who works or performs a service for another from whom he or she receives compensation. It is significant to note that the common law's development of the master-servant doctrine was principally concerned with establishing a tortious liability in the master for the acts of the servant and, indeed, the principle of respondeat superior plays more than a small part in the current malpractice crisis. . . . That my colleagues have ignored a significant component of the hospital-housestaff relationship namely the former's vicarious liability for the actions of the latter, is a convenient introduction to another aspect of these cases which requires greater discussion — the facts.

All housestaff officers are M.D.'s. All fellows and residents are licensed physicians in every State of the Union. . . . The records before us demonstrate . . . that housestaff officers, without immediate supervision of any kind, continually deal in matters literally of the ultimate significance. That they do is a function, no doubt, of their hours. The housestaff work round-the-clock, 7 days a week, 52 weeks a year. No other physicians do. They perform their services, on an individual basis, for periods lasting, at times, well over 100 hours a week, in shifts that often exceed 50 consecutive hours. They singly staff emergency rooms, frequently at times when their supposed "teachers" are not even in the facility. That accounts for the record facts which demonstrate that, without supervision, a housestaff officer can be called upon and, in fact, has been called upon, to open the chest wall of a 3-year-old child; hold the heart of a patient in his hands; remove breast tissues, kidneys, veins; deliver babies; . . . administer closely controlled and potentially lethal medications; and perform a host of similar procedures. . . . In return for those services, the hospital pays that housestaff officer what my colleagues call a "stipend." It exceeds, in some cases of multiple residencies, $20,000 a year. From that "stipend," the hospital withholds Federal and state taxes, contributes to social security, and provides for health insurance. . . . For those services the housestaff receives, absent unusual circumstances not before us, no degree, no grades, no examinations. Housestaff officers perform those services on (and in) individuals who would hardly take comfort in the notion that the individual in whose hands their life itself may repose is not primarily interested in performing that service for the hospital and patient but, rather, is primarily a student of the matter. [T]he Association of American Medical Colleges . . . [reports that] approximately 80 percent of a housestaff officer's time is spent "in direct patient care activities." Certainly, there is a didactic component to the work of any initiate, but simply because an individual is "learning" while performing this service cannot possibly be said to mark that individual as "primarily a student and, therefore, not an employee" for purposes of our statute.

I turn briefly to a consideration of the limited factors upon which my colleagues purport to rely: (a) The "Essentials," which describe the standards for approved internships and residencies, indicate that the primary function is educational. . . . The "Essentials" constitute, in part, a set of guidelines and instructions to hospitals which would seek to become training institutions. . . . [They mandate] . . . "Employment Agreements" which "should specify at a minimum . . . the salary . . . vacation periods . . . hours of duty," etc., of housestaff officers. . . . [The AMA's "Guidelines for Housestaff Contracts or Agreements" require] fair and equitable conditions of employment for all those performing the duties of interns residents and fellows. . . . It recognizes "The inherent right of a member of the housestaff to contract and negotiate freely with the institution, individually or collectively, for terms and conditions of employment and training should not be denied or infringed. No contract should require or proscribe that members of the housestaff shall or shall not be members of an association or union." [T]here is some support for the proposition that the primary interest of the housestaff's representational aims is the improvement of patient care . . . [and] that the primary value attached to an individual residency or subspecialty is the quality of the institution providing that program, and the opportunity of exposure to a wide range of medical experience. . . . There is, on the other hand, absolutely no support for a statement which implies that the so-called "stipend" (the AMA calls it "salary," the study initiated in part by AAMC calls it a "wage," the IRS calls it "payment for services rendered") is not a considerable source of concern. . . . I fail to perceive how the fact that an individual . . . chooses a residency program based on its quality and the opportunity for extensive training bears relevance to the question whether, having done so, he or she is an "employee" under the Act. It is, for example, fairly common knowledge that physicians engaged in private practice for many years take up residencies both within their certified specialty (to keep abreast of developments) and outside their certified specialty (to expand upon their skills). . . .

Section 2(12) of the Act sets forth the definition of a "professional employee" as:

> (a) any employee engaged in work . . .
>
> (iv) requiring knowledge of an advanced type in a field of science or learning customarily acquired by a prolonged course of specialized intellectual instruction and study in an institution of higher learning or a hospital . . . or
>
> (b). any employee, who
>
> (i) has completed the courses of specialized intellectual instruction and study described in clause (iv) of paragraph (a), and
>
> (ii) is performing related work under the supervision of a professional person to qualify himself to become a professional employee as defined in paragraph (a).

. . . Section 2(12) was, in part, designed to cover housestaff specifically.

In the words of the House Conference Report . . . , the section was designed to embrace "such persons as legal, engineering, scientific and medical personnel together with their junior professional assistants," and, as the language of Section 2(12)(b) so clearly states, included in the definition of professional employee are individuals who have completed courses of specialized instruction and are performing related work under the supervision of Section 2(12)(a) professionals. The definition fits, precisely, housestaff officers.

A large segment of the committee hearings on the recent amendments was devoted to the testimony, statements, and accompanying documents of representatives of the housestaff in support of the amendments. . . . At no time during the course of the hearings was even a mention made that housestaff officers, because "students," might not be entitled to coverage under the Act. [A]ny reasonably diligent reading of the legislative history surrounding the amendments would make it clear that coverage of housestaff, in some context, was an assumption on the part of Congress. [The] floor manager of the Senate bill indicated . . . that one of the conditions the bill was designed to redress was the "notoriously underpaid . . . average annual salary for all hospital employees — including doctors. . . . According to [the] president of the Physicians National Housestaff Association, the average house staff officer — intern, resident, or fellow — works 70 to 100 hours per week, and earns about $10,000 per year. His hourly wage, then ranges from $1.92 to $2.74."

4. THE UNIONIZATION OF DOCTORS

a. Unionization of Housestaff

Following the decision in *Cedars-Sinai,* housestaff organizations sought to persuade Congress to clarify that housestaff were employees entitled to organize under the protection of the National Labor Relations Act. Witnesses and members of Congress considered whether a collective bargaining relationship is necessarily inconsistent with an educational process. Members of Congress sympathetic to the hospitals pressed the housestaff to provide a conceptual definition of the appropriate scope of bargaining. Housestaff responded by pointing to a history of successful negotiation with hospitals where unions had been organized. See Hospital Housestaff as Professional Employees: Hearings before the Subcommittee on Labor Management Relations of the House Committee on Education and Labor, 95th Cong., 1st Sess., 288-289 (1977). The head of the American Association of Medical Colleges testified that collective bargaining undermined the inherently unequal relation between housestaff and teaching hospitals, but did not cite specific problems in prior collective bargaining with housestaff in several states. Id. at 34-35. The Committee concluded that the evidence "establishes that collective bargaining between hospitals and housestaff . . . result[s] in better medical education for housestaff and better care for hospital patients." Coverage of Medical Housestaff Under the National Labor Relations Act. Report of the Committee on Education and Labor, Rep. No. 95-980, 95th Cong., 2d Sess., 5, (1978). Nonetheless, Congress did not clarify that housestaff are employees entitled to the protection of the Act.

In Physicians National Housestaff Association v. Fanning, 642 F.2d 492 (D.C. Cir. 1980), *cert. denied,* 450 U.S. 917 (1981), a sharply divided court held that the courts had no power to review the Board's determination that housestaff were not employees because it did not constitute a "plain violation of a mandatory provision of the NLRA." The majority also noted that Congress did not adopt the statutory clarification sought by the housestaff in 1978.

Prior to the *Cedars-Sinai* decision, housestaff in Nebraska, New York, Pennsylvania, Massachusetts, and Michigan were regulated as employees under state labor laws. Housestaff unions continued to operate under the framework of the state labor laws when they were denied protection under the NLRA. In 1976 the Board held that "Federal preemption of the health care field [precludes] States from exercising their power to regulate in this area. . . . *Cedars-Sinai* . . . has not put hospital residents and interns beyond the reach of national labor policy, but has rather held that to extend them collective-bargaining rights would be contrary to that very policy." Kansas City General Hospital (*Kansas City II*), 225 NLRB 108, 109 (1976). NLRB v. Committee of Interns and Residents, 566 F.2d 810 (2d Cir. 1977), *cert. denied,* 435 U.S. 904 (1978), upheld this ruling.

In the 1990s, housestaff unions continue to represent interns and residents in areas in which they had already established contractual relationships with hospitals. However, housestaff unionization has not expanded to new areas and hospitals. Since neither federal nor state law protects housestaff rights to organize and bargain collectively, people who seek to organize have no protection against dismissal or other forms of discipline. Teaching hospitals can refuse to bargain collectively, even if a majority of the housestaff seek to do so. See S. Caswell, The Movement that Died: Housestaff Unionization in the Private Sector, 31 Labor L.J. 332 (1986).

States retain authority to regulate labor relations in the public sector. California's Public Employee Review Board has rejected a hospital's claim that housestaff are students, not employees. Physicians National Housestaff Association v. Regents of the University of California, reported in 1 Labor Lawyer 448 (1985).

b. Other Physician Unions

In the mid-1980s, almost one quarter of physicians work as employees of hospitals, the government, or in other settings such as HMOs and group practices. As more doctors cease to be independent agents contracting with patients and become employees of large bureaucratic organizations, interest in unionization grows. In part physicians are concerned that as employees, they earn significantly less than doctors in private practice. But more often, doctors state that they are motivated to unionize by a desire to promote quality patient care and resist unwarranted employer demands for cost control or profitability. See S. Marcus, Trade Unionism for Doctors: An Idea Whose Time Has Come, 311 N. Engl. J. Med. 1508 (1984). K. Stickler and

M. Nelson, Doctors and Unions: Is Collective Bargaining the Cure for Physicians' Labor Pains?, 13 Employee Rel. L.J. 4 (1987).

c. Physician Unions and Antitrust Liability

Physicians who organize may risk liability under the antitrust laws. Agreements among competitors to fix prices are a per se violation of the federal antitrust laws. See discussion Chapter 8. However, labor unions are immune from antitrust liability if they act in their own self-interest. U.S. v. Hutcheson, 312 U.S. 219, 231 (1941). A labor dispute must involve an employer-employee relationship, not "independent businessmen." Columbia River Packers Association v. Hinton, 315 U.S. 143, 146-147 (1942). These conflicting standards raise many uncertainties as to when physicians, especially private practitioners, can bargain collectively without violating the antitrust laws.

d. Physicians as Supervisors

For physicians, as for nurses, the distinction between employees and supervisors seriously constrains doctors' ability to unionize. In NLRB v. Yeshiva University, 444 U.S. 672 (1980), the Supreme Court upheld a Board rule that professors could not unionize because they exercised managerial authority through work on university committees. See discussion, M. Angel, Professionals and Unionization, 66 Minn. L. Rev. 383 (1982).

In FHP Inc., 274 NLRB 1141 (1985), the Board held that physicians and dentists working for an HMO could not unionize because their duties included "managerial" tasks through service on committees that monitored quality of care. The Board said:

> To be sure, the committees are not involved, for example, in setting base salaries or formulating premiums to be charged FHP subscribers. These decisions are made at the corporate level. Similarly, hiring decisions are made not on the basis of any of the standing or ad hoc committee recommendations, but by the provider director on the basis of departmental need and the recommendations of the recruiting division, the department chairmen, and area chiefs. Nonetheless, the record convincingly demonstrates that many of the decisions made at the committee level, which include managing the organization's protocol system, overseeing its medical records system, setting its medical prescription policy, reviewing and modifying the benefits and working conditions of its staff, establishing procedures and staff training for medical emergencies, and minimizing the institution's risk of medical malpractice liability, lie at the core of the HMO's operations. Accordingly, we conclude that the committees perform managerial functions within the meaning of the *Yeshiva* decision. [Id. at 1143.]

In Montefiore Hospital and Medical Center and New York State Federation of Physicians and Dentists, 261 NLRB 569 (1982), the Board rejected the hospital's claim that physicians exercised supervisory authority through participation in committee work at the medical school and in the teaching hospitals. The Board found that managerial authority was exercised by the central administration, heads of various medical departments, and chiefs of hospital services. Unlike the university setting, where the faculty of each school makes collegial decisions, "the medical and dental departments of the Medical Center are governed by the department chairmen or directors, and administered by them with the aid of subordinate supervisors called, variously, directors, chairmen, deputy chairmen, and chiefs of services." Id. at 571.

Physicians thus face a quandary. To unionize successfully, they must demonstrate that they are employees who work for wages at a site determined by the employer and that the employer controls and directs services as to place, time, and detail. On the one hand, a prime motivation for unionization is to gain greater control over patient care. On the other hand, if physicians gain such control they will be deemed supervisors, denied the protection of the labor laws, and subjected to the risk of antitrust liability.

5. SOME LEGAL IMPEDIMENTS TO THE UNIONIZATION OF NURSES

NLRB v. North Shore University Hospital

724 F.2d 269 (2nd Cir. 1983)

This case involves a petition for enforcement by the National Labor Relations Board of an order directing respondent North Shore University Hospital to bargain with New York State Nurses Association ("SNA") as the certified bargaining representative of the nonsupervisory registered nurses employed by the Hospital.. . . At an election conducted by the Board among North Shore Hospital's nonsupervisory nurses, . . . SNA, a professional organization of registered nurses, was selected as a bargaining representative by a vote of 368 to 96. The Hospital filed objections to the election, asserting that SNA was not qualified to be a bargaining representative "because its actions are controlled, directed and/or influenced by persons who occupy supervisory positions within health care institutions," including North Shore Hospital. [The Board rejected the hospital's argument and ordered it to bargain.] . . . We deny enforcement and remand.

SNA . . . operates a variety of programs related to nursing and the care of the sick. One of these programs, Economic and General Welfare ("EGW"), includes a collective bargaining component for member nurses. At the time of the hearing below, SNA had some 29,000 members, 25,000 of whom were represented by SNA for collective bargaining purposes in approximately 115 bargaining units at public and private health care facilities throughout New York State. SNA admits both supervisors and nonsupervisory nurses to membership, all members having equal privileges.

SNA is governed by a thirteen-member board of directors elected by the membership. SNA's executive and program staff is made up of full-time employees, including program directors, regional coordinators, nursing representatives, and labor relations representatives. . . . The SNA staff provides bargaining units of nurses with technical assistance in the form of suggested model rules or guidelines with respect to the organization of bargaining units. After discussing with SNA staff its own particular needs, a unit adopts its own rules.

While unit nurses do not submit bargaining proposals to the SNA for approval, they frequently develop specific proposals in their initial meetings with SNA staff members. Contract negotiations are conducted by a negotiating committee elected from the unit membership. The SNA representative assists and frequently functions as the primary negotiator on behalf of the unit, although a member of the local unit may handle negotiations relating to a particular proposal.

The authority of SNA staff to negotiate on behalf of the unit is limited by the ultimate power of the unit to adopt or reject negotiating proposals. [T]he legal issues before us involve the role of supervisors in SNA. Since SNA is a professional organization of registered nurses performing numerous functions of interest to nurses in addition to collective bargaining, it is to be expected that nurses who join early in their careers and subsequently become supervisors are likely to retain membership in SNA.

The record shows that supervisors are very active in SNA's affairs. . . . [Nonetheless, the Administrative Law Judge (ALJ)] rejected North Shore's claim that SNA is so dominated by supervisors that it should not be certified. Applying the Board's test set out in Sierra Vista Hospital, Inc., 241 NLRB 631 (1979), the ALJ held that the Hospital had not carried the "burden . . . of showing that danger of a conflict of interest interfering with the collective bargaining process is clear and present." . . . The Board affirmed.

We are confronted here with a situation in which two normally consistent policies of the Act conflict. On the one hand, the freedom of choice by the employees to select a particular bargaining representative or none at all is a core policy of the Act. . . . On the other, Section 8(a)(2) of the Act limits the influence of agents of the employer such as supervisors upon such bargaining representatives to ensure that collective bargaining is truly at arms length. . . .

All agree that certain degrees of supervisory influence within an organization may be so great that it will be unable to qualify as a bargaining representative. . . . Indeed, a major purpose of Section 8(a)(2), appears to have been the elimination of the celebrated "company-dominated union," . . . once prevalent as an anti-union device but now only an occasional curiosity. . . . Although the company union may be largely a thing of the past, the policy against it remains, and the question before us is the extent to which, as a consequence of that policy, supervisory influence may disqualify a multipurpose professional organization from representing rank and file employees in collective bargaining.

We agree with the Board that the fact that supervisors are members of such an organization does not automatically disqualify it as a statutory bargaining representative. We also agree that unless there is "clear and present danger" of "a conflict of interest interfering with the collective bargaining process," resort to disqualification is inappropriate. . . . However, we disagree with the Board's application of the *Sierra Vista* test . . . because it limits the inquiry as to a conflict of interest to proof of explicit supervisory interference in the case of the particular bargaining unit before it. While that narrow inquiry may be appropriate in the case of an organization representing the employees of one employer in an industrial context, it is inadequate to effectuate the policies of the Act in the case of a multipurpose professional organization representing thousands of employees in numerous bargaining units. We believe that in the latter case the inquiry must extend to all relevant circumstances. . . .

We conclude that the governing structure and actual practices are important for several reasons. First, supervisors who participate actively in a professional organization which represents (or is seeking to represent) rank and file employees who serve under them, are by the very nature of their relationship to their employer and to the professional organization subject to conflicting pressures. Since these are the two most important entities affecting their career, the existence of a conflict of interest both within the organization and on the job is indisputable. It is the existence of the conflict, moreover, not whether in particular instances a supervisor resolves it in favor of the organization, the employees, or the employer, which is of importance. . . .

Second, supervisors as a class have interests of their own, and an organization which is itself governed in part by supervisors will tend to reflect at least in part those interests. For example, the authority of supervisors vis-à-vis rank and file employees is usually a major issue in collective bargaining. An organization in which supervisors play a significant governing role will have difficulty in isolating and reflecting only the views of the rank and file on that issue. Staff of the professional organization who are employed at the pleasure of a board of directors containing supervisors cannot easily cast aside the knowledge that supervisory employees have a say in their own employment when they advise employees on bargaining positions and negotiate on their behalf. Moreover, it is tunnel vision to assume that this influence will be of importance only when a supervisor of employees in a particular unit is a member of the board of directors of the certified bargaining representative. Third, evidence of explicit interference in collective bargaining of the kind demanded by the Board may not be available. . . . When supervisors and employees are not members in a common union, the former can usually influence union affairs only through job-related activities. Where active membership is shared, such influence may be internalized in the normal course of union affairs and not be subject to direct proof. For example, supervisors may not only have control over an employee's working conditions but may also be able to affect the employee's role in the professional organization. Indeed, the more pervasive that influence is, the more difficult it may be to prove simply because the rank and file acquiesces. . . .

Fourth, where supervisors are active in the internal affairs of a bargaining representative, actual violations of Section 8(a)(2) attributable to employers seem inevitable. Consider, for example, Professor Gorman's description of the Board's present case law on the subject:

> In itself, retention of union membership by supervisors is not illegal. But it is illegal for supervisors to serve as union officials or on a union bargaining team, . . . or . . . even to vote in elections for union officers, since the supervisors might have the balance of power in a close election and could therefore select union officials who will later deal with them in their capacity as employer representatives.
>
> . . . The Board has held that it is unlawful for a supervisor to vote in an election of a delegate to be sent by the local union to the annual convention of the international, since that delegate may at the international meeting shape a policy which will affect the local in its dealings with the employer. It has even been suggested that the supervisor/union-member may not speak out on contentious issues at union meetings, since this will stifle the expression of opposing views by rank-and-file employees who may fear for their job security at the hands of the supervisor. . . . [R. Gorman, Labor Law, 199-200 (1976).]

We believe it reasonably obvious that . . . certifying SNA as a bargaining representative without more will inexorably lead to systematic violations of Section 8(a)(2) chargeable to North Shore Hospital. Neither the Board nor SNA deny that the active role of supervisors in SNA affairs may cause the Hospital to violate Section 8(a)(2). Rather, they argue that the activities of supervisors in SNA are not so egregious as to override the free choice of the Hospital's nurses. . . . This argument might well be persuasive if either the Board or SNA demonstrated any readiness to help prevent such violations. Instead, however, they profess their own lack of responsibility and state that it is up to the Hospital and the Hospital alone to prevent its supervisors from violating Section 8(a)(2) through their activities in SNA.

We reject this cavalier view of the Board's role under the Act. Having primary enforcement responsibility and full power to bring charges on its own, the Board ought not acquiesce in situations in which violations seem so probable. . . . We by no means suggest either that a professional organization such as SNA cannot have a collective bargaining component or that the Board may not take the multiple goals of such organizations into account in fashioning appropriate rules under Section 8(a)(2). . . . SNA is hardly a company-dominated union. . . . The degree to which the Act requires a restructuring of a professional organization such as SNA is for the Board in the first instance to decide. It must, however, look at all the circumstances, including the structure of the organization and the role of supervisors in its governance. Where that role is of significance, the Board should determine the appropriate methods of insulating the collective bargaining component and of preventing supervisors from violating Section 8(a)(2) through activities within the organization. . . .

NOTE ON THE ROLE OF NURSES' ASSOCIATIONS IN ORGANIZING NURSES

For reasons of professional self-image and history, when nurses consider unionization they usually prefer to be represented by their professional association, which can, they hope, reconcile the values and methodology of professionalism and unionization. As the main case illustrates, the labor law makes it difficult for nurses to make this choice.

The Board's decision in *Sierra Vista III,* cited in the main case, held that if nurses chose to be represented by their state nurses' association, the group would not be disqualified unless the employer "meet[s] the 'heavy burden' of showing that the participation of supervisors presents a 'clear and present danger' of conflict of interest which compromises the labor organization's bargaining integrity." French Hospital Medical Center, 254 NLRB 711 (1981).

On remand of the *North Shore* case, the Board declined to establish guidelines to clarify when a nurses association will be allowed to represent nurses. Furthermore, other circuit courts have continued to enforce the *Sierra Vista III* standard. See NLRB v. Walker County Medical Center, 722 F.2d 1535 (11th Cir. 1984). Hence, hospitals, unions, NLRB regional representatives, and administrative law judges all confront tremendous uncertainty.

In response to the *North Shore* decisions, the New York State Nurses Association reorganized itself to insulate its collective bargaining function from supervisory influence. It created a unit, the Council of Nursing Practitioners (CNP), with membership restricted to nonsupervisory nurses. Ultimate bargaining authority rests with the CNP. Highland Hospital v. NLRB, 861 F.2d 56 (2nd Cir. 1988), upheld a Board order requiring a hospital to negotiate with the newly constituted NYSNA. The court rejected the hospital's claim that the presence of supervisory nurses on the NYSNA board of directors precluded the organization from representing nurses. "[T]he board of directors is not involved in, nor can it interfere with, collective bargaining matters." Id. at 59.

Whether or not nurses are represented by a state nurses association, it is often difficult to determine whether a nurse, either registered or practical, is a supervisor. LPNs frequently have significant responsibility in directing the work of aids and, especially in nursing homes, are often the person on the premises with greatest authority. But these workers, like RNs, are simultaneously subject to enormous medical and administrative control. Two companion opinions by Judge Posner explore these issues. NLRB v. Res-Care, Inc., 705 F.2d 1461 (7th Cir. 1983), held that a group of LPNs were not supervisors, despite their authority over aides. By contrast, NLRB v. American Medical Services, Inc., 705 F.2d 1472 (7th Cir. 1983), reversed a Board order allowing a unit of nurses, on very similar facts. The court relied, in part, on "the evident difference between the . . . ratio of supervisors to employees if the Board's position is upheld. . . . Since . . . the purpose of excluding supervisors from the protection of the . . . act is to give the employer a solid cadre of employees who owe undivided loyalty to him, this discrepancy in ratios in two facilities that are similar except in size raises a warning flag." 705 F.2d 1473.

One hospital attorney observes that under *North Shore's* "all-relevant circumstances" standard, "employers are given the opportunity to protract representation proceedings, to threaten to petition the Board for revocation of the organization's certification, and to engage in fishing expeditions which inquire into the inner workings of the labor organization." D. Dyleski-Najjar, Professional Unions in the Health Care Industry, 17 Loy. U. Chi. L.J. 383, 403 (1986).

At an abstract level it is easy enough to understand that the interests of both unions and employers are compromised when a single individual plays a dual role as both supervisor and union leader. Try to think concretely what this means in the hospital context. Characterize the interests of employers, nurse employees, unions, and nurse supervisors. What sorts of rules could the NLRB adopt to assure that supervisors do not exercise inappropriate power in professional organizations that represent nurses?

6. BARGAINING ON ISSUES OF PATIENT CARE

Both nurses and doctors are more likely to engage in strikes or job actions over issues of working conditions related to patient care than over economic issues. Bargaining demands focus on levels of staffing, the need for equipment and translators, excessive work hours that undermine ability to provide quality care, resistance to demands that employees perform tasks for which they are not trained, efforts to increase support staff, and participation in quality review or joint study committees. R. U. Miller, The Impact of Collective Bargaining on Hospitals, 114-117 (1979).

Most hospital administrators will not discuss such issues or accept contractual limitations on management prerogatives. The Executive Committee of the American Hospital Association states:

> The staffing of a hospital must be an objective process and should not be controlled by a group with special interests. . . . Nurses as an organized group are not legally responsible for patient care. Only management has the responsibility

> to determine the number of employees, their qualifications, and their assignments within the institution so as to be consistent with the best patient care and the most effective utilization of personnel. [Quoted in Miller, Id.]

The labor law largely supports this position. Professor Howard Lesnick describes the concept of work reflected in the labor law.

> The dominant view conceives of work as an exchange relationship. Work is a burden, i.e. the giving up of "leisure" in return for compensation. The utility of the work is defined by the user, initially the employer as the direct purchaser of labor, ultimately the consumer. The employer decides what it contracts to buy; the employee "fills the job." The worker has a role defined by the job and does not own the job. The value of work for the worker is only as a means toward self-sufficiency separate from work. The worker has no legitimate interest in the product, but only in the pay and working conditions, which affect him or her personally. [Unpublished draft.]

Lesnick protests this conception of work, saying, "Work is not merely the sale of a sale-able piece of oneself, in return for self sufficiency; it is an expression of one's energy, one's capacity and desire to be useful, one's responsibility and connection to fellow humans." Id. See also Lesnick, The Consciousness of Work and the Values of American Labor Law, 32 Buff. L. Rev. 833 (1983). In the context of medical services, particularly the work of skilled professionals, it is difficult to conceive that administrators, rather than doctors, nurses and other hands-on providers of care, have sole power to define the content of work.

In Good Samaritan Hospital & Health Center, 265 NLRB 618 (1982), two occupational therapists alleged that they were wrongfully dismissed for engaging in concerted activities protected under §7 of the NLRA. For several months, the employees had protested the professional competence, therapeutic philosophy, and ethics of the newly hired director of the Developmental Learning Program. The Board dismissed their complaints noting that "they readily conceded they were concerned with the quality of care offered by the program and the welfare of the children. . . . [T]heir energies were not directed to improve their lot as employees, but were instead an effort on their part to affect the ultimate direction, philosophy, and managerial policies. . . . As such, their criticisms and recommendations related to disputes outside the objectives of the mutual aid or protection provisions of the National Labor Relations Act." Id. at 626.

Lutheran Social Services of Minnesota Inc., 250 NLRB 35 (1980), reached the same result on similar facts and also criticizes the manner in which the employees expressed their concerns. "[T]heir behavior appears to have been essentially aimless and undirected, consisting of unremitting complaining about the value of management policies and the competence and good faith of their managers and coworkers. . . ." Id. at 43.

By contrast, the Board ordered the reinstatement of a head nurse who was discharged for activities "disloyal" to the employer when she joined a group that submitted evidence of serious deficiencies in the hospital to a JCAH survey accreditation team. The Second Circuit upheld the Board's order, and rejected the hospital's defense that the submission of evidence to the JCAH was solely in the interests of patient welfare, and hence unrelated to working conditions. The court observed that "in the health care field such issues often appear to be inextricably intertwined." Misericordia Hospital Medical Center v. NLRB, 623 F.2d 808 (2d Cir. 1980).

Similarly, in NLRB v. Mount Desert Island Hospital, 695 F.2d 634 (1st Cir. 1982), the court upheld a Board finding that a nurse had engaged in protected activity when, after filing complaints with the administrators and talking with fellow workers, he wrote a letter to the local paper asserting that inadequate staffing undermined patient care. The hospital contended that a letter signed only by one person could not constitute "concerted action." The court found that the "letter may be considered a direct overture for further concerted efforts to improve working conditions. . . ." Shortly after the letter was published, thirty other employees met with the editor of the Times and substantiated Grange's complaints about working conditions. Within three weeks, over one hundred employees signed Grange's petition. Id. at 639-640. The court also rejected the hospital's claim that the nurse's action was malicious in "needlessly" tarnishing the hospital's reputation. See also Community Hospital of Roanoke Valley, Inc. v. NLRB, 538 F.2d 607 (4th Cir. 1976), holding that a nurse's TV interview protesting hospital staffing levels was related to working conditions, not fabricated or disloyal, and hence protected.

Unionization has in fact placed little restraint on management prerogatives and discretion. Miller, supra at 124. It is not clear whether this is because of management resistance, because unions have focused on traditional economic concerns, or because the labor law defines these issues as within the sole authority of hospital administrators. See L. Hoffman, Housestaff Activism: The Emergence of Patient-Care Demands, 7 J. Health Polit. Policy L. 421 (1982).

D. Discrimination and Medical Work

Minorities and women are disproportionately represented in the hospital workforce. In 1977, 76 percent of all hospital workers were female, compared to 40 percent of all workers. Blacks comprised 18.9 percent of all hospital employees compared to 10.8 percent of all workers. The medical care workforce is sharply segregated along racial and sexual lines. Physicians, at the top of the medical care hierarchy, are predominantly white and male, although during the 1980s, the proportion of women physicians grew. In 1977, 89 percent of physicians were male, and 91 percent were white. RNs, next in the hierarchy, are almost exclusively (97 percent) female and are racially integrated (89 percent white). LPNs are also predominantly female (97 percent), and racially integrated (79 percent white). Aides and orderlies are 86 percent female, and 74 percent are white. Technicians and business office clericals are racially and sexually integrated, though white men tend to dominate the higher status, better paid positions. Maintenance workers are almost exclusively male and racially integrated. U.S. Bureau of Labor Statistics, Employment and Earnings, 161, 153, Tables 23 and 30 (Jan. 1978). See V. Navarro, Women in Health Care, 292 N. Engl. J. Med. 398 (1975).

This section examines antidiscrimination law in the medical care context. Do persistent racial and sexual segregation and hierarchy in the medical care workforce demonstrate that the antidiscrimination laws are ineffectual, or are there alternative explanations, other than discrimination, that account for these race and sex based disparities?

1. EXPLICIT RACE AND GENDER DISCRIMINATION

Mississippi University for Women v. Hogan

458 U.S. 718 (1981)

Justice O'Connor delivered the opinion of the Court.

This case presents the narrow issue of whether a state statute that excludes males from enrolling in a state-supported professional nursing school violates the Equal Protection Clause of the Fourteenth Amendment.

The facts are not in dispute. In 1884, the Mississippi Legislature created the Mississippi Industrial Institute and College for the Education of White Girls of the State of Mississippi, now the oldest state-supported all-female college in the United States. . . . The school, known today as Mississippi University for Women (MUW), has from its inception limited its enrollment to women. . . .

Respondent, Joe Hogan, is a registered nurse but does not hold a baccalaureate degree in nursing. Since 1974, he has worked as a nursing supervisor in a medical center in Columbus, the city in which MUW is located. In 1979, Hogan applied for admission to the MUW School of nursing's baccalaureate program. Although he was otherwise qualified, he was denied admission to the School of Nursing solely because of his sex. . . .

Because the challenged policy expressly discriminates among applicants on the basis of gender, it is subject to scrutiny under the Equal Protection Clause of the Fourteenth Amendment. . . . That this statutory policy discriminates against males rather than against females does not exempt it from scrutiny or reduce the standard of review. . . . Our decisions also establish that the party seeking to uphold a statute that classifies individuals on the basis of their gender must carry the burden of showing an "exceedingly persuasive justification" for the classification. . . . The burden is met only by showing at least that the classification serves "important governmental objectives and that the discriminatory means employed" are "substantially related to the achievement of those objectives."

Although the test for determining the validity of a gender-based classification is straightforward, it must be applied free of fixed notions concerning the roles and abilities of males and females. Care must be taken in ascertaining whether the statutory objective itself reflects archaic and stereotypic notions. Thus, if the statutory objective is to exclude or "protect" members of one gender because they are presumed to suffer from an inherent handicap or to be innately inferior, the objective itself is illegitimate. . . .

If the State's objective is legitimate and important, we next determine whether the requisite direct, substantial relationship between objective and means is present. The purpose of requiring that close relationship is to assure that the validity of a classification is determined through reasoned analysis rather than through the mechanical application of traditional, often inaccurate, assumptions about the proper roles of men and women. The need for the requirement is amply revealed by reference to the broad range of statutes already invalidated by this Court, statutes that relied upon the simplistic, outdated assumption that gender could be used as a "proxy for other, more germane bases of classification," . . . to establish a link between objective and classification. . . .

The State's primary justification for maintaining the single-sex admissions policy of MUW's School of Nursing is that it compensates for discrimination against women and, therefore, constitutes educational affirmative action. . . . As applied to the School of Nursing, we find the State's argument unpersuasive.

. . . Mississippi has made no showing that women lacked opportunities to obtain training in the field of nursing or to attain positions of leadership in that field when the MUW School of Nursing opened its door or that women currently are deprived of such opportunities. In fact, in 1970, the year before the School of Nursing's first class enrolled, women earned 94 percent of the nursing baccalaureate degrees conferred in Mississippi and 98.6 percent of the degrees earned nationwide. . . . When MUW's School of Nursing began operation, nearly 98 percent of all employed registered nurses were female. . . .

Rather than compensate for discriminatory barriers faced by women, MUW's policy of excluding males from admission to the School of Nursing tends to perpetuate the stereotyped view of nursing as an exclusively woman's job. . . . MUW's admissions policy lends credibility to the old view that women, not men, should become nurses, and makes the assumption that nursing is a field for women a self-fulfilling prophecy. . . .

Policies that explicitly differentiate on the basis of race or sex are rare. Is the *Hogan* decision likely to increase the numbers of men entering the nursing profession? Is an increase in the number of male nurses likely to produce increased authority and compensation for nurses as a whole?

Are there circumstances in which hospitals should be allowed to draw explicit sex-based distinctions in the assignment of medical and nursing personnel? These issues are most often litigated under Title VII of the Civil Rights Act of 1964, which prohibits employers from discriminating on the basis of race or sex. The Act permits sex based differentiations where sex is a "bona fide occupational qualification, (BFOQ)." 42 U.S.C. §2000e-2(a) requires that to establish sex as a BFOQ, an employer must demonstrate that the challenged policy is reasonably related to the essence of its business and that there is a factual basis for believing that it is impossible or impractical to deal with persons on an individual basis. Backus v. Baptist Medical Center, 510 F. Supp. 1191 (1981), *vacated,* 671 F.2d 1100 (1982), considered the claim of a male nurse who challenged a hospital policy that only female nurses could be assigned work with obstetrical patients. The district court accepted the hospital's claims that "the majority of women patients will object to intimate contact with a member of the opposite sex. . . . [Furthermore] a male nurse would necessitate the presence of a female nurse to protect the hospital from charges of molestation. This unnecessary duplication of man-power would result in higher salary costs." 510 F. Supp at 1194. Do you find these arguments persuasive? Are they applicable to male physicians, as well as male nurses? If not, why? The Circuit Court held the case moot because the plaintiff voluntarily left his job after he lost in the district court.

Many courts have considered whether Title VII applies when a hospital denies a physician staff privileges on allegedly discriminatory grounds. Most hold that Title VII applies to defendants who significantly affect access of any individual to employment opportunities, whether or not they are technically employers. The federal law, in broad terms, prohibits employers from discriminating against "any individual" and bars discrimination in relation to "privileges of employment" as well as employment itself. See Sibley Memorial Hospital v. Wilson, 488 F.2d 1338 (D.C. Circ. 1973); Gomez v. Alexian Brothers Hospital, 698 F.2d 1019, 1021 (9th Circ. 1983); Doe v. St. Joseph's Hospital, 788 F.2d 411 (7th Circ. 1986); Pardazi v. Cullman Medical Center, 838 F.2d 1155 (11th Cir. 1988); Zaklama v. Mt. Sinai Medical Center, 842 F.2d 291 (11th Cir. 1988). By contrast the Seventh Circuit decided that a nurse referral agency is neither an employer nor a union, and hence is not subject to Title VII. Shrock v. Altru Nurses Registry, 810 F.2d 658 (7th Cir. 1987).

Employers are prohibited from retaliating against employees who oppose discrimination. Wrighten v. Metropolitan Hospital Inc., 726 F.2d 1346 (9th Cir. 1984), upheld the claim of a black nurse who alleged that she had been fired because she complained about the adequacy of care provided to black patients.

In 1978, Congress amended Title VII to prohibit discriminatory treatment of pregnant workers. Employers are not required to treat pregnant workers more favorably than others, but they may not treat them worse. So, for example, if the employer offers leaves for temporary disabilities, such leaves must also be offered to pregnant women, if they are disabled. Hayes v. Shelby Memorial Hospital, 726 F.2d 1543 (11th Cir. 1984), found that the employer violated the act when it fired a pregnant radiology technician. The hospital did not demonstrate that the worker would be exposed to levels of radiation that would be dangerous to the fetus, and failed to consider less discriminatory alternatives to firing the worker. Maddox v. Grandview Care Center, Inc., 780 F.2d 987 (11th Cir. 1986) upheld a lower court judgment for a nurse's assistant who was denied a six month leave of absence recommended by her physician. The defendant nursing home allowed only a three month maternity leave, but permitted employees with other medical conditions to take unpaid leaves for indefinite periods if recommended by their physician and approved by their supervisor. For an excellent analysis of the ways in which employers may deal with occupational hazards to reproductive capacity without running afoul of the antidiscrimination laws see, W. Williams, Firing the Woman to Protect the Fetus: The Reconciliation of Fetal Protection with Employment Opportunity Goals under Title VII, 69 Geo. L.J. 641 (1981).

2. EXPLICIT DISCRIMINATION AGAINST THE PHYSICALLY AND MENTALLY HANDICAPPED

Discrimination against these groups is, by contrast, common in medical education and employment. Section 504 of the Rehabilitation Act of 1973 provides that: "No otherwise qualified handicapped individual in the United States . . . shall, solely by reason of his handicap, be excluded from the participation in, be denied the benefits of, or be subjected to discrimination under any program or activity receiving Federal financial assistance." Southeastern Community College v. Davis, 442 U.S. 397 (1979), rejected the claim of a hearing-impaired woman who was denied admission to a registered nurse training program. The plaintiff had worked for several years as an LPN, and the school refused her application, apparently on grounds that her hearing impairment would present such a safety hazard to patients that she would not be able to complete the clinical portion of her training or to become licensed. The trial court dismissed her claim, stating that her handicap prevented her from being "otherwise qualified" to work as a nurse. The Fourth Circuit reversed and would have required the college to first consider her qualifications without regard to her disability. If her handicap impeded her ability to meet essential requirements, the appellate court would have required consideration whether accommodations could be made to enable her to meet program requirements. Only if accommodations were not reasonably feasible could the applicant be denied admission to the program. The Supreme Court reversed, holding that Section 504 "requires only that an otherwise qualified handicapped individual not be excluded from participation in a federally funded program solely by reason of his handicap. . . ." 442 U.S. at 407. The Court also held that admissions criteria must be legitimate and necessary, but offered little guidance as to how such standards are to be evaluated.

Does a hospital discriminate on the basis of handicap if it fires or refuses to hire people who test HIV positive or who have AIDS? School Board of Nassau County v. Arline, 107 S. Ct. 1123 (1987), rejected a Justice Department interpretation of Section 504 that would have allowed employers to discriminate against people with infectious disease because they are perceived by others as dangerous. The plaintiff, a school teacher with chronic tuberculosis, was fired, without inquiry whether she was able to do her work. The Court said:

> The fact that some persons who have contagious diseases may pose a serious health threat to others under certain circumstances does not justify excluding from the coverage of the Act all persons with actual or perceived contagious diseases. Such exclusion would mean that those accused of being contagious would never have the opportunity to have their condition evaluated in light of medical evidence and a determination made as to whether they were "otherwise qualified." Rather, they would be vulnerable to discrimination on the basis of mythology — precisely the type of injury Congress sought to prevent. [107 S. Ct. at 1130.]

Individualized hearings are required to determine whether the individual is "otherwise qualified." In the context of employment of a person handicapped with a contagious disease, the Court held that this inquiry should include:

> (findings of) facts, based on reasonable medical judgments given the state of medical knowledge, about (a) the nature of the risk (how the disease is transmitted), (b) the duration of the risk (how long the carrier is infectious), (c) the severity of the risk (what is the potential harm to third parties), and (d) the probabilities the disease will be transmitted and will cause varying degrees of harm. . . .
>
> In making these findings, courts normally should defer to the reasonable medical judgments of public health officials. The next step in the "otherwise-qualified" inquiry is for the court to evaluate, in light of these medical findings,

whether the employer could reasonably accommodate the employee. . . . [107 S. Ct. at 1132.]

Recall the facts presented in Chapter 1 about the transmission of AIDS and consider whether and when an employer could legitimately fire or refuse to hire an employee who tests HIV positive or who has AIDS.

3. FACIALLY NEUTRAL POLICIES WITH DISPARATE SEXUAL OR RACIAL IMPACT

Such policies are widespread in health care, but very few health care workers have challenged such policies under Title VII. Townsend v. Nassau County Medical Center, 558 F.2d 117 (2d Cir. 1977), *cert. denied,* 434 U.S. 1015 (1978), rejected the claim of a black woman technician. Margaret Townsend had performed well as a technician for two years, when the hospital instituted a requirement that people filling her job must have a bachelor of science degree. The hospital allowed incumbents to retain their jobs, without a degree, if they passed a standardized exam. Ms. Townsend was not able to do so. She challenged both the degree requirement and the exam as racially discriminatory, in that far fewer black people in the relevant labor market met the new requirements. The district court held that Title VII mandates that an employer must recognize the *actual* demonstrated job skills of a minority employee, whether those skills are acquired through practical experience or through formal training, and ruled that the requirements could not be applied to exclude a black employee "from a position for which she has demonstrated eminent qualifications." 558 F.2d at 121. The court of appeals reversed, holding that "The requirement of a college degree, particularly in the sciences, seems to be in the modern day of advanced scientific method, a neutral requirement for the protection of the public." 558 F.2d at 125.

As the case illustrates, it is difficult to challenge a neutral policy with racially or sexually disparate impact, particularly in positions that require scientific knowledge and training beyond the ken of ordinary people and judges. See E. Bertholett, Application of Title VII to Jobs in High Places, 95 Harv. L. Rev. 945 (1982).

4. EQUAL PAY FOR EQUAL WORK

The Equal Pay Act of 1963 prohibits employers from paying men and women at different rates for "equal work" defined as requiring "equal skill, efforts, responsibility and performed under similar working conditions." 29 U.S.C. §206(d)(1) (1988). The Act has been interpreted narrowly to require the plaintiff to show that the work of men and women is equal, with respect to each of these four elements.

Traditionally hospitals employed two categories of aides — women, who were called aides, and men, who were called orderlies — and paid men significantly more. The job qualifications for both positions were identical — generally a tenth grade education, cleanliness and a desire to work with people. The job requirements were also identical — providing routine personal care and housekeeping services to patients. Prior to the Equal Pay Act, these pay differentials were explained by a presumption that men, but not women, needed greater pay to support their families, and by sex differentials in wage rates paid in the larger wage labor market. When the Equal Pay Act made these justifications illegitimate, many hospitals sought to preserve the wage differentiation by creating minor differences in the job descriptions of men and women. For example, men, but not women, were trained to insert catheters. Or men, but not women, would be expected to "assume leadership" in the event of a fire or other emergency. Or, most commonly, it was assumed that men, but not women, could do heavy lifting or provide security.

Dozens of cases scrutinized whether these differences justified pay differentials or, as most courts found, were a pretext for gender discrimination. See cases collected in B. Babcock, A. Friedman, E. Norton & S. Ross, Sex Discrimination in the United States (1974). After litigating dozens of similar claims involving aides and orderlies, the Secretary of Labor sought to promulgate general standards prohibiting pay differentiation among these workers in all hospitals. Courts rejected this effort and required that the claims continue to be adjudicated on a case by case basis. See, for instance, Brennan v. Price William Hospital Corp., 503 F.2d 282 (4th Cir. 1974), *cert. denied,* 420 U.S. 972 (1975).

5. EQUAL PAY FOR COMPARABLE WORK

Nursing and other patient care work has traditionally been done by women. Like other personal service work done by women in the market and the home, nursing is not well paid. Wage rates for RNs today compare unfavorably with earnings of male-dominated trade groups, such as carpenters, printers, bus drivers, and police officers, even though educational requirements for nurses are higher. See discussion S. Moskowitz, Pay Equity and American Nurses: A Legal Analysis, 27 St. Louis U.L.J. 801 (1983).

Since World War II, federal, state, and private agencies have sought to establish "objective" criteria by which managers can evaluate the skill, effort, responsibility, and worth of the work that people do. Moskowitz reviews the job evaluation literature and reports that "[i]n Minnesota, RNs and vocational education instructors were assigned the same number of job evaluation points, but nurses were paid $537 less per month. In San Jose, California, nurses received $839 per month while electrical foremen received $1168 per month for work rated equal. RNs in the State of Washington earned $1368 per month for work that was rated higher than that of highway engineers, who earned $1980 per month." Id. at 816-819.

Until 1981, there was some uncertainty whether Title VII of the Civil Rights Act of 1964 provided a remedy to women who alleged that they were paid discriminatorily unequal wages for work that was of comparable value to that done by men, or whether wage claims could only be challenged under the Equal Pay Act standards requiring that the work done be substantially similar. In Washington County v. Gunther, 452 U.S. 161 (1981), the Supreme Court held that Title VII's prohibition on sex discrimination bars pay discrimination, whether or not the women can show that they do work that is "equal" to men under the Equal Pay Act's standards. Women have not succeeded in establishing Title VII sex discrimination claims based on evidence that an employer pays women less for work of comparable value to that done by men. For example, AFSCME v. Washington, 770 F.2d 1401 (9th Cir. 1985), rejected a Title VII sex discrimination claim on behalf of 15,000 employees of the State of Washington, despite overwhelming evidence that women employees received lower pay than men employees for comparable work.

Nurses, both before and after *Gunther,* have sought wage increases through litigation under Title VII. In Lemons v. City and County of Denver, 620 F.2d 228 (D. Colo. 1978), *cert. denied,* 449 U.S. 888 (1980), nurses demonstrated, through expert testimony and job evaluation studies undertaken by the defendants, that they were paid significantly less than male-dominated jobs requiring similar, or less, effort, skill, and responsibility. The trial court's decision, rejecting their claim, captures the realpolitik of the opposition to comparable worth.

> This case . . . is pregnant with the possibility of disrupting the entire economic system of the United States of America. . . .
>
> The entire theory of the plaintiffs' case is that . . . there is occupational discrimination which has come down through the centuries and that Congress intended that the Courts should take over the restructuring of the economy of the United States of America. Plaintiffs say, and I don't quarrel with this . . . that their skills are such that in a truly egalitarian society, they would receive more money. . . .
>
> The plaintiffs here say they want their pay to be compared with other occupations. Of course they do. If that were done, it would give them more pay. But I can find nothing in the law that requires that. It would be nice for the plaintiffs. It would be completely disruptive of our way of life, and we've got enough disruptions now.
>
> I am unable to believe that the Congress of the United States has mandated that the job of every person in the United States be evaluated skill-wise, productive-wise, and otherwise to the job of every other person, and they have a completely new pay scale set up by some group of experts or pseudo experts. Let me assure you that you that you could never find any two experts who would be in complete agreement.

> And if the Congress thinks that some bureaucracy should be set up to fix the pay of everybody in the United States, I wish them well the first time they confront George Meany. I will guarantee you that isn't going to work. . . .
>
> Congress cannot, and never has been able, to repeal the law of supply and demand. And the situation, unfortunate that it may be, is that the supply of nurses is very large as compared to the demand, and it puts the nurses in a somewhat disadvantageous negotiation position. But, the discrimination, as I see it, is not a discrimination in the nursing profession against females.
>
> Plaintiffs' very statistical evidence demonstrates that if there is discrimination within the nursing profession, it is in favor of females because females outnumber males by a tremendous percentage. [17 F.E.P. Cases 906 (D. Colo. 1978).]

Which of these points are most persuasive? Are there good answers to them?

Other nurses have focused on their wage rates in contrast to related male-dominated health personnel groups. Nurses in Madison, Wisconsin, showed that their wages were significantly less than male-dominated occupations such as public health sanitarians, physicians assistants, and psychiatric social workers. Expert job evaluators supported the nurses' assertions and their testimony was not rebutted. Yet the court, relying on market forces, rejected the nurses' claim. Briggs v. City of Madison, 536 F. Supp. 435 (W.D. Wis. 1982).

C H A P T E R

VIII

New Competitive Ideologies and Organizations

For most of our history, many, perhaps most, people have believed that principles other than free market competition should determine the nature and cost of medical care. Many people still see essential medical services as different from other goods and services, and believe that medical care should not be distributed solely on the basis of ability and willingness to pay. Because many people have never had means of paying for medical care, hospitals were organized as charitable institutions. Concepts of professionalism, discussed in Chapter 7, reject the assumption of free market competition in medical care. "Professionalism" encompasses noble ideals of service and care, as well as authoritarian, defensive paternalism. As health insurance developed in the 1930s, it initially sought to make insurance available to the entire community, not simply those best able to pay. Widespread purchase and provision of insurance in turn undermine classic free market arrangements. Finally, traditions of service and charity, among both physicians and hospitals, suggest a departure from standard market assumptions. Since the 1970s, these assumptions about medicine have been challenged. This chapter explores the conceptual debates about whether medical care should be restructured to be more competitive, examines some of the new, more competitive arrangements in health care, and describes the role of the law in encouraging or discouraging such approaches.

The first section introduces the subject with three strong statements, two urging greater competition in medicine and medical insurance, and the third defending government regulation. People who seek to apply free market principles to medical care and medical insurance markets advocate divergent approaches, and this chapter addresses each in turn. Section B examines reforms to encourage formation of arrangements to provide defined packages of services and to compete with one another and with fee-for-service providers. Section C looks at programs to require greater patient cost sharing to encourage individuals to take a more active role in shaping the cost and nature of the services they need and receive. Finally, Section D examines the application of the antitrust laws to medical care. In addition to these large themes, profit making organizations increasingly challenge the traditional hegemony of the nonprofit institutions, and these developments are discussed in Section E. Section F discusses Medicare and Medicaid fraud and abuse and development of alternative health care delivery arrangements.

A. Competition and Regulation

Stanford economist, Alain Enthoven, offers an early and intellectually influential, proposal to restructure markets for medical care and insurance. For a more recent statement of his proposal, see A. Enthoven & R. Kronick, A Consumer-Choice Health Plan for the 1990s, 320 N. Engl. J. Med. 29, 94 (1989).

Enthoven, Consumer Choice Health Plan

298 N. Engl. J. Med. 650 (1978)

[T]o achieve comprehensive care of good quality for all, at a cost we can afford, we must change the fundamental structure of the system of health-care financing and delivery. Instead of today's fragmented system dominated by the cost-increasing incentives of fee-for-service, we need a health-care economy made up predominantly, though not exclusively, of competing organized systems. In such systems, physicians would accept responsibility for providing comprehensive health-care services to defined populations, largely for a prospective per capita payment, or some other form of payment that rewards economy in the use of health-care resources.

To date, we have not had a great deal of experience with alternative forms of organization and payment of physicians that reward economy in the use of resources. The tax laws, Medicare, and lack of competition have discouraged their development. So we are not in a good position to prescribe how this can best be done. We should seek to learn more about the possibilities by establishing an overall system that rewards desirable innovation — i.e., by a fair market test among competing alternatives in which systems that do a better job for a lower cost survive and grow. Many types of systems might succeed in such a competition. . . .

INFORMED CHOICE AMONG COMPETING ALTERNATIVES

[Consumer Choice Health Plan] CCHP is designed to assure that all people have a choice among competing alternatives, that they have good information on which to base their choice, and that competition emphasizes quality of benefits and total cost. CCHP would resemble the Federal Employees Health Benefits Program (FEHBP) and similar plans. It would extend to the whole population and to all qualifying health plans FEHBP's proved principles of competition, multiple choice, private underwriting and management of health plans, periodic government-supervised open enrollment and equal premiums for all similar enrollees selecting the same plan and benefits.

EQUITY AND INCENTIVES FOR ECONOMIZING CHOICES

CCHP seeks to correct inequities and cost-increasing incentives in the tax laws, Medicare and Medicaid. Today, the tax laws exclude employer contributions to health insurance, no matter how large, from the employee's gross income. . . . [CCHP would replace] the present exclusion and deduction with a refundable tax credit that is the same for the high-income and the low-income person. In other words, the employer contribution would be included in taxable income, but the resulting tax would be reduced by a tax credit. . . . In CCHP, the tax credit would be based on actuarial cost — i.e., the average total cost of covered benefits for persons in each actuarial category (e.g., men 45 to 64 years of age). Thus, persons in higher-risk groups having higher predicted medical need would get larger tax credits. But people would not get extra subsidies for joining more costly health plans.

In CCHP, Medicaid would be replaced by a system of vouchers for premium payments. . . . Medicare would be changed to give each beneficiary the right to have the average cost for his actuarial category paid to the qualified plan of his choice as a fixed prospective periodic payment.

Thus, CCHP would take money now used to subsidize people's choice of more costly systems of care, and use it to raise the floor under the least well covered. It would give people an incentive to seek out systems that provide care economically by letting them keep all the savings. While government assures that people have enough money to join a good plan, above the subsidy-level people would be using their own net after-tax money, which should motivate them to seek value for it. . . . CCHP can be thought of in two related parts: a financing system and rules to create a socially desirable competition.

THE FINANCING SYSTEM

. . . The flow of government subsidies to individuals to help them buy health insurance in CCHP would be based on actuarial cost — i.e., the average total costs of covered benefits (insured and out-of-pocket) in the base year, updated each year by a suitable price index, for persons in each actuarial category. For persons not covered by Medicare, the actuarial categories might be the simple and familiar three-part structure of "individual, individual plus one dependent, and individual plus two or more dependents." However, in a competitive situation, this classification might give health plans too strong an incentive to attempt to select preferred risks by design of benefit packages (e.g., good maternity benefits to attract healthy young families), location of facilities, or emphasis in specialty mix (strength in pediatrics, weakness in cardiology). Carried to a logical extreme, such a system could lead to poor care for high-risk persons. . . . So experience might show that a more complex set of actuarial categories is desirable. . . .

In CCHP, premiums would be set by each health plan for each actuarial category and benefit package, on the basis of its own costs and its own judgment of what it can charge in a competitive market. Thus, persons in more costly actuarial categories would pay higher premiums. This step is desirable because we want competing plans to be motivated to serve them and is made socially acceptable by giving such people higher subsidies through tax credits or vouchers. . . .

RULES TO CREATE A SOCIALLY DESIRABLE COMPETITION: CRITERIA FOR QUALIFIED HEALTH PLANS

To qualify to receive tax credits, vouchers or Medicare payments, a health plan would have to operate according to a set of rules intended to create a fair and socially desirable competition based on quality and cost effectiveness. . . .

OPEN ENROLLMENT

Each plan must participate in a periodic government-run open enrollment in which it must accept all enrollees who choose it, without regard to age, sex, race, religion, national origin, or, with possible minor exceptions, prior health conditions. Each September, for example, every family would receive an informative booklet published by the administrative agency. The book would give an understandable presentation of the costs, benefits, and limitations of each qualified health plan in the area. During October, each head of household would make an election for the coming year. . . . This step would greatly enhance competition by giving each person a choice from among competing plans, and it would assure that every person could enroll in a qualified plan.

The enrollment process should be run by a government agency for several reasons. First of all, an impartial regulatory agency is needed to assure that the information presented is complete, balanced, and fair. Secondly, such an agency is needed to assure that every eligible person is truly given an opportunity to enroll in the plan of his choice. Thirdly, this apportionment obviates the need for each health plan to have its own salesmen, reducing cost and possibly preventing the marketing abuses. . . .

COMMUNITY RATING

A qualified plan must charge the same premium to all persons in the same actuarial category enrolled for the same benefits in the same area, to preclude prohibitive rates for poor risks and to spread health-care costs over the whole population. . . .

LOW OPTION

Qualified plans must offer a low option limited to the basic benefits. . . . This requirement is to prevent plans from limiting membership to the well-to-do by offering only plans with costly supplemental benefits.

A LIMIT ON EACH PERSON'S (OR FAMILY'S) OUT-OF-POCKET COSTS

Qualified plans must publish a clearly stated annual limit on individual (or family) out-of-pocket outlays for covered benefits (e.g., $1500 per year). Out-of-pocket outlays include deductibles, copayments, and any differences between indemnity payments and the actual cost of covered services. Beyond the limit, the plan must pay all costs for covered benefits. This requirement would help assure that plans do not compete by offering inadequate benefits that would leave the seriously ill uninsured and a burden on the public sector. It would provide full protection against catastrophic medical expenses and prevent medical bankruptcies.

Qualified plans would be permitted to require that their members obtain all their covered benefits from participating providers with whom they have made agreements concerning fees and utilization controls (except for out-of-area emergency treatment). Indeed, the pressure of economic competition would gradually force health plans to make such agreements. But if a plan did not have an agreement with a participating provider in a needed specialty, it would nevertheless have to pay the cost and "hold the consumer harmless" within the agreed cost-sharing limits. . . .

PUBLIC POLICY TOWARD DELIVERY-SYSTEM REFORM

CCHP would create a competitive economy whose rules were fair to cost-effective organized systems. It would correct the biases against them in the tax laws, Medicare, Medicaid, employer-employee financing arrangements, and elsewhere, and it would give them the opportunity to reach their whole potential markets through the government-run open enrollment. It would allow them to pass on to consumers the full benefit of their savings in the form of reduced premiums, which would help them to attract new members. But CCHP would not, in itself, create those systems. If such systems are to come into being, many local efforts to organize them will be required. Such initiatives might be led, as they have been in the past and are being today, by employers, unions, universities, consumer co-operatives, foundations, insurance companies, physician groups, hospitals, and local governments. If additional public policies to encourage such efforts prove to be needed, they should be the subject of separate legislation. . . .

CONCLUSIONS

CCHP's design principles were equity, practicality, and rational economics. [It] . . . offers the *medical profession* the surest basis for maintaining its autonomy. Without an effective system of economic competition to control and legitimize costs, a system of direct government economic controls is inevitable. Such controls would inevitably be based on arbitrary numerical standards applied across the board without respect for individual preferences or quality. They would involve increasing paper work of a frustrating and unproductive kind. The Medicare regulations give a taste of what is in store down that road. The politicizing of the negotiating process over physician fees would inevitably be damaging and unpalatable. By contrast in an effective system of economic competition, such as that proposed in CCHP, medical-care costs could be controlled by the judgment of physicians. Individual preferences would be respected. For this system to work, physicians would have to accept responsibility for managing the total health-care costs of their enrolled population groups. . . .

In addition to offering the best prospect for bringing costs under control, CCHP offers substantial attractions to various important groups in society. This characteristic should give it broad political appeal. For the *poor,* it offers continuity of subsidized health plan coverage that is independent of job or Medicaid eligibility, access to health plans that serve the middle class. . . . CCHP would be especially helpful to the working poor. For *workers,* it offers an expanded range of choice, improved efficiency, and reduced cost through competition and assured continuity of coverage in the face of job changes or unemployment. Medicare beneficiaries would be able to obtain protection against catastrophic expense and reduced or eliminated cost sharing by joining an efficient health plan. For the well-to-do, CCHP offers a finite "controllable" government commitment to personal health-care services versus today's open-ended commitment, less of a tax increase than for some of the main alternatives, less of a tax burden in the long run than would be entailed by the status quo, and a private-sector solution with a limited government role. For hospital administrators, CCHP could mean relief from burdensome, frustrating government regulations and a chance to succeed by offering better services at lower cost rather than today's increasing emphasis on beating the regulations. CCHP offers private health insurers continued existence and a meaningful role.

Prof. Clark Havighurst of Duke Law School is one of the most prolific advocates of competitive approaches to health care financing and delivery. This early, influential article articulates the approach he favors and his differences with both those who favor government regulation, and those, such as Enthoven, who favor significant governmental intervention to encourage more competitive structures. For a comprehensive statement of Havighurst's views, see his law school case book, Health Care Law and Policy (1988). For an overview and critique of pro-competitive approaches see Marmor, Boyer & Greenberg, Medical Care and Pro-competitive Reform, 34 Vand. L. Rev. 1003 (1981); Rosenblatt, Health Care, Markets, and Democratic Values, 34 Vand. L. Rev. 1067 (1981).

Havighurst & Hackbarth, Private Cost Containment

300 N. Engl. J. Med. 1298-1305 (1979)

Market advocates [such as Enthoven] have often appeared to rely on group-practice HMOs as the primary vehicle with which to introduce competition and increased cost consciousness into health services. Because of the emphasis that such HMOs have received . . . , there is now a common tendency to equate the market strategy with their development. But the federal law's encouragement of one set of desirable initiatives has had the effect of discouraging others that might serve the public as well or better.

Although HMOs offer many important improvements over traditional mechanisms, they may sacrifice the productivity, commitment, and personal element that characterize traditional medicine at its best. Prepaid groups are also difficult to start and cannot quickly exert a powerful competitive influence, and many areas may be unable to support enough groups to make competition meaningful. Finally, HMOs have become a rallying point for government interventionists, who prefer to dictate to consumers and providers, rather than to enhance their freedom of choice. For all these reasons, it is desirable to identify new opportunities for experimentation and change that lie on the broad — and largely unexplored spectrum — from traditional financing mechanisms to federally subsidized group-practice HMO's. . . .

POSSIBLE INSURER STRATEGIES

Before private insurers are embraced as appropriate vehicles for cost containment, it is necessary to decide how the insurance contract can accommodate emerging concerns about costs without overstepping the limits of the insurer's appropriate role. Private-sector cost containment is in large measure an administrative problem that must be addressed in a competitive environment. Both providers and consumers must be satisfied with a plan's various elements, which should include not only the price charged or paid, but also fairness and freedom from undue administrative problems. Numerous conflicting interests must be addressed, and the plans that are most successful in accommodating these conflicting interests will be most successful in the marketplace. Plans that are too cumbersome will not and should not survive in a competitive market.

Insurer cost containment must not occur by controlling medical practice. Instead, in accord with traditional insurance concepts, cost containment should simply define the limits of insurance coverage. Exclusions from coverage that are strategically imposed for cost-containment purposes could affect any of several of the insurance policy's dimensions. Monetary exclusions, including deductibles, co-payment requirements, and limits on the amounts payable in particular circumstances, are one set of possibilities. Another possible approach is to exclude particular treatments or procedures, or to include them only if certain conditions are met. Still another cost-containment strategy would be to exclude from coverage (or include on less advantageous terms) services rendered by providers who refuse to accept the insurer's administrative requirements or fee schedule or who are simply not known to be efficient or co-operative. Insurance purchasers, comparing premiums with the coverage given, might rationally choose policies with any of these types of selective coverage, thereby accepting, in return for a lower premium, some financial risk or some restriction on their free choice of provider. . . .

It is important to recognize that a coverage limitation in an insurance policy is nothing more than that. An exclusion from coverage does not necessarily imply anything about the appropriateness or inappropriateness of the excluded treatments or procedures, or the competence or efficiency of any providers whose services are not covered. All that is involved is a voluntary contractual limitation on the right of the insured to draw on the common fund. Because we are not dealing, for the moment, with patients who are indigent, it can be assumed that the patient can usually pay for any additional care that he and his physician agree is desirable. Therefore, any service exclusions that plans might adopt should not become the subject of a debate over what is or is not good medical practice or over the medical "need" for the excluded service in particular circumstances. Likewise, exclusion of individual providers from a plan's coverage cannot be legitimately called into question so long as the market is competitive and therefore offers providers alternative opportunities. Competing plans must ordinarily be presumed to supply what consumers want.

The concern that a coverage limitation might sometimes impose a real hardship on the insured must not be overstated, for the object in designing coverage should be to include anything that is both essential and expensive. Although this object may not be perfectly achieved at reasonable cost, the rare cases of actual inability to pay for noncovered but necessary treatment should be easily handled by the health-care system's remaining capacity for extending free care. Whereas a governmental requirement to assure some coverage of catastrophic expenses may seem necessary to prevent "free-riding" on the health-care system's charitable impulses, it is not inappropriate to rely implicitly to some residual extent on providers to buffer any serious side effects of competing insurers' cost-containment efforts. Physicians should recognize that insurer-sponsored exclusions from coverage or limitations on freedom of choice may well be in the best interests of insured groups, and that it is within the power and traditional responsibility of providers to prevent the rare case of severe hardship to an individual. . . .

SELECTIVITY IN BENEFIT PROVISIONS

One strategy for offsetting moral hazard would be to include in insurance policies many more details on the services covered and the terms of coverage than are now included. . . .

Exclusion of a particular service from coverage may be appropriate for many reasons unrelated to medical need or circumstances. In large measure, the need for insurance against a particular risk is a function of the income level of the insured, as well as his savings and preferences about risk-bearing. . . . The effect of any exclusion from coverage is, of course, to require the physician and patient to undertake a benefit-cost assessment, taking all the immediate circumstances into account. The physician would be expected to act in the time-honored capacity of professional adviser and fiduciary, with responsibility for the patient's financial situation as well as his health. In our view, this form of cost containment could be highly attractive. Carefully analyzed, this approach makes cost containment the ultimate responsibility not of the insurer, which merely defines and enforces coverage limitations, but of the physician-fiduciary acting in consultation with the patient.

With this conceptual framework established, it is possible to suggest some specific exclusions from coverage that the insurer and insured might jointly decide to be rational, especially if the tax laws were changed to eliminate the incentive to overinsure. A likely development would be an increase in the size of annual deductibles, to perhaps as much as 10 per cent of income. Most physician-patient encounters would then take place without insurance in the picture. Of course, more comprehensive coverage would be appropriate for subsidized low-income persons, since they could not be expected to bear a substantial self-insurance risk.

Even if a major shift to higher deductibles occurred, serious cost-containment problems would still exist beyond the threshold. This challenge could also be addressed by selectivity in coverage. For example, a plan might exclude (or include only with a very large co-payment) experimental treatments and unproved technology, highly discretionary items, and hospital stays beyond some minimum (in cases without special complications). In setting these limits, different plans could be expected to reach different conclusions. Far from signifying a need for a regulatory or professional arbiter of correctness, such differences of opinion are the essence of the democratic marketplace, where change in technology and in the standards of medical practice are most appropriately tested. . . .

The effectiveness of detailed coverage limitations would depend heavily on provider co-operation. In traditional open-panel insurance plans, such co-operation has been difficult to obtain. Physicians have frequently helped patients make maximum use of their insurance coverage, ordering unnecessary hospitalization and stretching diagnoses to bring treatments within the insurance policy. Thus, unless insurers can obtain provider co-operation in the administration of coverage limitations, those forms of cost containment cannot work.

The most straightforward way of enlisting provider co-operation is through provider-participation agreements that spell out in detail the physician's and the plan's respective responsibilities. Participation agreements have been widely used in service plans in the past and are used under Medicare and Medicaid. It would seem easy enough to adapt them to give individual providers specific responsibilities in the cost-containment effort, such as a duty to seek prior authorization or predetermination of benefits. . . .

Some physicians may fear that limits on private insurers' coverage, if administered along the lines suggested, would be indistinguishable from governmental controls. Yet there are profound differences that should make the market alternative attractive. In the first place, insurers would not use administrative controls unless their cost was less than the net benefit derived; government programs, not facing competition, operate under no such constraint and frequently squander resources unproductively. Secondly, participation in a given plan would be voluntary, not compulsory, and providers would have to be persuaded to participate. . . . Thirdly, the crucial distinction between regulation and coverage limitation — that a coverage limitation does not interfere with or second-guess medical judgment — would probably be more scrupulously observed in a private system.

SELECTIVITY TOWARD PROVIDERS OF COVERED SERVICES

A different strategy by which health insurers could control costs involves selectivity not primarily in terms of benefits but in terms of providers whose services are covered. The essential element in this strategy is a health plan's ability to deny to certain providers the right to draw on the insurance fund. [T]he insurance premium would reflect the cost experience of the covered providers. In effect, therefore, the insurer would be marketing the group's particular ability to deliver good care for less money. In contrast, traditional insurance, covering care rendered by any provider, averages the high-cost and low-cost providers together in arriving at experience-rated premiums. . . .

Whereas certain types of physician-sponsored [health insurance plans] are promising vehicles for carrying out the market strategy, other types are barriers to its implementation and present severe antitrust problems. . . . [Those] closely associated with organized medicine cannot be regarded as among the initiatives that are key to the market solution, even though they may have been stimulated by competitive threats from [other insurers]. Although all physician-sponsored [insurance programs], as joint ventures organized by competitors, must bear scrutiny under the Sherman Act's prohibition of combinations in restraint of trade, some will appear better than others. A plan of the closed-panel variety, while eliminating some competition among the participating providers, has potential competitive benefits as well and would violate the law only if it threatened to dominate the market. On the other hand, a profession-sponsored open-panel plan serving a defensive purpose for the profession as a whole raises serious antitrust concerns. . . .

THE ISSUE OF FREE CHOICE

[T]he profession has given "free choice" undue emphasis and has used it to legitimize anticompetitive policies and practices. Perceiving a danger to the profession if its ranks should be divided into competing closed panels, the profession coined the code phrase "free choice of physician" and adroitly persuaded itself and others of this value's overriding importance. The campaign for a competitive market in health services requires that the issue of free choice be considered in proper perspective.

A consumer who chooses one closed panel over another or over a plan offering unrestricted choice is exercising a free choice. The only legitimate questions are whether the consumer is offered a reasonable range of choices and whether he has an adequate chance to change plans if he decides that he has made a mistake. An annual opportunity to change plans would seem a sufficient response to the latter question. Minimal regulation can assure that consumers are not duped into selecting utterly inappropriate or financially irresponsible plans; moreover, if they feel the need, patients can purchase care outside the plan. . . .

THE MONOPSONY PROBLEM

If insurers or other health plans can discriminate among providers on the basis of quality, price, and co-operation with cost-containment efforts, they will be able to use their strategic bargaining position to deprive individual practitioners of their accustomed power to set their fees unilaterally or with regard only to the receptivity of the ignorant and (usually) insured patient. Faced with an insurer-developed fee schedule and participation agreement, a physician would have to decide whether to accede or to seek better terms elsewhere. As long as a sufficient number of buyers is competing for his services, the physician cannot complain if the competitive market places a lower value on his services than he does.

In some markets, however, a single insurer might be so dominant that it could treat providers unfairly, using excessive buying power — monopsony power, as economists call it — to drive fees below competitive levels and to dictate practices. Providers are understandably nervous about insurer dominations, and they are entitled to careful and principled attention to their concerns from antitrust enforcers and other market advocates. The antitrust laws . . . should be available to combat exploitation by dominant economic interests wherever it occurs. . . .

More important, any plan that attempts to exploit providers will simply trigger the development of alternative plans that, by paying more, can attract the better doctors and give better care, leaving the low-cost plan at an appropriate competitive disadvantage. Freedom to join (or organize) a competing plan is thus the ultimate protection for providers, as it is for consumers. . . .

CONCLUSIONS

That we cannot predict exactly what would happen in a competitive market is no argument for rejecting the market alternative. Indeed, its unpredictability is the best argument for choosing the market approach; if we knew what people would choose, we could legislate that result and be done with it. Even if one believed, as many seem to, that changing consumer incentives and restoring competitive conditions would not affect outcomes appreciably, that is not an argument against making the recommended changes. Once competitive conditions are restored, the result, whatever it is, will be the product of a functioning marketplace, something wholly lacking in the present state of affairs. The need for comprehensive regulation will then be much harder to establish, since it will not be clear why private choices should be second-guessed. The important factor is not so much the result itself — for example, the share of the gross national product dedicated to health care — as the process by which that result is reached. We must establish a process that can be trusted to reveal consumers' preferences and to adapt as those preferences change. The competitive market is more likely to meet those requirements than the political process is. . . .

Bruce Vladeck wrote the following article while he was Commissioner of Health for the State of New Jersey and supervising implementation of the nation's first experiment in diagnostic based hospital reimbursement. That experiment soon thereafter became the basis for the most dramatic reform in Medicare since the program was adopted in 1965. See Chapter 3. Mr. Vladeck left the public sector to become the Executive Director of the United Hospital Fund, the trade association of New York City's voluntary hospitals.

Vladeck, The Market vs. Regulation: The Case for Regulation

59 Milbank Mem. Fund Q. 209 (1981)

Consumers have sought the kinds of health insurance they have, not because they wish to act irrationally in the aggregate economic sense, but precisely because they don't wish to be forced to make rational trade-offs when they are confronted with medical care consumption decisions. No matter how we draw our curves or shape our abstract arguments, the elemental fact is that medical care is about living and dying, something considered by many to be of a rather different character from the purchase of tomatoes. The primary characteristic of most consumers of medical care most of the time is that they are scared. They are scared of dying, or disfigurement, or permanent disability; and these are serious matters. It is hardly fair to expect any of us to make rational decisions about matters of such import. As a society, we may be prepared to pay a substantial economic premium to insulate people from having to make such decisions.

This argument is flawed, the proponents of a greater role for markets will say, because most encounters between individual consumers and health care providers do not involve life and death situations; indeed, most physician visits and even most hospitalizations involve conditions that will go away on their own in the absence of medical intervention. That is probably true, but it is also probably irrelevant. The real question is not . . . what we are prepared to spend to reduce in the fourth decimal place the extremely low probability of a very highly disvalued event. Rather, it is a question of how much we are prepared to spend to be able to seek reassurance — of a variety of kinds in a variety of circumstances — when we are scared, or anxious, or lonely, when we are not dying.

EQUITY

Whether or not the content of medical care is effective from the perspective of narrowly drawn cost-benefit analyses, it is something we value highly. Indeed, it is something we value so highly that as a society we are committed to providing it to all, even if some can't afford to pay for it from their own pockets. . . . Everyone learns in the first week of Economics I that the one thing markets don't do very well is insure equity. Equity considerations are thus always the major arguments for public intervention in a market economy. What is often ignored, however, is that the very same equity concerns often require some degree of regulation in the form of government intervention. It is not enough, as market advocates would contend, simply to redistribute income. To begin with, as a society we are prepared to distribute access to services, not to redistribute cash income. More to the point, narrow economic incentives will not satisfactorily distribute even services.

One of the most important characteristics of poor people, but one economists tend to ignore when they so blindly consign questions of equity to the outer fringes of nonmarket areas, is that almost by definition poor people fare less well in markets of any kind, even when they are given purchasing power. . . . Most people receiving direct government subsidies for medical care have limited access to that care not merely because of low incomes per se but rather because of low income arising from certain kinds of social or ethnic status. Even when incomes are relatively more equal, these socioethnic disparities make access to health care difficult. The poor in the United States are characteristically old, or black, or hispanic, or young members of families with a single parent. At all income levels, people in these categories have special problems with health care services. . . .

It is not so long ago that the widespread extension of community-rated health insurance was seen as a great social advance, precisely because it provided for greater equity in access to health services through insurance than a free market would permit. . . . Competition among insurance plans, unless it were constrained by an enormous and pervasive regulatory system, could not help but encourage "creaming" of the lowest-risk population groups. Conversely, it might be suggested that standardized health insurance at a universal community rate with progressive subsidies to help the poor purchase such insurance would be conceptually indistinguishable, in many ways, from what used to be called national health insurance.

PUBLIC PURSE

Given our predispositions in this country away from public ownership (or direct public provision) of services and toward market solutions whenever they are thought to be available, the primary way in which Americans have sought to ensure access to health services for old and poor people is through subsidies in the form of Medicare and Medicaid. But that approach creates the most important political rationale for extensive regulation of the health care sector. Put most simply, the dollars we are talking about controlling are tax dollars; and the public needs to be rather protective of how its tax dollars are spent.

At the most elemental level, any industry that receives more than 40 percent of its revenue from government should simply accept at the outset that it is going to have to undergo a substantial loss of autonomy. Put more positively, we have an obligation to be at least as careful in our expenditure of tax dollars for health care as we are in our expenditure of tax dollars for highways, welfare, or sanitation. Whatever their cause, excessive hospital costs waste tax dollars as efficiently as more obviously unnecessary projects. . . .

The historical record seems very clear to me. Extensive regulation of health care providers is the price we pay for not having national health insurance. Given a political stalemate in society which precludes development of a health insurance system like that in every other modern society, we have chosen to subsidize particular groups while consciously refusing to make major structural changes in the health care industry. Fee-for-service health care and reasonable cost, however, lead to inordinate public expense — unless there is substantial and effective regulation of fees and services. Equal access for the poor and elderly will feed cost inflation unless costs are directly controlled.

A somewhat more subtle, but equally critical, point links these concepts of equity and protection of the public purse. Government is always the provider or insurer of last resort. To the extent that our society is unwilling to deny life-saving or disability-preventing medical care to those without other resources, there is a role for government in arranging for their care. The more competitive the private insurance market, the more such people there will be — because insurers avoid bad risks and have a marketing strategy of selling low-cost, low-benefit programs to those with the lowest income (but the greatest probability of needing services) — and thus the greater the burden on public funds. . . .

SLAYING DRAGONS

In evaluating the competing claims for regulation and competition in health care, there is also the small matter of empirical evidence. The standard to which regulation is generally compared, that of the "efficient" performance of perfect theoretical markets, is almost purely a theoretical construct. Apart from a few markets for agricultural commodities, there are almost no true markets left in modern society; and one can even raise historical questions about how many ever really existed. It was Adam Smith, after all, who warned of the inevitable tendencies to monopoly, mercantilism, and other exercises of economic power. As a regulator, I'm growing tired of being beaten over the head by defunct economists.

Dispute rages over the fine points, but there is no question that state-operated hospital cost-containment programs work . . .

. . . Close examination of most of the currently trumpeted procompetitive plans would reveal how much regulatory content of their own they would require. In these plans, the focus of regulation is shifted from providers to insurers, but a powerful, external guiding hand remains. In order to make reality look more like the textbook theories, we would need lots of regulation anyway.

DESTRUCTIVE COMPETITION

One of the curious facts about the argument for increased competition in the health care sector is that there has been so much competition for so long, although of a kind that is less than perfectly desirable. Specifically, note the classic patterns of competition among hospitals, which are widely thought to have resulted in substantial excess capacity and enormous overinvestment in dubiously useful technology. In a market structure in which consumers do not make basic consumption decisions about hospital services themselves, in which they are forced to rely on the preferences and decisions of physicians, competition among institutions for physicians' favor is bound to be inordinately expensive and destructive. One could argue that the sorts of destructive competition we have seen among hospitals result from the nature of health insurance coverage. But that argument ignores the way in which people and physicians actually perceive and care about the hospitals with which they do business. . . . The so-called technological imperative in medical practice may not be a technological or professional/scientific phenomenon at all, but rather a competitive one. . . .

Competition among health insurers is, in fact, a major source of the expansion of comprehensive first-dollar health insurance. Moreover, . . . the structure of the real health insurance market strongly discourages cost containment. Forcing insurers to sell packages that would make consumers more price sensitive would require extensive new regulation.

THE GOLDEN MEAN

Traditionally, the possible social arrangements for the control of certain kinds of essential services have been defined as markets on the one hand and public ownership or direct public provision on the other. The sorts of regulatory phenomena we see in health care, or utilities, or other segments of American life are uniquely American, a sort of compromise between the two historical ideological poles. Moderation of this kind, suggested Aristotle, is a principal characteristic of effective democracy.

I do not imply that regulation is a "golden" mean between markets and public ownership, but I would suggest that there may be something of value inherent in the regulatory process itself that has been sought and then preserved by those who have made public policy. When it works correctly — and it doesn't always — regulation of the kind we practice in this country tends to involve the oversight of an industry by informed, sometimes judicious, and certainly meddlesome experts. As a general rule, regulators have some professional training and background in the industry they are regulating; and, as a result, they may be more prone to protect the industry's interests than those of the anonymous consumer. (However, when the service involved is thought to be essential, there is something to be said for the industry's interest as well; the public convenience and necessity may be served by the continued existence of even a very inefficient airline, railroad, or hospital.) In contrast to the functioning of an ideal market, regulation is extraordinarily cumbersome, time consuming, and inefficient; but it has the virtues of its weaknesses. The most important of these virtues are due process, stability, and accountability.

DUE PROCESS

Whatever else one may or may not say about the regulatory process as it is practiced in most jurisdictions, it is certainly characterized by a high degree of formal due process. Given the interests involved, that may very well be a desirable attribute. In a pure market, individual physicians or individual nursing homes, for example, might well be badly battered by the forces of market competition in a way that was unfair from the perspective of anything but economic efficiency. Formal fairness is a value of some significance in and of itself, and I do think the regulatory process compares quite favorably to most competitive processes in its ability to provide for it. Anyone who has ever sat through a heated hearing on a contested certificate-of-need (CON) application or read the transcript of a hearing of a state hospital rate-setting commission should recognize that public notices, public meetings, adversary procedures, formal records, and the constraints of appeals processes sometimes lead to better decisions and at least sometimes produce decisions favoring the economically or politically weaker parties.

STABILITY

Another thing which regulatory processes are good at providing, and which they are frequently criticized for, is a high degree of stability. . . . Again, the health sector may be a bit different from the kinds of sectors in which one is more comfortable talking about markets. We have all heard that some substantial proportion of private firms fail in any given year; for a healthy market economy, a high degree of attrition among unsuccessful competitors is not only necessary but also desirable. Imagine, on the other hand, a world in which a quarter of the nursing homes, a quarter of the hospitals, or a quarter of the health insurers or HMOs went bankrupt in any given year. . . . When one is talking about something like the assurance of access to health care services for thousands of people, a degree of stability over and above that characteristic of competitive markets is probably highly desirable. Nor does it make sense from the viewpoint of public policy or narrow economic efficiency to let the market play out until Chrysler-style bailouts become necessary to insure the stability of firms. . . .

ACCOUNTABILITY

Whatever the failures in the process, governmental regulators do retain a substantial degree of political accountability to the general public. That accountability may be imperfect and highly attenuated; yet it is often strong and direct. . . .

One of the things that has been wrong with the discussion of regulation versus competition in the health sector has been the failure to address this very basic characteristic of regulation: that it is an essentially political process. Market strategies are, of course, essentially political processes as well. They just tend to promote the political interests of different groups from those whose interests are served by regulation. . . .

Regulation, in its most basic terms, constitutes the imposition of influence and power by those with a political majority on those who have customarily exercised power in a given sector of economic activity. Of course, the critics of regulation are immediately going to respond that most regulatory processes have more effectively served the interests of those already in power, particularly the providers of service, than of consumers. That is probably accurate. Upon obtaining any short-term profits at all, any rational, self-interested, utility-maximizing capitalist will immediately invest those profits in political influence. This . . . is the major shortcoming and major tension of representative democracy in a market society: market power too often is translated into political power. But, when there is no consumer sovereignty to begin with, surely consumers stand a better chance of getting their interests served in a competitive political environment than in an historically uncompetitive and anticompetitive market for health services. . . .

B. Organization and Financing of Medical Care: Alternatives to Fee-for-Service

Alternative delivery systems require substantial legal work. Lawyers draft the contracts that define the rights and responsibilities of subscribers, employers, physicians, hospitals, and insurers. As you read these materials, think about the issues that, as counsel to any of these parties, you would seek to address through contractual provisions. What do you want? What are you willing to compromise? What regulatory issues must you address? As a provider's lawyer, what must you do to assure Medicaid or Medicare reimbursement? How can you avoid federal criminal sanctions against fraud and abuse? Do state prohibitions on the corporate practice of medicine affect formation of alternative insurance and delivery arrangements? When should/can an organization incorporate in a profit form, a non-profit form, as an insurance company, or as a service benefit corporation? How does corporate structure affect malpractice liability? Regulatory policy in this area has changed rapidly in recent years. What state or federal laws might you seek, as counsel for any of these groups? What policy arguments support claims for new regulation or freedom from existing regulatory restraints? Antitrust issues have generated most litigation in the development of alternative delivery systems; they are addressed in Section D-3-b, infra.

1. THE ACRONYMS OF ALTERNATIVE DELIVERY

Professor Frances H. Miller diagrams common arrangements for financing and delivery of health care. Traditional indemnity insurance, discussed in the Introduction and Chapter 3, is presented in Figure 8.1.

The service benefit plans — that is, Blue Cross and Blue Shield — are distinguished by their contractual relations with participating hospitals and doctors (Figure 8.2).

Under a third common arrangement, the health maintenance organization or HMO, the organization promises to provide a defined package of inpa-

FIGURE 8.1

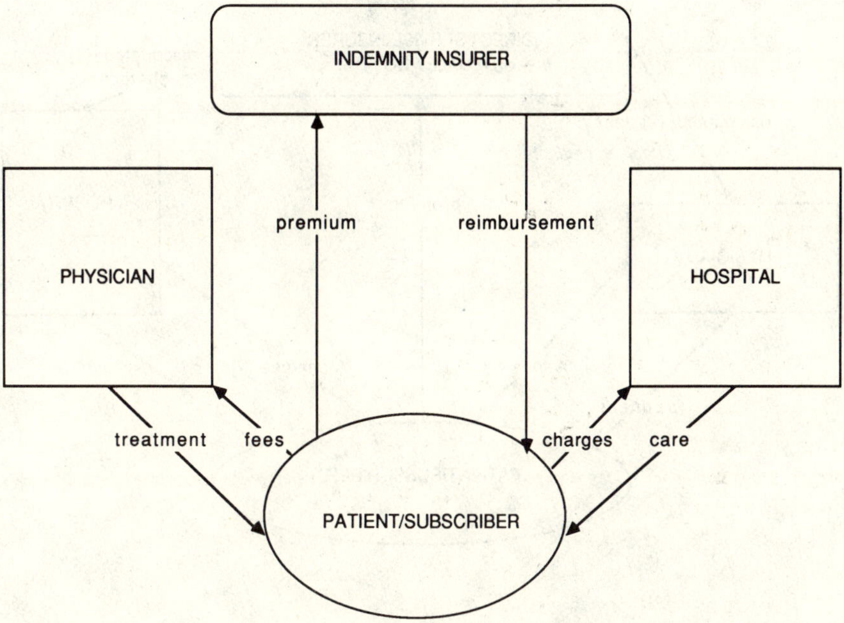

tient and outpatient services, in return for a fixed payment. Because the organization may not obtain new payments from the patient simply because more services are used, unnecessary care is discouraged. Some HMOs own their own hospitals; other do not. Some employ staff physicians, while others pay doctors on a fee-for-service or other basis. Some, known as "closed-panel HMOs," limit the doctors who its members may use, while other "open-panel HMOs" do not. The key definitional characteristic of an HMO is that it provides its members a defined package of care (Figure 8.3).

An independent practice association, IPA, is similar to Blue Cross and Blue Shield, in that it contracts with hospitals and doctors and agrees to pay for services that enrollees obtain from participating providers. It is distinct from the Blues in that IPAs usually contract with a more select group of providers. In addition, IPA payments to physicians are often contingent upon the costs of an individual physician or of the program (Figure 8.4).

A preferred provider organization (PPO) contracts with "preferred" providers, who agree to accept discounted fees and to be subject to constraints against unnecessary utilization. If a person insured by a PPO receives care from a "preferred" provider, the insurance premium covers the full cost of care. If the insured chooses to obtain care from a noncontracting provider, PPO coverage functions as indemnity insurance that pays a portion of the medical bill (Figure 8.5).

These five forms of insurance are not sharply distinct. In many areas, tra-

FIGURE 8.2

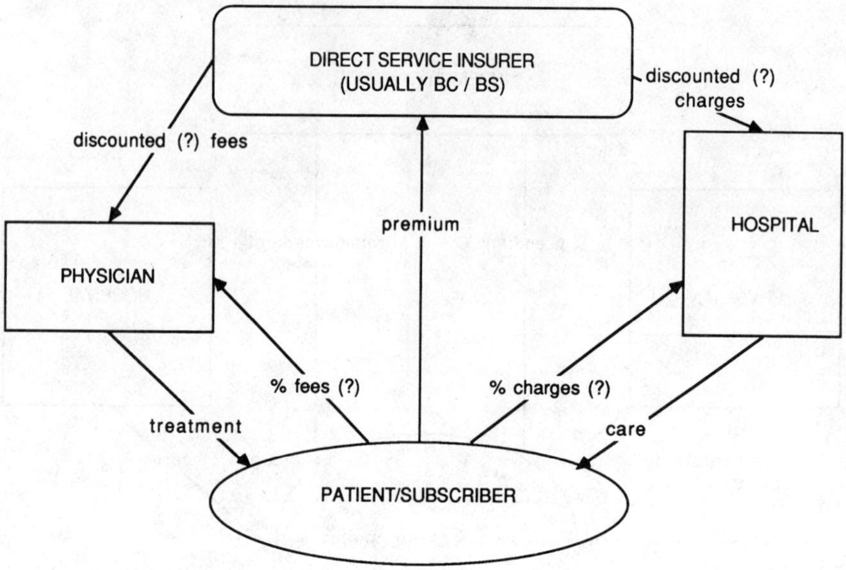

FIGURE 8.3

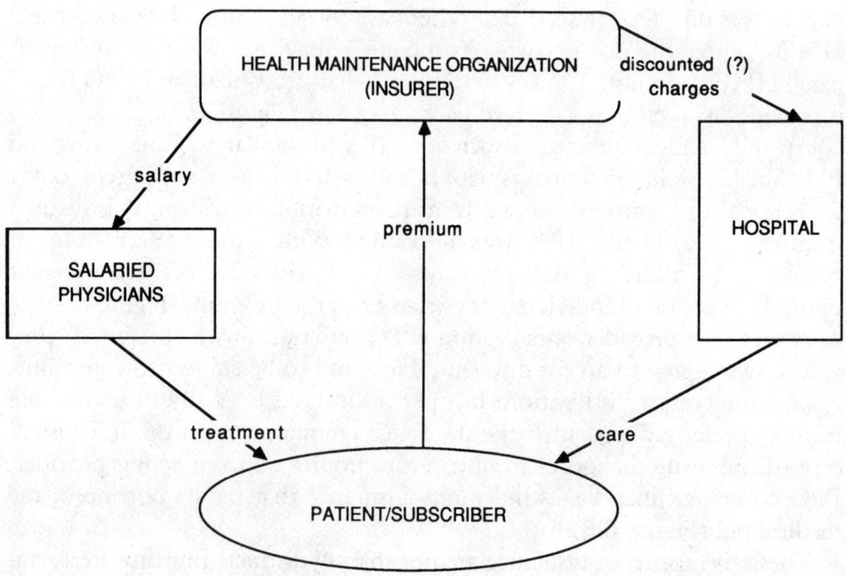

FIGURE 8.4

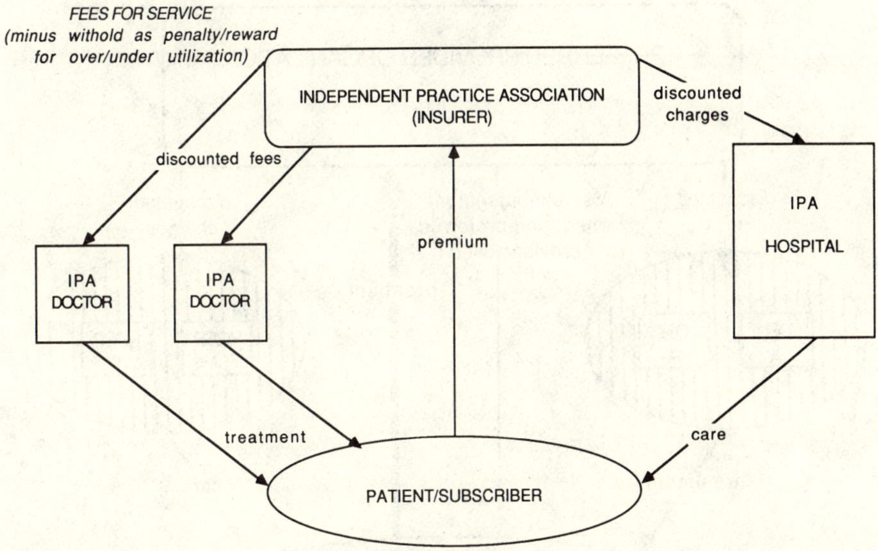

ditional Blue and indemnity insurers now require various forms of utilization control. A Blue plan that limits the providers allowed to participate in it is similar to a PPO. An open-panel HMO that pays doctors on a fee-for-service basis, is virtually indistinguishable from a PPO.

HMOs, IPAs, and PPOs are referred to generically as "alternative delivery systems" (ADS). Theoretically, the central distinction between fee-for-service insurance and ADS is that only the latter are "at risk" if the costs of services provided exceed premiums collected. Hence, the ADS have an incentive to keep costs down and ensure that no unnecessary care is provided. By contrast, if the costs of an indemnity insurer or a Blue plan exceed projections, rates can be adjusted upward the following year. In fact, rising health costs, and in some states, insurance department regulation, constrain all insurers' ability to pass on costs. The core peril of fee-for-service medicine is the financial incentive for unnecessary and costly care. By contrast, the core hazard of an ADS is that quality and caution will be sacrificed to cost restraint.

2. EARLY HMO DEVELOPMENT

HMOs are the oldest common form of ADS. Three large HMOs were founded in the 1930s: the Group Health Association (GHA) of Washington, D.C., the Kaiser-Permanente Medical Care Program, centered in California, and the Health Insurance Plan (HIP) of Greater New York. Industrialist Henry J. Kaiser sought a stable, efficient means of providing medical care to his

FIGURE 8.5

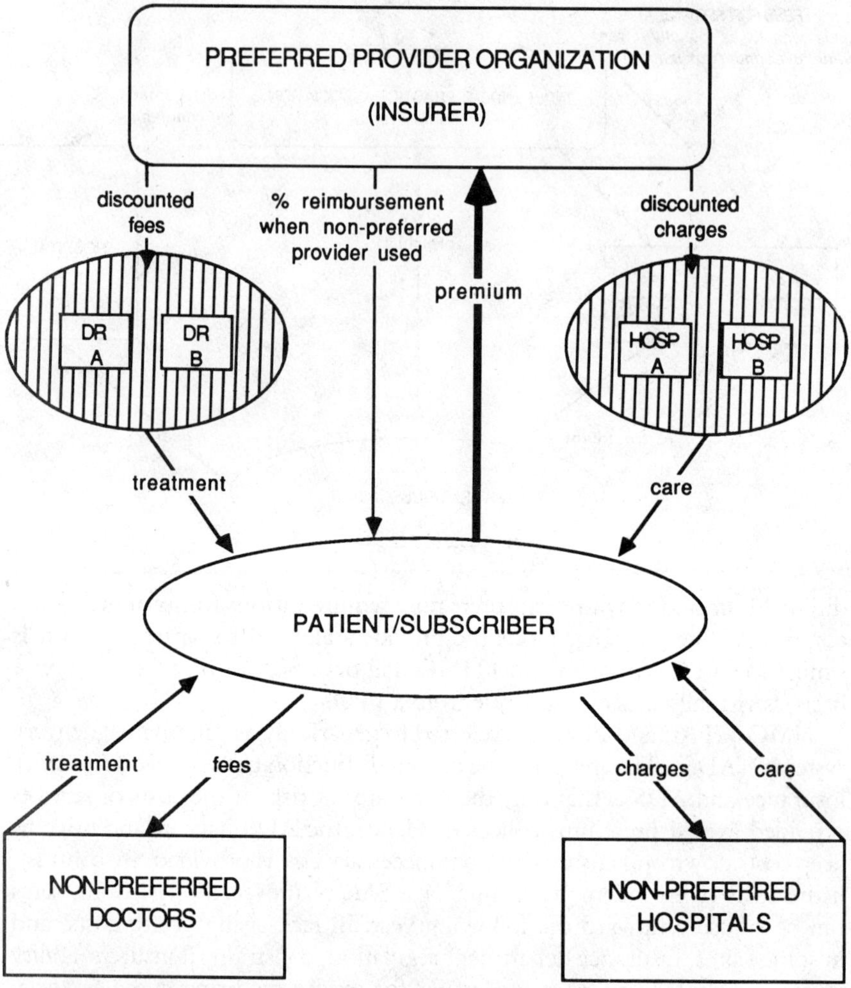

employees. GHA and HIP were both founded by consumer credit unions that perceived the connection between illness and debt. See L. Brown, Politics and Health Care Organization: HMOs as Federal Policy (1983).

Until the 1980s, the most conspicuous fact about HMOs was their small numbers (about 235 in 1980) and the small percentage of the population they enrolled (about 4 percent). Id. at 1. HMOs are costly, complex organizations that are difficult to build and maintain. Large capital investments are required before an HMO can open its doors and market its service. While many groups potentially have the interest and ability to sponsor an HMO — employers, unions, medical schools, insurance companies, governments, fee-for-service group practices, or existing HMOs — the challenge remains difficult. Some fledgling HMOs faced opposition from traditional fee-for-service providers. C. Havighurst, Deregulating the Health Care Industry at 214-224 (1982). Finally, some consumers prefer to retain existing patient-physician relations or the freedom to choose a physician or hospital at time of illness.

3. EARLY EXPERIENCE OF ABUSE IN MEDICAID HMOs

In 1971, then California Governor Ronald Reagan launched a major program to restrain Medicaid costs by providing care, on a pre-paid capitation basis. California quickly contracted with 24 HMOs, most of which had been newly formed. These organizations then sought to persuade Medicaid eligibles to give up their right to have fee-for-service payments and enroll in an HMO that would provide them comprehensive care. Schneider & Stern, Health Maintenance Organizations and the Poor: Problems and Prospects, 70 N.W.U.L. Rev. 90, 106, 135 (1975) provide a contemporaneous evaluation.

> Evidence of fraudulent and misleading solicitation practices is so conspicuous and so pervasive that they cannot be dismissed as aberrational. The more people they enrolled, the more money they made. . . . Methods of solicitation utilized by dishonest HMO solicitors ranged from the ingenious to the absurd. They included: (a) appearing at the doorstep in doctor and nurse uniforms claiming they were representatives of the Welfare Department and telling recipients that unless they switched over to the new HMO their Medicaid coverage would be terminated; (b) telling recipients that could still continue to see their own doctor, but by signing up for the HMO they would be entitled to an additional new . . . medical benefit . . . ; (c) offering free fried chicken dinners for every member of the household who enrolled; . . . (f) claiming that they were going door-to-door to get signatures for a petition to oust Governor Reagan.
>
> [Once individuals were enrolled], many recipients found promised service inaccessible or unavailable. The most flagrant and tragic abuses stemmed from the unavailability of emergency care. Although all HMOs were required to provide 24-hour emergency services . . . , the reality of the situation was often quite different. In a number of cases, enrollees who attempted to call the 24-hour emergency number printed on their HMO card found there was simply no answer at the other end. . . . In other instances, enrollees who, in an emergency, attempted to utilize the 24-hour emergency clinic listed on their card were confronted upon arrival with nonexistence of the facility (not open yet or just closed down), or with the total inability of the staff to deal with a real emergency. . . . Enrollees had similar difficulties obtaining services of specialists. . . .

4. THE HMO ACT OF 1973

This legislation, 42 U.S.C.A. §300e-9 (1982), was adopted to 1) encourage the development of Health Maintenance Organizations and 2) assure that HMOs were structured to promote quality and access while restraining costs. The Act sought to overcome three major impediments to the development of HMOs. First, it provided grants and subsidized loans to meet the substantial start up costs of organizations structured to meet federal requirements. Second, to market their services HMOs must have access to consumers with purchasing power. The Act requires that employers of more than 25 people offer their employees the option of joining any qualified HMO in its service area. The employer is not required to subsidize the cost of premiums more for workers who enroll in an HMO, nor is it allowed to pay less. See Health Care Plan Inc. v. Bahou, 61 N.Y.2d 814, 462 N.E.2d 128 (1984). Finally, in many states, laws prohibiting the corporate practice of medicine, or requiring medical society approval for a new form of health insurance, inhibit HMO growth. These laws were preempted.

In response to the California experience, Congress adopted several requirements to promote quality and assure access. The Act specified a minimum benefit package that must be offered to consumers and a supplemental benefit package that must be offered for an additional fee. It required that HMO enrollment fees be set on the basis of community rating, rather than experience rating. To discourage HMOs from "skimming," by enrolling only those people who were unlikely to need health services, the Act required each qualified HMO to have a 30-day open enrollment period each year. It required that if an HMO did not provide services within fixed periods of time, enrollees could obtain them from outside the plan and send the bill to the HMO. The Act contains minimal provisions requiring opportunities for membership participation in HMO governance. To prevent formation of HMOs that serve only populations vulnerable to exploitation, the Act mandates that the enrollee population be "broadly representative" of the community served and limits the number of Medicaid and Medicare enrollees to no more than 50 percent of the total enrollee population.

Federal financial support for HMO development ended in the early 1980s. HMOs still seek federal qualification to increase access to markets and to reassure consumers. HMO developers chafed at the protective requirements of the federal act. Congress has reduced the package of basic benefits that HMOs are required to provide. In 1981, the community rating requirement was significantly relaxed.

The requirement that each qualified HMO hold an open enrollment period of 30 days every year was the most controversial provision of the original statute. It could be waived for any organization demonstrating that compliance would be a serious hardship. Nonetheless, HMO promoters argued that this obligation undermined their ability to compete with insurance programs that were free to refuse coverage to people judged to be bad risks. In Congress, those who defended open enrollment presented evidence showing that many plans had complied without significant cost. Nonetheless, in 1981, the open enrollment requirement was abolished. (See S. Rep. No. 127, 97th Cong., 1st Sess. 1981.) The Senators who dissented from the Committee Report amending the open enrollment provision observed, "open enrollment is a cornerstone of HMO's potential contribution to competition in health care. Through open enrollment, the benefits of HMO membership are extended to all members of the community, fostering competition between HMOs and other insurance carriers." S. Rep. No. 127 97th Cong. lst Sess. at 60.

5. THE GROWTH OF ALTERNATIVE DELIVERY SYSTEMS IN THE 1980s

Two forces produced rapid growth in all forms of ADS in this decade. First, employers made more aggressive efforts to control health insurance costs. Second, in an effort to save Medicare and Medicaid costs, the federal and state governments promoted more competitive approaches to financing and providing care.

One survey shows that over 27 percent of the nation's employees with group health insurance were enrolled in either an HMO or a PPO plan in 1987. By contrast, a 1981 survey of large and mid-sized employers found approximately 4 percent of the surveyed enrollees in these plans. HMOs and PPOs are most popular in the West. HMOs are weakest in the South, serving only about 8 percent of employees. PPOs are weakest in the East, where they have attracted less than 1 percent of employees. Overall, in 1987, 16 percent of employees were enrolled in HMOs; 11 percent were enrolled in PPOs; 32 percent were enrolled in some form of managed fee-for-service; and 41 percent were insured by unmanaged fee-for-service policies. Gabel et al., The Changing World of Group Health Insurance, 7 Health Affairs 48, 52-54 (1988).

The legal rights of individuals enrolled in ADS have yet to be fully defined. A 1989 suit against U.S. Health Care, Inc., alleges that the HMOs failure to disclose the financial arrangements with physicians that encourage them to deny specialist referrals violates both the Pennsylvania consumer protection act and the federal Racketeer Influenced and Corrupt Organizations law (RICO). See Garcia, U.S. Healthcare Sued in Challenge of HMO Procedure, Wall St. J., Jan. 3, 1989, B4. A 25-year-old member of a Milwaukee HMO voiced similar complaints when she discovered that she suffers from a rare lung disease that is fatal within two years unless treated with a drug that her HMO, following Medicare practice, defines as experimental. Had she enrolled in either Blue Cross/Blue Shield or in other area HMOs the costly drug would have been covered. Green, HMO Won't Fund Dying Patient's "Experimental" Drug Therapy, AMA News, Jan. 13, 1989. A2.

6. EMPLOYER SELF-INSURANCE AND ALTERNATIVE DELIVERY

One important co-factor encouraging employers to seek alternative means of providing health insurance to their employees is the move toward self-insurance. As one insurance executive observes, "employers who wanted lower costs and more relevant data moved their ongoing responsibility for their health-care plan from the personnel or human-resource officer, to the financial officer, where CFOs and CEOs became more directly involved in evaluating benefits and costs." Bubb, Startling Resurgence in Costs Requires New National Policy, 12 Financier 28, 29 (1988). Rising costs generate interest in both self-insurance and alternative arrangements offered by the Blues and commercial insurers.

Jensen & Gabel, The Erosion of Purchased Health Insurance

25 Inquiry 328 (1988)

The passage of ERISA in 1974 marked the seminal point in the growth of self-insurance. The intent of the act was to ensure that workers entitled to private pensions when they leave the work force do, in fact, receive them. One unanticipated effect of ERISA was its exemption of employee welfare benefit plans from traditional state regulation. . . . This exemption offers a number of incentives for a firm to self-insure.

First, self-insured plans are not subject to state premium taxes. . . . Second, self-insured plans are exempt from state-mandated benefit laws. . . . Third, self-insured plans are exempt from state laws regarding capital and financial reserve requirements. . . . Fourth, self-insured firms need not contribute to state risk pools, which sell insurance to people insurers consider uninsurable. . . . Fifth, self-insured firms are assured full access to claims data and can easily find out what services enrollees purchase under the plan, from whom they purchase them, how much is spent on various categories of care, and other aspects of plan utilization. . . . Sixth, self-insurance allows the firms to pay claims as they are submitted, rather than prospectively in the form of premiums. Thus, the firms may hold the claims reserves, which can be used as working capital in the event of unanticipated cash flow problems. . . .

Enrollment in self-insured plans nearly doubled between 1981 and 1985 among medium and large private sector firms. Forty-two percent of employees were covered by a self-insured plan in 1985, up from only 22 percent in 1981. Close to half of the five-year increase occurred in 1984. . . .

[S]elf-insured coverage was more expensive than both commercial and

Blue Cross and Blue Shield coverage in 1981 and . . . 1985. Increases in the costs of commercial coverage out-paced those for Blue Cross and Blue Shield Plans. . . . Self-insured plans were more likely to incorporate cost containment [provisions] . . . and HMOs frequently were introduced at the time the firm adopted self-insurance. Thus, many employers may have viewed self-insurance as part of a package of cost-saving tools that included a redesign of offered benefits as well as a new funding mechanism. Perhaps the primary appeal of self-insurance is the perception that the employer controls the destiny of the firm's increasingly costly health benefit package rather than a state legislature or an insurance company.

[G]roup health insurance appears to be evolving into two separate but unequal systems — one under state scrutiny, the other not. There are strong indications that the transformation of health insurance and health insurers will continue.

Chapter 2 considers whether states may regulate self-insurance programs. ERISA largely precludes state regulation of these programs, while providing minimal federal oversight. It is unclear whether ERISA allows states to regulate employer-sponsored plans that purchase stop-loss coverage through conventional insurance markets or that contract with insurers to administer their health insurance plan. Insurance Board under Social Insurance Plan of Bethlehem Steel Corp. v. Muir, 819 F.2d 408 (3rd Cir. 1987).

7. STATE INSURANCE AND CORPORATE REGULATION

Blue Cross and Blue Shield enabling laws commonly require these organizations to offer participation agreements to all qualified providers. Antidiscrimination clauses in state insurance laws prohibit insurers from unfairly discriminating among covered individuals or providers. See Chapter 2. Do or should such provisions preclude the Blues or insurers from adopting a PPO program? Do or should they apply to hospitals, physicians, or other developers who create a PPO program? During the 1980s, over 20 states passed legislation specifically authorizing creation of PPOs. Rand Corp., Report to DHHS and the FTC, State Laws and Regulations Governing Preferred Provider Organizations, at Table 2 (1986). For instance, Montana's preferred provider statute allows a broad range of insurers to negotiate and contract with health care providers. It requires disclosure of information about cost and coverage, and payment for emergency services when the insured "cannot reasonably reach a preferred provider," and prior approval of the insurance commissioner. Mont. Code Ann. §§33-22-1701-1706 (1987). New Hampshire authorizes "health insurers" to issue preferred provider contracts, including rate differentiations on the basis of economic, geographic or professional considerations. N.H. Rev. Stat. Ann., Sec. 420-C (1987).

8. ALTERNATIVE DELIVERY SYSTEMS FOR MEDICAID AND MEDICARE IN THE 1980s

Since the 1970s, federal policy has encouraged enrollment of Medicaid beneficiaries in mainstream HMOs that also serve middle class patients and are certified under the federal act. However, few Medicaid beneficiaries have joined such HMOs, primarily because the HMOs consider Medicaid capitation rates inadequate. In the mid-1980s, fewer than one in four federally qualified HMOs accepted Medicaid beneficiaries. See Dallek, Commentary, 36 Case W. Res. L. Rev. 969, 972 (1986); Rosenblatt, Medicaid Primary Care Case Management, the Doctor-Patient Relationship, and the Politics of Privatization, 36 Case W. Res. L. Rev. 915, 937 (1986).

Nonetheless, during the 1980s, state Medicaid programs increasingly sought to enroll people eligible for Medicaid in programs of "managed care." Rand Rosenblatt describes these developments. Id. at 918-919, 943-948.

> [T]he concept of "primary care case management" emerged from several sources as a major cost containment strategy in the Medicaid program. Under this model, the patient chooses or is assigned to a particular primary care provider, who then controls the patient's access to hospitals, specialists, and most of the rest of the health care system. The primary care provider or "case manager" is given a direct financial incentive to control costs, since in most plans the provider's income will decrease if he or she approves expensive specialist or hospital care.
>
> The rapid adoption of primary care case management (PCCM) by more than 20 state Medicaid programs presents a moment of some opportunity and great peril for the poor. The opportunity lies in the fact that under PCCM, the state Medicaid agency actually undertakes to enroll Medicaid patients with particular physicians who have contractually promised to provide them with adequate care as part of a prepaid, organized system. If these arrangements are adequately funded and regulated, they could overcome Medicaid patients' longstanding difficulties in finding doctors who will accept them, improve the quality of care through a variety of monitoring programs by professionals and patients, and deter unnecessary costs. . . . The peril lies in the fact that PCCM, like all pre-paid, at-risk payment systems, creates a financial incentive to "contain costs" and maximize provider income by denying adequate care. . . .

This development became possible in the 1980s because of changes in federal law.

> Prior to 1981, states wishing to implement PCCM or other at-risk health care faced two major restrictions in the federal Medicaid statute. The first were re-

strictions on state Medicaid contracts with "at-risk" providers such as HMOs, embodied in §1903(m) of the Social Security Act. Under this provision, states were permitted to enroll Medicaid recipients in prepaid, capitated health plans only if Medicare and Medicaid enrollment did not exceed 50 percent of the total enrollment and if the plans were federally qualified HMOs or were based at federally funded community health centers. The HMO restrictions had been developed in response to [the California experience of the 1970s.] . . . The second was the Medicaid recipient's right to freedom of choice of any qualified provider who agreed to supply services, embodied in §1902(a)(23) of the Social Security Act. The Secretary of Health and Human Services . . . [has] authority under §1115 of the Social Security Act to waive these requirements to enable the states to carry out demonstration projects. Relatively few states had pursued such projects before 1981, perhaps because they required a formal research design and evaluation. Taken together, the provisions on at-risk contracting and freedom of choice insured that Medicaid recipients could only be offered voluntary enrollment in plans that also served privately insured patients and that met federal regulatory standards.

The Omnibus Budget Reconciliation Act of 1981 (OBRA) . . . allowed the states to contract with plans that were not federally qualified HMOs if they met certain requirements as to accessibility of services and financial solvency. . . . [In addition] . . . §1915(b) of the Social Security Act authorized the Secretary to waive the requirements of *both* §1902 . . . *and* §1903(m) . . . to implement a case management system. . . . In the next session's Tax Equity and Fiscal Responsibility Act of 1982 (TEFRA), Congress quickly deleted the Secretary's authority to waive the provisions of §1903(m), explaining that it has been "an erroneous statutory reference.". . . The waiver provisions as finally enacted — §1915(b) of the Social Security Act . . . [require] that in reviewing waivers the Secretary was now to consider not only whether care was cost-effective and efficient, but also whether the waiver proposal would "substantially impair access to . . . [medical] services of adequate quality where medically necessary." Moreover, the Secretary was directed to "monitor the implementation of waivers . . . to assure that the requirements . . . are being met. . . ."

The Secretary has freely granted waivers for Medicaid managed care programs and problems have resulted. Dallek, Id. at 974-975, offers this description.

A case in point is Health Power, Ohio's largest Medicaid HMO, which began servicing Medicaid recipients in Columbus in [1984. The Ohio PSRO evaluated] . . . the care received by the HMO's 10,000 patients. The audit found that patient charts were "illegible" and "indecipherable," laboratory reports were "sporadic" and "in total disarray," and EKGs were "ordered, put in the chart, and never interpreted." Moreover, referrals to specialists were "sporadic and poorly documented," and not one of the medical records reviewed showed that therapy or rehabilitation had been ordered.

The auditors found that at one Health Power clinic, two physicians were seeing 400 patients per day. . . . "[D]octors simply rotated through 20 examination rooms." The audit team medical director concluded that "[t]he program

> was chaos, total unadulterated chaos. In that mess, you couldn't tell diddly-squat. There was no quality assurance there that I could find." At the time, the state failed to act on the audit findings. In fact, it gave Health Power a $25,000 grant a few months later to expand operations to Dayton and Cincinnati.
>
> Health Power did accomplish a dramatic reduction in hospital utilization; its enrollees were hospitalized at a rate less than any other HMO population in the state. This reduction resulted in a $1 million bonus for the HMO and its clinics for the first seven months of the HMO operation.

In 1982, Arizona became the last state to join Medicaid when it adopted the nation's largest alternative delivery system for individuals eligible for Medicaid. It obtained a federal waiver to allow it to create a program premised on competitive bidding and for-profit management, under which all eligible individuals would be enrolled in HMOs created to serve them. A newly created corporation, a subsidiary of McDonnell Douglas, won the initial bid to administer the program. By broad concensus, the initial years of the Arizona program were a disaster in terms of access, costs, and quality of care. In 1985, the state terminated this contract and assumed greater oversight responsibility. In the late 1980s, assessments of the quality of the Arizona program are mixed. For an enthusiastic review, see Gov. Bruce Babbit & J. Rose, Building a Better Mousetrap; Health Care Reform and the Arizona Program, 3 Yale J. on Reg. 243 (1986). For a more skeptical assessment, see Rosenblatt & Dallek, supra.

The Medicare program, which serves a far more powerful, organized, and articulate constituency has moved more cautiously in authorizing payments to alternative delivery systems. Since 1965, Medicare has paid HMOs for services provided to Medicare beneficiaries, but did not restrict the other providers from whom beneficiaries could seek care. In 1973, Medicare allowed capitation payments, under which beneficiaries were "locked in" to an HMO, but restricted payments to organizations that met the standards of the federal act. In areas such as California and Minneapolis where a large proportion of the population is enrolled in HMOs, the experience of Medicare patients has, by and large, been good. Inspired by these successes, in 1985 the federal government liberalized the terms upon which individuals eligible for Medicare could enroll in alternative delivery systems. See 50 Fed. Reg. 1314 (Jan. 10, 1985), adopting regulations to implement Pub. L. No. 98-248, §114 (1982). See J. Igelhart, Medicare Turns to HMOs, 312 N. Engl. J. Med. 132 (1983). Between 1982 and 1987 the number of Medicare beneficiaries enrolled in HMOs grew from 200,000 to 900,000. Senate Special Comm. on Aging, Minority Staff Rep., Medicare and HMOs: A First Look with Disturbing Findings ii (1987).

Scandals — again reminiscent of the early California experience — occurred in some Medicare HMOs, and many who had been enthusiastic about ADS for Medicare patients perceived the need for greater regulatory oversight. See J. Igelhart, Second Thought About HMOs for Medicare Patients,

316 N. Engl. J. Med. 1497 (1987). For a detailed examination of the problems and rights of Medicare beneficiaries enrolled in HMOs, see M. Parks & J. Waxman, The Medicare/HMO Partnership: Some Problems for Beneficiaries, 21 Clearinghouse Rev. 236 (1987).

Despite the dangers, some managed-care programs for Medicaid and Medicare beneficiaries seem to have delivered quality care, produced high levels of patient satisfaction, and, at the same time, reduced costs. Rosenblatt describes positive PCCM programs for Medicaid beneficiaries.

> [T]he experience of other states — notably Wisconsin and Michigan — demonstrates the positive contributions that can be made by active involvement of Medicaid recipients and their advocates and allies in PCCM programs. In Wisconsin, a coalition of [consumer groups] . . . have made impressive efforts to monitor the operation of the state's program requiring AFDC recipients to enroll in HMOs and to suggest constructive improvements. In the wake of a tragic death of a five-month-old child covered by Medicaid in December 1985, apparently caused by confusion about HMO coverage of emergency care, and the extensive press coverage of this and similar incidents, Wisconsin agreed to significant changes in its HMO contracts for Medicaid patients proposed by consumers and their advocates. These changes included clearer explanations for consumers of emergency care, HMO liability for all subsequent care related to telephone calls to which the HMO fails to respond in thirty minutes, and HMO payment for appropriate diagnostic tests needed to determine if an emergency exists. . . .
>
> Michigan represents what is probably the most serious large-scale effort to reconcile PCCM with the ideals of patient-centered care through financial incentives and recipient and advocate participation. First, rather than impose the strong negative financial incentive of capitation on all providers, Michigan has a carefully graduated system, with full risk capitation for all Medicaid services extended only to large HMOs with a sizeable enrollment and administrative capacity. . . .
>
> In addition to carefully designed financial incentives, Michigan relies heavily on recipient, advocate, and provider participation in policymaking and program implementation. After an initial period of exclusion and opposition, welfare rights organizations and clients were given prominent places on the projects' advisory boards. Moreover, an organization representing Medicaid clients, the Michigan League of Human Services, has a contract with the state agency to monitor the implementation of PPSP. Its contract includes marketing, client enrollment, geographic accessibility, twenty-four hour availability of services, referrals and second opinions, and protection of clients' rights. . . .
>
> The contrasting experiences of Wisconsin, Michigan, Arizona, and Kentucky suggest that rigid dichotomies between "public" and participatory administration on the one hand and "market competition" and financial incentives on the other are unnecessary and counterproductive. . . .
>
> The development of Medicaid PCCM programs can and should be seen as part of a larger debate over the future of the American welfare state. Without this larger context, it is hard to understand the deep commitment of key federal and state officials to unregulated private management of Medicaid in the face

of well-known risks of financial irregularity and low quality care. . . . But the Medicaid PCCM experience suggests that the general concept of "privatization" does not so much resolve questions about redistribution and government role as cast them in a new language for continued controversy. . . .

[T]he purposes of a privatizing strategy can differ sharply. The purposes may range from use of the private sector as a means of realizing governmental goals (such as delivery of health care to the poor) to "radical privatization, [requiring] drastic withdrawal of government" from previous functions such as welfare or environmental regulation. These different purposes have also been described as the "empowerment" side of privatization, in which government funding is used to strengthen private providers of public needs, as opposed to "loadshedding," in which the government withdraws from both service financing and service delivery. . . . [Bruce Vladeck draws a similar distinction] between true health care cost containment, which attempts to reduce the amount of resources employed to produce a given volume of services, and "ersatz cost containment" which, like "loadshedding," seeks only to reduce outlays by a particular payer (and which usually increases expenditures by other payers and even increases unit costs). [Id. at 962-966.]

9. THE IMPACT OF ADS ON COST, QUALITY, AND ACCESS

There is great debate about the impact of these new forms of health care financing. Frech & Ginsburg in Competition Among Health Insurers, Revisited, 13 J. Health Polit. Policy Law 279 (1988), and Altman & Rodwin in Halfway Competitive Markets and Ineffective Regulation: The American Health Care System, 13 J. Health Polit. Policy Law 323 (1988), reach markedly different conclusions. Frech and Ginsburg find that the increase in alternatives spurs competition and, therefore, must cause health costs to drop. Altman and Rodwin review the same developments, find little or no savings, and conclude that without significant new government regulation, medical care costs will continue to balloon.

Frech and Ginsburg conclude that although "[m]anaged care increases administrative costs, . . . employers ordering managed care believe that the insurance-induced overuse of services has declined." Id. at 283. Altman and Rodwin agree that these private-sector initiatives have added important incentives for changes in medical practice. Yet the most "significant change is that [firms] are becoming involved in 'managing' the delivery of medical care — an activity similar in character to regulation." Id. at 329. According to Altman and Rodwin, such initiatives "have not had a significant bearing on total spending for health care." Id. at 329.

Altman and Rodwin assert that HMOs produce little in financial savings. Instead of offering lower premiums to undercut fee-for-service programs, HMOs charge premiums equal to traditional insurers so as to offer more extensive benefits. They also aim to win upper-income low-risk customers instead of high-risk lower-income ones who tend to have greater medical expenses. Consequently, more costly fee-for-service plans pick up the expenses, reinforcing inflation.

Frech and Ginsburg claim that the addition of HMOs and PPOs to the market encourages competition and are optimistic that the general trend towards greater competition and creation of new forms of health financing will eventually build a more cost-efficient health care system.

C. Patient Cost Sharing

W. Hsiao, Restructuring Medicare Benefits in Conference on the Future of Medicare

Subcomm. on Health, Comm. on Ways and Means, U.S. House of Representatives, 98th Cong., 1st Sess. 38-46 (1983)

Because Medicare provides broad coverage of hospital care and physicians' services, participants in the program are made to feel better off for having this insurance policy. This results in two effects: so-called moral hazard and a price effect. Moral hazard relates to specific behavioral responses to the incentives created by insurance coverage. Because of the availability of insurance, people may alter aspects of their lifestyles that will adversely affect their health, in the knowledge that they would be cared for if they become ill. For example, they may decide not to stop smoking or to lose weight, which they might have done if they or their families had been directly responsible for the financial consequences of associated illnesses.

Related to this, Medicare causes medical care prices to seem lower than the actual value of the resources employed. This so-called price effect will also provide a motivation for Medicare beneficiaries to obtain more services than they would if they had to pay the full cost. The price effect would not be very important if the consumption of medical services were determined only by medical need. The influence of economic factors, such as insurance coverage, on utilization levels has been well documented, however. . . .

[T]here are a number of strong arguments for incorporating cost-sharing provisions into insurance programs. Medicare's experience, however, has demonstrated that the behavioral responses of both beneficiaries and providers can largely offset the intended benefits of cost-sharing. Such responses can now be seen as a result of the faulty design of the Medicare benefit structure and of the market imperfections that were not well understood in the mid-1960s when Medicare was enacted.

A major flaw of Medicare's benefit structure is that it violates the primary purpose of insurance: to protect the beneficiary from financial ruin. The cost-sharing provisions of [Medicare] leave beneficiaries to face unlimited liabilities in the event of catastrophic illness. . . . Consequently, the risk of substantial financial loss, however small it might be, would encourage beneficiaries to buy supplementary insurance coverages. This flaw in Medicare's benefit structure helped to create the demand for Medigap insurance.

Two-thirds of Medicare beneficiaries have voluntarily purchased this coverage. Medigap premium rates are high. . . . By assuming financial responsibility for cost-sharing amounts, Medigap works to offset the cost-consciousness that Medicare's cost-sharing provisions were intended to encourage. Medicare benefits, therefore, must be restructured before the cost-sharing provisions will function in the manner intended.

A second major flaw in the Medicare cost-sharing provisions is that they were designed under the assumption that beneficiaries will have adequate information about the relative cost of services rendered by different providers as well as the alternative modes of care that would be available in treating an illness. The reality, however, is that patients lack adequate information about the fees charged by physicians and prices charged by hospitals. Such information is not readily available. More importantly, it is usually the physician who makes the decisions about what tests should be done, what procedures should be performed, and where the patient should be hospitalized. . . . Both patients and physicians lack comparative information about the cost of tests, medical procedures, and hospital care, as well as their effectiveness. As a result, even when cost-sharing is paid directly by the patient (that is, unsupplemented by private insurance) neither the patient nor the physician may be able to invest the resources required to obtain the data necessary to make well-informed choices. . . .

Within the same market area, there is substantial variation in the prices charged by hospitals and physicians for what appear to be the same services. There are many reasons for these charge differences. Some result from real product differences that may lead to different health outcomes. Others result from differences in amenities or other factors that affect the cost of the service but may not influence the outcome.

Some differences in charges arise because of the differences in technical competence among providers. . . . Higher fees, however, are not necessarily associated with better medical care. Many less successful physicians are able to charge high fees because patients lack sufficient knowledge to evaluate doctors' technical capabilities. Moreover, patients and physicians alike find it difficult to obtain accurate information on physicians' charges. Often, the cost of obtaining information will be very high because the patient has to sample the services of a physician before he can obtain sufficient information about both his charges and his competence. Consequently, patients often base their selection of doctors on factors other than price.

Other charge differences are due to the different amenities of the providers, such as air-conditioned buildings, carpeted floors, and gourmet cooking. Some physicians may have higher costs because they have more attractive waiting rooms, more courteous secretaries, designer dressing gowns, well located offices, and so forth. These differences will not necessarily affect the health conditions of patients, yet they will increase the satisfaction of patients when they get care. Lastly, both hospitals and physicians have different production costs because of the variation in their managerial capabilities and in the scope of their activities. . . .

The primary purpose of any insurance plan is to protect the insured from financial catastrophe. The current benefit structure, as we have noted, fails to serve this purpose when it leaves beneficiaries with unlimited liabilities. This flaw can be remedied by limiting the patient's share of the medical costs. Equity considerations, however, necessitate that the limit be linked to beneficiaries' family income. In order to achieve federal savings from an increase in cost sharing, as well as an equitable distribution of the cost sharing burden, we have developed a set of proposed revisions.

The cost-sharing provisions in the proposed plan are designed to encourage patients to select the least costly provider. The Federal Government would classify hospitals into three broad categories. In each region (such as a health service area), hospitals would be grouped into high, intermediate, and low cost facilities, based on the prior year's average cost for selected diagnosis related groups (DRGs). . . . Patients would then pay a different co-insurance rate depending on the cost category of the hospital in which their care was received. These "price" comparisons of area hospitals should be widely disseminated to the consumers and physicians.

Some patients may have to be hospitalized in higher cost facilities for sound reasons. Under our system, these patients would have to pay a higher co-insurance rate, but their liabilities would be limited by a ceiling. Some patients may choose to go to higher cost facilities for convenience, better amenities, or because a particular physician uses that facility. If they made that choice, however, they would have to pay more.

Our proposed plan would also require the Federal Government to classify physicians into three broad price categories: high, intermediate, and low. The amount of cost sharing would then vary according to the price category of the physician from whom care is received. The criteria for the classification would be based on the fees charged for selected commonly performed procedures. The classification of physicians would again be done by service area, and the category to which each physician belongs would be widely disseminated to all consumers.

Rosenblatt, Health Care, Markets, and Democratic Values

34 Vand. L. Rev. 1067, 1079-1082 (1981)

Market advocates attempt to structure the patient's relationship to health care as an economic transaction, namely, as an exchange of a commodity for money in a competitive market setting. A primary justification for increasing market competition in health care is to promote efficiency in the use and delivery of services. Some proponents argue that market competition also has value in its own right as a uniquely legitimate method of defining and promoting efficiency. It is argued that collective social decisions, however made, are inherently coercive and inevitably inefficient. Market mechanisms are said to promote only the value of individual liberty, which enables consumers to express their own preferences by their economic "votes"; otherwise, these mechanisms are considered to be value-neutral.

Despite its considerable superficial appeal, this position is misguided. The distribution of health services through competitive markets promotes at least three major and related nonneutral values. First, in a competitive market individuals are encouraged to make decisions about health care primarily from an economic perspective, as opposed to a broader, more realistic view. Second, individuals also are encouraged to perceive health care choices and health itself as an individual matter, rather than as a matter based upon a close interrelationship between individual decisions and social patterns concerning nutrition, work, environmental quality, economic opportunity, and many other factors. Last, in a competitive market, individuals in their role as citizens or government officials are encouraged to believe that the proper goal of most government policy is to encourage voluntary market transactions. As a result, issues of equality become confined to the special and limited sphere of redistributing purchasing power, the purpose of which is to permit deserving low income persons to participate in the free market. These three values may be defensible, but they certainly are not neutral, at least not in the sense of simply allowing individuals to express their own preferences. On the contrary, they are designed to exert influence over what those preferences might be, as well as to limit the kinds of social settings in which preferences can be expressed and satisfied. . . .

Most advocates of the market approach to health care assert that the central advantage of their plans is the encouragement of cost-benefit decisions by various decisionmakers in the context of economic constraint. The meanings of the terms "cost," "benefit," "health," and "health care" in the pro-market literature usually are assumed to be obvious. Cost typically is understood to mean the monetary equivalent of providing a unit of service such as a diagnostic test, surgical procedure, or hospital day. Benefit normally is assumed to represent one or another quantifiable measure of treatment outcome such as mortality rate, length of stay in the hospital, or probability of cure. For some purposes, or in some contexts, these criteria may be adequate. The market advocates rarely, however, specify the conditions, contexts, or purposes that justify these criteria. On the contrary, the pro-market literature is replete with summary references to studies that cast doubt on the effectiveness or efficiency of a wide range of procedures and practices, together with a general endorsement of cost-benefit decisions as the major virtue of competitive markets. This approach radically over-simplifies the way in which patients, considered as whole individuals, actually experience the costs and benefits of health and health care.

Health can be understood rather simply as the absence of disease and death, and health care as a "curative defence" against both. When this is the accepted criterion, a particular medical procedure can be evaluated in terms of whether it contributes to reduced morbidity and mortality — disease and death respectively. Health care, however, also must be understood as a caring rather than purely a curative activity, the goal of which is to reduce pain and anxiety and increase the patient's sense of self-determination and quality of life. In some contexts, these two goals may come into conflict: whereas intensive, high-technology treatment needed to keep a terminal patient alive may delay death and hence promote health in the first sense, it may at the same time reduce the patient to a miserable object and thereby undermine health care in the second sense. In most contexts, however, the two senses of health are usually interdependent and mutually supportive. A patient who is being treated with dignity, who feels emotionally supported and assisted in making decisions, is more likely to have a favorable outcome in terms of disease and death as well. From this perspective, a central need of health care reform is not more refined quantitative cost-benefit analyses, but rather a restructuring of the patient-provider relationship that ideally could increase the sense of self-determination and satisfaction for both.

The market advocates recognize that much of modern health care has both a caring and a curing function. While conceding that caring services are of "undeniable value," the market advocates also argue that this value is very difficult to measure in quantitative or statistical terms. Because of our inability to measure the benefit generated by caring services, Enthoven argues that "we cannot give a clear answer to the question of whether or not we are getting much health improvement for [the] large increases in [health] spending." In other words, although the market advocates in theory recognize the importance and value of caring services, as a practical matter these benefits are excluded from the cost-benefit analysis. The rationale for this de facto exclusion is that since the benefits of many types of health care are not clear in curative or statistical terms, they are best treated as matters of individual consumption to be paid for out of patients' own current assets, instead of from collective funds such as government programs or insurance.

It is interesting that some market advocates on occasion claim that price competition will enable the patient to exercise self-determination over the professional and self-interested biases of physicians. According to Enthoven, the professional view of quality of care is "the maximum that medical care can do to prolong life or alleviate suffering, costs not considered." Enthoven argues, however, that consumers do not in fact share this view. In other areas of life, people routinely take risks — they "drive cars [and] fly in airplanes . . . not to mention smoke and drink excessively." Enthoven questions, therefore, why people should be expected to prefer minimal risk, regardless of cost, when considering medical care.

> People's preferences for risk reductions, compared with the benefits they would receive from other uses of resources ought to be considered. . . . Even from the point of view of health, at some point dollars are better spent on other things, such as food and housing, rather than more medical care. Some terminal patients may not want a few more days or weeks of suffering life.
>
> The best quality care is not that care which ekes out the last possible day of life expectancy [or, presumably, degree of risk reduction]. Rather, the best quality of care reflects society's preferences in the use of resources. It is being provided when the extra health benefits yielded by expenditure of another dollar of resources on medical care are valued by consumers the same as they value the benefits obtained from the same expenditure in other activities. . . .

The striking feature of this passage is its assumption that the market is the best means of achieving individual self-determination. Few would quarrel with the need to help individual patients, their families, and society as a whole grapple with the profound problems inherent in maintaining life or reducing risk at great expense, which expense necessarily impinges upon numerous alternative uses of scarce resources. The question, however, is whether the market approach actually would contribute to resolving these problems.

Enthoven uses the example of the terminal patient who may not desire life-prolonging treatment as a case in support of his thesis. Under current financing arrangements, most insurance policies would cover the expenses of such care, assuming these costs did not exceed some stated dollar or service limit. In these circumstances, the decision whether to prolong life would be made on quality of life grounds, without consideration of monetary cost to the patient. A market approach presumably would add the factor of economic cost in some form to the decision. Havighurst, for example, advocates the marketing of cheaper insurance policies that would exclude one or another form of costly care for catastrophic illnesses. As Enthoven suggests, the consumer would be permitted in such a market to opt for greater financial risk in return for more cash to expend on immediate consumption. It is more likely, however, that the vast majority of patients faced with the decision whether to incur a $25,000 liability for continued treatment, for example, would not feel that their capacity for self-determination had been expanded, nor would they be consoled by the knowledge that they had exercised their self-determination in the prior choice of premium.

Note: Patient Cost Sharing

Extent of Cost Sharing. Deductibles and co-insurance in employee benefit plans and in Medicare increased dramatically in the 1980s. The proportion of private plans with inpatient deductibles increased from 30 percent in 1982 to 63 percent in 1984. Altman & Rodwin, Halfway Competitive Markets and Ineffective Regulation: The American Health Care System, 13 J. Health Pol. Poly. & L. 323 (1988). Between 1982 and 1984 the percentage of insurance plans requiring a front-end deductible for surgical fees increased from 34 percent to 59 percent, and the percentage paying the full after-deduction balance of surgical fees decreased from 42 percent to 26 percent. Goldsmith, Death of a Paradigm: The Challenge of Competition, 3 Health Affairs 5, 12 (1984). In 1981, Medicare met only 45 percent of all health expenditures of the elderly. On average the aged spent $1154 per person, out-of-pocket, for health services. Conference on the Future of Medicare 126 (1983). In 1984, the elderly spent an estimated 15 percent of their average income for out-of-pocket expenses, the same percentage as in 1966. Office of Technology Assessment, Payment for Physician Services: Strategies for Medicare 4 (1986).

Both distributive and behavioral consequences must be considered in evaluating cost-sharing proposals. An unambiguous effect of patients' cost sharing is to shift costs from the insurance program to the patient. Cost sharing is popular with both public and private insurance programs because it "saves" money. But unless cost sharing promotes behavioral change, costs are not saved but simply shifted from the program to the patient.

In the 1980s, growing numbers of insured people confronted ever larger out-of-pocket costs at time of injury or illness. Chapter 2, Sec. B(4). Controlled studies suggest that cost sharing does not discourage the use or reduce the cost of acute or inpatient care, though it does discourage the use of routine preventive services.

Proponents of patients' cost-sharing claim that it will produce behavioral changes in both patients and providers and will thereby reduce overall costs by promoting the use of lower-cost providers. Does cost-sharing encourage people to shop for physicians in a way that rewards quality or reduces cost? Professor Rand Rosenblatt describes the dynamic as to cost.

> [I]t is often impossible to determine the price of a medical treatment in advance. Diagnostic work usually must be done first, and by the time the patient receives a reliable estimate of the overall price, a considerable investment in time and money already has been made. To begin shopping for a new physician at this point would entail new office visits, new tests, additional work time lost, travel expenses, and personal aggravation. Indeed, the costs incurred in these added efforts quite conceivably could exceed any competitive advantage that the patient might obtain in the treatment price. On the other hand, attempts to shop at an earlier stage — for example, by visiting several doctors and seeking a variety of estimates based upon potential yet unknown diagnoses — would still involve considerable time, office fees, and a bewildering range of speculative options. Moreover, if the symptoms are at all uncomfortable, as they often are, the individual competition model becomes still more unrealistic. [Health Care, Markets, and Democratic Values, 34 Vand. L. Rev. 1067, 1080 (1981).]

It is even less clear how cost-sharing could promote quality and appropriate levels of health care. Although patients face difficulties in identifying the price of the service they need, they are better able to compare price than to evaluate the quality and appropriateness of recommended care. Much could and should be done to enhance patients' ability to evaluate the quality and appropriateness of medical care and to encourage them to seek independent evaluations, particularly for high-risk, elective interventions. See Chapters 5 and 6.

D. ANTITRUST AND THE ORGANIZATION OF MEDICAL CARE DELIVERY

1. INTRODUCTION TO ANTITRUST PRINCIPLES

Until the late 1970s, antitrust law was rarely applied to medical care arrangements, which were rather built on assumptions antithetical to free market competition, including ideals of professionalism and service, and state involvement in licensing and regulation. In one important early case, the AMA and its Washington, D.C., affiliate were convicted of a criminal violation of the Sherman Act when they conspired to prevent Group Health Association, an early health maintenance organization, from obtaining and keeping staff doctors. AMA v. United States, 130 F. 233 (D.C. Cir. 1942), *aff'd*, 317 U.S. 519 (1943). The AMA cited ethical objections to contract practice and prepayment. The Court, while recognizing doctors' right to establish standards of professional conduct and to effect agreements for self-discipline and control, distinguished efforts to destroy competing professional organizations. United States v. Oregon State Medical Society, 343 U.S. 326 (1952), rejected a challenge to medical society efforts to boycott doctors who participated in another early HMO. In dicta the Court "recognized that forms of competition usual in the business world may be demoralizing to the ethical standards of a profession." 343 U.S. at 336. Until the 1970s, there was little other effort to apply antitrust to medical care.

Application of antitrust laws to medical care financing and delivery has mushroomed in recent years. This dramatic change was precipitated by several factors. A general intellectual and cultural climate supported deregulation and increased competition. Legal scholars provided the conceptual tools to allow courts to break the doctrinal barriers that traditionally limited the application of antitrust laws to medical care.

This section begins with a general description of the substantive requirements of antitrust law. Part 2 examines the evisceration of doctrines that previously prevented application of the antitrust law to medical care. Two concepts have been most important in limiting the application of antitrust to health care arrangements: 1) the notion that professional services, and in particular medical services, are special in some way that makes full application of free market competition inappropriate, and 2) the idea that state government should be free to promote values other than free market competition. Part 3 explores the concrete application of antitrust laws to several common medical care arrangements, including denial of hospital staff privileges, limits on insurance reimbursement, and denial of membership in private professional associations.

This section introduces the legal principles that determine whether common arrangements in medical care violate the federal antitrust law. Antitrust law *assumes* that competition is good and that practices which "unreasonably" impede it are illegal. Historically the central concerns of health policy have been access, costs, and quality. Consider whether the concerns of antitrust law and of health policy complement one another.

Health Care Committee, American Bar Association, An Antitrust Overview

The Antitrust Health Care Handbook (1988)

A. APPLICATION OF THE ANTITRUST LAWS TO THE HEALTH CARE INDUSTRY

Prior to the mid-1970s it was widely believed that federal antitrust laws did not apply to any significant extent to activities of health care providers. It was conventional wisdom that most health care activities did not affect interstate commerce and that, in any event, the health care industry was not subject to the antitrust laws because it was a "learned profession" which was regulated by the states.

Beginning in 1975, however, the Supreme Court made it clear that health care providers and institutions can be subject to the federal antitrust laws because their activities may either occur in interstate commerce or have a substantial effect on interstate commerce, that there is no exemption for "learned professions" and that, in order for state regulation to supplant federal antitrust law, the activity or practice at issue must be mandated by the state. Despite its somewhat unique features, therefore, the health care industry is clearly subject to the antitrust laws.

B. THE PURPOSE OF THE ANTITRUST LAWS

The principal purpose of the federal antitrust laws is to promote free competition by prohibiting acts or practices that interfere with free competition. The antitrust laws — as "the referee of the game of competition" — ensure that improper conduct does not intervene to deny each business enterprise a full and equal opportunity to compete. As the Supreme Court stated in Northern Pacific Railway v. United States:

> The Sherman Act was designed to be a comprehensive charter of economic liberty aimed at preserving free and unfettered competition as the rule of trade. It rests on the premise that the unrestrained interaction of competitive forces will yield the best allocation of our economic resources, the lowest prices, the highest quality and the greatest material progress, while at the same time providing an environment conducive to the preservation of our democratic political and social institutions. But even were that premise open to question, the policy unequivocally laid down by the Act is competition.

The principal beneficiary of free competition is the consumer whose interests the antitrust laws are intended to serve. In the health care industry, the consumer interest often is represented by two separate entities — the individual who receives the service (i.e., the patient) and the entity that pays for the service (i.e., the payor).

C. *PRINCIPAL FEDERAL ANTITRUST STATUTES*

1. The Sherman Act:
   a. Section 1 of the Sherman Act prohibits contracts, combinations and conspiracies in restraint of trade.
   b. Section 2 prohibits monopolization, attempted monopolization and conspiracies to monopolize.
2. The Clayton Act (and the Robinson-Patman Act which amends it):
   a. Section 2 of the Clayton Act (known as the Robinson-Patman Act) prohibits discrimination in price between different purchasers in the sale of commodities of like grade and quality where the discrimination may lessen competition:
   b. Section 3 prohibits exclusive dealing arrangements, requirements contracts and tying arrangements involving the sale of a commodity where the effect may be to substantially lessen competition; and
   c. Section 7 prohibits mergers, acquisitions or joint ventures that may substantially lessen competition or tend to create a monopoly in any line of commerce in any section of the country.
3. The Federal Trade Commission Act:
   a. Section 5 of the Act prohibits unfair methods of competition, which has been held to include all Sherman Act and Clayton Act violations; and
   b. unfair deceptive acts or practices, which includes false or misleading advertising or misrepresentations to the public.
4. State antitrust laws which are patterned to varying degrees upon the federal antitrust laws.

A given act or practice may violate one or more of the antitrust laws. The essential task for a health care attorney, administrator, or provider is not to keep the precise distinctions between the various acts in mind, but rather to learn to recognize situations that may present risks under any of the antitrust laws. For this reason, the Handbook discusses general antitrust principles and is organized around categories of practices hospitals are likely to encounter.

D. ENFORCEMENT AND PENALTIES

The federal antitrust laws are enforced by the Antitrust Division of the Department of Justice, which may bring either criminal or civil actions, and the Federal Trade Commission, which is limited to bringing civil actions. In addition, any person (i.e., a private plaintiff) who is injured by reason of a violation of the antitrust laws may bring a civil suit to enjoin a particular act or practice or to recover threefold damages (i.e., a private treble damage action). A prevailing private plaintiff recovers reasonable attorney's fees and costs from the defendant, but a prevailing defendant does not recover attorney's fees and costs from an unsuccessful plaintiff. Potential private plaintiffs include (1) individuals, such as physicians, dentists or other providers; (2) business entities such as competing health care institutions, suppliers, or third-party payors; or (3) governmental bodies, such as states.

E. BASIC ANTITRUST PRINCIPLES

1. *The Concept of Agreement*

Section 1 of the Sherman Act prohibits contracts, combinations or conspiracies that unreasonably restrain trade. This means that two or more independent entities, persons or businesses must act in combination in order for there to be a violation of Section 1. They must reach an agreement that has either an anticompetitive purpose or an unreasonable anticompetitive effect. The agreement can be expressed, implied, tacit, or the product of coercion. Although there need not be a formal agreement, a conscious commitment to a common scheme is necessary. Whether conduct results from independent decisions of parties rather than from their joint agreement often is a question of fact decided by the jury.

2. *Standards of Legality: Rule of Reason and Per Se*

Agreements or practices may be lawful in some circumstances and unlawful in others depending on the intent of the parties, the justifications for the practice, and the extent to which competition is actually affected. These agreements or practices are analyzed under the "rule of reason" in order to assess the restraining effect in the market. Such restraints like exclusive contracts or restrictions on staff privileges are covered by the rule of reason and are not unlawful unless they are shown to have some substantial adverse effect on competition.

The rule of reason is best explained by Justice Brandeis in Chicago Board of Trade v. United States:

> Every agreement concerning trade, every regulation of trade, restrains. To bind, to restrain, is of their very essence. The true test of legality is whether the restraint imposed is such as merely regulates and perhaps thereby promotes competition or whether it is such as may suppress or even destroy competition. To determine that question the court must ordinarily consider the facts peculiar to the business to which the restraint is applied; its condition before and after the restraint was imposed; the nature of the restraint and its effect, actual or probable. The history of the restraint, the evil believed to exist, the reason for adopting the particular remedy, the purpose or end sought to be attained, are all relevant facts.

In health care antitrust cases, courts typically have looked to the purpose of the restriction to see whether it is reasonably related to legitimate objectives such as quality of care or whether it is motivated by an anticompetitive intent to damage or eliminate a competitor from the market. Courts also have looked to the effect of the restriction in the market. To constitute an unreasonable restraint of trade, the restriction must result in the substantial foreclosure of competition of a particular product or service in a particular geographic area. In short, an adverse effect on the quality, price or availability of services must be shown.

While most restraints of trade are analyzed in terms of the reasonableness of their nature, purpose and effect, some agreements or practices have such a pernicious effect on competition that they are presumed conclusively to be unreasonable and are per se unlawful without any further inquiry into the precise harm or business justification. Although exceptions may be found, per se violations typically include:

a. *Price-fixing:* Agreements with a substantial effect on price, even those that only indirectly affect price.

b. *Market Allocations:* An allocation or division of markets or customers by geographic area or by product among two or more actual or potential competitors.

c. *Group Boycotts:* An unjustified collaborative action designed to injure or exclude a business from access to the market. A group boycott by competitors of the party boycotted may be per se unlawful, but more recent cases have applied a rule of reason analysis.

d. *Tying Arrangements:* An agreement by a seller to sell one (the tying) product or service only on the condition that the buyer purchase a second (the tied) product or service. A tying arrangement is per se unlawful if the seller of the tying product or service has sufficient economic power to force the purchase of the tied product or service.

3. *The Relevant Market*

The relevant market is an important antitrust concept which has been critical in many health care antitrust cases. Under the rule of reason, the legality of a practice is determined by its effect on competition in a relevant market. Similarly, the legality of mergers and joint ventures are determined by their potential effects in a relevant market. The relevant market has two dimensions; the products or services involved and the geographic area of competition.

A product market includes all products or services that have a significant, positive cross-elasticity of demand or, in other words, all products or services that consumers consider reasonable substitutes for one another. For example, a relevant product market might be defined as the cluster of services that constitute in-patient general acute care hospital services or it might be based upon one or more medical specialties or subspecialties, such as open heart surgery.

The relevant geographic market is the area of effective competition that the seller encounters when it offers the product or service for sale. In many health care cases, the geographic market is limited by the distance that patients will travel to obtain a particular service. Often this is a county or multicounty area. For example, if the hospitals in one city raised their billed charges (i.e., their prices) for a particular service and, as a result, the residents of that city could and would travel to a nearby city for treatment, the two cities would probably be included in the geographic market.

4. *Monopoly Power*

"Monopoly power" is the power to exclude competitors or control price within a relevant market. Monopoly power often is defined in terms of market share in the relevant market. Therefore, once the relevant market has been defined the number of competitors in the market and their market shares must be determined in order to determine whether, and to what degree, any of them possess monopoly power. It should be noted, however, that monopoly power is not necessary to establish attempted monopolization.

As a practical matter, monopoly power usually *but not always* requires more than 60 percent of the relevant market. At one end, 90 percent has been held clearly sufficient and, at the other end, 33 percent clearly insufficient to convey monopoly power. Market share is not the only factor to consider. Such factors as technological superiority, the relative size of competitors, barriers to entry into the market, pricing trends and practices, the homogeneity of products, and stability of market shares over time also should be considered in determining whether market power exists.

5. *Monopolization and Attempted Monopolization*

To establish unlawful monopolization, the plaintiff must show that the defendant possesses monopoly power in the relevant market and that such power was obtained by willful acquisition as distinguished from growth or development as a consequence of a superior product, business acumen or historic accident. Mere possession of monopoly power is not unlawful unless it is achieved or maintained through exclusionary, anticompetitive or predatory conduct.

To establish attempted monopolization, the defendant must have a specific intent to monopolize the relevant market and sufficient market power to establish a dangerous probability of success. As a general rule, 30 percent of a market is insufficient to establish a dangerous probability of success.

6. *Mergers and Acquisitions*

Section 7 of the Clayton Act prohibits anticompetitive mergers, acquisitions and joint ventures. Section 7 prohibits acquisitions in any section of the country (i.e., relevant geographic market) in any line of commerce (i.e., relevant product market) where "the effect of such acquisition may be substantially to lessen competition, or tend to create a monopoly."

Mergers are categorized as horizontal, vertical or conglomerate depending upon the relationship, if any, of the parties to the transaction. A merger between firms that compete in a relevant market is a horizontal merger. A vertical merger is between firms that stand in a supplier/purchaser relationship. Conglomerate mergers are all other mergers. Such mergers extend the product, service, or geographic area of the acquiring firm beyond those in which it currently competes.

As an aid to determining when a merger violates Section 7, the Antitrust Division of the Department of Justice has issued Guidelines indicating the circumstances under which the Division may challenge a merger or acquisition.

2. TRADITIONAL IMPEDIMENTS TO APPLYING ANTITRUST PRINCIPLES TO MEDICAL CARE

a. The "Learned Profession" Exemption

Traditional concepts of professionalism posit that the complexity of professional knowledge and service mean that professionals should not be subject to lay control, whether exercised through bureaucratic or market mechanisms. Professional ethics include notions of public service. In addition, when professionals provide personal services, often of an intensely important nature, these concepts dictate that no "third party" should be allowed to interfere with the loyalty and intimacy of the relationship. These ideas were reflected in the medical profession's longstanding reluctance to accept prepaid health insurance, and in the historic legal bans on the corporate practice of medicine. See Introduction and Chapter 7.

Despite one early case rejecting physicians' claims that the professional nature of their service immunized them from scrutiny under the antitrust laws, AMA v. United States, 317 U.S. 519 (1943), affirmed the criminal conviction of the AMA and its Washington, D.C., affiliate. The Court rejected the defendants' claim that ethical standards required them to deny AMA membership to doctors who consulted with the Group Health Association, one of the first HMOs. Medical society membership was usually prerequisite to obtaining admitting privileges at local hospitals. Despite this early precedent, few antitrust claims were asserted against professional people until 1975. In that year the Court held that a Virginia state bar rule requiring lawyers to charge a minimum price for specified services was not immune from antitrust challenge. Goldfarb v. Virginia State Bar, 421 U.S. 773.

In *Goldfarb*, lawyers sought to invoke "professional ethics" to defend a practice of setting a minimum fee lawyers were required to charge for routine legal services . The Court rejected the claim that in a price-fixing case "professional ethics" could justify a practice that otherwise violated the antitrust law. The Court did, however, recognize that the "public service aspect, and other features of the professions, may require that a particular practice, which could properly be viewed as a violation of the Sherman Act in another context, be treated differently." 421 U.S. at 788, n.17.

Arizona v. Maricopa County Medical Society, 457 U.S. 332 (1982), rejected physicians' claims that the professional nature of their service required modification of traditional antitrust principles in a price-fixing case. The Medical Society had created a preferred provider organization in which physicians decided for the insurance company what maximum fees to charge patients who used doctors participating in the plan. In holding the plan per se illegal, the Court assumed that the "schedules impose a meaningful limit on physicians' charges, and that the advance agreement by the doctors to accept the maxima enables the insurance carriers to limit and to calculate more efficiently the risks they underwrite and therefore serves as an effective cost-containment mechanism that has saved patients and insurers millions of dollars." 457 U.S. at 342.

> The doctors . . . argue that the *per se* rule does not govern this case because the agreements at issue are horizontal and fix maximum prices, are among members of a profession, are in an industry with which the judiciary has little antitrust experience, and are alleged to have procompetitive justifications. . . .
>
> [T]he fact that doctors — rather than nonprofessionals — are the parties to the price-fixing agreements [does not] support the respondents' position. . . . The price-fixing agreements in this case . . . are not premised on public service or ethical norms. The respondents do not argue . . . that the quality of the professional service that their members provide is enhanced by the price restraint. The respondents' claim for relief from the *per se* rule is simply that the doctors' agreement not to charge certain insureds more than a fixed price facilitates the successful marketing of an attractive insurance plan. But the claim that the price restraint will make it easier for customers to pay does not distin-

guish the medical profession from any other provider of goods or services. [457, U.S. at 351.]

The substantive antitrust principles governing physician and insurer actions to constrain costs or create new health financing arrangements are discussed infra, Sec. D-3-b. As you read these materials, consider the basis for the distinction the Court suggests between professional activities "premised on public service" and the activity challenged in *Maricopa*. Is an effort to make medical care available at reasonable cost a form of public service? Must providers be excluded from such efforts? What forms of arguably anticompetitive activity might be defended as "premised on public service"?

Medical societies traditionally restricted dissemination of price information and banned physician advertising. American Medical Association v. Federal Trade Commission, 638 F.2d 443 (2nd Cir. 1980), *aff'd,* 455 U.S. 676 (1982), upheld an FTC order condemning these "ethical" rules as anticompetitive. The FTC did, however, allow the AMA to adopt guidelines prohibiting unsubstantiated, false, and deceptive representations by its members. 16 C.F.R. §13.330.

Federal Trade Commission v. Indiana Federation of Dentists, 476 U.S. 447 (1986), upheld an FTC order against Indiana dentists who sought to invoke "ethical" norms to defend their refusal to submit X-rays that Blue Shield sought in an effort to control unnecessary services and excess costs. The Court rejected the dentists' claim, but in dicta observed that, "[w]e have been slow to condemn rules adopted by professional associations as unreasonable per se. . . ." 476 U.S. at 458.

b. The McCarran-Ferguson Act

The McCarran-Ferguson Act, 15 U.S.C.A. §§1011-1015 (1976), was enacted in 1945 in response to the decision in United States v. South-Eastern Underwriters Association, 322 U.S. 533 (1944), holding that the business of insurance is interstate commerce subject to the Sherman Act. The McCarran-Ferguson Act provides:

> Congress hereby declares that the continued regulation and taxation by the several States of the business of insurance is in the public interest, and that silence on the part of the Congress shall not be construed to impose any barrier to the regulation or taxation of such business by the several States.
>
> Section 2.(a) The business of insurance, and every person engaged therein, shall be subject to the laws of the several States which relate to the regulation or taxation of such business.
>
> (b) No Act of Congress shall be construed to invalidate, impair, or supersede any law enacted by any State for the purpose of regulating the business of insurance, or which imposes a fee or tax upon such business, unless such Act specifically relates to the business of insurance: Provided,

> That the Sherman Act shall be applicable to the business of insurance to the extent that such business is not regulated by State Law. . . .

In 1979, the Supreme Court sharply limited the immunity provided by the McCarran-Ferguson Act. In Group Life and Health Insurance Co. v. Royal Drug Co., 440 U.S. 205 (1979), a drugstore sought to challenge an arrangement under which Blue Shield entered into contracts with participating pharmacies under which they agreed to provide drugs to Blue Shield subscribers for a fixed price paid directly by Blue Shield. All pharmacies were entitled to enter into participation agreements. When a subscriber selected a nonparticipating pharmacy, Blue Shield paid 75 percent of drug charges. In structure, the arrangement is identical to the common agreements between Blue Cross and participating hospitals. The arrangement had been approved by the state Insurance Commissioner.

The Court held, five to four, that, under the McCarran-Ferguson Act, this arrangement was not immune from antitrust scrutiny. The majority, per Justice Stewart, observed that the Act's exemption is for

> "the business of insurance," not the "business of insurance companies.". . . The primary elements of an insurance contract are the spreading and underwriting of a policyholder's risk. . . . The Pharmacy Agreements . . . do not involve any underwriting or spreading of risk, but are merely arrangements for the purchase of goods and services by Blue Shield. . . . The Pharmacy Agreements are thus legally indistinguishable from countless other business arrangements that may be made by insurance companies to keep their costs low and thereby also keep low the level of premiums charged to their policyholders. . . . [Id. at 214-215.]
>
> Another commonly understood aspect of the business of insurance relates to the contract between the insurer and the insured. . . . The Pharmacy Agreements are not "between insurer and insured." They are separate contractual arrangements between Blue Shield and pharmacies engaged in the sale and distribution of goods and services other than insurance. . . . [Id. at 215-216.]

Justice Brennan, joined by Justices Marshall and Powell and the Chief Justice, dissented. They observed that Congress, in 1945, rejected "bills before it which would have limited the "business of insurance" to a narrow range of specified insurance company practices, but chose instead the more general language which ultimately became law. . . ." Id. at 235.

> [W]hen the McCarran-Ferguson Act became law, service-benefit plans similar to the Blue Shield plan at issue here were a widespread and well recognized form of insurance, subject to regulation in most of the States. Congress itself treated these important programs as insurance. [T]he legislative history makes it abundantly clear that numerous horizontal agreements between insurance companies which do not technically involve the underwriting of risk were regarded by Congress as within the scope of the Act's exemption for the "business

> of insurance." For example, rate agreements among insurers, a conspicuous congressional illustration . . . do not themselves spread risk. . . .
>
> Some kind of provider agreement becomes a necessity if a service-benefits insurer is to meet its obligations to the insureds. The policy before us in this case, for example, promises payment of benefits in drugs. Thus, some arrangement must be made to provide those drugs for subscribers. Such an arrangement obtains the very benefits promised in the policy; it does not simply relate to the general operation of the company. [Id. at 242-244.]

Subsequently, in Union Labor Life Insurance Co. v. Pireno, 458 U.S. 119 (1982), the Court held another common health insurance arrangement not immune from antitrust scrutiny under the McCarran-Ferguson Act. The insurer contracted with the state Chiropractic Association to advise them whether services provided to insured individuals were necessary and reasonably priced. A chiropractor, whose claims were sometimes denied, challenged the arrangement as a conspiracy to fix prices.

Justice Brennan delivered the opinion of the Court, holding that the arrangement was not part of the "business of insurance." The standard for determining whether a practice is part of the business of insurance is

> first, whether the practice has the effect of transferring or spreading a policyholder's risk; second, whether the practice is an integral part of the policy relationship between the insurer and the insured; and third, whether the practice is limited to entities within the insurance industry. [T]he challenged peer review arrangement is logically and temporally unconnected to the transfer of risk accomplished by [the] insurance policies. The transfer of risk from insured to insurer is effected by means of the contract between the parties — the insurance policy — and that transfer is complete at the time that the contract is entered. . . . [458 U.S. 130.]

Justice Rehnquist, Chief Justice Berger, and Justice O'Connor dissented, protesting that, "[T]he Court today exposes to antitrust liability an aspect of the business of insurance designed to promote fair and efficient claims settlement. [T]he contractual relationship between the insurer and the insured [is] the essence of the 'business of insurance'." 458 U.S. at 135.

> Central to this contractual relationship is the process of claims adjustment — the determination of the actual payments to be made to the insured for losses covered by the insurance contract. The key representation of the insurance company and the principal expectation of the policyholder is that prompt payment will be made when the event insured against actually occurs. . . . It is the claims adjustor — in this case petitioners' Peer Review Committee — which determines whether and to what extent an insured's losses will be covered. . . . Few insurance matters could be of greater importance to policyholders than whether their claims will be paid, and it is the Peer Review Committee which in effect makes that determination. . . . [Id. at 136-137.]

The ideological divisions in these cases are curious. Justice Brennan wrote for the majority in *Pireno*, treating the majority opinion in *Royal Drug* as a given, despite his earlier trenchant dissent. Justices Marshall and Powell joined Brennan in this flip-flop from one case to the next. Justice Rehnquist switched in the other direction, joining the majority in *Royal Drug*, and dissenting in *Pireno*. How do you interpret the politics of these decisions?

The Court's decisions in these cases have been sharply criticized as a misinterpretation of the intent of the Congress that adopted the McCarran-Ferguson Act. See Law & Ensminger, Negotiating Physicians' Fees: Individual Patients or Society? (A Case Study in Federalism), 61 N.Y.U.L. Rev. 1, 60-74 (1986); Kimball & Heaney, Emasculation of the McCarran-Ferguson Act: A Study in Judicial Activism, 1985 Utah L. Rev. 1.

Whether or not these cases were "correct" as a technical matter of statutory interpretation, they have acquired a life of their own. Many common arrangements between health insurers, providers, and insureds are now subject to antitrust scrutiny. Congress could clarify the meaning of the McCarran-Ferguson Act. Several factors explain why it has not done so. Most important, as we shall see in the next section, courts have generally found that the arrangements challenged in these cases, while now subject to antitrust scrutiny, do not violate the antitrust laws. Second, the 1980s were a period of great optimism about the power of pro-competitive responses to social problems and corresponding skepticism about the efficacy of state regulation. Third, state regulation of insurance has often not been vigorous or effective. Finally, the subject is complex and raises controversial issues in relation to both competition vs. regulation and state vs. federal authority.

Few insurance practices have been held to meet the immunity standards of *Royal Drug* and *Pireno*. But Health Care Equalization Comm. Iowa Chiropractic Society v. Iowa Medical Society, 851 F.2d 1020 (8th Cir. 1988), held that Blue Cross/Blue Shield contracts with subscribers excluding coverage for chiropractic services were part of the "business of insurance" and hence immune from antitrust scrutiny under the McCarran-Ferguson Act.

c. State Action

In 1943, the Supreme Court recognized in Parker v. Brown, 317 U.S. 341, 351, that:

> [i]n a dual system of government in which, under the Constitution, the states are sovereign, save only as Congress may constitutionally subtract from their authority, an unexpressed purpose to nullify a state's control over its officers and agents is not lightly to be attributed to Congress.

Antitrust Professors Areeda and Turner observe: "To have held the Sherman Act applicable to the states could have removed the authority of the states to . . . regulate for the protection of the public, or to adopt other than a regime of competition even though peculiar local conditions required a different course which a busy national Congress was unlikely to consider. . . . The existence of a state action immunity enables states . . . to define areas inappropriate for market control." 1 Antitrust Law at 69, 73. Particularly in relation to health care and insurance, the United States has often chosen social arrangements, such as community rating, that reflect virtues other than competition and efficiency.

The *Parker* doctrine, like the McCarran-Ferguson Act, affirmed traditional state power to choose social arrangements other than competition. The competitive faith that animated the Court's 1979 decision in *Royal Drug* also produced a series of cases sharply restricting the power of states to choose noncompetitive social arrangements. Professor Handler comments that from 1943 to 1975, "[t]he Parker v. Brown rule was simple and easy to understand, and it provided certainty. It evoked very little litigation; only a handful of cases reached the courts. . . ." Reforming the Antitrust Laws, 82 Colum. L. Rev. 1287, 1330 (1982). Since 1975, the Court has restricted state authority to regulate in ways that conflict with the Sherman Act, and has required that state regulation take bureaucratically intrusive forms in order to enjoy immunity.

In medical care, the state action immunity issue has arisen most often in relation to the issue of staff privileges.

Patrick v. Burget

108 S. Ct. 1658 (1988)

Justice MARSHALL delivered the opinion of the Court.

The question presented in this case is whether the state action doctrine of Parker v. Brown, 317 U.S. 341 (1943), protects physicians in the State of Oregon from federal antitrust liability for their activities on hospital peer-review committees.

Astoria, Oregon, where the events giving rise to this lawsuit took place, is a city of approximately 10,000 people, located in the northwest corner of the State. The only hospital in Astoria is the Columbia Memorial Hospital (CMH). Astoria also is the home of a private group-medical practice called the Astoria Clinic. At all times relevant to this case, a majority of the staff members at the CMH were employees or partners of the Astoria Clinic. Petitioner Timothy Patrick is a general and vascular surgeon. He became an employee of the Astoria Clinic and a member of the CMH's medical staff in 1972. One year later, the partners of the Clinic, who are the respondents in this case, invited petitioner to become a partner of the Clinic. Petitioner declined this offer and instead began an independent practice in competition with the surgical practice of the Clinic. Petitioner continued to serve on the medical staff of the CMH.

After petitioner established his independent practice, the physicians associated with the Astoria Clinic consistently refused to have professional dealings with him. . . .

In 1979 . . . a partner at the Clinic, complained to the executive committee of the CMH's medical staff about an incident in which petitioner had left a patient in the care of a recently hired associate, who then left the patient unattended. The executive committee decided to refer this complaint, along with information about other cases handled by petitioner, to the state Board of Medical Examiners (BOME). Respondent Franklin Russell, another partner at the Clinic, chaired the committee of the BOME that investigated these matters. The members of the BOME committee criticized petitioner's medical practices to the full BOME, which then issued a letter of reprimand that had been drafted by Russell. . . . Two years later the executive committee of the CMH's medical staff . . . recommend[ed] the termination of petitioner's privileges on the ground that petitioner's care of his patients was below the standards of the hospital. Petitioner demanded a hearing. . . . Before the committee rendered its decision, petitioner resigned from the hospital staff rather than risk termination.

During the course of the hospital peer-review proceedings, petitioner filed this lawsuit [alleging] that the partners of the Astoria Clinic had violated Sections 1 and 2 of the Sherman Act. . . . Specifically, petitioner contended that the Clinic partners had initiated and participated in the hospital peer-review proceedings to reduce competition from petitioner rather than to improve patient care. Respondents denied this assertion, and the District Court submitted the dispute to the jury with instructions that it could rule in favor of petitioner only if it found that respondents' conduct was the result of a specific intent to injure or destroy competition.

The jury returned a verdict against respondents. . . . It awarded damages of $650,000. . . . The District Court, as required by law, . . . trebled the antitrust damages.

The Court of Appeals for the Ninth Circuit reversed. . . . It found that there was substantial evidence that respondents had acted in bad faith in the peer-review process. The court held, however, that even if respondents had used the peer-review process to disadvantage a competitor rather than to improve patient care, their conduct in the peer-review proceedings was immune from antitrust scrutiny. The court reasoned that the peer-review activities of physicians in Oregon fall within the state action exemption from antitrust liability because Oregon has articulated a policy in favor of peer review and actively supervises the peer-review process. . . . We now reverse. . . .

The Court . . .[has] sought to ensure that private parties could claim state action immunity from Sherman Act liability only when their anticompetitive acts were truly the product of state regulation. We accordingly established a rigorous two-pronged test to determine whether anticompetitive conduct engaged in by private parties should be deemed state action and thus shielded from the antitrust laws. See California Retail Liquor Dealers Association v. Midcal Aluminum, Inc., 445 U.S. 97 (1980). First, "the challenged restraint must be 'one clearly articulated and affirmatively expressed as state policy.'" Id. at 105. Second, the anticompetitive conduct "must be 'actively supervised' by the State itself." Id. at 105. Only if an anticompetitive act of a private party meets both of these requirements is it fairly attributable to the State.

In this case, we need not consider the "clear articulation" prong of the *Midcal* test, because the "active supervision" requirement is not satisfied. . . . The requirement is designed to ensure that the state action doctrine will shelter only the particular anticompetitive acts of private parties that, in the judgment of the State, actually further state regulatory policies. . . . To accomplish this purpose, the active supervision requirement mandates that the State exercise ultimate control over the challenged anticompetitive conduct. . . . The mere presence of some state involvement or monitoring does not suffice. . . . The active supervision prong of the *Midcal* test requires that state officials have and exercise power to review particular anticompetitive acts of private parties and disapprove those that fail to accord with state policy. . . .

Respondents in this case contend that the State of Oregon actively supervises the peer-review process through the state Health Division, the BOME, and the state judicial system. . . . [However, none] of these actors reviews — or even could review — private decisions regarding hospital privileges to determine whether such decisions comport with state regulatory policy and to correct abuses. . . . Hospitals in Oregon are under a statutory obligation to establish peer-review procedures and to review those procedures on a regular basis. . . . The Health Division's statutory authority over peer review relates only to a hospital's procedures; that authority does not encompass the actual decisions made by hospital peer-review committees. . . .

Similarly, the BOME does not engage in active supervision over private peer-review decisions. The principal function of the BOME is to regulate the licensing of physicians in the State. As respondents note, Oregon hospitals are required by statute to notify the BOME promptly of a decision to terminate or restrict privileges. . . . Neither this statutory provision nor any other, however, indicates that the BOME has the power to disapprove private privilege decisions. . . .

The only remaining alleged supervisory authority in this case is the state judiciary. [T]he Court of Appeals [held] that Oregon's courts directly review privilege-termination decisions and that this judicial review constitutes active state supervision. [J]udicial review of privilege-termination decisions in Oregon, if such review exists at all, falls short of satisfying the active supervision requirement. . . .

[T]he Oregon courts have indicated that even if they were to provide judicial review of hospital peer-review proceedings, the review would be of a very limited nature. The Oregon Supreme Court . . . stated that a court "should [not] decide the merits of plaintiff's dismissal" and that "[i]t would be unwise for a court to do more than to make sure that some sort of reasonable procedure was afforded and that there was evidence from which it could be found that plaintiff's conduct posed a threat to patient care." . . . This kind of review would fail to satisfy the state action doctrine's requirement of active supervision. . . .

Because we conclude that no state actor in Oregon actively supervises hospital peer-review decisions, we hold that the state action doctrine does not protect the peer-review activities challenged in this case from application of the federal antitrust laws. In so holding, we are not unmindful . . . that effective peer review is essential to the provision of quality medical care and that any threat of antitrust liability will prevent physicians from participating openly and actively in peer-review proceedings. This argument, however, essentially challenges the wisdom of applying the antitrust laws to the sphere of medical care, and as such is properly directed to the legislative branch. . . .

i. The Staff Privileges Cases

The Eleventh Circuit distinguished *Patrick* in a similar case. Bolt v. Halifax Hospital Medical Center, 851 F.2d 1273 (11th Cir. 1988), *petition for reh'g en banc granted*, 861 F.2d 1234 (1988). The court rejected the hospital's claim that it was legally incapable of conspiring with the members of its medical staff. But the court held that the decision terminating plaintiff's staff privileges was immune from antitrust scrutiny on state action grounds.

> The purpose of the active state supervision requirement is to ensure that the conduct in question is in fact a product of state regulation. A state may choose to regulate private economic activity through a state agency; it may just as readily choose to regulate such activity through its courts. Indeed, regulation through the judiciary may be more likely to ensure accurate implementation of the state's policy, for courts are especially well suited to divine, interpret, and enforce legislative policy. . . .
>
> That judicial review may be provided without express legislative authorization does not make that review any less a form of regulation by the state. It is sufficient if the legislature clearly articulates a policy and then acquiesces in the courts' implementation of that policy. . . .
>
> Of course, judicial review cannot constitute active state supervision unless it is available on an established basis and is of a sufficiently probing nature. To be sufficiently probing, the scope of judicial review must first of all encompass the fairness of procedures used in reaching the decision. Furthermore, it must involve consideration of whether the decision had a sufficient basis in fact. Our review of the Florida case law convinces us that such review is available in the Florida courts. [Id. at 1282.]

The Health Care Quality Improvement Act of 1986, 42 U.S.C.A. §§11101-11152 (Supp. 1987), immunizes peer review action from liability if the action was taken 1) in the reasonable belief that it was in the furtherance of quality health care, 2) after effort to obtain the facts, 3) after notice and a hearing or other "fair" procedures, and 4) in the belief that the action was warranted. Id. at 11112(a). The law presumes that these four standards have been met and requires a physician who has been disciplined to prove otherwise. Perhaps most significantly, it allows defendants, in suits challenging the actions of the professional review board, to recover attorneys' fees and other defense costs if they substantially prevail. See Chapter 5.

The Act does not change other "immunities under law," id. at 11115(a), including the state action immunity. States may thus immunize peer review action that does not meet the federal standards. How would you draft a state law to encourage physician participation in peer review, by providing antitrust immunity, without allowing destructive anticompetitive behavior?

ii. Antitrust Immunity for Local Governments and Public Hospitals

Municipalities have never enjoyed the full measure of sovereignty of states. In the late 1970s, a series of Supreme Court cases applied the stringent *Midcal* standards to local governments. See Community Communications Co. v. City of Boulder, 455 U.S. 40 (1982), collecting cases. The movement to apply the antitrust laws to municipalities threatened to undermine their ability to govern and to deliver essential public services. In the 1980s, both the Court and the Congress acted to provide local government greater latitude to engage in conduct that the antitrust laws would open to challenge if done by a private party.

Town of Hallie v. City of Eau Claire, 471 U.S. 34 (1985), held that: a) a state statute that expressly permits, but does not compel, anticompetitive conduct can immunize a municipality from antitrust scrutiny and b) a municipality need not show that the anticompetitive behavior is actively supervised by the state. The Court explained, "Where a private party is engaging in the anticompetitive activity, there is a real danger that he is acting to further his own interests, rather than the governmental interests of the state. Where the actor is a municipality, there is little or no danger that it is involved in a *private* price-fixing arrangement. . . . Once it is clear that the state authorization exists, there is no need to require the State to supervise actively the municipality's execution of what is a properly delegated function." 471 U.S. at 47.

In addition, the Local Government Antitrust Act of 1984, 15 U.S.C. §§34-36 (Supp. 1988), provides that "no damages, interests on damages, costs, or attorney's fees may be recovered [in an antitrust case] . . . from any local government, or official or employee thereof acting in an official capacity." Id. at §35. The federal statute, hence, limits antitrust relief against local governmental agencies to injunctive remedies. The *Hallie* doctrine, if applicable, wholly immunizes the anticompetitive municipal action.

Most courts have held that the Act protects public hospitals, as well as municipalities. See, for instance, Palm Springs Medical Clinic, Inc. v. Desert Hospital, 628 F. Supp. 454 (C.D. Cal. 1986); Wicker, CRNA v. Union County General Hospital, 673 F. Supp. 177 (N.D. Miss. 1987). Sandcrest Outpatient Services v. Cumberland County Hospital System, 853 F.2d 1139 (4th Cir. 1988), extended the Act's protection to a private management company administering a public hospital under contract, where the hospital board retained final authority to approve or disapprove the manager's actions. Medic Air Corp. v. Air Ambulance Authority, 843 F.2d 1187 (9th Cir. 1988), held that state law affirmatively authorized the county board of health to enter into an exclusive dealing contract with an air ambulance service, but that the private entity that held the contract could nonetheless be challenged for predatory pricing and conspiracy to restrain trade in other aspects of its business.

Whether a public hospital enjoys the broader immunity provided by the *Hallie* doctrine depends upon whether the anticompetitive conduct was expressly authorized by state law. Costal Neuro-Psychiatric Associates v. Onslow Memorial Hospital, 795 F.2d 340 (4th Cir. 1986), refused to allow a challenge to a public hospital's exclusive dealing contract, noting that state law required public hospitals to determine who should be granted staff privileges. The court found that the hospital had engaged in anticompetitive activity, but had done so under a law passed to promote greater hospital self-governance. 795 F.2d 342. By contrast, Wicker v. Union County General Hospital, 673 F. Supp. 177 (N.D. Miss. 1987), held that a statute authorizing the public hospital to determine who should be granted physician staff privileges did not affirmatively authorize, and hence immunize, a decision denying admitting privileges to a nurse anesthesiologist.

iii. Commentary on New State Action Standards

The recent Supreme Court decisions limiting *Parker* immunity have sparked significant scholarly commentary. John S. Wiley questions the assumption that state regulatory schemes condoning arrangements that would otherwise violate the Sherman Act promote democratic values, efficiency, or consumer welfare. He observes that such laws are often promoted by special economic interests and commonly delegate decision making authority to those interests. Further, the "'active supervision' requirement is pointless and costly. It condemns . . . [state sponsored] cartel effort only for involving too few hearings and bureaucrats, not for being illegitimate at its core. [E]ncouraging a more cumbersome regulatory maze lacks federal purpose.

[T]hrowing more bureaucrats at the problem [will not] make some revised regulatory structure a metaphysically 'truer' expression of authentic state will." Revision and Apology in Antitrust Federalism, 96 Yale L.J. 1277, 1282 (1987). See also, A Capture Theory of Antitrust Federalism, 99 Harv. L. Rev. 713 (1986). Merrick Garland, by contrast, argues that current Supreme Court doctrine does not exhibit a "trend toward greater federal intrusion," or a distrust of state regulation, but rather only condemns state regulation that delegates "to private parties the power to restrain market competition." Antitrust and State Action: Economic Efficiency and the Political Process, 96 Yale L.J. 486, 487 (1987), and Antitrust and Federalism: A Reply to Professor Wiley, 96 Yale L.J. 1291 (1987). Garland argues that recent Supreme Court decisions have struck a near perfect balance between state and federal interests.

The debate, while fascinating, fails to address important issues that emerge in health policy. Are tightly supervised state regulation, most often controlled by a private interest cartel, and federally enforced competition the only social arrangements available? Can "democratic" values be achieved only through "state" processes, or do "private" organizations also promote (or undermine) democratic values? Can democratic processes sometimes choose values other than "efficiency," or is such an ostensible choice certain to be the work of a special interest cartel? Whether state action immunities should be broad or narrow might depend, in part, on the consequences of applying the antitrust laws to common arrangements in health care. As you read the material in the following section, consider the impact of a decade of active antitrust litigation in medical care.

d. Erosion of Other Barriers to Antitrust Enforcement

i. Interstate Commerce

The federal antitrust law applies only to activity that has a substantial effect on interstate commerce. Markets for medical service and insurance were once considered local. Hospital Building Co. v. Trustees of Rex Hospital, 425 U.S. 738 (1976), held that a restraint on competition, even in a local hospital market, can affect interstate commerce and thus meet the jurisdictional requirements of the antitrust laws. The restraint at issue allegedly affected the interstate flow of a hospital's medicines and supplies, third-party payment, management fees, and construction financing. In the late 1980s, lower federal courts have continued to apply more demanding standards of impact on interstate commerce to bar claims of potential antitrust plaintiffs. See, for instance, Mitchell v. Frank R. Howard Memorial Hospital, 853 F.2d 762

(9th Cir. 1988); and Jaffee v. Horton Memorial Hospital, 680 F. Supp. 125 (S.D.N.Y. 1988).

Circuits have split on whether the plaintiff in a staff privileges case must show that the alleged restraint of competition affects commerce or simply that the general business activities of the defendant hospital affect interstate commerce. See, for instance, Seglin v. Esau, 769 F.2d 1274 (7th Cir. 1985) (activities infected by the restraint must affect interstate commerce); and Shahawy v. Harrison, 778 F.2d 636 (11th Cir. 1985) (it is sufficient if the defendants' general business affects interstate commerce).

ii. Health Planning

Chapter 3, Sec. D describes the state and federal health planning processes that have, since the late 1960s, sought to regulate and control the supply of health care facilities. In 1974, Congress recognized that "the health care industry does not respond to classic marketplace forces," and adopted an extensive health planning program. See H.R. Conf. Rep. No. 93-1640, 93rd Cong., 2d Sess. 39 (1974). In 1979, however, Congress introduced a note of ambiguity into the regulatory process mandated by the health planning act. While imposing significant new regulatory controls, Congress also noted that "competition and consumer choice" were to be favored in making regulatory decisions in the health industry whenever they "can constructively serve . . . to advance the purposes of quality assurance, cost effectiveness, and access" to health care. 42 U.S.C.A. §300k-2(a)(17) (1982). In the late 1980s, the federal role in health planning ended, although most states have continued to administer certificate of need programs.

In National Gerimedical Hospital and Gerontology Center v. Blue Cross, 452 U.S. 378 (1981), Blue Cross voluntarily cooperated with the local Health Systems Agency, created under the federal health planning law, by limiting reimbursement to a hospital constructed after the planning agency denied it permission to build. Blue Cross argued that its action gave teeth to the planning program mandated by Congress and that when the antitrust laws and the health planning act conflicted, the more recent and specific law should be read to repeal the antitrust law. The Court held that those who participate in the health planning process are immune from antitrust scrutiny only to the extent that the health planning law specifically mandated anticompetitive conduct.

Since *National Gerimedical* the Circuits have split on the degree of ongoing state supervision necessary to immunize actions taken pursuant to the state health planning process. Phoenix Baptist Hospital and Medical Center v. Samaritan Health Services, 688 F.2d 847 (9th Cir. 1982), *cert. denied*, 462 U.S. 1123 (1983), characterized the state CON process as a "statutory division of markets" and concluded that actions taken in response to the process satisfied *Midcal's* two-prong test. By contrast, a state action immunity claim was rejected in a merger case where there was a stringent certificate of need review process, but no continuing state supervision. North Carolina v. P.I.A. Asheville, Inc. 740 F.2d 274 (4th Cir. 1984), *cert. denied*, 471 U.S. 1003 (1985).

Even where state action immunity claims are rejected, plaintiffs denied a certificate of need may have difficulty establishing a substantive antitrust violation against health planning decisions. See, for instance, Huron Valley Hospital v. City of Pontiac, 849 F.2d 262 (6th Cir. 1988) upholding a summary judgment in favor of defendants who had denied plaintiffs a certificate of need in order to "reserve all medical-surgical acute care hospital services in the area to the hospitals already in existence in the area." Id. at 263.

3. APPLYING ANTITRUST PRINCIPLES TO TRADITIONAL HEALTH CARE RELATIONS

a. Staff Privileges

Cases involving staff privileges pose a sharp challenge for the application of antitrust doctrine to medical services. The National Health Lawyer's Association reports that in 1986, staff privileges cases are the largest single category of antitrust suits in the health care field — 40 percent of cases filed.

The Outsider's Perspective. Most hospitals are accurately characterized as "doctors' workshops," functionally controlled by a small group of physicians who act to promote their own economic and ideological interests. Most hospitals do not provide a full range of services to meet their patients' needs, including osteopathic, chiropractic, or massage therapy. Many do not offer low technology, patient-controlled, childbirth or reproductive health services. See Chap. 10. Rather than expand capacity to meet patient needs, insiders deny disfavored providers access to hospitals. Insiders sometimes also deny privileges to potential competitors simply to maintain the volume of service the insiders can provide and to enable them to keep fees high.

Outsiders denied staff privileges believe that their services are as valuable as those provided by insiders. A person denied staff privileges on grounds of alleged incompetence suffers a devastating blow to his or her self-image and economic well being. A successful antitrust claim can vindicate reputation, reorder professional relations, and generate money damages. An antitrust suit offers an outsider the best hope of vindication, albeit at the cost of attorneys' fees.

The Insider's Perspective. Most hospitals are accurately characterized as "doctors' workshops," functionally controlled by a relatively small group of able physicians with power to make a hospital financially stable or bankrupt. Whether they think of themselves as "rational economic actors" or as responsible citizens, they deny staff privileges to individuals who undermine the longterm stability of the hospital. Individuals seeking entry may be talented practitioners who want work in a saturated market, or they may be unskilled, unscrupulous people, who can destroy a hospital's reputation for excellence. Insider doctors value credentials, team spirit, skill, and capacity to bring patients and income to the institution. Insiders understand that granting admitting privileges to people who lack these qualities — faith healers, chiropractors, nurse-midwives, drug addicts, competent rebels, or superfluous specialists — threatens the interests of the hospital and of patients. Further, because unused skills atrophy, insiders seek to limit supply of specialists to allow each practitioner to work at capacity. Public financing programs, tort law, and the press place increasing pressure on insiders to take responsibility to assure that other practitioners with admitting privileges are responsible and competent.

Fear of antitrust litigation, however, deters participation in the processes of peer review and staff privileges decision-making, which are essential to protect these insider values. A physician's malpractice insurance does not ordinarily cover antitrust damage judgments or the attorney's fees necessary to defend against such a claim. Physicians cannot allow hospital lawyers to defend them against antitrust claims, as the interests of hospital and physician may conflict.

The Antitrust Law Perspective. When practitioners cooperate to deny staff privileges to competitors, the action can reasonably be characterized as a conspiracy amongst horizontal competitors, as a denial of access to essential facilities, or as a boycott, all of which are illegal *per se* under the Sherman Act. Boycotts are most plainly illegal if the market is highly concentrated and if the defendant does not offer efficiency or quality justifications for its actions. Despite the *per se* label, the materials that follow show that courts and commentators have been reluctant to condemn all staff privileges decisions.

A Traditional Regulatory Perspective. Because of the vital human importance of medical care, public officials — state and federal legislators, insurance and health administrators — seek to assure minimally adequate service. Decisions about who should be allowed to care for hospitalized patients are both important and controversial. Public officials lack the expertise and practical knowledge to make such judgments and hence seek to delegate responsibility for such decisions to organized groups of physicians, sometimes, but not always, with regulatory oversight.

A Consumer Perspective. Since the 1960s, informed consumers have understood the importance of hospital staff privileges. Both the Neighborhood Health Centers, funded by the Office of Economic Opportunity, and HMOs have been inhibited because many hospitals have denied admitting privileges to their physicians, however well qualified they may be. Consumer groups have pressured the Joint Commission on Accreditation of Hospitals to use its power to make staff privileges available to doctors working in Neighborhood Health Centers. See, Worthington and Silver, Regulation of the Quality of Care in Hospitals, 1975 J.L. & Cont. Probs. 35. Consumers have also sought legislative and regulatory changes to open hospital privileges to midwives and other alternative providers. Consumers have used antitrust remedies to protect doctors who have worked with them from retaliatory denials of staff privileges. See, for instance, Feminist Women's Health Center v. Mohammad, 586 F.2d 530 (5th Cir. 1978) (abortion clinic challenges an insider policy denying staff privileges to physicians who provide outpatient abortion services).

At the same time, the consumer perspective has not embraced the notion that all who declare themselves practitioners should be allowed to care for hospitalized patients. Rather, consumers have protested hospitals' failure to limit admitting privileges to reasonably competent people. See, for instance, S. Law & S. Polan, Pain and Profit: The Politics of Malpractice 51-77. In 1986, Dr. Sydney Wolff, head of Ralph Nader's Health Research Group, was the lead witness in support of AMA-promoted legislation to protect doctors who engage in peer review from liability under the antitrust laws.

The two cases that follow are highly condensed statements of the ambiguities expressed by the courts.

Miller v. Indiana Hospital

843 F.2d 139 (3rd Cir. 1988)

In this antitrust case filed by a physician against a hospital and members of its administrative and medical staff, the district court entered summary judgment for the defendants based on its conclusion that the hospital's decision to terminate the physician's staff privileges was supported by "substantial evidence" of the physician's unprofessional conduct. . . .

Plaintiff . . . is a licensed physician and surgeon specializing in urology. . . . He established a practice in Indiana, Pennsylvania, in 1959 after obtaining staff privileges in the Department of Surgery at Indiana Hospital . . . the only general hospital in . . . [the county]. . . .

Miller purchased land and built a five-office medical building. . . . [He sought to create a family practice to provide services] . . . "at lower cost than the same services at the hospital." . . .

In 1977, a patient under Miller's care at the hospital died. [T]he hospital's executive committee . . . recommend[ed] to the hospital's board of directors that Miller's staff privileges be revoked. Following Miller's demand [a hearing was held which] . . . lasted for three days, produced over twenty-two hundred pages of transcript testimony and exhibits, and resulted in a recommendation that Miller's staff privileges be revoked.

Specifically, the hearing committee found that Miller had exhibited "disruptive, insulting, intimidating, disrespectful, disparaging, abusive, and other improper behavior" toward various members of the staff; that he had acted improperly in the case of the deceased patient by failing to request a medical consultation, by failing to order certain tests, and by making improper entries in the patient's record [etc]. . . .

Miller filed an action against the hospital in [state court alleging] . . . breach of contract, defects in the hearing proceedings, and Fourteenth Amendment due process violations. . . . [The state courts found] that "the charges against [Miller] were supported by sufficient evidence" and that Miller "was dismissed in a fair and impartial manner in accordance with the hospital bylaws." Miller v. Indiana Hospital, 277 Pa. Super. 370, 380, 419 A.2d 1191, 1196 (1980). . . .

In 1981, Miller filed the present action [against the hospital] in federal district court in which he . . . alleged . . . violations of both federal and state antitrust laws. [T]he respective parties moved for summary judgment. . . . The hospital argues that because this court stated in Weiss v. York Hospital, 745 F.2d 786, 820 (3d Cir. 1984), *cert. denied,* 470 U.S. 1060 (1985), that a medical staff "is . . . entitled to exclude individual doctors . . . on the basis of their lack of professional competence or unprofessional conduct," the threshold inquiry in an antitrust staff privilege case is the professional competency of the individual physician. The hospital misreads *Weiss.* Nothing in that case suggests that the usual antitrust inquiry may be avoided merely because the conspiracy alleged involves a hospital. . . .

[T]he substantial evidence test used by the district court . . . is derived from administrative law and reflects the deference that a judicial body owes to the administrators entrusted with regulatory authority. . . . That test has no place in an antitrust case where Congress has given the jury the responsibility of resolving disputed fact issues. . . .

Miller contends that his hospital staff privileges were revoked and his applications for reinstatement denied because defendants wished to stifle his competition. . . . Defendants' argument that they revoked Miller's staff privileges because of his professional incompetence and unprofessional conduct is a defense they may present before the jury which, if convinced, will absolve them of any antitrust liability. It is inappropriate and unprecedented, however, to pretermit the jury's consideration of the parties' various contentions under the rubric of the substantial evidence test. [T]he substantial evidence test effectively eliminates any application of the antitrust laws to defendants' actions. It is apparent therefore that the district court erred as a matter of law in applying a substantial evidence test to determine if there were genuine issues of material fact to withstand summary judgment. . . .

Miller concedes for the purpose of this appeal that a rule of reason analysis is applicable to the hospital's conduct. The hospital argues that its conduct was patently reasonable because Miller, after a full hearing approved by the state court, was found to have demonstrated professional incompetence and unprofessional conduct. However, Miller has produced evidence which, if believed by the jury, would show that, in fact, the hospital's revocation of his privileges, although ostensibly for professional incompetence and unprofessional conduct, was motivated by the anticompetitive purpose of destroying Miller's competition or prospective competition. . . .

Wilk v. American Medical Association, American Hospital Association, the Joint Commission on Accreditation of Hospitals and Others

719 F.2d 207 (7th Cir. 1983)

. . . Plaintiffs, five licensed chiropractors, charged defendants-appellees with violating Sections 1 and 2 of the Sherman Act. . . . Plaintiffs alleged that defendants engaged in a combination and conspiracy to eliminate the chiropractic profession through refusing to deal with plaintiffs and other chiropractors. . . .

Plaintiffs' principal ground of appeal is that the court's instructions gave the jury to understand, incorrectly, that a boycott by defendants, resulting in a diminution of competition between chiropractors and medical doctors, was lawful if the boycott was the product of a genuine belief by medical doctors that chiropractic is dangerous quackery. Because the district court embraced this incorrect view of the law, plaintiffs contend, it received in evidence, erroneously and over objection, much prejudicial material concerning the alleged evils of chiropractic. . . .

Chiropractic is a health care service. Its primary therapeutic tool is spinal manipulation. . . . In [the] . . . states where plaintiffs have practiced, there were no laws in effect during the time relevant to this lawsuit that prohibited chiropractors from furnishing care in a hospital under the supervision of a medical staff member. . . .

Principle 3 of the AMA Principles of Medical Ethics in effect during the alleged boycott provided: "A physician should practice a method of healing founded on a scientific basis; and he should not voluntarily professionally associate with anyone who violates this principle." . . . [In 1963, the AMA established a "Committee on Quackery," which] . . . considered "its prime mission to be, first, the containment of chiropractic and ultimately, the elimination of chiropractic." . . .

In plaintiffs' view of the Sherman Act, it was irrelevant whether the stated reasons, namely, ethical considerations springing from belief that chiropractic is dangerous quackery, were the true reasons or whether the true reasons were economic. [D]efendants were insistent that under the Sherman Act, available defenses were that their conduct had been undertaken in the interest of public health, safety, and welfare, and that their conduct had been noncommercial.

The trial was dominated by defendants' efforts to persuade the jury that they had acted in the good faith belief that chiropractic is dangerous quackery. Evidence intended to show that chiropractic is indeed dangerous quackery was introduced to support the proposition that defendants' belief was genuine. . . .

[T]he able and experienced district judge suffered from the uncertainty which marks the law of boycotts by professionals: specifically, what legal justification, if any, exists for such boycotts when their effect is to restrain competition. [T]he jury was plainly led to believe that if the money motive was present but was not "primary" or "principal," even the most classical anticompetitive conduct would not constitute a per se violation. The jury may well have found that a generalized public interest motive was dominant with one defendant or another. If so, the jury was required by the instructions to withhold the per se violation label even from conduct — comparable to horizontal price-fixing, for example — to which the label would otherwise clearly attach. This was error. . . . It can fairly be said that the Supreme Court of the United States has been persistent and firm in its support of the per se doctrine. . . .

The trial court should not have [allowed] . . . the jury . . . to find a per se violation . . . because . . . the evidence of the "patient care motive" required that rule of reason analysis be applied. . . . Particularly when a conspiracy of this sort is alleged in the context of a profession, the nature and extent of its anticompetitive effect are too uncertain to be amenable to per se treatment, as contrasted with treatment under the rule of reason. . . . [The Supreme] Court has taken pains to preserve the possibility that a particular practice which could be viewed as a violation of the Sherman Act in another context, should be viewed and treated differently in the circumstances peculiar to a learned profession. [A]n agreement to fix prices will not escape per se treatment simply because it is entered into by professionals and accompanied by ethical protestations. But a canon of medical ethics purporting, surely not frivolously, to address the importance of scientific method gives rise to questions of sufficient delicacy and novelty at least to escape per se treatment. . . .

[T]he instructions as given failed to convey that the single standard is whether the challenged agreement is one that promotes competition or one that suppresses competition. [I]t is effect or consequence which controls, not intent or motive. . . . In short, the instructions given cannot be defended successfully as an adequate approximation of a rule of reason test geared simply, clearly, and exclusively to the question whether the challenged conduct promoted or suppressed competition between medical doctors and chiropractors. . . . From the jury's viewpoint, the result was ambiguity, an uncertain trumpet. . . .

If it should be determined eventually in this case that the Sherman Act was violated, that determination should not rest on insistence that the Act is indifferent to, or even hostile to, the value of permitting medical doctors to honor in their practice what they perceive to be scientific method, or indifferent to or hostile to the value of encouragement, from within the profession, to its members to honor scientific method by declining to associate with those thought to dishonor it. A value independent of the values attributed to unrestrained competition must enter the equation. . . .

The jury should be instructed in appropriate language to the following effect: the burden of persuasion is on the plaintiffs to show that the effect of Principle 3 and the implementing conduct has been to restrict competition rather than to promote it. If the plaintiffs have met this burden, the burden of persuasion is on the defendants to show: (1) that they genuinely entertained a concern for what they perceive as scientific method in the care of each person with whom they have entered into a doctor-patient relationship; (2) that this concern is objectively reasonable; (3) that this concern has been the dominant motivating factor in defendants' promulgation of Principle 3 and in the conduct intended to implement it; and (4) that this concern for scientific method in patient care could not have been adequately satisfied in a manner less restrictive of competition. . . .

There is another important respect in which the instructions were inadequate and prejudicial to plaintiffs: they failed to distinguish sharply enough between the "public interest motive" and the "patient care motive." The patient care motive could explain nothing more than the refusal by the medical doctors, and the hospitals staffed by medical doctors, to associate with chiropractors in the treatment of patients. It could not explain, for example, defendants' efforts to . . . [obtain laws] to eliminate chiropractic. . . . It is true that medical doctors are better qualified than most members of the public to form an opinion whether chiropractic poses a threat to public health, safety, and welfare. They are free to attempt to persuade legislatures and administrative agencies. But a generalized concern for the health, safety, and welfare of members of the public as to whom a medical doctor has assumed no specific professional responsibility, however genuine and well-informed such a concern may be, affords no legal justification for economic measures to diminish competition with some medical doctors by chiropractors. . . .

We conclude that the instructions to the jury were prejudicially erroneous in two respects. The overriding question in the case was whether, in applying the rule of reason, the jury was to be allowed to consider any factor whatever beyond the effect of defendants' conduct on competition. The district court elected to permit the jury to go beyond that single test and to consider the defendants' motives. But it failed to confine that consideration sharply to defendants' patient care motive, as contrasted with their generalized public interest motive. And, with respect to the patient care motive, the court failed to convey clearly and understandably the manner in which the jury was to weigh it, particularly as to the least restrictive means requirement. . . .

b. Staff Privileges Cases

i. Courts Fragment

If the principles of these cases seem unclear, it is because they are. A practitioner denied staff privileges can allege three *per se* violations of the antitrust laws: 1) a group boycott under Section 1 of the Sherman Act; 2) monopolization or attempted monopolization in violation of Section 2 of the Sherman Act, if the hospital possesses monopoly power or is an "essential facility"; or 3) a claim of illegal tying or exclusive dealing, if the denial is a consequence of the hospitals' tying or exclusive dealing contract with another group or individual.

Concerted Action. To establish concerted action under Section 1, a plaintiff must show an agreement between two or more separate actors. A corporation and its individual officers, directors, or agents comprise a single entity and therefore are not capable of conspiring with one another. However, if a physician has an "independent stake" that goes beyond a desire to enhance the corporation's welfare, then the physicians may be seen as separate entities capable of conspiring with one another, or with the hospital.

Some courts have held that individual medical staff members act in their own economic interest in excluding a practitioner from the staff. Weiss v. York Hospital 745 F.2d 786, 814 (3rd Cir. 1984), *cert. denied,* 470 U.S. 1060 (1985), found that "the medical staff itself is a combination as a matter of law," a "walking conspiracy." The court however rejected the claim that the hospital conspired with the medical staff. Other courts, finding that no decision-maker had an "independent personal stake" in the plaintiff's exclusion, have dismissed claims of conspiracy between the hospital and physicians on the medical staff. See, for instance, Feldman v. Jackson Memorial Hospital, 571 F. Supp. 1000 (S.D. Fla. 1983), *aff'd,* 752 F.2d 647 (11th Cir. 1983), *cert. denied,* 472 U.S. 1029 (1985).

Nanavati v. Burdette Tomlin Memorial Hospital, 857 F.2d 96 (3rd Cir. 1987), considered antitrust claims in the continuing saga of the dispute between Dr. Nanavati and this hospital. See Chap. 5, Section D(2). Dr. Nanavati alleged that Dr. Sorensen, the hospital, and its Executive Committee conspired to boycott patient referrals to him. The jury rendered a judgment in favor of Dr. Sorensen, but found that the hospital and its Executive Committee had conspired to deny him referrals because of "unprofessional behavior or violation of other public service or other ethical norms." 857 F.2d 116. The trial court entered judgment not withstanding the jury verdict, for the hospital and executive committee. The Court of Appeals affirmed, holding that the hospital could not conspire with its executive committee. It also affirmed the judgment for the executive committee, finding that even though many doctors on the hospital staff had expressed an intent to boycott referrals to Dr. Nanavati, none of these individuals had been joined as defendants or were members of the Executive Committee. 857 F.2d at 119-120.

Concern for Quality of Care. Many courts have relied upon quality of care concerns to uphold actions denying staff privileges to either individual physicians or classes of licensed practitioners. Kaczanowki v. Medical Center Hospital of Vermont, 612 F. Supp. 688 (D. Vt. 1985), granted a summary judgment upholding a medical staff decision denying staff privileges to licensed podiatrists. Cooper v. Forsyth County Hospital Authority Inc., 604 F. Supp. 685 (M.D.N.C. 1985), *cert. denied,* 107 S. Ct. 474 (1986), did the same.

On the other hand, both *Miller* and *Wilk* suggest a more limited role for quality of care concerns in antitrust challenges to denial of staff privileges. On remand in *Wilk,* the District Court found that the defendants "genuinely entertained a concern for scientific method in the care of patients" and that concern for patients was the "dominant motivating factor" behind their actions. Nonetheless, defendants failed to meet the burden of proving that concern was "objectively reasonable." At the same time, the court rejected the notion that the courtroom was a legitimate forum for deciding whether chiropractic is scientific or whether the decision was a judicial endorsement of chiropractic. The AMA was ordered to stop "restricting, regulating or impeding" its members or hospitals from associating with chiropractors and required to mail the court order to all its members, and to publish it in the Journal of the American Medical Association. 671 F. Supp. 1465 (D. Ill. 1987).

The Supreme Court has suggested in dicta that the legality of arrangements challenged under the antitrust laws may not turn upon good motive or desire to improve patient care. See Jefferson Parish Hospital District No. 2 v. Hyde, 466 U.S. 2 (1984); and F.T.C. v. Indiana Federation of Dentists, 476 U.S. 447 (1986), both discussed infra.

ii. Commentators Suggest Solutions

Clark Havighurst recommends application of an "essential-facilities doctrine" to staff privileges cases. He would impose liability only when 1) the hospital is an essential resource, access to which is necessary for the competitor to compete effectively; and 2) the privileges decision was controlled by the applicant's competitors, that is, the medical staff, rather than the hospital's governing board. Doctors and Hospitals: An Antitrust Perspective on Traditional Relationships, 1984 Duke L.J. 1071.

P. Kissam, W. Webber, L. Bigus, and L. Holzgraefe in Antitrust and Hospital Privileges: Testing the Conventional Wisdom, 70 Calif. L. Rev. 595 (1982), urge that staff privileges cases be resolved by determining whether defendants have an anticompetitive intent. J. Miles and M. Philp would require the plaintiff to prove that 1) she or he is unable to obtain privileges at another hospital in the relevant geographic market and that 2) the exclusion unreasonably restrains competition in the physician services market. If plaintiffs met this burden, defendants could claim an affirmative defense by establishing procompetitive effects in the hospital services market. If both sides met their burdens, the plaintiff would lose. Hospitals Caught in the Antitrust Net: An Overview, 24 Duq. L. Rev. 489, 525 (1985).

iii. Tying and Exclusive Dealing Contracts

The only Supreme Court case considering the merits of an antitrust challenge to a hospital decision denying staff privileges involved an anesthesiologist who was rejected for privileges at a hospital that had an exclusive dealing contract with an anesthesia group. The physician alleged that the hospital illegally tied patients' purchase of anesthesia services to their consumption of surgical procedures. Jefferson Parish Hospital District No. 2 v. Hyde, 466 U.S. 2 (1984), unanimously held no per se violation. The Court divided sharply on the analysis applied. Five Justices would retain the modified per se rule against tying where the seller has market power in the relevant market and uses that power to "force" the buyer to purchase the tied product. They found sufficient demand for anesthesia services to identify a product market separate and distinct from other hospital services, but concluded that patients in the relevant market were not forced to purchase anesthesiological services as a result of the exclusive contract because there were many other hospitals in the relevant market. Thus the hospital did not have enough market power either to prevent other anesthesiologists from practicing their specialty or to force patients to use its anesthesiologists. The four concurring Justices would analyze tying arrangements under a rule of reason analysis and condemn them only: if there are two separate products (or services) not sold in conjunction with one another; the seller has market power in the tying product; the market for the tied product is concentrated with high entry barriers; and the seller's forcing the buyer to accept the tie is an exercise of market power that reduces output in the tied product market.

Addressing the role that motives play in antitrust analysis, the plurality opinion said:

> [a]n examination of the reason or reasons why petitioners denied respondent staff privileges will not provide the answer to the question whether the package of services they offered to their patients is an illegal tying arrangement. As a matter of antitrust law, petitioners may give their anesthesiology business to Roux because he is the best doctor available, because he is willing to work long hours, or because he is the son-in-law of the hospital administrator without violating the per se rule against tying. Without evidence that petitioners are using market power to force [this anesthesiologist] upon patients there is no basis to view the arrangement as unreasonably restraining competition what-

> ever the reasons for its creation. Conversely, with such evidence, the per se rule against tying may apply. Thus we reject the view of the District Court that the legality of an arrangement of this kind turns on whether it was adopted for the purpose of improving patient care." [466 U.S. at 25, n.41.]

One article observes, "The *Hyde* analysis is sufficiently ambiguous that exclusive hospital-physician contracts should remain a fertile ground for antitrust litigation." Miles & Philp, Hospitals Caught in the Antitrust Net: An Overview, 24 Duq. L. Rev. 489, 534 (1985).

Exclusive dealing contracts are quite common; in 1985 over 70 percent of American hospitals used some form of exclusive contract. Is a decision denying general medical staff privileges different from one denying admitting privileges to particular doctors or groups of practitioners? Often the impetus for use of an exclusive contract, and thus the decision not to grant the applicant privileges, comes from the hospital rather than from the medical staff.

While many cases have challenged exclusive dealing contracts, few have succeeded. Collins v. Associated Pathologists, 844 F.2d 474 (7th Cir. 1988), is illustrative and collects recent cases. The circuit affirmed a summary judgment against a pathologist who challenged a hospital's exclusive dealing arrangement with a rival group. The court found that there was no tying arrangement because there is no market for pathology services separate from the market for hospital services. Id. at 477. Further, the contract did not unreasonably restrain trade because the relevant product was pathologists and not pathological services and hence the relevant market is a national one, upon which the defendant had a minimal impact. Id. at 479. In addition, the exclusive contract did not constitute a boycott because since the contract was not illegal *per se,* the boycott pursuant to it was likewise not illegal. Finally, more than the existence of an issue of triable fact is needed to survive a motion for summary judgment. The court concluded that in some antitrust cases, "use of summary judgment is not only permitted but encouraged." 844 F.2d at 475. By contrast, a successful challenge to an exclusive dealing contract involved particularly egregious circumstances in which physician anesthesiologists persuaded a hospital to give them an exclusive contract, explicitly arguing that their incomes were threatened by a nurse anesthesiologist who was highly successful and popular with both patients and surgeons. Oltz v. Saint Peter's Community Hospital, 861 F.2d 1440 (9th Cir. 1988).

c. Price Fixing or Cost Containment?

Organizations that agree to finance medical care in return for a fee or premium must set a price for insured services and describe the terms upon which payment is made. Familiar insurance arrangements and new forms of managed care raise knotty issues under the antitrust laws. Characterizing relationships is a critical step in antitrust analysis. Three issues that antitrust courts have regarded as important in characterizing health care financing arrangements are 1) whether an agreement is horizontal or vertical, 2) whether an agreement is a conspiracy amongst independent competitors or an integrated package of service and financing, and 3) the measurement and relevance of market power.

Agreements among actors who compete with one another in the same geographic and product market — for instance, among doctors, among hospitals, or among insurers — are considered horizontal. In general, horizontal agreements amongst competitors are more likely to be illegal under the antitrust laws than vertical or other agreements. But as the following cases and notes illustrate, it is often difficult to characterize particular arrangements and determine the legal standards applicable to evaluating them.

Arizona v. Maricopa County Medical Society

457 U.S. 332 (1982)

Justice STEVENS delivered the opinion of the Court.

[The defendant physicians established a preferred provider arrangement under which doctors agreed to accept, as payment in full, fees set by the plan. Patients who sought services from participating doctors paid fixed fees, while those who sought services from non-participating doctors negotiated fees on an individual basis.]

Section 1 of the Sherman Act of 1890 literally prohibits every agreement "in restraint of trade." . . . [We have] recognized that Congress could not have intended a literal interpretation of the word "every" . . . [and] have analyzed most restraints under the so-called "rule of reason." As its name suggests, the rule of reason requires the fact finder to decide whether under all the circumstances of the case the restrictive practice imposes an unreasonable restraint on competition.

The elaborate inquiry into the reasonableness of a challenged business practice entails significant costs. Litigation of the effect or purpose of a practice often is extensive and complex. . . . Judges often lack the expert understanding of industrial market structures and behavior to determine with any confidence a practice's effect on competition. . . . The costs of judging business practices under the rule of reason, however, have been reduced by the recognition of per se rules. Once experience with a particular kind of restraint enables the Court to predict with confidence that the rule of reason will condemn it, it has applied a conclusive presumption that the restraint is unreasonable.

. . . By 1927, the Court was able to state that "it has . . . often been decided and always assumed that uniform price-fixing by those controlling in any substantial manner a trade or business in interstate commerce is prohibited by the Sherman Law." . . .

> Maximum and minimum price fixing may have different consequences in many situations. But schemes to fix maximum prices, by substituting the perhaps erroneous judgment of a seller for the forces of the competitive market, may severely intrude upon the ability of buyers to compete and survive in that market. . . . Maximum prices may be fixed too low for the dealer to furnish services . . . which consumers desire and for which they are willing to pay. Maximum price fixing may channel distribution through a few large or specifically advantaged dealers. . . . Moreover, if the actual price charged under a maximum price scheme is nearly always the fixed maximum price . . . , the scheme tends to acquire all the attributes of an arrangement fixing minimum prices. . . .

[Prior cases] place horizontal agreements to fix maximum prices on the same legal — even if not economic — footing as agreements to fix minimum or uniform prices. The per se rule "is grounded on faith in price competition as a market force (and not) on a policy of low selling prices at the price of eliminating competition." . . . In this case the rule is violated by a price restraint that tends to provide the same economic rewards to all practitioners regardless of their skill, their experience, their training, or their willingness to employ innovative and difficult procedures in individual cases. Such a restraint also may discourage entry into the market and may deter experimentation and new developments by individual entrepreneurs. It may be a masquerade for an agreement to fix uniform prices, or it may in the future take on that character.

We are equally unpersuaded by the argument that we should not apply the per se rule in this case because the judiciary has little antitrust experience in the health care industry. . . . [We have held] that "[w]hatever may be its peculiar problems and characteristics, the Sherman Act, so far as price-fixing agreements are concerned, establishes one uniform rule applicable to all industries alike." . . .

The respondents' principal argument is that the per se rule is inapplicable because their agreements are alleged to have procompetitive justifications. . . . [They] contend that their fee schedules are procompetitive because they make it possible to provide consumers of health care with a uniquely desirable form of insurance coverage that could not otherwise exist. . . . It is true that a binding assurance of complete insurance coverage — as well as most of the respondents' potential for lower insurance premiums — can be obtained only if the insurer and the doctor agree in advance on the maximum fee that the doctor will accept as full payment for a particular service. Even if a fee schedule is therefore desirable, it is not necessary that the doctors do the price fixing. . . .

Our adherence to the per se rule is [also] grounded . . . on a recognition of the respective roles of the Judiciary and the Congress in regulating the economy. . . . Given its generality, our enforcement of the Sherman Act has required the Court to provide much of its substantive content. By articulating the rules of law with some clarity and by adhering to rules that are justified in their general application, however, we enhance the legislative prerogative to amend the law. The respondents' arguments against application of the per se rule in this case therefore are better directed to the Legislature. . . .

The foundations are not analogous to partnerships or other joint arrangements in which persons who would otherwise be competitors pool their capital and share the risks of loss as well as the opportunities for profit. In such joint ventures, the partnership is regarded as a single firm competing with other sellers in the market. The agreement under attack is an agreement among hundreds of competing doctors concerning the price at which each will offer his own services to a substantial number of consumers. It is true that some are surgeons, some anesthesiologists, and some psychiatrists, but the doctors do not sell a package of three kinds of services. If a clinic offered complete medical coverage for a flat fee, the cooperating doctors would have the type of partnership arrangement in which a price-fixing agreement among the doctors would be perfectly proper. But the fee agreements disclosed by the record in this case are among independent competing entrepreneurs. They fit squarely into the horizontal price-fixing mold.

Justices BLACKMUN and O'CONNOR did not participate in the decision of this case.

Justice POWELL, with whom The Chief Justice and Justice REHNQUIST join, dissenting.

The medical care plan condemned by the Court today is a comparatively new method of providing insured medical services at predetermined maximum costs. It involves no coercion. Medical insurance companies, physicians, and patients alike are free to participate or not as they choose. On its face, the plan seems to be in the public interest. . . .

On summary judgment, the record and all inferences therefrom must be viewed in the light most favorable to the respondents. . . . The respondents' contention that the "consumers" of medical services are benefited substantially by the plan is given short shrift. . . .

[T]he foundation arrangement forecloses no competition. Unlike the classic cartel agreement, the foundation plan does not instruct potential competitors: "Deal with consumers on the following terms and no others." Rather, physicians who participate in the foundation plan are free both to associate with other medical insurance plans — at any fee level, high or low — and directly to serve uninsured patients — at any fee level, high or low. Similarly, insurers that participate in the foundation plan also remain at liberty to do business outside the plan with any physician — foundation member or not — at any fee level. Nor are physicians locked into a plan for more than one year's membership. . . . Thus freedom to compete, as well as freedom to withdraw, is preserved. . . .

Second, on this record we must find that insurers represent consumer interests. Normally consumers search for high quality at low prices. But once a consumer is insured — i.e., has chosen a medical insurance plan — he is largely indifferent to the amount that his physician charges if the coverage is full, as under the foundation-sponsored plan.

The insurer, however, is not indifferent. To keep insurance premiums at a competitive level and to remain profitable, insurers — including those who have contracts with the foundations — step into the consumer's shoes with his incentive to contain medical costs. Indeed, insurers may be the only parties who have the effective power to restrain medical costs, given the difficulty that patients experience in comparing price and quality for a professional service such as medical care. . . .

[O]n the record before us, we must infer that the foundation plan — open as it is to insurers, physicians, and the public — has in fact benefited consumers by "enabl[ing] the insurance carriers to limit and to calculate more efficiently the risks they underwrite." . . .

It is settled law that once an arrangement has been labeled as "price fixing" it is to be condemned per se. But it is equally well settled that this characterization is not to be applied as a talisman to every arrangement that involves a literal fixing of prices. Many lawful contracts, mergers, and partnerships fix prices. . . . The inquiry in an antitrust case is not simply one of "determining whether two or more potential competitors have literally 'fixed' a 'price.' . . . [Rather], it is necessary to characterize the challenged conduct as falling within or without that category of behavior to which we apply the label 'per se price fixing.' That will often, but not always, be a simple matter." . . .

Before characterizing an arrangement as a per se price-fixing agreement meriting condemnation, a court should determine whether it is a "naked restrain[t] of trade with no purpose except stifling of competition." . . . Such a determination is necessary because "departure from the rule-of-reason standard must be based upon demonstrable economic effect rather than . . . upon formalistic line drawing." . . . As part of this inquiry, a court must determine whether the procompetitive economies that the arrangement purportedly makes possible are substantial and realizable in the absence of such an agreement. . . .

The Court, in defending its holding, also suggests that "respondents' arguments against application of the per se rule . . . are better directed to the Legislature." . . . This is curious advice. The Sherman Act does not mention per se rules. . . . Since the enactment of the Sherman Act in 1890, it has been the duty of courts to interpret and apply its general mandate — and to do so for the benefit of consumers. . . .

Except in emergencies, Massachusetts Blue Shield makes payments only to physicians who sign participation agreements with it. Those agreements require that physicians accept Blue Shield fees as payment in full. The Massachusetts Medical Society challenged the arrangement, relying upon the Sherman Act, as interpreted in Arizona v. Maricopa County Medical Society. The district court upheld their claim. See Chap. 3-D for a discussion of the various arrangements insurers make for paying physicians.

Kartell v. Blue Shield of Massachusetts

749 F.2d 922 (1st Cir. 1984), cert. denied, *471 U.S. 1029 (1985)*

BREYER, Circuit Judge.

. . . The district court found that, because of the large number of subscribers, doctors are under "heavy economic pressure" to take them as patients and to agree to Blue Shield's system for charging the cost of their care. The court believed that the effect of this payment system, when combined with Blue Shield's size and buying power, was to produce an unreasonably rigid and unjustifiably low set of prices. In the court's view, the fact that doctors cannot charge Blue Shield subscribers more than the Blue Shield payment-schedule amounts interferes with the doctors' freedom to set higher prices for more expensive services and discourages them from developing and offering patients more expensive (and perhaps qualitatively better) services. For these and related reasons, the district court held that Blue Shield . . . unreasonably restrains trade, and thereby violates Sherman Act. . . .

To find an unlawful restraint, one would have to look at Blue Shield as if it were a "third force," intervening in the marketplace in a manner that prevents willing buyers and sellers from independently coming together to strike price/quality bargains. Antitrust law typically frowns upon behavior that impedes the striking of such independent bargains. The persuasive power of the district court's analysis disappears, however, once one looks at Blue Shield, not as an inhibitory "third force," but as itself the purchaser of the doctors' services. . . . Antitrust law rarely stops the buyer of a service from trying to determine the price or characteristics of the product that will be sold. . . .

Several circuits have held in antitrust cases that insurer activity closely analogous to that present here amounts to purchasing, albeit for the account of others. . . . To understand that reasoning, consider some highly simplified examples. Suppose a father buys toys for his son — toys the son picks out. Or suppose a landlord hires a painter to paint his tenant's apartment, to the tenant's specifications. Is it not obviously lawful for the father (the landlord) to make clear to the seller that the father (the landlord) is in charge and will pay the bill? Why can he not then forbid the seller to charge the child (the tenant) anything over and above what the father (the landlord) pays — at least if the seller wants the buyer's business? [I]f it is lawful for the buyer to buy for the third party in the first place, how can it be unlawful to bargain for a price term that will stick?

Given this argument, it is not surprising the courts have unanimously upheld contracts analogous in various degrees to the one at issue here — contracts in which those who directly provide goods or services to insureds have agreed to cap or forego completely additional charges to those insureds in return for direct payment by the insurer. . . . Scholarly commentators believe that these cases were correctly decided. . . .

Two arguments might be made in an effort to distinguish these cases. First, the doctors may claim that Blue Shield is not, in essence, a buyer. Traditionally, doctors have opposed financial arrangements that involved the "selling" of their services to anyone but the patient. . . . The relevant antitrust facts are that Blue Shield pays the bill and seeks to set the amount of the charge. Those facts . . . convince us that Blue Shield's activities here are like those of a buyer. Whether for ethical, medical, or related professional purposes Blue Shield is, or is not, considered a buyer is beside the point. We here consider only one specific argued application of the antitrust laws and we do not suggest how Blue Shield ought to be characterized in any other context. Second, the doctors seek to distinguish these precedents by pointing to an important district court finding . . . that Blue Shield is a buyer with significant "market power" — i.e., the power to force prices below the level that a freely competitive market would otherwise set. They argue that Blue Shield's "market power" makes a significant difference. We do not agree. . . .

To resolve this argument about the existence of market power — an issue hotly debated by the expert economists who testified at trial — would force us to evaluate a record that the district court described as "two competing mountains of mostly meaningless papers." Rather than do so, we shall assume that Blue Shield possesses significant market power. We shall also assume, but purely for the sake of argument, that Blue Shield uses that power to obtain "lower than competitive" prices.

We next ask whether Blue Shield's assumed market power makes a significant legal difference. As a matter of pure logic, to distinguish the examples previously mentioned one must accept at least one of the following three propositions: One must believe either (1) that the law forbids a buyer with market power to bargain for "uncompetitive" or "unreasonable" prices, or (2) that such a buyer cannot buy for the account of others, or (3) that there is some relevant difference between obtaining such price for oneself and obtaining that price for others for whom one can lawfully buy. In our view, each of these propositions is false, as a matter either of law or of logic. First, the antitrust laws interfere with a firm's freedom to set even uncompetitive prices only in special circumstances, where, for example, a price is below incremental cost. . . . Ordinarily, however, even a monopolist is free to exploit whatever market power it may possess when that exploitation takes the form of charging uncompetitive prices. . . .

Second, as we previously mentioned, there is no law forbidding a legitimate insurance company from itself buying the goods or services needed to make its customer whole. . . . The rising costs of medical care, the possibility that patients cannot readily evaluate (as competitive buyers) competing offers of medical service, the desirability of lowering insurance costs and premiums, the availability of state regulation to prevent abuse — all convince us that we ought not create new potentially far-reaching law on the subject. . . .

Third, to reject the first two propositions is, as a matter of logic, to reject the third. If it is lawful for a monopoly buyer to buy for the account of another, how can it be unlawful for him to insist that no additional charge be made to that other? . . .

[Physicians] argue that Blue Shield's pricing system is insufficiently sensitive to service differences, or that it encourages high costs, or does not give the patients what they really need. . . . The short — and conclusive — answer to these arguments is that normally the choice of what to seek to buy and what to offer to pay is the buyer's. And, even if the buyer has monopoly power, an antitrust court (which might, in appropriate circumstances, restructure the market) will not interfere with a buyer's (nonpredatory) determination of price. . . .

[T]he arguments that Blue Shield's payments for doctors' services are "too low" are [also unpersuasive.] . . . A legitimate buyer is entitled to use its market power to keep prices down. The claim that Blue Shield's price scheme is "too rigid" because it ignores qualitative differences among physicians is properly addressed to Blue Shield or to a regulator, not to a court. There is no suggestion that Blue Shield's fee schedule reflects, for example, an effort by, say, one group of doctors to stop other doctors from competing with them. Here, Blue Shield and the doctors "sit on opposite sides of the bargaining table." [T]he district court rested its decision in large part upon the Supreme Court's recent case, Arizona v. Maricopa County Medical Society. . . . *Maricopa,* however, involved a horizontal agreement among competing doctors about what to charge. A horizontal agreement among competitors is typically unlawful because the competitors prevent themselves from making independent decisions about the terms as to which they will bargain. . . .

Ball Memorial Hospital v. Mutual Hospital Insurance, Inc.

784 F.2d 1325 (7th Cir. 1986)

EASTERBROOK, Circuit Judge.

The provision of health care financing services has become increasingly competitive. Hospitals and physicians (the providers of service) have begun to offer financing packages, much as automobile manufacturers sometimes finance their own products. In health care, where the need for service often depends on events beyond anyone's control, financing often is combined with insurance to spread the risks.

One package is the preferred provider organization (PPO). In exchange for a stated monthly payment, the hospital promises to pay the costs of patients who use particular providers. Patients who use providers other than the "preferred" ones must pay part or all of the fees themselves. . . . A PPO plan specifies in advance the fee it will pay a provider for any given medical service.

The plaintiffs in this case are 80 acute-care hospitals (the Hospitals). All 80 provide care on a fee-for-service basis. . . . Some of the 80 also offer PPO plans; others are preparing to do so. . . .

The Blues have been losing market share in Indiana for some years. . . . Just how "large" the Blues are turns out not to matter, so we do not pursue the question. . . . All agree that however large the Blues may be, they are losing business. Concerned about this, the Blues decided to offer a PPO of their own, in addition to their traditional service benefit plans. . . . The Blues asked for bids from all acute-care hospitals in Indiana and invited each to bid a percentage discount from its regular fees. . . . The hospitals that offer PPO plans saw the Blues' decision as a threat to their success. All hospitals saw a PPO plan as a threat to revenues — those who participated in the plan might collect less per service rendered, and those outside the plan might lose volume.

Ninety-one of Indiana's 115 acute-care hospitals submitted bids, and the Blues signed up 61 of the 91. . . . All [hospitals] remain eligible to participate in the regular service benefit plan offered by the Blues, which is the Blues' most popular product. All hospitals in Indiana also may provide services to patients covered by the Blues' PPO, but the Blues will reimburse only 75 percent of the hospitals' fees; the patients must pay the rest. The Blues will reimburse 100 percent of the agreed charges when insureds use hospitals within the PPO. . . .

The Hospitals [sought] . . . injunctive relief against the Blues' proposed PPO under Sections 1 and 2 of the Sherman Act. . . . [After hearing] . . . the district court denied the [hospitals'] request for a preliminary injunction . . . [finding] that the Blues do not have the power to restrict output in the market or to raise price because they furnish a fungible product that other people can and do supply easily.

The court treated the product as "health care financing." The Blues, other insurance companies, hospitals offering PPOs, HMOs, and self-insuring employers all offer methods of financing health care. . . . The market in health care financing is competitive, the court concluded, not only because customers can switch readily but also because new suppliers can enter quickly and existing ones can expand their sales quickly. More than 1000 firms are licensed to sell health insurance in Indiana, and more than 500 sell this insurance currently. According to the district court, all can expand on a moment's notice. . . .

Buyers' willingness to switch and sellers' ability to enter and expand rapidly, the district court concluded, means that "a firm's share of premium revenues reflects no more than its ability to compete successfully in meeting consumer demands." . . . The Blues cannot exclude competitors, cannot raise prices without losing business quickly; the Blues' size therefore indicates only their success in offering the package of price and service that customers prefer, not any market power.

The district court also found that PPO plans "contain cost by promoting price competition among hospitals." . . . The PPO program will enable the Blues to offer lower premiums, the court found; it estimated the savings at 10 to 20 percent for 1985. . . . It may be cheaper to operate one hospital at 95 percent of capacity and another at 55 percent, rather than each at 75 percent; the less-used hospital can close a wing and reduce its staff.

In light of its conclusions on the benefits of PPOs, the district court thought that a preliminary injunction would injure rather than promote the public interest. . . . The Hospitals insist that the public interest is on their side and that they are likely to prevail on the merits. . . .

Market power is a necessary ingredient in every case under the Rule of Reason. . . . Unless the defendants possess market power, it is unnecessary to ask whether their conduct may be beneficial to consumers. Firms without power bear no burden of justification. The Hospitals say that the Blues have a large share of the market for medical insurance in Indiana, and that this establishes market power. In many cases a firm's share of current sales does indicate power. . . . When a firm (or group of firms) controls a significant percentage of the productive assets in the market, the remaining firms may not have the capacity to increase their sales quickly to make up for any reduction by the dominant firm or group of firms.

In other cases, however, a firm's share of current sales does not reflect an ability to reduce the total output in the market, and therefore it does not convey power over price. . . . If firms are able to enter, expand, or import sufficiently quickly, that may counteract a reduction in output by existing firms. [T]he lower the barriers to entry, and the shorter the lags of new entry, the less power existing firms have. . . .

The district court found that each of the factors suggesting that market share does not imply market power is present in the market for medical insurance. . . . The Blues do not own any assets that block or delay entry. The insurance industry is not like the steel industry, in which a firm must take years to build a costly plant before having anything to sell. The "productive asset" of the insurance business is money, which may be supplied on a moment's notice, plus the ability to spread risk, which many firms possess and which has no geographic boundary. . . . The conclusion that the Blues face vigorous and effective competition is not clearly erroneous. [T]he Blues lack market power and are therefore entitled to adopt a PPO plan without further scrutiny under the Sherman Act.

The Hospitals try to avoid this conclusion by urging that Section 2 of the Sherman Act imposes an additional test — that the Blues act without anticompetitive intent. [T]he Hospitals insist that any firm with a large market share has an obligation not to augment that share at the expense of rivals and may not drive hard bargains.

Although the district court did not make findings concerning the Blues' intent, the Hospitals say that the record reeks of bad intent. . . . In January 1983 the Blues circulated an internal report stating in part . . . , "[we are] in a unique position to serve as a broker between what might appear to be the conflicting interests of financially threatened providers and cost conscious group purchasers. . . . We also control an overwhelming share of the marketplace in key areas. . . . In short, the time seems right for an aggressive new stance in the financing of health care benefits. . . . The growth of competitive forces poses a grave threat, and will grow worse without counteraction."

Res ipsa loquitur, the Hospitals say. If the Blues lack market power, how come their own planning documents talk this way? The Hospitals say that the district court should have inferred power from intent, and that given this intent to prevent competition the district court also was required to enjoin the adoption of the PPO. . . .

[A]n argument about evil intent in antitrust requires us to ask: "intent to do what?" The Hospitals seem to think that intent to get the best price is a bad intent. . . . The Blues are a single firm, and the acts of single firms are judged by a different standard under Section 2.

Competition is a ruthless process. A firm that reduces cost and expands sales injures rivals — sometimes fatally. The firm that slashes costs the most captures the greatest sales and inflicts the greatest injury. The deeper the injury to rivals, the greater the potential benefit. These injuries to rivals are byproducts of vigorous competition, and the antitrust laws are not balm for rivals' wounds. . . . So "intent to harm rivals" is not a useful standard in antitrust. Vigorous competitors intend to harm rivals, to do all the business if they can. To penalize this intent is to penalize competition. . . .

d. Price Fixing and the Antitrust Laws

i. Horizontal Agreements Among Providers

As Arizona v. Maricopa County Medical Society makes plain, horizontal agreements to set prices are illegal *per se*. Thus competing providers not integrated into a joint venture may not be directly involved in negotiations which produce fee schedules. In many areas physicians or hospitals seek to offer new forms of health care financing. A substantial literature, both academic and trade, considers how they might do so without violating the antitrust law. See, for instance, J. Harrison, Price Fixing, the Professions, and Ancillary Restraints: Coping with Maricopa County, 1982 U. Ill. L. Rev. 925; Note, Preferred Provider Organizations and Provider Contracting: New Analyses under the Sherman Act, 37 Hastings L.J. 377 (1985). The simplest method is for competing providers to be divorced from the process by which fees are formulated and for the plan to negotiate each independent provider's contract individually.

In FTC v. Indiana Federation of Dentists, 476 U.S. 447 (1986), the Court upheld a Federal Trade Commission order against a group of dentists who refused to submit X-rays to insurers for review of the necessity of services provided. Following the FTC, the Court declined to characterize the arrangement as illegal *per se,* but found it invalid under a rule of reason analysis.

> The Federation's policy takes the form of a horizontal agreement among the participating dentists to withhold from their customers a particular service that they desire — the forwarding of x rays to insurance companies along with claim forms. . . . A refusal to compete with respect to the package of services offered to customers, no less than a refusal to compete with respect to the price term of an agreement, impairs the ability of the market to advance social welfare by ensuring the provision of desired goods and services to consumers at a price approximating the marginal cost of providing them. Absent some countervailing procompetitive virtue . . . such an agreement limiting consumer choice by impeding the "ordinary give and take of the market place," . . . cannot be sustained under the Rule of Reason. No credible argument has been advanced for the proposition that making it more costly for the insurers and patients who are the dentists' customers to obtain information needed for evaluating the dentists' diagnoses has any such procompetitive effect. [476 U.S. 459.]

ii. The Blue Plans as Horizontal Conspiracies

Blue Shield and Blue Cross were initially created and controlled by physicians and hospitals, and their founders continue to exercise important influence in the formulation of plan policy. In 1981, the Federal Trade Commission issued Guidelines informing local Blue Shield Plans of the restructuring necessary to avoid prosecution by the federal agency. The FTC Guidelines state that a plan is "physician controlled" when

> a physician group has the formal or informal ability to set overall plan policies by dominating its decision making processes. Such overall control is likely to exist when a physician group selects a majority of the voting members of the plan's governing body. It appears unlikely that a group selecting less than one-fourth of the seats on a plan's governing body would be found to control the

> plan, without additional evidence that the group dominates the plan's decision making process by other means. Absent such overall physician control, a plan is treated as a single entity that is separate from the physician group. [Physician Agreements to Control Medical Prepayment Plans, 46 Fed. Reg. 48,982 (1981).]

Even if a Blue Shield Plan conforms to FTC Guidelines, an individual practitioner who feels aggrieved by Blue Shield practices may institute suit arguing that, whatever the formal arrangements, a particular group of physicians still retains de facto control of plan policy. If a group of physicians in fact controls the insurer, any practices that disfavor competing providers can be challenged as illegal *per se* under *Maricopa*. In Addino v. Genessee Valley Medical Care, Inc., 593 F.Supp. 892 (W.D.N.Y. 1984), podiatrists argued that Blue Shield's actions setting rates paid for medical services were *per se* illegal under Section 1 of the Sherman Act because, even though the plan's Board was dominated by lay people, physicians retained control of the nominating committee and medical advisory committee, and thus exercised de facto control of plan policy. The court upheld the podiatrists' claim of *per se*, structural, illegality on a motion for summary judgment. Similarly, Virginia Academy of Clinical Psychologists v. Blue Shield, 624 F.2d 476 (4th Cir. 1980), *cert. denied*, 450 U.S. 916 (1981), found that, in denying reimbursement to psychologists, Blue Shield was a combination of physicians, controlled by physician members. By contrast, Pennsylvania Dental Association v. Medical Service Association of Pennsylvania, 574 F. Supp. 457 (M.D. Pa. 1983), *aff'd without opinion*, 722 F.2d 731 (3rd Cir. 1983), found insufficient evidence of physician control to support dentists' charge that a Blue Shield plan was physician controlled.

Physicians often have significant control over the malpractice insurance companies established in the 1970s when commercial insurers became unreliable sources of coverage. See discussion in Chapter 5. Nurse Midwifery Associates v. Hibbett, 549 F. Supp. 1185 (M.D. Tenn. 1982), challenged such a malpractice insurer's decision denying coverage to a physician who provided backup services to nurse-midwives. Plaintiffs alleged that an individual physician, who was also president of the malpractice insurer, terminated coverage to eliminate competition from nurse-midwives. Because the midwives were unable to obtain alternative obstetrical backup, they went out of business in 1980, while their case was pending in preliminary stages. The district court denied defendants' motion for summary judgment; in 1990 the case is still awaiting trial.

Are the Blue plans caught in a bind? If they are aggressive in constraining costs, providers, as in *Kartell*, will accuse them of predatory pricing. But if they oblige the demands of most providers, anyone not favored will accuse them of being an agent of the doctors or hospitals. Does antitrust law encourage the Blue plans to pay whatever is necessary to avoid trouble from anyone who threatens to sue? Are those the incentives the law should provide these organizations? Does antitrust law provide insurers other cost constraining incentives?

iii. Non-Horizontal Coercion or Agreement

Contracts between parties who compete in different markets, such as insurers and providers, are not horizontal. Such agreements are not illegal *per se,* but are instead judged under the rule of reason. Continental TV v. GTE Sylvania, Inc., 433 U.S. 36 (1977). A non-horizontal agreement can have anticompetitive effects upon the market for health insurance or upon the market for medical care. Courts are sharply divided on the standards for judging when a vertical agreement violates the antitrust laws.

As *Royal Drug, Kartell,* and *Ball* illustrate, the Blue plans are frequently targets of antitrust suits in which competing insurers or nonparticipating providers allege that a vertical agreement between the Blue plan and participating providers violates the antitrust laws. Many courts have adopted the approach of the First Circuit in *Kartell,* rejecting such claims of vertical price restraint simply by characterizing the relationship between the Blue plan and providers as one of buyer and seller. If Blue Shield is merely a buyer negotiating the best possible terms with sellers, there is no restraint to analyze. Of course a buyer can agree with a seller as to the price the buyer will pay and at which the seller will sell. Courts do not need to consider the competitive impact upon the markets for medical services or for medical insurance. See, for instance, Group Life & Health Insurance Co. v. Royal Drug Co., 737 F.2d 922 (5th Cir. 1984) (upholding the program described in *Royal Drug,* supra); Medical Arts Pharmacy of Stamford, Inc. v. Blue Cross & Blue Shield of Connecticut, 675 F.2d 502 (2nd Cir. 1982) (Blue Cross is purchaser of prescribed drugs from participating pharmacies); Barry v. Blue Cross of California, 805 F.2d 866 (9th Cir. 1986) (rejects physician complaints about a Blue Cross preferred provider program that paid more to doctors who agreed to participate and to limit patient referrals to other participating doctors).

By contrast, in St. Bernard General Hospital Inc. v. Hospital Service Association of New Orleans, Inc., 712 F.2d 978 (5th Cir. 1983), *cert. denied,* 466 U.S. 970 (1984), the court found evidence sufficient to support treble damage claims for price-fixing and group boycott in a Blue plan's differential treatment of participating and nonparticipating hospitals. Both types of hospitals were entitled to payment, at the same cost-based rates, for services rendered to subscribers. Participating hospitals were entitled to select some members of the Blue Cross board and were required to provide financial support to Blue Cross in the event of insolvency. Only nonprofit hospitals could be participating hospitals. The profit-making hospitals complained because Blue Cross reimbursed them only for costs, and not for profits.

In Reazin v. Blue Cross and Blue Shield of Kansas, Inc., 663 F. Supp. 1360 (D. Kan. 1987), Blue Cross terminated the participating provider status of the largest teaching hospital in the Wichita area. Blue Cross had sought to market its own HMO and PPO, and informed hospitals that, if they joined competing HMOs or PPOs, they would no longer be eligible to participate in Blue Cross. The Wichita teaching hospital participated in a joint venture with the Hospital Corporation of America, the most successful HMO in the Wichita area. The court upheld the jury's finding that the Blue plan had conspired with competing hospitals to terminate the teaching hospital's provider status in violation of Section 1. The court also found a violation of Section 2, based on the Blues' market power, including the ability to exclude competitors and to control price.

Rhode Island Blue Shield attempted to keep a new open panel HMO out of the state by informing Blue Shield participating physicians that their fees would be reduced by 20 percent if they also participated in the new HMO. The trial court found that the Blues possessed significant market power, and the jury entered a verdict against them. The trial court entered a judgment for the Blues notwithstanding a jury verdict holding that they were entitled to become the low cost producer of insurance by bargaining for low physician fees. The "inevitable" harm to Ocean State resulting from this use of their bargaining power was a natural consequence of competition, not the result of an antitrust violation. Ocean State Physicians Health Plan, Inc. v. Blue Cross and Blue Shield of Rhode Island, 692 F. Supp. 52, 71 (D. R.I. 1988).

Are you persuaded by the *Kartell* court's analogy between purchasers of medical insurance and children or tenants? The analogy casts the patient/consumer in a passive role, dependent upon the protection of the father/landlord/insurer. Is this characterization dangerous, or is it rather a useful expedient to reaching a sensible result?

iv. Integrated Packages vs. Agreements Among Competitors

An HMO that employs salaried physicians integrates both insurance and service delivery functions into the same corporate entity. A fully integrated organization cannot offend Section 1 of the Sherman Act because a single corporate entity cannot "conspire" with itself to restrain trade.

Programs such as IPAs, PPOs, traditional Blue plans, and some indemnity insurance, allowing a broad spectrum of practitioners to participate, impose vertical price restraints. If providers and insurers are integrated in an organization that shares risks, they are no longer considered independent competitors capable of conspiring with one another. While some type of risk-spreading is essential, complete merger of previously separate entities is not required. See, Greaney & Sindelar, Physician-Sponsored Joint Ventures: An Antitrust Analysis of Preferred Provider Organizations, 18 Rutgers L.J. 513 (1987).

v. The Measurement and Relevance of Market Power

Whether an entity has "market power" is relevant to determining a Sherman Act violation, particularly under Section 2. Analysis of market power may focus on either the market for medical services or the market for prepaid health insurance.

"Monopoly" usually refers to a seller's "power to control market prices or exclude competition." United States v. Grinnell Corp., 384 U.S. 563, 571 (1966). "Monopsony" describes "a situation in which the relevant market for a factor of protection is dominated by a single purchaser." In re Permian Basin Area Rates Cases, 390 U.S. 747, 794, n.64 (1968). For example, competing health insurers sometimes allege that powerful Blue plans exercise monopoly power in the market for health insurance, while physicians and hospitals allege that the Blues exercise monopsony power in the market for medical care.

Is the *Ball* court realistic in holding that the Blues do not exercise monopoly power because other health insurers can enter the Indiana market "on a moment's notice"? The court fails to note that under Indiana law several regulatory requirements must be met before a new entity can transact business as either an insurance company or a PPO. Indiana Code Ann. §27-8-7-1 to 27-8-7-21. Public notice must be given and interested parties within the state are entitled to a hearing to determine whether the new organization should be authorized to do business. Insurance companies must meet capitalization requirements, while PPOs must establish contractual relations with providers. Consumers often have strong ties of loyalty to their current physicians, and both consumers and employers often have strong brand loyalty to large scale, well established organizations such as the Blues. See Kirsch, *Ball Memorial Hospital:* Section 2 Sherman Act Analysis in the Alternative Health Care Delivery Market, 14 Am. J. L. Med. 249, 265-278 (1988).

As *Ball* makes plain, bigness is not itself illegal, and even monopolists and monopsonists are entitled to drive hard bargains. However, entities with market power may not engage in "predatory conduct." Predatory conduct is selling below cost, eliminating efficient competitors, raising prices to supra-competitive levels, while barriers restrain re-entry. It is often difficult for a court to distinguish between a legitimate hard bargain and an illegal predatory practice.

vi. Insurer Discrimination Against Alternative Providers

Insurers, both the Blue plans and commercial companies, have traditionally been reluctant to reimburse certain groups of health care providers, such as podiatrists, chiropractors, nurse-midwives, and psychologists. In part, that reluctance stems from a desire to restrain costs and premiums by limiting the range of services for which payment will be made. In addition, antipathy towards alternative providers may be a product of traditional ways of thinking and close relations with the medical profession, particularly in the case of Blue Shield. As we have seen, alternative providers have had significant success in using the antitrust laws to challenge decisions denying them hospital staff privileges. Can alternative providers use the antitrust laws to force insurers to provide them reimbursement?

The antitrust law provides few remedies for providers denied insurance reimbursement. As the Supreme Court said in U.S. v. Colgate, 250 U.S. 300, 307 (1919), "In the absence of any purpose to create or maintain a monopoly, the [Sherman Act] does not restrict the long recognized right of a trader or manufacturer engaged in an entirely private business, freely to exercise his own independent discretion as to the parties with whom he will deal. And, of course, he may announce in advance the circumstances under which he will refuse to sell." In Aspen Skiing Co. v. Aspen Highlands Skiing Corp., 472 U.S. 585 (1985), the Court tempered the right not to deal by prohibiting the owner of one of two ski resorts in the Aspen area, owning three of the four mountains, from withdrawing from an arrangement with the other resort whereby skiers could buy multi-area tickets and ski at all four mountains. Although even a monopolist has no duty to engage in joint programs with competitors, the right to refuse to deal recognized in *Colgate* is qualified where the intent of the challenged conduct is "exclusionary," "anticompetitive," or "predatory," and the effect is to deprive consumers of what they want, and the defendant has not justified its action by showing that it promotes competition or efficiency. The Court emphasized that the "absence of an unqualified duty to cooperate does not mean that every time a firm declines to participate in a particular cooperative venture, that decision may not . . . give rise to liability in certain circumstances." Id. at 601.

In several cases alternative health care providers have sought to use the antitrust laws to challenge insurer decisions denying them reimbursement. In most cases, claims have rested on the assertion that the Blue plan was in fact controlled by physicians or hospitals, who were in direct competition with the aggrieved alternative provider. See discussion, supra. In Trident Neuro-Imaging Laboratory v. Blue Cross and Blue Shield, 568 F. Supp. 1474 (D.S.C. 1983), physician-directed private clinics that own CAT scanners alleged that the Blues had conspired with the local Health Systems Agency and hospitals with CAT scanners to exclude physicians with CAT scanners from competition. The court held there was sufficient evidence of conspiracy to boycott physician-owned scanners to withstand a defense motion for summary judgment, but a jury ultimately held for the defendant.

e. Private Credentialing Organizations

As with staff privileges decisions, antitrust treatment of private credentialing and accrediting organizations poses a fundamental challenge. The hallmark of professionalism is that organized members of the profession determine who should be admitted to their ranks and which institutions should be allowed to educate them. Chapter 7. On the one hand, reliance on these organizations is deeply ingrained in the organization of medical care in the United States. On the other hand, in antitrust terms, these organizations look very much like horizontal conspiracies amongst competitors to restrain the kinds and quality of services available.

Koefoot v. American College of Surgeons

652 F. Supp. 882 (N.D. Ill. 1986)

[Plaintiff, a surgeon practicing at several hospitals in rural Nebraska, was expelled from the American College of Surgeons for violating its rule against itinerant surgery, which requires certified surgeons to either provide post-operative care for their patients or arrange for another certified surgeon to do so.]

. . . The plaintiffs have articulated four separate antitrust theories in their trial brief. They are: 1) that the itinerant surgery rule constitutes a horizontal allocation of markets because it gives ACS surgeons a mechanism by which they can block entry into their markets; 2) that the rule creates a tie-in between two separate services — surgery and post-operative care; 3) that the rule constitutes a boycott of non-surgeon physicians; and 4) that the application of the rule to Dr. Koefoot constitutes a boycott of him. . . .

The two centerpiece issues are: first, whether this action is to be tried under the per se rule, the rule of reason, or a combination of the two, and second, whether the legality of the itinerant surgery rule may be allowed to turn "on whether it was adopted for the purpose of improving patient care." Jefferson Parish Hospital District No. 2 v. Hyde, 466 U.S. 2, n.41 (1984). [T]he Court concludes that the per se approach would be inappropriate for this case and that the trial must be conducted under the rule of reason. . . .

[Defendants sought to show that patients are harmed when post-operative care is delegated to a person other than a qualified surgeon and that many of Dr. Koefoot's patients had been injured by his failure to provide, or arrange for a qualified surgeon to provide, post-operative care. Defendants argued that evidence that their rule prevented harm to patients tended to rebut plaintiff's claim that they were motivated by anticompetitive animus.]

[E]vidence that itinerant surgery is harmful is two steps removed from being relevant in an antitrust trial. This "harm" evidence is relevant only because motive evidence is relevant. . . . "Harm" evidence is, however, . . . much more prejudicial since it is likely to distract the jury from the true antitrust issues. For these reasons . . . the Court will severely limit both the quantity and quality of the "harm" evidence. As the Supreme Court has noted, the fact that consumers may be lead "to make unwise and even dangerous choices" is not a defense to an antitrust challenge. . . .

The defendants intend to argue to the jury that "[i]t is patently procompetitive for a professional association to adopt a rule that improves the quality of care provided to consumers.". . . To present this argument the defendants contend that they must be allowed to present their evidence that itinerant surgery is harmful to patients. The Court's response is straightfoward — the defendants will not need to use "harm" evidence to support their argument because their argument is itself completely improper. . . .

The second procompetitive benefit that the ACS asserts . . . is the surgical seal of approval placed upon ACS fellows. . . . The defendants contend that the FACS label itself is procompetitive because it provides consumers with a ready means to locate the "better" care they presumably desire. To establish this procompetitive use of the FACS label, the defendants insist that they must be allowed the opportunity to prove that itinerant surgery represents adherence to a lesser standard of care, i.e. that it is detrimental to patient well being. . . . Defendants have, once again, confused the goal of free market competition with their often expressed goal of improving patient care. [T]he possible precompetitive informational effect of the FACS label in the instant case does not depend on a finding that itinerant surgery is either good or bad for patients. . . . The defendants, again, are attempting to convince the jury that the itinerant surgery rule is procompetitive because it results in better patient care. As the Court has taken great pains to explain, that is not a proper antitrust argument.

There is a possible procompetitive effect provided by the FACS label that is independent of a value judgment on the merits of itinerant surgery. If a label enables consumers to more quickly find a product or service that they desire, then the label increases efficiency by reducing needless delay. A way for the ACS to prove that the FACS label has procompetitive value is not for it to prove that itinerant surgery is harmful, but rather for it to prove that the FACS label provides consumers with a shorthand method of locating something they already desire, which in this case would be post-operative care rendered by a surgeon. [On remand, the jury found for the defendant.]

NOTES AND QUESTIONS

Here are some questions about *Koefoot* that the authors of this casebook cannot answer. We pose them to underscore the Alice in Wonderland inquiries that antitrust doctrine generates. Can you explain, in simple terms, the role of motive in this analysis? As attorney for either Koefoot or the ACS, how would you probe the defendant's motive? Is the "market power" of the ACS important to resolution of plaintiff's claims? Should it be? What is the market in which the ACS operates, and how is it measured? The court suggests that the ACS membership requirements may be procompetitive if membership "provides consumers a shorthand method of locating something they already desire." Why should a professional association's ability to set standards be limited to meeting the preconceived preferences of uninformed consumers? How does the court imagine that consumers form and express "desires" for particular sorts of surgical care? As a trial lawyer how would you go about proving consumer preference for particular kinds of surgical care?

Kreuzer v. American Academy of Periodontology, 735 F.2d 1479 (D.C. Cir. 1984), considered an antitrust challenge to a professional association rule limiting membership to people who limit their practice to periodontics. The court rejected the defendants' claim that their membership rule could be upheld if it were adopted with a good intent of promoting quality patient care. Even if the membership requirement in fact promotes quality care, the court held that the defendants had failed to demonstrate that their rule "is the least restrictive method available to achieve the asserted goal."

C. Havighurst and W. King in Private Credentialing of Health Care Personnel: an Antitrust Perspective; Part One, 9 Am. J.L. Med. 131 (1983) and Part Two, 9 Am. J.L. Med. 263 (1983), argue that some professional credentialing associations are procompetitive, in that they permit the production of information and opinion that would otherwise not be available, but that the scale and sponsorship of other intraprofessional efforts cause them to have an anticompetitive effect restricting the diversity of views available to consumers. J. Rankin and B. Hubberd reply that the existing voluntary system for accrediting and credentialing has "worked well, stood the test of time and rendered substantial benefits to the health care profession and the public at large." Private Credentialing of Health Care Personnel: A Pragmatic Response to Academic Theory, 10 Am. J.L. Med. 189, 200 (1984).

For an argument that the standard accreditation processes of American law schools, the American Bar Association, and the Association of American Law Schools violate the Sherman Act, see First, Competition in the Legal Education Industry, 53 N.Y.U.L. Rev. 311 (1978).

E. The Profit Making in Health Care

Ginzberg, For-Profit Medicine

319 N. Engl. J. Med. 757 (1988)

Only a few years after the advocates of the new corporations prophesied that the nation's health care system would soon be dominated by a few "SuperMeds," the four largest for-profit hospital chains — Hospital Corporation of America, Humana, National Medical Enterprises, and American Medical International — began scaling down their operations and spinning off substantial segments. . . .

[T]he introduction of Medicare and Medicaid (which turned most of those admitted to hospitals into paying patients) created the preconditions for the establishment and growth of the for-profit hospital chains. In the decade after [1965] . . . , the number of nonprofit acute care hospital beds increased . . . by 28 percent. During the same decade the for-profit hospital sector grew . . . [by 55 percent].

The for-profit chains bought or constructed hospitals in states with favorable reimbursement environments. . . . In 1985, 60.7 percent of the acute care beds of the for-profit chains were located in just five states: California, Florida, Louisiana, Tennessee and Texas. The for-profit hospitals tended to be located in affluent suburbs, where the pressure to provide charity care was reduced, and in general they avoided high-cost, low-profit services such as operating outpatient departments and emergency rooms or running teaching programs. . . .

With strong assistance from the investment banking community, which is always on the lookout for promising initiatives, Wall Street looked favorably on the for-profit hospital chains, and for a number of years the results justified its enthusiasm. . . . As the for-profits developed a strong track record of rapid growth, high profits, and substantial appreciation in the value of their stocks, they, their friends on Wall Street, and increasing numbers of health care analysts sought to explain their remarkable performance. These explanations rested on five broad assumptions. . . . [Profit-making hospital chains can exploit economies of scale, provide a strong management structure, develop and install strong planning and control systems, introduce tight controls on the use of nursing and support personnel. Finally, they can] respond more quickly and effectively to the expressed and latent demands of patients for a more pleasant, more supportive environment that offered more attractive accommodations, better food, more liberal visiting hours and other amenities. . . .

The for-profit chains did well in the 1970s by virtue of the strong cash flows that underpinned their rapid growth. But the 1980s brought a softening in the demand for inpatient care . . . and a tightening of reimbursement policies. . . . The for-profit chains were lifted and lowered by the changing tide. . . . They had for the most part failed to attract to their staffs the best-established and most prestigious members of the medical profession, who had the key role in determining where patients were admitted. [T]he fact that most for-profit hospitals lacked graduate training programs meant that they were less well positioned to attract patients who required tertiary care. . . . Many of the competitive weaknesses of the for-profit hospital chains had been obscured during the upbeat 1970s, but they came to the fore in the less favorable hospital environment of the 1980s.

Jeff C. Goldsmith, an early and staunch advocate of competition, offers a similarly pessimistic assessment, observing that investment-owned firms were "the first major casualties of competition. . . . During 1987, eight investor-owned firms declared bankruptcy or suspended debt payments, while the four largest firms pared back unsuccessful ventures and reduced their hospital holdings. . . . Many signs point to an intensification of the problems that damaged the investor-owned hospital sector in the next few years. . . ." Competition's Impact: A Report from the Front, 7 Health Affairs 162, 165 (1988). See also M. Freudenheim, Stock Drops on Hospital Buyout, N.Y. Times, D.4, Nov. 22, 1988, describing a management buyout of the Hospital Corporation of America and sale of 104 hospitals to an employee stock ownership fund.

NOTE: WHAT DIFFERENCE DOES PROFIT/NON-PROFIT FORM MAKE?

Owners of a profit making enterprise have a personal claim on profits if income exceeds expenses. A nonprofit enterprise is controlled by people who are not entitled to such payments. This core difference has a profound impact upon the ways in which the organization can raise capital; only a profit making enterprise can sell stocks to individuals who hope to profit on their investment. Capital financing is discussed in Chapter 3.

Beyond this, there is substantial dispute about the extent to which corporate form affects organizational behavior. Many hospitals formally organized in the nonprofit form function as physician cooperatives operated primarily for the benefit of the doctors that control them, providing a shelter within which physicians may operate profitable businesses, such as laboratories. Other hospitals organized in nonprofit form function as poly-corporate enterprises in which hospital administrators control a group of medical enterprises, containing both for profit and nonprofit corporate entities. See P. Starr, Social Transformation of American Medicine 160-180 (1982). In 1986, the Institute of Medicine, National Academy of Science, issued a major report on the development of profit making enterprises in medical care. For-Profit Enterprise in Health Care 103 (B. Gray ed. 1986). It observes that profit making has always existed in health care, in that hospital suppliers and drug companies have traditionally operated in this form. However, these organizations have not been directly involved in patient care. Id. at xviii.

A core finding of the Institute study is that profit making hospitals provide less free care than nonprofits, and both provide less than public hospitals. More significantly, the growth of profit making organizations, both hospitals and free standing centers, makes it more difficult for nonprofits to cross-subsidize care for people unable to pay. Id. at 102-120. The study also finds that investor ownership is not necessarily incompatible with quality of care. However, the committee notes that this may change if hospitals become able to bypass physicians and market directly to consumers. The experience of profit making nursing homes is not reassuring. Id. at 138.

H. Hansmann in The Role of Nonprofit Enterprises, 89 Yale L.J. 835 (1980), examines theories underlying nonprofit structure. H. Hansmann in The Rationale for Exempting Nonprofit Organizations from Corporate Income Taxation, 91 Yale L.J. 54 (1981), argues that tax exemption helps compensate nonprofit organizations for constraints on ability to raise capital. R.C. Clark in Does the Nonprofit Form Fit the Hospital Industry?, 93 Harv. L. Rev. 1416 (1980), argues that nonprofit status does not address problems of market failure, including the perceived inability of patients to judge quality. A. Etziono and P. Doty in Profit in Not-for-Profit Corporations: The Example of Health Care, 91 Pol. Sci. Q. 433 (1976), argue that nonprofit form does not eliminate "profit-making abuses." T. Marmor et al. in A New Look at Nonprofits: Health Care Policy in a Competitive Age, 3 Yale J. on Reg. 313 (1986), argue that organizational form is less significant than the "shift in the character of American medicine — a rise of commercialism and a decline of a professional ethos — that cuts across organizational forms."

As a constitutional matter, the choice whether to prohibit, allow, or encourage profit making enterprise in health care is for the legislature. In 1987, the Rhode Island Supreme Court considered the constitutionality of a law prohibiting licensing of health care facilities that issue publicly traded stock. The court found that the legislative purpose was "to avert the apparent decline of available health care to poor people, . . . [an] objective solidly within the police power of the state and thus legitimate." See In re: Advisory Opinion Regarding House of Representatives Bill 85-H-7748 (No. 86-269-MP, R.I. Sup. Ct. Jan 5, 1987).

The nonprofit status of HMOs has been controversial under both federal and state laws. Under Minnesota law, nonprofit organizations are tax-exempt only if they provide some services to people who are unable to pay. Share v. Commissioner of Revenue, 363 N.W.2d 47 (Minn. 1985), held that a federally qualified health maintenance organization did not qualify for tax exemption, even though it was organized in nonprofit form and provided services to a cross section of the community, including individuals eligible for Medicaid and Medicare. Like most HMOs, the organization provided no services for which it was not paid and received all but 1 percent of its income from user fees. See also De Modena v. Kaiser Foundation Health Plan Inc. 743 F.2d 1391 (9th Cir. 1984), which held that the Kaiser Health Plan is a nonprofit organization, exempt from liability under the Robinson-Patman Act, despite its close relation with the Permanente Medical Groups, which are for-profit corporations consisting of doctors who provide medical care for members.

Conclusion. Have the visions articulated by Havighurst and Enthoven been realized? The 1980s saw a dramatic increase in enrollment in the kinds of prepaid health plans that Enthoven favors, but the comprehensive program that he advocated was not adopted. The 1980s also saw a dramatic increase in the formation of alternative delivery organizations and the application of antitrust principles advocated by Havighurst. It is also plain that these developments have not reduced health care costs. While Havighurst rejected cost containment as a goal in its own right, others see that as important and have looked to procompetitive strategies as a means of controlling cost.

Government officials and employers who have adopted procompetitive strategies for containing costs express alarm that costs continue to rise. The Chair of the Allied-Signal Corp. observes:

> Allied-Signal took a series of steps to mitigate the rise beginning in 1982. It increased employee cost-sharing. . . . In addition, the company offered more than 100 Health Maintenance Organizations nationwide, and later established Preferred Provider arrangements in Phoenix and Kansas City, two of its larger locations, in an effort to curb expenditures. By 1987, approximately 27,000, or 30 percent, of Allied-Signal's active employees were enrolled in HMOs.
>
> Our efforts met with early success. From 1984 to 1987, the company's average health-care costs increased less than 6 percent annually, a lower rate than the medical-care CPI for the comparable period. But in early 1987, costs began to increase rapidly. By the end of the year they had increased 39 percent over the previous year, to $355 million. Company projections indicated costs of more than $600 million by 1990. [Hennessy, Business' Bargaining Power Can Limit Runaway Costs, 12 Financier 34 (1988).]

An insurance executive expresses alarm at resurgence of costs in 1987. "Utilization and intensity of services have picked up and health-insurance premiums are now generally increasing by 20-35 percent on renewals. The frightening thing about this recent acceleration in costs is that it has not been accompanied by a recession. [I]n 1987 almost every health-insurance carrier saw skyrocketing loss rations. Virtually all health insurers lost money last year; numbers have exited the business, and rates are going up again in 1988 — with increased calls for Government intervention, often led by the employer." Startling Resurgence in Costs Requires New National Policy, 12 Financier 28, 29 (1988).

F. Medicare and Medicaid Fraud and Abuse and Alternative Delivery Systems

U.S. v. Greber

760 F.2d 68 (3rd Cir. 1985)

In this appeal, defendant argues that payments made to a physician for professional services in connection with tests performed by a laboratory cannot be the basis of Medicare fraud. We . . . hold that if one purpose of the payment was to induce future referrals, the medicare statute has been violated. . . .

Defendant is an osteopathic physician who is board certified in cardiology. In addition to hospital staff and teaching positions, he was the president of Cardio-Med, Inc., an organization which he formed. The company provides physicians with diagnostic services, one of which uses a Holter-monitor. . . . Cardio-Med billed Medicare for the monitor service and, when payment was received, forwarded a portion to the referring physician. . . .

[T]he indictment charged defendant with having tendered remuneration or kickbacks to the referring physicians in violation of 42 U.S.C. §1395nn(b)(2)(B) (1982), [and] . . . alleged that defendant made false statements to Medicare in violation of 18 U.S.C. §1001 (1982). Defendant submitted claim forms representing that the Holter-monitors had been operated for eight hours or more when in fact the devices had been used for a much shorter time. Medicare required at least eight hours of operation to qualify for payment. . . . The proof as to the Medicare fraud counts was that defendant had paid . . . physicians "interpretation fees" . . . even though defendant had actually evaluated the monitoring data. . . .

Congress, concerned with the growing problem of fraud and abuse in the system, wished to strengthen the penalties to enhance the deterrent effect of the statute. . . . A particular concern was the practice of giving "kickbacks" to encourage the referral of work. Testimony before the Congressional committee was that "physicians often determine which laboratories would do the test work for their Medicaid patients by the amount of the kickbacks and rebates offered by the laboratory. . . . Kickbacks take a number of forms including cash, long-term credit arrangements, gifts, supplies and equipment, and the furnishing of business machines.". . .

To remedy the deficiencies in the statute and achieve more certainty, the present version of 42 U.S.C. §1395nn(b)(2) was enacted. It provides:

> Whoever knowingly and willfully offers or pays any remuneration (including any kickback, bribe or rebate) directly or indirectly, overtly or covertly in cash or in kind to induce such person —

> (B) to purchase, lease order, or arrange for or recommend purchasing . . . or ordering any . . . service or item for which payment may be made . . . under this title, shall be guilty of a felony. . . .

Defendant contends that . . . absent a showing that the only purpose behind the fee was to improperly induce future services, compensating a physician for services actually rendered could not be a violation of the statute. . . .

The language and purpose of the statute support the government's view. Even if the physician performs some service for the money received, the potential for unnecessary drain on the Medicare system remains. The statute is aimed at the inducement factor.

The text refers to "any remuneration." That includes not only sums for which no actual service was performed but also those amounts for which some professional time was expended. "Remunerates" is defined as "to pay an equivalent for service." Webster Third New International Dictionary (1966). By including such items as kickbacks and bribes, the statute expands "remuneration" to cover situations where no service is performed. That a particular payment was remuneration (which implies that a service was rendered) rather than a kickback, does not foreclose the possibility that a violation nevertheless could exist. . . . If the payments were intended to induce the physician to use Cardio-Med's services, the statute was violated, even if the payments were also intended to compensate for professional services.

NOTES: FRAUD AND ABUSE

As the *Greber* case suggests, the range of practices prohibited by the fraud and abuse provisions is potentially broad and could condemn both traditional organizational arrangements in health care, and alternative delivery systems. Do the financing arrangements at the University of Pennsylvania Medical School, described by Sparer, Chapter 7, raise problems under the federal statute? May a hospital offer discounted office space, low interest loans, or other financial inducements to convince physicians to relocate their practice to the hospital's community? To refer patients to the hospital? To discharge patients promptly? As a matter of policy, should a hospital be allowed to do so? Does a hospital or physician violate the statute if they offer to waive deductibles and co-insurance payments? For an analysis suggesting that the answers to these questions are unclear, both as a matter of statutory interpretation and as a matter of policy, see Note The Medicare-Medicaid Anti-Fraud and Abuse Amendments: Their Impact on the Present Health Care System, 36 Emory L.J. 691 (1987).

In West Allis Memorial Hospital v. Bowen, 832 F.2d 251 (7th Cir. 1988), a hospital complained that its competitor waived Medicare deductibles and co-insurance. The plaintiff asserted that it would implement a similar program of its own, but feared prosecution under the anti-fraud provisions if it did so. The court held that the hospital had no standing and refused to offer an advisory opinion whether the practice was permitted under the statute.

In 1987, Congress responded to industry objections to the vagueness of the statute and directed the Office of the Inspector General to draft regulations (commonly referred to as "safe harbor regulations") specifying acts that would *not* be deemed to violate the illegal remuneration statute. Congress ordered OIG to publish such proposed regulations by August 1988.

The Secretary's proposed "safe harbor" regulations would immunize several types of health professional and provider practice. 54 Fed. Reg. 3088 (1989), to be codified at 42 C.F.R. pt. 1001.

Investment interests. Professionals or providers who hold investment in and receive dividend income from companies to whom or to whose products they have referred patients are immune from prosecution if the company in which investments are made is sufficiently large that the return on the investment is tangentially related to referral decisions.

Space and equipment rental arrangements are immune from prosecution when they contemplate a fixed periodic rental payment for at least one year, at fair market value.

Personal Service Agreements are exempt from prosecution if they have a term of at least one year, are set out in writing, specify the services to be provided, and fix the aggregate compensation of the parties in advance, at fair market value, without adjustments for the numbers of reimbursable referrals made by the party being compensated.

Sale of practice is exempt if it is completed within a year of any agreement in contemplation of sale, and, if the seller will not be in a position to make referrals to the purchaser within a year of the agreement.

Waiver of Medicare deductibles and coinsurance payments is protected to the extent that they apply only to inpatient hospital care, are only for the deductible amount, are available to all Medicare patients regardless of diagnosis, and do not raise costs to any federal program.

Group Purchasing Organizations can receive payments from the vendor of goods or services so long as each of the members of the group for whom the GPO acts has a written agreement with the GPO specifying the amount the GPO can receive from each vendor and this information is disclosed to the Secretary upon request.

Even though health care costs continued to rise in the 1980s, there is substantial evidence that both regulatory and competitive strategies caused them to rise more slowly. One study, which controlled for changes in volume of services, found that between 1980 and 1984 hospital costs covered by Medicare's DRG payments were 12.5 percent lower than they would have been in the absence of rate regulation, and in the four states covered by all-payer rate regulation, hospital costs were between 11 percent and 15 percent lower than they would otherwise have been. In contrast, changes in the proportion of people enrolled in HMOs reduced hospital costs by less than one percent. The savings achieved by the shift in Medicare payment are likely to be a one-time occurrence. Evidence on the effects of all-payer rate regulation suggests that there can be year-to-year reductions in hospitals' costs relative to cost growth in states without regulation. J. Hadley and K. Swartz, The Impacts on Hospital Costs Between 1980 and 1984 of Hospital Rate Regulation, Competition, and Changes in Health Insurance Coverage, 26 Inquiry 35 (1989). However, hospitals in the all-payer states protest that rising labor costs and uninsured patients, combined with rate restrictions, have pushed them to the point of bankruptcy. Johnson, Three States Weigh New Hospital Price-Setting Rules, N. Y. Times, May 24, 1989, A1.

C H A P T E R

IX

Organ Transplantation

There are medical procedures so humanly compelling that it is sometimes difficult to apply the usual legal rules to them. The transplantation of an organ from a corpse to the body of a living (although sometimes dying) person, perhaps the most spectacular procedure in medicine, is a dramatic example. Because of their "life from death" drama, heart transplants especially catch the public's imagination and have formed a staple for newspapers, magazines, and TV reports on medicine for the past two decades. In this regard, organ transplants have provided some of the most celebrated examples of human experimentation in the history of medicine. The first successful human kidney transplant from an unrelated donor was performed in Boston in 1962, the first heart transplant in South Africa in 1967, and the first permanent artificial heart in Salt Lake City in 1982. More than 4000 heart transplants are now performed annually worldwide — a spectacular number, but trivial when one realizes that this many people die of heart disease in the U.S. every day.

The procedure of removing organs from individuals for transplant to others has forced society to adopt a new way of defining death itself. We have moved from total reliance on a definition centered on respiration and circulation (heartbeat) to one that includes the total and irreversible loss of brain function, even if respiration is artificially maintained. Most states have enacted laws on brain death, and all states have enacted laws to facilitate organ donation.

The power of transplantation to shape our views of legitimate human experimentation and our definition of death would alone be sufficient to warrant the attention of law students to organ transplants. But there is much more here. Organ transplantation is the most expensive procedure in medicine by almost any measure and thus raises the issues of access, cost, and quality control in a stark context. Both national and state task forces were established in the mid-1980s to help shape public policy concerning the delivery of organ transplants. The reason for such singular attention was summarized by the Massachusetts Task Force on Organ Transplantation (1984):

— those needing them are easily identified, need them quickly to survive, and have often been able to get their plight highly publicized;

— transplants are viewed by the public as lifesaving;
— the transplant procedure is extremely expensive, so that its general provision may have a significant impact on the health care system, and this is the first time rationing a medical procedure has been seriously discussed by public officials; and
— denial of a transplant on the basis of inability to pay seems to unfairly restrict the procedure to the wealthy, and seems to place a specific price on life. Id. at 5.

In this chapter we explore issues unique to transplants to see how transplantation affects the way we view ourselves and one another (and thus how we view what appropriate medical care is), how public policy can affect the introduction of an extreme and expensive medical technology, how transplant technology might be rationed, and how even more powerful technologies on the horizon (like fully implantable artificial hearts) might affect all of these issues. These materials challenge us to apply the lessons of all the preceding chapters to the rational use of organ transplants in our health care system. They also provide a useful supplement to the chapter on Medical Technology by illustrating how intense our desire can be to adopt and adapt to what Lewis Thomas describes as only "half-way technology." See Chapter 4, A(1).

We begin by reviewing the complex issues involved in organ procurement, including the use of live donors, the use of deceased donors, and the need for a new definition of death that would permit removing organs from "brain dead" corpses whose respiration is artificially maintained. We then explore the regulatory problems related to introducing this extreme and expensive procedure into medicine, including issues of cost, quality, and access. Finally, we review in some detail the genesis of the artificial heart and the issues this most spectacular of all medical technologies raises regarding human experimentation, consent, governmental regulation, resource allocation, and rationing.

A. Organ Procurement

1. ORGANS FROM LIVING DONORS

One of the unique things about organ transplantation is the necessity for two individuals to be involved: the donor and the recipient. Initial transplants in the United States and abroad involved the kidney, a paired organ. Because individuals have two kidneys and only need one to live well, live donation (at least among tissue-compatible relatives) is possible. Nevertheless, performing major surgery on an individual who is not sick (the donor) remains troublesome, and most physicians prefer to use cadaver donors. As difficult as the psychological problems are involving adults, the psychological and legal issues raised when the proposed donor is a minor or is mentally-impaired, are even more complex.

Strunk v. Strunk

445 S.W.2d 145 (Ken. Ct. App. 1969)

OSBORNE, Judge.

The specific question involved upon this appeal is: Does a court of equity have the power to permit a kidney to be removed from an incompetent ward of the state upon petition of his committee, who is also his mother, for the purpose of being transplanted into the body of his brother, who is dying of a fatal kidney disease? We are of the opinion it does.

The facts of the case are as follows: Arthur L. Strunk, 54 years of age, and Ava Strunk, 52 years of age, of Williamstown, Kentucky, are the parents of two sons. Tommy Strunk is 28 years of age, married, an employee of the Penn State Railroad and a part-time student at the University of Cincinnati. Tommy is now suffering from chronic glomerulus nephritis, a fatal kidney disease. He is now being kept alive by frequent treatment on an artificial kidney, a procedure which cannot be continued much longer.

Jerry Strunk is 27 years of age, incompetent, and through proper legal proceedings has been committed to the Frankfort State Hospital and School, which is a state institution maintained for the feeble-minded. He has an I.Q. of approximately 35, which corresponds with the mental age of approximately six years. He is further handicapped by a speech defect, which makes it difficult for him to communicate with persons who are not well acquainted with him. When it was determined that Tommy, in order to survive, would have to have a kidney the doctors considered the possibility of using a kidney from a cadaver if and when one became available or one from a live donor if this could be made available. The entire family, his mother, father and a number of collateral relatives were tested. Because of incompatibility of blood type or tissue none were medically acceptable as live donors. As a last resort, Jerry was tested and found to be highly acceptable. This immediately presented the legal problem as to what, if anything, could be done by the family, especially the mother and the father to procure a transplant from Jerry to Tommy. The mother as a committee petitioned the county court for authority to proceed with the operation. The court found that the operation was necessary, that under the peculiar circumstances of this case it would not only be beneficial to Tommy but also beneficial to Jerry because Jerry was greatly dependent upon Tommy, emotionally and psychologically, and that his well-being would be jeopardized more severely by the loss of his brother than by the removal of a kidney.

Appeal was taken to the Franklin Circuit Court where the chancellor reviewed the record, examined the testimony of the witnesses and adopted the findings of the county court.

A psychiatrist, in attendance to Jerry, who testified in the case, stated in his opinion the death of Tommy under these circumstances would have "an extremely traumatic effect upon him" (Jerry).

The Department of Mental Health of this Commonwealth has entered the case as amicus curiae. . . . Its recommendations are as follows: . . .

> Jerry Strunk, a mental defective, has emotions and reactions on a scale comparable to that of a normal person. He identifies with his brother Tom; Tom is his model, his tie with his family. Tom's life is vital to the continuity of Jerry's improvement at Frankfort State Hospital and School. The testimony of the hospital representative reflected the importance to Jerry of his visits with his family and the constant inquiries Jerry made about Tom's coming to see him. Jerry is aware he plays a role in the relief of this tension. We the Department of Mental Health must take all possible steps to prevent the occurrence of any guilt feelings Jerry would have if Tom were to die.
>
> The necessity of Tom's life to Jerry's treatment and eventual rehabilitation is clearer in view of the fact that Tom is his only living sibling and at the death of their parents, now in their fifties, Jerry will have no concerned, intimate communication so necessary to his stability and optimal functioning. . . .
>
> Throughout the legal proceedings, Jerry has been represented by a guardian ad litem, who has continually questioned the power of the state to authorize the removal of an organ from the body of an incompetent who is a ward of the state. We are fully cognizant of the fact that the question before us is unique. Insofar as we have been able to learn, no similar set of facts has come before the highest court of any of the states of this nation or the federal courts. . . .
>
> It is a universal rule of equity that where a person is not equal to protecting himself in a particular case, the court will protect him. As part of the inherent power of equity, a court of equity has full and complete jurisdiction over the persons of those who labor under any legal disability and also over their property. . . .

The right to act for the incompetent in all cases has become recognized in this country as the doctrine of substituted judgment and is broad enough not only to cover property but also to cover all matters touching on the well-being of the ward. The doctrine has been recognized in American courts since 1844. . . .

The medical practice of transferring tissue from one part of the human body to another (autografting) and from one human being to another (homografting) is rapidly becoming a common clinical practice. . . . The chance of success in the transfer of these organs is greatly increased when the donor and the donee are genetically related. . . .

The renal transplant is becoming the most common of the organ transplants. This is because the normal body has two functioning kidneys, one of which it can reasonably do without, thereby making it possible for one person to donate a kidney to another. Testimony in this record shows that there have been over 2500 kidney transplants performed in the United States up to this date. The process can be effected under present techniques with minimal danger to both the donor and the donee. Doctors Hamburger and Crosneir describe the risk to the donor as follows:

> This discussion is limited to renal transplantation, since it is inconceivable that any vital organ other than the kidney might ever be removed from a healthy living donor for transplantation purposes. The immediate operative risk of unilateral nephrectomy in a healthy subject has been calculated as approximately 0.05 per cent. The long-term risk is more difficult to estimate, since the various types of renal disease do not appear to be more frequent or more severe in individuals with solitary kidneys than in normal subjects. On the other hand, the development of surgical problems, trauma, or neoplasms, with the possible necessity of nephrectomy, do increase the long-term risks in living donors; the long-term risk, on this basis, has been estimated at 0.07 per cent. . . . These data must, however, be considered in the light of statistical life expectancy which, in a healthy 35 year old adult, goes from 99.3 percent to 99.1 percent during the next five succeeding years; this is an increase in risk equal to that incurred by driving a car for 16 miles every working day. . . . The risks incurred by the donor are therefore very limited. . . .

Review of our case law leads us to believe that the power given to a committee under KRS 387.230 would not extend so far as to allow a committee to subject his ward to the serious surgical techniques here under consideration unless the life of his ward be in jeopardy. Nor do we believe the powers delegated to the county court by virtue of the above statutes would reach so far as to permit the procedure which we are dealing with here.

We are of the opinion that a chancery court does have sufficient inherent power to authorize the operation. The circuit court having found that the operative procedures in this instance are to the best interest of Jerry Strunk and this finding having been based upon substantial evidence, we are of the opinion the judgment should be affirmed. We do not deem it significant that this case reached the circuit court by way of appeal as opposed to a direct proceeding in that court.

Judgment affirmed.

HILL, C. J., MILLIKEN and REED, JJ., concur.

NEIKIRK, PALMORE and STEINFELD, JJ., dissent.

STEINFELD, Judge (dissenting).

Apparently because of my indelible recollection of a government which, to the everlasting shame of its citizens, embarked on a program of genocide and experimentation with human bodies I have been more troubled in reaching a decision in this case than in any other. My sympathies and emotions are torn between a compassion to aid an ailing young man and a duty to fully protect unfortunate members of society.

The opinion of the majority is predicated upon the authority of an equity court to speak for one who cannot speak for himself. However, it is my opinion that in considering such right in this instance we must first look to the power and authority vested in the committee. . . . The authority and duty have been to protect and maintain the ward, to secure that to which he is entitled and preserve that which he has. . . .

The majority opinion is predicated upon the finding of the circuit court that there will be psychological benefits to the ward but points out that the incompetent has the mentality of a six-year-old child. It is common knowledge beyond dispute that the loss of a close relative or a friend to a six-year-old child is not of major impact. Opinions concerning psychological trauma are at best most nebulous. Furthermore, there are no guarantees that the transplant will become a surgical success, it being well known that body rejection of transplanted organs is frequent. The life of the incompetent is not in danger, but the surgical procedure advocated creates some peril.

It is written in Prince v. Massachusetts, 321 U.S. 158, 64 S. Ct. 438, 88 L. Ed. 645 (1944), that "Parents may be free to become martyrs themselves. But it does not follow they are free, in identical circumstances, to make martyrs of their children before they have reached the age of full and legal discretion when they can make that choice for themselves." The ability to fully understand and consent is a prerequisite to the donation of a part of the human body. Cf. Bonner v. Moran, 75 U.S. App. D.C. 156, 126 F.2d 121, 139 A.L.R. 1366 (1941), in which a fifteen-year-old infant's consent to removal of a skin patch for the benefit of another was held legally ineffective.

Unquestionably the attitudes and attempts of the committee and members of the family of the two young men whose critical problems now confront us are commendable, natural and beyond reproach. However, they refer us to nothing indicating that they are privileged to authorize the removal of one of the kidneys of the incompetent for the purpose of donation, and they cite no statutory or other authority vesting such right in the courts. The proof shows that less compatible donors are available and that the kidney of a cadaver could be used, although the odds of operational success are not as great in such case as they would be with the fully compatible donor brother.

I am unwilling to hold that the gates should be open to permit the removal of an organ from an incompetent for transplant, at least until such time as it is conclusively demonstrated that it will be of significant benefit to the incompetent. The evidence here does not rise to that pinnacle. To hold that committees, guardians or courts have such awesome power even in the persuasive case before us, could establish legal precedent, the dire result of which we cannot fathom. Regretfully I must say no.

NEIKIRK and PALMORE, JJ., join with me in this dissent.

Head v. Colloton

331 N.W.2d 870 (Iowa 1983)

McCormick, Justice.

This appeal presents a question concerning the right of access of a member of the general public to a hospital's record of the identity of a potential bone marrow donor. . . .

Plaintiff William Head is a leukemia victim who is currently undergoing chemotherapy in a Texas clinic. His illness is in relapse, and the prognosis is grim.

The University of Iowa Hospitals and Clinics include a bone marrow transplant unit. That unit maintains a bone marrow transplant registry, listing persons whose blood has been tissue-typed by the hospital. The tissue typing reveals blood antigen characteristics which must be known for determining whether a donor's bone marrow will be a suitable match-up for the bone marrow of a donee. A bone marrow transplant consists of removing bone marrow from a healthy person and infusing it into the body of a patient in the hope it will generate healthy white blood cells. The procedure is experimental between unrelated persons.

Late in 1982, plaintiff phoned the transplant unit and, through a series of conversations with a staff member, learned that the hospital's registry included the name of a woman who might, upon further testing, prove to be a suitable donor to him. Only one in approximately 6000 persons would have blood with the necessary antigen characteristics.

The tissue typing of the woman, referred to in the record as "Mrs. X," had not been done for reasons of her own health but to determine her suitability as a blood platelet donor to a member of her family who was ill. The hospital subsequently placed her name in its platelet donor registry. Then, when it later established an experimental program involving bone marrow transplants between unrelated persons, the hospital, without Mrs. X's knowledge or consent, placed her name in the bone marrow transplant registry. When the hospital established the new program, its institutional review board approved a procedure for contacting persons listed on the registry to determine whether they would act as donors. The procedure involved sending a letter informing the person of the program, its nature and goals, and inviting the person's participation in it. If the letter was not answered, a staff member was authorized to telephone the person and ask a series of general questions designed to determine whether the person would volunteer as a donor.

After plaintiff's contact with the bone marrow unit, the unit staff on December 31, 1982, sent Mrs. X the general letter informing her about the program and encouraging her to participate in it. When no response to the letter was received, a staff member telephoned Mrs. X on January 10, 1983, and asked her the series of questions. In responding to those questions, Mrs. X said she was not interested in being a bone marrow donor. When asked if she might ever be interested in being a donor, she said, "Well, if it was for family, yes. Otherwise, no." Despite plaintiff's subsequent request that the hospital make a specific inquiry of Mrs. X in plaintiff's behalf or to disclose her identity to him so he could contact her, the hospital refused to contact her or to disclose her identity to plaintiff. He then brought the present action.

Defendants John Colloton and Lloyd J. Filer are hospital employees with access to the bone marrow transplant registry. Plaintiff asked for a mandatory injunction to require them to disclose the name and identity of the potential donor either to the court or to his attorney. He proposed that the court or counsel then be permitted to write the woman to notify her of plaintiff's need and her possible suitability as a donor, asking her if she would consider being a donor to plaintiff.

After hearing evidence on the issue, the court ordered defendants to send the requested letter. This court sustained defendants' application for interlocutory review and issued a stay of the order.

This case involves application of the provisions of chapter 68A, Iowa's public records statute. Under section 68A.1, "public records" include "all records and documents of or belonging to this state. . . ." §68A.1. Defendants concede that the records of the University of Iowa hospital, a state hospital, are public records within the meaning of this provision. Thus the bone marrow donor registry is a public record. Section 68A.2 provides for public access to all public records [except]

> 2. Hospital records and medical records of the condition, diagnosis, care, or treatment of a patient or former patient, including outpatient. . . .

The evidence shows the hospital believed Mrs. X became a patient when she submitted to tissue typing. . . .

We conclude that the hospital record of Mrs. X is the hospital record of the "condition, diagnosis, care or treatment of a patient, or former patient" within the meaning of section 68A.7(2). Therefore the record is confidential. . . .

Finally, plaintiff contends it is significant that the remedy he sought and the trial court awarded fell short of disclosure of Mrs. X's identity. He suggests the interests of the parties under chapter 68A are satisfied by this remedy. We find, instead, that the remedy the trial court fashioned was not authorized by the statute. If public access is available at all under chapter 68A, it is right of general public access. The statute does not permit the singling out of one member of the public for special access on special terms.

Reversed.

Notes on Transplantation without Donor Consent

(1) *Strunk* is the first case in which a transplant was authorized by a court without the donor's consent. Several years later, a Connecticut court approved a kidney transplant involving seven-year-old identical twins. A psychiatrist testified that a successful operation would be of "immense benefit to the donor in that the donor would be better off in a family that was happy than in a family that was distressed. . . ." Instead of relying exclusively on this strained testimony, the court held that the "natural parents of a minor should have the right to give their consent to an isograft kidney transplantation procedure when their motivation and reasoning are favorably reviewed by community representation which includes a court of equity." Hart v. Brown, 29 Conn. Sup. 368, A.2d 386, 391 (1972).

(2) In only two cases (both involving mentally handicapped donors) have the courts rejected a petition by the parents. In the first case, from Louisiana, the court rejected a petition to permit the use of a 17-year-old with a mental age of four as a donor for his 32-year-old sister. The court found that while the brother was the best donor, he was not the only one; and also that since dialysis was available, the procedure was not immediately necessary to preserve the sister's life. Finally, in distinguishing *Strunk,* the court found that the law of Louisiana "is designed to promote and protect the ultimate best interests of the minor." The argument that the brother might benefit from the transplant was rejected as "highly speculative . . . and highly unlikely." In re Richardson, 284 So. 2d 185 (La. App. 1973).

In the Wisconsin case, permission was sought to transplant a kidney from a 39-year-old catatonic schizophrenic (who had a mental age of 12 and who had been institutionalized for 16 years) into his 38-year-old sister, who was the mother of six. Other family members were potential donors, but either they themselves or their physicians objected to their use. The court concluded that since the donor could not consent, the procedure could not be done on him. The court held that guardians have a duty of loyalty to their wards and must act in their "best interests"; and there was no evidence that the transplant would benefit the donor: "An incompetent particularly should have his own interests protected. Certainly no advantage should be taken of him. In the absence of real consent on his part, and in a situation where no benefit to him has been established, we fail to find any authority for the county court, or this court, to approve the operation." In re Pescinski, 67 Wis. 2d 4, 226 N.W.2d 180 (1975). Would the *Strunk* court have arrived at the same conclusion? See Robertson, Organ Donations by Incompetents and the Substituted Judgment Doctrine, 76 Colum. L. Rev. 48 (1976).

(3) In *Strunk,* the Director of the Renal Division of the University of Kentucky Medical Center testified that if something should later happen to the retarded donor's remaining kidney, based on selection criteria at the medical center, the donor would not be eligible for either hemodialysis or trans-

plantation. Savage, Organ Transplantation with an Incompetent Donor: Kentucky Resolves the Dilemma of Strunk v. Strunk, 58 Ken. L.J. 129, 146 (1970). Is it fair or just to permit the use of a kidney from an individual unable to consent to its use for transplant, if that individual (should his remaining kidney cease functioning) would be ineligible for effective medical treatment because of his mental handicap? It should be noted that since 1972, mental handicap is no longer a bar to dialysis, but it remains a major factor in transplantation decisions. Should the combination of potential benefit and standard medical procedure make the consent issue trivial for the recipient? What issues would be raised by a proposal to tissue type all residents of institutions for the mentally retarded for possible use as organ and tissue donors? Would *Head* have been decided differently if the potential donor had been mentally retarded and institutionalized, and the potential recipient agreed to visit the donor for the rest of his life?

Courts will not, of course, compel "donations" of bone marrow from competent adult family members. McFall v. Shimp, 10 Pa. D. & C.3d 90 (1978) (rejecting a request to compel a cousin to donate bone marrow to a person dying of leukemia).

(4) In 1974, Massachusetts Supreme Judicial Court Single Justice Francis Quirico decided the case of Nathan v. Farinelli, S.J.C., No. 74-87, in which court permission was sought to transplant bone marrow from a six-year-old child, Toni Farinelli, to her 10-year-old brother, William, who was suffering from the usually fatal disease of aplastic anemia. Unlike previously appointed guardians ad litem for the donor, this one, Attorney Garrick Cole, refused to consent for Toni on the basis that the procedure was not in her best interests and that the hospital had refused to indemnify her if she was harmed. Psychiatric testimony was that postulating a "benefit" to Toni based on her likely future feelings of altruism would be pure speculation. The court thus concluded that it could not be determined that the procedure was in Toni's "best interests." In addition, because of possible conflicts of interests, it concluded that the parents could not properly determine what course Toni might prefer. The court redefined the role of the judge in such declaratory judgment cases: to determine "whether the parents' decision to allow Toni to participate as a donor . . . is fair and reasonable in the particular circumstances of this case." Id. The Court concluded that, based on the urgency of William's physical condition, his need for a transplant, and the probable and possible consequences to the donor, that the procedure was "fair and reasonable as to Toni." Id.

The court nonetheless asked the hospital to explore the availability of insurance to cover any damages Toni might suffer as a result of her participation. The transplant was performed, and it was unsuccessful. The parents and physicians petitioned to perform a second transplant, even though the probability of success had dropped from about 30 percent to less than 1 percent, and insurance had not been secured for Toni. The court granted this petition as well. William died before the second bone marrow transplant could be performed. Are all these cases really being decided by upholding the power of the family to protect its own members? On use of live donors generally see Adams, Live Organs Donors and Informed Consent, 8 J. Leg. Med. 555 (1987).

2. ORGAN PROCUREMENT AND THE DEFINITION OF DEATH

A Definition of Irreversible Coma: Report of the Ad Hoc Committee of the Harvard Medical School to Examine the Definition of Brain Death

205 J.A.M.A. 337-340 (1968)

Our primary purpose is to define irreversible coma as a new criterion for death. There are two reasons why there is need for a definition: (1) Improvements in resuscitative and supportive measures have led to increased efforts to save those who are desperately injured. Sometimes these efforts have only partial success so that the result is an individual whose heart continues to beat but whose brain is irreversibly damaged. The burden is great on patients who suffer permanent loss of intellect, on their families, on the hospitals, and on those in need of hospital beds already occupied by these comatose patients. (2) Obsolete criteria for the definition of death can lead to controversy in obtaining organs for transplantation. . . .

CHARACTERISTICS OF IRREVERSIBLE COMA

An organ, brain or other, that no longer functions and has no possibility of functioning again is for all practical purposes dead. Our first problem is to determine the characteristics of a *permanently* nonfunctioning brain.

A patient in this state appears to be in deep coma. The condition can be satisfactorily diagnosed by points 1, 2, and 3 to follow. The electroencephalogram (point 4) provides confirmatory data, and when available it should be utilized. . . .

1. *Unreceptivity and Unresponsitivity.* — There is a total unawareness to externally applied stimuli and inner need and complete unresponsiveness — our definition of irreversible coma. Even the most intensely painful stimuli evoke no vocal or other response, not even a groan, withdrawal of a limb, or quickening of respiration.

2. *No Movements or Breathing.* — Observation covering a period of at least one hour by physicians is adequate to satisfy the criteria of no spontaneous muscular movements or spontaneous respiration or response to stimuli such as pain, touch, sound, or light. After the patient is on a mechanical respirator, the total absence of spontaneous breathing may be established by

turning off the respirator for three minutes and observing whether there is any effort on the part of the subject to breathe. . . .

3. *No reflexes.* — Irreversible coma with abolition of central nervous system activity is evidenced in part by the absence of elicitable reflexes. The pupil will be fixed and dilated and will not respond to a direct source of bright light. . . . Ocular movement (to head turning and to irrigation of the ears with ice water) and blinking are absent. . . .

4. *Flat Electroencephalogram.* — Of great confirmatory value is the flat or isoelectric EEG. . . .

All of the above tests shall be repeated at least 24 hours later with no change.

The validity of such data as indications of irreversible cerebral damage depends on the exclusion of two conditions: hypothermia (temperature below 90 F [32.2 C]) or central nervous system depressants, such as barbiturates.

The patient's condition can be determined only by a physician. When the patient is hopelessly damaged as defined above, the family and all colleagues who have participated in major decisions concerning the patient, and all nurses involved, should be so informed. Death is to be declared and *then* the respirator turned off. The decision to do this and the responsibility for it are to be taken by the physician-in-charge, in consultation with one or more physicians who have been directly involved in the case. It is unsound and undesirable to force the family to make the decision.

LEGAL COMMENTARY

. . . At present, the law of the United States, in all 50 states and in the federal courts, treats the question of human death as a question of fact to be decided in every case. When any doubt exists, the courts seek medical expert testimony concerning the time of death of the particular individual involved. However, the law makes the assumption that the medical criteria for determining death are settled and not in doubt among physicians. Furthermore, the law assumes that the traditional method among physicians for determination of death is to ascertain the absence of all vital signs. To this extent, *Black's Law Dictionary* (fourth edition, 1951) defines death as

> The cessation of life; the ceasing to exist; *defined by physicians* as a total stoppage of the circulation of the blood, and a cessation of the animal and vital functions consequent thereupon, such as respiration, pulsation, etc. [italics added].

In this report, . . . we suggest that responsible medical opinion is ready to adopt new criteria for pronouncing death to have occurred in an individual sustaining irreversible coma as a result of permanent brain damage. If this position is adopted by the medical community, it can form the basis for change in the current legal concept of death. No statutory change in the law should be necessary since the law treats this question essentially as one of fact to be determined by physicians. The only circumstance in which it would be necessary that legislation be offered in the various states to define "death" by law would be in the event that great controversy were engendered surrounding the subject and physicians were unable to agree on the new medical criteria.

It is recommended as a part of these procedures that judgment of the existence of these criteria is solely a medical issue. It is suggested that the physician in charge of the patient consult with one or more other physicians directly involved in the case before the patient is declared dead on the basis of these criteria. In this way, the responsibility is shared over a wider range of medical opinion, thus providing an important degree of protection against later questions which might be raised about the particular case. It is further suggested that the decision to declare the person dead, and then to turn off the respirator, be made by physicians not involved in any later effort to transplant organs or tissue from the deceased individual. This is advisable in order to avoid any appearance of self-interest by the physicians involved. . . .

Notes on Brain Death

(1) Since 1969, various individuals and groups, including the American Bar Association (ABA), in 1975, and the American Medical Association (AMA), in 1979, have proposed that uniform legislation on brain death be adopted in each of the 50 states. Currently, more than 40 states have adopted "brain death" legislation, using many different approaches. Legislation was not needed before these varying statutes were adopted, but uniform legislation certainly seems desirable now to help disspell confusion.

Viewing uniformity as more important than the language of their particular models, representatives of the ABA, the AMA, and the National Conference of Commissioners on Uniform State Laws (NCCUSL) met in May, 1980, and agreed upon a common model. The NCCUSL adopted the new proposal in August, 1980, the AMA in October, 1980, and ABA in February, 1981. This model, which was also endorsed by the President's Commission for the Study of Ethical Problems in Medicine and Biomedical and Behavioral Research (Defining Death [1981]) reads,

> An individual who has sustained either (1) irreversible cessation of circulatory and respiratory functions, or (2) irreversible cessation of all functions of the entire brain, including the brain stem, is dead. A determination of death must be made in accordance with accepted medical standards. Id. at 2.

The model gives the physician two alternative criteria for determining death and leaves the application of such criteria in individual cases to accepted medical standards. It is a conservative definition, requiring death of the *entire* brain, and so does not apply to patients (like Karen Ann Quinlan, see Chapter 6 (D)) in persistent vegetative states. See Cranford & Smith, Some Critical Distinctions between Brain Death and the Persistent Vegetative State, 6 Ethics in Science & Med. 199 (1979).

Alexander Capron and Leon Kass proposed a conceptually similar version of a model law in 1972. They suggested that there are four conceptual levels on which a statutory definition of death can operate: (1) the basic concept or idea; (2) general physiological standards; (3) operational criteria; and (4) specific tests or procedures. The model act chooses level (2), leaving (1) for another day, and (3) and (4) to the medical profession. This seems appropriate, since legislating in areas (3) and (4) would necessitate almost yearly changes in the law if it is to keep pace with advances in medical technology and diagnostic ability. Capron & Kass, A Statutory Definition of the Standards for Determining Human Death: An Appraisal and a Proposal, 121 U. Penn. L. Rev. 87 (1972). What would you advise a physician in a state with no brain death statute regarding "the law" of using brain death criteria for declaring death?

(2) Robert Veatch has suggested we consider redefining death completely, basing it not on biological activity but on a concept of personhood. He calls for a definition of death based on "irreversible cessation of spontaneous cerebral functions." R. Veatch, Death, Dying and the Biological Revolution 45-58 (rev. ed. 1989). Does this make sense? Should we try to apply "brain death" criteria to the beginning of life as well by making brain activity (instead of viability) the time at which the state's interest in fetal life becomes compelling?

(3) There are some unique medical and scientific problems in accurately diagnosing brain death in children under the age of five. However, there are no unique legal problems in determining brain death in this population: the key, as it is in adults, is to apply accepted medical criteria properly. Such criteria have been proposed and widely endorsed. Task Force for the Determination of Brain Death in Children, Guidelines for the Determination of Brain Death in Children, 21 Ann. Neurol. 616 (1987).

(4) The donor for the first human heart transplant in the U.S. was an anencephalic (no higher brain function) newborn who was immersed in ice water until the infant's heart stopped beating. Efforts to use anencephalic newborns for kidney donation have largely been a failure. But in 1987 debate was renewed on using their hearts. The "problem" is that although anencephalic neonates have no higher brain function, as long as they are able to breathe on their own, they do possess brain stem function and thus are not dead under current brain death standards. Waiting the one to seven days usually required for the infants to die under traditional criteria almost always means that their organs will be useless for transplant. Should these standards be changed? Should anencephalics be declared a "new category" that are "born dead" even though they are breathing? What impact might this have? See, for instance, Capron, Anencephalic Donors: Separate the Dead from the

Dying, 17 Hastings Cent. Rep. 5 (Feb. 1987); and Truog & Fletcher, Anencephalic Newborns: Can Organs be Transplanted before Brain Death? 321 N. Engl. J. Med. 388 (1989).

3. HARVESTING ORGANS FROM THE DEAD

Strachan v. John F. Kennedy Memorial Hospital

109 N.J. 523, 538 A.2d 346 (1988)

CLIFFORD, J.

. . . Plaintiffs' son's body had been maintained on a life-support system, a respirator, even after the parents had demanded that the system be removed, following the unanimous conclusion of several physicians that the young man was brain dead.

A majority of the Appellate Division, reversing a judgment for plaintiffs after jury verdicts, determined that defendants, a hospital and its administrator, were guilty of "no actionable wrongdoing associated with withholding or mishandling the dead body.". . . The pertinent facts may be summarized as follows.

At approximately 4:30 P.M. on Friday, April 25, 1980, twenty-year-old Jeffrey Strachan shot himself in the head in an apparent suicide attempt. He was rushed to John F. Kennedy Memorial Hospital (the Hospital), an acute care facility and one of the defendants in this case. At 5:25 that afternoon Dr. Hummel, the emergency room physician, diagnosed Jeffrey as brain dead. . . .

Examination later that evening by Dr. Cohen, a neurosurgeon and one of the attending physicians, confirmed that Jeffrey was brain dead. . . . Dr. Cohen asked plaintiffs to consider donating Jeffrey's organs. He noted on the medical chart that the staff should proceed to "harvest" Jeffrey's organs if the parents gave their permission (the obvious implication being that there was no doubt about Jeffrey's status: he was dead). Because plaintiffs were uncertain about what to do, they deferred a decision and agreed to return in the morning. . . .

Plaintiffs returned the next morning, Saturday, April 26. They informed a Dr. Pinsler . . . of their decision not to donate any of Jeffrey's organs. They also requested that he be taken off the respirator. Dr. Pinsler advised plaintiffs to "think it over some more." Plaintiffs also discussed their request with Dr. Cohen. When Mr. Strachan asked a nurse when the machine would be turned off, he was informed that the hospital administrator had not given any order for the removal of the machinery, and that the removal could not be effected without such an order.

After speaking with Mr. Strachan that evening Dr. Venkat, also a neurosurgeon and an associate of Dr. Cohen, examined Jeffrey and agreed that the young man was brain dead. He noted plaintiffs' request to turn off the respirator, and indicated on the chart that "as soon as the hospital administrator tells us the procedure, we will do so."

Assistant administrator and nursing director Jeanette Licorice communicated with defendant Pirolli, the hospital administrator, late that same evening. Pirolli in turn called the Hospital's general counsel, Edward Sullivan, for advice. Sullivan suggested that the Hospital obtain plaintiffs' consent for removal of the respirator. He also indicated that the Hospital should run two electroencephalograms (EEGs), twenty-four hours apart, to get a "clear understanding of what the boy's condition is." He suggested to Pirolli that a court order might be obtained as an alternative to a medical decision to turn off the respirator. Another possible solution offered by Sullivan was the convening of a Prognosis Committee to assist the physicians in the decision to pronounce the patient dead.

The results of the two EEGs confirmed that Jeffrey was indeed brain dead. The Hospital authorities did not convene a Prognosis Committee. Dr. Weinstein, also a neurosurgeon engaged in practice with Drs. Cohen and Venkat, made an entry on Jeffrey's chart for Monday, April 28, 1980, indicting: "patient officially brain dead and by hospital regulations we may discontinue respiration [with] family's permission." Plaintiffs signed a release requesting Jeffrey's removal from life-support systems. The release provided:

> We have been advised by the attending physicians of our son, Jeffrey Strachan, that he has been declared "brain dead." It is therefore requested that all life support-life-support-death devices [sic] be discontinued as soon as possible.
>
> In making this request we are fully aware of our legal responsibilities and further hold harmless John F. Kennedy Memorial Hospital and the attending physicians with regard to discontinuance of life support devices.

At 4:05 P.M., Dr. Weinstein disconnected the respirator. Dr. Santoro pronounced Jeffrey dead and executed a death certificate, after which Jeffrey's body was turned over to his family for burial.

Plaintiffs thereafter instituted this action against the Hospital, administrator Pirolli, the physicians involved, and the Delaware Valley Transplant Program and its representative Stephen Sammut. The action against the physicians, the transplant program, and Sammut was voluntarily dismissed prior to trial, and the case proceeded against the Hospital and administrator Pirolli only. At the conclusion of trial the court instructed the jury on the bases of liability, including *respondeat superior,* under which the Hospital would be liable if Pirolli were found liable. The court then submitted the matter to the jury with special interrogatories, including the following:

> 1(a) Did defendant, Augustine R. Pirolli, have a duty to have procedures in place for the removal of Jeffrey Strachan from the life support systems when

> requested by his parents, and willfully and wantonly fail to do so, as alleged by the plaintiffs? . . .
> 2(a) [same question] . . . and negligently failed to do so, as alleged by the plaintiffs?
> 2(b) Was this failure a proximate cause of the infliction of additional severe emotional stress upon the plaintiffs?
> 3(a) Did the defendant, Augustine R. Pirolli, willfully and wantonly hold the body of Jeffrey Strachan so as to prevent his proper burial? . . .
> 4(a) Did the defendant, Augustine R. Pirolli, negligently hold the body of Jeffrey Strachan so as to prevent his proper burial?
> 4(b) Did this holding result in additional mental distress to the plaintiffs?

The jury responded affirmatively to both parts of questions 2 and 4, and awarded plaintiffs $70,000 each, for total verdicts of $140,000. As indicated, a divided Appellate Division reversed.

II

The foregoing interrogatories, which track the trial court's charge, suggest that there were two separate causes of action, based on separate duties owed by defendants to plaintiffs, on which the jury could make separate determinations: one resting on a duty to have in place procedures for the removal of plaintiffs' son from the life-support system on plaintiffs' request, the other based on a duty to release to the parents their son's dead body. This was error. The circumstances of the case projected but one duty: to act reasonably in honoring the family's legitimate request to turn over their son's body.

Quite apart from the substantive question of whether courts should impose on hospitals a duty to have certain procedures in place is the problem of the trial court's having left to the jury the issue of whether such a duty exists. A prerequisite to recovery on a negligence theory is a duty owed by defendant to plaintiff. . . . Although the jury in this case was asked to determine whether defendants were under such a duty, the question of whether a duty exists is a matter of law properly decided by the court, not the jury, . . . and is largely a question of fairness or policy. "The inquiry involves a weighing of the relationship of the parties, the nature of the risk, and the public interest in the proposed solution." . . .

We are disinclined, as a matter of sound public policy, to announce an absolute duty, henceforth to be adhered to by all affected hospitals, to have in place *procedures* for the removal of a dead body from a life-support mechanism on the request of the next of kin. Cf. Kirker v. Orange County, 519 So. 2d 682 (Fla. Dist. Ct. App. 1988) (Allegations of negligence against defendant county, of which medical examiner's office was an agency, charging failure to provide proper procedures for corneal removal and failure to generate and maintain accurate records of such procedures "do not rise to level of willful, wanton or malicious behavior such as would sustain an action for emotional distress."). The imposition of a paperwork duty does little to advance either the mission of health-care providers or the needs of society. If "procedures" are to be viewed as more than mere "paperwork" and considered indispensable in this area — in the nature of a standard that governs the medical community — then those procedures should be designed and imposed by those most directly involved, the physicians and hospitals themselves. That is the business of the medical community itself, not of this Court.

That is not to say, however, that the absence of such procedures may not be relevant on the issue of whether these defendants fulfilled the obligation that surely they had: to act reasonably in the face of plaintiffs' request to turn over the body. . . .

Plaintiffs' right of recovery . . . depends on when Jeffrey's death occurred. Jeffrey was pronounced brain dead by the emergency room physician at 5:25 P.M. on Friday. That assessment was confirmed by a neurosurgeon that evening, and again confirmed by other doctors and by the results of additional testing throughout the weekend. The evidence is overwhelming that Jeffrey was deemed brain dead considerably earlier than Monday at 4:10 P.M. when Dr. Santoro pronounced him dead and executed a death certificate. Thus the question comes down to whether our legal definition of death should include brain death.

Traditionally, death was defined as the irreversible cessation of cardiopulmonary function. . . . This definition, however, came under attack as failing to reflect advances in medical technology. Because cardiac and respiratory activity can be mechanically maintained for some time, definitions of "death" have increasingly focused on the cessation of brain functions. . . . Once the brain is dead, no technology exists to restore its function. . . .

Technological advances have also made possible the performance of organ transplants on a regular basis. For organs to be preserved for transplant, the donor's cardiopulmonary system must continue functioning until the organs can be removed. Under the traditional definition of death, such a donor would be considered as still alive because the heart continues to beat and the lungs continue to perform the respiratory function. In a very real sense, then, a break from the traditional definition of death is a necessary condition to the existence of transplant programs, for otherwise the organ-removal process might be deemed to have "killed" the donor. . . .

In response to these concerns, many states have adopted new definitions of death, incorporating brain death. The Uniform Determination of Death Act (UDDA) provides:

> *§1. [Determination of Death]*
> An individual who has sustained either (1) irreversible cessation of circulatory and respiratory functions, or (2) irreversible cessation of all functions of the entire brain, including the brain stem, is dead. A determination of death must be made in accordance with accepted medical standards. . . .

We therefore conclude that section one of the UDDA provides the appropriate legal definition of death. That some of the developments in refining that definition and implementing it elsewhere came to pass after the critical events of the case before us is of small moment, given this Court's 1976 reference in *Quinlan,* with obvious approval, to "brain death" as satisfying the criterion for "death" and as "representing . . . prevailing and accepted medical standards." See 70 N.J. at 27-28, 355 A. 2d 647. We therefore conclude that there was ample support in the evidence for the jury's conclusion that defendants had "negligently [held] the body of Jeffrey Strachan so as to prevent his proper burial." (Answer to Interrogatory 4(a).) . . .

[T]here can be no doubt that on deeming Jeffrey brain dead, the doctors considered Jeffrey "dead." The failure of defendants to honor the family members' request posed a plain affront to their dignity and autonomy and exposed them to unnecessary distress at a time of profound grief.

The record in this case reveals particularly compelling evidence of distress. Although plaintiffs were told that their son was brain dead and nothing further could be done for him, for three days after requesting that their son be disconnected from the respirator plaintiffs continued to see him lying in bed, with tubes in his body, his eyes taped shut, and foam in his mouth. His body remained warm to the touch. Had Jeffrey's body been removed from the respirator when his parents requested, a scene fraught with grief and heartache would have been avoided, and plaintiffs would have been spared additional suffering.

Because Jeffrey was no longer alive, defendants breached no duty owed him by their failure to turn off the respirator. Jeffrey suffered no harm as a result of defendants' negligence. Plaintiffs' distress, therefore, was not the result of witnessing another's injury, but rather the result of a breach of duty owed directly to plaintiffs. Perhaps the confusion stems from the fact that the duty owed to plaintiffs related to the handling of Jeffrey's body, but that does not render this a "bystander" case. If, for example, a hospital negligently reported to a patient's parents that the patient's condition was considerably worse than in fact it was, the parents' distress would flow from the breach of a duty owed to them, not one owed to their child. . . .

The requirement of physical injury is grounded on the notion that emotional distress claims are too easily fabricated without such a limitation. . . .

We need look no further than the long-recognized exception for negligent handling of a corpse, see *Muniz,* supra, 153 N.J. Super. at 80, 379 A.2d 57, or the especial likelihood that this claim is genuine, see *Berman,* supra, 80 N.J. at 433-434, 404 A.2d 8, to conclude that plaintiffs need not demonstrate any physical manifestations of their emotional distress here. The result at trial was consistent with the stated principles.

IV

We have determined that there was ample evidence to support the jury's conclusion that defendants violated their duty to honor plaintiffs' legitimate request to turn over their son's dead body. So much of the Appellate Division judgment as reversed the trial court judgment in favor of plaintiffs on that claim is reversed. Because we do not recognize a separate cause of action based on defendants' failure to have had in place procedures for the removal of life-support systems, we affirm so much of the judgment below as upset the trial-level judgment in plaintiffs' favor on that claim.

Ordinarily that would result in our reinstating the jury verdict of $70,000 for plaintiffs on the first-stated claim. Under the circumstances, however, we can have no confidence in the assumption that had the jurors been properly instructed on a single cause of action rather than on two separate and distinct negligence claims, they would have concluded that the total recoverable damages amounted to $70,000. We therefore remand for a retrial on damages only on the claim for failure to have released the dead body.

Judgment affirmed in part, reversed in part. The cause is remanded to the trial court for retrial on damages only, consistent with this opinion.

State of Florida v. Powell

497 So. 2d 1188 (Fla. 1986)

OVERTON, Justice.

This is a petition to review a circuit court order finding unconstitutional section 732.9185, Florida Statutes (1983), which authorizes medical examiners to remove corneal tissue from decedents during statutorily required autopsies when such tissue is needed for transplantation. The statute prohibits the removal of the corneal tissue if the next of kin objects, but does not require that the decedent's next of kin be notified of the procedure. The Fifth District Court of Appeal certified that this case presents a question of great public importance requiring immediate resolution by this Court. We accept jurisdiction pursuant to article V, section 3(b)(5), Florida Constitution. . . . The challenged statute provides:

> Corneal removal by medical examiners. —
>
> (1) In any case in which a patient is in need of corneal tissue for a transplant, a district medical examiner or an appropriately qualified designee with training in ophthalmologic techniques may, upon request of any eye bank authorized under §732.918, provide the cornea of a decedent whenever all of the following conditions are met:
>
> (a) A decedent who may provide a suitable cornea for the transplant is under the jurisdiction of the medical examiner and an autopsy is required in accordance with §406.11.
>
> (b) No objection by the next of kin of the decedent is known by the medical examiner.
>
> (c) The removal of the cornea will not interfere with the subsequent course of an investigation or autopsy.
>
> (2) Neither the district medical examiner nor his appropriately quali-

> fied designee nor any eye bank authorized under §732.918 may be held liable in any civil or criminal action for failure to obtain consent of the next of kin.

The trial court decided this case by summary judgment. The facts are not in dispute. On June 15, 1983, James White drowned while swimming at the city beach in Dunellon, Florida. Associate Medical Examiner Dr. Thomas Techman, who is an appellant in this cause, performed an autopsy on James' body at Leesburg Community Hospital. On July 11, 1983, Anthony Powell died in a motor vehicle accident in Marion County. Medical Examiner Dr. William H. Shutze, who is also an appellant in this cause, performed an autopsy on Anthony's body. In each instance, under the authority of section 732.9185, the medical examiner removed corneal tissue from the decedent without giving notice to or obtaining consent from the parents of the decedent. . . .

In its judgment, the trial court noted that section 732.9185 "has as its purpose the commendable and laudable objective of providing high quality cornea tissue to those in need of same," but declared the statute unconstitutional on the grounds that it (1) deprives survivors of their fundamental personal and property right to dispose of their deceased next of kin in the same condition as lawful autopsies left them, without procedural or substantive due process of law; (2) creates an invidious classification which deprives survivors of their right to equal protection; and (3) permits a taking of private property by state action for a non-public purpose, in violation of article X, section 6(a), of the Florida Constitution. The court concluded that the state has no compelling interest in non-consensual removal of appellees' decedents' corneal tissue that outweighs the survivors' right to dispose of their sons' bodies in the condition death left them. For the reasons expressed below, we reject these findings. . . .

The unrebutted evidence in this record establishes that the State of Florida spends approximately $138 million each year to provide its blind with the basic necessities of life. At present, approximately ten percent of Florida's blind citizens are candidates for cornea transplantation, which has become a highly effective procedure for restoring sight to the functionally blind. As advances are made in the field, the number of surgical candidates will increase, thereby raising the demand for suitable corneal tissue. The increasing number of elderly persons in our population has also created a great demand for corneas because corneal blindness often is age-related. Further, an affidavit in the record states:

> Corneal transplants are particularly important in newborns. The brain does not learn to see if the cornea is not clear. There is a critical period in the first few months of life when the brain "learns to see." If the cornea is not clear, the brain not only does not "learn to see," but the brain loses its ability to "learn to see." Hence, corneal transplant in children must be made as soon as practic-

> able after the problem is discovered. Without the medical examiner legislation, there would be virtually no corneal tissue available for infants and these children would remain forever blind.

The record reflects that the key to successful corneal transplantation is the availability of high-quality corneal tissue and that corneal tissue removed more than ten hours after death is generally unsuitable for transplantation. The implementation of section 732.9185 in 1977 has, indisputably, increased both the supply and quality of tissue available for transplantation. Statistics show that, in 1976, only 500 corneas were obtained in Florida for transplantation while, in 1985, more than 3000 persons in Florida had their sight restored through corneal transplantation surgery. . . .

An autopsy is a surgical dissection of the body; it necessarily results in a massive intrusion into the decedent. This record reflects that cornea removal, by comparison, requires an infinitesimally small intrusion which does not affect the decedent's appearance. With or without cornea removal, the decedent's eyes must be capped to maintain a normal appearance.

Our review of section 732.9185 reveals certain safeguards which are apparently designed to limit cornea removal to instances in which the public's interest is greatest and the impact on the next of kin the least: corneas may be removed only if the decedent is under the jurisdiction of the medical examiner; an autopsy is mandated by Florida law; and the removal will not interfere with the autopsy or an investigation of the death. Further, medical examiners may not automatically remove tissue from all decedents subject to autopsy; rather, a request must be made by an eye bank based on a present need for the tissue.

We conclude that this record clearly establishes that this statute reasonably achieves the permissible legislative objective of providing sight to many of Florida's blind citizens.

We next address the trial court's finding that section 732.9185 deprives appellees of a fundamental property right. All authorities generally agree that the next of kin have no property right in the remains of a decedent. . . .

Under the facts and circumstances of these cases, we find no taking of private property by state action for a non-public purpose in violation of article X, section 6, of the Florida Constitution. . . .

The record contains no evidence that the appellees' objections to the removal of corneal tissues for human transplants are based on any "fundamental tenets of their religious beliefs." . . .

In conclusion, we hold that section 732.9185 is constitutional because it rationally promotes the permissible state objective of restoring sight to the blind. In so holding, we note that laws regarding the removal of human tissues for transplantation implicate moral, ethical, theological, philosophical, and economic concerns which do not readily lend themselves to analysis within a traditional legal framework. Applying constitutional standards of review to section 732.9185 obscures the fact that at the heart of the issue lies

a policy question which calls for a delicate balancing of societal needs and individual concerns more appropriately accomplished by the legislature. . . .
McDonald, C.J., and Adkins, Boyd, Ehrlich and Barkett, JJ., concur.

Shaw, J., dissents.

Two general questions, with numerous subsidiary questions, are whether the conditions precedent to cornea removal were present and whether the provisions of section 732.9185 were followed. The issue of the constitutionality of sections 406.11 and 732.9185, as applied, is inchoate at this stage of the proceeding.

The legislature is apparently of the view, contrary to the majority, that a decedent's next of kin have the right to possess and control the decedent's body and that both the decedent and next of kin may control the removal and donation of human organs. The various provisions of chapter 245, Florida Statutes (1981), titled Disposition of Dead Bodies, are grounded on the right of the next of kin to claim control and possession of dead bodies. Section 245.07 appears to rule out the state's use of dead bodies for the advancement of medical science unless the bodies are unclaimed or donated under section 245.11. On the question of the donation and removal of organs, chapter 732, part X, Florida Statutes (1985), authorizes and establishes programs whereby both the decedent and survivors may donate organs of a decedent. Section 732.912 is particularly pertinent. Subsection (1) authorizes the donation of organs by will; subsection (2) authorizes the donation of a decedent's organs by next of kin in a priority order and also recognizes the right of next of kin to veto the removal or donation of organs. Moreover, section 732.9185(1)(b) itself recognizes the right of the next of kin to veto the donation of the cornea. The crucial point is that part X of chapter 732 is grounded on the right of the decedent and next of kin to control the removal and disposition of organs taken from the body of the decedent. If this is not so, part X is grounded on air. It is a conundrum in that it is simply not legally possible nor permissible to donate or control the donation of an article which does not belong to the donor.

I agree that these cases present issues of great public importance which may, at some point, require this court's attention. At this point, however, there is substantial doubt that sections 406.11 and 732.9185 have been correctly interpreted and applied by the cognizant authorities in Marion County. The issues presented by these suits, particularly the counts requesting a declaratory judgment of the rights, duties, and privileges of the next of kin, are likely to be with us a long time and to become even more intense as medical science advances and organ transplants increase in number. I am simply not prepared to rush to judgment on issues as important as these based on a summary judgment. These issues are important, but we are not a legislative body rushing to enact emergency legislation to meet an urgent state need before the end of a legislative session. These cases should be remanded with instructions that the trial go forward and a record be developed.

Notes on Organ Harvesting

(1) It is difficult to dispute the Florida Supreme Court's conclusion that "restoring sight to the blind" is a legitimate state purpose. But isn't actual saving of life (as is involved in heart and liver transplants) even more legitimate, even "compelling"? Would a state statute that permitted physicians and hospitals to take the organs from deceased persons (such as Jeffrey Strachan) without the consent of the next-of-kin be constitutional if its purpose was to "save lives"? Is there a difference between corneas and hearts that explains why many states have laws similar to Florida's, but why no state has a law that permits the taking of other organs without consent of either the "donor" or the next-of-kin?

(2) The general practice in the United States is to seek the consent of the next-of-kin for organ donation, even in cases in which the individual himself or herself has executed an authorization under the Uniform Anatomical Gift Act (which authorization is legally sufficient). Since 1970, all 50 states have had some version of the Uniform Anatomical Gift Act in place. Its key provision is section 2:

> ***Section** 2.* [*Persons Who May Execute an Anatomical Gift.*]
>
> (a) Any individual of sound mind and 18 years of age or more may give all or any part of his body for any purpose specified in section 3, the gift to take effect upon death.
>
> (b) Any of the following persons, in order of priority stated, when persons in prior classes are not available at the time of death, and in the absence of actual notice of contrary indications by the decedent or actual notice of opposition by a member of the same or a prior class, may give all or any part of the decedent's body for any purpose specified in section 3:
>
> (1) the spouse,
> (2) an adult son or daughter,
> (3) either parent,
> (4) an adult brother or sister,
> (5) a guardian of the person of the decedent at the time of his death,
> (6) any other person authorized or under obligation to dispose of the body.
>
> (c) If the donee has actual notice of contrary indications by the decedent or that a gift by a member of a class is opposed by a member of the same or a prior class, the donee shall not accept the gift. The persons authorized by subsection (b) may make the gift after or immediately before death.

(3) Surveys have indicated that physicians and hospitals are unwilling to act on donations without the added consent of the family. Roger Evans describes the results of his survey for the federal government:

> When donor documentation is available, family consent is still required. . . . People we talked to in 47 states said that surgeons require family approval.

> When presented with the hypothetical situation in which the decedent's relatives could not be located, only 11 of the 47 states responding said they would probably proceed with organ removal. Three major reasons were given for requiring family consent despite valid donor documentation. In 28 states people said they rely on family confirmation in order to avoid legal disputes. Ethical considerations . . . is a factor in 25 states where medical personnel feel that it is morally wrong to ignore objections raised by survivors. Finally, 15 states cited fear of bad publicity. Only four states take full advantages of the provisions of the anatomical gift acts. [Organ Transplants, Testimony before the Subcomm. on Investigations and Oversight of the Comm. on Science and Technology, U.S. House of Representatives, April, 1983, No. 16, at 380 (98th Cong. 1st sess.).]

Even if donor cards were honored, however, it could not solve the "organ shortage" since even in states that provide an opportunity for individuals to fill out an organ donor card when obtaining or renewing their driver's license, only between 1.5 percent and 8.5 percent of all people fill out such a card. The only exception is Colorado, where 60 percent of all licensed drivers have designated themselves as organ donors. Id. at 379.

(4) The failure of the Uniform Anatomical Gift Act has prompted a number of proposals for amendment and new approaches. One, which has been universally rejected in the U.S., but has been adopted in some European countries, is "presumed consent," wherein the deceased is "presumed" to have consented to donate his or her organs in the absence of a document refusing such consent. Dukeminier & Sanders, Organ Transplantation: A Proposal for Routine Salvaging of Cadaver Organs, 279 N. Engl. J. Med. 413 (1968). And see R.H. Blank, Rationing Medicine 44-45 (1988). As philosopher Tristram Engelhardt notes, "Free societies are characterized by the commitment to live with tragedies that result from the decisions of free individuals not to participate in the beneficent endeavors of others." Engelhardt, Allocating Scarce Medical Resources and the Viability of Organ Transplantation, 311 N. Engl. J. Med. 66, 70 (1984). Another unsuccessful proposal has been to encourage the sale of organs, on the theory that the marketplace can produce sufficient organs (especially kidneys) if individuals are permitted to sell one of their own to those in need. Unlawful sales, however, continue. In early 1989, for example, five people in Florida were accused of fraudulently obtaining corneas from 47 corpses and selling them for profit. Medical examiners assumed the corneas were going to a regional tissue bank, but many were sold to a Saudi Arabian hospital for $650 each (corneas can be suitable for transplant for up to two weeks). N.Y. Times, Jan. 12, 1989 at A24. This scam was, of course, greatly aided by Florida's cornea procurement law. Should the market be permitted to operate in human organs and tissue? Would the ability to buy and sell increase the supply, or would it disgust many people who now donate their organs and tissues, dissuading them from participating at all?

A final proposal, to require hospital personnel to inquire of the family of a brain-dead patient whether or not they would like to donate the individual's organs, has found wide acceptance. More than 40 states, as of 1989, had adopted so-called "required request" legislation. The federal government also requires that all hospitals who are recipients of Medicare funds put a "required request" system in place. No matter how one views this issue, it should be astonishing that the problems with organ procurement are still viewed by some as *legal* problems (and thus susceptible to a legal solution) rather than as complex interpersonal problems involved in death and the doctor-patient-family relationship not susceptible to legal cure.

4. PROCURING TISSUE FOR TRANSPLANT FROM ABORTED FETUSES

Annas & Elias, The Politics of Transplantation of Human Fetal Tissue

320 N. Engl. J. Med. 1079-1082 (1989)

Research involving human fetal tissue has been the subject of intense political debate in this country for almost two decades. . . .

The most recent series of disputes began in October 1987, when the National Institutes of Health (NIH) submitted a request to the assistant secretary for health in which the NIH sought approval to fund the transplantation of human fetal tissue into the brain of a patient with Parkinson's disease. In March 1988, Assistant Secretary Robert Windom asked that the NIH establish a special advisory panel to study 10 questions about fetal-tissue research. And in May a moratorium was announced on the use of fetuses from elective abortions in federally funded research.

The 21-member Human Tissue Fetal Transplant Research Panel subsequently created by the NIH invited more than 50 people, including the representatives of 16 groups, to present their views in public sessions. On December 5, the panel finalized its report,[1] and on December 14 the advisory committee to the NIH director adopted it unanimously. Wisely, the panel separated questions concerning the use of fetal tissue from those involving abortion — a legally and ethically appropriate move, but perhaps ultimately a politically untenable one. While the panel was still deliberating, the White House sent draft regulations to the secretary of health and human services that proposed a prohibition of the use of federal funds in any research

[1.] Consultants of the Advisory Committee to the Director of the National Institutes of Health. Report of the human fetal tissue transplant panel. Washington, D.C.: National Institutes of Health, 1988.

involving fetal tissues.[2] Nonetheless, the new secretary, Louis Sullivan, has told Congress that the issues could be separated, and he will study the panel's report before making a decision.[3] The final decision will provide an early signal of President Bush's willingness to let the politics of abortion dictate the course of the research that is done by government scientists and funded with federal money.

The panel's task was somewhat simplified by its decision to limit discussion to the use of tissue from dead fetuses and its rejection of any intrafamilial donations or payment for fetal tissue — rulings consistent with an October 1988 amendment to the National Organ Transplant Act. The panel concluded that although it was of "moral relevance" that the fetal tissue be obtained from an induced abortion (rather than a spontaneous abortion or an interrupted ectopic pregnancy), the use of the tissue in research was "acceptable public policy" because "abortion is legal and . . . the research in question is intended to achieve significant medical goals." This conclusion was accepted on a vote of 15 to 2, and included recommendations that the decision to abort be kept independent of the decision to retrieve and use fetal tissue, that recipients be informed of the tissue's fetal origins, and that fetal tissue be accorded the same respect given other cadaveric human tissue. In answer to the remaining questions, the panel adopted the following recommendations: the decision to abort must be made before the use of the tissue is discussed; anonymity should be maintained between donor and recipient; the timing and method of the abortion should not be influenced by the potential use of the fetal tissues; and the consent of the pregnant woman is necessary and sufficient for the use of tissue unless the father objects. The panel also concluded that "there is sufficient evidence from animal experimentation to justify proceeding with human clinical trials in Parkinson's disease and juvenile diabetes."

Many of these recommendations were adopted unanimously, and no more than two panel members dissented from any of them. The most illuminating part of the report, however, was not its bland prose, but the dissent and the responses it evoked, because these exchanges encapsulated the national debate.

In their dissent, attorney James Bopp and Professor James Burtchaell argued that research with fetuses aborted electively is "ethically compromised" by the lack of authentic informed consent, the incentives it offers for more abortions, and its complicity with the abortion. The consent issue involves the standard argument that a woman who decides to abort her fetus forfeits all rights and interests in the fetus and its remains.[4] The incentive argument

[2.] Boffey PM. Aides at White House draft ban on use of fetal tissue. New York Times. September 9, 1988:A10.

[3.] Tolchin M. Bush choice backed for health chief after an apology. New York Times. February 24, 1989:12.

[4.] Burtchaell JT. University policy on experimental use of aborted fetal tissue. IRB 1988; 10(4):7-11.

posits that many women are ambivalent about abortion, and that such ambivalence may be tipped in favor of abortion if the women are informed that some good may come of it.[5] The complicity argument, as stated by the dissenters, is primarily an emotional appeal based on an analogy to Nazi experimentation.

Professor John Robertson's response was joined by nine other panel members. He noted that a woman does not lose or forfeit all interest in an aborted fetus simply by choosing abortion. If she did, he said, this "would lead to a policy of using fetal remains without parental consent or to a total ban on fetal transplants." The assertion that the number of abortions will increase is "highly speculative," and Robertson argued that even "some" increase in the number of abortions would not make fetal transplants unacceptable, because such logic would assume "that even a marginal increase in abortion should bar fetal tissue transplant research." Robertson rejected the complicity argument completely, noting first that society's mere willingness to use the organs of persons killed in automobile accidents or murdered does not mean that society or transplant surgeons are accomplices in automobile accidents or murder. Finally, the Nazi analogy fails because those experiments were conducted on live, unconsenting patients, who suffered greatly from them, whereas research on fetal tissue involves only the dead remains of lawfully aborted fetuses, which cannot be harmed, and such research is done only with consent.

The dissenters' primary argument was that federal funding of fetal research would "institutionalize" governmental complicity with the "abortion industry," — a superficially appealing claim, perhaps, except that the federal government already profits directly from those who perform abortions, by taxing their earnings.

Those with serious misgivings about the use of dead fetal tissue are surely correct when they point out that dead fetuses cannot be equated with dead hamsters or human kidneys. Nonetheless, it is difficult to justify the use of the organs and tissues of dead children in transplantation without permitting the transplantation of tissue from dead fetuses. Some who object may be reacting not to the use of the fetus, but to the role of the not-to-be mother, and it can be argued that the panel did not address this role adequately. Kathleen Nolan has argued that the image of the "devouring mother" is an especially powerful and destructive one in our view of women as mothers. In her words,

> by allowing tissue retrieval, [these women] seem to "fail to protect" the dead fetus, letting it fall prey to the needs of others. Subliminally this threatens unconscious beliefs about the role of women as mothers. . . .

[5.] Bopp J. Use of fetal tissue will increase the number of abortions. National Right to Life News. November 17, 1988:4.

> No matter that the fetus is dead — mothers should still fend off the scavengers.[6]

The images of research physicians as scavengers and of mothers as indifferent to the fate of their deceased children are disturbing to many. But the fetus lacks the status of a child[7] and, after death, has no protectable interests of its own. At the same time, like a dead adult, the dead fetus is not abandoned property and should be treated with respect because of what it is and what it symbolizes. The mother's real role, like that of any surviving relative, is not to "consent" to burial or the use of body parts in transplantation. Rather, as the next of kin, she has the legal authority to dispose of the body in the customary manner (usually burial or cremation) and to object to any use of the body inconsistent with such customs, because of the mental anguish that such untraditional or disrespectful use of the body may cause her.[8]. Treating fetal remains with "respect" may mean not putting the fetus on public display, but when the choices include burial, incineration, or use in legitimate research, the third can be as respectful of the remains as the first two.

The report of the Stanford University Medical Center Committee on Ethics, which appears elsewhere in this issue of the *Journal,* [9] is fundamentally consistent with the report of the NIH panel. Together, these documents show wide agreement in the medical community on the major issues involved in the use of fetal tissue. One troubling difference must be noted, however. The Stanford report attempts to sidestep the question of elective abortion by recommending that "if tissue from spontaneous abortions can satisfy the medical demands for both quantity and quality of tissue, it would be preferable to avoid the ethical problems of using induced abortions." The use of tissues from fetuses aborted spontaneously is particularly problematic. It is now well established that about half of such fetuses aborted in the first trimester and 20 percent of those aborted in the second trimester are chromosomally abnormal. Moreover, a variety of microorganisms have been associated with spontaneous abortions, including cytomegalovirus, herpes simplex types 1 and 2, rubella, toxoplasma, and *Ureaplasma urealyticum.* It would be indefensible to transplant abnormal or infected fetal tissue that could increase both the risk of a transplant failure and that of infection in the recipient. Tissue from spontaneously aborted fetuses should not be used for transplantation into a human subject. . . . The politics of abortion have thus led us to focus on the tangential question of the tissue's source rather than

[6.] Nolan K. *Genug ist genug:* a fetus is not a kidney. Hastings Cent. Rep. 1988; 18(6):13-9.

[7.] Freedman B. The ethics of using human fetal tissue. IRB 1988; 10(6):1-4.

[8.] Strachan v. John F. Kennedy Memorial Hospital, 538 A.2d 346 (N.J. 1988).

[9.] Greely H.T., Hamm T., Johnson R., et al. The ethical use of human fetal tissue in medicine. N. Engl. J. Med. 1989; 320:1093-6.

the central question of its benefits to sick people. The subjects of the proposed transplant research are not the fetuses (which are dead), but the tissue recipients. . . .

B. Legal Regulation of Organ Transplantation: Cost, Quality, and Access

1. ACCESS TO ORGAN TRANSPLANTATION

Annas, The Prostitute, the Playboy, and the Poet: Rationing Schemes for Organ Transplantation

75 Am. J. Public Health 187-189 (1985)

In the public debate about the availability of heart and liver transplants, the issue of rationing on a massive scale has been credibly raised for the first time in United States medical care. In an era of scarce resources, the eventual arrival of such a discussion was, of course, inevitable. Unless we decide to ban heart and liver transplantation, or make them available to everyone, some rationing scheme must be used to choose among potential transplant candidates. The debate has existed throughout the history of medical ethics. Traditionally it has been stated as a choice between saving one of two patients, both of whom require the immediate assistance of the only available physician to survive.

National attention was focused on decisions regarding the rationing of kidney dialysis machines when they were first used on a limited basis in the late 1960s. . . .

In Seattle, Washington, an anonymous screening committee was set up to pick who among competing candidates would receive the life-saving technology. One lay member of the screening committee is quoted as saying:

> The choices were hard . . . I remember voting against a young woman who was a known prostitute. I found I couldn't vote for her, rather than another candidate, a young wife and mother. I also voted against a young man who, until he learned he had renal failure, had been a ne'er do-well, a real playboy. He promised he would reform his character, go back to school, and so on, if only he were selected for treatment. But I felt I'd lived long enough to know that a person like that won't really do what he was promising at the time.

When the biases and selection criteria of the committee were made public, there was a general negative reaction against this type of arbitrary device. Two experts reacted to the "numbing accounts of how close to the surface lie the prejudices and mindless cliches that pollute the committee's deliberations," by concluding that the committee was "measuring persons in accordance with its own middle-class values." The committee process, they noted, ruled out "creative nonconformists" and made the Pacific Northwest "no place for a Henry David Thoreau with bad kidneys."

To avoid having to make such explicit, arbitrary, "social worth" determinations, the Congress, in 1972, enacted legislation that provided federal funds for virtually all kidney dialysis and kidney transplantation procedures in the United States. This decision, however, simply served to postpone the time when identical decisions will have to be made about candidates for heart and liver transplantation in a society that does not provide sufficient financial and medical resources to provide all "suitable" candidates with the operation.

There are four major approaches to rationing scarce medical resources: the market approach; the selection committee approach; the lottery approach; and the "customary" approach.

THE MARKET APPROACH

The market approach would provide an organ to everyone who could pay for it with their own funds or private insurance. It puts a very high value on individual rights, and a very low value on equality and fairness. It has properly been criticized on a number of bases, including that the transplant technologies have been developed and are supported with public funds, that medical resources used for transplantation will not be available for higher priority care, and that financial success alone is an insufficient justification for demanding a medical procedure. Most telling is its complete lack of concern for fairness and equity. . . . Rationing by financial ability says we do not believe in equality, but believe that a price can and should be placed on human life and that it should be paid by the individual whose life is at stake. Neither belief is tolerable in a society in which income is inequitably distributed.

THE COMMITTEE SELECTION PROCESS

The Seattle Selection Committee is a model of the committee process. Ethics Committees set up in some hospitals to decide whether or not certain handicapped newborn infants should be given medical care may represent another. These committees have developed because it was seen as unworkable or unwise to explicitly set forth the criteria on which selection decisions would be made. But only two results are possible, as Professor Guido Calabrezi has pointed out: either a pattern of decision-making will develop or it will not. If a pattern does develop (e.g., in Seattle, the imposition of middle-class values), then it can be articulated and those decision "rules" codified and used directly, without resort to the committee. If a pattern does not develop, the committee is vulnerable to the charge that it is acting arbitrarily, or dishonestly, and therefore cannot be permitted to continue to make such important decisions.

In the end, public designation of a committee to make selection decisions on vague criteria will fail because it too closely involves the state and all members of society in explicitly preferring specific individuals over others, and in devaluing the interests those others have in living. It thus directly undermines, as surely as the market system does, society's view of equality and the value of human life.

THE LOTTERY APPROACH

The lottery approach is the ultimate equalizer which puts equality ahead of every other value. This makes it extremely attractive, since all comers have an equal chance at selection regardless of race, color, creed, or financial status. On the other hand, it offends our notions of efficiency and fairness since it makes *no* distinctions among such things as the strength of the desires of the candidates, their potential survival, and their quality of life. In this sense it is a mindless method of trying to solve society's dilemma which is caused by its unwillingness or inability to spend enough resources to make a lottery unnecessary. By making this macro spending decision evident to all, it also undermines society's view of the pricelessness of human life. A first-come, first-served system is a type of natural lottery since referral to a transplant program is generally random in time. Nonetheless, higher income groups have quicker access to referral networks and thus have an inherent advantage over the poor in a strict first-come, first-served system.

THE CUSTOMARY APPROACH

Society has traditionally attempted to avoid explicitly recognizing that we are making a choice not to save individual lives because it is too expensive to do so. As long as such decisions are not explicitly acknowledged, they can be tolerated by society. . . . The customary approach permits individual physicians to select their patients on the basis of medical criteria or clinical suitability. This, however, contains much hidden social worth criteria. For example, one criterion, common in the transplant literature, requires an individual to have sufficient family support for successful aftercare. This discriminates against individuals without families and those who have become alienated from their families. The criterion may be relevant, but it is hardly medical.

Similar observations can be made about medical criteria that include IQ, mental illness, criminal records, employment, indigency, alcoholism, drug addiction, or geographical location. Age is perhaps more difficult, since it may be impressionistically related to outcome. But it is not medically logical to assume that an individual who is 49 years old is necessarily a better medical candidate for a transplant than one who is 50 years old. Unless specific examination of the characteristics of older persons that make them less desirable candidates is undertaken, such a cut off is arbitrary, and thus devalues the lives of older citizens. The same can be said of blanket exclusions of alcoholics and drug addicts.

In short, the customary approach has one great advantage for society and one great disadvantage: it gives us the illusion that we do not have to make choices; but the cost is mass deception, and when this deception is uncovered, we must deal with it either by universal entitlement or by choosing another method of patient selection.

A COMBINATION OF APPROACHES

A socially acceptable approach must be fair, efficient, and reflective of important social values. The most important values at stake in organ transplantation are fairness itself, equity in the sense of equality, and the value of life. To promote efficiency, it is important that no one receive a transplant unless they want one and are likely to obtain significant benefit from it in the sense of years of life at a reasonable level of functioning.

Accordingly, it is appropriate for there to be an initial screening process that is based *exclusively* on medical criteria designed to measure the probability of a successful transplant, i.e., one in which the patient survives for at least a number of years and is rehabilitated. There is room in medical criteria for social worth judgments, but there is probably no way to avoid this completely. For example, it has been noted that "in many respects social and medical criteria are inextricably intertwined" and that therefore medical criteria might "exclude the poor and disadvantaged because health and socioeconomic status are highly interdependent." . . .

To prevent the gulf between the haves and have nots from widening, we must make every reasonable attempt to develop medical criteria that are objective and independent of social worth categories. One minimal way to approach this is to require that medical screening be reviewed and approved by an ethics committee with significant public representation, filed with a public agency, and made readily available to the public for comment. . . .

As this implies, after the medical screening is performed, there may be more acceptable candidates in the "pool" than there are organs or surgical teams to go around. Selection among waiting candidates will then be necessary. This situation occurs now in kidney transplantation, but since the organ matching is much more sophisticated than in hearts and livers (permitting much more precise matching of organ and recipient), and since dialysis permits individuals to wait almost indefinitely for an organ without risking death, the situations are not close enough to permit use of the same matching criteria. On the other hand, to the extent that organs are specifically tissue- and size-matched and fairly distributed to the best matched candidate, the organ distribution system itself will resemble a natural lottery.

When a pool of acceptable candidates is developed, a decision about who gets the next available, suitable organ must be made. We must choose between using a conscious, value-laden, social worth selection criterion (including a committee to make the actual choice), or some type of random device. In view of the unacceptability and arbitrariness of social worth criteria being applied, implicitly or explicitly, by committee, this method is neither viable nor proper. On the other hand, strict adherence to a lottery might create a situation where an individual who has only a one-in-four chance of living five years with a transplant (but who could survive another six months without one) would get an organ before an individual who could survive as long or longer, but who will die within days or hours if he or she is not immediately transplanted. Accordingly, the most reasonable approach seems to be to allocate organs on a first-come, first-served basis to members of the pool but permit individuals to "jump" the queue if the second level selection committee believes they are in immediate danger of death (but still have a reasonable prospect for long-term survival with a transplant) and the person who would otherwise get the organ can survive long enough to be reasonably assured that he or she will be able to get another organ.

The first-come, first-served method of basic selection (after a medical screen) seems the preferred method because it most closely approximates the randomness of a straight lottery without the obviousness of making equity the only promoted value. Some unfairness is introduced by the fact that the more wealthy and medically astute will likely get into the pool first, and thus be ahead in line, but this advantage should decrease sharply as public awareness of the system grows. The possibility of unfairness is also inherent in permitting individuals to jump the queue, but some flexibility needs to be retained in the system to permit it to respond to reasonable contingencies.

We will have to face the fact that should the resources devoted to organ transplantation be limited (as they are now and are likely to be in the future), at some point it is likely that significant numbers of individuals will die in the pool waiting for a transplant. Three things can be done to avoid this: 1) medical criteria can be made stricter, perhaps by adding a more rigorous notion of "quality" of life to longevity and prospects for rehabilitation; 2) resources devoted to transplantation and organ procurement can be increased; or 3) individuals can be persuaded not to attempt to join the pool.

Of these three options, only the third has the promise of both conserving resources and promoting autonomy. While most persons medically eligible for a transplant would probably want one, some would not — at least if they understood all that was involved, including the need for a lifetime commitment to daily immunosuppression medications, and periodic medical monitoring for rejection symptoms. Accordingly, it makes public policy sense to publicize the risks and side effects of transplantation, and to require careful explanations of the procedure be given to prospective patients *before* they undergo medical screening. It is likely that by the time patients come to the transplant center they have made up their minds and would do almost anything to get the transplant. Nonetheless, if there are patients who, when confronted with all the facts, would voluntarily elect not to proceed, we enhance both their own freedom and the efficiency and cost-effectiveness of the transplantation system by screening them out as early as possible. . . .

Note on the ESRD Act

The End Stage Renal Disease Act was passed with almost no debate as an amendment to H.R. 1, the Social Security Amendments of 1972, effectively extending kidney dialysis and transplant coverage under Medicare to more than 90 percent of the population (coverage included those over 65 as well as those under this age who were insured by social security) "medically determined to have chronic renal disease" and to require dialysis or transplant. In a dramatic move, in November, 1971, a New York resident testified and was dialyzed in a demonstration before the House Ways and Means Committee. The brief Senate debate centered on trading money for identified lives, and whether one particular disease should be singled out for special treatment. For a complete description of the legislative history, see Rettig, The Policy Debate on Patient Care Financing for Victims of End-Stage Renal Disease, 40 L. Contemp. Prob. 195 (1976).

The End Stage Renal Disease Act represents the so-called "disease-by-disease" approach to national health insurance. In retrospect, it is easy to see that we did not adopt this model, but still useful to try to understand why kidney disease was singled out for such special, unique federal consideration. Dialysis is life saving for people who need it, but this is true of many other treatments as well that we do not pay for. And our experience can usefully be compared to that of England under their national health program. The U.K. has only 30 patients per million population on dialysis (compared to ten times that number in the U.S.), and very few over the age of 55. Office of Technology Assessment, Life-Sustaining Technology and the Elderly 263 (1987). One difference is said to be that in England dialysis is not looked upon as a "legal right," whereas in the U.S. it is. It is said that the notion that "ESRD patients ought legally to be entitled to treatment is regarded in the U.K. by policymakers with a mixture of contempt and horror." Id.

Ethicist Arthur Caplan has argued, however, that we are focusing on the wrong lessons from ESRD and that it never was a good model for anything to do with national health insurance. Unlike almost everything else currently existing in medicine, Caplan notes, funding and development of dialysis occurred simultaneously, without planning and without knowing what the ultimate technology would look like or cost.

> The issue facing any national health insurance program is the stance it will adopt toward new and evolving medical therapies. The problem is that our knowledge of technological evolution is so poor that it is hard to classify or analyze the state of particular developments. Since need and demand are not the sole determinants of cost, our ignorance about the way in which various

> modes of medical therapy evolve is a major stumbling block for anticipating the ultimate cost of any national health insurance program. [Caplan, Kidneys, Ethics, and Politics: Policy Lessons of the ESRD Experience, 6 J. Health Polit. Policy Law 488, 499-500 (1981).]

By 1980, there were more than 50,000 individuals receiving dialysis under the ESRD program at a cost of approximately $1 billion. In 1987 the figures were 80,000 recipients at a cost of approximately $2 billion. Looked at another way, less than .2 percent of the Medicare population accounted for approximately 5 percent of total Medicare funds. The average age of individuals on dialysis has gone from about 40 to over 50. Transplantation is preferable in terms of quality of life and survival to dialysis, and last year more than 8000 kidney transplants were performed. Nonetheless, fewer than 15 percent of all individuals on dialysis are considered reasonable medical candidates for a transplant. See Kolata, Dialysis After Nearly a Decade, 208 Science 473 (1980); Blagg, The End-Stage Renal Disease Program: Here are Some of the Data, 257 J.A.M.A. 662 (1987); Luke, Renal Replacement Therapy, 308 N. Engl. J. Med. 1593 (1983); and Vollmer, Whal & Blagg, Survival with Dialysis and Transplantation in Patients with End-Stage Renal Disease, 308 N. Engl. J. Med. 1553 (1983).

2. REGULATION OF HEART TRANSPLANTS

After an unseemly flurry of 150 "me too" transplants at 60 medical centers around the world following Christiaan Barnard's initial heart transplant in South Africa in 1967, all but three centers ceased doing heart transplants because of the devastatingly poor results: University of Cape Town, the Medical College of Virginia, and Stanford. No public or private insurance payment was available for these procedures because they were experimental. But it was clear that someday they would be effective in treating at least some patients, so a major public policy question became how heart transplants should be introduced into the U.S. health care system. One possible model, of course, was to follow the kidney transplant model, but no politicians seriously advocated this. In 1980, the Board of Trustees at the Massachusetts General Hospital, took the position that no heart transplants be done at their institution "at the present time" because the results did not justify the extreme expense. Stanford, on the other hand, pressed forward with its research program, and sought public payment for heart transplant procedures on the basis that they were no longer experimental. See B. Jennett, High Technology Medicine 84-89 (1984). Medical writer Richard Knox picks up the story in 1980 when HHS announced its first attempt to influence the introduction of this new medical technology.

The reigning imperative of American medicine has been: *If it works, do it.* Or as many physicians might put it: *If it helps, how can it be withheld?* Up to now the government has taken a similar stance, asking only three questions about a new medical technology before deciding whether to pay for it out of Medicare and Medicaid funds: Is it safe? Is it effective? Does it have wide acceptance in the medical community?

No longer. Using heart transplantation as a starting point, the government has embarked on a new and utterly uncharted course. Patricia Roberts Harris, Secretary of the Department of Health and Human Services (HHS), announced on 12 June that HHS will require new technologies to pass muster on the basis of their "social consequences" before "financing their wide distribution," . . . this assessment will be a sort of environmental impact statement for medical innovation, encompassing such boundless issues as a new procedure's cost-effectiveness and cost-benefit ratios, its ethical implications, and its "long-term effects on society." Voluminously detailed regulations embodying the requirement and setting forth its rationale are being drafted now. It will be the first time in the 15-year history of Medicare the government has attempted to define what is meant by the statutory requirement that the program pay only for "reasonable and necessary" medical care — including such controversy-fraught issues as "necessary for whom?" and "reasonable under what circumstances?"

As she announced plans for developing the all-encompassing new reimbursement tests, Harris declared that heart transplantation — a technology that holds symbolic first place in any ranking of therapies for aggressiveness, intensity, and derring-do — will be "the prototype" for such an assessment. [Knox, Heart Transplants: To Pay or Not to Pay, 209 Science 570 (1980).]

U.S. General Accounting Office, Heart Transplants
8, 10 (1989)

Heart transplantation has become a recognized treatment for end-stage heart disease. During fiscal year 1988, 109 hospitals performed 1,529 heart transplants in the United States, a significant increase from the 172 transplants performed by 12 hospitals in 1983. However, as transplants have become an accepted treatment, health care providers, insurers, the government, and the public have raised concerns as to equitable access to transplantation, the cost and payment for heart transplants, and the diffusion of transplant technology. . . .

On December 6, 1967, a few days after the world's first human heart transplant, a medical team in Brooklyn, New York, performed the first heart transplant in the United States. The recipient, a 17-day-old baby, died after 6-1/2 hours. On January 6, 1968, the second heart transplant in the United States was performed in Stanford, California. The patient survived for 15 days. By December 1970, 167 heart transplants had been recorded by the

National Heart, Lung, and Blood Institute, of which 105 were performed in the United States.

In these early heart transplants, acute rejection and life-threatening infections were consistent problems; these resulted in high death rates. By 1971, most heart transplant teams discontinued transplants. As a result, only 13 heart transplants were performed that year in the United States, compared with 54 in 1968. Only Stanford University Hospital and the Medical College of Virginia remained active in heart transplantation.

The number of heart transplants did not significantly increase until the early 1980s, when cyclosporine, an immunosuppressive medication, was introduced. The drug helps fight the body's rejection of a transplanted organ, thereby improving the patient's chance of survival. A recent study indicated that about 73 percent of heart transplant recipients have survived at least 5 years.

With better survival rates, heart transplants increased significantly. From 1983 to 1986, the number of transplants almost doubled each year, increasing from 172 in 1983 to 1,368 in 1986. In 1987 the number (1,512) increased at a lesser rate. . . .

To address these issues, HCFA funded the National Heart Transplantation Study. On the basis of study recommendations that the procedure was efficacious, Medicare began reimbursing for heart transplants performed at designated hospitals in April 1987. This decision was made retroactive to October 1986.

The Congress passed the National Organ Transplant Act of 1984 (P.L. 98-507) to address the issues of organ donation and procurement. This act (1) directed the HHS Secretary to establish the Organ Procurement and Transplantation Network and the Task Force on Organ Transplantation to study and make recommendations to improve the field of transplantation; (2) prohibited the transfer for valuable consideration or purchase of donor organs by any person, if it affects interstate commerce; and (3) authorized grants to organ procurement organizations (OPOS) for establishment, initial operation, and expansion. OPOS coordinate organ procurement activities, including the recovery of donor organs, preserving and making arrangements to transport the organs, and providing education to encourage donations.

HHS awarded contracts to the United Network for Organ Sharing (UNOS) to operate the Transplantation Network and maintain a registry of organ transplants. For the registry, UNOS collects demographic data on all transplant recipients and follows their postoperative progress. In its 1986 report, the congressionally mandated Task Force on Organ Transplantation recommended that HCFA require hospitals, as a condition of Medicare participation, to establish policies to identify potential donors and request organ donation from the next of kin. Later that year, the Congress passed the Omnibus Budget Reconciliation Act of 1986, Public Law 99-509; among other things, the act required all hospitals participating in Medicare and Medicaid to establish written protocols for identifying potential organ donors and assuring families the option to donate or decline donation. The act also required hospitals performing organ transplants to be members of, and abide by the rules of, the Transplantation Network. UNOS developed policies governing membership criteria, allocation of organs, and standards of quality.

NOTE ON REGULATION OF HEART TRANSPLANTS

(1) The HHS study was announced in the Federal Register in January, 1981, and later awarded to the Battelle Human Affairs Research Centers in Seattle, Washington. The study, under the direction of Roger Evans, was made public in the summer of 1986. During this four and a half year period, there was an incredible growth in heart transplants, with almost 100 hospitals offering to perform this procedure. See, for instance, Evans, Anderson & Perry, The National Heart Transplantation Study: An Overview, 2 Heart Transplantation 85 (1982). The growth, coupled with the lack of action on the federal level while HHS officials said they were waiting for the Battelle Report, meant that individual states were forced to confront heart transplantation on their own.

(2) A number of states, most notably Ohio, Massachusetts, and New York, took strong regulatory steps to try to make sure heart transplantation was introduced in a reasonable manner. Using the determination of need (DON) mechanism, a public task force was established in Massachusetts to make recommendations on how transplantation technology should be introduced, who should have access to it, and who should pay for it. The task force's major recommendation centered on the need for a public social assessment of organ transplantation prior to making a financial commitment to it. The task force called for a three-year demonstration period of limited transplantation during which data would be collected on its clinical, social, economic, and ethical aspects. Thereafter a public body would determine the size and direction of "Phase II." During Phase I, hospitals performing transplants would do so within their existing budgets (the only allowable cost increases would be for the organ itself and new immunosuppression drugs). Hospitals would also agree to extensive and uniform data collection for evaluation. Special attention would be provided to consent procedures, including patient selection criteria and procedures. Patient selection could not take income or ability to pay into account, but should instead rely entirely on "clinical suitability" with organs going to those "who can benefit the most from them in terms of probability of surviving the procedure for a significant period of time with reasonable prospects for rehabilitation." If the pool of qualified candidates is larger than the number of organs available, patients should be given them on a first-come, first-served basis. Finally, if more than one hospital were granted a certificate of need, they should be required to work together, using uniform procedures for patient selection, in a "consortium"

model. Report of the Massachusetts Task Force on Organ Transplantation (Mass. Dept. Public Health, 1984). On New York's approach, see New York State Task Force on Life and the Law, Transplantation in New York State (1988). And see generally, Lindsey & McGlynn, State Coverage for Organ Transplantation: A Framework for Decision Making, 22 Health Serv. Res. 881 (1988).

(3) The Massachusetts approach has been criticized as over regulated and overly influential on the rest of the country. Havighurst & King, Liver Transplantation in Massachusetts: Public Policymaking as Morality Play, 19 Indiana L. Rev. 955 (1986). Advocates of the free market found two aspects of the Massachusetts Task Force Report inexplicable.

The first was the Task Force's insistence that if transplants could not be made available independent of ability to pay, they should not be performed at all:

> The OTTF appears content with a state policy that could deny a transplant to a dying person who had made explicit financial provision for it. The best explanation for this complacency in the face of a denial of lifesaving medical care may be simply that the OTTF members had lost the capacity to conceive of the purchase of health services as a private matter. If so, their attitude reveals a great deal about the political culture of Massachusetts and its approach to health care. [Id. at 976.]

Secondly, the notion that to protect against tradeoffs in the health care system, the burden of proof should be placed on hospitals to show that any decreases in services as a result of liver or heart transplantation were from "lower priority" services was seen as a regulatory shell game made necessary by past overregulation: "Such an allocation of the burden of proof would apparently require a hospital to prove its own past inefficiency and waste of public resources in order to qualify for the establishment of a transplant program; a well-run hospital doing only things highly beneficial to patients need not apply. Such paradoxes are common under regulation." Id. at 973. This assessment is inaccurate — it is the priority of the services terminated, not inefficiency in delivering them, that is at issue. Nonetheless, the real problem is that hospitals would contend that *no* services were curtailed to do transplants, making the recommendation irrelevant unless followed up by an independent audit of services. See generally Overcast & Evans, Technology Assessment, Public Policy and Transplantation: A Restrained Appraisal of the Massachusetts Task Force Approach, 13 Law, Med. & Health Care 106 (1985); Annas, The Dog and His Shadow: A Response to Overcast and Evans, 13 Law, Med. & Health Care 112 (1985); and the following articles in the February, 1985 issue of Law, Med. & Health Care, which is a symposium issue on the Task Force Report: Casscells, A Clinician's View of Massachusetts Task Force on Organ Transplantation; Pauly, Equity and Cost; Caplan, If There is a Will is There a Way?; Miller, Reflections on Organ Transplantation in the United Kingdom; and Jonsen, Organ Transplants and the Principle of Fairness. See also Organ Substitution Technology (D. Mathieu, ed. 1988); Human Organ Transplantation (Cowan et al. eds., 1987), and a review essay on this book and critical assessment of the Massachusetts Task Force's approach, Bovbjerg, Human Organ Transplantation, 9 J. Legal Med. 467 (1988).

(4) Other than the unique provisions of the Massachusetts Determination of Need law, the National Task Force on Organ Transplantation adopted much of the approach and language of the Massachusetts Task Force in its recommendations. The National Task Force concentrated primarily on developing mechanisms to make organ transplants available to all who could benefit from them in a way that was fair and independent of ability to pay. To avoid explicitly calling for the type of program set up for kidney transplants and dialysis, suggestions were made for limiting the number of centers doing heart and liver transplants (based on volume and survival rates). On the issue of organ supply, however, the National Task Force was much more forceful and detailed in its recommendations than the Massachusetts Task Force. It recommended making the retrieval of organs "routine" and allocating them in a uniform and fair manner that was consistent throughout the country. The "required request" approach and the use of uniform standards for donee identification were adopted by Congress in the Omnibus Budget Reconciliation Act of 1986, and took effect in October, 1987. The idea is for the approximately 120 organ procurement agencies in the United States to use the same standards and to move toward a single, national system for organ sharing that guarantees equitable access to organs. These recommendations are based, at least in part, on the National Task Force's view that, at least after they are donated, human organs are a "national resource" and should be treated as such. In the Task Force's words:

> 1. The Task Force recommends that each donated organ be considered a national resource to be used for the public good; the public must participate in the decisions of how this resource can be used to best serve the public interest. . . .
>
> 3. The Task Force recommends that selection of patients both for waiting lists and for allocation of organs be based on medical criteria that are publicly stated and fairly applied. . . .
>
> 4. The Task Force recommends that non-immigrant aliens comprise not more than 10 percent of the total number of kidney transplant recipients at each transplant center. . . .
>
> 5. The Task Force rejects the commercialization of organ transplantation. . . . [Report of the Task Force on Organ Transplantation, Organ Transplantation: Issues and Recommendations, DHHS, 9-10 (1986).]

How does treating organs as a "national resource" affect the way we think about them?

(5) Primarily on the basis of the Battelle Report, HHS finally promulgated regulations designed to insure coverage for heart transplants for those

eligible for Medicare on April 6, 1987 (52 Fed. Reg. 10935-51). Those eligible are individuals over the age of 65 (almost never suitable candidates for a heart transplant) and those who have been disabled for two years or more. There will probably be fewer than 100 transplant candidates a year, but since most Medicaid programs and many private insurers follow Medicare's lead regarding reimbursement for new procedures, the regulations are likely to be very influential.

The primary thrust of the regulations is to limit, for the first time in Medicare's history, Medicare payment for a procedure to designated medical centers. In order to qualify for Medicare payment, a facility must meet specific requirements, including the following:

Experience: The facility must have, since January 1, 1982, performed 12 or more heart transplants "in each of the two preceding 12 month periods, and 12 patients prior to that but since January 1, 1982."

Performance: The overall survival rate must at least equal Stanford's: "Initially the facility must demonstrate actual survival rates of 73 percent for one year and 65 percent for two years for patients who have had a heart transplant since January 1, 1982 at the facility."

Both experience and performance statistics must be for individual hospitals; consortia among hospitals are not eligible for Medicare center designation. The legal basis for using selected centers (rather than all centers) was found in linking the operative words "medically reasonable and necessary" with qualified facilities, that is, "heart transplants are medically reasonable and necessary when performed in facilities that meet certain criteria." Does this approach make sense for all "extreme and expensive" medical interventions? See generally Besharov & Silver, Rationing Access to Advanced Medical Techniques, 8 J. Legal Med. 507 (1987).

UNOS has decided to adopt the Medicare requirements for membership, and requires an established transplant program to meet minimum volume and survival rates. In 1988, 131 hospitals had heart transplant programs; 69 performed fewer than 12 transplants, and another 22 performed no heart transplants at all. GAO, Heart Transplants 14 (1989). And see generally Special Issue on Organ Transplantation 14 J. Health Polit. Policy Law 1-229 (1989 Blumstein and Sloan eds.), especially Rettig, The Politics of Organ Transplantation: A Parable of Our Time at 191-228.

3. FINANCING TRANSPLANTS AT THE STATE LEVEL

Montoya v. Johnston

654 F. Supp. 511 (W. D. Tex. 1987)

WALTER S. SMITH, JR., District Judge.

This action for injunctive relief came before the Court on February 18, 1987. . . .

The Plaintiffs, Janette Montoya and Jenny Blizzard, ages six months and six years respectively, both suffer from "end-stage" liver disease. As a result of the Plaintiffs' conditions, physicians have indicated that both children are in need of a liver transplant in order to survive. Presently, the cost of a liver transplant in Texas is approximately $200,000. Furthermore, those needing a transplant are not placed on an "active transplant list" unless a $100,000 prepayment is made or a private insuror or government benefits program guarantees payment for the transplant. Although both children are eligible for Medicaid, a problem has arisen in that the Texas Medicaid program will not pay more than $50,000 for the transplants. Effective July 1, 1986, the Texas Department of Human Services ("TDHS") placed a $50,000 cap on inpatient hospital expenses that Medicaid would pay for medical service for one person during a 12-month period. Plaintiffs have filed suit against the officials of the TDHS alleging that the $50,000 annual Medicaid cap functionally excludes liver transplants from Medicaid coverage and constitutes an arbitrary denial of services to otherwise eligible recipients. Specifically, the Plaintiffs base their claim on 42 U.S.C. §1983 and allege violations of rights guaranteed under the Medical Assistance Program (Medicaid). . . .

Applying the principles articulated in *Beal* [Beal v. Doe, 432 U.S. 438 (1977)] to this case, the issue becomes whether the Plaintiffs' liver transplants in this case constitute medically necessary treatment. If the Court finds that the transplants do constitute medically necessary treatment, it would be inconsistent with the objectives of the Act for Texas to refuse to fund the transplants. . . .

In this case, the Plaintiffs have submitted affidavits from the childrens' physicians which state that liver transplants are not considered experimental. As such, having reviewed the doctors' affidavits and having heard the argument of counsel, the Court finds that the liver transplants necessary to sustain the Plaintiffs' lives are not experimental.

Furthermore, the Court is of the opinion that the liver transplants in this instance are medically appropriate. The best indicator for determining the medical appropriateness of treatment rests with a patient's physician. *Rush,* 625 F.2d at 526. Dr. William Belknap, M.D., treating physician for Jenny Blizzard, states in his affidavit that "[h]er condition is critical. In my professional opinion, her chances of survival without a liver transplant are zero."

The Court will next address whether the Texas Medicaid program may prohibit treatment which has been found to be "medically necessary." The Court begins its analysis of this issue by noting that Medicaid regulations prohibit certain types of restrictions within state plans:

> The Medicaid agency may not arbitrarily deny or reduce the amount, duration or scope of a required service . . . to an otherwise eligible recipient solely because of the diagnosis, type of illness or condition. . . .

Texas voluntarily entered the federal Medicaid cooperative program and voluntarily recognized liver transplants as a covered service under Medicaid. Accordingly, Texas must comply with the federal standards which prohibit the arbitrary and/or unreasonable denial of services to otherwise eligible recipients. In this suit, the Court finds that the $50,000 Medicaid cap is arbitrary and unreasonable in that it functionally excludes the Plaintiffs' liver transplants from medicaid coverage. In support of its finding, the Court notes that Jenny Blizzard and Janette Montoya will not be put on an "active transplant list" unless a $100,000 down payment is made or a government benefits program guarantees payment for the transplants. If Medicaid were to guarantee payment, the final bill would be in excess of the $50,000 cap since liver transplants cost approximately $200,000. Therefore, if the Court did not allow the $50,000 limit to be exceeded in this case, the Plaintiffs would be ineligible to be put on the "active transplant list" and would be functionally denied Medicaid coverage although liver transplants are a covered item under the Texas Medicaid program and the Plaintiffs are eligible Medicaid recipients.

The Texas Department of Human Services opposes exceeding the $50,000 cap claiming that there are limited funds in the Medicaid budget and that funding these procedures diverts funds from less risky and more beneficial uses as far as total recipients are concerned. The Court, however, notes that in a recent fiscal year only 95 of the approximately one million Medicaid patients in Texas exceeded the sum of $50,000. Therefore, since only approximately .000095 percent of all Texas Medicaid claims previously exceeded the sum of $50,000 annually, it would appear that exceeding the limit in Plaintiffs' cases would only have an extremely minimal effect, if any, on the funds available for other recipients. As such, the Court is of the opinion that a greater benefit is achieved in permitting funding for the transplants than in refusing to exceed the $50,000 cap. Furthermore, the Court is also of the opinion that a temporary restraining order, and preliminary and permanent injunction should be immediately issued requiring the Defendants in their official capacities to take any and all necessary steps to effectuate liver transplants for Janette Montoya and Jenny Blizzard. . . .

It is so ordered.

Notes on State Funding of Transplants

(1) Litigants have been very successful in suing state Medicaid programs for coverage of "life saving" transplants. As the Fourth Circuit has said when balanced against a life, the Commonwealth's interest "was measured only in money and was inconsequential by comparison." Todd v. Sorrell, 841 F.2d 87 (1988). But isn't this *always* the case when a decision is made not to fund a life saving or life sustaining technology? Does this mean that all such technologies *must* be funded? Almost all of the two dozen cases on this subject have so decided. See Medicaid Transplant Litigation Proliferates, Clearinghouse Rev. 20-21 (May 1987); and Johnson, Vermont Case may Upset Transplant Policy, N.Y. Times, Jan. 15, 1989, at 34 (state court rules that Vermont Medicaid must pay for liver transplant of a 57-year-old although its rules excluded all persons over the age of 18). COBRA required that Medicaid programs seeking federal matching funds for transplants after January, 1987, promulgate regulations specifying criteria for patient selection and facility designation. As of 1988, about half the state Medicaid programs covered heart transplants and about two-thirds covered liver transplants for children. The Eighth Circuit has concluded that state Medicaid programs may exclude organ transplants from coverage. Ellis v. Patterson, 859 F.2d 52 (1988).

(2) There have been a series of so-called "media-abetted" transplants in which individuals are put on television to either raise money to pay for a transplant or to encourage people to donate an organ for their transplant. This is highly questionable behavior, since it inequitably puts a premium on individuals who do well on television and can command a sympathetic audience, and penalizes those who do not have access to the media. On the other hand, the generous response such individuals have generally encountered speaks well for the charity of our citizens. Nonetheless, focusing on the high cost of these procedures obscures issues of their validity, usefulness, proper role in medicine, and patient selection criteria. Rather than deal with such issues on a national level, President Reagan, for example, preferred the private charity route. He wrote a check for $1000 to the "Tabatha Foster Fund" in early 1988 to help defray the costs of her multiple organ transplant. USA Today, Jan. 26, 1988 at 3A. A more useful national policy would have been one that evaluated the chances for success of this almost unique five-organ transplant, and discouraged or prevented its being performed in the first place. Reagan also contributed $1000 to Ronnie DeSillers, who died while a search was in progress for a record-setting fourth liver to transplant, when any reasonable allocation policy would restrict the total number of organs an individual can obtain from the national pool to one or two (at least if others were waiting who had not previously received transplants).

(3) It is actually "easy" for a state to make the decision to fund transplants, since comparatively few are done on Medicaid patients in any event, and although individual cost is high, total cost to the system is relatively low.

Thus the decision of Oregon not to fund transplants for Medicaid and to substitute expanded coverage of basic medical services for low income children and pregnant women is somewhat surprising. It indicates that states are at least starting to talk about "rationing" and making hard choices. See Welch & Larson, The Oregon Decision to Curtail Funding for Organ Transplantation, 319 N. Engl. J. Med. 171 (1988). See R.H. Blank, Rationing Medicine (1988). Can we justify rationing medical care just for the poor? Is it fair for the poor to be organ donors but not recipients?

C. The Case of the Artificial Heart

The artificial heart is a case study within a case study. As we have seen, the total amount of money that can be spent on human organ transplants is limited by (among other things) the supply of human organs to transplant. Thus, as we approach 2000 human heart transplants a year, we near the limit of the total number of human hearts we will be able to obtain in the U.S. Artificial organs (like kidney dialysis), of course, have no such naturally imposed limitation. In fact, it has been reasonably estimated that 35,000 to 50,000 individuals a year could benefit from a fully implantable artificial heart. Even if the cost could be kept to an average of $100,000 each (a highly unlikely prospect), this would total $5 billion annually, almost the entire research budget of the National Institutes of Health. Universal coverage could, as it did in dialysis, eliminate fairness problems in patient selection, but the cost would be high, and the likely effect would be to implant the device in more and more marginal candidates, with less benefit to recipients, and at higher cost.

What lessons from the experience with human heart transplantation can we as a society apply to artificial hearts? Or is this technology so seductive that it will take on a "life of its own" that puts it beyond all regulatory control? The first artificial heart was implanted by Denton Cooley in 1969; it is also the only time to date that such an implant has led to a lawsuit. That suit provides a useful place to begin our discussion.

1. ISSUES IN HUMAN EXPERIMENTATION AND RESEARCH

J. Thorwald, The Patients

405-406 (1971)

RECOLLECTIONS OF A HOUSTON REPORTER:

Cooley came out to a conference, casual as always. Liotta followed. And then Cooley exploded his bombshell — he knew quite well that it was a big bomb. He declared that in the past several months Liotta and he had developed an artificial heart. Whereupon he distributed pictures of it. He added that they had tested it on animals and kept a calf alive on it for forty-four hours. (This sounded strange to me, for I knew Liotta only as an employee subordinate to DeBakey.) Cooley then told us that the whole operation had not been intended as a violent medical shock-troop enterprise to use the artificial heart. Rather, he had entered the operating room intending to perform a heart muscle repair on Haskell Karp. During the operation it had become evident that Karp's heart was so badly damaged that it could not be restarted. Only a transplant could have saved him. But, Cooley continued, we knew what the heart donor situation was. He didn't have any. And so in a desperate attempt to save Karp's life they had resorted to the artificial pump in order to keep him going until a donor could be found.

The pump was working amazingly well. Karp had awakened like a man with his own heart, and Cooley was hoping that the artificial heart would continue to function for many hours. Of course, no one could predict how long it would go on, and therefore there was now one urgent task: to find a heart donor for Karp. He begged us to do everything we could to publicize his appeal for a heart donor with Karp's blood group, O Rh-positive.

So that is how the story was published in the newspapers. And on Good Friday and Saturday morning we had the medical sensation of the year: the first human being with a pumping machine inside his chest instead of his own heart. Cooley was leading the pack again, and there was no question about it — we would do everything we could to find a heart donor for Haskell Karp. We were also handed pictures of Karp in his hospital bed.

Karp v. Cooley

349 F. Supp. 827 (S.D. Tex. 1972)

SINGLETON, District Judge.

After nine days of trial in the above-captioned malpractice suit based on diversity jurisdiction, the joint motion of defendants Cooley and Liotta for a directed verdict was granted. Fed. R. Civ. P.50(a). The granting of said directed verdict is based on the following facts and conclusions. . . .

Haskell Karp had a medical history revealing past coronary problems. He had scarlet fever at the age of fifteen. In 1959, at the age of thirty-seven, he had his first heart attack. . . . On Monday, March 3, 1969, Mrs. Karp telephoned Dr. Cooley long-distance to set a day when he might see Mr. Karp. Two days later, Wednesday, March 3, 1969, Haskell Karp, 47, accompanied by his wife, was admitted into St. Luke's Episcopal Hospital, Houston, Texas. Upon admission, Mr. Karp signed (as was later established at trial by a handwriting expert) an authorization for medical and/or surgical treatment (TR. EX.1) which reads:

> I hereby authorize the physician or physicians in charge of Haskell (None) Karp to administer any treatment; or to administer such anesthetics; and perform such operations as may be deemed necessary or advisable in the diagnosis and treatment of this patient.
> Date *3/5/69* Signed */s/ Haskell Karp*
> Witness */s/ Wauneta F. Tappan*

Mr. Karp remained as a patient in the hospital for several weeks being examined and treated by several doctors associated with the hospital. During this period of time, Dr. Cooley suggested that Mr. Karp's desire for a more active and productive life-style could best be achieved by a heart transplant. Mr. Karp rejected this suggestion and preferred to undergo ventriculoplasty surgery (wedge procedure) which Dr. Cooley had developed. . . . This surgery necessitates the excision of part of the diseased tissues in the left ventricle in order that the remaining tissue and heart muscle can function at its optimal level. . . .

As regards the informed consent issue, Dr. Cooley testified that he discussed various aspects of the surgery in question with Mr. Karp on at least three occasions: once the week before April 4, again at 10:30 P.M. on the night of April 2, and a brief chat on April 3. According to Dr. Cooley's testimony, of these the most significant was that of April 2. On that occasion, Dr. Cooley explained to Mr. Karp that the ventriculoplasty surgery could be performed on Friday, April 4, 1969. Dr. Cooley testified he explained the risks, grave dangers and backup procedures involved therein. Further, he explained to Mr. Karp that there was a "70-30" chance of his surviving the ventriculoplasty operation. Dr. Cooley explained, as was stated in the written consent form, that if death appeared imminent that his heart would be removed and a mechanical heart substitute (sometimes referred to as the Cooley-Liotta mechanical heart) inserted. Dr. Cooley testified that he told Mr. Karp the mechanical heart substitute would not be permanent but would be replaced as soon as possible by a human heart transplant, but that at that time there was no heart donor available, nor any prospect of one. Dr. Cooley also testified that he promised Mr. Karp he would do all that is humanly possible to insure his well-being and improve his patient's, that is, Mr. Karp's condition. At that time, Mr. Karp gave him his verbal consent to the surgery. . . .

Dr. Cooley testified that neither good medical standards nor his own personal practice would permit him to tell a patient that his condition was without hope and that he was going to die. . . .

Mr. Henry C. Reinhard, a St. Luke's Hospital administrator, testified that Thursday, April 3, 1969, he went to Mr. Karp's room where he found Mr. Karp alone and asked him if he had any questions regarding the surgical consent. . . . Mr. Reinhard witnessed, as Mrs. Karp had previously done, the following consent form:

> I, Haskell Karp, request and authorize Dr. Denton A. Cooley and such other surgeons as he may designate to perform upon me, in St. Luke's Episcopal Hospital of Houston, Texas, cardiac surgery for advanced cardiac decompensation and myocardial insufficiency as a result of numerous coronary occlusions. The risk of this surgery has been explained to me. In the event cardiac function cannot be restored by excision of destroyed heart muscle and plastic reconstruction of the ventricle and death seems imminent, I authorize Dr. Cooley and his staff to remove my diseased heart and insert a mechanical cardiac substitute. I understand that this mechanical device will not be permanent and ultimately will require replacement by a heart transplant. I realize that this device has been tested in the laboratory but has not been used to sustain a human being and that no assurance of success can be made. I expect the surgeons to exercise every effort to preserve my life through any of these means. No assurance has been made by anyone as to the results that may be obtained.
>
> I understand that the operating surgeon will be occupied solely with the surgery and that the administration of the anesthetic(s) is an independent function. I hereby request and authorize Dr. Arthur S. Keats, or others he may designate, to administer such anesthetics as he or they may deem advisable.
>
> I hereby consent to the photographing of the operation to be performed, including appropriate portions of my body, for medical, scientific, and educational purposes.
>
> WITNESSES: Signature /s/ Haskell Karp
>
> HASKELL KARP
>
> /s/ Mrs. Haskell Karp
>
> Mrs. Haskell Karp (wife)
>
> /s/ Henry C. Reinhard Jr.
>
> Henry C. Reinhard, Jr.

In the early afternoon of April 4, 1969, Mr. Karp was rolled into the hall of the surgical ward. . . .

Dr. Cooley performed the wedge procedure on Mr. Karp's left ventricle. This surgery revealed that Mr. Karp's heart had extensive scarring and damage. Approximately 35 percent of the left ventricle was removed. After the surgery had been completed in its normal and customary fashion, the heart began to fibrillate. This was corrected by electrically shocking the heart. However, according to the only medical testimony given on the subject, the strength of the heart's contractions were not sufficient to sustain life in Mr. Karp. Therefore, according to back-up procedures outlined in the written consent form, Dr. Cooley, assisted by Dr. Liotta, removed the heart and implanted the mechanical heart substitute.

Mr. Karp regained consciousness and lived on the mechanical heart substitute for approximately 64 hours. During this period of time Dr. Cooley and Mrs. Karp made public appeals through the news media for a human heart donor. On April 7, 1969, at 6:30 A.M., Mr. Karp underwent surgery to remove the mechanical heart and to replace it with a human heart. His urine output was low after the first surgery, and after the second, he became anuric despite all measures to reverse the condition. Mr. Karp died on April 8, 1969, at 3:15 P.M.

. . . Upon a review of all the evidence produced, it could not be concluded by a jury that Dr. Cooley had violated the medical standard in this community by the information he gave or did not give to Mr. Karp concerning his surgery. Therefore, the defendant Cooley fell within the guidelines set out in Wilson v. Scott, 412 S.W.2d 299, 301 (Tex. 1967). . . . Texas law would require that a jury be instructed that Mr. Karp is charged with reading the consent even if in fact he did not. . . . Under Texas law the jury would also have to have been instructed that Mrs. Karp's consent to the surgery was not required. Indeed, Mrs. Karp could not legally grant consent to surgery to be performed on her husband and, therefore, any information given to her or withheld from her could not have affected the informed consent of her husband. . . . Accordingly, as to any issue of informed consent, a verdict must be directed for Dr. Cooley.

Note on First-of-Their-Kind Organ Transplants

(1) This decision was affirmed on appeal, Karp v. Cooley, 493 F.2d 408 (5th Cir. 1974), on the basis that the lack of consent of Mrs. Karp to the procedure was of "no significance under Texas law"; that Mr. Karp was near death in any event, so there was no causal connection between any failure of informed consent and death; and finally that there was no evidence that Karp would not have consented had all the risks been disclosed. As to the charge of unlawful experimentation, the court concluded simply: "The record contains no evidence that Mr. Karp's treatment was other than therapeutic and we agree that in this context an action for experimentation must be measured by traditional malpractice evidentiary standards." Id at 423-424. Does this mean that "life saving" procedures are "therapeutic" (nonexperimental) by

definition? That informed consent is irrelevant because potentially life-saving procedures are inherently so "coercive"? See also Chapter 6(C)(2).

(2) The informed consent procedures in *Karp* can be compared to those used in other first-of-their-kind transplants. The first patient to survive the implantation of an artificial heart valve, Mary Richardson, for example, was not even told about the implant prior to the procedure on her. Instead she was led to believe that the operation was merely a repeat of a more routine one that had previously been performed. Her surgeon, Dwight Harkin, not only did not tell her about the procedure (even after the operation), but inaccurately denied that she could hear the clicking sound made by her artificial valve. She did not actually see the type of artificial valve that was used in the procedure until she left the hospital and was confronted by a group of newspaper photographers and a nurse who held the valve in her hands. J. Thorwald, The Patients 47-70 (1971).

Ruth Tucker, the first recipient of a human kidney, was informed about the nature of the procedure before the operation. But her surgeon, Richard Lawler, refused to tell her that the operation had been a failure. Instead, he made this information known at a medical meeting, and it was transmitted to Ms. Tucker by a reporter, who came to her house to get her reaction to the doctor's report on her case. She is quoted as having said, "What a way to get your death sentence — from a newspaper reporter." Id. at 93-101.

The first recipient of chimpanzee kidneys, Jefferson Davis, a black patient in a New Orleans charity hospital, indicated that he didn't think he had any choice but to accept. In his words, to his surgeon, Dr. Keith Reemtsma, "You told me it gonna be animal kidneys. Well, I ain't got no choice." His wife indicated even less knowledge, "They said, the doctors, that they'd do a transplant, but they never said it'd be a monkey, a chimp, you know. I didn't know that until they did it. When it came out in the papers . . . that's the first I knew about it." Id. at 205-206.

The recipient of the first heart transplant, Boyd Rush, had a similar experience. His sister signed the following consent form:

> I hereby give full permission for left leg amputation and heart surgery on Boyd Rush. I understand that any clots present will be removed from the heart to stop them from going to still more arteries of his body. I further understand that his heart is in extremely poor condition. If for any unanticipated reason the heart should fail completely during either operation and it should be impossible to start it, I agree to the insertion of a *suitable heart transplant* if such should be available at the time. I further understand that hundreds of heart transplants have been performed in laboratories throughout the world but that any heart transplant would represent the *initial transplant in man*. [Emphasis supplied.] [Id. at 242-250.]

At the time of the operation no human donor was available so surgeon James D. Hardy performed the heart transplant using a large chimpanzee as a donor. The words "suitable heart" were thought to be broad enough to justify this. The operation was unsuccessful, and the furor in the medical community that it evoked helped insure that the first human heart transplant would not take place in the United States.

The first recipient of a human heart was told about the proposed procedure, but not about the risks it entailed and the probability of success. Instead Dr. Christiaan Barnard purposely led Louis Washkansky to believe that the procedure had an 80 percent success probability, instead of telling him that the 80 percent referred only to his chances of coming out of the operation alive, not to getting better as a result of it. In Dr. Barnard's words:

> He had not asked for odds or any details. . . . He was ready to accept it because he was at the end of the line, waiting for a transfer. What else was there to say? Either you got it, or you folded up. . . . Since then many people have said it was very brave of Mr. Washkansky to accept a heart transplant. They really mean it would be brave for them to accept a heart transplant — not Washkansky. *For a dying man, it is not a difficult decision because he is at the end.* If a lion chases you to the bank of the river filled with crocodiles, you will leap into the water convinced you have a chance to swim to the other side. But you would never accept such odds if there were no lion. [Emphasis supplied.] [C. Barnard, One Life 311 (1969).]

Multiple organ transplants present a parallel example. The first cases involved transplantation of the stomach, small intestine, colon, pancreas, and liver. The longest-lived patient to date lived 193 days (a 3½-year-old female). Commenting on these procedures, transplant surgeon Francis Moore observed:

> The surgical enthusiasm of the authors is clear, desirable, even essential, and to be expected . . . One read that "the procedure is well-bourne." . . . Possibly I should have the unhappy duty of pointing out that there was a 50 percent immediate mortality here and that both surviving patients showed multiple anastomotic leaks, focal sepsis, and a number of other surgical complications; if this is tolerating the operative procedure very well, one wonders what it would look like if the procedures were not well tolerated. . . . There can be no question that this procedure should be withheld from other patients for the immediate future, until such time as these two research groups have perfected an animal model. . . .
>
> What about the "desperate remedies" phenomenon here? We read too often in the medical literature that some patient was so desperately ill that almost anything was welcomed by the patient, the family, and the physicians. This sort of hyperbolic "desperate remedies" pressure on physicians and patients (and the reading public) should be looked on with skepticism. There must be some likelihood of success before the desperate remedy becomes more than a desperate search for an opportunity to try a new procedure awaiting trial. . . . [Moore, The Desperate Case: CARE (Costs, Applicability, Research, Ethics), 261 J.A.M.A. 1483-1484 (1989).]

2. THE FIRST PERMANENT ARTIFICIAL HEART: THE CASE OF BARNEY CLARK

Special Consent for Artificial Heart Device Implantation and Related Procedures [Excerpts from the Clark Consent Form]

After Barney Clark 195-201 (M. Shaw ed. 1987)

It is the judgment of physicians and others who have evaluated my diagnostic tests that, although no specific life span can be estimated, it is probable that I will die much sooner than most others of my age and that while alive I will continue to be severely restricted due to my failing heart. I further understand that there are no further medical therapies that will arrest the course of this deterioration of my heart. Replacement of my natural heart is the only treatment. While prolongation of life beyond that expected for my condition by use of a mechanical heart has not been proven in humans, nevertheless I am willing to submit to its implantation on an experimental basis in order to determine if it will help people with my condition. . . .

With these considerations in mind, and with the further understanding and recognition of the additional matters contained in this document, I hereby authorize Dr. William C. DeVries, who is referred to hereafter in this special consent as "my physician," and such assistants and associates as he may designate, to implant a mechanical artificial heart in place of my diseased natural heart. . . .

2.1 I hereby request and authorize my physician to proceed with the implantation of an experimental total artificial heart device. I *recognize that the ventricles* (the larger two of the heart's four pumping chambers) *from my own natural heart will be removed* and a mechanical heart device will be placed within my chest in the space formerly occupied by my own natural heart, and that this mechanical device will require my body to be attached to an air-driving system by two plastic six-foot long air tubes to pump my blood through my mechanical heart and circulate it through my body. I am aware that my life style will be significantly different with an artificial heart. My activity will be *severely limited* because of the drive lines. The external drive systems will not necessarily require me to be bedridden but at best would allow me to move from room to room, and may allow brief periods of being outside and riding in a car or van if it is capable of carrying the external drive system. I may be able to carry on many life functions in a normal manner (e.g. toilet activity, eating, reading and desk work). It is possible, however, that I may have to remain bedridden due to pain, weakness or other problems.

2.2 I further understand that due to the positioning and nature of the artificial heart if it is installed, that in addition to the surgery necessary for the original installation, additional chest surgeries may be required in the event the device needs to be replaced or repaired which will be explained to me and will be done with a new consent form signed by me for each such procedure and that in all likelihood, general anesthesia with its attendant risks would be necessary in connection with such procedures.

2.3 I also understand that if the artificial heart device is installed that I can anticipate considerable postoperative pain and discomfort similar to or greater than that which would be experienced following the usual type of cardiovascular surgery, and that additional or prolonged discomfort and pain may result in the event of further surgery. I also understand that the use of the artificial heart may necessitate additional instrumentation and studies in order that adequate information may be obtained concerning its functioning, and such instrumentation and studies are expected to consist of or be similar to those involved in cardiac catheterization but may include other procedures, with attendant risks, discomfort and inconvenience. Each of these new procedures will have a consent form which must be signed before they are performed. . . .

16. I understand I am free at any time to withdraw my consent to participate in this experimental project, recognizing that the exercise of such an option after the artificial heart is in place may result in my death.

17. I have also reviewed with my physician and those with whom I live the considerable financial implications, including costs of surgery, hospitalization, continuing instrumentation, studies, monitoring and living with the artificial heart would impose upon me, and I am willing to accept these responsibilities. The University of Utah accepts no financial obligation for any harm or injury arising from this experiment. It is understood that none of the foregoing is intended to release my physicians, or the hospital, or their agents from liability for negligence. . . .

If-you-have-any-questions-regarding-this-experiment-you-may-contact Dr. William DeVries.

I have signed the foregoing Special Consent at least 24 hours previously, and have had the opportunity to further consider the risks of the procedure. After such additional consideration, it is still my desire to have my physician proceed with the implantation of an artificial heart, and I hereby confirm and ratify this Special consent.

D. Breo, Extraordinary Care

198-206 (1986)

The slow recuperation of Barney Clark, DDS, the man with a plastic heart, has been an ordeal not only for the 62-year-old dentist but also for his medical team at the U. of Utah Medical Center.

Physicians and patient alike, however, agree on the main point — the historic operation was worth it.

In a videotaped interview released to reporters March 2, 1983, Dr. Clark was asked by his surgeon, William C. DeVries, MD, "What would you advise the next potential recipient of an artificial heart?" The famous patient replied, "Well, I would tell them that it's worth it if the alternative is they either die or they have it done. . . . All in all, it has been a pleasure to be able to help people, and then, you people have learned something."

Despite Dr. Clark's optimistic approval, however, his physicians describe a roller-coastal clinical recovery that still is not resolved fully.

Ironically, Dr. Clark's artificial heart has performed almost flawlessly, with the single exception of a broken mitral valve that occurred last December. His main problems since the implant have been weak lungs, weak kidneys, and an organic brain syndrome that at one point left him virtually comatose. The key to his future recovery appears to be more his brain and mental intactness than his artificial heart and normal cardiac output.

The stakes are high because not only is Dr. Clark dependent upon the artificial heart, but also the artificial heart program is dependent upon Dr. Clark's recovery.

To Chase N. Peterson, MD, vice president for health sciences at the U. of Utah and the man who met the news media on behalf of the medical team, the returns are already in:

"Dr. Clark," he says, "has already proven a favorable risk-benefit ratio for the implantation of an artificial heart. His risk was exactly six minutes. That's what he had to lose, because if he had not received the artificial heart when he did, he would have been dead in six minutes. His benefit so far is 100 days (March 11, when Dr. Peterson was interviewed). So we risked six minutes of Dr. Clark's former life to give him at least 100 more days.

Claudia Berenson, MD, the psychiatrist who has seen Dr. Clark most days since the operation, notes, however, that "In some ways, Dr. Clark was sicker after the operation than before. The seizures and organic brain syndrome he suffered within a week of the heart's implantation put him out of mental commission for almost 10 weeks. He could not think clearly enough to participate in his own recovery. He was confused and disoriented and when his awareness would briefly return, he would often remark, 'My mind is shot. Maybe I would be better off dead.' Sometimes, he would just say, 'Maybe I'd be better off (dead).' Other times, he was more emphatic (about wanting to die). Dr. Clark's mental difficulties did not fully resolve until Feb. 15. I want to emphasize that his brain syndrome was *organic*, relating to his seizures, and was not a reaction to the surgery. Today, he is intact mentally."

Dr. DeVries, the surgeon who performed the implant, plans to send Dr. Clark home soon, but he cautions, "Until we do, our job is not over. The medical team sees no reason to celebrate until we are convinced that Dr. Clark can lead a useful life." . . .

"We don't want to exploit ourselves or turn this whole thing into a circus. We need guidance on how much news the press would like to know, deserves to know, and needs to know. They don't teach these things in medical school. What's right when you're dealing with the press? Do you talk only with the scientific publications? The local papers? Your friends? The people you have come to trust? Everybody? These are important questions because the way the press performs will affect all of us. . . .

One thing that has worked almost without fail is Dr. Clark's aluminum and plastic heart, the Jarvik-7 that has registered about 14 million beats since being implanted Dec. 2.

"We've learned that the artificial heart works in a human," Dr. Peterson says. "In fact, it works very well, even in the presence of other severe illnesses. And it has worked so far without causing either a clot or an infection, which are two of our biggest fears."

Dr. Berenson says that at first Dr. Clark was disturbed by the "pounding" of his artificial heart. "Until you get used to it," she adds, "it's a little like having a jackhammer inside you. You can put your hand on Dr. Clark's arm or leg and feel the vibration. He used to complain about the 'pounding,' but he eventually got used to it, just like a person with a consistent heart murmur or a person with a heart pacemaker adjusts to the sound. As long as the sound is consistent, it becomes reassuring."

The psychiatrist sticks by her earlier assessment that "we loaded the dice for success when we selected Dr. Clark. He's not only tough, he's highly motivated. During his 2½-minute videotaped interview Dr. Clark clearly was suffering from respiratory distress, as indicated by his pursed-lip breathing. Another reason for his discomfort, though, Dr. Berenson suggests, "is that Dr. Clark very much wants to succeed. He wants to put forth the best possible image, both for himself and the medical center, and he may have been trying a little too hard." . . .

"He's my patient, but he's also become a friend," Dr. DeVries says. "We've seen him through the implant, the air leaks, the seizures, the broken-valve operation, the nosebleed operation, and now, the pneumonia. And still, he's in fair condition. A remarkable man.

"It's not yet time to celebrate. But we're waiting. On Christmas Day, my children and Dr. Joyce's children came to Dr. Clark's room and sang Christmas carols. I could see the joy in his eyes. He was really happy.

"Now, if we can only get him out on the golf course."

[Dr. Clark died on March 23, 1983.]

Note on Experiments with the Artificial Heart

(1) Many people, including the Jarvik 7's designer, Robert Jarvik, had said that they did not believe the device should be used on a human being

until it was fully implantable and thus portable and possibly forgettable. Dr. DeVries disagreed:

> Many people have asked us the question as to — it's not fully implantable, why then would you do it? Why not wait ten years, when it's implantable, and then do it? But the key is informed consent. Why should I let people die, when I can give them a chance to live — if they're willing to accept the limitations of the external pumping system? [Quoted in Altman, The Ordeal of a Human Experiment, N.Y. Times, May 14, 1985, at C3.]

See generally Annas, Death and the Magic Machine: Informed Consent to the Artificial Heart, 9 W. N. Eng. L. Rev. 89 (1987). Is informed consent alone sufficient justification to implant an artificial heart in a dying adult? What about in a dying child?

(2) Like Cooley, did DeVries view this operation as "therapy"? Are playing a round of golf or going home therapeutic goals or experimental goals? What problems are raised by "life saving" transplants and implants that are objectively experimental but are treated as therapy by the physician and patient? See generally After Barney Clark (M. Shaw ed. 1984); and Berenson & Grosser, Total Artificial Heart Implantation, 41 Arch. Gen. Psychiatry 910 (1984).

(3) What role should public policy play in the development of technologies like the artificial heart? Is this type of technology "regulatable"? Could Medicare and Medicaid refuse to pay for artificial hearts if they "work"? How could they be distinguished from heart and liver transplants? See Status of the Artificial Heart Program: Hearings Before the Subcomm. on Investigations and Oversight of the House Comm. on Science and Technology, 99th Conf., 2nd Sess. (1986).

3. SOCIAL POLICY ASSESSMENTS OF THE ARTIFICIAL HEART

Artificial Heart Assessment Panel, National Heart and Lung Institute, The Totally Implantable Artificial Heart

5-11 (1973)

The idea of replacing the heart of a human being with a machine is not an easy one to grasp. Viewing it merely as one more life-saving medical advance clearly misses some of the point, for the human heart symbolizes fundamental aspects of the human condition, and its replacement poses problems beyond those usually found in the fields of medicine and medical ethics. Indeed, some of the problems extend well beyond our powers of prediction, conceptualization, and analysis, and may lie in the realm of symbolism and the irrational. . . . Some of the speculative questions concerning the artificial heart may be grouped under the general rubric of the problem of the "man-machine symbiosis" — that is, the extent to which technological processes should be imposed upon, or substituted for, the natural processes of human beings. The problem of "fabricating man" which surfaces in many contexts — recall the computer "Hal" in the film 2001: A Space Odyssey and Harold Benson in Michael Crichton's The Terminal Man — is a generic philosophical one with immense practical implications. . . . The heart has held pre-eminence in poetry and in common speech as the seat of bravery, love, joy, and generosity. Will its replacement by a mechanical pump and motor not merely place technology deep in man's bosom but place man more deeply in the bosom of technology? . . . The challenge of replacing the human heart with a machine may symbolize for the technologists a form of ultimate accomplishment, like going to the moon. The view of human destiny as involving pursuit of technological success for its own sake seems to be deeply fixed in human nature as it has evolved in the twentieth century. In the process of decision-making, government has only infrequently seemed sensitive to larger concerns, and has seemed consistently to prefer remedies premised on the development of new technology over the curbing of old technology or the alteration of institutions or conduct. Only recently has reexamination of the premises underlying the technological imperative begun to appear in the nation's intellectual life. . . . The artificial heart, if it becomes a reality, may also symbolize a kind of ultimate victory in the age-old battle of man against death. . . . Just as the preservation of life is increasingly regarded as an appropriate object of medicine and technology only if there are assurances about the quality of life preserved, a limit to the governmental or societal commitment to the preservation of the life of individual citizens may be recognized. . . . As the technological means of prolonging life become more sophisticated and more expensive, life may come to take on more of the nature of a "good" which, like consumer goods, is enjoyed by the patient and valued differently by different individuals, depending upon their age, health, psychological and economic well-being. . . . The specific role of government in relation to the preservation of human life is also provocatively raised by other circumstances. There is an interesting dichotomy in society's attitude towards the protection of what Thomas Schelling calls "statistical lives" and its attitude when specific, identifiable lives are at stake. We willingly accept a significant statistical risk of death as a price of many activities which the human community values highly. For example, bridge building, tunnel excavation, and use of the automobile are certain to result in fatal accidents. In these and many other circumstances, human lives are traded for desired societal benefits. On the other hand, when specific identifiable lives are in jeopardy, society seems bound to try to preserve these lives even at very high cost. This dichotomy suggests that society may be more interested in preserving the myth that life is sacred than in saving lives themselves. . . .

NOTES ON THE FUTURE

(1) The panel's reference to 2001 recalls Arthur C. Clarke's speculations on human evolution as expressed in his book and movie of that name. HAL's antagonist, David Bowman reviews theories that as scientific knowledge advances, man will devise methods to "get rid of the fragile, disease-and-accident-prone homes that nature had given them, and which doomed them to inevitable death. They would replace their natural bodies as they wore out — or perhaps even before that — by constructions of metal and plastic, and would thus achieve immortality. . . ." Id. at 173. Is this our future? Will replaceable organs give way to an entirely replaceable body; and will "brain transfers" to robot bodies eventually be replaced with brain impulse transfers to computer chips? What is the future of our species? What should it be? How does medical technology affect and transform our views of human nature itself?

The problem of death is clearly the centerpiece for all our discussions of the artificial heart. Novelist Don Delillo has argued persuasively in a fictional context that we have only three ways to deal with death in our culture: denial, religion, and technology. As to technology, he has his narrator, Murray, tell Jack:

> You could put your faith in technology. It got you here, it can get you out. This is the whole point of technology. It creates an appetite for immortality on the one hand. It threatens universal extinction on the other. . . . It's what we invented to conceal the terrible secret of our decaying bodies. But it's also life, it provides new organs for those that wear out. New devices, new techniques every day. Lasers, masers, ultrasound. Give yourself up to it Jack, believe in it. They'll insert you in a gleaming tube, irradiate your body with the basic stuff of the universe. Light, energy, dreams. God's own goodness. [D. Delillo, White Noise 285 (1986).]

To this thought, Jack replies simply, "I don't think I want to see any doctors for awhile, Murray, thanks." Id.

(2) The 1973 Panel Report was followed by a series of other panels, each convened to decide whether or not to proceed with funding the artificial heart. All have recommended continuation of the program. The program was begun in 1964, and original estimates called for the first totally implantable artificial heart to be in clinical use by 1970. In 1973, the development of a nuclear powered heart was terminated and emphasis put on developing an electrical engine to power the heart (rather than the pneumatically-driven approach exemplified by the Jarvik 7). In that year as well, focus was shifted to a left ventricular assist device designed to functionally augment the left ventricle — the main pumping chamber of the heart. Since 1980, work at NIH has been concentrated on making a tether-free ventricular assist system capable of functioning in humans for two years without mechanical failure.

A 1985 NIH Panel recommended that research on the implantable ventricular assist device should continue, and that "The fully implantable, long-term, total artificial heart should become a part of the targeted program and should be actively pursued." The Working Group on Mechanical Circulatory Support of the National Heart, Lung and Blood Institute. Artificial Heart and Assist Devices: Directions, Needs, Costs, Societal and Ethical Issues (1985).

In 1973, the Panel examining the artificial heart based its assessments on production of a heart that could perform flawlessly for ten years. In the report of the 1985 panel, the assessment was based on ability to perform for five years without replacement. How long should such an artificial heart be capable of performing before it is worth implanting in a human being? How should the quality of life of recipients be assessed? Should artificial hearts be part of any "adequate benefit package" under a program of national health insurance? Should they be available to Medicaid and Medicare recipients? On what basis should such decisions be made?

(3) On February 12, 1988, the Journal of the American Medical Association devoted an entire issue to the artificial heart. This event can properly be viewed as marking the end of an era for the use of the Jarvik-7 and comparable pneumatically driven devices as permanent implants, although William DeVries apparently still believes that in proper circumstances it might be justified to perform an additional experiment. His articles in the issue chronicle, among other things, the first four permanent implants. DeVries, The Permanent Artificial Heart: Four Case Reports, 259 J.A.M.A. 849 (1988). Although dead as a permanent device (at least until a more portable or permanently implantable device is developed), a number of centers continue to use the device as a "bridge to transplant," even though this has little ethical justification in an era of heart shortage for human transplants (at least if individuals on artificial hearts are given priority for the next human heart). In fact, so long as the total number of human heart transplants is limited by the availability of human hearts, temporary artificial hearts can save no net lives, but can only change the identity of those who receive human heart transplants (by preferring those on temporary devices). Even if those on temporary devices did as well as those who had not suffered this insult to their bodies (and there is little evidence for this), temporary artificial hearts would still be a uniquely wasteful technology: it would dramatically increase the cost of heart transplantation (approximately doubling it) without any net gain in lives saved, that is, it is an expensive and useless technology in today's world. See Relman, Artificial Hearts — Permanent and Temporary, 314 N. Engl. J. Med. 644 (1986).

(4) In May, 1988, the National Institutes of Health decided not to continue to fund the development of the artificial heart. The New York Times greeted this announcement with the following editorial on May 16, 1988 at A16, entitled The Dracula of Medical Technology:

> The federal project to create an implantable artificial heart is dead. During its 24-year life this Dracula of a program sucked $240 million out of the National Heart, Lung and Blood Institute. At long last, the institute has found the resolve to drive a stake through its voracious creation. "The human body just couldn't seem to tolerate it," explains Claude Lenfant, the director of the institute.
>
> Starting with Barney Clark in 1982, artificial hearts have been implanted in four courageous patients in the United States and one abroad. Recipients would become such supermen, the technology's enthusiasts had predicted, that they'd have to be barred from marathon races. But the crude machines, with their noisy pumps, simply wore out the human body and spirit. All patients suffered life of poor quality, often punctuated by strokes or seizures. . . . The lesson of the artificial heart is achingly familiar: In medicine, diligent prevention is always better than heroic cure. But try telling that to a government that would rather develop transplants than teach people not to smoke.

The obituary for the artificial heart was, however, premature. The heart indeed has a "life of its own." Senators Orrin Hatch and Edward Kennedy fought the decision, and threatened to enact unprecedented legislation that would prohibit the NIH from cutting existing programs by more than 10 percent. Both Utah and Massachusetts have economic ties to the artificial heart. NIH Director James B. Wyngaarden then insisted that the money for the artificial heart be restored. He explained, "A provision requiring us to meet all existing commitments before making new funding would be devastating . . . downward negotiations [in research budgets] are now common [and] the legislation would have been a disaster." Culliton, Politics of the Heart, 241 Science 283 (1988). Science correspondent Barbara J. Culliton summarized the "negotiations" between the Senate and NIH:

> The crucial question raised by this incident over the artificial heart is whether Congress is taking an increasingly heavy hand in what scientists regard as the micromanagement of NIH by outsiders. It is hard to know, but many NIH leaders are not happy that they were forced to make such an unambiguous and public retreat. And although there are legitimate arguments pro and con over the scientific merits of the heart institute's decision, the fact is that it retreated for political reasons. . . . The NIH's struggle for freedom from political interference has been going on for years. For its side, NIH has the power of scientific reasoning; Congress has plain power. It is not a level playing field. [Id.]

The New York Times, of course, was not happy with this turn of events, and wrote in another editorial, entitled ~~Senators~~ Doctors Kennedy and Hatch: "The artificial heart represents medical technology at its most mindless. Even if the machine could be made to work, it would bring limited benefit to a few at a vast cost, just the opposite of what medicine should achieve. . . . Senators Kennedy and Hatch have second-guessed Dr. Lenfant

[Director of the Heart, Lung and Blood Institute] in a way that lards their own pork barrels." N.Y. Times, July 15, 1988 at A30.

J. Swazey, R. Fox & J. Watkins: The Artificial Heart: A Case Study of Social and Ethical Issues Posed by Advanced Medical Technology

27-30 (1989)

"MADE IN THE U.S.A.": THE SOCIAL AND CULTURAL CONTEXT OF THE ARTIFICIAL HEART EXPERIMENT

Findings

If any one theme came to dominate our perspective on the artificial heart story, it is what we believe to be its quintessentially American character. This is not to say that the development and testing of an artificial heart could occur only in America, and indeed such work has been underway in several other countries. However, there is a very American cast to the scope and pace of work on total and partial artificial hearts in the United States since the 1950s, to the ways the devices and those involved with them, especially in the case of the Jarvik heart, have acted and have been perceived and portrayed, and to the types of ethical and social policy concerns that the total artificial heart, in particular, has evoked. As a case study, the artificial heart reemphasizes the importance of recognizing and understanding the social and cultural contexts of medical research and care.

Commentary

Focusing particularly on the development and clinical uses of the Jarvik 7 device, the American tapestry of the artificial heart story has many constituents, several of which we have noted in previous parts of the report. There is, for example, the mix of and tensions between academic and corporate medicine, government funded university-based research and development and R & D lodged in private for-profit sectors, the new alliances between universities and industry, and debate on many fronts about the roles of the media in reporting and shaping "news."

The types and combinations of bioethical, legal, and social policy concerns that have been raised about artificial hearts, particularly during the early clinical phases of their use as experimental permanent devices and as "rescue medicine" interventions for patients awaiting a heart transplant, also have particularly American aspects. This is seen in the content of ethical debate about the human experimentation dimensions of implants, which have focused on issues of autonomy and informed consent, the special vulnerability of the dying patient as research subject, risks and benefits, quality of life, and the moral and legal implications of "turning the key" to end the experiment. Temporary "emergency" use of the device as a bridge to transplant also has stirred ethical debate. Its components have included informed consent issues, the adequacy of IRB and FDA approvals and monitoring, use of risky experimental devices with little in the way of evaluative clinical research, and allocation of resource questions with respect to the imbalance between donor hearts and transplant candidates. And, for over 20 years, a series of studies for the NIH's artificial heart program have raised questions about what we will or should do, societally, if a safe and effective artificial heart is developed.

These "what if it works?" issues, sometimes framed with reference to the history of chronic dialysis, have centered on the individual and aggregate costs of artificial heart implants for perhaps thousands of persons a year, how access to the device should be determined, and by whom the costs should be borne. More immediately, with respect to the Jarvik heart as a permanent device, some felt that the greatest worry about its clinical use was that it might work. The prospect of even a few patients tethered for years to their pneumatic power consoles evoked deep concerns about the quality of life and rigorous care and monitoring demands that recipients and their families would experience.

The ways that the media reported and portrayed the artificial heart, including the scope, amount, and duration of coverage, provide a rich source of information about the attributes that this innovation, and the people and places connected with it, are seen to embody. When we analyzed a small sample of our press files, for example, we found the following "Americana" patterns in the ways that some of the lead figures (Drs. DeVries, Jarvik, Kolff, and Lansing [head of the Humana Heart Institute], and artificial heart recipients Barney Clark, William Schroeder, Jack Burcham, and Murray Haydon, and their families) were recurrently characterized. These depictions represent highly traditional American values, virtues, and images, which often have a mythic and legendary quality:

- Small town, community feeling.
- Traditional conceptions of male and female, husband and wife roles.
- Celebration of family (many children and grandchildren; idyllic marriage).
- Work ethic as a virtue.
- Individualism, in the form of self-reliance, self-confidence, inner strength, and the determined pursuit of a goal.
- An "admirable tension" between work ethic and individualism, on the one hand, and familial and community values, on the other (particularly in the case of the super-dedicated doctors).
- Youthful, robust, gifted, irrepressible, pioneering and inventive, restive, innovative spirits.

- Dedication to a larger-than-self, collective, "for humanity" purpose.
- Patriotism: community, military service, school, church, "civic religion."
- Emphasis on achievement, competition, and success (humble origins; hard work; desire to excel; young dreams; attainment of respect, wealth, occupational and professional reputation and recognition; community leadership; "winning").
- Grace, gallantry, and equanimity in the face of life, and death.

One of the most striking sociocultural differences we encountered between the artificial heart and other therapeutic innovations we have studied firsthand was the largely latent ways that Mormonism influenced and was reflected in the Jarvik heart's development and first clinical use. Mormonism has been an especially interesting facet of the artificial heart story because, as O'Dea has written, it is "in many respects the most American of religions."

> [Mormonism] has been "an America in miniature." The chief processes of American history have been repeated within the smaller context of the peculiar Mormon experience. . . . When we add to these historical processes the fact that in its values Mormonism offers an analogous spectacle of distinction and similarity, the strange combination of peculiarity and typicality stands out as the most striking Mormon characteristic.

When we discussed our initial impressions about the influence of Mormon religion and culture with members of the artificial heart team in Utah, they argued that it was American values, not the Mormon faith, which had helped shape the artificial heart story. But this, we observed, was precisely the point: Mormonism is a blend of at once religious and secular sociocultural values. Thus, the themes noted above in press stories about the artificial heart express congruent Mormon and American value patterns. So, too, does the eulogy delivered by Elder Neal Maxwell, a member of the Mormon Church's Council of Twelve, at Barney Clark's funeral. "True scientific research," Elder Maxwell observed, "is but the carefully ordered expression of that mortal drive and hunger and quest to know more of what God knows." Dr. Clark's days with an artificial heart, he said, were "a unique second salute to God in gratitude for the gift of mortal life. . . . To a world increasingly filled with hopelessness and despair, he stood quietly but resolutely for an entirely different view of life." As we encountered the artificial heart story in Utah, then, we found that "in largely implicit and unintended ways, Mormonism played a role in shaping the heart team's values, vocabulary, and imagery; its conception of itself; its leadership and organization; and its relationships — to colleagues, to its special patient Barney Clark and his family, to the IRB, to the press, and to the American public. Mormonism in this sense added certain special dimensions of meaning and mission to the implantation of the artificial heart in Barney Clark.

The history of American culture, to take another set of characteristics vividly exemplified by the artificial heart experiment, has been marked by strong "dream of progress" convictions and an often boundless optimism about the fruits of science and technology. In contrast to the more Gallicly somber beliefs of a René Dubos about our pursuit of the mirage of health, for example, there is the "we shall overcome" optimism expressed (at times) by a Lewis Thomas, strongly convinced that there is a finite list of human diseases which, with the development of a truly scientific medicine, we will be able to fully understand and effectively prevent or treat.

The visions of "spare parts" medicine and "bionic man" represented by the artificial heart belong to a much cruder, more mechanistic genre than Thomas' vision of the conquest of disease through the fruits of basic biomedical research. But, both visions are part of the same culturally patterned beliefs in our eventual ability to conquer illness and infirmity and perfect imperfect human bodies. This belief, to be sure, antedates American culture, and it is not untainted by strands of pessimism or fears, but it has been more pronounced and played out more fully here than in other societies.

The conviction that an artificial heart can, should, and will be perfected thus is a hypertrophied exemplar of American beliefs and values about the yield of science and technology. As enacted in the artificial heart story, these convictions are ridden with hubris — an arrogance about our ability to "slay the dragon" of nature that is not unique to the artificial heart. As Reiser has written, "The machines we build are highly directive. For we build into them not only mechanical or electronic powers but our own aspirations. . . . Machines . . . can become key agents of a view developed through the Scientific Revolution that nature should be mastered, not lived with. What greater act of domination could we as humans devise than to substitute a machine for the most conspicuous agent of life, the heart?"

K. Vonnegut, Jr., Fortitude, reprinted in Wampeters, Foma, & Granfalloons (opinions)

43-44 (1968)

Little: Oh, my God — oh, my God —

Frankenstein: Yeah. Those are her kidneys over there. That's her liver, of course. There you got her pancreas.

Little: Amazing. Dr. Frankenstein, after seeing this, I wonder if I've even been *practicing* medicine, if I've ever even *been* to medical school. *(Pointing)* That's her *heart*?

Frankenstein: That's a Westinghouse heart. They make a damn good heart, if you ever need one. They make a kidney I wouldn't touch with a ten-foot pole.

Little: That heart is probably worth more than the whole township where I practice.

Frankenstein: That pancreas is worth your whole state. *Vermont*?

Little: Vermont.

Frankenstein: What we paid for the pancreas — yeah, we could have bought Vermont for that. Nobody'd ever made a pancreas before, and we had to have one in ten days or lose the patient. So we told all the big organ manufacturers, "OK, you guys got to have a crash program for a pancreas. Put every man you got on the job. We don't care what it costs, as long as we get a pancreas by next Tuesday."

Little: And they succeeded.

Frankenstein: The patient's still alive, isn't she? Believe me, those are some expensive sweetbreads.

Little: But the patient could afford them.

Frankenstein: You don't live like this on Blue Cross.

PROBLEM ON ALLOCATING ARTIFICIAL HEARTS

Assume that after an adequate artificial heart is developed, Congress determines that it is not financially feasible to make this technology available to everyone, and it is politically impossible to outlaw it altogether. Accordingly, Congress enacts a statute that limits the total number of artificial hearts implanted in the U.S. to 10,000 annually, requires that all such implants be paid for by the federal government. Any physician not so certified who performs an implant shall have his or her license to practice medicine revoked. The statute further provides that patient eligibility shall be determined by statutory and medical criteria, and patients selected from a waiting list by lottery as follows:

(1) To be placed on the National Waiting List for Artificial Hearts, the candidate must meet the following criteria: He or she must

(a) be more than 15 years old but less than 70 years old;

(b) be capable of living at least 10 additional years if the implant procedure is successful; and

(c) not be a chronic alcoholic or a drug addict.

(2) Individuals certified as meeting the criteria in part (1) by a physician certified by the National Health Agency as a qualified thoracic surgeon shall have their names immediately placed on the National Waiting List for Artificial Hearts. Individuals will be selected from this list at random at the rate of 200 a week. Individuals will be notified of their selection by telegram which will indicate the date and place of the implant procedure. All transportation costs will be paid by the National Health Service. Individuals shall remain on the list

until they die or until such time as they fail to meet any of criteria set forth in part (1).

Would such a statute be constitutional? See Annas, Allocation of Artificial Hearts in 2002: Minerva v. National Health Agency, 3 Am. J. Law Med. 59 (1977). If you were on the staff of the Congressional Committee responsible for this legislation, what recommendations would you make to improve it?

C H A P T E R

X

Reproductive Health Services

A significant portion of health service today seeks to help people to bear children or to avoid pregnancy. Because of the human importance of reproduction, and the potential for conflict among the people and interests involved, state regulation of reproduction has been extensive and tremendously controversial. It impacts family policy, the status of women, religious concerns, the relation between church and state, and the allocation of power between state and federal governments and between courts and legislatures. Our purpose here is not to survey the whole range of complex issues that relate to human reproduction, but rather to focus on the role that the law has assigned to medicine in resolving multi-faceted social issues in relation to abortion, prenatal care, coercive requirements governing the actions of pregnant women, and sterilization.

One particular issue, surrogate motherhood, has generated a great deal of public controversy. Nonetheless it will not be addressed here because it does not raise questions of medical care or health policy. Mary Beth Whitehead and William Stern entered in to a contract, facilitated by a commercial agency, under which she agreed to be inseminated by him, to bear a child, and to relinquish her claims to it, in exchange for a fee. After the baby was born, she changed her mind. The trial court awarded permanent custody to Mr. Stern, permitted Ms. Stern to adopt Baby M., and permanently terminated all of Ms. Whitehead's parental rights. In the matter of Baby M., 217 N.J. Super. 313, 525 A.2d 1128 (1987). The New Jersey Supreme Court affirmed the award of custody to Mr. Stern, but reversed the trial court's termination of Ms. Whitehead's visitation rights and its order permitting Ms. Stern to adopt the baby. It remanded the case to a new trial judge for a determination of appropriate visitation rights for Ms. Whitehead. 109 N.J. 396, 537 A.2d 1227 (1988). For excellent and diverse analysis of the interests in conflict see: Colloquy, In re Baby M, 76 Georgetown L.J. 1717-1844 (1988); Forum on Surrogate Motherhood: Politics and Privacy, 16 L. Med. Health Care 1 (1988); M. Field, Surrogate Motherhood: The Legal and Human Issues (1988).

A. Legal Policy in Relation to Medical Care for Mothers and Babies

1. PATTERNS OF INFANT MORTALITY

Infant mortality data is widely regarded as an important gauge of both child health and the general health of a population. Throughout the world, the numbers of babies per thousand who died before their first birthday has declined significantly in the twentieth century. The infant mortality figures for the United States appear below in Table 10.1.

Since the 1940s, three main factors have contributed to this decline. Antibiotics allow treatment of infectious diseases that were once fatal to young children. Second, advances have been made in the capacity to save infants born prematurely or with serious handicaps. Finally, broader availability of contraception and abortion mean that fewer women at high risk are forced to bear children. Grossman & Jacobowitz, Variations in Infant Mortality Rates Among Counties of the United States: The Roles of Public Policies and Programs, 18 Demography 695 (1981).

Nonetheless, in 1985 the U.S. infant mortality rate placed it nineteenth in the world, behind such countries as Spain and Singapore. Even when only the white U.S. infant mortality rate is compared with overall rates in other nations, the U.S. ranked only fourteenth, behind Hong Kong and Japan. Moreover, when only the U.S. black infant mortality rate is considered, the nation ranked twenty-eighth, behind countries with fewer medical and economic resources, such as Cuba and Bulgaria. The U.S. rate was equal to that of Costa Rica.

Despite improvements in overall infant mortality statistics, sharp racial disparities remain. In 1985, black infants were nearly twice as likely as white

TABLE 10.1
Infant Mortality

1915–1919	95.7
1920–1924	76.7
1930–1934	60.4
1940	47.0
1950	29.2
1960	26.0
1970	20.0
1980	12.6
1980	12.6
1985	10.6

Vital Statistics of the United States, Mortality, Part A, 1, except 1985, which is Id., Part B, 87.

infants to die before their first birthday. Babies born to teen-age mothers were three times as likely to die before their first birthday as those born to women in their twenties. At every maternal age, black newborns are significantly more likely to die than white babies. Geronimus, The Effects of Race, Residence, and Prenatal Care on the Relationship of Maternal Age to Neonatal Mortality, 76 J. Am. Pub. Health Assn. 1416 (1986).

Medical and health experts divide discussion of infant mortality into two distinct phases: neonatal mortality (deaths within the first twenty-eight days of life) and postneonatal mortality (deaths among infants between one month and twelve months). Two-thirds of all infant deaths occur during the neonatal period. Post-neonatal death rate tends to be associated with the quality of an infant's home life, including housing, sanitation, food, access to health care, and other items associated with socioeconomic status. Postneonatal mortality has dropped for both white and black infants in recent years, with a more rapid decline for blacks.

In 1985 the United States experienced an *increase* in the proportion of babies born at low birthweight, the proportion born prematurely, and the proportion born to women who had received no prenatal care. Black neonatal mortality rates increased, and the overall decline in infant mortality rates stopped. See data collected in Children's Defense Fund, The Health of America's Children: Maternal and Child Health Data Book, 3-6 (1988). (Hereinafter, 1988 CDF Report.)

2. RELATIONS AMONG INFANT MORTALITY, LOW BIRTH WEIGHT AND ACCESS TO PRENATAL CARE

Low birthweight is the leading factor associated with neonatal mortality. A low birthweight baby is 40 times more likely to die during the neonatal period and 20 times more likely to die during the first year as a normal weight infant. Low birthweight can result from prematurity, poor fetal weight gain during a pregnancy of a given duration, or both. The higher infant mortality rates among children of black women and teenagers are largely explained by high proportions of low birthweight infants among these groups. Congenital problems, which account for 20 percent of infant deaths, are distributed equally along racial lines.

Low birthweight also increases a child's risk of illness and is associated with neurodevelopmental handicaps, lower-respiratory-tract infections, learning disorders, behavior problems, visual and hearing problems, autism, cerebral palsy, epilepsy, and complications of neonatal intensive care interventions.

Low birth weight, and the infant deaths and disabilities that result from it, is largely preventable. Some factors that increase risk should be addressed before a woman becomes pregnant: such as reproductive education to alert high risk women to the dangers of closely spaced pregnancies, programs to discourage unsought pregnancy among young teen-agers, and programs to help women end drug, alcohol, or nicotine dependence. Once a woman is pregnant, many studies document a close correlation between low birth weight and lack of early quality prenatal care. After extensive review of the data, the Institute of Medicine concludes, "the overwhelming weight of the evidence indicates that prenatal care reduces low birthweight and that the effect is greatest among high-risk women." Institute of Medicine, Division of Health Promotion and Disease Prevention, Preventing Low Birthweight at 8 (1985). (Hereinafter 1985 Institute of Medicine Rpt.) See also, American Academy of Pediatrics Task Force on Infant Mortality, Statement on Infant Mortality, 78 Pediatrics 1155 (1986).

Some studies have sought to determine whether the clear correlation between prenatal care and improved infant health is coincidental or causative. Do women who are motivated and able to obtain prenatal care also possess other characteristics that improve birth outcomes, wholly apart from the medical care they receive? For example, it seems plausible that a woman who quits smoking and drinks milk when she becomes pregnant is also more likely to obtain prenatal care. Does prenatal care itself contribute to improved infant health? Controlled studies suggest that prenatal care does reduce the risk of low birth weight and infant mortality, though it is less clear what specific services produce this favorable result. 1985 Institute of Medicine Rpt. at 8; Dott & Fort, The Effect of Availability and Utilization of Prenatal Care and Hospital Services on Infant Mortality Rates, 123 Am. J. Ob. Gyn. 854 (1975). See also National Health Law Program, The Cost-Effectiveness of Prenatal Care, 19 Clearinghouse Rev. 259 (1985). J. Murrah and M. Bernfield in The Differential Effect of Prenatal Care on the Incidence of Low Birth Weight Among Blacks and Whites in a Prepaid Health Care Plan, 319 N. Engl. J. Med. 1385 (1988), studied HMO patients, matched for age and education. Black mothers used prenatal care less and had a higher incidence of infants with low birth weights. The difference in the use of prenatal care, however, accounted for less than 15 percent of the difference in the incidence of low birth weight. Nonetheless, the authors conclude that even in a low risk population, prenatal care is highly cost beneficial, and more beneficial for blacks than for whites.

While most women obtain some prenatal care, an extensive nationwide study by the General Accounting Office found that about 63 percent of the women studied received inadequate prenatal care, which began late and did not meet generally recognized minimal standards. Insufficient prenatal care was a problem for women of all ages, of all races, and from all sizes of communities, U.S. GAO, Prenatal Care: Medicaid Recipients and Uninsured Women Obtain Insufficient Care 3 (1987). (Hereinafter, GAO Study.)

3. COMMON BARRIERS TO ACCESS TO PRENATAL AND CHILDBIRTH CARE

Three barriers to prenatal care predominate in virtually every demographic group of women — lack of money to pay for care, lack of transportation, and unawareness of pregnancy. GAO Study at 3.

a. Lack of Health Insurance

In 1984, 17 percent of all American women did not have insurance for prenatal or obstetrical care. Among women who are covered by private insurance policies, about 9 percent have policies that exclude coverage for maternity care. Alan Guttmacher Institute, Blessed Events and the Bottom Line: Financing Maternity Care in the U.S. 20 (1987). Historically, many insurance policies excluded coverage for routine prenatal care and normal deliveries. In the mid-1970s, the Supreme Court held that such discrimination against pregnant women was not a form of sex discrimination prohibited by the Constitution or by Title VII of the Civil Rights Act of 1964. Congress responded by enacting the Pregnancy Discrimination Act of 1978 prohibiting employers from discriminating on the basis of pregnancy. See Newport News Shipbuilding and Dry Dock Co. v. Equal Employment Opportunity Commission, 462 U.S. 669 (1983). However, the law has many exceptions. It only applies to employment-related group insurance policies. It only applies to the employee and spouse, and does not require coverage for other dependents, such as teenage daughters. Finally, the federal act does not protect people employed in firms with 15 or fewer employees.

b. Inadequate Insurance Coverage and lack of access to care

Many private insurance policies provide no coverage for routine outpatient care, including prenatal services. In most areas, Medicaid reimbursement for prenatal care and deliveries is significantly lower than charges or private insurance reimbursement, and is insufficient to motivate obstetricians to provide care.

The GAO Study documents that the wide disparities between Medicaid reimbursement and physician charges and private insurance rates cause most private physicians to refuse to provide prenatal or delivery services to poor women. Nonetheless, the GAO recommends against increasing reimbursement, because few women who obtained insufficient care cited difficulty in finding a doctor as the most important barrier to earlier or more frequent care. Fifty-two percent of the Medicaid recipients obtained their prenatal care from hospital clinics or local health department clinics. Id. at 55.

While in most communities women covered by private or public insurance can find a source of prenatal care, some cannot. The GAO documented that in Los Angeles women waited two to sixteen weeks, with an average wait of three to four weeks, to obtain a prenatal care appointment at the county hospital. In Charleston, West Virginia, in each of the past four years the city's only prenatal care clinic was closed for a period of months; GAO investigators could find no private physician in the Charleston area willing to care for women eligible for Medicaid. GAO Report at 41. In 1987, Medicaid recipients in California filed suit alleging that low reimbursement and bureaucratic red tape make it impossible to find practitioners to provide prenatal or dental services. Plaintiffs allege that in 12 California counties no obstetrician accepts Medicaid patients. Plaintiffs claim that this de facto denial of service violates federal law. Clark v. Kizer, No. S-87-1700 LKK JAM (E.D. Cal. 1987).

c. Lack of Transportation

Lack of transportation services to obtain prenatal care is a particular problem for women in rural areas and middle-size cities. GAO Report at 40. A study of the prenatal care received by a cross section of women in Detroit found that the women who received the most prenatal care had access to the most expensive forms of transportation, that is, car or taxi, while those who received the least relied on public transport. Poland, et al., Barriers to Receiving Adequate Prenatal Care, 157 Am J. Ob. Gyn. 297, 300 (1987). (Hereinafter, Detroit.)

d. Ambivalence about Pregnancy

The Detroit study found that, next to insurance coverage, the most significant predictor of adequate prenatal care was the initial attitude toward pregnancy and the month in which pregnancy was suspected. Id. The GAO Report reaches a similar conclusion. Not surprisingly, women who have ambivalent or negative attitudes towards pregnancy are less likely to obtain adequate prenatal care. Abortion clinics routinely ask that women who come seeking an abortion participate in a process of "option counseling" designed to assure that the woman has thought through her decision and is not unduly pressured by external forces. See Sec. B-1, infra. Prenatal care programs virtually never offer such a service. Are the two situations different? If they are similar, should abortion clinics abandon their practice of option counseling and simply assume that a woman who seeks service at an abortion clinic knows her own mind, or should prenatal care programs offer option counseling?

e. Drug Dependence

Many pregnant women, like Americans generally, are addicted to substances such as crack, heroin, cocaine, alcohol, cigarettes and coffee. All are known to increase the risks of low birthweight and other problems in pregnancy. Between 5 and 10 percent of pregnant women drink heavily. H. Rosett & L. Weiner, Alcohol and the Fetus 29 (1984). The Detroit study found that almost 31 percent of the women in the "poor care" group were addicted to illegal drugs, primarily heroin, compared with 7 percent of the women in the adequate care group. Id. at 300. A national study in 1988 found that 11 percent of pregnant women had used illegal drugs during pregnancy. Drug use in pregnancy "cuts across racial and socioeconomic lines and maternal age groups, especially since cocaine has become so popular." J. Brody, Widespread Abuse of Drugs by Pregnant Women is Found, N.Y. Times, Aug. 30, 1988, A1.

Since 1986, addiction to crack (a cocaine-based drug ingested through smoking) has risen dramatically, particularly among women and in poor communities, and now exceeds heroin addiction. People become addicted to crack more easily than to heroin, and it produces even more dramatic adverse medical and social consequences, including addicted newborns. See Kerr, Addiction's Hidden Toll: Poor Families in Turmoil, N. Y. Times, June 23, 1988, A1.

Few programs help pregnant women overcome dependence on nicotine, alcohol, or other drugs. A 1986 study by the U.S. Department of Health and Human Services found only six programs in the United States designed to treat women who have problems with substance addictions, including illegal drugs. Healthy Mothers, Healthy Babies: A Compendium of Program Ideas for Serving Low-Income Women, 63 (1986). See Schachter, Help is Hard to Find for Addict Mothers: Drug Use "Epidemic" Overwhelms Services, L. A. Times, Dec. 12, 1986, Pt.II at 1. Fetal growth retardation can be overcome by providing antismoking assistance to pregnant women. Sexton, A Clinical Trial of Change in Maternal Smoking and Its Effect on Birth Weight, 251 J.A.M.A. 911 (1984). For a comprehensive discussion of legal remedies to challenge discrimination against pregnant women by addiction treatment programs, see McNulty, Combatting Pregnancy Discrimination in Access to Substance Abuse Treatment for Low-Income Women, 23 Clearinghouse Rev. 21 (1989).

4. SPECIAL FUNDING PROGRAMS FOR PRENATAL CARE

a. The Cost-Benefits of Prenatal Care

There is a broad consensus that prenatal care for high risk women saves both lives and money. The Children's Defense Fund asserts, "During this decade, if current trends prevail, the nation will have spent at least $2.5 billion in first-year costs alone to care for the excess numbers of low-birthrate infants who need extensive medical care and whose tragic situations could have been averted had the nation moved more rapidly to reduce the incidence of low birthrate." 1988 CDF Report, supra at 33.

In 1978, the Surgeon General of the United States, citing both health and cost concerns, established the "1990 Infant Health Objectives for the Nation," setting targets for reduction in the incidence of low birthweight and infant mortality. The goal was to reduce the infant mortality rate to no more than nine deaths per 1000 live births, with no county and no racial or ethnic subgroup having an infant mortality rate in excess of twelve deaths per 1000 live births.

The Institute of Medicine estimates the cost savings that could be produced by expanded prenatal care. They urge that such services be targeted to high risk groups and explain,

> if the expanded use of prenatal care reduced the low birthweight rate in the target group from 11.5 percent to only 10.76 percent, the increased expenditures for prenatal services would be approximately equal to a single year of cost savings in direct medical care expenditures for the low birthweight infants born to the target population. If the rate were reduced to the 1990 goal set by the Surgeon General, every additional dollar spent for prenatal care within the target group would save $3.38 in the total cost of caring for low birthweight infants, because there would be fewer low birthweight infants requiring expensive medical care. [Institute of Medicine Report, supra at 17.]

In 1988, federal officials acknowledge that the goals will not be met by 1990. U.S. Falling Short on Its Infant Health Goals, N.Y. Times, July 10, 1988, A17.

The Congressional Office of Technology Assessment estimates that for every low-weight birth that is averted by earlier or more frequent prenatal care, the health care system saves between $14,000 and $30,000 in hospitalization costs associated with low birthweight in the first year of life. Healthy Children, Investing in the Future at 85 (1988).

b. Medicaid Expansions

Responding to this broad consensus, Congress has expanded Medicaid coverage for pregnant women and young children.

- The Deficit Reduction Act of 1984 (P.L. 98-369) and the Consolidated Omnibus Budget Reconciliation Act of 1986 (P.L. 99-272) expanded Medicaid to *require* state coverage of all pregnant women and children younger than five with family incomes and resources below their states'

Aid to Families with Dependent Children (AFDC) financial eligibility levels, regardless of whether they live in one- or two-parent families.

- The 1986 Act also *permits* states to extend Medicaid to pregnant women and children younger than five with family incomes above their states' AFDC financial eligibility levels but below the federal poverty level. In addition it *permits* states to claim federal reimbursement for services provided to presumptively eligible pregnant women, while their application for Medicaid is being processed.
- The Omnibus Budget Reconciliation Act of 1987 (P.L. 100-203) *permits* states to extend Medicaid coverage to all poor children younger than eight, and to extend Medicaid to infants and pregnant women with family incomes below 185 percent of the federal poverty level, that is, $17,926 a year for a family of three. It also *requires* state coverage through age six of the children added to Medicaid by the 1984 Act.
- The Medicare Catastrophic Health Insurance Amendments of 1988 *require* states to cover women and infants up to 75 percent of poverty effective in July 1989, and up to 100 percent of poverty, effective a year later.

As of 1988, 31 states had opted to provide Medicaid coverage to women and infants with incomes above normal state Medicaid eligibility levels, although coverage did not begin in some until 1989. Some states with large high-risk populations — such as Texas and Wisconsin — have not picked up the option for expanded Medicaid eligibility.

However, mounting evidence suggests that expanding Medicaid eligibility is often not sufficient, in itself, to make adequate prenatal and delivery services available to high risk women and children. Frequently the Medicaid application process is so slow and complex that it precludes entry into prenatal care in the first trimester of pregnancy. Expanding beneficiary eligibility does not produce corresponding increases in the providers willing to render care. Low reimbursement and bureaucratic red tape deter physician participation. Proposed Medicaid Infant Mortality Amendments of 1988 would have addressed these problems by allowing reimbursement for outreach activities, requiring states to implement "presumptive eligibility" programs for poor pregnant women, requiring states to reimburse providers at levels sufficient to assure that maternity care is reasonably available, and mandating uninterrupted coverage through the postpartum period. The bill was not adopted in 1988.

A comprehensive study by the Institute of Medicine, Academy of Science, expresses skepticism about this basic approach. "[I]n the long run, the best prospects for improving use of prenatal care — and reversing current declines — lie in reorganizing the nation's maternity care system. Although a new system may include some elements of the existing one, the Committee specifically recommends against the current practice of making incremental changes in programs already in place. Instead, it argues for fundamental reform. . . . A deeper commitment to family planning services and education should accompany improvements in the maternity care system." Prenatal Care: Reaching Mothers, Reaching Infants. at 12 (1988).

c. Federal Maternal and Child Health Block Grants

Since 1935, the federal Title V Maternal and Child Health program has offered states block grants to provide maternal and child health services. Title V is not an entitlement program guaranteeing eligible people a defined set of services. Rather, states have broad discretion to make grants directly to public and private providers of health and health-related services, including free or subsidized prenatal care, health education, outreach to pregnant women, and transportation. The law restricts provision of inpatient services to "high risk women," but does not define who they are. See Albino v. City of Chicago, 578 F. Supp. 1487 (N.D. Ill. 1983), holding that Cook County Hospital cannot be denied Title V funds for services provided to high risk women who are not eligible for Medicaid. Relative to Medicaid, Title V is a very small program. In 1986, $388 million federal dollars were allocated to states under Title V, for maternal and child health services, as opposed to over three billion in Medicaid expenditures for poor children.

Nonetheless, the maternity and infant care projects (MIC) funded under Title V are widely recognized for the quality and comprehensive services they offer and the positive impact they have had in reducing infant mortality. See, for instance, Wallace, Status of Infant and Perinatal Morbidity and Mortality: A Review of the Literature, 93 Pub. Health. Rep. 386 (1978), and GAO Report at 65. Funding for Title V programs has been sharply limited through the 1980s. See Rosenbaum, The Maternal and Child Health Block Grant Act of 1981: Teaching an Old Program New Tricks, 17 Clearinghouse Rev. 400 (1983). G. Loos et al., Probable Future Funding Priorities in Maternal and Child Health: A Modified Delphi National Survey, 9 J. Health Polit. Policy and Law 683 (1985).

d. State Programs

Several states, responding to the cost-benefit considerations presented above and to the tragedy of preventable infant death and disability, have adopted special programs to provide prenatal and maternity care. The Appendix to the GAO Report describes special programs in several states, most funded with Title V and state funds. For example, Georgia's Hospital Care for Pregnant Women Act requires that each county assume responsibility for financing the costs of childbirth for indigent women. Terrell County v. Albany Dougherty Hospital Authority, 256 Ga. 627, 352 S.E.2d 378 (1987), held that the act is not unconstitutionally vague and requires a county to pay for services provided to a woman at the public hospital in another county. See generally Leu, Legislative Research Bureau Report: A Proposal to Strengthen State Measures for the Reduction of Infant Mortality, 23 Harv. J. on Legis. 559 (1986).

e. Employer Initiatives

Employers, concerned about rising health care costs, have also initiated programs encouraging prenatal services. For example, the Sunbeam Corporation, which administers a self-insured program, found that in 1984 four cases of premature low weight babies accounted for half of the costs of its employee health insurance program. Many of the pregnant women covered by their program in Coushatta, Louisiana and Holly Springs, Mississippi, did not have physicians. (Holly Springs is the community where Campbell v. Mincy arose. See Chap 1.) When the company instituted its own prenatal care program in 1986, average costs per maternity dropped from $27,242 to $3000. See Freudenheim, In Pursuit of the Punctual Baby, N. Y. Times, Dec. 28, 1988, D1. Participation in the program is mandatory for pregnant Sunbeam employees. Is that troubling? Is it legal?

5. CONCEPTS OF QUALITY PRENATAL AND CHILDBIRTH CARE AND THE ROLE OF THE LAW

Hemminki, Content of Prenatal Care in the United States: A Historic Perspective

26 Med. Care 199 (1988)

[Dr. Elina Hemminki, Visiting Scientist in Biometry of the National Institute of Child Health and Human Development of the National Institutes of Health, evaluated the content of prenatal care in the U.S. through questionnaires to physicians and patients, review of professional standards and literature, and commercial advertising in obstetric journals and other occasional surveys.]

Several functions have been ascribed to prenatal care: its purpose is to provide information, health education, and support to pregnant women; to find the women with problems; to prepare mothers and fathers for delivery and child care; and in some countries and places, to provide financial and social benefits. The aspect that is emphasized varies among countries and facilities. . . .

Since 1959, the American College of Obstetricians and Gynecologists (ACOG) has put out a series of professional standards, including recommendations for prenatal care. . . .

Frequent visits were recommended: a visit every 4 weeks until 28 weeks, then every 2 weeks . . . until 36 weeks, and then weekly. Identification of problems in the first visit has emphasized laboratory and other examination. . . . Advice on how to question general health, pregnancy, family, social, and nutritional histories were not emphasized until the 1982 standards. The laboratory examinations suggested were listed in detail. Checklists to identify risk pregnancy concentrated on clinical problems. . . . Blood pressure, weight measurements, and urinalysis were recommended at every visit. . . . In the 1959 and 1965 standards, the chest x-ray was recommended as part of a routine examination in the first visit. X-ray pelvimetry was recommended at term if a narrow pelvis was suspected. . . .

Recommendations for action if problems were found were limited. [O]nly in the 1977 standards were referrals explicitly mentioned.

The 1959 and 1965 standards were brief in regard to health education. They point out areas that should be discussed with the woman, but did not advise what to say. Only the care of breasts was described briefly, and in the 1965 revisions, explicit advice on the danger of medications was given. . . . Starting with the 1974 standards, explicit advice on diet, weight gain, and caloric intake were given. Weight reduction was advised against during pregnancy. . . . Childbirth education classes were recommended in all standards more or less enthusiastically. . . . Other aspects of health education, such as exercise, rest, emotional problems, hygiene, sex, medication, smoking, alcohol and drug abuse were listed without specific management advice. . . .

The 1977 standards discussed non-medical problems in more depth than the others. Areas such as financial problems, unwanted pregnancies, family problems, attitude toward pregnancy, and teenage pregnancy were reviewed. This is the only report in which any advice was given regarding the monetary costs of pregnancy; it recommended discrete referrals to other programs or practitioners. However, examples of potential special-assistance programs were not given. . . .

Advice on prenatal care in *Williams Obstetrics,* an extensively used textbook on obstetrics, was similar to that of the ACOG recommendations. (Four editions: 1951, 1961, 1971 and 1980 were studied.) [I]n the 1951 and 1961 editions recommendations for restricting weight gain were even stricter than in the ACOG standards. The highest recommended gain was 20-25 pounds . . . and 18 pounds . . . was suggested. The weight limit was supposed to be strictly enforced. The two later editions, although still considering 20-25 pounds to be a favorable range, were more concerned about poor weight gain than about excess eating.

Expert advice and practice did not totally conform with each other. . . . Blood pressure was measured less frequently than recommended in the

ACOG standards. Laboratory tests were made in 35-58 percent of the visits. . . . Multivitamins were commonly used, even though both ACOG standards and *Williams Obstetrics* had clear reservations about their use. Diuretics were used long after the expert advice had condemned them. The expert advice had strict limits for weight gain, but some physicians had even stricter limits. The 1982 ACOG standards did not recommend salt restriction for normal pregnancies, but in practice it was commonly used.

The data available on the content of prenatal care . . . suggest that screening has received the most emphasis . . . [particularly of] biologic . . . indicators such as laboratory values and physical measurements. Expert recommendations have offered little guidance for providing health education/counseling and social support. . . .

Comparison of the expert advice and the results from surveys on practice, showed that they do not always coincide. But apparently expert advice can be used to describe general attitudes common to many practitioners providing prenatal care. Some practitioners have their own habits, which probably change slower than those of the experts. [N]onconformity of the practitioners is not necessarily bad, because expert opinions have often been wrong. . . . For example, the 1965 ACOG recommendations advised chest x-ray to all women, but only a small proportion of women had it.

The general assumption has been that prenatal care is beneficial and special attempts have been made to get all women to receive it. . . . This assumption of benefits has been so widespread that usually prenatal care programs have been introduced without evaluation of effectiveness. . . .

Quantity and type of food have been central in health education. Experts recommended strict weight-gain restrictions and apparently many practitioners did their best to prevent women from eating. Appetite suppressants were advertised, and apparently they also were used. The fact that the 1974 ACOG standards explicitly advised against weight reduction during pregnancy, suggests that such practice had also occurred. Present United States expert opinions are ambivalent on limiting weight gain. [I]n 1980 many women were given upper limits for weight gain, and often they were lower than that recommended as average. . . .

Contact with health-care system and physicians increase the risk of drug use, and . . . women who made many prenatal visits had used more drugs than women who made fewer visits. . . .

Omissions are more difficult to document, but very likely they have also occurred. The mean time spent with the physician in prenatal visits was 11 minutes. . . . If support given to pregnant women is an important element in prenatal care, its scarcity may be a drawback in American prenatal care. It may be important for the woman to believe that she is taken care of, esteemed, and helped. Time, understanding, social, and financial help are ways to convey the importance of her pregnancy to the woman herself. . . .

6. PATTERNS OF MATERNITY CARE: HISTORIC DEVELOPMENT AND FUTURE OPTIONS

a. The Medicalization of Childbirth

In the first half of the twentieth century the proportion of American babies born in the hospital increased from 10 percent to 90 percent. Many factors explain this dramatic change. Prior to the twentieth century, women gave birth in a woman-centered environment, attended by a midwife, family, and neighbors. If a male physician entered the lying-in chamber, he had to negotiate a female support group who acted as the woman's advocate. At the same time, childbirth was dangerous, painful, and frightening. A woman describes her third birth in 1885, saying, "Between oceans of pain there stretched continents of fear; fear of death and dread of suffering beyond bearing." Quoted in J. W. Leavitt, Brought to Bed: Childbearing in America, 1750-1950 33 (1986). This home and women-centered pattern of childbirth declined as more women found themselves living far from their kin. Agonizing births in unrelenting succession led women to seek out male practitioners whose medical armamentarium promised some degree of relief and safety from birth's chronic threats. At the same time, the declining power of religious ideas about the meaning of pain, suffering, and death transformed women's expectations. A new breed of women, born around the turn of the century, expected safety and certainty in their birth experiences. Birth was removed from the bare hands of women and an omnipotent God, and picked up in the surgical gloves of scientific medicine. See also M. Edwards & M. Waldorf, Reclaiming Childbirth: History and Heroines of American Childbirth Reform 153 (1984); P. Eakins, The American Way of Birth (1986).

The medical profession also encouraged changes in maternity care. In 1920, Dr. Joseph B. DeLee published an influential article stating that routine care for normal childbirth required that the woman be sedated through labor, the baby removed from the unconscious mother by forceps, an incision (an episiotomy) be made to facilitate use of the forceps, and the placenta be removed by injecting a drug (ergot). The Prophylactic Forceps Operation, 1 Am. J. Obstet. Gynecol. 32 (1920). Because the anesthetized woman might thrash about and injure herself, her arms and legs had to be restrained. Dr. DeLee compared labor to crushing a baby's head in a door and driving a pitch fork up a woman's body. Using these analogies, he concluded that labor itself was abnormal. "In both cases, the cause of the damage, the fall on the pitchfork and the crushing of the door, is pathogenic, that is, disease-producing, and anything pathogenic is pathologic or abnormal." Id. at 34.

The growing obstetrical specialty found this analysis persuasive. The birth process prescribed by Dr. DeLee requires both hospitalization and physician care. No doubt most obstetricians sincerely believed that the birthing process prescribed best met the needs of both women and babies. Surgical intervention saved some women and babies who would have suffered death or injury. On the other hand, in retrospect, it is plain that the "routine" suggested for normal cases made labor far more difficult for both mother and child and caused unnecessary pain and injury to many.

In the 1920s, the obstetricians enlisted the power of the state to prohibit midwifery or strictly limit the midwife's authority. See Brack, Displaced: The Midwife by the Male Physician, 1 J. Women and Health 18 (1976). The obstetrician's vision of optimal patient care coincided with professional self-interest. Until the 1930s, midwives and obstetricians were in direct economic competition for both prenatal and birthing services. But perhaps more important than immediate economic concerns, obstetricians in hospital-based teaching programs needed a broad population of patients to assure a minimal number of "interesting," that is, acute cases for training sophisticated specialists. Professional prestige of a training program rested largely on its accomplishment in treating the acute and unusual. The virtual disappearance of the nurse midwife was not a necessary consequence of the rise in obstetrical skill and professionalization. Europe experienced similar changes in birth practices in the early twentieth century. But there programs for the education and registration of midwives were instituted, generally under the control and supervision of physicians. In England in 1913, three physicians, all members of a medical society, refused to respond to a midwife's call for assistance in an emergency, because of the society's "ethical" requirement that no member would attend such cases without immediate payment of a higher than usual fee. The midwife had previously sent each doctor a letter informing him that the mother was insured and payment would be forthcoming. The mother died. English law responded by prohibiting a physician from denying backup support in such circumstances. J. Donnison, Midwives and Medical Men 185 (1977).

b. The Sheppard-Towner Act

This legislation, adopted by Congress in 1921, was the first federally funded health care program in the United States. It provided states matching funds to establish prenatal and child health centers. In these centers, women trained in nutrition, sanitation, and the care of children provided support and education to expectant mothers, under the supervision of public health nurses, midwives, and a few physicians, most of whom were women. Earlier, Progressive women and feminists had established local programs, on which the federal initiative was modeled, and persuaded Congress to adopt the Act. One leading feminist, Florence Kelley, said, "Of all the activities in which I have shared during more than forty years of striving, none is, I am convinced, of such fundamental importance as the Sheppard-Towner Act." S. Rothman, Woman's Proper Place at 136-152 (1978).

The Sheppard-Towner Act assumed that prenatal and child health services should be provided by trained lay women. The program sought to make such care a universal, public service, like public education. The Act required community sponsors to recruit local doctors to provide advice and backup services. It prohibited sponsored programs from providing treatment to women or children who were ill, but rather required that they be referred to private physicians or other agencies. For several years, in many communities the program enjoyed enthusiastic and influential support and achieved some success.

Nonetheless, "[b]y 1929, the medical profession had mounted a highly effective campaign that eliminated the program and made obsolete its assumptions about the proper methods of delivering health care. The defeat of Sheppard-Towner marked the end of female expertise in the field of health care and, at the same time, shifted the provision of preventive health services from the public to the private sector. Women trained in hygiene working in state-supported clinics gave way to physicians engaged in private practice." Id. at 136-152.

In 1921, the AMA had attempted, without success, to prevent enactment of Sheppard-Towner. After the Act was adopted, the AMA increasingly encouraged its general practitioner membership to offer preventative care. Through the 1920s, doctors shifted their practices from the sickrooms of patients' homes to the office, instituting systems of advance appointments and routine examinations of the healthy. Local medical societies offered physicians instruction in routine prenatal and well-child care. But there is little reason to believe that the doctors' concepts of hygiene and nutrition were better founded than those of the women who staffed the clinics that they sought to supplant.

The new and rapidly growing obstetrical profession raised the more powerful challenge to the Sheppard-Towner program. Initially many local obstetricians supported these programs, provided them advice, and found them a useful source of referral of difficult cases. But obstetricians increasingly came to see pregnancy as a potentially acutely dangerous disease. These specialists argued that in promoting healthy birth outcomes, nutrition and social support are far less important than medical monitoring for toxemia and other acute conditions of pregnancy. The obstetricians joined the AMA in urging Congress to end Sheppard-Towner and redirecting federal funds to improve medical research and education for obstetricians. In 1929, Congress repealed its first federal medical care program.

c. The Partial Demedicalization of Childbirth

In the 1940s, American women and physicians were influenced by an English book, Grantly Dick-Read's Childbirth Without Fear. In the 1950s, the trend toward "prepared childbirth" was furthered by books and classes in the French Lamaze method of childbirth preparation. However, women's active preparation for childbirth remained uncommon until the rise of the feminist and consumer health movements of the late 1960s. While some obstetricians resisted, many have supported childbirth education and increased patient participation in the process. For some, support for prepared, participatory childbirth reflects respect for women's self-determination, while others recognize that education and preparation enable the woman to "help" the physician, on his terms. Hospitals, sometimes acting on information gathered through market research, increasingly offer a more homelike environment for labor, delivery and recovery, midwifery services, and expanded education for women and other family members. See Sullivan, Hospitals Wooing Parents-to-Be, Philadelphia Inquirer, July 6, 1988, at B-2.

While educated and prepared childbirth has increased, so too have the "standard" technological processes, such as internal and external fetal monitoring, that restrict laboring women's mobility and thereby undermine women's ability to use their own resources to promote healthy labor and birth. See Chapter 4.

Further, the growth in prepared and participatory childbirth has been largely a middle class phenomenon. Many factors contribute to this. Clinics serving low income women are less likely to offer referrals for these services than are the private physicians serving middle class women. Medicaid reimbursement, which in most states is wholly inadequate to cover even the basic physiologic services of prenatal care and delivery, does not provide reimbursement for education and childbirth preparation. Low income women themselves are less likely to know about and to request such services.

d. Contemporary Barriers to Midwifery Practice

Three principal obstacles prevent broader availability of midwifery birthing services in the 1980s: restrictive licensing provisions, lack of reimbursement, and inability to obtain hospital admitting privileges or physician backup service. In all but a few states these barriers have been overcome, to a greater or lesser degree, during the 1970s. See discussion: G. Robinson, Midwifery and Malpractice Insurance: A Profession Fights for Survival, 134 U. Pa. L. Rev. 1001 (1986).

In most places, physician supervision is the condition of the midwife's ability to practice, to be paid, and to care for patients in the hospital. Midwives take sharply conflicting attitudes toward this state of affairs. Some maintain that the basic philosophy of midwifery and obstetrics are so diametrically opposed that a midwife can practice her profession and serve her patients well only by working independently of physicians. As a practical matter, such midwives are excluded from hospital practice and can only offer home care and birth. See, for instance, Ina May Gaskin and the Farm Midwives, Spiritual Midwifery (1975) and S. Armes, Immaculate Deception (1975). Other midwives seek cooperative, mutually respectful relations with obstetricians and provide a hospital-based service, with integrated physician backup. See, for instance, B. Brennan & J. Heilman, The Complete Book of Midwifery (1977).

Medicaid requires that states pay for "services furnished by a nurse midwife . . . which [she] is legally authorized to perform under State law." 42 U.S.C. §1396(a) (17) (1980 Supp.). Nurse midwife reimbursement is thereby limited by the varying practices of each state. The Civilian Health and Medical Program of the Uniformed Services (CHAMPUS) provides reimbursement for all "covered care independent of physician referral and supervision," provided by licensed midwives. 32 C.F.R. §199.12 (1981). Seventeen states require private health insurers to reimburse for nurse-midwife care if the condition treated or the service provided is otherwise covered by the policy. Robinson, supra at 1010-1012. Most private insurers now cover midwifery services, though many Blue plans do not. Hackley, Independent Reimbursement for Third-party Payors to Nurse-Midwives, 26 J. Nurse-Midwifery 15 (1981).

e. The Future of Prenatal Care?

Why should obstetrics and gynecology — specialties with a strong emphasis on surgical technique — provide leadership in relation to prenatal care?

Many of the services most important in prenatal care are more central in the training of nurses, midwives, and family practitioners than in the training of obstetricians. Pregnant women need nutrition counseling and access to social programs providing nutritional supplementation; emotional support to reduce stress and to help women resolve conflicting obligations to her partner, other children, job, or education; counseling to reduce anxiety about pregnancy, delivery, and childcare; services to aid women in overcoming chemical dependency; referral services to enable women to find community services necessary to prepare for a new child.

Scattered evidence suggests that, even for high risk women, programs providing such supportive services achieve more favorable birth outcomes. See, for instance, Heins et al. Social Support in Improving Perinatal Outcome: The Resource Mothers Program, 70 Obstet. Gynecol. 263 (1987). (A controlled study of first-time teen mothers. Half were assigned an older nonprofessional woman, chosen for warmth, child raising experience, and knowledge of community service, and the other half were not. The teens who were offered the support of the experienced mothers had significantly fewer low birth weight infants.) Several studies and experimental programs have demonstrated the positive effect of introducing midwife prenatal and delivery care in poor, high risk populations. For example, in the 18 months following the introduction of such a pilot program in Madera County California, the prematurity rate dropped from 11 percent to 6.6 percent; in Holmes County, Mississippi, such a program reduced infant mortality rates from 39 per 1000 live births to 20 per 1000 live births in two years. See Testimony of Sally Tom, Government Liaison, American Academy of Nurse Midwives, Spending Reduction Proposals (Part II): Hearings Before the Senate Comm. on Finance, 97th Cong., 1st Sess., 340-342 (1981). Low birthweight figures were cut nearly by half after implementation of a nurse-midwifery program providing prenatal care to low income women in four Georgia counties. Reid and Morris, Perinatal Care and Cost Effectiveness: Changes in Health Expenditures and Birth Outcome Following Establishment of a Nurse-Midwife Program, 17 Med. Care 495 (1979).

An adequate diet is a critical factor in encouraging the growth of healthy babies. Basic welfare and food stamp allocations do not allow many low income American women to obtain an adequate diet, particularly when pregnant. The federal Special Supplemental Food Program for Women, Infants and Children (WIC) provides all states federal funds to provide food, nutrition education, counseling, and health care to pregnant and postpartum women, and to infants and children. Only pregnant women who are in a prenatal care program are eligible for WIC. Because of inadequate funding, in 1987 only 40.4 percent of eligible women and children received WIC services. CDF Report, supra at 52.

While it is possible that prenatal care will place increasing emphasis on supportive social, educational, and nutritional services, other developments are imaginable. The growth of obstetrical technology to monitor, image, test, and treat the fetus, combined with increased reliance upon cesarean delivery, suggests a future in which prenatal care might involve more advanced and intrusive techniques and technologies.

B. Legal Definition of the Role of Medicine in the Control of Human Reproduction

This section traces the influence of the medical profession on legal policy in relation to abortion, explores the role that the Supreme Court has assigned to physicians in defining the parameters of constitutional rights, and describes how contraceptive and abortion services are delivered and financed. Deep opposition to abortion in the twentieth century is premised upon a moral/religious view of the fetus as a human being and upon a social/religious belief that sex should be limited to reproduction. There is virtually no opposition to abortion from a medical or public health perspective. For example, in 1989, the press revealed that the Surgeon General would not release a report that the President had asked him to prepare on the adverse psychological and physical consequences of abortion, because after thorough investigation it was not possible to document adverse effects. Polchin, Koop's Stand on Abortion's Effects Surprises Friends and Foes Alike, N.Y. Times, Jan. 11, 1989, A20, Col. 5. Therefore, in focusing on the medical and public health aspects of abortion, this section is necessarily pro-choice.

1. LEGAL CONCEPTS OF PHYSICIAN ROLE IN REPRODUCTIVE DECISION MAKING

Roe v. Wade

410 U.S. 113 (1973)

[Pregnant women challenged the constitutionality of the Texas criminal abortion laws which proscribe procuring or attempting an abortion except on medical advice for the purpose of saving the mother's life. The Court held that the law violates the Due Process Clause of the Fourteenth Amendment, which protects the right to privacy, including a woman's qualified right to terminate her pregnancy. Though the State cannot override that right, it has legitimate interests in protecting both the pregnant woman's health and the potentiality of human life. Both of these interests grow and reach a "compelling" point at various stages of the woman's approach to term.]

Blackmun, J.

. . . Texas first enacted a criminal abortion statute in 1854. . . . It perhaps is not generally appreciated that the restrictive criminal abortion laws in effect in a majority of States today are of relatively recent vintage. . . .

[A]t common law, at the time of the adoption of our Constitution, and throughout the major portion of the 19th century, abortion was viewed with less disfavor than under most American statutes currently in effect. [A] woman enjoyed a substantially broader right to terminate a pregnancy than she does in most States today. . . .

THE POSITION OF THE AMERICAN MEDICAL ASSOCIATION

The anti-abortion mood prevalent in this country in the late 19th century was shared by the medical profession. Indeed, the attitude of the profession may have played a significant role in the enactment of stringent criminal abortion legislation during that period.

. . . [In 1859, the AMA] adopted resolutions protesting "against such unwarrantable destruction of human life," calling upon state legislatures to revise their abortion laws, and requesting the cooperation of state medical societies "in pressing the subject." . . .

In 1871 . . . the [AMA recommended] that it "be unlawful and unprofessional for any physician to induce abortion or premature labor, without the concurrent opinion of at least one respectable consulting physician, and then always with a view to the safety of the child — if that be possible," and calling "the attention of the clergy of all denominations to the perverted views of morality entertained by a large class of females — aye, and men also, on this important question."

Except for periodic condemnation of the criminal abortionist, no further formal AMA action took place until 1967. In that year, the [House of Delegates adopted] . . . a stated policy of opposition to induced abortion, except when there is "documented medical evidence" of a threat to the health or life of the mother, or that the child "may be born with incapacitating physical deformity or mental deficiency," or that a pregnancy "resulting from legally established statutory or forcible rape or incest may constitute a threat to the mental or physical health of the patient," two other physicians "chosen because of their recognized professional competency have examined the patient and have concurred in writing," and the procedure "is performed in a hospital accredited by the Joint Commission on Accreditation of Hospitals." . . .

In 1970, [the AMA] . . . noted "polarization of the medical profession on this controversial issue"; . . . "the remarkable shift in testimony" in six months, felt to be influenced "by the rapid changes in state laws and by the judicial decisions which tend to make abortion more freely available"; and a feeling "that this trend will continue." [The House of Delegates adopted resolutions emphasizing] "the best interests of the patient," "sound clinical judgment," and "informed patient consent," in contrast to "mere acquiescence to the patient's demand." The resolutions asserted that abortion is a medical procedure that should be performed by a licensed physician in an accredited hospital only after consultation with two other physicians and in conformity with state law, and that no party to the procedure should be required to violate personally held moral principles. . . .

[The Court's description of the technological changes that made abortion safer than childbirth are set forth in Chapter 4. Discussion of constitutional privacy decisions is omitted.]

This right of privacy . . . is broad enough to encompass a woman's decision whether or not to terminate her pregnancy. The detriment that the State would impose upon the pregnant woman by denying this choice altogether is apparent. Specific and direct harm medically diagnosable even in early pregnancy may be involved. Maternity, or additional offspring, may force upon the woman a distressful life and future. Psychological harm may be imminent. Mental and physical health may be taxed by child care. There is also the distress, for all concerned, associated with the unwanted child, and there is the problem of bringing a child into a family already unable, psychologically and otherwise, to care for it. In other cases, as in this one, the additional difficulties and continuing stigma of unwed motherhood may be involved. All these are factors the woman and her responsible physician necessarily will consider in consultation.

On the basis of elements such as these, appellant and some amici argue that the woman's right is absolute and that she is entitled to terminate her pregnancy at whatever time, in whatever way, and for whatever reason she alone chooses. With this we do not agree. . . . The Court's decisions recognizing a right of privacy also acknowledge that some state regulation in areas protected by that right is appropriate. As noted above, a State may properly assert important interests in safeguarding health, in maintaining medical standards, and in protecting potential life. At some point in pregnancy, these respective interests become sufficiently compelling to sustain regulation of the factors that govern the abortion decision. . . .

[B]y adopting one theory of life, Texas may [not] override the rights of the pregnant woman that are at stake. [T]he State does have an important and legitimate interest in preserving and protecting the health of the pregnant woman . . . and . . . still another important and legitimate interest in protecting the potentiality of human life. These interests are separate and distinct. Each grows in substantiality as the woman approaches term and, at a point during pregnancy, each becomes "compelling." With respect to the State's important and legitimate interest in the health of the mother, the "compelling" point, in the light of present medical knowledge, is at approximately the end of the first trimester. This is so because of the now-established medical fact . . . that until the end of the first trimester mortality in abortion may be less than mortality in normal childbirth. It follows that, from and after this point, a State may regulate the abortion procedure to the extent that the regulation reasonably relates to the preservation and protection of maternal health. Examples of permissible state regulation in this area are requirements as to the qualifications of the person who is to perform the abortion; as to the licensure of that person; as to the facility in which the procedure is to be performed, that is, whether it must be a hospital or may be a clinic or some other place of less-than-hospital status; as to the licensing of the facility; and the like.

This means, on the other hand, that, for the period of pregnancy prior to this "compelling" point, the attending physician, in consultation with his patient, is free to determine, without regulation by the State, that, in his medical judgment, the patient's pregnancy should be terminated. If that decision is reached, the judgment may be effectuated by an abortion free of interference by the State.

With respect to the State's important and legitimate interest in potential life, the "compelling" point is at viability. This is so because the fetus then presumably has the capability of meaningful life outside the mother's womb. State regulation protective of fetal life after viability thus has both logical and biological justifications. If the State is interested in protecting fetal life after viability, it may go so far as to proscribe abortion during that period, except when it is necessary to preserve the life or health of the mother. . . .

Doe v. Bolton

410 U.S. 179 (1973)

[Georgia law proscribed an abortion except as performed by a licensed physician when necessary in "his best clinical judgment" because continued pregnancy would endanger a pregnant woman's life or injure her health; the fetus would likely be born with a serious defect; or the pregnancy resulted from rape. In addition, the statute required that: (1) the abortion be performed in a hospital accredited by the Joint Commission on Accreditation of Hospitals (JCAH); (2) the procedure be approved by the hospital staff abortion committee; and (3) the performing physician's judgment be confirmed by independent examinations of the patient by two other licensed physicians. Appellant Doe, an indigent married Georgia citizen, who was denied an abortion after eight weeks of pregnancy for failure to meet any of these requirements, sought declaratory and injunctive relief, contending that the Georgia laws were unconstitutional.]

Mr. Justice BLACKMUN delivered the opinion of the Court.

The statutes in question are . . . patterned upon the American Law Institute's Model Penal Code. . . . The ALI proposal has served as the model for recent legislation in approximately one-fourth of our States. . . .

Appellants argue that . . . Georgia statutes . . . [are] unconstitutionally vague. [I]t still remains a crime for a physician to perform an abortion except when . . . it is "based upon his best clinical judgment that an abortion is necessary." The appellants contend that the word "necessary" does not warn the physician of what conduct is proscribed. . . .

The vagueness argument is set at rest by the decision in United States v. Vuitch, 402 U.S. 62,71-72, (1971), where the issue was raised with respect to a District of Columbia statute making abortions criminal "unless the same were done as necessary for the preservation of the mother's life or health and under the direction of a competent licensed practitioner of medicine." That statute has been construed to bear upon psychological as well as physical well being. This being so, the Court concluded that the term "health" presented no problem of vagueness. "Indeed, where a particular operation is necessary for a patient's physical or mental health is a judgment that physicians are obviously called upon to make routinely whenever surgery is considered." . . . This conclusion is equally applicable here. Whether, in the words of the Georgia statute, "an abortion is necessary" is a professional judgment that the Georgia physician will be called upon to make routinely. [T]he medical judgment may be exercised in the light of all factors — physical, emotional, psychological, familial, and the woman's age — relevant to the well-being of the patient. All these factors may relate to health. This allows the attending physician the room he needs to make his best medical judgment. And it is room that operates for the benefit, not the disadvantage, of the pregnant woman.

. . . The appellants next . . . attack [the other requirements] not only on the ground that they unduly restrict the woman's right of privacy, but also on procedural due process and equal protection grounds. The physician-appellants also argue that, by subjecting a doctor's individual medical judgment to committee approval and to confirming consultations, the statute impermissibly restricts the physician's right to practice his profession and deprives him of due process.

1. JCAH ACCREDITATION

The Joint Commission on Accreditation of Hospitals is an organization without governmental sponsorship or overtones. No question whatever is raised concerning the integrity of the organization or the high purpose of the accreditation process. That process, however, has to do with hospital standards generally and has no present particularized concern with abortion as a medical or surgical procedure. In Georgia, there is no restriction on the performance of nonabortion surgery in a hospital not yet accredited by the JCAH so long as other requirements imposed by the State, such as licensing of the hospital and of the operating surgeon, are met. Furthermore, accreditation by the Commission is not granted until a hospital has been in operation at least one year.

We hold that the JCAH-accreditation requirement does not withstand constitutional scrutiny in the present context. It is a requirement that simply is not "based on differences that are reasonably related to the purposes of the Act in which it is found." . . .

This is not say that Georgia may not or should not, from and after the end of the first trimester, adopt standards for licensing all facilities where abortions may be performed so long as those standards are legitimately related to the objective the State seeks to accomplish. . . . Appellants and various amici have presented us with a mass of data purporting to demonstrate that some facilities other than hospitals are entirely adequate to perform abortions if they possess these qualifications. The State, on the other hand, has not presented persuasive data to show that only hospitals meet its acknowledged interest in insuring the quality of the operation and the full protection of the patient. We feel compelled to agree with appellants that the State must show more than it has in order to prove that only the full resources of a licensed hospital, rather than those of some other appropriately licensed institution, satisfy these health interests. We hold that the hospital requirement of the Georgia law, because it fails to exclude the first trimester of pregnancy. . . .

2. COMMITTEE APPROVAL

Appellants attack the discretion the statute leaves to the committee. The most concrete argument they advance is their suggestion that it is still a badge of infamy "in many minds" to bear an illegitimate child, and that the Georgia system enables the committee members' personal views as to extramarital sex relations, and punishment therefor, to govern their decisions. This approach obviously is one founded on suspicion and one that discloses a lack of confidence in the integrity of physicians. To say that physicians will be guided in their hospital committee decisions by their predilections on extramarital sex unduly narrows the issue to pregnancy outside marriage. . . . The appellants' suggestion is necessarily somewhat degrading to the conscientious physician, particularly the obstetrician, whose professional activity is concerned with the physical and mental welfare, the woes, the emotions, and the concern of his female patients. He, perhaps more than anyone else, is knowledgeable in this area of patient care, and he is aware of human frailty, so-called "error," and needs. The good physician — despite the presence of rascals in the medical profession, as in all others, we trust that most physicians are "good" — will have sympathy and understanding for the pregnant patient that probably are not exceeded by those who participate in other areas of professional counseling.

It is perhaps worth noting that the abortion committee has a function of its own. It is a committee of the hospital and it is composed of members of the institution's medical staff. The membership usually is a changing one. In this way, its work burden is shared and is more readily accepted. The committee's function is protective. It enables the hospital appropriately to be advised that its posture and activities are in accord with legal requirements. It is to be remembered that the hospital is an entity and that it, too, has legal rights and legal obligations.

Saying all this, however, does not settle the issue of the constitutional propriety of the committee requirement. Viewing the Georgia statute as a whole, we see no constitutionally justifiable pertinence in the structure for the advance approval by the abortion committee. With regard to the protection of potential life, the medical judgment is already completed prior to the committee stage, and review by a committee once removed from diagnosis is basically redundant. We are not cited to any other surgical procedure made subject to committee approval as a matter of state criminal law. The woman's right to receive medical care in accordance with her licensed physician's best judgment and the physician's right to administer it are substantially limited by this statutorily imposed overview. And the hospital itself is otherwise fully protected. [T]he hospital is free not to admit a patient for an abortion. It is even free not to have an abortion committee. Further a physician or any other employee has the right to refrain, for moral or religious reasons, from participating in the abortion procedure. These provisions obviously are in the statute in order to afford appropriate protection to the individual and to the denominational hospital.

3. *TWO-DOCTOR CONCURRENCE*

. . . [The statute requires] confirmation by two Georgia-licensed physicians in addition to the recommendation of the pregnant woman's own consultant (making under the statute, a total of six physicians involved, including the three on the hospital's abortion committee). We conclude that this provision, too, must fall.

The statute's emphasis . . . is on the attending physician's "best clinical judgment that an abortion is necessary." That should be sufficient. [N]o other voluntary medical or surgical procedure for which Georgia requires confirmation by two other physicians has been cited to us. If a physician is licensed by the State, he is recognized by the State as capable of exercising acceptable clinical judgment. If he fails in this, professional censure and deprivation of his license are available remedies. Required acquiescence by co-practitioners has no rational connection with a patient's needs and unduly infringes on the physician's right to practice. The attending physician will know when a consultation is advisable — the doubtful situation, the need for assurance when the medical decision is a delicate one, and the like. Physicians have followed this routine historically and know its usefulness and benefit for all concerned. It is still true today that "[r]eliance must be placed upon the assurance given by his license, issued by an authority competent to judge in that respect, that he (the physician) possesses the requisite qualifications." . . .

Akron v. Akron Center for Reproductive Health, Inc.

462 U.S. 416 (1983)

[*Opinions on informed consent*]

[Abortion providers challenged an ordinance that (1) requires all abortions after the first trimester of pregnancy to be performed in a hospital; (2) prohibits a physician from performing an abortion on an unmarried minor under the age of 15 unless he or she obtains the consent of one of her parents or unless the minor obtains an order from a court having jurisdiction over her that the abortion be performed; (3) requires that the attending physician inform his patient of the status of her pregnancy, the development of her fetus, the date of possible viability, the physical and emotional complications that may result from an abortion, and the availability of agencies to provide her with assistance and information with respect to birth control, adoption, and childbirth, and also inform her of the particular risks associated with her pregnancy and the abortion technique to be employed; (4) prohibits a physician from performing an abortion until 24 hours after the pregnant woman signs a consent form; and (5) requires physicians performing abortions to ensure that fetal remains are disposed of in a "humane and sanitary manner." A violation of the ordinance is punishable as a misdemeanor.]

Justice Powell

. . . [Previously] . . . we upheld a Missouri law requiring a pregnant woman to "certif[y] in writing her consent to the abortion and that her consent is informed and freely given and is not the result of coercion.". . . We explained:

> The decision to abort . . . is an important, and often a stressful one, and it is desirable and imperative that it be made with full knowledge of its nature and consequences. The woman is the one primarily concerned, and her awareness of the decision and its significance may be assured, constitutionally, by the State to the extent of requiring her prior written consent.

We rejected the view that "informed consent" was too vague a term, construing it to mean "the giving of information to the patient as to just what would be done and as to its consequences. To ascribe more meaning than this might well confine the attending physician in an undesired and uncomfortable straitjacket in the practice of his profession."

The validity of an informed consent requirement thus rests on the State's interest in protecting the health of the pregnant woman. The decision to have an abortion has "implications far broader than those associated with most other kinds of medical treatment," . . . and thus the State legitimately may seek to ensure that it has been made "in the light of all attendant circumstances — psychological and emotional as well as physical — that might be relevant to the well-being of the patient." . . . This does not mean, however, that a State has unreviewable authority to decide what information a woman must be given before she chooses to have an abortion. It remains primarily the responsibility of the physician to ensure that appropriate information is conveyed to his patient, depending on her particular circumstances. [T]he State's interest in ensuring that this information be given will not justify abortion regulations designed to influence the woman's informed choice between abortion or childbirth.

Viewing the city's regulations in this light, we believe that [this law] attempts to extend the State's interest in ensuring "informed consent" beyond permissible limits. First, it is fair to say that much of the information required is designed not to inform the woman's consent but rather to persuade her to withhold it altogether. [It] requires the physician to inform his patient that "the unborn child is a human life from the moment of conception," a requirement inconsistent with the Court's holding in Roe v. Wade that a State may not adopt one theory of when life begins to justify its regulation of abortions. . . . Moreover, . . . Subsection (5), that begins with the dubious statement that "abortion is a major surgical procedure" and proceeds to describe numerous possible physical and psychological complications of abortion, is a "parade of horribles" intended to suggest that abortion is a particularly dangerous procedure.

An additional, and equally decisive, objection [to the law] . . . is its intrusion upon the discretion of the pregnant woman's physician. This provision specifies a litany of information that the physician must recite to each woman regardless of whether in his judgment the information is relevant to her personal decision. For example, even if the physician believes that some of the risks outlined . . . are nonexistent for a particular patient, he remains obligated to describe them to her. . . . By insisting upon recitation of a lengthy and inflexible list of information, Akron unreasonably has placed "obstacles in the path of the doctor upon whom (the woman is) entitled to rely for advice in connection with her decision."

[The law also requires] . . . that the disclosure be made by the "attending physician." The [lower] court found that "the practice of all three plaintiff clinics has been for the counseling to be conducted by persons other than the doctor who performs the abortion," . . . and determined that Akron had not justified requiring the physician personally to describe the health risks. Akron challenges this holding as contrary to our cases that emphasize the importance of the physician-patient relationship. In Akron's view . . . the "attending physician" requirement "does no more than seek to ensure that there is in fact a true physician-patient relationship even for the woman who goes to an abortion clinic.". . . Requiring physicians personally to discuss the abortion decision, its health risks, and consequences with each patient may in some cases add to the cost of providing abortions, though the record here does not suggest that ethical physicians will charge more for adhering to this typical element of the physician-patient relationship. Yet . . . we have "stressed repeatedly the central role of the physician, both in consulting with the woman about whether or not to have an abortion, and in determining how any abortion was to be carried out.". . . Moreover, we have left no doubt that, to ensure the safety of the abortion procedure, the States may mandate that only physicians perform abortions. . . . We are not convinced, however, that there is as vital a state need for insisting that the physician performing the abortion, or for that matter any physician, personally counsel the patient in the absence of a request. The State's interest is in ensuring that the woman's consent is informed and unpressured; the critical factor is whether she obtains the necessary information and counseling from a qualified person, not the identity of the person from whom she obtains it. . . .

Justice O'CONNOR, with whom Justice WHITE and Justice REHNQUIST join, dissenting.

. . . Our recent cases indicate that a regulation imposed on "a lawful abortion 'is not unconstitutional unless it unduly burdens the right to seek an abortion.'" In my view, this "unduly burdensome" standard should be applied to the challenged regulations throughout the entire pregnancy without reference to the particular "stage" of pregnancy involved. If the particular regulation does not "unduly burden" the fundamental right, then our evaluation of that regulation is limited to our determination that the regulation rationally relates to a legitimate state purpose. Irrespective of what we may believe is wise or prudent policy in this difficult area, "the Constitution does not constitute us as 'Platonic Guardians' nor does it vest in this Court the authority to strike down laws because they do not meet our standards of desirable social policy, 'wisdom,' or 'common sense.'". . .

"*Roe* did not declare an unqualified 'constitutional right to an abortion.'" Rather, the *Roe* right is intended to protect against state action "drastically limiting the availability and safety of the desired service," against the imposition of an "absolute obstacle" on the abortion decision, or against "official interference" and "coercive restraint" imposed on the abortion decision. . . .

We have approved informed consent provisions in the past even though the physician was required to deliver certain information to the patient. . . . The city of Akron is merely attempting to ensure that the decision to abort is made in light of that knowledge that the City deems relevant to informed choice. As such, these regulations do not impermissibly affect any privacy right under the Fourteenth Amendment. . . .

Akron v. Akron Center for Reproductive Health, Inc.

462 U.S. 416 (1983)

[*Opinions on hospitalization requirements*]
BLACKMUN, J.

. . . The ordinance requires that any abortion performed "upon a pregnant woman subsequent to the end of the first trimester of her pregnancy" must be "performed in a hospital.". . . The ordinance thus prevents the performance of abortions in outpatient facilities that are not part of an acute-care, full-service hospital. . . .

[A] State's interest in health regulation becomes compelling at approximately the end of the first trimester. The existence of a compelling state interest in health, however, is only the beginning of the inquiry. The State's regulation may be upheld only if it is reasonably designed to further that state interest. And the Court in *Roe* did not hold that it always is reasonable for a State to adopt an abortion regulation that applies to the entire second trimester. A State necessarily must have latitude in adopting regulations of general applicability in this sensitive area. But if it appears that during a substantial portion of the second trimester the State's regulation "depart[s] from accepted medical practice," . . . the regulation may not be upheld simply because it may be reasonable for the remaining portion of the trimester. Rather, the State is obligated to make a reasonable effort to limit the effect of its regulations to the period in the trimester during which its health interest will be furthered.

There can be no doubt that . . . [the] second-trimester hospitalization requirement places a significant obstacle in the path of women seeking an abortion. A primary burden created by the requirement is additional cost to the woman. . . . [A] second-trimester abortion costs more than twice as much in a hospital as in a clinic. . . . Moreover, . . . second-trimester abortions were rarely performed in Akron hospitals. . . . Thus, a second-trimester hospitalization requirement may force women to travel to find available facilities, resulting in both financial expense and additional health risk. . . .

Akron does not contend that [the rule] . . . imposes only an insignificant burden on women's access to abortion, but rather defends it as a reasonable health regulation. This position had strong support at the time of Roe v. Wade, as hospitalization for second-trimester abortions was recommended by the American Public Health Association (APHA), . . . and the American College of Obstetricians and Gynecologists (ACOG). . . . Since then, however, the safety of second-trimester abortions has increased dramatically. . . . The Court of Appeals found that . . . experience indicates that [an abortion] may be performed safely on an outpatient basis in appropriate nonhospital facilities. The evidence is strong enough to have convinced the APHA to abandon its prior recommendation of hospitalization for all second-trimester abortions. . . . Similarly, the ACOG no longer suggests that all second-trimester abortions be performed in a hospital. It recommends that abortions performed in a physician's office or outpatient clinic be limited to 14 weeks of pregnancy, but it indicates that abortions may be performed safely in "a hospital-based or in a free-standing ambulatory surgical facility, or in an outpatient clinic meeting the criteria required for a free-standing surgical facility," until 18 weeks of pregnancy. . . .

"[P]resent medical knowledge," convincingly undercuts Akron's justification for requiring that all second-trimester abortions be performed in a hospital. . . .

O'Connor, J.

I find no justification for the trimester approach used by the Court to analyze this restriction. I would apply [an] "unduly burdensome" test and find that the hospitalization requirement does not impose an undue burden on that decision.

The Court's reliance on increased abortion costs and decreased availability is misplaced. [T]here is no evidence in this case to show that the two Akron hospitals that performed second-trimester abortions denied an abortion to any woman. . . . Further, almost any state regulation, including the licensing requirements that the Court would allow, . . . inevitably and necessarily entails increased costs for any abortion. . . . A health regulation, such as the hospitalization requirement, simply does not rise to the level of "official interference" with the abortion decision. . . .

Health-related factors that may legitimately be considered by the State go well beyond what various medical organizations have to say about the physical safety of a particular procedure. . . .

Webster v. Reproductive Health Services

109 S. Ct. 3040

Chief Justice REHNQUIST announced the judgment of the Court and delivered the opinion . . . in which Justice WHITE and Justice KENNEDY join.

This appeal concerns the constitutionality of a Missouri statute regulating the performance of abortions. . . .

I

. . . The first provision, or preamble, contains "findings" by the state legislature that "[t]he life of each human being begins at conception." . . . Among its other provisions, the Act requires that, prior to performing an abortion on any woman whom a physician has reason to believe is 20 or more weeks pregnant, the physician ascertain whether the fetus is viable by performing "such medical examinations and tests as are necessary to make a finding of the gestational age, weight, and lung maturity of the unborn child." The Act also prohibits the use of public employees and facilities to perform or assist abortions not necessary to save the mother's life, and it prohibits the use of public funds, employees, or facilities for the purpose of "encouraging or counseling" a woman to have an abortion not necessary to save her life. . . .

II . . .

A . . .

The State contends that the preamble itself is precatory and imposes no substantive restrictions on abortions, and that appellees therefore do not have standing to challenge it. Appellees, on the other hand, insist that the preamble is an operative part of the Act intended to guide the interpretation of other provisions of the Act. They maintain, for example, that the preamble's definition of life may prevent physicians in public hospitals from dispensing certain forms of contraceptives, such as the intrauterine device.

. . . Certainly the preamble does not by its terms regulate abortion or any other aspect of appellees' medical practice. The Court has emphasized that Roe v. Wade "implies no limitation on the authority of a State to make a value judgment favoring childbirth over abortion." Maher v. Roe, 432 U.S.

at 474. The preamble can be read simply to express that sort of value judgment.

We think extent to which the preamble's language might be used to interpret other state statutes or regulations is something that only the courts of Missouri can definitively decide. . . . It will be time enough for federal courts to address the meaning of the preamble should it be applied to restrict the activities of appellees in some concrete way. . . .

B

Section 188.210 provides that "[i]t shall be unlawful for any public employee within the scope of his employment to perform or assist an abortion, not necessary to save the life of the mother," while §188.215 makes it "unlawful for any public facility to be used for the purpose of performing or assisting an abortion not necessary to save the life of the mother.". . .

In Maher v. Roe, supra, the Court upheld a Connecticut welfare regulation under which Medicaid recipients received payments for medical services related to childbirth, but not for nontherapeutic abortions. . . .

The Court of Appeals distinguished these cases on the ground that [t]o prevent access to a public facility does more than demonstrate a political choice in favor of childbirth; it clearly narrows and in some cases forecloses the availability of abortion to women." 851 F.2d, at 1081. The court reasoned that the ban on the use of public facilities "could prevent a woman's chosen doctor from performing an abortion because of his unprivileged status at other hospitals or because a private hospital adopted a similar anti-abortion stance." Ibid. It also thought that "[s]uch a rule could increase the cost of obtaining an abortion and delay the timing of it as well." Ibid.

We think that this analysis is much like that which we rejected in *Maher*, *Poelker*, and *McRae*. As in those cases, the State's decision here to use public facilities and staff to encourage childbirth over abortion "places no governmental obstacle in the path of a woman who chooses to terminate her pregnancy." . . . The challenged provisions only restrict a woman's ability to obtain an abortion to the extent that she chooses to use a physician affiliated with a public hospital. . . . Having held that the State's refusal to fund abortions does not violate Roe v. Wade, it strains logic to reach a contrary result for the use of public facilities and employees. . . .

The Court of Appeals sought to distinguish our cases on the additional ground that "[t]he evidence here showed that all of the public facility's costs in providing abortion services are recouped when the patient pays." 851 F.2d, at 1083. Absent any expenditure of public funds, the court thought that Missouri was "expressing" more than "its preference for childbirth over abortions," but rather was creating an "obstacle to exercise of the right to choose an abortion [that could not] stand absent a compelling state interest." Ibid. We disagree.

. . . Nothing in the Constitution requires States to enter or remain in the business of performing abortions. Nor, as appellees suggest, do private physicians and their patients have some kind of constitutional right of access to public facilities for the performance of abortions. . . .

D

Section 188.029 of the Missouri Act provides:

> Before a physician performs an abortion on a woman he has reason to believe is carrying an unborn child of twenty or more weeks gestational age, the physician shall first determine if the unborn child is viable by using and exercising that degree of care, skill, and proficiency commonly exercised by the ordinarily skillful, careful, and prudent physician engaged in similar practice under the same or similar conditions. In making this determination of viability, the physician shall perform or cause to be performed such medical examinations and tests as are necessary to make a finding of the gestational age, weight, and lung maturity of the unborn child and shall enter such findings and determination of viability in the medical record of the mother.

. . . The State emphasizes the language of the first sentence, which speaks in terms of the physician's determination of viability being made by the standards of ordinary skill in the medical profession. Appellees stress the language of the second sentence, which prescribes such "tests as are necessary" to make a finding of gestational age, fetal weight, and lung maturity.

The Court of Appeals read §188.029 as requiring that after 20 weeks "doctors *must* perform tests to find gestational age, fetal weight and lung maturity." 851 F.2d, at 1075, n.5. The court indicated that the tests needed to determine fetal weight at 20 weeks are "unreliable and inaccurate" and would add \$125 and \$250 to the cost of an abortion. Ibid. It also stated that "amniocentesis, the only method available to determine lung maturity, is contrary to accepted medical practice until 28–30 weeks of gestation, expensive, and imposes significant health risks for both the pregnant woman and the fetus." Ibid.

We must first determine the meaning of §188.029 under Missouri law. Our usual practice is to defer to the lower court's construction of a state statute, but we believe the Court of Appeals has "fallen into plain error" in this case. . . .

We think the viability-testing provision makes sense only if the second sentence is read to require only those tests that are useful to making subsidiary findings as to viability. . . .

The viability-testing provision of the Missouri Act is concerned with promoting the State's interest in potential human life rather than in maternal health. [It] creates what is essentially a presumption of viability at 20 weeks, which the physician must rebut with tests indicating that the fetus is not viable prior to performing an abortion. It also directs the physician's determination as to viability by specifying consideration, if feasible, of gestational age, fetal weight, and lung capacity. The District Court found that "the medical evidence is uncontradicted that a 20-week fetus is *not* viable," and that "23½ to 24 weeks gestation is the earliest point in pregnancy where a reasonable possibility of viability exists." 662 F. Supp., at 420. But it also found that there may be a 4-week error in estimating gestational age, id., at 421, which supports testing at 20 weeks.

In Roe v. Wade, the Court recognized that the State has "important and legitimate" interests in protecting maternal health and in the potentiality of human life. . . . Planned Parenthood of Central Missouri v. Danforth, 428 U.S. 52, 64 (1976), [held] that "the determination of whether a particular fetus is viable is, and must be, a matter for the judgement of the responsible attending physician." 439 U.S. at 396. . . .

To the extent that §188.029 regulates the method for determining viability, it undoubtedly does superimpose state regulation on the medical determination of whether a particular fetus is viable. The Court of Appeals and the District Court thought it unconstitutional for this reason. To the extent that the viability tests increase the cost of what are in fact second-trimester abortions, their validity may also be questioned under *Akron,* where the Court held that a requirement that second trimester abortions must be performed in hospitals was invalid because it substantially increased the expense of those procedures.

We think that the doubt cast upon the Missouri statute by these cases is not so much a flaw in the statute as it is a reflection of the fact that the rigid trimester analysis of the course of a pregnancy enunciated in *Roe* has resulted in subsequent cases . . . making constitutional law in this area a virtual Procrustean bed. . . .

Stare decisis is a cornerstone of our legal system, but it has less power in constitutional cases, where save for constitutional amendments, this Court is the only body able to make needed changes. We have not refrained from reconsideration of a prior construction of the Constitution that has proved "unsound in principle and unworkable in practice." We think the *Roe* trimester framework falls into that category.

In the first place, the rigid *Roe* framework is hardly consistent with the notion of a Constitution cast in general terms, as ours is, and usually speaking in general principles, as ours does. The key elements of the *Roe* framework — trimesters and viability — are not found in the text of the Constitution or in any place else one would expect to find a constitutional principle. Since the bounds of the inquiry are essentially indeterminate, the result has been a web of legal rules that have become increasingly intricate, resembling a code of regulations rather than a body of constitutional doctrine. . . .

In the second place, we do not see why the State's interest in protecting potential human life should come into existence only at the point of viability, and that there should therefore be a rigid line allowing state regulation after viability but prohibiting it before viability. . . .

. . . The State here has chosen viability as the point at which its interest in potential human life must be safeguarded. . . . It is true that the tests in question increase the expense of abortion, and regulate the discretion of the physician in determining the viability of the fetus. Since the tests will undoubtedly show in many cases that the fetus is not viable, the tests will have been performed for what were in fact second-trimester abortions. But we are satisfied that the requirement of these tests permissibly furthers the State's interest in protecting potential human life, and we therefore believe §188.029 to be constitutional. . . .

The dissent also accuses us, *inter alia,* of cowardice and illegitimacy in dealing with "the most politically divisive domestic legal issue of our time." There is no doubt that our holding today will allow some governmental regulation of abortion that would have been prohibited under the language of [prior] cases. . . . But the goal of constitutional adjudication is surely not to remove inexorably "politically divisive" issues from the ambit of the legislative process, whereby the people through their elected representatives deal with matters of concern to them. The goal of constitutional adjudication is to hold true the balance between that which the Constitution puts beyond the reach of the democratic process and that which it does not. We think we have done that today. The dissent's suggestion that legislative bodies, in a Nation where more than half of our population is women, will treat our decision today as an invitation to enact abortion regulation reminiscent of the dark ages not only misreads our views but does scant justice to those who serve in such bodies and the people who elect them.

III

Both appellants and the United States as *Amicus Curiae* have urged that we overrule our decision in Roe v. Wade. The facts of the present case, however, differ from those at issue in *Roe*. . . . To the extent indicated in our opinion, we would modify and narrow *Roe* and succeeding cases.

Justice O'CONNOR, concurring in part and concurring in the judgment. . . .

I

Nothing in the record before us or the opinions below indicates that subsections 1(1) and 1(2) of the preamble to Missouri's abortion regulation statute will affect a woman's decision to have an abortion. . . . I agree with the Court, therefore, that all of these intimations of unconstitutionality are simply too hypothetical to support the use of declaratory judgment procedures and injunctive remedies in this case.

Similarly, it seems to me to follow directly from our previous decisions concerning state or federal funding of abortions that appellees' facial challenge to the constitutionality of Missouri's ban on the utilization of public facilities and the participation of public employees in the performance of abortions not necessary to save the life of the mother, cannot succeed. . . . Appellees and *amici* suggest that the State could try to enforce the ban against private hospitals using public water and sewage lines, or against private hospitals leasing state-owned equipment or state land. Whether some or all of these or other applications of §188.215 would be constitutional need not be decided here.

II

In its interpretation of Missouri's "determination of viability" provision, the plurality has proceeded in a manner unnecessary to deciding the question at hand. I agree with the plurality that it was plain error for the Court of Appeals to interpret the second sentence of Mo. Rev. Stat. §188.029 as meaning that "doctors *must* perform tests to find gestational age, fetal weight and lung maturity. . . ."

Unlike the plurality, I do not understand these viability testing requirements to conflict with any of the Court's past decisions concerning state regulation of abortion. Therefore, there is no necessity to accept the state's invitation to reexamine the constitutional validity of Roe v. Wade. . . .

I do not think the second sentence of §188.029, as interpreted by the Court, imposes a degree of state regulation on the medical determination of viability that in any way conflicts with prior decisions of this Court. As the plurality recognizes, the requirement that, where not imprudent, physicians perform examinations and tests useful to making subsidiary findings to determine viability "promot[es] the State's interest in potential human life rather than in maternal health." No decision of this Court has held that the State may not directly promote its interest in potential life when viability is possible. . . .

It is clear to me that requiring the performance of examinations and tests useful to determining whether a fetus is viable, when viability is possible, and when it would not be medically imprudent to do so, does not impose an undue burden on a woman's abortion decision. [T]he cost of examinations and tests that could usefully and prudently be performed when a woman is 20–40 weeks pregnant to determine whether the fetus is viable would only marginally, if at all, increase the cost of an abortion. . . .

. . . As the Court recognized in *Thornburgh,* the State's compelling interest in potential life postviability renders its interest in determining the critical point of viability equally compelling. Under the Court's precedents, the same cannot be said for the *Akron* second-trimester hospitalization requirement. As I understand the Court's opinion in *Akron,* therefore, the plurality's suggestion today that *Akron* casts doubt on the validity of §188.029, even as the Court has interpreted it, is without foundation and cannot provide a basis for reevaluating *Roe*. . . .

Justice SCALIA, concurring in part and concurring in the judgment.

. . . I share Justice BLACKMUN's view, that [the plurality decision] would overrule Roe v. Wade. I think that should be done, but would do it more explicitly.

The outcome of today's case will doubtless be heralded as a triumph of judicial statesmanship. It is not that, unless it is statesmanlike needlessly to prolong this Court's self-awarded sovereignty over a field where it has little proper business since the answers to most of the cruel questions posed are political and not juridical — a sovereignty which therefore quite properly, but to the great damage of the Court, makes it the object of the sort of organized public pressure that political institutions in a democracy ought to receive.

. . . We have not disposed of this case on some statutory or procedural ground, but have decided, and could not avoid deciding, whether the Missouri statute meets the requirements of the United States Constitution. The only choice available is whether, in deciding that constitutional question, we should use Roe v. Wade as the benchmark, or something else. . . .

The real question, then, is whether there are valid reasons to go beyond the most stingy possible holding today. It seems to me there are not only valid but compelling ones. Ordinarily, speaking no more broadly than is absolutely required avoids throwing settled law into confusion; doing so today preserves a chaos that is evident to anyone who can read and count. Alone sufficient to justify a broad holding is the fact that our retaining control, through *Roe,* of what I believe to be, and many of our citizens recognize to be, a political issue, continuously distorts the public perception of the role of this Court. We can now look forward to at least another Term with carts full of mail from the public, and streets full of demonstrators, urging us — their unelected and life-tenured judges who have been awarded those extraordinary, undemocratic characteristics precisely in order that we might follow the law despite the popular will — to follow the popular will. Indeed, I expect we can look forward to even more of that than before, given our indecisive decision today. And if these reasons for taking the unexceptional course of reaching a broader holding are not enough, then consider the nature of the constitutional question we avoid: In most cases, we do no harm by not speaking more broadly than the decision requires. Anyone affected by the conduct that the avoided holding would have prohibited will be able to challenge it himself, and have his day in court to make the argument. Not so with respect to the harm that many States believed, pre-*Roe,* and many may continue to believe, is caused by largely unrestricted abortion. That will continue to occur if the States have the constitutional power to prohibit it, and would do so, but we skillfully avoid telling them so. Perhaps those abortions cannot constitutionally be proscribed. That is surely an arguable question, the question that reconsideration of Roe v. Wade entails. But what is not at all arguable, it seems to me, is that we should decide now and not insist that we be run into a corner before we grudgingly yield up our judgment. . . .

. . . The result of our vote today is that we will not reconsider that prior opinion, even if most of the Justices think it is wrong, unless we have before us a statute that in fact contradicts it — and even then (under our newly discovered "no-broader-than-necessary" requirement) only minor problematical aspects of *Roe* will be reconsidered, unless one expects State legislatures to adopt provisions whose compliance with *Roe* cannot even be argued with a straight face. It thus appears that the mansion of constitutionalized abortion-law, constructed overnight in Roe v. Wade, must be disassembled door-jamb by door-jamb, and never entirely brought down, no matter how wrong it may be.

Justice BLACKMUN, with whom Justice BRENNAN and Justice MARSHALL join, concurring in part and dissenting in part.

Today, Roe v. Wade, and the fundamental constitutional right of women to decide whether to terminate a pregnancy, survive but are not secure. Although the Court extricates itself from this case without making a single, even incremental, change in the law of abortion, the plurality and Justice SCALIA would overrule *Roe* (the first silently, the other explicitly) and would return to the States virtually unfettered authority to control the quintessentially intimate, personal, and life-directing decision whether to carry a fetus to term. Although today, no less than yesterday, the Constitution and the decisions of this Court prohibit a State from enacting laws that inhibit women from the meaningful exercise of that right, a plurality of this Court implicitly invites every state legislature to enact more and more restrictive abortion regulations in order to provoke more and more test cases, in the hope that sometime down the line the Court will return the law of procreative freedom to the severe limitations that generally prevailed in this country before January 22, 1973. Never in my memory has a plurality announced a judgment of this Court that so foments disregard for the law and for our standing decisions.

Nor in my memory has a plurality gone about its business in such a deceptive fashion. At every level of its review, from its effort to read the real meaning out of the Missouri statute, to its intended evisceration of precedents and its deafening silence about the constitutional protections that it would jettison, the plurality obscures the portent of its analysis. With feigned restraint, the plurality announces that its analysis leaves *Roe* "undisturbed," albeit "modif[ied] and narrow[ed]." But this disclaimer is totally meaningless. The plurality opinion is filled with winks, and nods, and knowing glances to those who would do away with *Roe* explicitly, but turns a stone face to anyone in search of what the plurality conceives as the scope of a woman's right under the Due Process Clause to terminate a pregnancy free from the coercive and brooding influence of the State. The simple truth is that *Roe* would not survive the plurality's analysis, and that the plurality provides no substitute for *Roe*'s protective umbrella.

I fear for the future. I fear for the liberty and equality of the millions of women who have lived and come of age in the 16 years since *Roe* was decided. I fear for the integrity of, and public esteem for, this Court. . . .

In the plurality's view, the viability-testing provision imposes a burden on second-trimester abortions as a way of furthering the State's interest in protecting the potential life of the fetus. Since under the *Roe* framework, the State may not fully regulate abortion in the interest of potential life (as opposed to maternal health) until the third trimester, the plurality finds it necessary, in order to save the Missouri testing provision, to throw out *Roe*'s trimester framework. In flat contradiction to *Roe,* the plurality concludes that the State's interest in potential life is compelling before viability, and upholds the testing provision because it "permissibly furthers" that state interest.

A

At the outset, I note that in its haste to limit abortion rights, the plurality compounds the errors of its analysis by needlessly reaching out to address constitutional questions that are not actually presented.

. . . The statute's plain language requires the physician to undertake whatever tests are necessary to determine gestational age, weight, and lung maturity, regardless of whether these tests are necessary to a finding of viability, and regardless of whether the tests subject the pregnant woman or the fetus to additional health risks or add substantially to the cost of an abortion.

Had the plurality read the statute as written, it would have had no cause to reconsider the *Roe* framework. As properly construed, the viability-testing provision does not pass constitutional muster under even a rational-basis standard, the least restrictive level of review applied by this Court. By mandating tests to determine fetal weight and lung maturity for every fetus thought to be more than 20 weeks gestational age, the statute requires physicians to undertake procedures, such as amniocentesis, that, in the situation presented, have no medical justification, impose significant additional health risks on both the pregnant woman and the fetus, and bear no rational relation to the State's interest in protecting fetal life. As written, §188.029 is an arbitrary imposition of discomfort, risk, and expense, furthering no discernible interest except to make the procurement of an abortion as arduous and difficult as possible. Thus, were it not for the plurality's tortured effort to avoid the plain import of §188.029, it could have struck down the testing provision as patently irrational irrespective of the *Roe* framework. . . .

No one contests that under the *Roe* framework the State, in order to promote its interest in potential human life, may regulate and even proscribe non-therapeutic abortions once the fetus becomes viable. . . . Nothing in *Roe,* or any of its progeny, holds that a State may not effectuate its compelling interest in the potential life of a viable fetus by seeking to ensure that no viable fetus is mistakenly aborted because of the inherent lack of precision in estimates of gestational age. A requirement that a physician make a finding of viability, one way or the other, for every fetus that falls within the range of possible viability does no more than preserve the State's recognized authority. Although, as the plurality correctly points out, such a testing requirement would have the effect of imposing additional costs on second-trimester abortions where the tests indicated that the fetus was not viable, these costs would be merely incidental to, and a necessary accommodation of, the State's unquestioned right to prohibit non-therapeutic abortions after the point of viability. In short, the testing provision, as construed by the plurality is consistent with the *Roe* framework and could be upheld effortlessly under current doctrine.

How ironic it is, then, and disingenuous, that the plurality scolds the Court of Appeals for adopting a construction of the statute that fails to avoid constitutional difficulties. By distorting the statute, the plurality manages to avoid invalidating the testing provision on what should have been noncontroversial constitutional grounds; having done so, however, the plurality rushes headlong into a much deeper constitutional thicket. . . . Evidently, from the plurality's perspective, the real problem with the Court of Appeal's construction of §188.029 is not that it raised a constitutional difficulty, but that it raised the wrong constitutional difficulty — one not implicating *Roe*. The plurality has remedied that, traditional canons of construction and judicial forbearance notwithstanding.

B

Having set up the conflict between §188.029 and the *Roe* trimester framework, the plurality summarily discards *Roe*'s analytic core as "'unsound in principle and unworkable in practice.'" This is so, the plurality claims, because the key elements of the framework do not appear in the text of the Constitution, because the framework more closely resembles a regulatory code than a body of constitutional doctrine, and because under the framework the State's interest in potential human life is considered compelling only after viability, when, in fact, that interest is equally compelling throughout pregnancy. The plurality does not bother to explain these alleged flaws in *Roe*. Bald assertion masquerades as reasoning. The object, quite clearly, is not to persuade, but to prevail.

1

The plurality opinion is far more remarkable for the arguments that it does not advance than for those that it does. The plurality does not even mention, much less join, the true jurisprudential debate underlying this case: whether the Constitution includes an "unenumerated" general right to privacy as recognized in many of our decisions . . . and, more specifically, whether and to what extent such a right to privacy extends to matters of childbearing and family life, including abortion. . . . These are questions of unsurpassed significance in this Court's interpretation of the Constitution, and mark the battleground upon which this case was fought. . . .

But rather than arguing that the text of the Constitution makes no mention of the right to privacy, the plurality complains that the critical elements of the *Roe* framework — trimesters and viability — do not appear in the Constitution and are, therefore, somehow inconsistent with a Constitution cast in general terms. Were this a true concern, we would have to abandon most of our constitutional jurisprudence. As the plurality well knows, or should know, the "critical elements" of countless constitutional doctrines nowhere appear in the Constitution's text. The Constitution makes no mention, for example, of the First Amendment's "actual malice" standard for proving certain libels, or of the standard for determining when speech is obscene. Similarly, the Constitution makes no mention of the rational-basis test, or the specific verbal formulations of intermediate and strict scrutiny by which this Court evaluates claims under the Equal Protection Clause. The reason is simple. Like the *Roe* framework, these tests or standards are not, and do not purport to be, rights protected by the Constitution. Rather, they are judge-made methods for evaluating and measuring the strength and scope of constitutional rights or for balancing the constitutional rights of individuals against the competing interests of government.

. . . As we recently reaffirmed in Thornburgh v. American College of Obstetricians and Gynecologists, few decisions are "more basic to individual dignity and autonomy" or more appropriate to that "certain private sphere of individual liberty" that the Constitution reserves from the intrusive reach of government than the right to make the uniquely personal, intimate, and self-defining decision whether to end a pregnancy. It is this general principle, the "'moral fact that a person belongs to himself and not others nor to society as a whole,'" that is found in the Constitution. The trimester framework simply defines and limits that right to privacy in the abortion context to accommodate, not destroy, a State's legitimate interest in protecting the health of pregnant women and in preserving potential human life. Fashioning such accommodations between individual rights and the legitimate interests of government, establishing benchmarks and standards with which to evaluate the competing claims of individuals and government, lies at the very heart of constitutional adjudication. . . .

2

The plurality next alleges that the result of the trimester framework has "been a web of legal rules that have become increasingly intricate, resembling a code of regulations rather than a body of constitutional doctrine." Again, if this were a true and genuine concern, we would have to abandon vast areas of our constitutional jurisprudence. . . . Are these distinctions any finer, or more "regulatory," than the distinctions we have often drawn in our First Amendment jurisprudence, where, for example, we have held that a "release time" program permitting public-school students to leave school grounds during school hours to receive religious instruction does not violate the Establishment Clause, even though a release-time program permitting religious instruction on school grounds does violate the Clause? Our Fourth Amendment jurisprudence recognizes factual distinctions no less intricate. . . .

That numerous constitutional doctrines result in narrow differentiations between similar circumstances does not mean that this Court has abandoned adjudication in favor of regulation. Rather, these careful distinctions reflect the process of constitutional adjudication itself, which is often highly fact-specific, requiring such determinations as whether state laws are "unduly burdensome" or "reasonable" or bears a "rational" or "necessary" relation to asserted state interests. . . .

. . . If, in delicate and complicated areas of constitutional law, our legal judgments "have become increasingly intricate," it is not, as the plurality contends, because we have overstepped our judicial role. Quite the opposite: the rules are intricate because we have remained conscientious in our duty to do justice carefully, especially when fundamental rights rise or fall with our decisions.

3

Finally, the plurality asserts that the trimester framework cannot stand because the State's interest in potential life is compelling throughout pregnancy, not merely after viability. The opinion contains not one word of rationale for its view of the State's interest. This "it-is-so-because-we-say-so" jurisprudence constitutes nothing other than an attempted exercise of brute force; reason, much less persuasion, has no place. . . .

For my own part, I remain convinced, as six other Members of this Court 16 years ago were convinced, that the *Roe* framework, and the viability standard in particular, fairly, sensibly, and effectively functions to safeguard the constitutional liberties of pregnant women while recognizing and accommodating the State's interest in potential human life. The viability line reflects the biological facts and truths of fetal development; it marks that threshold moment prior to which a fetus cannot survive separate from the woman and cannot reasonably and objectively be regarded as a subject of rights or interests distinct from, or paramount to, those of the pregnant woman. At the same time, the viability standard takes account of the undeniable fact that as the fetus evolves into its postnatal form, and as it loses its dependence on the uterine environment, the State's interest in the fetus' potential human life, and in fostering a regard for human life in general, becomes compelling. As a practical matter, because viability follows "quickening" — the point at which a woman feels movement in her womb — and because viability occurs no earlier than 23 weeks gestational age, it establishes an easily applicable standard for regulating abortion while providing a pregnant woman ample time to exercise her fundamental right with her responsible physician to terminate her pregnancy.[9] Although I have stated previously for a majority of

9. Notably, neither the plurality nor Justice O'CONNOR advance the now familiar catchphrase criticism of the *Roe* framework that because the point of viability will recede with advances in medical technology, *Roe* "is clearly on a collision course with itself." See *Akron*, 462 U.S., at 458 (dissenting opinion). This critique has no medical foundation. As the medical literature and the *amicus* briefs filed in this case conclusively demonstrate, "there is an 'anatomic threshold' for fetal viability of about 23–24 weeks gestation." Brief for American Medical Association, et al. as *Amici Curiae*. Prior to that time, the crucial organs are not sufficiently mature to provide the mutually sustaining functions that are prerequisite to ex-

this Court that "[c]onstitutional rights do not always have easily ascertainable boundaries," to seek and establish those boundaries remains the special responsibility of this Court. In *Roe,* we discharged that responsibility as logic and science compelled. The plurality today advances not one reasonable argument as to why our judgment in that case was wrong and should be abandoned.

C

Having contrived an opportunity to reconsider the *Roe* framework, and then having discarded that framework, the plurality finds the testing provision unobjectionable because it "permissibly furthers the State's interest in protecting potential human life." This newly minted standard is circular and totally meaningless. Whether a challenged abortion regulation "permissibly furthers" a legitimate state interest is the *question* that courts must answer in abortion cases, not the standard for courts to apply. In keeping with the rest of its opinion, the plurality makes no attempt to explain or to justify its new standard, either in the abstract or as applied in this case. Nor could it. The "permissibly furthers" standard has no independent meaning, and consists of nothing other than what a majority of this Court may believe at any given moment in any given case. The plurality's novel test appears to be nothing more than a dressed-up version of rational-basis review, this Court's most lenient level of scrutiny. One thing is clear, however: were the plurality's "permissibly furthers" standard adopted by the Court, for all practical purposes, *Roe* would be overruled.

The "permissibly furthers" standard completely disregards the irreducible minimum of *Roe:* the Court's recognition that a woman has a limited fundamental constitutional right to decide whether to terminate a pregnancy. That right receives no meaningful recognition in the plurality's written opinion. Since, in the plurality's view, the State's interest in potential life is compelling as of the moment of conception, and is therefore served only if abortion is abolished, every hindrance to a woman's ability to obtain an abortion must be "permissible." Indeed, the more severe the hindrance, the more effectively (and permissibly) the State's interest would be furthered. . . .

. . . The plurality repudiates every principle for which *Roe* stands; in good conscience, it cannot possibly believe that *Roe* lies "undisturbed" merely because this case does not call upon the Court to reconsider the Texas statute, or one like it. If the Constitution permits a State to enact any statute that

---

trauterine survival, or viability. Moreover, "no technology exists to bridge the development gap between the three-day embryo culture and the 24th week of gestation." Fetal Extrauterine Survivability, Report to the New York State Task Force on Life and Law 10 (1988). Nor does the medical community believe that the development of any such technology is possible in the foreseeable future. Id., at 12. In other words, the threshold of fetal viability is, and will remain, no different from what it was at the time *Roe* was decided. Predictions to the contrary are pure science fiction. See Brief for A Group of American Law Professors as *Amici Curiae* 23–25.

reasonably furthers its interest in potential life, and if that interest arises as of conception, why would the Texas statute fail to pass muster? One suspects that the plurality agrees. It is impossible to read the plurality opinion and especially its final paragraph, without recognizing its implicit invitation to every State to enact more and more restrictive abortion laws, and to assert their interest in potential life as of the moment of conception. All these laws will satisfy the plurality's non-scrutiny, until sometime, a new regime of old dissenters and new appointees will declare what the plurality intends: that *Roe* is no longer good law.

D

Thus, "not with a bang, but a whimper," the plurality discards a landmark case of the last generation, and casts into darkness the hopes and visions of every woman in this country who had come to believe that the Constitution guaranteed her the right to exercise some control over her unique ability to bear children. The plurality does so either oblivious or insensitive to the fact that millions of women, and their families, have ordered their lives around the right to reproductive choice, and that this right has become vital to the full participation of women in the economic and political walks of American life. . . .

The result, as we know from experience, would be that every year hundreds of thousands of women, in desperation, would defy the law, and place their health and safety in the unclean and unsympathetic hands of back-alley abortionists, or they would attempt to perform abortions upon themselves, with disastrous results. Every year, many women, especially poor and minority women, would die or suffer debilitating physical trauma, all in the name of enforced morality or religious dictates or lack of compassion, as it may be.

Of the aspirations and settled understandings of American women, of the inevitable and brutal consequences of what it is doing, the tough-approach plurality utters not a word. This silence is callous. It is also profoundly destructive of this Court as an institution. To overturn a constitutional decision is a rare and grave undertaking. To overturn a constitutional decision that secured a fundamental personal liberty to millions of persons would be unprecedented in our 200 years of constitutional history. Although the doctrine of *stare decisis* applies with somewhat diminished force in constitutional cases generally, even in ordinary constitutional cases "any departure from *stare decisis* demands special justification." . . . This requirement of justification applies with unique force where, as here, the Court's abrogation of precedent would destroy people's firm belief, based on past decisions of this Court, that they possess an unabridgeable right to undertake certain conduct.

. . . Today's decision involves the most politically divisive domestic legal issue of our time. By refusing to explain or to justify its proposed revolutionary revision in the law of abortion, and by refusing to abide not only by our precedents, but also by our canons for reconsidering those precedents, the plurality invites charges of cowardice and illegitimacy to our door. I cannot say that these would be undeserved.

II

For today, at least, the law of abortion stands undisturbed. For today, the women of this Nation still retain the liberty to control their destinies. But the signs are evident and very ominous, and a chill wind blows.

Justice STEVENS, concurring in part and dissenting in part.

Having joined Part II-C of the Court's opinion, I shall not comment on §188.205 of the Missouri statute. With respect to the challenged portions of §§188.210 and 188.215, I agree with Justice BLACKMUN, ante, at 2–5, n.1 (concurring in part and dissenting in part), that the record identifies a sufficient number of unconstitutional applications to support the Court of Appeals' judgment invalidating those provisions. The reasons why I would also affirm that court's invalidation of §188.029, the viability testing provision, and §§1.205.1(1)(2) of the preamble,[1] require separate explanation.

[Justice Stevens dissented from the holdings with respect to the preamble and the viability testing requirements on grounds that they reflect a particular, religiously based, doctrine and therefore violate the Establishment Clause of the First Amendment.]

a. PHYSICIANS' ROLES IN THE ENACTMENT OF RESTRICTIVE ABORTION LAWS

The Court recognized in Roe v. Wade that physicians were key actors in the late nineteenth-century campaigns to prohibit abortion in the United States. The evidence recited suggests that doctors acted to protect the health of women and to advance a particular moral attitude toward the fetus. More recent histories paint a more complex picture. John Mohr, Abortion in America: The Origins and Evolution of a National Policy 1800-1900, 147-170 (1978), argues that the regular allopathic medical profession sought these restrictive laws to promote the authority of regular doctors and to restrict their irregular competitors. In the nineteenth century, abortions were generally performed by "irregulars" — midwives, professional abortionists, em-

1. The State prefers to refer to subsections (1) and (2) of §1.205 as "prefactory statements with no substantive effect." Brief for Appellants 9; see id., at 21; see also 851 F.2d 1071, 1076(CAS 1988). It is true that §1.205 is codifed in Chapter 1, Laws in Force and Construction of Statutes, of Title I, Laws and Statutes, of the Missouri Revised Statutes, while all other provisions at issue are codifed in Chapter 188, Regulation of Abortions, of Title XII, Public Health and Welfare. But because §1.205 appeared at the beginning of House Bill No. 1596, see ante, at 1–2, it is entirely appropriate to consider it as a preamble relevant to those regulations.

pirical medics, herbalists, and other practitioners. Physicians did not wish to provide abortion services, but, at the same time, sought to consolidate all of medical practice under their control. L. Gordon, Woman's Body Woman's Right, 59-60 (1976), also argues that allopathic physicians' campaign to consolidate authority over the practice of medicine provided the central impetus behind the criminalization of abortion.

A second important factor motivating the enactment of restrictive abortion laws can be found in the shifting nature of the women who sought abortion. In the late nineteenth century, abortions were no longer sought solely because of illegitimacy or adultery. Rather, "respectable" women began to seek abortions to limit family size. Mohr, supra at 86-102. Some physicians sought criminal restrictions on abortions because birthrates were declining among white Yankee Protestants relative to Catholics and nonwhites. Id. at 166-167; Gordon, supra at 138.

b. Physicians' Roles in the Twentieth Century Legalization of Abortion

In the 1960s, physicians initially led the effort to liberalize abortion laws in the United States. Many doctors witnessed the devastating consequences to women when abortion is denied or when women obtained illegal abortions. In the late 1960s, leadership of the campaign for legal abortion shifted to the women's movement, which emphasized women's "right to choose" and control of their bodies, rather than physician discretion. Even as abortion laws have been liberalized, doctors have been among the most influential voices defending reproductive freedom. They understandably seek to avoid the risk that criminal sanctions will be applied to the personal/professional/ethical/medical judgments that they must make in caring for women who seek abortions. K. Luker, Abortion and the Politics of Motherhood, Chapter 4 (1984); F. Jaffe, B. Lindheim & P. Lee, Abortion Politics (1981).

c. The Supreme Court's Concept of the Physician's Role in Abortion Decision-Making

Justice Blackmun, in Roe v. Wade, observes and relies upon the fact that in the first trimester of pregnancy abortion is safer for the women than pregnancy and childbirth. In 1974, for white women, the risk of death from childbirth was 20 times greater than the risk of abortion, while for black women the risk was 15 times greater. See discussion of data in McRae v. Califano, 491 F. Supp. 630, 634-638 (E.D. N.Y., 1980). Further, when abortion is legally available, the death rates decrease as the medical profession becomes more practiced in offering the service, and more abortions are done earlier during pregnancy. Ciba Foundation Symposium, 115 Abortion: Medical Progress and Social Implications at 36 (1985). In the U.S., increased availability of legal abortion in the 1970s reduced deaths among women of childbearing age, allowed development of safer abortion techniques, and increased provision of low-cost outpatient gynecologic services. See Cates, Legal Abortion: The Public Health Record, 215 Science 1586 (1982).

In *Roe* and *Bolton* why does the Court emphasize the physician's determination that an abortion is medically necessary, rather than the woman's determination whether she is willing and able to bear a child? More recently, the Court has described the abortion choice as the woman's.

> Our cases long have recognized that the Constitution embodies a promise that a certain private sphere of individual liberty will be kept largely beyond the reach of government. . . . That promise extends to women as well as to men. Few decisions are more personal and intimate, more properly private, or more basic to individual dignity and autonomy, than a woman's decision — with the guidance of her physician . . . — whether to end her pregnancy. A woman's right to make that choice freely is fundamental. Any other result, in our view, would protect inadequately a central part of the sphere of liberty that our law guarantees equally to all. [Thornburgh v. American College of Obstetricians and Gynecologists, 106 S. Ct. 2169 (1986) (Blackmun, J., for the Court).]

When might a physician determine that an abortion was medically necessary, even though the woman sought to continue the pregnancy? When might a physician determine that an abortion was not medically necessary, even though the woman had decided that she was not able or willing to bear a child? These issues were explored in testimony before a federal district court when Congress prohibited the use of federal funds to finance abortions for women eligible for Medicaid, except when the physician certifies that an abortion is necessary to save the life of the woman. (Medicaid and abortion funding is discussed more generally in Chapter 2.) Lawyers for pregnant women, attorneys for the federal government, and guardians ad litem for fetuses questioned dozens of physicians to explore the issue of an abortion that is necessary because "the life of the mother would be endangered if the fetus were carried to term." McRae v. Califano, 491 F. Supp. 630, 667, n. 33 (E.D. N.Y. 1979). The physicians testified that the pregnancy-related conditions that threaten women's lives arise during the last weeks of pregnancy. Early in pregnancy, it is possible to predict that certain women are at higher statistical risk. But it is not possible to identify the individual women who will eventually encounter those risks. By the time the risks arise, it is often too late to prevent death or serious injury to the patient. Id. at 665.

The physicians also testified that the woman's attitude toward her pregnancy is an extremely important factor in determining whether pregnancy poses a threat to her life or health. A woman who is unable and unwilling to bear a child will experience tremendous stress in pregnancy, which will in turn adversely affect her medical condition. Id. at 668-673 and 690. On the other hand, the physicians testified that if a woman desired to attempt to bear a child, most would never advise that an abortion was "medically necessary," whatever her medical situation. Many factors — diabetes, obesity, high blood pressure, cancer, or mental illness — make pregnancy difficult. But, if the pregnancy is desired and the woman is able to work to maintain it, the physicians testified that even in these difficult cases they regard the basic choice as belonging to the women, informed by the physicians' knowledge of the likely consequences of pregnancy. Id. at 671-672.

In *Bolton* Justice Blackmun expresses confidence that "the good physician . . . will have sympathy and understanding for the pregnant patient. . . ." Id. at 197. Justice Blackmun also assumes that "a physician . . . has the right to refrain, for moral or religious reasons, from participating in the abortion procedure." Id. at 197-198. If a physician is morally opposed to abortion in all circumstances, how can he or she exercise sympathetic judgment in determining whether an abortion in necessary for a particular woman who seeks one? In 1985, most obstetricians and gynecologists in the United States did not perform a single abortion. During that year, 30 percent of all pregnancies ended in abortion. Thus it is apparent that even women who have an established relationship with a gynecologist, must often look elsewhere for abortion services. See C. Weisman, et al., Abortion Attitudes and Performance Among Male and Female Obstetrician-Gynecologists, 18 Family Planning Perspectives 67, 69 (1986).

In Thornburgh v. A.C.O.G., supra, the Court struck down a Pennsylvania "informed consent" statute similar to that invalidated in the *Akron* case, though somewhat less detailed. Justice Blackmun, for the majority, said that requiring the physician to recite a mandatory, often irrelevant, litany is "nothing less than an outright attempt to wedge the Commonwealth's message discouraging abortion into the privacy of the informed-consent dialogue between the woman and her physician. . . . Forcing the physician or counselor to present the materials . . . makes him or her in effect an agent of the State in treating the woman and places his or her imprimatur upon . . . the materials. . . . All this is, or comes close to being, state medicine imposed upon the woman, not the professionally medical guidance she seeks. . . ." 106 S. Ct. 2179-2180 (1986). Justice White, dissenting, responds:

> Were the Court serious about the need for strict scrutiny of the regulations that infringe on the "judgment" of medical professionals, "structure" their relations with their patients, and amount to "state medicine," there is no telling how many state and federal statutes (not to mention principles of state tort law) governing the practice of medicine might be condemned. And of course, there would be no reason why a concern for professional freedom could be confined to the medical profession: nothing in the Constitution indicates a preference for the liberty of doctors over that of lawyers, accountants, bakers, or brick-makers.

> The rationale for state efforts to regulate the practice of a profession or vocation is simple: the government is entitled not to trust members of a profession to police themselves, and accordingly the legislature may for the most part impose such restrictions on the practice of a profession or business as it may find necessary to the protection of the public. This is precisely the rationale for infringing the professional freedom of doctors by imposing disclosure requirements upon them: "Respect for the patient's right of self-determination on particular therapy demands a standard set by law for physicians rather than one which physicians may or may not impose upon themselves." Canterbury v. Spence, 464 F.2d at 784. Unless one is willing to recast entirely the law with respect to the legitimacy of state regulation of professional conduct, the obvious rationality of the policy of promoting informed patient choice on the subject of abortion must defeat any claim that the disclosure requirements imposed by Pennsylvania are invalid because they infringe on "professional freedom" or on the "physician-patient relationship." [106 S. Ct. at 2200-2201.]

As a practical matter, does it matter that the Supreme Court articulated the constitutionally protected abortion decision as one to be made by the physician, in consultation with his patient, rather than as a woman's right? Even if we focus on the woman's right to be free from state interference in choosing abortion, plainly she can only effectuate that choice if she can find a physician willing to serve her. Further, the evidence is that doctors who perform abortions assume that it is the woman, not the physician, who must determine whether or not she should bear a child. Given these facts, does the Supreme Court's characterization of the abortion choice as a physician's judgment have any consequence? See Asaro, The Judicial Portrayal of the Physician in Abortion and Sterilization Decisions: The Use and Abuse of Medical Discretion, 6 Harv. Women's L.J. 51 (1983).

In the 1970s, some key Justices described clinic-based abortion practice with evident distaste. See Belotti v. Baird, 443 U.S. 622, n.21 (1979) (Powell); and Planned Parenthood v. Danforth, 428 U.S. 52 (1976) (Stewart). Justice Stewart provided the following account:

> The counseling . . . occurs entirely on the day the abortion is to be performed. . . . It lasts for two hours and takes place in groups that include both minors and adults who are strangers to one another. . . . The physician takes no part in this counseling process. . . . Counseling is typically limited to a description of abortion procedures, possible complications, and birth control techniques. . . .
>
> The abortion itself takes five to seven minutes. . . . The physician has no prior contact with the minor, and on the days that abortions are being performed at the [clinic], the physician . . . may be performing abortions on many other adults and minors. . . . On busy days patients are scheduled in separate groups, consisting usually of five patients. . . . After the abortion [the physician] spends a brief period with the minor and others in the group in the recovery room. . . ." [Id. at 91-92.]

What, if anything, is wrong with this process? Note that in *Akron,* Justice Powell wrote the majority decision upholding clinic based practice in which physicians delegate counseling functions to nurses and trained lay people.

d. Omnibus Antiabortion Legislation

The statute struck down in Akron v. Akron Center for Reproductive Health is one of dozens of state and local efforts to test the limits of their power to restrict access to abortion. These omnibus laws are drafted and promoted by national antiabortion organizations. In Thornburgh v. ACOG, supra, the majority noted that the statute before it was Pennsylvania's fourth attempt to pass a comprehensive law restricting access to abortion. The majority noted that the law "aimed at limiting abortions, was patterned after a model statute developed by a Chicago-based nonprofit anti-abortion organization." 476 U.S. 9 at 752. Justice White, dissenting, protests that, "[t]he history of the state legislature's decade-long effort to pass a constitutional abortion statute is recounted as if it were evidence of some sinister conspiracy. [T]he legislature's willingness to pursue permissible policies through means that go to the limits allowed by existing precedents is no sign of *mens rea.*" Id. at 798. Is a history of enactment of unconstitutional restrictions on access to abortion probative of the constitutionality of the most recent attempt?

Problem: The Current Constitutionality of State Requirements that only Physicians can Perform Abortions

In Connecticut v. Menillo, 423 U.S. 9 (1975), an untrained lay person challenged his criminal conviction for illegally performing an abortion. The Court said, "the rationale of our decision [in Roe v. Wade] supports continued enforceability of criminal abortion statutes against nonphysicians. [T]he insufficiency of the State's interest in maternal health is predicated upon the first trimester abortion's being as safe for the woman as normal childbirth at term, and that predicate holds true only if the abortion is performed by medically competent personnel under conditions insuring maximum safety for the woman." Id. at 10-11. In the *Akron* case the Court observes that "we have left no doubt that, to ensure the safety of the abortion procedure, the States may mandate that only physicians perform abortion. . . ." 462 U.S. at 432.

You are working as counsel to the health center described in Sermchief v.

Gonzales, 660 S.W.2d 683 (Mo. 1983), Chapter 7. The clinic has many patients and few physicians. The medical director believes that the nurse practitioners, some of whom have many years experience doing procedures more complex than abortion, would, with training, be perfectly competent to perform abortions in the first trimester. Requiring physicians to perform all abortions limits the doctors' ability to provide more difficult services to acutely ill patients. Further, the rule that only physicians can perform abortions makes it more difficult for the clinic to recruit physicians, who are not interested in spending a significant portion of the work day providing a service that is so simple and unchallenging.

First, prepare a memo describing the physicians' power to delegate authority to perform abortions to nurses. Be as clear as you can about what sort of supervision the physicians must provide.

Second, despite your best efforts the state Board of Medical Licensing has learned that nurses are performing abortions and threatens to discipline everyone involved. The medical director of the clinic asks you to explore the possibility of a constitutional challenge. Evaluate the legal strength of the arguments you might make. What sorts of evidence would you seek to present to support your legal claims. Anticipate the legal and factual claims you might expect from the state. As *Akron* makes plain the Supreme Court has often relied on the expert advice of medical professional organizations. What positions would you expect the AMA or ACOG to take?

2. PATTERNS OF DELIVERY OF REPRODUCTIVE HEALTH SERVICES IN THE UNITED STATES

J. Rosoff, Not Just Teenagers

20 Fam. Plann. Perspect. 52 (1988)

This issue is devoted to an Alan Guttmacher Institute (AGI) study of how the United States compares with 19 other Western democracies in rates of births, abortions and pregnancies — especially unintended pregnancies — and contraceptive use. The study also examines how contraceptive use in these countries is affected by their public policies and programs related to reproduction and family planning. The focus is on adults; the study thus extends a previous AGI comparison of developed countries that had examined the reproductive and contraceptive behavior of adolescents. In that investigation, the AGI researchers had found that U.S. teenagers have much lower rates of contraceptive use and much higher rates of childbearing, abortion and pregnancy than do adolescents in other developed countries, even though the levels of adolescent sexual activity appear to be quite similar in all of the countries studied. What the new study shows is that this contrast in behavior not only appears among American adolescents but shows up as well among older U.S. women, especially those in their 20s.

For example, although its birthrate is only a little above the average for the group, the United States has one of the highest pregnancy rates of the 20 countries investigated; indeed, the rate is lower than only those of Greece and Ireland. Reflecting this elevated pregnancy rate are the country's very high abortion rate and high level of unintended births. Both the U.S. rates of abortion *and* unintended births are about five times those of the Netherlands, which is at the bottom of the range. Because so many U.S. women resort to contraceptive sterilization before they turn 30, the contrast between the United States and the other countries is especially marked among women under age 25.

Compared with most of the other countries, the United States has a low level of contraceptive use — especially use of the two most effective reversible methods, the pill and the IUD (even before the IUD was removed from the U.S. market). Furthermore, U.S. women are more likely than those in most of the other countries to report using no method at all.

What are some of the reasons for these contrasts?

• Typically, contraceptive care is integrated into the primary health services of the countries, making it available at many convenient and familiar locations. Not so in the United States.

• In many of the countries where the use of effective contraceptive methods is high and pregnancy and abortion rates are low, contraceptive care is delivered mainly through family physicians rather than medical specialists. These family physicians are especially likely to prescribe oral contraceptives, the most effective reversible method. In the United States — where pill use is lower than in most of the other countries examined and pregnancy and abortion rates are high — contraceptive services are delivered largely by medical specialists (obstetrician-gynecologists). These specialists are distributed unevenly geographically and charge more for their services than do family physicians.

• Family planning clinics in most of the countries other than the United States are meant to serve primarily first-time contraceptive users (usually young people) and other groups (such as immigrants), who may require special counseling, evening or weekend hours, female clinic personnel or a wide range of method choices. In contrast, U.S. clinics are designed primarily to provide free or subsidized services to people too poor to purchase contraceptive care from private physicians. Many U.S. women who attend clinics would prefer to go to a private doctor for family planning services, but cannot afford to do so. Others who could benefit from the personal counseling or other special arrangements offered by clinics may find such facilities unattractive in the belief that they provide a lower standard of medical care. In other countries, the choice of a clinic or doctor is determined by the needs of the patient; in the United States, it is determined by the patient's financial resources.

• A narrower range of contraceptive methods is available in the United States than in many of the other countries. Not only has the loss of most IUDs restricted the choices of U.S. couples, but methods available elsewhere — like the morning-after pill, the steroidal implant, injectable steroids, the cervical cap, new and presumably safer pill formulations, and more easily reversible means of tubal sterilization — are not yet marketed in the United States, partly because of liability considerations and partly because of the controversy surrounding abortion.

• In most of the countries studied, but not in the United States, contraceptives are available to everyone for free or at very low cost.

• There is considerably greater dissemination of information about contraception and sexuality in some of the other countries, through advertising, publicity, education in the schools or enlistment of pharmacists as distributors of appropriate literature. Use of the condom, the most effective of the nonprescription methods (and the only method that is also effective in preventing STDs, including AIDS) tends to be more widespread in the countries where this method is widely advertised.

Thus, family planning services in the United States are more expensive, are less conveniently located and are provided in less familiar settings than they are in many other developed countries, where pregnancy and abortion rates are lower. A finding of both the current research and the earlier study of teenagers is that use of the most effective methods is greater in countries where there is the broadest dissemination of information about contraceptive methods and about the locations where they can be obtained. Such information is both provided and assimilated much more easily where open, tolerant attitudes toward sex prevail.

a. The Organization and Financing of Contraceptive Services

Higher income women generally obtain contraceptive services from private physicians, while lower income women rely upon clinics. In 1983, 5106 clinics offered family planning services in the U.S. Over half of these are organized by local health departments; 13 percent are sponsored by Planned Parenthood, 7 percent by hospitals and the rest by a variety of other agencies. About one-third of American women live in counties in which there is no clinic providing family planning service, and that figure increased slightly between 1975 and 1983. In counties where family planning clinics exist, they serve only about one-half of the low income women who are at risk of pregnancy. See A. Torres et al., Family Planning Clinic Services in U.S. Counties, 1983, 19 Fam. Plann. Perspect. 54 (1987).

Family planning services are financed through Medicaid, private insurance, federal funds provided under Title X of the Public Health Service Act, patient fees, and state and local grants. Medicaid and Title X are the largest sources of public support for family planning. Through the Reagan years, the Administration sought to restrict the funds provided through Title X. Between 1980 and 1985, public support for contraceptive services declined by 12 percent in constant dollars. R. Gold et al. Public Funding of Contraceptive, Sterilization and Abortion Services, 1985, 18 Fam. Plann. Perspect. 259 (1986).

Title X is the popular name for the Family Planning Services and Population Research Act of 1970, Pub. L. No. 91-572, 84 Stat. 1506, codified at 42 U.S.C. §300-300a-8. It provides block grants to states, which in turn allocate funds to qualified providers of family planning services. Qualified agencies must meet a variety of standards, including a requirement that federal funds be matched with resources from other sources. In enacting Title X, Congress sought "to make comprehensive, voluntary family planning services, and information relating thereto, readily available to all persons. . . ." 116 Cong. Rec. 24094 (1970). Section 1008 of Title X provides that: "None of the funds appropriated under this subchapter shall be used in programs where abortion is a method of family planning." 42 U.S.C. §300a-6 (1982).

In 1988, the Department of Health and Human Services issued regulations seeking to curtail any relationship between Title X agencies and organizations providing abortion services. The regulations define "Title X project funds" to include all of the resources of an agency, whether or not received from the federal government under Title X. In essence, the regulations would terminate Title X grants to organizations that provide abortions with funds from other sources. They prohibit Title X agencies from offering referral for abortion, or, in essence, from discussing abortion. Title X agencies are required to offer pregnant women a "list of available providers that promote the welfare of mother and unborn child," even if the woman seeks a referral for abortion. Planned Parenthood Federation of America v. Bowen, 687 F. Supp. 540 (D. Colo. 1988), struck down the regulations as unauthorized by the statute and unconstitutional. The court found that they "violate (1) a woman's Fifth Amendment liberty interest in choosing whether to have an abortion, (2) her First Amendment right to receive necessary medical information to vindicate her Fifth Amendment liberty interest, and (3) a physician's or other treating practitioner's First Amendment right to disseminate necessary medical information to patients." 687 F. Supp. at 547. Commonwealth of Massachusetts v. Bowen, 679 F. Supp. 137 (D. Mass. 1988), reached similar conclusions. State of New York v. Bowen, 690 F. Supp. 1216 (S.D.N.Y. 1988), held that the regulations were within the discretion of the agency and that the government is constitutionally free to use its funding programs to express its preference for childbirth.

b. The Organization and Financing of Abortion Services

In 1985, over half of the pregnancies in the U.S. were unintended. Just under 1.6 million abortions were performed, making this the most common surgical procedure. About 30 percent of pregnancies ended in abortion, and each year about three percent of women of childbearing age have an abortion. Sixty percent of abortions are performed in specialized abortion clinics. The number of clinics providing abortion services declined by about 5 percent between 1982 and 1985. The vast majority of U.S. counties — 82 percent — have no physician or clinic that provides abortion services. These counties are home to 30 percent of all women aged 15 to 44. Further, in many counties that have a physician who provided at least one abortion in 1985, very few women obtain abortions. A local physician might serve only his or her established patients or might provide abortions only under limited or rare circumstances. From 1982 to 1985, the proportion of counties with no abortion provider rose from 78 percent to 82 percent. Not surprisingly, about 6 percent of abortions are performed outside of a woman's home state. The proportion was as high as 57 percent for Wyoming residents and 47 percent for those of West Virginia, and was more than 25 percent for residents of four other states.

In 1973, most abortions were done in the hospital. Through the 1980s, the proportion of abortions done on an inpatient basis decreased, and by 1985 only 13 percent of abortions were done in the hospital. In addition, most hospitals that provide abortions now offer them on an outpatient basis. Of all abortions performed in 1985, only 3 percent involved an overnight stay in the hospital.

Most women pay for abortions with cash, in advance. In 1985, the average cost of an abortion was $213, and the charges for a first trimester abortion ranged from $75 to almost $900. During the 1980s, the cost of an abortion rose less rapidly than the costs of other medical care. Between 1983 and 1986, the average amount paid for a first trimester nonhospital abortion rose by 7 percent, while the consumer price index for medical care rose by 21 percent.

Since the Supreme Court decision in Harris v. McRae, 448 U.S. 297 (1980), virtually no federal funds have financed abortions for low income women. See discussion, Chapter 2. However, in 1985, 14 states and the District of Columbia continued to use their own funds to finance abortions for low income women. In eight states and the District of Columbia, the legislature or executive chose to fund abortion services for poor women and, in the other six, state courts have interpreted state constitutional provisions to require even-handed funding for abortion. The states that continue to fund abortions for low income women include several states with very large populations of low income women, such as New York, California, New Jersey, Michigan, Massachusetts, and Connecticut. This note is drawn from

Henshaw et al., Abortion Services in the United States, 1984 and 1985, 19 Fam. Plann. Perspect. 63 (1987); and Jones et al., Unintended Pregnancy, Contraceptive Practice and Family Planning Services in Developed Countries, 20 Fam. Plann. Perspect. 53 (1988).

C. Legal and Medical Coercion in Reproductive Health Services

1. COERCIVE TREATMENT IN PREGNANCY

a. Some Cases

In November, 1985, Pamela Rae Stewart Monson gave birth to a son. Her placenta separated from the uterine wall. The baby was born with serious brain damage and died in January. In September, 1986, Ms. Stewart was arrested and jailed. Her bond was set at $10,000. After seven days in jail, she was released on $2,500 bond. J. Schacter, Woman Accused of Contributing to Baby's Demise During Pregnancy, L. A. Times, Oct. 1, 1986, Pt. II, 1.

Pamela Stewart was charged under California Penal Code, §270, a child support statute enacted in 1872 to enforce fathers' obligations to provide financial support for their children. It prohibits the willful omission of "necessary clothing, food, shelter or medical attendance." In 1925 it was extended to punish fathers who failed to support "a child conceived but not yet born," and, in 1974, extended to mothers.

The state alleged that she failed to follow physician orders, including failure to maintain bedrest, engaging in sexual intercourse with her husband, active care of her two children, delay in reporting to the hospital when vaginal bleeding was observed. (Media commentary focused on allegations that Ms. Stewart used amphetamines on the day of delivery. She and her husband denied the charges, asserting rather that she had taken an antihistamine. No one claimed that the drug use, even if true, caused the placenta to separate, which in turn damaged the baby's brain.)

The California Chapter of the American College of Obstetrics and Gynecology protested the prosecution saying, "California ACOG strives to promote healthy mothers and healthy babies. It does not condone unhealthy behavior, but ACOG believes criminal charges for a mother's behavior during pregnancy which may be harmful to the fetus is inappropriate and counterproductive. Such prosecution is contrary to public interest as it will inhibit many women from seeking prenatal care at all or prompt others not to provide accurate information to medical personnel for fear of incriminating themselves." The indictment was dismissed on pre-trial motion, on grounds that the statute did not encompass the conduct alleged. J. Warren, Infant Death Case: Mother Innocent of Prenatal Crime, L. A. Times, Feb. 27, 1987, Pt. 1, p. 3. col. 3.

More commonly, courts are asked to order a cesarean section when a physician believes it necessary and the mother refuses consent. Kolder et al., Court Ordered Obstetrical Interventions, 316 N. Engl. J. Med. 1192 (1987). [Hereinafter Kolder.] Among 21 cases in which court orders were sought, the orders were obtained in 86 percent; in 88 percent of these cases, the orders were received within six hours. In six of the 21 cases the prediction that the fetus was in serious distress proved to be inaccurate. Id. at 1195. Almost all the women involved were black, Asian, or Hispanic, and all were poor. Id. at 1196.

Mrs. Jessie Mae Jefferson of Butts County Georgia, followed her physician's advice through pregnancy, but refused, on religious grounds, to submit to a cesarean section. Her doctors sought a court order, testifying that it was 99 percent certain that the child could not survive a vaginal delivery and that the mother's chance of surviving was not better that 50 percent. The Georgia Department of Human Resources sought temporary custody of the fetus on grounds that it was not receiving proper parental care. Jefferson v. Griffin Spalding Hospital Authority, 247 Ga. 86, 274 S.E.2d 457 (1981), held that "as a matter of fact the child is a human being fully capable of sustaining life independent of the mother. 274 5.E.2d at 458. [T]his child is without the proper parental care and subsistence necessary for his or her physical life and health." Id. at 459. The court appointed a guardian to consent to a cesarian section, but before it could be performed, a healthy baby was born vaginally. Mother Nature Overrules Supreme Court, 17 Bull. Ga. Med. Assn. 1 (1981).

Angie C., a 27-year-old Washington woman had had bone cancer since she was 13. She underwent extensive treatment over the years, including the amputation of her leg. In her mid-twenties she was married, and her cancer seemed to be in remission. She became pregnant. Twenty-five weeks into the pregnancy, a routine prenatal exam revealed a lung tumor and the doctors told her that she might have only days to live. The woman believed, reasonably, that a 25 week fetus had little chance of survival. The hospital sought a court ordered cesarean section, over the objections of the woman, her husband, her parents, and her physicians. The hospital's expert testified that there was a 50 to 60 percent chance that a fetus of this age would survive and less than a 20 percent chance that it would be born with a handicap. They also acknowledged that the operation would hasten the mother's death, and were not pressed on the chances of a fetus whose mother had experienced such a difficult pregnancy. The operation was ordered and performed. Within hours both infant and mother died. In Re. A.C., 533 A.2d 611 (D.C. App. 1987). [The court *en banc* has agreed to review the decision ordering the operation.] See Annas, She's Going to Die: The Case of Angela C., 18 Hastings Cent. Rep. 23 (1988).

Angie C's mother describes these events. Five days after the sudden diagnosis, the family received a telephone call saying that she was not doing well. They called a priest, arranged for last rites. "Only a few minutes later the hospital staff told us we were needed at a short meeting. They did not tell us it was a court hearing. It took all day. Poor Angie, first she's told she's dying and the next thing everybody abandons her and leaves her alone in her room. . . . Then even before the hearing was over they started prepping her for surgery. She was already in so much pain. We told the judge she didn't want the surgery, that we didn't want her to suffer anymore, that we didn't think the baby would live. But they didn't listen. After the surgery and after they told her the baby was dead, I think Angie just gave up." "Drama in the Womb: A Matter of Life and Death Winds Up in Court," L.A. Times, Dec. 25, 1987, Part V-A, p. 5. Her father asked, "For 14 years our daughter was considered terminally ill and what right did the court have to decide that her life was over?" Id. Professor Robert Burt comments, the judge

> so rigorously obliterated Angela Carder from these proceedings — by refusing to see her and by referring to her as if she were already dead — in order to alleviate the tension he felt, the cognitive dissonance he was experiencing, in choosing between two tragically incommensurate goals: to save a mother or an infant. In order to make this choice, however, the judge not only removed himself from any interaction with the mother. He also imagined himself so remote from the infant as to deprive it of any recognizable flesh-and-blood embodiment. He transformed the fetus into a lifeless abstraction, an embodiment of Life rather than a living, breathing human being. . . . The hospital administrators implicitly understood the tradition of medical authoritarianism. . . . They believed, that is, that medical decisions must be based on unquestionable authority — on data that is so rigorously based on scientific evidence that it cannot be questioned. . . . But the hospital administrators also understood that this portrait of medical practice is now outdated; and so, since they could not rely on unquestionably correct data and could no longer invoke the social status of physicians to mask the uncertainty of their data, the hospital administrators turned to the last bastion of unquestionable authority in our society: The Judge, the embodiment of the Law. [Burt, Uncertainty and Medical Authority in the World of Jay Katz, 16 L. Med. Health Care 190 (1988).]

In 1986, two brain-dead women were kept alive on life support systems to incubate not-yet-viable fetuses. There was no indication of the mother's wishes in either case. In one case, the parents objected, but the father, who planned to marry the woman, sought to maintain her life. The Santa Clara, California, court ordered that life systems be maintained, and a healthy baby was born. "Brain Dead Woman Gives Birth," Washington Post, July 31, 1986, A16. In the second case, both the parents and husband objected to maintaining life support systems, but a man who claimed he was the father persuaded a court to order support until a one pound one-and-a-half-ounce baby was born. Baby is Weak After Birth to Brain-Dead Woman, N. Y. Times, August 16, 1986, A6.

In Taft v. Taft, 388 Mass. 331, 446 N.E.2d 395 (1983), the physician of a woman in her fourth month of pregnancy recommended that her cervix be sutured to "hold her pregnancy." She objected, on religious grounds. Her husband persuaded a lower court to order her to have it done. The Massachusetts Supreme Court reversed, holding that compulsory surgery violated her rights to privacy and to free exercise of religion.

A 35-year-old mother of 10 was about to deliver her eleventh child. Her physicians believed that the umbilical cord was wrapped around the neck of the baby and that it would not survive unless delivered by cesarean section. The mother resisted. Civil Court Judge, Margaret Taylor refused to order surgery, holding that pregnant women, like other people, have a right to decide whether to undergo surgery. The mother delivered a healthy child vaginally. T. Lewin, Courts Acting to Force Care of the Unborn, N.Y. Times, Nov. 23, 1987, A1.

b. Physician Attitudes and the Public/Private Dichotomy

While the California Chapter of the American College of Obstetricians and Gynecologists opposed criminal prosecution for failure to follow physician orders, a 1987 survey of the heads of fellowship programs in maternal-fetal medicine found that: 26 percent approve of state surveillance of pregnant women to assure compliance with physician orders; 46 percent support detention of women who refused medical advice and thereby endanger fetal life; 22 percent believe that home birth should be illegal. Kolder at 1194.

A common view in American obstetrical practice in the 1980s focuses on the worst possible outcome in a situation of uncertainty and takes action to prevent that outcome, regardless of the probability that the adverse result will occur. Brody & Thompson, The Maximum Strategy in Modern Obstetrics, 12 J. Fam. Prac. 977 (1981). This approach, sometimes fueled by fear of malpractice liability, is highly controversial. See Rhoden, The Judge in the Delivery room: The Emergence of Court-Ordered Caesareans, 74 Cal. L. Rev. 1951, 1962-1965 (1986) (hereinafter *Rhoden*).

Given these attitudes, it is likely that physicians often pressure pregnant women to "consent" to treatments and behaviors that the women initially resist. In a democratic society, is it preferable that these negotiations between patients and physicians take place in the "privacy" of the hospital or that they be subject to the scrutiny and supervision of the law? Which context is more empowering to women? To physicians? Or perhaps it makes no difference. For an argument that physicians should not look to the law to legitimate coercive treatment and that courts should not provide that legitimacy, see Annas, Protecting the Liberty of Pregnant Patients, 316 N. Engl. J. Med.

1213 (1987). Professor Martha Field, Controlling the Woman to Protect the Fetus, 17-2 L. Med. Health Care 1 (1989), argues powerfully against any coercive action based on women's decisions and behavior in pregnancy. Professor John Robertson supports "post-birth criminal or civil sanctions for culpable maternal behavior that seriously injures offspring." Letter, 317 N. Engl. J. Med. 1223 (1987). Robertson & Schulman, Pregnancy and Prenatal Harm to Offspring: The Case of Mothers with PKU, 17 Hastings Cent. Rept. 22 (1987). See generally Rhoden.

c. One Imperfect Analogy: Child Abuse and Neglect

Although parents have broad discretion to raise their children according to the dictates of their own consciences, the state's authority to protect children from parental neglect and abuse is well established. See generally Areen, Cases and Materials in Family Law, Chapter 7 (1985). Parents' right to reject recommended medical treatment for their children is discussed, Chap. 6.

Some courts and commentators argue that child neglect law provides a model for determining when the state should order a woman to undergo surgery, or take other actions, for the benefit of her fetus. John Robertson asserts, "The mother has, if she conceives and chooses not to abort, a legal and moral duty to bring the child into the world as healthy as is reasonably possible." J. Robertson, Procreative Liberty and the Control of Conception, Pregnancy, and Childbirth, 69 Va. L. Rev. 405, 438 (1983). J.E.B. Myers, Abuse and Neglect of the Unborn: Can the State Intervene?, 23 Duq. L. Rev. 1, 26-31 (1982), argues that, after fetal viability, courts should balance interests in child protection and parental autonomy, as in neglect and abuse cases, but giving somewhat greater weight to the mother's interest in physical autonomy. The power of the child abuse analogy is that it both respects broad parental discretion and autonomy, and, at the same time, insists that parents owe children a certain minimal level of care.

Other commentators reject the analogy between the duty parents owe to children and the duty a pregnant woman owes to a fetus. Nancy Rhoden argues that the analogy ignores the intrusion upon a woman's physical integrity. Rhoden at 1960-1968. Note, Maternal Rights and Fetal Wrongs: The Case Against the Criminalization of "Fetal Abuse," 101 Harv. L. Rev. 994, 1006 (1988), asserts that, "Broad fetal abuse statutes that are patterned on child abuse statutes . . . would be void for vagueness because they do not define the specific forms of abuse that constitute crimes and thus would not give notice to mothers of the scope of their duties toward their fetuses. [T]his vagueness is somewhat ameliorated in the child abuse context by years of judicial interpretation that puts individuals on notice of forbidden acts. . . ."

One core difficulty in the analogy between neglect of children and neglect of a fetus lies in the remedies available if a parent fails to meet minimal standards. If a parent neglects or abuses a child, the community can take responsibility for providing care and protection. While the loss to the parent may be grave, the parent nonetheless remains free to live his or her life. By contrast, because it is not possible to separate the fetus from the mother, the community cannot assume responsibility for providing care, but can only coerce the mother. Substantial intrusion may be required to impose the will of the state upon a resistant woman. In some cases, effectuating coercive orders may require that women be incarcerated for the entire pregnancy. As a practical matter it is easier to enforce a coerced judgment that a woman should have a cesarean section. But forced surgery is a very large intrusion.

d. A Second Imperfect Analogy: Abortion

The abortion cases hold that only when the fetus is capable of life outside the woman's body, may the state act to protect it, and then only so long as the woman's life or health is not jeopardized and the physician is allowed latitude to make judgments about the woman's interests and the viability of the fetus. Section B, supra. Since the woman has the right to destroy a fetus at any point prior to viability, must she also have the right to make other decisions posing a lesser risk to the fetus?

One difficulty with reliance upon the abortion analogy is that, in the parenting context, the greater authority — to deny life to a potential child — does not necessarily include the lesser — to damage a child one has chosen to bear. Rush, Prenatal Caretaking: Limits of State Intervention with and Without *Roe,* 39 U. Fla. L. Rev. 55, 64 (1987). The "state's willingness to protect fetal health and the mother's right to abort . . . can exist simultaneously." Stearns, Maternal Duties During Pregnancy: Toward a Conceptual Framework, 21 N. Eng. L. Rev. 595, 604 (1986).

The abortion analogy poses a second, practical, difficulty in that the trimester analysis of Roe v. Wade may not provide a sensible framework for thinking about the duties that a woman might owe to her unborn child. The developing fetus is most vulnerable in the first trimester of pregnancy, when the woman's right to terminate the pregnancy is broadest.

e. Yet Another Imperfect Analogy: The Right to Refuse Medical Treatment

The individual's right to refuse medical treatment and parents' right to reject expert recommendations of medical treatment for their children are discussed in Chapter 6. A competent person's right to refuse medical treatment encompasses the right to reject intrusions, such as donation of a kidney or bone marrow, that could save the life of another. Parents are not legally compelled to undergo surgery for the benefit of their children, even if the child's life depends upon it and the risk to the parent is slight. See discussion Regan, Rewriting Roe v. Wade, 77 Mich. L. Rev. 1569 (1977).

Rhoden, supra argues that these principles should define the duty that pregnant women owe to their fetuses and that courts should never compel cesarian sections or other medical invasions of pregnant women. John Robertson supports mandatory cesareans, as well as coercive orders compelling a parent to "donate" blood, bone marrow, or even organs, depending on the degree of risk. Robertson, The Right to Procreate and In Utero Fetal Therapy, 3 J. Leg. Med. 333, 354-355 (1982).

PROBLEM: A LEGISLATIVE DRAFTING EXERCISE

Draft a statute defining standards that pregnant women must meet for the protection of their fetus, and specifying the remedies available to enforce compliance or to punish noncompliance. A legislature considering such a statute would want to hear a variety of perspectives on these difficult issues, such as opinions of obstetricians, pediatricians, judges, district attorneys, women's groups, child welfare authorities, constitutional lawyers, and religious organizations. There are likely to be sharp differences of opinion within these interested groups. First, take roles within these various groups to hammer out an organizational position and then bring the institutional positions together to seek resolution in the legislative process.

2. COERCED STERILIZATION

a. EUGENIC STERILIZATION

In 1927, the Supreme Court considered a Virginia program providing for the involuntary sterilization of people found to be "the probable potential parent of socially inadequate offspring." Justice Holmes, writing for the Supreme Court, upheld the program.

> Carrie Buck is a feeble minded white woman who was committed to the State Colony. . . . She is the daughter of a feeble minded mother in the same institution and the mother of an illegitimate feeble minded child. . . We have seen more than once that the public welfare may call upon the best citizens for their lives. It would be strange if it could not call upon those who already sap the strength of the State for these lesser sacrifices, often not felt to be such by those concerned, in order to prevent our being swamped with incompetence. It is better for all the world, if instead of waiting to execute degenerate offspring for crime, or to let them starve for their imbecility, society can prevent those

> who are manifestly unfit from continuing their kind. . . . Three generations of imbeciles are enough [Buck v. Bell, 274 U.S. 200, 205-207 (1927).]

Carrie Buck left the institution after she was sterilized and lived with her husband until his death. "[T]hrough her adult life she regularly displayed intelligence and kindness. . . . She was an avid reader, and even in her last weeks was able to converse lucidly, recalling events from her childhood." Her daughter, Vivian, who was an infant when she was judged "feeble minded," was listed on the honor roll in her first two years of school. She died at age 8. Lombardo, Three Generations, No Imbeciles: New Light on Buck v. Bell, 60 N.Y.U. L. Rev. 30 (1985).

Skinner v. Oklahoma, 316 U.S. 535 (1942), considered a program for the mandatory sterilization of recidivist criminals except those convicted of white-collar crimes. The Court held that the distinction violated Equal Protection principles.

> We are dealing here with legislation which involves one of the basic civil rights of man. Marriage and procreation are fundamental to the very existence and survival of the race. The power to sterilize, if exercised, may have subtle, far-reaching and devastating effects. In evil or reckless hands it can cause races or types which are inimical to the dominant group to wither and disappear. There is no redemption for the individual whom the law touches. Any experiment which the State conducts is to his irreparable injury. He is forever deprived of a basic liberty. [316 U.S. at 541.]

While many states retain statutes authorizing eugenic sterilization, it seems that it is no longer common in the United States. It has become increasingly clear that the assumptions of Buck v. Bell are not scientifically grounded. See, for instance, Murdock, Sterilization of the Retarded: A Problem or a Solution, 62 Cal. L. Rev. 917 (1974). The policies of the Nazi government underscored the dangers of eugenic sterilization. Popular attitudes are closer to the views expressed in *Skinner*, rather than those expressed in Buck v. Bell. But while official eugenic sterilization is no longer common, problems of coercion, often motivated by eugenic beliefs, persist.

b. Coerced Consent

In 1973, two black women, ages 12 and 14, were sterilized before either of them, or their parents, were fully informed about the nature of the operation. A sister, Katie Relf, age 15, locked herself in a room to escape sterilization. A federal suit alleged that the federal government had failed to assure that federal Medicaid funds were used only for voluntary sterilizations. The district court found, "An indefinite number of poor people have been improperly coerced into accepting a sterilization operation under the threat that various federally supported welfare benefits would be withdrawn unless they submitted to irreversible sterilizations. Patients receiving Medicaid assistance at childbirth are evidently the most frequent targets of this pressure." Relf v. Weinberger, 372 F. Supp. 1196, 1199 (D.D.C. 1974).

In response to this suit, the federal agency issued regulations specifying the informed consent that must be obtained if a sterilization is to be financed with Medicaid funds. The regulations require a 72-hour waiting period between the time of consent and the operation, and prohibit sterilization of women under age 21. 42 C.F.R. §§50-201 to 50.206. Voe v. Califano, 434 F. Supp. 1058 (D. Conn. 1977), upheld the constitutionality of the minors provision. While *Medicaid funds* cannot be used to finance involuntary sterilizations, physicians remain free to condition their "private" services upon a requirement that the patient "consent" to be sterilized. Walker v. Pierce, Chapter 1.

It is not clear that the federal regulations have been enforced. In the late 1970s, when Ralph Nader and various women's health organizations sought to monitor compliance, violations were common. See S. Law, Sterilization Comes Easier for the Disadvantaged, 23 N.Y.U.L. Bull. 15 (1977). The most common problems involve women in labor, particularly those who do not speak English. Many factors encourage doctors to press poor women to "consent" to sterilization: widespread belief that poor women should not have more children, residency and specialty board certification requirements of surgical experience, financial incentives. In the 1980s, few public or private resources monitor sterilization consent.

The incidence of surgical sterilization has continued to rise. Low income women, those with little education, and Hispanics and Blacks, are most likely to be sterilized. T. Shapiro, Population Control Politics: Women, Sterilization and Reproductive Freedom (1985); F. DeStafano et al., Demographic Trends in Tubal Sterilization: United States, 1970-1978, 72 Am. J. Pub. Health 480 (1982).

c. "Best Interest" Sterilization of Retarded People

Many states have enacted laws authorizing the involuntary sterilization of individuals who a court determines are severely retarded, sexually active, unable to use other forms of contraception, and unable to care for their offspring. These statutes have been upheld against constitutional challenge. See In re Sterilization of Moore, 289 N.C. 95, 221 S.E.2d 307 (1976); North Carolina Association of Retarded Children v. North Carolina, 420 F. Supp. 451 (M.D.N.C. 1976).

Until 1978, most state court judges ruled that they had no authority to approve sterilization of a retarded person without a specific statutory process.

In part, judges feared that they might be held liable in a federal civil rights action. But Stump v. Sparkman, 435 U.S. 349 (1978), held that judicial actions authorizing sterilization of retarded people are immune from subsequent scrutiny, unless they are taken in violation of a specific state law.

Since that time state courts have exercised greater latitude in authorizing sterilization of retarded people. Matter of Guardianship of Hayes, 93 Wash. 2d 228, 608 P.2d 635 (1980), held that

> the Superior Court has jurisdiction to entertain and act upon a request for an order authorizing sterilization. [I]n the absence of controlling legislation, the court may grant such a petition in the rare and unusual case that sterilization is in the best interest of the retarded person. [I]n the question of sterilization the interests of the parents of a retarded person cannot be presumed to be identical to those of the child. The problem of parental consent to sterilization is of great concern to professionals in the field of mental health, and the overwhelming weight of opinion of those who have studied the problem appears to be that consent of a parent or guardian is a questionable or inadequate basis for sterilization. . . . Substantial medical evidence must be adduced, and the burden on the proponent of sterilization will be to show by clear, cogent and convincing evidence that such a procedure is in the best interest of the retarded person.

Massachusetts took a different approach, holding that court may authorize sterilization, but must "endeavor, as accurately as possible, to determine the wants and needs of this ward as they relate to the sterilization procedure. . . . No sterilization is to be compelled on the basis of any State or parental interest." Matter of Moe, 385 Mass. App. 555, 432 N.E. 2d 712 (1982). The dissenting judge said, "The court speaks of human dignity in connection with the free choice to be sterilized. It is difficult to think of an experience more degrading to human dignity than a sterilization ordered by a judge who is empowered by the court to read the heart and mind of the incompetent ward and forever bar the ward from bringing forth a child." 432 N.E. 2d at 724.

In California, a statute specifically prohibited judges from authorizing the sterilization of mentally incompetent people. Mildred G. v. Valerie N., 40 Cal. 3d 143, 219 Cal. Rptr. 387, 707 P.2d 760 (1985), held the statute unconstitutional. "True protection of procreative choice can be accomplished only if the state permits the court-supervised substituted judgment of the conservator to be exercised on behalf of a conservatee who is unable to personally exercise this right. Limiting the exercise of that judgment by denying the right to effective contraception through sterilization to this class of conservatees denies them a right held not only by conservatees who are competent to consent but by all other women. . . ." 219 Cal. Rptr. at 404, 707 P.2d at 777. Judge Rose Bird dissented, saying, "[P]recisely because choice and consent are meaningless concepts when applied to such a person, the majority's invocation of the theory of procreative choice and the fiction of substituted consent cannot withstand constitutional scrutiny. The majority opinion opens the door to abusive sterilization practices which will serve the convenience of conservators, parents, and service providers rather than incompetent conservatees. The ugly history of sterilization abuse against developmentally disabled persons in the name of seemingly enlightened social policies counsels a different choice." 219 Cal. Rptr. 409, 707 P.2d 781-782.

Table of Cases

Principal cases appear in italics.

Index